ERC
T-S
Sage - H7Y
Salt

ERC
T-S
Sage - H7Y

HOLT
SOCIAL
STUDIES

World Geography

Christopher L. Salter

HOLT, RINEHART AND WINSTON

A Harcourt Education Company

Orlando • **Austin** • New York • San Diego • London

Author

Dr. Christopher L. Salter

Dr. Christopher L. "Kit" Salter is Professor Emeritus of geography and former Chair of the Department of Geography at the University of Missouri. He did his undergraduate work at Oberlin College and received both his M.A. and Ph.D. degrees in geography from the University of California at Berkeley.

Dr. Salter is one of the country's leading figures in geography education. In the 1980s he helped found the national Geographic Alliance network to promote geography education in all 50 states. In the 1990s Dr. Salter was Co-Chair of the National Geography Standards Project, a group of distinguished geographers who created *Geography for Life* in 1994, the document outlining national standards in geography. In 1990 Dr. Salter received the National Geographic Society's first-ever Distinguished Geography Educator Award. In 1992 he received the George Miller Award for distinguished service in geography education from the National Council for Geographic Education. In 2006 Dr. Salter was awarded Lifetime Achievement Honors by the Association of American Geographers for his transformation of geography education.

Over the years, Dr. Salter has written or edited more than 150 articles and books on cultural geography, China, field work, and geography education. His primary interests lie in the study of the human and physical forces that create the cultural landscape, both nationally and globally.

ISBN-13 978-0-03-099503-3
ISBN-10 0-03-099503-5

3 4 5 6 7 8 9 032 13 12 11 10 09 08

Making This Book Work for You

Studying geography will be easy for you with this textbook. Take a few minutes now to become familiar with the easy-to-use structure and special features of your book. See how it will make geography come alive for you!

Unit

Each unit begins with a satellite image, a regional atlas, and a table with facts about each country. Use these pages to get an overview of the region you will study.

Regional Atlas

The maps in the regional atlas show some of the key physical and human features of the region.

Facts about Countries See which countries are included in each region and learn some important facts about them with these helpful tables.

Maps *(continued)*

Interactive Maps

Geography Skills With map zone geography skills, you can go online to find interactive versions of the key maps in this book. Explore these interactive maps to learn and practice important map skills and bring geography to life.

To use map zone interactive maps online:

1. Go to go.hrw.com.
2. Enter the KEYWORD shown on the interactive map.
3. Press return!

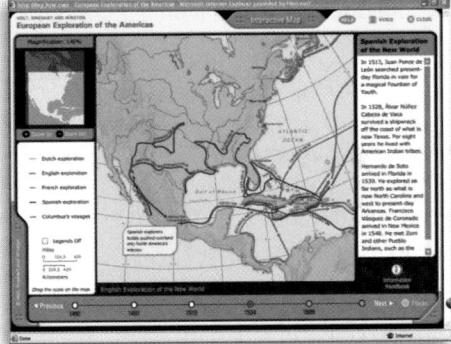

Interactive Maps

Geography Skills

Maps

The *World Almanac and Book of Facts is* America's largest-selling reference book of all time, with more than 81 million copies sold since 1868.

FACTS ABOUT THE WORLD

Study the latest facts and figures about the world.

FACTS ABOUT COUNTRIES

Study the latest facts and figures about countries.

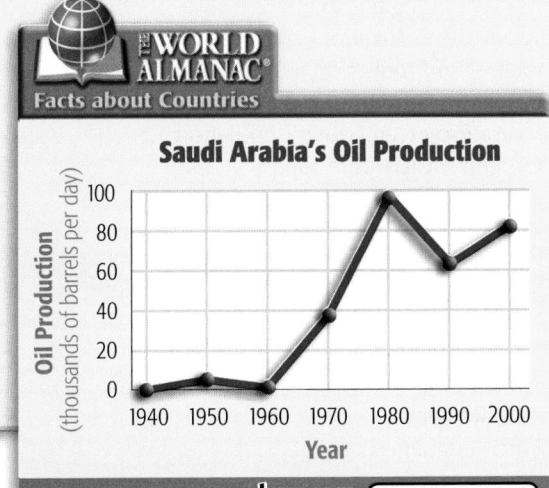

Charts and Graphs

Use charts and graphs to analyze geographic information.

Charts and Graphs

Quick Facts and Infographics

Analyze visual information to learn about geography.

Primary Sources

Learn about the world through important documents and personal accounts.

BIOGRAPHIES

Meet the people who have influenced the world and learn about their lives.

Literature

Learn about the world's geography through literature.

Satellite View

See the world through satellite images and explore what these images reveal.

Social Studies Skills

Learn, practice, and apply the skills you need to study and analyze geography.

CONNECTING TO . . .

Explore the connections between geography and other subjects.

TECHNOLOGY

SCIENCE

MATH

THE ARTS

HISTORY

ECONOMICS

Writing Workshop

Learn to write about geography.

Features

Reference

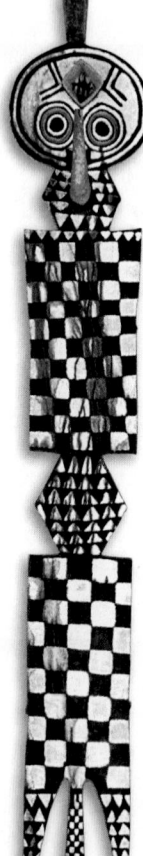

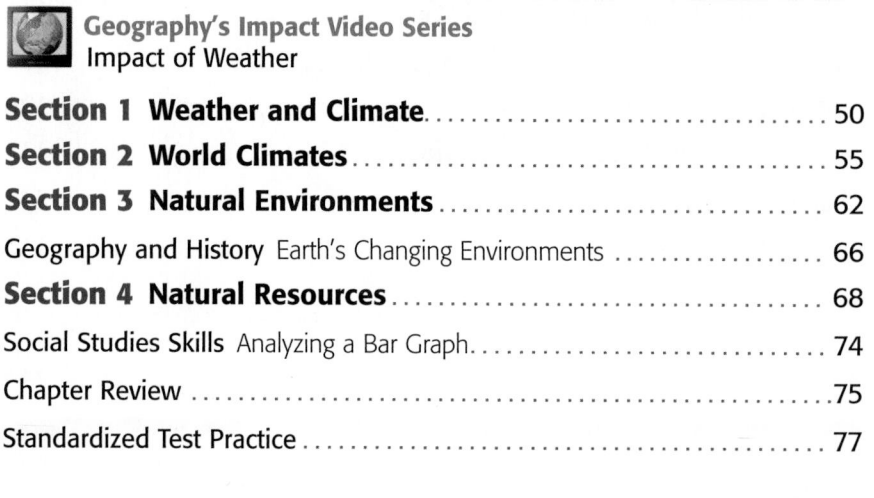
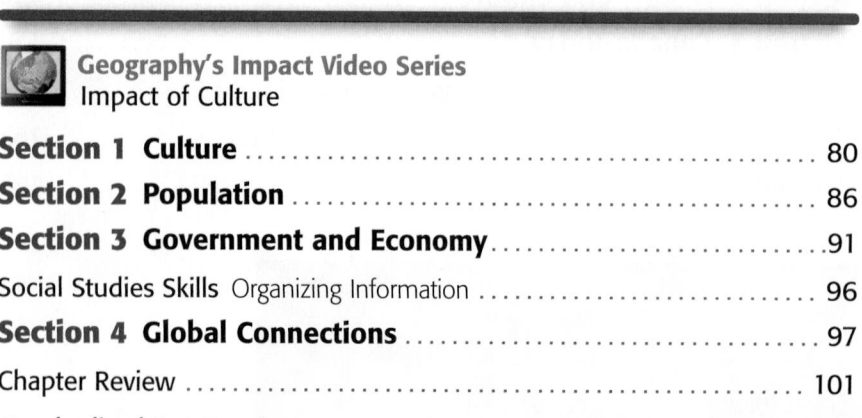

Contents

UNIT 1 Introduction to Geography

Reviewers

Academic Reviewers

Elizabeth Chako, Ph.D.
Department of Geography
The George Washington University

Altha J. Cravey, Ph.D.
Department of Geography
University of North Carolina

Eugene Cruz-Uribe, Ph.D.
Department of History
Northern Arizona University

Toyin Falola, Ph.D.
Department of History
University of Texas

Sandy Freitag, Ph.D.
Director, Monterey Bay History
    and Cultures Project
Division of Social Sciences
University of California,
    Santa Cruz

Oliver Froehling, Ph.D.
Department of Geography
University of Kentucky

Reuel Hanks, Ph.D.
Department of Geography
Oklahoma State University

Phil Klein, Ph.D.
Department of Geography
University of Northern Colorado

B. Ikubolajeh Logan, Ph.D.
Department of Geography
Pennsylvania State University

Marc Van De Mieroop, Ph.D.
Department of History
Columbia University
New York, New York

Christopher Merrett, Ph.D.
Department of History
Western Illinois University

Thomas R. Paradise, Ph.D.
Department of Geosciences
University of Arkansas

Jesse P.H. Poon, Ph.D.
Department of Geography
University at Buffalo–SUNY

Robert Schoch, Ph.D.
CGS Division of Natural Science
Boston University

Derek Shanahan, Ph.D.
Department of Geography
Millersville University
Millersville, Pennsylvania

David Shoenbrun, Ph.D.
Department of History
Northwestern University
Evanston, Illinois

Sean Terry, Ph.D.
Department of Interdisciplinary
    Studies, Geography and
    Environmental Studies
Drury University
Springfield, Missouri

Educational Reviewers

Dennis Neel Durbin
Dyersburg High School
Dyersburg, Tennessee

Carla Freel
Hoover Middle School
Merced, California

Tina Nelson
Deer Park Middle School
Randallstown, Maryland

Don Polston
Lebanon Middle School
Lebanon, Indiana

Robert Valdez
Pioneer Middle School
Tustin, California

Teacher Review Panel

Heather Green
LaVergne Middle School
LaVergne, Tennessee

John Griffin
Wilbur Middle School
Wichita, Kansas

Rosemary Hall
Derby Middle School
Birmingham, Michigan

Rose King
Yeatman-Liddell School
St. Louis, Missouri

Mary Liebl
Wichita Public Schools USD 259
Wichita, Kansas

Jennifer Smith
Lake Wood Middle School
Overland Park, Kansas

Melinda Stephani
Wake County Schools
Raleigh, North Carolina

Chapter

Each regional chapter begins with a preview of what you will learn and a map of the region. Special instruction is also given in reading and skills.

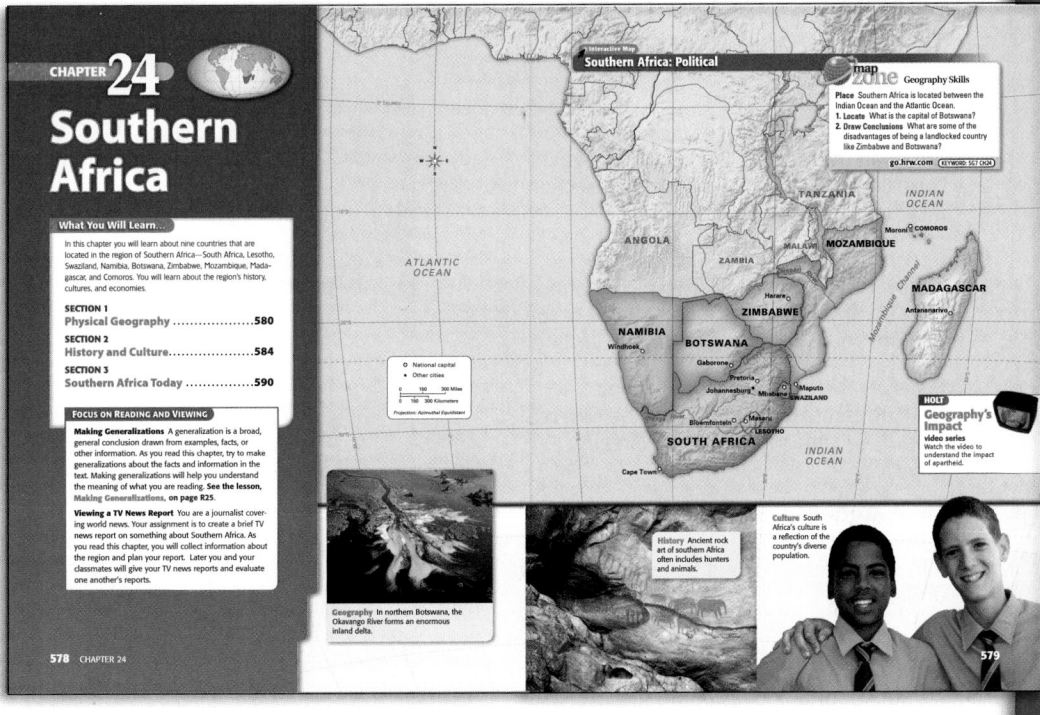

Reading Social Studies

Chapter reading lessons give you skills and practice to help you read the textbook. More help with each lesson can be found in the back of the book. Margin notes and questions in the chapter make sure you understand the reading skill.

Social Studies Skills

The Social Studies Skills lessons give you an opportunity to learn, practice, and apply an important skill. Chapter Review questions then follow up on what you learned.

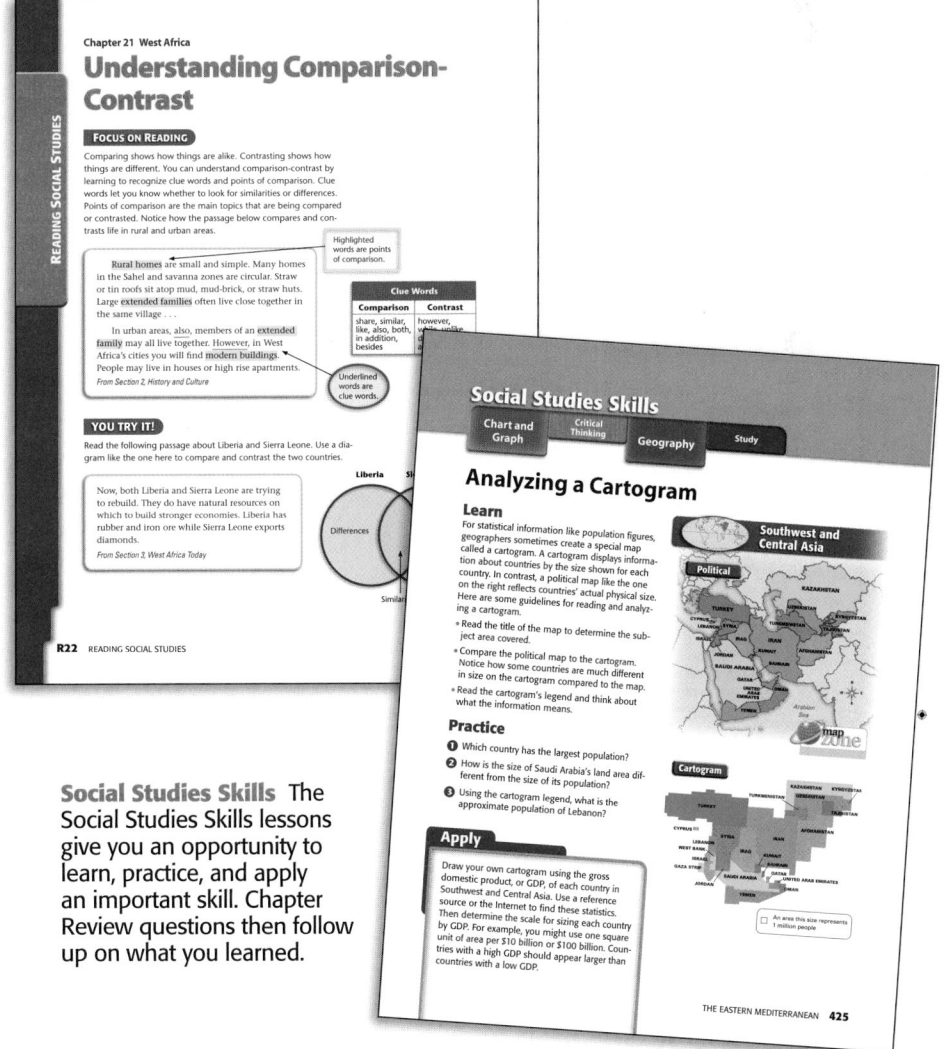

MAKING THIS BOOK WORK FOR YOU

Section

The section opener pages include Main Ideas, an overarching Big Idea, and Key Terms and Places. In addition, each section includes these special features:

If YOU Lived There . . . Each section begins with a situation for you to respond to, placing you in a place that relates to the content you will be studying in the section.

Building Background The Building Background connects what will be covered in each section with what you already know.

Short Sections of Content The information in each section is organized into small chunks of text that you can easily understand.

Taking Notes Suggested graphic organizers help you read and take notes on the important ideas in the section.

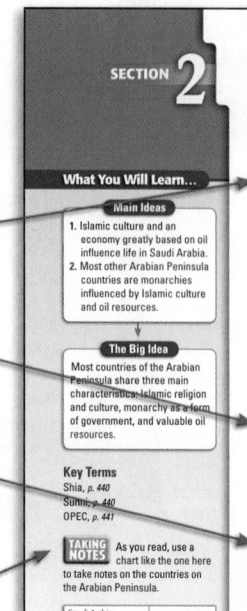

SECTION 2

The Arabian Peninsula

What You Will Learn...

Main Ideas

1. Islamic culture and an economy greatly based on oil influence life in Saudi Arabia.
2. Most other Arabian Peninsula countries are monarchies influenced by Islamic culture and oil resources.

The Big Idea

Most countries of the Arabian Peninsula share three main characteristics—Islamic religion and culture, monarchy as a form of government, and valuable oil resources.

Key Terms

Shia, *p. 440*
Sunni, *p. 440*
OPEC, *p. 441*

TAKING NOTES As you read, use a chart like the one here to take notes on the countries on the Arabian Peninsula.

Saudi Arabia	
Kuwait	
Bahrain	
Qatar	
United Arab Emirates	
Oman	
Yemen	

If YOU lived there...

You are a financial adviser to the ruler of Oman. Your country has been making quite a bit of money from oil exports. However, you worry that your economy is too dependent on oil. You think Oman's leaders should consider expanding the economy. Oman is a small country, but it has beautiful beaches, historic palaces and mosques, and colorful markets.

How would you suggest expanding the economy?

BUILDING BACKGROUND Oman and all the countries of the Arabian Peninsula have valuable oil resources. In addition to oil, these countries share two basic characteristics: Islamic religion and monarchy as a form of government. The largest country, and the one with the most influence in the region, is Saudi Arabia.

Saudi Arabia

Saudi Arabia is by far the largest of the countries of the Arabian Peninsula. It is also a major religious and cultural center and has one of the region's strongest economies.

People and Customs

Nearly all Saudis are Arabs and speak Arabic. Their culture is strongly influenced by Islam, a religion founded in Saudi Arabia by Muhammad. Islam is based on submitting to God and on messages Muslims believe God gave to Muhammad. These messages are writen in the Qur'an, the holy book of Islam.

Nearly all Saudis follow one of two main branches of Islam. **Shia** Muslims believe that true interpretation of Islamic teaching can only come from certain religious and political leaders called imams. **Sunni** Muslims believe in the ability of the majority of the community to interpret Islamic teachings. About 85 percent of Saudi Muslims are Sunni.

With about 9 million people, Istanbul, shown here, is Turkey's largest city.

electronics. About 40 percent of Turkey's labor force works in agriculture. Grains, cotton, sugar beets, and hazelnuts are major crops.

Turkey is rich in natural resources, which include oil, coal, and iron ore. Water is also a valuable resource in the region. Turkey has spent billions of dollars building dams to increase its water supply. On one hand, these dams provide hydroelectricity. On the other hand, some of these dams have restricted the flow of river water into neighboring countries.

READING CHECK Finding Main Ideas What kind of government does Turkey have?

SUMMARY AND PREVIEW In this section you learned about Turkey's history, people, government, and economy. Next, you will learn about Israel.

go.hrw.com
Online Quiz
KEYWORD: SG7 HP17

Section 2 Assessment

Reviewing Ideas, Terms, and Places
1. **a. Recall** What city did both the Romans and Ottoman Turks capture?
   b. Explain In what ways did Atatürk try to modernize Turkey?
2. **a. Recall** What ethnic group makes up 20 percent of Turkey's population?
   b. Draw Conclusions What makes Turkey *secular*?
   c. Elaborate Why do you think Turkey wants to be a member of the European Union?

Critical Thinking
3. **Summarizing** Using the information in your notes, summarize Turkey's history and Turkey today.

Turkey's History	Turkey Today

FOCUS ON WRITING
4. **Describing Turkey** A description of Turkey might include details about its people, culture, government, and economy. Take notes on the details you think are important and interesting.

Turkey Today

Turkey's government meets in the capital of Ankara, but **Istanbul** is Turkey's largest city. Istanbul's location will serve as an economic bridge to Europe as Turkey plans to join the European Union.

Government

Turkey's legislature is called the National Assembly. A president and a prime minister share executive power.

Although most of its people are Muslim, Turkey is a secular state. **Secular** means that religion is kept separate from government. For example, the religion of Islam allows a man to have up to four wives. However, by Turkish law a man is permitted to have just one wife. In recent years Islamic political parties have attempted to increase Islam's role in Turkish society.

Economy and Resources

As a member of the European Union, Turkey's economy and people would benefit by increased trade with Europe. Turkey's economy includes modern factories as well as village farming and craft making.

Among the most important industries are textiles and clothing, cement, and

Reading Check Questions end each section of content so you can check to make sure you understand what you just studied.

Summary and Preview The Summary and Preview connects what you studied in the section to what you will study in the next section.

Section Assessment Finally, the section assessment boxes make sure that you understand the main ideas of the section. We also provide assessment practice online!

Features

Your book includes many features that will help you learn about geography, such as Close-up and Satellite View.

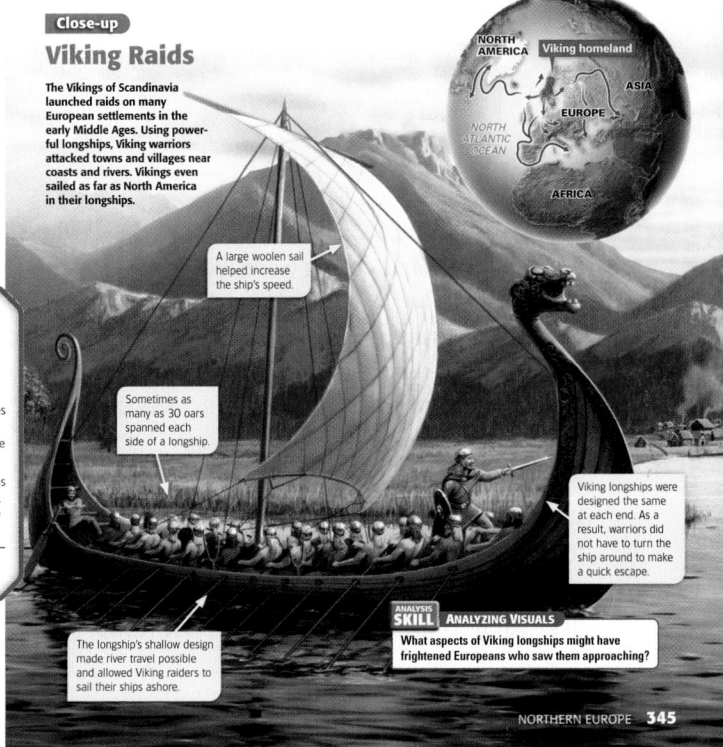

Viking Raids

The Vikings of Scandinavia launched raids on many European settlements in the early Middle Ages. Using powerful longships, Viking warriors attacked towns and villages near coasts and rivers. Vikings even sailed as far as North America in their longships.

NORTH AMERICA — Viking homeland — ASIA — EUROPE — NORTH ATLANTIC OCEAN — AFRICA

A large woolen sail helped increase the ship's speed.

Sometimes as many as 30 oars spanned each side of a longship.

Viking longships were designed the same at each end. As a result, warriors did not have to turn the ship around to make a quick escape.

ANALYSIS SKILL ANALYZING VISUALS
What aspects of Viking longships might have frightened Europeans who saw them approaching?

The longship's shallow design made river travel possible and allowed Viking raiders to sail their ships ashore.

NORTHERN EUROPE **345**

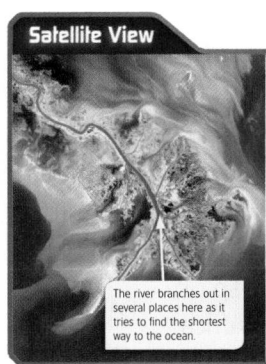

Satellite View

The Mississippi River Delta

From its source in Minnesota, the Mississippi River flows south across the central United States. It ends at the tip of Louisiana, which is shown here. This satellite image shows the area where the Mississippi River meets the Gulf of Mexico. This area is called a delta. A river's delta is formed from sediment that a river carries downstream to the ocean. Sediment is usually made up of rocks, soil, sand, and dead plants. Each year, the Mississippi dumps more than 400 million tons of sediment into the Gulf of Mexico.

The light blue and green areas in this image are shallow areas of sediment. The deeper water of the Gulf of Mexico is dark blue. Also, notice that much of the delta land looks fragile. This is new land that the river has built up by depositing sediment.

Making Inferences What natural hazards might people living in the Mississippi Delta experience?

The river branches out in several places here as it tries to find the shortest way to the ocean.

Satellite View See and explore the world through satellite images.

Close-up These features help you see how people live and what places look like around the world.

Chapter Review

At the end of each chapter, the Chapter Review will help you review key concepts, analyze information critically, complete activities, and show what you have learned.

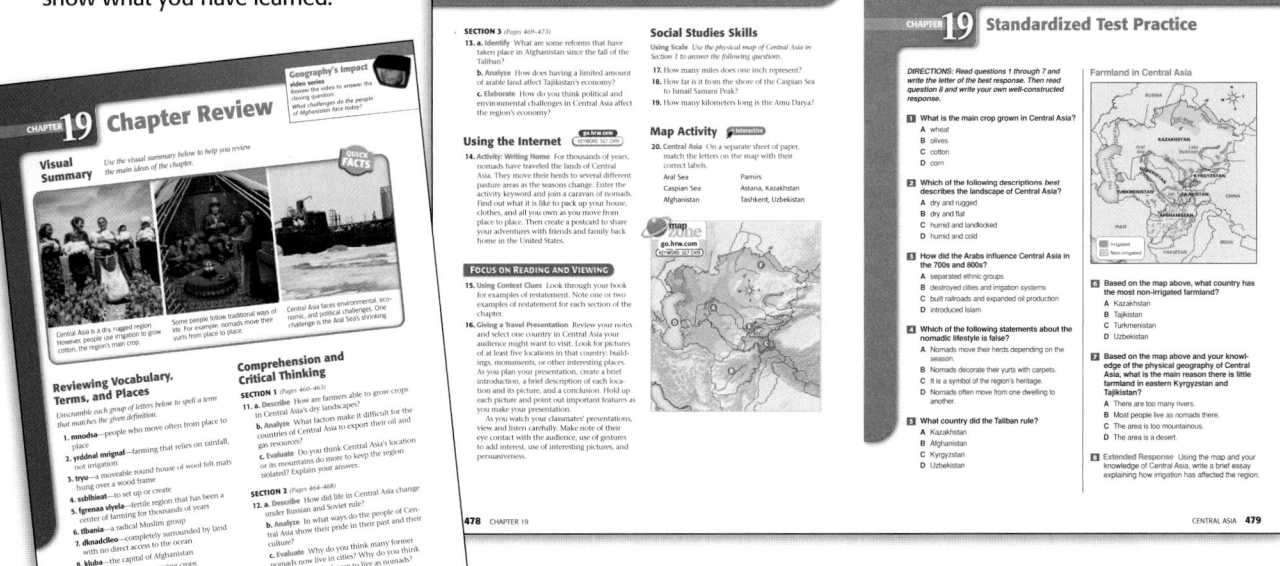

Standardized Test Practice Practice for standardized tests with the last page of each chapter before moving on to another region of the world!

MAKING THIS BOOK WORK FOR YOU **xxxi**

Scavenger Hunt

Are you ready to explore the world of geography? *Holt Social Studies: World Geography* is your ticket to this exciting world. Before you begin your journey, complete this scavenger hunt to get to know your book and discover what's inside.

On a separate sheet of paper, fill in the blanks to complete each sentence below. In each answer, one letter will be in a yellow box. When you have answered every question, copy these letters in order to reveal the answer to the question at the bottom of the page.

1 According to the Table of Contents, the title of Chapter 3 is Climate, Environment, and ☐☐☐☐☐☐☐☐☐. What else can you find in the Table of Contents?

2 Section 2 of Chapter 10 is called ☐☐☐☐☐☐.

3 Look up Benito Juárez in the Biographical Dictionary. He was the president of ☐☐☐☐☐☐. On what page will you read about him?

4 The second key term listed on page 426 is ☐☐☐☐☐☐.

5 On page 590, the main ideas are followed by The ☐☐☐ Idea. How do the main ideas connect to what is covered in this section?

6 The title of the map on page 539 is East Africa: ☐☐☐☐☐☐☐☐.

7 The Case Study feature on pages 370–371 is called The Breakup of ☐☐☐☐☐☐☐☐☐☐. What other features can you find in the book?

8 In the English and Spanish Glossary, the second word in the definition of cartography is ☐☐☐☐☐☐☐.

9 The Skills lesson on page 660 is called Analyzing ☐☐☐☐☐☐☐ ☐☐ ☐☐☐☐. What are the four types of skills lessons shown at the top of the page?

10 The subject of the Writing Workshop on Page 104 is ☐☐☐☐☐☐☐☐☐☐ a Process.

Fact!

About how many people live in the world today?

☐☐☐ ☐☐☐☐☐☐

Regions of the World

Regions of the World

Geographers divide the world into regions for study. Each region has something about it that makes it unique and different from other regions. The map on the next page shows the major regions of the world. Explore this map to begin your study of geography.

How to Use the Map

The map on the next page is a special kind of map. It has transparent overlays that show different features and regions of the world. You can look at each overlay separately, or you can look at them together to see how they are connected. Just follow the steps below.

❶ **The Base Map** Start by lifting up all the transparent overlays and looking at only the base map. It shows the world's major oceans and seven continents, or large landmasses. What are the names of these continents? Where is each one located? Which oceans border each continent?

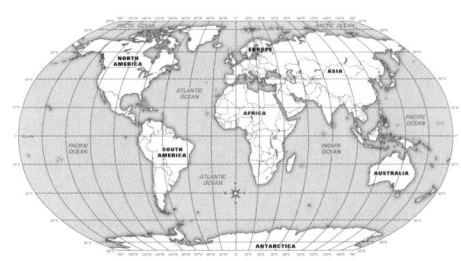

❷ **The First Overlay** Cover the base map with the first transparent overlay. It shows some of the world's major physical features, like rivers and mountains. First, study the rivers. Which rivers are shown? On which continents are they located? Next, look at the mountains. What mountain ranges can you see, and where are they?

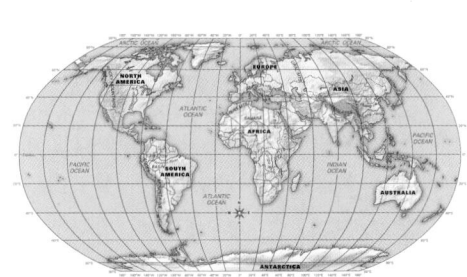

❸ **The Second Overlay** Now cover the base map and first overlay with the second overlay. It shows the major regions of the world. The name of each region is listed at the bottom. Now, put it all together. What are the five regions shown? Which continents do they include, and where are they located? What are some major mountains and rivers found in each region? What oceans surround them? Finally, where are these major world regions located in relation to one another?

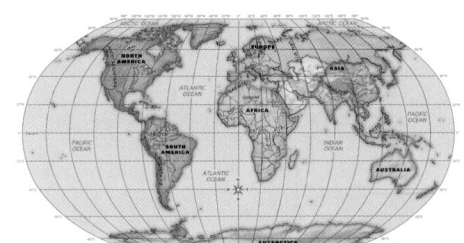

Regions of the World

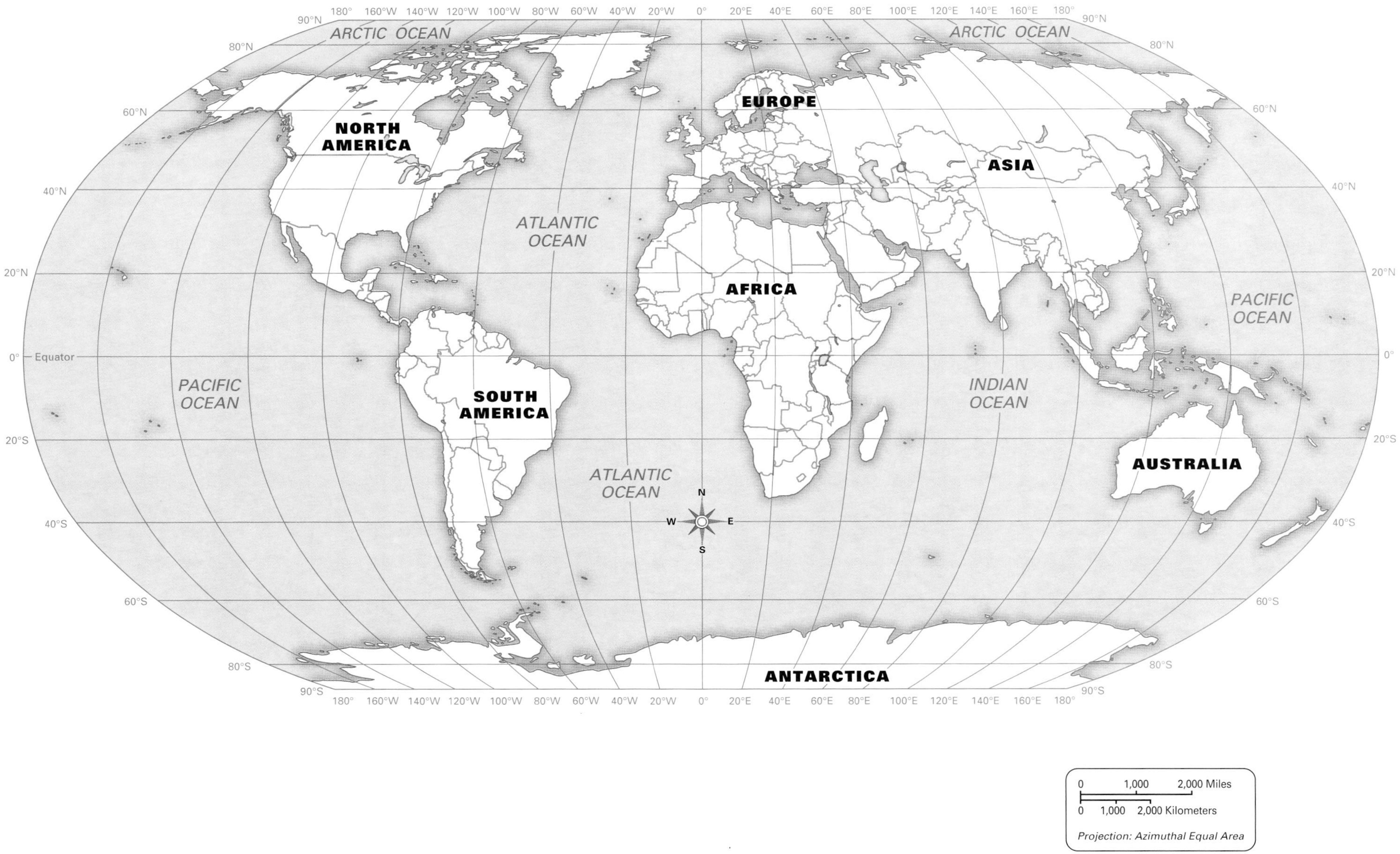

NORTH AMERICA

SOUTH AMERICA

EUROPE

ASIA

AFRICA

AUSTRALIA

ANTARCTICA

ARCTIC OCEAN

ATLANTIC OCEAN

PACIFIC OCEAN

INDIAN OCEAN

PACIFIC OCEAN

ATLANTIC OCEAN

Equator

0°

20°N

40°N

60°N

80°N

90°N

20°S

40°S

60°S

80°S

90°S

180°

160°W

140°W

120°W

100°W

80°W

60°W

40°W

20°W

0°

20°E

40°E

60°E

80°E

100°E

120°E

140°E

160°E

180°

N

E

S

W

0   1,000   2,000 Miles

0   1,000   2,000 Kilometers

Projection: Azimuthal Equal Area

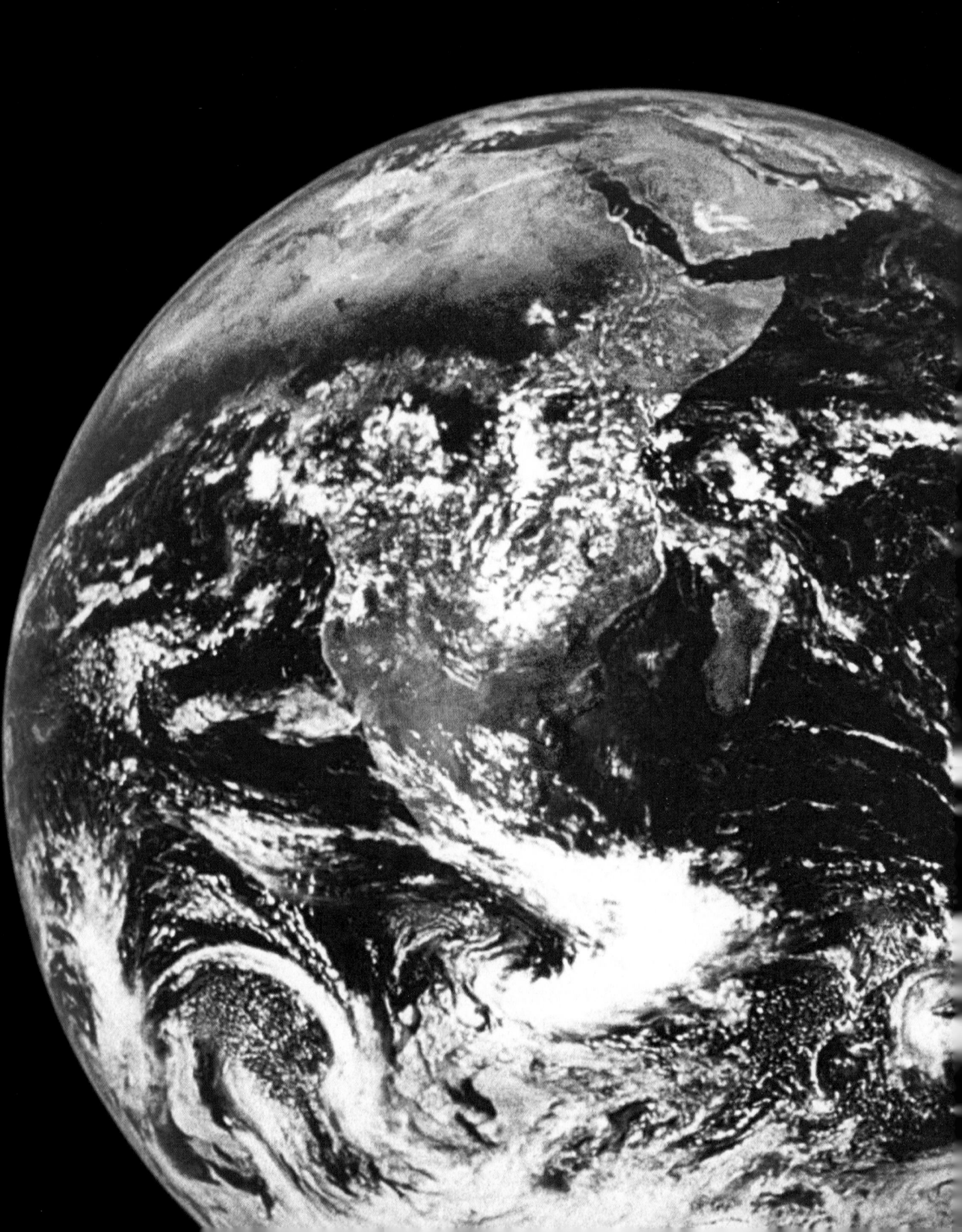

Geography and Map Skills Handbook

Contents

Throughout this textbook, you will be studying the world's people, places, and landscapes. One of the main tools you will use is the map—the primary tool of geographers. To help you begin your studies, this Geography and Map Skills Handbook explains some of the basic features of maps. For example, it explains how maps are made, how to read them, and how they can show the round surface of Earth on a flat piece of paper. This handbook will also introduce you to some of the types of maps you will study later in this book. In addition, you will learn about the different kinds of features on Earth and about how geographers use themes and elements to study the world.

✳Interactive Maps

Geography Skills With map zone geography skills, you can go online to find interactive versions of the key maps in this book. Explore these interactive maps to learn and practice important map skills and bring geography to life.

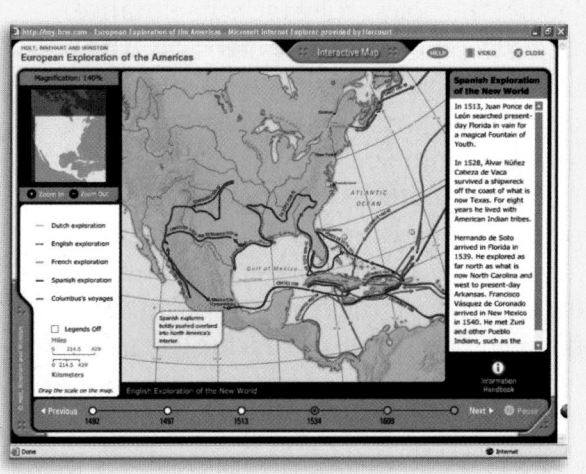

To use map zone interactive maps online:

1. Go to go.hrw.com.
2. Enter the KEYWORD shown on the interactive map.
3. Press return!

Mapping the Earth
Using Latitude and Longitude

A **globe** is a scale model of the Earth. It is useful for showing the entire Earth or studying large areas of Earth's surface.

To study the world, geographers use a pattern of imaginary lines that circles the globe in east-west and north-south directions. It is called a **grid**. The intersection of these imaginary lines helps us find places on Earth.

The east-west lines in the grid are lines of **latitude**, which you can see on the diagram. Lines of latitude are called **parallels** because they are always parallel to each other. These imaginary lines measure distance north and south of the **equator**. The equator is an imaginary line that circles the globe halfway between the North and South Poles. Parallels measure distance from the equator in **degrees**. The symbol for degrees is °. Degrees are further divided into **minutes**. The symbol for minutes is ´. There are 60 minutes in a degree. Parallels north of the equator are labeled with an N. Those south of the equator are labeled with an S.

The north-south imaginary lines are lines of **longitude**. Lines of longitude are called **meridians**. These imaginary lines pass through the poles. They measure distance east and west of the **prime meridian**. The prime meridian is an imaginary line that runs through Greenwich, England. It represents 0° longitude.

Lines of latitude range from 0°, for locations on the equator, to 90°N or 90°S, for locations at the poles. Lines of longitude range from 0° on the prime meridian to 180° on a meridian in the mid-Pacific Ocean. Meridians west of the prime meridian to 180° are labeled with a W. Those east of the prime meridian to 180° are labeled with an E. Using latitude and longitude, geographers can identify the exact location of any place on Earth.

Lines of Latitude

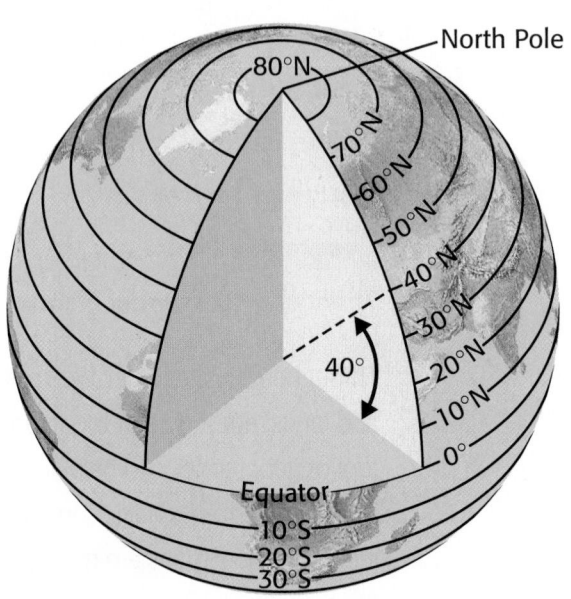

Lines of Longitude

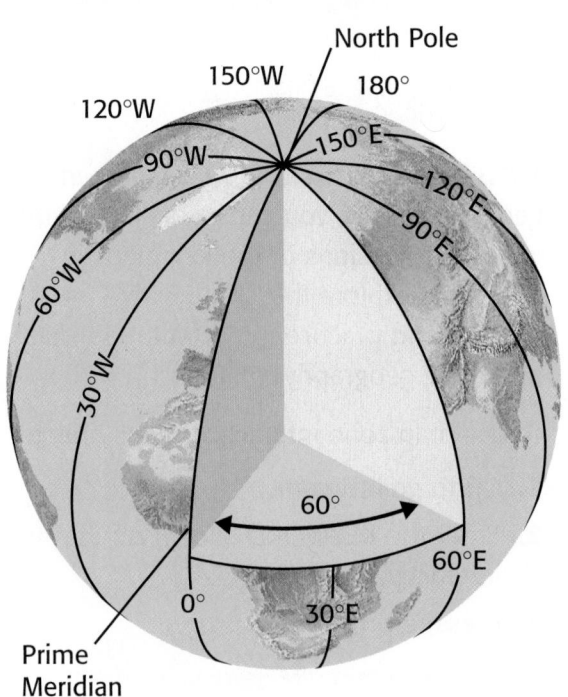

The equator divides the globe into two halves, called **hemispheres**. The half north of the equator is the Northern Hemisphere. The southern half is the Southern Hemisphere. The prime meridian and the 180° meridian divide the world into the Eastern Hemisphere and the Western Hemisphere. Look at the diagrams on this page. They show each of these four hemispheres.

Earth's land surface is divided into seven large landmasses, called **continents**. These continents are also shown on the diagrams on this page. Landmasses smaller than continents and completely surrounded by water are called **islands**.

Geographers organize Earth's water surface into major regions too. The largest is the world ocean. Geographers divide the world ocean into the Pacific Ocean, the Atlantic Ocean, the Indian Ocean, and the Arctic Ocean. Lakes and seas are smaller bodies of water.

Northern Hemisphere

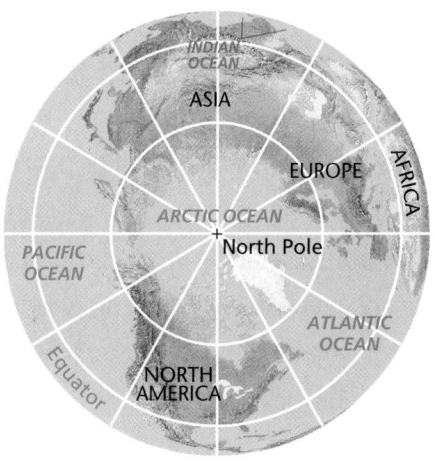

Southern Hemisphere

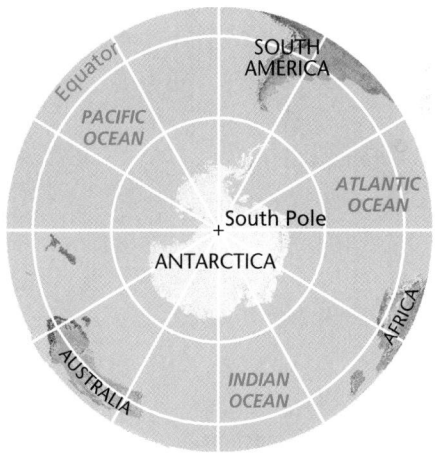

Western Hemisphere

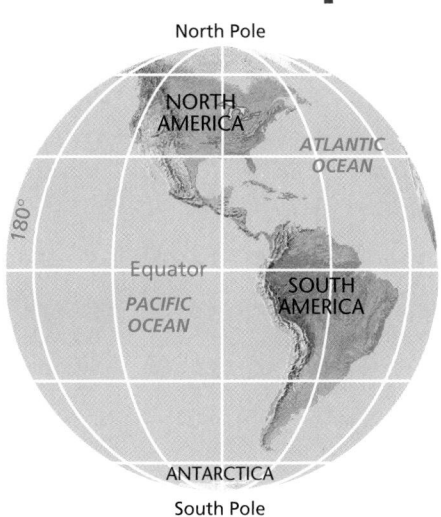

Eastern Hemisphere

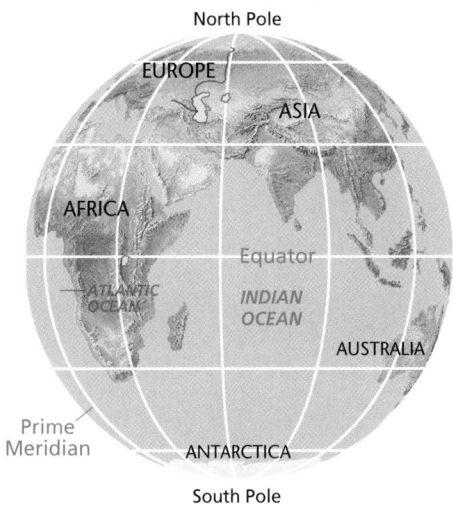

Mapmaking
Understanding Map Projections

A **map** is a flat diagram of all or part of Earth's surface. Mapmakers have created different ways of showing our round planet on flat maps. These different ways are called **map projections**. Because Earth is round, there is no way to show it accurately on a flat map. All flat maps are distorted in some way. Mapmakers must choose the type of map projection that is best for their purposes. Many map projections are one of three kinds: cylindrical, conic, or flat-plane.

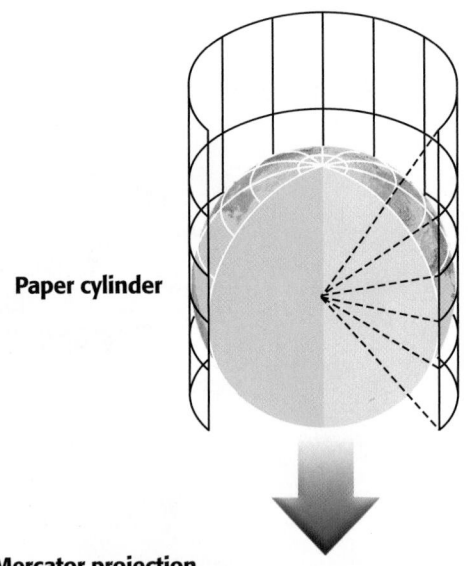

Paper cylinder

Cylindrical Projections

Cylindrical projections are based on a cylinder wrapped around the globe. The cylinder touches the globe only at the equator. The meridians are pulled apart and are parallel to each other instead of meeting at the poles. This causes landmasses near the poles to appear larger than they really are. The map below is a Mercator projection, one type of cylindrical projection. The Mercator projection is useful for navigators because it shows true direction and shape. However, it distorts the size of land areas near the poles.

Mercator projection

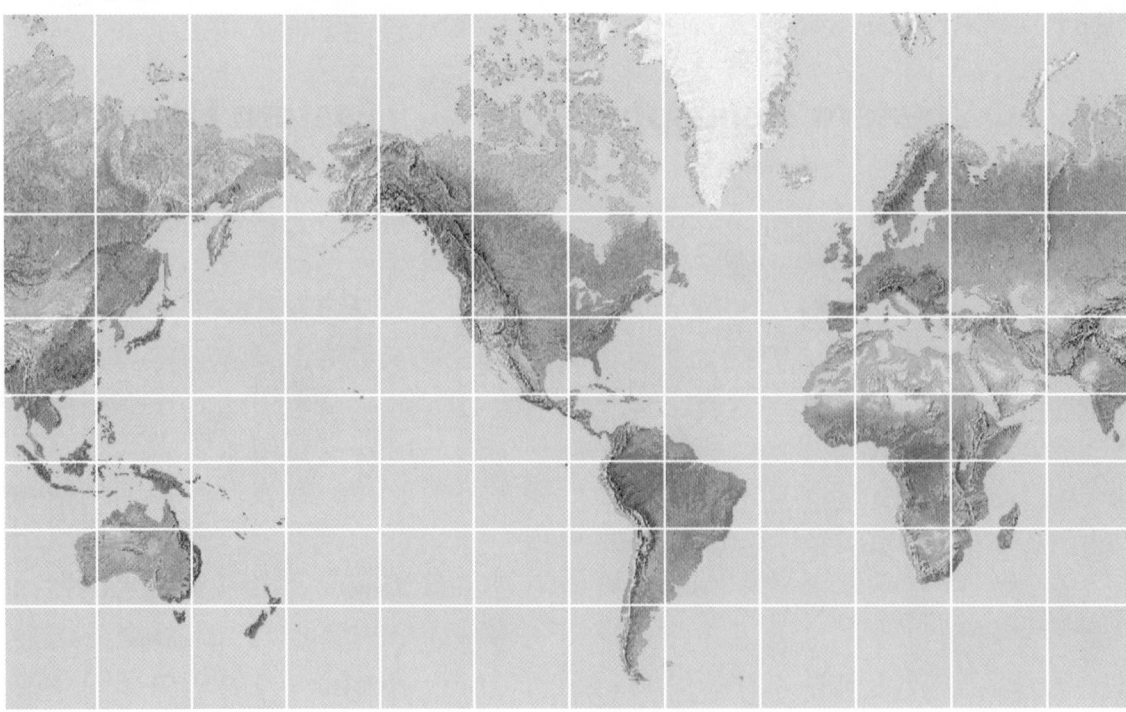

Conic Projections

Conic projections are based on a cone placed over the globe. A conic projection is most accurate along the lines of latitude where it touches the globe. It retains almost true shape and size. Conic projections are most useful for showing areas that have long east-west dimensions, such as the United States.

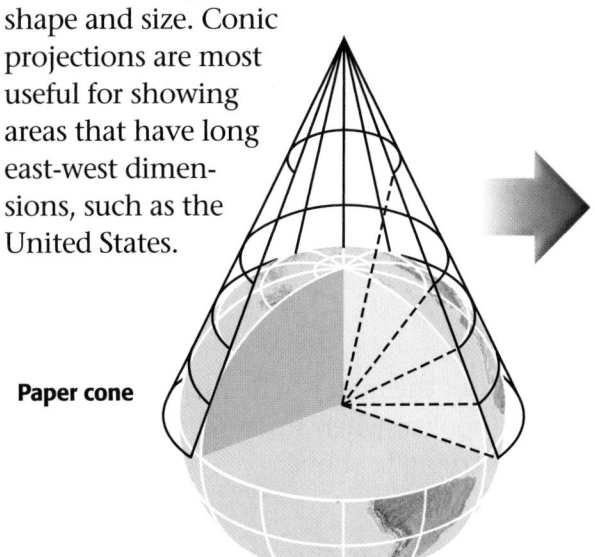

Paper cone

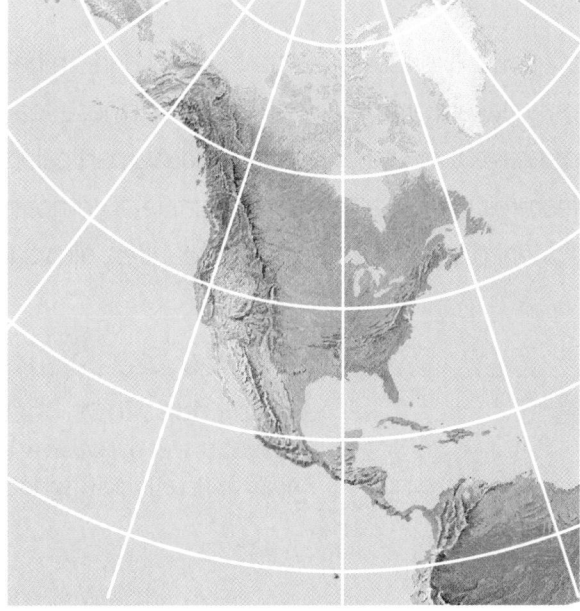

Conic projection

Flat-plane Projections

Flat-plane projections are based on a plane touching the globe at one point, such as at the North Pole or South Pole. A flat-plane projection is useful for showing true direction for airplane pilots and ship navigators. It also shows true area. However, it distorts the true shapes of landmasses.

Flat plane

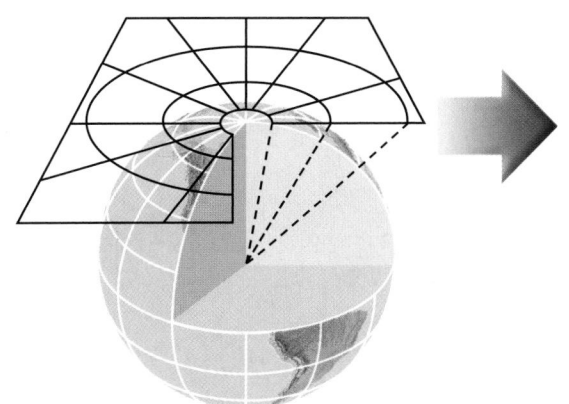

Flat-plane projection

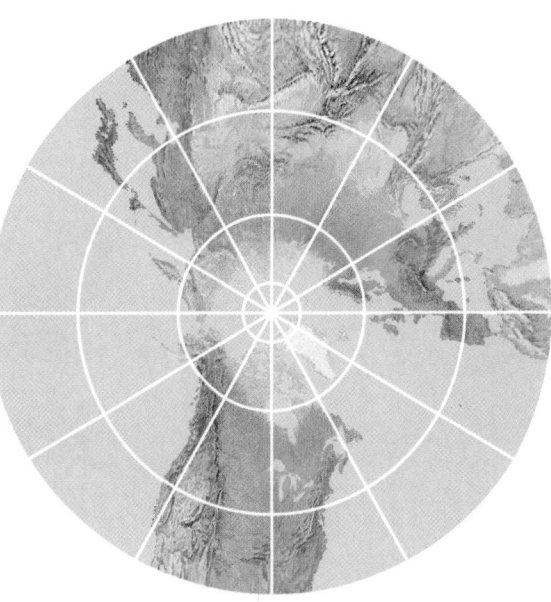

Map Essentials
How to Read a Map

Maps are like messages sent out in code. To help us translate the code, mapmakers provide certain features. These features help us understand the message they are presenting about a particular part of the world. Of these features, almost all maps have a title, a compass rose, a scale, and a legend. The map below has these four features, plus a fifth—a locator map.

❶ Title

A map's **title** shows what the subject of the map is. The map title is usually the first thing you should look at when studying a map, because it tells you what the map is trying to show.

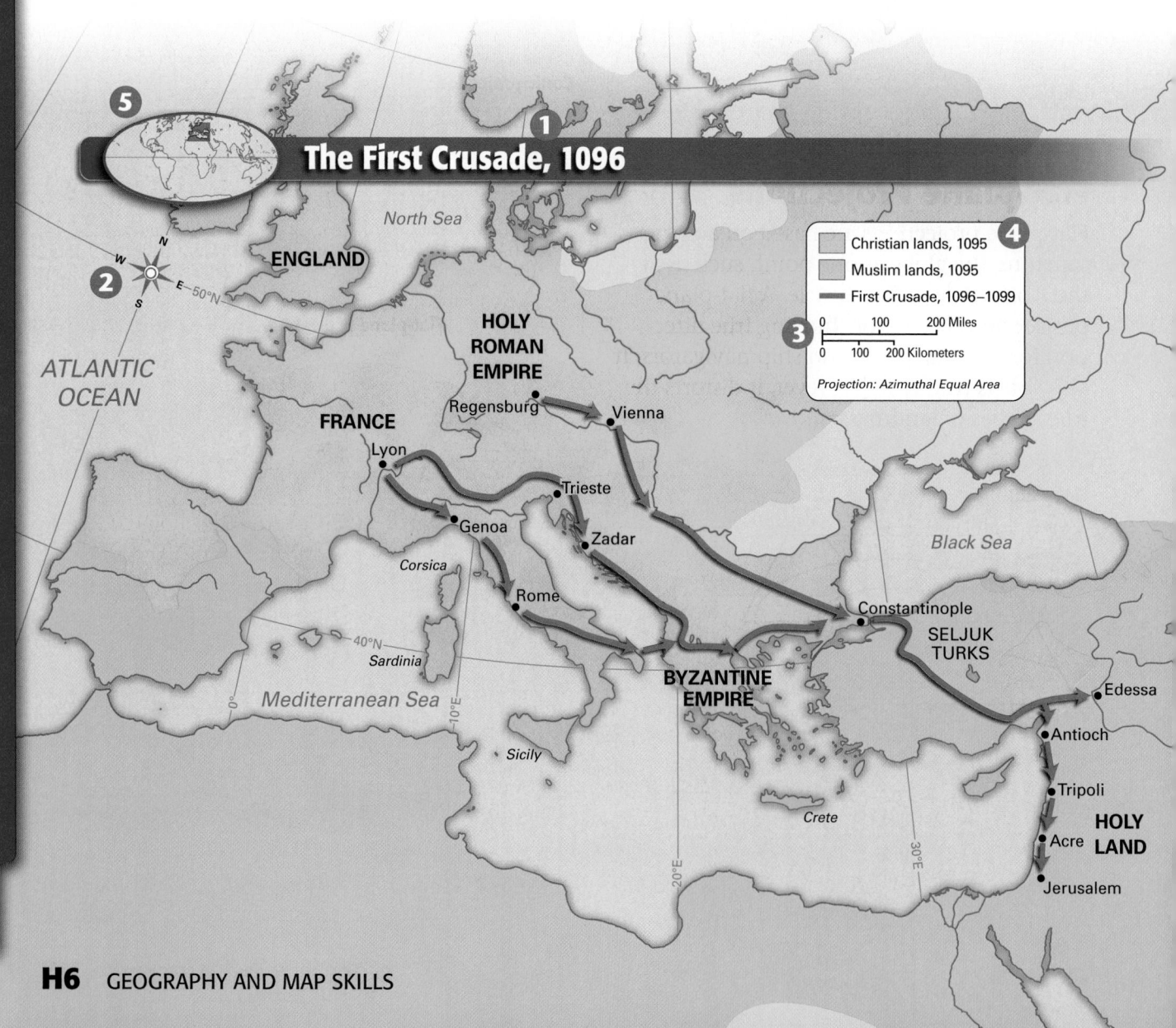

The First Crusade, 1096

North Sea

ENGLAND

ATLANTIC
OCEAN

HOLY
ROMAN
EMPIRE

FRANCE

Regensburg   Vienna

Lyon

Trieste

Genoa

Corsica

Rome

Zadar

Sardinia

Mediterranean Sea

Sicily

BYZANTINE
EMPIRE

Crete

Black Sea

Constantinople

SELJUK
TURKS

Edessa

Antioch

Tripoli

Acre   HOLY
LAND

Jerusalem

Christian lands, 1095
Muslim lands, 1095
First Crusade, 1096–1099

0   100   200 Miles
0   100   200 Kilometers

Projection: Azimuthal Equal Area

② Compass Rose

A directional indicator shows which way north, south, east, and west lie on the map. Some mapmakers use a "north arrow," which points toward the North Pole. Remember, "north" is not always at the top of a map. The way a map is drawn and the location of directions on that map depend on the perspective of the mapmaker. Most maps in this textbook indicate direction by using a compass rose. A **compass rose** has arrows that point to all four principal directions.

③ Scale

Mapmakers use scales to represent the distances between points on a map. Scales may appear on maps in several different forms. The maps in this textbook provide a **bar scale**. Scales give distances in miles and kilometers.

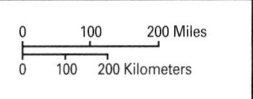

To find the distance between two points on the map, place a piece of paper so that the edge connects the two points. Mark the location of each point on the paper with a line or dot. Then, compare the distance between the two dots with the map's bar scale. The number on the top of the scale gives the distance in miles. The number on the bottom gives the distance in kilometers. Because the distances are given in large intervals, you may have to approximate the actual distance on the scale.

④ Legend

The **legend**, or key, explains what the symbols on the map represent. Point symbols are used to specify the location of things, such as cities, that do not take up much space on the map. Some legends show colors that represent certain features like empires or other regions. Other maps might have legends with symbols or colors that represent features such as roads. Legends can also show economic resources, land use, population density, and climate.

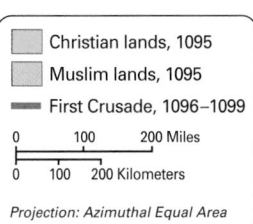

⑤ Locator Map

A **locator map** shows where in the world the area on the map is located. The area shown on the main map is shown in red on the locator map. The locator map also shows surrounding areas so the map reader can see how the information on the map relates to neighboring lands.

Working with Maps
Using Different Kinds of Maps

As you study the world's regions and countries, you will use a variety of maps. Political maps and physical maps are two of the most common types of maps you will study. In addition, you will use special-purpose maps. These maps might show climate, population, resources, ancient empires, or other topics.

Political Maps

Political maps show the major political features of a region. These features include country borders, capital cities, and other places. Political maps use different colors to represent countries, and capital cities are often shown with a special star symbol.

Caribbean South America: Political

ATLANTIC OCEAN

Barranquilla
Cartagena
Maracaibo
Caracas
Valencia
TRINIDAD AND TOBAGO
Lake Maracaibo
PANAMA
Orinoco River
VENEZUELA
Georgetown
Medellín
Paramaribo
PACIFIC OCEAN
Cayenne
GUYANA
Bogotá
FRENCH GUIANA
(FRANCE)
SURINAME
Cali
Orinoco River
COLOMBIA
0° Equator
Rio Negro
ECUADOR
Putumayo River
PERU
Amazon River

⦾ National capital
★ Other capitals
• Other cities

0   100   200 Miles
0   100   200 Kilometers
Projection: Azimuthal Equal-Area

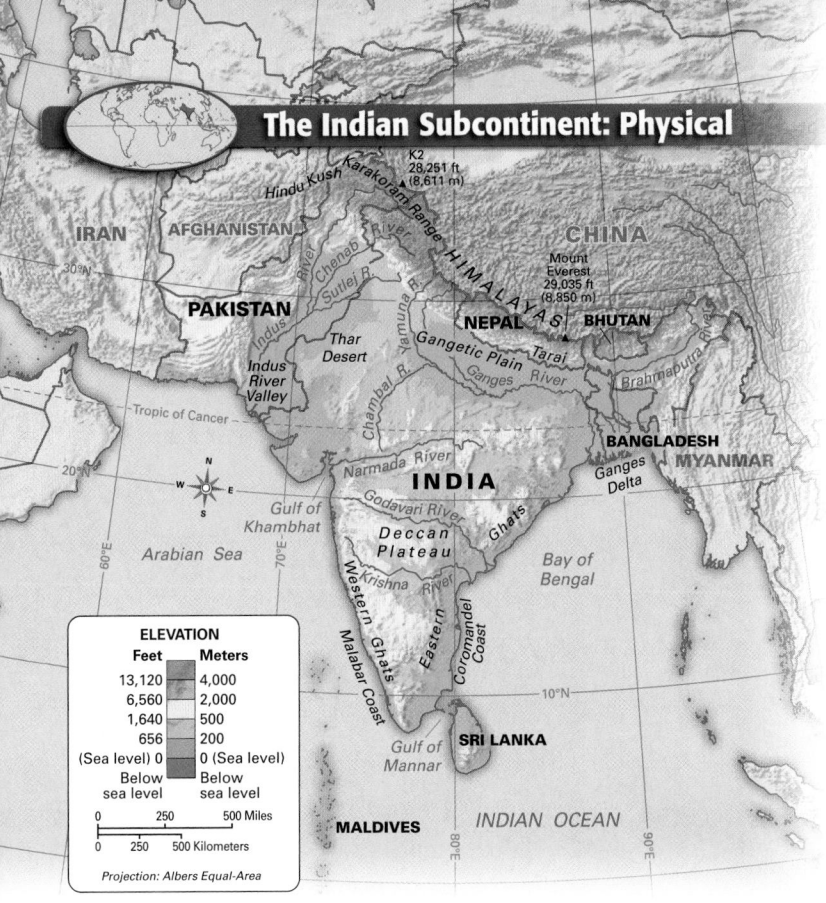

The Indian Subcontinent: Physical

ELEVATION

Feet	Meters
13,120	4,000
6,560	2,000
1,640	500
656	200
(Sea level) 0	0 (Sea level)
Below sea level	Below sea level

0   250   500 Miles
0   250   500 Kilometers

Projection: Albers Equal-Area

Physical Maps

Physical maps show the major physical features of a region. These features may include mountain ranges, rivers, oceans, islands, deserts, and plains. Often, these maps use different colors to represent different elevations of land. As a result, the map reader can easily see which areas are high elevations, like mountains, and which areas are lower.

Special-Purpose Maps

Special-purpose maps focus on one special topic, such as climate, resources, or population. These maps present information on the topic that is particularly important in the region. Depending on the type of special-purpose map, the information may be shown with different colors, arrows, dots, or other symbols.

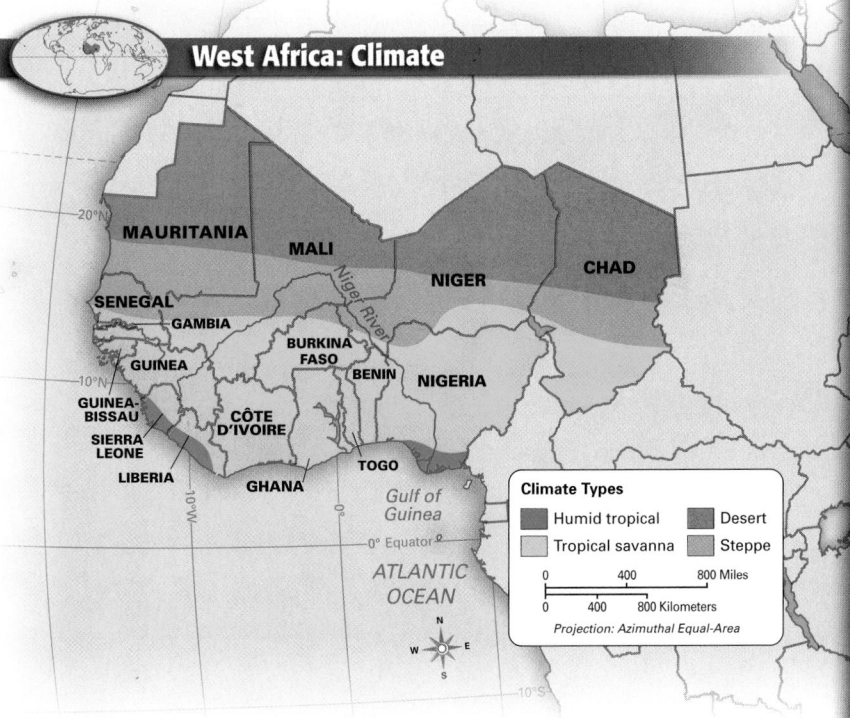

West Africa: Climate

Climate Types
- Humid tropical
- Tropical savanna
- Desert
- Steppe

0   400   800 Miles
0   400   800 Kilometers

Projection: Azimuthal Equal-Area

Using Maps in Geography The different kinds of maps in this textbook will help you study and understand geography. By working with these maps, you will see what the physical geography of places is like, where people live, and how the world has changed over time.

Geographic Dictionary

OCEAN
a large body of water

CORAL REEF
an ocean ridge made up of
skeletal remains of tiny sea animals

GULF
a large part of
the ocean that
extends into land

PENINSULA
an area of land that sticks
out into a lake or ocean

BAY
part of a large
body of water
that is smaller
than a gulf

ISLAND
an area of land
surrounded entirely
by water

ISTHMUS
a narrow piece of land
connecting two larger
land areas

DELTA
an area where a
river deposits soil
into the ocean

STRAIT
a narrow body of
water connecting two
larger bodies of water

SINKHOLE
a circular depression
formed when the roof
of a cave collapses

WETLAND
an area of land
covered by
shallow water

RIVER
a natural flow of
water that runs
through the land

LAKE
an inland body
of water

FOREST
an area of densely
wooded land

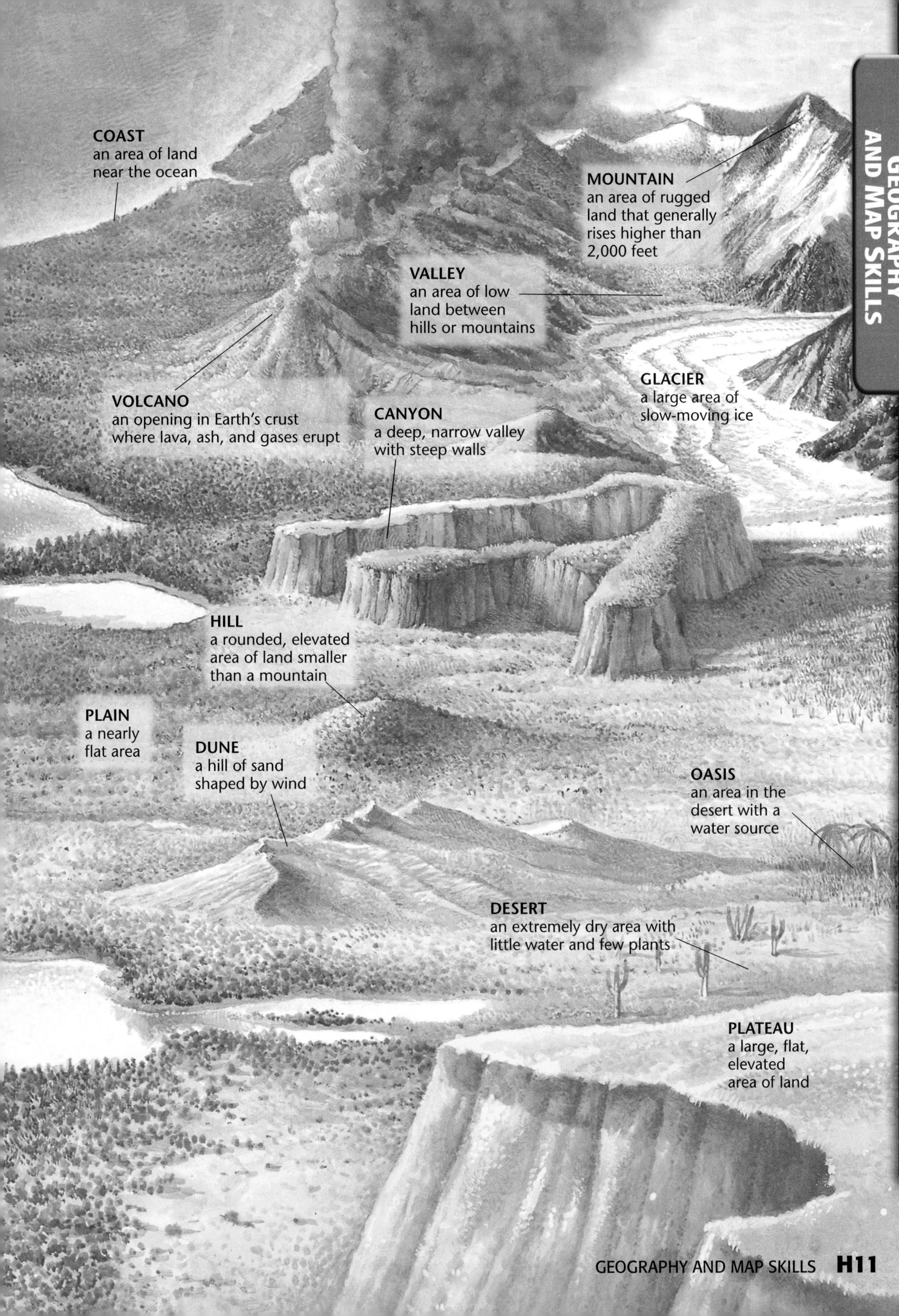

COAST
an area of land
near the ocean

MOUNTAIN
an area of rugged
land that generally
rises higher than
2,000 feet

VALLEY
an area of low
land between
hills or mountains

GLACIER
a large area of
slow-moving ice

VOLCANO
an opening in Earth's crust
where lava, ash, and gases erupt

CANYON
a deep, narrow valley
with steep walls

HILL
a rounded, elevated
area of land smaller
than a mountain

PLAIN
a nearly
flat area

DUNE
a hill of sand
shaped by wind

OASIS
an area in the
desert with a
water source

DESERT
an extremely dry area with
little water and few plants

PLATEAU
a large, flat,
elevated
area of land

Themes and Essential Elements of Geography

by Dr. Christopher L. Salter

To study the world, geographers have identified 5 key themes, 6 essential elements, and 18 geography standards.

"How should we teach and learn about geography?" Professional geographers have worked hard over the years to answer this important question.

In 1984 a group of geographers identified the 5 Themes of Geography. These themes did a wonderful job of laying the groundwork for good classroom geography. Teachers used the 5 Themes in class, and geographers taught workshops on how to apply them in the world.

By the early 1990s, however, some geographers felt the 5 Themes were too broad. They created the 18 Geography Standards and the 6 Essential Elements. The 18 Geography Standards include more detailed information about what geography is, and the 6 Essential Elements are like a bridge between the 5 Themes and 18 Standards.

Look at the chart to the right. It shows how each of the 5 Themes connects to the Essential Elements and Standards. For example, the theme of Location is related to The World in Spatial Terms and the first three Standards. Study the chart carefully to see how the other themes, elements, and Standards are related.

The last Essential Element and the last two Standards cover The Uses of Geography. These key parts of geography were not covered by the 5 Themes. They will help you see how geography has influenced the past, present, and future.

5 Themes of Geography

Location The theme of location describes where something is.

Place Place describes the features that make a site unique.

Regions Regions are areas that share common characteristics.

Movement This theme looks at how and why people and things move.

Human-Environment Interaction People interact with their environment in many ways.

6 Essential Elements

18 Geography Standards

I. The World in Spatial Terms

1. How to use maps and other tools
2. How to use mental maps to organize information
3. How to analyze the spatial organization of people, places, and environments

II. Places and Regions

4. The physical and human characteristics of places
5. How people create regions to interpret Earth
6. How culture and experience influence people's perceptions of places and regions

III. Physical Systems

7. The physical processes that shape Earth's surface
8. The distribution of ecosystems on Earth

IV. Human Systems

9. The characteristics, distribution, and migration of human populations
10. The complexity of Earth's cultural mosaics
11. The patterns and networks of economic interdependence on Earth
12. The patterns of human settlement
13. The forces of cooperation and conflict

V. Environment and Society

14. How human actions modify the physical environment
15. How physical systems affect human systems
16. The distribution and meaning of resources

VI. The Uses of Geography

17. How to apply geography to interpret the past
18. How to apply geography to interpret the present and plan for the future

Become an Active Reader

by Dr. Kylene Beers

Did you ever think you would begin reading your social studies book by reading about *reading*? Actually, it makes better sense than you might think. You would probably make sure you knew some soccer skills and strategies before playing in a game. Similarly, you need to know something about reading skills and strategies before reading your social studies book. In other words, you need to make sure you know what-ever you need to know in order to read this book successfully.

Tip #1

Read Everything on the Page!

You can't follow the directions on the cake-mix box if you don't know where the directions are! Cake-mix boxes always have directions on them telling you how many eggs to add or how long to bake the cake. But, if you can't find that information, it doesn't matter that it is there.

Likewise, this book is filled with information that will help you understand what you are reading. If you don't study that information, however, it might as well not be there. Let's take a look at some of the places where you'll find important information in this book.

The Chapter Opener
The chapter opener gives you a brief overview of what you will learn in the chapter. You can use this information to prepare to read the chapter.

The Section Openers
Before you begin to read each section, preview the information under What You Will Learn. There you'll find the main ideas of the section and key terms that are important in it. Knowing what you are looking for before you start reading can improve your understanding.

Boldfaced Words
Those words are important and are defined somewhere on the page where they appear—either right there in the sentence or over in the side margin.

Maps, Charts, and Artwork
These things are not there just to take up space or look good! Study them and read the information beside them. It will help you understand the information in the chapter.

Questions at the End of Sections
At the end of each section, you will find questions that will help you decide whether you need to go back and re-read any parts before moving on. If you can't answer a question, that is your cue to go back and re-read.

Questions at the End of the Chapter
Answer the questions at the end of each chapter, even if your teacher doesn't ask you to. These questions are there to help you figure out what you need to review.

Tip #2

Use the Reading Skills and Strategies in Your Textbook

Good readers use a number of skills and strategies to make sure they understand what they are reading. In this textbook you will find help with important reading skills and strategies such as "Using Prior Knowledge," and "Understanding Main Ideas."

We teach the reading skills and strategies in several ways. Use these activities and lessons and you will become a better reader.

- First, on the opening page of every chapter we identify and explain the reading skill or strategy you will focus on as you work through the chapter. In fact, these activities are called "Focus on Reading."

- Second, as you can see in the example at right, we tell you where to go for more help. The back of the book has a reading handbook with a full-page practice lesson to match the reading skill or strategy in every chapter.

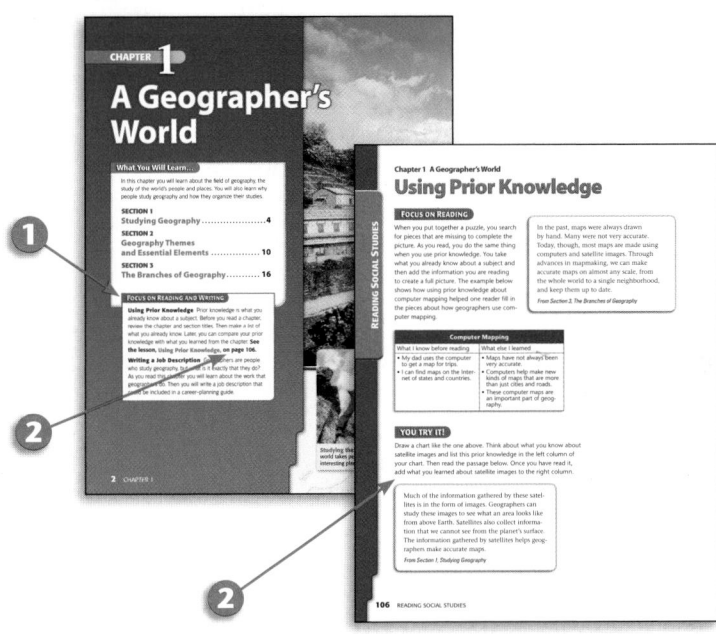

or British citizens migrated to ...lia in search of cheap land.

World Population Trends

In the last 200 years Earth's population has exploded. For thousands of years world population growth was low and relatively steady. About 2,000 years ago, the world had some 300 million people. By 1800 there were almost 1 billion people. Since 1800, better health care and improved food production have supported tremendous population growth. In 1999 the world's population passed 6 billion people.

Population trends are an important part of the study of the world's people. Two important population trends are clear

FOCUS ON READING

What is the main idea of this paragraph? What facts are used to support that idea?

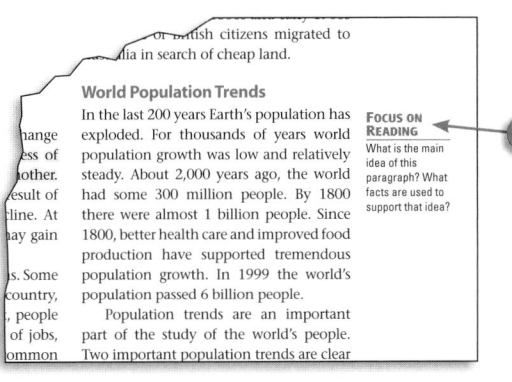

- Finally, we provide another practice activity in the Chapter Review at the end of every chapter. That activity gives you one more chance to make sure you know how to use the reading skill or strategy.

- Third, we give you short practice activities and examples as you read the chapter. These activities and examples show up in the margin of your book. Again, look for the words, "Focus on Reading."

10. Organizing Information Practice or... information by creating a graphic organizer for Section 3. Use the main ideas on the first page of the section for your large circles. Then write the subtopics under each main idea. Finally, identify supporting details for each subtopic.

15. ...
    dens...
16. Which
    people
    square

FOCUS ON READING AND WRITING

Understanding Main Ideas *Read the paragraph below carefully, then write out the main idea of the paragraph.*

11. The ancient Greeks were the first to practice democracy. Since then many countries have adopted democratic government. The United Kingdom, South Korea, and Ghana all practice democracy. Democracy is the most widely used government in the world today.

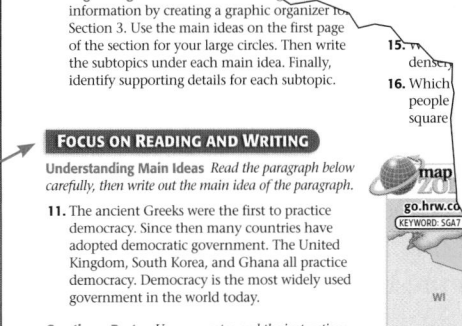

Tip #3

Pay Attention to Vocabulary

It is no fun to read something when you don't know what the words mean, but you can't learn new words if you only use or read the words you already know. In this book, we know we have probably used some words you don't know. But, we have followed a pattern as we have used more difficult words.

- First, at the beginning of each section you will find a list of key terms that you will need to know. Be on the lookout for those words as you read through the section. You will find that we have defined those words right there in the paragraph where they are used. Look for a word that is in boldface with its definition highlighted in yellow.

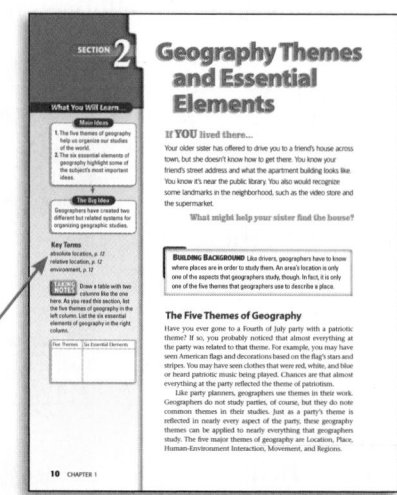

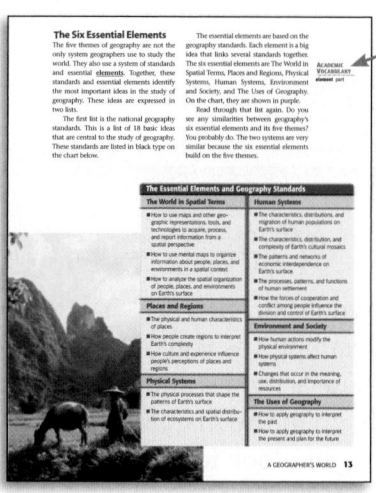

- Second, when we use a word that is important in all classes, not just social studies, we define it in the margin under the heading Academic Vocabulary. You will run into these academic words in other textbooks, so you should learn what they mean while reading this book.

Tip #4

Read Like a Skilled Reader

You won't be able to climb to the top of Mount Everest if you do not train! If you want to make it to the top of Mount Everest then you must start training to climb that huge mountain.

Training is also necessary to become a good reader. You will never get better at reading your social studies book—or any book for that matter—unless you spend some time thinking about how to be a better reader.

Skilled readers do the following:

1. They preview what they are supposed to read before they actually begin reading. When previewing, they look for vocabulary words, titles of sections, information in the margin, or maps or charts they should study.

2. They get ready to take some notes while reading by dividing their notebook paper into two parts. They title one side "Notes from the Chapter" and the other side "Questions or Comments I Have."

3. As they read, they complete their notes.

4. They read like **active readers**. The Active Reading list below shows you what that means.

5. Finally, they use clues in the text to help them figure out where the text is going. The best clues are called signal words. These are words that help you identify chronological order, causes and effects, or comparisons and contrasts.

Chronological Order Signal Words: *first, second, third, before, after, later, next, following that, earlier, subsequently, finally*

Cause and Effect Signal Words: *because of, due to, as a result of, the reason for, therefore, consequently, so, basis for*

Comparison/Contrast Signal Words: *likewise, also, as well as, similarly, on the other hand*

Active Reading

There are three ways to read a book: You can be a turn-the-pages-no-matter-what type of reader. These readers just keep on turning pages whether or not they understand what they are reading. Or, you can be a stop-watch-and-listen kind of reader. These readers know that if they wait long enough, someone will tell them what they need to know. Or, you can be an active reader. These readers know that it is up to them to figure out what the text means. Active readers do the following as they read:

Predict what will happen next based on what has already happened. When your predictions don't match what happens in the text, re-read the confusing parts.

Question what is happening as you read. Constantly ask yourself why things have happened, what things mean, and what caused certain events. Jot down notes about the questions you can't answer.

Summarize what you are reading frequently. Do not try to summarize the entire chapter! Read a bit and then summarize it. Then read on.

Connect what is happening in the section you're reading to what you have already read.

Clarify your understanding. Be sure that you understand what you are reading by stopping occasionally to ask yourself whether you are confused by anything. Sometimes you might need to re-read to clarify. Other times you might need to read further and collect more information before you can understand. Still other times you might need to ask the teacher to help you with what is confusing you.

Visualize what is happening in the text. In other words, try to see the events or places in your mind. It might help you to draw maps, make charts, or jot down notes about what you are reading as you try to visualize the action in the text.

Social Studies Words

As you read this textbook, you will be more successful if you learn the meanings of the words on this page. You will come across these words many times in your social studies classes, like geography and history. Read through these words now to become familiar with them before you begin your studies.

Social Studies Words

WORDS ABOUT TIME

AD	refers to dates after the birth of Jesus
BC	refers to dates before Jesus's birth
BCE	refers to dates before Jesus's birth, stands for "before the common era"
CE	refers to dates after Jesus's birth, stands for "common era"
century	a period of 100 years
decade	a period of 10 years
era	a period of time
millennium	a period of 1,000 years

WORDS ABOUT THE WORLD

climate	the weather conditions in a certain area over a long period of time
geography	the study of the world's people, places, and landscapes
physical features	features on Earth's surface, such as mountains and rivers
region	an area with one or more features that make it different from surrounding areas
resources	materials found on Earth that people need and value

WORDS ABOUT PEOPLE

anthropology	the study of people and cultures
archaeology	the study of the past based on what people left behind
citizen	a person who lives under the control of a government
civilization	the way of life of people in a particular place or time
culture	the knowledge, beliefs, customs, and values of a group of people
custom	a repeated practice or tradition
economics	the study of the production and use of goods and services
economy	any system in which people make and exchange goods and services
government	the body of officials and groups that run an area
history	the study of the past
politics	the process of running a government
religion	a system of beliefs in one or more gods or spirits
society	a group of people who share common traditions
trade	the exchange of goods or services

Academic Words

What are academic words? They are important words used in all of your classes, not just social studies. You will see these words in other textbooks, so you should learn what they mean while reading this book. Review this list now. You will use these words again in the chapters of this book.

Academic Words

abstract	expressing a quality or idea without reference to an actual thing
affect	to change or influence
agreement	a decision reached by two or more people or groups
aspects	parts
cause	to make something happen
circumstances	conditions that influence an event or activity
concrete	specific, real
consequences	the effects of a particular event or events
contemporary	modern
criteria	rules for defining
development	the process of growing or improving
distinct	clearly different and separate
distribute	to divide among a group of people
effect	the results of an action or decision
efficient	productive and not wasteful
element	part
establish	to set up or create
execute	to perform, carry out
factor	cause
features	characteristics
function	use or purpose
impact	effect, result
implement	to put in place
implications	consequences
incentive	something that leads people to follow a certain course of action
influence	change, or have an effect on
innovation	a new idea or way of doing something
method	a way of doing something
motive	a reason for doing something
neutral	unbiased, not favoring either side in a conflict
policy	rule, course of action
primary	main, most important
procedure	a series of steps taken to accomplish a task
process	a series of steps by which a task is accomplished
purpose	the reason something is done
reaction	a response to something
role	a part or function
structure	the way something is set up or organized
traditional	customary, time-honored
values	ideas that people hold dear and try to live by
vary	to be different

Multiple Choice

A multiple-choice test item is a question or an incomplete statement with several answer choices. To answer a multiple-choice test item, select the choice that best answers the question or that best completes the statement.

Learn

Use these strategies to answer multiple-choice test items:

1 Carefully read the question or incomplete statement.

2 Look for words that affect the meaning, such as *all, always, best, every, most, never, not,* or *only.* For example, in Item 1 to the right, the word *all* tells you to look for the answer in which all three choices are correct.

3 Read *all* the choices before selecting an answer—even if the first choice seems right.

4 In your mind, cross off any of the answer choices that you know for certain are wrong.

5 Consider the choices that are left and select the *best* answer. If you are not sure, select the choice that makes the most sense.

Read the questions and write the letter of the best response.

1 Which of the following are *all* physical features of geography?

   A landforms, climates, people
   B landforms, climates, soils
   C landscapes, climates, plants
   D landscapes, communities, soils

2 A region is an area that has

   A one or more common features.
   B no people living in it.
   C few physical features.
   D set physical boundaries.

Practice

Read the questions and write the letter of the best response.

1 Which of the following is part of the study of human geography?

   A bodies of water
   B communities
   C landforms
   D plants

2 The economy of North Korea is *best* described as a

   A command economy.
   B developed economy.
   C market economy.
   D traditional economy.

Primary Sources

Primary sources are materials, often called documents, created by people who lived during the times you are reading about. Examples of primary sources include text documents, such as letters and diaries, and visual documents, such as photographs.

Learn

Use these strategies to answer test questions about primary sources:

1 Note the document's title and source line. This information can tell you the document's author, date, and purpose.

2 Skim the document. Get an idea of its main focus.

3 Read the question about the document. Note what information you are being asked to find.

4 Read or examine the document carefully. As you do, identify the main idea and key details.

5 Compare the question and answer choices to the document. Look for similar words. Then read between the lines. Use your critical-thinking skills to draw conclusions.

6 Review the question and select the best answer.

Read the passage below. Use the passage to select the best answer to the question that follows.

Geography for Life

"Geography is a field of study that enables us to find answers to questions about the world around us—about where things are and how and why they got there…With a strong grasp of geography, people are better equipped to solve issues at not only the local level but also the global level."

— from *Geography for Life*, by the Geography Education Standards Project

1 Which statement below *best* summarizes the main idea of the above passage?

A Geography helps people to read and make maps.

B Geography helps people to get where they are going.

C Geography helps people to understand the world better and to solve problems.

D Geography helps people explore Earth.

Practice

Read the passage from the primary source, "The Charter of the United Nations," in Chapter 4. Use the passage to answer the following questions.

1 What does the passage state is a central goal of the United Nations?

A democracy

B peace

C power

D war

2 Based on the passage, why might the UN send troops into a region?

A to punish a country

B to conquer a country

C to obtain valuable resources

D to protect a member country

Charts and Graphs

Charts and graphs are tables or drawings that present and organize information or data. Some standardized tests include questions about charts and graphs. These questions require you to interpret the information or data in the chart or graph to answer the question.

Learn

Use these strategies to answer test questions about charts and graphs:

1 Read the title of the chart or graph. Identify the subject and purpose of the information shown.

2 Read all the other labels. Note the types of information the chart or graph is showing and how the information is organized.

3 Analyze the information or data. Look for patterns, changes over time, and similarities or differences. For example, in the graph at right, world population growth rises dramatically after 1900.

4 Read the question carefully. Note key words in the question.

5 Review the chart or graph to find the correct answer.

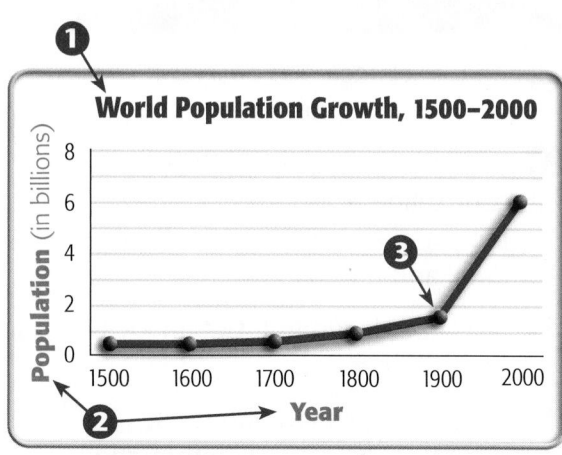

World Population Growth, 1500–2000

Source: *Atlas of World Population History*

1 Based on the graph above, during which period did the world population <u>increase</u> the <u>most</u>?

A 1600 to 1700

B 1700 to 1800

C 1800 to 1900

D 1900 to 2000

Practice

Examine the chart at right. Use the chart to answer the question below.

1 Which country in the Ring of Fire had two major volcanic eruptions?

A Colombia

B Indonesia

C Philippines

D United States

THE WORLD ALMANAC Facts about the World — **Major Eruptions in the Ring of Fire**

Volcano	Year
Tambora, Indonesia	1815
Krakatau, Indonesia	1883
Mount Saint Helens, United States	1980
Nevado del Ruiz, Colombia	1985
Mount Pinatubo, Philippines	1991

Maps

Standardized tests may include questions that refer to information in maps. These maps might show political features such as cities and states, physical features such as mountains and plains, or information such as climate, land use, or settlement patterns.

Learn

Use these strategies to answer questions about maps.

1 Read the map title to identify the map's subject and purpose. The map below shows levels of government freedom around the world.

2 Study the legend. It explains information in the map, such as what different colors or symbols mean.

3 Note the map's direction and scale. The scale shows the distance between points in the map.

4 Examine the map closely. Read all the labels and study the other information, such as colors, borders, or symbols.

5 Read the question about the map.

6 Review the map to find the answer.

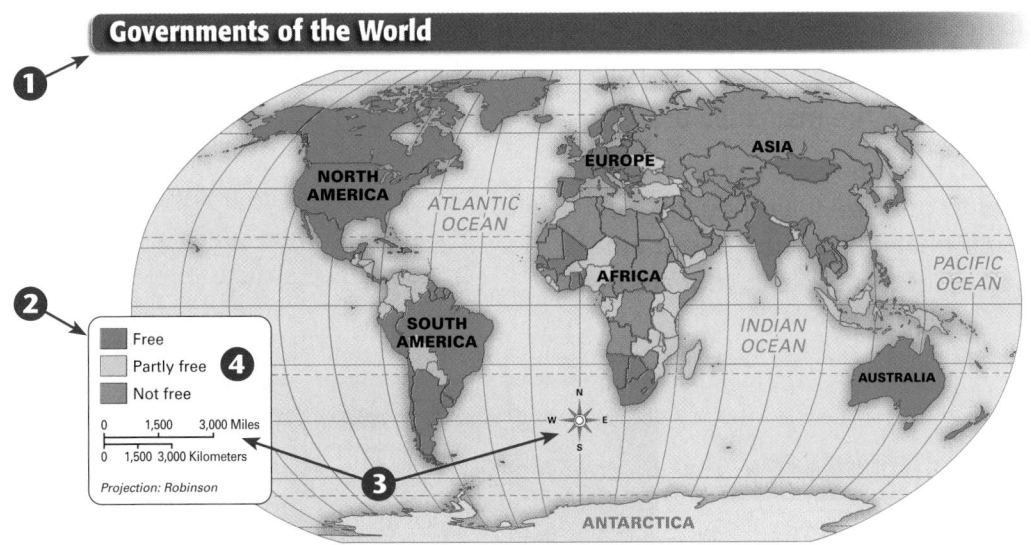

Governments of the World

Source: *Freedom House*

Practice

Examine the map above. Use the information in the map to answer the following questions.

1 Which two continents have the least government freedom?
- **A** Africa and Asia
- **B** Africa and Europe
- **C** Australia and Europe
- **D** Europe and Asia

2 The continents with the most freedom are Australia and
- **A** Africa.
- **B** Europe.
- **C** North America.
- **D** South America.

Extended Response

Extended response questions usually require you to examine a document, such as a letter, chart, or map. You then use the information in the document to write an extended answer, often a paragraph or more in length.

Learn

Use these strategies to answer extended response questions:

1 Read the directions and question carefully to determine the purpose of your answer. For example, are you to explain, identify causes, summarize, or compare? To help determine the purpose, look for key words such as *compare, contrast, describe, discuss, explain, interpret, predict,* or *summarize.*

2 Read the title of the document. Identify its subject and purpose.

3 Study the document carefully. Read all the text. Identify the main idea or focus.

4 If allowed, make notes on another sheet of paper to organize your thoughts. Jot down information from the document that you want to include in your answer.

5 Use the question to create a topic sentence. For example, for the practice question below, a topic sentence might be, "Earth's tilt and revolution cause the seasons to change at about the same time each year in the Northern Hemisphere."

6 Create an outline or graphic organizer to help organize your main points. Review the document to find details or examples to support each point.

7 Write your answer in complete sentences. Start with your topic sentence. Then refer to your outline or organizer as you write. Be sure to include details or examples from the document.

8 Last, proofread your answer. Check for correct grammar, spelling, punctuation, and sentence structure.

Practice

Read question 1 and write your own well-constructed extended response.

1 **Extended Response** Use the diagram to explain the change of the seasons in the Northern Hemisphere. Provide an explanation for each season—winter, spring, summer, and fall.

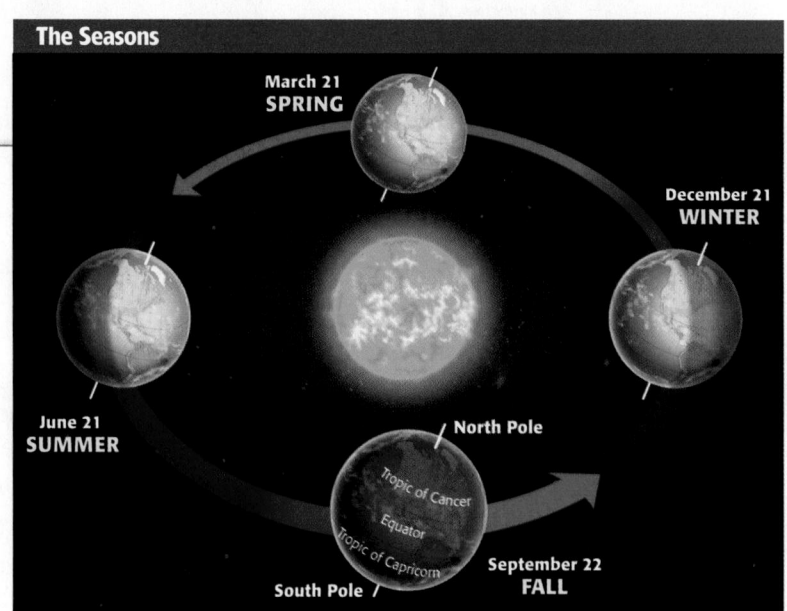

The Seasons

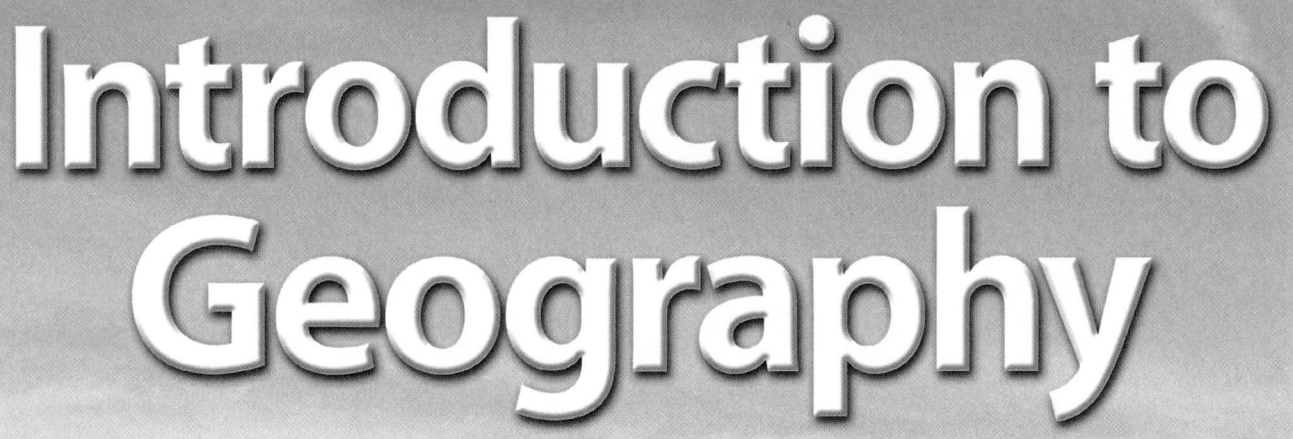

Introduction to Geography

Deserts

Huge deserts, such as the Sahara in North Africa, are visible from space and appear yellow and brown.

Oceans

About 71 percent of Earth's surface is covered by vast amounts of salt water, which form the world's oceans.

Introduction to Geography

Explore the Satellite Image
Human-made machines that orbit Earth, called satellites, send back images of our planet like this one. What can you learn about Earth from studying this satellite image?

Frozen Lands

Earth's icy poles are frozen year-round and appear a brilliant white from space. These frozen lands contain much of Earth's freshwater.

665.00'

A Geographer's World

What You Will Learn...

In this chapter you will learn about the field of geography, the study of the world's people and places. You will also learn why people study geography and how they organize their studies.

FOCUS ON READING AND WRITING

Using Prior Knowledge Prior knowledge is what you already know about a subject. Before you read a chapter, review the chapter and section titles. Then make a list of what you already know. Later, you can compare your prior knowledge with what you learned from the chapter. **See the lesson, Using Prior Knowledge, on page R2.**

Writing a Job Description Geographers are people who study geography, but what is it exactly that they do? As you read this chapter you will learn about the work that geographers do. Then you will write a job description that could be included in a career-planning guide.

Studying the World Exploring the world takes people to exciting and interesting places.

This village is in the country of Nepal. It rests high in the Himalayas, the highest mountains in the world.

What is the land around the village like? How can you tell that people live in this area?

HOLT

Geography's Impact
video series
Watch the video to understand the impact of studying geography.

Human Geography Geography is also the study of people. It asks where people live, what they eat, what they wear, and even what kinds of animals they keep.

Physical Geography Geography is the study of the world's land features, such as this windswept rock formation in Arizona.

3

Studying Geography

What You Will Learn...

Main Ideas

1. Geography is the study of the world, its people, and the landscapes they create.
2. Geographers look at the world in many different ways.
3. Maps and other tools help geographers study the planet.

The Big Idea

The study of geography and the use of geographic tools helps us view the world in new ways.

Key Terms

geography, *p. 4*
landscape, *p. 4*
social science, *p. 5*
region, *p. 6*
map, *p. 8*
globe, *p. 8*

TAKING NOTES Draw a large circle like the one below in your notebook. As you read this section, write a definition of geography at the top of the circle. Below that, list details about what geographers do.

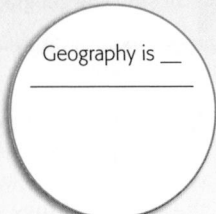

Geography is __

If **YOU** lived there...

You have just moved to Miami, Florida, from your old home in Pennsylvania. Everything seems very different—from the weather and the trees to the way people dress and talk. Even the streets and buildings look different. One day you get an e-mail from a friend at your old school. "What's it like living there?" he asks.

How will you describe your new home?

BUILDING BACKGROUND Often, when you are telling someone about a place they have never been, what you are describing is the place's geography. What the place looks like, what kind of weather it has, and how people live there are all parts of its geography.

What Is Geography?

Think about the place where you live. What does the land look like? Are there tall mountains nearby, or is the land so flat that you can see for miles? Is the ground covered with bright green grass and trees, or is the area part of a sandy desert?

Now think about the weather in your area. What is it like? Does it get really hot in the summer? Do you see snow every winter? How much does it rain? Do tornadoes ever strike?

Finally, think about the people who live in your town or city. Do they live mostly in apartments or houses? Do most people own cars, or do they get around town on buses or trains? What kinds of jobs do adults in your town have? Were most of the people you know born in your town, or did they move there?

The things that you have been thinking about are part of your area's geography. **Geography** is the study of the world, its people, and the landscapes they create. To a geographer, a place's **landscape** is all the human and physical features that make it unique. When they study the world's landscapes, geographers ask questions much like the ones you just asked yourself.

Geography as a Science

Many of the questions that geographers ask deal with how the world works. They want to know what causes mountains to form and what creates tornadoes. To answer questions like these, geographers have to think and act like scientists.

As scientists, geographers look at data, or information, that they gather about places. Gathering data can sometimes lead geographers to fascinating places. They might have to crawl deep into caves or climb tall mountains to make observations and take measurements. At other times, geographers study sets of images collected by satellites orbiting high above Earth.

However geographers gather their data, they have to study it carefully. Like other scientists, geographers must examine their findings in great detail before they can learn what all the information means.

Geography as a Social Science

Not everything that geographers study can be measured in numbers, however. Some geographers study people and their lives. For example, they may ask why countries change their governments or why people in a place speak a certain language. This kind of information cannot be measured.

Because it deals with people and how they live, geography is sometimes called a social science. A **social science** is a field that studies people and the relationships among them.

The geographers who study people do not dig in caves or climb mountains. Instead, they visit places and talk to the people who live there. They want to learn about people's lives and communities.

READING CHECK **Analyzing** In what ways is geography both a science and a social science?

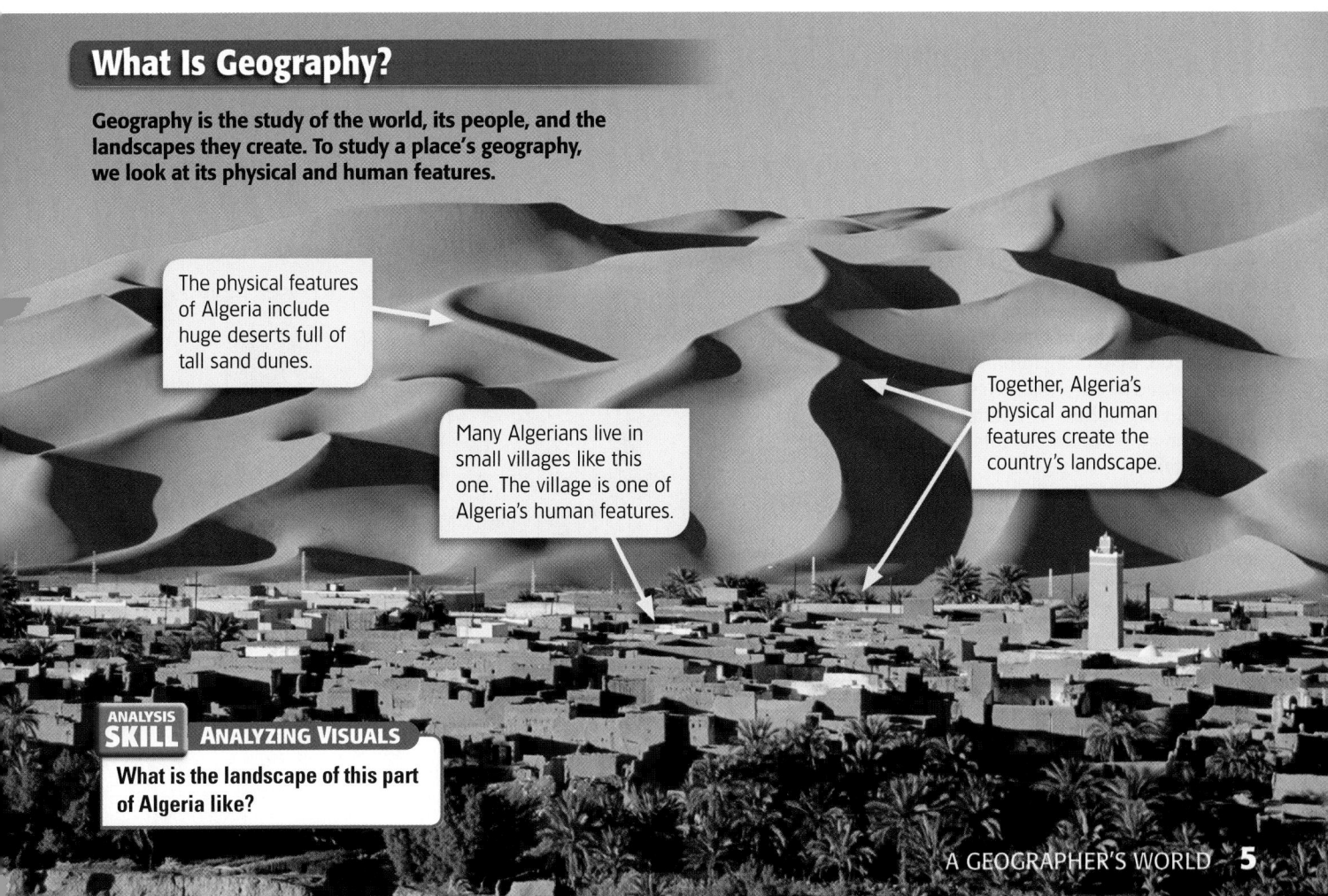

What Is Geography?

Geography is the study of the world, its people, and the landscapes they create. To study a place's geography, we look at its physical and human features.

The physical features of Algeria include huge deserts full of tall sand dunes.

Many Algerians live in small villages like this one. The village is one of Algeria's human features.

Together, Algeria's physical and human features create the country's landscape.

ANALYSIS SKILL **ANALYZING VISUALS**

What is the landscape of this part of Algeria like?

Looking at the World

Whether they study volcanoes and storms or people and cities, geographers have to look carefully at the world around them. To fully understand how the world works, geographers often look at places at three different levels.

Local Level

Some geographers study issues at a local level. They ask the same types of questions we asked at the beginning of this chapter: How do people in a town or community live? What is the local government like? How do the people who live there get around? What do they eat?

By asking these questions, geographers can figure out why people live and work the way they do. They can also help people improve their lives. For example, they can help town leaders figure out the best place to build new schools, shopping centers, or sports complexes. They can also help the people who live in the city or town plan for future changes.

Regional Level

Sometimes, though, geographers want to study a bigger chunk of the world. To do this, they divide the world into regions. A **region** is a part of the world that has one or more common features that distinguish it from surrounding areas.

Some regions are defined by physical characteristics such as mountain ranges, climates, or plants native to the area. As a result, these types of regions are often easy to identify. The Rocky Mountains of the western United States, for example, make up a physical region. Another example of this kind of region is the Sahara, a huge desert in northern Africa.

Other regions may not be so easy to define, however. These regions are based on the human characteristics of a place, such as language, religion, or history. A place in which most people share these kinds of characteristics can also be seen as a region. For example, most people in Scandinavia, a region in northern Europe, speak similar languages and practice the same religion.

Looking at the World

Geographers look at the world at many levels. At each level, they ask different questions and discover different types of information. By putting information gathered at different levels together, geographers can better understand a place and its role in the world.

ANALYZING VISUALS Based on these photos, what are some questions a geographer might ask about London?

Local Level This busy neighborhood in London, England, is a local area. A geographer here might study local foods, housing, or clothing.

Regions come in all shapes and sizes. Some are small, like the neighborhood called Chinatown in San Francisco. Other regions are huge, like the Americas. This huge region includes two continents, North America and South America. The size of the area does not matter, as long as the area shares some characteristics. These shared characteristics define the region.

Geographers divide the world into regions for many reasons. The world is a huge place and home to billions of people. Studying so large an area can be extremely difficult. Dividing the world into regions makes it easier to study. A small area is much easier to examine than a large area.

Other geographers study regions to see how people interact with one another. For example, they may study a city such as London, England, to learn how the city's people govern themselves. Then they can compare what they learn about one region to what they learn about another region. In this way, they can learn more about life and landscapes in both places.

Global Level

Sometimes geographers do not want to study the world just at a regional level. Instead they want to learn how people interact globally, or around the world. To do so, geographers ask how events and ideas from one region of the world affect people in other regions. In other words, they study the world on a global level.

Geographers who study the world on a global level try to find relationships among people who live far apart. They may, for example, examine the products that a country exports to see how those products are used in other countries.

In recent decades, worldwide trade and communication have increased. As a result, we need to understand how our actions affect people around the world. Through their studies, geographers provide us with information that helps us figure out how to live in a rapidly changing world.

READING CHECK **Finding Main Ideas** At what levels do geographers study the world?

Regional Level As a major city, London is also a region. At this level, a geographer might study the city's population or transportation systems.

Global Level London is one of the world's main financial centers. Here a geographer might study how London's economy affects the world.

Geographers use many tools to study the world. Each tool provides part of the information a geographer needs to learn what a place is like.

ANALYZING VISUALS What information could you learn from each of these tools?

High School Soccer Participation

Participation in High School Soccer

- More than 9%
- 5–9%
- 3–5%
- Fewer than 3%
- Data not available

A geographer can use a globe to see where a place, such as the United States, is located.

Maps usually give geographers more information about a place than globes do. This map, for example, shows rates of soccer participation in the United States.

The Geographer's Tools

Have you ever seen a carpenter building or repairing a house? If so, you know that builders need many tools to do their jobs correctly. In the same way, geographers need many tools to study the world.

Maps and Globes

FOCUS ON READING

What do you already know about maps and globes?

The tools that geographers use most often in their work are maps and globes. A **map** is a flat drawing that shows all or part of Earth's surface. A **globe** is a spherical, or ball-shaped, model of the entire planet.

Both maps and globes show what the world looks like. They can show where mountains, deserts, and oceans are. They can also identify and describe the world's countries and major cities.

There are, however, major differences between maps and globes. Because a globe is spherical like Earth, it can show the world as it really is.

A map, though, is flat. It is not possible to show a spherical area perfectly on a flat surface. To understand what this means, think about an orange. If you took the peel off of an orange, could you make it lie completely flat? No, you could not, unless you stretched or tore the peel first.

The same principle is true with maps. To draw Earth on a flat surface, people have to distort, or alter, some details. For example, places on a map might look to be farther apart than they really are, or their shapes or sizes might be changed slightly.

Still, maps have many advantages over globes. Flat maps are easier to work with than globes. Also, it is easier to show small areas like cities on maps than on globes.

In addition, maps usually show more information than globes. Because globes are more expensive to make, they do not usually show anything more than where places are and what features they have.

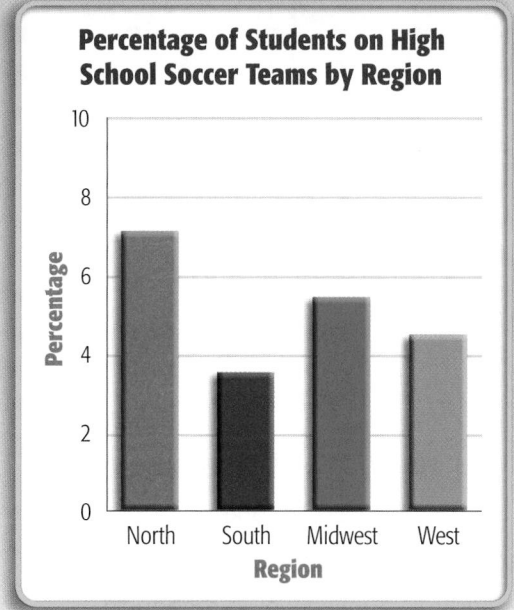

Percentage of Students on High School Soccer Teams by Region

Charts and graphs are also tools geographers can use to study information. They are often used when geographers want to compare numbers, such as the number of students who play soccer in each region of the country.

Maps, on the other hand, can show all sorts of information. Besides showing land use and cities, maps can include a great deal of information about a place. A map might show what languages people speak or where their ancestors came from. Maps like the one on the opposite page can even show how many students in an area play soccer.

Satellite Images

Maps and globes are not the only tools that geographers use in their work. As you have already read, many geographers study information gathered by satellites.

Much of the information gathered by these satellites is in the form of images. Geographers can study these images to see what an area looks like from above Earth. Satellites also collect information that we cannot see from the planet's surface. The information gathered by satellites helps geographers make accurate maps.

Other Tools

Geographers also use many other tools. For example, they use computer programs to create, update, and compare maps. They also use measuring devices to record data. In some cases, the best tools a geographer can use are a notebook and tape recorder to take notes while talking to people. Armed with the proper tools, geographers learn about the world's people and places.

READING CHECK **Summarizing** What are some of the geographer's basic tools?

SUMMARY AND PREVIEW Geography is the study of the world, its people, and its landscapes. In the next section, you will learn about two systems geographers use to organize their studies.

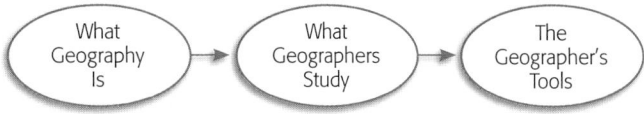

Section 1 Assessment

go.hrw.com
Online Quiz
KEYWORD: SG7 HP1

Reviewing Ideas, Terms, and Places

1. a. **Define** What is **geography**?
   b. **Explain** Why is geography considered a science?
2. a. **Identify** What is a **region**? Give two examples.
   b. **Elaborate** What global issues do geographers study?
3. a. **Describe** How do geographers use satellite images?
   b. **Compare and Contrast** How are maps and globes similar? How are they different?

Critical Thinking

4. **Summarizing** Draw three ovals like the ones shown here. Use your notes to fill the ovals with information about geography, geographers, and their tools.

What Geography Is → What Geographers Study → The Geographer's Tools

FOCUS ON WRITING

5. **Describing the Subject** Based on what you have learned, what might attract people to work in geography? In your notebook, list some details about geography that might make people interested in working in the subject.

A GEOGRAPHER'S WORLD **9**

Geography Themes and Essential Elements

What You Will Learn...

Main Ideas

1. The five themes of geography help us organize our studies of the world.
2. The six essential elements of geography highlight some of the subject's most important ideas.

The Big Idea

Geographers have created two different but related systems for organizing geographic studies.

Key Terms

absolute location, *p. 12*
relative location, *p. 12*
environment, *p. 12*

TAKING NOTES Draw a table with two columns like the one here. As you read this section, list the five themes of geography in the left column. List the six essential elements of geography in the right column.

Five Themes	Six Essential Elements

If YOU lived there...

Your older sister has offered to drive you to a friend's house across town, but she doesn't know how to get there. You know your friend's street address and what the apartment building looks like. You know it's near the public library. You also would recognize some landmarks in the neighborhood, such as the video store and the supermarket.

What might help your sister find the house?

BUILDING BACKGROUND Like drivers, geographers have to know where places are in order to study them. An area's location is only one of the aspects that geographers study, though. In fact, it is only one of the five themes that geographers use to describe a place.

The Five Themes of Geography

Have you ever gone to a Fourth of July party with a patriotic theme? If so, you probably noticed that almost everything at the party was related to that theme. For example, you may have seen American flags and decorations based on the flag's stars and stripes. You may have seen clothes that were red, white, and blue or heard patriotic music being played. Chances are that almost everything at the party reflected the theme of patriotism.

Like party planners, geographers use themes in their work. Geographers do not study parties, of course, but they do note common themes in their studies. Just as a party's theme is reflected in nearly every aspect of the party, these geography themes can be applied to nearly everything that geographers study. The five major themes of geography are Location, Place, Human-Environment Interaction, Movement, and Regions.

The Five Themes of Geography

Geographers use five major themes, or ideas, to organize and guide their studies.

go.hrw.com   KEYWORD: SG7 CH1

Location The theme of location describes where something is. The mountain shown above, Mount Rainier, is in west-central Washington.

Place Place describes the features that make a site unique. For example, Washington, D.C., is our nation's capital and has many great monuments.

UNITED STATES

Regions Regions are areas that share common characteristics. The Mojave Desert, shown here, is defined by its distinctive climate and plant life.

Movement This theme looks at how and why people and things move. Airports like this one in Dallas, Texas, help people move around the world.

Human-Environment Interaction People interact with their environments in many ways. Some, like this man in Florida, use the land to grow crops.

ANALYSIS SKILL   ANALYZING VISUALS

Which of the five themes deals with the relationships between people and their surroundings?

Location

Every point on Earth has a location, a description of where it is. This location can be expressed in many ways. Sometimes a site's location is expressed in specific, or absolute, terms, such as an address. For example, the White House is located at 1600 Pennsylvania Avenue in the city of Washington, D.C. A specific description like this one is called an **absolute location**. Other times, the site's location is expressed in general terms. For example, Canada is north of the United States. This general description of where a place lies is called its **relative location**.

Place

Another theme, Place, is closely related to Location. However, Place does not refer simply to where an area is. It refers to the area's landscape, the features that define the area and make it different from other places. Such features could include land, climate, and people. Together, they give a place its own character.

Human-Environment Interaction

FOCUS ON READING
What do you know about environments?

In addition to looking at the features of places, geographers examine how those features interact. In particular, they want to understand how people interact with their environment—how people and their physical environment affect each other. An area's **environment** includes its land, water, climate, plants, and animals.

People interact with their environment every day in all sorts of ways. They clear forests to plant crops, level fields to build cities, and dam rivers to prevent floods. At the same time, physical environments affect how people live. People in cold areas, for example, build houses with thick walls and wear heavy clothing to keep warm. People who live near oceans look for ways to protect themselves from storms.

Movement

People are constantly moving. They move within cities, between cities, and between countries. Geographers want to know why and how people move. For example, they ask if people are moving to find work or to live in a more pleasant area. Geographers also study the roads and routes that make movement so common.

Regions

You have already learned how geographers divide the world into many regions to help the study of geography. Creating regions also makes it easier to compare places. Comparisons help geographers learn why each place has developed the way it has.

READING CHECK Finding Main Ideas What are the five themes of geography?

The six essential elements are used by geographers to organize their studies and are closely related to the geography standards. Each element includes several of the standards, as listed in the chart.

ANALYZING VISUALS How many of the six essential elements can you see illustrated in this photo?

The Six Essential Elements

The five themes of geography are not the only system geographers use to study the world. They also use a system of standards and essential **elements**. Together, these standards and essential elements identify the most important ideas in the study of geography. These ideas are expressed in two lists.

The first list is the national geography standards. This is a list of 18 basic ideas that are central to the study of geography. These standards are listed in black type on the chart below.

The essential elements are based on the geography standards. Each element is a big idea that links several standards together. The six essential elements are The World in Spatial Terms, Places and Regions, Physical Systems, Human Systems, Environment and Society, and The Uses of Geography. On the chart, they are shown in purple.

Read through that list again. Do you see any similarities between geography's six essential elements and its five themes? You probably do. The two systems are very similar because the six essential elements build on the five themes.

ACADEMIC VOCABULARY
element part

The Essential Elements and Geography Standards

The World in Spatial Terms

- How to use maps and other geographic representations, tools, and technologies to acquire, process, and report information from a spatial perspective
- How to use mental maps to organize information about people, places, and environments in a spatial context
- How to analyze the spatial organization of people, places, and environments on Earth's surface

Places and Regions

- The physical and human characteristics of places
- How people create regions to interpret Earth's complexity
- How culture and experience influence people's perceptions of places and regions

Physical Systems

- The physical processes that shape the patterns of Earth's surface
- The characteristics and spatial distribution of ecosystems on Earth's surface

Human Systems

- The characteristics, distributions, and migration of human populations on Earth's surface
- The characteristics, distribution, and complexity of Earth's cultural mosaics
- The patterns and networks of economic interdependence on Earth's surface
- The processes, patterns, and functions of human settlement
- How the forces of cooperation and conflict among people influence the division and control of Earth's surface

Environment and Society

- How human actions modify the physical environment
- How physical systems affect human systems
- Changes that occur in the meaning, use, distribution, and importance of resources

The Uses of Geography

- How to apply geography to interpret the past
- How to apply geography to interpret the present and plan for the future

BOOK
Geography for Life

The six essential elements were first outlined in a book called Geography for Life. *In that book, the authors—a diverse group of geographers and teachers from around the United States— explained why the study of geography is important.*

❝Geography *is* for life in every sense of that expression: lifelong, life-sustaining, and life-enhancing. Geography is a field of study that enables us to find answers to questions about the world around us—about where things are and how and why they got there.❞

❝Geography focuses attention on exciting and interesting things, on fascinating people and places, on things worth knowing because they are absorbing and because knowing about them lets humans make better-informed and, therefore, wiser decisions.❞

❝With a strong grasp of geography, people are better equipped to solve issues at not only the local level but also the global level.❞

–from *Geography for Life,*
by the Geography Education Standards Project

ANALYSIS SKILL ANALYZING PRIMARY SOURCES

Why do the authors of these passages think that people should study geography?

For example, the element Places and Regions combines two of the five themes of geography—Place and Regions. Also, the element called Environment and Society deals with many of the same issues as the theme Human-Environment Interaction.

There are also some basic differences between the essential elements and the themes. For example, the last element, The Uses of Geography, deals with issues not covered in the five themes. This element examines how people can use geography to plan the landscapes in which they live.

Throughout this book, you will notice references to both the themes and the essential elements. As you read, use these themes and elements to help you organize your own study of geography.

READING CHECK **Summarizing** What are the six essential elements of geography?

SUMMARY AND PREVIEW You have just learned about the themes and elements of geography. Next, you will explore the branches into which the field is divided.

Section 2 Assessment

go.hrw.com
Online Quiz
KEYWORD: SG7 HP1

Reviewing Ideas, Terms, and Places

1. **a. Define** What is the difference between a place's **absolute location** and its **relative location**? Give one example of each type of location.
   b. Contrast How are the themes of Location and Place different?
   c. Elaborate How does using the five themes help geographers understand the places they study?
2. **a. Identify** Which of the five themes of geography is associated with airports, highways, and the migration of people from one place to another?
   b. Explain How are the geography standards and the six essential elements related?
   c. Compare How are the six essential elements similar to the five themes of geography?

Critical Thinking

3. **Categorizing** Draw a chart like the one below. Use your notes to list the five themes of geography, explain each of the themes, and list one feature of your city or town that relates to each.

Theme					
Explanation					
Feature					

FOCUS ON WRITING

4. **Including Themes and Essential Elements** The five themes and six essential elements are central to a geographer's job. How will you mention them in your job description? Write down some ideas.

Analyzing Satellite Images

Learn

In addition to maps and globes, satellite images are among the geographer's most valuable tools. Geographers use two basic types of these images. The first type is called true color. These images are like photographs taken from high above Earth's surface. The colors in these images are similar to what you would see from the ground. Vegetation, for example, appears green.

The other type of satellite image is called an infrared image. Infrared images are taken using a special type of light. These images are based on heat patterns, and so the colors on them are not what we might expect. Bodies of water appear black, for example, since they give off little heat.

Practice

Use the satellite images on this page to answer the following questions.

1 On which image is vegetation red?

2 Which image do you think probably looks more like Italy does from the ground?

Vegetation appears green.

Water appears blue.

True color satellite image of Italy

Vegetation appears red.

Water appears black.

Infrared satellite image of Italy

Apply

Search the Internet to find a satellite image of your state or region. Determine whether the image is true color or infrared. Then write three statements that describe what you see on the image.

The Branches of Geography

What You Will Learn...

Main Ideas

1. Physical geography is the study of landforms, water bodies, and other physical features.
2. Human geography focuses on people, their cultures, and the landscapes they create.
3. Other branches of geography examine specific aspects of the physical or human world.

The Big Idea

Geography is divided into two main branches—physical and human geography.

Key Terms

physical geography, *p. 16*
human geography, *p. 18*
cartography, *p. 19*
meteorology, *p. 20*

 **TAKING NOTES** Draw two large circles like the ones below in your notebook. As you read this section, take notes about one of the main branches of geography in each circle.

If YOU lived there...

You are talking to two friends about the vacations their families will take this summer. One friend says that his family is going to the Grand Canyon. He is very excited about seeing the spectacular landscapes in and around the canyon. Your other friend's family is going to visit Nashville, Tennessee. She is looking forward to trying new foods at the city's restaurants and touring its museums.

Which vacation sounds more interesting? Why?

BUILDING BACKGROUND Geography is the study of the world and its features. Some features are physical, like the Grand Canyon. Others are human, like restaurants and museums. The main branches of geography focus on these types of features.

Physical Geography

Think about a jigsaw puzzle. Seen as a whole, the puzzle shows a pretty or interesting picture. To see that picture, though, you have to put all the puzzle pieces together. Before you assemble them, the pieces do not give you a clear idea of what the puzzle will look like when it is assembled. After all, each piece contains only a tiny portion of the overall image.

In many ways, geography is like a huge puzzle. It is made up of many branches, or divisions. Each of these branches focuses on a single part of the world. Viewed separately, none of these branches shows us the whole world. Together, however, the many branches of geography improve our understanding of our planet and its people.

Geography's two main branches are physical geography and human geography. The first branch, **physical geography**, is the study of the world's physical features—its landforms, bodies of water, climates, soils, and plants. Every place in the world has its own unique combination of these features.

Physical Geography

The study of Earth's physical features, including rivers, mountains, oceans, weather, and other features, such as Victoria Falls in southern Africa

Human Geography

The study of Earth's people, including their ways of life, homes, cities, beliefs, and customs, like those of these children in Malawi, a country in central Africa

Geography

The study of Earth's physical and cultural features

The Physical World

What does it mean to say that physical geography is the study of physical features? Physical geographers want to know all about the different features found on our planet. They want to know where plains and mountain ranges are, how rivers flow across the landscape, and why different amounts of rain fall from place to place.

More importantly, however, physical geographers want to know what causes the different shapes on Earth. They want to know why mountain ranges rise up where they do and what causes rivers to flow in certain directions. They also want to know why various parts of the world have very different weather and climate patterns.

To answer these questions, physical geographers take detailed measurements. They study the heights of mountains and the temperatures of places. To track any changes that occur over time, physical geographers keep careful records of all the information they collect.

Uses of Physical Geography

Earth is made up of hundreds of types of physical features. Without a complete understanding of what these features are and the effect they have on the world's people and landscapes, we cannot fully understand our world. This is the major reason that geographers study the physical world—to learn how it works.

There are also other, more specific reasons for studying physical geography, though. Studying the changes that take place on our planet can help us prepare to live with those changes. For example, knowing what causes volcanoes to erupt can help us predict eruptions. Knowing what causes terrible storms can help us prepare for them. In this way, the work of physical geographers helps us adjust to the dangers and changes of our world.

READING CHECK **Analyzing** What are some features in your area that a physical geographer might study?

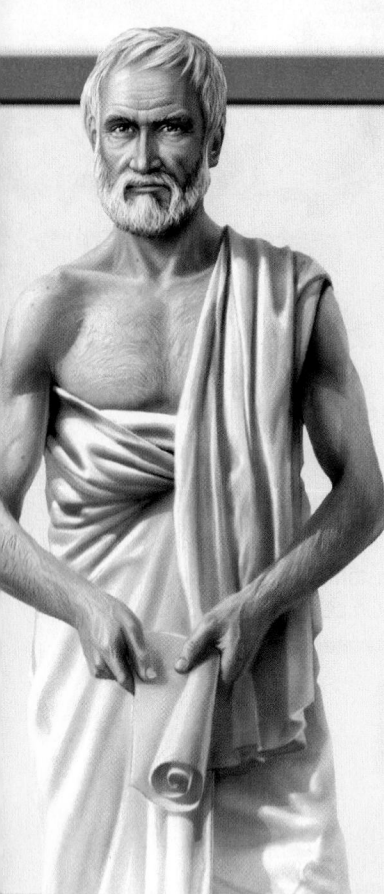

Eratosthenes
(c. 276–c. 194 BC)

Did you know that geography is over 2,000 years old? Actually, the study of the world is even older than that, but the first person ever to use the word *geography* lived then. His name was Eratosthenes (er-uh-TAHS-thuh-neez), and he was a Greek scientist and librarian. With no modern instruments of any kind, Eratosthenes figured out how large Earth is. He also drew a map that showed all of the lands that the Greeks knew about. Because of his many contributions to the field, Eratosthenes has been called the Father of Geography.

Generalizing Why is Eratosthenes called the Father of Geography?

Human Geography

The physical world is only one part of the puzzle of geography. People are also part of the world. **Human geography** is the study of the world's people, communities, and landscapes. It is the second major branch of geography.

The Human World

Put simply, human geographers study the world's people, past and present. They look at where people live and why. They ask why some parts of the world have more people than others, and why some places have almost no people at all.

Human geographers also study what people do. What jobs do people have? What crops do they grow? What makes them move from place to place? These are the types of questions that geographers ask about people around the world.

Because people's lives are so different around the world, no one can study every aspect of human geography. As a result, human geographers often specialize in a smaller area of study. Some may choose to study only the people and landscapes in a certain region. For example, a geographer may study only the lives of people who live in West Africa.

Other geographers choose not to limit their studies to one place. Instead, they may choose to examine only one aspect of people's lives. For example, a geographer could study only economics, politics, or city life. However, that geographer may compare economic patterns in various parts of the world to see how they differ.

Uses of Human Geography

Although every culture is different, people around the world have some common needs. All people need food and water. All people need shelter. All people need to deal with other people in order to survive.

Human geographers study how people in various places address their needs. They look at the foods people eat and the types of governments they form. The knowledge they gather can help us better understand people in other cultures. Sometimes this type of understanding can help people improve their landscapes and situations.

On a smaller scale, human geographers can help people design their cities and towns. By understanding where people go and what they need, geographers can help city planners place roads, shopping malls, and schools. Geographers also study the effect people have on the world. As a result, they often work with private groups and government agencies who want to protect the environment.

READING CHECK **Summarizing** What do human geographers study?

Other Fields of Geography

Physical geography and human geography are the two largest branches of the subject, but they are not the only ones. Many other fields of geography exist, each one devoted to studying one aspect of the world.

Most of these fields are smaller, more specialized areas of either physical or human geography. For example, economic geography—the study of how people make and spend money—is a branch of human geography. Another specialized branch of human geography is urban geography, the study of cities and how people live in them. Physical geography also includes many fields, such as the study of climates. Other fields of physical geography are the studies of soils and plants.

Cartography

One key field of geography is **cartography**, the science of making maps. You have already seen how important maps are to the study of geography. Without maps, geographers would not be able to study where things are in the world.

In the past, maps were always drawn by hand. Many were not very accurate. Today, though, most maps are made using computers and satellite images. Through advances in mapmaking, we can make accurate maps on almost any scale, from the whole world to a single neighborhood, and keep them up to date. These maps are not only used by geographers. For example, road maps are used by people who are planning long trips.

CONNECTING TO Technology

Computer Mapping

In the past, maps were drawn by hand. Making a map was a slow process. Even the simplest map took a long time to make. Today, however, cartographers have access to tools people in the past—even people who lived just 50 years ago—never imagined. The most important of these tools are computers.

Computers allow us to make maps quickly and easily. In addition, they let us make new types of maps that people could not make in the past.

The map shown here, for example, was drawn on a computer. It shows the number of computer users in the United States who were connected to the Internet on a particular day. Each of the lines that rises off of the map represents a city in which people were using the Internet. The color of the line indicates the number of computer users in that city. As you can see, this data resulted in a very complex map.

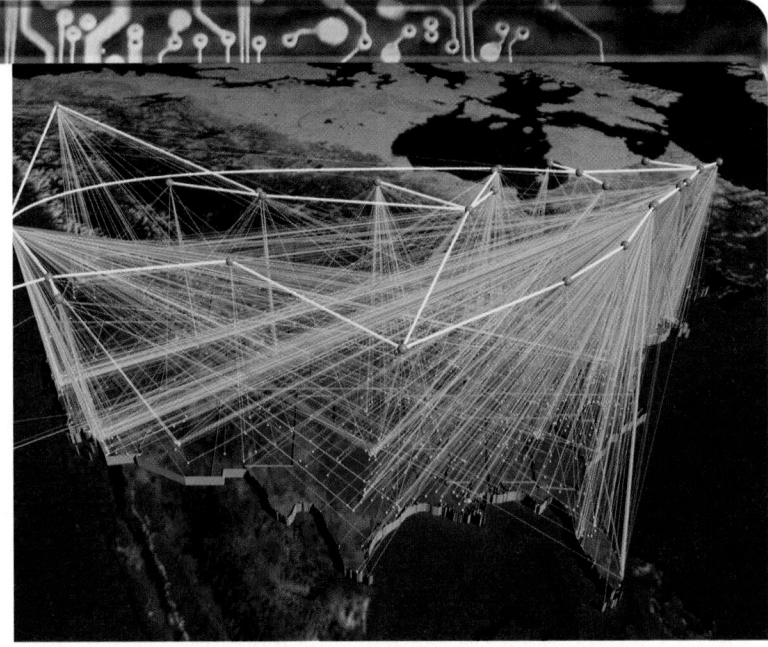

Making such a map required cartographers to sort through huge amounts of complex data. Such sorting would not have been possible without computers.

Contrasting How are today's maps different from those created in the past?

Meteorology is the study of weather. This meteorologist is using computers to follow and predict the movement of a powerful storm.

Meteorology

Have you ever seen the weather report on television? If so, you have seen the results of another branch of geography. This branch is called **meteorology**, the study of weather and what causes it.

Meteorologists study weather patterns in a particular area. Then they use the information to predict what the weather will be like in the coming days. Their work helps people plan what to wear and what to do on any given day. At the same time, their work can save lives by predicting the arrival of terrible storms. These predictions are among the most visible ways in which the work of geographers affects our lives every day.

READING CHECK Finding Main Ideas What are some major branches of geography?

Hydrology

FOCUS ON READING

What do you already know about drinking water?

Another important branch of geography is hydrology, the study of water on Earth. Geographers in this field study the world's river systems and rainfall patterns. They study what causes droughts and floods and how people in cities can get safe drinking water. They also work to measure and protect the world's supply of water.

SUMMARY AND PREVIEW In this section, you learned about two main branches of geography, physical and human. In the next chapter, you will learn more about the physical features that surround us and the processes that create them.

Section 3 Assessment

go.hrw.com
Online Quiz
KEYWORD: SG7 HP1

Reviewing Ideas, Terms, and Places

1. **a. Define** What is **physical geography**?
   b. Explain Why do we study physical geography?
2. **a. Identify** What are some things that people study as part of **human geography**?
   b. Summarize What are some ways in which the study of human geography can influence our lives?
   c. Evaluate Which do you think would be more interesting to study, physical geography or human geography? Why?
3. **a. Identify** What are two specialized fields of geography?
   b. Analyze How do cartographers contribute to the work of other geographers?

Critical Thinking

4. **Comparing and Contrasting** Draw a diagram like the one shown here. In the left circle, list three features of physical geography from your notes. In the right circle, list three features of human geography. Where the circles overlap, list one feature they share.

Physical   Human

FOCUS ON WRITING

5. **Choosing a Branch** Your job description should point out to people that there are many branches of geography. How will you note that?

Chapter Review

Geography's Impact
video series
Review the video to answer the closing question:
Why do you think it might be valuable to know the absolute location of a place?

Visual Summary

Use the visual summary below to help you review the main ideas of the chapter.

QUICK FACTS

Physical geography—the study of the world's physical features—is one main branch of geography.

Human geography—the study of the world's people and how they live—is the second main branch.

Geographers use many tools to study the world. The most valuable of these tools are maps.

Reviewing Vocabulary, Terms, and Places

Match the words in the columns with the correct definitions listed below.

1. geography
2. physical geography
3. human geography
4. element
5. meteorology
6. region
7. cartography
8. map
9. landscape
10. globe

a. a part of the world that has one or more common features that make it different from surrounding areas

b. a flat drawing of part of Earth's surface

c. a part

d. a spherical model of the planet

e. the study of the world's physical features

f. the study of weather and what causes it

g. the study of the world, its people, and the landscapes they create

h. the science of making maps

i. the physical and human features that define an area and make it different from other places

j. the study of people and communities

Comprehension and Critical Thinking

SECTION 1 *(Pages 4–9)*

11. a. **Identify** What are three levels at which a geographer might study the world? Which of these levels covers the largest area?

   b. **Compare and Contrast** How are maps and globes similar? How are they different?

   c. **Elaborate** How might satellite images and computers help geographers improve their knowledge of the world?

SECTION 2 *(Pages 10–14)*

12. a. Define What do geographers mean when they discuss an area's landscape?

b. Explain Why did geographers create the five themes and the six essential elements?

c. Predict How might the five themes and six essential elements help you in your study of geography?

SECTION 3 *(Pages 16–20)*

13. a. Identify What are the two main branches of geography? What does each include?

b. Summarize How can physical geography help people adjust to the dangers of the world?

c. Elaborate Why do geographers study both physical and human characteristics of places?

Using the Internet
go.hrw.com
KEYWORD: SG7 CH1

14. Activity: Using Maps What does your town or community look like? What can be found there? Maps can help you understand your community and learn about its features. Enter the activity keyword to learn more about maps and how they can help you better understand your community. Then search the Internet to find a map of your community. Use the map to find the locations of at least five important features. For example, you might locate your school, the library, a park, or major highways. Be creative and find other places you think your classmates should be aware of.

Social Studies Skills

Analyzing Satellite Images *Use the satellite images of Italy from the Social Studies Skills lesson in this chapter to answer the following questions.*

15. On which image do forests appear more clearly, the true-color or the infrared image?

16. What color do you think represents mountains on the infrared satellite image?

17. Why might geographers use satellite images like these while making maps of Italy?

18. Using Prior Knowledge Create a chart with three columns. In the first column list what you knew about geography before you read the chapter. In the second column list what you learned in the chapter. In the third column list questions that you now have about geography.

19. Writing Your Job Description Review your notes on the different jobs geographers do. Then write your job description. You should begin your description by explaining why the job is important. Then identify the job's tasks and responsibilities. Finally, tell what kind of person might do well as a geographer.

Map Activity

20. Sketch Map Draw a map that shows your school and the surrounding neighborhood. Your map does not have to be complicated, but you should include major features like streets and buildings. Use the map shown here as an example.

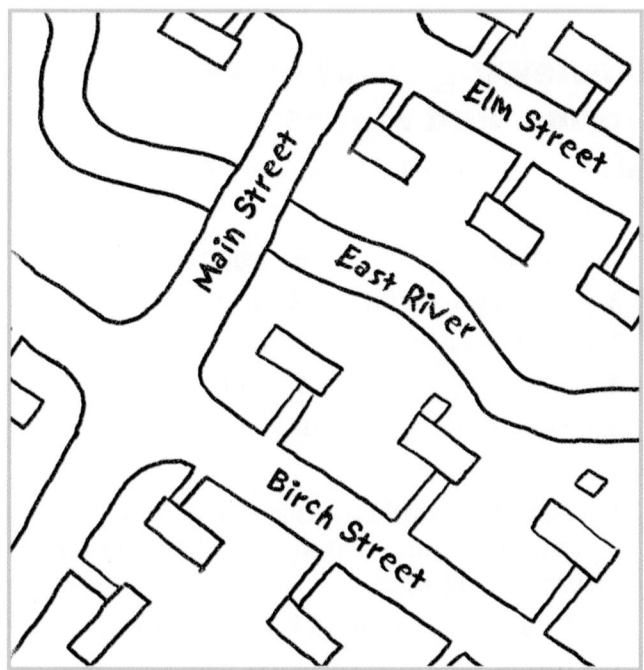

Standardized Test Practice

DIRECTIONS: *Read questions 1 through 7 and write the letter of the best response. Then read question 8 and write your own well-constructed response.*

1 Which of the following subjects would a human geographer study the most?

A mountains

B populations

C rivers

D volcanoes

2 The study of weather is called

A meteorology.

B hydrology.

C social science.

D cartography.

3 A region is an area that has

A one or more common features.

B no people living in it.

C few physical features.

D set physical boundaries.

4 How many essential elements of geography have geographers identified?

A two

B four

C six

D eight

5 The physical and human characteristics that define an area are its

A landscape.

B location.

C region.

D science.

The United States

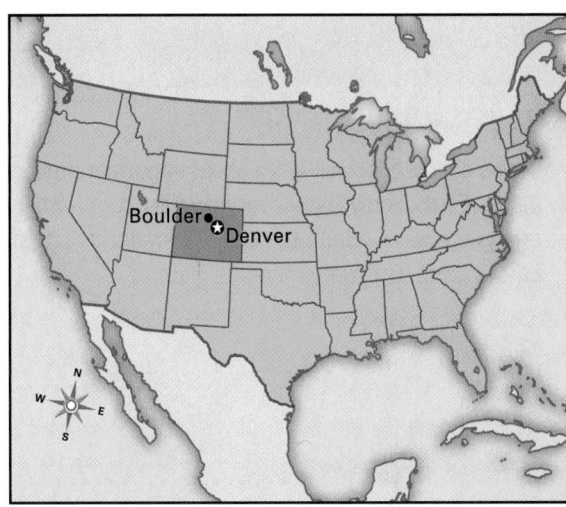

6 Which of the five themes of geography would a geographer most likely study using this map?

A movement

B location

C human-environment interaction

D landscape

7 The smallest level at which a geographer might study a place is

A microscopic.

B local.

C regional.

D global.

8 **Extended Response** Look at the map of the United States above. Do you think this map is more likely to be used by a physical geographer or by a human geographer? Give two reasons for your answer. Then write two statements about what a geographer could find on this map.

Planet Earth

What You Will Learn...

In this chapter you will learn about important processes on planet Earth. You will discover how Earth's movements affect the energy we receive from the sun, how water affects life, and how Earth's landforms were made.

FOCUS ON READING AND WRITING

Using Word Parts Sometimes you can figure out the meaning of a word by looking at its parts. A root is the base of the word. A prefix attaches to the beginning, and a suffix attaches to the ending. When you come across a word you don't know, check to see whether you recognize its parts. **See the lesson, Using Word Parts, on page R3.**

Writing a Haiku Join the poets who have celebrated our planet for centuries. Write a haiku, a short poem, about planet Earth. As you read the chapter, gather information about changes in the sun's energy, Earth's water supply, and shapes on the land. Then choose the most intriguing information to include in your haiku.

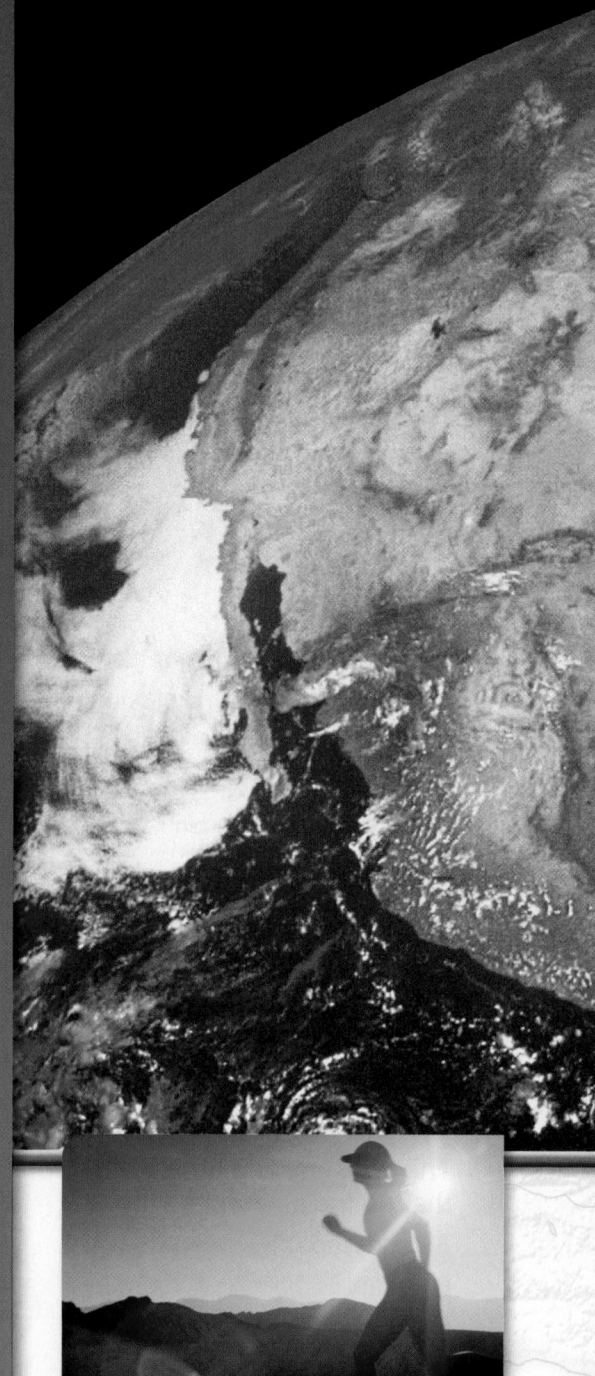

Energy from the Sun The planet's movement creates differences in the amount of energy Earth receives from the sun.

ANALYSIS SKILL **ANALYZING VISUALS**

Many of Earth's features are visible from space. This photo, taken from a satellite orbiting the planet, shows part of the North American continent.

Which of Earth's features are visible in this photo?

HOLT

Geography's Impact
video series
Watch the video to understand the impact of water on Earth.

Land Forces on and under Earth's surface have shaped the different landforms on our planet. Geographers study how mountains and other landforms were made.

Water on Earth Water is essential for life on Earth. Much of the planet's water supply is stored in Earth's oceans and ice caps.

25

Earth and the Sun's Energy

If YOU lived there...

You live in Chicago and have just won an exciting prize—a trip to Australia during winter vacation in January. As you prepare for the trip, your mother reminds you to pack shorts and a swimsuit. You are confused. In January you usually wear winter sweaters and a heavy jacket.

Why is the weather so different in Australia?

BUILDING BACKGROUND Seasonal differences in weather are an important result of Earth's constant movement. As the planet moves, we experience changes in the amount of energy we receive from the sun. Geographers study and explain why different places on Earth receive differing amounts of energy from the sun.

Earth's Movement

Energy from the sun helps crops grow, provides light, and warms Earth. It even influences the clothes we wear, the foods we eat, and the sports we play. All life on Earth requires **solar energy**, or energy from the sun, to survive. The amount of solar energy places on Earth receive changes constantly. Earth's rotation, revolution, and tilt, as well as latitude, all affect the amount of solar energy parts of the planet receive from the sun.

Rotation

Imagine that Earth has a rod running through it from the North Pole to the South Pole. This rod represents Earth's axis—an imaginary line around which a planet turns. As Earth spins on its axis, different parts of the planet face the sun. It takes Earth 24 hours, or one day, to complete this rotation. A **rotation** is one complete spin of Earth on its axis. As Earth rotates during this 24-hour period, it appears to us that the sun moves across the sky. The sun seems to rise in the east and set in the west. The

Solar Energy

Earth's tilt and rotation cause changes in the amount of energy we receive from the sun. As Earth rotates on its axis, energy from the sun creates periods of day and night. Earth's tilt causes some locations, especially those close to the equator, to receive more direct solar energy than others.

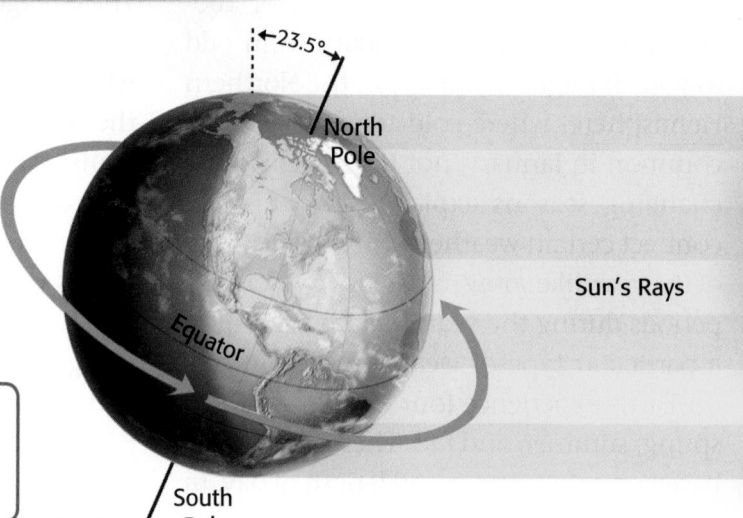

North Pole

Equator

Sun's Rays

South Pole

23.5°

sun, however, does not move. It is actually Earth's rotation that creates the sense of the sun's movement.

Earth's rotation also explains why day changes to night. As you can see in the illustration, solar energy strikes only the half of Earth facing the sun. Warmth and light from the sun create daytime. At the same time, the half of the planet facing away from the sun experiences the cooler temperatures and darkness of night. Earth's rotation causes regular shifts from day to night. As a result, levels of solar energy on Earth constantly change.

Revolution

As Earth spins on its axis, it also follows a path, or orbit, around the sun. Earth's orbit around the sun is not a perfect circle. Sometimes the orbit takes Earth closer to the sun, and at other times the orbit takes it farther away. It takes 365¼ days for Earth to complete one **revolution**, or trip around the sun. We base our calendar year on the time it takes Earth to complete its orbit around the sun. To allow for the fraction of a day, we add an extra day—February 29—to our calendar every four years.

Tilt and Latitude

Another **factor** affecting the amount of solar energy we receive is the planet's tilt. As the illustration shows, Earth's axis is not straight up and down. It is actually tilted at an angle of 23½ degrees from vertical. At any given time of year, some locations on Earth are tilting away from the sun, and others are tilting toward it. Places tilting toward the sun receive more solar energy and experience warmer temperatures. Those tilting away from the sun receive less solar energy and experience cooler temperatures.

A location's **latitude**, the distance north or south of Earth's equator, also affects the amount of solar energy it receives. Low-latitude areas, those near the equator like Hawaii, receive direct rays from the sun all year. These direct rays are more intense and produce warmer temperatures. Regions with high latitudes, like Antarctica, are farther from the equator. As a result, they receive indirect rays from the sun and have colder temperatures.

READING CHECK Finding Main Ideas What factors affect the solar energy Earth receives?

ACADEMIC VOCABULARY
factor cause

The Seasons

Does the thought of snow in July or 100-degree temperatures in January seem odd to you? It might if you live in the Northern Hemisphere, where cold temperatures are common in January, not July. The planet's changing seasons explain why we often connect certain weather with specific times of the year, like snow in January. Seasons are periods during the year that are known for a particular type of weather. Many places on Earth experience four seasons—winter, spring, summer, and fall. These seasons are based on temperature and length of day. In some parts of the world, however, seasons are based on the amount of rainfall.

FOCUS ON READING
The prefix *hemi-* means half. What does the word *hemisphere* mean?

Winter and Summer

The change in seasons is created by Earth's tilt. As you can see in the illustration below, while one of Earth's poles tilts away from the sun, the other tilts toward it. During winter part of Earth is tilted away from the sun, causing less direct solar energy, cool temperatures, and less daylight. Summer occurs when part of Earth is tilted toward the sun. This creates more direct solar energy, warmer temperatures, and longer periods of daylight.

Because of Earth's tilt, the Northern and Southern hemispheres experience opposite seasons. As the North Pole tilts toward the sun in summer, the South Pole tilts away

The Seasons: Northern Hemisphere

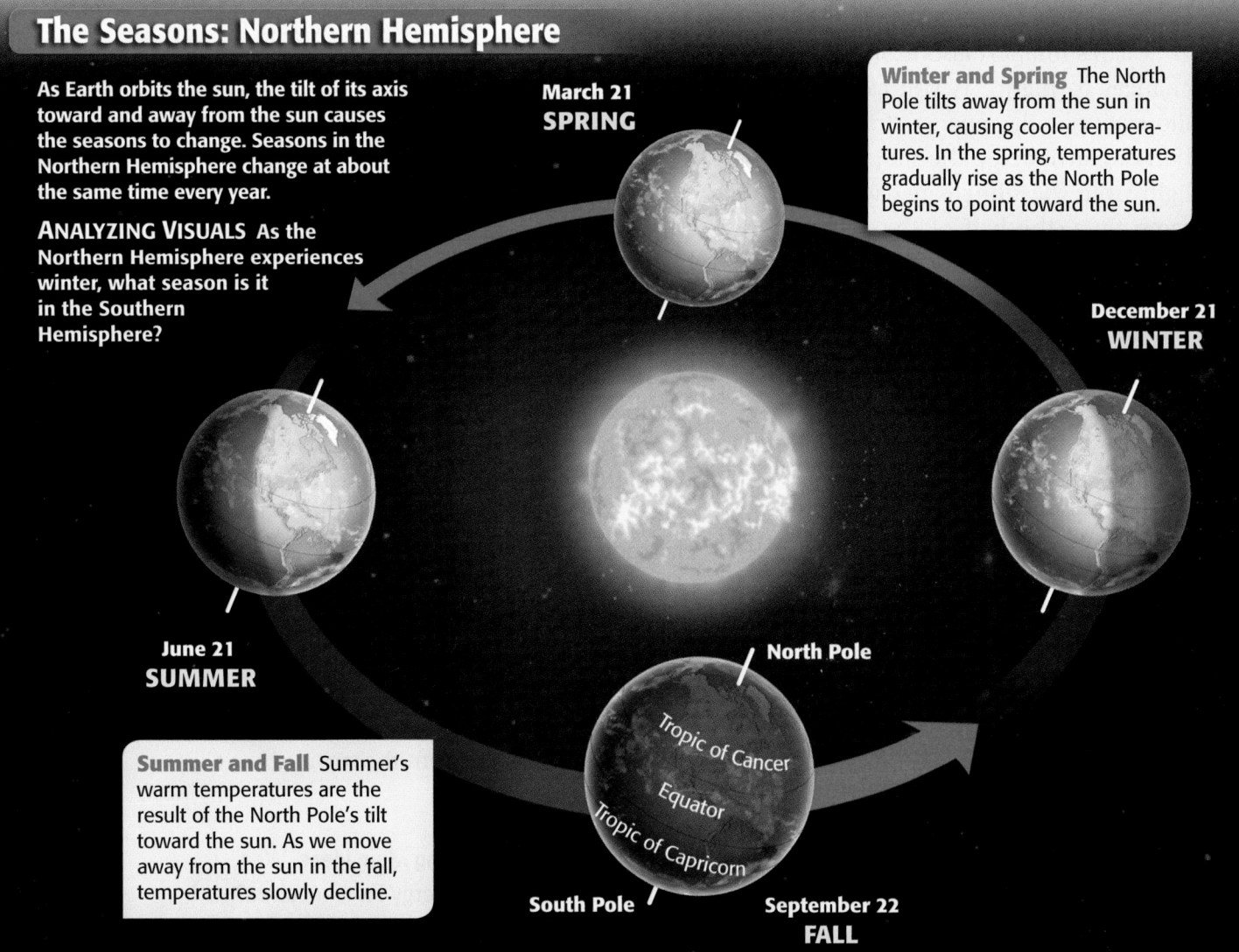

As Earth orbits the sun, the tilt of its axis toward and away from the sun causes the seasons to change. Seasons in the Northern Hemisphere change at about the same time every year.

ANALYZING VISUALS As the Northern Hemisphere experiences winter, what season is it in the Southern Hemisphere?

March 21
SPRING

Winter and Spring The North Pole tilts away from the sun in winter, causing cooler temperatures. In the spring, temperatures gradually rise as the North Pole begins to point toward the sun.

December 21
WINTER

June 21
SUMMER

Summer and Fall Summer's warm temperatures are the result of the North Pole's tilt toward the sun. As we move away from the sun in the fall, temperatures slowly decline.

North Pole

Tropic of Cancer

Equator

Tropic of Capricorn

South Pole

September 22
FALL

from it. As a result, the Southern Hemisphere experiences winter. Likewise, when it is spring in the Northern Hemisphere, it is fall in the Southern Hemisphere.

Spring and Fall

As Earth orbits the sun, there are periods when the poles tilt neither toward nor away from the sun. These periods mark spring and fall. During the spring, as part of Earth begins to tilt toward the sun, solar energy increases. Temperatures slowly start to rise, and days grow longer. In the fall the opposite occurs as winter approaches. Solar energy begins to decrease, causing cooler temperatures and shorter days.

Rainfall and Seasons

Some regions on Earth have seasons marked by rainfall rather than temperature. This is true in the **tropics**, regions close to the equator. At certain times of year, winds bring either dry or moist air to the tropics, creating wet and dry seasons. In India, for example, seasonal winds called monsoons bring heavy rains from June to October and dry air from November to January.

READING CHECK **Identifying Cause and Effect** What causes the seasons to change?

FOCUS ON CULTURE

The Midnight Sun

Can you imagine going to sleep late at night with the sun shining in the sky? People who live near the Arctic and Antarctic circles experience this every summer, when they can receive up to 24 hours of sunlight a day. The time-lapse photo below shows a typical sunset during this period—except the sun never really sets! This phenomenon is known as the midnight sun. For locations like Tromso, Norway, this means up to two months of constant daylight each summer. People living near Earth's poles often use the long daylight hours to work on outdoor projects in preparation for winter, when they can receive 24 hours of darkness a day.

Predicting How might people's daily lives be affected by the midnight sun?

SUMMARY AND PREVIEW Solar energy is crucial for all life on the planet. Earth's position and movements affect the amount of energy we receive from the sun and determine our seasons. Next, you will learn about Earth's water supply and its importance to us.

Section 1 Assessment

go.hrw.com
Online Quiz
KEYWORD: SG7 HP2

Reviewing Ideas, Terms, and Places

1. **a. Identify** What is **solar energy**, and how does it affect Earth?
   b. Analyze How do **rotation** and tilt each affect the amount of solar energy that different parts of Earth receive?
   c. Predict What might happen if Earth received less solar energy than it currently does?
2. **a. Describe** Name and describe Earth's seasons.
   b. Contrast How are seasons different in the Northern and Southern hemispheres?
   c. Elaborate How might the seasons affect human activities?

Critical Thinking

3. **Identifying Cause and Effect** Use your notes and the diagram to identify the causes of seasons.

Cause

Cause

Effect: Earth's changing seasons

FOCUS ON WRITING

4. **Describing the Seasons** What are the seasons like where you live? In your notebook, jot down a few notes that describe the changing seasons.

Water on Earth

What You Will Learn...

Main Ideas

1. Salt water and freshwater make up Earth's water supply.
2. In the water cycle, water circulates from Earth's surface to the atmosphere and back again.
3. Water plays an important role in people's lives.

The Big Idea

Water is a dominant feature on Earth's surface and is essential for life.

Key Terms

freshwater, *p. 31*
glaciers, *p. 31*
surface water, *p. 31*
precipitation, *p. 31*
groundwater, *p. 32*
water vapor, *p. 32*
water cycle, *p. 33*

TAKING NOTES As you read, take notes about Earth's water, the water cycle, and how water affects our lives. Use a diagram like the one below to organize your notes.

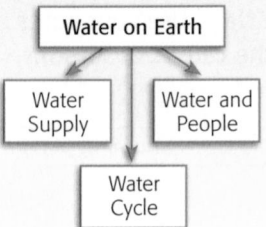

If YOU lived there...

You live in the desert Southwest, where heavy water use and a lack of rainfall have led to water shortages. Your city plans to begin a water conservation program that asks people to limit how much water they use. Many of your neighbors have complained that the program is unnecessary. Others support the plan to save water.

How do you feel about the city's water plan?

BUILDING BACKGROUND Although water covers much of Earth's surface, water shortages, like those in the American Southwest, are common all over the planet. Because water is vital to the survival of all living things, geographers study Earth's water supply.

Earth's Water Supply

Think of the different uses for water. We use water to cook and clean, we drink it, and we grow crops with it. Water is used for recreation, to generate electricity, and even to travel from place to place. Water is perhaps the most important and abundant resource on Earth. In fact, water covers some two-thirds of the planet. Understanding Earth's water supply and how it affects our lives is an important part of geography.

Earth's Distribution of Water

Earth's water supply is divided into two main types—salt water and freshwater. Humans, plants, and animals rely on Earth's freshwater supply for survival.

Salt Water

Although water covers much of the planet, we cannot use most of it. About 97 percent of the Earth's water is salt water. Because salt water contains high levels of salt and other minerals, it is unsafe to drink.

In general, salt water is found in Earth's oceans. Oceans are vast bodies of water covering some 71 percent of the planet's surface. Earth's oceans are made up of smaller bodies of water such as seas, gulfs, bays, and straits. Altogether, Earth's oceans cover some 139 million square miles (360 million square km) of the planet's surface.

Some of Earth's lakes contain salt water. The Great Salt Lake in Utah, for example, is a saltwater lake. As salt and other minerals have collected in the lake, which has no outlet, the water has become salty.

Freshwater

Since the water in Earth's oceans is too salty to use, we must rely on other sources for freshwater. **Freshwater**, or water without salt, makes up only about 3 percent of our total water supply. Much of that freshwater is locked in Earth's **glaciers**, large areas of slow-moving ice, and in the ice of the Antarctic and Arctic regions. Most of the freshwater we use everyday is found in lakes, in rivers, and under Earth's surface.

One form of freshwater is surface water. **Surface water** is water that is found in Earth's streams, rivers, and lakes. It may seem that there is a great deal of water in our lakes and rivers, but only a tiny amount of Earth's water supply—less than 1 percent—comes from surface water.

Streams and rivers are a common source of surface water. Streams form when precipitation collects in a narrow channel and flows toward the ocean. **Precipitation** is water that falls to Earth's surface as rain, snow, sleet, or hail. In turn, streams join together to form rivers. Any smaller stream or river that flows into a larger stream or river is called a tributary. For example, the Missouri River is the largest tributary of the Mississippi River.

Lakes are another important source of surface water. Some lakes were formed as rivers filled low-lying areas with water. Other lakes, like the Great Lakes along the U.S.–Canada border, were formed when glaciers carved deep holes in Earth's surface and deposited water as they melted.

Most of Earth's available freshwater is stored underground. As precipitation falls to Earth, much of it is absorbed into the ground, filling spaces in the soil and rock.

Salt Water Earth's oceans contain some 97 percent of the planet's water supply. Unfortunately, this water is too salty to drink.

Freshwater Freshwater from lakes, rivers, and streams makes up only a fraction of Earth's water supply.

Water found below Earth's surface is called **groundwater**. In some places on Earth, groundwater naturally bubbles from the ground as a spring. More often, however, people obtain groundwater by digging wells, or deep holes dug into the ground to reach the water.

READING CHECK **Contrasting** How is salt water different from freshwater?

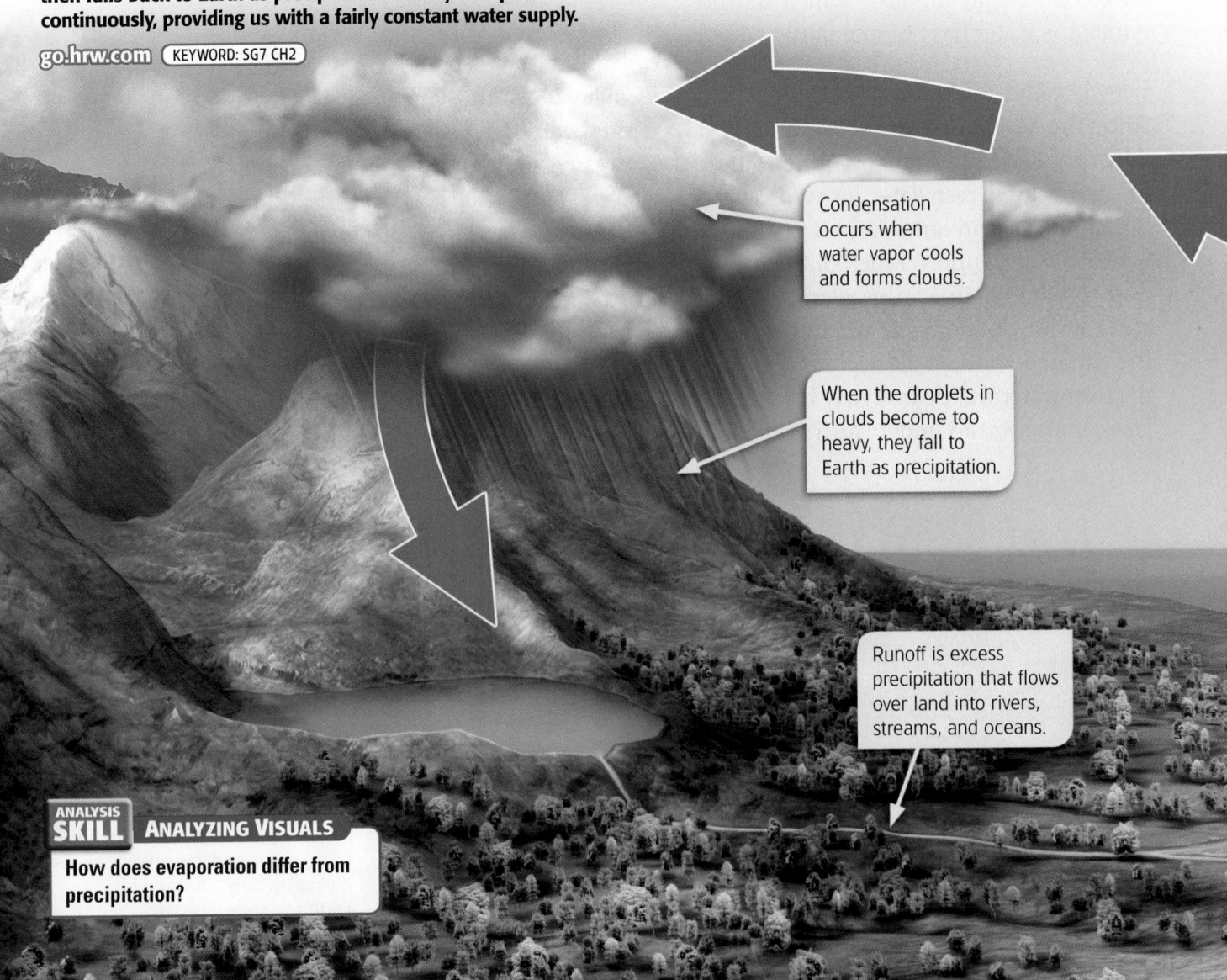

*Interactive
Close-up

The Water Cycle

Energy from the sun drives the water cycle. Surface water evaporates into Earth's atmosphere, where it condenses, then falls back to Earth as precipitation. This cycle repeats continuously, providing us with a fairly constant water supply.

go.hrw.com KEYWORD: SG7 CH2

Condensation occurs when water vapor cools and forms clouds.

When the droplets in clouds become too heavy, they fall to Earth as precipitation.

Runoff is excess precipitation that flows over land into rivers, streams, and oceans.

ANALYSIS
SKILL **ANALYZING VISUALS**

How does evaporation differ from precipitation?

The Water Cycle

When you think of water, you probably visualize a liquid—a flowing stream, a glass of ice-cold water, or a wave hitting the beach. But did you know that water is the only substance on Earth that occurs naturally as a solid, a liquid, and a gas? We see water as a solid in snow and ice and as a liquid in oceans and rivers. Water also occurs in the air as an invisible gas called **water vapor**.

Water is always moving. As water heats up and cools down, it moves from the planet's surface to the atmosphere, or the mass of air that surrounds Earth. One of the most important processes in nature is the water cycle. The **water cycle** is the movement of water from Earth's surface to the atmosphere and back.

The sun's energy drives the water cycle. As the sun heats water on Earth's surface, some of that water evaporates, or turns from liquid to gas, or water vapor. Water vapor then rises into the air. As the vapor rises, it cools. The cooling causes the water vapor to condense, or change from a vapor into tiny liquid droplets. These droplets join together to form clouds. If the droplets become heavy enough, precipitation occurs—that is, the water falls back to Earth as rain, snow, sleet, or hail.

When that precipitation falls back to Earth's surface, some of the water is absorbed into the soil as groundwater. Excess water, called runoff, flows over land and collects in streams, rivers, and oceans. Because the water cycle is constantly repeating, it allows us to maintain a fairly constant supply of water on Earth.

READING CHECK **Finding Main Ideas** What is the water cycle?

As energy from the sun heats water on Earth's surface, the water evaporates, or turns to water vapor, and rises to the atmosphere.

Water and People

How many times a day do you think about water? Many of us rarely give it a second thought, yet water is crucial for survival. Water problems such as the lack of water, polluted water, and flooding are concerns for people all around the world. Water also provides us with <u>countless</u> benefits, such as energy and recreation.

Water Problems

One of the greatest water problems people face is a lack of available freshwater. Many places face water shortages as a result of droughts, or long periods of lower-than-normal precipitation. Another cause of water shortages is overuse. In places like the southwestern United States, where the population has grown rapidly, the heavy demand for water has led to shortages.

Even where water is plentiful, it may not be clean enough to use. If chemicals and household wastes make their way into streams and rivers, they can contaminate the water supply. Polluted water can carry diseases. These diseases may harm humans, plants, and animals.

Flooding is another water problem that affects people around the world. Heavy rains often lead to flooding, which can damage property and threaten lives. One example of dangerous flooding occurred in Bangladesh in 2004. Floods there destroyed roads and schools and left some 25 million people homeless.

Water's Benefits

Water does more than just quench our thirst. It provides us with many benefits, such as food, power, and even recreation.

Water's most important benefit is that it provides us with food to eat. Everything we eat depends on water. For example, fruits and vegetables need water to grow.

FOCUS ON READING
Look at the word *countless* in this paragraph. The suffix *-less* means unable to. What does *countless* mean?

The Benefits of Water

Many people take advantage of the recreational and agricultural benefits that water provides.

Animals also need water to live and grow. As a result, we use water to farm and raise animals so that we will have food to eat.

Water is also an important source of energy. Using dams, we harness the power of moving water to produce electricity. Electricity provides power to air-condition or heat our homes, to run our washers and dryers, and to keep our food cold.

Water also provides us with recreation. Rivers, lakes, and oceans make it possible for us to swim, to fish, to surf, or to sail a boat. Although recreation is not critical for our survival, it does make our lives richer and more enjoyable.

READING CHECK **Summarizing** How does water affect people's lives?

SUMMARY AND PREVIEW In this section you learned that water is essential for life on Earth. Next, you will learn about the shapes on Earth's surface.

Section 2 Assessment

go.hrw.com
Online Quiz
KEYWORD: SG7 HP2

Reviewing Ideas, Terms, and Places

1. a. **Describe** Name and describe the different types of water that make up Earth's water supply.
   b. **Analyze** Why is only a small percentage of Earth's **freshwater** available to us?
   c. **Elaborate** In your opinion, which is more important—**surface water** or **groundwater**? Why?

2. a. **Recall** What drives the **water cycle**?
   b. **Make Inferences** From what bodies of water do you think most evaporation occurs? Why?

3. a. **Define** What is a drought?
   b. **Analyze** How does water support life on Earth?
   c. **Evaluate** What water problem do you think is most critical in your community? Why?

Critical Thinking

4. **Sequencing** Draw the graphic organizer at right. Then use your notes and the graphic organizer to identify the stages in Earth's water cycle.

FOCUS ON WRITING

5. **Learning about Water** Consider what you have learned about water in this section. How might you describe water in your haiku? What words might you use to describe Earth's water supply?

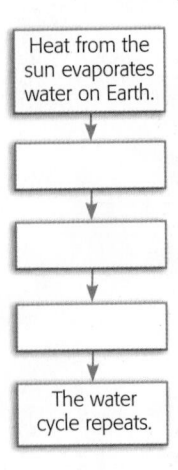

Heat from the sun evaporates water on Earth.

↓

↓

↓

The water cycle repeats.

The Land

If YOU lived there...

You live in the state of Washington. All your life, you have looked out at the beautiful, cone-shaped peaks of nearby mountains. One of them is Mount Saint Helens, an active volcano. You know that in 1980 it erupted violently, blowing a hole in the mountain and throwing ash and rock into the sky. Since then, scientists have watched the mountain carefully.

How do you feel about living near a volcano?

BUILDING BACKGROUND Over billions of years, many different forces have changed Earth's surface. Processes deep underground have built up landforms and even shifted the position of continents. Wind, water, and ice have also shaped the planet's landforms. Changes in Earth's surface continue to take place.

Landforms

Do you know the difference between a valley and a volcano? Can you tell a peninsula from a plateau? If you answered yes, then you are familiar with some of Earth's many landforms. **Landforms** are shapes on the planet's surface, such as hills or mountains. Landforms make up the landscapes that surround us, whether it's the rugged mountains of central Colorado or the flat plains of Oklahoma.

Earth's surface is covered with landforms of many different shapes and sizes. Some important landforms include:

- mountains, land that rises higher than 2,000 feet (610 m)
- valleys, areas of low land located between mountains or hills
- plains, stretches of mostly flat land
- islands, areas of land completely surrounded by water
- peninsulas, land surrounded by water on three sides

Because landforms play an important role in geography, many scientists study how landforms are made and how they affect human activity.

READING CHECK Summarizing What are some common landforms?

What You Will Learn...

Main Ideas

1. Earth's surface is covered by many different landforms.
2. Forces below Earth's surface build up our landforms.
3. Forces on the planet's surface shape Earth's landforms.
4. Landforms influence people's lives and culture.

The Big Idea

Processes below and on Earth's surface shape the planet's physical features.

Key Terms

landforms, *p. 35*
continents, *p. 36*
plate tectonics, *p. 36*
lava, *p. 37*
earthquakes, *p. 38*
weathering, *p. 39*
erosion, *p. 39*

TAKING NOTES As you read, use a diagram like the one below to take notes on Earth's landforms. In the circles, be sure to note how landforms are created, change, and affect people's lives.

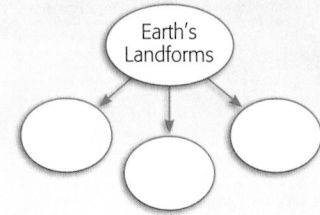

Forces below Earth's Surface

Geographers often study how landforms are made. One explanation for how landforms have been shaped involves forces below Earth's surface.

Earth's Plates

ACADEMIC VOCABULARY

structure the way something is set up or organized

To understand how these forces work, we must examine Earth's **structure**. The planet is made up of three layers. A solid inner core is surrounded by a liquid layer, or mantle. The solid outer layer of Earth is called the crust. The planet's **continents**, or large landmasses, are part of Earth's crust.

Geographers use the theory of plate tectonics to explain how forces below Earth's surface have shaped our landforms. The theory of **plate tectonics** suggests that Earth's surface is divided into a dozen or so slow-moving plates, or pieces of Earth's crust. As you can see in the image below,

some plates, like the Pacific plate, are quite large. Others, like the Nazca plate, are much smaller. These plates cover Earth's entire surface. Some plates are under the ocean. These are known as ocean plates. Other plates, known as continental plates, are under Earth's continents.

Why do these plates move? Energy deep inside the planet puts pressure on Earth's crust. As this pressure builds up, it forces the plates to shift. Earth's tectonic plates all move. However, they move in different directions and at different speeds.

The Movement of Continents

Earth's tectonic plates move slowly—up to several inches per year. The continents, which are part of Earth's plates, shift as the plates move. If we could look back some 200 million years, we would see that the continents have traveled great distances. This idea is known as continental drift.

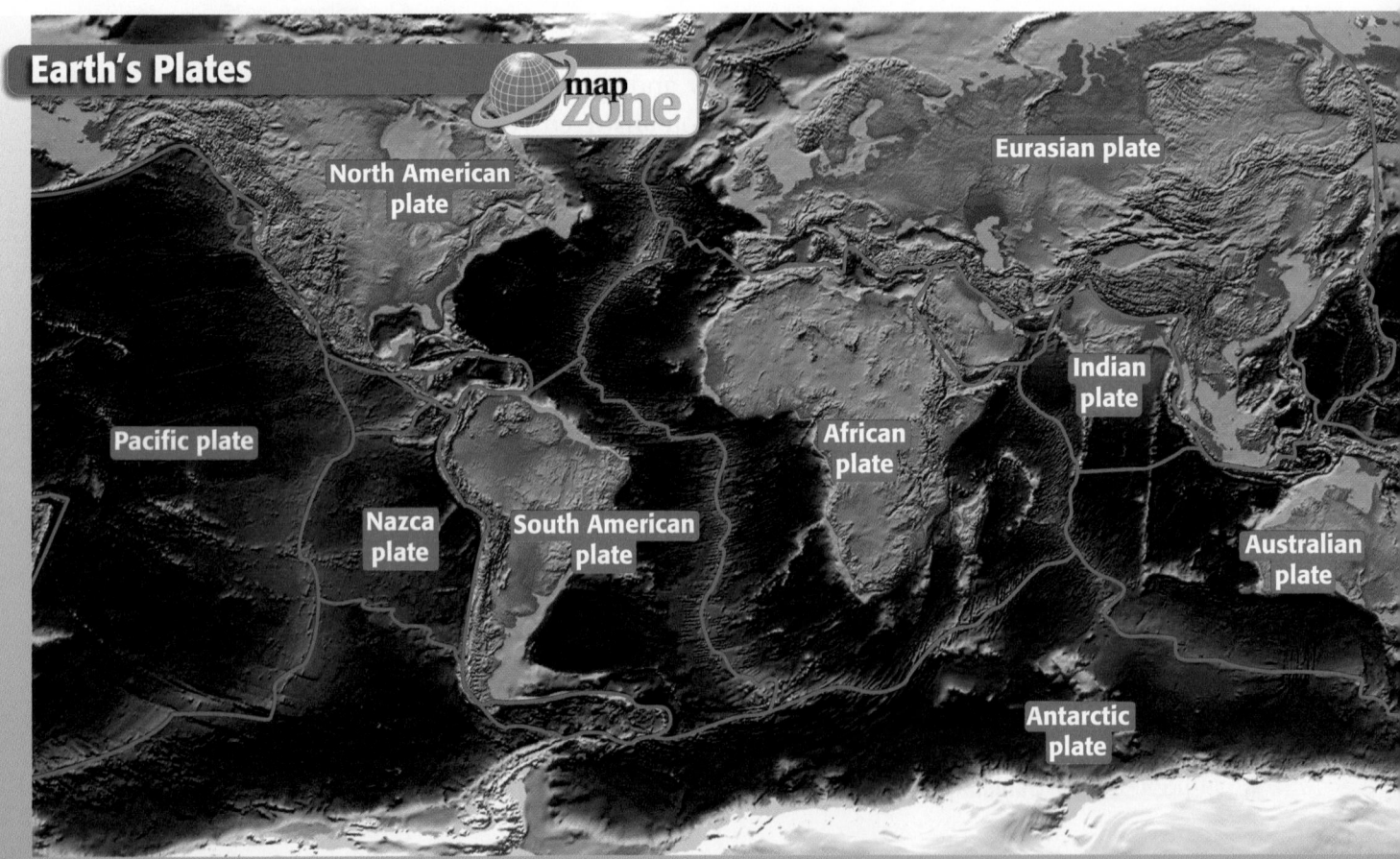

Earth's Plates

map zone

North American plate

Eurasian plate

Pacific plate

Indian plate

African plate

Nazca plate

South American plate

Australian plate

Antarctic plate

The theory of continental drift, first developed by Alfred Wegener, states that the continents were once united in a single supercontinent. According to this theory, Earth's plates shifted over millions of years. As a result, the continents slowly separated and moved to their present positions.

Earth's continents are still moving. Some plates move toward each other and collide. Other plates separate and move apart. Still others slide past one another. Over time, colliding, separating, and sliding plates have shaped Earth's landforms.

Plates Collide

As plates collide, the energy created from their collision produces distinct landforms. The collision of different types of plates creates different shapes on Earth's surface. Ocean trenches and mountain ranges are two examples of landforms produced by the collision of tectonic plates.

BIOGRAPHY

Alfred Wegener
(1880–1930)

German scientist Alfred Wegener's fascination with the similarities between the western coast of Africa and the eastern coast of South America led to his theory of continental drift. Wegener argued that the two continents had once been joined together. Years of plate movement broke the continents apart and moved them to their current locations. It was only after Wegener's death that his ideas became a central part of the theory of plate tectonics.

The theory of plate tectonics suggests that the plates that make up Earth's crust are moving, usually only a few inches per year. As Earth's plates collide, separate, and slide past each other, they create forces great enough to shape many of Earth's landforms.

ANALYZING VISUALS Looking at the map, what evidence indicates that plates have collided or separated?

When two ocean plates collide, one plate pushes under the other. This process creates ocean trenches. Ocean trenches are deep valleys in the ocean floor. Near Japan, for example, the Pacific plate is slowly moving under other plates. This collision has created several deep ocean trenches, including the world's deepest trench, the Mariana Trench.

Ocean plates and continental plates can also collide. When this occurs, the ocean plate drops beneath the continental plate. This action forces the land above to crumple and form a mountain range. The Andes in South America, for example, were formed when the South American and Nazca plates collided.

The collision of two continental plates also results in mountain-building. When continental plates collide, the land pushes up, sometimes to great heights. The world's highest mountain range, the Himalayas, formed when the Indian plate crashed into the Eurasian plate. In fact, the Himalayas are still growing as the two plates continue to crash into each other.

Plates Separate

A second type of plate movement causes plates to separate. As plates move apart, gaps between the plates allow magma, a liquid rock from the planet's interior, to rise to Earth's crust. **Lava**, or magma that reaches Earth's surface, emerges from the gap that has formed. As the lava cools, it builds a mid-ocean ridge, or underwater mountain. For example, the separation of the North American and Eurasian plates formed the largest underwater mountain, the Mid-Atlantic Ridge. If these mid-ocean ridges grow high enough, they can rise above the surface of the ocean, forming volcanic islands. Iceland, on the boundary of the Eurasian and North American plates, is an example of such an island.

FOCUS ON READING
The suffix *–sion* means the act of. What does the word *collision* mean?

Plates Slide

Tectonic plates also slide past each other. As plates pass by one another, they sometimes grind together. This grinding produces **earthquakes**—sudden, violent movements of Earth's crust. Earthquakes often take place along faults, or breaks in Earth's crust where movement occurs. In California, for example, the Pacific plate is sliding by the edge of the North American plate. This has created the San Andreas Fault zone, an area where earthquakes are quite common.

The San Andreas Fault zone is one of many areas that lie along the boundaries of the Pacific plate. The frequent movement of this plate produces many earthquakes and volcanic eruptions along its edges. In fact, the region around the Pacific plate, called the Ring of Fire, is home to most of the world's earthquakes and volcanoes.

READING CHECK Finding Main Ideas What forces below Earth's surface shape landforms?

Plate Movement

The movement of tectonic plates has produced many of Earth's landforms. Volcanoes, islands, and mountains often result from the separation or collision of Earth's plates.

ANALYZING VISUALS What type of landform is created by the collision of two continental plates?

The separation of plates can allow magma to rise up and create volcanic islands like Surtsey Island, near Iceland.

Plate A

Plate B

magma

Plate A

Plate B

The Himalayas in South Asia resulted from the collision of two massive continental plates.

Forces on Earth's Surface

For millions of years, the movement of Earth's tectonic plates has been building up landforms on Earth's surface. At the same time, other forces are working to change those very same landforms.

Imagine a small pile of dirt and rock on a table. If you poured water on the pile, it would move the dirt and rock from one place to another. Likewise, if you were to blow at the pile, the rock and dirt would also move. The same process happens in nature. Weather, water, and other forces change Earth's landforms by wearing them away or reshaping them.

Weathering

One force that wears away landforms is weathering. **Weathering is the process by which rock is broken down into smaller pieces.** Several factors cause rock to break down. In desert areas, daytime heating and nighttime cooling can cause rocks to crack. Water may get into cracks in rocks and freeze. The ice then expands with a force great enough to break the rock. Even the roots of trees can pry rocks apart.

Regardless of which weathering process is at work, rocks eventually break down. These small pieces of rock are known as sediment. Once weathering has taken place, wind, ice, and water often move sediment from one place to another.

Erosion

Another force that changes landforms is the process of erosion. **Erosion is the movement of sediment from one location to another.** Erosion can wear away or build up landforms. Wind, ice, and water all cause erosion.

Powerful winds often cause erosion. Winds lift sediment into the air and carry it across great distances. On beaches and in deserts, wind can deposit large amounts of sand to form dunes. Blowing sand can also wear down rock. The sand acts like sandpaper to polish and wear away at rocks. As you can see in the photo below, wind can have a dramatic effect on landforms.

Earth's glaciers also have the power to cause massive erosion. Glaciers, or large, slow-moving sheets of ice, build up when winter snows do not melt the following summer. Glaciers can be huge. Glaciers in Greenland and Antarctica, for example, are great sheets of ice up to two miles (3 km) thick. Some glaciers flow slowly downhill like rivers of ice. As they do so, they erode the land by carving large U-shaped valleys and sharp mountain peaks. As the ice flows downhill, it crushes rock into sediment and can move huge rocks long distances.

Wind Erosion

Landforms in Utah's Canyonlands National Park have been worn away mostly by thousands of years of powerful winds.

39

Water is the most common cause of erosion. Waves in oceans and lakes can wear away the shore, creating jagged coastlines, like those on the coast of Oregon. Rivers also cause erosion. Over many years, the flowing water can cut through rock, forming canyons, or narrow areas with steep walls. Arizona's Horseshoe Bend and Grand Canyon are examples of canyons created in this way.

Flowing water shapes other landforms as well. When water deposits sediment in new locations, it creates new landforms. For example, rivers create floodplains when they flood their banks and deposit sediment along the banks. Sediment that is carried by a river all the way out to sea creates a delta. The sediment settles to the bottom, where the river meets the sea. The Nile and Mississippi rivers have created two of the world's largest river deltas.

READING CHECK **Comparing** How are weathering and erosion similar?

Water Erosion

For millions of years, the Colorado River has worn away the rock at Horseshoe Bend in Arizona.

Landforms Influence Life

Why do you live where you do? Perhaps your family moved to the desert to avoid harsh winter weather. Or possibly one of your ancestors settled near a river delta because its fertile soil was ideal for growing crops. Maybe your family wanted to live near the ocean to start a fishing business. As these examples show, landforms exert a strong influence on people's lives. Earth's landforms affect our settlements and our culture. At the same time, we affect the landforms around us.

Earth's landforms can influence where people settle. People sometimes settle near certain landforms and avoid others. For example, many settlements are built near fertile river valleys or deltas. The earliest urban civilization, for example, was built in the valley between the Tigris and Euphrates rivers. Other times, landforms discourage people from settling in a certain place. Tall, rugged mountains, like the Himalayas, and harsh desert climates, like the Sahara, do not usually attract large settlements.

Landforms affect our culture in ways that we may not have noticed. Landforms often influence what jobs are available in a region. For example, rich mineral deposits in the mountains of Colorado led to the development of a mining industry there. Landforms even affect language. On the island of New Guinea in Southeast Asia, rugged mountains have kept the people so isolated that more than 700 languages are spoken on the island today.

People sometimes change landforms to suit their needs. People may choose to modify landforms in order to improve their lives. For example, engineers built the Panama Canal to make travel from the Atlantic Ocean to the Pacific Ocean easier. In Southeast Asia, people who farm on steep hillsides cut terraces into the slope to

Living with Landforms

The people of Rio de Janeiro, Brazil, have learned to adapt to the mountains and bays that dominate their landscape.

ANALYZING VISUALS How have people in Rio de Janiero adapted to their landscape?

create more level space to grow their crops. People have even built huge dams along rivers to divert water for use in nearby towns or farms.

READING CHECK **Analyzing** What are some examples of humans adjusting to and changing landforms?

SUMMARY AND PREVIEW Landforms are created by actions deep within the planet's surface, and they are changed by forces on Earth's surface, like weathering and erosion. In the next chapter you will learn how other forces, like weather and climate, affect Earth's people.

Section 3 Assessment

go.hrw.com
Online Quiz
KEYWORD: SG7 HP2

Reviewing Ideas, Terms, and Places

1. **a. Describe** What are some common **landforms**?
   b. Analyze Why do geographers study landforms?
2. **a. Identify** What is the theory of **plate tectonics**?
   b. Compare and Contrast How are the effects of colliding plates and separating plates similar and different?
   c. Predict How might Earth's surface change as tectonic plates continue to move?
3. **a. Recall** What is the process of **weathering**?
   b. Elaborate How does water affect sediment?
4. **a. Recall** How do landforms affect life on Earth?
   b. Predict How might people adapt to life in an area with steep mountains?

Critical Thinking

5. **Analyzing** Use your notes and the chart below to identify the different factors that alter Earth's landforms and the changes that they produce.

Factor	Change in Landform

FOCUS ON WRITING

6. **Writing about Earth's Land** Think of some vivid words you could use to describe Earth's landforms. As you think of them, add them to your notebook.

The Ring of Fire

Essential Elements

The World in Spatial Terms
Places and Regions
Physical Systems
Human Systems
Environment and Society
The Uses of Geography

Background Does "the Ring of Fire" sound like the title of a fantasy novel? It's actually the name of a region that circles the Pacific Ocean known for its fiery volcanoes and powerful earthquakes. The Ring of Fire stretches from the tip of South America all the way up to Alaska, and from Japan down to the islands east of Australia. Along this belt, the Pacific plate moves against several other tectonic plates. As a result, thousands of earthquakes occur there every year, and dozens of volcanoes erupt.

The Eruption of Mount Saint Helens One of the best-known volcanoes in the Ring of Fire is Mount Saint Helens in Washington State. Mount Saint Helens had been dormant, or quiet, since 1857. Then in March 1980, it began spitting out puffs of steam and ash. Officials warned people to leave the area. Scientists brought in equipment to measure the growing bulge in the mountainside. Everyone feared the volcano might erupt at any moment.

On May 18, after a sudden earthquake, Mount Saint Helens let loose a massive explosion of rock and lava. Heat from the blast melted snow on the mountain, which

Ring of Fire

map zone

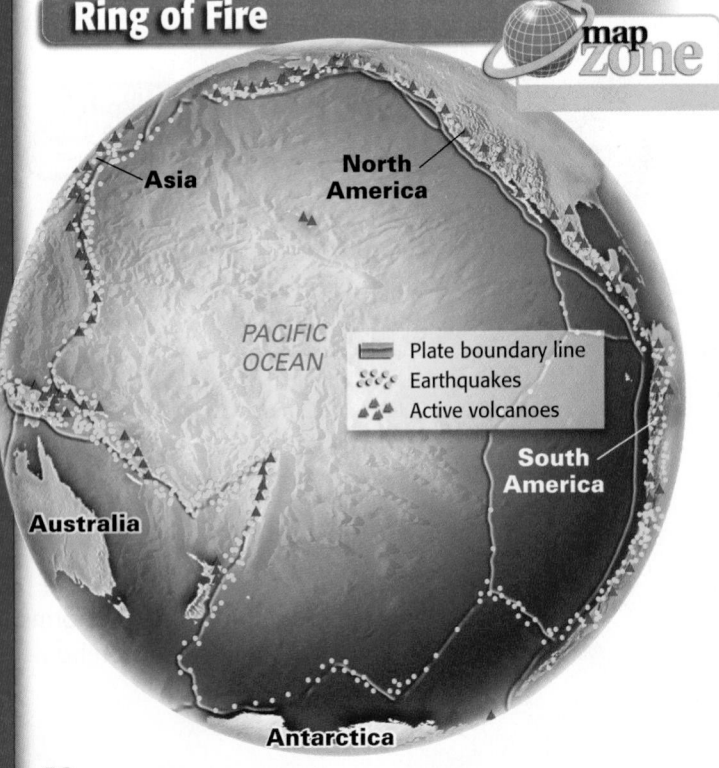

Asia
North America
PACIFIC OCEAN
South America
Australia
Antarctica

Plate boundary line
Earthquakes
Active volcanoes

THE WORLD ALMANAC
Facts about the World
Major Eruptions in the Ring of Fire

Volcano	Year
Tambora, Indonesia	1815
Krakatau, Indonesia	1883
Mount Saint Helens, United States	**1980**
Nevado del Ruiz, Colombia	1985
Mount Pinatubo, Philippines	1991

go.hrw.com KEYWORD: SG7 CH2

Mount Saint Helens, 1980
The 1980 eruption of Mount Saint Helens blew ash and hot gases miles into the air. Today, scientists study the volcano to learn more about predicting eruptions.

mixed with ash to create deadly mudflows. As the mud quickly poured downhill, it flattened forests, swept away cars, and destroyed buildings. Clouds of ash covered the land, killing crops, clogging waterways, and blanketing towns as far as 200 miles (330 km) away. When the volcano finally quieted down, 57 people had died. Damage totaled nearly $1 billion. If it were not for the early evacuation of the area, the destruction could have been much worse.

What It Means By studying Mount Saint Helens, scientists learned a great deal about stratovolcanoes. These are tall, steep, cone-shaped volcanoes that have violent eruptions. Stratovolcanoes often form in areas where tectonic plates collide.

Because stratovolcanoes often produce deadly eruptions, scientists try to predict when they might erupt. The lessons learned from Mount Saint Helens helped scientists

warn people about another stratovolcano, Mount Pinatubo in the Philippines. That eruption in 1991 was the second-largest of the 1900s. It was far from the deadliest, however. Careful observation and timely warnings saved thousands of lives.

The Ring of Fire will always remain a threat. However, the better we understand its volcanoes, the better prepared we'll be when they erupt.

Geography for Life Activity

1. How did the eruption of Mount Saint Helens affect the surrounding area?

2. Why do scientists monitor volcanic activity?

3. **Investigating the Effects of Volcanoes** Some volcanic eruptions affect environmental conditions around the world. Research the eruption of either Mount Saint Helens or the Philippines' Mount Pinatubo to find out how its eruption affected the global environment.

Using a Physical Map

Learn

Physical maps show important physical features, like oceans and mountains, in a particular area. They also indicate an area's elevation, or the height of the land in relation to sea level.

When you use a physical map, there are important pieces of information you should always examine.

- Identify physical features. Natural features, such as mountains, rivers, and lakes, are labeled on physical maps. Read the labels carefully to identify what physical features are present.

- Read the legend. On physical maps, the legend indicates scale as well as elevation. The different colors in the elevation key indicate how far above or below sea level a place is.

Practice

Use the physical map of India at right to answer the questions below.

1. What landforms and bodies of water are indicated on the map?

2. What is the highest elevation in India? Where is it located?

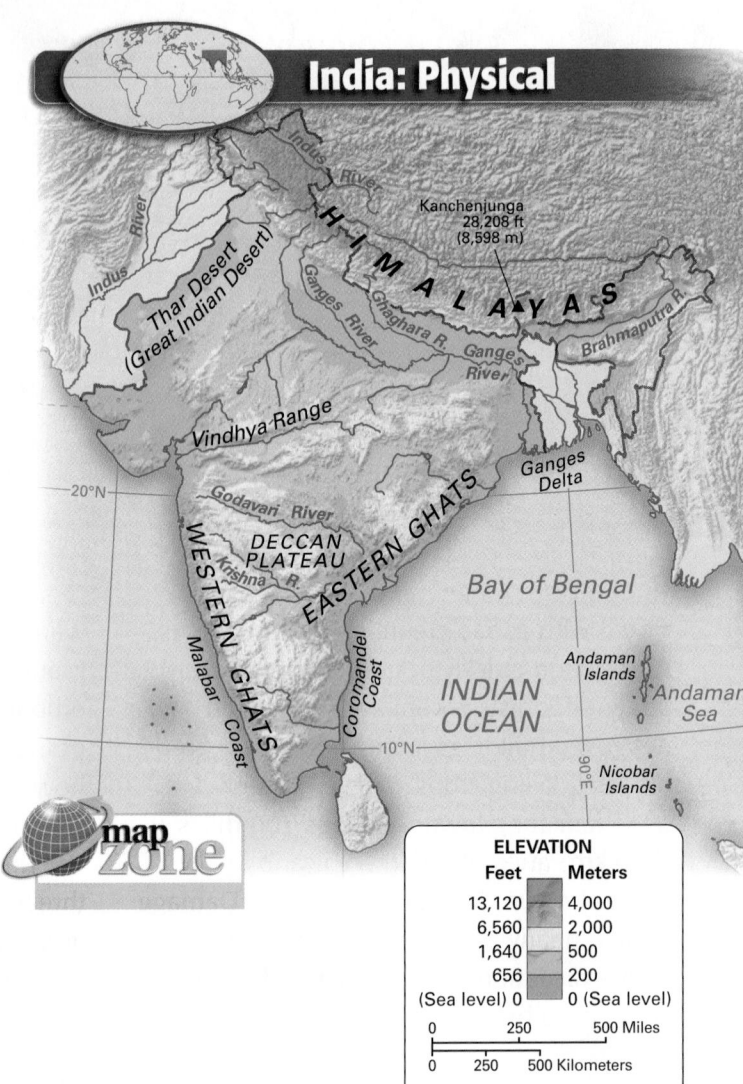

India: Physical

ELEVATION		
Feet		**Meters**
13,120		4,000
6,560		2,000
1,640		500
656		200
(Sea level) 0		0 (Sea level)

0   250   500 Miles

0   250   500 Kilometers

Projection: Lambert Conformal Conic

Apply

Locate the physical map of Africa in the atlas in the back of the book. Use the map to answer the questions below.

1. Which region has the highest elevation?

2. What bodies of water surround Africa?

3. What large island is located off the east coast of Africa?

Chapter Review

Geography's Impact
video series
Review the video to answer the closing question:
What are some reasons for water shortages, and what can be done to solve this problem?

Visual Summary

Use the visual summary below to help you review the main ideas of the chapter.

QUICK FACTS

The amount of solar energy Earth receives changes based on Earth's movement and position.

Water is crucial to life on Earth. Our abundant water supply is stored in oceans, in lakes, and underground.

Earth's various landforms are shaped by complex processes both under and on the planet's surface.

Reviewing Vocabulary, Terms, and Places

For each statement below, write T if it is true and F if it is false. If the statement is false, write the correct term that would make the sentence a true statement.

1. **Weathering** is the movement of sediment from one location to another.

2. Because high **latitude** areas receive indirect rays from the sun, they have cooler temperatures.

3. Most of our **groundwater** is stored in Earth's streams, rivers, and lakes.

4. It takes 365¼ days for Earth to complete one **rotation** around the sun.

5. Streams are formed when **precipitation** collects in narrow channels.

6. **Earthquakes** cause erosion as they flow downhill, carving valleys and mountain peaks.

7. The planet's tilt affects the amount of **erosion** Earth receives from the sun.

Comprehension and Critical Thinking

SECTION 1 *(Pages 26–29)*

8. **a. Identify** What factors influence the amount of energy that different places on Earth receive from the sun?

   b. Analyze Why do the Northern and Southern hemispheres experience opposite seasons?

   c. Predict What might happen to the amount of solar energy we receive if Earth's axis were straight up and down?

SECTION 2 *(Pages 30–34)*

9. **a. Describe** What different sources of water are available on Earth?

   b. Draw Conclusions How does the water cycle keep Earth's water supply relatively constant?

   c. Elaborate What water problems affect people around the world? What solutions can you think of for one of those problems?

10. a. Define What is a landform? What are some common types of landforms?

b. Analyze Why are Earth's landforms still changing?

c. Elaborate What physical features dominate the landscape in your community? How do they affect life there?

Using the Internet

go.hrw.com
KEYWORD: SG7 CH2

11. Activity: Researching Earth's Seasons Earth's seasons not only affect temperatures, they also affect how much daylight is available during specific times of the year. Enter the activity keyword to research Earth's seasons and view animations to see how seasons change. Then use the interactive worksheet to answer some questions about what you learned.

FOCUS ON READING AND WRITING

Using Word Parts *Use what you learned about prefixes, suffixes, and word roots to answer the questions below.*

12. Examine the word *separation*. What is the suffix? What is the root? What does separation mean?

13. The prefix *in-* means not. What do the words *invisible* and *inactive* mean?

14. The suffix *-ment* means action or process. What does the word *movement* mean?

Writing a Haiku *Use your notes and the directions below to write a haiku.*

15. Look back through the notes you made about planet Earth. Choose one aspect of Earth to describe in a haiku. Haikus are short, three-line poems. Traditional haikus consist of only 17 syllables—five in the first line, seven in the second line, and five in the third line. You may choose to write a traditional haiku, or you may choose to write a haiku with a different number of syllables. Be sure to use descriptive words to paint a picture of planet Earth.

Social Studies Skills

Using a Physical Map *Examine the physical map of the United States in the back of this book. Use it to answer the questions below.*

16. What physical feature extends along the Gulf of Mexico?

17. What mountain range in the West lies above 6,560 feet?

18. Where does the elevation drop below sea level?

Map Activity

Physical Map *Use the map below to answer the questions that follow.*

19. Which letter indicates a river?

20. Which letter on the map indicates the highest elevation?

21. The lowest elevation on the map is indicated by which letter?

22. An island is indicated by which letter?

23. Which letter indicates a large body of water?

24. Which letter indicates an area of land between 1,640 feet and 6,560 feet above sea level?

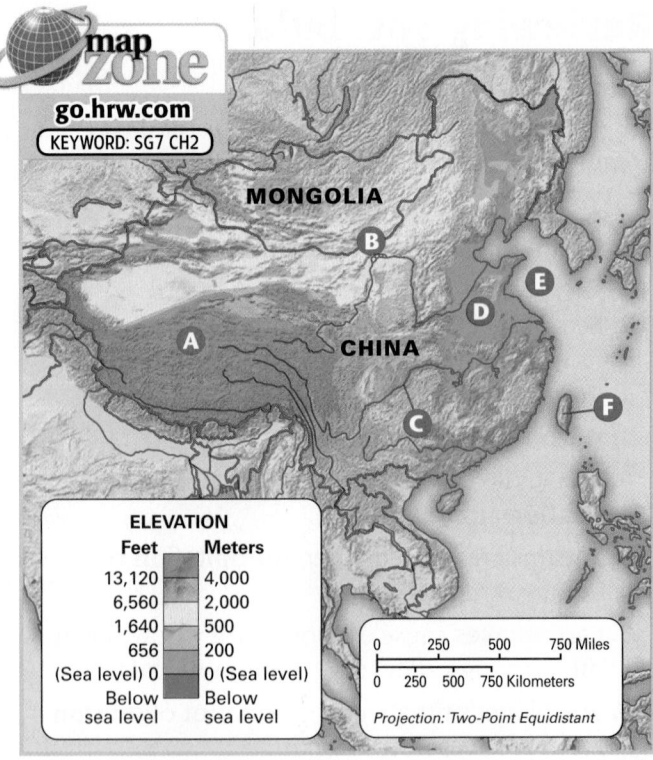

DIRECTIONS: Read questions 1 through 7 and write the letter of the best response. Then read question 8 and write your own well-constructed response.

1 **Which regions on Earth have seasons tied to the amount of rainfall?**

A polar regions

B the tropics

C the Northern Hemisphere

D high latitudes

2 **Most of Earth's water supply is made up of**

A groundwater.

B water vapor.

C freshwater.

D salt water.

3 **The theory of continental drift explains how**

A Earth's continents have moved thousands of miles.

B Earth's axis has moved to its current position.

C mountains and valleys are formed.

D sediment moves from one place to another.

4 **Which of the following is a cause of erosion?**

A evaporation

B ice

C plate collisions

D Earth's tilt

5 **Changes in solar energy that create day and night are a result of**

A the movement of tectonic plates.

B Earth's rotation.

C the revolution of Earth around the sun.

D Earth's tilt.

The Water Cycle

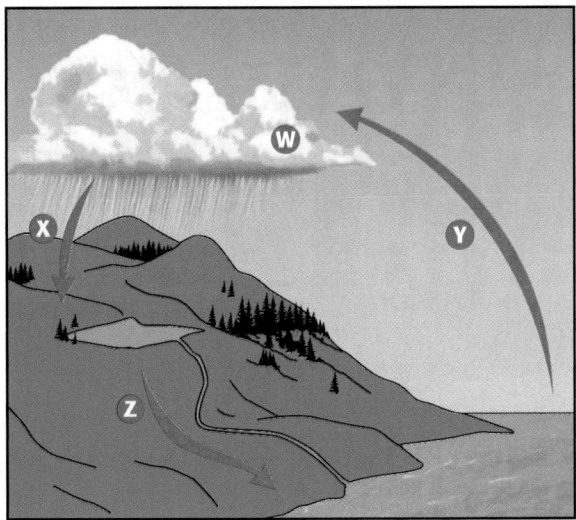

6 **In the illustration above, which letter *best* reflects the process of evaporation?**

A W

B X

C Y

D Z

7 **Which of the following is *most likely* a cause of water pollution?**

A River water is used to produce electricity.

B Heavy rainfall causes a river to overflow its banks.

C Chemicals from a factory seep into the local water supply.

D Groundwater is used faster than it can be replaced.

8 **Extended Response Question** Use the water cycle diagram above to explain how Earth's water cycle affects our water supply.

Climate, Environment, and Resources

What You Will Learn...

In this chapter you will learn about weather and climate. Climate is the weather conditions over a long period of time. You will also learn about how living things and the environment are connected and about the importance of Earth's natural resources.

FOCUS ON READING AND VIEWING

Understanding Cause and Effect A cause makes something happen. An effect is the result of a cause. Words such as *because, result, since,* and *therefore* can signal causes or effects. As you read, look for causes and effects to understand how things relate. **See the lesson, Understanding Cause and Effect, on page R4.**

Presenting and Viewing a Weather Report You have likely seen a TV weather report, which tells the current weather conditions and predicts future conditions. After reading this chapter, prepare a weather report for a season and place of your choosing. Present your report to the class and then view your classmates' reports.

Climate Earth has many climates, such as the dry climate of the region shown here.

ANALYSIS
SKILL **ANALYZING VISUALS**

This photo shows a severe thunderstorm. These storms produce violent weather, such as heavy rainfall and strong winds, which affects people's lives.

How do you think this storm might have affected the people who lived in this area?

HOLT

Geography's Impact
video series
Watch the video to understand the impact of weather.

Environments Living things, such as this koala, depend on their surroundings.

Natural Resources Earth provides many valuable and useful natural resources, such as oil.

Weather and Climate

What You Will Learn...

Main Ideas

1. While weather is short term, climate is a region's average weather over a long period.
2. The amount of sun at a given location is affected by Earth's tilt, movement, and shape.
3. Wind and water move heat around Earth, affecting how warm or wet a place is.
4. Mountains influence temperature and precipitation.

The Big Idea

The sun, location, wind, water, and mountains affect weather and climate.

Key Terms

weather, *p. 50*
climate, *p. 50*
prevailing winds, *p. 51*
ocean currents, *p. 52*
front, *p. 53*

TAKING NOTES As you read, use a chart like the one here to take notes about the factors that affect weather and climate.

Sun and Location	Wind and Water	Mountains

If YOU lived there...

You live in Buffalo, New York, at the eastern end of Lake Erie. One evening in January, you are watching the local TV news. The weather forecaster says, "A huge storm is brewing in the Midwest and moving east. As usual, winds from this storm will drop several feet of snow on Buffalo as they blow off Lake Erie."

Why will winds off the lake drop snow on Buffalo?

BUILDING BACKGROUND All life on Earth depends on the sun's energy and on the cycle of water from the land to the air and back again. In addition, sun and water work with other forces, such as wind, to create global patterns of weather and climate.

Understanding Weather and Climate

"Climate is what you expect; weather is what you get."
—Robert Heinlein, from *Time Enough for Love*

What is it like outside right now where you live? Is it hot, sunny, wet, cold? Is this what it is usually like outside for this time of year? The first two questions are about **weather**, the short-term changes in the air for a given place and time. The last question is about **climate**, a region's average weather conditions over a long period.

Weather is the temperature and precipitation from hour to hour or day to day. "Today is sunny, but tomorrow it might rain" is a statement about weather. Climate is the expected weather for a place based on data and experience. "Summer here is usually hot and muggy" is a statement about climate. The factors that shape weather and climate include the sun, location on Earth, wind, water, and mountains.

READING CHECK Finding Main Ideas How are weather and climate different from each other?

Sun and Location

Energy from the sun heats the planet. Different locations receive different amounts of sunlight, though. Thus, some locations are warmer than others. The differences are due to Earth's tilt, movement, and shape.

You have learned that Earth is tilted on its axis. The part of Earth tilted toward the sun receives more solar energy than the part tilted away from the sun. As the Earth revolves around the sun, the part of Earth that is tilted toward the sun changes during the year. This process creates the seasons. In general, temperatures in summer are warmer than in winter.

Earth's shape also affects the amount of sunlight different locations receive. Because Earth is a sphere, its surface is rounded. Therefore, solar rays are more direct and concentrated near the equator. Nearer the poles, the sun's rays are less direct and more spread out.

As a result, areas near the equator, called the lower latitudes, are mainly hot year-round. Areas near the poles, called the higher latitudes, are cold year-round. Areas about halfway between the equator and poles have more seasonal change. In general, the farther from the equator, or the higher the latitude, the colder the climate.

READING CHECK **Summarizing** How does Earth's tilt on its axis affect climate?

Wind and Water

Heat from the sun moves across Earth's surface. The reason is that air and water warmed by the sun are constantly on the move. You might have seen a gust of wind or a stream of water carrying dust or dirt. In a similar way, wind and water carry heat from place to place. As a result, they make different areas of Earth warmer or cooler.

Global Wind Systems

Prevailing winds blow in circular belts across Earth. These belts occur at about every 30° of latitude.

ANALYZING VISUALS Which direction do the prevailing winds blow across the United States?

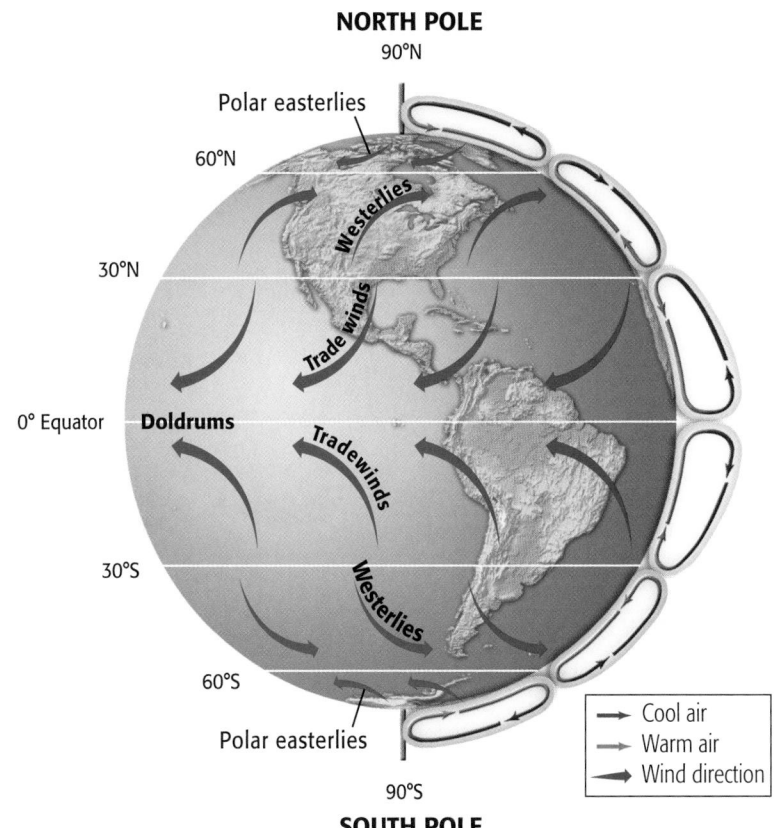

NORTH POLE
90°N
Polar easterlies
60°N
Westerlies
30°N
Trade winds
0° Equator Doldrums
Tradewinds
30°S
Westerlies
60°S
Polar easterlies
90°S
SOUTH POLE

→ Cool air
→ Warm air
→ Wind direction

Global Winds

Wind, or the sideways movement of air, blows in great streams around the planet. **Prevailing winds** are winds that blow in the same direction over large areas of Earth. The diagram above shows the patterns of Earth's prevailing winds.

To understand Earth's wind patterns, you need to think about the weight of air. Although you cannot feel it, air has weight. This weight changes with the temperature. Cold air is heavier than warm air. For this reason, when air cools, it gets heavier and sinks. When air warms, it gets lighter and rises. As warm air rises, cooler air moves in to take its place, creating wind.

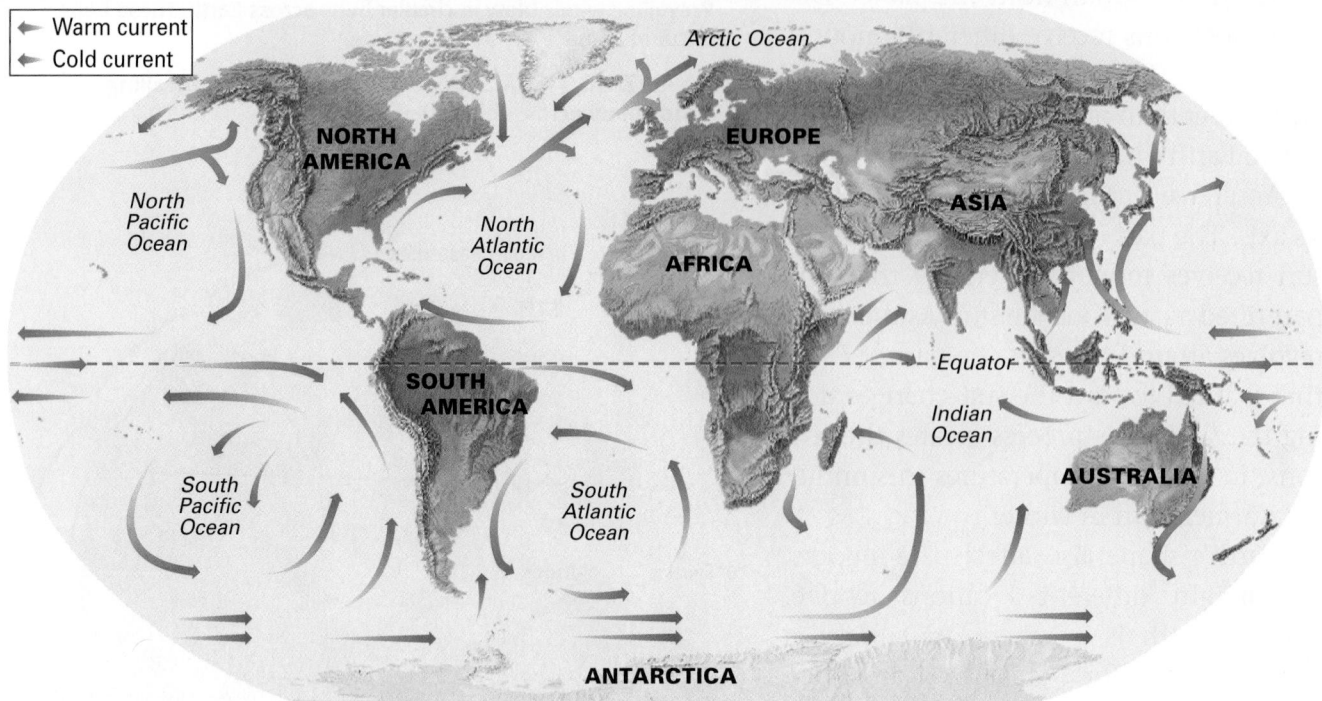

Warm current
Cold current

Arctic Ocean

NORTH AMERICA

EUROPE

ASIA

North Pacific Ocean

North Atlantic Ocean

AFRICA

SOUTH AMERICA

Equator

Indian Ocean

AUSTRALIA

South Pacific Ocean

South Atlantic Ocean

ANTARCTICA

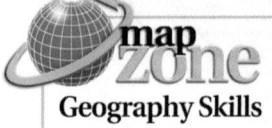

map zone
Geography Skills

Movement Ocean currents carry warm water from the equator toward the poles and cold water from the poles toward the equator. The currents affect temperature.

1. **Use the Map** Does a warm or cold ocean current flow along the lower west coast of North America?
2. **Explain** How do ocean currents move heat between warmer and colder areas of Earth?

On a global scale, this rising, sinking, and flowing of air creates Earth's prevailing wind patterns. At the equator, hot air rises and flows toward the poles. At the poles, cold air sinks and flows toward the equator. Meanwhile, Earth is rotating. Earth's rotation causes prevailing winds to curve east or west rather than flowing directly north or south.

FOCUS ON READING

What is the effect of Earth's rotation on prevailing winds?

Depending on their source, prevailing winds make a region warmer or colder. In addition, the source of the winds can make a region drier or wetter. Winds that form from warm air or pass over lots of water often carry moisture. In contrast, winds that form from cold air or pass over lots of land often are dry.

Ocean Currents

Like wind, **ocean currents**—large streams of surface seawater—move heat around Earth. Winds drive these currents. The map above shows how Earth's ocean currents carry warm or cool water to different areas. The water's temperature affects air temperature near it. Warm currents raise temperatures; cold currents lower them.

The Gulf Stream is a warm current that flows north along the U.S. East Coast. It then flows east across the Atlantic to become the North Atlantic Drift. As the warm current flows along northwestern Europe, it heats the air. Westerlies blow the warmed air across Europe. This process makes Europe warmer than it otherwise would be.

Large Bodies of Water

Large bodies of water, such as an ocean or sea, also affect climate. Water heats and cools more slowly than land does. For this reason, large bodies of water make the temperature of the land nearby milder. Thus, coastal areas, such as the California coast, usually do not have as wide temperature ranges as inland areas.

As an example, the state of Michigan is largely surrounded by the Great Lakes. The lakes make temperatures in the state milder than other places as far north.

Wind, Water, and Storms

If you watch weather reports, you will hear about storms moving across the United States. Tracking storms is important to us because the United States has so many of them. As you will see, some areas of the world have more storms than others do.

Most storms occur when two air masses collide. An air mass is a large body of air. The place where two air masses of different temperatures or moisture content meet is a **front**. Air masses frequently collide in regions like the United States, where the westerlies meet the polar easterlies.

Fronts can produce rain or snow as well as severe weather such as thunderstorms and icy blizzards. Thunderstorms produce rain, lightning, and thunder. In the United States, they are most common in spring and summer. Blizzards produce strong winds and large amounts of snow and are most common during winter.

Thunderstorms and blizzards can also produce tornadoes, another type of severe storm. A tornado is a small, rapidly twisting funnel of air that touches the ground. Tornadoes usually affect a limited area and last only a few minutes. However, they can be highly destructive, uprooting trees and tossing large vehicles through the air. Tornadoes can be extremely deadly as well.

In 1925 a tornado that crossed Missouri, Illinois, and Indiana left 695 people dead. It is the deadliest U.S. tornado on record.

The largest and most destructive storms, however, are hurricanes. These large, rotating storms form over tropical waters in the Atlantic Ocean, usually from late summer to fall. Did you know that hurricanes and typhoons are the same? Typhoons are just hurricanes that form in the Pacific Ocean.

Extreme Weather

Severe weather is often dangerous and destructive. In the top photo, rescuers search for people during a flood in Yardley, Pennsylvania. Below, a tornado races across a wheat field.

Snow

Warming dry air

Rain

Cooling moist air

Rain Shadow

Rain Shadow Effect

Most of the moisture in the ocean air falls on the mountainside facing the wind. LIttle moisture remains to fall on the other side, creating a rain shadow.

Mountains

Mountains can influence an area's climate by affecting both temperature and precipitation. Many high mountains are located in warm areas yet have snow at the top all year. How can this be? The reason is that temperature decreases with elevation—the height on Earth's surface above sea level.

Mountains also create wet and dry areas. Look at the diagram at left. A mountain forces air blowing against it to rise. As it rises, the air cools and precipitation falls as rain or snow. Thus, the side of the mountain facing the wind is often green and lush. However, little moisture remains for the other side. This effect creates a rain shadow, a dry area on the mountainside facing away from the direction of the wind.

READING CHECK Finding Main Ideas How does temperature change with elevation?

SUMMARY AND PREVIEW As you can see, the sun, location on Earth, wind, water, and mountains affect weather and climate. In the next section you will learn what the world's different climate regions are like.

Hurricanes produce drenching rain and strong winds that can reach speeds of 155 miles per hour (250 kph) or more. This is more than twice as fast as most people drive on highways. In addition, hurricanes form tall walls of water called storm surges. When a storm surge smashes into land, it can wipe out an entire coastal area.

READING CHECK Analyzing Why do coastal areas have milder climates than inland areas?

Section 1 Assessment

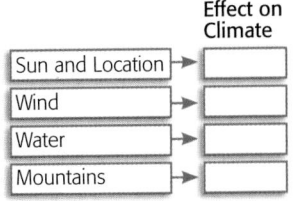
Reviewing Ideas, Terms, and Places

1. **a. Recall** What shapes **weather** and **climate**?
   b. Contrast How do weather and climate differ?
2. **a. Identify** What parts of Earth receive the most heat from the sun?
   b. Explain Why do the poles receive less solar energy than the equator does?
3. **a. Describe** What creates wind?
   b. Summarize How do **ocean currents** and large bodies of water affect climate?
4. **a. Define** What is a rain shadow?
   b. Explain Why might a mountaintop and a nearby valley have widely different temperatures?

Critical Thinking

5. **Identifying Cause and Effect** Draw a chart like this one. Use your notes to explain how each factor affects climate.

	Effect on Climate
Sun and Location	→
Wind	→
Water	→
Mountains	→

FOCUS ON VIEWING

6. **Writing about Weather and Climate** Jot down information to include in your weather report. For example, you might want to include a term such as *fronts* or describe certain types of storms such as hurricanes or tornadoes.

World Climates

If YOU lived there...

You live in Colorado and are on your first serious hike in the Rocky Mountains. Since it is July, it is hot in the campground in the valley. But your guide insists that you bring a heavy fleece jacket. By noon, you have climbed to 11,000 feet. You are surprised to see patches of snow in shady spots. Suddenly, you are very happy that you brought your jacket!

Why does it get colder as you climb higher?

BUILDING BACKGROUND While weather is the day-to-day changes in a certain area, climate is the average weather conditions over a long period. Earth's different climates depend partly on the amount of sunlight a region receives. Differences in climate also depend on factors such as wind, water, and elevation.

Major Climate Zones

In January, how will you dress for the weekend? In some places, you might get dressed to go skiing. In other places, you might head out in a swimsuit to go to the beach. What the seasons are like where you live depends on climate.

Earth is a patchwork of climates. Geographers identify these climates by looking at temperature, precipitation, and native plant life. Using these items, we can divide Earth into five general climate zones—tropical, temperate, polar, dry, and highland.

The first three climate zones relate to latitude. Tropical climates occur near the equator, in the low latitudes. Temperate climates occur about halfway between the equator and the poles, in the middle latitudes. Polar climates occur near the poles, in the high latitudes. The last two climate zones occur at many different latitudes. In addition, geographers divide some climate zones into more specific climate regions. The chart and map on the next two pages describe the world's climate regions.

READING CHECK Drawing Inferences Why do you think geographers consider native plant life when categorizing climates?

What You Will Learn...

Main Ideas

1. Geographers use temperature, precipitation, and plant life to identify climate zones.
2. Tropical climates are wet and warm, while dry climates receive little or no rain.
3. Temperate climates have the most seasonal change.
4. Polar climates are cold and dry, while highland climates change with elevation.

The Big Idea

Earth's five major climate zones are identified by temperature, precipitation, and plant life.

Key Terms

monsoons, *p. 58*
savannas, *p. 58*
steppes, *p. 59*
permafrost, *p. 61*

TAKING NOTES As you read, use a chart like the one here to help you note the characteristics of Earth's major climate zones.

Climate Zone	Characteristics

World Climate Regions

To explore the world's climate regions, start with the chart below. After reading about each climate region, locate the places on the map that have that climate. As you locate climates, look for patterns. For example, places near the equator tend to have warmer climates than places near the poles. See if you can identify some other climate patterns.

Tropical climate

	Climate	Where is it?	What is it like?	Plants
Tropical	HUMID TROPICAL	On and near the equator	Warm with high amounts of rain year-round; in a few places, monsoons create extreme wet seasons	Tropical rain forest
	TROPICAL SAVANNA	Higher latitudes in the tropics	Warm all year; distinct rainy and dry seasons; at least 20 inches (50 cm) of rain during the summer	Tall grasses and scattered trees
Dry	DESERT	Mainly center on 30° latitude; also in middle of continents, on west coasts, or in rain shadows	Sunny and dry; less than 10 inches (25 cm) of rain a year; hot in the tropics; cooler with wide daytime temperature ranges in middle latitudes	A few hardy plants, such as cacti
	STEPPE	Mainly bordering deserts and interiors of large continents	About 10–20 inches (25–50 cm) of precipitation a year; hot summers and cooler winters with wide temperature ranges during the day	Shorter grasses; some trees and shrubs by water
Temperate	MEDITERRANEAN	West coasts in middle latitudes	Dry, sunny, warm summers; mild, wetter winters; rain averages 15–20 inches (30–50 cm) a year	Scrub woodland and grassland
	HUMID SUBTROPICAL	East coasts in middle latitudes	Humid with hot summers and mild winters; rain year-round; in paths of hurricanes and typhoons	Mixed forest
	MARINE WEST COAST	West coasts in the upper-middle latitudes	Cloudy, mild summers and cool, rainy winters; strong ocean influence	Evergreen forests
	HUMID CONTINENTAL	East coasts and interiors of upper-middle latitudes	Four distinct seasons; long, cold winters and short, warm summers; average precipitation varies	Mixed forest

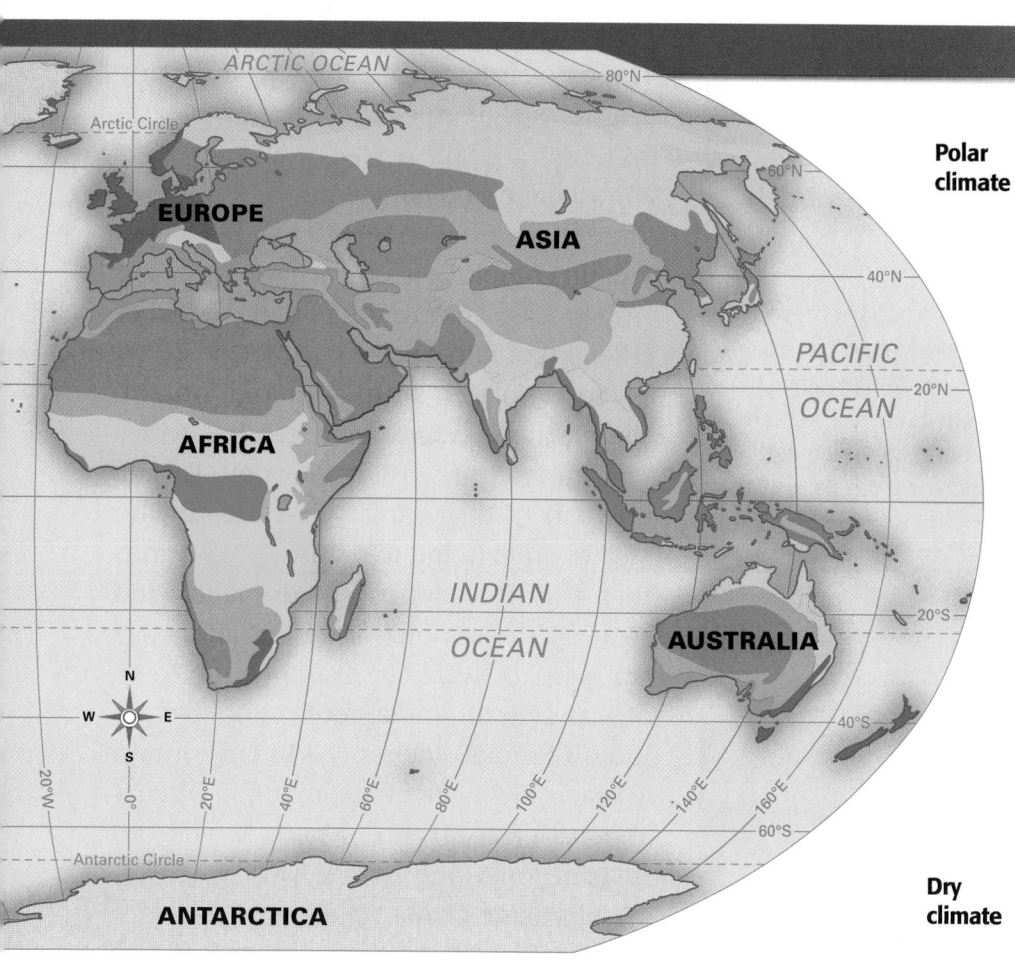

Polar climate

Dry climate

Climate		Where is it?	What is it like?	Plants
Polar	SUBARCTIC	Higher latitudes of the interior and east coasts of continents	Extremes of temperature; long, cold winters and short, warm summers; little precipitation	Northern evergreen forests
	TUNDRA	Coasts in high latitudes	Cold all year; very long, cold winters and very short, cool summers; little precipitation; permafrost	Moss, lichens, low shrubs
	ICE CAP	Polar regions	Freezing cold; snow and ice; little precipitation	No vegetation
Highland	HIGHLAND	High mountain regions	Wide range of temperatures and precipitation amounts, depending on elevation and location	Ranges from forest to tundra

Geography Skills

Regions Note how Earth's climate regions relate to different locations.

1. **Locate** Which climates are found mainly in the Northern Hemisphere?
2. **Identify** What climate does most of northern Africa have?
3. **Make Generalizations** Where are many of the world's driest climates found on Earth?
4. **Interpreting Charts** Examine the chart. Which two climates have the least amount of vegetation?

go.hrw.com KEYWORD: SG7 CH3

The Tuareg of the Sahara.

In the Sahara, the world's largest desert, temperatures can top 130°F (54°C). Yet the Tuareg (TWAH–reg) of North and West Africa call the Sahara home—and prefer it. The Tuareg have raised camels and other animals in the Sahara for more than 1,000 years. The animals graze on sparse desert plants. When the plants are gone, the Tuareg move on.

In camp, Tuareg families live in tents made from animal skins. Some wealthier Tuareg live in adobe homes. The men traditionally wear blue veils wrapped around their face and head. The veils help protect against windblown desert dust.

Summarizing How have the Tuareg adapted to life in a desert?

Tropical and Dry Climates

Are you the type of person who likes to go to extremes? Then tropical and dry climates might be for you. These climates include the wettest, driest, and hottest places on Earth.

Tropical Climates

Our tour of Earth's climates starts at the equator, in the heart of the tropics. This region extends from the Tropic of Cancer to the Tropic of Capricorn. Look back at the map to locate this region.

Humid Tropical Climate At the equator, the hot, damp air hangs like a thick, wet blanket. Sweat quickly coats your body.

Welcome to the humid tropical climate. This climate is warm, muggy, and rainy year-round. Temperatures average about 80°F (26°C). Showers or storms occur almost daily, and rainfall ranges from 70 to more than 450 inches (180 to 1,140 cm) a year. In comparison, only a few parts of the United States average more than 70 inches (180 cm) of rain a year.

Some places with a humid tropical climate have **monsoons**, seasonal winds that bring either dry or moist air. During one part of the year, a moist ocean wind creates an extreme wet season. The winds then shift direction, and a dry land wind creates a dry season. Monsoons affect several parts of Asia. For example, the town of Mawsynram, India, receives on average more than 450 inches (1,140 cm) of rain a year—all in about six months! That is about 37 feet (11 m) of rain. As you can imagine, flooding during wet seasons is common and can be severe.

The humid tropical climate's warm temperatures and heavy rainfall support tropical rain forests. These lush forests contain more types of plants and animals than anywhere else on Earth. The world's largest rain forest is in the Amazon River basin in South America. There you can find more than 50,000 species, including giant lily pads, poisonous tree frogs, and toucans.

Tropical Savanna Climate Moving north and south away from the equator, we find the tropical savanna climate. This climate has a long, hot, dry season followed by short periods of rain. Rainfall is much lower than at the equator but still high. Temperatures are hot in the summer, often as high as 90°F (32°C). Winters are cooler but rarely get cold.

This climate does not receive enough rainfall to support dense forests. Instead, it supports **savannas**—areas of tall grasses and scattered trees and shrubs.

Dry Climates

Leaving Earth's wettest places, we head to its driest. These climates are found in a number of locations on the planet.

Desert Climate Picture the sun baking down on a barren wasteland. This is the desert, Earth's hottest and driest climate. Deserts receive less than 10 inches (25 cm) of rain a year. Dry air and clear skies produce high daytime temperatures and rapid cooling at night. In some deserts, highs can top 130°F (54°C)! Under such conditions, only very hardy plants and animals can live. Many plants grow far apart so as not to compete for water. Others, such as cacti, store water in fleshy stems and leaves.

Steppe Climate Semidry grasslands or prairies—called **steppes** (STEPS)—often border deserts. Steppes receive slightly more rain than deserts do. Short grasses are the most common plants, but shrubs and trees grow along streams and rivers.

READING CHECK **Contrasting** What are some ways in which tropical and dry climates differ?

Temperate Climates

If you enjoy hot, sunny days as much as chilly, rainy ones, then temperate climates are for you. *Temperate* means "moderate" or "mild." These mild climates tend to have four seasons, with warm or hot summers and cool or cold winters.

Temperate climates occur in the middle latitudes, the regions halfway between the equator and the poles. Air masses from the tropics and the poles often meet in these regions, which creates a number of different temperate climates. You very likely live in one, because most Americans do.

Mediterranean Climate Named for the region of the Mediterranean Sea, this sunny, pleasant climate is found in many popular vacation areas. In a Mediterranean climate, summers are hot, dry, and sunny. Winters are mild and somewhat wet. Plant life includes shrubs and short trees with scattered larger trees. The Mediterranean climate occurs mainly in coastal areas. In the United States, much of California has this climate.

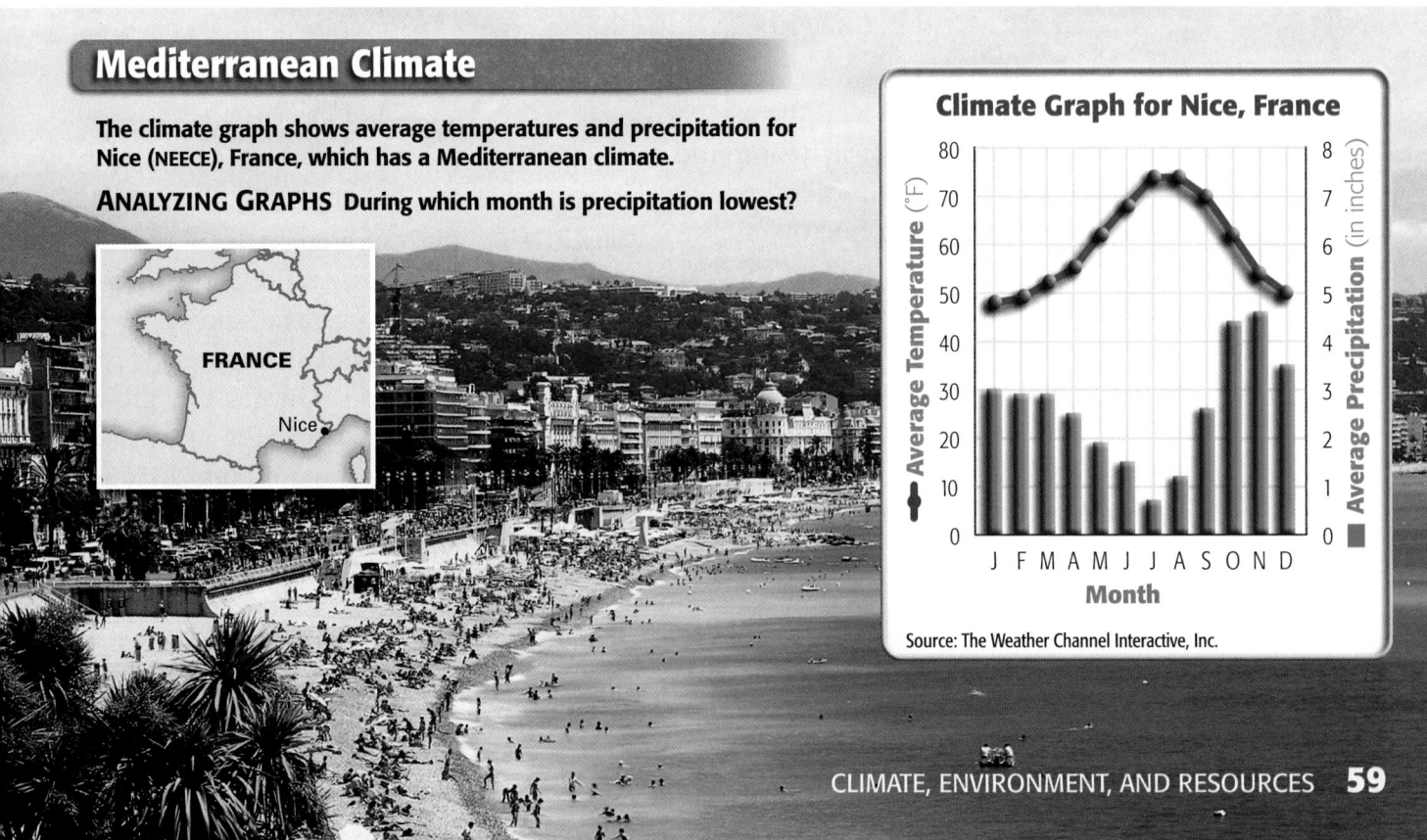

Mediterranean Climate

The climate graph shows average temperatures and precipitation for Nice (NEECE), France, which has a Mediterranean climate.

ANALYZING GRAPHS During which month is precipitation lowest?

FRANCE

Nice

Climate Graph for Nice, France

Source: The Weather Channel Interactive, Inc.

Highland Climates

Mount Kilimanjaro is the tallest mountain in Africa. Although Kilimanjaro is only about 200 miles (320 km) south of the equator, snow blankets its highest peak.

Kilimanjaro rises to 19,341 ft (5,895 m). The snow-covered summit has an ice cap climate.

Climate and plant life ranges from rain forest, to steppe, to desert, to tundra.

A tropical savanna climate is found around the base of Mount Kilimanjaro.

ANALYSIS SKILL **ANALYZING VISUALS**

Which type of tropical climate is found on Mount Kilimanjaro?

Humid Subtropical Climate The southeastern United States is an example of the humid subtropical climate. This climate occurs along east coasts near the tropics. In these areas, warm, moist air blows in from the ocean. Summers are hot and muggy. Winters are mild, with occasional frost and snow. Storms occur year-round. In addition, hurricanes can strike, bringing violent winds, heavy rain, and high seas.

A humid subtropical climate supports mixed forests. These forests include both deciduous trees, which lose their leaves each fall, and coniferous trees, which are green year-round. Coniferous trees are also known as evergreens.

Marine West Coast Climate Parts of North America's Pacific coast and of western Europe have a marine west coast climate. This climate occurs on west coasts where winds carry moisture in from the seas.

The moist air keeps temperatures mild year-round. Winters are foggy, cloudy, and rainy, while summers can be warm and sunny. Dense evergreen forests thrive in this climate.

Humid Continental Climate Closer to the poles, in the upper-middle latitudes, many inland and east coast areas have a humid continental climate. This climate has four **distinct** seasons. Summers are short and hot. Spring and fall are mild, and winters are long, cold, and in general, snowy.

This climate's rainfall supports vast grasslands and forests. Grasses can grow very tall, such as in parts of the American Great Plains. Forests contain both deciduous and coniferous trees, with coniferous forests occurring in the colder areas.

READING CHECK **Categorizing** Which of the temperate climates is too dry to support forests?

ACADEMIC VOCABULARY

distinct clearly different and separate

Polar and Highland Climates

Get ready to feel the chill as we end our tour in the polar and highland climates. The three polar climates are found in the high latitudes near the poles. The varied highland climate is found on mountains.

Subarctic Climate The subarctic climate and the tundra climate described below occur mainly in the Northern Hemisphere south of the Arctic Ocean. In the subarctic climate, winters are long and bitterly cold. Summers are short and cool. Temperatures stay below freezing for about half the year. The climate's moderate rainfall supports vast evergreen forests called taiga (TY-guh).

Tundra Climate The tundra climate occurs in coastal areas along the Arctic Ocean. As in the subarctic climate, winters are long and bitterly cold. Temperatures rise above freezing only during the short summer. Rainfall is light, and only plants such as mosses, lichens, and small shrubs grow.

In parts of the tundra, soil layers stay frozen all year. Permanently frozen layers of soil are called **permafrost**. Frozen earth absorbs water poorly, which creates ponds and marshes in summer. This moisture causes plants to burst forth in bloom.

Ice Cap Climate The harshest places on Earth may be the North and South poles. These regions have an ice cap climate. Temperatures are bone-numbingly cold, and lows of more than –120°F (–84°C) have been recorded. Snow and ice remain year-round, but precipitation is light. Not surprisingly, no vegetation grows. However, mammals such as penguins and polar bears thrive.

Highland Climates The highland climate includes polar climates plus others. In fact, this mountain climate is actually several climates in one. As you go up a mountain, the climate changes. Temperatures drop, and plant life grows sparser. Going up a mountain can be like going from the tropics to the poles. On very tall mountains, ice coats the summit year-round.

FOCUS ON READING

What is the effect of elevation on climate?

READING CHECK **Comparing** How are polar and highland climates similar?

SUMMARY AND PREVIEW As you can see, Earth has many climates, which we identify based on temperature, precipitation, and native plant life. In the next section you will read about how nature and all living things are connected.

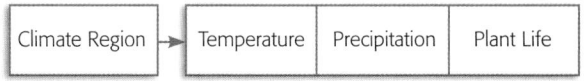

Section 2 Assessment

Reviewing Ideas, Terms, and Places

1. **a. Recall** Which three major climate zones occur at certain latitudes?
   b. Summarize How do geographers categorize Earth's different climates?
2. **a. Define** What are **monsoons**?
   b. Make Inferences In which type of dry climate do you think the fewest people live, and why?
3. **a. Identify** What are the four temperate climates?
   b. Draw Conclusions Why are places with a Mediterranean climate popular vacation spots?
4. **a. Describe** What are some effects of **permafrost**?
   b. Explain How are highland climates unique?

Critical Thinking

5. **Categorizing** Create a chart like the one below for each climate region. Then use your notes to describe each climate region's average temperatures, precipitation, and native plant life.

Climate Region	→	Temperature	Precipitation	Plant Life

FOCUS ON VIEWING

6. **Discussing World Climates** Add information about the climate of the place you have selected, such as average temperature and precipitation.

Natural Environments

What You Will Learn...

Main Ideas

1. The environment and life are interconnected and exist in a fragile balance.
2. Soils play an important role in the environment.

The Big Idea

Plants, animals, and the environment, including soil, interact and affect one another.

Key Terms

environment, *p. 62*
ecosystem, *p. 63*
habitat, *p. 64*
extinct, *p. 64*
humus, *p. 65*
desertification, *p. 65*

TAKING NOTES As you read, use a chart like the one below to help you take notes on the main topics in this section.

Limits and Connections in Nature	
Changes to Environments	
Soil and the Environment	

If **YOU** lived there...

When your family moved to the city, you were sure you would miss the woods and pond near your old house. Then one of your new friends at school told you there's a large park only a few blocks away. You wondered how interesting a city park could be. But you were surprised at the many plants and animals that live there.

What environments might you see in the park?

BUILDING BACKGROUND No matter where you live, you are part of a natural environment. From a desert to a rain forest to a city park, every environment is home to a unique community of plant and animal life. These plants and animals live in balance with nature.

The Environment and Life

If you saw a wild polar bear outside your school, you would likely be shocked. In most parts of the United States, polar bears live only in zoos. This is because plants and animals must live where they are suited to the **environment**, or surroundings. Polar bears are suited to very cold places with lots of ice, water, and fish. As you will see, living things and their environments are connected and affect each other in many ways.

Limits on Life

The environment limits life. As our tour of the world's climates showed, factors such as temperature, rainfall, and soil conditions limit where plants and animals can live. Palm trees cannot survive at the frigid North Pole. Ferns will quickly wilt and die in deserts, but they thrive in tropical rain forests.

At the same time, all plants and animals are adapted to specific environments. For example, kangaroo rats are adapted to dry desert environments. These small rodents can get all the water they need from food, so they seldom have to drink water.

Connections in Nature

The interconnections between living things and the environment form ecosystems. An **ecosystem** is a group of plants and animals that depend on each other for survival and the environment in which they live. Ecosystems can be any size and can occur wherever air, water, and soil support life. A garden pond, a city park, a prairie, and a rain forest are all examples of ecosystems.

The diagram below shows a forest ecosystem. Each part of this ecosystem fills a certain role. The sun provides energy to the plants, which use the energy to make their own food. The plants then serve as food, either directly or indirectly, for all other life in the forest. When the plants and animals die, their remains break down and provide nutrients for the soil and new plant growth. Thus, the cycle continues.

Close-up

A Forest Ecosystem

A forest is one type of ecosystem. The plants and animals in the forest depend on one another and the forest environment for survival.

1. Sunlight is the source of energy for most living things.

2. Plants use the energy in sunlight to make food. They serve as the basis for other life in the ecosystem.

3. Animals such as rabbits eat plants and gain some of their energy.

4. Predators, such as wolves and hawks, eat rabbits and other prey for energy.

5. Larger predators, such as mountain lions, compete for the prey that is available.

ANALYSIS SKILL ANALYZING VISUALS

What might happen in the forest ecosystem above if the number of rabbits fell significantly?

Changes to Environments

The interconnected parts of an ecosystem exist in a fragile balance. For this reason, a small change to one part can affect the whole system. A lack of rain in the forest ecosystem could kill off many of the plants that feed the rabbits. If the rabbits die, there will be less food for the wolves and mountain lions. Then they too may die.

Many actions can affect ecosystems. For example, people need places to live and food to eat, so they clear land for homes and farms. Clearing land has **consequences**, however. It can cause the soil to erode. In addition, the plants and animals that live in the area might be left without food and shelter.

Actions such as clearing land and polluting can destroy habitats. A **habitat** is the place where a plant or animal lives. The most diverse habitats on Earth are tropical rain forests. People are clearing Earth's rain forests for farmland, lumber, and other reasons, though. As a result, these diverse habitats are being lost.

ACADEMIC VOCABULARY

consequences the effects of a particular event or events

FOCUS ON READING

What are some causes of habitat destruction?

Extreme changes in ecosystems can cause species to die out, or become **extinct**. As an example, flightless birds called dodos once lived on Mauritius (maw-RI-shuhs), an island in the Indian Ocean. When people began settling on the island, their actions harmed the dodos' habitat. First seen in 1507, dodos were extinct by 1681.

Recognizing these problems, many countries are working to balance people's needs with the needs of the environment. The United States, for example, has passed many laws to limit pollution, manage forests, and protect valuable ecosystems.

READING CHECK **Drawing Inferences** How might one change affect an entire ecosystem?

Soil and the Environment

As you know, plants are the basis for all food that animals eat. Soils help determine what plants will grow and how well. Because soils support plant life, they play an important role in the environment.

CONNECTING TO Science

Soil Factory

The next time you see a fallen tree in the forest, do not think of it as a dead log. Think of it as a soil factory. A fallen tree is buzzing with the activity of countless insects, bacteria, and other organisms. These organisms invade the fallen log and start to break the wood down.

As the tree decays and crumbles, it turns into humus. Humus is a rich blend of organic material. The humus mixes with the soil and broken rock material. These added nutrients then enrich the soil, making it possible for new trees and plants to grow. Fallen trees provide as much as one-third of the organic material in forest soil.

Summarizing What causes a fallen tree to change into soil?

Fertile soils are rich in minerals and **humus** (HYOO-muhs), decayed plant or animal matter. These soils can support abundant plant life. Like air and water, fertile soil is essential for life. Without it, we could not grow much of the food we eat.

Soils can lose fertility in several ways. Erosion from wind or water can sweep topsoil away. Planting the same crops over and over can also rob soil of its fertility. When soil becomes worn out, it cannot support as many plants. In fragile dry environments this can lead to the spread of desertlike conditions, or **desertification**. The spread of desertlike conditions is a serious problem in many parts of the world.

READING CHECK **Analyzing** What do fertile soils contain, and why are these soils important?

SUMMARY AND PREVIEW Living things and the environment are connected, but changes can easily upset the balance in an ecosystem. Because they support plant life, soils are important parts of ecosystems. In the next section you will learn about Earth's many resources.

Soil Layers

The three layers of soil are the topsoil, subsoil, and broken rock. The thickness of each layer depends on the conditions in a specific location.

ANALYZING VISUALS In which layer of soil are most plant roots and insects found?

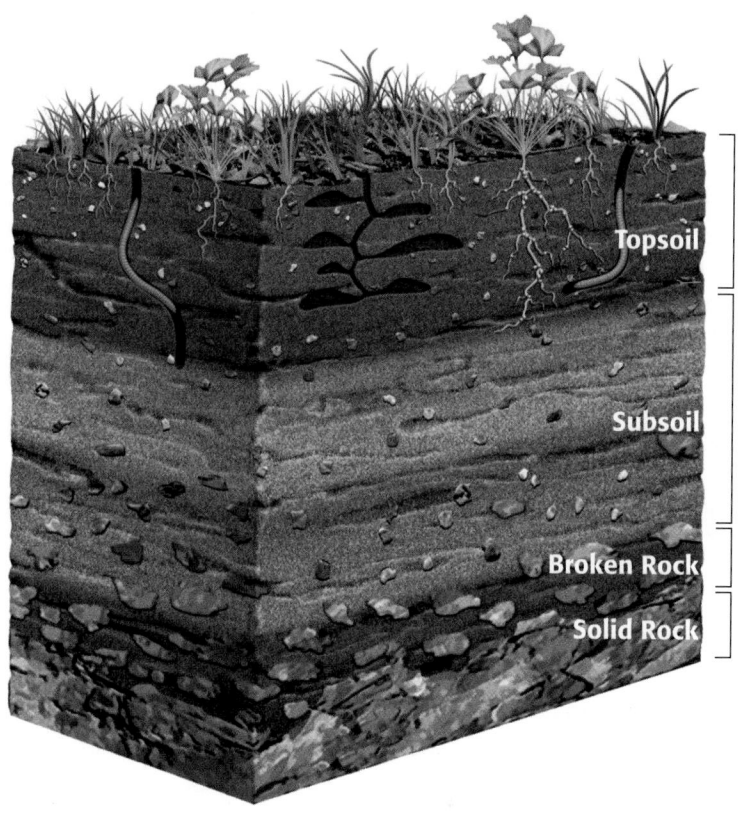

Topsoil

Subsoil

Broken Rock

Solid Rock

go.hrw.com
Online Quiz
KEYWORD: SG7 HP3

Section 3 Assessment

Reviewing Ideas, Terms, and Places

1. **a. Define** What is an **ecosystem**, and what are two examples of ecosystems?
   b. Summarize How do nature and people change ecosystems?
   c. Elaborate Why can plants and animals not live everywhere?
2. **a. Recall** What is **humus**, and why is it important to soil?
   b. Identify Cause and Effect What actions can cause **desertification**, and what might be some possible effects?
   c. Elaborate Why it is important for geographers and scientists to study soils?

Critical Thinking

3. **Identifying Cause and Effect** Review your notes. Then use a chart like this one to identify some of the causes and effects of changes to ecosystems.

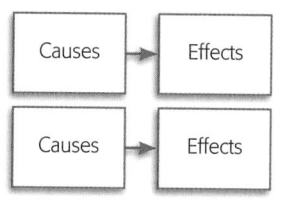

FOCUS ON VIEWING

4. **Writing about Natural Environments** Jot down ideas about how different types of weather might affect the environment of the place you chose. For example, how might lack of rain affect the area?

Earth's Changing Environments

PANGAEA

Pangaea About 250 million years ago, all of Earth's continents were connected, forming one giant landmass called Pangaea.

What was North America like 74 million years ago, when dinosaurs roamed Earth? You might be surprised to learn that it was a very different place. Earth's environments are always changing. The map at right shows North America in the age of dinosaurs. Back then, the climate was warm and humid, and large inland seas covered much of the land. The region's plants and animals were completely different. Slowly, however, things changed. Some major event, possibly an asteroid impact, wiped out the dinosaurs. Over time, North America's environments changed into the ones that exist today.

What Survived Dinosaurs, such as the plant-eating ceratopsian at left, are long gone. But insects, such as cockroaches and dragonflies, are still around.

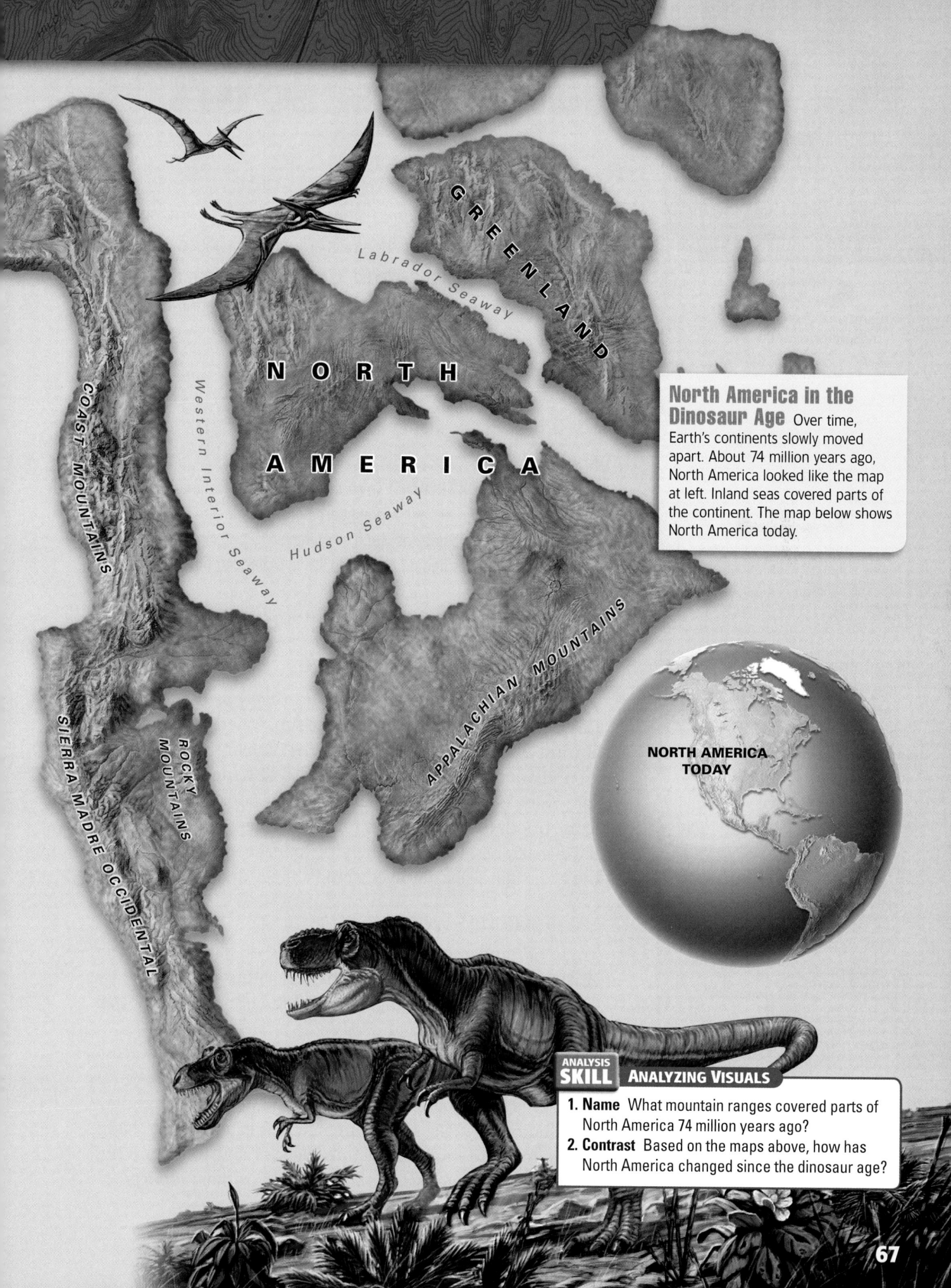

GREENLAND

Labrador Seaway

NORTH

AMERICA

COAST MOUNTAINS

Western Interior Seaway

Hudson Seaway

SIERRA MADRE OCCIDENTAL

ROCKY MOUNTAINS

APPALACHIAN MOUNTAINS

North America in the Dinosaur Age Over time, Earth's continents slowly moved apart. About 74 million years ago, North America looked like the map at left. Inland seas covered parts of the continent. The map below shows North America today.

NORTH AMERICA TODAY

ANALYSIS SKILL **ANALYZING VISUALS**

1. **Name** What mountain ranges covered parts of North America 74 million years ago?
2. **Contrast** Based on the maps above, how has North America changed since the dinosaur age?

67

Natural Resources

If YOU lived there...

You live in Southern California, where the climate is warm and dry. Every week, you water the grass around your house to keep it green. Now the city has declared a "drought emergency" because of a lack of rain. City officials have put limits on watering lawns and on other uses of water.

How can you help conserve scarce water?

What You Will Learn...

Main Ideas

1. Earth provides valuable resources for our use.
2. Energy resources provide fuel, heat, and electricity.
3. Mineral resources include metals, rocks, and salt.
4. Resources shape people's lives and countries' wealth.

The Big Idea

Earth's natural resources have many valuable uses, and their availability affects people in many ways.

Key Terms

natural resource, *p. 68*
renewable resources, *p. 69*
nonrenewable resources, *p. 69*
deforestation, *p. 69*
reforestation, *p. 69*
fossil fuels, *p. 69*
hydroelectric power, *p. 70*

TAKING NOTES As you read, use a chart like this one to take notes on Earth's resources.

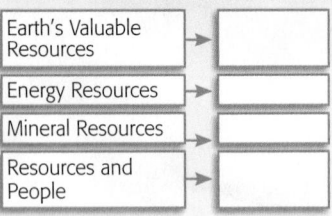

Earth's Valuable Resources	
Energy Resources	
Mineral Resources	
Resources and People	

BUILDING BACKGROUND In addition to plant and animal life, other resources in the environment greatly influence people. In fact, certain vital resources, such as water, soils, and minerals, may determine whether people choose to live in a place or how wealthy people are.

Earth's Valuable Resources

Think about the materials in nature that you use. You have learned about the many ways we use sun, water, and land. They are just a start, though. Look at the human-made products around you. They all required the use of natural materials in some way. We use trees to make paper for books. We use petroleum, or oil, to make plastics for cell phones. We use metals to make machines, which we then use to make many items. Without these materials, our lives would change drastically.

Using Natural Resources

Trees, oil, and metals are all examples of natural resources. A **natural resource** is any material in nature that people use and value. Earth's most important natural resources include air, water, soils, forests, and minerals.

Understanding how and why people use natural resources is an important part of geography. We use some natural resources just as they are, such as wind. Usually, though, we change natural resources to make something new. For example, we change metals to make products such as bicycles and watches. Thus, most natural resources are raw materials for other products.

Reforestation

Members of the Green Belt Movement plant trees in Kenya. Although trees are a renewable resource, some forests are being cut down faster than new trees can replace them. Reforestation helps protect Earth's valuable forestlands.

ANALYZING VISUALS How does reforestation help the environment?

Types of Natural Resources

We group natural resources into two types, those we can replace and those we cannot. **Renewable resources** are resources Earth replaces naturally. For example, when we cut down a tree, another tree can grow in its place. Renewable resources include water, soil, trees, plants, and animals. These resources can last forever if used wisely.

Other natural resources will run out one day. These **nonrenewable resources** are resources that cannot be replaced. For example, coal formed over millions of years. Once we use the coal up, it is gone.

Managing Natural Resources

People need to manage natural resources to protect them for the future. Consider how your life might change if we ran out of forests, for example. Although forests are renewable, we can cut down trees far faster than they can grow. The result is the clearing of trees, or **deforestation**.

By managing resources, however, we can repair and prevent resource loss. For example, some groups are engaged in **reforestation**, planting trees to replace lost forestland.

READING CHECK **Contrasting** How do renewable and nonrenewable resources differ?

BIOGRAPHY

Wangari Maathai
(1940–)

Can planting a tree improve people's lives? Wangari Maathai thinks so. Born in Kenya in East Africa, Maathai wanted to help people in her country, many of whom were poor. She asked herself what Kenyans could do to improve their lives. "Planting a tree was the best idea that I had," she says. In 1977 Maathai founded the Green Belt Movement to plant trees and protect forestland. The group has now planted more than 30 million trees across Kenya! These trees provide wood and prevent soil erosion. In 2004 Maathai was awarded the Nobel Peace Prize. She is the first African woman to receive this famous award.

Energy Resources

Every day you use plants and animals from the dinosaur age—in the form of energy resources. These resources power vehicles, produce heat, and generate electricity. They are some of our most important and valuable natural resources.

Nonrenewable Energy Resources

Most of the energy we use comes from **fossil fuels**, nonrenewable resources that formed from the remains of ancient plants and animals. The most important fossil fuels are coal, petroleum, and natural gas.

Coal has long been a reliable energy source for heat. However, burning coal causes some problems. It pollutes the air and can harm the land. For these reasons, people have used coal less as other fuel options became available.

FOCUS ON
READING
In the second
sentence on this
page, what cause
does the word
because signal?
What is the effect
of this cause?

Today we use coal mainly to create electricity at power plants, not to heat single buildings. Because coal is plentiful, people are looking for cleaner ways to burn it.

Petroleum, or oil, is a dark liquid used to make fuels and other products. When first removed from the ground, petroleum is called crude oil. This oil is shipped or piped to refineries, factories that process the crude oil to make products. Fuels made from oil include gasoline, diesel fuel, and jet fuel. Oil is also used to make petrochemicals, which are processed to make products such as plastics and cosmetics.

As with coal, burning oil-based fuels can pollute the air and land. In addition, oil spills can harm wildlife. Because we are so dependent on oil for energy, however, it is an extremely valuable resource.

The cleanest-burning fossil fuel is natural gas. We use it mainly for heating and cooking. For example, your kitchen stove may use natural gas. Some vehicles run on natural gas as well. These vehicles cause less pollution than those that run on gasoline.

Renewable Energy Resources

Unlike fossil fuels, renewable energy resources will not run out. They also are generally better for the environment. On the other hand, they are not available everywhere and can be costly.

The main alternative to fossil fuels is **hydroelectric power**—the production of electricity from waterpower. We obtain energy from moving water by damming rivers. The dams harness the power of moving water to generate electricity.

Hydroelectric power has both pros and cons. On the positive side, it produces power without polluting and lessens our use of fossil fuels. On the negative side, dams create lakes that replace existing resources, such as farmland, and disrupt wildlife habitats.

Another renewable energy source is wind. People have long used wind to power windmills. Today we use wind to power wind turbines, a type of modern windmill. At wind farms, hundreds of turbines create electricity in windy places.

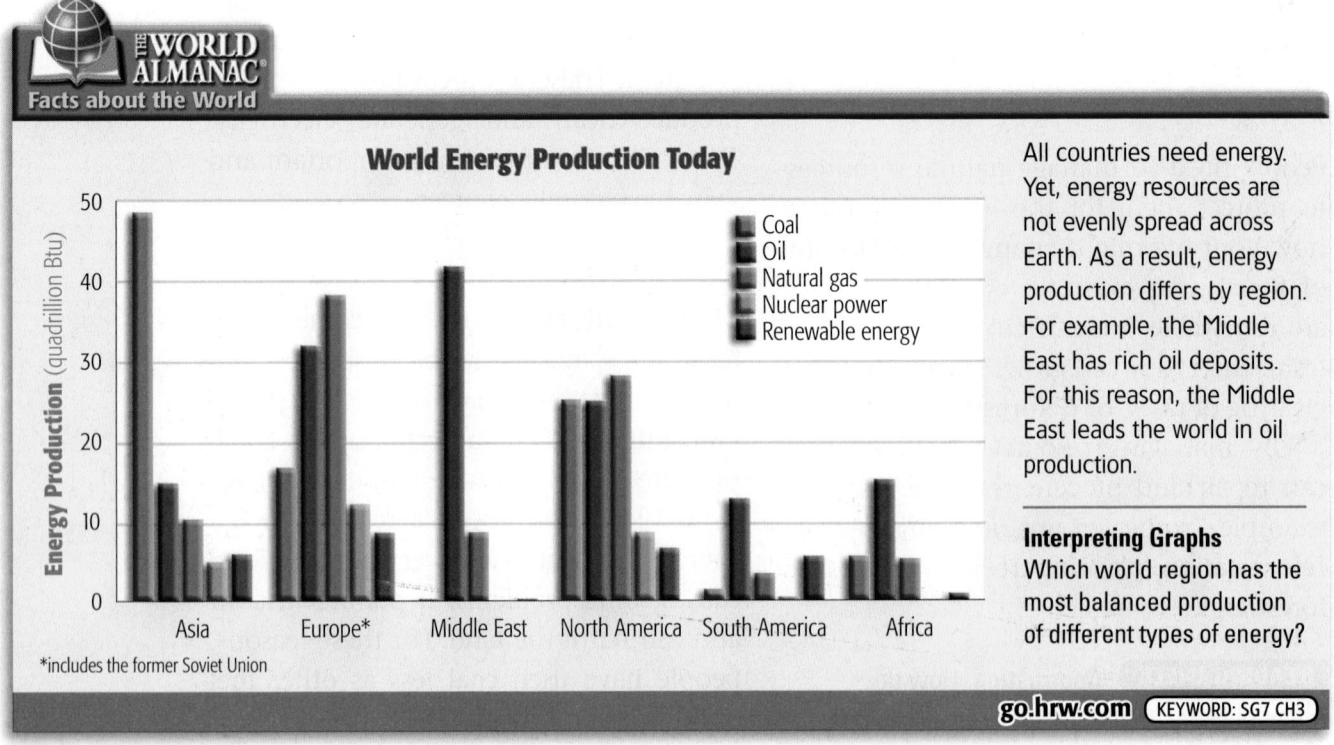

THE WORLD ALMANAC®
Facts about the World

World Energy Production Today

Legend:
- Coal
- Oil
- Natural gas
- Nuclear power
- Renewable energy

Y-axis: Energy Production (quadrillion Btu) — 0, 10, 20, 30, 40, 50

X-axis: Asia, Europe*, Middle East, North America, South America, Africa

*includes the former Soviet Union

All countries need energy. Yet, energy resources are not evenly spread across Earth. As a result, energy production differs by region. For example, the Middle East has rich oil deposits. For this reason, the Middle East leads the world in oil production.

Interpreting Graphs
Which world region has the most balanced production of different types of energy?

go.hrw.com   KEYWORD: SG7 CH3

A third source of renewable energy is heat from the sun and Earth. We can use solar power, or power from the sun, to heat water or homes. Using special solar panels, we turn solar energy into electricity. We can also use geothermal energy, or heat from within Earth. Geothermal power plants use steam and hot water located within Earth to create electricity.

Nuclear Energy

A final energy source is nuclear energy. We obtain this energy by splitting atoms, small particles of matter. This process uses the metal uranium, so some people consider nuclear energy a nonrenewable resource. Nuclear power does not pollute the air, but it does produce dangerous wastes. These wastes must be stored for thousands of years before they are safe. In addition, an accident at a nuclear power plant can have terrible effects.

READING CHECK **Drawing Inferences** Why might people look for alternatives to fossil fuels?

Mineral Resources

Like energy resources, mineral resources can be quite valuable. These resources include metals, salt, rocks, and gemstones.

Minerals fulfill countless needs. Look around you to see a few. Your school building likely includes steel, made from iron. The outer walls might be granite or limestone. The window glass is made from quartz, a mineral in sand. From staples to jewelry to coins, metals are everywhere.

Minerals are nonrenewable, so we need to conserve them. Recycling items such as aluminum cans will make the supply of these valuable resources last longer.

READING CHECK **Categorizing** What are the major types of mineral resources?

From the Ground to the Air

The photo shows a bauxite mine. Bauxite is used to make aluminum. This metal is used in many products, such as jet planes. See how many other products made from aluminum you can name.

Resources and People

Natural resources vary from place to place. The resources available in a region can shape life and wealth for the people there.

Resources and Daily Life

The natural resources available to people affect their lifestyles and needs. In the United States we have many different kinds of natural resources. We can choose among many different ways to dress, eat, live, travel, and entertain ourselves. People in places with fewer natural resources will likely have fewer choices and different needs than Americans.

For example, people who live in remote rain forests depend on forest resources for most of their needs. These people may craft containers by weaving plant fibers together. They may make canoes by hollowing out tree trunks. Instead of being concerned about money, they might be more concerned about food.

Products from Petroleum

This Ohio family shows some common products made from petroleum, or oil.

ANALYZING VISUALS What petroleum-based products can you identify in this photo?

Resources and Wealth

The availability of natural resources affects countries' economies as well. For example, the many natural resources available in the United States have helped it become one of the world's wealthiest countries. In contrast, countries with few natural resources often have weak economies.

Some countries have one or two valuable resources but few others. For example, Saudi Arabia is rich in oil but lacks water for growing food. As a result, Saudi Arabia must use its oil profits to import food.

READING CHECK Identifying Cause and Effect How can having few natural resources affect life and wealth in a region or country?

SUMMARY AND PREVIEW You can see that Earth's natural resources have many uses. Important natural resources include air, water, soils, forests, fuels, and minerals. In the next chapter you will read about the world's people and cultures.

go.hrw.com
Online Quiz
KEYWORD: SG7 HP3

Section 4 Assessment

Reviewing Ideas, Terms, and Places

1. **a. Define** What are **renewable resources** and **nonrenewable resources**?
   b. Explain Why is it important for people to manage Earth's natural resources?
   c. Develop What are some things you can do to help manage and conserve natural resources?
2. **a. Define** What are **fossil fuels**, and why are they significant?
   b. Summarize What are three examples of renewable energy resources?
   c. Predict How do you think life might change as we begin to run out of petroleum?
3. **a. Recall** What are the main types of mineral resources?
   b. Analyze What are some products that we get from mineral resources?

4. **a. Describe** How do resources affect people?
   b. Make Inferences How might a country with only one valuable resource develop its economy?

Critical Thinking

5. **Categorizing** Draw a chart like this one. Use your notes to identify and evaluate each energy resource.

Fossil Fuels	Renewable Energy	Nuclear Energy
Pros	Pros	Pros
Cons	Cons	Cons

FOCUS ON VIEWING

6. **Noting Details about Natural Resources** What natural resources does the place you chose have? Note ways to refer to some of these resources (or the lack of them) in your weather report.

from
The River

by Gary Paulsen

About the Reading *In the novel* The River, *a teenager named Brian has already proven his ability to survive in the wilderness. On this trip into the wilderness, he is accompanied by a man who wants to learn survival skills from him. With only a pocket knife and a transistor radio as tools, the two men meet challenges that at first appear too difficult to overcome. In the following passage from the novel, the men have just arrived in the wilderness.*

AS YOU READ Notice how Brian uses his senses to predict how some natural resources can help him survive.

He didn't just hear birds singing, not just a background sound of birds, but each bird. He listened to each bird. Located it, knew where it was by the sound, listened for the sound of alarm. He didn't just see clouds, but light clouds, scout clouds that came before the heavier clouds that could mean rain and maybe wind. ❶ The clouds were coming out of the northwest, and that meant that weather would come with them. Not could, but would. There would be rain. Tonight, late, there would be rain.

His eyes swept the clearing. . . There was a stump there that probably held grubs; hardwood there for a bow, and willows there for arrows; a game trail, . . . porcupines, raccoons, bear, wolves, moose, skunk would be moving on the trail and into the clearing. ❷ He flared his nostrils, smelled the air, pulled the air along the sides of his tongue in a hissing sound and tasted it, but there was nothing. Just summer smells. The tang of pines, soft air, some mustiness from rotting vegetation. No animals. ❸

GUIDED READING

WORD HELP

grubs soft, thick wormlike forms of insects
flared widened
tang sharp, biting smell
mustiness damp, stale smell

❶ Scout clouds are clouds that appear to be searching for other clouds to come.

❷ Brian notes that the stump likely holds grubs. He can eat the grubs for food.

❸ Brian does not smell any animals nearby.
Why might Brian want to know if animals are around?

Connecting Literature to Geography

1. **Predicting** Brian observes the clouds and can tell from their appearance and movement that rain is coming. What might be some ways that he can use his environment to prepare for the rain?

2. **Finding Main Ideas** The environment provides many resources that we can use, from wood to plants to animals. What resources does Brian identify around him that he can use to survive?

Social Studies Skills

Analyzing a Bar Graph

Learn

Bar graphs are drawings that use bars to show data in a clear, visual format. Use these guidelines to analyze bar graphs.

- Read the title to identify the graph's subject and purpose.

- Read the graph's other labels. Note what the graph is measuring and the units of measurement being used. For example, this bar graph is measuring precipitation by climate. The unit of measurement is inches. If the graph uses colors, note their purpose.

- Analyze and compare the data. As you do, note any increases or decreases and look for trends or changes over time.

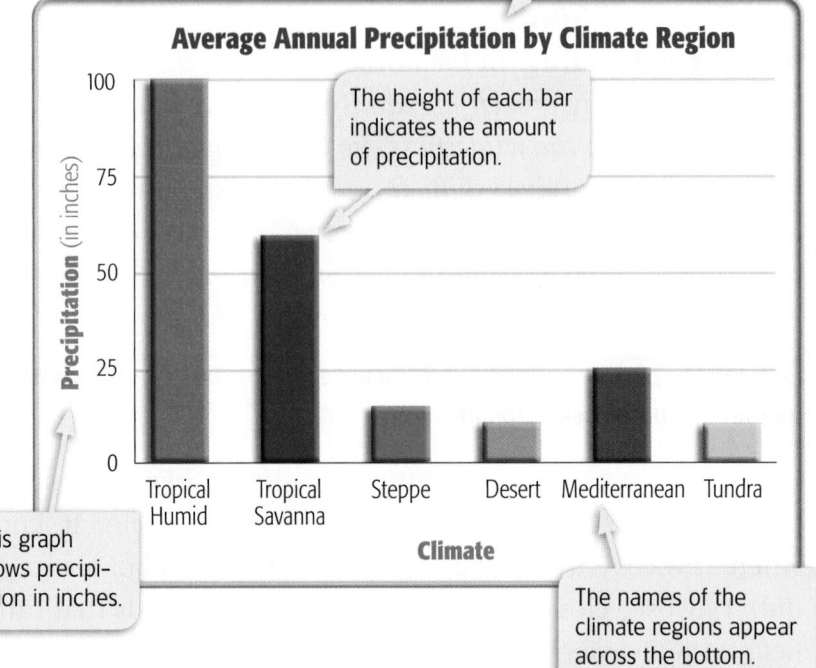

This bar graph compares the average annual precipitation of six climate regions.

Average Annual Precipitation by Climate Region

The height of each bar indicates the amount of precipitation.

This graph shows precipitation in inches.

The names of the climate regions appear across the bottom.

Practice

1 On the bar graph above, which climate region has the highest average annual precipitation?

2 Which two climate regions have about the same amount?

3 Which climate region receives an average of between 50 and 75 inches of precipitation each year?

Apply

Examine the World Energy Production Today bar graph in Section 4. Then use the graph to answer the following questions.

1. Which region produces the most oil?

2. Which three regions produce little or no nuclear power?

3. Based on the graph, what type of energy resource do most Asian countries likely use?

Chapter Review

Geography's Impact
video series
Review the video to answer the closing question:
How are climate and weather different, and how does the influence they have differ?

Visual Summary

Use the visual summary below to help you review the main ideas of the chapter.

QUICK FACTS

Earth has a wide range of climates, which we identify by precipitation, temperature, and native plant life.

Plants, animals, and the environment are interconnected and affect one another in many ways.

Earth's valuable natural resources, such as air, water, forests, and minerals, have many uses and affect people's lives.

Reviewing Vocabulary, Terms, and Places

Unscramble each group of letters below to spell a term that matches the given definition.

1. **usumh**—decayed plant or animal matter
2. **tahrewe**—changes or conditions in the air at a certain time and place
3. **netorietfaosr**—planting trees where forests were
4. **neticxt**—completely died out
5. **estpep**—semidry grassland or prairie
6. **sifeticatorined**—spread of desertlike conditions
7. **laitemc**—an area's weather patterns over a long period of time
8. **arsmofrtpe**—permanently frozen layers of soil
9. **snonomo**—winds that change direction with the seasons and create wet and dry periods
10. **vansanas**—areas of tall grasses and scattered shrubs and trees

Comprehension and Critical Thinking

SECTION 1 *(Pages 50–54)*

11. **a. Identify** What five factors affect climate?

   b. Analyze Is average annual precipitation an example of weather or climate?

   c. Evaluate Of the five factors that affect climate, which one do you think is the most important? Why?

SECTION 2 *(Pages 55–61)*

12. **a. Recall** What are the five major climate zones?

   b. Explain How does latitude relate to climate?

   c. Elaborate Why do you think the study of climate is important in geography?

SECTION 3 *(Pages 62–65)*

13. **a. Define** What is an ecosystem, and why does it exist in a fragile balance?

SECTION 3 (continued)

b. Explain Why are plants an important part of the environment?

c. Predict What might be some results of desertification?

SECTION 4 (Pages 68–72)

14. a. Define What are minerals?

b. Contrast How do nonrenewable resources and renewable resources differ?

c. Elaborate How might a scarcity of natural resources affect life in a region?

Using the Internet

go.hrw.com
KEYWORD: SG7 CH3

15. Activity: Experiencing Extremes Could you live in a place where for part of the year it is always dark and temperatures plummet to –104°F? What if you had to live in a place where it is always wet and stormy? Enter the activity keyword to learn more about some of the world's extreme climates. Then create a poster that describes some of those climates and the people, animals, and plants that live in them.

FOCUS ON READING AND VIEWING

Understanding Cause and Effect *Answer the following questions about causes and effects.*

16. What causes desertification?

17. What are the effects of abundant natural resources on a country's economy?

Presenting and Viewing a Weather Report *Use your weather report notes to complete the activity below.*

18. Select a place and a season. Then write a script for a weather report for that place during that season. Describe the current weather and predict the upcoming weather. During your presentation, use a professional, friendly tone of voice and make frequent eye contact with your audience. Then view your classmates' weather reports. Be prepared to give feedback on the content and their presentation techniques.

Social Studies Skills

Analyzing a Bar Graph *Examine the bar graph titled Average Annual Precipitation by Climate Region in the Social Studies Skills for this chapter. Then use the bar graph to answer the following questions.*

19. Which climate region receives an average of 100 inches of precipitation a year?

20. Which climate region receives an average of 25 inches of precipitation a year?

21. What is the difference in average annual precipitation between tropical humid climates and Mediterranean climates?

Map Activity

22. Prevailing Winds On a separate sheet of paper, match the letters on the map with their correct labels.

equator	South Pole	westerly
North Pole	trade wind	

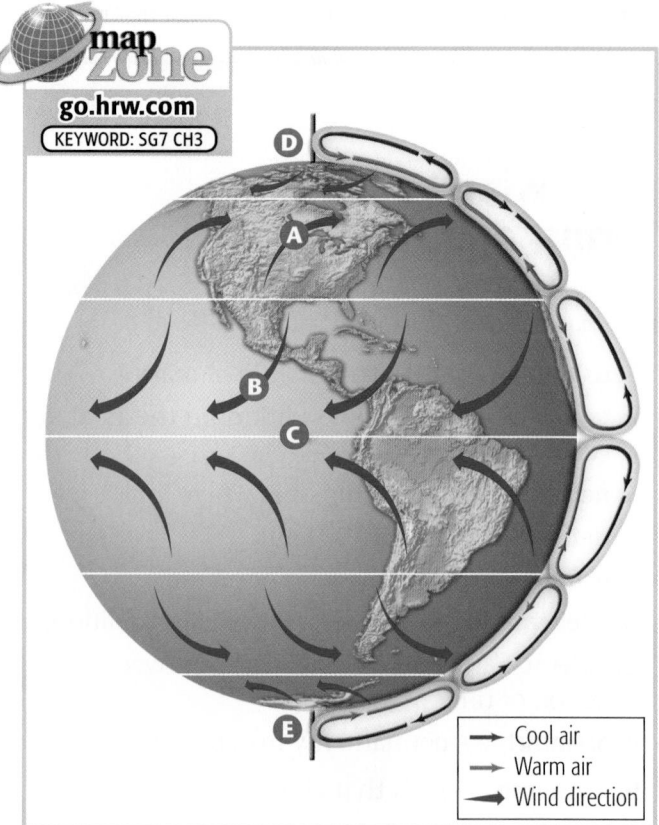

go.hrw.com
KEYWORD: SG7 CH3

→ Cool air
→ Warm air
→ Wind direction

DIRECTIONS: Read questions 1 through 7 and write the letter of the best response. Then read question 8 and write your own well-constructed response.

1 The cold winds that flow away from the North and South poles are the

A doldrums.

B polar easterlies.

C trade winds.

D westerlies.

2 Which climate zone occurs only in the upper latitudes?

A highland

B temperate

C tropical

D polar

3 Where are the most diverse habitats on Earth found?

A steppe

B tropical rain forest

C tropical savanna

D tundra

4 What is the cleanest burning fossil fuel?

A coal

B natural gas

C oil

D petroleum

5 Which renewable energy source uses the heat of Earth's interior to generate power?

A geothermal energy

B hydroelectric energy

C nuclear energy

D solar energy

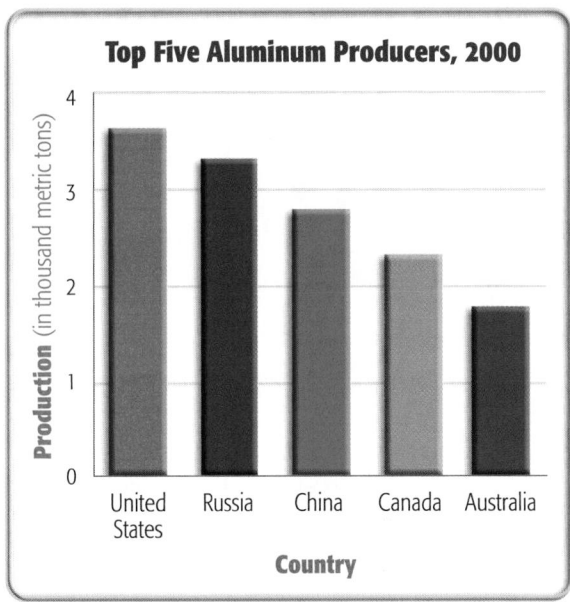

Top Five Aluminum Producers, 2000

Production (in thousand metric tons) vs. Country (United States, Russia, China, Canada, Australia)

6 Based on the graph above, which country produced about 2,750 metric tons of aluminum in 2000?

A Australia

B China

C Russia

D United States

7 Which of the following form over tropical waters and are Earth's largest and most destructive storms?

A blizzards

B hurricanes

C thunderstorms

D tornadoes

8 Extended Response   Forces such as the sun, latitude, wind, and water shape climate. Examine the World Climate Regions map in Section 2. Describe two climate patterns that you see on the map and explain how various forces combine to create the two patterns.

CHAPTER 4

The World's People

What You Will Learn...

In this chapter you will learn what culture is and how it changes over time. You will also study population and the different types of governments and economic systems used around the world. Finally, you will discover how global connections are bringing the world's people closer together.

FOCUS ON READING AND WRITING

Understanding Main Ideas A main idea is the central idea around which a paragraph or passage is organized. As you read, ask yourself what each paragraph is about. Look for a sentence or two that summarizes the main point of the entire paragraph. **See the lesson, Understanding Main Ideas, on page R5.**

Creating a Poster Think of some great posters you have seen—at the movies, in bus stations, or in the halls of your school. They likely all had a colorful image that captured your attention and a few words that explained the main idea. Read this chapter about the world's people. Then create a poster that includes words and images that summarize the chapter's main ideas.

Culture Thousands of different cultures make up our world. Clothing, language, and music are just some parts of culture.

ANALYSIS SKILL | **ANALYZING VISUALS**

Many of the world's people come together every four years to compete in the Olympics.

What indicates that some of the people in this photo are from different parts of the world?

HOLT

Geography's Impact
video series
Watch the video to learn the impact of culture.

Population Geographers study human populations like this one in India to learn where and why people live in certain places.

Global Connections Technology allows people in remote places around the world to communicate.

79

Culture

What You Will Learn...

Main Ideas

1. Culture is the set of beliefs, goals, and practices that a group of people share.
2. The world includes many different culture groups.
3. New ideas and events lead to changes in culture.

The Big Idea

Culture, a group's shared practices and beliefs, differs from group to group and changes over time.

Key Terms

culture, *p. 80*
culture trait, *p. 81*
culture region, *p. 82*
ethnic group, *p. 83*
cultural diversity, *p. 83*
cultural diffusion, *p. 85*

TAKING NOTES As you read, take notes on culture. Use a web diagram like the one below to organize your notes.

If YOU lived there...

You live in New York City, and your young cousin from out of state has come to visit. As you take her on a tour of the city, you point out the different cultural neighborhoods, like Chinatown, Little Italy, Spanish Harlem, and Koreatown. Your cousin isn't quite sure what culture means or why these neighborhoods are so different.

How can you explain what culture is?

BUILDING BACKGROUND For hundreds of years, immigrants from around the world have moved to the United States to make a new home here. They have brought with them all the things that make up culture—language, religion, beliefs, traditions, and more. As a result, the United States has one of the most diverse cultures in the world.

What Is Culture?

If you traveled around the world, you would experience many different sights and sounds. You would probably hear unique music, eat a variety of foods, listen to different languages, see distinctive landscapes, and learn new customs. You would see and take part in the variety of cultures that exist in our world.

A Way of Life

What exactly is culture? **Culture** is the set of beliefs, values, and practices that a group of people has in common. Culture includes many aspects of life, such as language and religion, that we may share with people around us. Everything in your day-to-day life is part of your culture, from the clothes you wear to the music you hear to the foods you eat.

On your world travels, you might notice that all societies share certain cultural features. All people have some kind of government, educate their children in some way, and create some type of art or music. However, not all societies practice their culture in the same way. For example, in Japan the school year begins in the spring, and students wear school uniforms. In the United States, however, the school year begins in the late

Culture Traits

These students in Japan and Kenya have some culture traits in common, like eating lunch at school. Other culture traits are different.

ANALYZING VISUALS What culture traits do these students share? Which are different?

summer, and most schools do not require uniforms. Differences like these are what make each culture unique.

Culture Traits

Cultural features like starting the school year in the spring or wearing uniforms are types of culture traits. A **culture trait** is an activity or behavior in which people often take part. The language you speak and the sports you play are some of your culture traits. Sometimes a culture trait is shared by people around the world. For example, all around the globe people participate in the game of soccer. In places as different as Germany, Nigeria, and Saudi Arabia, many people enjoy playing and watching soccer.

While some culture traits are shared around the world, others change from place to place. One example of this is how people around the world eat. In China most people use chopsticks to eat their food. In Europe, however, people use forks and spoons. In Ethiopia, many people use bread or their fingers to scoop their food.

Development of Culture

How do cultures develop? Culture traits are often learned or passed down from one generation to the next. Most culture traits develop within families as traditions, foods, or holiday customs are handed down over the years. Laws and moral codes are also passed down within societies. Many laws in the United States, for example, can be traced back to England in the 1600s and were brought by colonists to America.

Cultures also develop as people learn new culture traits. Immigrants who move to a new country, for example, might learn to speak the language or eat the foods of their adopted country.

Other factors, such as history and the environment, also affect how cultures develop. For example, historical events changed the language and religion of much of Central and South America. In the 1500s, when the Spanish conquered the region, they introduced their language and Roman Catholic faith. The environment in which we live can also shape culture.

FOCUS ON READING
What is the main idea of this paragraph?

For example, the desert environment of Africa's Sahara influences the way people who live there earn a living. Rather than grow crops, they herd animals that have adapted to the harsh environment. As you can see, history and the environment affect how cultures develop.

READING CHECK **Finding Main Ideas** What practices and customs make up culture?

Culture Groups

Earth is home to thousands of different cultures. People who share similar culture traits are members of the same culture group. Culture groups can be based on a variety of factors, such as age, language, or religion. American teenagers, for example, can be said to form a culture group based on location and age. They share similar tastes in music, clothing, and sports.

Culture Regions

When we refer to culture groups, we are speaking of people who share a common culture. At other times, however, we need to refer to the area, or region, where the culture group is found. A **culture region** is an area in which people have many shared culture traits.

In a specific culture region, people share certain culture traits, such as religious beliefs, language, or lifestyle. One well-known culture region is the Arab world. As you can see at right, an Arab culture region spreads across Southwest Asia and North Africa. In this region, most people write and speak Arabic and are Muslim. They also share other traits, such as foods, music, styles of clothing, and architecture.

Occasionally, a single culture region dominates an entire country. In Japan, for example, one primary culture dominates the country. Nearly everyone in Japan speaks the same language and follows the same practices. Many Japanese bow to their elders as a sign of respect and remove their shoes when they enter a home.

A single country may also include more than one culture region within its borders. Mexico is one of many countries that is made up of different culture regions. People in northern Mexico and southern Mexico, for example, have different culture traits. The culture of northern Mexico tends to be more modern, while traditional culture remains strong in southern Mexico.

A culture region may also stretch across country borders. As you have already learned, an Arab culture region dominates much of Southwest Asia and North Africa. Another example is the Kurdish culture region, home to the Kurds, a people that live throughout Turkey, Iran, and Iraq.

Arab Culture Region

Culture regions are based on shared culture traits. Southwest Asia and North Africa make up an Arab culture region based on ethnic heritage, a common language, and religion. Most people in this region are Arab, speak and write Arabic, and practice Islam.

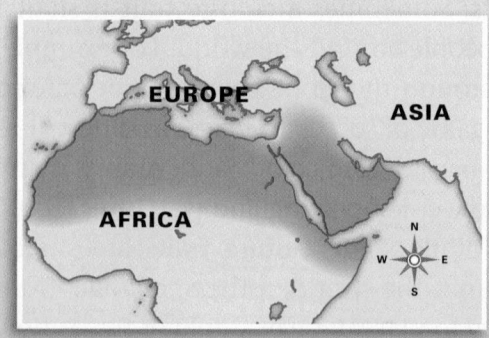

EUROPE

ASIA

AFRICA

N
W   E
S

Cultural Diversity

As you just learned, countries may contain several culture regions within their borders. Often, these culture regions are based on ethnic groups. An **ethnic group** is a group of people who share a common culture and ancestry. Members of ethnic groups often share certain culture traits such as religion, language, and even special foods.

Some countries are home to a variety of ethnic groups. For example, more than 100 different ethnic groups live in the East African country of Tanzania. Countries with many ethnic groups are culturally diverse. **Cultural diversity** is the state of having a variety of cultures in the same area. While cultural diversity creates an interesting mix of ideas, behaviors, and practices, it can also lead to conflict.

In some countries, ethnic groups have been in conflict. In Canada, for example, some French Canadians want to separate from the rest of Canada to preserve their language and culture. In the 1990s ethnic conflict in the African country of Rwanda led to extreme violence and bloodshed.

Although ethnic groups have clashed in some culturally diverse countries, they have cooperated in others. In the United States, for example, many different ethnic groups live side by side. Cities and towns often celebrate their ethnic heritage with festivals and parades, like the Saint Patrick's Day Parade in Boston or Philadelphia's Puerto Rican Festival.

READING CHECK **Making Inferences** Why might cultural diversity cause conflict?

Many people share Arab culture traits. An Algerian boy, above, and Palestinian girls, at left, share the same language and religion.

ANALYZING VISUALS What culture traits do you see in the photos?

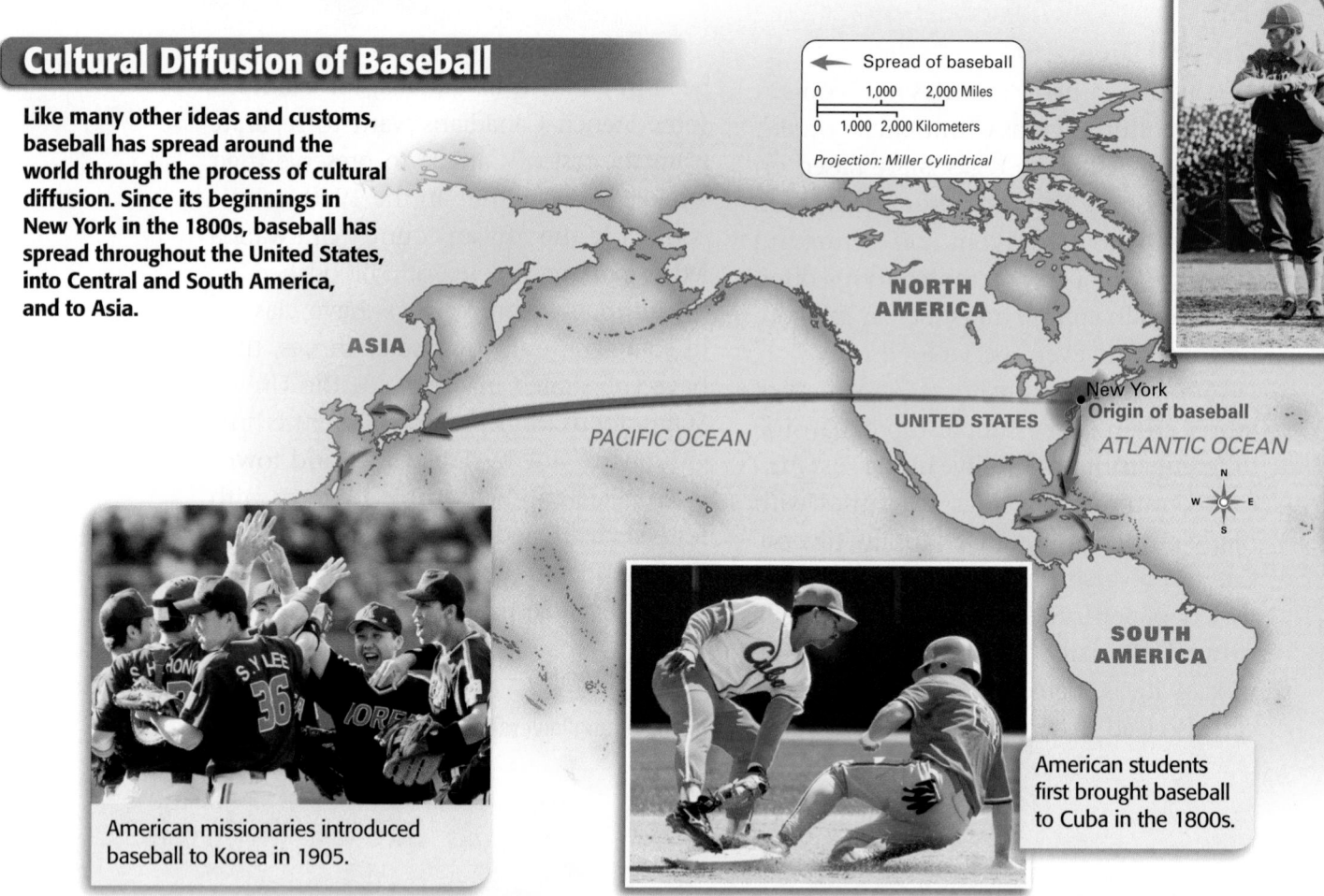

Cultural Diffusion of Baseball

Like many other ideas and customs, baseball has spread around the world through the process of cultural diffusion. Since its beginnings in New York in the 1800s, baseball has spread throughout the United States, into Central and South America, and to Asia.

Spread of baseball

0   1,000   2,000 Miles

0   1,000 2,000 Kilometers

Projection: Miller Cylindrical

ASIA

NORTH AMERICA

PACIFIC OCEAN

UNITED STATES

New York
Origin of baseball

ATLANTIC OCEAN

SOUTH AMERICA

American missionaries introduced baseball to Korea in 1905.

American students first brought baseball to Cuba in the 1800s.

Changes in Culture

You've read books or seen movies set in the time of the Civil War or in the Wild West of the late 1800s. Think about how our culture has changed since then. Clothing, food, music—all have changed drastically. When we study cultural change, we try to find out what caused the changes and how those changes spread from place to place.

How Cultures Change

Cultures change constantly. Some changes happen rapidly, while others take many years. What causes cultures to change? **Innovation** and contact with other people are two key causes of cultural change.

New ideas often bring about cultural changes. For example, when Alexander Graham Bell invented the telephone, it changed how people communicate with each other. Other innovations, such as motion pictures, changed how people spend their free time. More recently, the creation of the Internet dramatically altered the way people find information, communicate, and shop.

Cultures also change as societies come into contact with each other. For example, when the Spanish arrived in the Americas, they introduced firearms and horses to the region, changing the lifestyle of some Native American groups. At the same time, the Spaniards learned about new foods like potatoes and chocolate. These foods then became an important part of Europeans' diet. The Chinese had a similar influence on Korea and Japan, where they introduced Buddhism and written language.

ACADEMIC VOCABULARY

innovation
a new idea or way of doing something

84 CHAPTER 4

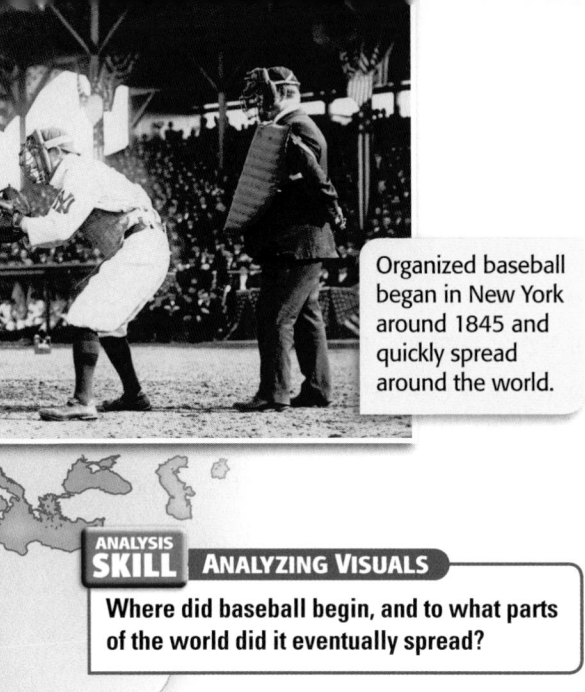

Organized baseball began in New York around 1845 and quickly spread around the world.

Where did baseball begin, and to what parts of the world did it eventually spread?

How Ideas Spread

You have probably noticed that a new slang word might spread from teenager to teenager and state to state. In the same way, clothing styles from New York or Paris might become popular all over the world. More serious cultural traits spread as well. Religious beliefs or ideas about government may spread from place to place. The spread of culture traits from one region to another is called **cultural diffusion**.

Cultural diffusion often occurs when people move from one place to another. For example, when Europeans settled in the Americas, they brought their culture along with them. As a result, English, French, Spanish, and Portuguese are all spoken in the Americas. American culture also spread as pioneers moved west, taking with them their form of government, religious beliefs, and customs.

Cultural diffusion also takes place as new ideas spread from place to place. As you can see on the map above, the game of baseball first began in New York, then spread throughout the United States. As more and more people learned the game, it spread even faster and farther. Baseball eventually spread around the world. Wearing blue jeans became part of our culture in a similar way. Blue jeans originated in the American West in the mid-1800s. They gradually became popular all over the country and the world.

READING CHECK **Finding Main Ideas** How do cultures change over time?

SUMMARY AND PREVIEW In this section you learned about the role that culture plays in our lives and how our cultures change. Next, you will learn about human populations and how we keep track of Earth's changing population.

Section 1 Assessment

Reviewing Ideas, Terms, and Places
1. **a. Define** What is **culture**?
   b. Analyze What influences the development of culture?
   c. Elaborate How might the world be different if we all shared the same culture?
2. **a. Identify** What are the different types of **culture regions**?
   b. Analyze How does **cultural diversity** affect societies?
3. **a. Describe** How does **cultural diffusion** take place?
   b. Make Inferences How can the spread of new ideas lead to cultural change?
   c. Evaluate Do you think that cultural diffusion has a positive or a negative effect? Explain your answer.

Critical Thinking
4. **Finding Main Ideas** Using your notes and a chart like the one here, explain the main idea of each aspect of culture in your own words.

Culture Traits	Culture Groups	Cultural Change

FOCUS ON WRITING

5. **Writing about Culture** What key words about culture can you include on your poster? What images might you include? Jot down your ideas in your notebook.

Population

What You Will Learn...

Main Ideas

1. The study of population patterns helps geographers learn about the world.
2. Population statistics and trends are important measures of population change.

The Big Idea

Population studies are an important part of geography.

Key Terms

population, *p. 86*
population density, *p. 86*
birthrate, *p. 88*
migration, *p. 89*

TAKING NOTES As you read, take notes on population. Use a graphic organizer like the one below to organize your notes on population patterns and population change.

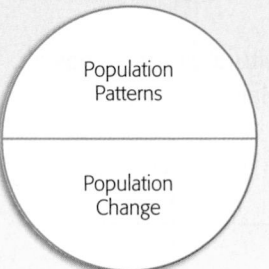

Population Patterns

Population Change

If **YOU** lived there...

You live in Mexico City, one of the largest and most crowded cities in the world. You realize just how crowded it is whenever you ride the subway at rush hour! You love the excitement of living in a big city. There is always something interesting to do. At the same time, the city has a lot of crime. Heavy traffic pollutes the air.

What do you like and dislike about living in a large city?

BUILDING BACKGROUND An important part of geographers' work is the study of human populations. Many geographers are interested in where people live, how many people live there, and what effects those people have on resources and the environment.

Population Patterns

How many people live in your community? Do you live in a small town, a huge city, or somewhere in between? Your community's **population**, or the total number of people in a given area, determines a great deal about the place in which you live. Population influences the variety of businesses, the types of transportation, and the number of schools in your community.

Because population has a huge impact on our lives, it is an important part of geography. Geographers who study human populations are particularly interested in patterns that emerge over time. They study such information as how many people live in an area, why people live where they do, and how populations change. Population patterns like these can tell us much about our world.

Population Density

Some places on Earth are crowded with people. Others are almost empty. One statistic geographers use to examine populations is **population density**, a measure of the number of people living in an area. Population density is expressed as persons per square mile or square kilometer.

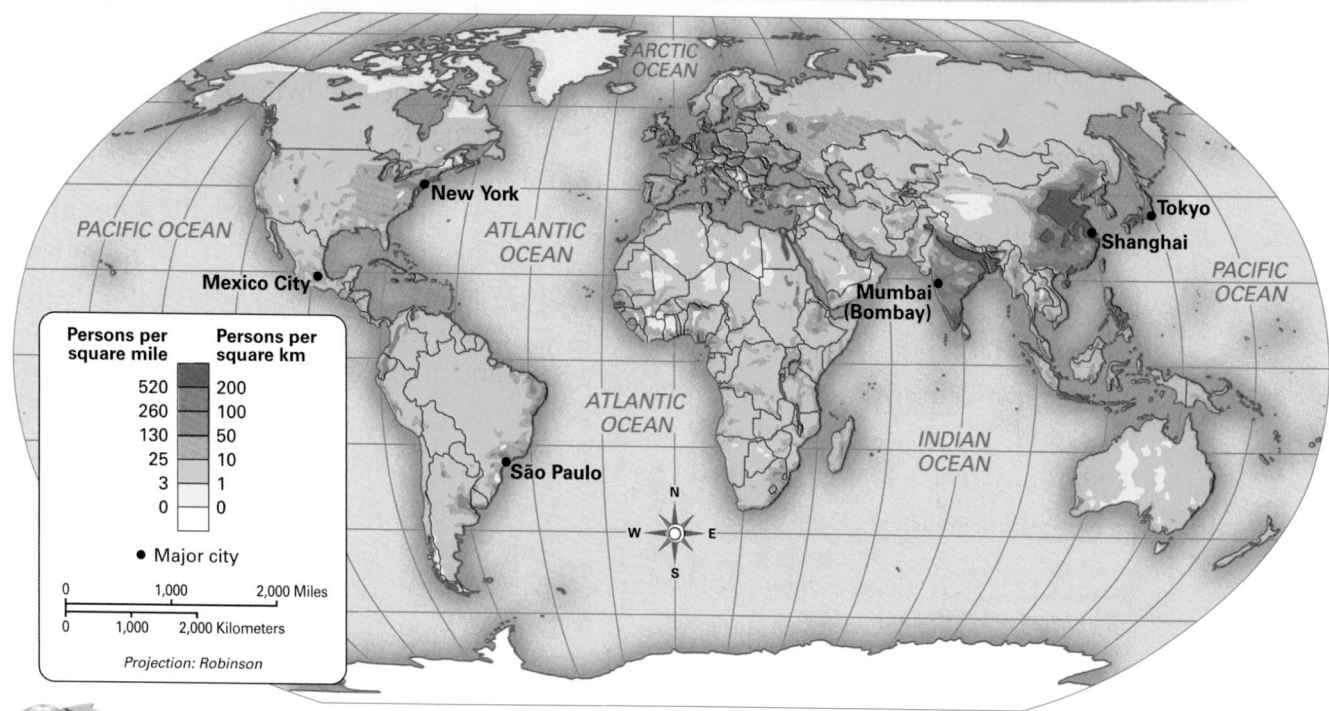

Geography Skills

Location While low population densities are common throughout much of the world, South and East Asia are two of the world's most densely populated regions.

1. Identify Which continent is the most densely populated? Which is the least densely populated?

2. Making Inferences Why might the population density of far North America be so low?

go.hrw.com   KEYWORD: SG7 CH4

Population density provides us with important information about a place. The more people per square mile in a region, the more crowded, or dense, it is. Japan, for example, has a population density of 880 people per square mile (340 per square km). That is a high population density. In many parts of Japan, people are crowded together in large cities, and space is very limited. In contrast, Australia has a very low population density. Only 6 people per square mile (2 per square km) live there. Australia has many wide-open spaces with very few people.

How do you think population density affects life in a particular place? In places with high population densities, the land is often expensive, roads are crowded, and buildings tend to be taller. On the other hand, places with low population densities tend to have more open spaces, less traffic, and more available land.

Where People Live

Can you tell where most of the world's people live by examining the population density map above? The reds and purples on the map indicate areas of very high population density, while the light yellow areas indicate sparse populations. When an area is thinly populated, it is often because the land does not provide a very good life. These areas may have rugged mountains or harsh deserts where people cannot grow crops. Some areas may be frozen all year long, making survival there very difficult.

For these reasons, very few people live in parts of far North America, Greenland, northern Asia, and Australia.

Notice on the map that some areas have large clusters of population. Such clusters can be found in East and South Asia, Europe, and eastern North America. Fertile soil, reliable sources of water, and a good agricultural climate make these good regions for settlement. For example, the North China Plain in East Asia is one of the most densely populated regions in the world. The area's plentiful agricultural land, many rivers, and mild climate have made it an ideal place to settle.

READING CHECK **Generalizing** What types of information can population density provide?

CONNECTING TO Math

Calculating Population Density

Population density measures the number of people living in an area. To calculate population density, divide a place's total population by its area in square miles (or square kilometers). For example, if your city has a population of 100,000 people and an area of 100 square miles, you would divide 100,000 by 100. This would give you a population density of 1,000 people per square mile ($100,000 ÷ 100 = 1,000$).

Analyzing If a city had a population of 615,000 and a total land area of 250 square miles, what would its population density be?

City	Population	Total Area (square miles)	Population Density (people per square mile)
Adelaide, Australia	1,032,585	336	3,073
Lima, Peru	8,043,521	1,029	7,816
Nairobi, Kenya	2,143,254	266	8,057

Population Change

The study of population is much more important than you might realize. The number of people living in an area affects all elements of life—the availability of housing and jobs, whether hospitals and schools open or close, even the amount of available food. Geographers track changes in populations by examining important statistics, studying the movement of people, and analyzing population trends.

Tracking Population Changes

Geographers examine three key statistics to learn about population changes. These statistics are important for studying a country's population over time.

Three key statistics—birthrate, death rate, and the rate of natural increase—track changes in population. Births add to a population. Deaths subtract from it. The annual number of births per 1,000 people is called the **birthrate**. Similarly, the death rate is the annual number of deaths per 1,000 people. The birthrate minus the death rate equals the percentage of natural increase, or the rate at which a population is changing. For example, Japan has a rate of natural increase of 0.02%. This means it has slightly more births than deaths and a very slight population increase.

Population growth rates differ from one place to another. In some countries, populations are growing very slowly or even shrinking. Many countries in Europe and North America have very low rates of natural increase. In Russia, for example, the birthrate is about 10.8 and the death rate is 16. The result is a negative rate of natural increase and a shrinking population.

In most countries around the world, however, populations are growing. Mali, for example, has a rate of natural increase of about 3 percent. While that may sound

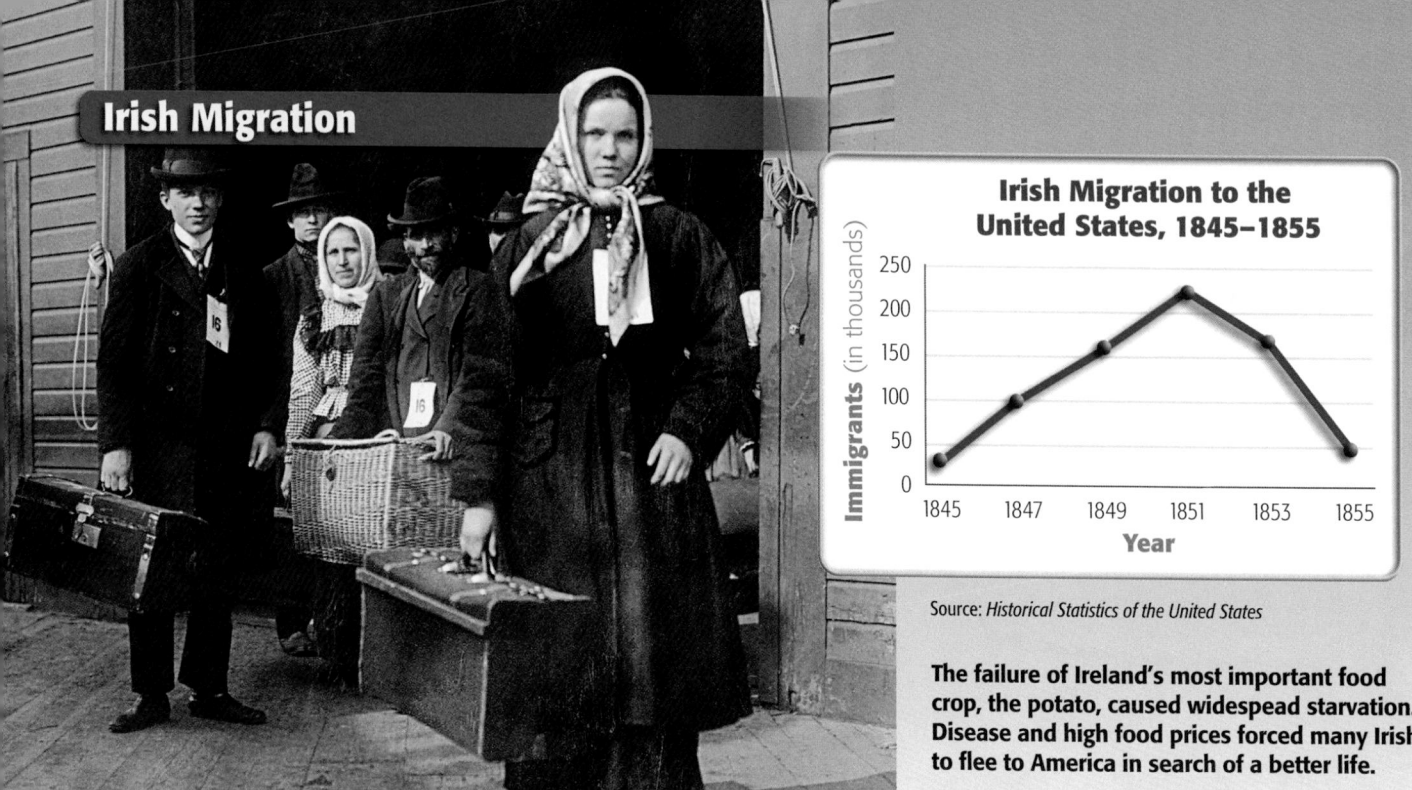

Irish Migration

Irish Migration to the United States, 1845–1855

Source: *Historical Statistics of the United States*

The failure of Ireland's most important food crop, the potato, caused widespead starvation. Disease and high food prices forced many Irish to flee to America in search of a better life.

ANALYZING GRAPHS In what year did Irish migration to the United States peak?

small, it means that Mali's population is expected to double in only 21 years! High population growth rates can pose some challenges, as governments try to provide enough jobs, education, and medical care for their rapidly growing populations.

Migration

A common cause of population change is migration. **Migration** is the process of moving from one place to live in another. As one country loses citizens as a result of migration, its population can decline. At the same time, another country may gain population as people settle there.

People migrate for many reasons. Some factors push people to leave their country, while other factors pull, or attract, people to new countries. Warfare, a lack of jobs, or a lack of good farmland are common push factors. For example, during the Irish potato famine of the mid-1800s, poverty and disease forced some 1.5 million people to leave Ireland. Opportunities for a better life often pull people to new countries. For example, in the 1800s and early 1900s thousands of British citizens migrated to Australia in search of cheap land.

World Population Trends

In the last 200 years Earth's population has exploded. For thousands of years world population growth was low and relatively steady. About 2,000 years ago, the world had some 300 million people. By 1800 there were almost 1 billion people. Since 1800, better health care and improved food production have supported tremendous population growth. In 1999 the world's population passed 6 billion people.

Population trends are an important part of the study of the world's people. Two important population trends are clear today. The first trend indicates that the population growth in some of the more industrialized nations has begun to slow.

FOCUS ON READING
What is the main idea of this paragraph? What facts are used to support that idea?

World Population Growth

Advances in food production and health care have dramatically lowered death rates. As a result, the global population has seen incredible growth over the last 200 years.

ANALYZING GRAPHS By how much did the world's population increase between 1800 and 2000?

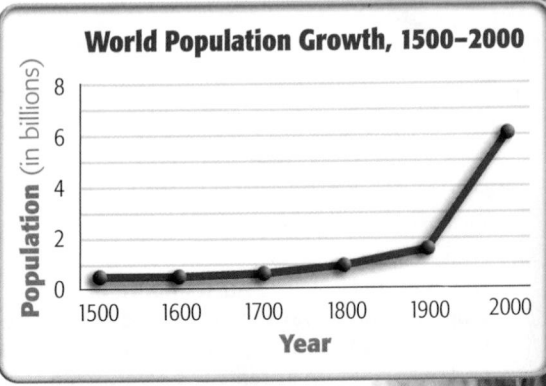

World Population Growth, 1500–2000

Source: *Atlas of World Population History*

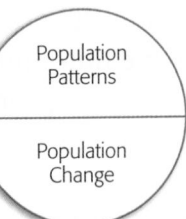

For example, Germany and France have low rates of natural increase. A second trend indicates that less industrialized countries, like Nigeria and Bangladesh, often have high growth rates. These trends affect a country's workforce and government aid.

READING CHECK Summarizing What population statistics do geographers study? Why?

SUMMARY AND PREVIEW In this section you have learned where people live, how crowded places are, and how population affects our world. Geographers study past and present population patterns in order to plan for the future. In the next section, you will learn how governments and economies affect people on Earth.

go.hrw.com
Online Quiz
KEYWORD: SG7 HP4

Section 2 Assessment

Reviewing Ideas, Terms, and Places

1. **a. Identify** What regions of the world have the highest levels of **population density**?
   b. Draw Conclusions What information can be learned by studying population density?
   c. Evaluate Would you prefer to live in a region with a dense or a sparse population? Why?
2. **a. Describe** What is natural increase? What can it tell us about a country?
   b. Analyze What effect does **migration** have on human populations?
   c. Predict What patterns do you think world population might have in the future?

Critical Thinking

3. **Summarizing** Draw a graphic organizer like the one here. Use your notes to write a sentence that summarizes each aspect of the study of population.

Population Patterns

Population Change

FOCUS ON WRITING

4. **Discussing Population** What effect does population have on our world? Write down some words and phrases that you might use on your poster to explain the importance of population.

Government and Economy

If YOU lived there...

You live in Raleigh, North Carolina. Your class at school is planning a presentation about life in the United States for a group of visitors from Japan. Your teacher wants you to discuss government and economics in the United States. As you prepare for your speech, you wonder what you should say.

How do government and economics affect your life?

> **BUILDING BACKGROUND** Although you probably don't think about them every day, your country's government and economy have a big influence on your life. That is true in every country in every part of the world. Governments and economic systems affect everything from a person's rights to the type of job he or she has.

Governments of the World

Can you imagine what life would be like if there were no rules? Without ways to establish order and ensure justice, life would be chaotic. That explains why societies have governments. Our governments make and enforce laws, regulate business and trade, and provide aid to people. Governments help shape the culture and economy of a country as well as the daily lives of the people who live there.

Democratic Governments

Many countries—including the United States, Canada, and Mexico—have democratic governments. A **democracy** is a form of government in which the people elect leaders and rule by majority. In most democratic countries, citizens are free to choose representatives to make and enforce the laws. Voters in the United States, for example, elect members of Congress, who make the laws, and the president, who enforces those laws.

What You Will Learn...

Main Ideas
1. The governments of the world include democracy, monarchy, dictatorship, and communism.
2. Different economic activities and systems exist throughout the world.
3. Geographers group the countries of the world based on their level of economic development.

The Big Idea
The world's countries have different governments and levels of economic development.

Key Terms
democracy, *p. 91*
communism, *p. 92*
market economy, *p. 94*
command economy, *p. 94*
gross domestic product (GDP), *p. 95*
developed countries, *p. 95*
developing countries, *p. 95*

TAKING NOTES As you read, use a chart like this one to take notes on the different types of governments and economies.

Government	Economy

Governments of the World

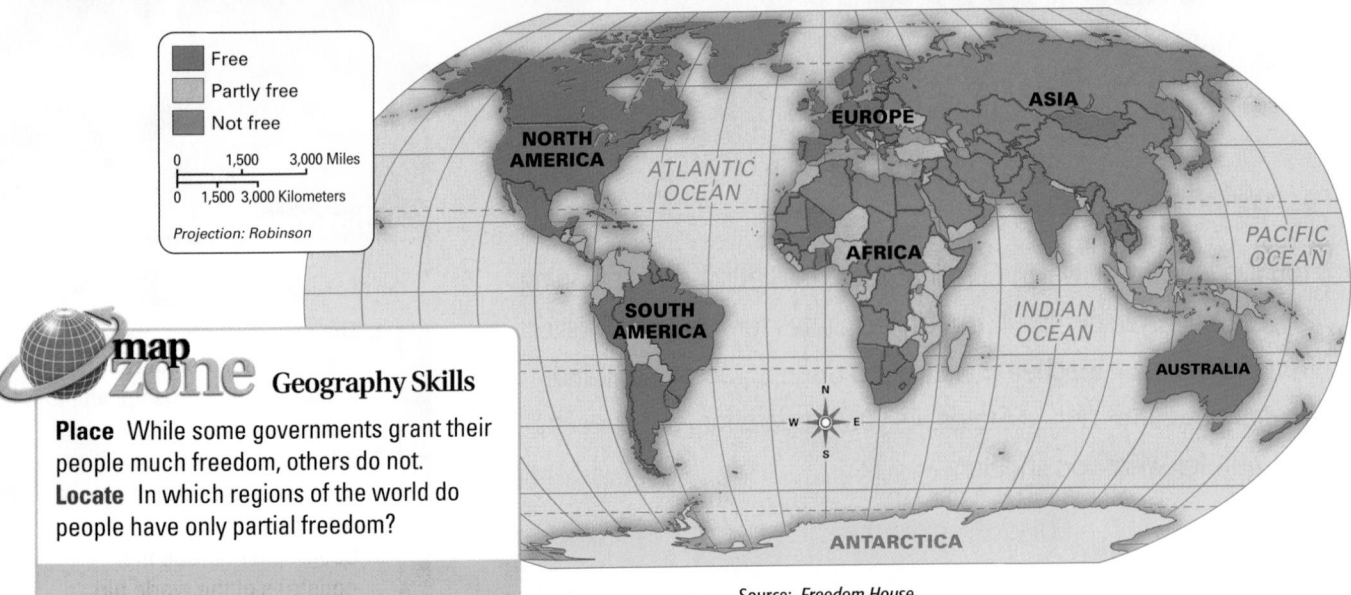

Free
Partly free
Not free

0   1,500   3,000 Miles
0   1,500 3,000 Kilometers

Projection: Robinson

map zone **Geography Skills**

Place While some governments grant their people much freedom, others do not.
Locate In which regions of the world do people have only partial freedom?

Source: *Freedom House*

Most democratic governments in the world work to protect the freedoms and rights of their people, such as the freedom of speech and the freedom of religion. Other democracies, however, restrict the rights and freedoms of their people. Not all democratic governments in the world are completely free.

Other Types of Government

Not all of the world's countries, however, are democracies. Several other types of government are found in the world today, including monarchies, dictatorships, and Communist states.

Monarchy is one of the oldest types of government in the world. A monarchy is ruled directly by a king or queen, the head of a royal family. Saudi Arabia is an example of a monarchy. The Saudi king has executive, legislative, and judicial powers. In some monarchies, power is in the hands of just one person. As a result, the people have little say in their government. Other monarchies, however, like Norway and Spain, use many democratic practices.

Dictatorship is a type of government in which a single, powerful ruler has total control. This leader, called a dictator, often rules by force. Iraq under Saddam Hussein was an example of a dictatorship. People who live under a dictatorship are not free. They have few rights and no say in their own government.

Yet another form of government is communism. **Communism** is a political system in which the government owns all property and dominates all aspects of life in a country. Leaders of most Communist governments are not elected by citizens. Rather, they are chosen by the Communist Party or by Communist leaders. In most Communist states, like Cuba and North Korea, the government strictly controls the country's economy and the daily life of its people. As a result, people in Communist states often have restricted rights and very little freedom.

READING CHECK **Supporting a Point of View** Why might people prefer to live in a democracy as opposed to a dictatorship?

Economies of the World

One important function of government is to monitor a country's economy. The economy is a system that includes all of the activities that people and businesses do to earn a living. Countries today use a mix of different economic activities and systems.

Economic Activity

Every country has some level of economic activity. Economic activities are ways in which people make a living. Some people farm, others manufacture goods, while still others provide services, such as driving a taxi or designing skyscrapers. Geographers divide these economic activities into four different levels.

The first level of economic activity, the primary industry, uses natural resources or raw materials. People in these industries earn a living by providing raw materials to others. Farming, fishing, and mining are all examples of primary industries. These activities provide raw materials such as grain, seafood, and coal for others to use.

Secondary industries perform the next step. They use natural resources or raw materials to manufacture other products. Manufacturing is the process in which raw materials are changed into finished goods. For example, people who make furniture might take wood and make products such as tables, chairs, or desks. Automobile manufacturers use steel, plastic, glass, and rubber to put together trucks and cars.

In the third level of activity, or tertiary industry, goods and services are exchanged. People in tertiary industries sell the furniture, automobiles, or other products made in secondary industries. Other people, like health care workers or mechanics, provide services rather than goods. Teachers, store clerks, doctors, and TV personalities are all engaged in this level of economic activity.

Economic Activity

Primary Industry

Primary industries use natural resources to make money. Here a farmer sells milk from dairy cows to earn a living.

Secondary Industry

Secondary economic activities use raw materials to produce or manufacture something new. In this case, the milk from dairy cows is used to make cheese.

Tertiary Industry

Tertiary economic activities provide services to people and businesses. This grocer selling cheese in a market is involved in a tertiary activity.

Quaternary Industry

Quaternary industries process and distribute information. Skilled workers research and gather information. Here, inspectors examine and test the quality of cheese.

The highest level of economic activity, quaternary industry, involves the research and distribution of information. People making a living at this level work with information rather than goods, and often have specialized knowledge and skills. Architects, lawyers, and scientists all work in quaternary industries.

Economic Systems

Just as economic activities are organized into different types, so are our economic systems. Economic systems can be divided into three types: traditional, market, and command. Most countries today use a mix of these economic systems.

One economic system is a **traditional** economy, a system in which people grow their own food and make their own goods. Trade may take place through barter, or the exchange of goods without the use of money. Rural and remote communities often have a mostly traditional economy.

ACADEMIC VOCABULARY
traditional
customary, time-honored

The most common economic system used around the world today is a market economy. A **market economy** is a system based on private ownership, free trade, and competition. Individuals and businesses are free to buy and sell what they wish. Prices are determined by the supply and demand for goods. This is sometimes called capitalism. The United States is one of many countries that use this system.

A third system is a **command economy**, a system in which the central government makes all economic decisions. The government decides what goods to produce, how much to produce, and what prices will be. While no country has a purely command economy, the economies of North Korea and Cuba are close to it. The Communist governments of these nations own and control most businesses.

READING CHECK **Summarizing** What economic systems are used in the world today?

THE WORLD ALMANAC
Facts about Countries
A Developed and a Developing Country

Australia	**Afghanistan**
Per Capita GDP (U.S. $): $32,900	Per Capita GDP (U.S. $): $800
Life Expectancy at Birth: 80.6	Life Expectancy at Birth: 43.8
Literacy Rate: 100%	Literacy Rate: 28%
Physicians Per 10,000 People: 24.7	Physicians Per 10,000 People: 1.9

Contrasting How does the quality of life in Afghanistan differ from that in Australia?

go.hrw.com KEYWORD: SG7 CH4

Economic Development

Economic systems and activities affect a country's economic development, or the level of economic growth and quality of life. Geographers often group countries into two basic categories—developed and developing countries—based on their level of economic development.

Economic Indicators

Geographers use economic indicators, or measures of a country's wealth, to decide if a country is developed or developing. One such measure is gross domestic product. **Gross domestic product (GDP)** is the value of all goods and services produced within a country in a single year. Another indicator is a country's per capita GDP, or the total GDP divided by the number of people in a country. As you can see in the chart, per capita GDP allows us to compare incomes among countries. Other indicators include the level of industrialization and overall quality of life. In other words, we look at the types of industries and technology a country has, in addition to its level of health care and education.

Developed and Developing Countries

Many of the world's wealthiest and most powerful nations are **developed countries**, countries with strong economies and a high quality of life. Developed countries like Germany and the United States have a high per capita GDP and high levels of industrialization. Their health care and education systems are among the best in the world. Many people in developed countries have access to technology.

The world's poorer nations are known as **developing countries**, countries with less productive economies and a lower quality of life. Almost two-thirds of the people in the world live in developing countries. These developing countries have a lower per capita GDP than developed countries. Most of their citizens work in farming or other primary industries. Although these countries typically have large cities, much of their population still lives in rural areas. People in developing countries usually have less access to health care or technology. Guatemala, Nigeria, and Afghanistan are all developing countries.

READING CHECK **Analyzing** What factors separate developed and developing countries?

SUMMARY AND PREVIEW The world's countries have different governments, economies, and levels of development. Next, you will learn how people are linked in a global community.

Section 3 Assessment

go.hrw.com
Online Quiz
KEYWORD: SG7 HP4

Reviewing Ideas, Terms, and Places

1. a. **Identify** What are some different types of government?
   b. **Elaborate** Under which type of government would you most want to live? Why?
2. a. **Describe** What are the levels of economic activity?
   b. **Evaluate** Which economic system do you think is best? Explain your answer.
3. a. **Define** What is **gross domestic product**?
   b. **Contrast** In what ways do **developed countries** differ from **developing countries**?

Critical Thinking

4. **Categorizing** Draw a chart like the one here. Use the chart and your notes to identify the different governments, economies, and levels of economic development in the world today.

Types of Government	Economic Systems	Economic Development

FOCUS ON WRITING

5. **Thinking about Government and Economy** What kind of images and words might you use to present the main ideas behind the world's governments and economies?

Social Studies Skills

Organizing Information

Learn

Remembering new information is easier if you organize it clearly. As you read and study, try to organize what you are learning. One way to do this is to create a graphic organizer. Follow these steps to create a graphic organizer as you read.

- Identify the main idea of the passage. Write the main idea in a circle at the top of your page.

- As you read, look for subtopics under the main idea. On your paper, draw a row of circles below the main idea, one for each subtopic. Write the subtopics in the circles.

- Below each subtopic, draw a big box. Look for facts and supporting details for each subtopic. List them in the box below the subtopic.

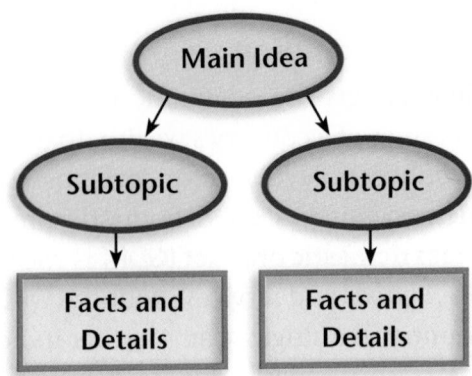

Practice

Read the passage below carefully. Then use the graphic organizer above to organize the information from the passage.

> Cultures change slowly over time. New ideas and new people can often lead to cultural change.
>
> Cultures often change as new ideas are introduced to a society. New ways of doing things, new inventions, and even new beliefs can all change a culture. One example of this is the spread of computer technology. As people adopted computers, they learned a new language and new work habits.
>
> Cultures also change when new people introduce their culture traits to a society. For example, as immigrants settle in the United States, they add new culture traits, like food, music, and clothing, to American culture.

Apply

Turn to Section 1 and read the passage titled Culture Regions. Draw a graphic organizer like the one above. Then follow the steps to organize the information you have read. The passage will have two or more subtopics. Add additional circles and rectangles for each additional subtopic you find.

Global Connections

If YOU lived there...

You live in Louisville, Kentucky, and you have never traveled out of the United States. However, when you got ready for school this morning, you put on a T-shirt made in Guatemala and jeans made in Malaysia. Your shoes came from China. You rode to school on a bus with parts manufactured in Mexico. At school, your class even took part in a discussion with students in Canada.

What makes your global connections possible?

BUILDING BACKGROUND Trade and technology have turned the world into a "global village." People around the world wear clothes, eat foods, and use goods made in other countries. Global connections are bringing people around the world closer than ever before.

Globalization

In just seconds an e-mail message sent by a teenager in India beams all the way to a friend in London. A band in Seattle releases a new CD that becomes popular in China. People from New York to Singapore respond to a crisis in Brazil. These are all examples of **globalization**, the process in which countries are increasingly linked to each other through culture and trade.

What caused globalization? Improvements in transportation and communication over the past 100 years have brought the world closer together. Airplanes, telecommunications, and the Internet allow us to communicate and travel the world with ease. As a result, global culture and trade have increased.

Popular Culture

What might you have in common with a teenager in Japan? You probably have more in common than you think. You may use similar technology, wear similar clothes, and watch many of the same movies. You share the same global popular culture.

What You Will Learn...

Main Ideas

1. Globalization links the world's countries together through culture and trade.
2. The world community works together to solve global conflicts and crises.

The Big Idea

Fast, easy global connections have made cultural exchange, trade, and a cooperative world community possible.

Key Terms

globalization, *p. 97*
popular culture, *p. 98*
interdependence, *p. 99*
United Nations (UN), *p. 99*
humanitarian aid, *p. 100*

TAKING NOTES As you read, take notes on globalization and the world community. Use a graphic organizer like the one below to take notes.

Globalization	World Community

More and more, people around the world are linked through popular culture. **Popular culture** refers to culture traits that are well known and widely accepted. Food, sports, music, and movies are all examples of our popular culture.

The United States has great influence on global popular culture. For example, American soft drinks are sold in almost every country in the world. Many popular American television shows are broadcast internationally. English has become the major global language. One-quarter of the world's people speak English. It has become the main language for international music, business, science, and education.

At the same time, the United States is influenced by global culture. Martial arts movies from Asia attract large audiences in the United States. Radio stations in the United States play music by African, Latin American, and European musicians. We even adopt many foreign words, like *sushi* and *plaza*, into English.

Close-up

A Global Economy

The growth of the global economy has affected many businesses, especially the automobile industry. Automakers can now buy parts from countries all around the world, depending on where they can get the best price.

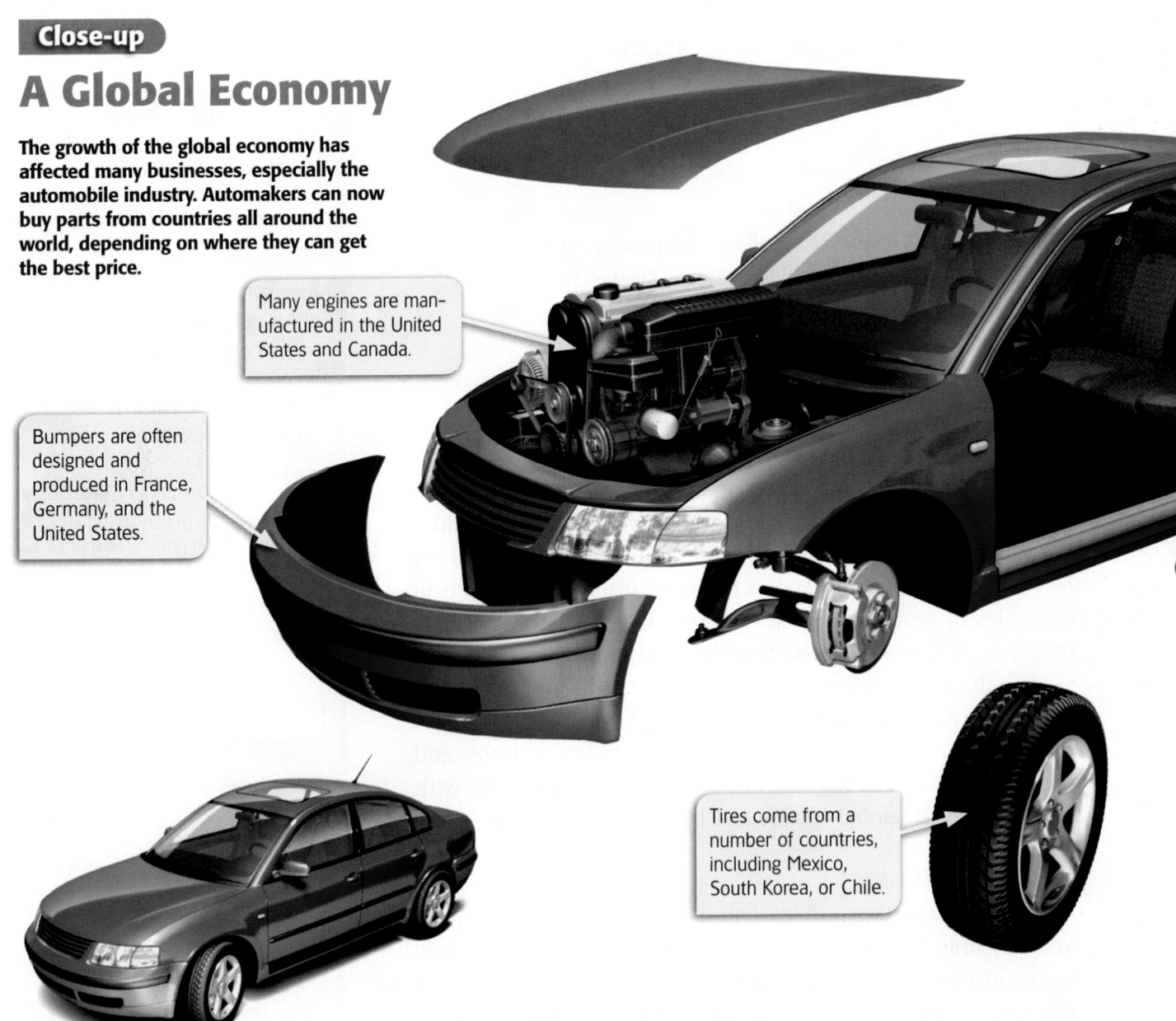

Many engines are man-ufactured in the United States and Canada.

Bumpers are often designed and produced in France, Germany, and the United States.

Tires come from a number of countries, including Mexico, South Korea, or Chile.

Global Trade

Globalization not only links the world's people, but it also connects businesses and affects trade. For centuries, societies have traded with each other. Improvements in transportation and communication have made global trade quicker and easier. For example, a shoe retailer in Chicago can order the sneakers she needs on a Web site from a company in China. The order can be flown to Chicago the next day and sold to customers that afternoon.

Many cars feature windows manufactured in Venezuela or the United States.

Seats are sometimes assembled in Japan from covers sewn in Mexico.

ANALYSIS SKILL ANALYZING VISUALS

From what different countries do automotive parts often originate?

The expansion of global trade has increased interdependence among the world's countries. **Interdependence** is a relationship between countries in which they rely on one another for resources, goods, or services. Many companies in one country often rely on goods and services produced in another country. For example, automakers in Europe might purchase auto parts made in the United States or Japan. Consumers also rely on goods produced elsewhere. For example, American shoppers buy bananas from Ecuador and tomatoes from Mexico. Global trade gives us access to goods from around the world.

READING CHECK **Finding Main Ideas** How has globalization affected the world?

A World Community

Some people call our world a global village. What do you think this means? Because of globalization, the world seems smaller. Places are more connected. What happens in one part of the world can affect the entire planet. Because of this, the world community works together to promote cooperation among countries in times of conflict and crisis.

The world community encourages cooperation by working to resolve global conflicts. From time to time, conflicts erupt among the countries of the world. Wars, trade disputes, and political disagreements can threaten the peace. Countries often join together to settle such conflicts. In 1945, for example, 51 nations created the United Nations. The **United Nations (UN)** is an organization of the world's countries that promotes peace and security around the globe.

The world community also promotes cooperation in times of crisis. A disaster may leave thousands of people in need.

FOCUS ON READING

What is the main idea of this paragraph? What facts are used to support that idea?

HISTORIC DOCUMENT
The Charter of the United Nations

Created in 1945, the United Nations is an organization of the world's countries that works to solve global problems. The Charter of the United Nations outlines the goals of the UN, some of which are included here.

We the Peoples of the United Nations Determined ...

to save succeeding generations from the scourge [terror] of war ...

to practice tolerance and live together in peace with one another as good neighbors, and

to unite our strength to maintain international peace and security, and

to ensure ... that armed forces shall not be used, save [except] in the common interest, and

to employ international machinery [systems] for the promotion of the economic and social advancement of all peoples,

Have Resolved to Combine our Efforts to Accomplish these Aims.

—*from the Charter of the United Nations*

ANALYSIS SKILL **ANALYZING PRIMARY SOURCES**

What are some of the goals of the United Nations?

Earthquakes, floods, and drought can cause crises around the world. Groups from many nations often come together to provide **humanitarian aid**, or assistance to people in distress.

Organizations representing countries around the globe work to help in times of crisis. For example, in 2004 a tsunami, or huge tidal wave, devastated parts of Southeast Asia. Many organizations, like the United Nations Children's Fund (UNICEF) and the International Red Cross, stepped in to provide humanitarian aid to the victims of the tsunami. Some groups lend aid to refugees, or people who have been forced to flee their homes. Groups like Doctors Without Borders give medical aid to those in need around the world.

READING CHECK **Analyzing** How has globalization promoted cooperation?

SUMMARY In this section you learned how globalization links the countries of the world through shared culture and trade. Globalization allows organizations around the world to work together. They often solve conflicts and provide humanitarian aid.

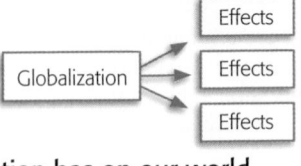
go.hrw.com
Online Quiz
KEYWORD: SG7 HP4

Section 4 Assessment

Reviewing Ideas, Terms, and Places
1. **a. Describe** What is **globalization**?
   b. Make Inferences How has **popular culture** influenced countries around the world?
   c. Evaluate In your opinion, has globalization hurt or helped the people of the world?
2. **a. Define** What is **humanitarian aid**?
   b. Draw Conclusions How has globalization promoted cooperation among countries?
   c. Predict What types of problems might lead to international cooperation?

Critical Thinking
3. **Identifying Cause and Effect** Use your notes and the graphic organizer at right to identify the effects that globalization has on our world.

Globalization → Effects / Effects / Effects

FOCUS ON WRITING
4. **Writing about Global Connections** What aspects of globalization might you include in your poster? Jot down your ideas in your notebook.

Chapter Review

Geography's Impact
video series
Review the video to answer the closing question:
Why do you think some peoples must work to preserve their cultures in the modern world?

Visual Summary

Use the visual summary below to help you review the main ideas of the chapter.

QUICK FACTS

The world has many different cultures, or shared beliefs and practices.

The world's people practice different economic activities and systems.

Globalization brings people around the world closer than ever before.

Reviewing Vocabulary, Terms, and Places

Choose one word from each word pair to correctly complete each sentence below.

1. Members of a/an _____ often share the same religion, traditions, and language. **(ethnic group/population)**

2. People in a _____ are free to buy and sell goods as they please. **(command economy/ market economy)**

3. Organizations like the International Red Cross provide _____ to people in need around the world. **(humanitarian aid/cultural diffusion)**

4. _____, the process of moving from one place to live in another, is a cause of population change. **(Population density/Migration)**

5. A country with a strong economy and a high standard of living is considered a _____. **(developed country/developing country)**

Comprehension and Critical Thinking

SECTION 1 *(Pages 80–85)*

6. **a. Describe** What is cultural diversity?

b. Analyze What causes cultures to change over time?

c. Elaborate Describe some of the culture traits practiced by people in your community.

SECTION 2 *(Pages 86–90)*

7. **a. Describe** What does population density tell us about a place?

b. Draw Conclusions Why do certain areas attract large populations?

c. Elaborate Why do you think it is important for geographers to study population trends?

SECTION 3 *(Pages 91–95)*

8. **a. Recall** What is a command economy?

SECTION 3 (continued)

b. Make Inferences Why might developing countries have only primary and secondary economic activities?

c. Evaluate Do you think government is important in our everyday lives? Why or why not?

SECTION 4 *(Pages 97–100)*

9. a. Describe How have connections among the world's countries improved?

b. Analyze What impact has globalization had on world trade and culture?

c. Evaluate What do you think has been the most important result of globalization? Why?

Social Studies Skills

10. Organizing Information Practice organizing information by creating a graphic organizer for Section 3. Use the main ideas on the first page of the section for your large circles. Then write the subtopics under each main idea. Finally, identify supporting details for each subtopic.

FOCUS ON READING AND WRITING

Understanding Main Ideas *Read the paragraph below carefully, then write out the main idea of the paragraph.*

11. The ancient Greeks were the first to practice democracy. Since then many countries have adopted democratic government. The United Kingdom, South Korea, and Ghana all practice democracy. Democracy is the most widely used government in the world today.

Creating a Poster *Use your notes and the instructions below to help you create a poster.*

12. Review your notes about the world's cultures, populations, governments, and economies. Then select a subject for your poster. On a large sheet of paper, write a title that identifies your topic. Decorate your poster with illustrations that relate to your main idea. Write a short caption explaining each image. Be sure to use words and images that will grab your audience's attention and clearly express your main idea.

Using the Internet

go.hrw.com
KEYWORD: SG7 CH4

13. Activity: Writing a Report Population changes have a huge impact on the world around us. Countries around the world must deal with shrinking populations, growing populations, and other population issues. Enter the activity keyword and explore the issues surrounding global population. Then imagine you have been asked to report on global population trends to the United Nations. Write a report in which you identify world population trends and their impact on the world today.

Map Activity ✴Interactive

Population Density *Use the map below to answer the questions that follow.*

14. What letter on the map indicates the least crowded area?

15. What letter on the map indicates the most densely crowded area?

16. Which letter indicates a region with 260–520 people per square mile (100–200 people per square km)?

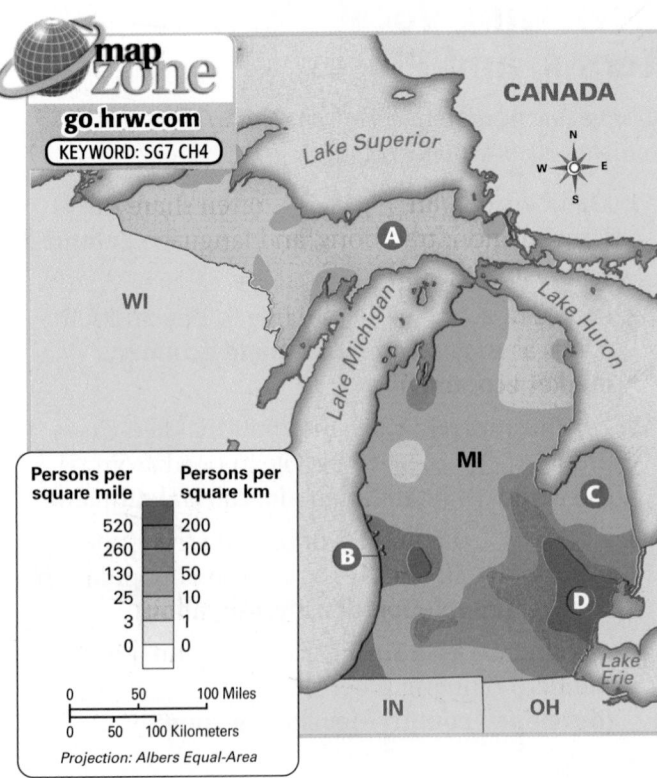

DIRECTIONS: Read questions 1 through 7 and write the letter of the best response. Then read question 8 and write your own well-constructed response.

1 Which of the following is *most likely* a culture trait?

A religion

B population density

C interdependence

D cultural diffusion

2 What developments led to the rapid increase in world population in the last 200 years?

A a decline in migration

B improvements in technology and communication

C a decrease in standard of living

D improvements in health care and agriculture

3 Which economic system is used in the United States?

A market economy

B command economy

C traditional economy

D domestic economy

4 A government in which a single, powerful ruler exerts complete control is a

A Communist state.

B democracy.

C dictatorship.

D republic.

5 Global connections have improved as a result of

A population growth.

B cultural diversity.

C the spread of democratic government.

D improvements in technology.

Developed and Developing Countries

Country	Per Capita GDP (U.S. $)	Life Expectancy at Birth	TVs per 1,000 People
Cameroon	$2,400	53.0	34
Singapore	$30,900	81.8	341
Ukraine	$7,600	67.9	433
Uruguay	$10,700	76.5	531

6 Which of the countries in the chart above is *most likely* a developed country?

A Cameroon

B Singapore

C Ukraine

D Uruguay

7 Which of the following is an example of economic interdependence?

A Cattle ranchers in Oklahoma sell beef to grocery stores in Maryland.

B Students in Germany use the Internet to communicate with scientists in Brazil.

C Construction companies in Canada build skyscrapers with steel imported from the United States.

D Immigrants from Russia settle in London.

8 Extended Response Using the data in the chart above, write a paragraph in which you compare and contrast the standard of living in Ukraine and Singapore.

Explaining a Process

Assignment
Write a paper explaining one
of these topics:
- how water recycles on Earth
- how agriculture developed

How does soil renewal work? How do cultures change? Often the first question we ask about something is how it works or what process it follows. One way we can answer these questions is by writing an explanation.

1. Prewrite

Choose a Process
- Choose one of the topics above to write about.
- Turn your topic into a big idea, or thesis. For example, your big idea might be "Water continually circulates from Earth's surface to the atmosphere and back."

> **TIP** **Organizing Information** Explanations should be in a logical order. You should arrange the steps in the process in chronological order, the order in which the steps take place.

Gather and Organize Information
- Look for information about your topic in your textbook, in the library, or on the Internet.
- Start a plan to organize support for your big idea. For example, look for the individual steps of the water cycle.

2. Write

Use a Writer's Framework

> **A Writer's Framework**
>
> **Introduction**
> - Start with an interesting fact or question.
> - Identify your big idea.
>
> **Body**
> - Create at least one paragraph for each point supporting the big idea. Add facts and details to explain each point.
> - Use chronological order or order of importance.
>
> **Conclusion**
> - Summarize your main points in your final paragraph.

3. Evaluate and Revise

Review and Improve Your Paper
- Re-read your paper and make sure you have followed the framework.
- Make the changes needed to improve your paper.

Evaluation Questions for an Explanation of a Process
1. Do you begin with an interesting fact or question?
2. Does your introduction identify your big idea? Does it provide any background information your readers might need?
3. Do you have at least one paragraph for each point you are using to support the big idea?
4. Do you include facts and details to explain and illustrate each point?
5. Do you use chronological order or order of importance to organize your main points?

4. Proofread and Publish

Give Your Explanation the Finishing Touch
- Make sure you have capitalized the first word in every sentence.
- Check for punctuation at the end of every sentence.
- Think of a way to share your explanation.

5. Practice and Apply

Use the steps and strategies outlined in this workshop to write your explanation. Share your paper with others and find out whether the explanation makes sense to them.

The Americas

The Great Lakes

Five huge lakes in North America known as the Great Lakes make up the largest group of fresh water lakes on Earth.

The Andes

Stretching along South America's western coast, the Andes are the longest mountain range in the world.

The Amazon

In the heart of South America, the Amazon rain forest is home to millions of plant and animal species.

The Americas

Explore the Satellite Image

Forests, mountains, and plains stretch from north to south across the Americas. How do you think the features you can see on this satellite image influence life in the Americas?

The Satellite's Path

>44'56.08<

>>>>>>>>>665.00'87<

567.476.348   +799   +803   +996   +355

456.094.

The Americas: Physical

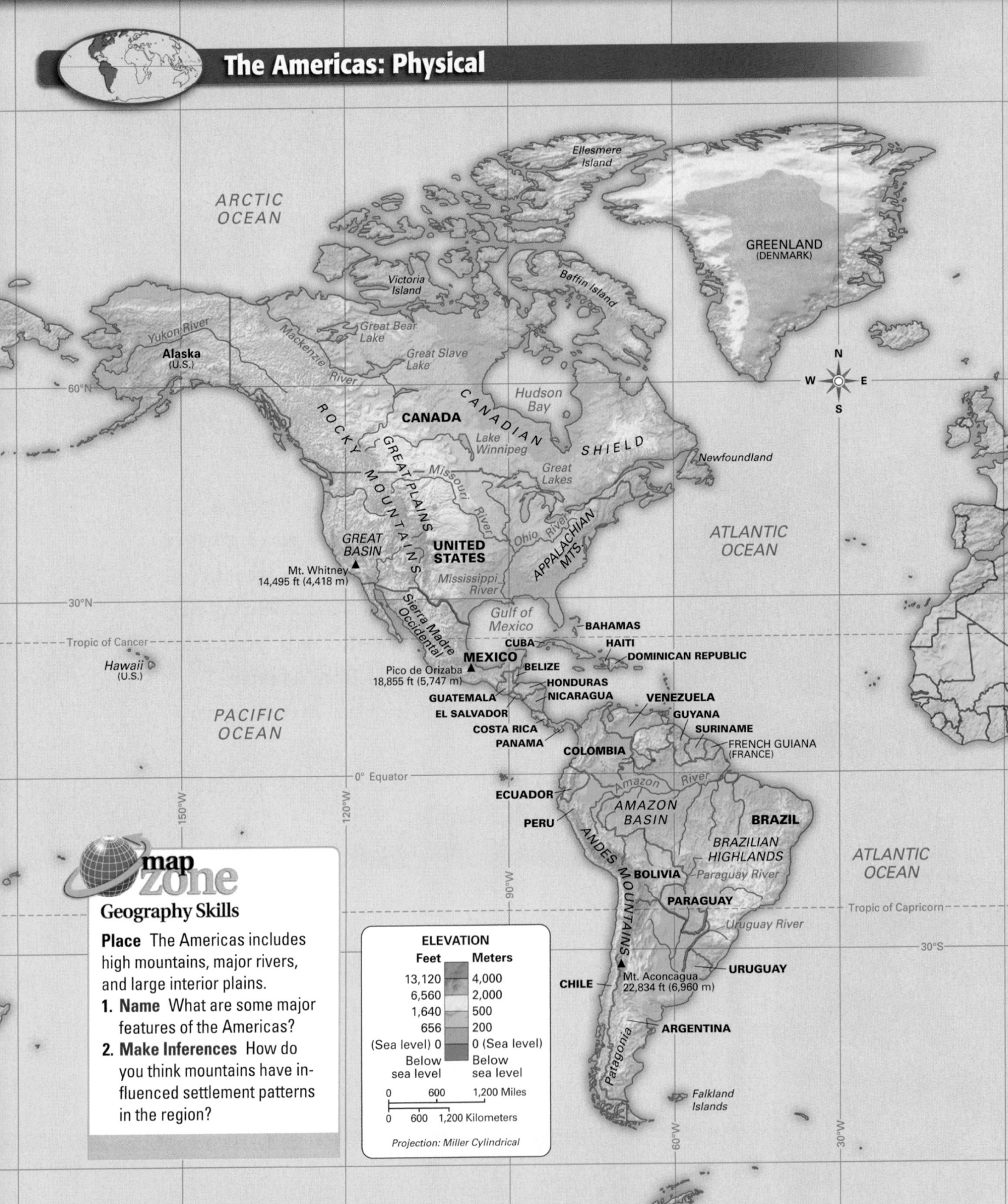

ELEVATION

Feet		Meters
13,120		4,000
6,560		2,000
1,640		500
656		200
(Sea level) 0		0 (Sea level)
Below sea level		Below sea level

0   600   1,200 Miles

0   600   1,200 Kilometers

Projection: Miller Cylindrical

Geography Skills

Place The Americas includes high mountains, major rivers, and large interior plains.

1. **Name** What are some major features of the Americas?

2. **Make Inferences** How do you think mountains have influenced settlement patterns in the region?

THE WORLD ALMANAC®
Facts about the World — Geographical Extremes: The Americas

Longest River	Amazon River, Brazil/Peru: 4,000 miles (6,435 km)
Highest Point	Mt. Aconcagua, Argentina: 22,834 feet (6,960 m)
Lowest Point	Death Valley, United States: 282 feet (86 m) below sea level
Highest Recorded Temperature	Death Valley, United States: 134°F (56.6°C)
Lowest Recorded Temperature	Snag, Canada: -81.4°F (-63°C)
Wettest Place	Lloro, Colombia: 523.6 inches (1,329.9 cm) average precipitation per year
Driest Place	Arica, Chile: .03 inches (.08 cm) average precipitation per year
Highest Waterfall	Angel Falls, Venezuela: 3,212 feet (979 m)
Most Tornadoes	United States: More than 1,000 per year

Death Valley, United States

go.hrw.com KEYWORD: SG7 UN2

Size Comparison: The United States and the Americas

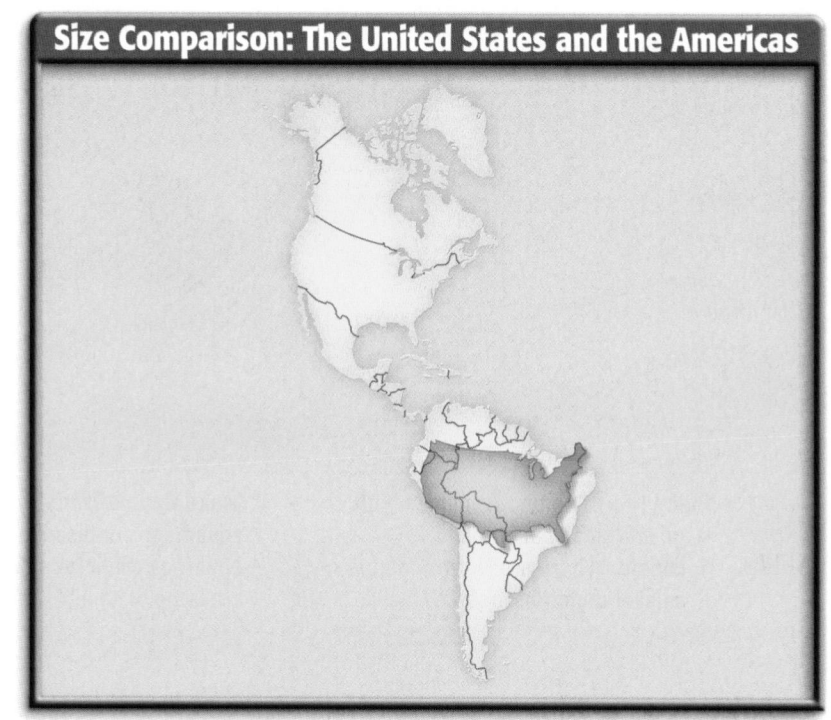

North America: Political

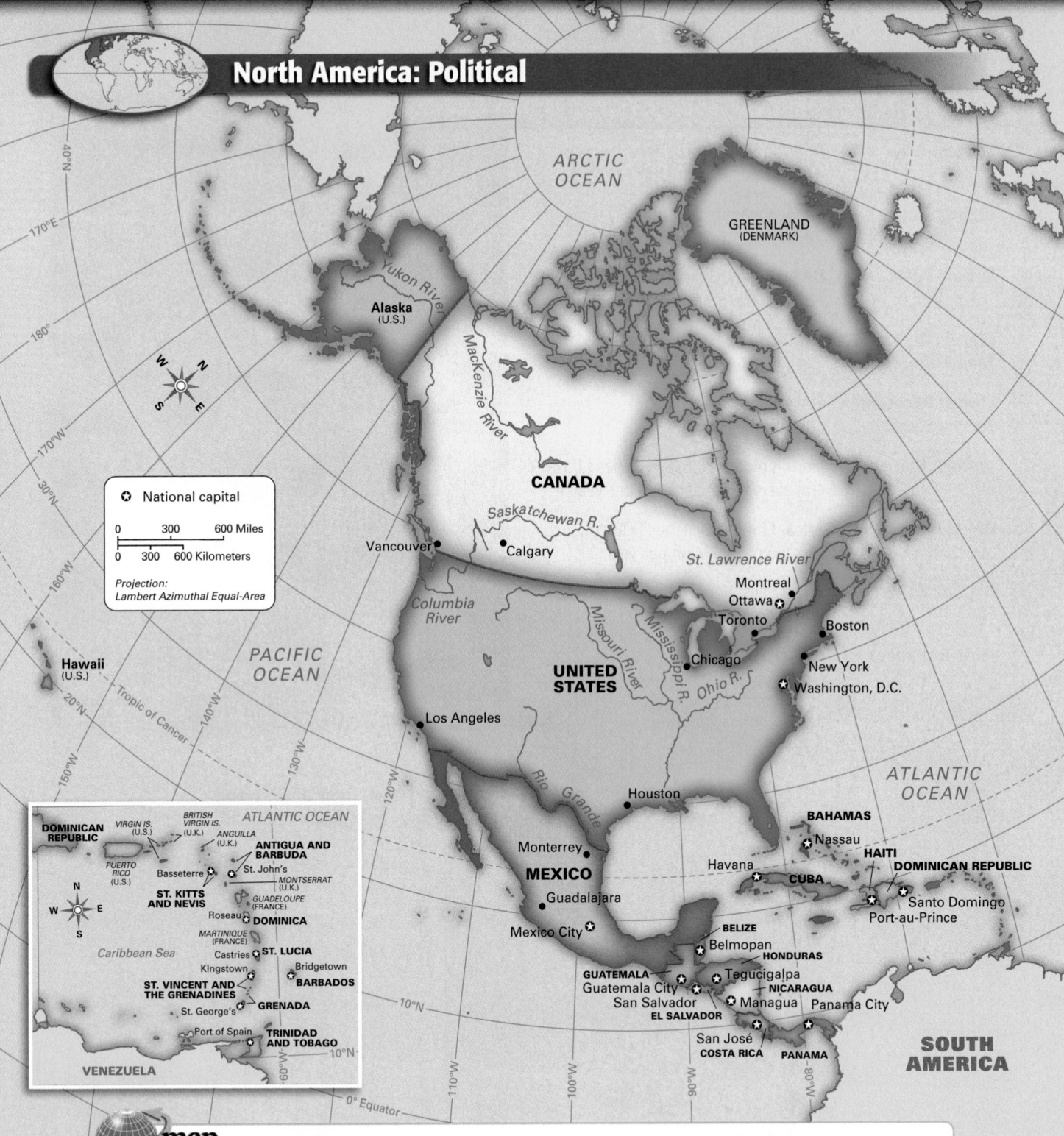

National capital

0   300   600 Miles
0   300   600 Kilometers

Projection:
Lambert Azimuthal Equal-Area

ARCTIC OCEAN

GREENLAND
(DENMARK)

Yukon River

Alaska
(U.S.)

MacKenzie River

CANADA

Saskatchewan R.

Vancouver

Calgary

St. Lawrence River

Montreal
Ottawa
Toronto

Boston

Columbia River

Missouri River

Mississippi R.

Chicago

New York
Washington, D.C.

PACIFIC OCEAN

Hawaii
(U.S.)

Tropic of Cancer

UNITED STATES

Ohio R.

Los Angeles

Rio Grande

Houston

ATLANTIC OCEAN

Monterrey

MEXICO

Guadalajara

Mexico City

BAHAMAS

Nassau

Havana

CUBA

HAITI

DOMINICAN REPUBLIC

Santo Domingo
Port-au-Prince

BELIZE
Belmopan
HONDURAS

GUATEMALA
Guatemala City
San Salvador
EL SALVADOR

Tegucigalpa
NICARAGUA
Managua
Panama City

San José
COSTA RICA
PANAMA

SOUTH AMERICA

Equator

Inset map:

ATLANTIC OCEAN

DOMINICAN REPUBLIC

VIRGIN IS. (U.S.)
BRITISH VIRGIN IS. (U.K.)
ANGUILLA (U.K.)

ANTIGUA AND BARBUDA

PUERTO RICO (U.S.)

Basseterre

St. John's

MONTSERRAT (U.K.)

ST. KITTS AND NEVIS

Roseau

GUADELOUPE (FRANCE)

DOMINICA

MARTINIQUE (FRANCE)

Castries
ST. LUCIA

Caribbean Sea

Kingstown

Bridgetown
BARBADOS

ST. VINCENT AND THE GRENADINES

GRENADA

St. George's

Port of Spain
TRINIDAD AND TOBAGO

VENEZUELA

map zone
Geography Skills

Place North America includes both large and small countries.
1. **Locate** Where are North America's smaller countries located?

2. **Make Generalizations** What are some advantages or disadvantages that countries might face because they are large or small?

South America: Political

Cartagena

Caracas

VENEZUELA

Georgetown
Paramaribo

GUYANA

Bogotá

SURINAME

French Guiana
(FRANCE)

COLOMBIA

Quito
ECUADOR
Guayaquil

0° Equator

*Galápagos
Islands*

Manaus

Amazon River

PERU

*PACIFIC
OCEAN*

10°N

10°S

Lima

BRAZIL

N
W E
S

Salvador

La Paz

BOLIVIA

Brasília

Sucre

*ATLANTIC
OCEAN*

20°S

Parana River

PARAGUAY

Rio de
Janeiro

Asunción

São Paulo

Tropic of Capricorn

CHILE

⊕ National capital

| 0 | 300 | 600 Miles |

| 0 | 300 | 600 Kilometers |

*Projection:
Lambert Azimuthal Equal-Area*

30°S

Córdoba

Santiago

URUGUAY

Buenos Aires
Montevideo

ARGENTINA

40°S

50°S

*Falkland
Islands*

*South Georgia
Island*

100°W 90°W 80°W 70°W 60°W 50°W 40°W 30°W 20°W

map zone

Geography Skills

Place South America includes 12 countries and one overseas department of France.

1. Name Which country is by far the largest in South America?

2. Compare Compare this map to the physical map of the Americas. What physical feature separates Chile and Argentina?

The Americas: Population

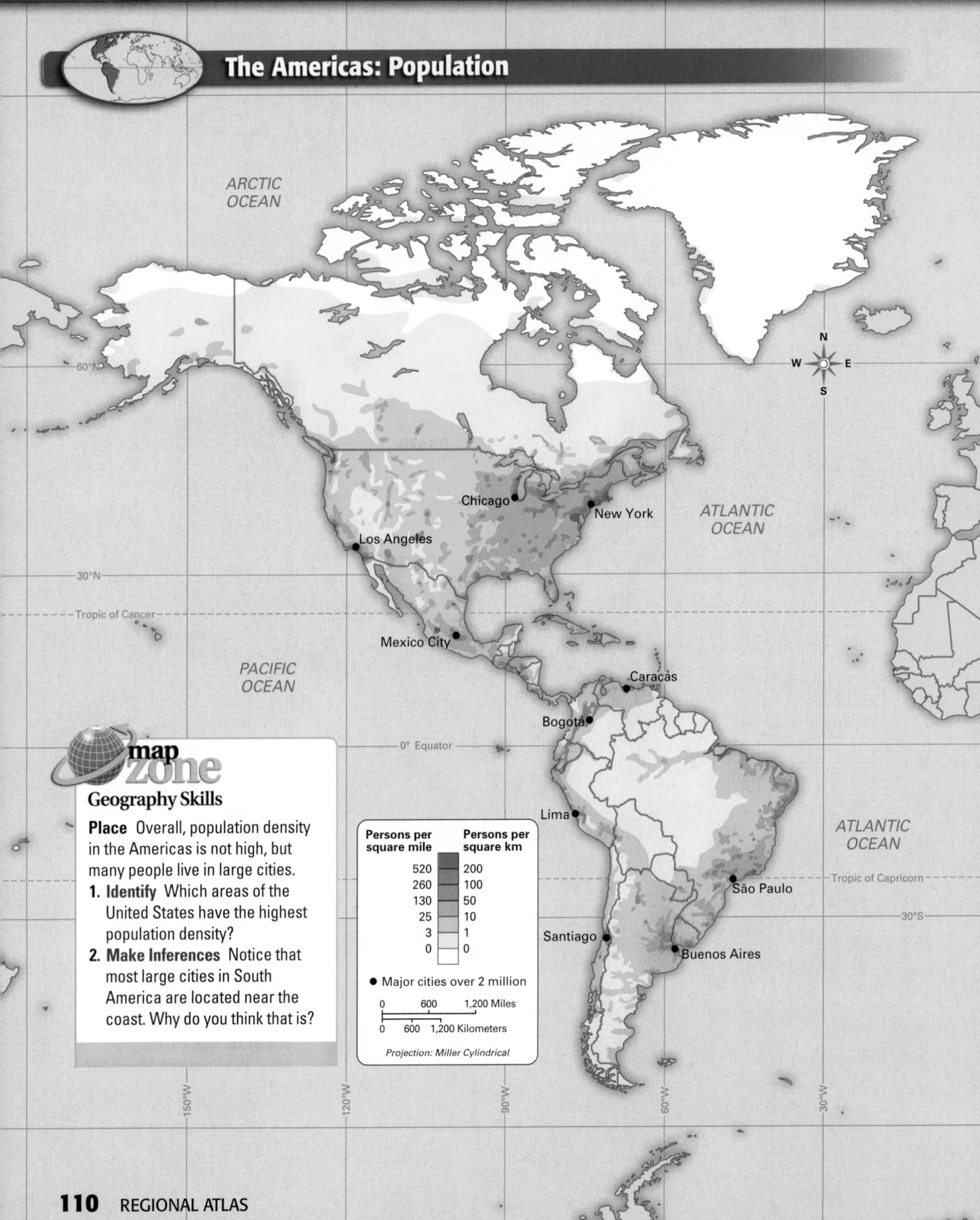

ARCTIC OCEAN

60°N

ATLANTIC OCEAN

N
W   E
S

Chicago
New York
Los Angeles

30°N

Tropic of Cancer

Mexico City

PACIFIC OCEAN

Caracas

Bogotá

0° Equator

map zone

Geography Skills

Place Overall, population density in the Americas is not high, but many people live in large cities.

1. **Identify** Which areas of the United States have the highest population density?

2. **Make Inferences** Notice that most large cities in South America are located near the coast. Why do you think that is?

Persons per square mile	Persons per square km
520	200
260	100
130	50
25	10
3	1
0	0

● Major cities over 2 million

0   600   1,200 Miles
0   600   1,200 Kilometers

Projection: Miller Cylindrical

Lima

ATLANTIC OCEAN

São Paulo

Tropic of Capricorn

30°S

Santiago

Buenos Aires

The Americas: Climate

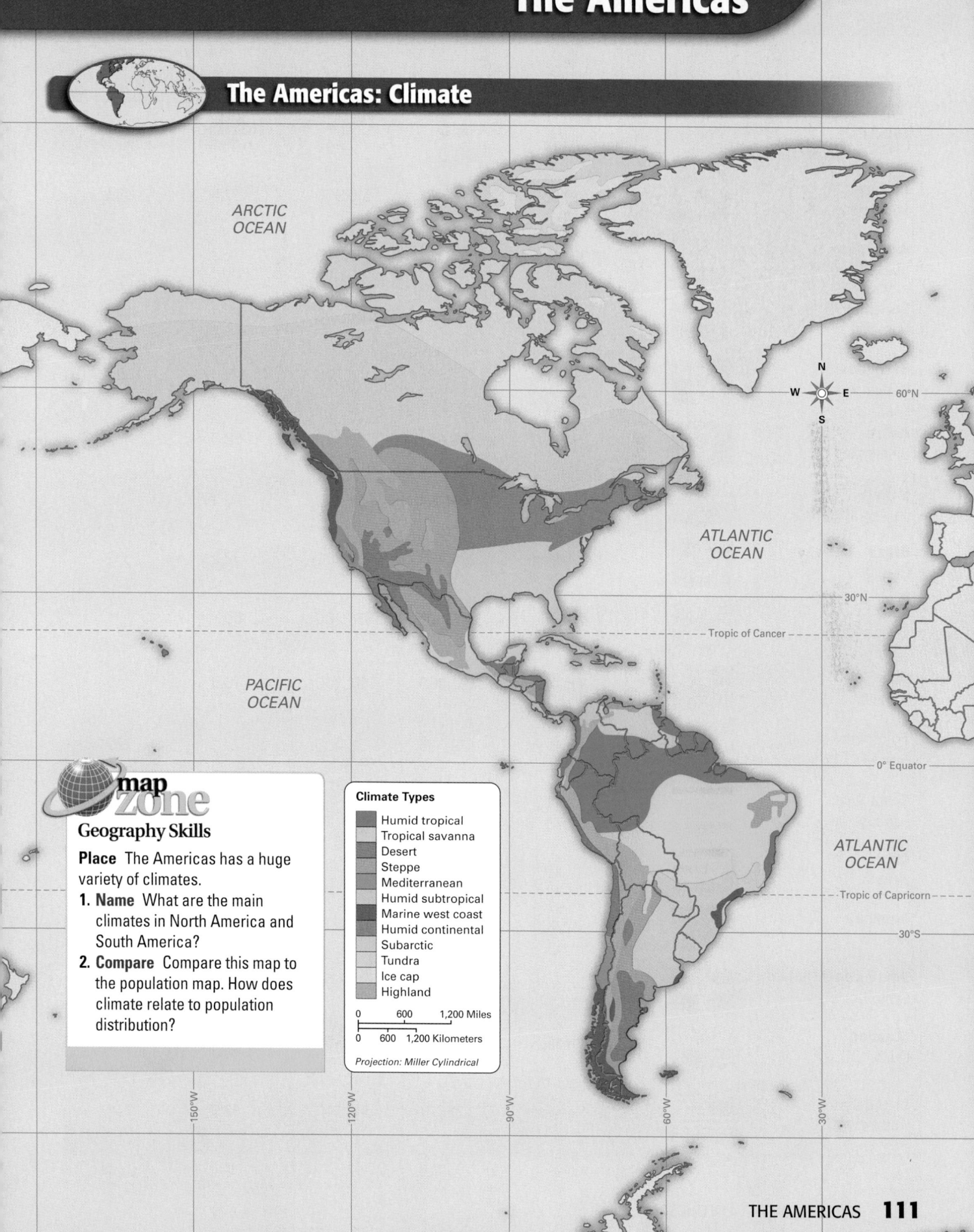

ARCTIC OCEAN

ATLANTIC OCEAN

N
W · E — 60°N
S

30°N

Tropic of Cancer

PACIFIC OCEAN

0° Equator

ATLANTIC OCEAN

Tropic of Capricorn

30°S

map zone

Geography Skills

Place The Americas has a huge variety of climates.

1. **Name** What are the main climates in North America and South America?

2. **Compare** Compare this map to the population map. How does climate relate to population distribution?

Climate Types

- Humid tropical
- Tropical savanna
- Desert
- Steppe
- Mediterranean
- Humid subtropical
- Marine west coast
- Humid continental
- Subarctic
- Tundra
- Ice cap
- Highland

0   600   1,200 Miles

0   600   1,200 Kilometers

Projection: Miller Cylindrical

150°W   120°W   90°W   60°W   30°W

The Americas

COUNTRY Capital	FLAG	POPULATION	AREA (sq mi)	PER CAPITA GDP (U.S. $)	LIFE EXPECTANCY AT BIRTH	TVS PER 1,000 PEOPLE
Antigua and Barbuda St. John's		69,500	171	$10,900	72.4	493
Argentina Buenos Aires		40.3 million	1,068,302	$15,000	76.3	293
Bahamas Nassau		305,600	5,382	$21,300	65.7	243
Barbados Bridgetown		280,900	166	$18,200	73.0	290
Belize Belmopan		294,400	8,867	$8,400	68.3	183
Bolivia La Paz, Sucre		9.1 million	424,164	$3,000	66.2	118
Brazil Brasília		190 million	3,286,488	$8,600	72.2	333
Canada Ottawa		33.4 million	3,855,101	$35,200	80.3	709
Chile Santiago		16.3 million	292,260	$12,700	76.9	240
Colombia Bogotá		44.4 million	439,736	$8,400	72.3	279
Costa Rica San José		4.1 million	19,730	$12,000	77.2	229
Cuba Havana		11.4 million	42,803	$3,900	77.6	248
Dominica Roseau		72,400	291	$3,800	75.1	232
Dominican Republic Santo Domingo		9.4 million	18,815	$8,000	73.1	96
Ecuador Quito		13.8 million	109,483	$4,500	76.6	213
United States Washington, D.C.		301.1 million	3,718,711	$43,500	78.0	844

COUNTRY Capital	FLAG	POPULATION	AREA (sq mi)	PER CAPITA GDP (U.S. $)	LIFE EXPECTANCY AT BIRTH	TVS PER 1,000 PEOPLE
El Salvador San Salvador		6.9 million	8,124	$4,900	71.8	191
Grenada Saint George's		89,900	133	$3,900	65.2	376
Guatemala Guatemala City		12.7 million	42,043	$4,900	69.7	61
Guyana Georgetown		769,100	83,000	$4,700	66.2	70
Haiti Port-au-Prince		8.7 million	10,714	$1,800	57.0	5
Honduras Tegucigalpa		7.5 million	43,278	$3,000	69.4	95
Jamaica Kingston		2.8 million	4,244	$4,600	73.1	191
Mexico Mexico City		108.7 million	761,606	$10,600	75.6	272
Nicaragua Managua		5.7 million	49,998	$3,000	70.9	69
Panama Panama City		3.2 million	30,193	$7,900	75.2	192
Paraguay Asunción		6.7 million	157,047	$4,700	75.3	205
Peru Lima		28.7 million	496,226	$6,400	70.1	147
Saint Kitts and Nevis Basseterre		39,300	101	$8,200	72.7	256
Saint Lucia Castries		170,600	238	$4,800	74.0	368
Saint Vincent and the Grenadines; Kingstown		118,100	150	$3,600	74.1	230
United States Washington, D.C.		301.1 million	3,718,711	$43,500	78.0	844

COUNTRY Capital	FLAG	POPULATION	AREA (sq mi)	PER CAPITA GDP (U.S. $)	LIFE EXPECTANCY AT BIRTH	TVS PER 1,000 PEOPLE
Suriname Paramaribo		470,800	63,039	$7,100	73.2	241
Trinidad and Tobago Port-of-Spain		1.1 million	1,980	$19,700	66.9	337
Uruguay Montevideo		3.5 million	68,039	$10,700	76.5	531
Venezuela Caracas		26 million	352,144	$6,900	74.8	185
United States Washington, D.C.		301.1 million	3,718,711	$43,500	78.0	844

ANALYSIS SKILL **ANALYZING TABLES**

1. Compare the information for the United States, Canada, Brazil, and Mexico. How do these four countries compare?
2. Which country has the lowest per capita GDP?

Largest Cities and Urban Populations

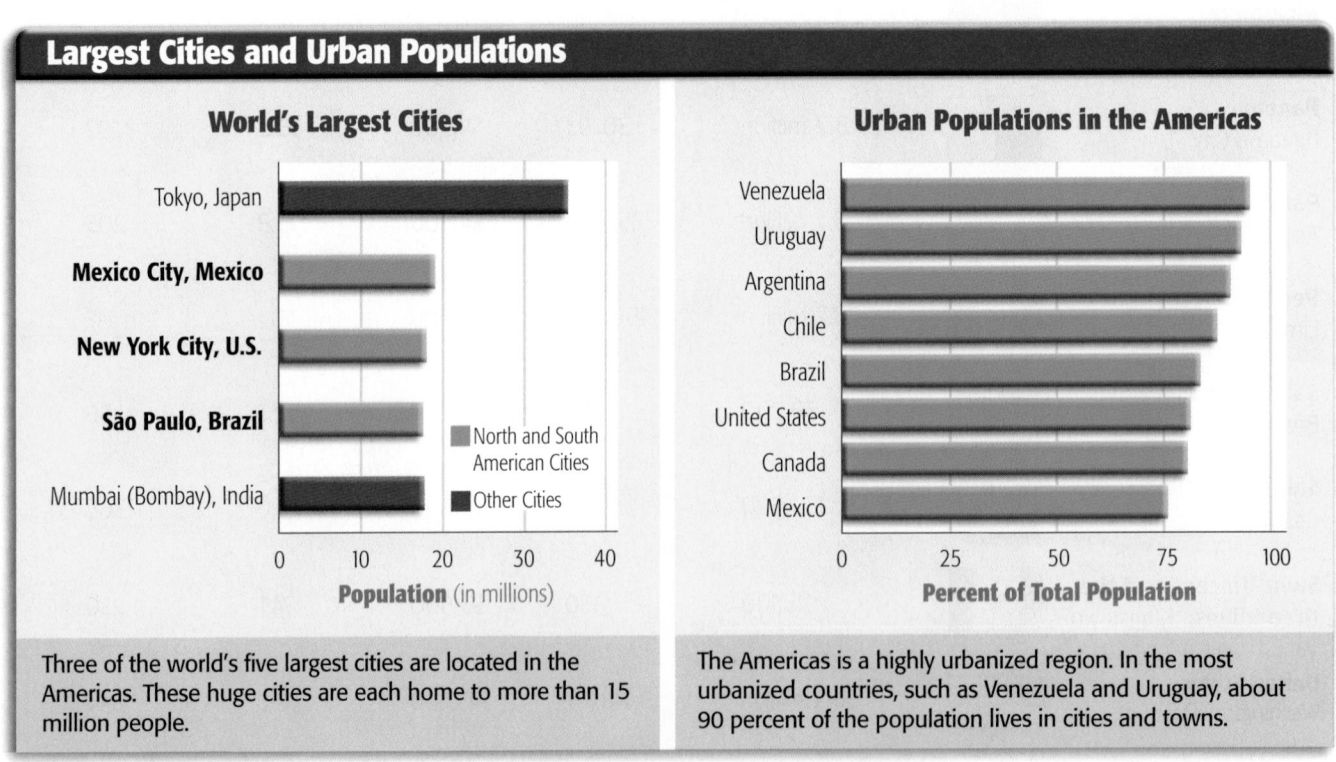

World's Largest Cities

Tokyo, Japan
Mexico City, Mexico
New York City, U.S.
São Paulo, Brazil
Mumbai (Bombay), India

■ North and South American Cities
■ Other Cities

Population (in millions)

Urban Populations in the Americas

Venezuela
Uruguay
Argentina
Chile
Brazil
United States
Canada
Mexico

Percent of Total Population

Three of the world's five largest cities are located in the Americas. These huge cities are each home to more than 15 million people.

The Americas is a highly urbanized region. In the most urbanized countries, such as Venezuela and Uruguay, about 90 percent of the population lives in cities and towns.

Major Food Exports of the Americas

Coffee Exports

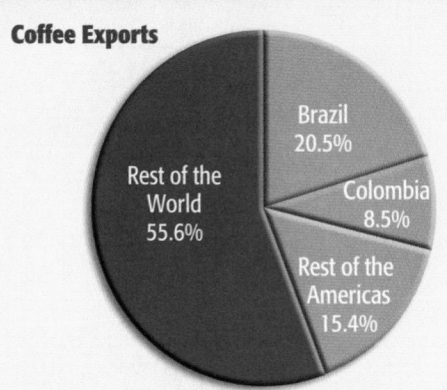

Brazil 20.5%
Rest of the World 55.6%
Colombia 8.5%
Rest of the Americas 15.4%

Wheat Exports

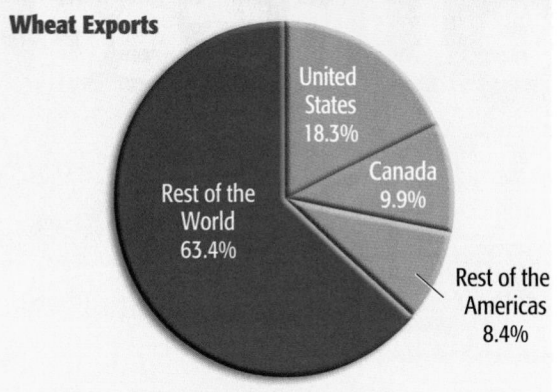

United States 18.3%
Canada 9.9%
Rest of the World 63.4%
Rest of the Americas 8.4%

Corn Exports

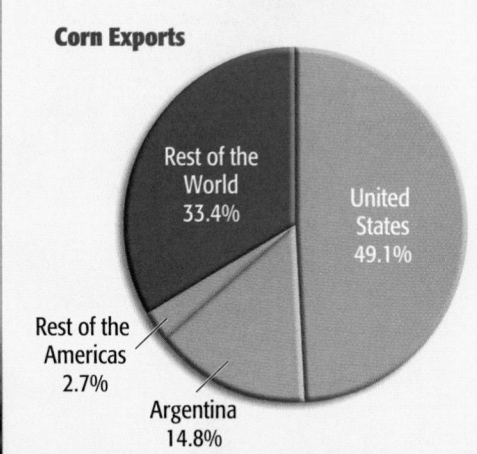

Rest of the World 33.4%
United States 49.1%
Rest of the Americas 2.7%
Argentina 14.8%

Banana Exports

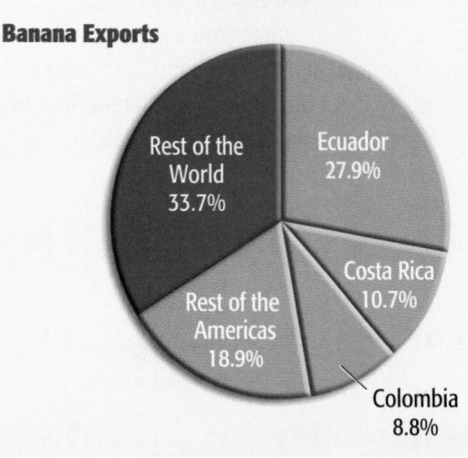

Rest of the World 33.7%
Ecuador 27.9%
Costa Rica 10.7%
Rest of the Americas 18.9%
Colombia 8.8%

The Americas is a major exporter of some crops, like coffee, wheat, corn, and bananas. While the United States leads in wheat and corn exports, other crops like coffee and bananas are exported from Central and South America.

ANALYSIS SKILL ANALYZING GRAPHS

1. What percentage of the world's corn exports come from the Americas?
2. Which countries in the Americas export the most coffee?

Workers harvest coffee beans in Costa Rica.

The United States

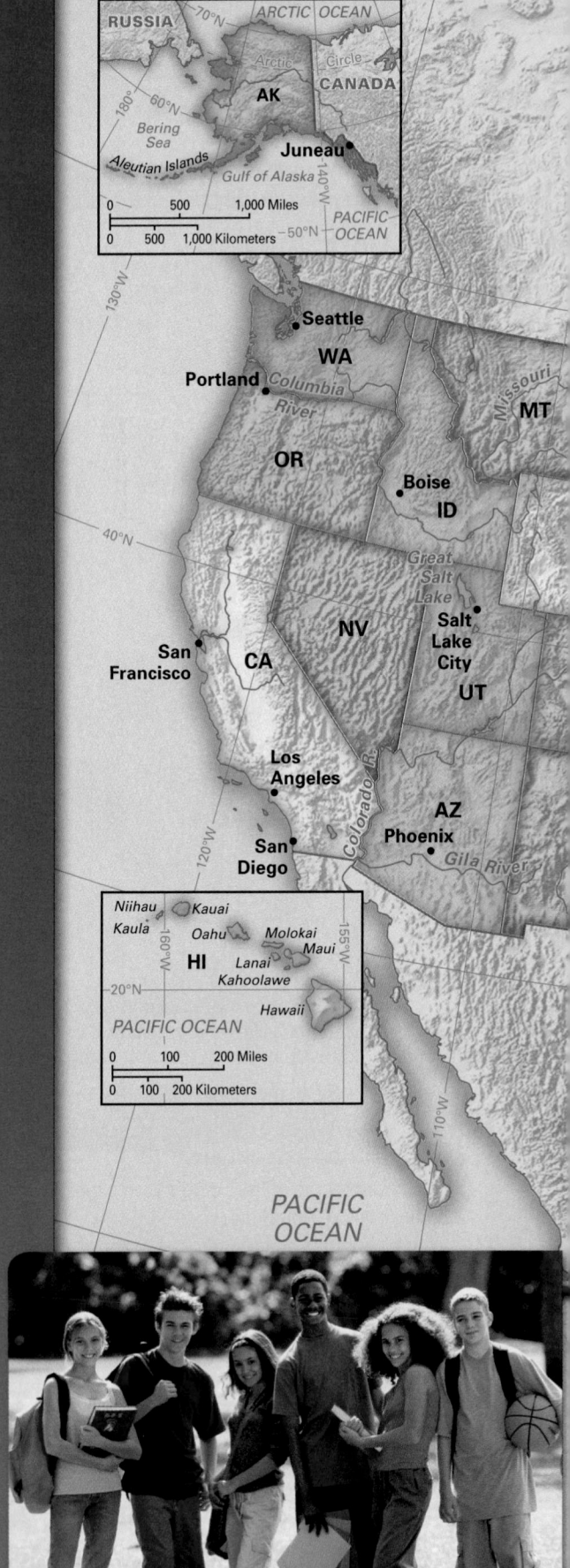

What You Will Learn...

In this chapter you will learn about the physical features, climates, and resources of the United States. You will also discover how democratic ideas and immigration have shaped the United States. Finally, you will learn about our country's different regions, diverse population, and the challenges we face as a nation.

FOCUS ON READING AND VIEWING

Categorizing A good way to make sense of what you read is to separate facts and details into groups, called categories. For example, you could sort facts about the United States into categories like natural resources, major cities, or rivers. As you read this chapter, look for ways to categorize details under each topic. **See the lesson, Categorizing, on page R6**.

Creating a Collage Artists create collages by gluing art and photographs onto a flat surface, such as a poster board. As you read this chapter, you will collect ideas for a collage about the United States. After you create your own collage, you will view and evaluate the collages of other students in your class.

Culture People of many different ethnic groups and cultures make up the population of the United States.

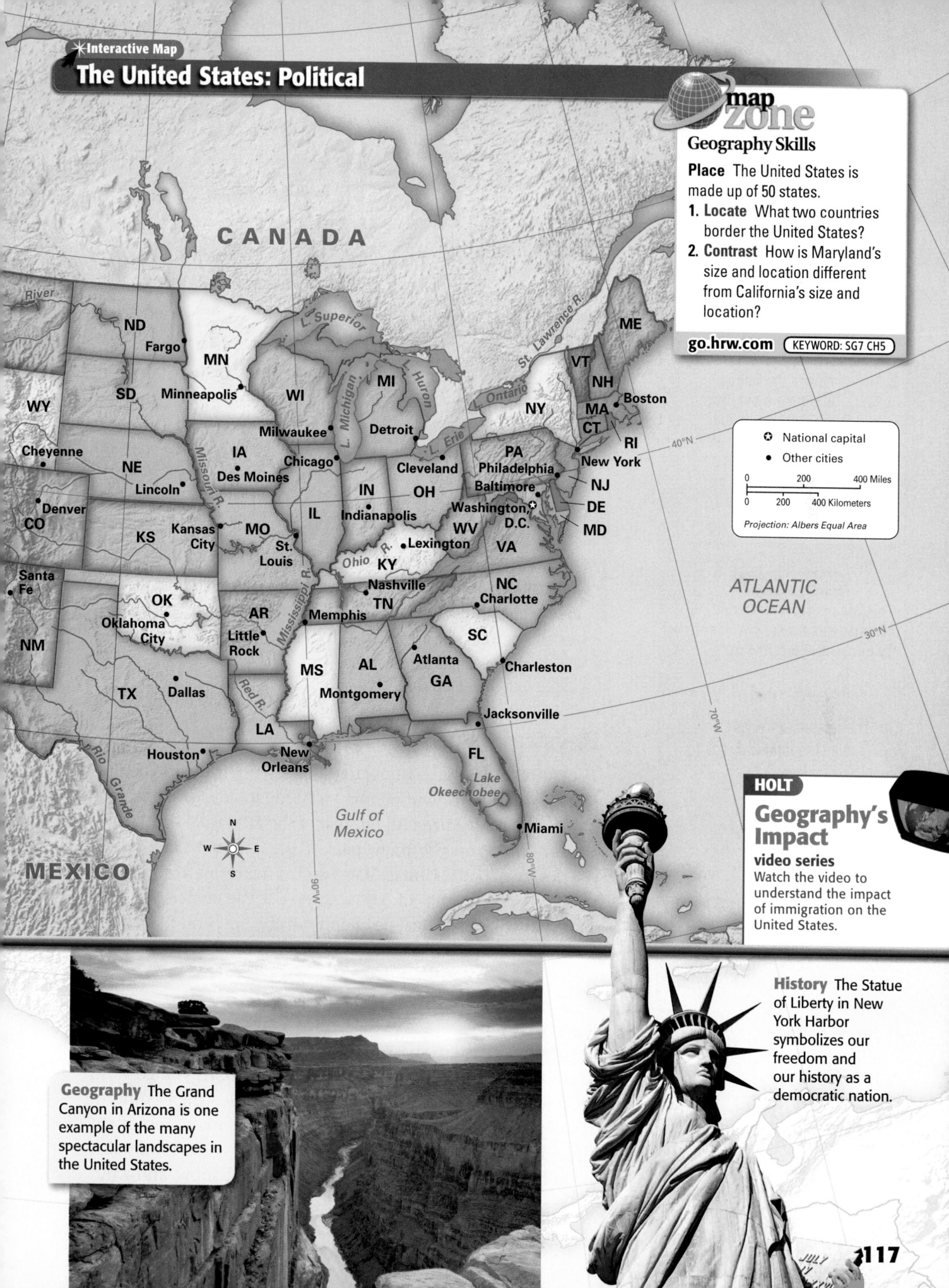

map Zone

Geography Skills

Place The United States is made up of 50 states.
1. **Locate** What two countries border the United States?
2. **Contrast** How is Maryland's size and location different from California's size and location?

go.hrw.com KEYWORD: SG7 CH5

CANADA

River

ND
Fargo
MN
Minneapolis
SD
WY
MI
L. Superior
WI
Milwaukee
L. Huron
L. Michigan
Detroit
L. Ontario
L. Erie
St. Lawrence R.
ME
VT
NH
Boston
NY
MA
CT
RI

40°N

Cheyenne
NE
IA
Des Moines
Chicago
Cleveland
IN
OH
Lincoln
Denver
CO
Missouri R.
KS
Kansas City
MO
St. Louis
IL
Indianapolis
PA
Philadelphia
Baltimore
Washington, D.C.
New York
NJ
DE
MD
WV
VA
Santa Fe
Ohio R.
Lexington
KY
Nashville
TN
Mississippi R.
NC
Charlotte

NM
OK
Oklahoma City
AR
Little Rock
Memphis
SC
Charleston

○ National capital
• Other cities

0   200   400 Miles
0   200   400 Kilometers
Projection: Albers Equal Area

ATLANTIC OCEAN

30°N

TX
Dallas
Red R.
MS
Montgomery
AL
Atlanta
GA
Jacksonville
LA
New Orleans
Houston
Rio Grande

70°W

FL

MEXICO

Gulf of Mexico
Lake Okeechobee
Miami

80°W
90°W

N
W   E
S

HOLT

Geography's Impact

video series
Watch the video to understand the impact of immigration on the United States.

Geography The Grand Canyon in Arizona is one example of the many spectacular landscapes in the United States.

History The Statue of Liberty in New York Harbor symbolizes our freedom and our history as a democratic nation.

117

Physical Geography

What You Will Learn...

Main Ideas

1. Major physical features of the United States include mountains, rivers, and plains.
2. The climate of the United States is wetter in the East and South and drier in the West.
3. The United States is rich in natural resources such as farmland, oil, forests, and minerals.

The Big Idea

The United States is a large country with diverse physical features, climates, and resources.

Key Terms and Places

Appalachian Mountains, *p. 118*
Great Lakes, *p. 119*
Mississippi River, *p. 119*
tributary, *p. 119*
Rocky Mountains, *p. 120*
continental divide, *p. 120*

TAKING NOTES As you read, look for information about the physical features, climate, and natural resources of the United States. Take notes in a graphic organizer like this one.

Physical Features	Climate	Natural Resources

If YOU lived there...

You live in St. Louis, Missouri, which is located on the Mississippi River. For the next few days, you will travel down the river on an old-fashioned steamboat. The Mississippi begins in Minnesota and flows south through 10 states in the heart of the United States. On your trip, you bring a video camera to film life along this great river.

What will you show in your video about the Mississippi?

BUILDING BACKGROUND The United States stretches from sea to sea across North America. To the north is Canada and to the south lies Mexico. Because it is so large, the United States has a great variety of landscapes and climates.

Physical Features

The United States is the third largest country in the world behind Russia and Canada. Our country is home to an incredible variety of physical features. All but two of the 50 states—Alaska and Hawaii—make up the main part of the country. Look at the physical map of the United States on the next page. It shows the main physical features of our country. Use the map as you read about America's physical geography in the East and South, the Interior Plains, and the West.

The East and South

If you were traveling across the United States, you might start on the country's eastern coast. This low area, which is flat and close to sea level, is called the Atlantic Coastal Plain. As you go west, the land gradually rises higher to a region called the Piedmont. The **Appalachian Mountains**, which are the main mountain range in the East, rise above the Piedmont. These mountains are very old. For many millions of years, rain, snow, and wind

ARCTIC OCEAN
BROOKS RANGE
Mount McKinley 20,320 ft (6,194 m)
AK
Arctic Circle
CANADA
Aleutian Islands
ALASKA RANGE
PACIFIC OCEAN
0   500   1,000 Miles
0   500   1,000 Kilometers

Niihau
Kaula
Kauai
Oahu
Molokai
Maui
Lanai
Kahoolawe
HI
Hawaii
PACIFIC OCEAN
0   100   200 Miles
0   100   200 Kilometers

CASCADE RANGE
Columbia River
SIERRA NEVADA
CENTRAL VALLEY
GREAT BASIN
Great Salt Lake
COLORADO PLATEAU
ROCKY MOUNTAINS
GREAT PLAINS
Missouri River
Mississippi River
Ohio River
UNITED STATES
INTERIOR PLAINS
CANADA
GREAT LAKES
Lake Superior
Lake Michigan
Lake Huron
Lake Ontario
Lake Erie
Niagara Falls
APPALACHIAN MOUNTAINS
PIEDMONT
ATLANTIC COASTAL PLAIN
ATLANTIC OCEAN
PACIFIC OCEAN
MEXICO
GULF COASTAL PLAIN
Gulf of Mexico
Florida Keys
Straits of Florida

PACIFIC OCEAN

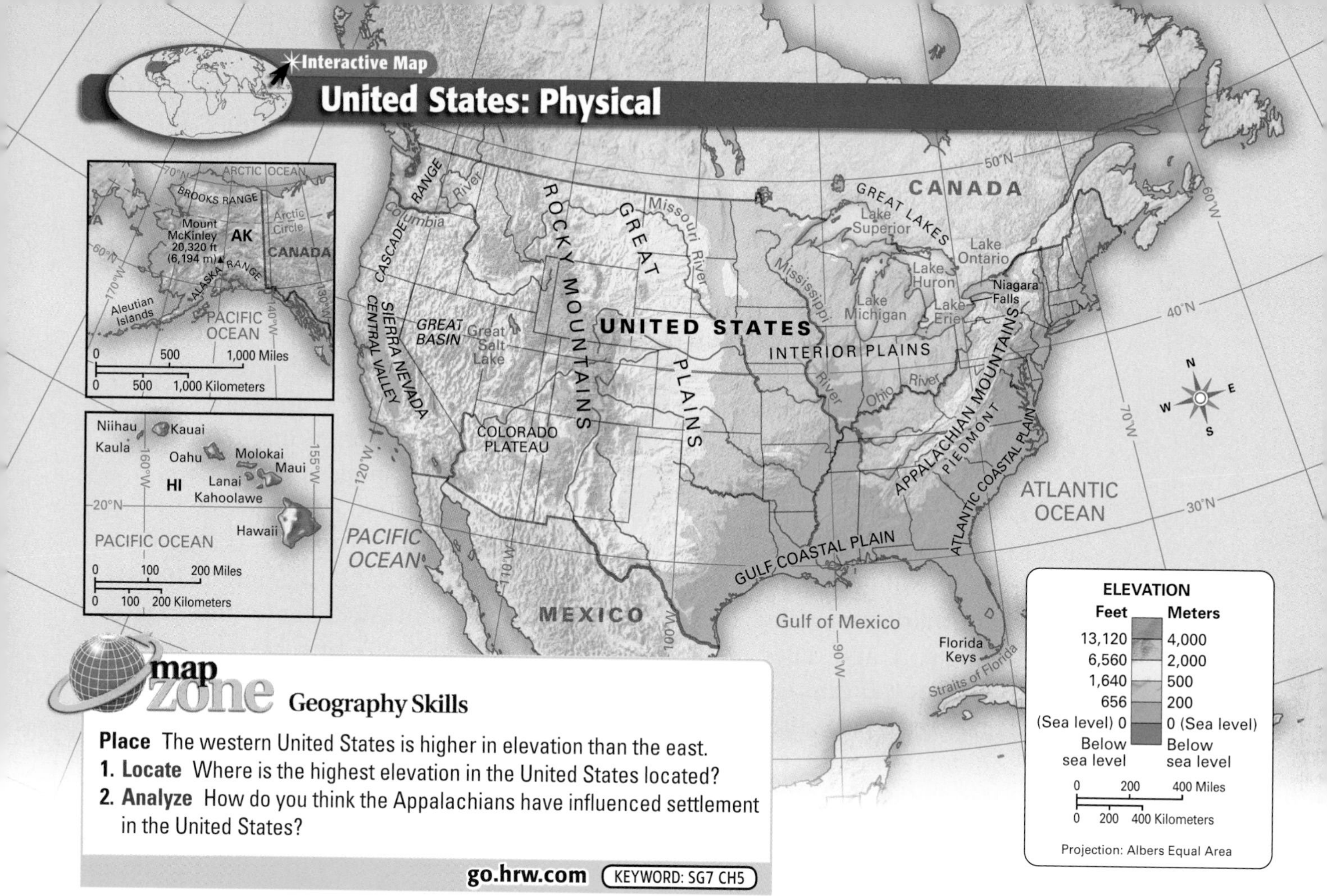

map zone Geography Skills

Place The western United States is higher in elevation than the east.
1. **Locate** Where is the highest elevation in the United States located?
2. **Analyze** How do you think the Appalachians have influenced settlement in the United States?

go.hrw.com   KEYWORD: SG7 CH5

ELEVATION

Feet	Meters
13,120	4,000
6,560	2,000
1,640	500
656	200
(Sea level) 0	0 (Sea level)
Below sea level	Below sea level

0   200   400 Miles
0   200   400 Kilometers
Projection: Albers Equal Area

have eroded and smoothed their peaks. As a result, the highest mountain in the Appalachians is about 6,700 feet (2,040 m).

The Interior Plains

As you travel west from the Appalachians, you come across the vast Interior Plains that stretch to the Great Plains just east of the Rocky Mountains. The Interior Plains are filled with hills, lakes, and rivers. The first major water feature that you see here is called the **Great Lakes**. These lakes make up the largest group of freshwater lakes in the world. The Great Lakes are also an important waterway for trade between the United States and Canada.

West of the Great Lakes lies North America's largest and most important river, the **Mississippi River**. Tributaries in the interior plains flow to the Mississippi. A **tributary** is a smaller stream or river that flows into a larger stream or river.

Appalachians The smooth peaks of the Appalachian Mountains dominate the landscape of western North Carolina.

Along the way, these rivers deposit rich silt. The silt creates fertile farmlands that cover most of the Interior Plains. The Missouri and Ohio rivers are huge tributaries of the Mississippi. They help drain the entire Interior Plains.

Look at the map on the previous page. Notice the land begins to increase in elevation west of the Interior Plains. This higher region is called the Great Plains. Vast areas of grasslands cover these plains.

The West

In the region called the West, several of the country's most rugged mountain ranges make up the **Rocky Mountains**. These enormous mountains, also called the Rockies, stretch as far as you can see. Many of the mountains' jagged peaks rise above 14,000 feet (4,270 m).

In the Rocky Mountains is a line of high peaks called the Continental Divide. A **continental divide** is an area of high ground that divides the flow of rivers towards opposite ends of a continent.

FOCUS ON READING

Into what two categories might you group the details on rivers?

Rivers east of the divide in the Rockies mostly flow eastward and empty into the Mississippi River. Most of the rivers west of the divide flow westward and empty into the Pacific Ocean.

Farther west, mountain ranges include the Cascade Range and the Sierra Nevada. Most of the mountains in the Cascades are dormant volcanoes. One mountain, Mount Saint Helens, is an active volcano. A tremendous eruption in 1980 blew off the mountain's peak and destroyed 150 square miles (390 sq km) of forest.

Mountains also stretch north along the Pacific coast. At 20,320 feet (6,194 m), Alaska's Mount McKinley is the highest mountain in North America.

Far out in the Pacific Ocean are the islands that make up the state of Hawaii. Volcanoes formed these islands millions of years ago. Today, hot lava and ash continue to erupt from the islands' volcanoes.

READING CHECK **Summarizing** What are the major physical features of the United States?

Satellite View

The river branches out in several places here as it tries to find the shortest way to the ocean.

The Mississippi River Delta

From its source in Minnesota, the Mississippi River flows south across the central United States. It ends at the tip of Louisiana, which is shown here. This satellite image shows the area where the Mississippi River meets the Gulf of Mexico. This area is called a delta. A river's delta is formed from sediment that a river carries downstream to the ocean. Sediment is usually made up of rocks, soil, sand, and dead plants. Each year, the Mississippi dumps more than 400 million tons of sediment into the Gulf of Mexico.

The light blue and green areas in this image are shallow areas of sediment. The deeper water of the Gulf of Mexico is dark blue. Also, notice that much of the delta land looks fragile. This is new land that the river has built up by depositing sediment.

Making Inferences What natural hazards might people living in the Mississippi Delta experience?

Interactive Map

United States: Climate

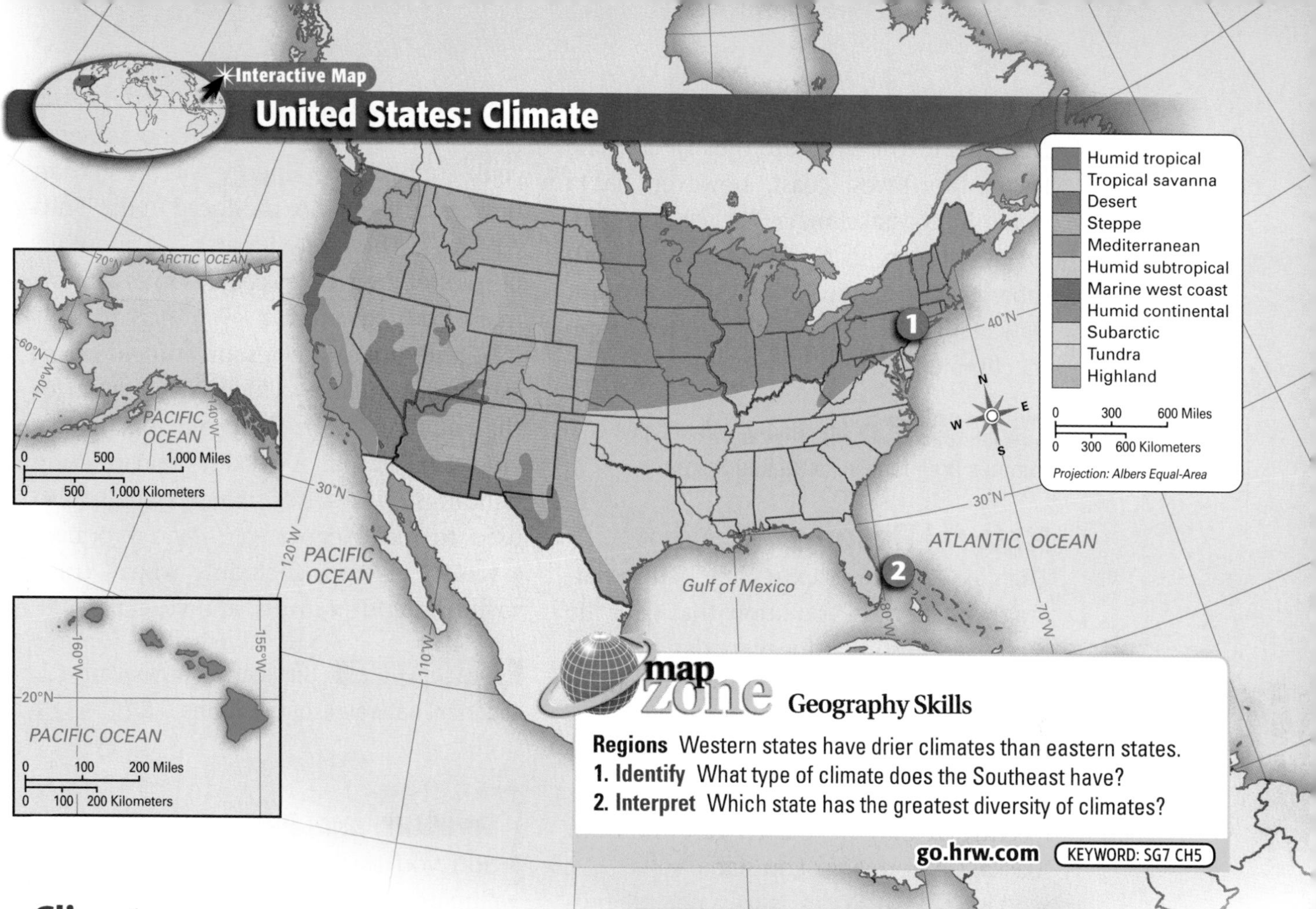

Humid tropical
Tropical savanna
Desert
Steppe
Mediterranean
Humid subtropical
Marine west coast
Humid continental
Subarctic
Tundra
Highland
0 300 600 Miles
0 300 600 Kilometers
Projection: Albers Equal-Area
ARCTIC OCEAN
PACIFIC OCEAN
0 500 1,000 Miles
0 500 1,000 Kilometers
60°N
170°W
140°W
30°N
40°N
120°W
110°W
80°W
70°W
PACIFIC OCEAN
ATLANTIC OCEAN
Gulf of Mexico
160°W
155°W
20°N
PACIFIC OCEAN
0 100 200 Miles
0 100 200 Kilometers
N
E
S
W
1
2

map zone Geography Skills

Regions Western states have drier climates than eastern states.

1. **Identify** What type of climate does the Southeast have?
2. **Interpret** Which state has the greatest diversity of climates?

go.hrw.com (KEYWORD: SG7 CH5)

Climate

Did you know that the United States has a greater variety of climates than any other country? Look at the map above to see the different climates of the United States.

The East and South

The eastern United States has three climate regions. In the Northeast, people live in a humid continental climate with snowy winters and warm, humid summers. Southerners, on the other hand, experience milder winters and the warm, humid summers of a humid subtropical climate. Most of Florida is warm all year.

The Interior Plains

Temperatures throughout the year can vary greatly in the Interior Plains. Summers are hot and dry in the Great Plains. However, most of the region has a humid continental climate with long, cold winters.

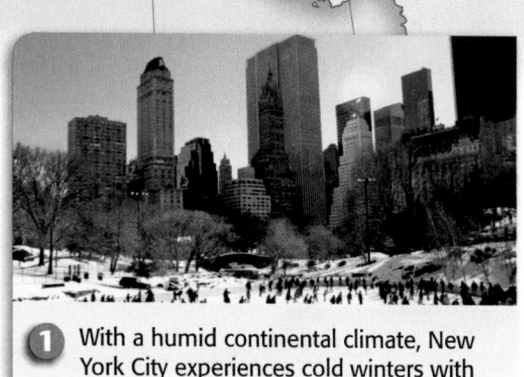

1 With a humid continental climate, New York City experiences cold winters with snowfall. In this climate people can ice skate during the winter.

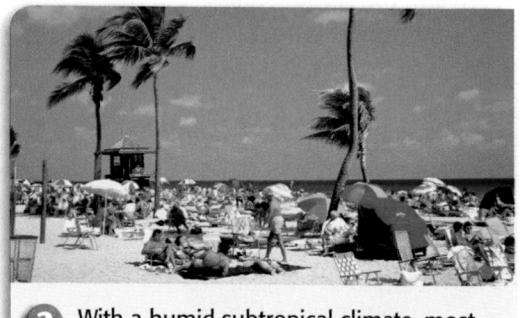

2 With a humid subtropical climate, most of Florida has warm sunny days during most of the year. In this climate people can enjoy the region's beaches.

The West

Climates in the West are mostly dry. The Pacific Northwest coast, however, has a wet, mild coastal climate. The region's coldest climates are in Alaska, which has both subarctic and tundra climates. In contrast, Hawaii is the only state with a warm, tropical climate.

READING CHECK **Identifying** What types of climates are found in the United States?

Natural Resources

The United States is extremely rich in natural resources. Do you know that your life is affected in some way every day by these natural resources? For example, if you ate bread today, it was probably made with wheat grown in the fertile soils of the Interior Plains. If you rode in a car or on a bus recently, it may have used gasoline from Alaska, California, or Louisiana.

The United States is a major oil producer but uses more oil than it produces. In fact, we import more than one half of the oil we need.

Valuable minerals are mined in the Appalachians and Rockies. One mineral, coal, supplies the energy for more than half of the electricity produced in the United States. The United States has about 25 percent of the world's coal reserves and is a major coal exporter.

Other important resources include forests and farmland, which cover much of the country. The trees in our forests provide lumber that is used in constructing buildings. Wood from these trees is also used to make paper. Farmland produces a variety of crops including wheat, corn, soybeans, cotton, fruits, and vegetables.

READING CHECK **Summarizing** What are important natural resources in the U.S.?

SUMMARY AND PREVIEW In this section you learned about the geography, climates, and natural resources of the United States. In the next section, you will learn about the history and culture of the United States.

Section 1 Assessment

go.hrw.com
Online Quiz
KEYWORD: SG7 HP5

Reviewing Ideas, Terms, and Places

1. **a. Define** What is a **tributary**?
   b. Contrast How are the **Appalachian Mountains** different from the **Rocky Mountains**?
   c. Elaborate Why are the **Great Lakes** an important waterway?
2. **a. Describe** What is the climate like in the Northeast?
   b. Draw Conclusions What would winter be like in Alaska?
3. **a. Recall** What kinds of crops are grown in the United States?
   b. Explain Why is coal an important resource?
   c. Predict What natural resources might not be as important to your daily life in the future?

Critical Thinking

4. **Categorizing** Copy the graphic organizer below. Use it to organize your notes on physical features, climate, and resources by region of the country.

East and South	Interior Plains	West

FOCUS ON VIEWING

5. **Thinking about Physical Geography** Jot down key words that describe the physical features and climate of the United States. Think of at least three objects or images you might use to illustrate physical features and climate.

Using a Political Map

Learn

Many types of maps are useful in studying geography. Political maps are one of the most frequently used types of maps. These maps show human cultural features such as cities, states, and countries. Look at the map's legend to figure out how these features are represented on the map.

Most political maps show national boundaries and state boundaries. The countries on political maps are sometimes shaded different colors to help you tell where the borders of each country are located.

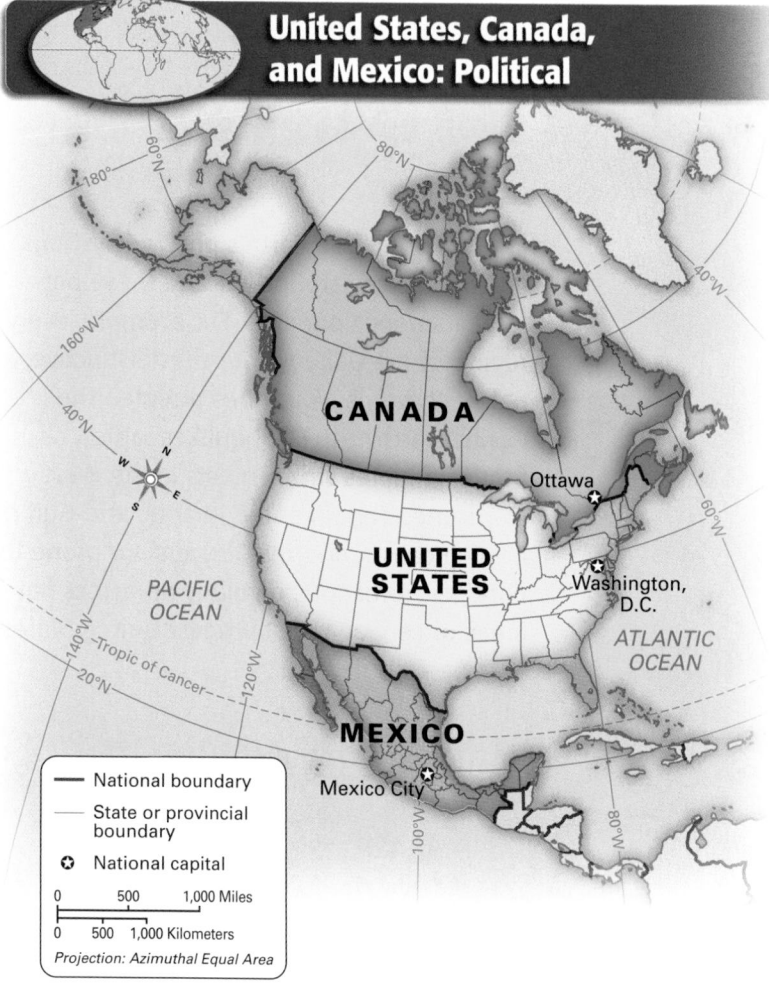

United States, Canada, and Mexico: Political

CANADA

Ottawa ✪

UNITED STATES

Washington, D.C. ✪

PACIFIC OCEAN

ATLANTIC OCEAN

MEXICO

Mexico City ✪

— National boundary

— State or provincial boundary

✪ National capital

0   500   1,000 Miles

0   500   1,000 Kilometers

Projection: Azimuthal Equal Area

Practice

Use the political map here to answer the following questions.

- What countries does this map show?
- How does the map show the difference between state boundaries and national boundaries?
- What is the capital of Canada?

Apply

Using an atlas or the Internet, find a political map of your state. Use that map to answer the following questions.

1. What is the state capital and where is it located?

2. What other states or countries border your state?

3. What are two other cities in your state besides the capital and the city you live in?

Natural Hazards
in the United States

Essential Elements

The World in Spatial Terms
Places and Regions
Physical Systems
Human Systems
Environment and Society
The Uses of Geography

Background Earth's physical systems create patterns around us, and these patterns influence our lives. For example, every region of the United States has distinctive natural hazards. Volcanoes threaten the Pacific Northwest. Earthquakes rattle California. Wildfires strike forests in the West. Hurricanes endanger the Atlantic and Gulf of Mexico coasts, and major rivers are prone to flooding. Tornadoes regularly rip across flat areas of central and southeast United States.

In fact, the United States lies in danger of getting hit by an average of six hurricanes a year. Formed by the warm waters of the Atlantic Ocean and Caribbean Sea and the collision of strong winds, hurricanes are the most powerful storms on Earth. Most hurricanes look like large doughnuts with a hole, or eye, in the middle of the storm. Around the eye, high winds and rain bands rotate counterclockwise. Once the hurricane moves over land or cold water it weakens.

Natural Hazards in the United States

Tornado Alley

Earthquakes	Volcanoes
Wildfires	Tornadoes
Hurricanes	Tornado Risk
Flood areas	Moderate
	High

map zone

After Hurricane Katrina hit New Orleans, people escaped the floodwaters by fleeing to rooftops and high-rise apartment buildings like this one.

Using satellite images like this one of Hurricane Katrina, scientists saw how large the storm was and warned people along the Gulf coast to evacuate.

Hurricane Katrina

On August 29, 2005, one of the most destructive hurricanes ever hit the United States. Hurricane Katrina devastated coastal regions of Louisiana, the city of New Orleans, and the entire coast of Mississippi.

With winds as high as 145 mph (235 km), Katrina destroyed hundreds of thousands of homes and businesses. In addition, the force of Katrina's storm surge pushed water from the Gulf of Mexico onto land to a height of about two stories tall. As a result, low-lying areas along the Gulf coast experienced massive flooding.

The storm surge also caused several levees that protected New Orleans from the waters of Lake Pontchartrain to break. The loss of these levees caused the lake's waters to flood most of the city. About 150,000 people who did not evacuate before the storm were left stranded in shelters, high-rise buildings, and on rooftops. Using boats and helicopters, emergency workers rescued thousands of the city's people. Total damages from the storm along the Gulf coast was estimated to be nearly $130 billion. More than 1,300 people died and over a million were displaced.

What It Means

Natural hazards can influence where we live, how we build our homes, and how we prepare for storms. In addition to hurricanes, other hazards affect the United States. For example, Tornado Alley is a region of the Great Plains that experiences a high number of tornadoes, or "twisters"—rapidly spinning columns of air that stay in contact with the ground. In Tornado Alley, special warning sirens go off when storms develop that might form a dangerous tornado.

Geography for Life Activity

1. How are hurricanes formed?

2. Many people train and volunteer as storm chasers. They may follow storms for hundreds of miles to gather scientific data, take photographs, or file news reports. What might be the risks and rewards of such activity? Would it interest you?

3. **Comparing Windstorms** Do some research to find out how tornadoes and hurricanes differ. Summarize the differences in a chart that includes information about how these storms start, where and when they tend to occur in the United States, and their wind strength.

History and Culture

What You Will Learn...

Main Ideas

1. The United States is the world's first modern democracy.
2. The people and culture of the United States are very diverse.

The Big Idea

Democratic ideas and immigration have shaped the history and culture of the United States.

Key Terms and Places

colony, *p. 126*
Boston, *p. 126*
New York, *p. 126*
plantation, *p. 127*
pioneers, *p. 128*
bilingual, *p. 130*

TAKING NOTES As you read, take notes on the history of the United States and its people and culture. Write your notes in a chart like this one.

History	People and Culture

If YOU lived there...

It is 1803, and President Jefferson just arranged the purchase of a huge area of land west of the Mississippi River. It almost doubles the size of the United States. Living on the frontier in Ohio, you are a skillful hunter and trapper. One day, you see a poster calling for volunteers to explore the new Louisiana Territory. An expedition is heading west soon. You think it would be exciting but dangerous.

Will you join the expedition to the West? Why or why not?

BUILDING BACKGROUND From 13 colonies on the Atlantic coast, the territory of the United States expanded all the way to the Pacific Ocean in about 75 years. Since then, America's democracy has attracted immigrants from almost every country in the world. Looking for new opportunities, these immigrants have made the country very diverse.

First Modern Democracy

Long before Italian explorer Christopher Columbus sailed to the Americas in 1492, native people lived on the land that is now the United States. These Native Americans developed many distinct cultures. Soon after Columbus and his crew explored the Americas, other Europeans began to set up colonies there.

The American Colonies

Europeans began settling in North America and setting up colonies in the 1500s. A **colony** is a territory inhabited and controlled by people from a foreign land. By the mid-1700s the British Empire included more than a dozen colonies along the Atlantic coast. New cities in the colonies such as **Boston** and **New York** became major seaports.

Some people living in the British colonies lived on plantations. A **plantation** is a large farm that grows mainly one crop. Many of the colonial plantations produced tobacco, rice, or cotton. Thousands of enslaved Africans were brought to the colonies and forced to work on plantations.

By the 1770s many colonists in America were unhappy with British rule. They wanted independence from Britain. In July 1776, the colonial representatives adopted the Declaration of Independence. The document stated that "all men are created equal" and have the right to "life, liberty, and the pursuit of happiness." Although not everyone in the colonies was considered equal, the Declaration was a great step toward equality and justice.

To win their independence, the American colonists fought the British in the Revolutionary War. First, colonists from Massachusetts fought in the early battles of the war in and around Boston. As the war spread west and south, soldiers from all the American colonies joined the fight against Britain.

In 1781 the American forces under General George Washington defeated the British army at the Battle of Yorktown in Virginia. With this defeat, Britain recognized the independence of the United States. As a consequence, Britain granted all its land east of the Mississippi River to the new nation.

Expansion and Industrial Growth

After independence, the United States gradually expanded west. Despite the challenges of crossing swift-moving rivers and traveling across rugged terrain and huge mountains, people moved west for land and plentiful resources.

BIOGRAPHY

George Washington
(1732–1799)

As the first president of the United States, George Washington is known as the Father of His Country. Washington was admired for his heroism and leadership as the commanding general during the Revolutionary War. Delegates to the Constitutional Convention chose him to preside over their meetings. Washington was then elected president in 1789 and served two terms.

Drawing Inferences Why do you think Washington was elected president?

Fight for Independence

This painting shows General George Washington leading American troops across the Delaware River to attack British forces.

These first settlers that traveled west were called **pioneers**. Many followed the 2,000-mile Oregon Trail west from Missouri to the Oregon Territory. Groups of families traveled together in wagons pulled by oxen or mules. The trip was harsh. Food, supplies, and water were scarce.

ACADEMIC VOCABULARY

development the process of growing or improving

While many pioneers headed west seeking land, others went in search of gold. The discovery of gold in California in the late 1840s had a major impact on the country. Tens of thousands of people moved to California.

By 1850 the population of the United States exceeded 23 million and the country stretched all the way to the Pacific Ocean. As the United States expanded, the nation's economy also grew. By the late 1800s, the country was a major producer of goods like steel, oil, and textiles, or cloth products. The steel industry grew around cities that were located near coal and iron ore deposits. Most of those new industrial cities were in the Northeast and Midwest. The country's economy also benefited from the **development** of waterways and railroads. This development helped industry and people move farther into the interior.

Attracted by a strong economy, millions of people immigrated, or came to, the United States for better jobs and land. Immigration from European countries was especially heavy in the late 1800s and early 1900s. As a result of this historical pattern of immigration, the United States is a culturally diverse nation today.

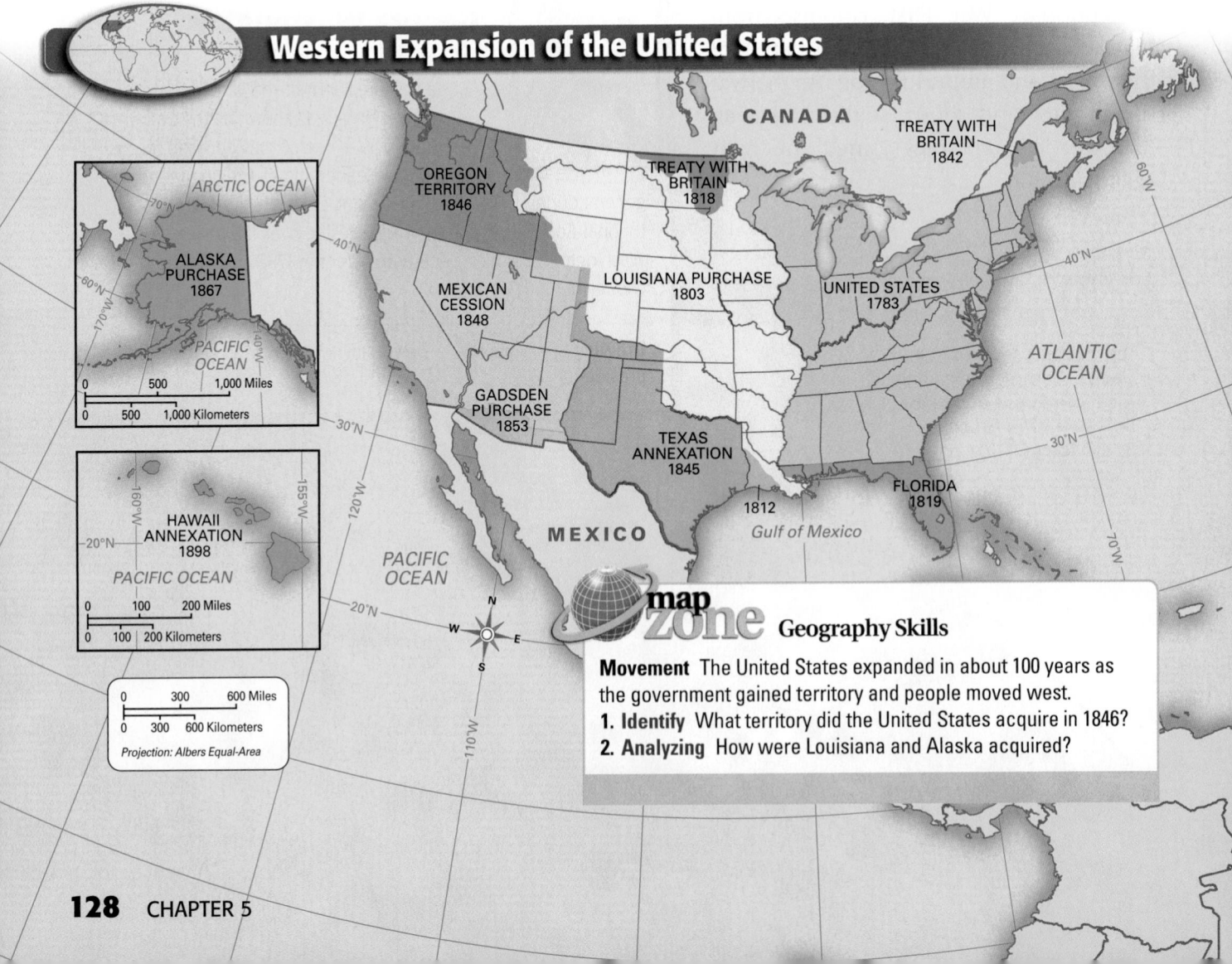

Western Expansion of the United States

map zone Geography Skills

Movement The United States expanded in about 100 years as the government gained territory and people moved west.
1. **Identify** What territory did the United States acquire in 1846?
2. **Analyzing** How were Louisiana and Alaska acquired?

Wars and Peace

The United States fought in several wars during the 1900s. Many Americans died in two major wars, World Wars I and II. After World War II, the United States and the Soviet Union became rivals in what was known as the Cold War. The Cold War lasted until the early 1990s, when the Soviet Union collapsed. U.S. troops also served in long wars in Korea in the 1950s and in Vietnam in the 1960s and 1970s. In 1991, the U.S. fought Iraq in the Persian Gulf War. More recently, the U.S. invaded Iraq in 2003 and is helping Iraqis rebuild their country today.

Today the United States is a member of many international organizations. The headquarters of one such organization, the United Nations (UN), is located in New York City. About 190 countries are UN members. The United States is one of the most powerful members.

Government and Citizenship

The United States has a limited, democratic government based on the U.S. Constitution. This document spells out the powers and functions of the branches of the federal government. The federal government includes an elected president and Congress. In general, the federal government handles issues affecting the whole country, but many powers are left to the 50 state governments. Counties and cities also have their own local governments. Many of these local governments provide services to the community such as trash collection, road building, electricity, and public transportation.

Rights and Responsibilities

American citizens have many rights and responsibilities, including the right to vote. Starting at age 18, U.S. citizens are allowed to vote. They are also encouraged

HISTORIC DOCUMENT
The Constitution

On September 17, 1787, state delegates gathered in Philadelphia to create a constitution, a written statement of the powers and functions of the new government of the United States. The Preamble, or introduction, to the U.S. Constitution is shown below. It states the document's general purpose.

" **We the People** of the United States, in order to form a more perfect Union, establish justice, insure domestic tranquillity, provide for the common defense, promote the general welfare, and secure the blessings of liberty to ourselves and our posterity, do ordain and establish this Constitution for the United States of America. "

Americans wanted peace within the United States and a national military force.

They wanted to ensure freedoms for themselves and for future generations.

ANALYSIS SKILL **ANALYZING PRIMARY SOURCES**

How do you think the ideas that appear in the Preamble affect your daily life?

to play an active role in government. For example, Americans can call or write their public officials to ask them to help solve problems in their communities. Without people participating in their government, the democratic process suffers.

READING CHECK Sequencing What were some major events in the history of the United States?

People and Culture

About 7 out of 10 Americans are descended from European immigrants. However, the United States is also home to people of many other cultures and ethnic groups. As a result, the United States is a diverse nation where many languages are spoken and different religions and customs are practiced. The blending of these different cultures has helped produce a unique American culture.

Ethnic Groups in the United States

FOCUS ON READING
What details would be included under a category called *ethnic groups*?

Some ethnic groups in the United States include Native Americans, African Americans, Hispanic Americans, and Asian Americans. As you can see on the maps on the next page, higher percentages of these ethnic groups are concentrated in different areas of the United States.

For thousands of years, Native Americans were the only people living in the Americas. Today, most Native Americans live in the western United States. Many Native Americans are concentrated in Arizona and New Mexico.

Even though African Americans live in every region of the country, some areas of the United States have a higher percentage of African Americans. For example, a higher percentage of African Americans live in southern states. Many large cities also have a high percentage of African Americans. On the other hand, descendants of people who came from Asian countries, or Asian Americans, are mostly concentrated in California.

Many Hispanic Americans originally migrated to the United States from Mexico, Cuba, and other Latin American countries. As you can see on the map of Hispanic Americans, a higher percentage of Hispanic Americans live in the southwestern states. These states border Mexico.

Language

What language or languages do you hear as you walk through the hall of your school? Since most people in the United States speak English, you probably hear English spoken every day. However, in many parts of the country, English is just one of many languages you might hear. Are you or is someone you know bilingual? People who speak two languages are **bilingual**.

After English, Spanish is the most widely spoken language in the United States. About 30 million Americans speak Spanish. Many of these people live in areas near Spanish-speaking countries like Mexico and Cuba.

Today more than 50 million U.S. residents speak a language in addition to English. These languages include Spanish, French, Chinese, Russian, Arabic, Navajo, and many others.

Religion

Americans also practice many religious faiths. Most people are Christians. However, some are Jewish or Muslim. A small percentage of Americans are Hindu or Buddhist. What religions are practiced in your community? Your community might have Christian churches, Jewish synagogues, and Islamic mosques, as well as other places of worship. Religious variety adds to our country's cultural diversity.

With so many different religions, many religious holidays are celebrated in the United States. These holidays include the Christian holidays of Christmas and Easter and the Jewish celebrations of Hanukkah, Yom Kippur, and Rosh Hashanah. Some African Americans also celebrate Kwanzaa, a holiday that is based on a traditional African festival. Muslims celebrate the end of the month of Ramadan with a large feast called 'Id al-Fitr.

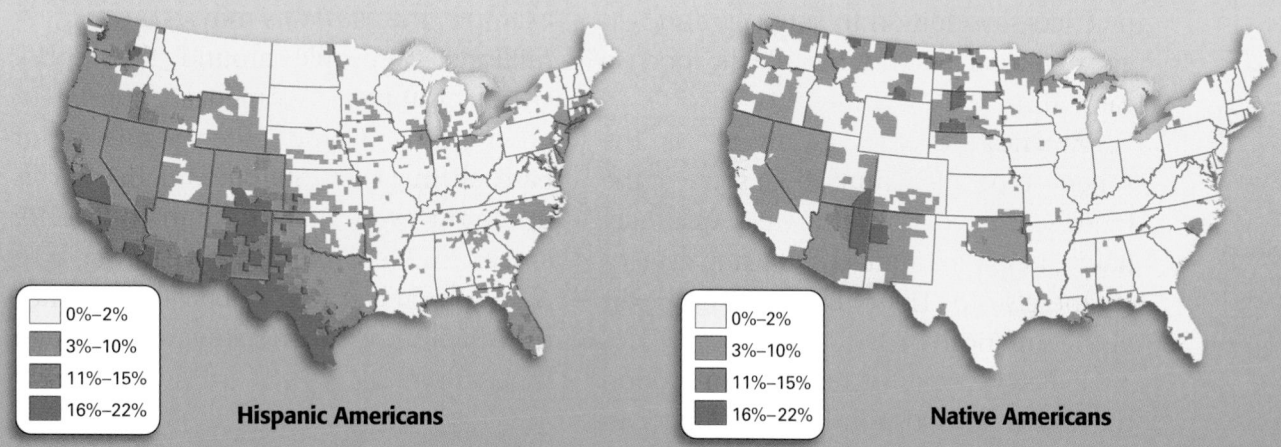

0%–2%	
3%–10%	
11%–15%	
16%–22%	**Hispanic Americans**

0%–2%	
3%–10%	
11%–15%	
16%–22%	**Native Americans**

Diverse America

People of different ethnic groups enjoy a concert in Miami, Florida. Like most large American cities, Miami has a very diverse population. More than half of all Hispanic Americans of Cuban descent live in Miami.

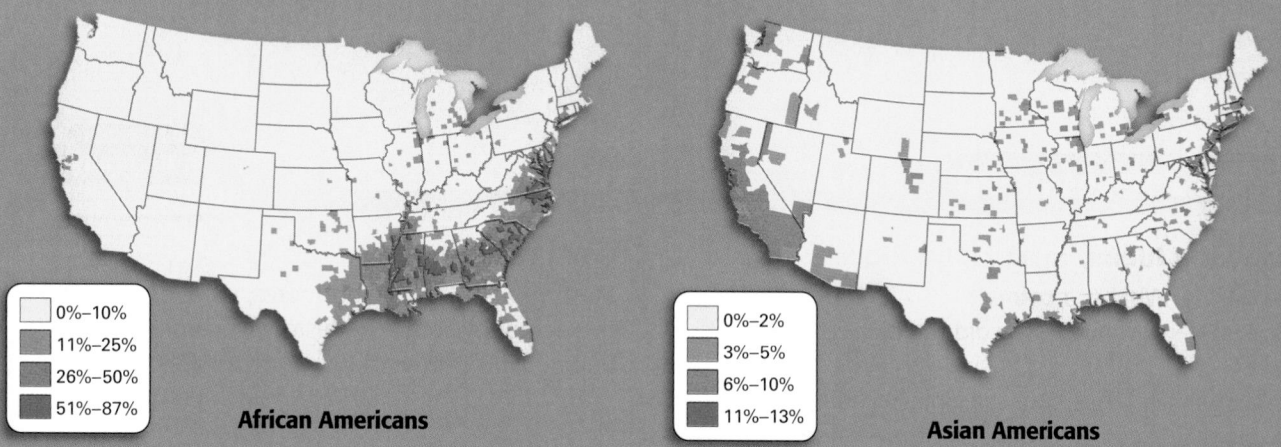

0%–10%	
11%–25%	
26%–50%	
51%–87%	**African Americans**

0%–2%	
3%–5%	
6%–10%	
11%–13%	**Asian Americans**

Source: U.S. Census Bureau, 2000

map zone
Geography Skills

Regions These maps show population information from the U.S. Census. Every 10 years, Americans answer census questions about their race or ethnic group.

1. **Locate** In what region of the United States does the highest percentage of African Americans live?
2. **Analyze** Why do you think many Hispanic Americans live in the southwestern United States?

Foods and Music

Diversity shows itself through cultural practices. In addition to language and religion, cultural practices include the food we eat and the music we listen to.

America's food is as diverse as the American people. Think about some of the foods you have eaten this week. You may have eaten Mexican tacos, Italian pasta, or Japanese sushi. These dishes are now part of the American diet.

Different types of music from around the world have also influenced American culture. For example, salsa music from Latin America is popular in the United States today. Many American musicians now combine elements of salsa into their pop songs. However, music that originated in the United States is also popular in other countries. American musical styles include blues, jazz, rock, and hip hop.

American Popular Culture

As the most powerful country in the world, the United States has tremendous influence around the world. American popular culture, such as movies, television programs, and sports, is popular elsewhere. For example, the *Star Wars* movies are seen by millions of people around the world. Other examples of American culture in other places include the popularity of baseball in Japan, Starbucks coffee shops in almost every major city in the world, and an MTV channel available throughout Asia. As you can see, Americans influence the rest of the world in many ways through their culture.

READING CHECK **Generalizing** How has cultural diversity enriched life in the United States?

SUMMARY AND PREVIEW The history of the United States has helped shape the democratic nation it is today. Drawn to the United States because of its democracy, immigrants from around the world have shaped American culture. In the next section, you will learn about the different regions of the United States and the issues the country is facing today.

Section 2 Assessment

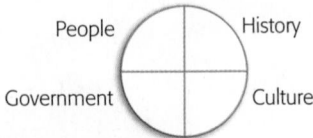

go.hrw.com
Online Quiz
KEYWORD: SG7 HP5

Reviewing Ideas, Terms, and Places

1. a. **Define** What is a **colony**?
   b. **Make Inferences** Why did the pioneers move west?
   c. **Elaborate** What is an example of the rights and responsibilities that American citizens have?
2. a. **Recall** What language other than English is widely spoken in the United States?
   b. **Summarize** What are some religions practiced in the United States?
   c. **Predict** How do you think American culture will be different in the future, and what influences do you think will bring about the changes?

Critical Thinking

3. **Summarizing** Using your notes, write one descriptive sentence about the history, government, people, and culture of the United States.

```
          People  |  History
        ----------+----------
      Government   |  Culture
```

FOCUS ON VIEWING

4. **Thinking about History and Culture** How would you describe the history and culture of the United States? Identify two images for your collage.

from
Bearstone

by Will Hobbs

In this book, a Native American boy named Cloyd learns more about his ancestors.

About the Reading *In* Bearstone, *writer Will Hobbs tells about an orphaned Native American boy named Cloyd who lives on a Colorado farm. While roaming the nearby canyons, Cloyd finds a relic from his ancestors. The relic is a stone in the shape of a turquoise bear, which becomes his Bearstone, the title of this story.*

AS YOU READ Identify what the mountains mean to Cloyd.

. . . This was a shining new world. To the north and east, peaks still covered with snow shone in the cloudless blue sky. He'd never seen mountains so sharp and rugged, so fierce and splendid. Below him, an eagle soared high above the old man's field. It was a good sign.

Then he remembered his grandmother's parting words as he left for Colorado. She told him something he'd never heard before: their band of Weminuche Utes ❶ hadn't always lived at White Mesa. ❷ Colorado, especially the mountains above Durango, had been their home until gold was discovered there and the white men wanted them out of the way. Summers the people used to hunt and fish in the high mountains, she'd said; they knew every stream, places so out of the way that white men still hadn't seen them. 'So don't feel bad about going to Durango,' she told him.

Cloyd regarded the distant peaks with new strength, a fierce kind of pride he'd never felt before. These were the mountains where his people used to live.

GUIDED READING

WORD HELP

band a group of Native American families

❶ Weminuche Utes are a band of Utes, a Native American cultural group.

❷ White Mesa is a Ute community in Utah where Cloyd lived before he moved to Colorado.

Connecting Literature to Geography

1. **Describing** What details in the first paragraph show us that Cloyd feels happy and at home in these mountains? Which details describe the physical features of these mountains?

2. **Making Inferences** Why did Cloyd's grandmother think he shouldn't feel bad about going to Durango? How does this fact affect his feelings about the mountains of Colorado?

The United States Today

What You Will Learn...

Main Ideas

1. The United States has four regions—the Northeast, South, Midwest, and West.
2. The United States has a strong economy and a powerful military but is facing the challenge of world terrorism.

The Big Idea

The United States has four main regions and faces opportunities and challenges.

Key Terms and Places

megalopolis, *p. 135*
Washington, D.C., *p. 135*
Detroit, *p. 137*
Chicago, *p. 137*
Seattle, *p. 138*
terrorism, *p. 140*

 **TAKING NOTES** As you read, take notes on the United States today. Organize your notes in a chart like the one below.

Regions	Economy, Military, and Terrorism

If YOU lived there...

You and your family run a small resort hotel in Fort Lauderdale, on the east coast of Florida. You love the sunny weather and the beaches there. Now your family is thinking about moving the business to another region where the tourist industry is important. They have looked at ski lodges in Colorado, lake cottages in Michigan, and hotels on the coast of Maine.

How will you decide among these different regions?

BUILDING BACKGROUND Geography, history, climate, and population give each region of the United States its own style. Some differences between the regions are more visible than others. For example, people in each region speak with different accents and have their favorite foods. Even with some differences, however, Americans are linked by a sense of unity in confronting important issues.

Regions of the United States

Because the United States is such a large country, geographers often divide it into four main regions. These are the Northeast, South, Midwest, and the West. You can see the four regions on the map on the next page. Find the region where you live. You probably know more about your own region than you do the three others. The population, resources, and economies of the four regions are similar in some ways and unique in others.

The Northeast

The Northeast shares a border with Canada. The economy in this region is heavily dependent on banks, investment firms, and insurance companies. Education also contributes to the economy. The area's respected universities include Harvard and Yale.

Interactive Map

Regions of the United States

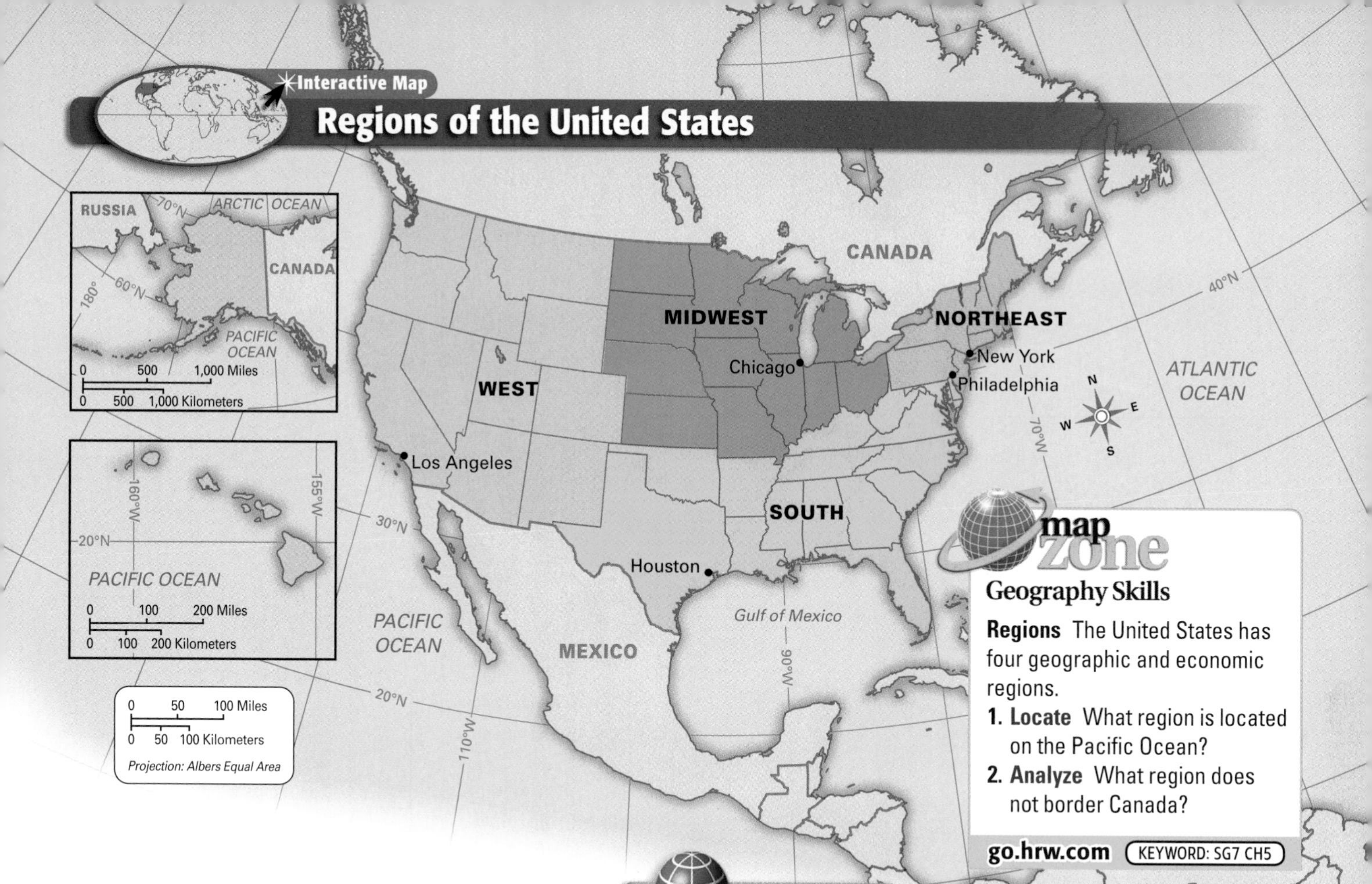
RUSSIA
ARCTIC OCEAN
CANADA
70°N
60°N
180°
PACIFIC OCEAN
0 500 1,000 Miles
0 500 1,000 Kilometers
160°W
155°W
20°N
PACIFIC OCEAN
0 100 200 Miles
0 100 200 Kilometers
0 50 100 Miles
0 50 100 Kilometers
Projection: Albers Equal Area
CANADA
MIDWEST
NORTHEAST
WEST
SOUTH
Chicago
New York
Philadelphia
Los Angeles
Houston
ATLANTIC OCEAN
PACIFIC OCEAN
Gulf of Mexico
MEXICO
40°N
30°N
20°N
70°W
90°W
110°W
N
E
S
W

map zone

Geography Skills

Regions The United States has four geographic and economic regions.

1. **Locate** What region is located on the Pacific Ocean?
2. **Analyze** What region does not border Canada?

go.hrw.com (KEYWORD: SG7 CH5)

Some natural resources of the Northeast states include rich farmland and huge pockets of coal. Used in the steelmaking process, coal remains very important to the region's economy. The steel industry helped make Pittsburgh, in western Pennsylvania, the largest industrial city in the Appalachians.

Today fishing remains an important industry in the Northeast. Major seaports allow companies to ship their products to markets around the world. Cool, shallow waters off the Atlantic coast are good fishing areas. Cod and shellfish such as lobster are the most valuable seafood.

The Northeast is the most densely populated region of the United States. Much of the Northeast is a **megalopolis**, a string of large cities that have grown together. This area stretches along the Atlantic coast from Boston to **Washington, D.C.** The three other major cities in the megalopolis are New York, Philadelphia, and Baltimore.

THE WORLD ALMANAC® Facts about Countries

Population of Major U.S. Cities

	City	Population
1	New York	8,143,197
2	Los Angeles	3,844,829
3	Chicago	2,842,518
4	Houston	2,016,582
5	Philadelphia	1,463,281

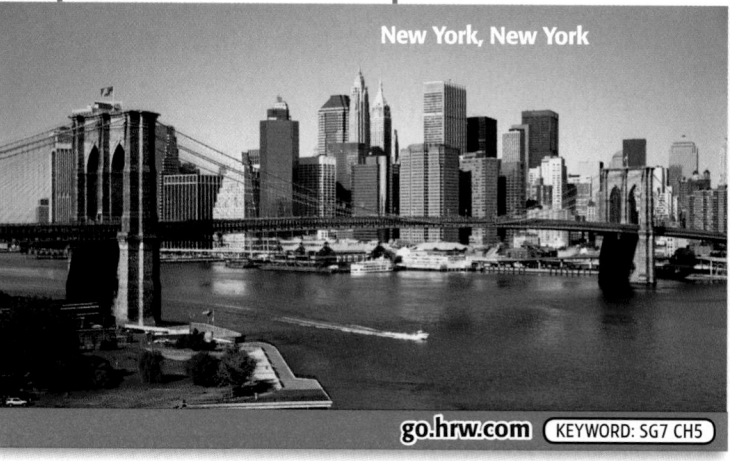

New York, New York

go.hrw.com (KEYWORD: SG7 CH5)

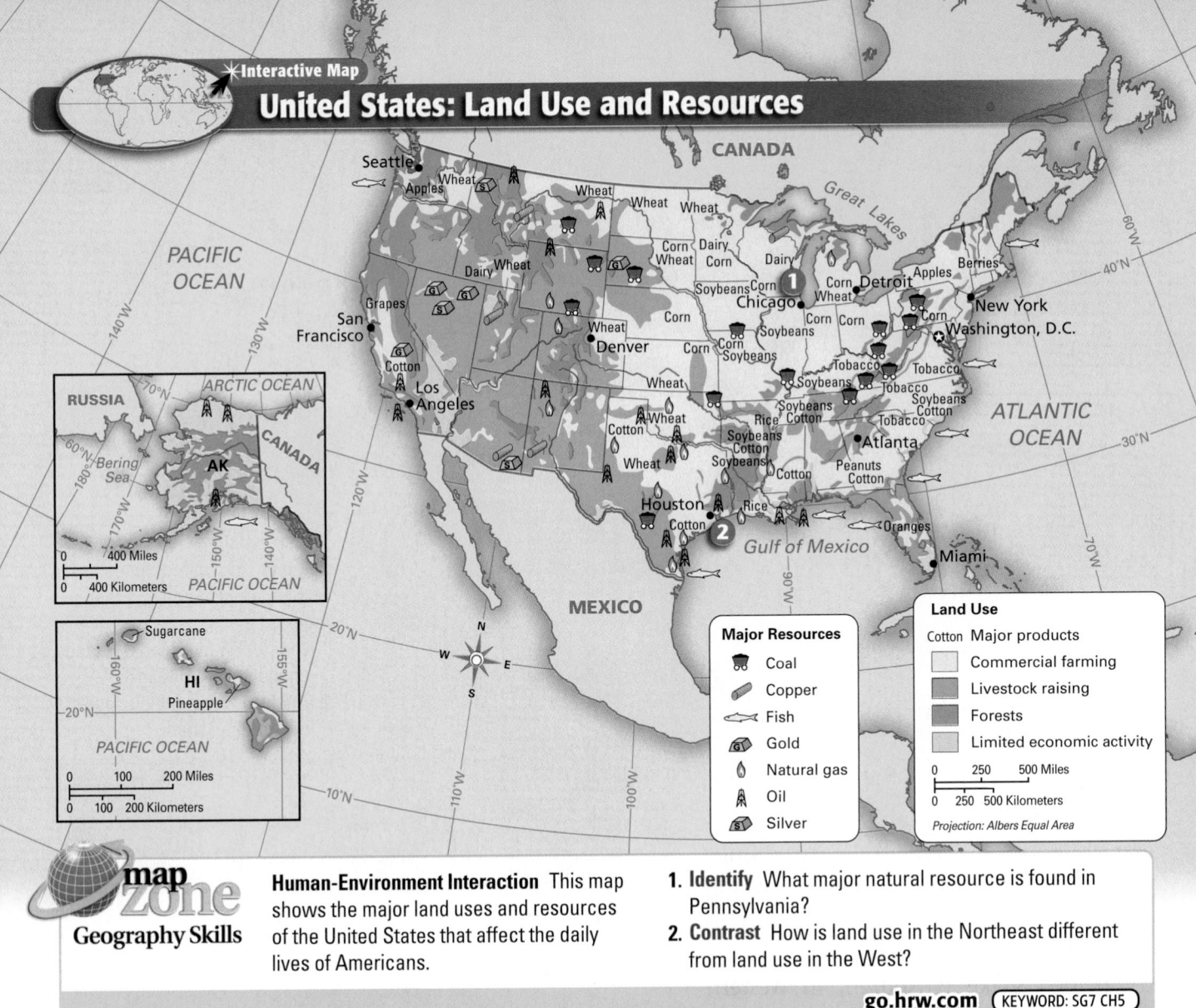

United States: Land Use and Resources

Interactive Map

Major Resources
- Coal
- Copper
- Fish
- Gold
- Natural gas
- Oil
- Silver

Land Use

Cotton Major products
- Commercial farming
- Livestock raising
- Forests
- Limited economic activity

0   250   500 Miles
0   250   500 Kilometers

Projection: Albers Equal Area

map zone
Geography Skills

Human-Environment Interaction This map shows the major land uses and resources of the United States that affect the daily lives of Americans.

1. **Identify** What major natural resource is found in Pennsylvania?
2. **Contrast** How is land use in the Northeast different from land use in the West?

go.hrw.com   KEYWORD: SG7 CH5

At least 40 million people live in this urban area. All of these cities were founded during the colonial era. They grew because they were important seaports. Today these cities are industrial and financial centers.

The South

The South is a region that includes long coastlines along the Atlantic Ocean and the Gulf of Mexico. Along the coastal plains rich soils provide farmers with abundant crops of cotton, tobacco, and citrus fruit.

In recent years, the South has become more urban and industrial and is one of the country's fastest-growing regions. The South's cities, such as Atlanta, have grown along with the economy. The Atlanta metropolitan area has grown from a population of only about 1 million in 1960 to more than 4 million today.

Other places in the South have also experienced growth in population and industry. The Research Triangle in North Carolina is an area of high-tech companies and several large universities. The Texas Gulf Coast and the lower Mississippi River area have huge oil refineries and petrochemical plants. Their products, which include gasoline, are mostly shipped from the ports of Houston and New Orleans.

136 CHAPTER 5

1 Farms with fertile soils like this one in Wisconsin cover much of the rural Midwest.

2 Large white containers, shown here at the Port of Houston, store oil from the Gulf Coast.

Millions of Americans vacation in the South, which makes the travel industry profitable in the region. Warm weather and beautiful beaches draw many vacationers to resorts in the South. You may not think of weather and beaches when you think about industry, but you should. Resort areas are an industry because they provide jobs and help local economies grow.

Many cities in the South trade goods and services with Mexico and countries in Central and South America. This trade is possible because several of the southern states are located near these countries. For example, Miami is an important trading port and travel connection with Caribbean countries, Mexico, and South America. Atlanta, Houston, and Dallas are also major transportation centers.

The Midwest

The Midwest is one of the most productive farming regions in the world. The Mississippi River and many of its tributaries carry materials that help create the region's rich soils, which are good for farming. Midwestern farmers grow mostly corn, wheat, and soybeans. Farmers in the region also raise livestock such as dairy cows.

The core of the Midwest's corn-growing region stretches from Ohio to Nebraska. Much of the corn is used to feed livestock, such as beef cattle and hogs.

To the north of the corn-growing region is an area of dairy farms. States with dairy farms are major producers of milk, cheese, and other dairy products. This area includes Wisconsin and most of Michigan and Minnesota. Much of the dairy farm region is pasture, but farmers also grow crops to feed dairy cows.

Many of the Midwest's farm and factory products are shipped to markets by water routes, such as those along the Ohio and Mississippi rivers. The other is through the Great Lakes and the Saint Lawrence Seaway to the Atlantic Ocean.

Most major cities in the Midwest are located on rivers or the Great Lakes. As a result, they are important transportation centers. Farm products, coal, and iron ore are easily shipped to these cities from nearby farms and mines. These natural resources support industries such as automobile manufacturing. For example, **Detroit**, Michigan, is the country's leading automobile producer.

One of the busiest shipping ports on the Great Lakes is **Chicago**, Illinois. The city also has one of the world's busiest airports. Chicago's industries attracted many immigrants in the late 1800s. People moved here to work in the city's steel mills. Today Chicago is the nation's third-largest city.

FOCUS ON READING

As you read about the Midwest, sort the details into three categories.

The West

The West is the largest region in the United States. Many western states have large open spaces with few people. The West is not all open spaces, however. Many large cities are on the Pacific coast.

One state on the coast, California, is home to more than 10 percent of the U.S. population. California's mild climate and wealth of resources attract people to the state. Most Californians live in Los Angeles, San Diego, and the San Francisco Bay area. The center of the country's entertainment industry, Hollywood, is in Los Angeles. Farming and the technology industry are also important to California's economy.

The economy of other states in the West is dependent on ranching and growing wheat. Wheat is grown mostly in Montana, Idaho, and Washington.

Much of the farmland in the West must be irrigated, or watered. One method of irrigation uses long sprinkler systems mounted on huge wheels. The wheels rotate slowly. This sprinkler system waters the area within a circle. From the air, parts of the irrigated Great Plains resemble a series of green circles.

The West also has rich deposits of coal, oil, gold, silver, copper, and other minerals. However, mining these minerals can cause problems. For example, coal miners in parts of the Great Plains use a **process** called strip mining, which strips away soil and rock. This kind of mining leads to soil erosion and other problems. Today laws require miners to restore mined areas.

In Oregon and Washington, forestry and fishing are two of the most important economic activities. **Seattle** is Washington's largest city. The Seattle area is home to many important industries, including a major computer software company. More than half of the people in Oregon live in and around Portland.

Alaska's economy is largely based on oil, forests, and fish. As in Washington and Oregon, people debate over developing

ACADEMIC VOCABULARY

process a series of steps by which a task is accomplished

Olympic National Park

One of the largest sections of coastal wilderness in the United States, shown here, stretches along the Pacific coast in Washington's Olympic National Park.

these resources. For example, some people want to limit oil drilling in wild areas of Alaska. Others want to expand drilling to produce more oil.

Hawaii's natural beauty, mild climate, and fertile soils are its most important resources. The islands' major crops are sugarcane and pineapples. Millions of tourists visit the islands each year.

READING CHECK **Comparing** How is the economy of the West different from the economy of the South?

Economy, Military, and Terrorism

The United States is the world's only superpower. It has both the largest economy and the most powerful military in the world. Those two strengths bring great opportunities to the United States. However, they also bring great challenges.

Economic and Military Power

The United States has many valuable natural resources. Modern technology and plentiful jobs make the United States a land of opportunity. With so many opportunities, the United States can support itself without relying on other countries. This independence has helped make the United States the world's largest economy.

Even with a strong economy, the United States benefits by trading with other countries. Major trading partners include Canada, Mexico, China, Japan, and Europe. The United States trades mostly with its neighbors, Canada and Mexico. In 1992 the United States, Mexico, and Canada signed the North American Free Trade Agreement, or NAFTA. This agreement made trade easier and cheaper between the three countries.

Rebirth in New York

This artist's sketch shows the new building that will stand where the World Trade Center once stood in New York.

With so much wealth, the United States can afford a powerful military. The main job of the U.S. armed forces is to protect our country. The U.S. military also has the opportunity to help other countries defend themselves.

Terrorism

On September 11, 2001, the United States suffered the deadliest terrorist attack in the country's history. Terrorists hijacked four American jets. They crashed two into the World Trade Center and one into the Pentagon. These attacks were a violent reminder that some people do not want the United States to be strong.

They want to disrupt our country's economy with **terrorism**, or violent attacks that cause fear.

In response to the terrorist attacks, U.S. President George W. Bush declared war on terrorism. He sent forces to Afghanistan, to kill or capture members of a terrorist group called al Qaeda. The United States also helped a new democratic government take power in Afghanistan. The United States then turned its attention to Iraq. President Bush believed that Iraqi leader Saddam Hussein was another threat to Americans. In 2003 Bush ordered U.S. troops to invade Iraq and remove Saddam from power.

Today world leaders are working with the United States to combat terrorism. In the United States, the Department of Homeland Security, a government agency, coordinates efforts to protect the country from any other terrorist attacks. Many other countries have increased security within their borders, especially at international airports.

Many Americans will never forget the people who lost their lives on September 11. In New York, a permanent memorial and building will stand at the former World Trade Center site. The main building, Freedom Tower, will be 70 stories tall. When completed in 2009, the tower will serve as a symbol of hope for New York and the country as a whole.

READING CHECK **Making Connections** What is the connection between the military and economic strength of the United States and the threat of terrorism?

SUMMARY AND PREVIEW In this section, you learned about the landscapes and economic activities of the different regions of the United States. You also learned that trade and terrorism are important issues in the country. In the next chapter, you will learn about Canada, our neighbor to the north of the United States.

Section 3 Assessment

go.hrw.com
Online Quiz
KEYWORD: SG7 HP5

Reviewing Ideas, Terms, and Places

1. **a. Define** What is a **megalopolis**? What major cities are part of the largest megalopolis in the United States?
   b. Compare and Contrast How is land use in the Midwest similar to and different from land use in the South?
   c. Elaborate How are the regions of the United States different from one another?
2. **a. Define** What is **terrorism**? What terrorist attack occurred in September 2001?
   b. Explain What makes the United States a superpower?
   c. Elaborate What steps are the United States and other countries taking in an attempt to combat world terrorism?

Critical Thinking

3. **Finding Main Ideas** Use your notes to help you list at least one main idea about the population, resources, and economy of each region.

	Northeast	South	Midwest	West
Population				
Resources				
Economy				

FOCUS ON VIEWING

4. **Thinking about the United States Today** You have read about the regions of the United States, as well as issues facing the country today. What key words, images, and objects might represent what you have learned?

Chapter Review

Geography's Impact
video series
Review the video to answer the closing question:
What do you think it would be like to live in a country that had no cultural diversity?

Visual Summary

Use the visual summary below to help you review the main ideas of the chapter.

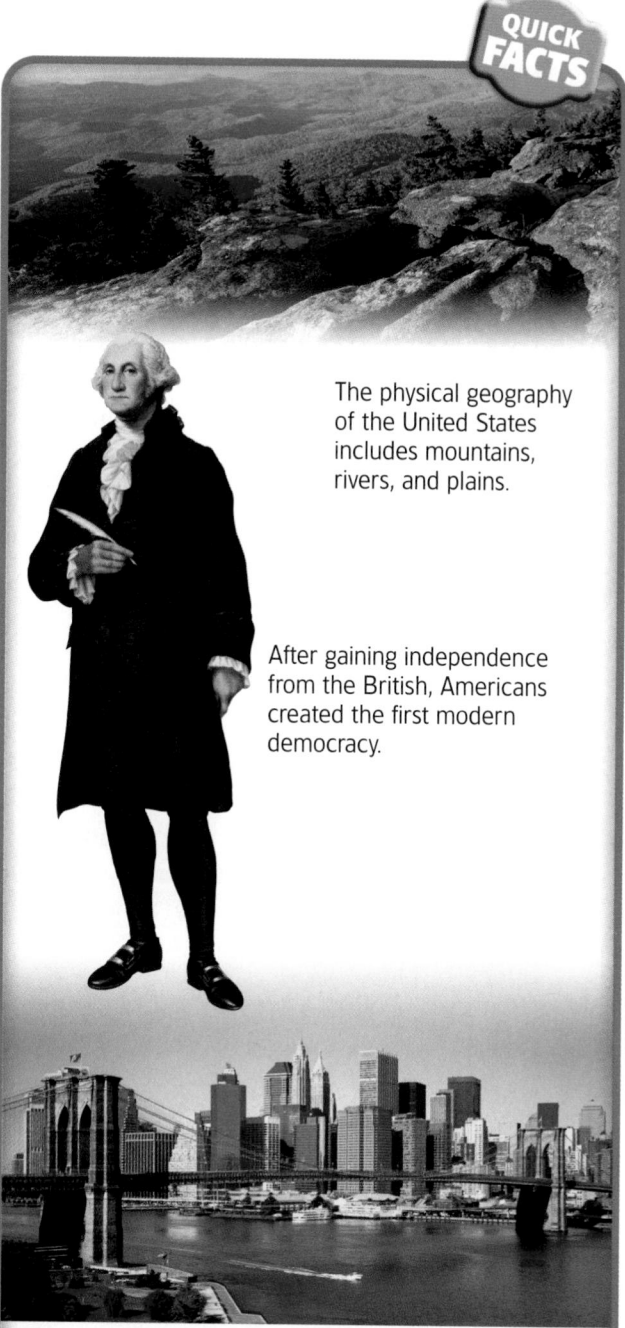

QUICK FACTS

The physical geography of the United States includes mountains, rivers, and plains.

After gaining independence from the British, Americans created the first modern democracy.

The United States has four geographic and economic regions—the Northeast, South, Midwest, and the West.

Reviewing Vocabulary, Terms, and Places

Match the terms or places with their definitions or descriptions.

a. Boston
b. Great Lakes
c. tributary
d. Rocky Mountains
e. colony
f. Appalachian Mountains
g. pioneers
h. bilingual
i. megalopolis
j. Washington, D.C.
k. Chicago
l. terrorism

1. a string of cities that have grown together
2. major seaport in the British colonies
3. stream or river that flows into a larger stream or river
4. violent attacks that cause fear
5. first settlers
6. largest freshwater lake system in the world
7. major mountain range in the West
8. capital of the United States
9. third-largest city in the United States
10. major mountain range in the East
11. having the ability to speak two languages
12. territory controlled by people from a foreign land

Comprehension and Critical Thinking

SECTION 1 *(Pages 118–122)*

13. a. Identify What river drains the entire Interior Plains and is the longest river in North America?

SECTION 1 *(continued)*

b. Contrast How is the physical geography of the Appalachians different from that of the Rocky Mountains? Why is this true?

c. Elaborate What natural resources affect your daily life?

SECTION 2 *(Pages 126–132)*

14. a. Define Who were the pioneers?

b. Draw Conclusions Why do you think people immigrate to the United States?

c. Elaborate How do you think American culture has been able to influence people and culture around the world?

SECTION 3 *(Pages 134–140)*

15. a. Recall What are the four regions of the United States?

b. Compare Is corn grown mostly in the Midwest or the South?

c. Elaborate How should the United States protect itself from terrorism?

Using the Internet

go.hrw.com
KEYWORD: SG7 CH5

16. Activity: Making a Brochure The United States is a country with a diverse population. This diversity is seen in many of the holidays Americans celebrate. Enter the activity keyword and research some of the holidays celebrated in the United States. Take notes on what you find. Then use your notes to create an illustrated brochure that discusses at least three holidays. Be sure to include information on the history, background, and traditions of each holiday.

Social Studies Skills

Reading a Political Map Look at the political map of the United States at the beginning of this chapter. Then answer the following questions.

17. What four states border Mexico?

18. What river forms the boundary between Illinois and Missouri?

FOCUS ON READING AND VIEWING

19. Categorizing For each category below, list details from the chapter.

Geography	People	Regions

20. Creating a Collage Using the ideas you developed for your collage on the United States, collect the pictures and objects you need. Make sure any objects you want to use can be attached to a poster board. Next, decide how to organize the pictures and objects. You might, for example, organize them by region or by time period. After you have attached your images and objects to the poster board, create a label to identify each grouping. Finally, write a title for the entire collage. When the class collages are displayed, be prepared to evaluate other collages on their organization and originality.

Map Activity

21. The United States On a sheet of paper, match the letters on the map with their correct labels.

Great Lakes   Rocky Mountains

Mississippi River   Pacific Ocean

Atlantic Ocean

Alaska

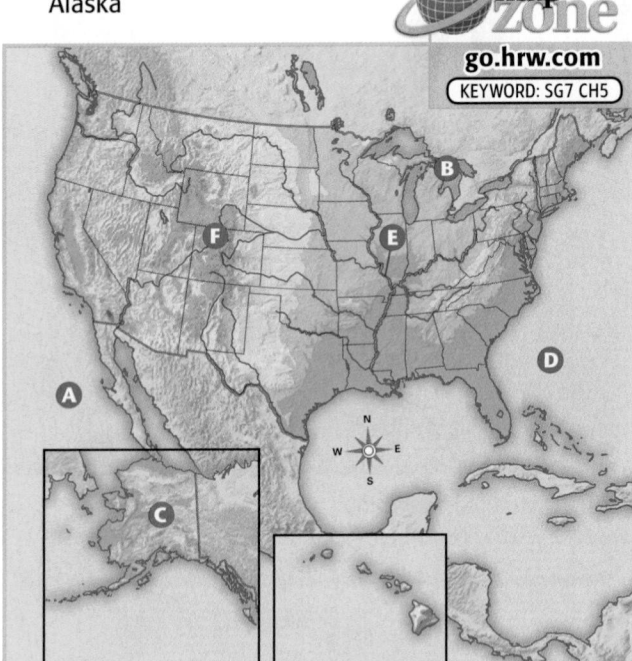

go.hrw.com
KEYWORD: SG7 CH5

Standardized Test Practice

DIRECTIONS: Read questions 1 through 7 and write the letter of the best response. Question 8 will require a brief essay.

1 What physical feature does the Mississippi River and its tributaries drain?

A Piedmont

B Rocky Mountains

C Interior Plains

D Great Lakes

2 What country did the United States gain independence from?

A Britain

B France

C Canada

D Mexico

3 Many pioneers moved west hoping to find

A silver.

B diamonds.

C coal.

D gold.

4 People who are bilingual speak how many languages?

A one

B five

C two

D three

5 NAFTA is a trade agreement among the United States, Mexico, and

A Brazil.

B Canada.

C Britain.

D Australia.

Regions of the United States

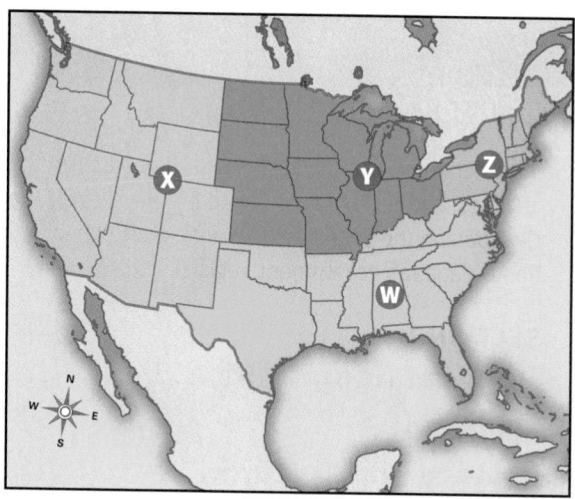

6 Based on the map above, which region is the Midwest?

A X

B W

C Z

D Y

7 Which region is known for its dense population?

A Z

B W

C Y

D X

8 **Extended Response** Look at the map of U.S. regions and the chart of major U.S. cities in Section 3. Write a short essay describing the population, resources, and economies of each region of the United States.

Canada

What You Will Learn...

In this chapter you will learn about the physical features, climates, and resources of Canada. You will study the history of Canada and the country's different cultures. Finally, you will learn about Canada's government, regions, and economy.

FOCUS ON READING AND SPEAKING

Understanding Lists Identifying a list of the interesting facts that you read about may help you understand the topic you are studying. For example, you could identify facts about Canada's physical features, regions, government, or economy. As you read this chapter, look for lists of facts. **See the lesson, Understanding Lists, on page R7.**

Creating a Radio Ad You are a member of the Canadian tourism board and your job is to develop a radio ad to attract visitors to Canada. Read about Canada in this chapter. Then, write a script for a one minute radio ad. Be ready to present your ad to the class.

Map legend:
- ⊙ National capital
- ★ Provincial capitals
- ● Other cities

0 ___ 250 ___ 500 Miles
0 ___ 250 ___ 500 Kilometers

Projection:
Lambert Azimuthal Equal-Area

ARCTIC OCEAN

Alaska (UNITED STATES)

YUKON TERRITORY
★ Whitehorse

NORTHWEST TERRITORIES
Yellowknife ●

BRITISH COLUMBIA

ALBERTA
Edmonton ★

Vancouver Island

Calgary ●

Vancouver ●
Victoria ★

PACIFIC OCEAN

Culture Ice hockey is Canada's national sport. Many Canadians grow up playing on frozen lakes.

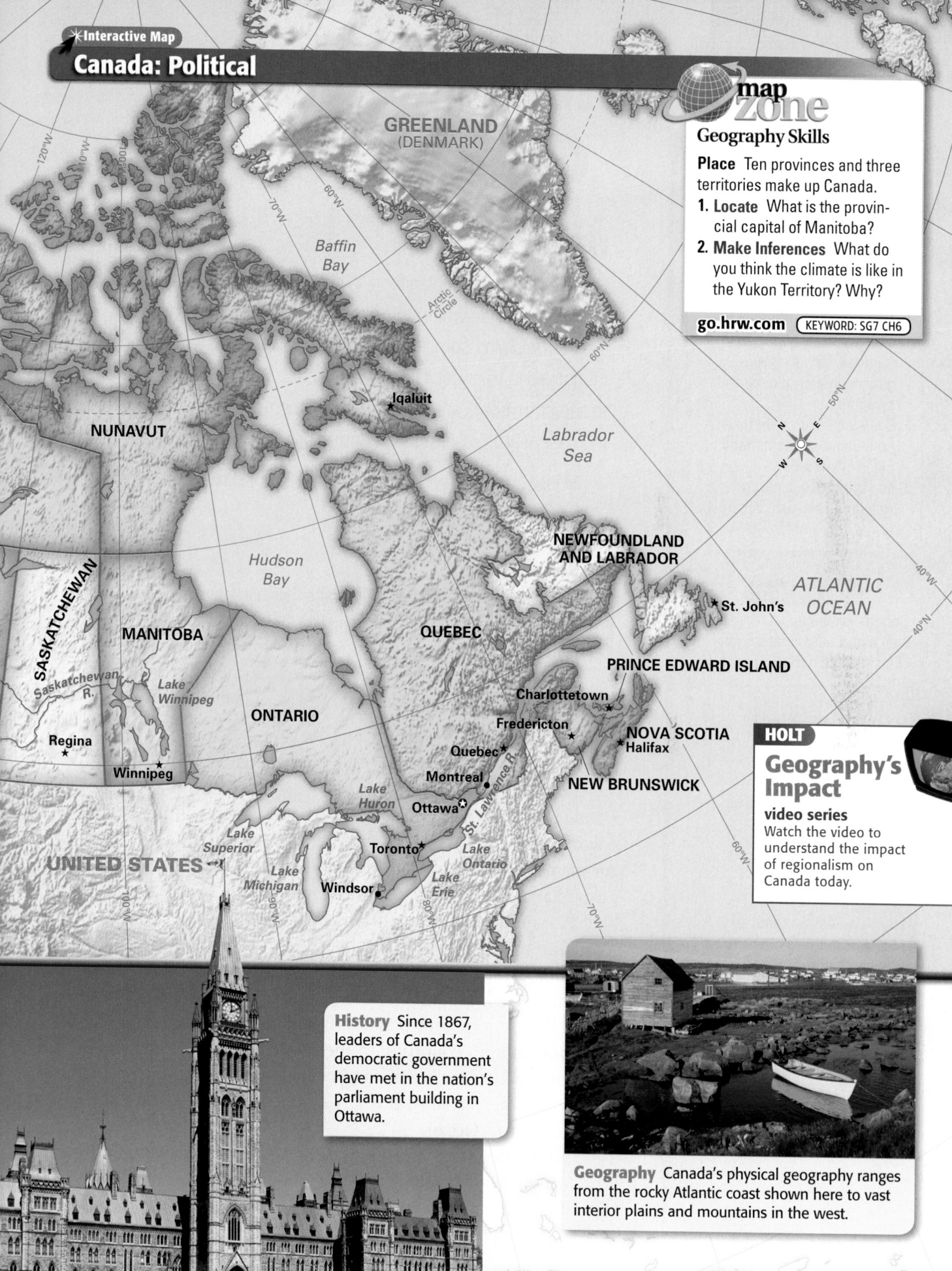

GREENLAND
(DENMARK)

Baffin
Bay

Arctic
Circle

Iqaluit

NUNAVUT

Labrador
Sea

Hudson
Bay

NEWFOUNDLAND
AND LABRADOR

★St. John's

ATLANTIC
OCEAN

SASKATCHEWAN

MANITOBA

QUEBEC

PRINCE EDWARD ISLAND

Saskatchewan
R.

Lake
Winnipeg

Charlottetown★

★Regina

ONTARIO

Fredericton★

NOVA SCOTIA

★Winnipeg

Quebec★

★Halifax

Montreal

NEW BRUNSWICK

Ottawa✪

St. Lawrence R.

Lake
Huron

UNITED STATES

Lake
Superior

Toronto★

Lake
Michigan

Lake
Ontario

Windsor

Lake
Erie

map zone

Geography Skills

Place Ten provinces and three territories make up Canada.
1. **Locate** What is the provincial capital of Manitoba?
2. **Make Inferences** What do you think the climate is like in the Yukon Territory? Why?

go.hrw.com KEYWORD: SG7 CH6

HOLT
Geography's Impact
video series
Watch the video to understand the impact of regionalism on Canada today.

History Since 1867, leaders of Canada's democratic government have met in the nation's parliament building in Ottawa.

Geography Canada's physical geography ranges from the rocky Atlantic coast shown here to vast interior plains and mountains in the west.

Physical Geography

What You Will Learn...

Main Ideas

1. A huge country, Canada has a wide variety of physical features, including rugged mountains, plains, and swamps.
2. Because of its northerly location, Canada is dominated by cold climates.
3. Canada is rich in natural resources like fish, minerals, fertile soil, and forests.

The Big Idea

Canada is a huge country with a northerly location, cold climates, and rich resources.

Key Terms and Places

Rocky Mountains, *p. 146*
St. Lawrence River, *p. 146*
Niagara Falls, *p. 146*
Canadian Shield, *p. 147*
Grand Banks, *p. 148*
pulp, *p. 149*
newsprint, *p. 149*

TAKING NOTES As you read, take notes on Canada's physical features, climates, and resources in three separate lists.

Physical Features	Climates	Resources
1.	1.	1.
2.	2.	2.

If YOU lived there...

You live in Winnipeg, Manitoba, in central Canada. Your hiking club is trying to decide where to go on a trip this summer. Since you live on the plains, some people want to visit the rugged Rocky Mountains in the west. Others want to travel north to Hudson Bay to see polar bears and other wildlife. Others would rather hike in the east near the Great Lakes and Niagara Falls.

Which place will you choose for this year's trip?

BUILDING BACKGROUND A long international boundary separates Canada and the United States. With the exception of the St. Lawrence River and the Great Lakes, there is no actual physical boundary between the two countries. Rivers, lakes, prairies, and mountain ranges cross the border.

Physical Features

Did you know that Canada is the second-largest country in the world? Russia is the only country in the world that is larger than Canada. The United States is the third-largest country in the world and shares many physical features with Canada.

As you look at the map on the following page, see if you can find the physical features that the United States and Canada share. You may notice that mountains along the Pacific coast and the **Rocky Mountains** extend north into western Canada from the western United States. Broad plains stretch across the interiors of both countries. In the east, the two countries share a natural border formed by the **St. Lawrence River**. An important international waterway, the St. Lawrence links the Great Lakes to the Atlantic Ocean.

The United States and Canada also share a spectacular physical feature called **Niagara Falls**. The falls are located on the Niagara River between the province of Ontario and New York State.

Created by the waters of the Niagara River, the falls flow between two of the Great Lakes—Lake Erie and Lake Ontario. The falls here plunge an average of 162 feet (50 m) down a huge ledge. That is higher than many 15-story buildings!

Canada has a region of rocky uplands, lakes, and swamps called the **Canadian Shield**. See on the map how this feature curves around Hudson Bay. The Shield covers about half the country.

Farther north, Canada stretches all the way up to the Arctic Ocean. The land here is covered with ice year-round. Ellesmere Island is very rugged with snow-covered mountains and jagged coastlines. Very few people live this far north, but wildlife such as the polar bear and the Arctic wolf have adapted to the harsh environment.

READING CHECK **Summarizing** What are the major physical features of Canada?

Interactive Map

Canada: Physical

Geography Skills

Place Canada is located between the United States and the Arctic Ocean.

1. **Locate** What mountain range has the highest elevation?
2. **Draw Conclusions** How does Canada's northerly location affect its climate?

go.hrw.com   KEYWORD: SG7 CH6

ELEVATION

Feet	Meters
13,120	4,000
6,560	2,000
1,640	500
656	200
(Sea level) 0	0 (Sea level)
Below sea level	Below sea level

Projection: Lambert Azimuthal Equal-Area

Mist rises over Niagara Falls where the Niagara River forms a natural boundary between the United States and Canada.

Climate

FOCUS ON READING

What climates would you include in a list of the climates of Canada?

Canada's location greatly influences the country's climate. Canada is located far from the equator at much higher latitudes than the United States. This more northerly location gives Canada cool to freezing temperatures year-round.

The farther north you go in Canada, the colder it gets. The coldest areas of Canada are located close to the Arctic Circle. Much of central and northern Canada has a subarctic climate. The far north has tundra and ice cap climates. About half of Canada lies in these extremely cold climates.

The central and eastern parts of southern Canada have a much different climate. It is humid and relatively mild. However, the mildest area of Canada is along the coast of British Columbia. This location on the Pacific coast brings rainy winters and mild temperatures. Inland areas of southern Canada are colder and drier.

READING CHECK **Categorizing** What are Canada's climates?

Resources

Canada is incredibly rich in natural resources such as fish, minerals, and forests. Canada's Atlantic and Pacific coastal waters are among the world's richest fishing areas. Off the Atlantic coast lies a large fishing ground near Newfoundland and Labrador called the **Grand Banks**. Here, cold waters from the Labrador Sea meet the warm waters of the Gulf Stream. These conditions are ideal for the growth of tiny organisms, or plankton, that fish like to eat. As a result, large schools of fish gather at the Grand Banks. However, recent overfishing of this region has left many fishers in Canada unemployed.

Minerals are also valuable resources in Canada. The Canadian Shield contains many mineral deposits. Canada is a main source of the world's nickel, zinc, and uranium. Lead, copper, gold, and silver are also important resources. Saskatchewan has large deposits of potash, a mineral used to make fertilizer. Alberta produces most of Canada's oil and natural gas.

Banff National Park

Some of Canada's most spectacular scenery is found here in the Rockies at Banff National Park.

The city of Windsor, Ontario, lies across the Detroit River from Detroit, Michigan.

Agriculture in Ontario

In this satellite image, crop fields in different stages of growth appear scattered throughout the province of Ontario. These rectangular fields of vegetation appear red at their height of growth and white after the crops are harvested. Rich soils and a mild climate in this region, which lies north of Lake Erie, make it one of Canada's most fertile regions. Crops grown here include wheat, soybeans, corn, and a variety of vegetables. Some of these crops are exported to the United States through the Canadian port of Windsor to Detroit, Michigan, just across the Detroit River. Both cities appear in this image as shades of blue and brown.

Drawing Conclusions What is the economy of southern Ontario based on?

Vast areas of forests stretch across most of Canada from Labrador to the Pacific coast. These trees provide lumber and pulp. **Pulp**—softened wood fibers—is used to make paper. The United States, the United Kingdom, and Japan get much of their newsprint from Canada. **Newsprint** is cheap paper used mainly for newspapers.

READING CHECK **Drawing Conclusions** How do Canada's major resources affect its economy?

SUMMARY AND PREVIEW In this section, you learned that Canada shares many physical features with the United States. However, Canada's geography is also different. Due to its northerly location, Canada has a cold climate. Fish, minerals, fertile soil, and forests are all important natural resources. In the next section, you will learn about the history and culture of Canada.

Section 1 Assessment

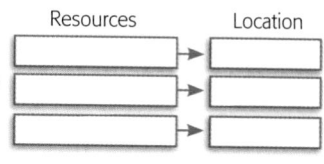

go.hrw.com
Online Quiz
KEYWORD: SG7 HP6

Reviewing Ideas, Terms, and Places

1. **a. Recall** What river links the Great Lakes to the Atlantic Ocean?
   b. Explain What physical features does **Niagara Falls** flow between?
   c. Develop If you were to live in Canada, where would you not want to live?
2. **a. Describe** How is Canada's climate related to its northerly location?
   b. Draw Conclusions Where would you expect to find Canada's coldest climate? Why?
3. **a. Define** What is the **Grand Banks**?
   b. Interpret How are Canada's forests a valuable resource?

Critical Thinking

4. **Generalizing** Using your notes on Canada's resources, identify the location of each type of resource.

Resources		Location
	→	
	→	
	→	

FOCUS ON SPEAKING

5. **Writing about Physical Geography** What information about Canada's physical features, climate, and resources might visitors find appealing? Jot down what descriptions you want to include in your radio ad.

History and Culture

What You Will Learn...

Main Ideas

1. Beginning in the 1600s, Europeans settled the region that would later become Canada.
2. Immigration and migration to cities have shaped Canadian culture.

The Big Idea

Canada's history and culture reflect Native Canadian and European settlement, immigration, and migration to cities.

Key Terms and Places

provinces, *p. 152*
Quebec, *p. 152*
British Columbia, *p. 152*
Toronto, *p. 154*

TAKING NOTES As you read, take notes on early settlement, building of the railroad, immigration, and migration to cities. Organize your notes in a diagram like this one.

History and Culture

If **YOU** lived there...

You own a general store in Calgary, Alberta, in the early 1880s. Your town is a center for agriculture and ranching on the prairies around you. Still, it sometimes feels very isolated. You miss your family in Ontario. Now the news comes that the Canadian Pacific Railway will soon reach Calgary. It will connect the town with all of central and eastern Canada.

How will the railroad change your life?

BUILDING BACKGROUND Canada is a close neighbor with the United States. The two countries are linked by a common language and a history of British colonial rule. But the two countries developed in different ways. Canada's diverse population developed its own culture and way of life.

History

As the ice sheets of the ice ages melted, people moved into all areas of what is now Canada. As they did elsewhere in the Americas, these ancient settlers adapted to the physical environment.

Canada's History

New France
Known as the Father of New France, explorer Samuel de Champlain established Quebec in 1608.

Native Canadians
Thousands of years ago, Indians and Inuit settled Canada.

Native Canadians

Indians and the Inuit (IH-nu-wuht) people were the first Canadians. Over the years, some of these native peoples divided into groups that became known as the First Nations. One group living on Canada's vast interior plains, the Cree, were skilled bison hunters. In the far north the Inuit adapted to the region's extreme cold, where farming was impossible. By hunting seals, whales, walruses, and other animals, the Inuit could feed, clothe, and house themselves. Today about 400,000 Indians and Inuit live in Canada.

European Settlement

Other people migrated to Canada from Europe. The first Europeans in Canada were the Vikings, or Norse. They settled on Newfoundland Island in about AD 1000, but later abandoned their settlements. In the late 1400s other Europeans arrived and explored Canada. Soon more explorers and fishermen from western Europe began crossing the Atlantic.

Trade quickly developed between the Europeans and Native Canadians. Europeans valued the furs that Native Canadians supplied. The Canadians wanted European metal goods like axes and guns. Through trading, they began to also exchange foods, clothing, and methods of travel.

New France

France was the first European country to successfully settle parts of what would become Canada. The French **established** Quebec City in 1608. They called their new territories New France. At its height, New France included much of eastern Canada and the central United States.

New France was important for several reasons. It was part of the French Empire, which provided money and goods to French settlers. It also served as a base to spread French culture.

France had to compete with Britain, another European colonial power, for control of Canada. To defend their interests against the British, the French built trade and diplomatic relationships with Native Canadians. They exported furs, fish, and other products from New France to other parts of their empire. In addition, the French sent manufactured goods from France to New France. French missionaries also went to New France to convert people to Christianity.

All of these efforts protected French interests in New France for 150 years, until the British finally defeated the French. Although it did not last, New France shaped Canada's cultural makeup. The descendants of French settlers form one of Canada's major ethnic groups today.

ACADEMIC VOCABULARY
establish to set up or create

British Settlement
The British built forts throughout Canada like this one in Halifax, Nova Scotia.

Dominion of Canada
After 1867, Canadians created their own government and a mounted police force patrolled the border with the United States.

British Conquest

In the mid-1700s, the rivalry between France and England turned to war. The conflict was called the French and Indian War. This was the war that resulted in the British taking control of New France away from the French. A small number of French went back to France. However, the great majority stayed. For most of them, few changes occurred in their daily activities. They farmed the same land, prayed in the same churches, and continued to speak French. Few English-speaking settlers came to what is now called **Quebec**.

Canadian Pacific Railroad

Since 1885, the Canadian Pacific Railway has snaked through the Canadian Rockies on its way to the Pacific coast.

The British divided Quebec into two colonies. Lower Canada was mostly French-speaking, and Upper Canada was mostly English-speaking. The boundary between Upper and Lower Canada forms part of the border between the provinces of Quebec and Ontario today. **Provinces** are administrative divisions of a country. To the east, the colony of Nova Scotia (noh-vuh SKOH-shuh) was also divided. A new colony called New Brunswick was created where many of the British settlers lived.

Creation of Canada

For several decades these new colonies developed separately from each other. The colonists viewed themselves as different from other parts of the British Empire. Therefore, the British Parliament created the Dominion of Canada in 1867. A dominion is a territory or area of influence. For Canadians, the creation of the Dominion was a step toward independence from Britain. The motto of the new Dominion was "from sea to sea."

How would Canadians create a nation from sea to sea? With railroads. When the Dominion was established, Ontario and Quebec were already well served by railroads. **British Columbia**, on the Pacific coast, was not. To connect British Columbia with the provinces in the east, the Canadians built a transcontinental railroad. Completed in 1885, the Canadian Pacific Railway was Canada's first transcontinental railroad.

After the Canadian Pacific Railway linked the original Canadian provinces to British Columbia, Canada acquired vast lands in the north. Much of this land was bought from the Hudson's Bay Company, a large British fur-trading business. Most of the people living in the north were Native Canadians and people of mixed European and native ancestry. With the building

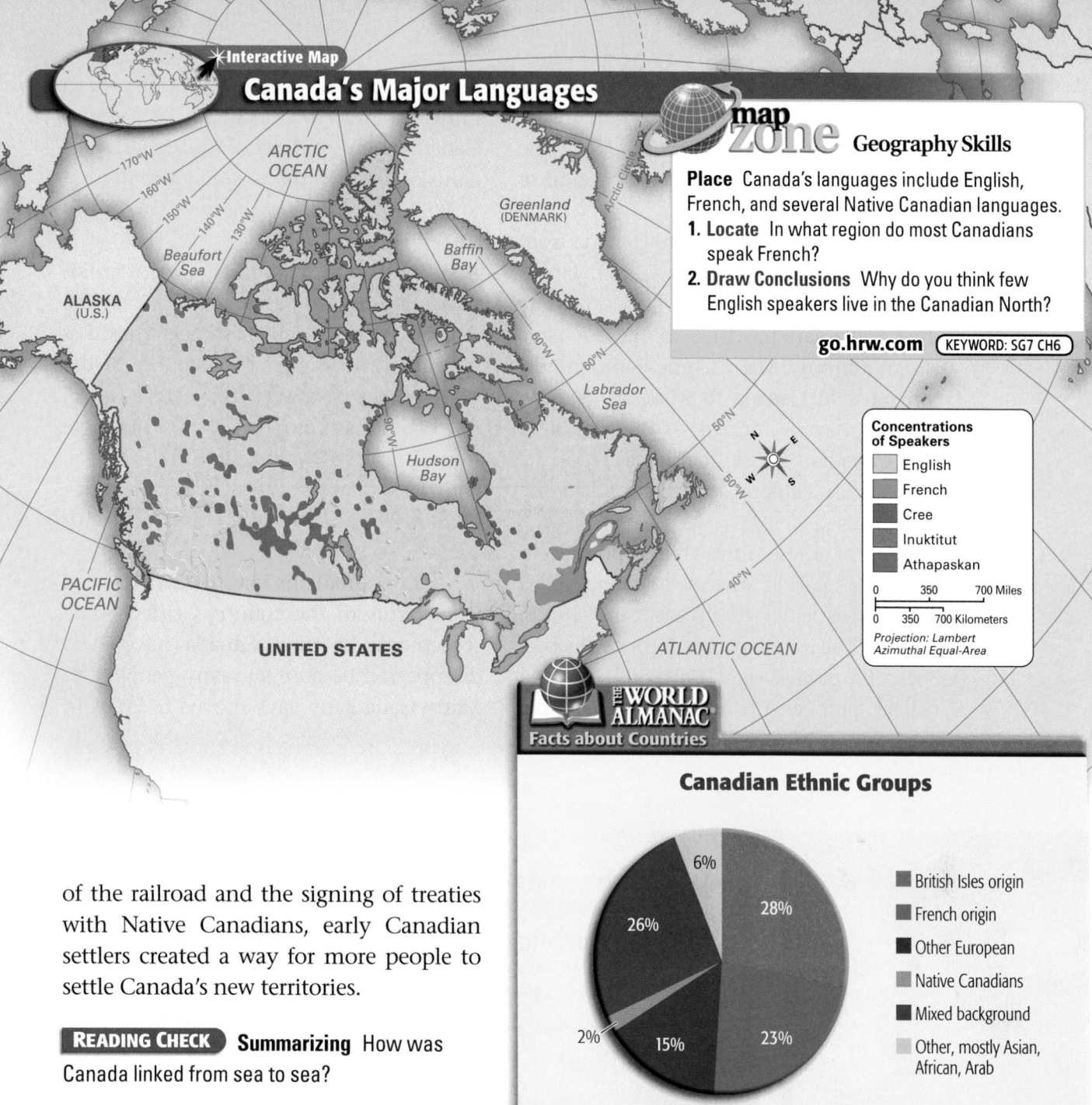

Canada's Major Languages

ARCTIC
OCEAN

170°W
160°W
150°W
140°W
130°W

Greenland
(DENMARK)

Baffin
Bay

ALASKA
(U.S.)

Beaufort
Sea

Labrador
Sea

Hudson
Bay

PACIFIC
OCEAN

UNITED STATES

ATLANTIC OCEAN

map zone Geography Skills

Place Canada's languages include English, French, and several Native Canadian languages.
1. **Locate** In what region do most Canadians speak French?
2. **Draw Conclusions** Why do you think few English speakers live in the Canadian North?

go.hrw.com KEYWORD: SG7 CH6

Concentrations of Speakers
- English
- French
- Cree
- Inuktitut
- Athapaskan

0   350   700 Miles
0 350 700 Kilometers
Projection: Lambert
Azimuthal Equal-Area

THE WORLD ALMANAC
Facts about Countries

Canadian Ethnic Groups

6%
28%
26%
23%
2%
15%

- British Isles origin
- French origin
- Other European
- Native Canadians
- Mixed background
- Other, mostly Asian, African, Arab

go.hrw.com KEYWORD: SG7 CH6

of the railroad and the signing of treaties with Native Canadians, early Canadian settlers created a way for more people to settle Canada's new territories.

READING CHECK **Summarizing** How was Canada linked from sea to sea?

Culture

Canada's people reflect a history of British and French colonial rule. In addition, the country has experienced waves of immigration. The country is home to a great variety of people who belong to different ethnic groups and cultures. Although individual groups still keep their own cultural ways, many Canadians have tried to create a single national identity.

Immigration

During the late 1800s and early 1900s, many immigrants came to Canada from Europe. Most were from Britain, Russia, and Germany. Some people also came from the United States. While most of these immigrants farmed, others worked in mines, forests, and factories.

Other immigrants were lured to Canada in 1897 by the discovery of gold in the Yukon Territory. Many people from the United States migrated north in search of Canada's gold.

Immigrants also came to Canada from Asian countries, especially China, Japan, and India. British Columbia became the first Canadian province to have a large Asian minority. Many Chinese immigrants migrated to Canada to work on the railroads. Chinese immigrants built most of the Canadian Pacific Railway, one of the railroad lines linking eastern Canada to the Pacific coast.

All of these immigrants played an important part in an economic boom that Canada experienced in the early 1900s. During these prosperous times, Quebec, New Brunswick, and Ontario produced wheat, pulp, and paper. British Columbia and Ontario supplied the country with minerals and hydroelectricity. As a result, Canadians enjoyed one of the highest standards of living in the world by the 1940s.

Movement to Cities

After World War II, another wave of immigrants from Europe arrived in Canada. Many settled in Canada's large cities. For example, **Toronto** has become one of the most culturally diverse cities in the world. The Europeans were joined by other people from Africa, the Caribbean, Latin America, and particularly Asia. Asian businesspeople have brought a great deal of wealth to Canada's economy.

Many Canadians have recently moved from farms to the country's cities. Some settlements in rural Canada have even disappeared because so many people left. Many Canadians have moved to cities in

FOCUS ON READING
What details of this paragraph could you add to a list of countries from which immigrants came?

Toronto

With about 5 million people, Toronto is Canada's largest city.

ANALYZING VISUALS How is Toronto's history reflected in this city square?

Vancouver's Chinatown

If you walked around Vancouver, British Columbia, you would quickly realize when you entered the neighborhood of Chinatown. First you would notice that most signs are in Chinese and you would hear some people speaking Chinese. Then you would realize most restaurants serve Chinese food, and shops sell colorful silk clothing, herbs, and art imported from China. If you were in the city for the Chinese New Year, you would probably see a parade of people in traditional Chinese dress. Vancouver's Chinatown is a unique place where Chinese culture is kept alive in Canada today.

Drawing Conclusions How is Vancouver's Chinatown a unique neighborhood?

Ontario to find jobs. Others moved to Vancouver, British Columbia, for its good job opportunities, mild climate, and location near plentiful resources. Resources such as oil, gas, potash, and uranium have provided wealth to many cities in the Western Provinces. However, the political and economic center of power remains in the cities of Ottawa, Toronto, and Montreal.

READING CHECK **Analyzing** How has immigration changed Canada?

SUMMARY AND PREVIEW In this section, you learned that Canada was greatly influenced by British and French settlement, the building of the railroad to the Pacific coast, immigration, and movement to cities. In the next section you will learn about Canada's regions and economy today.

Section 2 Assessment

go.hrw.com
Online Quiz
KEYWORD: SG7 HP6

Reviewing Ideas, Terms, and Places

1. **a. Recall** What is a **province**?
   b. Summarize How did Britain gain control of New France from the French?
   c. Elaborate How do you think the Canadian Pacific Railway changed Canada?
2. **a. Identify** What immigrant group helped build the railroads?
   b. Draw Conclusions Why did people migrate to Canada?
   c. Elaborate Why do you think many Canadians moved from farms to the cities?

Critical Thinking

3. **Analyzing** Draw a diagram like the one below. Using your notes, write a sentence in each box about how each topic influenced the next topic.

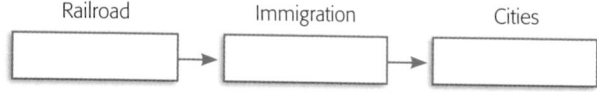

Railroad → Immigration → Cities

FOCUS ON SPEAKING

4. **Adding Details** Add information about the history and culture of Canada to your notes. Which details would most interest potential visitors?

Canada Today

What You Will Learn...

Main Ideas

1. Canada has a democratic government with a prime minister and a parliament.
2. Canada has four distinct geographic and cultural regions.
3. Canada's economy is largely based on trade with the United States.

The Big Idea

Canada's democratic government oversees the country's regions and economy.

Key Terms and Places

regionalism, *p. 157*
maritime, *p. 157*
Montreal, *p. 158*
Ottawa, *p. 159*
Vancouver, *p. 160*

TAKING NOTES As you read, take notes on Canada's four regions. Organize your notes in a chart like this one.

Eastern Provinces	Heartland	Western Provinces	Canadian North

If YOU lived there...

You and your family live in Toronto, Ontario. Your parents, who are architects, have been offered an important project in Montreal. If they accept it, you would live there for two years. Montreal is a major city in French–speaking Quebec. You would have to learn a new language. In Montreal, most street signs and advertisements are written in French.

How do you feel about moving to a city with a different language and culture?

BUILDING BACKGROUND Canada today has been shaped by both history and geography. Canada's first European settlers were French, but the British eventually controlled the territory. Differences in culture still remain, however. In addition, the four regions of Canada are separated by vast distances, economic activities, and culture.

Canada's Government

"Peace, order, and good government" is a statement from Canada's constitution that Canadians greatly value. Canadians are proud of their democratic government, which is led by a prime minister. Similar to a president, a prime minister is the head of a country's government.

Canada's prime minister oversees the country's parliament, Canada's governing body. Parliament consists of the House of Commons and the Senate. Canadians elect members of the House of Commons. However, senators are appointed by the prime minister.

Canada's 10 provincial governments are each led by a premier. These provincial governments are much like our state governments. Canada's central government is similar to our federal government. The Canadian federal system lets people keep their feelings of loyalty to their own province.

READING CHECK **Comparing** How is Canada's government similar to that of the United States?

Canada's Regions

Canada's physical geography separates the country into different regions. For example, people living on the Pacific coast in British Columbia are isolated from Canadians living in the eastern provinces on the Atlantic coast. Just as geographic distance separates much of Canada, differences in culture also define regions.

Regionalism

The cultural differences between English-speaking and French-speaking Canadians have led to problems. English is the main language in most of Canada. In Quebec, however, French is the main language. When Canadians from different regions discuss important issues, they are often influenced by regionalism. **Regionalism** refers to the strong connection that people feel toward the region in which they live.

In some places, this connection is stronger than people's connection to their country as a whole. To better understand regionalism in Canada, we will now explore each region of the country. As you read, refer to the map below to locate each region.

The Eastern Provinces

The region called the Eastern Provinces is a region that lies on the Atlantic coast of Canada. The provinces of New Brunswick, Nova Scotia, and Prince Edward Island are often called the Maritime Provinces. **Maritime** means on or near the sea. The province of Newfoundland and Labrador is usually not considered one of the Maritime Provinces. It includes the island of Newfoundland and a large region of the mainland called Labrador.

A short growing season limits farming in the Eastern Provinces. However, farmers in Prince Edward Island grow potatoes.

Interactive Map

Regions of Canada

Legend:
- The Eastern Provinces
- The Heartland
- The Western Provinces
- The Canadian North

0   500   1,000 Miles
0   500   1,000 Kilometers

Projection: Lambert Azimuthal Equal-Area

map zone

Geography Skills

Regions Canada has four distinct regions.
1. **Locate** What region is located on the Atlantic coast?
2. **Draw Conclusions** Why do you think few people live in the Canadian North?

go.hrw.com   KEYWORD: SG7 CH6

Quebec's Winter Carnival

At the annual Winter Carnival in the city of Quebec, millions of Canadians and visitors from around the world brave below-freezing temperatures to celebrate French Canadian culture.

The Inuit people traditionally used dogsleds as a means of transportation. Today dogsledding is a popular sport in Canada and a highlight of the carnival.

Most of the economy in Canada's Eastern Provinces is related to the forestry and fishing industries.

Many people in the Eastern Provinces are descendants of immigrants from the British Isles. In addition, French-speaking families have moved from Quebec to New Brunswick. Most of the region's people live in coastal cities. Many cities have industrial plants and serve as fishing and shipping ports. Along the Atlantic coast lies Halifax, Nova Scotia, the region's largest city.

The Heartland

FOCUS ON READING

In the paragraphs under The Heartland sort the facts into different lists.

Inland from the Eastern Provinces are Quebec and Ontario, which together are sometimes referred to as the Heartland. More than half of all Canadians live in these two provinces. In fact, the chain of cities that extends from Windsor, Ontario, to the city of Quebec is the country's most urbanized region.

The provincial capital of Quebec is also called Quebec. The city's older section has narrow streets, stone walls, and French-style architecture. **Montreal** is Canada's second-largest city and one of the largest French-speaking cities in the world. About 3.5 million people live in the Montreal metropolitan area. It is the financial and industrial center of the province. Winters in Montreal are very cold. To deal with this harsh environment, Montreal's people use underground passages and overhead tunnels to move between buildings in the city's downtown.

In Canada many residents of Quebec, called Quebecois (kay-buh-KWAH), believe their province should be given a special status. Quebecois argue that this status would recognize the cultural differences between their province and the rest of Canada. Some even want Quebec to become an independent country.

Many of the city's buildings reflect French architecture.

From the clues you see in this scene, what do you think is unique about French Canadian culture?

Ice sculptures created by Canadian and international artists line the carnival's grounds.

The carnival's mascot is a snowman who wears a traditional Canadian sash and hat.

On the other hand, many English-speaking Canadians think Quebec already has too many privileges. Most Canadians, however, still support a united Canada. Strong feelings of regionalism will continue to be an important issue.

With an even larger population than Quebec, the province of Ontario is Canada's leading manufacturing province. Hamilton, Ontario, is the center of Canada's steel industry. Canada exports much of its steel to the United States.

Ontario's capital, Toronto, is a major center for industry, finance, education, and culture. Toronto's residents come from many different parts of the world, including China, Europe, and India.

Canada's national capital, **Ottawa**, is also in Ontario. In Ottawa many people speak both English and French. The city is known for its grand government buildings, parks, and several universities.

The Western Provinces

West of Ontario are the prairie provinces of Manitoba, Saskatchewan, and Alberta. On the Pacific coast is the province of British Columbia. Together, these four provinces make up Canada's Western Provinces.

More people live in Quebec than in all of the prairie provinces combined. The southern grasslands of these provinces are part of a rich wheat belt. Farms here produce far more wheat than Canadians need. The extra wheat is exported. Oil and natural gas production is a very important economic activity in Alberta. The beauty of the Canadian Rockies attracts many visitors to national parks in western Alberta and eastern British Columbia.

British Columbia is Canada's westernmost province and home to almost 4 million people. This mountainous province has rich natural resources, including forests, salmon, and valuable minerals.

Even in June, snow covers the small town of Pond Inlet, Nunavut. The Inuit here travel by snowmobile and enjoy ice fishing.

Nearly half of British Columbia's population lives in and around the coastal city of **Vancouver**. The city's location on the Pacific coast helps it to trade with countries in Asia.

The Canadian North

Northern Canada is extremely cold due to its location close to the Arctic Circle. The region called the Canadian North includes the Yukon Territory, the Northwest Territories, and Nunavut (NOO-nuh-voot). These three territories cover more than a third of Canada but are home to only about 100,000 people.

Nunavut is a new territory created for the native Inuit people who live there. Nunavut means "Our Land" in the Inuit language. Even though Nunavut is part of Canada, the people there have their own **distinct** culture and government. About 30,000 people live in Nunavut.

The physical geography of the Canadian North includes forests and tundra. The frozen waters of the Arctic Ocean separate

ACADEMIC
VOCABULARY

distinct separate

isolated towns and villages. During some parts of the winter, sunlight is limited to only a few hours.

READING CHECK **Drawing Conclusions** How does geography affect the location of economic activities in the Western Provinces?

Canada's Economy

As you learned in Section 1, Canada has many valuable natural resources. Canada's economy is based on the industries associated with these resources. In addition, Canada's economy also benefits from trade.

Industries

Canada is one of the world's leading mineral producers. Canadians mine valuable titanium, zinc, iron ore, gold, and coal. Canada's iron and steel industry uses iron ore to manufacture products like planes, automobiles and household appliances. However, most Canadians work in the services industry. For example, tourism is

Canada's fastest-growing services industry. Canada's economy also benefits from the millions of dollars visitors spend in the country each year.

Trade

Canada's economy depends on trade. Many of Canada's natural resources that you have learned about are exported to countries around the world. Canada's leading trading partner is the United States.

As the world's largest trading relationship, Canada and the United States rely heavily on each other. About 60 percent of Canada's imported goods are from the United States. About 85 percent of Canada's exports, such as lumber, goes to the United States.

However, the United States placed tariffs, or added fees, on Canadian timber. American lumber companies accused Canada of selling their lumber at unfairly low prices. Canada argued that the tariffs were unfair according to the North American Free Trade Agreement (NAFTA).

The export of cattle to the United States is another area of dispute between the two countries. When a Canadian cow was discovered with mad cow disease in 2003, the United States banned the import of all cattle from Canada. Canadian ranchers now claim that all their cows are free of the disease. After a two-year ban, the United States imports Canadian cattle and beef again.

READING CHECK Summarizing What goods does Canada export?

SUMMARY AND PREVIEW In this section you learned that Canada has distinct regions based on geography and culture. The U.S. and Canada share a common history, a border, and the English language. Next, you will learn about the country of Mexico.

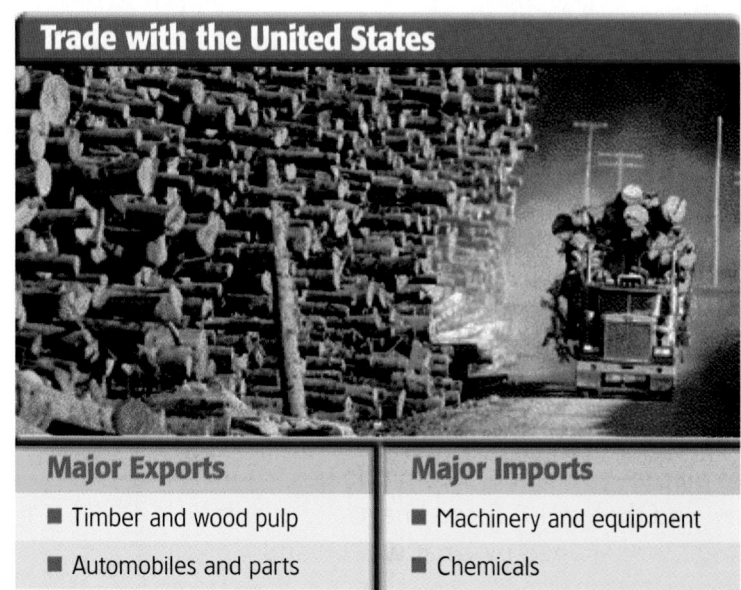

Trade with the United States

Major Exports	Major Imports
■ Timber and wood pulp	■ Machinery and equipment
■ Automobiles and parts	■ Chemicals
■ Aircraft	■ Consumer goods

Section 3 Assessment

go.hrw.com
Online Quiz
KEYWORD: SG7 HP6

Reviewing Ideas, Terms, and Places

1. **a. Recall** What office heads Canada's government?
   b. Summarize How is Canada's parliament structured?
2. **a. Define** What is **regionalism**?
   b. Contrast How are Canada's Western Provinces different from the Canadian North?
   c. Evaluate Why do you think the Quebecois want to break away from Canada?
3. **a. Describe** How are Canada's natural resources important to the country's economy?
   b. Draw Conclusions Why do Canada and the United States rely on each other as trading partners?

Critical Thinking

4. **Comparing and Contrasting** Use your notes to complete this chart. List the similarities and differences between the Eastern Provinces and Western Provinces.

Similarities	Differences
1.	1.
2.	

FOCUS ON SPEAKING

5. **Presenting Canada Today** Add details about Canada today to your notes. Consider which images you will use to persuade your audience to visit Canada after they listen to your ad.

Using Mental Maps and Sketch Maps

Learn

We create maps in our heads of all kinds of places—our schools, communities, country, and the world. These images, or mental maps, are shaped by what we see and experience.

We use mental maps of places when we draw sketch maps. A sketch map uses very simple shapes to show the relationship between places and the relative size of places. Notice the sketch map of the world shown here. It may not look like any other map in your book, but it does give you an idea of what the world looks like.

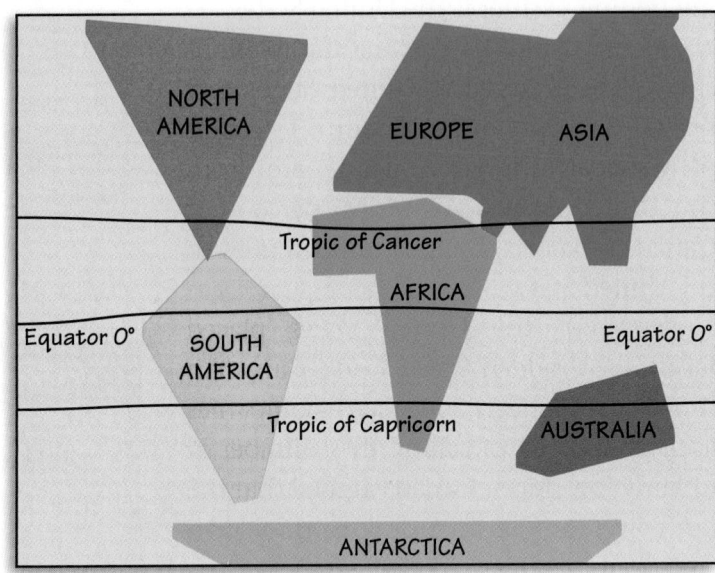

Practice

Does your mental map of the world look like the sketch map here? It is alright if they do not look exactly alike. Now think about the places in your own neighborhood. Use your mental map to draw a sketch map of your neighborhood. Then use your sketch map to answer the following questions.

- What are the most important features of your map?
- What is the largest building in your neighborhood?
- What labels did you use on your map?

Apply

Draw a sketch map of Canada. Make sure to include the cities and physical features you learned about in this chapter. Then exchange your map with another student. Ask your partner to make corrections to your map if he or she does not understand it.

Chapter Review

Geography's Impact
video series
Review the video to answer the closing question:
Why did the people of Nunavut want their own territory?

Visual Summary

Use the visual summary below to help you review the main ideas of the chapter.

QUICK FACTS

Canada has cold climates and its physical features include rugged mountains.

Native Canadian and European settlement has influenced Canadian culture.

Canada has distinctive cultural regions today.

Reviewing Vocabulary, Terms, and Places

Choose the letter of the answer that best completes each statement below.

1. A physical feature of rocky uplands, lakes, and swamps in Canada is called the
   a. Niagara Falls.
   b. Great Lakes.
   c. Grand Banks.
   d. Canadian Shield.

2. Which part of Canada did the French settle?
   a. Ontario
   b. New Brunswick
   c. Quebec
   d. British Colombia

3. What province was the first to have a large Asian population?
   a. Manitoba
   b. British Columbia
   c. Quebec
   d. Saskatchewan

4. A strong connection that people feel toward their region is called
   a. maritime.
   b. province.
   c. heartland.
   d. regionalism.

Comprehension and Critical Thinking

SECTION 1 *(Pages 146–149)*

5. a. **Define** What is pulp?
   b. **Make Inferences** What is the coldest area in Canada?
   c. **Evaluate** What makes the Grand Banks an ideal fishing ground?

SECTION 2 *(Pages 150–155)*

6. a. **Identify** Who were the first Canadians?
   b. **Draw Conclusions** Why did Canadians build a rail line across Canada?
   c. **Predict** Do you think Canada's cities will increase or decrease in population in the future? Explain your answers.

SECTION 3 *(Pages 156–161)*

7. a. **Recall** What kind of government does Canada have?

   b. Compare and Contrast How are the Eastern Provinces different than the Western Provinces?

   c. Evaluate Why do the Quebecois see themselves as different from other Canadians?

Using the Internet

8. **Activity: Writing Newspaper Articles** You are a reporter for The Quebec Chronicle assigned to write articles for the next issue of the newspaper. Enter the activity keyword to meet the people of Quebec and find background information for your articles covering Quebec. Use the links provided to conduct your research and then write three short articles. Go to press using the interactive template and publish your Canadian newspaper.

FOCUS ON READING AND SPEAKING

9. **Understanding Lists** Use your notes about Canada to create a list of important facts from each section. Organize your lists using this chart.

Physical Geography	History and Culture	Canada Today

10. **Creating a Tourism Ad** Now that you have collected notes on Canada's geography, history, and culture, choose the information you think will be most appealing to visitors. Write a one minute radio script, using descriptive and persuasive language to convince your audience to visit Canada. Describe Canada in a way that will capture your audience's imagination. Ask the class to listen carefully as you read your radio ad to them. Then ask the class to evaluate your ad on how persuasive it was or was not.

Social Studies Skills

11. **Using Mental Maps and Sketch Maps** Without looking at a map of Canada think about what the Eastern Provinces look like. Then create a sketch map of the Eastern Provinces. Make sure to include a compass rose and important physical features.

Map Activity

12. **Canada** On a separate sheet of paper, match the letters on the map with their correct labels.

Rocky Mountains   Manitoba

Nunavut   St. Lawrence River

Vancouver

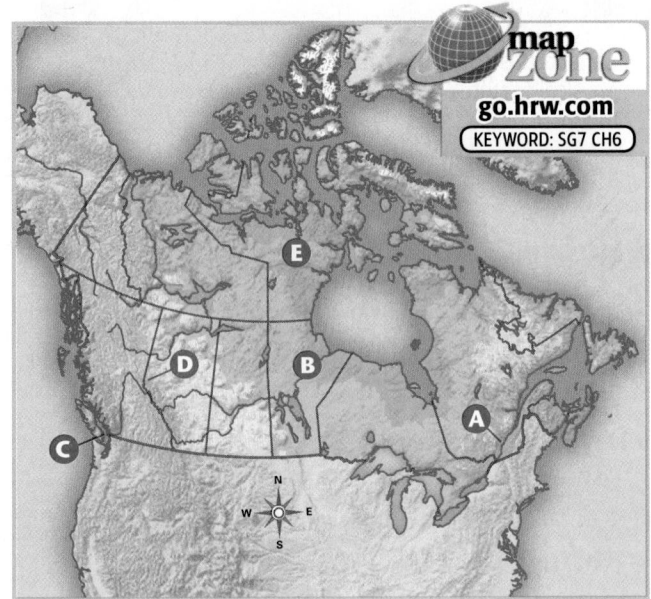

go.hrw.com
KEYWORD: SG7 CH6

Standardized Test Practice

DIRECTIONS: Read questions 1 through 7 and write the letter of the best response. Then read question 8 and write your own well-constructed response.

1 The United States and Canada share which physical feature?

A Canadian Shield

B Rocky Mountains

C Hudson Bay

D Saskatchewan River

2 What resource in Canada provides pulp and newsprint?

A forests

B nickel

C potash

D fish

3 Many Canadians moved from farms to cities to find

A gold.

B good schools.

C jobs.

D better weather.

4 Canada's prime minister oversees the country's

A railroads.

B parliament.

C provincial governments.

D city governments.

5 Canada's capital, Ottawa, is located in

A Northwest Territories.

B Nova Scotia.

C Ontario.

D British Columbia.

Climate of British Columbia

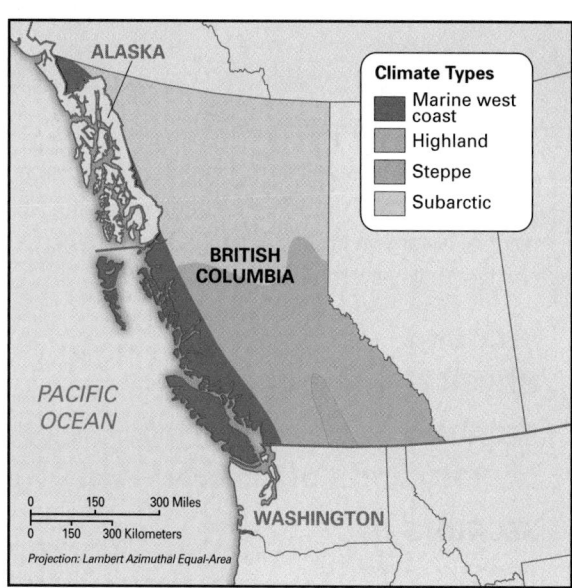

6 Based on the map above, which climate type does the Pacific coast of British Columbia experience?

A subarctic

B marine west coast

C highland

D steppe

7 About 60 percent of Canada's imported goods come from which country?

A Mexico

B Greenland

C Russia

D United States

8 Extended Response Look at the political map of Canada at the beginning of this chapter. Using information from the map, explain why the United States and Canada are major trading partners.

CHAPTER 7

Mexico

What You Will Learn…

In this chapter you will learn about Mexico's physical geography. You will also study the influence of early cultures and Spanish colonial history on Mexico's culture. Today, Mexico is experiencing changes in its government and economy.

FOCUS ON READING AND WRITING

Predicting Predicting is trying to guess what will happen next. As you read a chapter, stop along the way and consider what you have read. Does the text provide any clues about what will happen next? If it does, see if you can make a prediction about the text. **See the lesson, Predicting, on page R9.**

Writing an "I Am" Poem Countries have a tale to tell, just like people do. As you read this chapter, gather details about Mexico—how it looks, what its history was like, and what it is like today. Then write an "I Am" poem from the point of view of Mexico telling what you have learned.

Culture Brightly costumed dancers perform a traditional dance in Cancún.

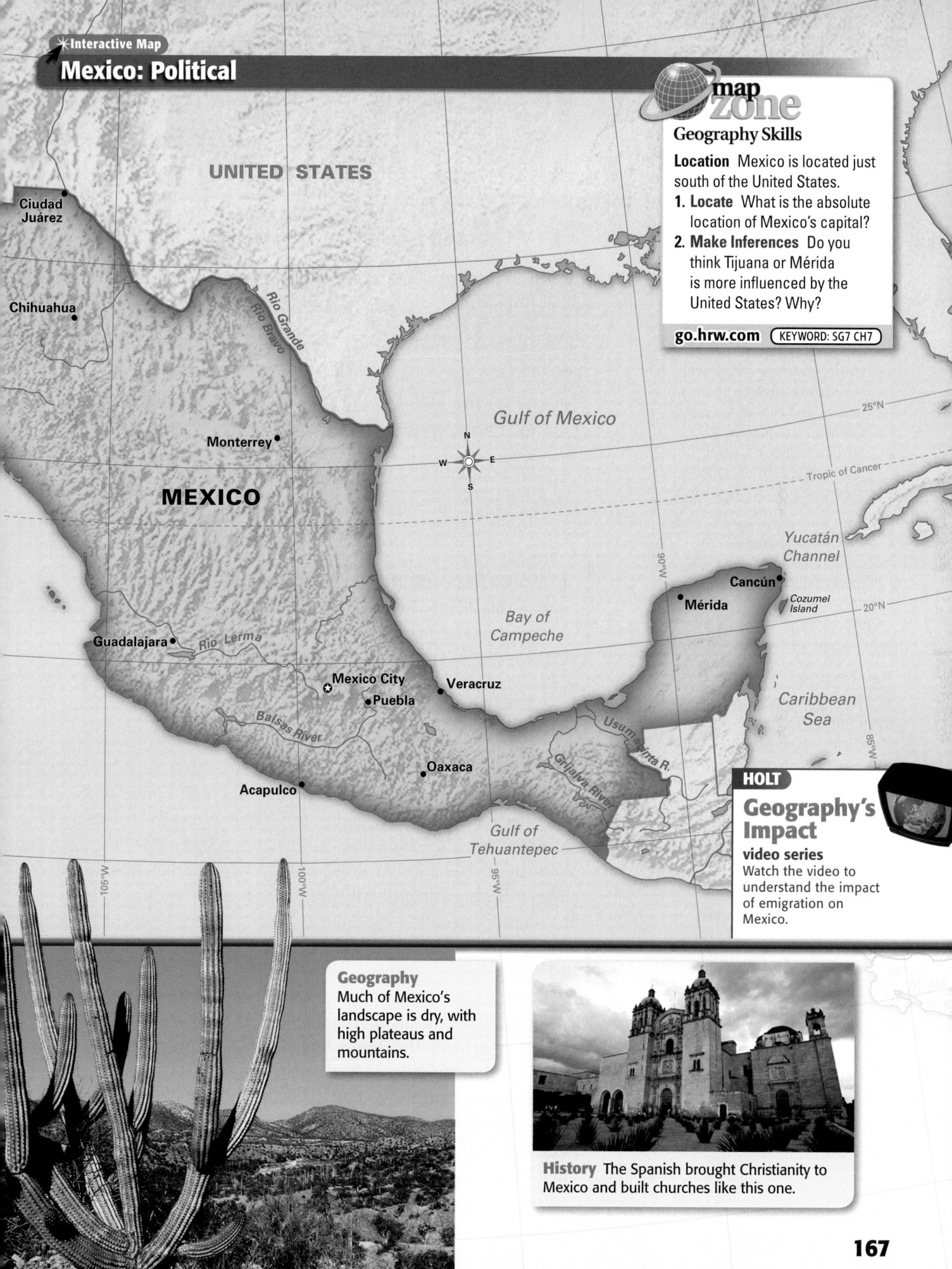

map zone

Geography Skills

Location Mexico is located just south of the United States.

1. **Locate** What is the absolute location of Mexico's capital?
2. **Make Inferences** Do you think Tijuana or Mérida is more influenced by the United States? Why?

go.hrw.com KEYWORD: SG7 CH7

UNITED STATES

Ciudad Juárez

Chihuahua

Rio Grande / Rio Bravo

Monterrey

MEXICO

Guadalajara

Rio Lerma

Mexico City

Puebla

Balsas River

Acapulco

Oaxaca

Gulf of Mexico

25°N

Tropic of Cancer

Yucatán Channel

Cancún

Mérida

Cozumel Island

20°N

Bay of Campeche

Veracruz

Usumacinta R.

Grijalva River

Caribbean Sea

Gulf of Tehuantepec

105°W

100°W

96°W

90°W

98°W

HOLT

Geography's Impact

video series
Watch the video to understand the impact of emigration on Mexico.

Geography
Much of Mexico's landscape is dry, with high plateaus and mountains.

History The Spanish brought Christianity to Mexico and built churches like this one.

167

Physical Geography

What You Will Learn...

Main Ideas

1. Mexico's physical features include plateaus, mountains, and coastal lowlands.
2. Mexico's climate and vegetation include deserts, tropical forests, and cool highlands.
3. Key natural resources in Mexico include oil, silver, gold, and scenic landscapes.

The Big Idea

Mexico is a large country with different natural environments in its northern, central, and southern regions.

Key Terms and Places

Río Bravo (Rio Grande), *p. 168*
peninsula, *p. 168*
Baja California, *p. 168*
Gulf of Mexico, *p. 168*
Yucatán Peninsula, *p. 168*
Sierra Madre, *p. 169*

TAKING NOTES As you read, use a graphic organizer like the one below to take notes on Mexico's physical geography.

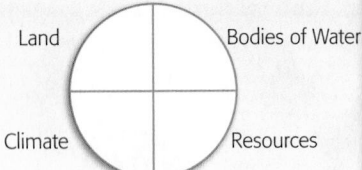

Land | Bodies of Water
Climate | Resources

If YOU lived there...

You live on Mexico's Pacific coast. Sunny weather and good beaches bring tourists year-round. Now you are on your way to visit a cousin in Puebla, in the highlands. To get there, you will have to take a bus along the winding roads of the steep Sierra Madre Occidental. This rugged mountain range runs along the coast. You have never been to the interior of Mexico before.

What landscapes will you see on your trip?

BUILDING BACKGROUND Mexico is part of Latin America, a region in the Western Hemisphere where Spanish and Portuguese culture shaped life. Mexico is also part of North America, along with the United States and Canada. Unlike its northern neighbors, Mexico's landscape consists mainly of highlands and coastal plains.

Physical Features

Mexico, our neighbor to the south, shares a long border with the United States. Forming part of this border is one of Mexico's few major rivers, the **Río Bravo**. In the United States this river is called the Rio Grande. At other places along the U.S.–Mexico border it is impossible to tell where one country ends and the other country begins.

Bodies of Water

As you can see on the map, except for its border with the United States, Mexico is mostly surrounded by water. Mexico's border in the west is the Pacific Ocean. Stretching south into the Pacific Ocean from northern Mexico is a narrow **peninsula**, or piece of land surrounded on three sides by water, called **Baja California**. To the east, Mexico's border is the **Gulf of Mexico**. The Gulf of Mexico is separated from the Caribbean Sea by a part of Mexico called the **Yucatán** (yoo-kah-TAHN) **Peninsula**.

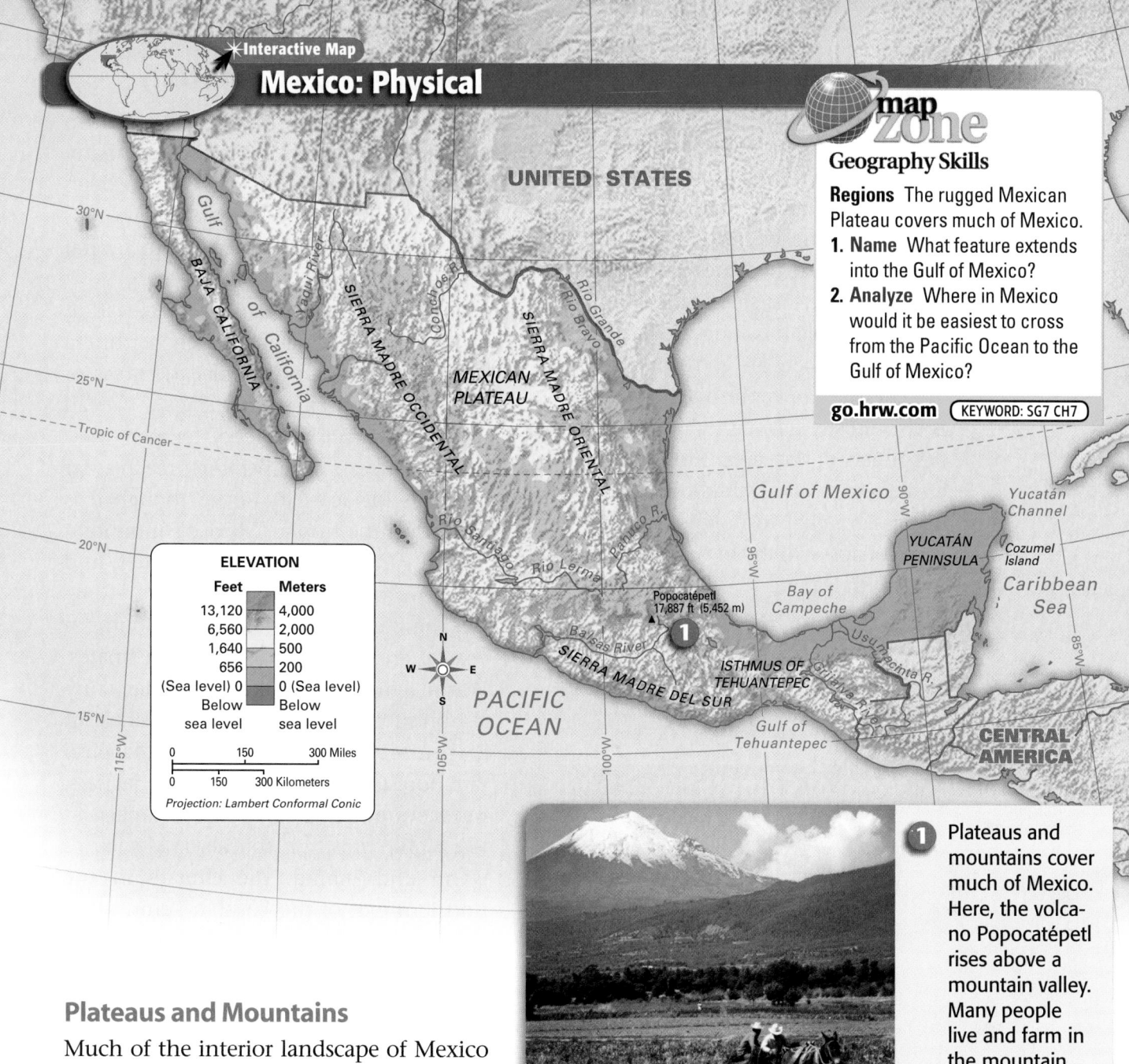

map zone

Geography Skills

Regions The rugged Mexican Plateau covers much of Mexico.

1. **Name** What feature extends into the Gulf of Mexico?
2. **Analyze** Where in Mexico would it be easiest to cross from the Pacific Ocean to the Gulf of Mexico?

go.hrw.com [KEYWORD: SG7 CH7]

UNITED STATES

Gulf of California

BAJA CALIFORNIA

SIERRA MADRE OCCIDENTAL

SIERRA MADRE ORIENTAL

MEXICAN PLATEAU

Yaqui River

Conchos R.

Rio Grande

Rio Bravo

Rio Santiago

Rio Lerma

Panuco R.

Gulf of Mexico

YUCATÁN PENINSULA

Yucatán Channel

Cozumel Island

Caribbean Sea

Popocatépetl 17,887 ft (5,452 m)

Bay of Campeche

Balsas River

Usumacinta R.

Grijalva River

SIERRA MADRE DEL SUR

ISTHMUS OF TEHUANTEPEC

PACIFIC OCEAN

Gulf of Tehuantepec

CENTRAL AMERICA

ELEVATION

Feet	Meters
13,120	4,000
6,560	2,000
1,640	500
656	200
(Sea level) 0	0 (Sea level)
Below sea level	Below sea level

0   150   300 Miles

0   150   300 Kilometers

Projection: Lambert Conformal Conic

1 Plateaus and mountains cover much of Mexico. Here, the volcano Popocatépetl rises above a mountain valley. Many people live and farm in the mountain valleys.

Plateaus and Mountains

Much of the interior landscape of Mexico consists of a high, mostly rugged region called the Mexican Plateau. The plateau's lowest point is more than a half mile above sea level. Its highest point is close to two miles above sea level. The entire plateau spreads between two mountain ranges that rise still higher. One range, the Sierra Madre Oriental, lies in the east. The other, the Sierra Madre Occidental, lies in the west. Together, these two mountain ranges and another shorter one in southern Mexico make up the **Sierra Madre** (SYER-rah MAH-dray), or "mother range."

Between the two ranges in the south lies the Valley of Mexico. Mexico City, the country's capital, is located there. The mountains south of Mexico City include towering, snowcapped volcanoes. Volcanic eruptions, as well as earthquakes, are a threat there. The volcano Popocatépetl (poh-puh-cah-TE-pet-uhl) near Mexico City has been active as recently as 2000.

FOCUS ON READING

What do you think the text will discuss next?

Coastal Lowlands

From the highlands in central Mexico, the land slopes down to the coasts. Beautiful, sunny beaches stretch all along Mexico's eastern and western coasts. The plain that runs along the west coast is fairly wide in the north. It becomes narrower in the south. On the east side of the country, the Gulf coastal plain is wide and flat. The soils and climate there are good for farming.

ACADEMIC VOCABULARY

vary to be different

The Yucatán Peninsula in the southeast is also mostly flat. Limestone rock underlies much of the area. Erosion there has created caves and sinkholes, steep-sided depressions that form when the roof of a cave collapses. Many of these sinkholes are filled with water.

READING CHECK **Summarizing** What are Mexico's major physical features?

Climate and Vegetation

From snowcapped mountain peaks to warm, sunny beaches, Mexico has many different climates. You can see Mexico's climate regions on the map below. This great variety of climates results in several different types of vegetation.

In some areas, changes in elevation cause climates to **vary** widely within a short distance. For example, the areas of high elevation on the Mexican Plateau can have surprisingly cool temperatures. At times, freezing temperatures reach as far south as Mexico City—even though it is located in the tropics. Mexico's mountain valleys generally have mild climates, and many people have settled there.

The valleys along Mexico's southern coastal areas also have pleasant climates. Warm temperatures and a summer rainy season support the forests that cover about 25 percent of Mexico's land area. Tropical rain forests provide a home for jaguars, monkeys, anteaters, and other animals.

While most of southern Mexico is warm and humid, the climate in the northern part of the Yucatán Peninsula is hot and dry. The main vegetation there is scrub forest.

✴Interactive Map
Mexico: Climate

Climate Types

■ Humid tropical
■ Tropical savanna
■ Desert
■ Steppe
■ Highland

0   200   400 Miles
0   200   400 Kilometers

Projection: Lambert Conformal Conic

Gulf of California

25°N

Tropic of Cancer

PACIFIC OCEAN

20°N

15°N

110°W   105°W   100°W   95°W

Gulf of Mexico

map zone Geography Skills

Regions Mexico's climate regions range from dry to tropical.
1. **Locate** Where is Mexico's desert climate located?
2. **Interpret** What part of Mexico probably gets the most rain?

go.hrw.com (KEYWORD: SG7 CH7)

A Tropical Climate
A tropical savanna climate supports lush vegetation along Mexico's southern beaches.

Like the Yucatán Peninsula in the south, most of northern Mexico is dry. The deserts in Baja California and the northern part of the plateau get little rainfall. Desert plants and dry grasslands are common in the north. Cougars, coyotes, and deer live in some areas of the desert.

READING CHECK **Analyzing** Why does Mexico City sometimes experience freezing temperatures even though it is in the tropics?

Natural Resources

Mexico is rich in natural resources. One of its most important resources is petroleum, or oil. Oil reserves are found mainly under the southern and Gulf coastal plains as well as offshore in the Gulf of Mexico. Mexico sells much of its oil to the United States.

Before oil was discovered in Mexico, minerals were the country's most valuable resource. Some gold and silver mines that were begun many centuries ago are still in operation. In addition, new mines have been developed in Mexico's mountains. Today Mexico's mines produce more silver than any other country in the world. Mexican mines also yield large amounts of copper, gold, lead, and zinc.

Another important resource is water. The refreshing water surrounding Mexico draws many tourists to the country's scenic beaches. Unfortunately, water is limited in many parts of Mexico. Water scarcity is a serious issue.

READING CHECK **Finding Main Ideas** What is one of Mexico's most important resources?

SUMMARY AND PREVIEW The natural environments of Mexico range from arid plateaus in the north to humid, forested mountains in the south. Next, you will study the history and culture of Mexico.

go.hrw.com
Online Quiz
KEYWORD: SG7 HP7

Section 1 Assessment

Reviewing Ideas, Terms, and Places

1. **a. Describe** What is the interior of Mexico like?
   b. Analyze Do you think the **Yucatán Peninsula** is a good place for farming? Explain your answer.
2. **a. Recall** What is the climate like in the northern part of the Yucatán Peninsula?
   b. Explain Why can climates sometimes vary widely within a short distance?
   c. Elaborate How do you think climate and vegetation affect where people live in Mexico?
3. **a. Identify** Where are Mexico's oil reserves located?
   b. Make Inferences What problems might water scarcity cause for Mexican citizens?
   c. Elaborate How are Mexico's location, climate, and physical features also natural resources?

Critical Thinking

4. **Categorizing** Draw a chart like the one here. Using your notes, list the geographical features found in northern Mexico and southern Mexico.

	Geography
Northern Mexico	
Southern Mexico	

FOCUS ON WRITING

5. **Telling What Mexico Looks Like** What features of Mexico's physical geography will you include in your "I Am" poem? Write notes about the physical features, climate and vegetation, and natural resources of Mexico.

History and Culture

Main Ideas

1. Early cultures of Mexico included the Olmec, the Maya, and the Aztec.
2. Mexico's period as a Spanish colony and its struggles since independence have shaped its culture.
3. Spanish and native cultures have influenced Mexico's customs and traditions today.

The Big Idea

Native American cultures and Spanish colonization shaped Mexican history and culture.

Key Terms

empire, *p. 173*
mestizos, *p. 174*
missions, *p. 174*
haciendas, *p. 174*

TAKING NOTES As you read, use a graphic organizer like the one below to help you organize your notes on Mexico's history and culture.

	Event or Detail
Early Cultures	
Colonial Times and Independence	
Culture	

If **YOU** lived there...

You belong to one of the native Indian peoples in southern Mexico in the early 1500s. Years ago, the Aztec rulers went to war against your people. They took many captives. They have always treated you cruelly. Now some strangers have come from across the sea. They want your people to help them conquer the Aztecs.

Will you help the strangers fight the Aztecs? Why or why not?

BUILDING BACKGROUND Mexico was home to several of the earliest advanced cultures in the Americas. Early farmers there developed crops that became staples in much of North America. Mexico also has valuable minerals, which drew Spanish conquerors and colonists. Spanish culture blended with native Mexican cultures.

Early Cultures

People first came to Mexico many thousands of years ago. As early as 5,000 years ago, they were growing beans, peppers, and squash. They also domesticated an early form of corn. Farming allowed these people to build the first permanent settlements in the Americas.

Early Cultures of Mexico

Olmec

- The Olmec made sculptures of giant stone heads.
- The heads may have represented rulers or gods.

Olmec

By about 1500 BC the Olmec people in Mexico were living in small villages. The Olmec lived on the humid southern coast of the Gulf of Mexico, where they built temples and giant statues. They also traded carved stones like jade and obsidian with other cultures in eastern Mexico.

Maya

A few hundred years later, the Maya built on the achievements of the Olmec. Between about AD 250 and 900, the Maya built large cities in Mexico and Central America. In these cities they built stone temples to worship their gods. They studied the stars and developed a detailed calendar. They also kept written records that scholars still study today to learn about Maya history. However, scholars do not fully understand why Maya civilization suddenly collapsed sometime after 900.

Aztec

After the decline of the Maya civilization, people called the Aztecs moved to central Mexico from the north. In 1325 they built their capital on an island in a lake. Known as Tenochtitlán (tay-nawch-teet-LAHN), this capital grew into one of the largest and most impressive cities of its time.

The Aztecs also built a large, powerful empire. An **empire** is a land with different territories and peoples under a single ruler.

CONNECTING TO Technology

Chinampas

The Aztecs practiced a form of raised-field farming in the swampy lake areas of central Mexico. They called these raised fields *chinampas*. To make them, Aztec farmers piled earth on rafts anchored to trees in the lake. There they grew the corn, beans, and squash that most people ate.

Analyzing Why do you think the Aztecs decided to build raised fields for their crops?

The Aztecs planted trees in the lake to anchor the rafts.

The Aztecs built their empire through conquest. They defeated their neighboring tribes in war. Then they forced the other people to pay taxes and to provide war captives for sacrifice to the Aztec gods.

READING CHECK **Summarizing** What were some achievements of Mexico's early cultures?

Maya

- The Maya had a trade network between cities.

- This Maya pyramid stands in Uxmal.

Aztec

- The Aztecs built the first empire in the Americas.

- Aztec artisans made art like this turquoise mask.

Colonial Mexico and Independence

FOCUS ON READING
What do you think will happen to the Aztec Empire?

In spite of its great size and power, the Aztec Empire did not last long after the first Europeans landed in Mexico. In 1519 Hernán Cortés, a Spanish soldier, arrived in Mexico with about 600 men. These conquistadors (kahn-KEES-tuh-dawrz), or conquerors, gained allies from other tribes in the region. They also had guns and horses, which the Aztecs had never seen before. The new weapons terrified the Aztecs and gave the Spanish an advantage.

The Spanish also unknowingly brought European diseases such as smallpox. The Aztecs had no resistance to these diseases, so many of them died. Greatly weakened by disease, the Aztecs were defeated. In 1521 Cortés claimed the land for Spain.

Colonial Times

After the conquest, Spanish and American Indian peoples and cultures mixed. This mixing formed a new Mexican identity. Spaniards called people of mixed European and Indian ancestry **mestizos** (me-STEE-zohs). When Africans were brought to America as slaves, they added to this mix of peoples. The Spaniards called people of mixed European and African ancestry mulattoes (muh-LAH-tohs). Africans and American Indians also intermarried.

Life in colonial Mexico was greatly influenced by the Roman Catholic Church. Large areas of northern Mexico were left to the church to explore and to rule. Church outposts known as **missions** were scattered throughout the area. Priests at the missions learned native languages and taught the Indians Spanish. They also worked to convert the American Indians to Catholicism.

In addition to spreading Christianity, the Spaniards wanted to find gold and silver in Mexico. American Indians and enslaved Africans did most of the hard physical labor in the mines. As a result, many died from disease and overwork.

Like mining, agriculture became an important part of the colonial economy. After the conquest, the Spanish monarch granted **haciendas** (hah-see-EN-duhs), or huge expanses of farm or ranch land, to some favored people of Spanish ancestry. Peasants, usually Indians, lived and worked on these haciendas. The haciendas made their owners very wealthy.

Hidalgo Calls for Independence

Miguel Hidalgo (center, in black) calls for independence from Spain in 1810. The famous Mexican painter Juan O'Gorman painted this image.

ANALYZING VISUALS What kinds of people joined Hidalgo in his revolt?

Independence

Spain ruled Mexico for almost 300 years before the people of Mexico demanded independence. The revolt against Spanish rule was led by a Catholic priest named Miguel Hidalgo. In 1810, he gave a famous speech calling for the common people to rise up against the Spanish. Hidalgo was killed in 1811, but fighting continued until Mexico won its independence in 1821.

Later Struggles

Fifteen years after Mexico gained its independence, a large area, Texas, broke away. Eventually, Texas joined the United States. As a result, Mexico and the United States fought over Texas and the location of their shared border. This conflict led to the Mexican-American War, in which Mexico lost nearly half its territory to the United States.

In the mid-1800s, Mexico faced other challenges. During this time, the popular president Benito Juárez helped Mexico survive a French invasion. He also made reforms that reduced the privileges of the church and the army.

In spite of these reforms, in the early 1900s the president helped the hacienda owners take land from peasants. Also, foreign companies owned huge amounts of land in Mexico and, in turn, influenced Mexican politics. Many Mexicans thought the president gave these large landowners too many privileges.

As a result, the Mexican Revolution broke out in 1910. The fighting lasted 10 years. One major result of the Mexican Revolution was land reform. The newly formed government took land from the large landowners and gave it back to the peasant villages.

READING CHECK **Sequencing** What events occurred after Mexico gained independence?

BIOGRAPHY

Benito Juárez
(1806–1872)

Benito Juárez was Mexico's first president of Indian heritage. A wise and passionate leader, Juárez stood up for the rights of all Mexicans. As the minister of justice, he got rid of special courts for members of the church and the military. As president, he passed reforms that laid the foundation for a democratic government. Today he is considered a national hero in Mexico.

Drawing Conclusions How may Juárez's heritage have affected his efforts for Mexico's citizens?

Culture

Mexico's history has **influenced** its culture. For example, one major influence from history is language. Most Mexicans speak Spanish because of the Spanish influence in colonial times. Another influence from Spain is religion. About 90 percent of all Mexicans are Roman Catholic.

However, Mexico's culture also reflects its American Indian heritage. For example, many people still speak American Indian languages. In Mexico, a person's language is tied to his or her ethnic group. Speaking an American Indian language identifies a person as Indian.

Mexicans also have some unique cultural practices that combine elements of Spanish influence with the influence of Mexican Indians. An example of this combining can be seen in a holiday called Day of the Dead. This holiday is a day to remember and honor dead ancestors.

ACADEMIC VOCABULARY
influence change or have an effect on

Day of the Dead

Everyone is sad when a loved one dies. But during Day of the Dead, Mexicans celebrate death as part of life. This attitude comes from the Mexican Indian belief that the souls of the dead return every year to visit their living relatives. To prepare for this visit, Mexican families gather in graveyards. They clean up around their loved one's grave and decorate it with flowers and candles. They also set out food and drink for the celebration. Favorite foods often include sugar candy skulls, chocolate coffins, and sweet breads shaped like bones.

Summarizing Why do Mexicans celebrate Day of the Dead?

Mexicans celebrate Day of the Dead on November 1 and 2. These dates are similar to the dates that the Catholic Church honors the dead with All Souls' Day. The holiday also reflects native customs and beliefs about hopes of life after death.

READING CHECK **Categorizing** What aspects of Mexican culture show the influence of Spanish rule?

SUMMARY AND PREVIEW Mexico's early cultures formed great civilizations, but after the conquest of the Aztec Empire, power in Mexico shifted to Spain. Spain ruled Mexico for nearly 300 years before Mexico gained independence. Mexico's history and its mix of Indian and Spanish backgrounds have influenced the country's culture. In the next section you will learn about life in Mexico today.

Section 2 Assessment

go.hrw.com
Online Quiz
KEYWORD: SG7 HP7

Reviewing Ideas, Terms, and Places

1. **a. Recall** Where in Mexico did the Olmec live?
   b. Explain How did the Aztecs build and rule their **empire**?
   c. Elaborate Why do you think scholars are not sure what caused the end of Maya civilization?
2. **a. Identify** Who began the revolt that led to Mexico's independence?
   b. Explain What was Mexico like in colonial times?
   c. Predict How may history have been different if the Aztecs had defeated the Spanish?
3. **a. Identify** What Mexican holiday honors dead ancestors?
   b. Summarize How did Mexico's colonial past shape its culture?

Critical Thinking

4. **Sequencing** Draw a diagram like the one below. Then, using your notes, list the major events in Mexico's history in the order they happened.

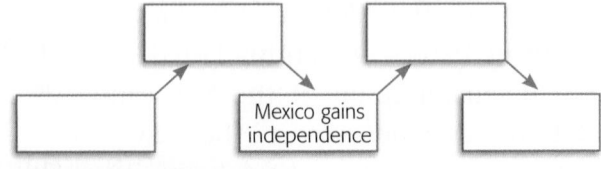
Mexico gains independence

FOCUS ON WRITING

5. **Learning about History and Culture** Mexico's history is full of fascinating stories. In your notebook, jot down ideas about people and stories from Mexico's history.

Social Studies Skills

| Chart and Graph | Critical Thinking | Geography | Study |

Taking Notes

Learn

Taking notes can help you remember what you have learned from your textbook or in class. To be effective, your notes must be clear and organized. One good way to organize your notes is in a chart like the one here. Use the following steps to help you take useful notes:

- Before you read: Divide a page in your notebook into two columns as shown.

- While you read: Write down your notes in phrases or sentences in the large column on the right.

- After you read: Review your notes. Then in the small column on the left, jot down ideas, key terms, or questions in your own words based on the notes you took.

Recall	Notes
New Mexican identity	- Spanish and American Indian cultures mixed. - mestizos - Africans came as slaves.
Influence on Catholic Church	- Life in colonial Mexico was influenced by the Roman Catholic Church. - missions - Priests taught Spanish.
Economy: mining and agriculture	- Spaniards were interested in gold and silver. - American Indians and enslaved Africans worked in mines. - Agriculture was important. - haciendas

Practice

Answer the following questions about taking notes.

1 Where should you write your notes while you read or listen in class?

2 How can jotting down key ideas, terms, and questions help you clarify your notes after you take them?

Apply

Look back at Section 1 of this chapter. Divide your paper into two columns and take notes on the section using the suggestions above. Then answer the following questions.

1. What ideas or questions did you write in the Recall column on the left?

2. What are some advantages of taking notes?

Mexico Today

If YOU lived there...

For many years, your family has lived in a small village in southern Mexico. Jobs are scarce there. Your older brother and sisters talk about moving to a larger city. Big cities may provide some more opportunities, but they can be crowded and noisy. Many people from your village have already gone to the city.

How do you feel about moving to the city?

BUILDING BACKGROUND After Mexico gained independence, many government leaders did not rule democratically. For years the Mexican people had little say in their government. But changes in the 1990s and 2000s led toward more democracy and prosperity.

Government and Economy

Today people in Mexico can vote in certain elections for the first time. People can find jobs in cities and buy their families a home. More children are able to attend school. In recent years, changes in Mexico's government and economy have made improvements like these possible.

Government

Mexico has a democratic government. However, Mexico is not like the United States where different political parties have always competed for power. In Mexico the same political party controlled the government for 71 years. But this control ended in 2000 when Mexicans elected Vicente Fox their president. Fox represented a different political party.

For many years, Mexico's government controlled most of the country's economic activity. Today the government has less control of the economy.

Economy

Mexico is a developing country. It has struggled with debts to foreign banks, unemployment, and inflation. **Inflation** is a rise in prices that occurs when currency loses its buying power.

Although living standards in Mexico are lower than in many other countries, Mexico's economy is growing. The North American Free Trade Agreement (NAFTA), which took effect in 1994, has made trade among Mexico, the United States, and Canada easier. Mexico's agricultural and industrial exports have increased since NAFTA went into effect.

Agriculture Agriculture has long been a key part of the Mexican economy. This is true even though just 12 percent of the land can grow crops. Many farmers in Mexico practice **slash-and-burn agriculture**, which is the practice of burning forest in order to clear land for planting.

The high market demand for food in the United States has encouraged many farmers in Mexico to grow cash crops. A **cash crop** is a crop that farmers grow mainly to sell for a profit. Trucks bring cash crops like fruits and vegetables from Mexico to the United States.

Industry Oil is also an important export for Mexico. Many Mexicans work in the oil, mining, and manufacturing industries. These industries are growing.

The fastest-growing industrial centers in Mexico lie along the U.S. border. Because wages are relatively low in Mexico, many U.S. and foreign companies have built factories in Mexico. Mexican workers in these factories assemble goods for export to the United States and other countries. Some Mexican workers also come to the United States to look for jobs that pay more than they can make at home.

Tourism Tourism is another important part of Mexico's economy. Many tourists visit old colonial cities and Maya and Aztec monuments. Coastal cities and resorts such as Cancún and Acapulco are also popular with tourists.

READING CHECK **Summarizing** How is the government's role in the economy changing?

Satellite View

Smoke

Fire

Slash-and-Burn Agriculture

Many people in Mexico are subsistence farmers. They do not own much land and grow only enough food to feed their families. To gain more land, farmers in southern Mexico burn patches of forest. The fires clear the trees and kill weeds, and ash from the fires fertilizes the soil. However, growing the same crops year after year drains valuable nutrients from the soil. The farmers then have to burn new forest land.

In the satellite image here, agricultural fires appear as red dots. As you can see, the fires create a lot of smoke. Wind then blows the smoke great distances. Every few years, when the conditions are right, smoke from agricultural fires in Mexico reaches as far as the southern United States. The smoke can cause health problems for some people.

Analyzing What direction was the wind blowing in this image?

Northern Mexico Northern Mexico's land is generally too dry to be much good for farming, but ranching is an important part of the region's economy.

ANALYSIS SKILL **ANALYZING INFORMATION**

How do you think life in greater Mexico City differs from life in northern Mexico?

Central Mexico The architecture and cobblestone streets of many towns in central Mexico reflect the region's Spanish colonial heritage.

Mexico's Culture Regions

Although all Mexicans share some cultural characteristics, we can divide Mexico into four regions based on regional differences. These four culture regions differ from each other in their population, resources, climate, and other features.

Greater Mexico City

Greater Mexico City includes the capital and about 50 smaller cities near it. With a population of more than 19 million, **Mexico City** is the world's second-largest city and one of the most densely populated urban areas. Thousands of people move there every year looking for work.

While this region does provide job and educational opportunities not so easily found in the rest of the country, its huge population causes problems. For example, Mexico City is very polluted. Factories and cars release exhaust and other pollutants into the air. The surrounding mountains trap the resulting **smog**—a mixture of smoke, chemicals, and fog. Smog can cause health problems like eye irritation and breathing difficulties.

Another problem that comes from crowding is poverty. Wealth and poverty exist side by side in Mexico City. The city has large urban slums. The slums often exist right next to modern office buildings, apartments, museums, or universities.

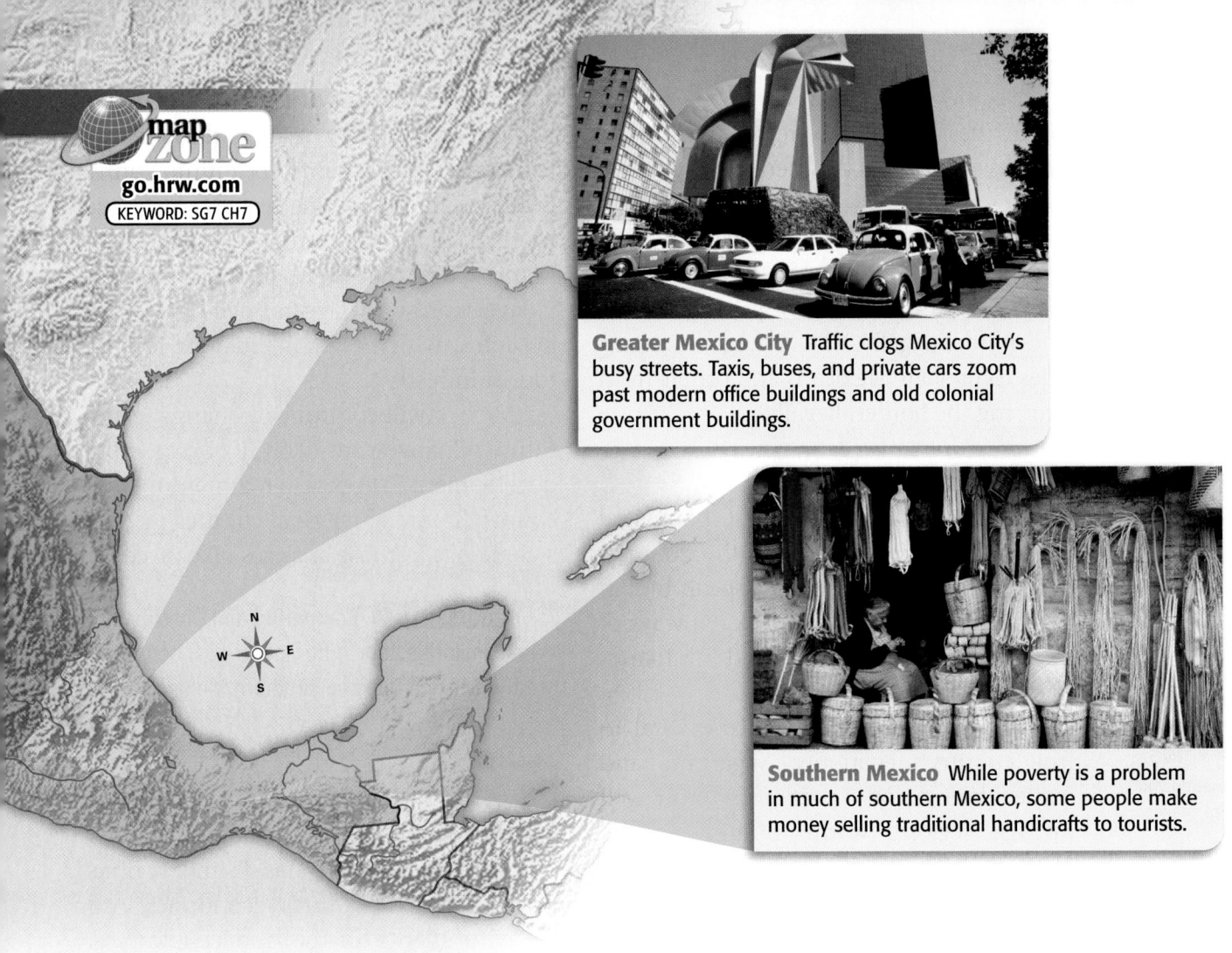

map zone
go.hrw.com
KEYWORD: SG7 CH7

Greater Mexico City Traffic clogs Mexico City's busy streets. Taxis, buses, and private cars zoom past modern office buildings and old colonial government buildings.

Southern Mexico While poverty is a problem in much of southern Mexico, some people make money selling traditional handicrafts to tourists.

Central Mexico

North of greater Mexico City lies Mexico's central region. Many cities in this region were established as mining or ranching centers during the colonial period. Mexico's colonial heritage can still be seen today in these cities and towns. For example, small towns often have a colonial-style church near a main central square. The central square, or plaza, has served for hundreds of years as a community meeting spot and market area.

In addition to small colonial towns, central Mexico has many fertile valleys and small family farms. Farmers in this region grow vegetables, corn, and wheat for sale, mostly to cities in Mexico.

While central Mexico has always been a mining center, in recent years the region has also attracted new industries from overcrowded Mexico City. As a result, some cities in the region, such as Guadalajara, are growing rapidly.

Northern Mexico

Northern Mexico has become one of the country's richest and most modern areas. Trade with the United States has helped the region's economy grow. Monterrey and Tijuana are now major cities there. Many U.S.- and foreign-owned factories called **maquiladoras** (mah-kee-lah-DORH-ahs) have been built along Mexico's long border with the United States.

ACADEMIC VOCABULARY
affect to change or influence

Northern Mexico's closeness to the border has **affected** the region's culture as well as its economy. American television, music, and other forms of entertainment are popular there. Many Mexicans cross the border to shop, work, or live in the United States. While many people cross the border legally, the U.S. government tries to prevent Mexicans and others from crossing the border illegally.

Southern Mexico

Southern Mexico is the least populated and industrialized region of the country. Many people in this region speak Indian languages and practice traditional ways of life. Subsistence farming and slash-and-burn agriculture are common.

FOCUS ON READING
What do you think makes southern Mexico vital to the country's economy?

However, southern Mexico is vital to the country's economy. Sugarcane and coffee, two major export crops, grow well in the region's warm, humid climate. Also, oil production along the Gulf coast has increased in recent years. The oil business has brought more industry and population growth to this coastal area of southern Mexico.

Another place in southern Mexico that has grown in recent years is the Yucatán Peninsula. Maya ruins, beautiful sunny beaches, and clear blue water have made tourism a major industry in this area. Many cities that were just tiny fishing villages only 20 years ago are now booming with new construction for the tourist industry.

Mexico will continue to change in the future. Changes are likely to bring more development. However, maintaining the country's unique regional cultures may be a challenge as those changes take place.

READING CHECK Comparing and Contrasting What similarities and differences exist between greater Mexico City and southern Mexico?

SUMMARY AND PREVIEW Mexico has a democratic government and a growing economy. It also has distinct regions with different cultures, economies, and environments. In the next chapter you will learn about the countries to the south of Mexico.

Section 3 Assessment

Reviewing Ideas, Terms, and Places

1. **a. Define** What is the term for the practice of burning forest in order to clear land for planting?
   b. Compare and Contrast How is Mexico's government similar to and different from the government of the United States?
2. **a. Identify** What is an environmental problem found in **Mexico City**?
   b. Make Inferences What conditions in Mexico lead some Mexicans to cross the border into the United States?
   c. Develop If you were to start a business in Mexico, what type of business would you start and where would you start it? Explain your decisions.

Critical Thinking

3. **Finding Main Ideas** Review your notes on Mexico's economy. Then use a chart like this one to show what parts of the economy are important in each region.

Greater Mexico City	Central Mexico	Northern Mexico	Southern Mexico

FOCUS ON WRITING

4. **Describing Mexico Today** Write some details about the four culture regions of Mexico. Which details will you include in your poem?

Chapter Review

Geography's Impact
video series
Review the video to answer the closing question:
Do you think emigration from Mexico to the United States hurts or helps Mexico? Why?

Visual Summary

Use the visual summary below to help you review the main ideas of the chapter.

QUICK FACTS

The physical geography of Mexico includes a high region of plateaus and mountains.

The Spanish conquered the Aztecs and ruled Mexico for about 300 years until the Mexicans gained independence.

Greater Mexico City, one of Mexico's four culture regions, is the center of Mexico's government and economy.

Reviewing Vocabulary, Terms, and Places

Unscramble each group of letters below to spell a term that matches the given definition.

1. **pmreie**—a land with different territories and peoples under a single ruler

2. **tflinnaoi**—a rise in prices that occurs when currency loses its buying power

3. **mogs**—a mixture of smoke, chemicals, and fog

4. **snipluane**—a piece of land surrounded on three sides by water

5. **ztosemsi**—people of mixed European and Indian ancestry

6. **hacs rpoc**—a crop that farmers grow mainly to sell for a profit

7. **ssnmiosi**—church outposts

8. **dqamiuarsloa**—U.S.- and foreign-owned factories in Mexico

9. **ndhceiasa**—expanses of farm or ranch land

Comprehension and Critical Thinking

SECTION 1 *(Pages 168–171)*

10. **a. Define** What is the Mexican Plateau? What forms its edges?

   b. Contrast How does the climate of Mexico City differ from the climate in the south?

   c. Evaluate What do you think would be Mexico's most important resource if it did not have oil? Explain your answer.

SECTION 2 *(Pages 172–176)*

11. **a. Recall** What early civilization did the Spanish conquer when they came to Mexico?

   b. Analyze How did Spanish rule influence Mexico's culture?

   c. Evaluate Which war—the war for independence, the Mexican War, or the Mexican Revolution—do you think changed Mexico the most? Explain your answer.

SECTION 3 *(Pages 178–182)*

12. **a. Describe** What are Mexico's four culture regions? Describe a feature of each.

    b. Analyze What regions do you think are the most popular with tourists? Explain your answer.

    c. Evaluate What are two major drawbacks of slash-and-burn agriculture?

Using the Internet

go.hrw.com
KEYWORD: SG7 CH7

13. **Activity: Writing a Description** Colorful textiles, paintings, and pottery are just some of the many crafts made throughout Mexico. Each region in Mexico has its own style of crafts and folk art. Enter the activity keyword to visit some of the different regions of Mexico and explore their arts and crafts. Pick a favorite object from each region. Learn about its use, its design, how it was made, and the people who made it. Then write a brief paragraph that describes each object and its unique characteristics.

Social Studies Skills

14. **Taking Notes** Look back at the information in Section 3 about Mexico's government and economy. Then use a chart like this one to take notes on the information in your book.

Recall	Notes

15. **Predicting** Now you can use your skills in predicting to think about events that might happen in the future. Reread the text in your book about Mexico's economy. Write three to four sentences about how you think the economy might change in the future.

16. **Writing an "I Am" Poem** Now it is time to write your poem. Title your poem "I am Mexico" and make it six lines long. Each line will tell one or more details about the country. For example, one line might state, "I have towering, snow-capped volcanoes." Make sure at least one line deals with physical geography, one line with history and culture, and one line with Mexico today. Your poem does not need to rhyme, but you should try to use vivid language.

Map Activity

17. **Mexico** On a separate sheet of paper, match the letters on the map with their correct labels.

Gulf of Mexico	Baja California
Río Bravo (Rio Grande)	Tijuana
Yucatán Peninsula	Mexico City

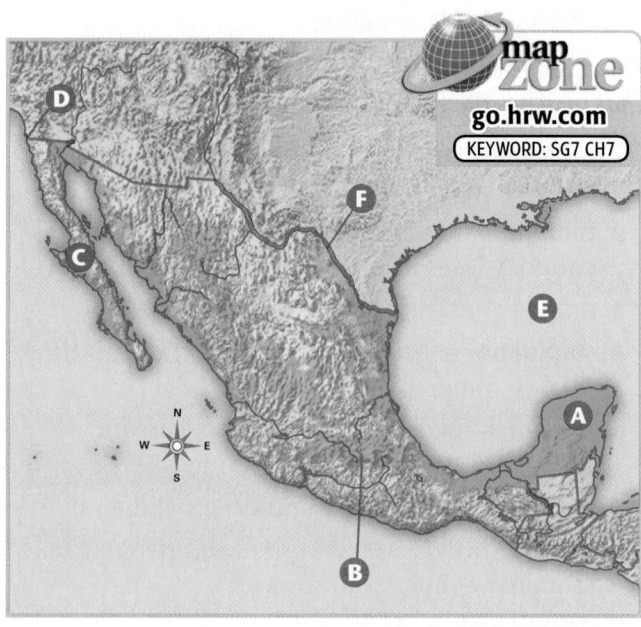

go.hrw.com
KEYWORD: SG7 CH7

Standardized Test Practice

DIRECTIONS: Read questions 1 through 6 and write the letter of the best response. Then read question 7 and write your own well-constructed response.

1 **What physical features make up much of central Mexico?**

A plateaus and mountains

B peninsulas

C beaches and lowlands

D sinkholes

2 **What early culture in Mexico did the Spanish conquer?**

A Olmec

B Maya

C Aztec

D conquistador

3 **Which of the following was a way in which the Spanish affected Mexico during colonial times?**

A granted land to the native people

B set up missions and taught about Christianity

C started the Mexican Revolution

D gave away half of Mexico to the United States

4 **Where are Mexico's fastest-growing industrial centers?**

A on the Gulf coast

B in Mexico City

C on the Yucatán Peninsula

D along the U.S. border

5 **What factor helps classify Mexico as a developing country?**

A high unemployment

B few political parties

C an economy based on oil and tourism

D relatively high living standards

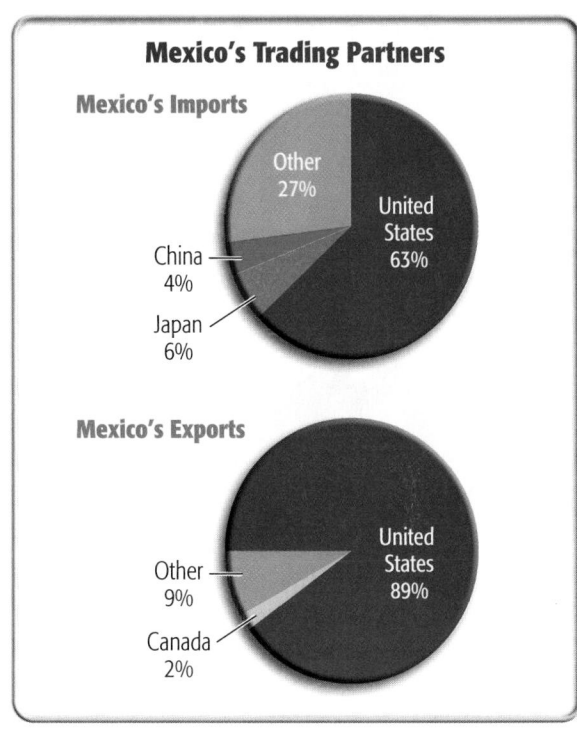

Mexico's Trading Partners

Mexico's Imports

Other 27%
United States 63%
China 4%
Japan 6%

Mexico's Exports

United States 89%
Other 9%
Canada 2%

Source: *World Almanac and Book of Facts,* 2005

6 **Based on the graphs above, which of the following statements is false?**

A The United States is Mexico's biggest trading partner.

B The United States imports 63% of its goods from Mexico.

C 89% of Mexico's exports go to the United States.

D Imports from Japan make up 6% of Mexico's total imports.

7 Extended Response Look at the graphs above and the information in Section 3. Then write a brief essay explaining how NAFTA has influenced Mexico.

CHAPTER 8

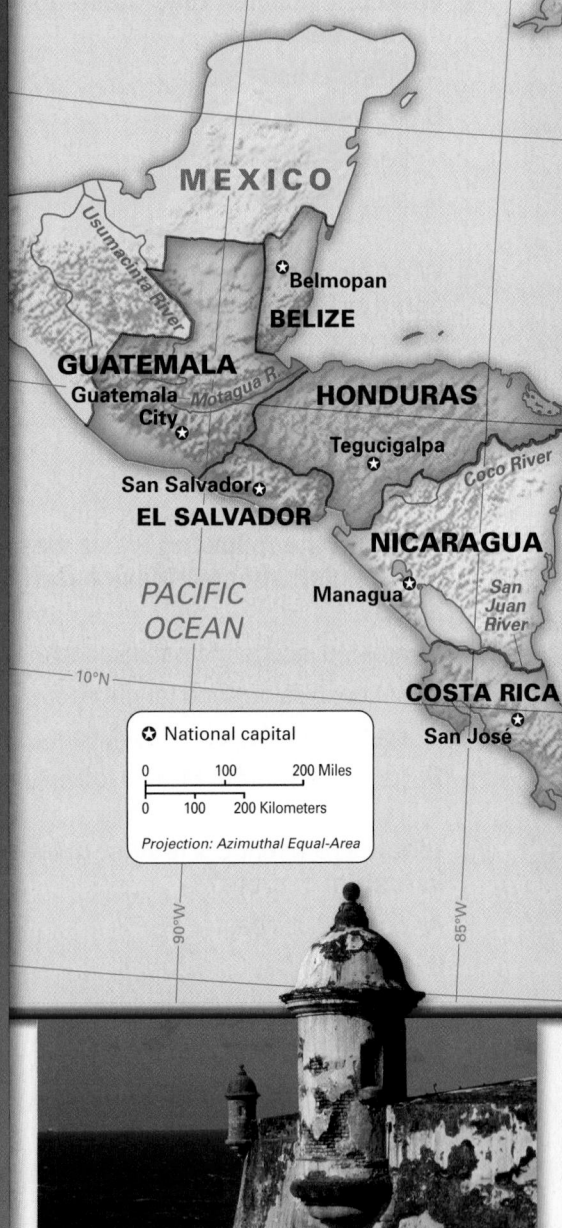

Central America and the Caribbean

What You Will Learn...

In this chapter you will learn about the beautiful physical landscapes of Central America and the Caribbean. You will also study the history of the region along with the people who live there and the way they live today.

FOCUS ON READING AND WRITING

Understanding Comparison-Contrast When you compare, you look for ways in which things are alike. When you contrast, you look for ways in which things are different. As you read the chapter, look for ways you can compare and contrast information. **See the lesson, Understanding Comparison-Contrast, on page R9.**

Creating a Travel Guide People use travel guides to learn more about places they want to visit. As you read about Central America and the Caribbean in this chapter, you will collect information about places tourists might visit. Then you will create your own travel guide for visitors to one of these vacation spots.

History The Spanish built forts like this one in Puerto Rico to defend their islands and protect the harbors from pirates.

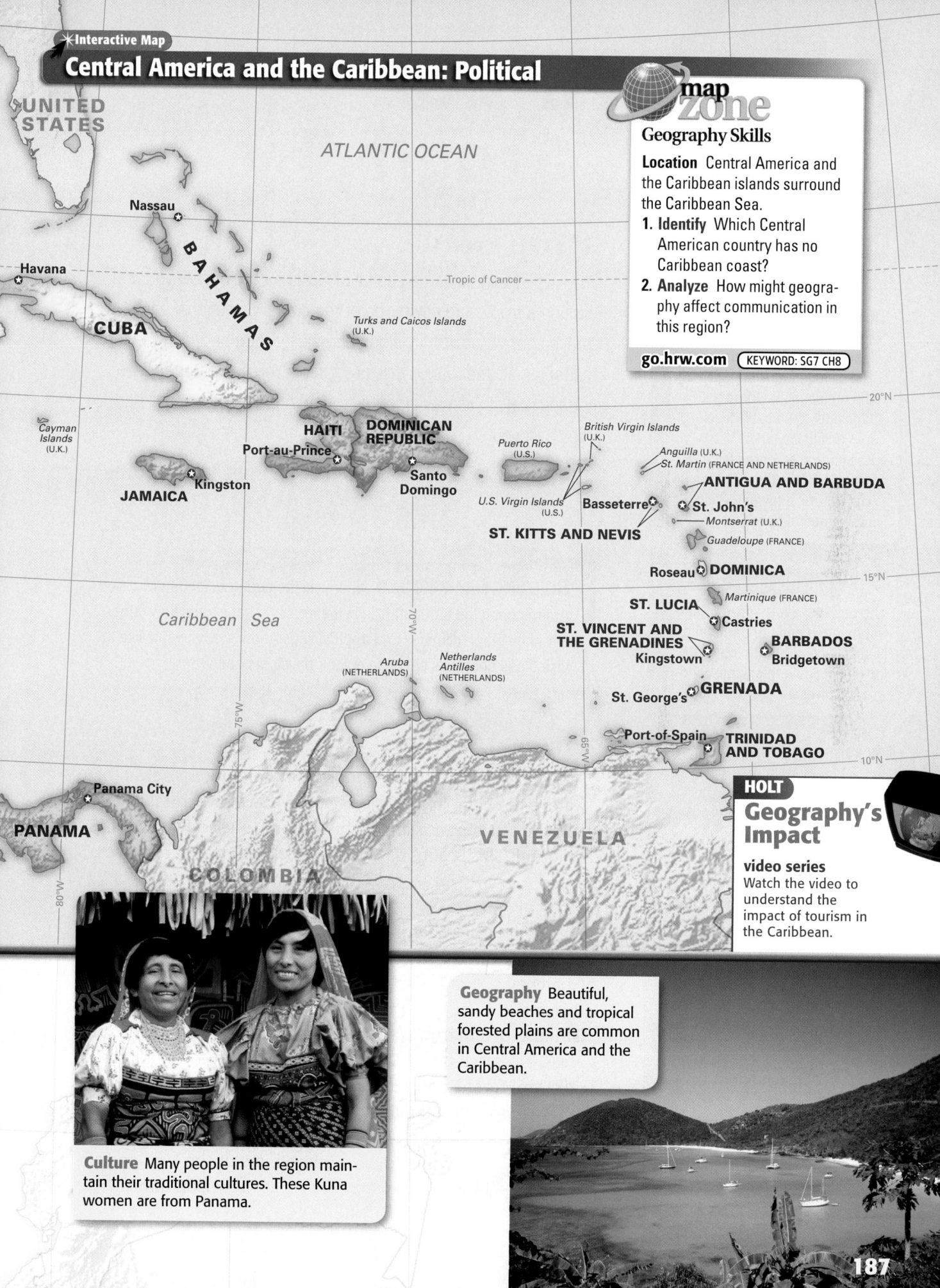

map zone

Geography Skills

Location Central America and the Caribbean islands surround the Caribbean Sea.

1. **Identify** Which Central American country has no Caribbean coast?
2. **Analyze** How might geography affect communication in this region?

go.hrw.com   KEYWORD: SG7 CH8

UNITED STATES

ATLANTIC OCEAN

Nassau

Havana

BAHAMAS

CUBA

Tropic of Cancer

Turks and Caicos Islands (U.K.)

20°N

Cayman Islands (U.K.)

HAITI

Port-au-Prince

DOMINICAN REPUBLIC

Santo Domingo

Puerto Rico (U.S.)

British Virgin Islands (U.K.)

Anguilla (U.K.)
St. Martin (FRANCE AND NETHERLANDS)

ANTIGUA AND BARBUDA

Kingston

JAMAICA

U.S. Virgin Islands (U.S.)

Basseterre

St. John's

Montserrat (U.K.)

ST. KITTS AND NEVIS

Guadeloupe (FRANCE)

Roseau DOMINICA

15°N

Caribbean Sea

70°W

ST. LUCIA

Martinique (FRANCE)

Castries

ST. VINCENT AND THE GRENADINES

Kingstown

BARBADOS

Bridgetown

Aruba (NETHERLANDS)

Netherlands Antilles (NETHERLANDS)

St. George's GRENADA

75°W

65°W

Port-of-Spain

TRINIDAD AND TOBAGO

10°N

Panama City

80°W

PANAMA

VENEZUELA

COLOMBIA

HOLT

Geography's Impact

video series
Watch the video to understand the impact of tourism in the Caribbean.

Geography Beautiful, sandy beaches and tropical forested plains are common in Central America and the Caribbean.

Culture Many people in the region maintain their traditional cultures. These Kuna women are from Panama.

Physical Geography

What You Will Learn...

Main Ideas

1. Physical features of the region include volcanic highlands and coastal plains.
2. The climate and vegetation of the region include forested highlands, tropical forests, and humid lowlands.
3. Key natural resources in the region include rich soils for agriculture, a few minerals, and beautiful beaches.

The Big Idea

The physical geography of Central America and the Caribbean islands includes warm coastal lowlands, cooler highlands, and tropical forests.

Key Terms and Places

isthmus, *p. 188*
Caribbean Sea, *p. 188*
archipelago, *p. 189*
Greater Antilles, *p. 189*
Lesser Antilles, *p. 189*
cloud forest, *p. 190*

TAKING NOTES As you read, use a chart like this one to take notes on the physical geography of the region.

Physical Features	
Climate and Vegetation	
Resources	

If YOU lived there...

You live in San José, the capital of Costa Rica. But now you are visiting a tropical forest in one of the country's national parks. You make your way carefully along a swinging rope bridge in the forest canopy—40 feet above the forest floor! You see a huge green iguana making its way along a branch. A brilliantly colored parrot flies past you.

What other creatures might you see in the forest?

BUILDING BACKGROUND Nearly all the countries of Central America and the Caribbean lie in the tropics. That means they generally have warm climates and tropical vegetation. Many people like to visit these countries because of their physical beauty.

Physical Features

Sandy beaches, volcanic mountains, rain forests, clear blue water—these are images many people have of Central America and the Caribbean islands. This region's physical geography is beautiful. This beauty is one of the region's greatest resources.

Central America

The region called Central America is actually the southern part of North America. Seven countries make up this region: Belize, Guatemala, Honduras, El Salvador, Nicaragua, Costa Rica, and Panama. As you can see on the map, Central America is an **isthmus**, or a narrow strip of land that connects two larger land areas. No place on this isthmus is more than about 125 miles (200 km) from either the Pacific Ocean or the **Caribbean Sea**.

A chain of mountains and volcanoes separates the Pacific and Caribbean coastal plains, and only a few short rivers flow through Central America. The ruggedness of the land and the lack of good water routes make travel in the region difficult.

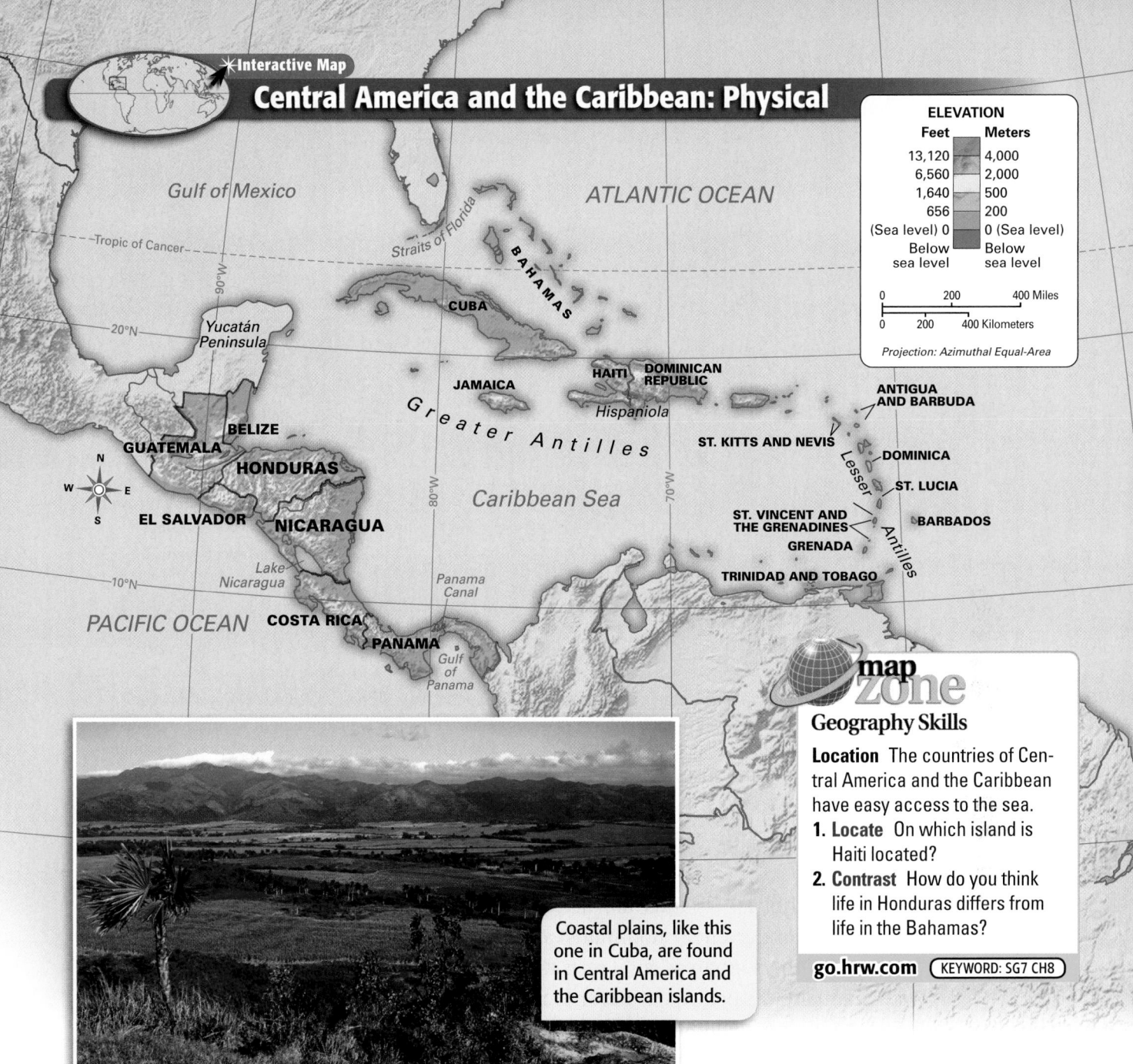

Central America and the Caribbean: Physical

ELEVATION

Feet		Meters
13,120		4,000
6,560		2,000
1,640		500
656		200
(Sea level) 0		0 (Sea level)
Below sea level		Below sea level

0   200   400 Miles
0   200   400 Kilometers

Projection: Azimuthal Equal-Area

Gulf of Mexico

ATLANTIC OCEAN

Tropic of Cancer

Straits of Florida

BAHAMAS

CUBA

20°N

Yucatán Peninsula

JAMAICA

HAITI   DOMINICAN REPUBLIC

Hispaniola

Greater Antilles

ANTIGUA AND BARBUDA

BELIZE

GUATEMALA

ST. KITTS AND NEVIS

DOMINICA

HONDURAS

Caribbean Sea

Lesser Antilles

ST. LUCIA

EL SALVADOR

NICARAGUA

BARBADOS

ST. VINCENT AND THE GRENADINES

GRENADA

Lake Nicaragua

Panama Canal

10°N

TRINIDAD AND TOBAGO

PACIFIC OCEAN   COSTA RICA

PANAMA

Gulf of Panama

Coastal plains, like this one in Cuba, are found in Central America and the Caribbean islands.

map zone

Geography Skills

Location The countries of Central America and the Caribbean have easy access to the sea.

1. **Locate** On which island is Haiti located?
2. **Contrast** How do you think life in Honduras differs from life in the Bahamas?

go.hrw.com   KEYWORD: SG7 CH8

The Caribbean Islands

Across the Caribbean Sea from Central America lie hundreds of islands known as the Caribbean islands. They make up an **archipelago** (ahr-kuh-PE-luh-goh), or large group of islands. Arranged in a long curve, the Caribbean islands stretch from the southern tip of Florida to northern South America. They divide the Caribbean Sea from the Atlantic Ocean.

There are two main island groups in the Caribbean. The four large islands of Cuba, Jamaica, Hispaniola, and Puerto Rico make up the **Greater Antilles** (an-TI-leez). Many smaller islands form the **Lesser Antilles**. They stretch from the Virgin Islands to Trinidad and Tobago. A third island group, the Bahamas, lies in the Atlantic Ocean southeast of Florida. It includes nearly 700 islands and thousands of reefs.

FOCUS ON READING

How are the Greater and Lesser Antilles different?

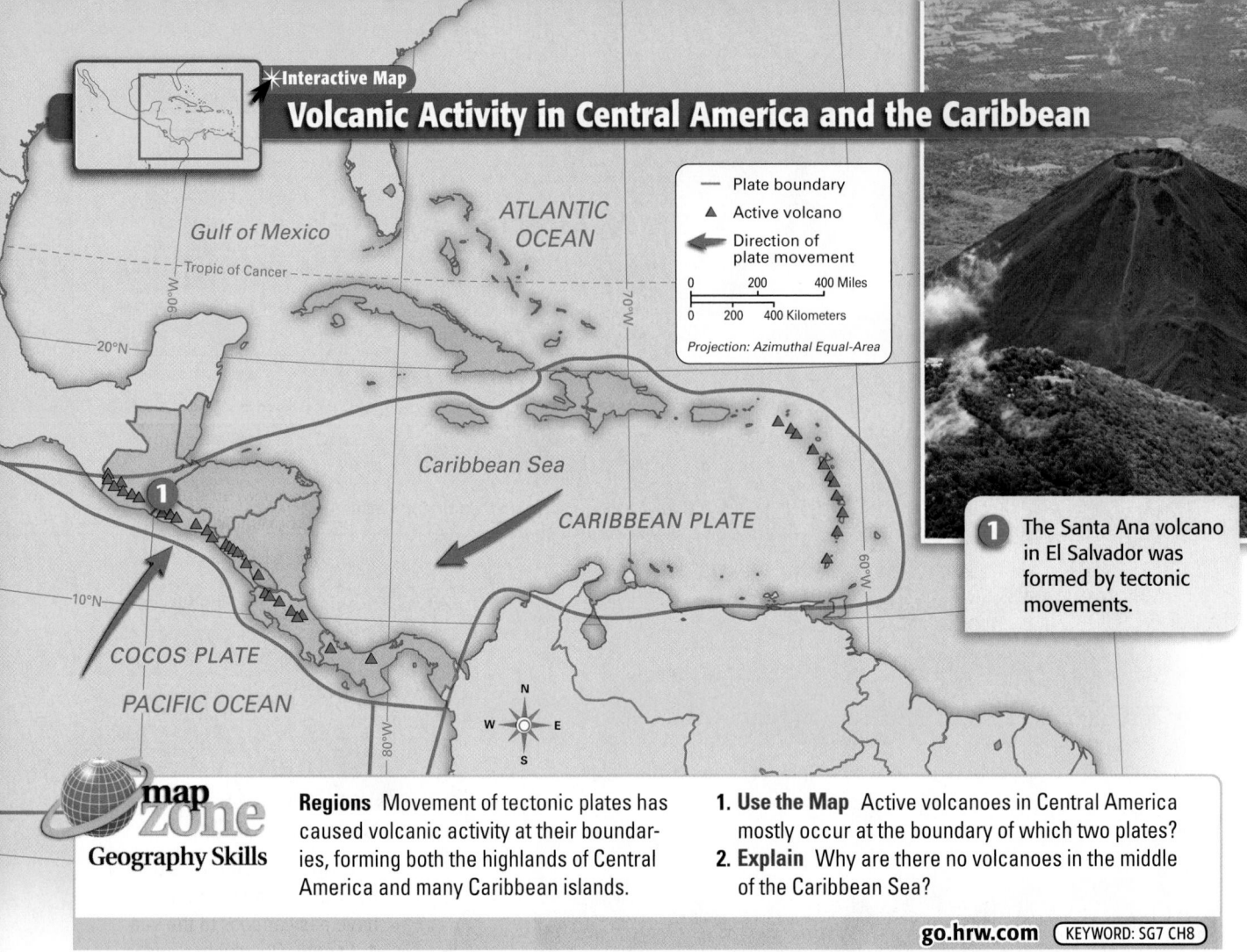

Volcanic Activity in Central America and the Caribbean

★Interactive Map

ATLANTIC OCEAN

Gulf of Mexico

Tropic of Cancer

20°N

Caribbean Sea

CARIBBEAN PLATE

COCOS PLATE

PACIFIC OCEAN

10°N

— Plate boundary
▲ Active volcano
← Direction of plate movement

0   200   400 Miles
0   200   400 Kilometers
Projection: Azimuthal Equal-Area

1 The Santa Ana volcano in El Salvador was formed by tectonic movements.

map zone
Geography Skills

Regions Movement of tectonic plates has caused volcanic activity at their boundaries, forming both the highlands of Central America and many Caribbean islands.

1. Use the Map Active volcanoes in Central America mostly occur at the boundary of which two plates?
2. Explain Why are there no volcanoes in the middle of the Caribbean Sea?

go.hrw.com KEYWORD: SG7 CH8

Many Caribbean islands are actually the tops of underwater mountains and volcanoes. Others began as coral reefs that were gradually pushed up to become flat limestone islands. Colliding tectonic plates have pushed this region's land up out of the sea over several million years. You can see these tectonic plates on the map above. Notice how the land follows the boundaries of the plates. Earthquakes and volcanic eruptions occur frequently as these plates shift. When such events do occur, they can cause great damage to the region and its people.

READING CHECK **Comparing** What physical features do Central America and the Caribbean islands have in common?

Climate and Vegetation

Central America and the Caribbean islands are generally sunny and warm. Humid tropical and tropical savanna climates are common in the islands and on Central America's coastal plains. On the Pacific coast, much of the area's original savanna vegetation has been cleared. It has been replaced by plantations and ranches. The opposite coast, along the Caribbean, has areas of tropical rain forest.

Inland mountain areas contain cool, humid climates. Some mountainous parts of Central America are covered with dense cloud forest. A **cloud forest** is a moist, high-elevation tropical forest where low clouds are common. These forests are home to numerous plant and animal species.

Temperatures in most of Central America and the Caribbean do not change much from day to night or from summer to winter. Instead, the change in seasons is marked by a change in rainfall. Winters in the region are generally dry, while it rains nearly every day during the summers.

From summer to fall, hurricanes are a threat in the region. These tropical storms bring violent winds, heavy rain, and high seas. Most hurricanes occur between June and November. Their winds and flooding can cause destruction and loss of life.

READING CHECK **Generalizing** Where would one find the coolest temperatures in the region?

Resources

The region's best resources are its land and climate. These factors make tourism an important industry. They also influence agriculture. Agriculture in the region can be profitable where volcanic ash has enriched the soil. Coffee, bananas, sugarcane, and cotton grow well and are major crops. Timber is exported from the rain forests.

Although its land and climate make good agricultural resources, the region has few mineral resources. Energy resources are also limited. Central America and the Caribbean islands must rely on energy imports, which limits their development.

READING CHECK **Analyzing** Why would having few energy resources limit economic development?

SUMMARY AND PREVIEW Central America and the Caribbean islands share volcanic physical features and a warm, tropical climate good for agriculture. In the next section you will learn about the history and culture of Central America.

Satellite View

Strong hurricane winds spin around a calm center point called the eye.

Hurricane Isabel

Hurricanes are rotating storms that bring heavy rain and winds that can reach speeds higher than 155 miles per hour (249 kph). This image shows Hurricane Isabel sweeping through the Caribbean Sea in 2003. Strong hurricanes like this one can shatter houses and hurl cars through the air.

Analyzing How can you tell the storm is rotating?

Section 1 Assessment

go.hrw.com
Online Quiz
KEYWORD: SG7 HP8

Reviewing Ideas, Terms, and Places

1. **a. Define** What is an **isthmus**?
   b. Explain How has tectonic activity affected Central America and the Caribbean islands?
2. **a. Describe** What is a **cloud forest**?
   b. Make Inferences Why do temperatures in the region change little from summer to winter?
3. **a. Recall** What crops grow well in the region?
   b. Evaluate Do you think tourists who want to go to the beach are more likely to visit Guatemala or the Bahamas? Explain your answer.

Critical Thinking

4. **Categorizing** Draw a diagram like the one here. Using your notes, write descriptive phrases about the physical features, climate, and resources of both places.

Central America	Caribbean Islands

FOCUS ON WRITING

5. **Writing about Geography** What information about the physical geography of the region might interest readers of your travel guide? Jot down some ideas.

Central America

If YOU lived there...

You live in El Salvador, in a town that is still living with the effects of a civil war 20 years ago. Your parents and your older neighbors still speak about those years with fear. One effect of the war was damage to the economy. Many people have gone to Mexico to try to make a better life. Now your parents are talking about going there to look for work. But you are not sure.

How do you feel about leaving your home?

What You Will Learn...

Main Ideas

1. The history of Central America was mostly influenced by Spain.
2. The culture of Central America is a mixture of Native American and European traditions.
3. The countries of Central America today have challenges and opportunities.

The Big Idea

Central America's native traditions and colonial history have created a mixed culture, unstable governments, and uncertain economies.

Key Terms and Places

ecotourism, *p. 196*
civil war, *p. 196*
Panama Canal, *p. 197*

TAKING NOTES As you read, use a graphic organizer like the one here to help you organize your notes on Central America.

History	
Culture	
The Region Today	

BUILDING BACKGROUND All the countries of Central America were once colonies of European nations. Years of colonial rule made it hard for most of these countries to establish strong economies or democratic governments. Today things are slowly improving.

History

Many countries of Central America have a shared history. This shared history has been influenced by the Maya, the Spanish, and the United States.

Early History

In several Central American countries, the Maya were building large cities with pyramids and temples by about AD 250. The Maya abandoned most of their cities around 900, but the ruins of many ancient cities still stand in the region today. People of Maya descent still live in Guatemala and Belize. In fact, many ancient Maya customs still influence modern life there.

Hundreds of years later, in the early 1500s, most of Central America came under European control. Spain claimed most of the region. Britain claimed what is now Belize and also occupied part of Nicaragua's coast. The Spanish established large plantations in their colonies to grow crops like tobacco and sugarcane. They made Central American Indians work on the plantations or in gold mines elsewhere in the Americas. In addition, Europeans brought many enslaved Africans to the region to work on plantations and in mines.

One-Crop Economies

The economies of many Central American countries relied on only one crop—bananas. The U.S.-based United Fruit Company was the biggest banana exporter and the largest employer in the region for many years. The old photo below shows the company's hiring hall in Guatemala.

ANALYZING VISUALS Why do workers place cushions between bananas?

Central America Since Independence

The Spanish colonies of Central America declared independence from Spain in 1821, but much of the region remained joined together as the United Provinces of Central America. The countries of Costa Rica, Nicaragua, Honduras, El Salvador, and Guatemala separated from each other in 1838 to 1839. Panama remained part of Colombia until 1903. Belize did not gain independence from Britain until 1981.

For most countries in Central America, independence brought little change. The Spanish officials left, but wealthy landowners continued to run the countries and their economies. The plantation crops of bananas and coffee supported Central American economies.

In the early to mid-1900s, one landowner in particular, the U.S.-based United Fruit Company, controlled most of the banana production in Central America. To help its business, the company developed railroads and port facilities. This kind of development helped transportation and communications in the region.

Many people resented the role of foreign companies, however. They thought it was wrong that only a few people should own so much land while many people struggled to make a living. In the mid- to late 1900s, demands for reforms led to armed struggles in Guatemala, El Salvador, and Nicaragua. Only in recent years have these countries achieved peace.

READING CHECK **Evaluating** How did Spain influence the region's history?

Culture

Central America's colonial history has influenced its culture. The region's people, languages, religion, and festivals reflect both Spanish and native practices.

People and Languages

Most of the people in Central America are mestizos, or people of mixed European and Indian ancestry. Various Indian peoples descended from the ancient Maya live in places such as the Guatemalan Highlands.

People of African ancestry also make up a significant minority in this region. They live mostly along the Caribbean coast.

In some countries in Central America, many people still speak the native Indian languages. In places that were colonized by England, English is spoken. For example, it is the official language of Belize. In most countries, however, Spanish is the official language. The Spanish colonization of Central America left this lasting mark on the region.

A Market in Guatemala

Villages in Guatemala and all over Central America hold weekly markets. On market day, people come from all around to buy and sell food and other items. The market is also an important gathering spot for the community. Scenes like this one are typical in the region.

The Catholic church is a major influence in most towns.

Patterns on women's clothing are unique to the village where the woman lives.

Religion, Festivals, and Food

Many Central Americans practice a religion brought to the region by Europeans. Most people are Roman Catholic because Spanish missionaries taught the Indians about Catholicism. However, Indian traditions have influenced Catholicism in return. Also, Protestant Christians are becoming a large minority in places such as Belize.

Religion has influenced celebrations in towns throughout the region. For example, to celebrate special saints' feast days, some people carry images of the saint in parades through the streets. Easter is a particularly important holiday. Some towns decorate whole streets with designs made of flowers and colorful sawdust.

During festivals, people eat **traditional** foods. Central America shares some of its traditional foods, like corn, with Mexico. The region is also known for tomatoes, hot peppers, and cacao (kuh-KOW), which is the source of chocolate.

READING CHECK **Contrasting** How is Belize culturally different from the rest of the region?

ACADEMIC VOCABULARY

traditional
customary, time-honored

Tourists contribute to the local economy when they buy crafts.

People often spend all day at the market and need to eat lunch there.

ANALYSIS **SKILL** **ANALYZING VISUALS**

How do the contributions of tourists and Guatemalans affect the local economy differently?

Central America Today

The countries of Central America share similar histories and cultures. However, they all face their own economic and political challenges today. In 2005 Costa Rica, the Dominican Republic, El Salvador, Guatemala, Honduras, and Nicaragua signed the Central American Free Trade Agreement (CAFTA) with the United States. The goal of this agreement is to increase trade among the countries.

Guatemala

Guatemala is the most populous country in Central America. More than 12 million people live there. Although most of the people in Guatemala are mestizos, nearly half of them are Central American Indians. Many speak Maya languages.

Most people in Guatemala live in small villages in the highlands. Fighting between rebels and government forces there killed some 200,000 people between 1960 and 1996. Guatemalans are still recovering from this conflict.

Coffee, which grows well in the cool highlands, is Guatemala's most important crop. The country also is a major producer of cardamom, a spice used in Asian foods.

Belize

Belize has the smallest population in Central America. The country does not have much land for agriculture, either. But **ecotourism**—the practice of using an area's natural environment to attract tourists—has become popular lately. Tourists come to see the country's coral reefs, Maya ruins, and coastal resorts.

Honduras

Honduras is a mountainous country. Most people live in mountain valleys and along the northern coast. The rugged land makes transportation difficult and provides little land where crops can grow. However, citrus fruits and bananas are important exports.

El Salvador

In El Salvador, a few rich families own much of the best land while most people live in poverty. These conditions were a reason behind a long civil war in the 1980s. A **civil war** is a conflict between two or more groups within a country. The war killed many people and hurt the economy.

El Salvador's people have been working to rebuild their country since the end of the war in 1992. One advantage they have in this rebuilding effort is the country's fertile soil. People are able to grow and export crops such as coffee and sugarcane.

Nicaragua

Nicaragua has also been rebuilding since the end of a civil war. In 1979, a group called the Sandinistas overthrew a dictator.

Many Nicaraguans supported the Sandinistas, but rebel forces aided by the United States fought the Sandinistas for power. The civil war ended in 1990 when elections ended the rule of the Sandinistas. Nicaragua is now a democracy.

Costa Rica

Unlike most other Central American countries, Costa Rica has a history of peace. It also has a stable, democratic government. The country does not even have an army. Peace has helped Costa Rica make progress in reducing poverty.

Agricultural products like coffee and bananas are important to Costa Rica's economy. Also, many tourists visit Costa Rica's rich tropical rain forests.

Panama

Panama is the narrowest, southernmost country of Central America. Most people live in areas near the **Panama Canal**. Canal fees and local industries make the canal area the country's most prosperous region.

The Panama Canal provides a link between the Pacific Ocean, the Caribbean Sea, and the Atlantic Ocean. The United States finished building the canal in 1914. For years the Panama canal played an important role in the economy and politics of the region. The United States controlled the canal until 1999. Then, as agreed to in a treaty, Panama finally gained full control of the canal.

READING CHECK **Drawing Inferences** Why do you think Panama might want control of the canal?

FOCUS ON READING

What word in the paragraphs on Costa Rica signals contrast?

SUMMARY AND PREVIEW Native peoples, European colonizers, and the United States have influenced Central America's history and culture. Today most countries are developing stable governments. Their economies rely on tourism and agriculture. In the next section you will learn about the main influences on the Caribbean islands and life there today.

Section 2 Assessment

go.hrw.com
Online Quiz
KEYWORD: SG7 HP8

Reviewing Ideas, Terms, and Places

1. **a. Recall** What parts of Central America did the British claim?
   b. Analyze How did independence affect most Central American countries?
   c. Elaborate What benefits and drawbacks might there be to the United Fruit Company's owning so much land?
2. **a. Identify** What language do most people in Central America speak?
   b. Explain How have native cultures influenced cultural practices in the region today?
3. **a. Define** What is a **civil war,** and where in Central America has a civil war been fought?
   b. Explain Why might some people practice **ecotourism**?
   c. Elaborate Why is the **Panama Canal** important to Panama? Why is it important to other countries?

Critical Thinking

4. **Summarizing** Copy the graphic organizer below. Using your notes, write at least one important fact about each Central American country today.

Guatemala	
Belize	
Honduras	
El Salvador	
Nicaragua	
Costa Rica	
Panama	

FOCUS ON WRITING

5. **Describing Central America** Note details about the history, culture, and life today of people in Central America. Which details will appeal to people who are thinking of visiting the region?

The Panama Canal

The Panama Canal links the Atlantic and Pacific oceans. Built in the early 1900s, workers on the canal faced tropical diseases and the dangers of blasting through solid rock. The result of their efforts was an amazing feat of engineering. Today some 13,000 to 14,000 ships pass through the canal each year.

Routes Before and After the Panama Canal

mapzone

San Francisco
New York
NORTH AMERICA

ATLANTIC OCEAN

5,200 MILES (8,368 KM)

Panama Canal

PACIFIC OCEAN

13,000 MILES (20,921 KM)

SOUTH AMERICA

The Panama Canal shortens a trip from the east coast of the United States to the west coast by about 8,000 miles (15,000 km).

— Route around South America

— Route through the Panama Canal

| 0 | 750 | 1,500 Miles |
| 0 | 750 | 1,500 Kilometers |

Projection: Azimuthal Equal-Area

N W E S

Crossing a Continent

The Panama Canal takes ships from sea level, across a mountain range, and back to sea level.

Caribbean Sea

Gatún Locks

Pedro Miguel Locks

Miraflores Locks

Gatún Lake

Pacific Ocean

Trains help guide large ships through the canal.

These locks act as doors to different compartments of the canal. Underground pumps raise and lower the water in each compartment like an elevator.

ANALYSIS SKILL **ANALYZING VISUALS**

1. Why was Panama a good location for a canal?
2. Why must ships be raised and lowered in order to get through the canal?

The Caribbean Islands

Main Ideas

1. The history of the Caribbean islands includes European colonization followed by independence.
2. The culture of the Caribbean islands shows signs of past colonialism and slavery.
3. Today the Caribbean islands have distinctive governments with economies that depend on agriculture and tourism.

The Big Idea

The Caribbean islands have a rich history and culture influenced by European colonization.

Key Terms and Places

dialect, *p. 202*
commonwealth, *p. 203*
refugee, *p. 203*
Havana, *p. 204*
cooperative, *p. 204*

TAKING NOTES As you read, use a diagram like the one below to help you organize your notes on the Caribbean islands.

History	Culture	The Region Today

If YOU lived there...

You are a young sailor on Christopher Columbus's second voyage to the New World. The year is 1493. Now that your ship is in the Caribbean Sea, you are sailing from island to island. You have seen volcanoes and waterfalls and fierce natives. Columbus has decided to establish a trading post on one of the islands. You are part of the crew who will stay there.

What do you expect in your new home?

BUILDING BACKGROUND In the late 1400s and early 1500s, European nations began to compete for colonies. Sailing for Spain, Christopher Columbus made four voyages to the Americas. He and his men discovered and explored many islands.

History

When Christopher Columbus discovered America in 1492, he actually discovered the Caribbean islands. These islands now include 13 independent countries. The countries themselves show the influence of those first European explorers.

Early History

Christopher Columbus first sailed into the Caribbean Sea from Spain in 1492. He thought he had reached the Indies, or the islands near India. Therefore, he called the Caribbean islands the West Indies and the people who lived there Indians.

Spain had little interest in the smaller Caribbean islands, but the English, French, Dutch, and Danish did. In the 1600s and 1700s, these countries established colonies on the islands. They built huge sugarcane plantations that required many workers. Most Caribbean Indians had died from disease, so Europeans brought Africans to work as slaves. Soon Africans and people of African descent outnumbered Europeans on many islands.

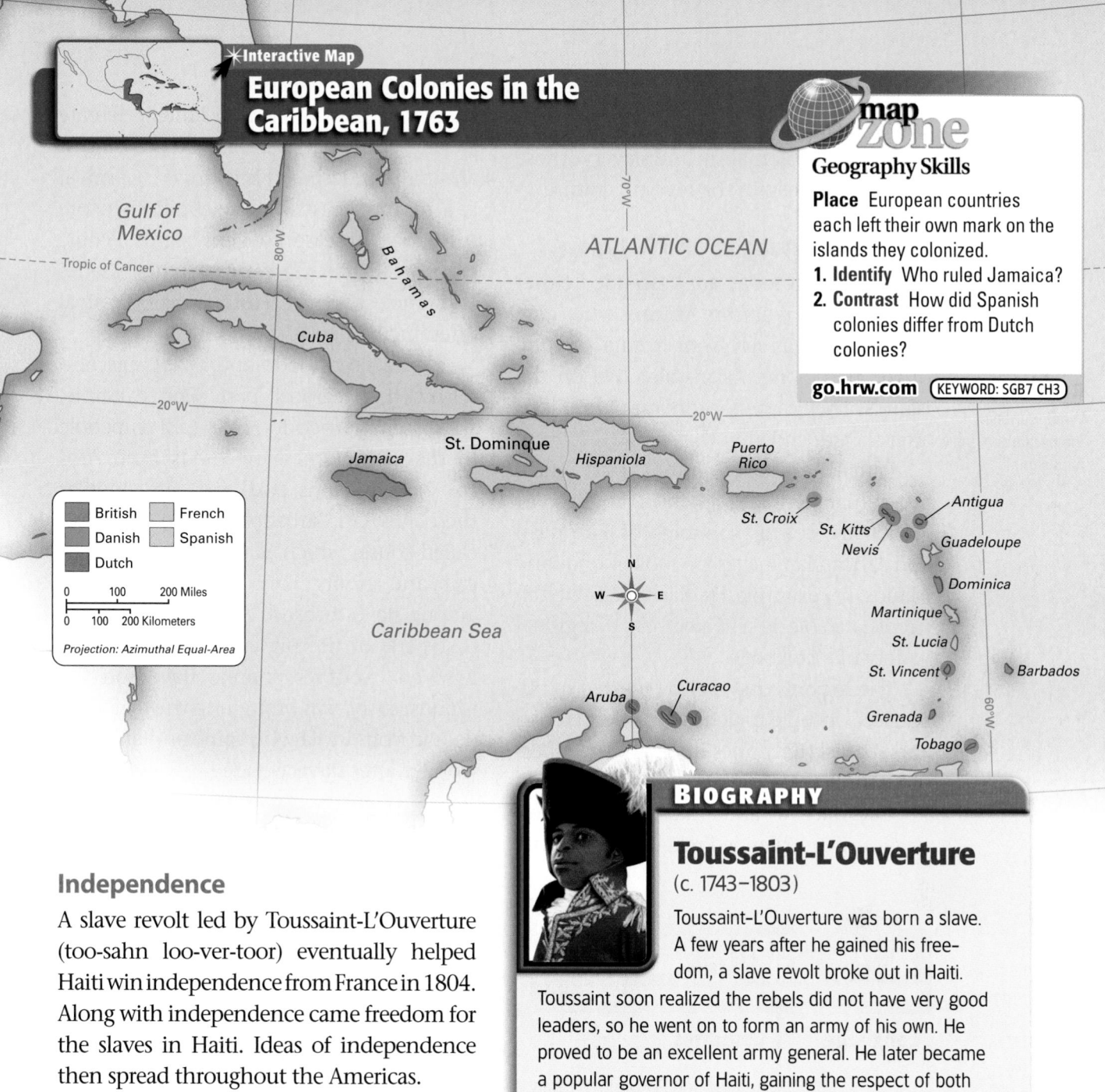

European Colonies in the Caribbean, 1763

*Interactive Map

Gulf of Mexico

Tropic of Cancer

ATLANTIC OCEAN

Bahamas

Cuba

Jamaica

St. Dominque

Hispaniola

Puerto Rico

St. Croix

St. Kitts
Nevis

Antigua

Guadeloupe

Dominica

Martinique

St. Lucia

St. Vincent

Barbados

Grenada

Tobago

Aruba

Curacao

Caribbean Sea

British **French**
Danish **Spanish**
Dutch

0   100   200 Miles
0 100   200 Kilometers

Projection: Azimuthal Equal-Area

N W E S

map zone

Geography Skills

Place European countries each left their own mark on the islands they colonized.
1. **Identify** Who ruled Jamaica?
2. **Contrast** How did Spanish colonies differ from Dutch colonies?

go.hrw.com (KEYWORD: SGB7 CH3)

BIOGRAPHY

Toussaint-L'Ouverture
(c. 1743–1803)

Toussaint-L'Ouverture was born a slave. A few years after he gained his freedom, a slave revolt broke out in Haiti. Toussaint soon realized the rebels did not have very good leaders, so he went on to form an army of his own. He proved to be an excellent army general. He later became a popular governor of Haiti, gaining the respect of both black and white people on the island.

Independence

A slave revolt led by Toussaint-L'Ouverture (too-sahn loo-ver-toor) eventually helped Haiti win independence from France in 1804. Along with independence came freedom for the slaves in Haiti. Ideas of independence then spread throughout the Americas.

By the mid-1800s, the Dominican Republic had gained independence. The United States won Cuba from Spain, but Cuba gained independence in 1902. The other Caribbean countries did not gain independence until more than 40 years later, after World War II. At that time, the Europeans transferred political power peacefully to most of the islands.

Many Caribbean islands still are not independent countries. For example, the islands of Martinique and Guadeloupe are still French possessions. Each has its own elected government and is also represented in the French government. Most people on these islands seem not to wish for independence from their ruling countries.

READING CHECK **Identifying Points of View** Why might an island's people not be interested in gaining independence?

Culture

Today nearly all Caribbean islands show signs of past colonialism and slavery. These signs can be seen in the region's culture.

People, Languages, and Religion

FOCUS ON READING

What words in the paragraph on food signal comparison?

Most islanders today are descended either from Europeans or from Africans who came to the region as slaves, or from a mixture of the two. Some Asians also live on the islands. They came to work on plantations after slavery ended in the region.

Languages spoken in the region reflect a colonial heritage. Spanish, English, or French as well as mixtures of European and African languages are spoken on many islands. For example, Haitians speak French Creole. Creole is a **dialect**, or a regional variety of a language.

The region's past is also reflected in the religions people practice. Former French and Spanish territories have large numbers of Catholics. People also practice a blend of Catholicism and traditional African religions. One blended religion is Santería.

Festivals and Food

People on the Caribbean islands celebrate a variety of holidays. One of the biggest and most widespread is Carnival. Carnival is a time of feasts and celebration before the Christian season of Lent begins. People usually celebrate Carnival with big parades and fancy costumes. Festivals like Carnival often include great music.

Caribbean food and cooking also reflect the region's past. For example, slave ships carried foods as well as people to the Caribbean. Now foods from Africa, such as yams and okra, are popular there. Also, in Barbados, people eat a dish called souse, which is made of pigs' tails, ears, and snouts. This dish was developed among slaves because slaveholders ate the best parts of the pig and gave slaves the leftovers. Another popular flavor on the islands, curry, was brought to the region by people from India who came as plantation workers after slavery ended.

READING CHECK **Generalizing** How does Caribbean culture reflect African influences?

THE WORLD ALMANAC
Facts about Countries **Languages of the Caribbean**

Language	Countries
English	Antigua and Barbuda, Barbados, Trinidad and Tobago
Creole English	Saint Kitts and Nevis, Grenada, Jamaica, Bahamas
Creole French	Haiti, Dominica, Saint Lucia
Spanish	Cuba, Puerto Rico, Dominican Republic

Interpreting Charts What language do people speak in Barbados?

go.hrw.com KEYWORD: SG7 CH8

Caribbean Music

The Caribbean islands have produced many unique styles of music. For example, Jamaica is famous as the birthplace of reggae. Merengue is the national music and dance of the Dominican Republic. Trinidad and Tobago is the home of steel-drum and calypso music.

Here, a band in the Grenadines performs on steel drums. Steel-drum bands can include as few as 4 or as many as 100 musicians. The instruments are actually metal barrels like the kind used for shipping oil. The end of each drum is hammered into a curved shape with multiple grooves and bumps. Hitting different-sized bumps results in different notes.

Drawing Inferences What role might trade have played in the development of steel-drum music?

The Caribbean Islands Today

Many Caribbean islands share a similar history and culture. However, today the islands' different economies, governments, and cultural landscapes encourage many different ways of life in the Caribbean.

Puerto Rico

Puerto Rico was a Spanish colony. Today it is a U.S. commonwealth. A **commonwealth** is a self-governing territory associated with another country. Although Puerto Ricans are U.S. citizens, they have no voting representation in the U.S. Congress. Puerto Ricans debate whether their island should remain a commonwealth. Some want it to become an American state. Others want it to become an independent country.

The link to the United States has been a big influence on Puerto Rico. U.S. aid and investment have helped make Puerto Rico's economy more developed than that of other Caribbean islands. However, wages remain lower and unemployment is still higher in Puerto Rico than in the United States. Many Puerto Ricans have moved to the United States to get better-paying jobs than they can find at home.

Haiti

Haiti occupies the mountainous western third of the island of Hispaniola. Port-au-Prince (pohr-toh-PRINS) is the capital and center of the country's limited industry. Agricultural products such as coffee and sugarcane are the country's main exports. Most Haitians farm small plots.

Haiti is the poorest country in the Americas. Its people have suffered under a string of corrupt governments during the last two centuries. Violence, political unrest, and poverty have created many political refugees. A **refugee** is someone who flees to another country, usually for political or economic reasons. Many Haitian refugees have come to the United States. Also, the United States has sent troops to Haiti on several occasions to help keep the peace.

Dominican Republic

The Dominican Republic occupies the eastern part of Hispaniola. The capital is Santo Domingo. Santo Domingo was the first permanent European settlement in the Western Hemisphere.

The Dominican Republic is not a rich country. However, its economy, health care, education, and housing are more developed than Haiti's. Agriculture is the basis of the economy in the Dominican Republic. The country's tourism industry has also grown in recent years. Beach resorts along the coast are popular with many tourists from Central and South America as well as from the United States.

Cuba

Cuba is the largest and most populous country in the Caribbean. It is located just 92 miles (148 km) south of Florida. **Havana**, the capital, is the country's largest and most important city.

Cuba has been run by a Communist government since Fidel Castro came to power in 1959. At that time, the government took over banks, large sugarcane plantations, and other businesses. Many of these businesses were owned by U.S. companies. Because of the takeovers, the U.S. government banned trade with Cuba and restricted travel there by U.S. citizens.

Today the government still controls the economy. Most of Cuba's farms are organized as cooperatives or government-owned plantations. A **cooperative** is an organization owned by its members and operated for their mutual benefit.

Besides controlling the economy, Cuba's government also controls all the newspapers, television, and radio stations. While many Cubans support these policies, others oppose them. Some people who oppose the government have become refugees in the United States. Many Cuban refugees have become U.S. citizens.

Cubans Divided

Government-sponsored rallies are a part of Cuban life. Meanwhile, some Cubans try to flee their country on tiny rafts.

ANALYZING VISUALS How can you tell that the people in the raft are trying to flee Cuba?

Other Islands

The rest of the Caribbean islands are small countries. Jamaica is the largest of the remaining Caribbean countries. The smallest country is Saint Kitts and Nevis. It is not even one-tenth the size of Rhode Island, the smallest U.S. state!

A number of Caribbean islands are not independent countries but territories of other countries. These territories include the U.S. and British Virgin Islands. The Netherlands and France also still have some Caribbean territories.

Some of these islands have enough land to grow some coffee, sugarcane, or spices. However, most islands' economies are based on tourism. Hundreds of people on the islands work in restaurants and hotels visited by tourists. While tourism has provided jobs and helped economies, not all of its effects have been positive. For example, new construction sometimes harms the same natural environment tourists come to the islands to enjoy.

READING CHECK **Contrasting** How are the governments of Puerto Rico and Cuba different?

Caribbean Tourism

Tourism has helped Caribbean economies. New developments, like this hotel in Saint Martin, have also changed many islands' landscapes.

SUMMARY AND PREVIEW The Caribbean islands were colonized by European countries, which influenced the culture of the islands. Today the islands have different types of governments but similar economies. Next, you will read about countries in South America that are also located near the Caribbean Sea.

Section 3 Assessment

go.hrw.com
Online Quiz
KEYWORD: SG7 HP8

Reviewing Ideas, Terms, and Places

1. a. Describe What crop was the basis of the colonial economy on the Caribbean islands?
b. Make Inferences Why do you think most smaller Caribbean countries were able to gain independence peacefully?

2. a. Define What is a **dialect**?
b. Explain In what ways have African influences shaped Caribbean culture?

3. a. Recall What is a **refugee**, and from what Caribbean countries have refugees come?
b. Make Inferences Why do you think many Cubans support their government's policies?
c. Evaluate What would be the benefits and drawbacks for Puerto Rico if it became a U.S. state?

Critical Thinking

4. Summarizing Look over your notes. Then use a diagram like this one to note specific influences on the region and where they came from in each circle. You may add more circles if you need to.

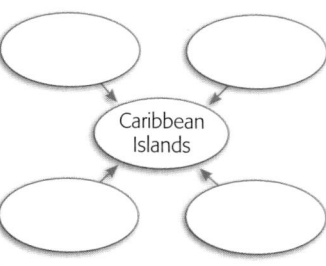

Caribbean Islands

FOCUS ON WRITING

5. Telling about the Caribbean Islands These islands have a fascinating history and a rich culture. Take notes about them for your travel guide.

Social Studies Skills

Chart and Graph | Critical Thinking | Geography | Study

Interpreting a Climate Graph

Learn

A climate graph is a visual representation of the climate in a certain region. The graph shows the average precipitation and average temperature for each month of the year.

Use the following tips to help you interpret a climate graph:

- The months of the year are labeled across the bottom of the graph.
- The measurements for monthly average temperatures are found on the left side of the graph.
- The measurements for monthly average precipitation are found on the right side of the graph.

Practice

Use the climate graph here to answer the following questions.

❶ What four months get the highest amount of precipitation?

❷ What months get fewer than two inches of precipitation?

❸ What is the average temperature in February?

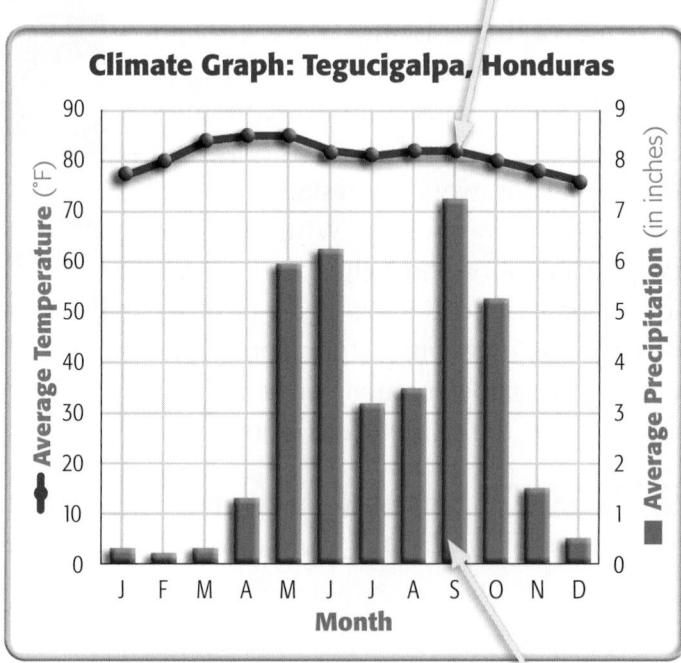

A line shows the average temperature each month.

Climate Graph: Tegucigalpa, Honduras

Source: The Weather Channel Interactive, Inc.

Bars show the average precipitation each month.

Apply

Using the Internet, an almanac, or a newspaper, look up the monthly average temperatures and precipitation for your home town. Then make your own climate graph using that information.

Chapter Review

Geography's Impact
video series
Review the video to answer the closing question:
Why do so many visitors to the Caribbean come from the United States and Canada?

Visual Summary

Use the visual summary below to help you review the main ideas of the chapter.

QUICK FACTS

The region's landscapes include warm coastal lowlands and cool highland regions with tropical forests.

Native cultures still influence Central America. Today governments and economies there are changing.

The Caribbean islands have a history of colonial rule. Today many countries' economies there depend on tourism.

Reviewing Vocabulary, Terms, and Places

Choose one word from each word pair to correctly complete each sentence below.

1. A(n) _____ is a narrow strip of land that connects two larger land areas. **(archipelago/ isthmus)**

2. A _____ is a self-governing territory associated with another country. **(commonwealth/ cooperative)**

3. A _____ is someone who flees to another country, usually for political or economic reasons. **(traditional/refugee)**

4. The United States controlled the _____ until 1999. **(Caribbean Sea/Panama Canal)**

5. The large islands of Cuba, Jamaica, Hispaniola, and Puerto Rico make up the _____. **(Greater Antilles/Lesser Antilles)**

6. _____ is found in the mountainous part of Central America. **(Cloud forest/Havana)**

Comprehension and Critical Thinking

SECTION 1 *(Pages 188–191)*

7. **a. Describe** What process has formed many of the Caribbean islands? Describe the effect this process has on the region today.

   b. Compare and Contrast How are summer and winter similar in Central America and the Caribbean? How are the seasons different?

   c. Elaborate What kinds of damage might hurricanes cause? What damage might earthquakes and volcanic eruptions cause?

SECTION 2 *(Pages 192–197)*

8. **a. Identify** In what Central American country is English the official language?

   b. Make Inferences Why do you think people of African ancestry live mainly along the coast?

   c. Elaborate How might recent political conflict have affected development in some countries?

9. a. Recall What country was the first to gain independence? Who led the revolt that led to independence?

b. Analyze How does tourism impact the smaller islands of the Caribbean?

c. Evaluate What might be some benefits and drawbacks of working for a cooperative?

Social Studies Skills

Interpreting a Climate Graph *Use the climate graph below to answer the questions that follow.*

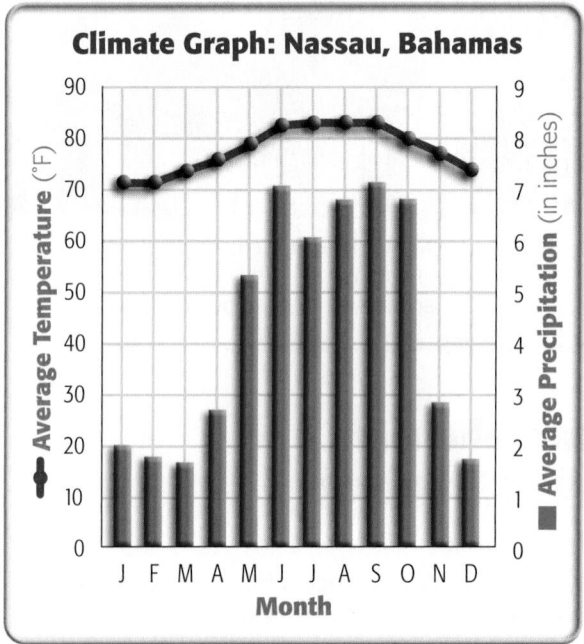

Climate Graph: Nassau, Bahamas

Source: The Weather Channel Interactive, Inc.

10. What two months get the most rainfall?

11. What is the average temperature in December?

Using the Internet

go.hrw.com
KEYWORD: SG7 CH8

12. Activity: Taking an Ecotour Ecotourism is all about visiting places to appreciate the environment. Enter the activity keyword to take your own Internet ecotour of Central America and the Caribbean islands. Visit the Web sites to learn more about some of the people and places you have read about in this chapter. Then create a postcard from a place you visited on your trip.

13. Understanding Comparison-Contrast Look back over the section on physical geography. Then write a paragraph of 3 to 4 sentences comparing and contrasting Central America with the Caribbean islands. Consider their physical features, climates, landscapes, and resources.

14. Creating a Travel Guide Choose one place in this region to be the subject of your travel guide. Then look over your notes for facts about that place to interest your reader. Your guide should begin with a paragraph describing the outstanding physical features of the place. Your second paragraph should identify interesting details about its history and culture. End with a sentence that might encourage your readers to visit. Include two images in your guide to show off the features of the place you have chosen.

Map Activity

15. Central America and the Caribbean On a separate sheet of paper, match the letters on the map with their correct labels.

Guatemala

Caribbean Sea

Panama

Puerto Rico

Havana, Cuba

Lesser Antilles

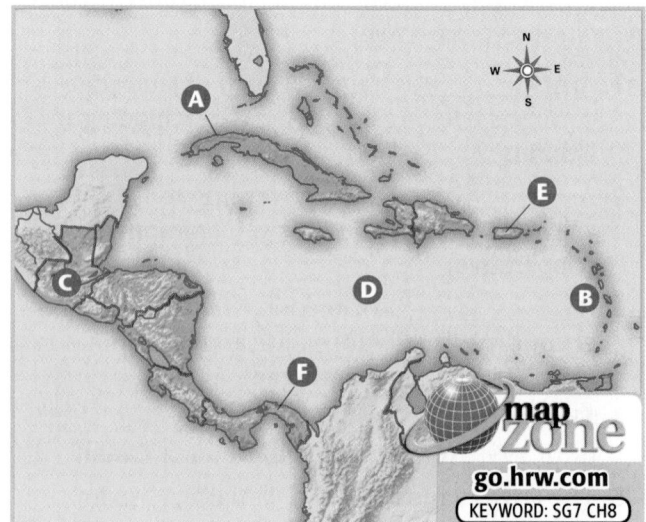

go.hrw.com
KEYWORD: SG7 CH8

DIRECTIONS: *Read questions 1 through 7 and write the letter of the best response. Then read question 8 and write your own well-constructed response.*

1 Which country is an example of an isthmus?

A Guatemala

B Bahamas

C Panama

D Cuba

2 Which European country established the most colonies in the Greater Antilles?

A France

B Spain

C England

D Netherlands

3 Which country has a Communist government?

A Cuba

B Puerto Rico

C Dominican Republic

D Haiti

4 Which of the following countries has remained at peace since independence?

A Guatemala

B El Salvador

C Nicaragua

D Costa Rica

5 Which of the following sentences about the region's economy is false?

A Coffee and bananas are major export crops.

B The region has good energy resources.

C The region's climate, land, and history attract many tourists.

D Most countries have limited economic development.

Languages of Central America

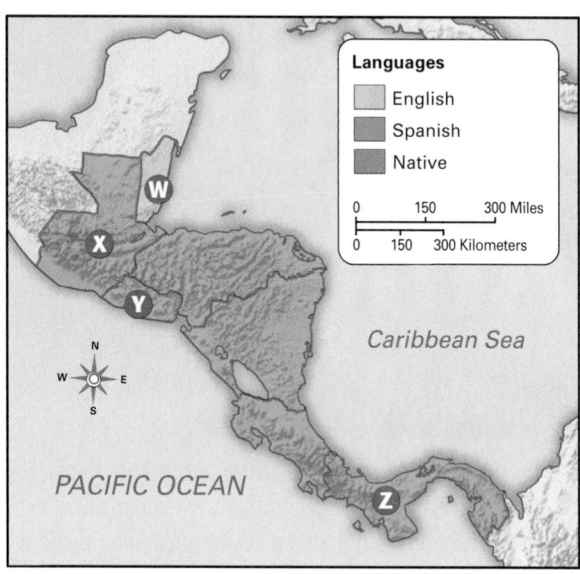

6 On the map above, which letter represents the country where English is spoken?

A W

B X

C Y

D Z

7 On the map above, which letters represent countries whose people speak either Spanish or a native language?

A W and X

B X and Y

C Y and Z

D X and Z

8 Extended Response Using the map above and your knowledge of Central America, write a description of influences on culture in Central America today.

Caribbean South America

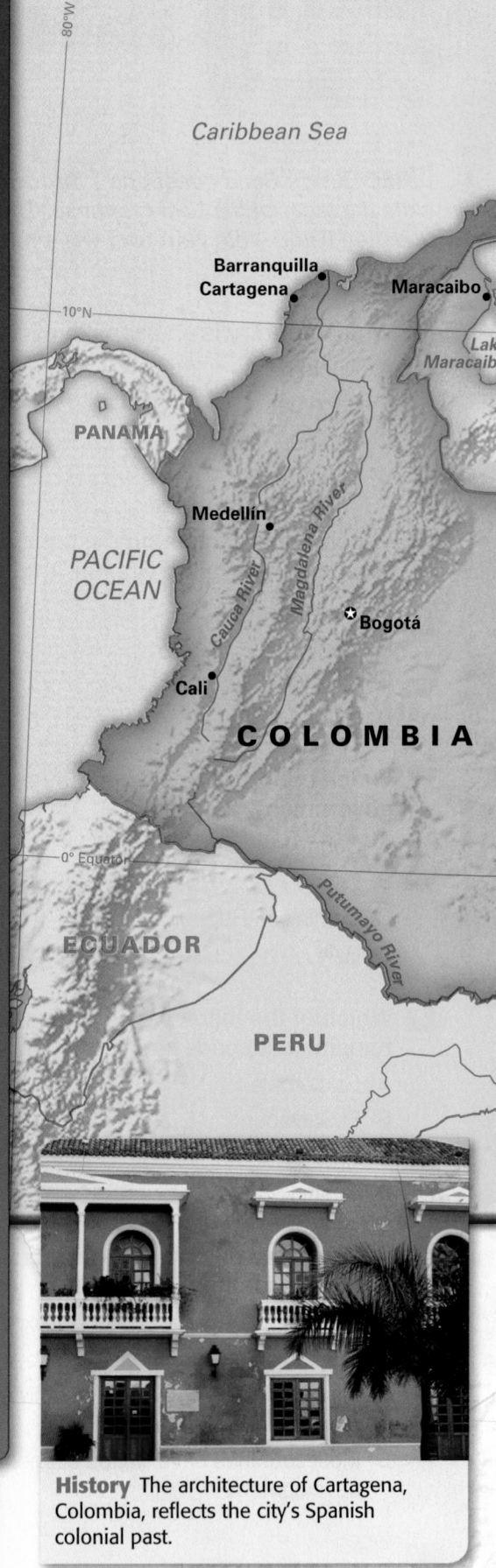

What You Will Learn...

In this chapter you will learn about the physical geography, history, and cultures of Colombia, Venezuela, Guyana, Suriname, and French Guiana. These countries make up the region of Caribbean South America.

FOCUS ON READING AND WRITING

Identifying Supporting Details Supporting details are the facts and examples that provide information to support the main ideas of a chapter, section, or paragraph. At the beginning of each section in this book, there is a list of main ideas. As you read this chapter, look for the details that support each section's main ideas. **See the lesson, Identifying Supporting Details, on page R10.**

Writing a Letter You live in a country in Caribbean South America. Your pen pal in the United States has asked you to write a letter telling her about life in your region. As you read this chapter, collect details to include in your letter. Your friend will want to know about your country as well as the whole region.

History The architecture of Cartagena, Colombia, reflects the city's Spanish colonial past.

Caribbean South America: Political

National capital ⊛
Other capitals ★
Other cities •

0   100   200 Miles
0   100   200 Kilometers
Projection: Azimuthal Equal-Area

ATLANTIC OCEAN

TRINIDAD AND TOBAGO

Caracas
Valencia

VENEZUELA

Orinoco River

Orinoco River

Georgetown

GUYANA

Paramaribo

Cayenne

SURINAME

FRENCH GUIANA (FRANCE)

N W E S

Rio Negro

BRAZIL

Amazon River

map zone

Geography Skills

Place Most of Caribbean South America is located on the Caribbean Sea.

1. **Identify** What is the capital of Venezuela?
2. **Contrast** How is Colombia's location different from Venezuela's location?

go.hrw.com   KEYWORD: SG7 CH9

HOLT

Geography's Impact
video series
Watch the video to learn about the impact of the Orinoco River.

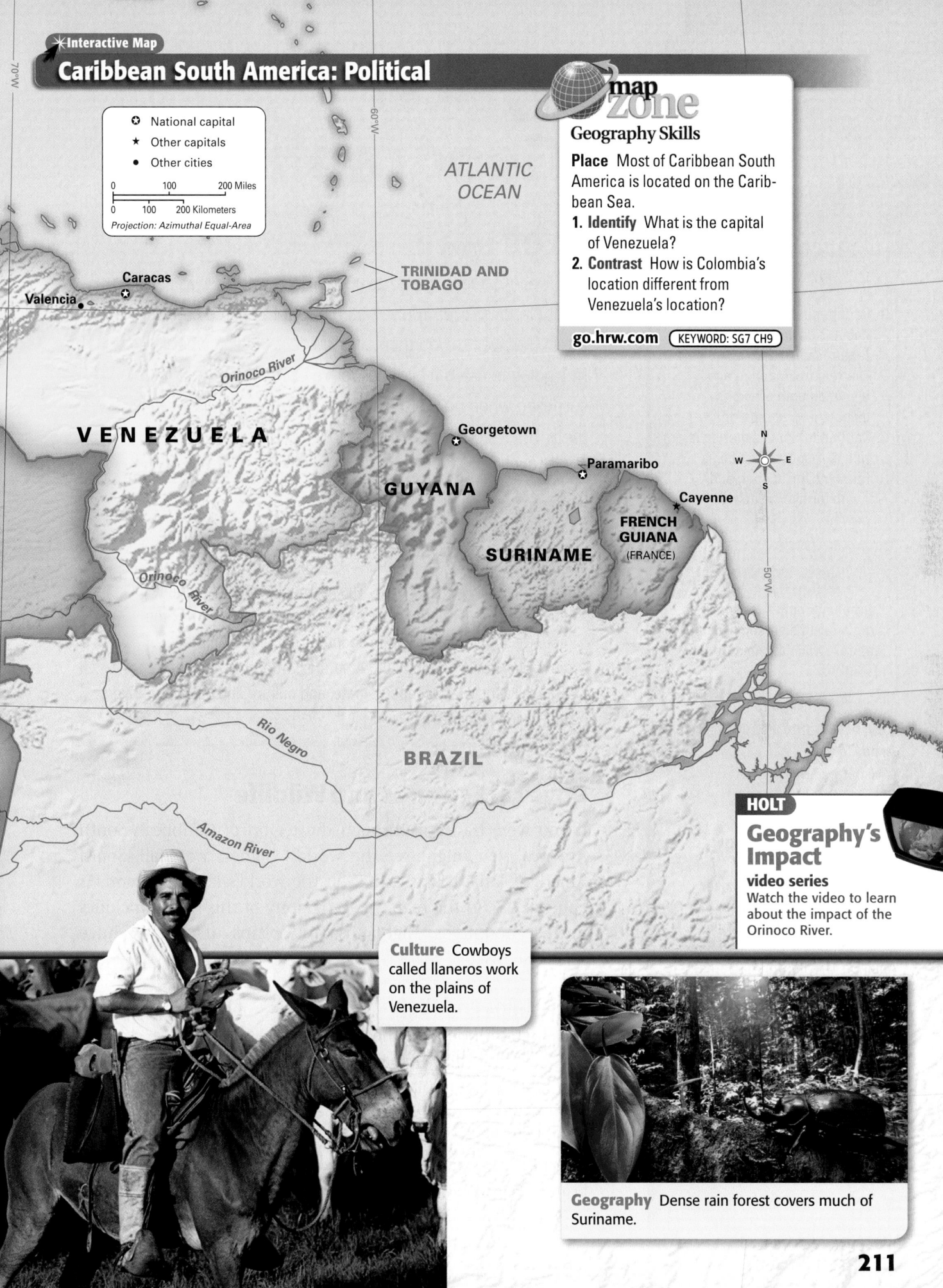

Culture Cowboys called llaneros work on the plains of Venezuela.

Geography Dense rain forest covers much of Suriname.

Physical Geography

If YOU lived there...

You live in Caracas, Venezuela, but this is your first visit to the great Orinoco River. You've heard about the fierce creatures that live in the river, so you think your guide is kidding when he says he's going to catch a piranha. You're expecting a monster and are surprised when he pulls up a small orange fish. It has many sharp teeth, but it's only seven inches long!

What other animals might you see in the region?

BUILDING BACKGROUND The narrow Isthmus of Panama joins the continent of South America at its northwestern corner, the country of Colombia. Like the countries of Central America, the five countries in Caribbean South America border the Caribbean Sea. They all vary in landscape, climate, and culture and have large rivers and rugged mountains.

Physical Features and Wildlife

If you were traveling through the region of Caribbean South America, you might see the world's highest waterfall, South America's largest lake, and even the world's largest rodent! As you can see on the map, the geography of this region includes rugged mountains, highlands, and plains drained by huge river systems.

Mountains and Highlands

The highest point in the region is in Colombia, a country larger than California and Texas combined. On the western side of Colombia the **Andes** (AN-deez) reach 18,000 feet (5,490 m). The Andes form a **cordillera** (kawr-duhl-YER-uh), a mountain system made up of roughly parallel ranges. Some of the Andes' snowcapped peaks are active volcanoes. Eruptions and earthquakes shake these mountains frequently.

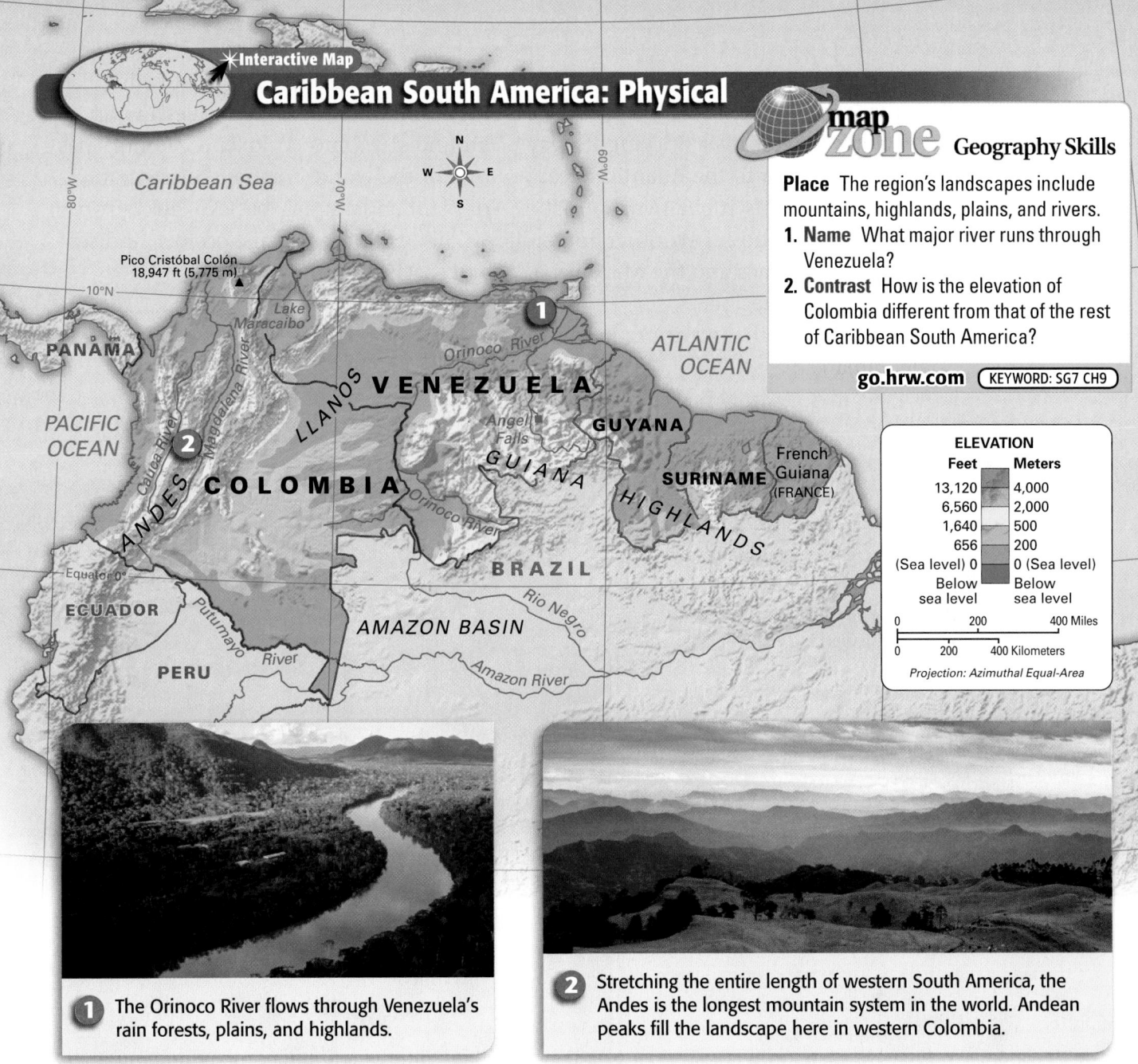

map zone Geography Skills

Place The region's landscapes include mountains, highlands, plains, and rivers.
1. **Name** What major river runs through Venezuela?
2. **Contrast** How is the elevation of Colombia different from that of the rest of Caribbean South America?

go.hrw.com KEYWORD: SG7 CH9

Caribbean Sea

Pico Cristóbal Colón 18,947 ft (5,775 m)

Lake Maracaibo

PANAMA

PACIFIC OCEAN

ANDES

Cauca River
Magdalena River

LLANOS

VENEZUELA

Orinoco River

ATLANTIC OCEAN

COLOMBIA

Angel Falls

GUYANA

GUIANA

SURINAME

French Guiana (FRANCE)

HIGHLANDS

Orinoco River

BRAZIL

Rio Negro

ECUADOR

Putumayo River

AMAZON BASIN

Amazon River

PERU

ELEVATION

Feet	Meters
13,120	4,000
6,560	2,000
1,640	500
656	200
(Sea level) 0	0 (Sea level)
Below sea level	Below sea level

0   200   400 Miles
0   200   400 Kilometers
Projection: Azimuthal Equal-Area

1 The Orinoco River flows through Venezuela's rain forests, plains, and highlands.

2 Stretching the entire length of western South America, the Andes is the longest mountain system in the world. Andean peaks fill the landscape here in western Colombia.

Lying on the Caribbean coast, Venezuela is located in the middle of the other countries in the region. Venezuela's highest elevation is in the **Guiana Highlands**, which stretch into Guyana and Suriname. For millions of years, wind and rain have eroded these highlands' plateaus. However, some of the steep-sided plateaus are capped by sandstone layers that have resisted erosion. These unusual flat-topped formations are sometimes called *tepuís* (tay-PWEEZ). The *tepuís* create a dramatic landscape as they rise about 3,000 to 6,000 feet (900 to 1,800 m) above the surrounding plains.

Plains, Rivers, and Wildlife

As you look at the map above, notice how much the elevation drops between the highlands and the Andes. This region of plains is known as the **Llanos** (YAH-nohs). The Llanos is mostly grassland with few trees. At a low elevation and not much vegetation, these plains flood easily.

FOCUS ON
READING
What details in
this paragraph
support this
section's first
main idea?

Flowing for about 1,600 miles (2,575 km), the **Orinoco** (OHR-ee-NOH-koh) **River** is the region's longest river. Snaking its way through Venezuela to the Atlantic Ocean, the Orinoco and its tributaries drain the plains and highlands. Two other important rivers, the Cauca and the Magdalena, drain the Andean region.

Caribbean South America is home to some remarkable wildlife. For example, hundreds of bird species, meat-eating fish called piranhas, and crocodiles live in or around the Orinoco River. Colombia has one of the world's highest concentrations of plant and animal species. The country's wildlife includes jaguars, ocelots, and several species of monkeys.

READING CHECK **Summarizing** What are the region's major physical features?

Venezuela's Canaima National Park

Covering almost 3 million acres of eastern Venezuela, Canaima National Park is one of the largest national parks in the world.

ANALYZING VISUALS What do you think attracts millions of people from around the world to visit Canaima National Park?

GUYANA

Angel Falls

Canaima National Park

Mt. Roraima ▲

Caroni River

VENEZUELA

BRAZIL

Dropping more than 3,200 feet (975 m), Angel Falls is the world's highest waterfall.

A rocky *tepuí* rises from the park's flat plains. Hundreds of these flat-topped mountains are scattered throughout the park.

The red-billed toucan is among the almost 500 species of birds that live in the park.

Climate and Vegetation

Caribbean South America's location near the equator means that most of the region has warm temperatures year-round. However, temperatures do vary with elevation. For example, in the Andes, as you go up in elevation, the temperature can drop rapidly—about four degrees Fahrenheit every 1,000 feet (305 m).

In contrast, the vast, flat landscape of the Llanos region has a tropical savanna climate. Here, both the wet and dry seasons provide favorable conditions for grasslands to grow.

Rain forests, another type of landscape, thrive in the humid tropical climate of southern Colombia. This area is a part of the Amazon Basin. Here, rain falls throughout the year, watering the forest's huge trees. These trees form a canopy where the vegetation is so dense that sunlight barely shines through to the jungle floor.

READING CHECK **Analyzing** What causes the region's temperatures to vary?

Resources

Good soil and moderate climates help make most of Caribbean South America a rich agricultural region. Major crops include rice, coffee, bananas, and sugarcane.

In addition, the region has other valuable resources, such as oil, iron ore, and coal. Both Venezuela and Colombia have large oil-rich areas. Forests throughout the region provide timber. While the seas provide plentiful fish and shrimp, the region's major rivers are used to generate hydroelectric power.

READING CHECK **Summarizing** How do geographic factors affect economic activities in Caribbean South America?

SUMMARY AND PREVIEW In this section you learned that the physical geography of Caribbean South America includes mountains, highlands, plains, and rivers. The region's location near the equator and its elevation affect the region's climate. In the next section you will learn about Colombia's history, people, and economy. You will also learn about the challenges Colombia is facing today, which include a civil war.

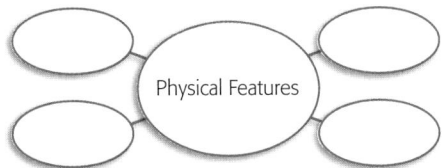
go.hrw.com
Online Quiz
KEYWORD: SG7 HP9

Section 1 Assessment

Reviewing Ideas, Terms, and Places

1. **a. Recall** Where are the **Andes** located?
   b. Explain How are the rock formations called *tepuís* unusual?
   c. Elaborate Why do the **Llanos** in Colombia and Venezuela flood easily?
2. **a. Describe** In the Andes, how does the temperature change with elevation?
   b. Make Inferences How does the region's location near the equator affect its climate?
3. **a. Identify** What is a major resource in both Venezuela and Colombia?
   b. Explain Which resource provides hydroelectric power?

Critical Thinking

4. **Categorizing** Use your notes to identify four types of physical features in the region. Write each type in one of the small circles of the diagram.

Physical Features

FOCUS ON WRITING

5. **Describing Physical Geography** Take notes about the physical features, wildlife, climate, vegetation, and resources of the region. After you decide which country you are living in, collect more details about it.

Colombia

If YOU lived there...

You live in the beautiful colonial city of Cartagena, on the coast of the Caribbean. Your family runs a small restaurant there. You're used to the city's wide beaches and old colonial buildings with wooden balconies that overhang the street. Now you are on your way to visit your cousins. They live on a cattle ranch on the inland plains region called the Llanos.

How do you think life on the ranch is different from yours?

BUILDING BACKGROUND Like most of the countries of Central and South America, Colombia was once a colony of Spain. Colombians gained their independence from Spain in 1819. The new country was then named after the explorer Christopher Columbus.

Colombia's History

Giant mounds of earth, mysterious statues, and tombs—these are the marks of the people who lived in Colombia more than 1,500 years ago. Colombia's history begins with these people. It also includes conquest by Spain and, later, independence.

The Chibcha

Have you heard of the legend of El Dorado (el duh-RAH-doh), or the Golden One? That legend about

This gold Chibcha artifact represents the ceremonial raft used by their king.

a land rich in gold was inspired by the Chibcha culture in Colombia. The Chibcha covered their new rulers in gold dust. Then they took each ruler to a lake to wash the gold off. As the new ruler washed, the Chibcha threw gold and emerald objects into the water. A well-developed civilization, they practiced pottery making, weaving, and metalworking. Their gold objects were among the finest in ancient America.

Spanish Conquest

In about 1500 Spanish explorers arrived on the Caribbean coast of South America. The Spaniards wanted to expand Spain's new empire. In doing so, the Spanish conquered the Chibcha and seized much of their treasure. Soon after claiming land for themselves, the Spaniards founded a colony and cities along the Caribbean coast.

One colonial city, **Cartagena**, was a major naval base and commercial port in the Spanish empire. By the 1600s Spaniards and their descendants had set up large estates in Colombia. Spanish estate owners forced South American Indians and enslaved Africans to work the land.

Independence

In the late 1700s people in Central and South America began struggling for independence from Spain. After independence was achieved, the republic of Gran Colombia was created. It included Colombia, Ecuador, Panama, and Venezuela. In 1830 the republic dissolved, and New Granada, which included Colombia and Panama, was created.

After independence, two different groups of Colombians debated over how Colombia should be run. One group wanted the Roman Catholic Church to participate in government and education. On the other hand, another group did not want the church involved in their lives.

CONNECTING TO History

Cartagena's Spanish Fort

Imagine you are a Spanish colonist living in Cartagena, Colombia, in the 1600s. Your city lies on the Caribbean coast and has been attacked by English pirates several times. They have stolen tons of silver and gold that were waiting shipment to Spain. How do you protect your city from these pirates? Build an enormous fort, of course! You make sure to design the fort's walls to deflect the cannonballs that the pirates shoot from their ships. Today this fort still stands on a peninsula outside Cartagena. A statue commemorates one of the heroes that defended the city from attack.

Drawing Conclusions Why did the Spanish want to defend Cartagena from the pirates?

Outbreaks of violence throughout the 1800s and 1900s killed thousands. Part of the problem had to do with the country's rugged geography, which isolated people in one region from those in another region. As a result, they developed separate economies and identities. Uniting these different groups into one country was hard.

READING CHECK **Drawing Conclusions** How did Spanish conquest shape Colombia's history and culture?

Different regions of Colombia are home to diverse ethnic groups.

ANALYZING VISUALS What are some of the goods sold in this market?

Colombians of African descent unload their goods at a local market near the Pacific coast.

Colombia Today

Colombia is Caribbean South America's most populous country. The national capital is **Bogotá**, a city located high in the eastern Andes. Although Colombia is rich in culture and resources, 40 years of civil war have been destructive to the country's economy.

People and Culture

Most Colombians live in the fertile valleys and river basins among the mountain ranges, where the climate is moderate and good for farming. Rivers, such as the Cauca and the Magdalena, flow down from the Andes to the Caribbean Sea. These rivers provide water and help connect settlements located between the mountains and the coast. Other Colombians live on cattle ranches scattered throughout the Llanos. Few people live in the tropical rainforest regions in the south.

Because the physical geography of Colombia isolates some regions of the country, the people of Colombia are often known by the region where they live. For example, those who live along the Caribbean coast are known for songs and dances influenced by African traditions.

FOCUS ON READING

In the first paragraph under Economy, find at least three details to support the idea stated in the first sentence.

Colombian culture is an interesting mix of influences:

• Music: traditional African songs and dances on the Caribbean coast and South American Indian music in remote areas of the Andes
• Sports: soccer, as well as a traditional Chibcha ring-toss game called *tejo*
• Religion: primarily Roman Catholicism
• Official language: Spanish
• Ethnic groups: 58 percent mestizo; also Spanish, African, and Indian descent

Economy

Colombia's economy relies on several valuable resources. Rich soil, steep slopes, and tall shade trees produce world-famous Colombian coffee. Other major export crops include bananas, sugarcane, and cotton. Many farms in Colombia produce flowers that are exported around the world. In fact, 80 percent of the country's flowers are shipped to the United States.

Colombia's economy depends on the country's valuable natural resources. Recently oil has become Colombia's major export. Other natural resources include iron ore, gold, and coal. Most of the world's emeralds also come from Colombia.

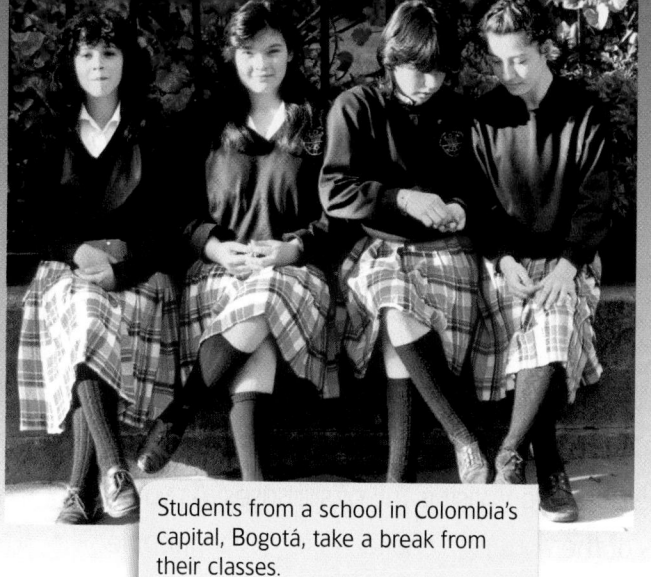

Students from a school in Colombia's capital, Bogotá, take a break from their classes.

Here in the Andes people travel from town to town on these colorful buses, called *chivas*.

Civil War

Civil war is a major problem in Colombia today. Many different groups have waged war with each other and with Colombia's government. For the past 40 years, these heavily armed militant groups have controlled large areas of the country.

One of these groups is an army of **guerrillas**, or members of an irregular military force. These guerrillas want to overthrow the government. The guerrillas, as well as other militant groups, have forced farmers off their land and caused thousands of Colombians to flee the country. All of these groups are also involved in growing crops of the illegal coca plant. This plant is used to make cocaine, a dangerous drug.

Because of the instability caused by civil war, the future of Colombia is uncertain. However, the Colombian government has passed new laws that make it harder for the guerrillas and other militant groups to operate freely. In addition, the United States provides assistance to Colombia's government. Colombia is one of the top recipients of U.S. foreign aid.

READING CHECK **Drawing Conclusions** How do you think civil war affects daily life in Colombia?

SUMMARY AND PREVIEW Colombia's history includes the Chibcha, Spanish conquest, and independence. Today, Colombia's people are dealing with a long civil war. Next, you will learn about Colombia's neighbor, Venezuela.

go.hrw.com
Online Quiz
KEYWORD: SG7 HP9

Section 2 Assessment

Reviewing Ideas, Terms, and Places
1. **a. Recall** Who were the Chibcha?
   b. Draw Conclusions Why did Spain want land in Colombia?
2. **a. Describe** What factors make Colombia ideal for growing coffee?
   b. Interpret In what part of the country do most Colombians live?
   c. Predict How might Colombia solve the problem of **guerrillas** trying to control the country?

Critical Thinking
3. **Analyzing** Using your notes, write a sentence about the topic of each box in a diagram like this one.

Music	→	
Sports	→	
Religion	→	
Language	→	

FOCUS ON WRITING
4. **Writing about Colombia** What information about the history, culture, and daily life of Colombia might your pen pal like to learn? Add these details to your notes.

Venezuela and the Guianas

If YOU lived there...

You've come from your home in eastern Venezuela to visit the nearby country of Suriname. Your visit is full of surprises. As you walk along the streets of the country's capital, Paramaribo, people are not speaking Spanish, but Dutch, English, and some languages you don't even recognize. You see Hindu temples and Muslim mosques alongside Christian churches.

Why is Suriname so different from Venezuela?

BUILDING BACKGROUND Venezuela, like Colombia, was once a Spanish colony, but the Guianas were colonized by other nations— Great Britain, the Netherlands, and France. When these countries gained independence, British Guiana became Guyana and Dutch Guiana became Suriname.

History and Culture of Venezuela

Venezuela was originally the home of many small tribes of South American Indians. Those groups were conquered by the Spanish in the early 1500s. Though Venezuela became independent from Spain in the early 1800s, those three centuries of Spanish rule shaped the country's history and culture.

Spanish Settlement and Colonial Rule

The Spanish came to Venezuela hoping to find gold and pearls. They forced the native Indians to search for these treasures, but they finally realized there was little gold to be found. Then the Spanish turned to agriculture, once again forcing the Indians to do the work. They grew indigo (IN-di-goh), a plant used to make a deep blue dye. Because the work was very hard, many of the Indians died. Then the Spanish began bringing enslaved Africans to take the Indians' places. Eventually, some of the slaves escaped, settling in remote areas of the country.

Venezuela's Independence

Each year, Venezuelans celebrate Simon Bolívar's efforts in achieving Venezuela's independence. Independence Day is filled with parades and parties.

Independence and Self-Rule

Partly because the colony was so poor, some people in Venezuela revolted against Spain. Simon Bolívar helped lead the fight against Spanish rule. Bolívar is considered a hero in many South American countries because he led wars of independence throughout the region. Bolívar helped win Venezuelan independence from Spain by 1821. However, Venezuela did not officially become independent until 1830.

Throughout the 1800s Venezuelans suffered from dictatorships and civil wars. Venezuela's military leaders ran the country. After oil was discovered in the early 1900s, some leaders kept the country's oil money for themselves. As a result, the people of Venezuela did not benefit from their country's oil wealth.

People and Culture

The people of Venezuela are descended from native Indians, Europeans, and Africans. The majority of Venezuelans are of mixed Indian and European descent. Indians make up only about 2 percent of the population. People of European descent tend to live in the large cities. People of African descent tend to live along the coast. Most Venezuelans are Spanish-speaking Roman Catholics, but the country's Indians speak 25 different languages and follow the religious practices of their ancestors.

Venezuelan culture includes dancing and sports. Venezuela's national dance, the *joropo*, is a lively foot-stomping couples' dance. Large crowds of Venezuelans attend rodeo events. Baseball and soccer are also popular throughout Venezuela.

READING CHECK **Summarizing** How did the Spanish contribute to Venezuela's history?

FOCUS ON READING

In the paragraphs under Venezuela Today, what details support the main idea that oil production plays a large role in Venezuela's economy and government?

Venezuela Today

Many Venezuelans make a living by farming and ranching. However, most wealthy Venezuelans have made money in the country's oil industry. In addition, Venezuela's government has also benefited from oil wealth.

Agriculture and Ranching

Rural areas of Venezuela are dotted by farms and ranches. Northern Venezuela has some small family farms as well as large commercial farms. **Llaneros** (yah-NAY-rohs)—or Venezuelan cowboys—herd cattle on the many ranches of the Llanos region. However, some small communities of Indians practice traditional agriculture.

Economy and Natural Resources

In the 1960s Venezuela began earning huge sums of money from oil production. This wealth allowed part of the population to buy luxuries. However, the vast majority of the population still lived in poverty. Many of Venezuela's poor people moved to the cities to try to find work. Some settled on the outskirts in communities of shacks. They had no running water, sewers, or electricity.

Venezuela's wealth attracted many immigrants from Europe and other South American countries. These immigrants, like most other Venezuelans, suffered in the 1980s when the price of oil dropped sharply. Without the money provided by high oil prices, the economy couldn't support the people. Oil prices recovered in the 1990s, and the Venezuelan economy continues to be based on oil production.

As you can see on the map on the next page, the Orinoco River basin and **Lake Maracaibo** (mah-rah-KY-boh) are rich in oil. Venezuela is the only South American member of the Organization of Petroleum

The Feast of Corpus Christi

One day each summer, men dressed as devils dance in the streets of the Venezuelan town of San Francisco de Yare. On this day, people here honor the Roman Catholic feast day of Corpus Christi. Spanish settlers brought the tradition of dressing up as devils to Venezuela. This tradition includes the making of elaborate, colorful masks that the dancers wear. These masks usually resemble pigs or jaguars. Dancing through the town's streets to the beat of drums, the dancers shake musical instruments called maracas. They believe their dancing, music, and scary masks will keep evil away from their town.

Summarizing How do some Venezuelans celebrate the Feast of Corpus Christi?

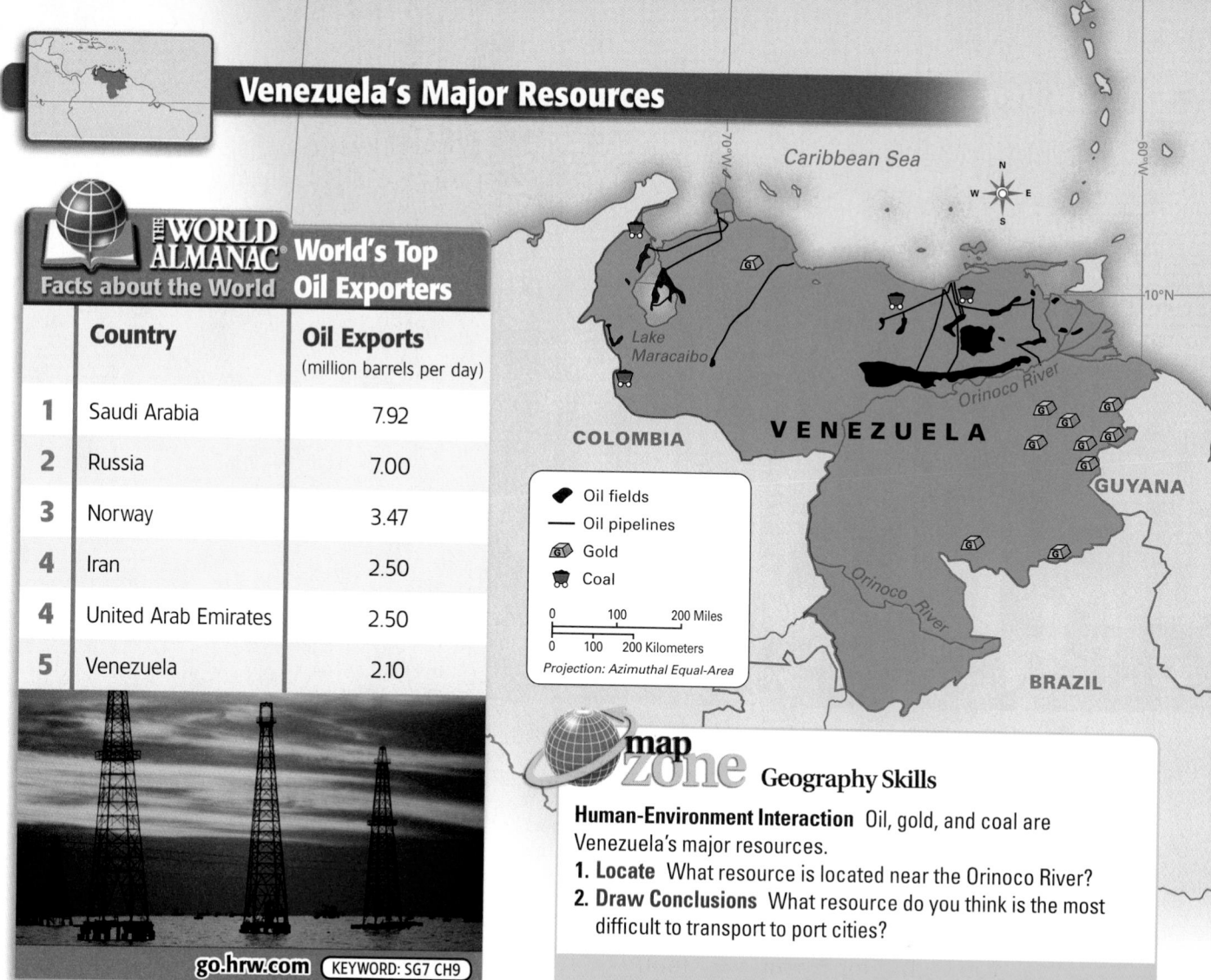

THE WORLD ALMANAC
Facts about the World

World's Top Oil Exporters

	Country	Oil Exports (million barrels per day)
1	Saudi Arabia	7.92
2	Russia	7.00
3	Norway	3.47
4	Iran	2.50
4	United Arab Emirates	2.50
5	Venezuela	2.10

go.hrw.com KEYWORD: SG7 CH9

map zone Geography Skills

Human-Environment Interaction Oil, gold, and coal are Venezuela's major resources.
1. **Locate** What resource is located near the Orinoco River?
2. **Draw Conclusions** What resource do you think is the most difficult to transport to port cities?

Exporting Countries (OPEC). The member countries in this organization attempt to control world oil production and keep oil prices from falling too low.

The Guiana Highlands in the southeast are rich in other minerals, such as iron ore for making steel. Gold is also mined in remote areas of the highlands. Dams on tributaries of the Orinoco River produce hydroelectricity.

Caracas (kah-RAH-kahs) is Venezuela's capital and the economic and cultural center of the country. It is a large city with a modern subway system, busy expressways, and tall office buildings. Still, neither Caracas nor Venezuela has escaped poverty.

Caracas is encircled by slums, and many Venezuelans living in the rural areas of the country are also poor.

Government

After years of suffering under military dictatorships, the people of Venezuela elected their first president in 1959. Since then, Venezuela's government has dealt with economic turmoil and political protests.

In 2002 Venezuela's president, Hugo Chavez, started to distribute the country's oil income equally among all Venezuelans. Before Chavez's presidency, only a small percentage of wealthy Venezuelans benefited from the country's oil income.

Caracas, Venezuela

With a population of more than 4 million, Venezuela's capital city, Caracas, is the country's financial and cultural center.

ANALYZING VISUALS Why do you think Caracas is located in this mountain valley?

Millions of Venezuelans went on strike to protest the president's actions as well as a failing economy. A **strike** is a group of workers stopping work until their demands are met. Some of Venezuela's workers went on strike for about two months. They wanted President Chavez to resign, but he refused. As a result of the strike, the Venezuelan economy suffered and the country's oil exports fell dramatically.

Many Venezuelans opposed to President Chavez called for a **referendum**, or recall vote. In 2004 Venezuelans voted for whether Chavez would remain in office or not. About 58 percent of Venezuelans voted for Chavez. Many of these voters believed he should use the country's oil wealth to help them. In his second term in office, Chavez adopted new **policies** to help end poverty, illiteracy, and hunger.

ACADEMIC
VOCABULARY
policy rule,
course of action

READING CHECK Identifying Cause and Effect What effect did the workers' strike have on Venezuela's economy?

The Guianas

The countries of Guyana, Suriname, and French Guiana are together known as the Guianas (gee-AH-nuhz). Dense tropical rain forests cover much of this region, which lies east of Venezuela.

Guyana

Guyana (gy-AH-nuh) comes from a South American Indian word that means "land of waters." About one-third of the country's population lives in Georgetown, the capital. Nearly all of Guyana's agricultural lands are located on the flat, fertile plains along the coast. Guyana's most important agricultural products are rice and sugar.

Guyana's population is diverse. About half of its people are descended from people who migrated to Guyana from India. These immigrants came to Guyana to work on the country's sugar plantations. Most Guyanese today farm small plots of land or run small businesses. About one-third of the population is descended from former African slaves. These people operate large businesses and hold most of the government positions.

Suriname

The resources and economy of Suriname (soohr-uh-NAHM) are similar to those of Guyana. Like Guyana, Suriname has a diverse population. The country's population includes South Asians, Africans, Chinese, Indonesians, and Creoles—people of mixed heritage. The capital, Paramaribo (pah-rah-MAH-ree-boh), is home to nearly half of the country's people.

French Guiana

French Guiana (gee-A-nuh) is a territory of France and sends representatives to the government in Paris. French Guiana's roughly 200,000 people live mostly in coastal areas. About two-thirds of the people are of African descent. Other groups include Europeans, Asians, and South American Indians. The country depends heavily on imports for its food and energy.

READING CHECK **Contrasting** How is French Guiana different from the rest of the Guianas?

Creole women carry gifts to a party in downtown Paramaribo. About 30 percent of Suriname's population is Creole.

SUMMARY AND PREVIEW In this section, you learned that Venezuela's history was largely shaped by Spanish settlement. Today Venezuela's economy is based on oil. You also learned that to the east, the Guianas are home to a diverse population. In the next chapter, you will learn about the history and people of Atlantic South America.

Section 3 Assessment

go.hrw.com
Online Quiz
KEYWORD: SG7 HP9

Reviewing Ideas, Terms, and Places

1. **a. Recall** What did Spanish settlers hope to find in Venezuela?
   b. Explain Who led Venezuela's revolt against Spain?
2. **a. Describe** What does the landscape of **Caracas** include?
   b. Explain How is oil important to Venezuela's economy?
   c. Elaborate Why did some Venezuelans go on **strike**?
3. **a. Describe** What are Guyana's agricultural lands and products like?
   b. Contrast How is population of the Guianas different from that of Colombia and Venezuela?

Critical Thinking

4. **Identifying Cause and Effect** Using your notes on Venezuela's natural resources and this diagram, list the effects of oil production on Venezuela's people, economy, and government.

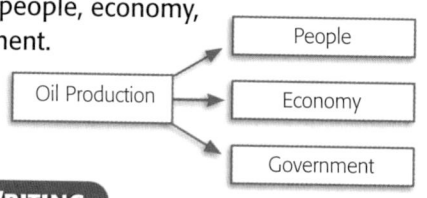

FOCUS ON WRITING

5. **Writing about Venezuela and the Guianas** Collect details about Venezuela and the Guianas for your letter. What is interesting about these cultures?

Social Studies Skills

Chart and Graph | Critical Thinking | Geography | Study

Using Latitude and Longitude

Learn

The pattern of imaginary lines that circle the globe in east-west and north-south directions is called a grid. Geographers measure the distances between the lines of the grid in degrees.

Look at the diagram to the right. As you can see, lines that run east to west are lines of latitude. These lines measure distance north and south of the equator. Lines that run north to south are lines of longitude. These lines measure distance east and west of the prime meridian.

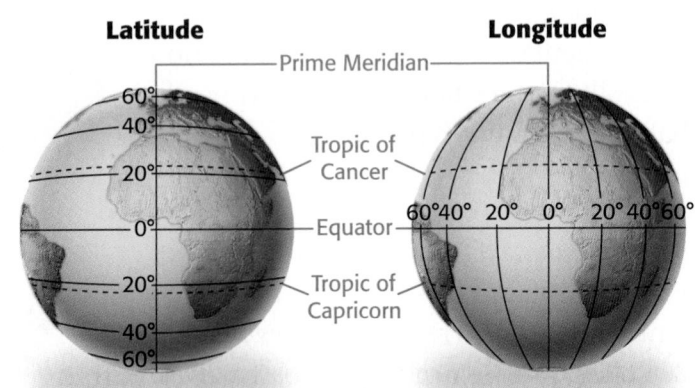

Practice

Look at the world map to the right. Use these guidelines to read latitude and longitude.

1 Pick a city on the map.

2 To find the latitude of the city you picked, first look at the equator. From there, look at the city's location. Then find the closest line of latitude to see how many degrees the city is north or south of the equator.

3 To find the longitude of the city, first look at the prime meridian. Then find the closest line of longitude to see how many degrees the city is east or west of the prime meridian.

World: Political

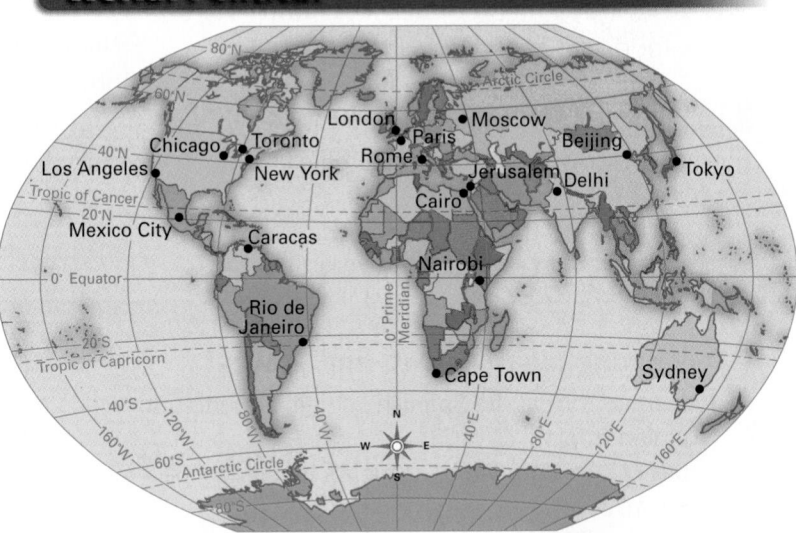

Apply

Using an atlas, find a map of the United States and a map of the world. On the map of the United States, find the line of latitude that is located near your hometown. Then look at a world map and follow this line of latitude across the world. Which countries share the same latitude as your hometown?

Chapter Review

Geography's Impact
video series
Review the video to answer the closing question:
What are some advantages and disadvantages of industries along the Orinoco River?

Visual Summary

Use the visual summary below to help you review the main ideas of the chapter.

QUICK FACTS

Caribbean South America's physical features include rivers, plains, mountains, and the world's highest waterfall.

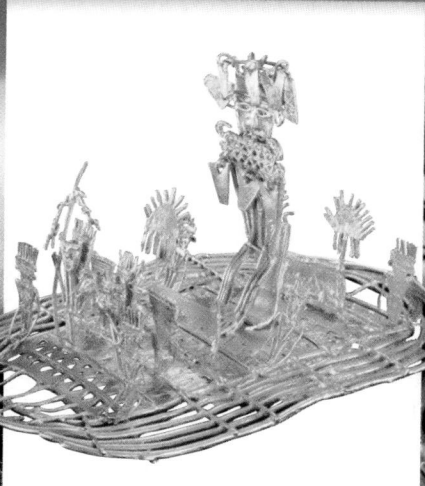

A country rich in history and culture, Colombia is enduring a civil war today.

Venezuela is an oil-rich nation that has a population of mostly mixed Indian and European descent.

Reviewing Vocabulary, Terms, and Places

For each statement below, write T if it is true and F if it is false.

1. The Andes is a river system.

2. The Orinoco River flows 1,300 miles (2,100 km) through Venezuela.

3. Caribbean South America's location near the equator means that the region is very cold.

4. The Chibcha were the first people to settle Colombia.

5. Colombian culture includes traditional African songs and dances.

6. Most Venezuelans are of mixed Indian and European descent.

7. Venezuela gained its independence from France.

8. Venezuela's economy depends on oil production.

Comprehension and Critical Thinking

SECTION 1 *(Pages 212–215)*

9. **a. Recall** What is the region's longest river?

   b. Analyze How does the temperature vary in the Andes?

   c. Evaluate Why do you think it would be hard to live in the rain forest of Colombia?

SECTION 2 *(Pages 216–219)*

10. **a. Describe** How did the Chibcha treat their ruler?

    b. Draw Conclusions What created a problem for all Colombians after independence?

    c. Elaborate Why do most Colombians live in fertile valleys and river basins?

SECTION 3 *(Pages 220–225)*

11. **a. Define** What is a strike?

SECTION 3 *(continued)*

b. Draw Conclusions Why did people from India immigrate to Guyana?

c. Predict Do you think Venezuela's government will continue to use oil wealth to help the country's people? Explain your answer.

Using the Internet

 go.hrw.com
KEYWORD: SG7 CH9

12. Activity: Writing a Journal Entry Ride with the llaneros! Pack your bags and prepare for a trek through the South American countryside. Explore the vast grasslands, visit villages, and learn about the life and work of the cowboys, or llaneros, of the Venezuelan plains. Enter the activity keyword. Then research and take notes about your adventure. Use the interactive template to write your journal entry. Describe what you have learned about the people and places you visited.

Social Studies Skills

13. Using Latitude and Longitude Look at the physical map in Section 1. Find the lines of latitude and longitude. What line of latitude, shown on the map, runs through both Venezuela and Colombia? Which country in Caribbean South America is partly located on the equator?

14. Identifying Supporting Details Look back over Section 2 on Colombia. Then make a list of details you find to support the section's main ideas. Make sure you include details about the Spanish conquest, independence, culture, resources, and civil war.

15. Writing a Letter By now you have information about the region and the country you have chosen to live in. Begin your letter to your pen pal by describing the most interesting physical and cultural features of the whole region. Then write a second paragraph telling your pen pal about the special physical and cultural features of the country you've chosen to live in. Try to keep your pen pal interested in reading by including fascinating details and descriptions.

Map Activity

16. Caribbean South America On a separate sheet of paper, match the letters on the map with their correct labels.

Llanos   Andes

Guiana Highlands   Orinoco River

Lake Maracaibo

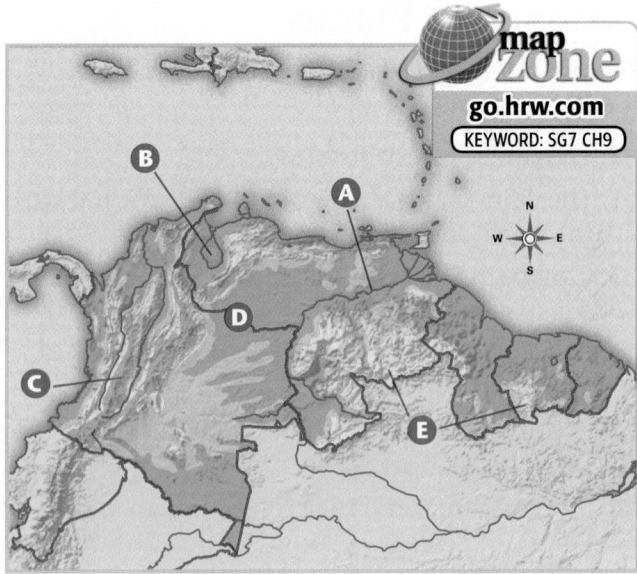

go.hrw.com
KEYWORD: SG7 CH9

DIRECTIONS: *Read questions 1 through 7 and write the letter of the best response. Then read question 8 and write your own well-constructed response.*

1 **Temperatures in Caribbean South America remain warm year-round because of the region's location near the**

A equator.

B Caribbean Sea.

C Amazon Basin.

D Tropic of Cancer.

2 **What valuable natural resource were the Chibcha known for using?**

A silver

B gold

C copper

D iron

3 **What Colombian city was a major naval base and commercial port in the Spanish empire?**

A Bogotá

B Cali

C Caracas

D Cartagena

4 **Venezuela's economy is based on**

A oil production.

B flower exports.

C small farms.

D silver mining.

5 **Simon Bolívar helped several South American countries gain independence from**

A Britain.

B Brazil.

C Spain.

D Mexico.

Volcanoes of Colombia

6 **Based on the map above, active volcanoes are located in Colombia's**

A rivers.

B mountains.

C plains.

D coastal areas.

7 **The physical geography of the Guianas includes**

A dense rain forests.

B deserts.

C the Orinoco River.

D the Andes.

8 **Extended Response** Look at the table of the world's oil exporters and the map of Venezuela's major resources in Section 3. Write a paragraph explaining why oil is Venezuela's most important resource. Identify at least two reasons.

Atlantic South America

What You Will Learn...

In this chapter you will learn about the plains and rain forest of Atlantic South America. You will also study the histories of the different countries and how different influences have shaped their cultures. In addition, you will learn about life, landscapes, and issues in Brazil, Argentina, Uruguay, and Paraguay today.

FOCUS ON READING AND WRITING

Using Context Clues As you read, you may find some unknown words. You can usually figure out what a word means by using context clues. Look at the words and sentences around the unknown word—its context—to figure out the definition. **See the lesson, Using Context Clues, on page R11.**

Creating a Web Site You are a Web designer at a travel agency. Read this chapter and then use what you learn to create a Web site about Atlantic South America. The goal of your Web site will be to convince viewers to visit the region.

PACIFIC OCEAN

110°W
100°W

0° Equator

20°S

⊘ National capital

● Other cities

0   300   600 Miles
0   300   600 Kilometers

Projection:
Lambert Azimuthal Equal-Area

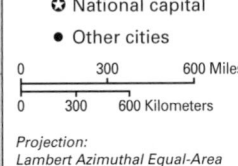
map zone

Geography Skills

Place Brazil and Argentina are South America's largest countries.
1. **Identify** What city lies on the Amazon River?
2. **Analyze** What would be some benefits of the location of Buenos Aires?

go.hrw.com KEYWORD: SG7 CH10

Culture During Carnival, Brazilians celebrate with music, dancing, and costumes.

VENEZUELA

GUYANA   SURINAME

COLOMBIA   FRENCH GUIANA
                        (FRANCE)

ECUADOR

Amazon River   •Manaus

PERU

B R A Z I L

N
W ⊕ E
S

BOLIVIA

•Salvador

✪Brasília

—Tropic of Capricorn—

CHILE   PARAGUAY

Asunción ✪

Paraná River

Rio de Janeiro•

São Paulo•

Córdoba•

URUGUAY

Buenos Aires ✪   ✪ Montevideo

ARGENTINA

ATLANTIC
OCEAN

0° Equator

10°S

20°S

30°S

40°S

50°S

Falkland
Islands

90°W 80°W 70°W 60°W 50°W 40°W 30°W

HOLT

Geography's Impact

video series
Watch the video to
understand the impact
of deforestation in the
Amazon Basin.

Geography The
Amazon Basin covers a
huge forested region in
northern Brazil.

History Colonial buildings, such as the Casa Rosada
in Buenos Aires, reflect the region's colonial heritage.

231

Physical Geography

If YOU lived there...

You live on the coast of Brazil, near the mouth of the Amazon River. Now you are taking your first trip up the river deep into the rain forest. The river is amazingly wide and calm. Trees on the riverbanks seem to soar to the sky. Your boat slows as you pass a small village. You notice that all the houses rest on poles that lift them 8 to 10 feet out of the water.

What would it be like to live in the rain forest?

BUILDING BACKGROUND While rugged mountains and highlands dominate the lansdcape of Caribbean South America, much of the Atlantic region is made up of broad interior plains. Landscapes in this region range from tropical rain forest to temperate, grassy plains.

Physical Features

The region of Atlantic South America includes four countries: Brazil, Argentina, Uruguay, and Paraguay. This large region covers about two-thirds of South America. Brazil alone occupies nearly half of the continent. Most of the physical features found in South America are found in these four countries.

Major River Systems

The world's largest river system, the Amazon, flows eastward across northern Brazil. The **Amazon River** is about 4,000 miles (6,440 km) long. It extends from the Andes Mountains in Peru to the Atlantic Ocean. Hundreds of tributaries flow into it, draining an area that includes parts of most South American countries.

Because of its huge drainage area, the Amazon carries more water than any other river in the world. About 20 percent of the water that runs off Earth's surface flows down the Amazon. Where it meets the Atlantic, this freshwater lowers the salt level of the Atlantic for more than 100 miles (160 km) from shore.

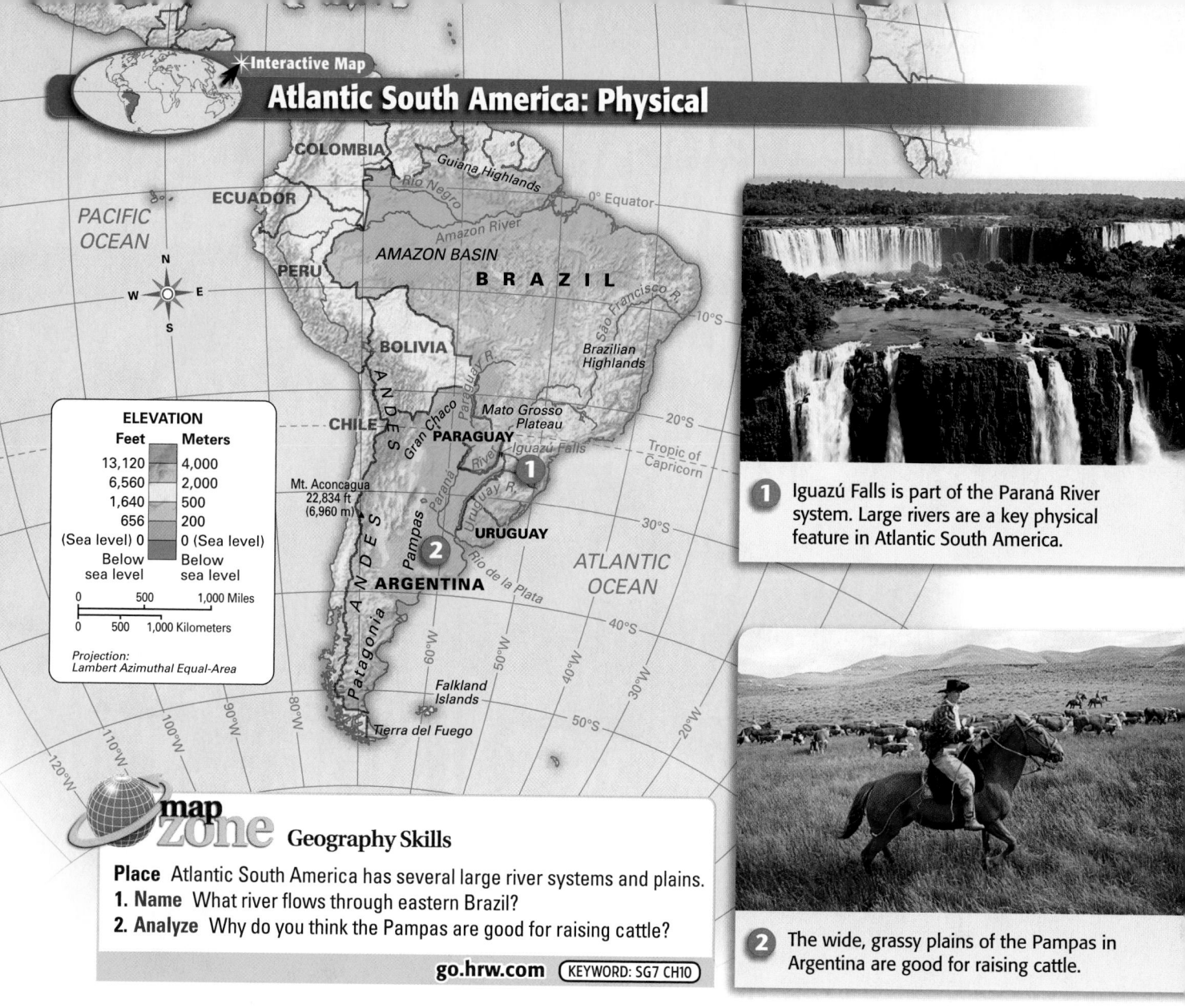

ELEVATION

Feet	Meters
13,120	4,000
6,560	2,000
1,640	500
656	200
(Sea level) 0	0 (Sea level)
Below sea level	Below sea level

Mt. Aconcagua 22,834 ft (6,960 m)

Projection: Lambert Azimuthal Equal-Area

map zone **Geography Skills**

Place Atlantic South America has several large river systems and plains.
1. **Name** What river flows through eastern Brazil?
2. **Analyze** Why do you think the Pampas are good for raising cattle?

go.hrw.com   KEYWORD: SG7 CH10

1 Iguazú Falls is part of the Paraná River system. Large rivers are a key physical feature in Atlantic South America.

2 The wide, grassy plains of the Pampas in Argentina are good for raising cattle.

The Paraná (pah-rah-NAH) River drains much of the central part of South America. Water from the Paraná River eventually flows into the **Río de la Plata** (REE-oh day lah PLAH-tah) and the Atlantic Ocean beyond. The Río de la Plata is an estuary. An **estuary** is a partially enclosed body of water where freshwater mixes with salty seawater.

Plains and Plateaus

As you can see on the map, this region's landforms mainly consist of plains and plateaus. The Amazon Basin in northern Brazil is a giant, flat floodplain. South of the Amazon Basin are the Brazilian Highlands, a rugged region of old, eroded mountains, and another area of high plains called the Mato Grosso Plateau.

Farther south, a low plains region known as the Gran Chaco (grahn CHAH-koh) stretches across parts of Paraguay and northern Argentina. In central Argentina are the wide, grassy plains of the **Pampas**. South of the Pampas is Patagonia—a region of dry plains and plateaus. All of these southern plains rise in the west to form the high Andes Mountains.

READING CHECK **Summarizing** What are the region's major landforms and rivers?

FOCUS ON READING

Where can you find the definition of *Pampas*?

The Amazon rain forest covers more than one-third of South America. Seen from the air, it looks like a big, green carpet. The top level of tree branches is called the canopy. Most action in the forest takes place in the canopy, but plenty of life also exists below.

Animals such as monkeys and sloths can spend their entire lives in the canopy.

People have cleared parts of the rain forest for farming, ranching, and logging.

Parts of the forest are flooded for half the year, and trees stand in water up to 40 feet (12 m) deep.

ANALYSIS SKILL **ANALYZING VISUALS**

What kinds of animals could not survive living in the canopy?

Climate and Vegetation

Atlantic South America has many climates. Generally, cool climates in southern and highland areas give way to tropical, moist climates in northern and coastal areas.

In southern Argentina Patagonia has a cool, desert climate. North of Patagonia, rich soils and a humid subtropical climate make parts of the Pampas good for farming. Farther north in Argentina, the Gran Chaco has a humid tropical climate. There, summer rains can turn some parts of the plains into marshlands.

North of Argentina, in Brazil, a large part of the central region has a tropical savanna climate with warm grasslands. The northeastern part of the country has a hot, dry climate, while the southeast is cooler and more humid.

In northern Brazil the Amazon Basin's humid tropical climate supports the world's largest tropical rain forest. Rain falls almost every day in this region. The Amazon rain forest contains the world's greatest variety of plant and animal life.

READING CHECK **Finding Main Ideas** What is the climate like in the rain forest?

Natural Resources

The Amazon rain forest is one of the region's greatest natural resources. It provides food, wood, rubber, plants for medicines, and other products. In recent years **deforestation**, or the clearing of trees, has become an issue in the forest.

The region's land is also a resource for commercial farming, which is found near coastal areas of Atlantic South America. In some areas, however, planting the same crop every year has caused **soil exhaustion**, which means the soil is infertile because it has lost nutrients needed by plants.

Atlantic South America also has good mineral and energy resources such as gold, silver, copper, iron, and oil. Dams on some of the region's large rivers also provide hydroelectric power.

READING CHECK **Summarizing** What resources does the rain forest provide?

SUMMARY AND PREVIEW Physical features of Atlantic South America include great river systems and plains. The Amazon rain forest makes up a huge part of the region. Next you will learn about Brazil, the country of the Amazon.

Section 1 Assessment

go.hrw.com
Online Quiz
KEYWORD: SG7 HP10

Reviewing Ideas, Terms, and Places

1. **a. Define** What is an **estuary**?
   b. Explain How does the **Amazon River** affect the Atlantic Ocean at the river's mouth?
   c. Elaborate What benefits do you think the rivers might bring to Atlantic South America?
2. **a. Recall** What kind of climate does Patagonia have?
   b. Make Inferences Why are temperatures in the south generally cooler than temperatures in the north?
3. **a. Identify** What resources does the rain forest provide?
   b. Analyze What is one benefit and one drawback of practicing commercial agriculture in the rain forest?
   c. Elaborate **Soil exhaustion** might lead to what kinds of additional problems?

Critical Thinking

4. **Categorizing** Look back over your notes. Then use a table like this one to organize the physical geography of Atlantic South America by country.

	Geography
Brazil	
Argentina	

FOCUS ON WRITING

5. **Describing Physical Geography** Jot down notes about the physical features, climate and vegetation, landscapes, and resources of this area. Identify one or two images you could use for your Web site.

Brazil

What You Will Learn...

Main Ideas

1. Brazil's history has been affected by Brazilian Indians, Portuguese settlers, and enslaved Africans.
2. Brazil's society reflects a mix of people and cultures.
3. Brazil today is experiencing population growth in its cities and new development in rain forest areas.

The Big Idea

The influence of Brazil's history can be seen all over the country in its people and culture.

Key Terms and Places

São Paulo, *p. 238*
megacity, *p. 238*
Rio de Janeiro, *p. 238*
favelas, *p. 239*
Brasília, *p. 239*
Manaus, *p. 239*

TAKING NOTES As you read, use a graphic organizer like this to take notes on Brazil's history, culture, and four different regions.

If YOU lived there...

You live in Rio de Janeiro, Brazil's second-largest city. For months your friends have been preparing for Carnival, the year's biggest holiday. During Carnival, people perform in glittery costumes and there is dancing all day and all night in the streets. The city is packed with tourists. It can be fun, but it is hectic! Your family is thinking of leaving Rio during Carnival so they can get some peace and quiet, but you may stay in Rio with a friend if you like.

Would you stay for Carnival? Why or why not?

BUILDING BACKGROUND Carnival is a tradition that is not unique to Brazil, but it has come to symbolize certain parts of Brazilian culture. Brazilian culture differs from cultures in the rest of South America in many ways. Brazil's unique history in the region is responsible for most of the cultural differences.

History

Brazil is the largest country in South America. Its population of more than 188 million is larger than the population of all of the other South American countries combined. Most Brazilians are descended from three groups of people who contributed in different ways throughout Brazil's history.

Colonial Brazil

The first people in Brazil were American Indians. They arrived in the region many thousands of years ago and developed a way of life based on hunting, fishing, and small-scale farming.

In 1500 Portuguese explorers became the first Europeans to find Brazil. Soon Portuguese settlers began to move there. Good climates and soils, particularly in the northeast, made Brazil a large sugar-growing colony. Colonists brought a third group of people—Africans—to work as slaves on the plantations. Sugar plantations made Portugal rich, but they also eventually replaced forests along the Atlantic coast.

Other parts of Brazil also contributed to the colonial economy. Inland, many Portuguese settlers created cattle ranches. In the late 1600s and early 1700s, people discovered gold and precious gems in the southeast. A mining boom drew people to Brazil from around the world. Finally, in the late 1800s southeastern Brazil became a major coffee-producing region.

Brazil Since Independence

Brazil gained independence from Portugal without a fight in 1822. However, independence did not change Brazil's economy much. For example, Brazil was the last country in the Americas to end slavery.

Since the end of Portuguese rule, Brazil has been governed at times by dictators and at other times by elected officials. Today the country has an elected president and legislature. Brazilians can participate in politics through voting.

READING CHECK **Summarizing** What was Brazil's colonial economy like?

People and Culture

The people who came to Brazil over the years brought their own traditions. These traditions blended to create a unique Brazilian culture.

People

More than half of Brazilians consider themselves of European descent. These people include descendants of original Portuguese settlers along with descendants of more recent immigrants from Spain, Germany, Italy, and Poland. Nearly 40 percent of Brazil's people are of mixed African and European descent. Brazil also has the largest Japanese population outside of Japan.

Because of its colonial heritage, Brazil's official language is Portuguese. In fact, since Brazil's population is so huge, there are more Portuguese-speakers in South America than there are Spanish-speakers, even though Spanish is spoken in almost every other country on the continent. Other Brazilians speak Spanish, English, French, Japanese, or native languages.

FOCUS ON READING
What context clues in this paragraph help you understand the meaning of *descent*?

Soccer in Brazil

To Brazilians, soccer is more than a game. It is part of being Brazilian. Professional stars are national heroes. The national team often plays in Rio de Janeiro, home of the world's largest soccer stadium. Some fans beat drums all through the games. But it is not just professional soccer that is popular. People all over Brazil play soccer—in cleared fields, on the beach, or in the street. Here, boys in Rio practice their skills.

Analyzing Why do you think soccer is so popular in Brazil?

Regions of Brazil

Brazil's regions differ from each other in their people, climates, economies, and landscapes.

ANALYZING VISUALS Which region appears to be the wealthiest?

1 The southeast has the country's largest cities, such as Rio de Janeiro.

Religion

Brazil has the largest population of Roman Catholics of any country in the world. About 75 percent of Brazilians are Catholic. In recent years Protestantism has grown in popularity, particularly among the urban poor. Some Brazilians practice macumba (mah-KOOM-bah), a religion that combines beliefs and practices of African and Indian religions with Christianity.

Festivals and Food

ACADEMIC VOCABULARY

aspects parts

Other **aspects** of Brazilian life also reflect the country's mix of cultures. For example, Brazilians celebrate Carnival before the Christian season of Lent. The celebration mixes traditions from Africa, Brazil, and Europe. During Carnival, Brazilians dance the samba, which was adapted from an African dance.

Immigrant influences can also be found in Brazilian foods. In parts of the country, an African seafood dish called vatapá (vah-tah-PAH) is popular. Many Brazilians also enjoy eating feijoada (fay-ZHWAH-dah), a stew of black beans and meat.

READING CHECK **Analyzing** How has cultural borrowing affected Brazilian culture?

Brazil Today

Brazil's large size creates opportunities and challenges for the country. For example, Brazil has the largest economy in South America and has modern and wealthy areas. However, many Brazilians are poor.

While some of the same issues and characteristics can be found throughout Brazil, other characteristics are unique to a particular region of the country. We can divide Brazil into four regions based on their people, economies, and landscapes.

The Southeast

Most people in Brazil live in the southeast. **São Paulo** is located there. More than 17 million people live in and around São Paulo. It is the largest urban area in South America and the fourth largest in the world. São Paulo is considered a **megacity**, or a giant urban area that includes surrounding cities and suburbs.

Rio de Janeiro, Brazil's second-largest city, lies northeast of São Paulo. Almost 11 million people live there. The city was the capital of Brazil from 1822 until 1960. Today Rio de Janeiro remains a major port city. Its spectacular setting and exciting culture are popular with tourists.

2 The dry northeast is Brazil's poorest region. Here, children attend school in the shade.

3 Rivers provide resources and transportation for people living in the Amazon region.

In addition to having the largest cities, the southeast is also Brazil's richest region. It is rich in natural resources and has most of the country's industries and productive farmland. It is one of the major coffee-growing regions of the world.

Although the southeast has a strong economy, it also has poverty. Cities in the region have huge slums called **favelas** (fah-VE-lahz). Many people who live in favelas have come to cities of the southeast from other regions of Brazil in search of jobs.

The Northeast

Immigrants to Brazil's large cities often come from the northeast, which is Brazil's poorest region. Many people there cannot read, and health care is poor. The region often suffers from droughts, which make farming and raising livestock difficult. The northeast has also had difficulty attracting industry. However, the region's beautiful beaches do attract tourists.

Other tourist attractions in northeastern Brazil are the region's many old colonial cities. These cities were built during the days of the sugar industry. They have brightly painted buildings, cobblestone streets, and elaborate Catholic churches.

The Interior

The interior region of Brazil is a frontier land. Its abundant land and mild climate could someday make it an important area for agriculture. For now, few people live in this region, except for those who reside in the country's capital, **Brasília**.

In the mid-1950s government officials hoped that building a new capital city in the Brazilian interior would help develop the region. Brasília has modern buildings and busy highways. More than 2 million people live in Brasília, although it was originally designed for only 500,000.

The Amazon

The Amazon region covers the northern part of Brazil. **Manaus**, which lies 1,000 miles (1,600 km) from the mouth of the Amazon, is a major port and industrial city. More than 1 million people live there. They rely on the river for transportation and communication.

Isolated Indian villages are scattered throughout the region's dense rain forest. Some of Brazil's Indians had little contact with outsiders until recently. Now, logging, mining, and new roads are bringing more people and development to this region.

Deforestation in the Amazon

Deforestation is changing the landscape of the Amazon rain forest. This satellite image shows new roads and cleared areas where people have taken resources from the forest.

Many people depend on the industries that result in deforestation. For example, people need wood for building and making paper. Also, farmers, loggers, and miners need to make a living. However, deforestation in the Amazon also threatens the survival of many plant and animal species. It also threatens hundreds of unique ecosystems.

Making Inferences What do you think might be some effects of building roads in the rain forest?

This new development provides needed income for some people. But it destroys large areas of the rain forest. It also creates tensions among the Brazilian Indians, new settlers, miners, and the government.

READING CHECK **Contrasting** How does the northeast of Brazil differ from the southeast?

SUMMARY AND PREVIEW In this section you read about Brazil—a huge country of many contrasts. Brazil reflects the mixing of people and cultures from its history. In the next section you will learn about Brazil's neighbors—Argentina, Uruguay, and Paraguay.

Section 2 Assessment

go.hrw.com
Online Quiz
KEYWORD: SG7 HP10

Reviewing Ideas, Terms, and Places

1. **a. Recall** What European country colonized Brazil?
   b. Make Inferences Why did the colonists bring Africans to work on plantations as slaves?
   c. Elaborate Why do you think the main basis of Brazil's colonial economy changed over the years?
2. **a. Identify** What religion is most common in Brazil?
   b. Explain Why is so much of Brazil's culture influenced by African traditions?
3. **a. Define** What is a **megacity**, and what is an example of a megacity in Brazil?
   b. Make Inferences Why might development in the Amazon cause tensions between Brazilian Indians and new settlers?
   c. Elaborate How might life change for a person who moves from the northeast to the southeast?

Critical Thinking

4. **Finding Main Ideas** Review your notes on Brazil. Then, write a main idea statement about each region. Use a graphic organizer like this one.

	Main Idea
The Southeast	
The Northeast	
The Interior	
The Amazon	

FOCUS ON WRITING

5. **Writing about Brazil** What information about the history, people, and culture of Brazil will draw readers to the country? What regions do you think they would like to visit? List details and ideas for possible images for your Web site.

Connecting Ideas

Learn

You have already used several types of graphic organizers in this book. Graphic organizers are drawings that help you organize information and connect ideas.

One type of graphic organizer is a word web. A word web like the one at right helps you organize specific facts and details around a main topic. Notice that information gets more detailed as it gets farther away from the main topic.

Practice

Use the word web here to answer the following questions. You may also want to look back at the information on Brazilian culture in your textbook.

❶ How can a graphic organizer help you connect ideas?

❷ What is the main topic of this word web?

❸ What three main ideas does this graphic organizer connect?

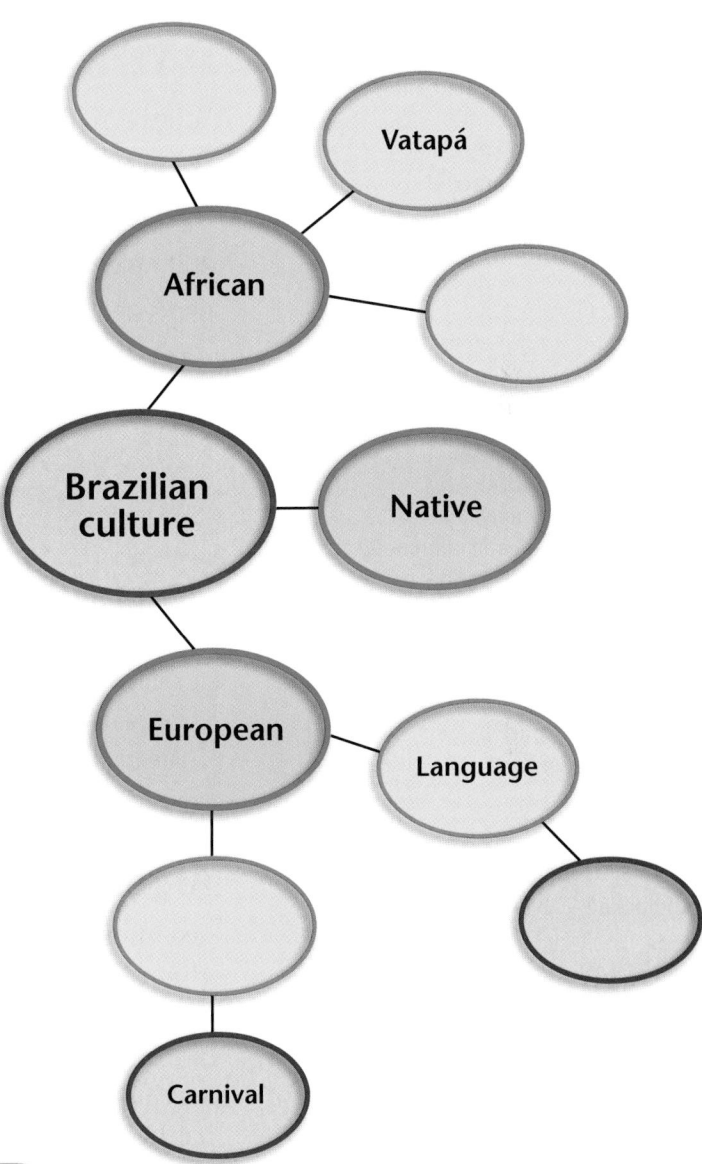

Apply

Copy the graphic organizer shown here in your notebook. Use the information on Brazilian culture in your textbook to fill in the blank circles with additional details about the main topic.

Argentina, Uruguay, and Paraguay

If **YOU** lived there...

You live in Montevideo, the capital of Uruguay. On weekends you like to visit the old part of the city and admire its beautiful buildings. You also enjoy walking along the banks of the Río de la Plata and watching fishers bring in their catch. Sometimes you visit the parks and beaches along the banks of the river.

How do you think the river has influenced Montevideo?

BUILDING BACKGROUND The southern countries of Atlantic South America—Argentina, Uruguay, and Paraguay—have all been influenced by their locations and European culture. Neither Spanish influence nor Indian culture is as strong in the southern part of South America as in other parts of the continent.

Argentina's History and Culture

Like most of South America, Argentina was originally home to groups of Indians. Groups living in the Pampas hunted wild game, while farther north Indians built irrigation systems for farming. However, unlike most of South America, Argentina has very few native peoples remaining. Instead, Argentina's culture has been mostly influenced by Europeans.

Early History

The first Europeans to come to Argentina were the Spanish. In the 1500s Spanish conquerors spread from the northern part of the continent into southern South America in search of silver and gold. They named the region Argentina. *Argentina* means "land of silver" or "silvery one."

Gauchos on the Pampas

Gauchos were a popular subject in Argentine art. In this painting from 1820, gauchos gather to watch a horse race.

ANALYZING VISUALS Why would horses be important to a gaucho?

The Spanish soon built settlements in Argentina. The Spanish monarch granted land to the colonists, who in turn built the settlements. These landowners were also given the right to force the Indians living there to work.

During the colonial era, the Pampas became an important agricultural region. Argentine cowboys, called **gauchos** (GOW-chohz), herded cattle and horses on the open grasslands. Although agriculture is still important on the Pampas, very few people in Argentina live as gauchos today.

In the early 1800s Argentina fought for independence from Spain. A period of violence and instability followed. Many Indians were killed or driven away by fighting during this time.

Modern Argentina

As the Indians were being killed off, more European influences dominated the region. New immigrants arrived from Italy, Germany, and Spain. Also, the British helped build railroads across the country. Railroads made it easier for Argentina to transport agricultural products for export to Europe. Beef exports, in particular, made the country rich.

Argentina remained one of South America's richest countries throughout the 1900s. However, the country also struggled under dictators and military governments during those years.

Some political leaders, like Eva Perón, were popular. But many leaders abused human rights. During the "Dirty War" in the 1970s, they tortured and killed many accused of disagreeing with the government. Both the country's people and its economy suffered. Finally, in the 1980s, Argentina's last military government gave up power to an elected government.

BIOGRAPHY

Eva Perón
(1919–1952)

Known affectionately as Evita, Eva Perón helped improve the living conditions of people in Argentina, particularly the poor.

As the wife of Argentina's president, Juan Perón, Evita established thousands of hospitals and schools throughout Argentina. She also helped women gain the right to vote. After years of battling cancer, Evita died at age 33. All of Argentina mourned her death for weeks.

Analyzing Why was Eva Perón able to help many people?

People and Culture

Argentina's historical ties to Europe still affect its culture. Most of Argentina's roughly 40 million people are descended from Spanish, Italian, or other European settlers. Argentine Indians and mestizos make up only about 3 percent of the population. Most Argentines are Roman Catholic.

Beef is still a part of Argentina's culture. A popular dish is parrilla (pah-REE-yah), which includes grilled sausage and steak. Supper is generally eaten late.

READING CHECK **Generalizing** What kind of governments did Argentina have in the 1900s?

Argentina Today

Today many more of Argentina's people live in **Buenos Aires** (BWAY-nohs EYE-rayz) than in any other city. Buenos Aires is the country's capital. It is also the second-largest urban area in South America. Much of Argentina's industry is located in and around Buenos Aires. Its location on the coast and near the Pampas has contributed to its economic development.

The Pampas are the country's most developed agricultural region. About 11 percent of Argentina's labor force works in agriculture. Large ranches and farms there produce beef, wheat, and corn for export to other countries.

Argentina's economy has always been affected by government policies. In the 1990s government leaders made economic reforms to help businesses grow. Argentina joined **Mercosur**—an organization that promotes trade and economic cooperation among the southern and eastern countries of South America. By the late 1900s and early 2000s, however, heavy debt and government spending brought Argentina into an economic crisis.

Argentina: Population

PARAGUAY

Tropic of Capricorn

CHILE

San Miguel de Tucumán

30°S

Córdoba

Mendoza

Rosario

BRAZIL

URUGUAY

Buenos Aires

PACIFIC OCEAN

ARGENTINA

ATLANTIC OCEAN

40°S

N W E S

• 10,000 people

0   300   600 Miles
0   300   600 Kilometers

Projection: Lambert Azimuthal Equal-Area

50°S

map zone **Geography Skills**

Place Buenos Aires is home to nearly a third of all Argentines.
1. **Interpreting Graphs** How many times bigger is Buenos Aires than Argentina's second-largest city?
2. **Analyze** What might be a benefit and a drawback of having most of the country's population in one area?

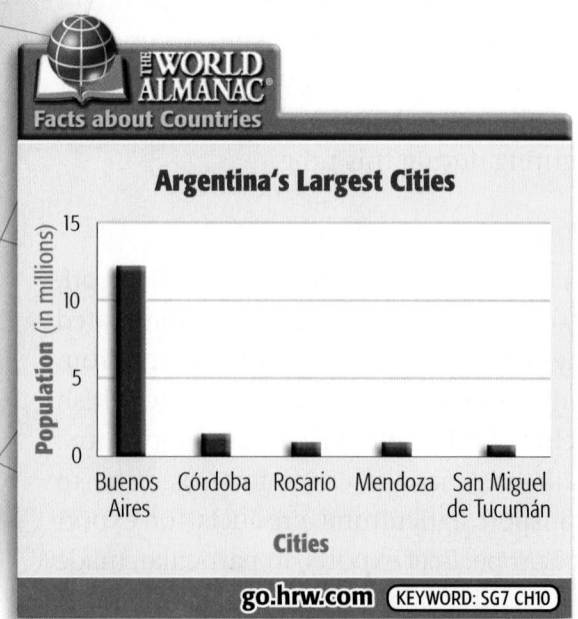

THE WORLD ALMANAC®
Facts about Countries

Argentina's Largest Cities

Population (in millions)

15

10

5

0

Buenos Aires   Córdoba   Rosario   Mendoza   San Miguel de Tucumán

Cities

go.hrw.com   KEYWORD: SG7 CH10

The economic crisis caused a political crisis. As a result, during 2001, Argentina's government changed hands four times as its leaders tried to solve the problems. By 2003 the economy had stabilized somewhat, but thousands of people's lives had changed forever. The crisis caused many people who once had professional careers to lose their jobs and join the informal economy. The **informal economy** is a part of the economy based on odd jobs that people perform without government regulation through taxes. Today many Argentines are still searching for ways to improve their economy.

READING CHECK Comparing and Contrasting What are some similarities and differences between Buenos Aires and the Pampas?

Uruguay

Tucked between Argentina and Brazil lies Uruguay. Its capital, Montevideo (mawn-tay-vee-DAY-oh), is located on the north shore of the Río de la Plata, not far from Buenos Aires. Uruguay has always been influenced by its larger neighbors.

Portugal claimed Uruguay during the colonial era, but the Spanish took over in the 1770s. By that time, few Uruguayan Indians remained. A few years later, in 1825, Uruguay declared independence from Spain. Since then, military governments have ruled Uruguay off and on. In general, however, the country has a strong tradition of respect for political freedom. Today Uruguay is a democracy.

People

As in Argentina, people of European descent make up the majority of Uruguay's population. Only about 12 percent of the population is mestizo, Indian, or of African descent. Roman Catholicism is the main religion in the country. Spanish is the official language, but many people also speak Portuguese because of Uruguay's location near Brazil.

More than 90 percent of Uruguay's people live in urban areas. More than a third of Uruguayans live in and near Montevideo. The country has a high literacy rate. In addition, many people there have good jobs and can afford a wide range of consumer goods and travel to Europe. However, many young people leave Uruguay to explore better economic opportunities elsewhere.

Economy

FOCUS ON READING

Where can you find the definition of *landlocked*?

Just as Uruguay's culture is tied to its neighbors, its economy is tied to the economies of Brazil and Argentina. In fact, more than half of Uruguay's foreign trade is with these two Mercosur partners. Beef is an important export. As in Argentina, ranchers graze livestock on inland plains.

Agriculture, along with some limited manufacturing, is the basis of Uruguay's economy. Uruguay has few mineral resources. One important source of energy is hydroelectric power. Developing poor rural areas in the interior, where resources are in short supply, is a big challenge.

READING CHECK **Compare** In what ways is Uruguay similar to Argentina?

Paraguay

Paraguay shares borders with Bolivia, Brazil, and Argentina. It is a landlocked country. **Landlocked** means completely surrounded by land with no direct access to the ocean. The Paraguay River divides the country into two regions. East of the river is the country's most productive farmland. Ranchers also graze livestock in some parts of western Paraguay.

Paraguay was claimed by Spanish settlers in the mid-1530s. It remained a Spanish colony until 1811, when it won independence. From independence until 1989, Paraguay was ruled off and on by dictators. Today the country has elected leaders and a democratic government.

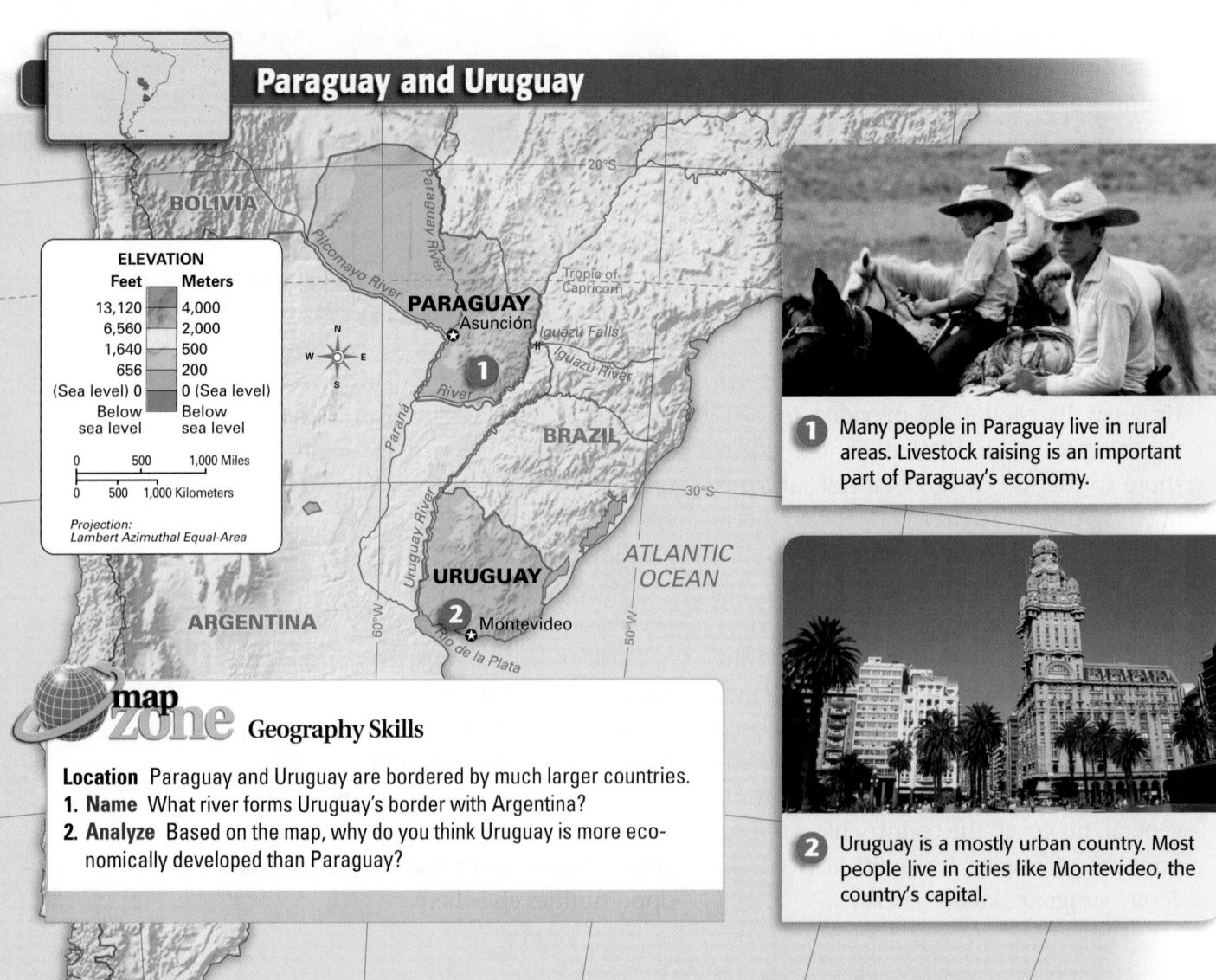

Paraguay and Uruguay

ELEVATION

Feet	Meters
13,120	4,000
6,560	2,000
1,640	500
656	200
(Sea level) 0	0 (Sea level)
Below sea level	Below sea level

0 500 1,000 Miles
0 500 1,000 Kilometers

Projection: Lambert Azimuthal Equal-Area

BOLIVIA

Pilcomayo River

Paraguay River

20°S

PARAGUAY
Asunción

Iguazú Falls

Iguazú River

Tropic of Capricorn

Paraná River

BRAZIL

Uruguay River

30°S

ATLANTIC OCEAN

URUGUAY
Montevideo

Río de la Plata

ARGENTINA

60°W

50°W

1 Many people in Paraguay live in rural areas. Livestock raising is an important part of Paraguay's economy.

2 Uruguay is a mostly urban country. Most people live in cities like Montevideo, the country's capital.

map zone **Geography Skills**

Location Paraguay and Uruguay are bordered by much larger countries.
1. **Name** What river forms Uruguay's border with Argentina?
2. **Analyze** Based on the map, why do you think Uruguay is more economically developed than Paraguay?

People

A great majority—about 95 percent—of Paraguayans are mestizos. Indians and people of mostly European descent make up the rest of the population. Paraguay has two official languages. Almost all people in Paraguay speak both Spanish and Guarani (gwah-ruh-NEE), an Indian language. As in Uruguay, most people are Roman Catholic.

Paraguay's capital and largest city is Asunción (ah-soon-SYOHN). The city is located along the Paraguay River near the border with Argentina.

Economy

Much of Paraguay's wealth is controlled by a few rich families and companies. These families and companies have tremendous influence over the country's government.

Agriculture is an important part of the economy. In fact, nearly half of the country's workers are farmers. Many of these farmers grow just enough food to feed themselves and their families. They grow crops such as corn, cotton, soybeans, and sugarcane. Paraguay also has many small businesses but not much industry.

Paraguay's future may be promising as the country learns how to use its resources more effectively. For example, the country has built large hydroelectric dams on the Paraná River. These dams provide more power than Paraguay needs, so Paraguay is able to sell the surplus electricity to Brazil and Argentina.

READING CHECK **Contrast** How are the people of Paraguay different from the people of Argentina and Uruguay?

SUMMARY AND PREVIEW The people of Paraguay, Argentina, and Uruguay share some aspects of their European heritage. Their economies are also closely tied. In the next chapter you will learn about these countries' neighbors to the west.

Section 3 Assessment

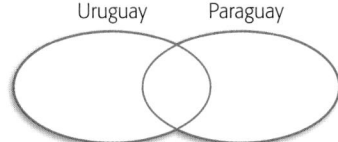

Reviewing Ideas, Terms, and Places

1. **a. Define** What is a **gaucho**?
   b. Explain Why is Argentina's population mostly of European descent?
2. **a. Identify** What is Argentina's biggest city?
   b. Make Inferences What benefits do you think being part of **Mercosur** brings to Argentina?
   c. Elaborate What are some benefits the **informal economy** provides, and what are some of its drawbacks?
3. **a. Recall** Where is Uruguay's capital located?
   b. Summarize How has Uruguay's location influenced its culture?
4. **a. Define** What does it mean to say a country is **landlocked**?
   b. Explain What is Paraguay's economy like?
   c. Predict What are some possible ways Paraguay may be able to improve its economy in the future?

Critical Thinking

5. **Comparing and Contrasting** Look over your notes on Uruguay and Paraguay. Then draw a diagram like the one here and use it to show similarities and differences between the two countries.

   Uruguay   Paraguay

FOCUS ON WRITING

6. **Thinking about Argentina, Uruguay, and Paraguay** Add details about these countries to your notes for your Web site. What information on history, culture, and specific locations will you include? For each country, think of one image that would best illustrate it.

from
The Gaucho Martín Fierro

by José Hernández

About the Reading *José Hernández spent part of his childhood on Argentina's Pampas. The gauchos lived freely on the plains there, herding cattle. In 1872 he published an epic poem about his days as an Argentine cowboy. The passage below is an excerpt.*

AS YOU READ Notice the emotion with which Hernández writes.

Even the poorest gaucho
had a string of matching horses;
he could always afford some amusement,
and people were ready for anything . . .
Looking out across the land
you'd see nothing but cattle and sky. ❶

When the branding-time came round
that was work to warm you up!
What a crowd! lassoing the running steers
and keen to hold and throw them . . . ❷
What a time that was! in those days surely
there were champions to be seen . . .

And the games that would get going
when we were all of us together!
We were always ready for them,
as at times like those
a lot of neighbors would turn up
to help out the regular hands.

Gauchos spent a lot of time alone on the plains, but sometimes they got together for games and amusement.

GUIDED READING

WORD HELP

lassoing catching with a rope
steers cattle
keen happy, eager

❶ Notice Hernández's description of the Pampas.

❷ Hernández describes the work of gauchos.

What were some activities of gauchos?

Connecting Literature to Geography

1. **Identifying Points of View** Hernández had happy memories of his days as a gaucho. What words and phrases demonstrate how Hernández felt?

2. **Analyzing** Although few people still work as gauchos, they are popular subjects in Argentine literature. What aspects of gaucho life do you think modern readers find appealing?

Chapter Review

Geography's Impact
video series
Review the video to answer the closing question:
What are some arguments for and against deforestation?

Visual Summary

Use the visual summary below to help you review the main ideas of the chapter.

QUICK FACTS

The lush Amazon rain forest covers a huge part of the region.

Brazil has many large cities as well as large rural areas.

Argentina, Uruguay, and Paraguay have large plains that are good for ranching.

Reviewing Vocabulary, Terms, and Places

For each group of terms below, write a sentence that shows how all the terms in the group are related.

1. estuary
   Río de la Plata
   Buenos Aires
2. megacity
   favelas
   aspects
3. gauchos
   Pampas
4. soil exhaustion
   deforestation
   Amazon River
5. Rio de Janeiro
   São Paulo
   Manaus

Comprehension and Critical Thinking

SECTION 1 *(Pages 232–235)*

6. **a. Recall** What kind of climate does the Amazon Basin have?

   b. Contrast How are northern Brazil and southern Argentina different?

   c. Elaborate How might the region's major physical features have influenced development and daily life in Atlantic South America?

SECTION 2 *(Pages 236–240)*

7. **a. Describe** What parts of Brazilian culture reflect African influences?

   b. Analyze What factors lead people from the northeast of Brazil to move to the southeast?

   c. Evaluate Is deforestation of the Amazon rain forest necessary? Explain your answer. What arguments might someone with a different opinion use?

8. a. Describe How is Argentina's culture different from the culture of most countries in South America?

b. Compare and Contrast What is one similarity and one difference between Uruguay and Paraguay?

c. Predict As Argentina's economy improves, what might happen to the informal economy there?

FOCUS ON READING AND WRITING

9. Using Context Clues Look through the chapter and pick out two difficult words that you had to figure out by using context clues. Then, note the context clues you used to help you figure out the definitions of the difficult words.

10. Creating a Web Site You can create a real Web site or a paper version of a Web site. First, look back through your notes and choose key ideas about each country to include. In designing your site, first include a home page that briefly describes the region. Indicate links for pages about each of the countries in the region.

Each of your country pages should include one short paragraph and one image. Remember to keep the pages simple—too much text might overwhelm your readers and send them off to another site!

Social Studies Skills

11. Connecting Ideas Draw a graphic organizer to help you organize information about the economy in Atlantic South America. One has been started for you below. You will need to add more ovals to contain the information.

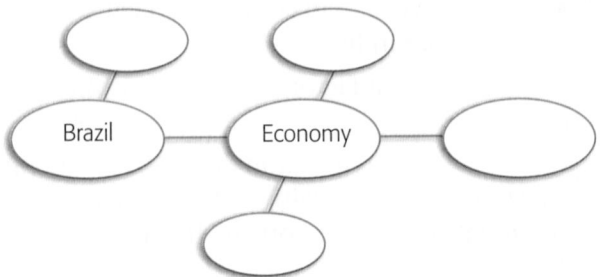

Using the Internet

go.hrw.com
KEYWORD: SG7 CH10

12. Activity: Creating a Poster The Amazon River is the world's second-longest river, and it crosses nearly half of South America. It also runs through the world's largest rain forest. Enter the activity keyword and explore the many aspects of the river, including its wildlife, the rain forest it cuts through, the people who live alongside it, and the environmental issues surrounding it. Use the information you find and the interactive template provided to create a poster about the amazing Amazon River.

Map Activity ★Interactive

13. Atlantic South America On a separate sheet of paper, match the letters on the map with their correct labels.

São Paulo	Pampas
Patagonia	Paraná River
Río de la Plata	Amazon River

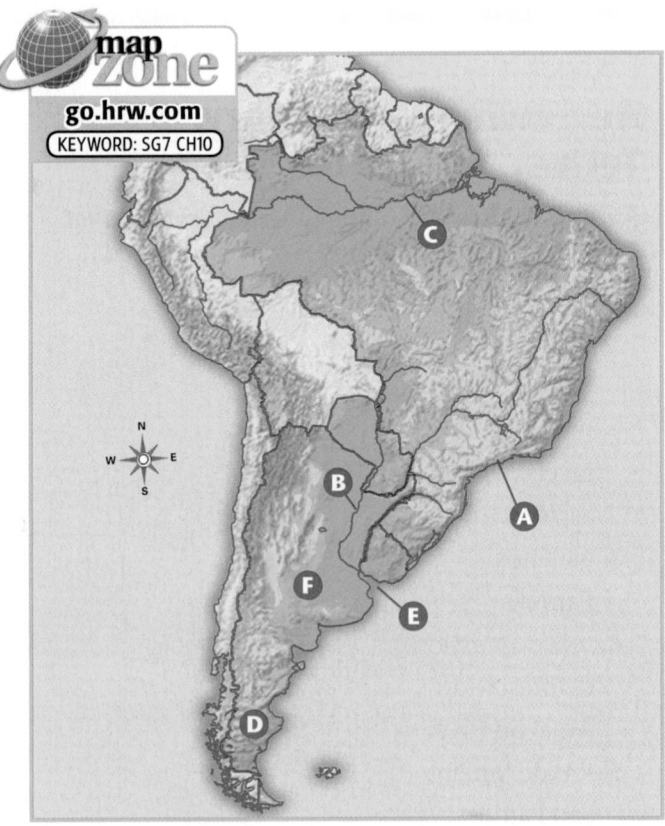

DIRECTIONS: Read questions 1 through 7 and write the letter of the best response. Then read question 8 and write your own well-constructed response.

1 In which country do most people speak Portuguese?

A Brazil

B Argentina

C Uruguay

D Paraguay

2 What major river flows through northwestern Brazil?

A Río de la Plata

B Uruguay River

C Paraná River

D Amazon River

3 Which of the following statements about Argentina is true?

A Most people are mestizos.

B Most people in Argentina live on the Pampas.

C Argentina is a member of Mercosur.

D Argentina has had a stable government and economy since 2000.

4 Which of the following was an effect of the "Dirty War" in Argentina?

A The country's economy suffered.

B Eva Perón became a popular political leader.

C Many Indians were killed on the Pampas.

D People elected military leaders to rule their country.

5 What is the most important part of the economy of Paraguay?

A mining

B agriculture

C manufacturing

D logging

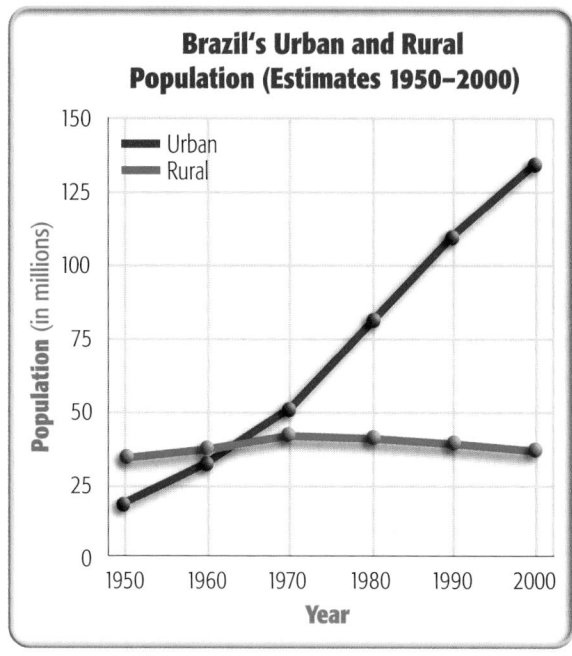

Source: Instituto Brasileiro de Geografia e Estatística

6 Based on the graph above, which of the following statements is false?

A Brazil's urban population is increasing while the rural population is decreasing.

B By 1960 more people in Brazil lived in urban areas than in rural areas.

C In 1950 more people in Brazil lived in rural areas than in urban areas.

D Brazil's total population is growing.

7 Based on the graph above, about how many people lived in urban areas of Brazil in 1990?

A 20 million

B 135 million

C 110 million

D 40 million

8 Extended Response Study the graph above and the information in your book about Brazil today. Then write a brief essay explaining how urban and rural landscapes in Brazil are changing. You will also want to discuss the causes and effects of this change.

Pacific South America

What You Will Learn...

In this chapter you will learn about the Andes mountains that dominate the physical geography of Pacific South America. You will also study the history and culture of the region. In addition, you will learn about some of the struggles and progress happening today in Ecuador, Peru, Bolivia, and Chile.

FOCUS ON READING AND SPEAKING

Making Inferences An inference is a kind of guess. Sometimes an author does not give you complete information, and you have to make an inference. As you read, try to fill in gaps in information. Make guesses about things the writer does not tell you directly. **See the lesson, Making Inferences, on page R12.**

Interviewing Interviews with experts are a great way to learn new information. As you read about Pacific South America, you will identify questions for an interview. Then, with a partner, you will create a script for an interview about the region. One of you will play the role of the interviewer, and one will play the regional expert.

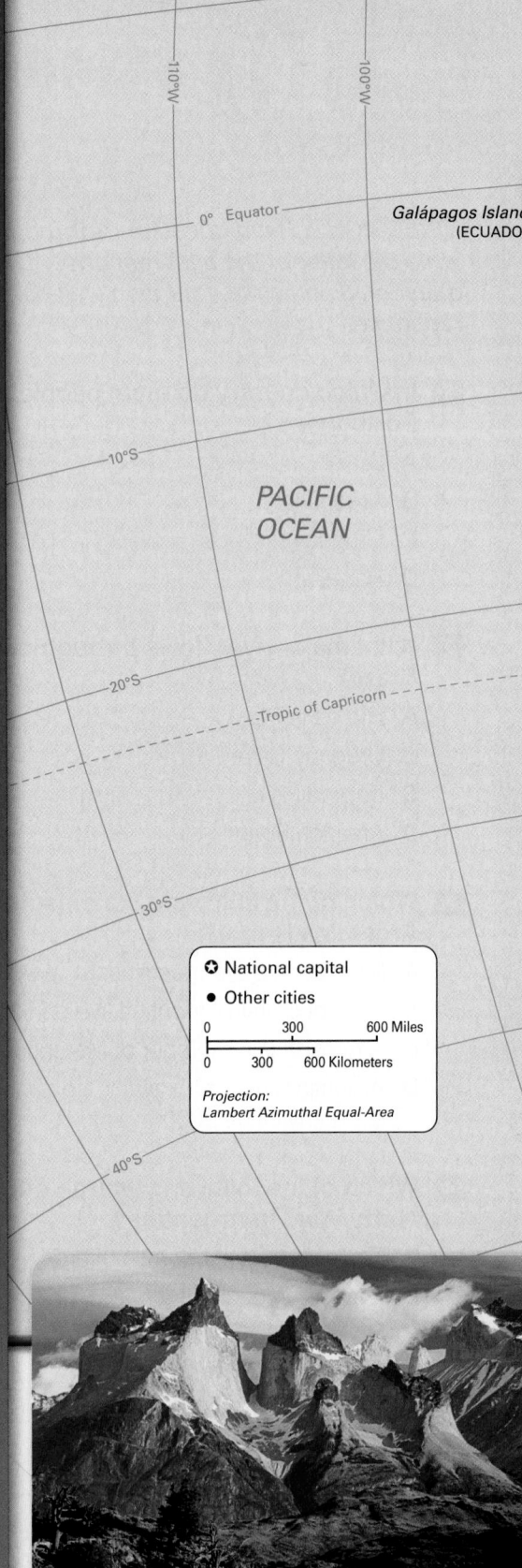

Galápagos Islands (ECUADOR)

PACIFIC OCEAN

⊗ National capital
● Other cities

0   300   600 Miles
0   300   600 Kilometers

Projection:
Lambert Azimuthal Equal-Area

Physical Geography The Andes are the second-highest mountain range in the world. These peaks are in a national park in Chile.

Pacific South America: Political

COLOMBIA

Quito ✪
ECUADOR
Guayaquil ●

Amazon River

Equator — 0°

PERU

Lima ✪   Cuzco ●

B R A Z I L

10°S

BOLIVIA
✪ La Paz
● Santa Cruz
✪ Sucre

CHILE   **PARAGUAY**

Tropic of Capricorn

20°S

Valparaíso ●
Santiago ✪

URUGUAY

ARGENTINA

*ATLANTIC
OCEAN*

30°S

map
zone

Geography Skills

Location The countries of Pacific South America lie on the western side of South America.

1. **Identify** Which country is landlocked?
2. **Analyze** How do you think Chile's shape affects life in that country?

go.hrw.com   KEYWORD: SG7 CH11

HOLT

Geography's Impact

video series
Watch the video to understand the impact of the Andes.

History Early cultures made beautiful gold and silver art.

Culture Many people who live in the Andes still wear traditional dress and speak native languages. These women are from Peru.

253

Physical Geography

What You Will Learn...

Main Ideas

1. The Andes are the main physical feature of Pacific South America.
2. The region's climate and vegetation change with elevation.
3. Key natural resources in the region include lumber, oil, and minerals.

The Big Idea

The Andes dominate Pacific South America's physical geography and influence the region's climate and resources.

Key Terms and Places

altiplano, *p. 255*
strait, *p. 255*
Atacama Desert, *p. 257*
El Niño, *p. 257*

TAKING NOTES As you read, use a diagram like the one here to help you organize your notes on the physical features, climates, and resources of Pacific South America.

Physical Features	Climate	Resources

If YOU lived there...

You and your family fish for herring in the cold waters off the coast of Peru. Last year, however, an event called El Niño changed both the weather and the water. El Niño made the nearby ocean warmer. Without cold water, all the herring disappeared. You caught almost no fish at all. El Niño also caused terrible weather on the mainland.

How might another El Niño affect you?

BUILDING BACKGROUND Although most of the countries of Pacific South America lie along the coast, their landscapes are dominated by the rugged mountain range called the Andes. These mountains influence climates in the region. Ocean winds and currents also affect coastal areas here.

Physical Features

The countries of Pacific South America stretch along the Pacific coast from the equator, for which the country of Ecuador is named, south almost to the Arctic Circle. One narrow country, Chile (CHEE-lay), is so long that it covers about half the Pacific coast by itself. Not all of the countries in Pacific South America have coastlines, however. Bolivia is landlocked. But all of the countries in this region do share one major physical feature—the high Andes mountains.

Mountains

The Andes run through Ecuador, Peru, Bolivia, and Chile. Some ridges and volcanic peaks in the Andes rise more than 20,000 feet (6,800 m) above sea level. Because two tectonic plates meet at the region's edge, earthquakes and volcanoes are a constant threat. Sometimes these earthquakes disturb Andean glaciers, sending ice and mud rushing down mountain slopes.

Landscapes in the Andes differ from south to north. In southern Chile, rugged mountain peaks are covered by ice caps. In the north, the Andes are more rounded than rugged, and there the range splits into two ridges. In southern Peru and Bolivia these ridges are quite far apart. A broad, high plateau called the **altiplano** lies between the ridges of the Andes.

Water and Islands

Andean glaciers are the source for many tributaries of the Amazon River. Other than the Amazon tributaries, the region has few major rivers. Rivers on the altiplano have no outlet to the sea. Water collects in two large lakes. One of these, Lake Titicaca, is the highest lake in the world that large ships can cross.

At the southern tip of the continent, the Strait of Magellan links the Atlantic and Pacific oceans. A **strait** is a narrow body of water connecting two larger bodies of water. The large island south of the strait is Tierra del Fuego, or "land of fire."

Chile and Ecuador both control large islands in the Pacific Ocean. Ecuador's volcanic Galápagos Islands have wildlife not found anywhere else in the world.

READING CHECK **Contrasting** How do the Andes differ from north to south?

★Interactive Map

Pacific South America: Physical

ELEVATION

Feet	Meters
13,120	4,000
6,560	2,000
1,640	500
656	200
(Sea level) 0	0 (Sea level)
Below sea level	Below sea level

0   400   800 Miles
0   400   800 Kilometers

Projection:
Lambert Azimuthal Equal-Area

map zone **Geography Skills**

Regions The Andes stretch all through the countries of Pacific South America.
1. **Identify** To what country do the Galápagos Islands belong?
2. **Interpret** How do you think the Andes affect life in the region?

go.hrw.com (KEYWORD: SG7 CH11)

1 Llamas graze on the high, dry altiplano. The climate on the altiplano is too dry for trees to grow.

255

Close-up

Climate Zones in the Andes

Five climate zones exist in the Andes. The different elevations support different types of plant and animal life.

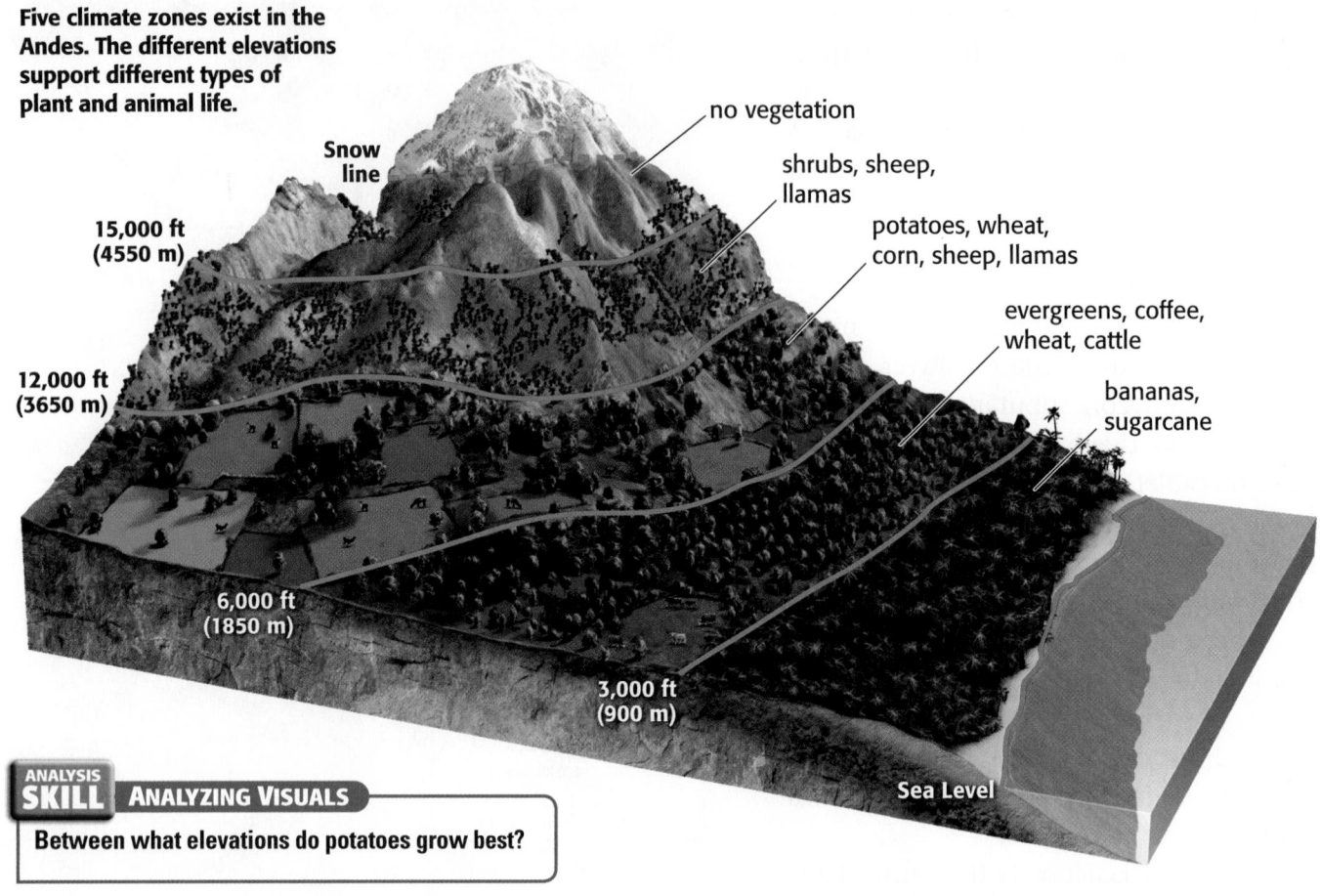

Snow line

15,000 ft (4550 m)

12,000 ft (3650 m)

6,000 ft (1850 m)

3,000 ft (900 m)

Sea Level

no vegetation

shrubs, sheep, llamas

potatoes, wheat, corn, sheep, llamas

evergreens, coffee, wheat, cattle

bananas, sugarcane

ANALYSIS SKILL **ANALYZING VISUALS**

Between what elevations do potatoes grow best?

Climate and Vegetation

FOCUS ON READING

What can you infer about the location of mountains in Ecuador?

Climate, vegetation, and landscapes all vary widely in Pacific South America. We usually think of latitude as the major factor that affects climate. However, in Pacific South America, elevation has the biggest effect on climate and vegetation.

Elevation

Mountain environments change with elevation. For this reason, we can identify five different climate zones in the Andes. You can see these different climate zones on the diagram above.

The lowest zone includes the hot and humid lower elevations near sea level. Crops such as sugarcane and bananas grow well there. This first zone is often found along the coast, but it is also found inland in eastern Ecuador and Peru and northern Bolivia. These regions are part of the Amazon basin. They have a humid tropical climate with thick, tropical rain forests.

As elevation increases, the air becomes cooler. The second elevation zone has moist climates with mountain forests. This zone is good for growing coffee. In addition, many of Pacific South America's large cities are located in this zone.

Higher up the mountains is a third, cooler zone of forests and grasslands. Farmers grow potatoes and wheat there. Many people in Pacific South America live and farm in this climate zone.

256 CHAPTER 11

At a certain elevation, the climate becomes too cool for trees to grow. This fourth climate zone above the tree line contains alpine meadows with grasslands and hardy shrubs. The altiplano region between the two ridges of the Andes lies mostly in this climate zone.

The fifth climate zone, in the highest elevations, is very cold. No vegetation grows in this zone because the ground is almost always covered with snow and ice.

Deserts

Pacific South America also has some climates that are not typical of any of the five climate zones. Instead of hot and humid climates, some coastal regions have desert climates.

Northern Chile contains the **Atacama Desert**. This desert is about 600 miles (965 km) long. Rain falls there less than five times a century, but fog and low clouds are common. They form when a cold current in the Pacific Ocean chills the warmer air above the ocean's surface. Cloud cover keeps the air near the ground from being warmed by the sun. As a result, coastal Chile is one of the cloudiest—and driest—places on Earth.

In Peru, some rivers cut through the dry coastal region. They bring snowmelt down from the Andes. Because they rely on melting snow, some of these rivers only appear at certain times of the year. The rivers have made some small settlements possible in these dry areas.

El Niño

About every two to seven years, this dry region experiences **El Niño**, an ocean and weather pattern that affects the Pacific coast. During an El Niño year, cool Pacific water near the coast warms. This change may cause extreme ocean and weather events that can have global effects.

As El Niño warms ocean waters, fish leave what is usually a rich fishing area. This change affects fishers. Also, El Niño **causes** heavy rains, and areas along the coast sometimes experience flooding. Some scientists think that air pollutants have made El Niño last longer and have more damaging effects.

READING CHECK **Finding Main Ideas** How does elevation affect climate and vegetation?

Natural Resources

The landscapes of Pacific South America provide many valuable natural resources. For example, forests in southern Chile and in eastern Peru and Ecuador provide lumber. Also, as you have read, the coastal waters of the Pacific Ocean are rich in fish.

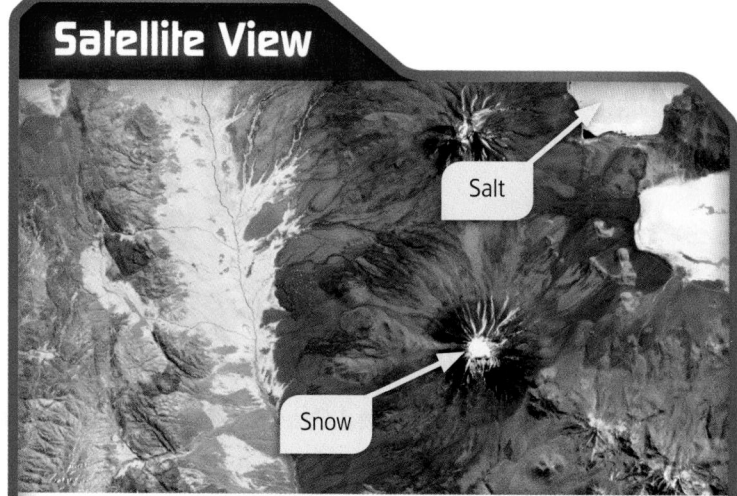

Satellite View

Salt

Snow

Atacama Desert

The Atacama Desert lies between the Pacific coast and the Andes in northern Chile. In this image you can see two snowcapped volcanoes. The salt in the top right part of the image is formed from minerals carried there by rivers that only appear during certain months of the year. These seasonal rivers also support some limited vegetation.

Drawing Conclusions Why do you think there is snow on the volcanoes even though the desert gets hardly any precipitation?

Bolivia: Resources

Gold · **Tin**
Lead · **Zinc**
Silver

0   100   200 Miles
0   100   200 Kilometers

Projection: Lambert
Azimuthal Equal-Area

BRAZIL

BOLIVIA

Madeira R.

Madre de Dios

Beni River

Guapore River

Mamoré River

Lake Titicaca

Lake Poopó

Pilcomayo River

−20°S

CHILE   ARGENTINA   PARAGUAY

N
W   E
S

map zone Geography Skills

Place Bolivia has many valuable mineral resources.
1. **Locate** Where are most of Bolivia's gold resources found?
2. **Interpret** What do you notice about the location of the mineral resources and the rivers?

In addition, the region has valuable oil and minerals. Ecuador in particular has large oil and gas reserves, and oil is the country's main export. Bolivia has some deposits of tin, gold, silver, lead, and zinc. Chile has copper deposits. In fact, Chile exports more copper than any other country in the world. Chile is also the site of the world's largest open pit mine.

Although the countries of Pacific South America have many valuable resources, one resource they do not have much of is good farmland. Many people farm, but the region's mostly cool, arid lands make it difficult to produce large crops for export.

READING CHECK **Categorizing** What types of resources do the countries of Pacific South America have?

SUMMARY AND PREVIEW The Andes are the main physical feature of Pacific South America. Next, you will learn how the Andes have affected the region's history and how they continue to affect life there today.

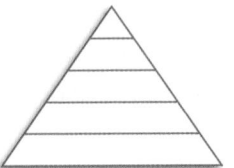

go.hrw.com
Online Quiz
KEYWORD: SG7 HP11

Section 1 Assessment

Reviewing Ideas, Terms, and Places

1. **a. Identify** What is the main physical feature of Pacific South America?
   b. Analyze How is Bolivia's location unique in the region?
2. **a. Define** What is **El Niño**, and what are some of its effects?
   b. Draw Conclusions Why are parts of Ecuador, in the tropics, cooler than parts of southern Chile?
3. **a. Identify** What country in this region has large oil reserves?
   b. Make Inferences Why do you think much of the region is not good for farming?
   c. Elaborate What effects do you think copper mining in Chile might have on the environment?

Critical Thinking

4. **Categorizing** Review your notes on climate. Then use a diagram like this one to describe the climate and vegetation in each of the five climate zones.

FOCUS ON SPEAKING

5. **Describing Physical Geography** Note information about the physical features, climate and vegetation, and resources of Pacific South America. Write two questions and answers you can use in your interview.

Social Studies Skills

Chart and Graph | Critical Thinking | Geography | Study

Interpreting an Elevation Profile

Learn

An elevation profile is a diagram that shows a side view of an area. This kind of diagram shows the physical features that lie along a line from point A to point B. Keep in mind that an elevation profile typically exaggerates vertical distances because vertical and horizontal distances are measured differently on elevation profiles. If they were not, even tall mountains would appear as tiny bumps.

> Vertical measurements are given on the sides of the diagram.

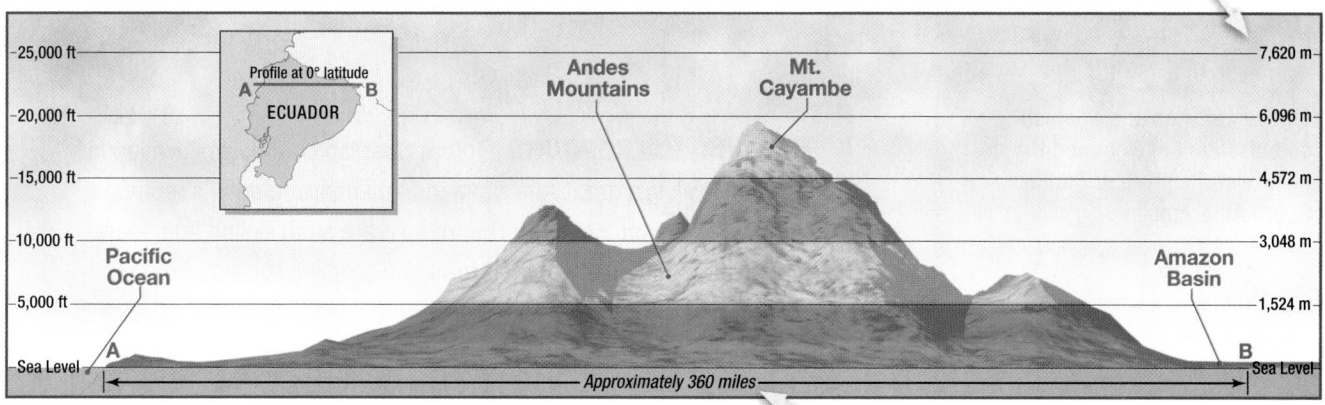

> The horizontal measurement is given along the bottom of the diagram.

Practice

Use the elevation profile above to answer the following questions.

1 What place does this elevation profile measure?

2 What is the highest point, and what is its elevation?

3 How can you tell that the vertical distance is exaggerated?

Apply

Look at the physical map of Pacific South America in Section 1 of this chapter. Choose a latitude line and create your own elevation profile for the land at that latitude. Be sure to pay attention to the scale and the legend so that you use correct measurements.

History and Culture

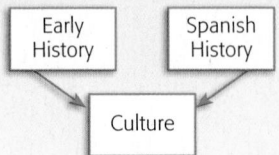
If YOU lived there...

You live in Cuzco, the capital of the Inca Empire. You are required to contribute labor to the empire, and you have been chosen to work on a construction project. Hauling the huge stones will be difficult, but the work will be rewarding. You can either choose to help build a magnificent temple to the sun god or you can help build a road from Cuzco to the far end of the empire.

Which project will you choose? Why?

BUILDING BACKGROUND Before Spanish conquerors arrived in the early 1500s, a great American Indian empire ruled this region. Cuzco was the Inca capital. The Incas were such skilled engineers and builders that many of their forts and temples still stand today.

History

Thousands of years ago, people in Pacific South America tried to farm on mountainsides as steep as bleachers. Other people tried to farm where there was almost no rain. These early cultures learned how to adapt to and modify their environments.

Early Cultures

Peru's first advanced civilization reached its height in about 900 BC in the Andes. These people built stone terraces into the steep mountainside so they could raise crops. In coastal areas, people created irrigation systems to store water and control flooding.

Agriculture supported large populations, towns, and culture. In the Bolivian highlands one early culture, the Tiahuanaco (tee-uh-wuh-NAH-koh), made huge stone carvings near a lakeshore. In another civilization on the coast, people scratched outlines of animals and other shapes into the surface of the Peruvian desert. These designs, known as the Nazca lines, are so large they can only be recognized from the sky.

An Inca City

The Inca city of Machu Picchu lay undiscovered high in the Andes until 1911.

ANALYZING VISUALS Why do you think Machu Picchu was undiscovered for almost 400 years?

The Inca Empire

Eventually, one group of people came to rule most of the region. By the early 1500s, these people, the Incas, controlled an area that stretched from northern Ecuador to central Chile. The Inca Empire was home to as many as 12 million people.

The huge Inca Empire was highly organized. Irrigation projects turned deserts into rich farmland. Thousands of miles of stone-paved roads connected the empire. Rope suspension bridges helped the Incas cross the steep Andean valleys.

As advanced as their civilization was, the Incas had no wheeled vehicles or horses. Instead, relay teams of runners carried messages from one end of the empire to the other. Working together, a team of runners could carry a message up to 150 miles (240 km) in one day. The runners did not carry any letters, however, because the Incas did not have a written language.

Spanish Rule

In spite of its great organization, however, the Inca Empire did not last long. A new Inca ruler, on his way to be crowned king, met the Spanish explorer Francisco Pizarro. Pizarro captured the Inca king, who ordered his people to bring enough gold and silver to fill a whole room. These riches were supposed to be a ransom for the king's freedom. Instead, Pizarro ordered the Inca king killed. Fighting broke out, and by 1535 the Spaniards had conquered the Inca Empire.

The new Spanish rulers often dealt harshly with the South American Indians of the fallen Inca Empire. Many Indians had to work in gold or silver mines or on the Spaniards' plantations. A Spanish **viceroy**, or governor, was appointed by the king of Spain to make sure the Indians followed the Spanish laws and customs that had replaced native traditions.

FOCUS ON READING

How do you think the South American Indians felt about the viceroy?

Independence

By the early 1800s, people in Pacific South America began to want independence. They began to revolt against Spanish rule. **Creoles**, American-born descendants of Europeans, were the main leaders of the revolts. The success of the revolts led to independence for Chile, Ecuador, Peru, and Bolivia by 1825.

READING CHECK **Evaluating** How did Inca civilization influence the history of the region?

Culture

Spanish and native cultures have both left their marks on Pacific South America. Most people in the region speak Spanish, and Spanish is the official language in all of the countries of the region.

However, people in many parts of the region also maintain much of their native culture. Millions of South American Indians speak native languages in addition to or instead of Spanish. In Bolivia, two native languages are official languages in addition to Spanish.

The people and customs of Pacific South America also reflect the region's Spanish and Indian heritage. For example, Bolivia's population has the highest percentage of South American Indians of any country on the continent. Many Bolivian Indians follow customs and lifestyles that have existed for many centuries. They often dress in traditional styles—full skirts and derby hats for the women and colorful, striped ponchos for the men.

Another part of the region's culture that reflects Spanish and Indian influences is religion. Most people in Pacific

Interactive Map

Languages in Pacific South America

map zone Geography Skills

Regions Spanish is an official language throughout the region, but many people speak native languages instead.
1. **Interpreting Graphs** Where do more people speak native languages than Spanish?
2. **Analyze** Why do you think many people do not speak Spanish?

go.hrw.com | KEYWORD: SG7 CH11

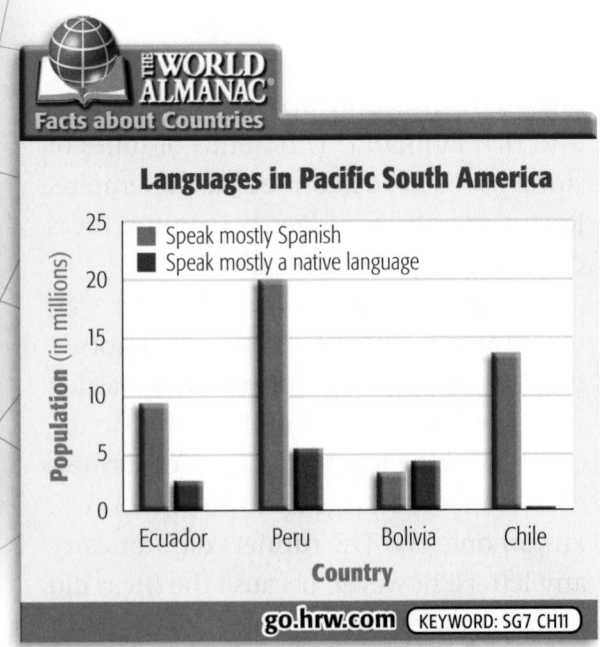

THE WORLD ALMANAC
Facts about Countries

Languages in Pacific South America

go.hrw.com | KEYWORD: SG7 CH11

Andean Culture

Performers bring native traditions to Carnival in Tarabuco, Bolivia. Carnival is a celebration before the Christian season of Lent.

ANALYZING VISUALS What do you think the climate is like in Tarabuco?

Men's striped ponchos differ in color depending on where they are from.

Music played on wooden flutes like these is popular in the Andes.

South America practice the religion of the Spanish—Roman Catholicism. Some people in the Andes, however, also still practice ancient religious customs. Every June, for example, people participate in a festival that was celebrated by the Incas to worship the sun. During festivals people wear traditional costumes, sometimes with wooden masks. They also play traditional instruments, such as wooden flutes.

READING CHECK Generalizing What traditional customs do people in the region still practice today?

SUMMARY AND PREVIEW Pacific South America was home to one of the greatest ancient civilizations in the Americas—the Inca. The Spanish conquered the Incas. Today the region's culture still reflects Inca and Spanish influences. Next, you will learn more about the governments and economies of Ecuador, Bolivia, Peru, and Chile today.

go.hrw.com
Section 2 Assessment
Online Quiz
KEYWORD: SG7 HP11

Reviewing Ideas, Terms, and Places

1. **a. Recall** What ancient empire built paved roads through the Andes?
   b. Explain What role did **Creoles** play in the history of Pacific South America?
   c. Predict How might the Inca Empire have been different if the Incas had had wheels and horses?
2. **a. Recall** What country has the highest percentage of South American Indians in its population?
   b. Make Generalizations What aspects of culture in Pacific South America reflect Spanish influence, and what aspects reflect Indian heritage?

Critical Thinking

3. **Sequencing** Look over your notes on the region's history. Then draw a graphic organizer like the one here and use it to put major historical events in chronological order.

Nazca lines drawn → ▢ → ▢ → ▢ → ▢

FOCUS ON SPEAKING

4. **Taking Notes on History and Culture** What information about the history and culture is important? Add two more questions, plus answers, to your notes.

Pacific South America Today

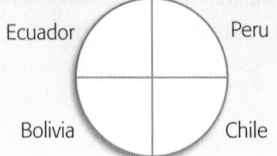

If YOU lived there...

You are at a political rally in Valparaíso, Chile. Your family owns a vineyard nearby, so government policies about the economy affect you personally. You listen carefully to the speakers at the rally. Some politicians are in favor of more free trade with countries in North America. Others speak about different issues, such as housing and education.

What would you like to ask the politicians?

BUILDING BACKGROUND All the countries of Pacific South America have faced similar issues in recent years. These include poverty, unstable governments, economic development, and how to encourage development and still protect the environment. Several of these countries are making progress, while others still have problems.

Ecuador Today

In recent decades, the countries of Pacific South America have all had some periods during which their governments were unstable. Ecuador, in particular, has faced recent instability. Widespread poverty is a constant threat to a stable government in this country.

Government

Ecuador is a democracy. However, the country has had 9 different presidents in 10 years. In 2005 the president fired the country's supreme court in order to replace the judges with new ones. This action did not please the Ecuadorian people. They thought the president was trying to gain too much power. Also, they were not happy that recent economic reforms had failed to improve housing, medical care, or education in the country. As a result, the Ecuadorian people and congress forced the president from power.

Economic Regions

Ecuador has three different economic regions. One region, the coastal lowlands, has agriculture and industry. The country's largest city, Guayaquil (gwy-ah-KEEL), is located there. It is Ecuador's major port and commercial center.

The Andean region of Ecuador is poorer. **Quito**, the national capital, is located there. Open-air markets and Spanish colonial buildings attract many tourists to Quito and other towns in the region.

A third region, the Amazon basin, has valuable oil deposits. The oil industry provides jobs that draw people to the region. Oil is also Ecuador's main export. But the oil industry has brought problems as well as benefits. The country's economy suffers if the world oil price drops. In addition, some citizens worry that drilling for oil could harm the rain forest.

READING CHECK **Generalizing** Why has Ecuador's government been unstable?

Bolivia Today

Like Ecuador, Bolivia is a poor country. Poverty has been a cause of political unrest in recent years.

Government

After years of military rule, Bolivia is a democracy. Bolivia's government is divided between two capital cities. The supreme court meets in Sucre (SOO-kray), but the congress meets in **La Paz**. Located at about 12,000 feet (3,660 m), La Paz is the highest capital city in the world. It is also Bolivia's main industrial center.

In the early 2000s, many Bolivians disagreed with the government's plans for how to best use the country's resources and fight poverty. National protests forced several presidents to resign. Then in 2005,

Bolivians elected an indigenous leader, Evo Morales, as president. He worked to improve the lives of Bolivia's poor.

Economy

Bolivia is the poorest country in South America. In the plains of eastern Bolivia there are few roads and little money for investment. However, foreign aid has provided funds for some development. In addition, the country has valuable resources, including metals and natural gas.

READING CHECK **Analyzing** Why might political revolts slow development?

CONNECTING TO Economics

The Informal Economy

Many people in the countries of Pacific South America are part of the informal economy. Street vendors, like the ones shown here in Quito, are common sights in the region's cities. People visit street vendors to buy items like snacks, small electronics, or clothing. The informal economy provides jobs for many people. However, it does not help the national economy because the participants do not pay taxes. Without income from taxes, the government cannot pay for services.

Analyzing How does the informal economy affect taxes?

Settlements around Lima

Lima has three main types of settlements. The wealthier people tend to live in houses and apartments in town. Poor people live mostly in slums or in recently built "young towns."

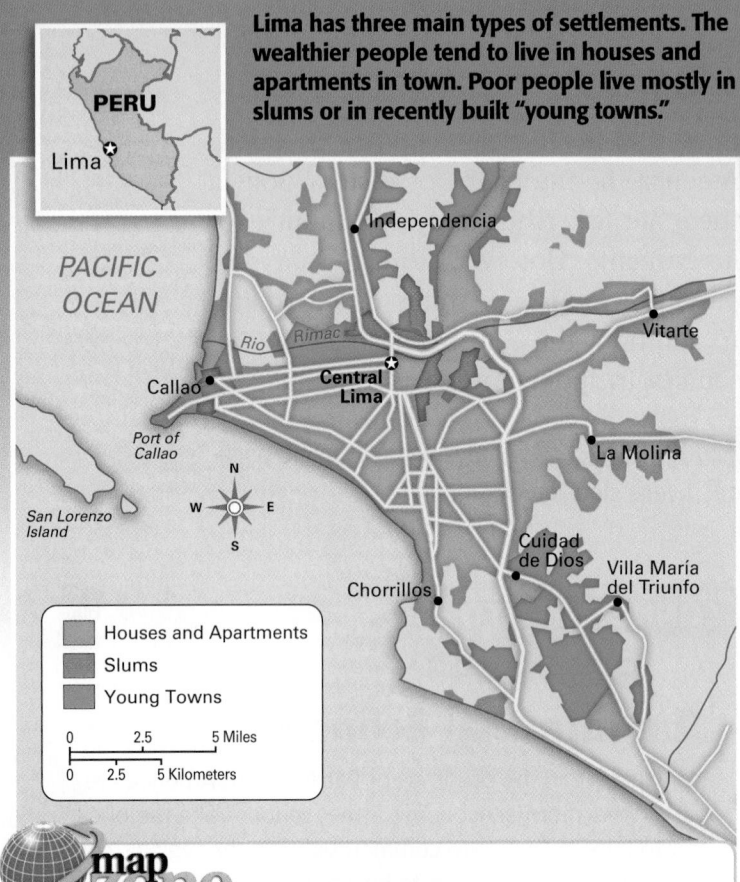

PERU

Lima

PACIFIC OCEAN

Independencia

Vitarte

Rio Rimac

Central Lima

Callao

Port of Callao

La Molina

San Lorenzo Island

N
W   E
S

Cuidad de Dios

Villa María del Triunfo

Chorrillos

Houses and Apartments
Slums
Young Towns

0   2.5   5 Miles
0   2.5   5 Kilometers

map zone Geography Skills

Human-Environment Interaction People have built three different basic types of housing in and around Lima.
1. **Use the Map** What is the most common type of housing?
2. **Draw Conclusions** Why are most young towns built far from central Lima?

Houses and Apartments Most housing in Lima is made up of high-rise apartments and private houses, some of which are from the colonial era.

industry, universities, and government jobs, which attract many people from the countryside to Lima.

Lima was the colonial capital of Peru, and the city still contains many beautiful old buildings from the colonial era. It has high-rise apartments and wide, tree-lined boulevards. However, as in many big urban areas, a lot of people there live in poverty.

In spite of the poverty, central Lima has few slum areas. This is because most poor people prefer to claim land on the outskirts of the city and build their own houses. Often they can get only poor building materials. They also have a hard time getting water and electricity from the city.

Settlements of new self-built houses are called "young towns" in Lima. Over time, as people improve and add to their houses, the new settlements develop into large, permanent suburbs. Many of the people in Lima's young towns are migrants from the highlands. Some came to Lima to escape violence in their home villages.

Peru Today

Peru is the largest and most populous country in Pacific South America. Today it is making some progress against political violence and poverty.

Lima

Peru's capital, **Lima** (LEE-muh), is the largest city in the region. Nearly one-third of all Peruvians live in Lima or the nearby port city of Callao (kah-YAH-oh). Lima has

Slums Just outside downtown and near the port area, many people live in slum housing. These buildings are permanent, but run-down.

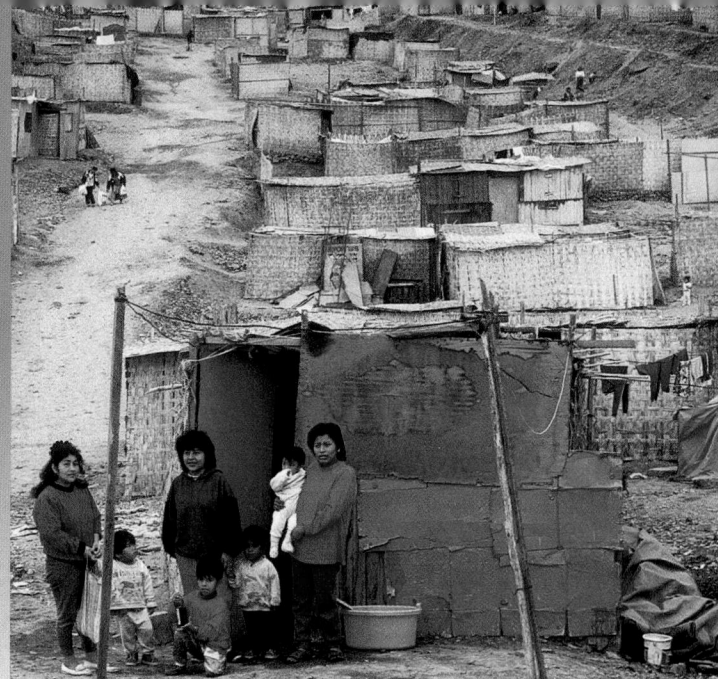

Young Towns Many poor people in recent years have taken over land on the outskirts of Lima and have built their own shelters.

Government

In the 1980s and 1990s, a terrorist group called the Shining Path was active. This group carried out deadly attacks because it opposed government policies. Some 70,000 people died in violence between the Shining Path and government forces, and Peru's economy suffered. However, after the arrest of the group's leaders, Peru's government began making progress against political violence and poverty. The country has an elected president and congress.

Resources

Peru's resources are key factors in its economic progress. Some mineral deposits are located near the coast, and hydroelectric projects on rivers provide energy. Peru's highlands are less developed than the coastal areas. However, many Peruvian Indians grow potatoes and corn there.

READING CHECK **Identifying Cause and Effect** How did the Shining Path affect Peru?

Chile Today

Like Peru, Chile has ended a long violent period. Chile now has a stable government and a growing economy.

Government

In 1970 Chileans elected a president who had some ideas influenced by communism. A few years later he was overthrown and died in a U.S.-backed military coup (KOO). A **coup** is a sudden overthrow of a government by a small group of people.

In the years after the coup, military rulers tried to crush their political enemies. Chile's military government was harsh and often violent. It imprisoned or killed thousands of people.

In the late 1980s the power of the rulers began to weaken. After more than 15 years, Chileans rejected the military dictatorship and created a new, democratic government. Chileans now enjoy many freedoms. Chile is one of the most stable countries in South America.

FOCUS ON READING

What can you infer about the reason for the end of the military government?

A man in Chile harvests grapes to be made into wine for export.

Resources and Economy

Chile's economy is the strongest in the region. Poverty rates have decreased, and Chile's prospects for the future seem bright. Small businesses and factories are growing quickly. More Chileans are finding work, and wages are rising.

About one-third of all Chileans live in central Chile. This region includes the capital, **Santiago**, and a nearby seaport, Valparaíso (bahl-pah-rah-EE-soh). Its mild Mediterranean climate allows farmers to grow many crops. For example, grapes grow well there, and Chilean fruit and wine are exported around the world.

Farming, fishing, forestry, and mining form the basis of Chile's economy. Copper mining is especially important. It accounts for more than one-third of Chile's exports.

Since international trade is key to Chile's economy, Chile wants to expand its trade links. Chile has signed a free trade agreement with the United States, and trade between the two countries has increased. Chile's other important trade partners are Argentina, Brazil, and China.

READING CHECK **Identifying Points of View** Why might Chile want to join a free trade group?

SUMMARY In recent years Ecuador, Peru, Bolivia, and Chile have struggled with political violence and poverty. However, Peru and Chile are recovering. Developing stronger economies and stable governments will remain key issue.

Section 3 Assessment

go.hrw.com
Online Quiz
KEYWORD: SG7 HP11

Reviewing Ideas, Terms, and Places

1. **a. Identify** What is Ecuador's largest city?
   b. Make Generalizations Why have Ecuadorians been unhappy with their government in recent years?
2. **a. Identify** What are Bolivia's two capital cities?
   b. Analyze Why might Bolivia's economy improve in the future?
3. **a. Recall** Why did many Peruvians move to Lima from the highlands in the 1980s?
   b. Elaborate What challenges do you think people who move to **Lima** from the highlands face?
4. **a. Define** What is a **coup**?
   b. Make Inferences What might happen to Chile's economy if the world price of copper drops?

Critical Thinking

5. **Solving Problems** Review your notes. Then, in a diagram like the one here, write one sentence about each country, explaining how that country is dealing with poverty or government instability.

Ecuador	
Bolivia	
Peru	
Chile	

FOCUS ON SPEAKING

6. **Thinking about Pacific South America Today** Add questions about each country in Pacific South America to your notes. How might you answer these questions in your interview? Write down the answer to each question.

Chapter Review

Geography's Impact
video series
Review the video to answer the closing question:
Why do descendants of the Incas still live in the difficult high altitudes of the Andes?

Visual Summary

Use the visual summary below to help you review the main ideas of the chapter.

QUICK FACTS

The high Andes affect the climates and landscapes of Pacific South America.

Many South American Indians maintain traditional customs and ways of life in the Andes.

Today the countries of Pacific South America are working toward development and improved economies.

Reviewing Vocabulary, Terms, and Places

Write each word defined below, circling each letter that is marked by a star. Then write the word these letters spell.

1. _ _ * _ _ _ _ _ _ _ _ _ _ _ _—a desert in northern Chile that is one of the cloudiest and driest places on Earth

2. * _ _ _ —the capital of Peru

3. _ _ _ _ * _—the capital of Ecuador

4. _ * _ _ _ _ _ _—a governor appointed by the king of Spain

5. _ _ _ * _ _ _—one of the capitals of Bolivia

6. _ _ _ _ _ * _—an American-born descendant of Europeans

7. _ _ _ _ * _ _—a narrow passageway that connects two large bodies of water

8. _ _ _ * _ _ _ _—an ocean and weather pattern that affects the Pacific coast

9. _ * _ _—a sudden overthrow of a government by a small group of people

Comprehension and Critical Thinking

SECTION 1 *(Pages 254–258)*

10. **a. Describe** What are climate and vegetation like on the altiplano?

   b. Compare and Contrast What are two differences and one similarity between the Atacama Desert and the altiplano?

   c. Evaluate What elevation zone would you choose to live in if you lived in Pacific South America? Why would you choose to live there?

SECTION 2 *(Pages 260–263)*

11. **a. Describe** How did the Incas organize their huge empire?

   b. Analyze How have Spanish and native cultures left their marks on culture in Pacific South America?

   c. Elaborate Why do you think Pizarro killed the Inca king even though he had received riches as ransom?

SECTION 3 *(Pages 264–268)*

12. a. Identify What country in Pacific South America has the healthiest economy?

b. Analyze What problems in Ecuador and Bolivia cause political unrest?

c. Evaluate What would be some benefits and drawbacks of moving from the highlands to one of Lima's "young towns"?

FOCUS ON READING AND SPEAKING

Making Inferences *Use the information in this chapter to answer the following questions.*

13. What is an inference?

14. What do you think contributes to people's ability to maintain traditional cultures in Pacific South America?

15. What can you infer about the size of the population in the Atacama Desert? What clues led you to make this inference?

16. Presenting an Interview Now that you have questions and answers, turn them into an interview. You and your partner should decide who will be the interviewer and who will be the expert. Then read through your script several times with your partner so that you both know it well enough to sound natural during the interview. Knowing your script well will allow you to make eye contact with your audience during the interview. Remember to use a lively and authoritative tone as you speak so that members of your audience will pay attention.

Using the Internet

go.hrw.com
KEYWORD: SG7 CH11

17. Activity: Analyzing Climate Chile has steep mountains, volcanoes, a desert, a rich river valley, and thick forests. These diverse areas contain many different climates. Enter the activity keyword and visit the links given to explore the many climates of Chile. Then test your knowledge by taking an online quiz.

Social Studies Skills

Interpreting an Elevation Profile *Use the elevation profile on the Social Studies Skills page to answer the following questions.*

18. What is the purpose of an elevation profile?

19. Where can you find the vertical measurements on an elevation profile?

20. What horizontal distance does the elevation profile measure?

21. What is the elevation of the Amazon basin?

Map Activity

22. Pacific South America On a separate sheet of paper, match the letters on the map with their correct labels.

Strait of Magellan	Santiago, Chile
Quito, Ecuador	Atacama Desert
Andes	La Paz, Bolivia

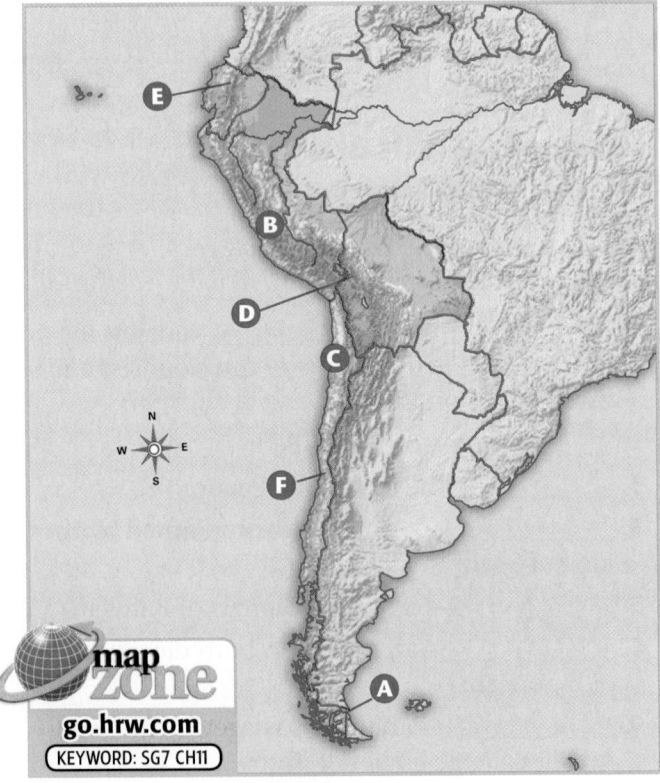

go.hrw.com
KEYWORD: SG7 CH11

DIRECTIONS: Read questions 1 through 7 and write the letter of the best response. Then read question 8 and write your own well-constructed response.

1 The main mountain range located in Pacific South America is called the

A altiplano.

B Andes.

C Strait of Magellan.

D Pampas.

2 Which of the following conditions is a result of El Niño?

A increased greenhouse gases

B more fish in a usually poor fishing area

C drought on the Pacific coast

D warmer waters near the Pacific coast

3 What early culture had a huge empire in Pacific South America in the early 1500s?

A Inca

B Aztec

C Tiahuanaco

D Nazca

4 Which of the following statements about culture in Pacific South America is false?

A Most people speak Spanish.

B Chile has a higher percentage of Indians than any other country in South America.

C Religion in the region often combines Catholic and ancient native customs.

D Wooden flutes and drums are traditional instruments.

5 Which country's main export is oil?

A Bolivia

B Chile

C Ecuador

D Peru

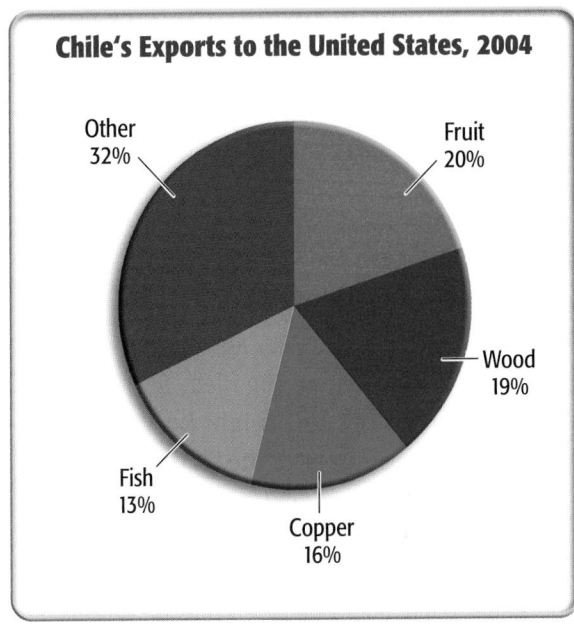

Chile's Exports to the United States, 2004

Other 32%
Fruit 20%
Wood 19%
Copper 16%
Fish 13%

Source: International Trade Administration, TradeStats Express

6 Based on the graph above, what one product is Chile's main export to the United States?

A fish

B wood

C fruit

D copper

7 What has been a major cause of political unrest in the region?

A dissatisfaction with economic policies

B arrest of the leaders of the Shining Path

C development of "young towns" in Peru

D high unemployment in Chile

8 Extended Response Using the graph above and your knowledge of Pacific South America today, compare and contrast the economic situations in each of the four countries.

Describing a Place

What are the physical features of a country? What is the weather like? What drives the economy? The answers to questions like these are often cold, hard facts and statistics. But they can bring life to a description of a place.

Assignment
Write a paper describing one of these places in the Americas:
- a city
- a country

1. Prewrite

Identify a Topic and Big Idea

- Choose one of the topics above to write about.
- Turn your topic into a big idea, or thesis. For example, your big idea might be, "Cuba's government greatly influences life in the country."

> **TIP** **Precise Language** Describe your place with specific nouns, verbs, adjectives, and adverbs. For example, rather than writing "Buenos Aires is big," write "Buenos Aires is the largest city in Argentina."

Gather and Organize Information

- Look for information about your place in the library or on the Internet. Organize your notes in groupings such as physical features, economy, or culture. Decide which facts about the place you are describing are most important or unique.

2. Write

Use a Writer's Framework

A Writer's Framework

Introduction
- Start with an interesting fact or question.
- Identify your big idea and provide any necessary background information.

Body
- Write at least one paragraph for each category. Include facts that help explain each detail.
- Write about each detail in order of importance.

Conclusion
- Summarize your description in your final paragraph.

3. Evaluate and Revise

Review and Improve Your Paper

- Re-read your paper and use the questions below to identify ways to revise your paper.
- Make the changes needed to improve your paper.

Evaluation Questions for a Description of a Place

1. Do you begin with an interesting fact or question?
2. Does your introduction identify your big idea? Do you provide background information to help your readers better understand your idea?
3. Do you have at least one paragraph for each category?
4. Do you use order of importance to organize the details of your description?
5. Are there more details you would like to know about your place? If so, what are they?

4. Proofread and Publish

Give Your Description the Finishing Touch

- Make sure you used commas correctly when listing more than two details in a sentence.
- Check your spelling of the names of places.
- Share your description with classmates or with students in another social studies class.

5. Practice and Apply

Use the steps and strategies outlined in this workshop to write your description of a place. Share your description with classmates. With your classmates, group the descriptions by country and then identify the places you would like to visit.

Europe and Russia

The Alps

The Alps, one of Europe's major mountain ranges, stretch across the heart of central Europe.

Islands and Peninsulas

Islands and peninsulas surround the edges of Europe, drawing people to the sea to work, travel, and trade.

Northern European Plain

Rolling across northern Europe is a vast lowland called the Northern European Plain.

Europe and Russia

Explore the Satellite Image
Land and sea are always close together in Europe. Islands and peninsulas are key features of this region. What can you learn about Europe's geography from this satellite image?

The Satellite's Path

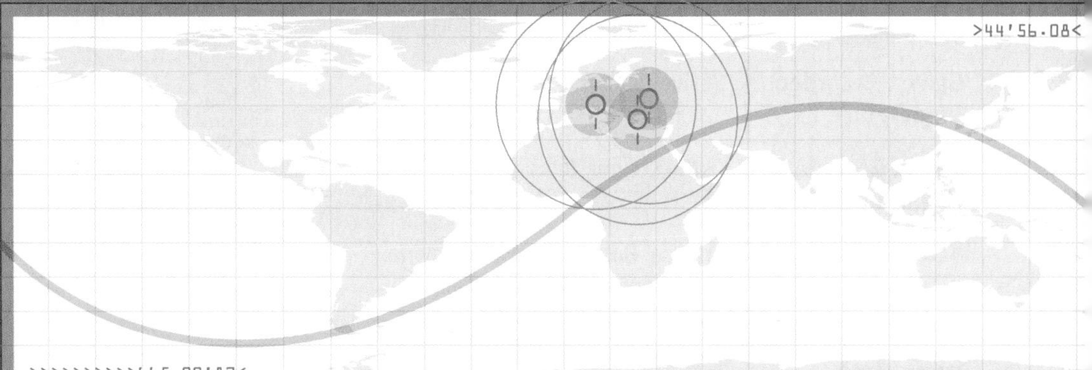

>44'56.08<

>>>>>>>>>665.00'87<

+355

567.476.348

+799

+996
+803

456.094.

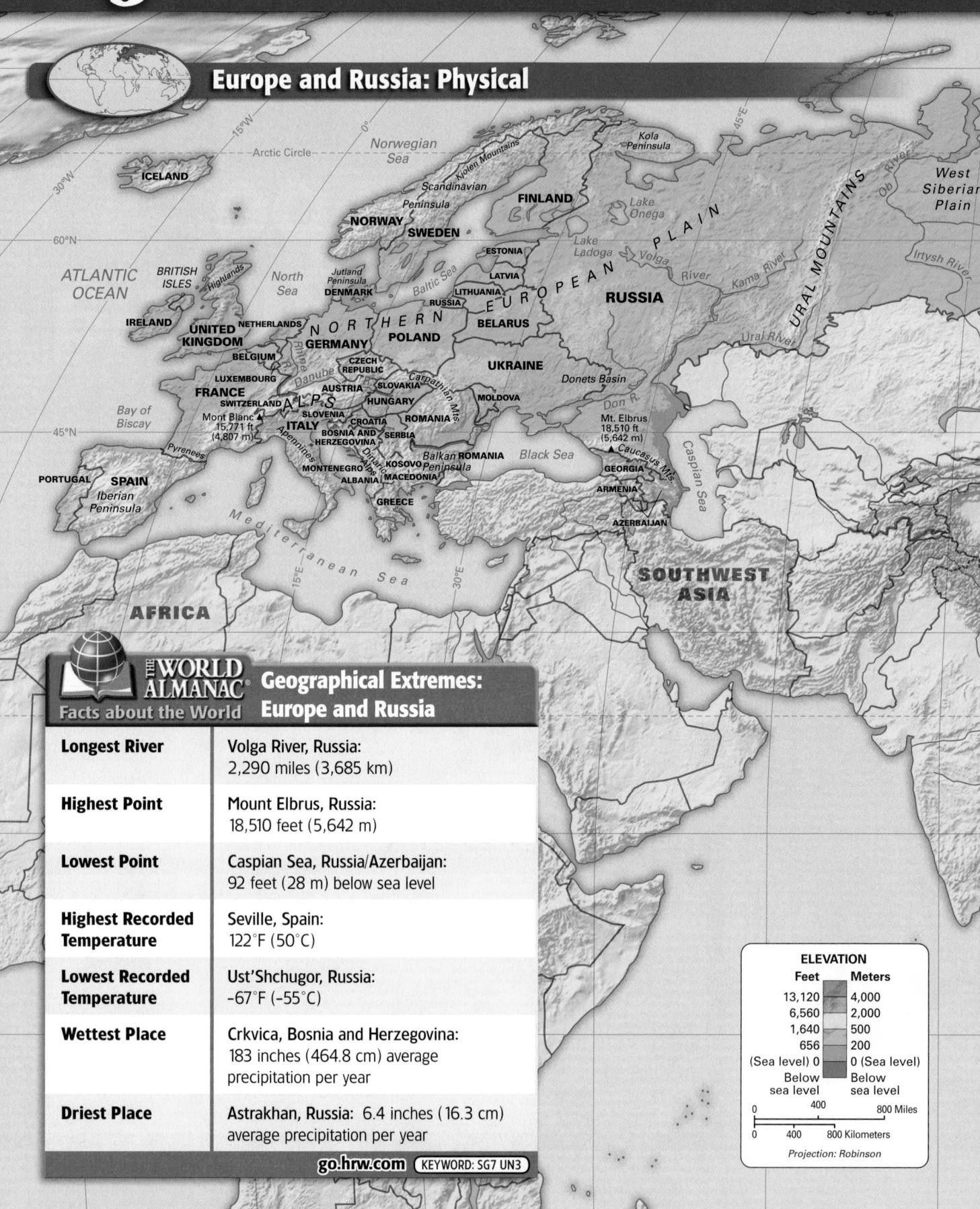

Europe and Russia: Physical

THE WORLD ALMANAC Facts about the World

Geographical Extremes: Europe and Russia

Longest River	Volga River, Russia: 2,290 miles (3,685 km)
Highest Point	Mount Elbrus, Russia: 18,510 feet (5,642 m)
Lowest Point	Caspian Sea, Russia/Azerbaijan: 92 feet (28 m) below sea level
Highest Recorded Temperature	Seville, Spain: 122°F (50°C)
Lowest Recorded Temperature	Ust'Shchugor, Russia: –67°F (–55°C)
Wettest Place	Crkvica, Bosnia and Herzegovina: 183 inches (464.8 cm) average precipitation per year
Driest Place	Astrakhan, Russia: 6.4 inches (16.3 cm) average precipitation per year

go.hrw.com KEYWORD: SG7 UN3

ELEVATION

Feet	Meters
13,120	4,000
6,560	2,000
1,640	500
656	200
(Sea level) 0	0 (Sea level)
Below sea level	Below sea level

0   400   800 Miles
0   400   800 Kilometers

Projection: Robinson

Europe and Russia

Taymyr Peninsula

Laptev Sea

New Siberian Islands

East Siberian Sea

ARCTIC OCEAN

75°N

165°W

Central Siberian Plateau

RUSSIA

S I B E R I A

Lena River

Kolyma R.

Kolyma Mountains

Bering Strait

60°N

Yenisey River

Kuznetsk Basin

Ob River

Angara River

Stanovoy Mts.

Sea of Okhotsk

Kamchatka Peninsula

Bering Sea

180°

Sayan Mts.

Yenisey River

Lake Baikal

Yablonovy Range

Amur River

Sakhalin Island

45°N

EAST ASIA

Kuril Islands

PACIFIC OCEAN

Sea of Japan (East Sea)

165°E

Size Comparison: The United States and Europe and Russia

N
W · E
S

Geography Skills

Place Europe is a small continent. Russia stretches from Eastern Europe across northern Asia.

1. **Name** What is the large region located in eastern Russia called?

2. **Make Inferences** Based on its latitude, what do you think the environment of Siberia is like?

Europe: Political

National capital
Other city

| 0 | 200 | 400 Miles |
| 0 | 200 | 400 Kilometers |

Projection: Azimuthal Equal-Area

ARCTIC OCEAN

Denmark Strait

70°N

Norwegian Sea

Arctic Circle

Reykjavik ICELAND

Faeroe Islands (DENMARK)

Shetland Islands (U.K.)

60°N

NORWAY

SWEDEN

FINLAND

Oslo

Stockholm

Helsinki

Tallinn

ESTONIA

Riga

LATVIA

North Sea

IRELAND

Dublin

DENMARK

Copenhagen

Baltic Sea

Kaliningrad (RUSSIA)

LITHUANIA

Vilnius

Minsk

BELARUS

RUSSIA

UNITED KINGDOM

50°N

London

NETHERLANDS

Amsterdam

Berlin

POLAND

Warsaw

ATLANTIC OCEAN

Brussels

BELGIUM

GERMANY

Rhine R.

Kiev

Dnieper River

Paris

LUXEMBOURG

Luxembourg

Prague

CZECH REPUBLIC

Danube R.

UKRAINE

FRANCE

LIECHTENSTEIN

SLOVAKIA

Bratislava

Vienna

MOLDOVA

Chişinău

Bern

SWITZERLAND

AUSTRIA

Budapest

HUNGARY

Ljubljana

SLOVENIA

Zagreb

ROMANIA

Bucharest

40°N

PORTUGAL

ANDORRA

MONACO

SAN MARINO

CROATIA

BOSNIA AND HERZEGOVINA

Belgrade

Sarajevo

SERBIA

Black Sea

Lisbon

Madrid

ITALY

Corsica (FRANCE)

VATICAN CITY

Rome

MONTENEGRO

Podgorica

Pristina

KOSOVO

Skopje

BULGARIA

Sofia

SPAIN

Balearic Islands (SPAIN)

Sardinia (ITALY)

Tirane

MACEDONIA

Adriatic Sea

Aegean Sea

ASIA

Strait of Gilbraltar

Gibraltar (U.K.)

0°

ALBANIA

GREECE

Athens

10°W

Sicily (ITALY)

20°E

30°E

AFRICA

MALTA

Valletta

Mediterranean Sea

Crete (GREECE)

map zone
Geography Skills

Place Europe includes many small countries.

1. Name Which European countries are island countries?

2. Make Generalizations Based on this map, which countries do you think might have the largest populations? Why?

Russia and the Caucasus: Political

ATLANTIC OCEAN

80°W · 100°W · 120°W · 140°W

60°W

40°W

20°W

0°

180°

160°W

Bering Strait

Arctic Circle

60°N

ARCTIC OCEAN

20°E · 40°E · 60°E · 80°E · 100°E · 120°E · 140°E · 160°E

80°N

Bering Sea

60°N

North Sea

Barents Sea

N E S W

Baltic Sea

Kaliningrad

St. Petersburg

EUROPE

Moscow

Nizhniy Novgorod

Volga River

Samara

Yekaterinburg

Ob River

Yenisey River

R U S S I A

Lena River

Sea of Okhotsk

Black Sea

GEORGIA

Tbilisi

ARMENIA

Yerevan

Baku

Caspian Sea

AZERBAIJAN

KAZAKHSTAN

Novosibirsk

Vladivostok

40°N

JAPAN

MONGOLIA

CHINA

PACIFIC OCEAN

Tropic of Cancer

20°N

Legend

- ✪ National capital
- • Other city

0 · 300 · 600 Miles
0 · 300 · 600 Kilometers

Projection: Two-Point Equidistant

map zone
Geography Skills

Place Russia is the largest country in the world.

1. Use the Map About how many miles is Russia from west to east?

2. Analyze Where does Russia have access to the ocean? How do you think that affects trade?

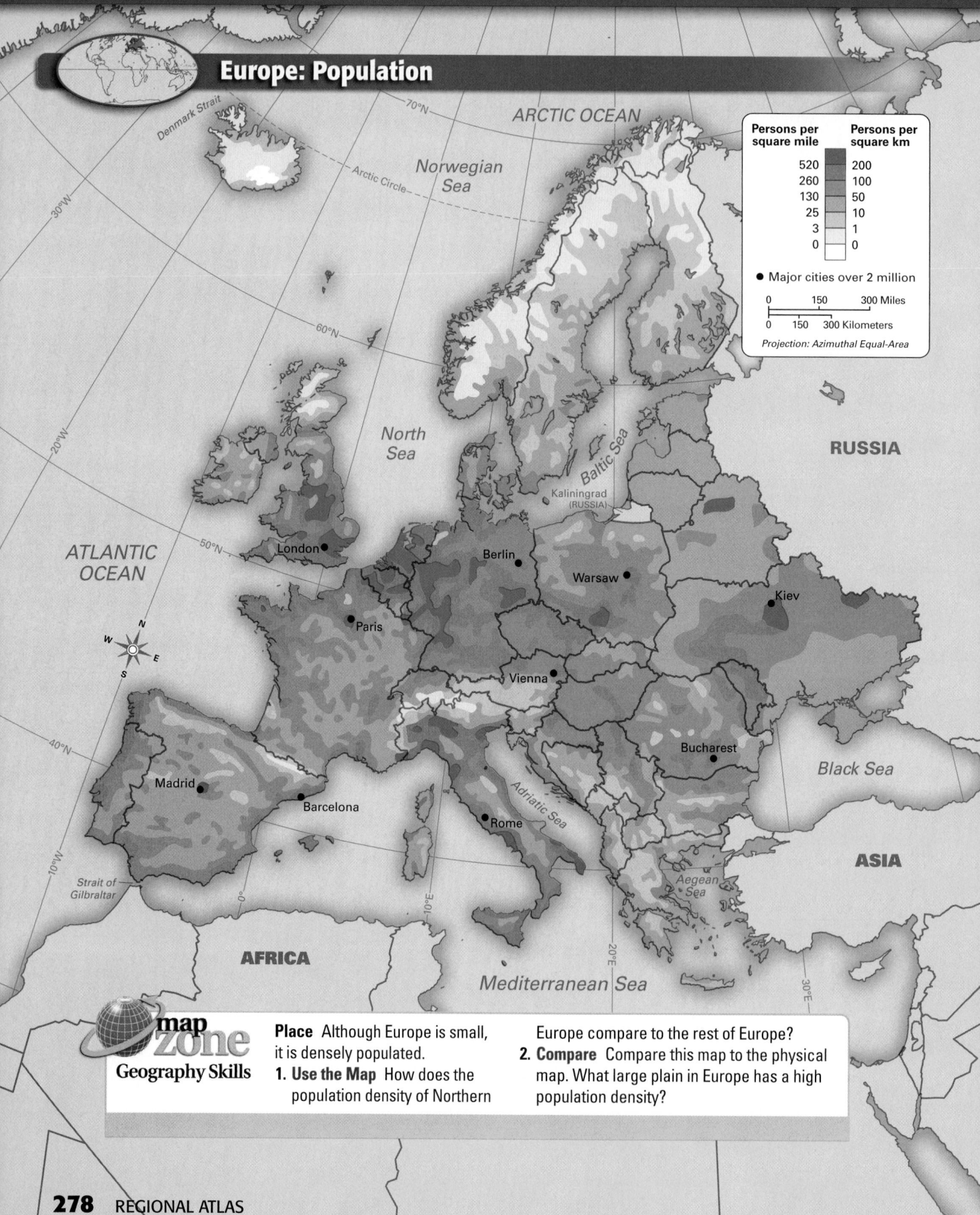

Europe: Population

Persons per square mile | **Persons per square km**
520 | 200
260 | 100
130 | 50
25 | 10
3 | 1
0 | 0

● Major cities over 2 million

0   150   300 Miles
0   150   300 Kilometers
Projection: Azimuthal Equal-Area

map zone
Geography Skills

Place Although Europe is small, it is densely populated.

1. Use the Map How does the population density of Northern Europe compare to the rest of Europe?

2. Compare Compare this map to the physical map. What large plain in Europe has a high population density?

Russia and the Caucasus: Climate

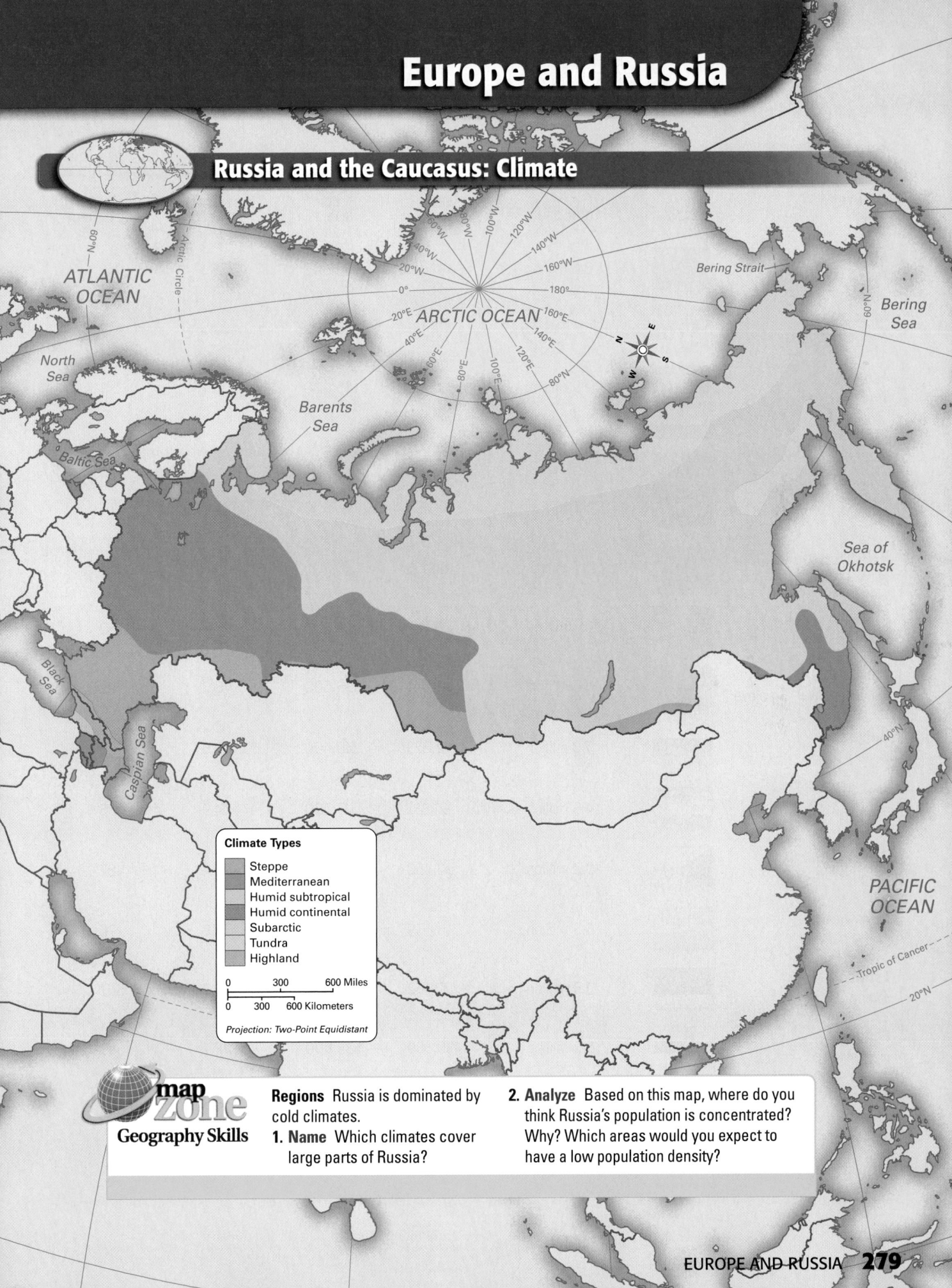

ATLANTIC OCEAN

ARCTIC OCEAN

Arctic Circle

60°N

80°W

100°W

120°W

140°W

160°W

20°W

40°W

0°

20°E

40°E

60°E

80°E

100°E

120°E

140°E

160°E

180°

60°N

80°N

40°N

20°N

N E S W

Bering Strait

Bering Sea

North Sea

Barents Sea

Baltic Sea

Black Sea

Caspian Sea

Sea of Okhotsk

PACIFIC OCEAN

Tropic of Cancer

Climate Types

- Steppe
- Mediterranean
- Humid subtropical
- Humid continental
- Subarctic
- Tundra
- Highland

0   300   600 Miles

0   300   600 Kilometers

Projection: Two-Point Equidistant

map zone
Geography Skills

Regions Russia is dominated by cold climates.

1. Name Which climates cover large parts of Russia?

2. Analyze Based on this map, where do you think Russia's population is concentrated? Why? Which areas would you expect to have a low population density?

Europe and Russia

COUNTRY / Capital	FLAG	POPULATION	AREA (sq mi)	PER CAPITA GDP (U.S. $)	LIFE EXPECTANCY AT BIRTH	TVS PER 1,000 PEOPLE
Albania / Tirana		3.6 million	11,100	$5,600	77.6	146
Andorra / Andorra la Vella		71,800	181	$38,800	83.5	440
Armenia / Yerevan		2.9 million	11,506	$5,400	72.1	241
Austria / Vienna		8.2 million	32,382	$35,500	79.2	526
Azerbaijan / Baku		8.1 million	33,436	$7,300	65.9	257
Belarus / Minsk		9.7 million	80,155	$7,800	70.0	331
Belgium / Brussels		10.4 million	11,787	$31,800	78.9	532
Bosnia and Herzegovina: Sarajevo		4.6 million	19,741	$5,500	78.2	112
Bulgaria / Sofia		7.3 million	42,823	$10,400	72.6	429
Croatia / Zagreb		4.5 million	21,831	$13,200	74.9	286
Czech Republic / Prague		10.2 million	30,450	$21,600	76.4	487
Denmark / Copenhagen		5.5 million	16,639	$37,000	77.9	776
Estonia / Tallinn		1.3 million	17,462	$19,600	72.3	567
Finland / Helsinki		5.2 million	130,559	$32,800	78.7	643
France / Paris		63.7 million	211,209	$30,100	79.9	620
United States / Washington, D.C.		301.1 million	3,718,711	$43,500	78.0	844

COUNTRY Capital	FLAG	POPULATION	AREA (sq mi)	PER CAPITA GDP (U.S. $)	LIFE EXPECTANCY AT BIRTH	TVS PER 1,000 PEOPLE
Georgia T'bilisi		4.6 million	26,911	$3,800	76.3	516
Germany Berlin		82.4 million	137,847	$31,400	78.9	581
Greece Athens		10.7 million	50,942	$23,500	79.4	480
Hungary Budapest		9.9 million	35,919	$17,300	72.9	447
Iceland Reykjavik		301,900	39,769	$38,100	80.4	505
Ireland Dublin		4.1 million	27,135	$43,600	77.9	406
Italy Rome		58.1 million	116,306	$29,700	79.9	492
Kosovo Pristina		2.1 million	4,203	$1,800	75.1	Not available
Latvia Riga		2.3 million	24,938	$15,400	71.6	757
Liechtenstein Vaduz		34,200	62	$25,000	79.8	469
Lithuania Vilnius		3.6 million	25,174	$15,100	74.4	422
Luxembourg Luxembourg		480,200	998	$68,800	79.0	599
Macedonia Skopje		2 million	9,781	$8,200	74.2	273
Malta Valletta		401,900	122	$20,300	79.2	549
Moldova Chişinau		4.3 million	13,067	$2,000	70.2	297
United States Washington, D.C.		301.1 million	3,718,711	$43,500	78.0	844

COUNTRY Capital	FLAG	POPULATION	AREA (sq mi)	PER CAPITA GDP (U.S. $)	LIFE EXPECTANCY AT BIRTH	TVS PER 1,000 PEOPLE
Monaco Monaco		32,700	1	$30,000	79.8	758
Montenegro Cetinje, Podgorica		684,700	5,415	$3,800	76.9	Not available
Netherlands Amsterdam		16.6 million	16,033	$31,700	79.1	540
Norway Oslo		4.6 million	125,182	$47,800	79.7	653
Poland Warsaw		38.5 million	120,728	$14,100	75.2	387
Portugal Lisbon		10.6 million	35,672	$19,100	77.9	567
Romania Bucharest		22.3 million	91,699	$8,800	71.9	312
Russia Moscow		141.4 million	6,592,772	$12,100	65.9	421
San Marino San Marino		29,600	24	$34,100	81.8	875
Serbia Belgrade		8.1 million	29,913	$10,400	75.3	277
Slovakia Bratislava		5.4 million	18,859	$17,700	74.9	418
Slovenia Ljubljana		2 million	7,827	$23,400	76.5	362
Spain Madrid		40.4 million	194,897	$27,000	79.8	555
Sweden Stockholm		9 million	173,732	$31,600	80.6	551
Switzerland Bern		7.6 million	15,942	$33,600	80.6	457
United States Washington, D.C.		301.1 million	3,718,711	$43,500	78.0	844

COUNTRY Capital	FLAG	POPULATION	AREA (sq mi)	PER CAPITA GDP (U.S. $)	LIFE EXPECTANCY AT BIRTH	TVS PER 1,000 PEOPLE
Ukraine Kiev		46.3 million	233,090	$7,600	67.9	433
United Kingdom London		60.8 million	94,526	$31,400	78.7	661
Vatican City Vatican City		821	0.17	Not available	Not available	Not available
United States Washington, D.C.		301.1 million	3,718,711	$43,500	78.0	844

World's Highest Per Capita GDPs

Luxembourg
Equatorial Guinea
United Arab Emirates
Norway
Ireland
United States
Andorra
Iceland
Denmark
Austria

European Countries
Other Countries

0 10 20 30 40 50 60 70

Per capita GDP
(in thousands of U.S. dollars)

Europe includes some of the wealthiest countries in the world. In fact, seven of the ten countries with the highest per capita GDPs are in Europe.

Densely Populated Countries: Europe

Country	Population Density (per square mile)
Netherlands	1,267
Belgium	889
United Kingdom	652
Germany	611
Italy	512
Switzerland	492
Denmark	334
Poland	328
United States	85

Many European countries are densely populated, especially when compared to the United States.

ANALYSIS SKILL   **ANALYZING INFORMATION**

1. What are the three most densely populated countries in Europe? How do their densities compare to that of the United States?
2. Which countries in Europe seem to have the lowest per capita GDPs? Look at the atlas political map. Where are these countries located in Europe?

Southern Europe

What You Will Learn...

In this chapter you will learn about four large countries located in Southern Europe—Greece, Italy, Spain, and Portugal. You will learn about the countries' long histories and the many groups that have influenced their societies. Finally, you will see how the countries' histories still affect their cultures and governments.

FOCUS ON READING AND WRITING

Asking Questions As you read a text, it can be helpful to ask yourself questions about what you are reading to be sure you understand it. One set of questions that you can use to test your understanding of a passage is the five Ws—who, what, when, where, and why. **See the lesson, Asking Questions, on page R13.**

Writing a News Report You are a newspaper reporter on special assignment in Southern Europe. Your editor has told you that many readers know about Southern Europe's past but not about the region today. After you read this chapter, you will write a news report about an imaginary event in a Southern European country today.

Geography Mountains cover large areas of Southern Europe. The Dolomites, shown here, are in northern Italy.

map zone **Geography Skills**

Place Southern Europe occupies three large peninsulas and thousands of small islands in the Mediterranean Sea.

1. **Identify** What is the capital of Greece?
2. **Interpret** Why do you think the region of Southern Europe is also called Mediterranean Europe?

go.hrw.com (KEYWORD: SG7 CH12)

HOLT

Geography's Impact
video series
Watch the video to understand the impact of the Olympics on Athens.

GERMANY

FRANCE

SWITZERLAND

AUSTRIA

EASTERN EUROPE

Milan

Venice

Po River

Genoa

ITALY

SAN MARINO

Florence

Tiber River

ANDORRA

Barcelona

VATICAN CITY

Rome

Adriatic Sea

Naples

Thessaloníki

Balearic Islands

Sardinia

Tyrrhenian Sea

GREECE

TURKEY

Ionian Sea

Aegean Sea

Palermo

Athens

ALGERIA

Sicily

MALTA

Crete

TUNISIA

Mediterranean Sea

10°E

20°E

History Greece was the home of Europe's first great civilization. The ruins in Delphi are more than 2,300 years old.

Culture Bullfights are popular events in parts of Spain. Bullfighters, called matadors, are honored members of society.

Physical Geography

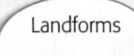
If **YOU** lived there...

You are in a busy fish market in a small town on the coast of Italy, near the Mediterranean Sea. It is early morning. Colorful fishing boats have just pulled into shore with their catch of fresh fish and seafood. They unload their nets of slippery octopus and wriggling shrimp. Others bring silvery sea bass. You are looking forward to lunch—perhaps a tasty fish soup or pasta dish.

How does the Mediterranean affect your life?

BUILDING BACKGROUND The Mediterranean Sea has shaped the geography, climate, and culture of Southern Europe. All of these countries have long coastlines, with good harbors and beautiful beaches. Because much of the interior is rugged and mountainous, the sea has also been a highway for trade and travel.

Physical Features

The continent of Europe has often been called a peninsula of peninsulas. Why do you think this is so? Look at the map of Europe in this book's Atlas to find out. Notice how Europe juts out from Asia like one big peninsula. Also, notice how smaller peninsulas extend into the many bodies of water that surround the continent.

Look at the map of Europe again. Do you see the three large peninsulas that extend south from Europe? From west to east, these are the Iberian Peninsula, the Italian Peninsula, and the Balkan Peninsula. Together with some large islands, they form the region of Southern Europe.

Southern Europe is also known as Mediterranean Europe. All of the countries of Southern Europe have long coastlines on the **Mediterranean Sea**. In addition to this common location on the Mediterranean, the countries of Southern Europe share many common physical features.

Landforms

The three peninsulas of Southern Europe are largely covered with rugged mountains. In Greece, for example, about three-fourths of the land is mountainous. Because much of the land is so rugged, farming and travel in Southern Europe can be a challenge.

The mountains of Southern Europe form several large ranges. On the Iberian Peninsula, the **Pyrenees** (PIR-uh-neez) form a boundary between Spain and France to the north. Italy has two major ranges. The **Apennines** (A-puh-nynz) run along the whole peninsula, and the **Alps**—Europe's highest mountains—are in the north. The Pindus Mountains cover much of Greece.

Southern Europe's mountains extend into the sea as well, where they rise above the water to form islands. The Aegean Sea east of Greece is home to more than 2,000 such islands. Southern Europe also has many larger islands formed by undersea mountains. These include Crete, which is south of Greece; Sicily, at the southern tip of Italy; and many others.

Not all of Southern Europe is rocky and mountainous, though. Some flat plains lie in the region. Most of these plains are along the coast and in the valleys of major rivers. It is here that most farming in Southern Europe takes place. It is also here that most of the region's people live.

FOCUS ON READING

As you read, ask yourself this question: Where are the Pyrenees?

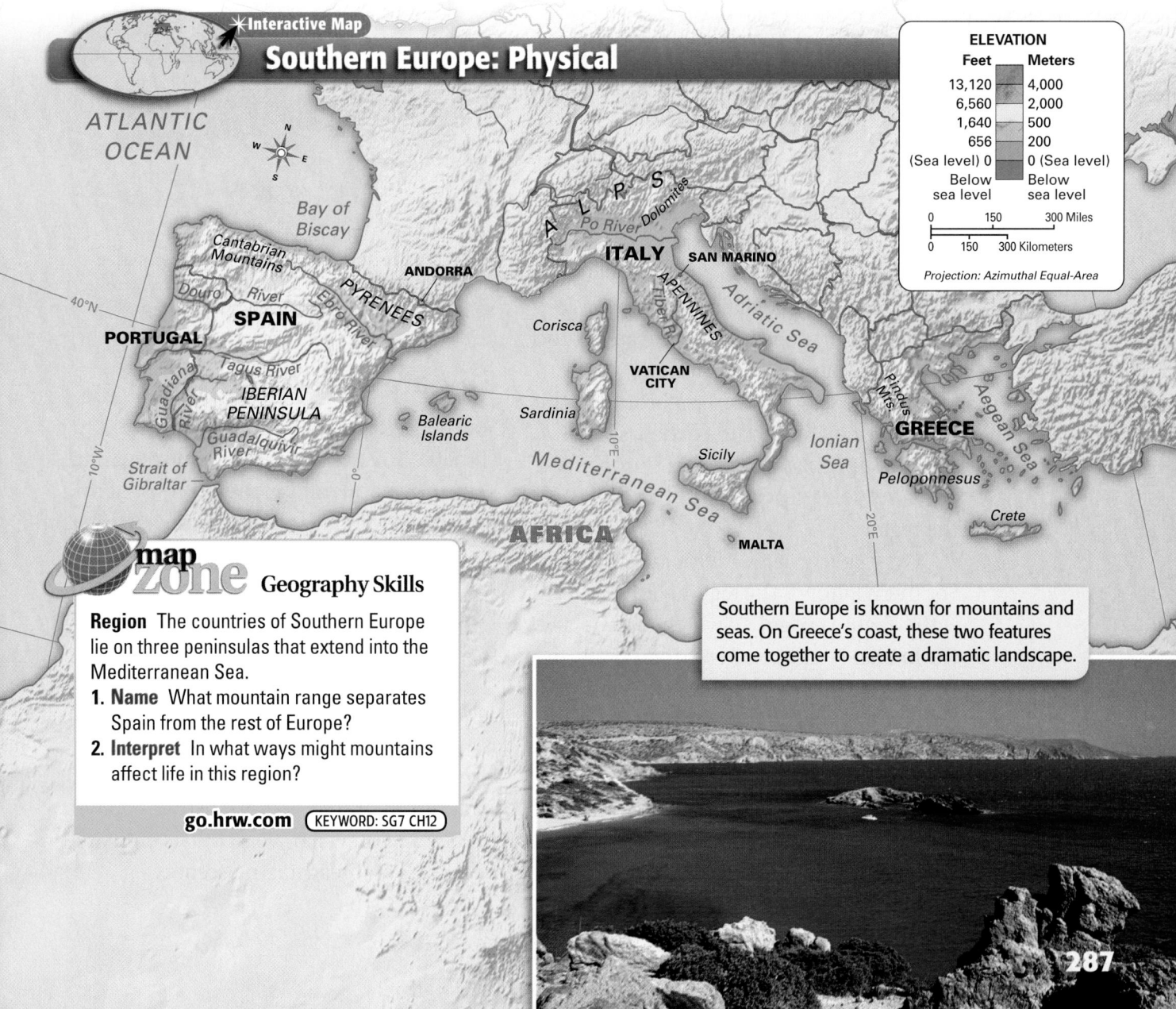

Southern Europe: Physical

Interactive Map

ELEVATION

Feet		Meters
13,120		4,000
6,560		2,000
1,640		500
656		200
(Sea level) 0		0 (Sea level)
Below sea level		Below sea level

0   150   300 Miles
0   150   300 Kilometers

Projection: Azimuthal Equal-Area

map zone Geography Skills

Region The countries of Southern Europe lie on three peninsulas that extend into the Mediterranean Sea.

1. **Name** What mountain range separates Spain from the rest of Europe?
2. **Interpret** In what ways might mountains affect life in this region?

go.hrw.com   **KEYWORD: SG7 CH12**

Southern Europe is known for mountains and seas. On Greece's coast, these two features come together to create a dramatic landscape.

287

Mediterranean Climate

Southern Europe is known for its Mediterranean climate, which features warm, dry summers and mild, wet winters. This climate affects nearly every aspect of life in the region.

1 **Agriculture** The climate of Southern Europe is ideal for growing many crops. Here, Portuguese farmers harvest grapes.

SPAIN

PORTUGAL

1

2

2 **Tourism** The region's mild and sunny climate draws millions of tourists to places like this beach in Ibiza, Spain.

Water Features

Since Southern Europe is mostly peninsulas and islands, water is central to the region's geography. No place in Southern Europe is very far from a major body of water. The largest of these bodies of water is the Mediterranean, but the Adriatic, Aegean, and Ionian seas are also important to the region. For many centuries, these seas have given the people of Southern Europe food and a relatively easy way to travel around the region.

Only a few large rivers run through Southern Europe. The region's longest river is the Tagus (TAY-guhs), which flows across the Iberian Peninsula. In northern Italy, the Po runs through one of Southern Europe's most fertile and densely populated areas. Other rivers run out of the mountains and into the many surrounding seas.

READING CHECK **Finding Main Ideas** What are the region's major features?

Climate and Resources

Southern Europe is famous for its pleasant climate. Most of the region enjoys warm, sunny days and mild nights for most of the year. Little rain falls in the summer, falling instead during the mild winter. In fact, the type of climate found across Southern Europe is called a **Mediterranean climate** because it is common in this region.

The region's climate is also one of its most valuable resources. The mild climate is ideal for growing a variety of crops, from citrus fruits and grapes to olives and wheat. In addition, millions of tourists are drawn to the region each year by its climate, beaches, and breathtaking scenery.

ITALY

3

GREECE

4

4 **Architecture** Climate also affects architecture in Southern Europe. Buildings, like these in Greece, are airy and made of light materials to reflect sunlight and heat.

ANALYSIS
SKILL **ANALYZING VISUALS**

What are four ways in which the Mediterranean climate affects life in Southern Europe?

3 **Vegetation** This field in Tuscany, a region of Italy, shows the variety of plants that thrive in Southern Europe's climate.

The sea is also an important resource in Southern Europe. Many of the region's largest cities are ports, which ship goods all over the world. In addition, the nearby seas are full of fish and shellfish, which provide the basis for profitable fishing industries.

READING CHECK **Generalizing** How is a mild climate important to Southern Europe?

SUMMARY AND PREVIEW In this section you learned about the physical features of Southern Europe. In the next section you will learn how those features affect life in one country—Greece.

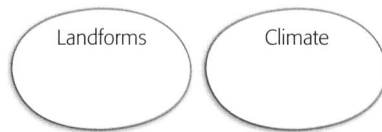

Section 1 Assessment

go.hrw.com
Online Quiz
KEYWORD: SG7 HP12

Reviewing Ideas, Terms, and Places
1. **a. Recall** Which three peninsulas are in Southern Europe?
   b. Explain Why is the sea important to Southern Europe?
   c. Elaborate Why do you think most people in Southern Europe live on coastal plains or in river valleys?
2. **a. Describe** What is the **Mediterranean climate** like?
   b. Generalize How is climate an important resource for the region?

Critical Thinking
3. **Finding Main Ideas** Draw a diagram like the one shown here.

Landforms   Climate

In the left oval, use your notes to explain how landforms affect life in Southern Europe. In the right oval, explain how climate affects life in the region.

FOCUS ON WRITING

4. **Describing the Setting** Your news report will be about an imaginary event someplace in Southern Europe. That event might happen on a beach, in the mountains, or on a farm. Write some ideas in your notebook.

Reading a Climate Map

Learn

Geographers use many different types of maps to study a region. One type that can be very useful is a climate map. Because climate affects so many aspects of people's lives, it is important to know which climates are found in a region.

Practice

Use the climate map of Europe below to answer the following questions.

❶ What does orange mean on this map?

❷ What city has a highland climate?

❸ What is the dominant climate in the countries of Southern Europe?

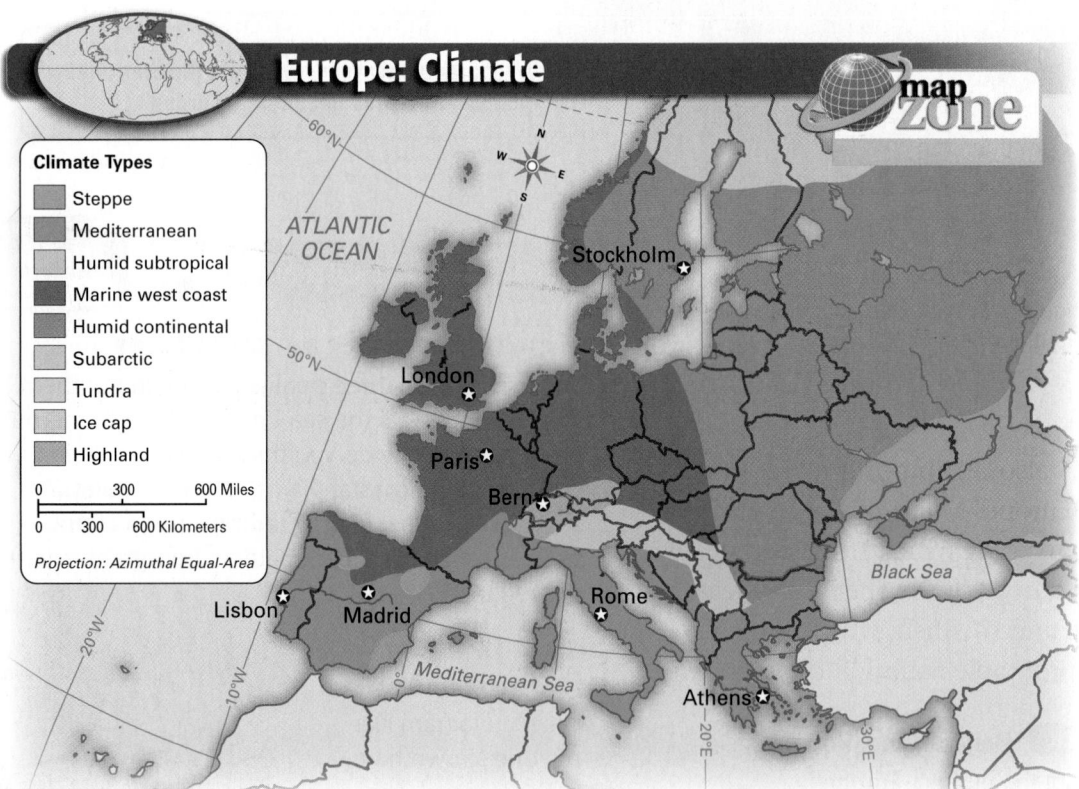

Europe: Climate

Climate Types
- Steppe
- Mediterranean
- Humid subtropical
- Marine west coast
- Humid continental
- Subarctic
- Tundra
- Ice cap
- Highland

0   300   600 Miles
0   300   600 Kilometers

Projection: Azimuthal Equal-Area

ATLANTIC OCEAN

Stockholm
London
Paris
Bern
Lisbon   Madrid
Rome
Black Sea
Mediterranean Sea
Athens

Apply

Choose one of the cities shown on the map above. Imagine that you are planning a trip to that city and need to know what the climate is like so you can prepare. Use the map to identify the type of climate found in your chosen city. Then use the library or the Internet to find out more about that type of climate. Write a short description of the climate and how you could prepare for it.

Greece

If YOU lived there...

You live in a small town on one of the many Greek islands. White houses perch on steep streets leading down to the sea. Many tourists come here by boat after visiting the busy capital city of Athens. They tell you about the beautiful ancient buildings they saw there. But your island has ancient statues and temple sites too. Still, some of your friends talk about moving to the city.

What might make people move to the city?

BUILDING BACKGROUND In recent years, many people have moved out of Greece's small towns and villages into cities, especially Athens. Now the capital of Greece, Athens is an ancient city. It was home to one of Europe's greatest civilizations, one whose influence is still felt today all around the world.

History

Greece is a country steeped in history. Home to one of the world's oldest civilizations, it has been called the birthplace of Western culture. Even today, remnants of ancient Greece can be found all over the country, and ideas from ancient thinkers continue to affect people's lives today.

Ancient Greece

Theater. Philosophy. Democracy. These are just a few of the ideas that the modern world owes to ancient Greece. The Greeks were pioneers in many fields, and their contributions still affect how we live and think.

In art, the Greeks created lifelike paintings and statues that served as examples for later artists to imitate. In architecture, they built stately temples of marble that continue to inspire architects around the world.

An ancient Greek jar

What You Will Learn...

Main Ideas

1. Early in its history, Greece was the home of a great civilization, but it was later ruled by foreign powers.
2. The Greek language, the Orthodox Church, and varied customs have helped shape Greece's culture.
3. In Greece today, many people are looking for new economic opportunities.

The Big Idea

The home of one of the Western world's oldest civilizations, Greece is trying to reclaim its place as a leading country in Europe.

Key Terms and Places

Orthodox Church, *p. 293*
Athens, *p. 294*

TAKING NOTES Draw a box like the one below. As you read, list details about Greek history and culture in the box.

Greece

CONNECTING TO Math

Proportion

The ancient Greeks were great admirers of mathematics. They thought math could be used in many areas of their lives. For example, they used it to design temples and other buildings.

Greek builders believed in a concept called the Golden Mean. This concept said that the height of a building should be a particular fraction of the building's width. If the building were too tall, they thought it would look flimsy. If it were too wide, it would look squat and ugly. As a result, these builders were very careful in planning their buildings. The Parthenon, the temple pictured below, was built using the Golden Mean. Many consider it to be the greatest of all Greek temples.

Generalizing How did mathematical ideas influence ancient Greek architecture?

They invented new forms of literature, including history and drama, and made advances in geometry and other branches of math that we still study. In philosophy, they created a system of reasoning that is the foundation for modern science. In government, they created democracy, which inspired the government embraced by most people around the world today.

No ancient civilization lasted forever, though. In the 300s BC Greece became a part of Alexander the Great's empire, which also included Egypt and much of Southwest Asia. Under Alexander, Greek culture spread throughout his empire.

FOCUS ON READING

As you read, ask yourself this question: Who conquered Greece in the 300s BC?

The Romans and the Turks

Alexander's empire did not last very long. When it broke up, Greece became part of another empire, the Roman Empire. For about 300 years, the Greeks lived under Roman rule.

After about AD 400 the Roman Empire was divided into two parts. Greece became part of the Eastern, or Byzantine, Empire. The rulers of the Byzantine Empire admired Greek culture and encouraged people to adopt the Greek language and customs. They also encouraged people to adopt their religion, Christianity.

Greece was part of the Byzantine Empire for about 1,000 years. In the 1300s and 1400s, however, Greece was taken over by the Ottoman Turks from central Asia. The Turks were Muslim, but they allowed the people of Greece to remain Christian. Some elements of Greek culture, though, began to fade. For example, many people began speaking Turkish instead of Greek.

Independent Greece

Many Greeks were not happy under Turkish rule. They wanted to be free of foreign influences. In the early 1800s, they rose up against the Turks. The rebellion seemed likely to fail, but the Greeks received help from other European countries and drove the Turks out. After the rebellion, Greece became a monarchy.

Greece's government has changed many times since independence. The country's first kings took steps toward restoring democracy, but for most of the 1900s the nation experienced instability. A military dictatorship ruled from 1967 to 1974. More recently, democracy has once again taken root in the country where it was born nearly 2,500 years ago.

READING CHECK **Sequencing** What groups have ruled Greece throughout history?

Culture

Over the course of its history, many factors have combined to shape Greece's culture. These factors include the Greek language, Christianity, and customs adopted from the many groups who have ruled Greece.

Language and Religion

The people of Greece today speak a form of the same language their ancestors spoke long ago. In fact, Greek is one of the oldest languages still spoken in Europe today. The language has changed greatly over time, but it was never lost.

Although the Greeks maintained their language, their ancient religions have long since disappeared. Today nearly everyone in Greece belongs to the **Orthodox Church**, a branch of Christianity that dates to the Byzantine Empire. Religion is important to the Greeks, and holidays such as Easter are popular times for celebration.

Customs

Greek customs reflect the country's long history and its physical geography. Greek food, for example, is influenced both by products native to Greece and by groups who have ruled Greece over time.

Ingredients such as lamb, olives, and vegetables are easily available in Greece because they grow well there. As a result, the Greeks use lots of these ingredients in their cooking. Greek cuisine was later enhanced with ideas borrowed from other people. From the Turks, the Greeks learned to cook with yogurt and honey, and from the Italians they learned about pasta.

Greek meals are often eaten at family gatherings. For centuries, family has been central to Greek culture. Even as Greece is becoming more modernized, the family has remained the cornerstone of society.

READING CHECK **Summarizing** What are two dominant elements of Greek culture?

Easter in Greece

Easter is one of the most sacred days of the year for Orthodox Christians. All over Greece, people celebrate Easter with festivals, feasts, and special rituals.

ANALYZING VISUALS What evidence in this photo suggests that Easter is a major celebration?

The priests carry containers of holy water. Later, they will sprinkle this holy water on crowds as part of a blessing.

Priests wear richly decorated robes as part of their Easter celebration.

Many Easter ceremonies are led by an archbishop, a high-ranking official in the Orthodox Church.

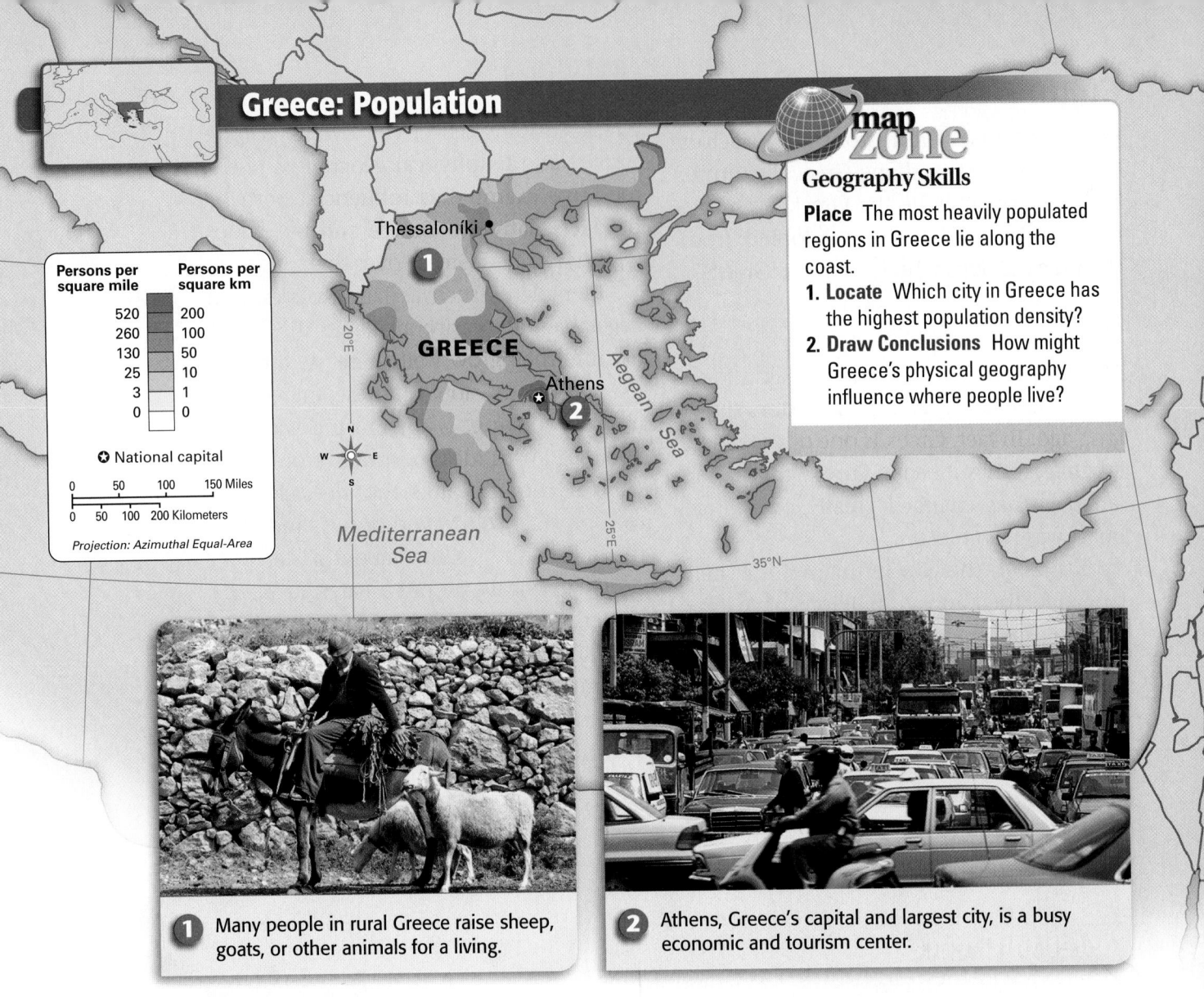

map zone

Geography Skills

Place The most heavily populated regions in Greece lie along the coast.

1. **Locate** Which city in Greece has the highest population density?
2. **Draw Conclusions** How might Greece's physical geography influence where people live?

Persons per square mile	Persons per square km
520	200
260	100
130	50
25	10
3	1
0	0

✪ National capital

0 50 100 150 Miles
0 50 100 200 Kilometers

Projection: Azimuthal Equal-Area

Thessaloníki

GREECE

Athens

Aegean Sea

Mediterranean Sea

① Many people in rural Greece raise sheep, goats, or other animals for a living.

② Athens, Greece's capital and largest city, is a busy economic and tourism center.

Greece Today

When many people think of Greece now, they think about the country's history. In fact, Greece's past often overshadows its present. Today, though, Greece is a largely urbanized society with a rapidly growing and diverse economy.

Urban and Rural Greece

About three-fifths of all people in Greece today live in cities. Of these cities, **Athens**—the nation's capital—is by far the largest. In fact, almost one-third of the country's entire population lives in or around the city of Athens.

Athens is a huge city where old and new mix. Modern skyscrapers rise high above the ancient ruins of Greek temples. Most of the country's industry is centered there. However, this industry has resulted in air pollution, which damages the ancient ruins and causes health problems.

Outside of the city, Greek life is very different. People in rural areas still live largely as people have lived for centuries. Many live in isolated mountain villages, where they grow crops and raise sheep and goats. Village life often centers around the village square. People meet there to discuss local events and make decisions.

Greece's Economy

Although Greece is experiencing rapid economic growth, it still lags behind some other European nations. This lag is largely caused by a lack of resources. Greece has few mineral resources, and only about one-fifth of its land can be farmed. The rest of the land is too rugged.

One industry in which Greece excels is shipping. Greece has one of the largest shipping fleets in the world. Greek ships can be found in ports all around the world, loaded with cargo from countries in Europe and other parts of the world.

Another profitable industry in Greece is tourism. Millions of people from around the world visit every year. Some are drawn to ancient ruins in Athens and other parts of the country. Others prefer the sunny, sandy beaches of Greece's many islands. The Greek government actively promotes this tourism, and more people visit the country every year. Largely due to this tourism, Greece's GDP—the value of all its goods and services—has risen steadily in recent years.

READING CHECK Finding Main Ideas What are the most important industries in Greece?

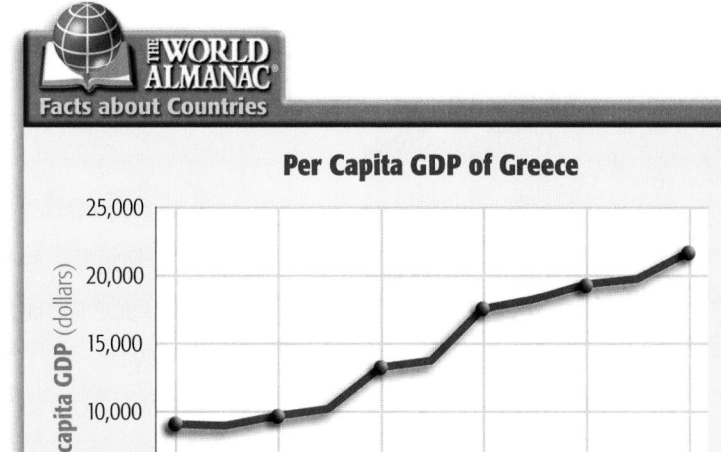

THE WORLD ALMANAC®
Facts about Countries

Per Capita GDP of Greece

Interpreting Graphs What was Greece's per capita GDP in 1994? What was it in 2004?

go.hrw.com KEYWORD: SG7 CH12

SUMMARY AND PREVIEW In this section you learned about Greece, a country with a long and varied history that still shapes its culture and economy today. In the next section you will learn about Italy, another country in the region that has been shaped by history.

Section 2 Assessment

go.hrw.com
Online Quiz
KEYWORD: SG7 HP12

Reviewing Ideas, Terms, and Places

1. **a. Identify** What were two major achievements of the ancient Greeks?
   b. Sequence What steps did the Greeks take to gain their independence?
2. **a. Define** What is the **Orthodox Church**?
   b. Generalize What is one way in which Greece's history affects its culture today?
3. **a. Describe** What is life like in **Athens** today?
   b. Explain Why is manufacturing not a major industry in Greece?
   c. Evaluate Would you rather live in Athens or in rural Greece? Why?

Critical Thinking

4. **Categorizing** Draw a table like the one here. Use the table to organize your notes into columns about Greece's history, its culture, and Greece today.

Greece		
History	Culture	Today

FOCUS ON WRITING

5. **Introducing Greece** If you choose Greece for the site of your news report, what would be a good topic? The movement of people to the cities? An event at a historic site? Jot down your ideas.

Italy

If **YOU** lived there...

You live in Rome, the historic heart of Italy. Wherever you walk in Rome, you see reminders of the city's long and rich history. It may be a 600-year-old church or a 2,000-year-old market. One of your favorite spots to visit is the Colosseum. When you sit inside this ancient arena, you can imagine fierce gladiators and wild animals fighting there long ago.

How does history affect life in Italy?

BUILDING BACKGROUND Italian history continues to affect life in Italy today, but its influence extends far beyond that one country. All around the world, people owe their ideas about art, government, law, and language to Italy and its people. Many of these ideas are ancient, but even today Italians help shape the world's culture.

History

Greece may have been the birthplace of the first civilization in Europe, but Italy was the home of the continent's greatest empire. For centuries, Italy was the heart of one of the largest and most powerful states the world has ever seen. Even after that state collapsed, Italy remained a major influence on Europe and other parts of the world.

Ancient Rome

The great civilization that developed in Italy was Rome. Built in the 700s BC as a tiny village, Rome grew to control nearly all the land around the Mediterranean Sea. At the height of the Roman Empire, the Romans controlled an empire that stretched from Britain in the northwest to the Persian Gulf. It included most of Europe as well as parts of southwest Asia and northern Africa.

Roman influences in the world can still be seen today. The Romans' art, architecture, and literature are still admired. Their laws and political ideas have influenced the governments and legal systems of many countries. In addition, the Romans helped spread Christianity, one of the world's major religions.

The Renaissance

The Roman Empire collapsed in the AD 400s, largely due to weak leadership and invasions from outside. With no central government to unite them, Italy's cities formed their own states. Each had its own laws, its own government, and its own army. Wars between them were common.

As time passed, the cities of Italy became major centers of trade. Merchants from these cities traveled to far-off places like China to bring goods back to Europe.

Many merchants became very rich from this trade. With the money they made, these merchants sponsored artists and architects. Their support of the arts helped lead to the Renaissance, a period of great creativity in Europe. It lasted from about 1350 through the 1500s. During the Renaissance artists and writers—many of them Italian—created some of the world's greatest works of art and literature.

Unified Italy

Italy remained divided into small states until the mid-1800s. At that time, a rise in nationalism, or strong patriotic feelings for a country, led people across Italy to fight for unification. As a result of their efforts, Italy became a unified kingdom in 1861.

In the 1920s a new government came to power. Under Benito Mussolini, Italy became a dictatorship. That dictatorship was short-lived, however. Mussolini joined Hitler to fight other countries of Europe in World War II. In 1945 Italy was defeated.

After World War II, Italy became a democracy. Since that time, power has rested in an elected Parliament and prime minister. Also since the end of the war, Italy has developed one of the strongest economies in Europe.

READING CHECK **Summarizing** What are some key periods in the history of Italy?

Italian History

The history of Italy stretches back nearly 3,000 years. This long span includes several key periods.

Ancient Rome

- According to legend, the city of Rome was built in the 700s BC.
- The Romans created a huge empire. At its height, the empire included parts of Europe, Southwest Asia, and northern Africa.
- Roman art, architecture, literature, and law still influence people today.
- Christianity arose and spread in the Roman Empire.

Roman statue

The Renaissance

- The Renaissance was a period of great advances in art, architecture, and literature.
- The Renaissance began in the 1300s in cities like Florence.
- From Italy, the Renaissance spread to other parts of Europe.
- Some of the world's greatest works of art were created at this time.

Leonardo da Vinci's *Mona Lisa*

Unified Italy

- Since the Middle Ages, Italy had been divided into small states.
- In the mid-1800s, increased feelings of nationalism led people across Italy to fight for unification.
- The fight for unification was led by Giuseppe Garibaldi.
- Italy was officially unified in 1861.

Giuseppe Garibaldi

Culture

For centuries, people around the world have admired and borrowed from Italian culture. Italy's culture has been shaped by many factors. Among these factors are the Roman Catholic Church, local traditions, and regional geography.

Religion

Most people in Italy belong to the Roman Catholic Church. Historically, the church has been the single strongest influence on Italian culture. This influence is strong in part because the **pope**, the spiritual head of the Roman Catholic Church, lives on the Italian Peninsula. He resides in **Vatican City**, an independent state located within the city of Rome.

ACADEMIC VOCABULARY

contemporary
modern

The lasting importance of the church can be seen in many ways in Italy. For example, the city of Rome alone is home to hundreds of Catholic churches from all periods of history. In addition, religious holidays and festivals are major events.

Local Traditions

In addition to religion, local traditions have influenced Italian culture. Italian food, for example, varies widely from region to region. These variations are based on local preferences and products. All over Italy, people eat many of the same foods—olives, tomatoes, rice, pasta. However, the ways in which people prepare this food differ. In the south, for example, people often serve pasta with tomato sauces. In the north, creamy sauces are much more common.

Other traditions reflect Italy's past. For example, Italy has always been known as a center of the arts. The people of Italy have long been trendsetters, shaping styles that are later adopted by other people. As a result, the Italians are leaders in many **contemporary** art forms. For example, Italy has produced some of the world's greatest painters, sculptors, authors, composers, fashion designers, and filmmakers.

READING CHECK **Finding Main Ideas** What are two major influences on Italian culture?

Major Cities of Italy

Milan, Rome, and Naples are the three largest cities in Italy. Because of their varied histories and locations, each city has a distinct landscape and culture.

ANALYZING VISUALS Which city would you most like to visit?

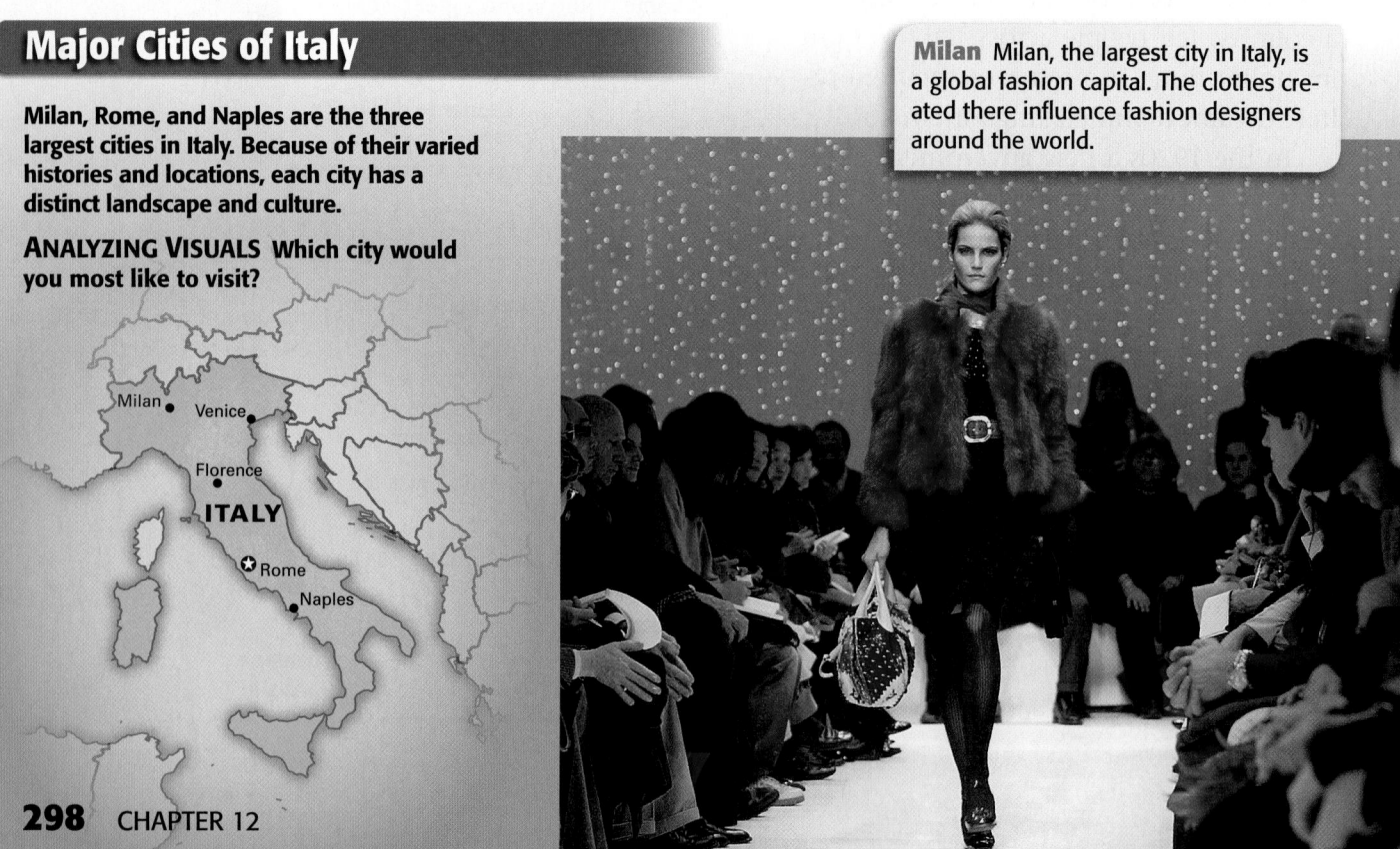

Milan Milan, the largest city in Italy, is a global fashion capital. The clothes created there influence fashion designers around the world.

Italy Today

A shared language, the Roman Catholic Church, and strong family ties help bind Italians together. At the same time, though, major differences exist in the northern and southern parts of the country.

Southern Italy

Southern Italy is the country's poorer half. Its economy has less industry than the north and depends heavily on agriculture. Farming is especially important in **Sicily**, an island at the peninsula's tip. Tourism is also vital to the south's economy. Among the region's attractions are its dazzling beaches and ancient Roman ruins.

In recent decades, Italy's government has tried to promote industry in the south. It has offered **incentives**, such as lower taxes, to private companies that will build factories there. Many of these government efforts center on the city of **Naples**, a busy port and the largest city in southern Italy. Thanks to government programs, Naples is now also an industrial center.

Northern Italy

In contrast to southern Italy, the northern part of the country has a strong economy. Northern Italy includes the country's most fertile farmlands, its major trade centers, and its most popular tourist destinations.

The Po River valley in northern Italy has the country's most productive farmland. For decades, the Po valley has been called the breadbasket of Italy because most of the country's crops are grown there. Despite its fertile soils, farmers cannot grow enough to support Italy's population. Italy has to import much of its food.

The north is also home to Italy's major industrial centers. Busy factories in such cities as Turin and Genoa make appliances, automobiles, and other goods for export. **Milan** is also a major industrial center as well as a worldwide center for fashion design. The location of these cities near central Europe helps companies sell their goods to foreign customers. Railroads, highways, and tunnels make the shipment of goods through the Alps easy.

ACADEMIC VOCABULARY

incentive something that leads people to follow a certain course of action

Rome Rome, the capital of Italy, is in the central part of the country. A major center of banking and industry, Rome is also one of the world's most popular tourist sites.

Naples Naples is the most important city in southern Italy. Less glamorous than many northern cities, it is a port and manufacturing center.

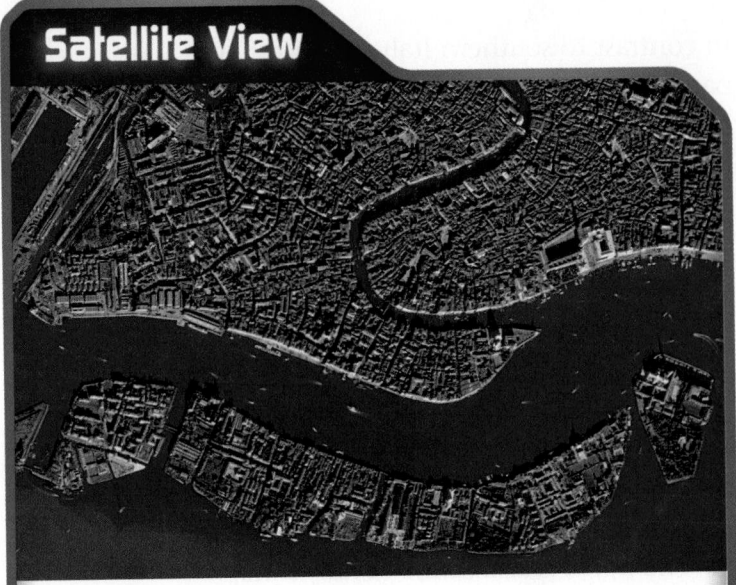

Venice

Venice, in northeastern Italy, is one of the country's most visited tourist attractions. Look at the image of Venice above, taken by an orbiting satellite. Does it look like other cities you have seen? What may not be obvious is that the paths that wind their way through the city are not roads, but canals. In fact, Venice has very few roads. This is because the city was built on islands—118 of them! People move about the city on boats that navigate along the canals. Every year, millions of tourists travel to Venice to see the sights as they are rowed along the scenic waterways.

Contrasting How is Venice unlike other cities you have studied?

Tens of millions of tourists visit the cities of northern Italy every year. They are drawn by the cities' rich histories and unique cultural features. Florence, for example, is a center of Italian art and culture. It was there that the Renaissance began in the 1300s. To the west of Florence is Pisa, famous for its Leaning Tower—the bell tower of the city's church. On the coast of the Adriatic Sea lies the city of Venice. Tourists are lured there by the romantic canals that serve as roads through the city.

Nestled in the center of the country is Italy's capital, **Rome**. With ties to both north and south, Rome does not fully belong to either region. From there, the country's leaders attempt to bring all the people of Italy together as one nation.

READING CHECK **Contrast** How are northern and southern Italy different?

SUMMARY AND PREVIEW In this section you read about Italy. The country's long history continues to affect life in Italy even today. Next, you will study two other countries whose pasts still affect life there—Spain and Portugal.

Section 3 Assessment

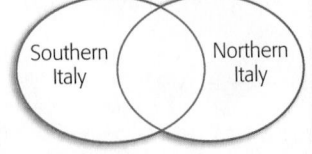

go.hrw.com
Online Quiz
KEYWORD: SG7 HP12

Reviewing Ideas, Terms, and Places

1. **a. Describe** What was Renaissance Italy like?
   b. Interpret How did nationalism influence Italian history?
2. **a. Identify** What religion has had a major impact on Italian culture?
   b. Explain How have local traditions helped shape Italian culture?
3. **a. Recall** What is the main economic activity of southern Italy?
   b. Contrast How are the economies of **Milan**, **Rome**, and **Naples** different?
   c. Rate If you could visit any one city in Italy, which would it be? Why?

Critical Thinking

4. **Comparing and Contrasting** Draw two circles like the ones here. Using your notes, list details about southern Italy in the left circle and about northern Italy in the right circle. Where the circles overlap, list common features of the two.

Southern Italy   Northern Italy

FOCUS ON WRITING

5. **Investigating Italy** What Italian event could you report on? Perhaps it could be a fashion show or a religious service at the Vatican. Make a list of events that could make an interesting report.

Spain and Portugal

If YOU lived there...

You have just moved to southern Spain from a town in the far north. You cannot help noticing that many of the buildings here look different from those in your hometown. Many of the buildings here have rounded arches over the doorways and tall towers in front of them. In addition, some are decorated with ornate tiles.

Why do you think the buildings look different?

> **BUILDING BACKGROUND** Throughout history, many different groups have ruled parts of Spain and Portugal. Each group brought elements of its own culture to the region. As a result, parts of the two countries have cultures unlike those found anywhere else.

History

The countries of Spain and Portugal share the Iberian Peninsula, or **Iberia**, the westernmost peninsula in Europe. Although the two are different in many ways, they share a common history.

Across the centuries, several powerful empires controlled all or part of the Iberian Peninsula. By 700 BC, the Phoenicians, from the eastern Mediterranean, had colonized coastal areas of what is now Spain. After the Phoenicians came the Greeks. A few centuries later, all of Iberia became part of the Roman Empire.

After the Roman Empire fell apart, Iberia was invaded by the Moors, a group of Muslims from North Africa. For about 600 years, much of the Iberian Peninsula was under Muslim rule.

Moorish structures, such as this tower outside of Lisbon, Portugal, can still be seen all over Iberia.

What You Will Learn...

Main Ideas

1. Over the centuries, Spain and Portugal have been part of many large and powerful empires.
2. The cultures of Spain and Portugal reflect their long histories.
3. Having been both rich and poor in the past, Spain and Portugal today have growing economies.

The Big Idea

Spain and Portugal have rich cultures, stable governments, and growing economies.

Key Terms and Places

Iberia, *p. 301*
parliamentary monarchy, *p. 304*
Madrid, *p. 304*
Barcelona, *p. 304*
Lisbon, *p. 304*

TAKING NOTES Draw a chart like the one shown here. As you read this section, take notes about Spain in the left column and notes about Portugal in the right.

Spain	Portugal

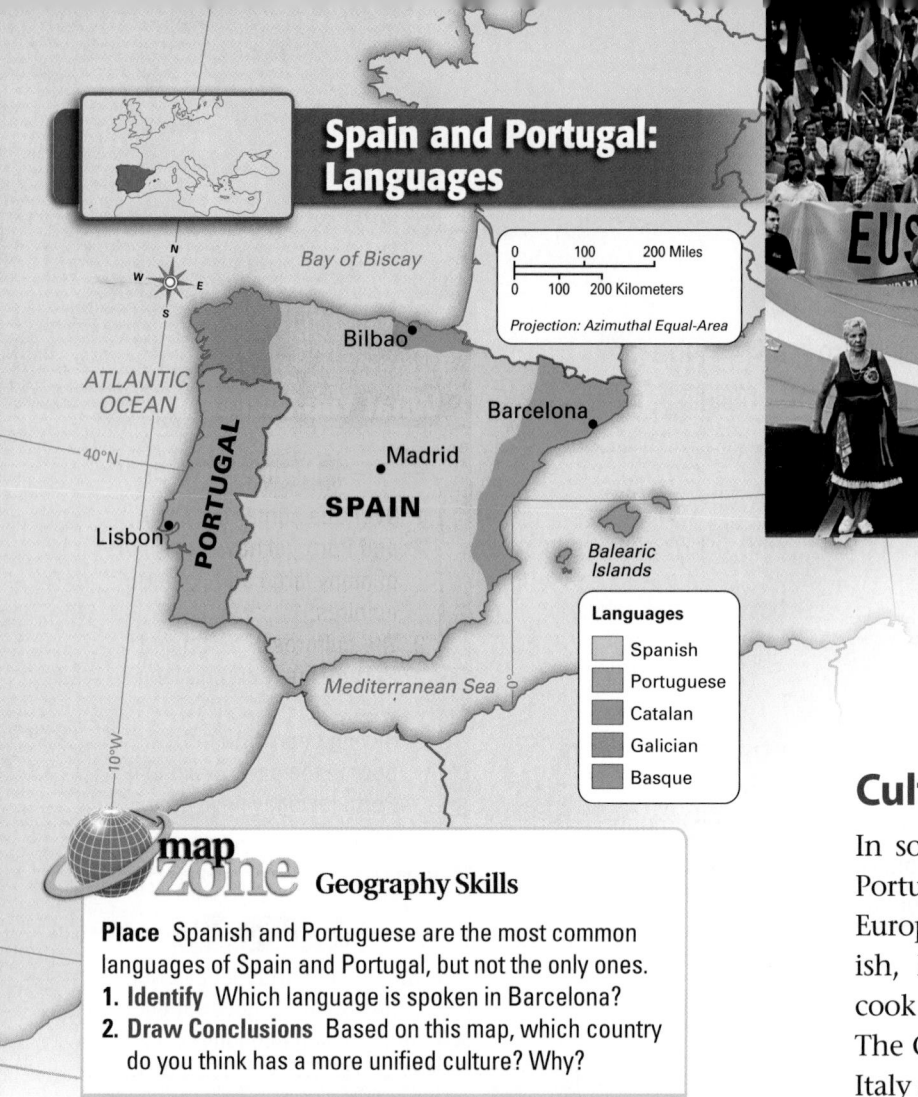

Spain and Portugal: Languages

Bay of Biscay

Bilbao

ATLANTIC
OCEAN

PORTUGAL

40°N

Barcelona

Madrid

SPAIN

Lisbon

Balearic
Islands

Mediterranean Sea

0   100   200 Miles
0   100   200 Kilometers
Projection: Azimuthal Equal-Area

Languages
- Spanish
- Portuguese
- Catalan
- Galician
- Basque

Many Basque speakers take part in rallies like this one in support of independence. The banner in this photo reads "Basque Nation Arise" in the Basque language.

map zone Geography Skills

Place Spanish and Portuguese are the most common languages of Spain and Portugal, but not the only ones.
1. **Identify** Which language is spoken in Barcelona?
2. **Draw Conclusions** Based on this map, which country do you think has a more unified culture? Why?

By the end of the 1400s, however, the Muslims were driven out of Iberia. The rulers of the Christian kingdoms of Spain and Portugal banded together to force non-Christians to leave Iberia. Those who refused to leave were made to convert or face severe punishments.

Spain and Portugal went on to build large empires that spanned the oceans. Both countries ruled huge territories in the Americas as well as smaller areas in Africa and Asia. These territories made the two kingdoms rich and powerful until most of their colonies broke away and became independent in the 1800s and 1900s.

READING CHECK **Summarizing** What empires have ruled Spain and Portugal?

Culture

In some ways, the cultures of Spain and Portugal are like those of other southern European countries. For example, the Spanish, Portuguese, Greeks, and Italians all cook with many of the same ingredients. The Catholic Church is very influential in Italy as well as Spain and Portugal. In other ways, Iberian cultures are unique.

Language

The most spoken languages in Iberia are, of course, Spanish and Portuguese. Various dialects of these languages are spoken in different parts of the peninsula. In addition, other languages are also spoken by many people in Iberia. The Catalan language of eastern Spain is similar to Spanish. Galician, which is spoken in northwest Spain, is more closely related to Portuguese.

In addition, the Basque (BASK) people of the Pyrenees have their own language, which is not related to either Spanish or Portuguese. The Basques also have their own customs and traditions, unlike those of the rest of Spain. As a result, many Basques have long wanted to form their own independent country.

Religion

Most people in both Spain and Portugal are Roman Catholic. People in both countries celebrate Christian holidays like Christmas and Easter. In addition, many towns hold fiestas, or festivals, in honor of their patron saints. At these festivals, people may gather to dance or to watch a bullfight.

Music and Art

Music and art have been central to Iberian culture for centuries. The Portuguese are famous for sad folk songs called fados. The Spanish are known for a style of song and dance called flamenco.

Many elements of Iberia's art and architecture reflect its Muslim past. Many buildings in the peninsula have elements of Muslim design, such as round arches and elaborate tilework.

READING CHECK **Comparing** What is one culture element that Spain and Portugal share?

Spain and Portugal Today

Like other countries in Western Europe, Spain and Portugal have rather strong economies. They do have some problems, however, problems that were largely brought on by past events.

Challenge of the Past

Spain and Portugal were once Europe's richest countries. Their wealth came from gold and silver found in their colonies.

When other countries in Europe began to build industrial economies, Spain and Portugal continued to rely on gold from their colonies. As those colonies became independent, that source of income was lost. As a result, Spain and Portugal were late in developing manufacturing.

Although Spain and Portugal are still poorer than other countries in Western Europe, they are growing rapidly. New industries such as tourism are making this new growth possible.

FOCUS ON READING

As you read, ask yourself this question: Why did Spain and Portugal fall behind other countries economically?

FOCUS ON CULTURE

Flamenco

Complex guitar rhythms, a heavy beat, and whirling dancers—these are all part of the traditional Spanish art form known as flamenco. The word *flamenco* refers both to a style of music and a style of dance. The most important instrument in the music is the guitar, which was itself a Spanish invention. Most of the time, the guitar is accompanied by other musical instruments and by singers.

When most people think of flamenco, however, they picture dancers. Flamenco dancers perform alone, in pairs, or in large groups. They wear brightly colored costumes as they perform complex steps. It is not unusual for dancers to clap their hands or snap their fingers to the beat or to play castanets as they dance. Castanets are small, hinged wooden instruments. The dancers clap the castanets together to make a clicking noise.

Finding Main Ideas What are the major elements of flamenco music and dancing?

Spanish culture blends old and new ideas. Here, modern vehicles drive by historic buildings in Barcelona.

In other ways, Spain has become a more modern country. Agriculture was once the major economic activity, but factories now create automobiles and other high-tech products. Cities such as **Madrid**—the capital—and **Barcelona** are centers of industry, tourism, and culture.

Portugal Today

Unlike Spain, Portugal is not a monarchy. It is a republic with elected leaders. As in Spain, the economy is based largely on industries centered in large cities, especially **Lisbon**. In many rural areas, though, people depend on agriculture. Farmers there grow many crops but are most famous for grapes and cork. Farmers harvest cork from the bark of a particular type of oak tree. Once it is dried, the cork is used to make bottle stoppers and other products.

READING CHECK **Contrasting** How are Spain and Portugal's governments different?

SUMMARY AND PREVIEW You have just learned about the countries of Southern Europe. Next, you will move north to study West-Central Europe.

Spain Today

The people of Spain have kept many aspects of their history alive. For example, Spain is still governed by a king, a descendant of the kings who ruled the country long ago. Unlike in the past, however, Spain today is a **parliamentary monarchy**, which means that the king rules with the help of an elected parliament.

Section 4 Assessment

go.hrw.com
Online Quiz
KEYWORD: SG7 HP12

Reviewing Ideas, Terms, and Places

1. **a. Recall** What is **Iberia**? What two countries are located there?
   b. Sequence What people have ruled Iberia, and in what order did they rule it?
2. **a. Identify** What is the most common religion in Spain and Portugal?
   b. Generalize How is Spain's history reflected in its architecture?
   c. Elaborate Why do you think many Basques want to become independent from Spain?
3. **a. Identify** What are two crops grown in Portugal?
   b. Analyze What is Spain's government like?

Critical Thinking

4. **Categorizing** Draw a diagram like the one here. Using your notes, record information about the cultures and economies of Spain and Portugal.

	Spain	Portugal
Culture		
Economy		

FOCUS ON WRITING

5. **Writing about Spain and Portugal** What details about Spain and Portugal will grab your readers' attention? Look back through your notes to choose the topic for your article.

Chapter Review

Geography's Impact
video series
Review the video to answer the closing question:
Why did the 2004 Olympics have so great an impact on Athens?

Visual Summary

Use the visual summary below to help you review the main ideas of the chapter.

QUICK FACTS

Greece
The birthplace of democracy, Greece is working to improve its economy.

Italy
Italy is one of Europe's leading cultural and economic countries.

Spain and Portugal
The rich cultures of Spain and Portugal are shaped by their histories.

Reviewing Vocabulary, Terms, and Places

Fill in the blanks with the correct term or location from this chapter.

1. The climate found in most of Southern Europe is the _____.

2. The _____ is the head of the Roman Catholic Church.

3. The highest mountains in Europe are the _____.

4. _____ is the capital of Greece.

5. A _____ is a government in which a king rules with the help of an elected body.

6. Italy's capital, _____, was the birthplace of an ancient civilization.

7. _____ is an independent state located within the city of Rome.

8. Spain and Portugal are located on a peninsula known as _____.

Comprehension and Critical Thinking

SECTION 1 *(Pages 286–289)*

9. **a.** **Describe** What are two physical features that all the countries of Southern Europe have in common?

   b. **Draw Conclusions** Why has Southern Europe's climate been called its most valuable resource?

   c. **Predict** How would daily life in Southern Europe be different if it were not a coastal region?

SECTION 2 *(Pages 291–295)*

10. **a.** **Identify** What is the largest city in Greece? How would you describe the city?

   b. **Generalize** How has Greece's economy changed in the last decade? What is largely responsible for this change?

   c. **Elaborate** How does Greek history still affect the country today?

SECTION 3 (Pages 296–300)

11. a. Recall Which region of Italy has the stronger economy? Why?

b. Sequence What periods followed the Roman Empire in Italy? What happened during those periods?

c. Elaborate What are some ways in which the Italians have influenced world culture?

SECTION 4 (Pages 301–304)

12. a. Identify Who are the Basques?

b. Compare and Contrast How are Spain and Portugal alike? How are they different?

c. Elaborate How do you think Iberia's history makes it different from other places in Europe?

FOCUS ON READING AND WRITING

Asking Questions *Read the passage below. After you read it, answer the questions below to be sure you have understood what you read.*

> " Spain is a democracy, but it has not always been. From 1939 to 1975, a dictator named Francisco Franco ruled the country. He came to power as a result of a bloody civil war and was unpopular with the Spanish people. "

13. Who is this paragraph about?

14. What did the people in this passage do?

15. When did the events described take place?

16. Where did the events described take place?

17. Why did the events happen?

Writing Your News Report *Use your notes and the instructions below to help you create your news report.*

18. If you have not yet chosen the event you will write about in your report, go through your notes and decide now. Create a plan for your report by answering these questions: What is the scene or setting of the event? Who is there? Why is it important enough to include in the news? What happened?

Start your news report with a dateline, for example: Rome, May 5, 2009. Begin your first paragraph with an interesting observation or detail. Explain the event in two or three short paragraphs. Close with an important piece of information or interesting detail.

Social Studies Skills

Reading a Climate Map *Use the climate map from the Social Studies Skills lesson of this chapter to answer the following questions.*

19. What type of climate does London have?

20. What climate is found only in the far north?

21. Where in Europe would you find a humid subtropical climate?

Using the Internet

22. Activity: Exploring Italian Cuisine Pizza. Pasta. Mozzarella. Olive oil. These are some of the most popular elements of Italian food, one of the world's favorites. Enter the activity keyword and learn more about the history and variety of Italian cooking. Then test your knowledge with the interactive activity.

Map Activity

23. Southern Europe On a separate sheet of paper, match the letters on the map with their correct labels.

Mediterranean Sea	Lisbon, Portugal
Athens, Greece	Po River
Sicily	Rome, Italy
Spain	Aegean Sea

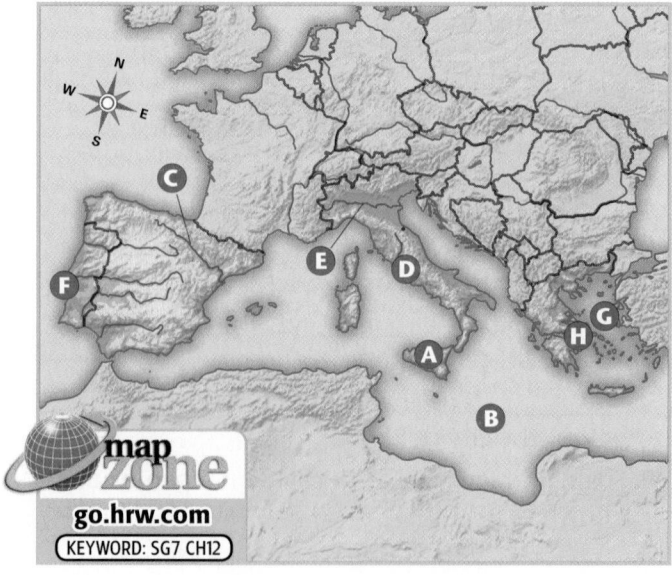

map zone

go.hrw.com
KEYWORD: SG7 CH12

DIRECTIONS: *Read questions 1 through 7 and write the letter of the best response. Then read question 8 and write your own well-constructed response.*

1 In which country of Southern Europe is the Eastern Orthodox Church dominant?

A Portugal

B Spain

C Italy

D Greece

2 Two of the most common foods in Southern European cooking are

A grapes and olives.

B corn and barley.

C beans and squash.

D beef and pork.

3 The form of government for which ancient Greece is best known is

A monarchy.

B dictatorship.

C democracy.

D parliamentary monarchy.

4 The Moors were Muslims who conquered

A Spain.

B Greece.

C Crete.

D Italy.

5 Which of these cities is in Portugal?

A Rome

B Athens

C Lisbon

D Madrid

Spain and Portugal: Climates

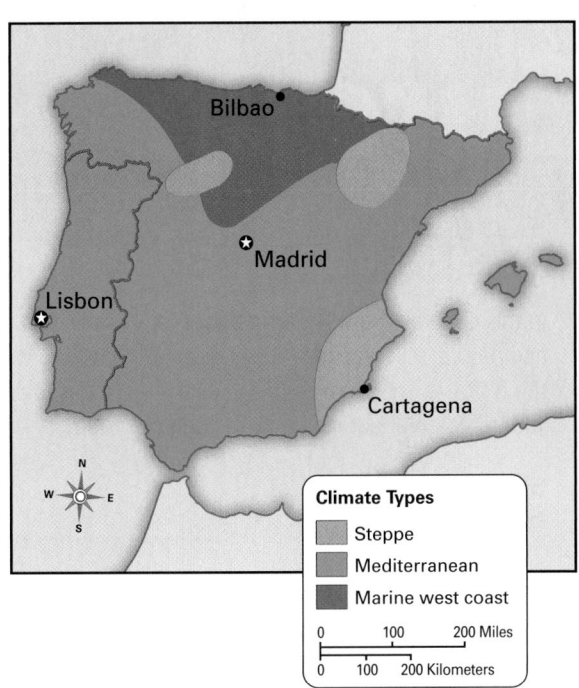

6 Based on the map above, which city in Spain lies in an area with a steppe climate?

A Bilbao

B Cartagena

C Lisbon

D Madrid

7 Based on the map on this page, which is the most common climate in Spain?

A Steppe

B Mediterranean

C Marine west coast

D Tropical

8 Extended response Climate influences many aspects of people's lives in Southern Europe. Write a short paragraph that describes the region's climate. At the end of the paragraph, list two ways in which climate affects how people live.

CHAPTER 13

West-Central Europe

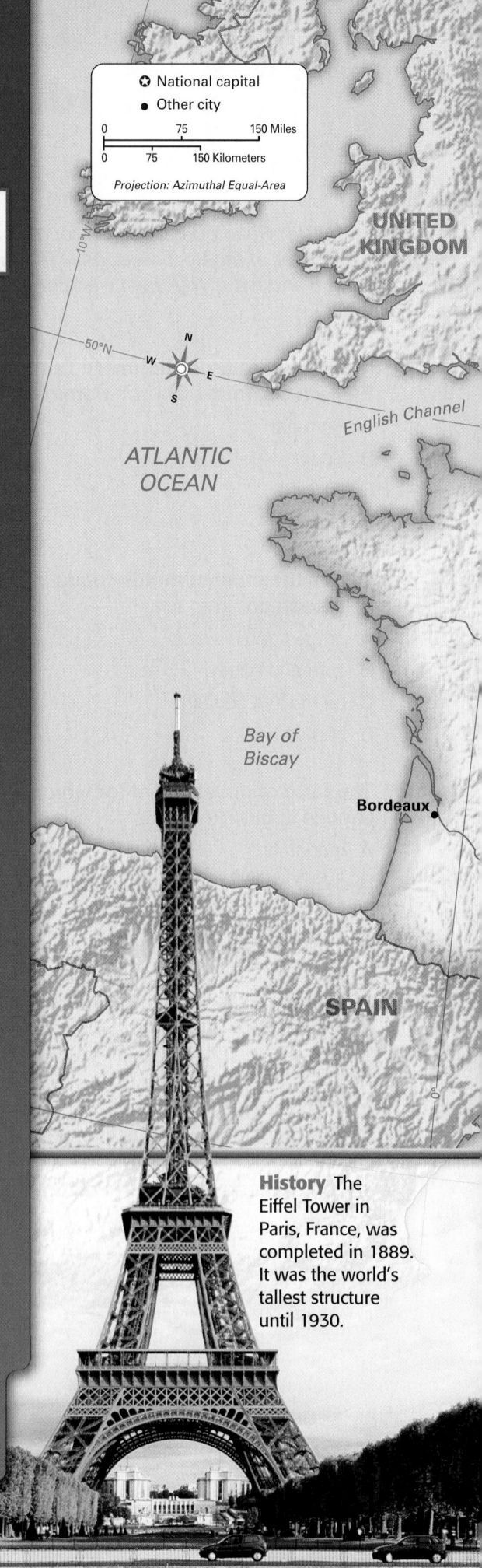

What You Will Learn...

In this chapter you will learn about the physical features, climate, and natural resources of West-Central Europe. You will also study the histories and cultures of the countries in this region. Finally, you will learn about life in these countries today.

FOCUS ON READING AND SPEAKING

Recognizing Word Origins Many of the words we use today came into English from other languages, such as Latin, French, or German. As you read this chapter, think about the origin, or sources, of words. Knowing a word's origin can help you remember the word's meaning. **See the lesson, Recognizing Word Origins, on page R14.**

Presenting a Persuasive Speech As you read about West-Central Europe, you will discover some issues. Issues are topics that people disagree about. Think about which of the issues seem important to you. Later, in a persuasive speech you will take a stand on one of these issues.

National capital
Other city

0   75   150 Miles
0   75   150 Kilometers

Projection: Azimuthal Equal-Area

UNITED KINGDOM

ATLANTIC OCEAN

English Channel

Bay of Biscay

Bordeaux

SPAIN

History The Eiffel Tower in Paris, France, was completed in 1889. It was the world's tallest structure until 1930.

West-Central Europe: Political

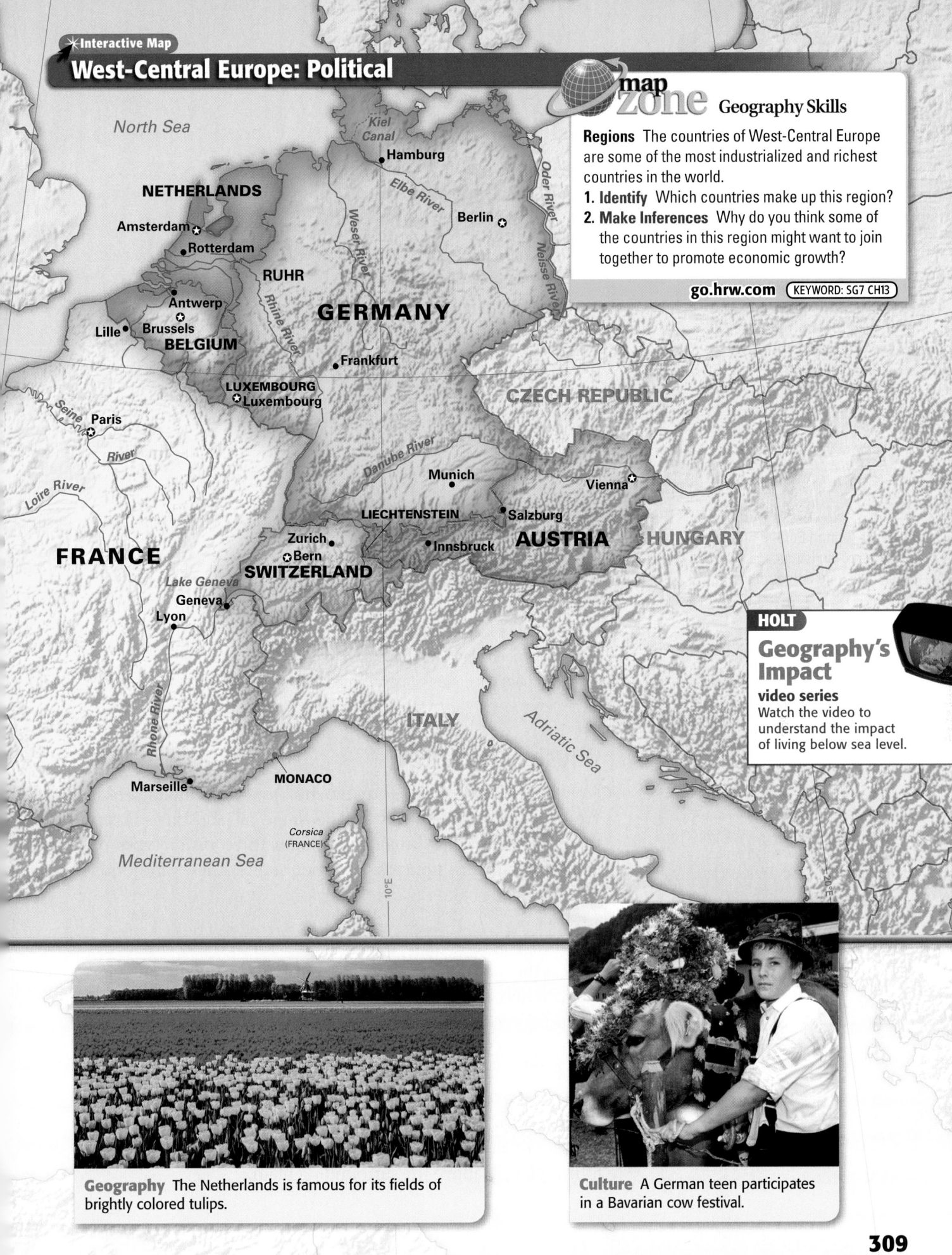

North Sea

Kiel Canal

Hamburg

NETHERLANDS

Amsterdam ✪

Rotterdam

Elbe River

Berlin ✪

Oder River

Neisse River

Weser River

RUHR

GERMANY

Rhine River

Antwerp ✪

Lille • • Brussels
BELGIUM

Frankfurt •

CZECH REPUBLIC

LUXEMBOURG
✪ Luxembourg

Seine River

Paris ✪

Loire River

Danube River

Munich •

Vienna ✪

LIECHTENSTEIN

Salzburg •

FRANCE

Zurich •
✪ Bern

SWITZERLAND

• Innsbruck

AUSTRIA

HUNGARY

Lake Geneva

Geneva •
Lyon •

Rhône River

ITALY

Adriatic Sea

Marseille •

MONACO

Corsica
(FRANCE)

Mediterranean Sea

10°E

20°E

map zone Geography Skills

Regions The countries of West-Central Europe are some of the most industrialized and richest countries in the world.
1. **Identify** Which countries make up this region?
2. **Make Inferences** Why do you think some of the countries in this region might want to join together to promote economic growth?

go.hrw.com   KEYWORD: SG7 CH13

HOLT

Geography's Impact
video series
Watch the video to understand the impact of living below sea level.

Geography The Netherlands is famous for its fields of brightly colored tulips.

Culture A German teen participates in a Bavarian cow festival.

309

Physical Geography

If YOU lived there...

You are a photographer planning a book about the landscapes of West-Central Europe. You are trying to decide where to find the best pictures of rich farmland, forested plateaus, and rugged mountains. So far, you are planning to show the colorful tulip fields of the Netherlands, the hilly Black Forest region of Germany, and the snow-covered Alps in Switzerland.

What other places might you want to show?

BUILDING BACKGROUND The countries of West-Central Europe are among the most prosperous and powerful countries in the world. The reasons include their mild climates, good farmland, many rivers, market economies, and stable governments. In addition, most of these countries cooperate as members of the European Union.

Physical Features

From fields of tulips, to sunny beaches, to icy mountain peaks, West-Central Europe offers a wide range of landscapes. Even though the region is small, it includes three major types of landforms—plains, uplands, and mountains. These landforms extend in wide bands across the region.

Plains, Uplands, and Mountains

Look at the map at right. Picture West-Central Europe as an open fan with Italy as the handle. The outer edge of this imaginary fan is a broad coastal plain called the **Northern European Plain**. This plain stretches from the Atlantic coast into Eastern Europe.

Most of this plain is flat or rolling and lies less than 500 feet (150 m) above sea level. In the Netherlands, parts of the plain dip below sea level. There, people must build walls to hold back the sea. In Brittany in northwestern France, the land rises to form a plateau above the surrounding plain.

The Northern European Plain provides the region's best farmland. Many people live on the plain, and the region's largest cities are located there.

The Central Uplands extend across the center of our imaginary fan. This area has many rounded hills, small plateaus, and valleys. In France, the uplands include the <u>Massif</u> Central (ma-SEEF sahn-TRAHL), a plateau region, and the Jura Mountains.

This range is on the French-Swiss border. In Germany, uplands cover much of the southern two-thirds of the country. Dense woodlands, such as the Black Forest, blanket many of the hills in this area.

The Central Uplands have many productive coalfields. As a result, the area is important for mining and industry. Some valleys provide fertile soil for farming, but most of the area is too rocky to farm.

FOCUS ON READING

Look up the origin of *massif* in a dictionary. How does its origin relate to the description of the Massif Central?

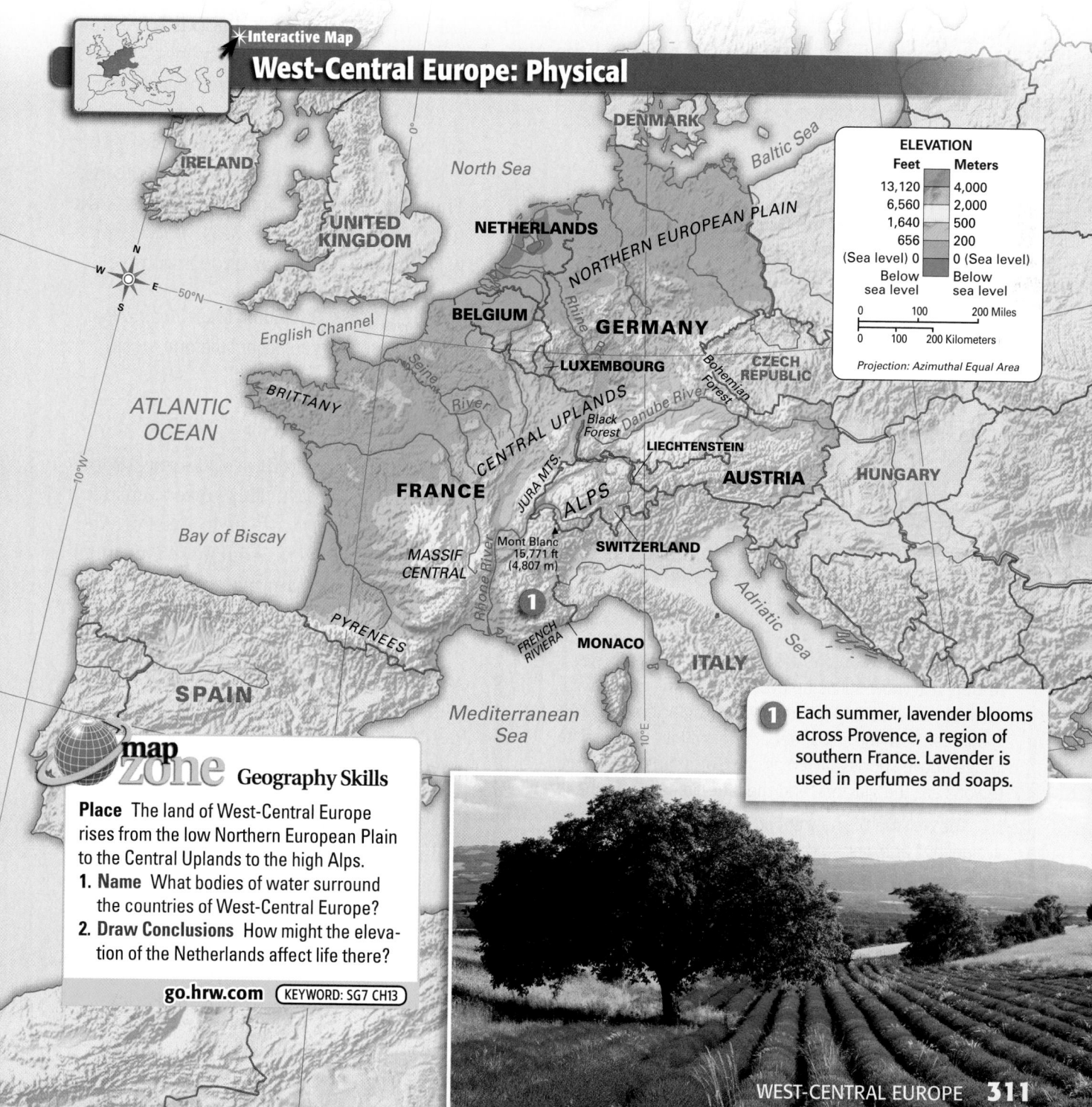

⭐Interactive Map

West-Central Europe: Physical

ELEVATION

Feet		Meters
13,120		4,000
6,560		2,000
1,640		500
656		200
(Sea level) 0		0 (Sea level)
Below sea level		Below sea level

0   100   200 Miles
0   100   200 Kilometers

Projection: Azimuthal Equal Area

DENMARK

IRELAND

North Sea

Baltic Sea

UNITED KINGDOM

NETHERLANDS

NORTHERN EUROPEAN PLAIN

BELGIUM

GERMANY

Rhine

English Channel

LUXEMBOURG

Bohemian Forest

CZECH REPUBLIC

ATLANTIC OCEAN

BRITTANY

Seine River

CENTRAL UPLANDS

Black Forest

Danube River

LIECHTENSTEIN

FRANCE

JURA MTS.

ALPS

AUSTRIA

HUNGARY

Bay of Biscay

MASSIF CENTRAL

Mont Blanc 15,771 ft (4,807 m)

Rhône River

SWITZERLAND

Adriatic Sea

①

PYRENEES

FRENCH RIVIERA

MONACO

ITALY

SPAIN

Mediterranean Sea

10°E

① Each summer, lavender blooms across Provence, a region of southern France. Lavender is used in perfumes and soaps.

map Zone Geography Skills

Place The land of West-Central Europe rises from the low Northern European Plain to the Central Uplands to the high Alps.
1. **Name** What bodies of water surround the countries of West-Central Europe?
2. **Draw Conclusions** How might the elevation of the Netherlands affect life there?

go.hrw.com (KEYWORD: SG7 CH13)

Along the inner part of our imaginary fan, the land rises dramatically to form the alpine mountain system. This system includes the Alps and the Pyrenees, which you read about in the last chapter.

As you have read, the Alps are Europe's highest mountain range. They stretch from southern France to the Balkan Peninsula. Several of the jagged peaks in the Alps soar to more than 14,000 feet (4,270 m). The highest peak is Mont Blanc (mawn BLAHN), which rises to 15,771 feet (4,807 m) in France. Because of the height of the Alps, large snowfields coat some peaks.

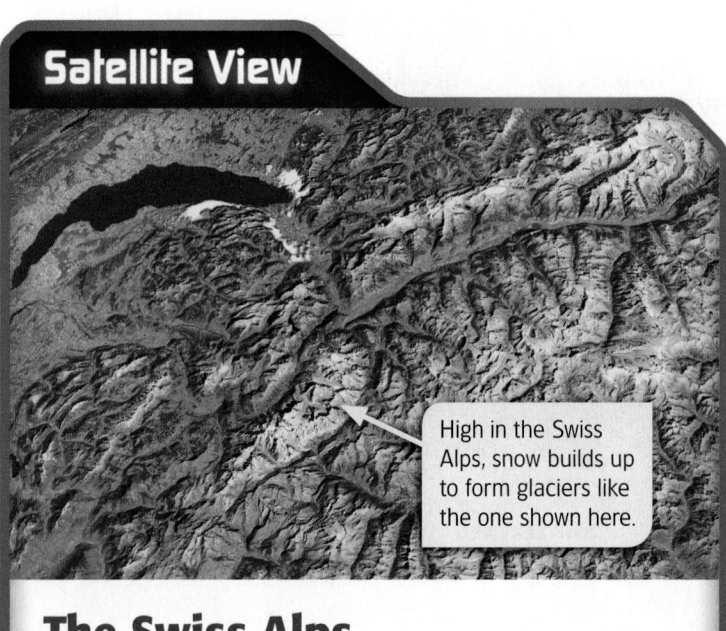

Satellite View

High in the Swiss Alps, snow builds up to form glaciers like the one shown here.

The Swiss Alps

At high elevations in the Alps, snow does not melt. For this reason, the snow builds up over time. As the snow builds up, it turns to ice and eventually forms glaciers. A glacier is a large, slow-moving sheet or river of ice. The satellite image above shows glaciers in the Swiss Alps. The white regions are the glaciers, and the blue areas are alpine lakes.

The buildup of snow and ice in the Alps can cause avalanches at lower elevations. An avalanche is a large mass of snow or other material that suddenly rushes down a mountainside. Avalanches pose a serious danger to people.

Analyzing Why do glaciers sometimes form at higher elevations in the Alps?

Water Features

Several bodies of water are important to West-Central Europe's physical geography. The **North Sea** and **English Channel** lie to the north. The Bay of Biscay and Atlantic Ocean lie to the west. The Mediterranean Sea borders France to the south.

Several rivers cross the region as well. Look at the map on the previous page to identify them. Two important rivers are the **Danube** (DAN-yoob) and the **Rhine** (RYN). For centuries people and goods have traveled these rivers, and many cities, farms, and industrial areas line their banks.

Several of West-Central Europe's rivers are navigable. A **navigable river** is one that is deep and wide enough for ships to use. These rivers and a system of canals link the region's interior to the seas. These waterways are important for trade and travel.

READING CHECK **Finding Main Ideas** What are the region's three major landform areas?

Climate and Resources

A warm ocean current flows along Europe's northwestern coast. This current creates a marine west coast climate in most of West-Central Europe. This climate makes much of the area a pleasant place to live. Though winters can get cold, summers are mild. Rain and storms occur often, though.

At higher elevations, such as in the Alps, the climate is colder and wetter. In contrast, southern France has a warm Mediterranean climate. Summers are dry and hot, and winters are mild and wet.

West-Central Europe's mild climate is a valuable natural resource. Mild temperatures, plenty of rain, and rich soil have made the region's farmlands highly productive. Farm crops include grapes, grains, and vegetables. In the uplands and Alps, pastures and valleys support livestock.

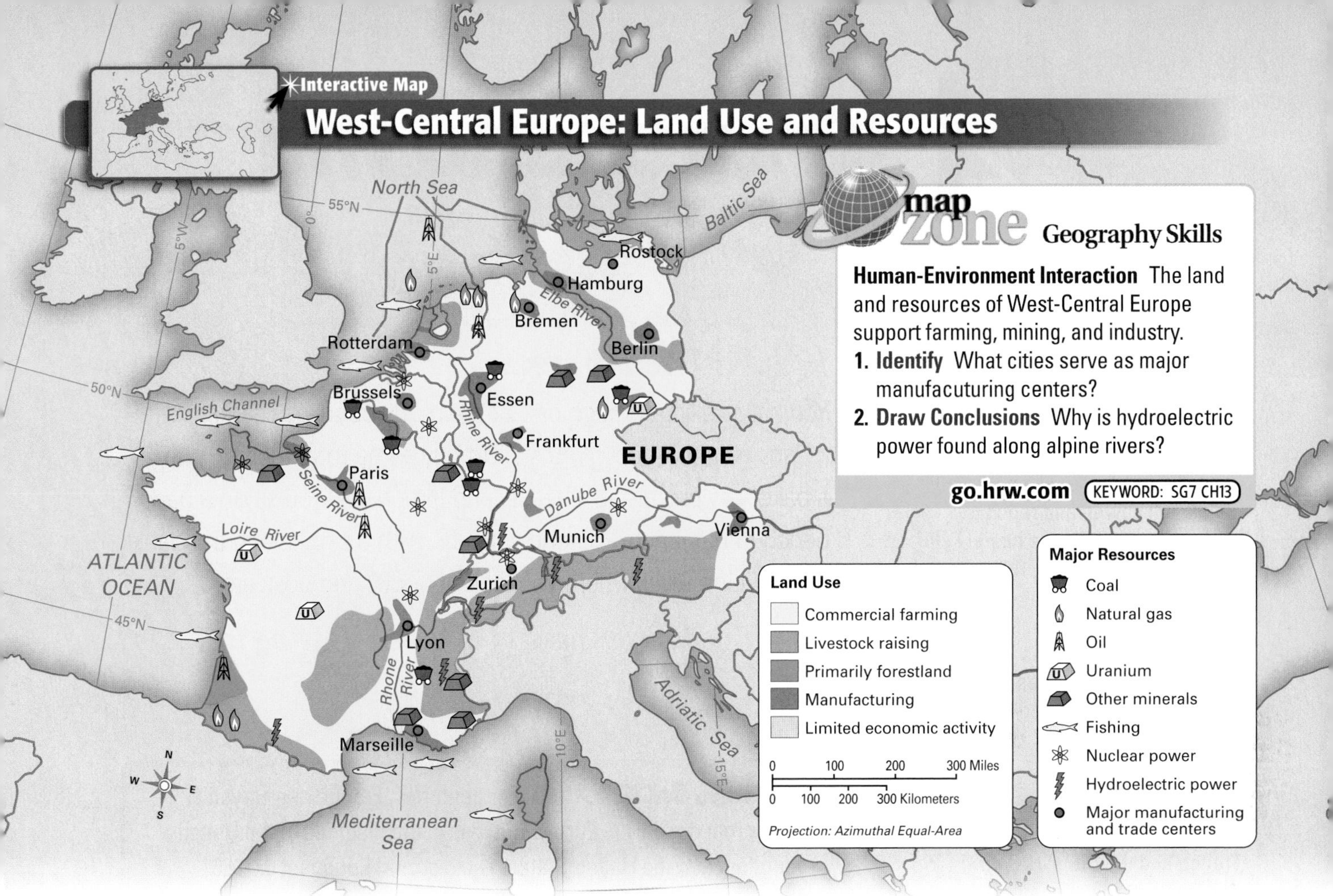

West-Central Europe: Land Use and Resources

North Sea
55°N
Rostock
Hamburg
Elbe River
Bremen
Rotterdam
Berlin
50°N
Brussels
Essen
English Channel
Rhine River
Frankfurt
EUROPE
Paris
Seine River
Danube River
Vienna
Loire River
Munich
ATLANTIC
OCEAN
45°N
Zurich
Lyon
Rhône River
Adriatic Sea
Marseille
N
W   E
S
Mediterranean
Sea
10°E
15°E

map zone

Geography Skills

Human-Environment Interaction The land and resources of West-Central Europe support farming, mining, and industry.
1. **Identify** What cities serve as major manufacuturing centers?
2. **Draw Conclusions** Why is hydroelectric power found along alpine rivers?

go.hrw.com (KEYWORD: SG7 CH13)

Land Use

☐ Commercial farming
▨ Livestock raising
▨ Primarily forestland
▨ Manufacturing
☐ Limited economic activity

0   100   200   300 Miles
0 100 200 300 Kilometers

Projection: Azimuthal Equal-Area

Major Resources

⛏ Coal
◊ Natural gas
⚙ Oil
Ⓤ Uranium
◈ Other minerals
🐟 Fishing
✳ Nuclear power
⚡ Hydroelectric power
● Major manufacturing and trade centers

Energy and mineral resources are not evenly distributed across the region, as the map shows. France has coal and iron ore, Germany also has coal, and the Netherlands has natural gas. Fast-flowing alpine rivers provide hydroelectric power. Even so, many countries must import fuels.

Another valuable natural resource is found in the breathtaking beauty of the Alps. Each year, tourists flock to the Alps to enjoy the scenery and to hike and ski.

READING CHECK **Summarizing** What natural resources contribute to the region's economy?

SUMMARY AND PREVIEW West-Central Europe includes low plains, uplands, and mountains. The climate is mild, and natural resources support farming, industry, and tourism. Next, you will read about France and the Benelux Countries.

go.hrw.com
Online Quiz
KEYWORD: SG7 HP13

Section 1 Assessment

Reviewing Ideas, Terms, and Places

1. **a. Describe** What are the main physical features of the **Northern European Plain**?
   b. Analyze How does having many **navigable** rivers benefit West-Central Europe?
2. **a. Recall** What is the region's main climate?
   b. Make Inferences How might an uneven distribution of mineral resources affect the region?

Critical Thinking

3. **Categorizing** Draw a fan like this one. Label each band with the landform area in West-Central Europe it represents. Using your notes, identify each area's physical features, climate, and resources.

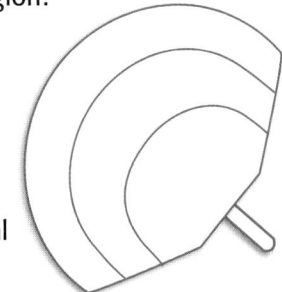

FOCUS ON SPEAKING

4. **Noting the Physical Geography** What issues related to land use and resources can you think of? Could mining coal or importing fuel be an issue? Jot down ideas.

France and the Benelux Countries

What You Will Learn...

Main Ideas

1. During its history France has been a kingdom, empire, colonial power, and republic.
2. The culture of France has contributed to the world's arts and ideas.
3. France today is a farming and manufacturing center.
4. The Benelux Countries have strong economies and high standards of living.

The Big Idea

France and the Benelux Countries have strong economies and rich cultural traditions.

Key Terms and Places

Paris, *p. 317*
Amsterdam, *p. 319*
The Hague, *p. 319*
Brussels, *p. 319*
cosmopolitan, *p. 319*

TAKING NOTES Draw a chart like the one below. As you read, list facts about each country.

France	
Belgium	
The Netherlands	
Luxembourg	

If YOU lived there...

You are strolling through one of the many open-air markets in a Paris neighborhood. You stop to buy some fruit, then go into a bakery to buy bread, cheese, and lemonade. You sit on a park bench to eat lunch. You end your day with a stroll along the banks of the Seine River, where you look at books and postcards.

Why do you think people enjoy living in Paris?

BUILDING BACKGROUND For centuries, France has played a major role not only in Europe but also in the histories of the United Kingdom and the United States. The Norman Conquest in 1066 brought French influences into English language, law, and culture. France later helped the American colonists win their independence.

History of France

In southwest France, Lascaux (lah-SKOH) Cave holds a treasure from the past. Inside, prehistoric paintings of bulls run and jump along the stone walls. More than 15,000 years old, these paintings show how long people have lived in what is now France.

Early History

In ancient times, France was part of a region called Gaul (GAWL). Centuries ago, Celtic peoples from eastern Europe settled in Gaul. In the 50s BC, the Romans conquered the region. They introduced Roman law. The Romans also established a Latin-based language that in time developed into French.

Roman rule in Gaul lasted until the AD 400s. The Franks, a Germanic people, then conquered much of Gaul. It is from the Franks that France gets its name. The Franks' greatest ruler was Charlemagne (SHAHR-luh-mayn), who built a powerful Christian empire. After he had conquered much of the old Roman Empire, the pope crowned him Emperor of the Romans in 800.

After Charlemagne's death, many invaders attacked the Franks. One such group, the Normans, settled in northwestern France. This area is called Normandy.

In 1066 the Normans conquered England. William the Conqueror, the duke of Normandy, became king of England. He now ruled England as well as part of France. In the 1300s England's king tried to claim the French throne to gain control of the rest of France. This event led to the Hundred Years' War (1337–1453). The French eventually drove out the English.

Revolution and Empire

From the 1500s to the 1700s, France built a colonial empire. The French established colonies in the Americas, Africa, and Asia. At this time, most French people lived in poverty and had few rights. For these reasons, in 1789 the French people overthrew their king in the French Revolution.

A few years later a brilliant general named Napoleon took power. In time, he conquered much of Europe. Then in 1815 several European powers joined forces and defeated Napoleon. They exiled him and chose a new king to rule France.

Modern History

During both World War I and World War II, German forces invaded France. After each war, France worked to rebuild its economy. In the 1950s it experienced rapid growth.

During the 1950s and 1960s, many of of the French colonies gained their independence. Some people from these former colonies then moved to France.

France is now a republic with a parliament and an elected president. France still controls several overseas territories, such as Martinique in the West Indies.

READING CHECK **Summarizing** Which foreign groups have affected France's history?

France's History

During its long history, France has gone from strong kingdom to great empire, to colonial world power, to modern republic.

Early History

- Early Celtic peoples settle in Gaul.
- The Romans conquer Gaul and rule the region for hundreds of years.
- The Franks conquer Gaul. The ruler Charlemagne builds a powerful empire.
- Normans settle in northwestern France. In 1066 they conquer England and take the throne.
- France and England fight the Hundred Years' War.

Charlemagne

Revolution and Empire

- In the 1500s France begins to build a colonial empire.
- In 1789 the people rise up in the French Revolution.
- In 1799 Napoleon takes control. He soon conquers much of Europe.
- European powers unite to defeat Napoleon in 1815.

Arc de Triomphe

Modern History

- German forces invade France during World War I and World War II.
- Many French colonies declare independence in the 1950s and 1960s.
- Today France is a republic with a president and a democratic government.

WWII German occupation

The Culture of France

During their long history, the French have developed a strong cultural identity. Today French culture is admired worldwide.

FOCUS ON READING
Use a dictionary to find the origin of *cuisine*. How does the word's origin relate to the meaning of *cuisine* today?

Language and Religion

A common heritage unites the French. Most people speak French and are Catholic. At the same time, many immigrants have settled in France. These immigrants have their own languages, religions, and customs. For example, many Algerian Muslims have moved to France. This immigration is making France more culturally diverse.

Customs

The French have a phrase that describes their attitude toward life—*joie de vivre* (zhwah duh VEEV-ruh), meaning "enjoyment of life." The French enjoy good food, good company, and good conversation.

An enjoyment of food has helped make French cooking some of the best in the world. French chefs and cooking schools have worldwide reputations. The French have also contributed to the language of food. Terms such as *café*, *cuisine* (cooking), and *menu* all come from the French.

The French also enjoy their festivals. The major national festival is Bastille Day, held on July 14. On that date in 1789 a mob destroyed the Bastille, a Paris prison symbolizing the French king's harsh rule. The event began the French Revolution.

Ideas and the Arts

The French have made major contributions to the arts and ideas. In the Middle Ages, the French built majestic cathedrals in the Gothic style. This style has high pointed ceilings, stained-glass windows, and tall towers that reach heavenward. Notre Dame Cathedral in Paris is an example.

Close-up

Paris

Some 2,000 years old, Paris grew up along the banks of the Seine (SEN) River. Known as "the City of Light" for its gleaming beauty, Paris shines as one of Europe's most cultured cities. Wide tree-lined avenues, historic squares, and lovely gardens and parks grace the city center.

Notre Dame is France's most famous cathedral. It is a masterpiece of Gothic architecture.

The Seine River winds through the heart of Paris. Beautiful bridges cross the river, and in places booksellers line its banks.

In the 1700s France was a center of the Enlightenment, a period in which people used reason to improve society. French Enlightenment ideas about government inspired the American Revolution and the development of modern democracy.

In the 1800s France was the center of one of the most famous art movements of the modern age—impressionism. This style of painting uses rippling light to create an impression of a scene. During the same period, French authors wrote classics such as *The Three Musketeers* by Alexandre Dumas (doo-mah). Today France is known for art and its fashion and film industries.

READING CHECK **Summarizing** What are some main features of French culture?

France Today

France is now West-Central Europe's largest country. It plays a leading role in Europe and in the European Union (EU).

Today about 75 percent of the French live in cities. **Paris**, the capital, is by far the largest city, with about 10 million people.

Fashionable with a quick pace, Paris is a center of business, finance, learning, and culture. It boasts world-class museums, art galleries, and restaurants as well as famous landmarks such as the Eiffel Tower and Notre Dame Cathedral.

Other major cities include Marseille (mar-SAY), a Mediterranean seaport, and Lyon (LYAWN), located on the Rhone River. A modern system of highways, canals, and high-speed trains links France's cities.

France has a strong economy. It is the EU's top agricultural producer, and its major crops include wheat and grapes. French workers are also highly productive. Rich soil and efficient workers have made France a major exporter of goods, such as its famous perfumes and wines.

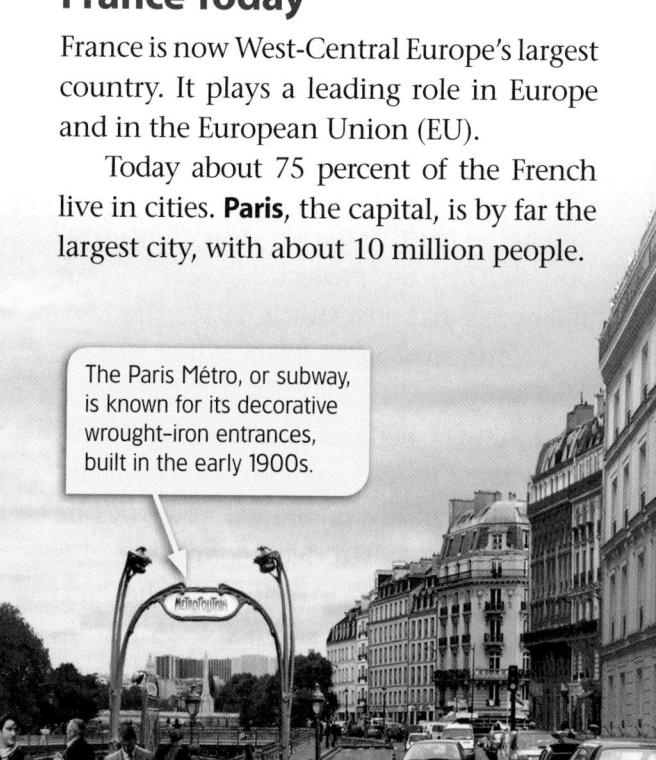

The Paris Métro, or subway, is known for its decorative wrought–iron entrances, built in the early 1900s.

Paris is known for its many sidewalk cafés, where people meet to eat, socialize, and relax.

ANALYSIS SKILL **ANALYZING VISUALS**

What examples do you see of the mixing of the new and the old in Paris?

Dutch Polders

More than 25 percent of the Netherlands lies below sea level. For centuries, the Dutch have reclaimed land from the sea. These reclaimed lands are called polders.

To create polders, the Dutch build dikes near the shoreline. They then use pumps to remove the water behind the dikes. A national system of dikes, dams, floodgates, and storm barriers now holds back the sea.

Unfortunately, creating polders has caused sinking lowlands and other environmental damage. The Dutch are working to address these problems. For example, they are considering restoring some of the polders to wetlands, lakes, and the seas.

Finding Main Ideas How have the Dutch modified their environment to live in a region that lies below sea level?

Tourism is also vital to the economy. Each year, millions of people visit Paris, the French Alps, and the sunny French Riviera, a resort area on the Mediterranean coast.

READING CHECK **Drawing Conclusions** Why do you think tourists might want to visit Paris?

The Benelux Countries

Belgium, the Netherlands, and Luxembourg are called the Benelux Countries. *Benelux* combines the first letters of each country's name. They are also called the Low Countries because of their elevation.

History

Many nations and empires dominated the Benelux region. In 1648 the Netherlands gained its independence. It ruled Belgium until 1830, and Luxembourg until 1867, when they gained independence.

In World War II, Germany occupied the Benelux Countries. After the war, they joined the North Atlantic Treaty Organization (NATO) for protection. NATO is an alliance of nations. In the 1950s the Benelux Countries joined the group of nations now known as the EU.

Today the Benelux Countries each have a parliament and ceremonial monarch. The tiny, densely populated countries lie between larger, stronger countries. This location has led to invasions but has also promoted trade. The Benelux Countries now have wealthy economies.

The Netherlands

Bordering the North Sea, the Netherlands is low and flat. Some of the land lies below sea level. The Netherlands includes the historical region of Holland and is sometimes called Holland. The people here are the Dutch, and the language they speak is also called Dutch.

Excellent harbors on the North Sea have made the Netherlands a center of international trade. The city of Rotterdam is one of the world's busiest seaports. It is also part of a highly industrial and urban, or city-based, area. This area includes **Amsterdam**, the capital, and **the Hague** (HAYG), the seat of government. Agriculture is also important to the Dutch economy, and Dutch cheese and tulips are world famous.

Belgium

Belgium is a highly urban country. More than 95 percent of the people of Belgium live in cities. The capital city, **Brussels**, serves as the headquarters for many international organizations, including the EU and NATO. The city of Brussels is as a result highly **cosmopolitan**, or characterized by many foreign influences.

Language divides Belgium. The coast and north are called Flanders. The people there speak Flemish. The southern interior is called Wallonia. The people there speak French and are called Walloons. These cultural differences have caused tensions.

Belgium is known for its cheeses, chocolate, cocoa, and lace. The city of Antwerp is a key port and diamond-cutting center.

Luxembourg

Luxembourg is a forested, hilly country. Although smaller than Rhode Island, it has one of the world's highest standards of living. Most of the people in Luxembourg are Roman Catholic and speak either French or German.

Luxembourg earns much of its income from services such as banking. The region also produces steel and chemicals. Its small cities are cosmopolitan centers of international business and government.

READING CHECK **Comparing** What do the Benelux Countries have in common?

SUMMARY AND PREVIEW As you have learned, France and the Benelux Countries are modern and urban with strong economies. Next, you will read about Germany and the Alpine Countries.

Section 2 Assessment

go.hrw.com
Online Quiz
KEYWORD: SG7 HP13

Reviewing Ideas, Terms, and Places

1. **a. Identify** Who was Charlemagne?
   b. Explain Why is Napoleon considered a significant figure in French history?
   c. Develop Why might the French be proud of their long history?
2. **a. Define** What is impressionism?
   b. Summarize What are some major contributions of French culture?
   c. Elaborate How has immigration influenced French culture?
3. **a. Describe** Why is **Paris** an important city?
   b. Summarize What is the French economy like?
4. **a. Describe** How does language divide Belgium?
   b. Draw Conclusions Why might **Brussels** be such a **cosmopolitan** city?

Critical Thinking

5. **Categorizing** Draw a chart like the one here. Use your notes and enter information into each category. Within each category, organize the information by country.

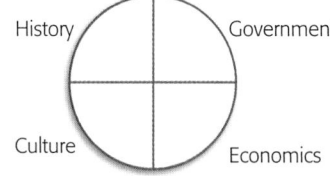
History | Government
Culture | Economics

FOCUS ON SPEAKING

6. **Describing France and the Benelux Countries** For each country, note one possible issue for your persuasive speech. For example, one issue might be language in Belgium. Should all Belgians have to speak the same language?

The European Union

How can smaller countries compete with larger ones? One way is by working together. Since the 1950s, countries across Europe have been working to build a united community. Today this organization is called the European Union (EU). It promotes political and economic cooperation among member nations. The chart on the next page shows how the EU has changed life in Europe.

Member Country

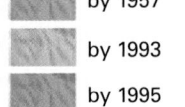

by 1957

by 1993

by 1995

by 2004

by 2007

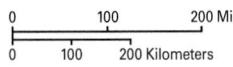

0   100   200 Miles

0   100   200 Kilometers

Projection: Lambert's Az. Equal Area

SWEDEN

DENMARK

IRELAND

UNITED KINGDOM

NETHERLANDS

BELGIUM

LUXEMBOURG

GERMANY

CZECH REPUBLIC

FRANCE

AUSTRIA

SLOVENIA

ITALY

PORTUGAL

SPAIN

MALTA

FINLAND

ESTONIA

LATVIA

LITHUANIA

OLAND

SLOVAKIA

HUNGARY

ROMANIA

BULGARIA

GREECE

CYPRUS

Benefits of Membership in the European Union

Trade

Before	After
■ European countries had to pay customs duties, or taxes, on goods they traded with other European countries. ■ Many European countries' economies were small compared to those of larger nations such as the United States.	■ EU countries are part of a common market. They can trade freely with each other without paying duties. ■ EU countries create a combined economy that is one of the largest in the world.

Currency

Before	After
■ Each European country had its own separate currency, or form of money. ■ European countries and their citizens had to exchange currencies to buy goods from other European countries.	■ Most EU countries share one currency, the euro. ■ EU countries and their citizens can use the euro to buy goods and trade throughout the EU.

Work and Travel

Before	After
■ Europeans had to have passports or other special permits to travel from one European country to another. ■ Europeans had to obtain permission to live and work in other countries in Europe.	■ Citizens of EU countries do not need passports or special permits to travel throughout most of the EU. ■ Citizens of EU countries can live and work anywhere in the EU without having to obtain permission.

The Euro The front sides of euro coins all have the same image, but the backs feature a unique symbol for each country. Euro bills show symbols of unity.

ANALYSIS SKILL **ANALYZING VISUALS**

1. **Name** Which six countries were the first to unite?
2. **Make Inferences** How do you think democracy's spread in Eastern Europe has affected the EU?
3. **Interpreting Charts** Based on the chart above, what are two benefits of EU membership?

Germany and the Alpine Countries

What You Will Learn...

Main Ideas

1. After a history of division and two world wars, Germany is now a unified country.
2. German culture, known for its contributions to music, literature, and science, is growing more diverse.
3. Germany today has Europe's largest economy, but eastern Germany faces challenges.
4. The Alpine Countries reflect German culture and have strong economies based on tourism and services.

The Big Idea

Germany and the Alpine Countries are prosperous countries with similar cultures.

Key Terms and Places

Berlin, *p. 323*
chancellor, *p. 325*
Vienna, *p. 327*
cantons, *p. 327*
Bern, *p. 327*

TAKING NOTES Draw a copy of the chart below. As you read, list facts about each country.

Germany	Alpine Countries

If YOU lived there...

You are walking with your grandfather through Berlin, Germany. He begins telling you about a time when Germany was divided into two countries—one democratic and one Communist. A large wall even divided the city of Berlin. Germans could not pass freely through the wall. You think of your friends who live in eastern Berlin. They would have been on the other side of the wall back then.

What do you think life in Berlin was like then?

BUILDING BACKGROUND Since the Middle Ages, Germany and France have been the dominant countries in West-Central Europe. Both are large and prosperous with hardworking people and good farmland. The two countries have often been at war, but today they are partners in building a cooperative European Union.

History of Germany

Some countries have had a strong influence on world events. Germany is one of these countries. From its location in the heart of Europe, Germany has shaped events across Europe and the world—for both good and bad.

Growth of a Nation

In ancient times, tribes from northern Europe settled in the land that is now Germany. The Romans called this region Germania, after the name of one of the tribes. Over time, many small German states developed in the region. Princes ruled these states. With the support of the Roman Catholic Church, these states became part of the Holy Roman Empire.

For hundreds of years, Germany remained a loose association of small states. Then in 1871, Prussia, the strongest state, united Germany into one nation. As a unified nation, Germany developed into an industrial and military world power.

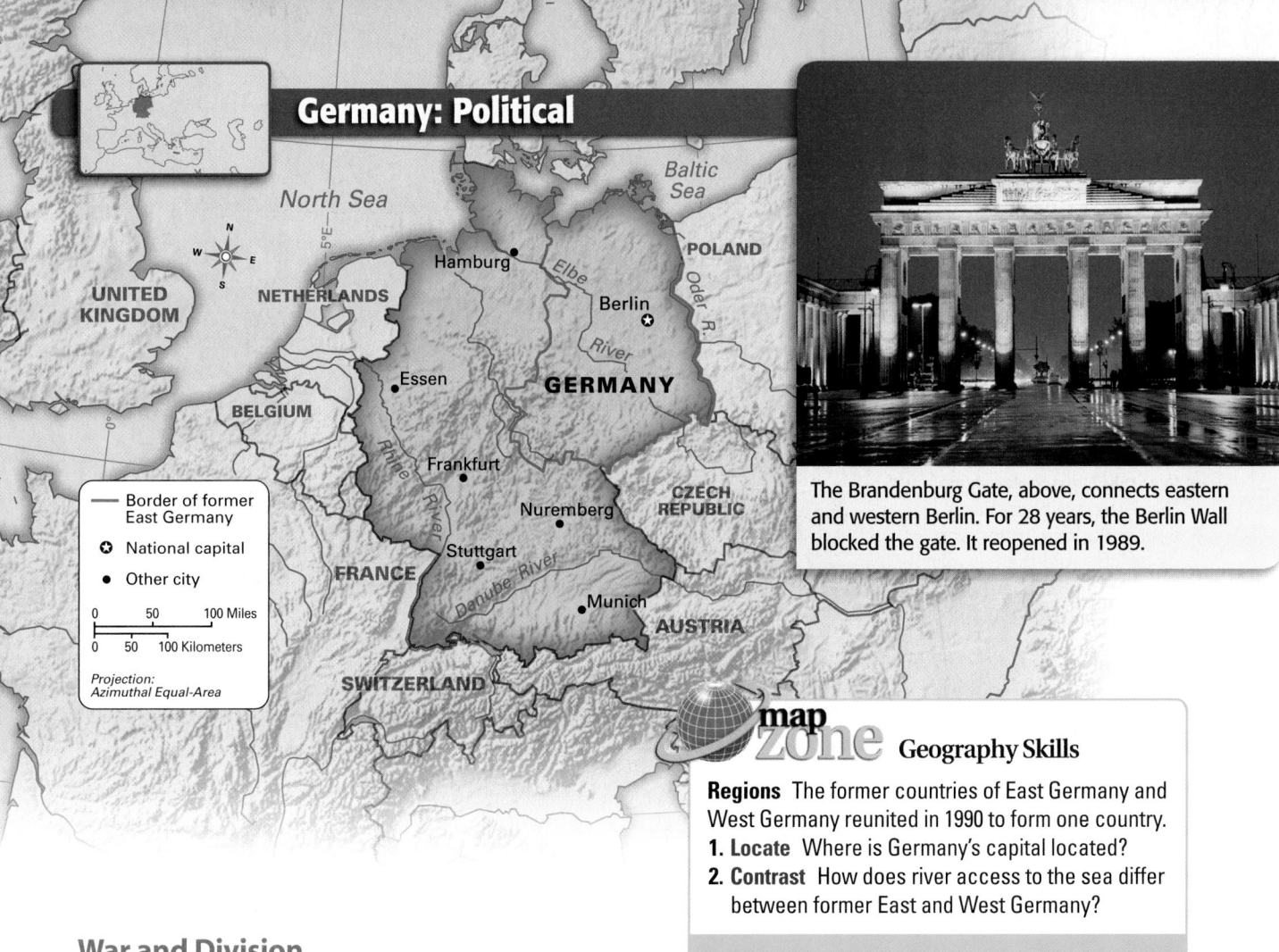

Germany: Political

North Sea

Baltic Sea

UNITED KINGDOM

NETHERLANDS

Hamburg

POLAND

Elbe

Berlin ✪

Oder R.

GERMANY

Essen

BELGIUM

River

Frankfurt

Rhine River

Nuremberg

CZECH REPUBLIC

Stuttgart

Danube River

FRANCE

Munich

AUSTRIA

SWITZERLAND

— Border of former East Germany

✪ National capital

• Other city

0   50   100 Miles
0   50   100 Kilometers

Projection:
Azimuthal Equal-Area

The Brandenburg Gate, above, connects eastern and western Berlin. For 28 years, the Berlin Wall blocked the gate. It reopened in 1989.

map zone Geography Skills

Regions The former countries of East Germany and West Germany reunited in 1990 to form one country.
1. **Locate** Where is Germany's capital located?
2. **Contrast** How does river access to the sea differ between former East and West Germany?

War and Division

In 1914–1918, Germany fought and lost World War I. Payments for war damages and a major depression severely hurt the German economy. Looking for a strong leader, Germans found Adolf Hitler and his Nazi Party. Hitler promised the Germans to restore their country to its former glory.

In 1939 Germany attacked Poland, starting World War II. Soon, Germany had conquered much of Europe. The Nazis also sought to kill all European Jews in what is called the Holocaust. Germany lost the war, though. By 1945 it lay in ruins, defeated.

After the war, British, French, and U.S. troops occupied West Germany. The Soviet Union's troops occupied East Germany. Over time, two countries emerged.

The city of **Berlin** was in Communist East Germany. Even so, West Germany kept control of the western part of the city.

In 1961 Communist leaders built the Berlin Wall. The Wall's **purpose** was to prevent East Germans from fleeing to West Berlin.

A Reunited Germany

After World War II, U.S. aid helped West Germany rebuild rapidly. It soon became an economic power. East Germany rebuilt as well, but its economy lagged. In addition, its people had limited freedoms.

In 1989 movements for democracy swept through Eastern Europe. Communist governments began collapsing. Joyful East Germans tore down the Berlin Wall. In 1990 East and West Germany reunited.

READING CHECK **Finding Main Ideas** What major challenges has Germany overcome?

ACADEMIC VOCABULARY
purpose the reason something is done

Germany's long history has enriched its culture. Historic castles dot the landscape, and long-held traditions continue. Blending with this history is a modern culture that includes a love of sports.

A Bavarian Castle King Ludwig II of Bavaria had the fairy-tale Neuschwanstein (noy-SHVAHN-shtyn) Castle built in the mid-1800s. The castle sits amid the Bavarian Alps in southern Germany.

Culture of Germany

Germans are known as hardworking and efficient people. At the same time, they enjoy their traditions and celebrating their cultural achievements.

People

Most Germans share a common heritage. About 90 percent are ethnic German, and most speak German. In recent years, significant numbers of immigrants have come to Germany to live and work as well. These immigrants include Turks, Italians, and refugees from Eastern Europe. Their influence is making German culture more diverse.

Religion

In 1517 Martin Luther, a German monk, helped start the Reformation. This religious reform movement led to the development of Protestant churches. Many Germanic states became Protestant; others remained Roman Catholic. Today in north and central Germany, most people are Protestant. In the south, most are Catholic. In eastern Germany, fewer Germans have religious ties, reflecting the area's Communist past.

Customs

Festivals and holidays tell us much about German culture. Religious festivals are very popular. For example, many areas hold festivals before the Christian season of Lent. In addition, Christmas is a major family event. The tradition of the Christmas tree even began in Germany.

Each region has local festivals as well. The best known is Oktoberfest in Bavaria, the region of southeast Germany. This festival is held each fall in Munich (MYOO-nik) to celebrate the region's food and drink.

The Arts and Sciences

Germany's contributions to the arts and sciences are widely admired. In music, Germany has produced famed classical composers, such as Johann Sebastian Bach and Ludwig van Beethoven. In literature, author Johann Wolfgang von Goethe (GOOH-tuh) ranks among Europe's most important writers. In science, Germans have made contributions in chemistry, engineering, medicine, and physics.

READING CHECK Summarizing What contributions have Germans made to world culture?

Most Austrians speak German and are Roman Catholic. The city of **Vienna** is Austria's capital and largest city. Located on the banks of the Danube, Vienna was once the center of Habsburg rule. Today historic palaces grace the city, which is a center of music and the fine arts.

Austria has a prosperous economy with little unemployment. Service industries, such as banking, are important and employ more than half of Austria's workforce. Tourism is important as well.

Switzerland

Since the 1600s Switzerland has been an independent country. Today it is a federal republic with 26 districts called **cantons**. Citizens are active in local government. In addition, all male citizens serve for a period in the militia, a citizen army.

Switzerland's location in the Alps has helped it remain **neutral** for centuries. To stay neutral, Switzerland has not joined the EU or NATO. The Swiss are active in international organizations, however.

As the map shows, the Swiss speak several languages. The main languages are German and French. Switzerland's capital, **Bern**, is centrally located to be near both German- and French-speaking regions.

Switzerland has one of the world's highest standards of living. It is famous for its banks, watches and other precision devices, and chocolate and cheese.

READING CHECK **Contrasting** How are the countries of Austria and Switzerland different?

SUMMARY AND PREVIEW You have read that Germany is an economic power with a rich culture, while the Alpine Countries are prosperous with beautiful mountain scenery. In the next chapter you will learn about Northern Europe.

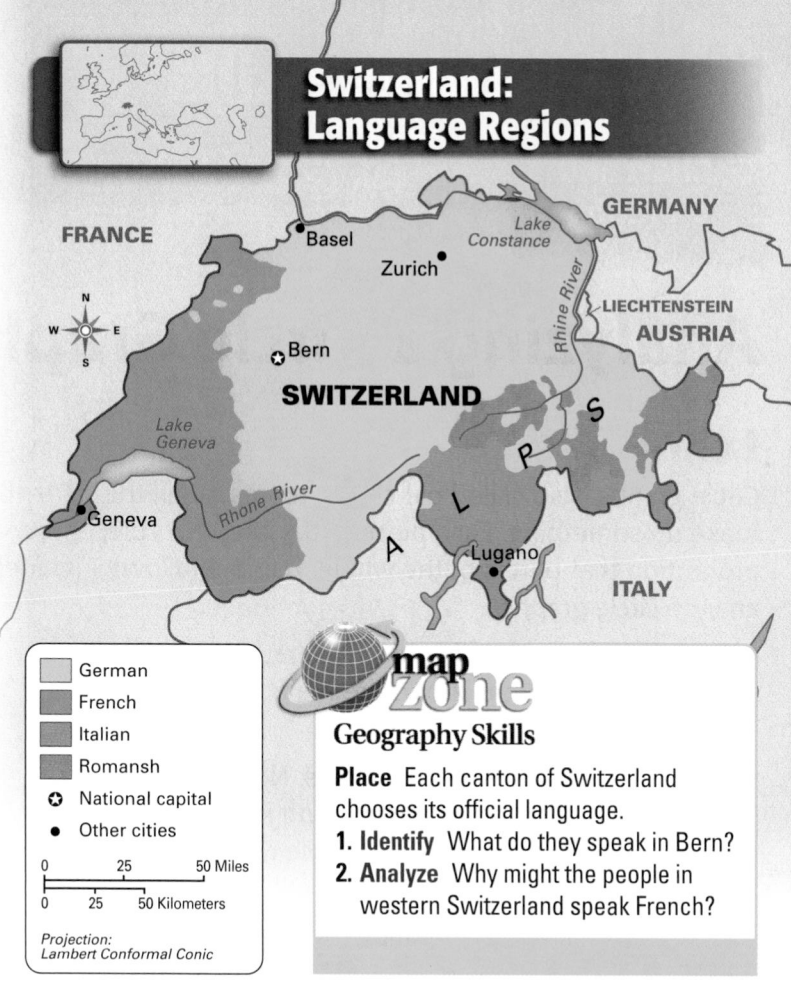

Switzerland: Language Regions

German
French
Italian
Romansh
✪ National capital
• Other cities

0   25   50 Miles
0   25   50 Kilometers

Projection:
Lambert Conformal Conic

map zone

Geography Skills

Place Each canton of Switzerland chooses its official language.
1. **Identify** What do they speak in Bern?
2. **Analyze** Why might the people in western Switzerland speak French?

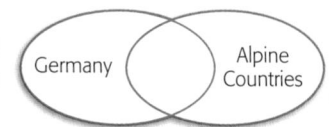

Section 3 Assessment

go.hrw.com
Online Quiz
KEYWORD: SG7 HP13

Reviewing Ideas, Terms, and Places

1. **a. Identify** Why is Adolf Hitler significant in history?
   b. Sequence What events led to German reunification?
2. **a. Recall** What are some popular festivals in Germany?
   b. Contrast How does religion differ across Germany?
3. **a. Describe** What is the role of Germany's **chancellor**?
   b. Explain Why has Germany's economy slowed?
4. **a. Define** What are **cantons**, and where are they found?
   b. Analyze How are the Alps a valuable resource?

Critical Thinking

5. **Comparing and Contrasting** Draw a Venn diagram like this one. Use your notes to list the differences and similarities.

   Germany   Alpine Countries

FOCUS ON SPEAKING

6. **Describing Germany and the Alpine Countries** For each country, note one issue for your speech. For example, you might argue that the Alps are the region's loveliest area.

Analyzing a Circle Graph

Learn

Circle graphs, also called pie charts, represent all the parts that make up something. Each piece of the circle, or "pie," shows what proportion that part is of the whole. Use the following guidelines to analyze circle graphs.

- Read the title to identify the circle graph's subject. The circle graph here shows the main languages spoken in Switzerland.

- Read the circle graph's other labels. Note what each part, or slice, of the circle graph represents. In the circle graph at right, each slice represents a different language.

- Analyze the data by comparing the size of the slices in the circle graph. Think about what the differences mean or imply.

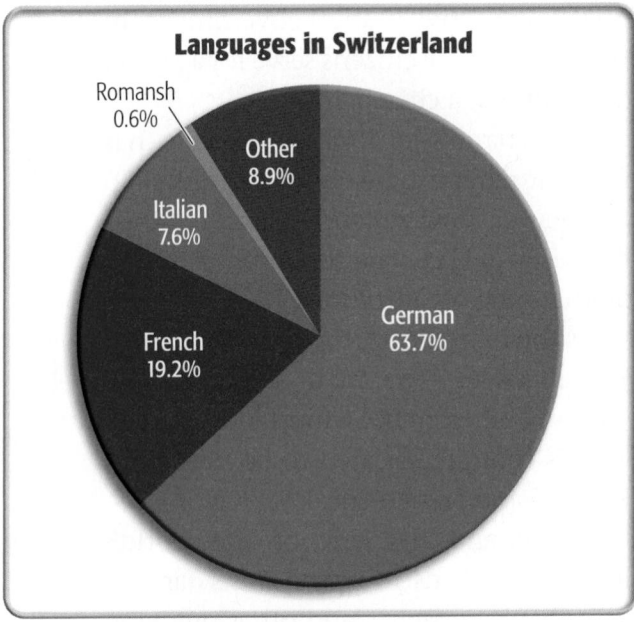

Languages in Switzerland

Romansh 0.6%
Other 8.9%
Italian 7.6%
German 63.7%
French 19.2%

Source: Central Intelligence Agency, *The World Factbook 2002*

Practice

❶ Based on the circle graph at right, what are the three main languages spoken in Switzerland?

❷ What language do less than 1 percent of the Swiss speak?

❸ What percentage of the Swiss speak other languages not listed individually?

Apply

To answer the following questions, use the circle graph titled France's Current Export Partners in the Standardized Test Practice.

1. To which country does France send the highest percentage of its exports?

2. How many of France's main export partners belong to the European Union?

3. What percentage of French exports go to the United States?

Geography's Impact
video series
Review the video to answer the closing question:
Do you think proximity to the sea has been more beneficial or harmful to the Netherlands?

Visual Summary

Use the visual summary below to help you review the main ideas of the chapter.

QUICK FACTS

France is a leading European nation and cultural center. The Benelux Countries are small, densely populated, and rich.

Germany is an industrial powerhouse with a rich culture. The landlocked Alpine Countries have stunning mountains.

Reviewing Vocabulary, Terms, and Places

Match each "I" statement below with the person, place, or thing that might have made the statement.

a. Berlin
b. Brussels
c. canton
d. chancellor
e. cosmopolitan city
f. Danube River
g. dike
h. navigable river
i. North Sea
j. Paris

1. "I am the capital of France and a center of business, finance, learning, and culture."
2. "I am an important waterway in the region of West-Central Europe."
3. "I am a prime minister in Germany."
4. "I am an earthen wall used to hold back water."
5. "I am a type of river that is wide and deep enough for ships to use."
6. "I am a district in Switzerland."
7. "I am a city that has many foreign influences."
8. "I am an international city and the capital of Belgium."
9. "I am a large body of water located to the north of the Benelux Countries and Germany."
10. "I was divided into two parts after World War II and am now the capital of Germany."

Comprehension and Critical Thinking

SECTION 1 *(Pages 310–313)*

11. **a. Recall** From southeast to northwest, what are the major landforms in West-Central Europe?

    b. Analyze How have geographic features supported trade and travel across the region of West-Central Europe?

    c. Elaborate How does West-Central Europe's mild climate serve as a valuable resource and contribute to the economy?

SECTION 2 *(Pages 314–319)*

12. a. Identify Where is the busiest seaport in the Netherlands located?

   b. Summarize What are some products and cultural features for which France is famous?

   c. Develop How have geographic features helped the Benelux Countries become centers of trade and international business?

SECTION 3 *(Pages 322–327)*

13. a. Recall What are three major events in German history, and when did each one occur?

   b. Analyze How is Switzerland's position in European affairs unique?

   c. Elaborate How has the royal Habsburg family shaped Austria's history?

Social Studies Skills

Analyzing a Circle Graph *Use the circle graph titled Languages in Switzerland in the Social Studies Skills to answer the following questions.*

14. Based on the circle graph, what percentage of the Swiss speak German?

15. What percentage of the Swiss speak French and Italian?

16. What fourth language do the Swiss speak?

FOCUS ON READING AND SPEAKING

17. Recognizing Word Origins Find the key term *cosmopolitan* in Section 2. Write the word's definition. Then use a good dictionary to research the word's origins. Explain how the word's origins relate to its definition.

18. Presenting a Persuasive Speech Choose one of the issues you identified as you read the chapter. Write an opinion statement about the issue, such as "The Dutch polders should be restored to wetlands." Next, list three facts or examples that support your opinion. Use the chapter and other sources to find information. Then use the list to write your short persuasive speech. Practice delivering your speech using an assured tone of voice and a confident posture.

Using the Internet

19. Activity: Researching Schools Imagine that your family is moving to Belgium or the Netherlands. In your new country you will be attending an international school. What kinds of classes will you have? What will your school day be like? What kinds of things might you see and do outside of school? Enter the activity keyword and select the country that interests you. Research schools and daily life there. Then complete the online worksheet to record what you have learned. Finally, compare the schools you researched to the school you attend today.

Map Activity

20. West-Central Europe On a separate sheet of paper, match the letters on the map with their correct labels.

Alps	Paris, France
Berlin, Germany	Pyrenees
North Sea	Vienna, Austria
Northern European Plain	

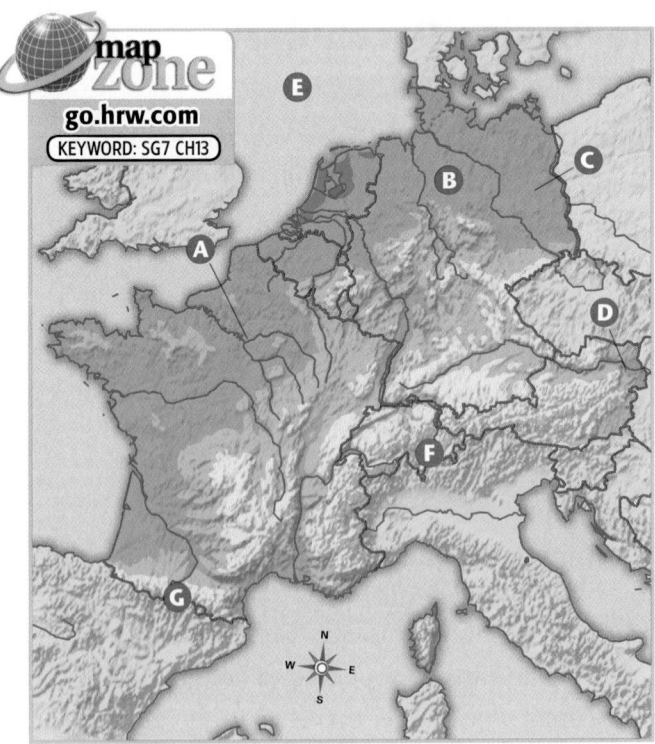

DIRECTIONS: *Read questions 1 through 7 and write the letter of the best response. Then read question 8 and write your own well-constructed response.*

1 The alpine mountain system includes the Alps and the

A Black Forest.

B Jura Mountains.

C Massif Central.

D Pyrenees.

2 What type of climate does *most* of West-Central Europe have?

A highland climate

B humid tropical climate

C marine west coast climate

D Mediterranean climate

3 Which three countries make up the Benelux Countries?

A Belgium, the Netherlands, and Luxembourg

B France, Belgium, and Luxembourg

C France, Germany, and Austria

D Germany, Austria, and Switzerland

4 Which French leader created a great empire only to be defeated in 1815?

A Adolf Hitler

B Charlemagne

C Napoleon

D William the Conqueror

5 What capital city in West-Central Europe was divided after World War II?

A Berlin

B Brussels

C Paris

D Vienna

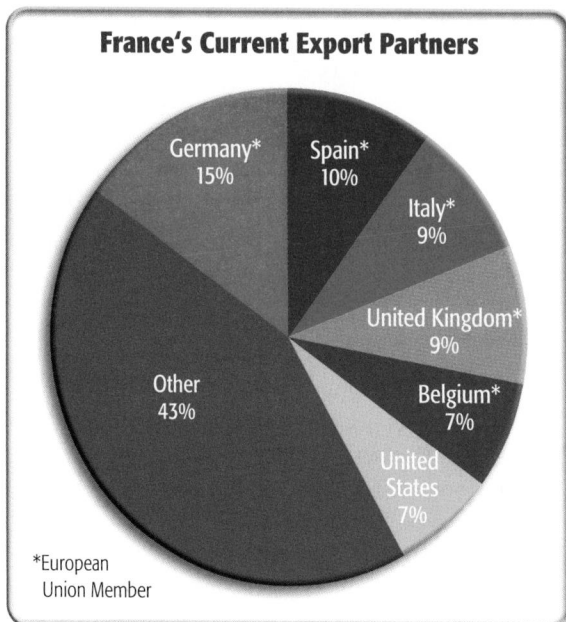

France's Current Export Partners

Germany* 15%
Spain* 10%
Italy* 9%
United Kingdom* 9%
Belgium* 7%
United States 7%
Other 43%

*European Union Member

Source: Central Intelligence Agency, *The World Factbook 2005*

6 Based on the graph above, what percentage of French goods went to France's top two export partners?

A 10%

B 15%

C 25%

D 30%

7 What is the main language spoken in both of the Alpine Countries?

A Dutch

B French

C German

D Italian

8 Extended Response   Examine the map of Germany in Section 3. Use the map to explain how the physical geography of former East and West Germany differed. Then analyze how you think each former country's physical geography affected its economy.

CHAPTER 14

Northern Europe

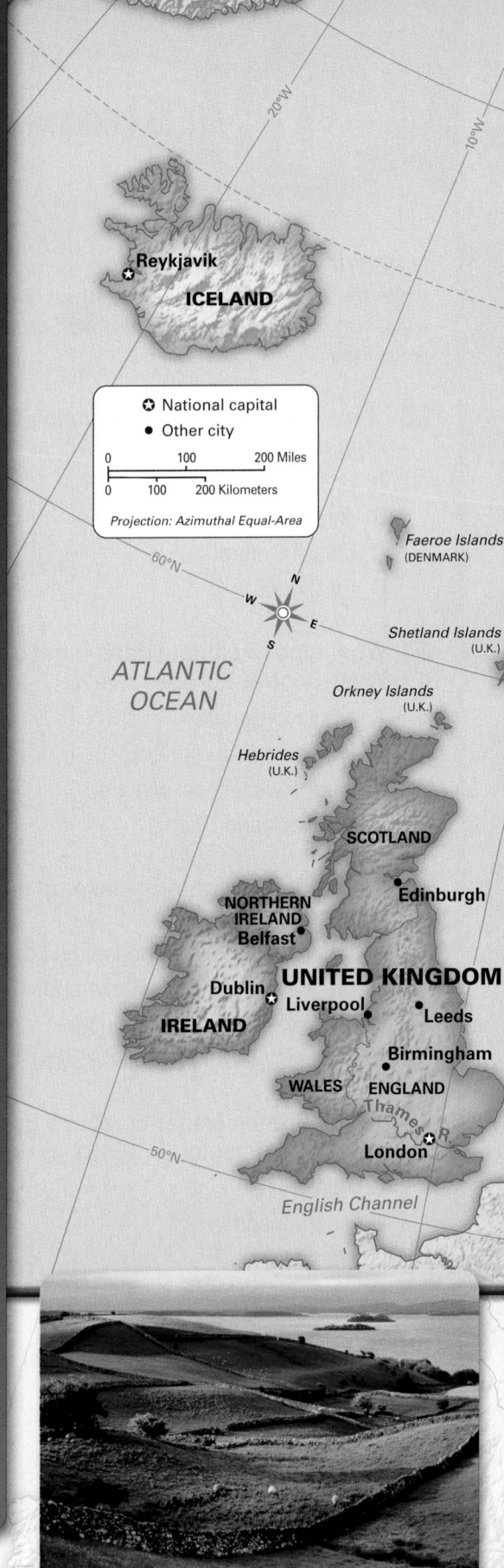

What You Will Learn...

In this chapter you will discover Northern Europe's unique and varied physical geography. You will also study the history and culture of Northern Europe's two main regions—the British Isles and Scandinavia. Finally, you will learn about the British Isles and Scandinavia today.

FOCUS ON READING AND WRITING

Using Context Clues—Synonyms As you read, you may occasionally encounter a word or phrase that you do not know. When that happens, use the words and sentences around the unfamiliar word—context clues—to help you determine the word's meaning. As you read this chapter, look for words that are synonyms, or words that mean the same as the unfamiliar word. **See the lesson, Using Context Clues—Synonyms, on page R15.**

Writing a Letter Letters are a great way to stay in touch with friends and family. As you read this chapter, gather information about Northern Europe. Then imagine you are traveling through this region. Write a letter to your friends and family at home in which you describe what you have learned on your travels.

Geography Fertile plains like this one in Ireland provide Northern Europe with much of its farmland.

70°N

ARCTIC
OCEAN

Tromso

Arctic Circle

Norwegian
Sea

FINLAND

SWEDEN

Gulf of Bothnia

NORWAY

Bergen

Helsinki

Gulf of Finland

Oslo

Stockholm

ESTONIA

Göteborg

RUSSIA

North
Sea

Baltic Sea

LATVIA

DENMARK

Copenhagen

LITHUANIA

RUSSIA

BELARUS

NETHERLANDS

GERMANY

POLAND

map
zone **Geography Skills**

Location Much of Northern Europe is separated from the rest of the continent by the English Channel and the North and Baltic seas.

1. Identify What countries extend north of the Arctic Circle?

2. Contrast How does Northern Europe differ physically from the rest of Europe?

go.hrw.com KEYWORD: SG7 CH14

HOLT

Geography's Impact
video series
Watch the video to understand the impact of volcanoes in Iceland.

History The Palace of Westminster in London has been home to the British Parliament for over 600 years.

Culture Skiing and other forms of outdoor recreation are popular throughout much of Scandinavia.

Physical Geography

Main Ideas

1. The physical features of Northern Europe include low mountain ranges and jagged coastlines.
2. Northern Europe's natural resources include energy sources, soils, and seas.
3. The climates of Northern Europe range from a mild coastal climate to a freezing ice cap climate.

The Big Idea

Northern Europe is a region of unique physical features, rich resources, and diverse climates.

Key Terms and Places

British Isles, *p. 334*
Scandinavia, *p. 334*
fjord, *p. 335*
geothermal energy, *p. 336*
North Atlantic Drift, *p. 336*

TAKING NOTES As you read, take notes on Northern Europe's physical features, natural resources, and climates. Record your notes in a chart like the one below.

Physical Features	Natural Resources	Climates

If YOU lived there...

Your family is planning to visit friends in Tromso, Norway. It is a city on the Norwegian Sea located 200 miles north of the Arctic Circle. You imagine a landscape covered in snow and ice. When you arrive, however, you discover green hills and ice-free harbors.

What might explain the mild climate?

BUILDING BACKGROUND Although located at high latitudes, Norway and the rest of Northern Europe have surprisingly mild temperatures. All the countries of Northern Europe are located on seas and oceans. As a result, they benefit from ocean currents that bring warm water north and keep the climate reasonably warm.

Physical Features

From Ireland's gently rolling hills to Iceland's icy glaciers and fiery volcanoes, Northern Europe is a land of great variety. Because of this variety, the physical geography of Northern Europe changes greatly from one location to another.

Two regions—the British Isles and Scandinavia—make up Northern Europe. To the southwest lie the **British Isles**, a group of islands located across the English Channel from the rest of Europe. Northeast of the British Isles is **Scandinavia**, a region of islands and peninsulas in far northern Europe. The island of Iceland, to the west, is often considered part of Scandinavia.

Hills and Mountains Rough, rocky hills and low mountains cover much of Northern Europe. Rugged hills stretch across much of Iceland, northern Scotland, and Scandinavia. The jagged Kjolen (CHUH-luhn) Mountains on the Scandinavian Peninsula divide Norway from Sweden. The rocky soil and uneven terrain in these parts of Northern Europe make farming there difficult. As a result, fewer people live there than in the rest of Northern Europe.

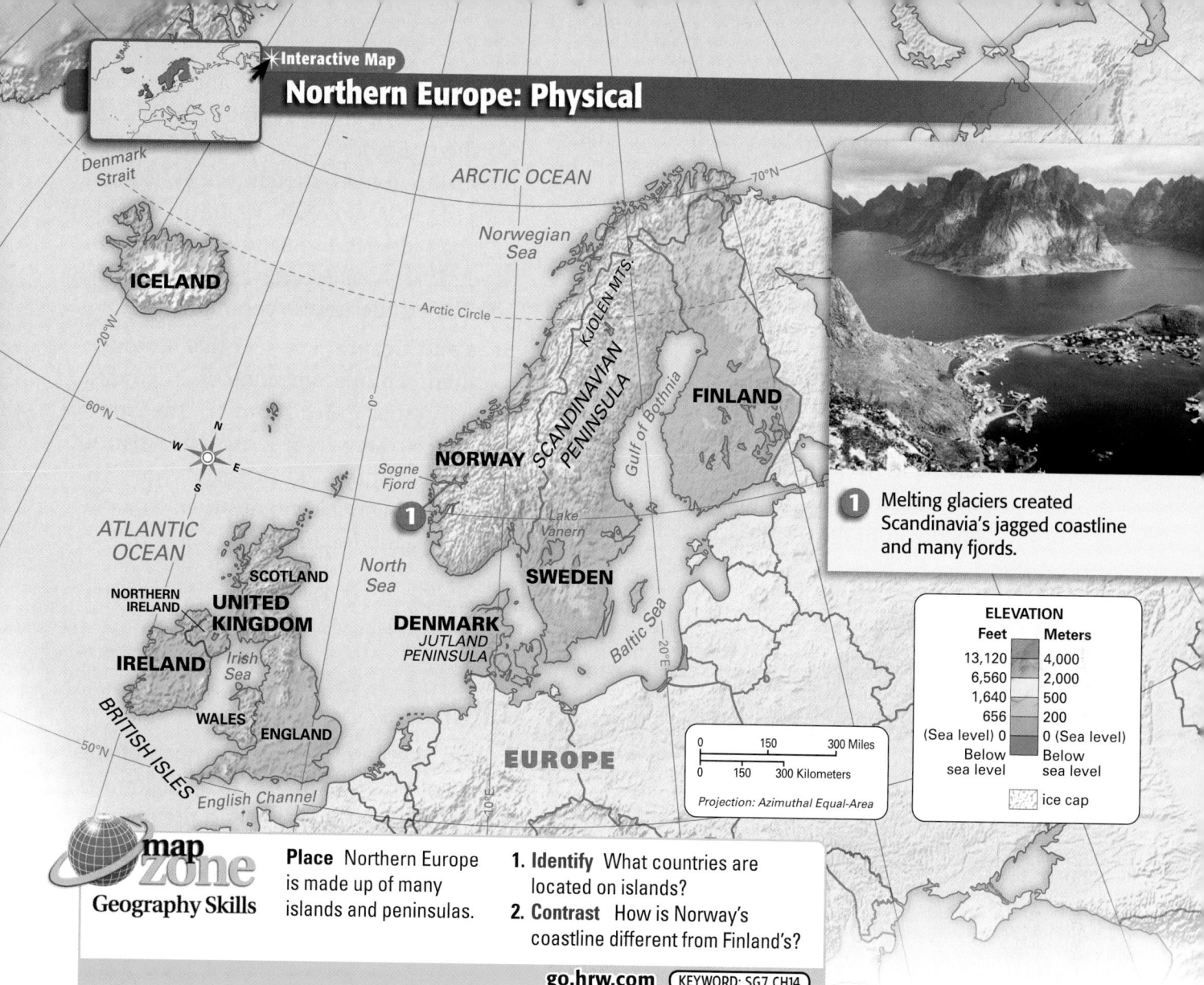

Northern Europe: Physical

ARCTIC OCEAN

Denmark Strait

Norwegian Sea

ICELAND

Arctic Circle

KJOLEN MTS.

SCANDINAVIAN PENINSULA

FINLAND

Gulf of Bothnia

NORWAY

Sogne Fjord

1

Lake Vanern

ATLANTIC OCEAN

SCOTLAND

NORTHERN IRELAND

UNITED KINGDOM

North Sea

SWEDEN

DENMARK
JUTLAND PENINSULA

Baltic Sea

IRELAND

Irish Sea

WALES

ENGLAND

BRITISH ISLES

English Channel

EUROPE

1 Melting glaciers created Scandinavia's jagged coastline and many fjords.

ELEVATION

Feet	Meters
13,120	4,000
6,560	2,000
1,640	500
656	200
(Sea level) 0	0 (Sea level)
Below sea level	Below sea level

ice cap

| 0 | 150 | 300 Miles |
| 0 | 150 | 300 Kilometers |

Projection: Azimuthal Equal-Area

map Zone
Geography Skills

Place Northern Europe is made up of many islands and peninsulas.

1. **Identify** What countries are located on islands?
2. **Contrast** How is Norway's coastline different from Finland's?

go.hrw.com KEYWORD: SG7 CH14

Farmland and Plains Fertile farmland and flat plains stretch across the southern parts of the British Isles and Scandinavia. Ireland's rolling, green hills provide rich farmland. Wide valleys in England and Denmark also have plenty of fertile soil.

Effects of Glaciers Slow-moving sheets of ice, or glaciers, have left their mark on Northern Europe's coastlines and lakes. As you can see on the map above, Norway's western coastline is very jagged. Millions of years ago, glaciers cut deep valleys into Norway's coastal mountains. As the glaciers melted, these valleys filled with water,

creating deep fjords. A **fjord** (fee-AWRD) is a narrow inlet of the sea set between high, rocky cliffs. Many fjords are very long and deep. Norway's Sogne (SAWNG-nuh) Fjord, for example, is over 100 miles (160 km) long and more than three-quarters of a mile (1.2 km) deep. Melting glaciers also carved thousands of lakes in Northern Europe. Sweden's Lake Vanern, along with many of the lakes in the British Isles, were carved by glaciers thousands of years ago.

READING CHECK **Summarizing** What are some physical features of Northern Europe?

Natural Resources

Natural resources have helped to make Northern Europe one of the wealthiest regions in the world. Northern Europe's **primary** resources are its energy resources, forests and soils, and surrounding seas.

ACADEMIC VOCABULARY

primary main, most important

Energy Northern Europe has a variety of energy resources. Norway and the United Kingdom benefit from oil and natural gas deposits under the North Sea. Hydroelectric energy is produced by the region's many lakes and rivers. In Iceland steam from hot springs produces **geothermal energy**, or energy from the heat of Earth's interior.

Forests and Soils Forests and soils are two other important natural resources in Northern Europe. Large areas of timber-producing forests stretch across Finland and the Scandinavian Peninsula. Fertile soils provide rich farmland for crops, such as wheat and potatoes. Livestock like sheep and dairy cattle are also common.

Seas and Oceans The seas that surround Northern Europe are another important natural resource. For centuries, the North Sea, the Norwegian Sea, and the Atlantic Ocean have provided rich stocks of fish. Today, fishing is a key industry in Norway, Denmark, and Iceland.

READING CHECK **Summarizing** What natural resources are found in Northern Europe?

Climates

Locate Northern Europe on a map of the world. Notice that much of the region lies near the Arctic Circle. Due to the region's high latitude, you might imagine that it would be quite cold during much of the year. In reality, however, the climates in Northern Europe are remarkably mild.

Northern Europe's mild climates are a result of the **North Atlantic Drift**, an ocean current that brings warm, moist air across the Atlantic Ocean. Warm waters from this ocean current keep most of the region warmer than other locations around the globe at similar latitudes.

Much of Northern Europe has a marine west coast climate. Denmark, the British Isles, and western Norway benefit from mild summers and frequent rainfall. Snow and frosts may occur in winter but do not usually last long.

Central Norway, Sweden, and southern Finland have a humid continental climate. This area has four true seasons with cold, snowy winters and mild summers.

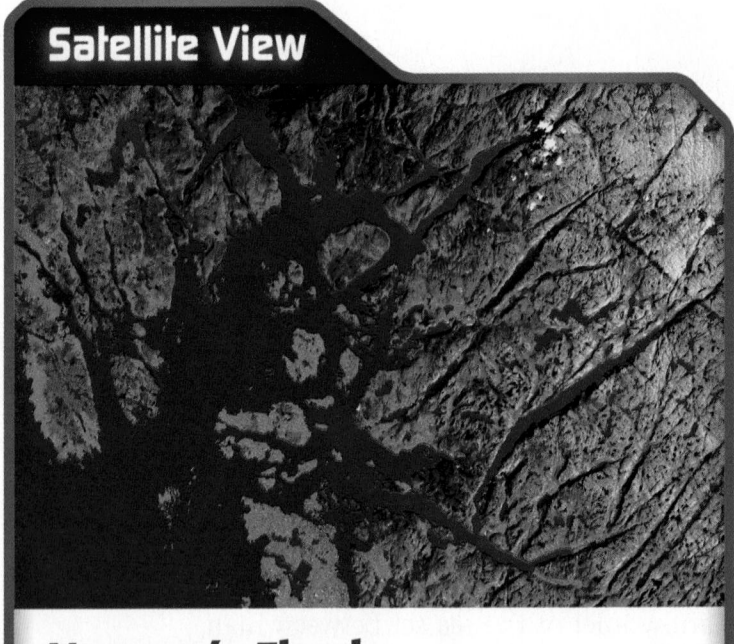

Satellite View

Norway's Fjords

Millions of years ago much of Norway was covered with glaciers. As the glaciers flowed slowly downhill, they carved long, winding channels, or fjords, into Norway's coastline.

As you can see in this satellite image, fjords cut many miles into Norway's interior, bringing warm waters from the North and Norwegian seas. As warm waters penetrate inland, they keep temperatures relatively mild. In fact, people have used these unfrozen fjords to travel during the winter when ice and snow made travel over land difficult.

Drawing Conclusions How do fjords benefit life in Norway?

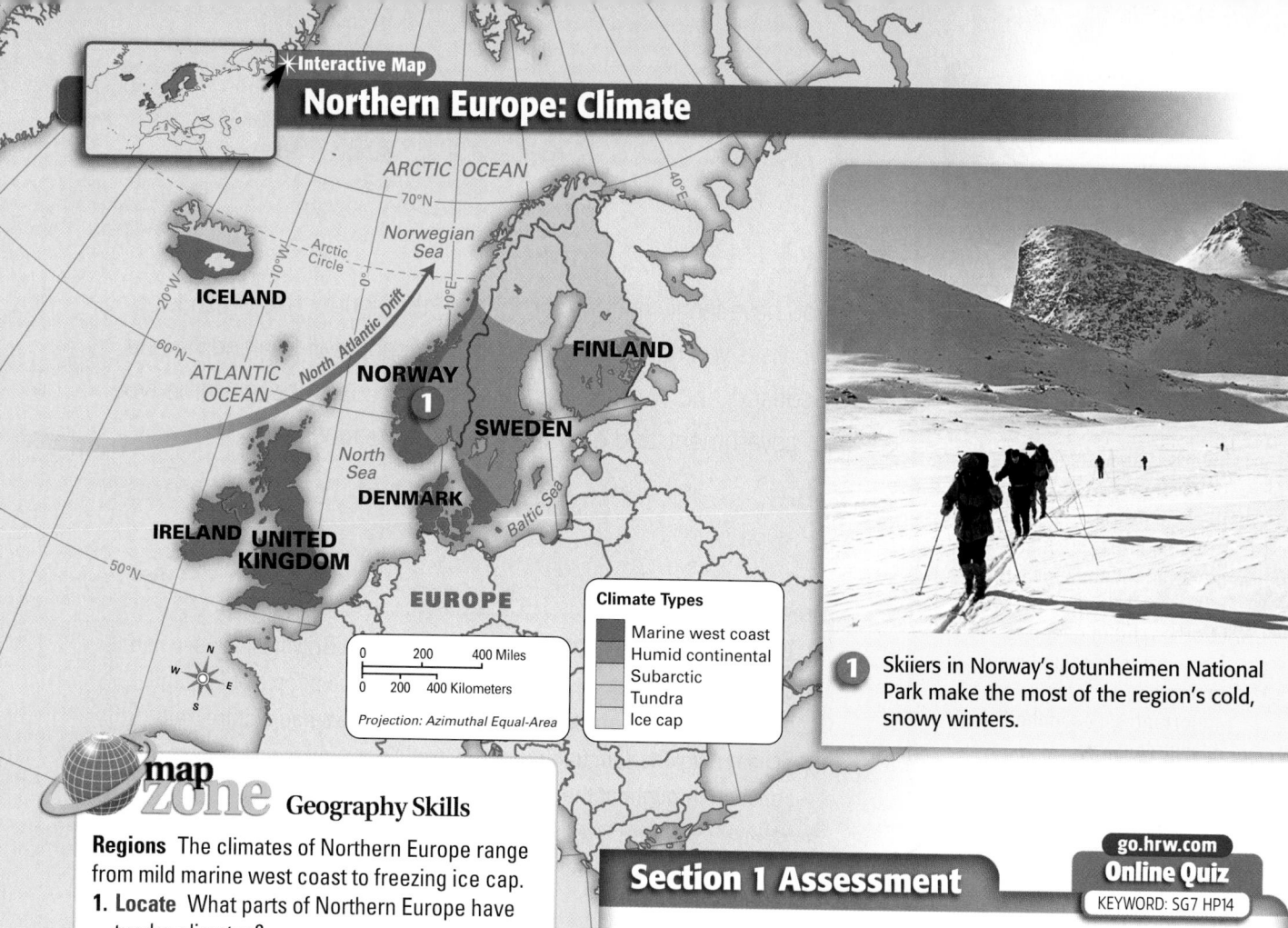

Northern Europe: Climate

Interactive Map

Climate Types
- Marine west coast
- Humid continental
- Subarctic
- Tundra
- Ice cap

0 200 400 Miles
0 200 400 Kilometers
Projection: Azimuthal Equal-Area

1 Skiiers in Norway's Jotunheimen National Park make the most of the region's cold, snowy winters.

map zone Geography Skills

Regions The climates of Northern Europe range from mild marine west coast to freezing ice cap.
1. **Locate** What parts of Northern Europe have tundra climates?
2. **Make Inferences** What allows much of Northern Europe to have mild climates?

go.hrw.com (KEYWORD: SG7 CH14)

Far to the north are colder climates. Subarctic regions, like those in Northern Scandinavia, have long, cold winters and short summers. Iceland's tundra and ice cap climates produce extremely cold temperatures all year.

READING CHECK Analyzing How does the North Atlantic Drift keep climates mild?

SUMMARY AND PREVIEW Northern Europe has many different physical features, natural resources, and climates. Next, you will learn about the history and culture of the British Isles.

Section 1 Assessment

go.hrw.com
Online Quiz
KEYWORD: SG7 HP14

Reviewing Ideas, Terms, and Places

1. **a. Describe** What are the physical features of this region?
   b. Analyze What role did glaciers play in shaping the physical geography of Northern Europe?
2. **a. Recall** What is **geothermal energy**?
   b. Make Inferences How do people in Northern Europe benefit from the surrounding seas?
3. **a. Identify** What climates exist in Northern Europe?
   b. Predict How might the climates of Northern Europe be different without the **North Atlantic Drift**?

Critical Thinking

4. **Comparing and Contrasting** Using your notes and a chart like the one below, compare and contrast the physical geography of the British Isles and Scandinavia.

	British Isles	Scandinavia
Physical Features		
Resources		
Climates		

FOCUS ON WRITING

5. **Describing the Physical Geography** Take notes on the physical features, resources, and climates of Northern Europe. In what season might you visit the region?

The British Isles

If YOU lived there...

You have family and friends that live throughout the British Isles. On visits you have discovered that the people of England, Ireland, Scotland, and Wales share the same language, use the same type of government, and eat many of the same foods.

Why might culture in the British Isles be similar?

BUILDING BACKGROUND The people of the British Isles have had close ties for thousands of years. As a result, the people of England, Scotland, Ireland, and Wales share many of the same culture traits. Similar religions, languages, literary traditions, and even holidays are common throughout the British Isles.

History

Two independent countries—the Republic of Ireland and the United Kingdom—make up the British Isles. The United Kingdom is a union of four small countries: England, Scotland, Wales, and Northern Ireland. Throughout their history, the people of the British Isles have been closely linked together.

What You Will Learn...

Main Ideas

1. Invaders and a global empire have shaped the history of the British Isles.
2. British culture, such as government and music, has influenced much of the world.
3. Efforts to bring peace to Northern Ireland and maintain strong economies are important issues in the British Isles today.

The Big Idea

Close cultural and historical ties link the people of the British Isles today.

Key Terms and Places

constitutional monarchy, *p. 340*
Magna Carta, *p. 340*
disarm, *p. 341*
London, *p. 342*
Dublin, *p. 342*

TAKING NOTES As you read, take notes on the history, culture, and issues of the British Isles today. Use a graphic organizer like the one below to organize your notes.

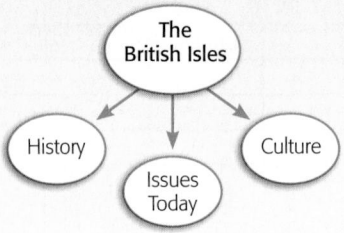

The British Isles
— History
— Issues Today
— Culture

Time Line

History of the British Isles

1558–1603 England becomes a world power during the reign of Queen Elizabeth I.

3100 BC ———— 1600

3100 BC Ancient settlers in England build Stonehenge.

Early History

The history of the British Isles dates back thousands of years. Early settlers built Stonehenge, an ancient monument, some 5,000 years ago. Around 450 BC, the Celts (KELTS) arrived in the British Isles and settled Scotland, Wales, and Ireland. Britain was even part of the ancient Roman Empire.

In the Middle Ages a series of invaders ruled the British Isles. The Angles, Saxons, and Vikings all established small kingdoms in Britain. Finally, in 1066, the Normans from northern France conquered England and established a strong kingdom there.

Over time, England grew in strength and power. It soon overshadowed its neighbors in the British Isles. By the 1500s strong rulers like Queen Elizabeth I had turned England into a world power.

Rise of the British Empire

A strong economy and mighty navy helped England build a vast empire. Over time, England joined with Wales and Scotland to create the United Kingdom of Great Britain. Eventually, Ireland was annexed too. England also launched an overseas empire. By the 1800s Britain had colonies in the Americas, India, and Australia.

The United Kingdom's economy soared in the 1700s and 1800s, thanks to the Industrial Revolution. Industries like iron, steel, and <u>textiles</u>, or cloth products, helped make the United Kingdom one of the world's richest countries.

Not everyone benefited, however. In the 1840s a severe food shortage devastated Ireland. Lack of support from the English government during the famine increased tensions between the two countries.

FOCUS ON READING
What does the word *textiles* mean? How can you tell?

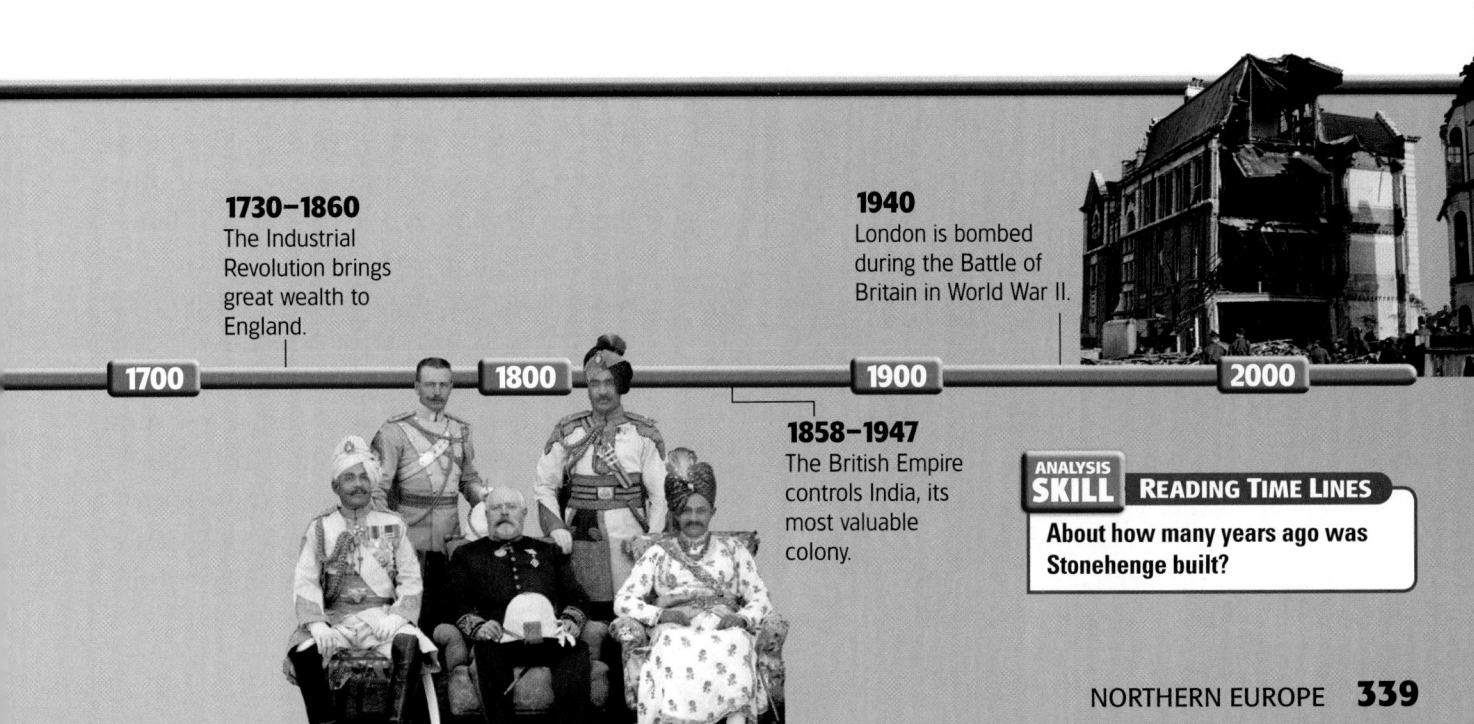

1730–1860
The Industrial Revolution brings great wealth to England.

1940
London is bombed during the Battle of Britain in World War II.

1700   1800   1900   2000

1858–1947
The British Empire controls India, its most valuable colony.

ANALYSIS SKILL **READING TIME LINES**

About how many years ago was Stonehenge built?

By the late 1800s the British Empire spanned the globe. Africa, Asia, Australia, and the Americas were all home to British colonies. At its height, the British Empire was the largest empire in history.

Decline of Empire

In the 1900s the British Empire began to fall apart. Both World War I and the Great Depression hurt the British economy. Rebellions in Ireland forced Britain to grant self-rule to all but the northern part of Ireland. In 1949 the Republic of Ireland gained full independence. Movements for independence also emerged in Britain's overseas colonies. After World War II, Great Britain gave up most of its colonies. The British Empire was no more.

READING CHECK **Sequencing** What major events mark the history of the British Isles?

Culture

For years the British ruled much of the world. As a result, the government, people, and popular culture of the British Isles have influenced people all around the globe.

Government

The government of the United Kingdom is a **constitutional monarchy**, a type of democracy in which a king or queen serves as head of state but a legislature makes the laws. The English first limited the power of monarchs in the Middle Ages. A document known as **Magna Carta**, or Great Charter, limited the powers of kings. It also required everyone to obey the law. Today, a prime minister leads the British government. Most members of Britain's legislative body, known as Parliament, are elected.

The Republic of Ireland has a president as head of state. The president, who has limited powers, appoints a prime minister. Together with the Irish parliament, the prime minister runs the government.

People

For hundreds of years, the countries of the British Isles have had close ties. As a result, the countries share many culture traits. One similarity is their common heritage. Many people in the British Isles can trace their heritage to the region's early settlers, such as the Celts, Angles, and Saxons. Sports like soccer and rugby are another shared trait among the people of Britain.

Although people in the British Isles share many culture traits, each region still maintains its own unique identity. This is particularly true in Ireland and Scotland. Unlike the rest of the British Isles, most Irish are Roman Catholic. Irish Gaelic, a Celtic language, is one of the country's official languages. The people of Scotland have also maintained their unique culture.

Culture

People in different regions of the British Isles hold fast to regional traditions and customs. Here, Scots proudly display two symbols of Scottish culture—bagpipes and kilts.

It is not unusual in Scotland to see people wearing kilts and playing bagpipes on special occasions.

Immigrants from all corners of the world have settled in Britain. Many immigrants from former British colonies, such as India and Jamaica, add to the rich culture of the British Isles.

Popular Culture

British popular culture influences people all around the globe. For example, English is the language of business, education, and the Internet in many places. British music and literature are also popular. Millions of people around the globe listen to music by bands like Ireland's U2 and England's The Beatles and read works by British authors like William Shakespeare.

READING CHECK **Summarizing** What parts of British culture have spread around the world?

British Isles Today

The British Isles face some challenges. Efforts to bring peace to Northern Ireland and to maintain a powerful economy are key issues in the British Isles today.

Northern Ireland

One of the toughest problems facing the British Isles today is conflict in Northern Ireland. Disputes between the people of Northern Ireland have a long history.

In the 1500s Protestants from England and Scotland began settling in Northern Ireland. Over time, they outnumbered Irish Catholics in the area. When Ireland became a separate state, Northern Ireland's Protestant majority chose to remain part of the United Kingdom.

Since then, many Catholics in Northern Ireland believe they have not been treated fairly by Protestants. Some Catholics hope

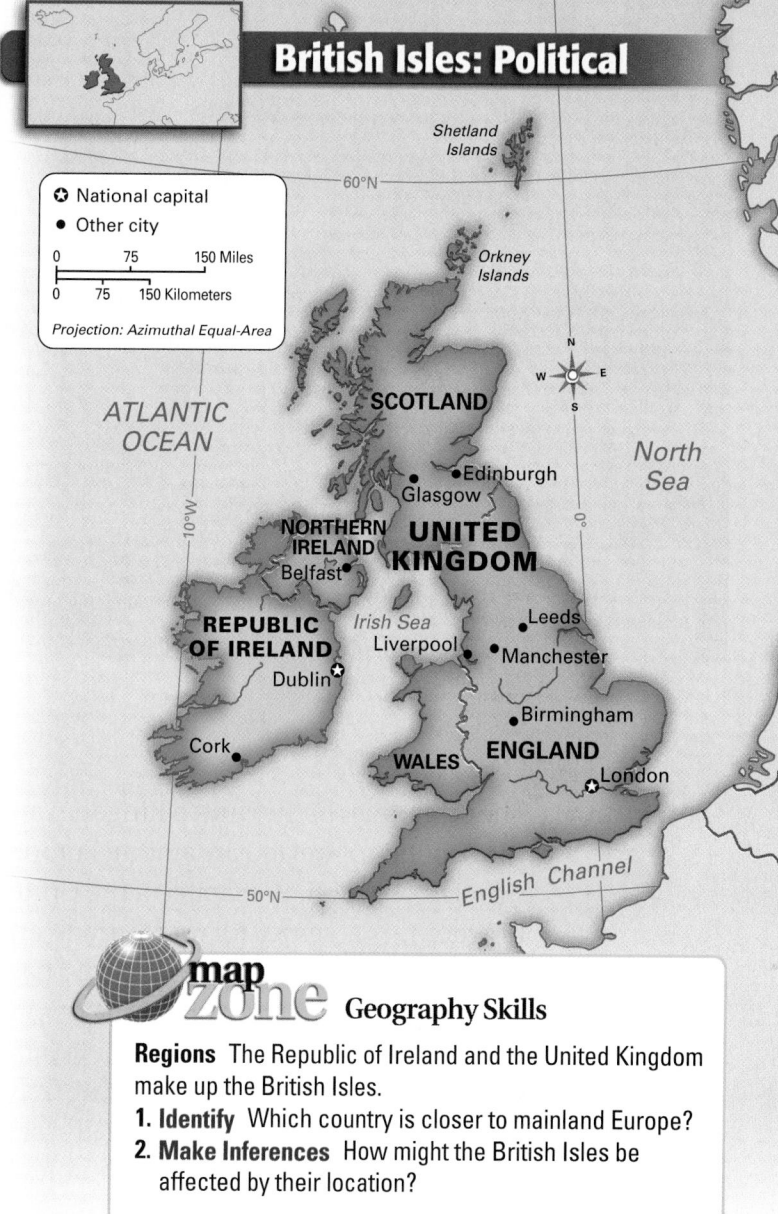

British Isles: Political

○ National capital
● Other city

0 75 150 Miles
0 75 150 Kilometers

Projection: Azimuthal Equal-Area

Shetland Islands

Orkney Islands

ATLANTIC OCEAN

SCOTLAND

• Edinburgh
Glasgow

North Sea

NORTHERN IRELAND
Belfast

UNITED KINGDOM

REPUBLIC OF IRELAND
Dublin ✪

Irish Sea
Liverpool

Leeds
Manchester

Cork

WALES

ENGLAND
• Birmingham
London ✪

English Channel

Geography Skills

Regions The Republic of Ireland and the United Kingdom make up the British Isles.

1. Identify Which country is closer to mainland Europe?

2. Make Inferences How might the British Isles be affected by their location?

to unite with the Republic of Ireland. For years the two sides have waged a bitter and violent struggle. In the late 1990s peace talks between the two warring sides began. An **agreement** eventually led to a cease-fire and the creation of a national assembly in Northern Ireland. However, the refusal of some groups to **disarm**, or give up all weapons, stalled the peace talks. Recently, however, hopes are once again high that peaceful relations between the groups will bring about a long-lasting peace.

ACADEMIC VOCABULARY

agreement a decision reached by two or more people or groups

The largest city in the British Isles, London serves as one of Europe's major financial centers.

The Economy

The economies of the United Kingdom and the Republic of Ireland are among Europe's strongest. **London**, the capital of the United Kingdom, is a center for world trade and industry. North Sea energy reserves have made the United Kingdom a major producer of oil and natural gas. In Ireland, computer equipment and software have become major industries, especially near **Dublin**, Ireland's capital. The economies of the United Kingdom and the Republic of Ireland also rely on service industries like banking, tourism, and insurance.

READING CHECK **Summarizing** What has been the cause of conflict in Northern Ireland?

SUMMARY AND PREVIEW You have learned about the rich history and culture of the British Isles. Next, you will learn about the countries of Scandinavia.

go.hrw.com
Online Quiz
KEYWORD: SG7 HP14

Section 2 Assessment

Reviewing Ideas, Terms, and Places

1. **a. Identify** What peoples invaded the British Isles?
   b. Make Inferences How did the Industrial Revolution strengthen the British Empire?
2. **a. Describe** What elements of British culture are found around the world?
   b. Explain How did **Magna Carta** affect British government?
3. **a. Define** What does **disarm** mean?
   b. Analyze What are the central issues of the conflict in Northern Ireland?
   c. Elaborate Why do you think the economy of the British Isles is so strong?

Critical Thinking

4. **Summarizing** Using your notes and a graphic organizer like the one here, summarize the history and culture of the British Isles in your own words.

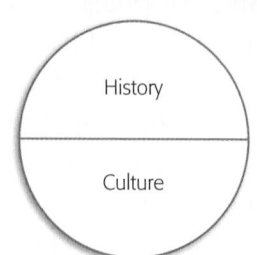

FOCUS ON WRITING

5. **Writing about the British Isles** What information about the British Isles do you think is most interesting? Take notes on what you could include in a letter to someone who has never visited the area.

Writing to Learn

Learn

Writing is an important tool for learning new information. When you write about what you read, you can better understand and remember information. For example, when you write a list of items you need from the grocery store, the act of writing can help you remember what to buy. Use the steps below to write to learn.

- Read the text carefully. Look for the main idea and important details.

- Think about the information you just read. Then summarize in your own words what you learned.

- Write a personal response to what you read. What do you think about the information? What questions might you have? How does this information affect you?

Practice

Use the steps you just learned to practice writing to learn. Read the paragraph below carefully, then complete a chart like the one here.

Tromso, Norway, is one of Europe's northern-most cities. Because of Earth's tilt and Tromso's location north of the Arctic Circle, the city experiences unusual conditions in both summer and winter. During the summer, the sun stays above the horizon continuously from late May to late July. In winter, residents of Tromso do not see the sun from November to January.

What I Learned	Personal Response

Apply

Read the information in Section 3 carefully. Then create a chart similar to the one above. In the first column, summarize the key ideas from the section in your own words. Use the second column to write your personal reaction to the information you learned.

Scandinavia

If **YOU** lived there...

You live in Copenhagen, the picturesque capital of Denmark. One of your favorite walks is along the waterfront, which is lined with colorful medieval buildings. Sailing boats of all sizes are anchored here. A famous statue in the harbor shows the Little Mermaid. But your favorite place of all is the huge amusement park called Tivoli Gardens, where you can enjoy fun and good food.

What sights would you show to a visitor?

What You Will Learn...

Main Ideas

1. The history of Scandinavia dates back to the time of the Vikings.
2. Scandinavia today is known for its peaceful and prosperous countries.

The Big Idea

Scandinavia has developed into one of the most stable and prosperous regions in Europe.

Key Terms and Places

Vikings, *p. 344*
Stockholm, *p. 346*
neutral, *p. 346*
uninhabitable, *p. 347*
Oslo, *p. 347*
Helsinki, *p. 347*
geysers, *p. 348*

TAKING NOTES As you read, take notes on the history of Scandinavia and the region today. Use a chart like the one below to help you organize your notes.

Scandinavia	
History	Region Today

BUILDING BACKGROUND After a long and warlike history, the modern countries of Scandinavia are models of peace and prosperity for the rest of Europe. Their cultures are similar in several ways, but each country has its own personality.

History

Hundreds of years ago, Scandinavia was home to warlike Vikings. The **Vikings** were Scandinavian warriors who raided Europe and the Mediterranean in the early Middle Ages. Excellent sailors, the Vikings used quick and powerful longboats to attack villages along coasts or rivers. The Vikings conquered the British Isles, Finland, and parts of France, Germany, and Russia. They were some of the most feared warriors of their time.

The Vikings were also great explorers. They established the first settlements in Iceland in the 800s and in Greenland in the 900s. A short time later, Vikings led by Leif Eriksson became the first Europeans to reach North America. The ruins of a Viking colony have been found in present-day Newfoundland, off the southeast coast of Canada.

In the 1100s the Viking raids ended. Powerful Scandinavian chiefs instead concentrated on strengthening their kingdoms. During the Middle Ages three kingdoms—Norway, Sweden, and Denmark—competed for power in the region.

Denmark was the first to gain the upper hand. By the late 1300s Denmark ruled a union of all the Scandinavian kingdoms and territories. Eventually, Sweden challenged Denmark's power.

In time, Sweden left the Danish-led union, taking Finland with it. Many years later, Sweden won control of Norway as well.

By the 1900s Scandinavian countries wanted their independence. Norway won its independence from Sweden in the early 1900s. Soon after, Finland became independent after centuries of foreign domination, or control, by Sweden and later by Russia. Iceland, then a Danish territory, declared its independence in 1944. To this day, however, Greenland remains a part of Denmark as a self-ruling territory.

READING CHECK **Analyzing** What historical ties do the countries of Scandinavia have?

FOCUS ON READING

What other word has the same meaning as *domination*? How can you tell?

Close-up

Viking Raids

The Vikings of Scandinavia launched raids on many European settlements in the early Middle Ages. Using powerful longships, Viking warriors attacked towns and villages near coasts and rivers. Vikings even sailed as far as North America in their longships.

A large woolen sail helped increase the ship's speed.

Sometimes as many as 30 oars spanned each side of a longship.

Viking longships were designed the same at each end. As a result, warriors did not have to turn the ship around to make a quick escape.

The longship's shallow design made river travel possible and allowed Viking raiders to sail their ships ashore.

ANALYSIS SKILL **ANALYZING VISUALS**

What aspects of Viking longships might have frightened Europeans who saw them approaching?

Scandinavia Today

Today the countries of Scandinavia have much in common. Similar political views, languages, and religion unite the region. The countries of Scandinavia have large, wealthy cities, strong economies, and well-educated workers. Scandinavians enjoy some of the world's highest standards of living. Each country provides its citizens with excellent social programs and services, such as free health care. Sweden, Denmark, Greenland, Norway, Finland, and Iceland are among the world's most peaceful, stable, and prosperous nations.

Sweden

Sweden is Scandinavia's largest and most populous country. Most Swedes live in the southern part of the country in large towns and cities. In fact, more than 80 percent of Swedes live in urban areas. **Stockholm**, Sweden's capital and largest city, is located on the east coast near the Baltic Sea. Often called a floating city, Stockholm is built on 14 islands and part of the mainland.

For almost 200 years, Sweden has been a neutral country. **Neutral** means that it has chosen not to take sides in an international conflict. Sweden does, however, play an active role in the United Nations as well as the European Union.

Denmark

Denmark, once the most powerful country in Scandinavia, is also the smallest. It is Scandinavia's most densely populated country, with some 333 people per square mile (128 per square km).

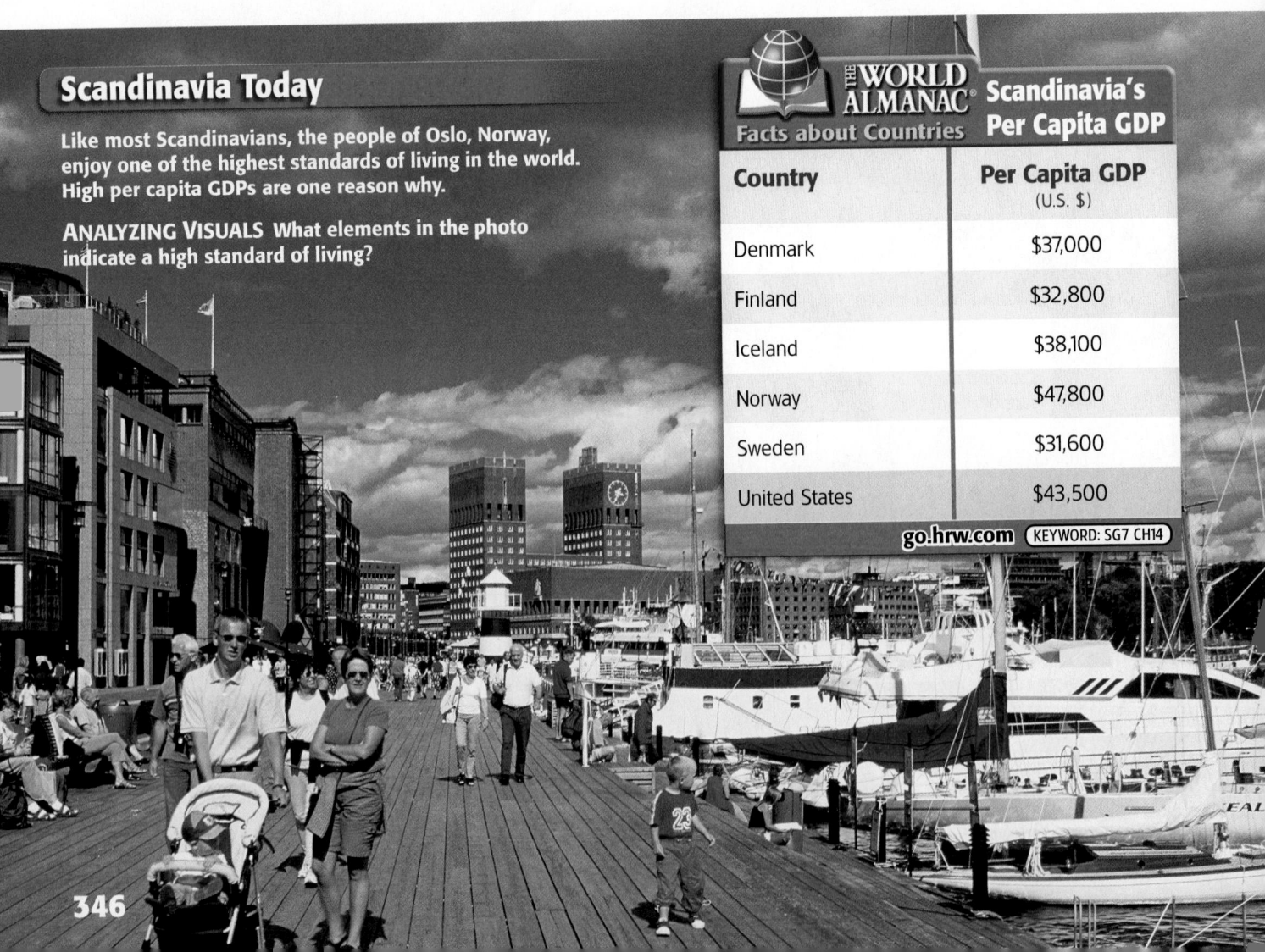

Scandinavia Today

Like most Scandinavians, the people of Oslo, Norway, enjoy one of the highest standards of living in the world. High per capita GDPs are one reason why.

ANALYZING VISUALS What elements in the photo indicate a high standard of living?

THE WORLD ALMANAC® Facts about Countries — **Scandinavia's Per Capita GDP**

Country	Per Capita GDP (U.S. $)
Denmark	$37,000
Finland	$32,800
Iceland	$38,100
Norway	$47,800
Sweden	$31,600
United States	$43,500

go.hrw.com KEYWORD: SG7 CH14

About 50 percent of Denmark's land is used for farming. Farm goods, especially meat and dairy products, are important Danish exports. Denmark also has modern industries, including iron, steel, textiles, and electronics industries.

Greenland

The island of Greenland is geographically part of North America. However, it is a territory of Denmark. A thick ice sheet covers about 80 percent of the island. Because of this, much of Greenland is **uninhabitable**, or not able to support human settlement. Most people live on the island's southwest coast where the climate is warmest.

Recently, a movement for complete independence from Denmark has gained popularity. However, economic problems make independence unlikely, as Greenland relies heavily on imports and economic aid from Denmark.

Norway

With one of the longest coastlines in the world, Norway takes advantage of its access to the sea. Fjords shelter Norway's many harbors. Its fishing and shipping fleets are among the largest in the world. **Oslo**, Norway's capital, is the country's leading seaport as well as its industrial center.

Norway has other valuable resources as well. Oil and natural gas provide Norway with the highest per capita GDP in Scandinavia. However, North Sea oil fields are expected to run dry over the next century. Despite strong economic ties to the rest of Europe, Norway's citizens have refused to join the European Union.

Finland

Finland is Scandinavia's easternmost country. It lies between Sweden and Russia. The capital and largest city is **Helsinki**, which is located on the southern coast.

FOCUS ON CULTURE

The Sami

The Sami (SAH-mee) people are a unique culture group that lives in far northern Norway, Sweden, Finland, and parts of Russia. They are descendants of Scandinavia's earliest settlers. Traditionally, Sami have earned a living herding reindeer, farming, and fishing. While today's Sami often work and live in modern cities and towns, they try to preserve many traditional Sami culture traits. The Sami language is taught in public schools, traditional reindeer grazing land is protected, and organizations promote Sami customs.

Making Inferences Why do you think the Sami are trying to preserve their traditions and customs?

As with other countries in the region, trade is important to Finland. Paper and other forest products are major exports. Shipbuilding and electronics are also important industries in Finland.

Iceland

Iceland is much greener than its name implies. Fertile farmland along the island's coast produces potatoes and vegetables and supports cattle and sheep.

Icelanders also make good use of their other natural resources. Fish from the rich waters of the Atlantic Ocean account for about 70 percent of Iceland's exports.

Iceland

Iceland's geysers and hot springs produce great amounts of energy. Geothermal plants like this one near the Blue Lagoon hot spring provide heat for buildings and homes throughout the country.

In addition, steam from hot springs and geysers produces geothermal energy. **Geysers** are springs that shoot hot water and steam into the air. Geothermal energy heats many of Iceland's buildings. Each year thousands of tourists flock to see Iceland's many geysers, volcanoes, and glaciers.

READING CHECK Comparing and Contrasting In what ways are the countries of Scandinavia similar and different?

SUMMARY AND PREVIEW Scandinavia today is a region of relative peace and stability. A common history and culture link the people of the region. Today, Scandinavia is one of the wealthiest regions in Europe and in the world. In the next chapter, you will learn about the unique geography, history, and culture of another European region— Eastern Europe.

Section 3 Assessment

go.hrw.com
Online Quiz
KEYWORD: SG7 HP14

Reviewing Ideas, Terms, and Places

1. **a. Identify** Who were the **Vikings**?
   b. Analyze What effect did the Vikings have on Scandinavian history?
   c. Evaluate Do you think the Vikings helped or hurt the future of Scandinavia? Explain your answer.
2. **a. Define** What does the term **neutral** mean?
   b. Compare What features do the countries of Scandinavia have in common today?
   c. Elaborate In which Scandinavian country would you prefer to live? Why?

Critical Thinking

3. **Finding Main Ideas** Use your notes and this chart to identify two main ideas about Scandinavia's history and two about its culture today.

History	Today

FOCUS ON WRITING

4. **Writing about Scandinavia** Where would you travel and what would you see in Scandinavia? Take notes on the details you might include in your letter.

Geography's Impact
video series
Review the video to answer the closing question:
How have Icelanders made good use of their island's volcanoes?

Visual Summary

Use the visual summary below to help you review the main ideas of the chapter.

QUICK FACTS

Low mountains and plentiful resources are key features of Northern Europe's physical geography.

The British Isles are known around the world for their rich history, vibrant culture, and healthy economies.

The countries of Scandinavia are among the most peaceful and prosperous in the world.

Reviewing Vocabulary, Terms, and Places

Write each word defined below, and circle each letter marked by a star. Then write the word these letters spell.

1. _ _ *_ _ _ _ —to give up all weapons

2. _ _ _ _ _ _ _ _ _ *—a decision reached by two or more people or groups

3. _ _ *_ _ _ —a narrow inlet of the sea set between high, rocky cliffs

4. _ *_ _ _ _ _ _ _ _ _ _ _ —a region in far Northern Europe that crosses the Arctic Circle

5. _ _ *_ _ _ _ —warriors from Northern Europe who raided much of Europe and the Mediterranean during the early Middle Ages

6. _ _ _ _ *_ _ _ _ _ _ _ _ _ _ —unable to support human settlement

7. _ _ *_ _ _ _ _ _ _ _ energy—energy produced by the heat of the planet's interior

8. _ _ _ *_ _ _ —the capital of the Republic of Ireland

9. _ _ _ *_ _ _ —main or most important

Comprehension and Critical Thinking

SECTION 1 *(Pages 334–337)*

10. **a.** **Identify** What are the major resources found in Northern Europe?

    b. **Analyze** Explain how the North Atlantic Drift is responsible for the relatively mild climates in Northern Europe.

    c. **Elaborate** In which region of Northern Europe would you prefer to live—the British Isles or Scandinavia? Why?

SECTION 2 *(Pages 338–342)*

11. **a.** **Describe** What culture traits do the people of the British Isles share in common?

    b. **Make Inferences** Why did the people of Ireland want to break away from the British Empire?

    c. **Predict** How might the conflict in Northern Ireland affect the future of the United Kingdom?

12. a. Recall What countries make up Scandinavia?

b. Compare and Contrast In what ways are the countries of Scandinavia similar and different?

c. Elaborate Why do you think Scandinavian countries today are so prosperous and stable?

Social Studies Skills

13. Writing to Learn Read the paragraph below carefully, then summarize it in your own words. Finally, write a personal response to what you learned in the paragraph.

> In the mid-1800s Ireland was devastated by a severe famine. For many Irish, the potato was a key part of their diet. When a disease infected potato crops around the country, millions were left without enough to eat. About 1.5 million Irish died as a result of the Irish Potato Famine.

FOCUS ON READING AND WRITING

Using Context Clues—Synonyms *Use context clues to determine the meaning of the underlined words in the sentences below.*

14. Wealthy in part because of its many natural resources, Scandinavia is one of the most affluent regions in Europe.

15. Thanks to the North Atlantic Drift, the British Isles are rarely affected by inclement, or harsh, weather.

16. Dissent, or disagreement, between Catholics and Protestants has caused years of conflict in Northern Ireland.

Writing a Letter *Use your notes from the chapter and the directions below to write a letter.*

17. Tell your friends and family members what you have seen on your travels in the British Isles and Scandinavia. You may want to organize the information by country. For example, you could start with a flight into London and end in Iceland. Include descriptions of fascinating physical features as well as any cities or cultural activities that are unusual or interesting.

Using the Internet

18. Activity: Creating a Poster What does a medieval king have to do with modern democracy? Magna Carta was signed in 1215 by King John I of England. It established the principle that no one, including the king, is above the law. It also opened the door to a more democratic government in England. Centuries later, emerging democracies in the United States and France looked to Magna Carta for guidance. Enter the activity keyword and learn more about Magna Carta and its relationship with modern democracy. Then create a poster to display some of the ways this document has influenced modern democratic governments.

Map Activity

19. Northern Europe On a separate sheet of paper, match the letters on the map with their correct labels.

Dublin	Oslo
English Channel	Reykjavik
Helsinki	Scandinavian Peninsula
London	Stockholm

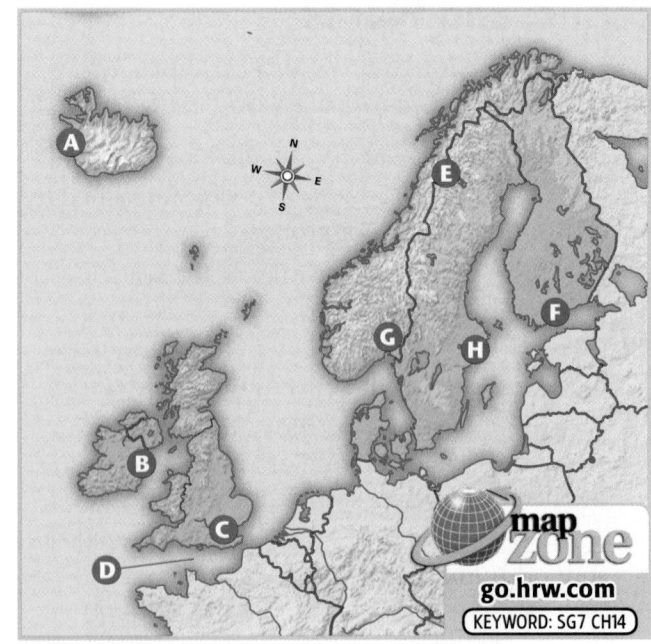

DIRECTIONS: Read questions 1 through 7 and write the letter of the best response. Then read question 8 and write your own well-constructed response.

1 What group of people from Northern Europe raided Europe between 800 and 1100?

A Anglo-Saxons

B Celts

C Sami

D Vikings

2 Which of the following accounts for the relatively mild climate throughout much of Northern Europe?

A Arctic Ocean

B few mountains or hills

C North Atlantic Drift

D seasonal monsoons

3 Which Northern European city is a major European economic center?

A Dublin

B Helsinki

C London

D Stockholm

4 What important energy source does Iceland use to heat buildings?

A geothermal energy

B hydroelectric energy

C natural gas

D solar energy

5 Since the early 1900s, disputes and even violence have disrupted life in

A Finland.

B Greenland.

C Northern Ireland.

D Scotland.

Scandinavia: Population Density

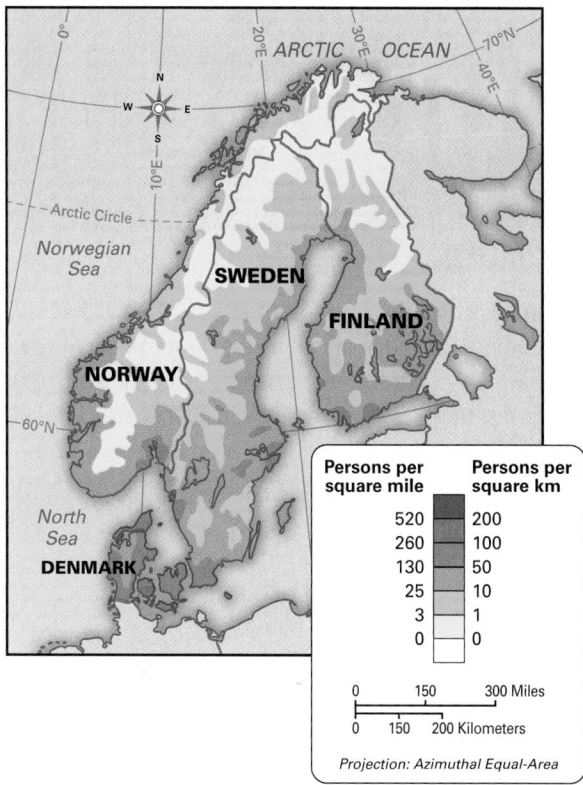

6 According to the map above, which part of Scandinavia is *least* densely populated?

A Northern Scandinavia

B Southern Scandinavia

C Eastern Scandinavia

D Western Scandinavia

7 Which of the following characteristics do the countries of Scandinavia have in common?

A high standards of living

B membership in the European Union

C status as neutral nations

D high unemployment rates

8 **Extended Response Question** Use the climate map in Section 1 and the map above to write a paragraph explaining how climate might affect settlement patterns in Scandinavia.

CHAPTER 15

Eastern Europe

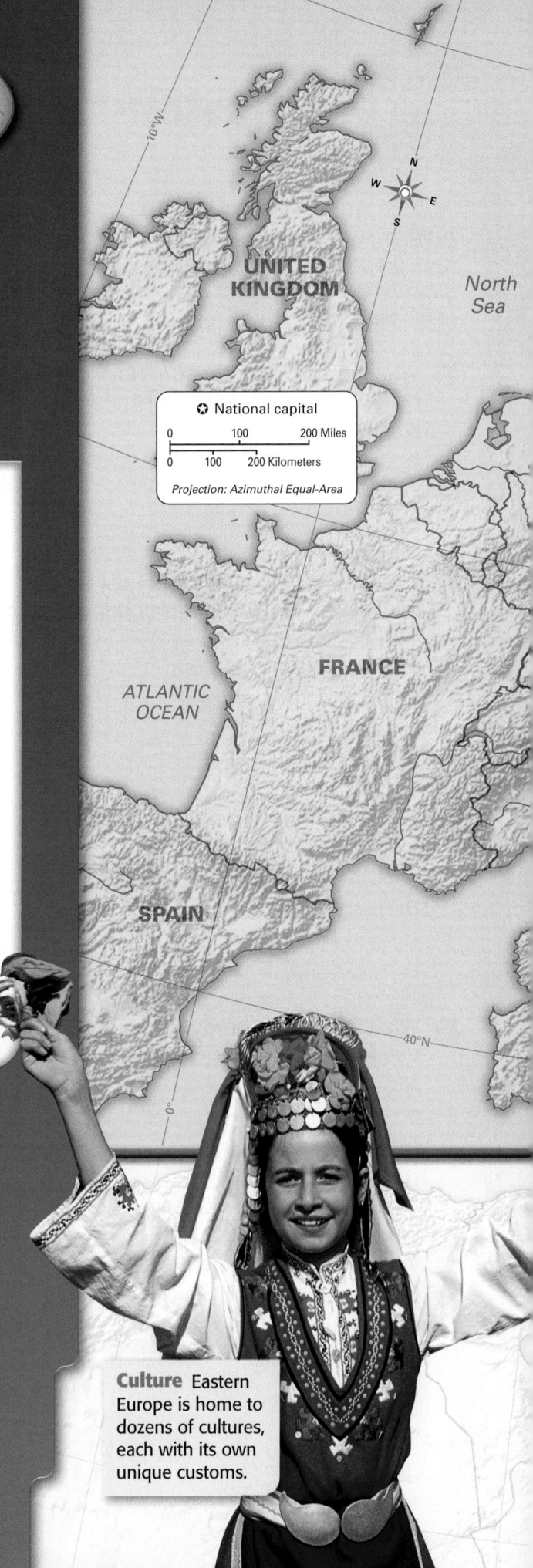

What You Will Learn...

In this chapter you will learn about the countries of Eastern Europe. Once dominated by the Soviet Union, these countries have experienced major changes since the early 1990s. In some cases, those changes have been peaceful and have led to great economic success. In other places, the changes resulted in war, economic hardship, and political problems.

FOCUS ON READING AND VIEWING

Understanding Problems and Solutions Writers sometimes organize information by stating a problem and then explaining the solution taken to solve it. To understand this type of writing, you need to identify both problems and solutions. **See the lesson, Understanding Problems and Solutions, on page R16.**

Presenting and Viewing Visual Reports After you read this chapter, you will present an oral report about one Eastern European country. You will also create a poster showing important features of the country. Finally, you will view and critique your classmates' reports and posters.

Culture Eastern Europe is home to dozens of cultures, each with its own unique customs.

map zone Geography Skills

Place Some of Eastern Europe's 20 countries are ancient, but others have been formed or changed more recently.

1. Name What is the region's largest country?

2. Make Generalizations Have you heard about any countries on this map in the news? What have you heard?

go.hrw.com KEYWORD: SG7 CH15

Tallinn
ESTONIA
Riga
LATVIA
Baltic Sea
LITHUANIA
Vilnius
Minsk
BELARUS
RUSSIA
GERMANY
POLAND
Warsaw
RUSSIA
Kiev
Prague
CZECH REPUBLIC
SLOVAKIA
Bratislava
UKRAINE
AUSTRIA
Budapest
HUNGARY
MOLDOVA
Chișinău
SLOVENIA
Ljubljana
Zagreb
CROATIA
ROMANIA
BOSNIA AND HERZEGOVINA
Belgrade
Bucharest
Danube River
Black Sea
Sarajevo
SERBIA
ITALY
Adriatic Sea
MONTENEGRO
KOSOVO
Pristina
BULGARIA
Podgorica
Sofia
Skopje
Tirana
MACEDONIA
ALBANIA
TURKEY
GREECE
Aegean Sea

20°E

50°N

30°E

HOLT

Geography's Impact

video series
Watch the video to understand the impact of ethnic conflict in Sarajevo.

Geography Like the Danube River shown here, many rivers flow through the mountains and plains of Eastern Europe.

History Buildings in cities like Prague, Czech Republic, are symbols of Eastern Europe's long history.

Physical Geography

What You Will Learn...

Main Ideas

1. The physical features of Eastern Europe include wide open plains, rugged mountain ranges, and many rivers.
2. The climate and vegetation of Eastern Europe differ widely in the north and the south.

The Big Idea

The physical geography of Eastern Europe varies greatly from place to place.

Key Places

Carpathians, *p. 354*
Balkan Peninsula, *p. 355*
Danube, *p. 356*
Chernobyl, *p. 357*

TAKING NOTES Draw a chart like the one below. As you read this section, use the chart to take notes about the landforms, climate, and vegetation of Eastern Europe.

Landforms	Climate	Vegetation

If **YOU** lived there...

You are traveling on a boat down the Danube River, one of the longest in Europe. As you float downstream, you pass through dozens of towns and cities. Outside of the cities, the banks are lined with huge castles, soaring churches, and busy farms. From time to time, other boats pass you, some loaded with passengers and some with goods.

Why do you think the Danube is so busy?

BUILDING BACKGROUND The physical geography of Eastern Europe varies widely from north to south. Many of the landforms you learned about in earlier chapters, including the Northern European Plain and the Alps, extend into this region.

Physical Features

Eastern Europe is a land of amazing contrasts. The northern parts of the region lie along the cold, often stormy shores of the Baltic Sea. In the south, however, are warm, sunny beaches along the Adriatic and Black seas. Jagged mountain peaks jut high into the sky in some places, while wildflowers dot the gently rolling hills of other parts of the region. These contrasts stem from the region's wide variety of landforms, water features, and climates.

Landforms

As you can see on the map, the landforms of Eastern Europe are arranged in a series of broad bands. In the north is the Northern European Plain. As you have already learned, this large plain stretches across most of Northern Europe.

South of the Northern European Plain is a low mountain range called the **Carpathians** (kahr-PAY-thee-uhnz). These rugged mountains are an extension of the Alps of West-Central Europe. They stretch in a long arc from the Alps to the Black Sea area.

South and west of the Carpathians is another plain, the Great Hungarian Plain. As its name suggests, this fertile area is located mostly within Hungary.

South of the plain are more mountains, the Dinaric (duh-NAR-ik) Alps and Balkan Mountains. These two ranges together cover most of the **Balkan Peninsula**, one of the largest peninsulas in Europe. It extends south into the Mediterranean Sea.

Water Features

Like the rest of the continent, Eastern Europe has many bodies of water that affect how people live. To the southwest is the Adriatic Sea, an important route for transportation and trade. To the east, the Black Sea serves the same <u>function</u>. In the far north is the Baltic Sea. It is another important trade route, though parts of the sea freeze over in the winter.

ACADEMIC VOCABULARY

function
use or purpose

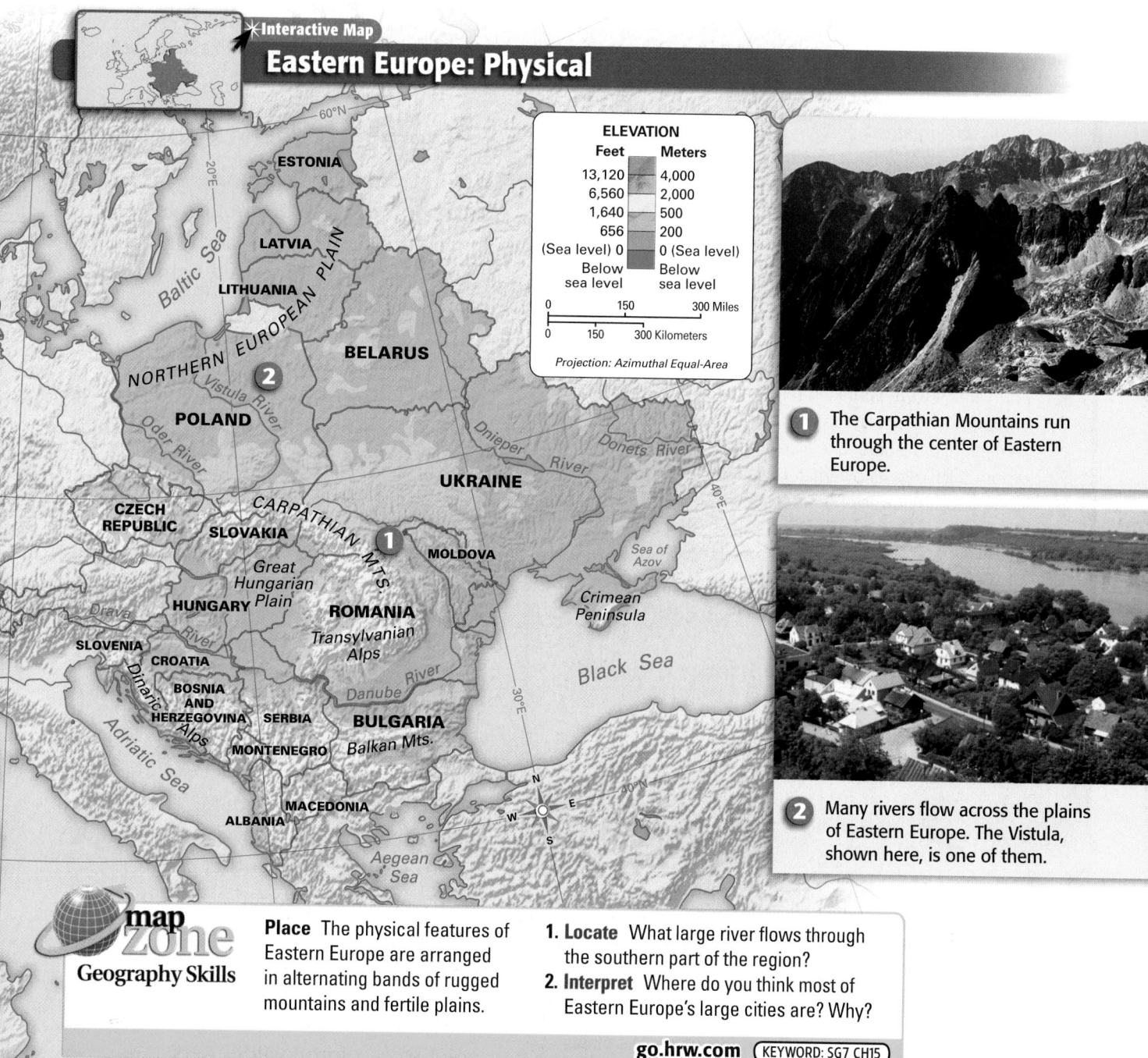

Interactive Map

Eastern Europe: Physical

ELEVATION

Feet		Meters
13,120		4,000
6,560		2,000
1,640		500
656		200
(Sea level) 0		0 (Sea level)
Below sea level		Below sea level

0   150   300 Miles
0   150   300 Kilometers

Projection: Azimuthal Equal-Area

ESTONIA
LATVIA
LITHUANIA
Baltic Sea
NORTHERN EUROPEAN PLAIN
BELARUS
Vistula River
POLAND
Oder River
CZECH REPUBLIC
SLOVAKIA
CARPATHIAN MTS.
UKRAINE
Dnieper River
Donets River
MOLDOVA
Sea of Azov
Great Hungarian Plain
HUNGARY
ROMANIA
Transylvanian Alps
Crimean Peninsula
SLOVENIA
Drava River
CROATIA
BOSNIA AND HERZEGOVINA
Dinaric Alps
SERBIA
Danube River
BULGARIA
Balkan Mts.
Black Sea
MONTENEGRO
Adriatic Sea
MACEDONIA
ALBANIA
Aegean Sea

N E W S

① The Carpathian Mountains run through the center of Eastern Europe.

② Many rivers flow across the plains of Eastern Europe. The Vistula, shown here, is one of them.

map zone
Geography Skills

Place The physical features of Eastern Europe are arranged in alternating bands of rugged mountains and fertile plains.

1. **Locate** What large river flows through the southern part of the region?
2. **Interpret** Where do you think most of Eastern Europe's large cities are? Why?

go.hrw.com   KEYWORD: SG7 CH15

In addition to these seas, Eastern Europe has several rivers that are vital paths for transportation and trade. The longest of these rivers, the **Danube** (DAN-yoob), begins in Germany and flows east across the Great Hungarian Plain. The river winds its way through nine countries before it finally empties into the Black Sea.

As you might expect, the Danube is central to the Eastern European economy. Some of the region's largest cities lie on the Danube's banks. Thousands of ships travel up and down the river every year, loaded with both goods and people. In addition, dams on the western parts of the river generate much of the region's electricity. Unfortunately, the high level of activity on the Danube has left it heavily polluted.

READING CHECK **Finding Main Ideas** What are the main bodies of water in Eastern Europe?

Climate and Vegetation

Like its landforms, the climates and natural vegetation of Eastern Europe vary widely. In fact, the climates and landscapes found across Eastern Europe determine which plants will grow there.

The Baltic Coast

The shores of the Baltic Sea are the coldest location in Eastern Europe. Winters there are long, cold, and harsh. This northern part of Eastern Europe receives less rain than other areas, but fog is common. In fact, some parts of the area have as few as 30 sunny days each year. The climate allows huge forests to grow there.

The Interior Plains

The interior plains of Eastern Europe are much milder than the far north. Winters there can be very cold, but summers are generally pleasant and mild. The western parts of these plains receive much more rain than those areas farther east.

Because of this variation in climate, the plains of Eastern Europe have many types of vegetation. Huge forests cover much of the north. South of these forests are open grassy plains. In the spring, these plains erupt with colorful wildflowers.

Primary Source

BOOK
The Plains of Ukraine

One of Russia's greatest novelists, Nikolai Gogol (gaw-guhl), was actually born in what is now Ukraine. Very fond of his homeland, he frequently wrote about its great beauty. In this passage from the short story "Taras Bulba," he describes a man's passage across the wide open fields of Ukraine.

❝No plough had ever passed over the immeasurable waves of wild growth; horses alone, hidden in it as in a forest, trod it down. Nothing in nature could be finer. The whole surface resembled a golden-green ocean, upon which were sprinkled millions of different flowers. Through the tall, slender stems of the grass peeped light-blue, dark-blue, and lilac star-thistles; the yellow broom thrust up its pyramidal head; the parasol-shaped white flower of the false flax shimmered on high. A wheat-ear, brought God knows whence, was filling out to ripening. Amongst the roots of this luxuriant vegetation ran partridges with outstretched necks. The air was filled with the notes of a thousand different birds.❞

—from "Taras Bulba," by Nikolai Gogol

ANALYSIS SKILL **ANALYZING PRIMARY SOURCES**

What features does Gogol describe on the plains of Ukraine?

Radiation Cleanup

A nuclear accident in 1986 leaked dangerous amounts of radiation into Eastern Europe's soil. Ukraine's government and scientists are still working to repair the damage.

Unfortunately, Eastern Europe's forests were greatly damaged by a terrible accident in 1986. A faulty reactor at the **Chernobyl** (chuhr-NOH-buhl) nuclear power plant in Ukraine exploded, releasing huge amounts of radiation into the air. This radiation poisoned millions of acres of forest and ruined soil across much of the region.

The Balkan Coast

Along the Adriatic Sea, the Balkan coast has a Mediterranean climate, with warm summers and mild winters. As a result, its beaches are popular tourist destinations.

Because a Mediterranean climate does not bring much rain, the Balkan coast does not have many forests. Instead, the land there is covered by shrubs and hardy trees that do not need much water.

READING CHECK **Contrasting** How do the climates and vegetation of Eastern Europe vary?

SUMMARY AND PREVIEW The landforms of Eastern Europe vary widely, as do its cultures. Next you will study the cultures of the northernmost parts of the region.

FOCUS ON READING

What problems did the Chernobyl accident cause for Eastern Europe?

Section 1 Assessment

Reviewing Ideas, Terms, and Places

1. **a. Identify** What are the major mountain ranges of Eastern Europe?
   b. Make Inferences How do you think the physical features of Eastern Europe influence where people live?
   c. Elaborate Why is the **Danube** so important to the people of Eastern Europe?
2. **a. Describe** What is the climate of the **Balkan Peninsula** like?
   b. Explain Why are there few trees in the far southern areas of Eastern Europe?
   c. Predict How do you think the lingering effects of the **Chernobyl** accident affect the plant life of Eastern Europe?

Critical Thinking

3. **Categorizing** Draw a chart like the one shown here. In each column, identify the landforms, climates, and vegetation of each area in Eastern Europe.

	Landforms	Climates	Vegetation
Baltic coast			
Interior plains			
Balkan coast			

FOCUS ON VIEWING

4. **Presenting Physical Geography** Until you decide what country you will report on, take notes about all of them. Make a list of the countries of Eastern Europe and the physical features found in each.

Poland and the Baltic Republics

What You Will Learn...

Main Ideas

1. History ties Poland and the Baltic Republics together.
2. The cultures of Poland and the Baltic Republics differ in language and religion but share common customs.
3. Economic growth is a major issue in the region today.

The Big Idea

The histories of Poland and the Baltic Republics, both as free states and as areas dominated by the Soviet Union, still shape life there.

Key Terms and Places

infrastructure, *p. 361*
Warsaw, *p. 361*

TAKING NOTES As you read, take notes about key events in the histories of Poland and the Baltic Republics, their cultures, and their economies today. You may want to organize your notes in a table like the one below.

Poland and the Baltics		
Key Events	Culture	Economy

If YOU lived there...

You live in the beautiful and historic city of Krakow, Poland. Over the centuries, terrible wars have damaged many Polish cities, but Krakow is fllled with cobblestone streets, romantic castles, and elaborate churches. The city is home to one of Europe's oldest shopping malls, the 500-year-old Cloth Hall. Glorious old Catholic churches also rise high above many parts of the city.

What does the city suggest about Polish history?

BUILDING BACKGROUND Located on the Northern European Plain, Poland and the Baltic Republics are caught between east and west. As a result, the region has often been a battlefield. On the other hand, this location at a cultural crossroads has helped each country develop its own distinctive culture, traditions, and customs.

History

The area around the Baltic Sea was settled in ancient times by many different groups. In time, these groups developed into the people who live in the region today. One group became the Estonians, one became the Latvians and Lithuanians, and one became the Polish. Each of these groups had its own language and culture. Over the centuries, however, shared historical events have helped tie all these people together.

Early History

By the Middle Ages, the people of the Baltics had formed many independent kingdoms. The kingdoms of Lithuania and Poland were large and strong. Together they ruled much of Eastern and Northern Europe. The smaller kingdoms of Latvia and Estonia, on the other hand, were not strong. In fact, they were often invaded by their more powerful neighbors. These invasions continued through the 1800s.

Eastern Europe under Soviet Influence, 1988

Extent of Soviet influence

0   100   200 Miles

0 100 200 Kilometers

Projection: Azimuthal Equal-Area

map zone

Geography Skills

Place From World War II until 1989, politics in Eastern Europe was dominated by the Soviet Union.

1. **Identify** Which modern countries were part of the Soviet Union?
2. **Name** What other countries have changed since 1988?

go.hrw.com KEYWORD: SG7 CH15

BIOGRAPHY

Pope John Paul II
(1920–2005)

Karol Wojtyla, later called Pope John Paul II, was born in Poland. Raised a Roman Catholic, he became a priest shortly after the Soviets took over the country. After becoming pope in 1978, he encouraged the Polish people to protest against their Communist government. Largely because of his efforts, Poland broke away from the Soviet Union in 1989.

The World Wars

Both World War I and World War II were devastating for the Baltic people. Much of the fighting in World War I took place in Poland. As a result, millions of Poles—both soldiers and civilians—died. Thousands more were killed in the Baltic countries.

World War II began when the Germans invaded Poland from the west. As the Germans pushed through Poland from the west, the army of the Soviet Union invaded Poland from the east. Once again, Poland suffered tremendously. Millions of people were killed, and property all over Poland was destroyed. Estonia, Latvia, and Lithuania also suffered. All three countries were occupied by the Soviet army.

Soviet Domination

As the map shows, the Soviet Union totally dominated Eastern Europe after World War II. Estonia, Latvia, and Lithuania became parts of the Soviet Union. Poland remained free, but the Soviets forced the Poles to accept a Communist government.

Many Eastern Europeans opposed Communist rule, and the Communist governments in the region eventually fell. Poland rejected Communism and elected new leaders in 1989. The Baltic Republics broke away from the Soviet Union in 1991 and became independent once more.

READING CHECK **Analyzing** How did the Soviet Union influence the region's history?

FOCUS ON READING
What problems were created in the Baltic region after World War II?

Culture

In some ways, the cultures of Poland and the Baltic Republics are very different from each other. For example, people in the area speak different languages and practice different religions. In other ways, however, their cultures are actually quite similar. Because the four countries lie near each other, common customs have taken root in all of them. People cook similar foods and enjoy the same types of entertainment.

CONNECTING TO the Arts

Baltic Embroidery

One of the crafts for which the people of the Baltic region are best known is embroidery. This type of decorative sewing lets people create beautiful designs. They use these designs on their clothing, tablecloths, and other cloth goods.

For centuries, people in the Baltic countries—both men and women—have embroidered the clothing they wear on special occasions, such as weddings. They use many colors of thread to sew intricate patterns of flowers, hearts, and geometric designs. Because the embroidery is done by hand, it can take hours of work to create a single garment.

Drawing Conclusions Why do you think people embroider only clothing for special occasions?

Cultural Differences

The most obvious differences between the cultures of the Baltic countries are their languages and religions. Because the countries were first settled by different groups, each has its own language today. Of these languages, only Latvian and Lithuanian are similar to each other. Polish is related to the languages of countries farther south. Estonian is similar to Finnish.

Trade patterns and invasions have affected religion in the area. Poland and Lithuania traded mostly with Roman Catholic countries, and so most people there are Catholic. Latvia and Estonia, on the other hand, were ruled for a long time by Sweden. Because the Swedish are mostly Lutheran, most people in Latvia and Estonia are Lutheran as well.

Cultural Similarities

Unlike language and religion, many of the customs practiced in the Baltic countries cross national boundaries. For example, people in these countries eat many of the same types of foods. Potatoes and sausage are very popular, as is seafood.

Other shared customs tie the Baltic countries together as well. For example, people in all three countries practice many of the same crafts. Among these crafts are pottery, painting, and embroidery.

Also common to the countries of the Baltic Sea area is a love of music and dance. For centuries, people of the Baltics have been famous for their musical abilities. Frédéric Chopin (1810–1849), for example, was a famous Polish pianist and composer. Today, people throughout Poland and the Baltic Republics gather at music festivals to hear popular and traditional tunes.

READING CHECK **Comparing** How are the cultures of the Baltic countries similar?

The Region Today

Estonia, Latvia, Lithuania, and Poland all still feel the effects of decades of Soviet rule. The economies of all four countries suffered because the Soviets did not build a decent infrastructure. An **infrastructure** is the set of resources, like roads, airports, and factories, that a country needs in order to support economic activities. The many factories built by the Soviets in Poland and the Baltics could not produce as many goods as those in Western Europe.

Today Poland and the Baltic Republics are working to rebuild and strengthen their economies. They are replacing the old and outdated factories built by the Soviets with new ones that take advantage of modern technology. As a result, cities like **Warsaw**, the capital of Poland, have become major industrial centers.

To further their economic growth, the countries of this region are also seeking new sources of income. One area in which they have found some success is tourism. Since the collapse of the Soviet Union in 1991, many Americans and Western Europeans have begun visiting. Polish cities like Warsaw and Krakow have long attracted tourists with their rich history and famous sites. Vilnius, Lithuania; Tallinn, Estonia; and Riga, Latvia, have also become tourist attractions. People are drawn to these cities by their fascinating cultures, cool summer climates, and historic sites.

READING CHECK **Generalizing** How has the region changed in recent years?

SUMMARY AND PREVIEW Poland and the Baltic Republics are still feeling the effects of decades of Soviet rule. In the next section, you will learn about more countries that feel the same effects.

Tourism in the Baltics

Baltic cities such as Tallinn, Estonia, draw many tourists each year. These tourists are attracted to the cities' many churches and cultural sites.

go.hrw.com
Online Quiz
KEYWORD: SG7 HP15

Section 2 Assessment

Reviewing Ideas, Terms, and Places

1. **a. Identify** What country ran the area after World War II?
   b. Draw Conclusions How do you think the two world wars affected the people of Poland?
2. **a. Describe** How do the languages spoken in Poland and the Baltic Republics reflect the region's history?
   b. Elaborate Why do you think that people across the region practice many of the same customs?
3. **a. Recall** What is one industry that has grown in the region since the fall of the Soviet Union?
   b. Explain How did Soviet rule hurt the area's economy?

Critical Thinking

4. **Identifying Cause and Effect** Draw a chart like the one shown here. In each box on the right, explain how the event affected the cultures or economies of the region.

Event	Effect
Soviet rule	
Breakup of the Soviet Union	
Growth of tourism	

FOCUS ON VIEWING

5. **Considering Poland and the Baltics** If you were to give your report about Poland or one of the Baltic Republics, what details would you include? Write down some ideas.

Inland Eastern Europe

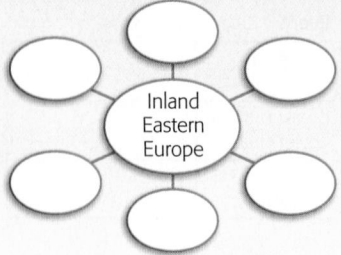
If **YOU** lived there...

You are a tourist visiting Budapest, the capital of Hungary. Early one morning, you stand on a bridge over the glittering water of the Danube River. You read in your guidebook that the two banks of the river were once separate cities. On the bank to your right, you see huge castles and churches standing on a tall hill. To your left is the Parliament building, obviously a much newer building.

What might have brought the cities together?

BUILDING BACKGROUND The city of Budapest, like many of the cities of inland Eastern Europe, has a long, colorful history. Various parts of the city reflect wildly different eras in its past. Medieval churches, for example, stand near huge imperial fortresses and Soviet-built warehouses, all relics of the region's history.

History and Culture

Located on the Northern European and Hungarian plains, inland Eastern Europe consists of six countries. They are the Czech (CHEK) Republic, Slovakia, Hungary, Ukraine, Belarus, and Moldova. Throughout history, many different peoples ruled these countries. Each ruling group influenced the culture and customs of the area.

Czech Republic and Slovakia

The area that now includes the Czech Republic and Slovakia was once home to many small kingdoms. People called the Slavs founded these kingdoms. The Slavs were people from Asia who moved into Europe by AD 1000. Eventually, strong neighbors such as Austria conquered the Slavic kingdoms.

After World War I, the victorious Allies took land away from Austria to form a new nation, Czechoslovakia. About fifty years later, in 1993, it split into the Czech Republic and Slovakia.

Because of their location, these two countries have long had ties with Western Europe. As a result, Western influences are common. For example, many people in the two countries are Roman Catholic. The architecture of cities like **Prague** (PRAHG), the capital of the Czech Republic, also reflects Western influences.

Hungary

In the 900s, a group of fierce invaders called the Magyars swept into what is now Hungary. Although they were conquered by the Austrians, the Magyars continued to shape Hungarian culture. The Hungarian language is based on the language spoken by the Magyars. In fact, people in Hungary today still refer to themselves as Magyars.

Ukraine, Belarus, and Moldova

The Slavs also settled Ukraine, Belarus, and Moldova. Later other groups, including the Vikings of Scandinavia, invaded and conquered the Slavs.

A group called the Rus (RUHS) built a settlement in what is now **Kiev**, Ukraine, in the 800s. The rulers of Kiev eventually created a huge empire.

In the late 1700s, that empire became part of Russia. When the Soviet Union was formed in 1922, Ukraine and Belarus were made Soviet republics. Moldova became a republic two years later. They did not become independent until the breakup of the Soviet Union in 1991.

The long history of Russian influence in the region is reflected in the countries' cultures. For example, most people in these countries are Orthodox Christians, like the people of Russia. In addition, Ukrainian and Belarusian languages are written in the Cyrillic, or Russian, alphabet.

READING CHECK **Analyzing** Which groups have influenced the history of the region?

The Kievan Empire

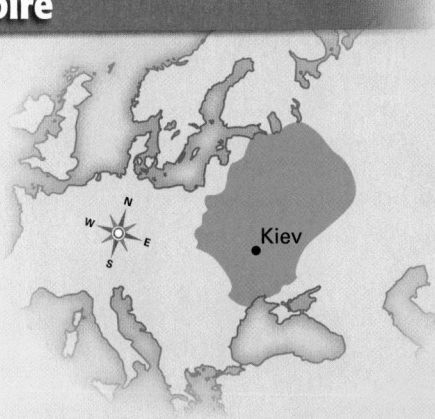

Kiev, now the capital of Ukraine, was once the capital of a large and powerful empire. At its height, the Kievan Empire stretched across much of Eastern Europe and Central Asia.

According to an old legend, the city of Kiev was built by three brothers and their sister. This monument built in the 1980s honors the city's legendary founders.

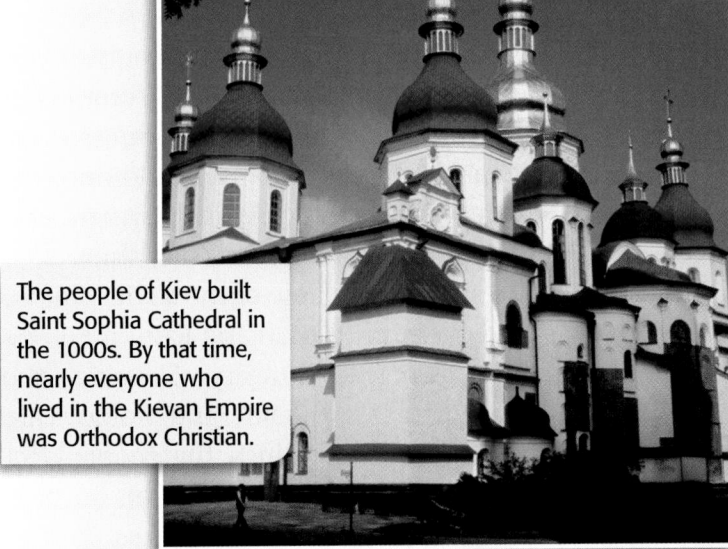

The people of Kiev built Saint Sophia Cathedral in the 1000s. By that time, nearly everyone who lived in the Kievan Empire was Orthodox Christian.

Close-up

Budapest

Budapest, Hungary, is one of the largest cities of Eastern Europe. The city's two parts, Buda and Pest, are separated by the Danube River.

Once the poorer half of the city, Pest has grown quickly. Hungary's Parliament meets here.

Only a few bridges link the two halves of Budapest.

Inland Eastern Europe Today

FOCUS ON READING

How might the CIS help solve problems in this region?

All of the countries of inland Eastern Europe were either part of the Soviet Union or run by Soviet-influenced governments. Since the end of Soviet domination, the people of inland Eastern Europe have largely overcome the problems created by the Soviets. Still, a few issues remain for the region's governments and economies.

Government

During the Soviet era, the countries of inland Eastern Europe had Communist governments. Under the Communists, people had few freedoms. In addition, the Soviets were poor economic planners, and their policies caused many hardships.

Since the collapse of the Soviet Union, the governments of inland Eastern Europe have changed. Hungary, Slovakia, the Czech Republic, Ukraine, and Moldova are now republics in which the people elect their leaders. Belarus also claims to be a republic, but it is really a dictatorship.

The countries of inland Eastern Europe belong to several international alliances. One such alliance, the **Commonwealth of Independent States**, or CIS, meets to discuss issues such as trade and immigration that affect former Soviet republics. The CIS is based in Minsk, the capital of Belarus. Ukraine and Moldova are also members, as are many countries in Asia.

The Czech Republic, Slovakia, Hungary, Romania, and Bulgaria are not part of the CIS. They have sought closer ties to the West than to the former Soviet Union. As a result, all five belong to the EU.

Economy

Economic development has been a major challenge for these countries since the collapse of the Soviet Union. The Czech Republic, Slovakia, Hungary, and Ukraine have been most successful. All four are thriving industrial centers. Ukraine, with rich, productive farmlands, grows grains, potatoes, and sugar beets.

Buda, the older half of the city, contains historic castles and churches.

The Danube is a key route for moving both goods and people in Eastern Europe.

ANALYSIS SKILL ANALYZING VISUALS

How do you think the Danube affects daily life in Budapest?

Cities

Life in inland Eastern Europe is centered around cities, especially national capitals. In each country, the capital is both a key economic center and a cultural one.

Three cities in the region are especially important—Prague, Kiev, and **Budapest**, the capital of Hungary. They are the most prosperous cities in the region and home to influential leaders and universities. In addition, the cities are popular tourist destinations. People from all over the world visit Eastern Europe to see these cities' architectural and cultural sites.

READING CHECK Generalizing What are the countries of inland Eastern Europe like today?

SUMMARY AND PREVIEW Inland Eastern Europe has been successful in facing the challenges left by Soviet influence. Next, you will learn about a region that has faced more challenges, the Balkans.

Section 3 Assessment

Reviewing Ideas, Terms, and Places

1. **a. Recall** In what country is **Prague** located?
   b. Sequence List the groups that ruled **Kiev** and the surrounding area in chronological order.
   c. Elaborate How has Hungary's history helped set it apart from other countries in inland Eastern Europe?
2. **a. Identify** What is the **Commonwealth of Independent States**? Which countries in this region are members?
   b. Draw Conclusions How have the economies of the region changed since the collapse of the Soviet Union?
   c. Develop Why do you think life is largely centered around cities in inland Eastern Europe?

Critical Thinking

3. **Generalizing** Draw a diagram like the one shown here. In the left oval, describe the government and economy of inland Eastern Europe under the Soviet Union. In the right oval, describe them since the Soviet Union's collapse.

Russia Today

FOCUS ON VIEWING

4. **Picturing Inland Eastern Europe** Which country sounds most interesting to you? Write down some details about it. Make a list of pictures you could use on your poster.

The Balkan Countries

What You Will Learn...

Main Ideas

1. The history of the Balkan countries is one of conquest and conflict.
2. The cultures of the Balkan countries are shaped by the many ethnic groups who live there.
3. Civil War and weak economies are major challenges to the region today.

The Big Idea

Life in the Balkans reflects the region's troubled past and its varied ethnic makeup.

Key Terms

ethnic cleansing, *p. 368*

TAKING NOTES Draw a chart like the one below. As you read, take notes about the histories, cultures, and current issues of the Balkan countries.

History		
Culture		
Issues		

If YOU lived there...

As part of your summer vacation, you are hiking across the Balkan Peninsula. As you hike through villages in the rugged mountains, you are amazed at the different churches you see. There are small Roman Catholic churches, huge Orthodox churches with onion-shaped domes, and Muslim mosques with tall minarets.

Why are there so many types of churches here?

BUILDING BACKGROUND The Balkan countries are possibly the most diverse area in Europe. In addition to practicing many religions, the people there speak many languages and have different customs. At times, the area's diversity has led to serious problems.

History

Like the rest of Eastern Europe, the Balkan Peninsula has been conquered and ruled by many different groups. The presence of these many groups continues to shape life in the area today.

Early History

By the 600s BC the ancient Greeks had founded colonies on the northern Black Sea coast. The area they settled is now part of Bulgaria and Romania. Later, the Romans conquered most of the area from the Adriatic Sea to the Danube River.

When the Roman Empire divided into west and east in the late AD 300s, the Balkan Peninsula became part of the Eastern, or Byzantine, Empire. Under Byzantine rule, many people of the Balkans became Orthodox Christians. More than 1,000 years later, Muslim Ottoman Turks conquered the Byzantine Empire. Under the Ottomans, many people became Muslims.

The Ottomans ruled the Balkan Peninsula until the 1800s. At that time, the people of the region rose up and drove the Ottomans out. They then created their own kingdoms.

World War I and After

Trouble between the Balkan kingdoms and their neighbors led to World War I. In the late 1800s the Austro-Hungarian Empire, which lay north of the Balkans, took over part of the peninsula. In protest, a man from Serbia shot the heir to the Austro-Hungarian throne, sparking the war.

After World War I, the Balkans changed dramatically. Europe's leaders divided the peninsula into new countries. Among these new countries was Yugoslavia, which combined many formerly independent countries under one government.

The nation of Yugoslavia lasted until the 1990s. The country eventually broke up, however, because of conflict between ethnic and religious groups.

READING CHECK **Summarizing** How did World War I affect the Balkan Peninsula?

Culture

Culturally, the Balkans are the most diverse area of Europe. This diversity is reflected in the large number of religions practiced and languages spoken there.

Religion

Most of the people of the Balkans, like most Europeans, are Christian. However, three types of Christianity are practiced in the area. Most Balkan Christians belong to the Orthodox Church. In the western part of the peninsula, there are many Roman Catholics. In addition, many countries also have large Protestant communities.

Christianity is not the only religion in the Balkans. Because of the Ottomans' long rule, Islam is also common. In fact, Albania is the only country in Europe in which most people are Muslims.

Religion in the Balkans

Buildings from many religions can be found around the Balkans. This Orthodox church is in Bulgaria.

THE WORLD ALMANAC
Facts about the World

Major Religions in the Balkans

Religion (y-axis): Roman Catholicism, Orthodox Christianity, Protestantism, Islam

Number of followers (in millions) — x-axis: 0, 5, 10, 15, 20, 25, 30, 35, 40

Analyzing Graphs What is the largest religion in the Balkans?

go.hrw.com **KEYWORD: SG7 CH15**

Language

People in the Balkans speak languages from three major groups. Most languages in the region belong to the Slavic family and are related to Russian. In Romania, though, people speak a language that developed from Latin. It is more closely related to French, Italian, and Spanish than to Slavic languages. In addition, some people in Romania speak Germanic languages.

Some languages of the Balkans are not related to these groups. For example, Albanian is unlike any other language in the world. In addition, a group called the Roma have a language of their own.

ACADEMIC VOCABULARY

implications
consequences

READING CHECK **Drawing Conclusions** Why is Balkan culture so diverse?

FOCUS ON CULTURE

The Roma

The Roma are a nomadic people. For centuries, they have roamed from place to place in horse-drawn wagons, working as blacksmiths, animal trainers, and musicians. Although Roma live all over the world, the largest concentration of them is in southeastern Europe.

For centuries, many other Europeans did not trust the Roma. They were suspicious of the Roma's nomadic lifestyle and could not understand their language. As a result, many Roma have been subject to prejudice and discrimination.

Summarizing What is traditional Roma life like?

The Balkans Today

The countries of the Balkan Peninsula, like most of Eastern Europe, were once run by Communist governments. Weak economic planning has left most of them poor and struggling to improve their economies. This area is still the poorest in Europe today.

Relations among religious and ethnic groups have had serious **implications** for the Balkans. When Yugoslavia broke apart, violence broke out among groups in some of the newly formed countries. Members of the largest religious or ethnic group in each country tried to get rid of all other groups who lived there. They threatened those who refused to leave with punishments or death. This kind of effort to remove all members of a group from a country or region is called **ethnic cleansing**.

The violence in the former Yugoslavia was so terrible that other countries stepped in to put an end to it. In 1995 countries around the world sent troops to Bosnia and Herzegovina to help bring an end to the fighting. The fighting between groups eventually ended, and in 2008, ten countries shared the Balkan Peninsula:

Albania The poorest country in Europe, Albania has struggled since the end of the Soviet period. High unemployment and crime rates have prevented the country's economy from improving.

Macedonia Once a part of Yugoslavia, Macedonia broke away in 1991. It was the first country to do so peacefully.

Slovenia Slovenia also broke from Yugoslavia in 1991. In 2004 it became the first Balkan country to join the EU.

Croatia When Croatia broke away from Yugoslavia, fighting broke out within the country. Ethnic Croats and Serbs fought over land for many years. In the end, many Serbs left Croatia, and peace was restored.

Mostar

Fighting between ethnic groups left the city of Mostar in Bosnia and Herzegovina in ruins. After the war, the people of Mostar had to rebuild their city.

ANALYZING VISUALS What does this photo suggest about life in Mostar today?

Bosnia and Herzegovina Since the end of ethnic and religious violence, peace has returned to Bosnia and Herzegovina. The people there are working to rebuild.

Serbia Serbia is the largest nation to emerge from the former Yugoslavia. Like other Balkan countries, Serbia has seen fighting among ethnic groups.

Kosovo Formerly a province of Serbia, Kosovo declared independence in 2008. Its population is mostly ethnic Albanian.

Montenegro The mountainous country of Montenegro separated peacefully from Serbia in June 2006.

Romania The largest of the Balkan states, Romania today is working to recover from years of bad government. Poor leaders have left its government and economy in ruins.

Bulgaria Since the fall of the Soviet Union, Bulgaria has changed dramatically. People there are working to develop a capitalist economy based on industry and tourism.

READING CHECK **Generalizing** What issues does the Balkan region face today?

SUMMARY AND PREVIEW The Soviet Union had a huge effect on Eastern Europe. Next, you will read about the Soviet Union and Russia.

FOCUS ON READING
What solutions are Bulgaria's leaders seeking to their economic problems?

Section 4 Assessment

go.hrw.com
Online Quiz
KEYWORD: SG7 HP15

Reviewing Ideas, Terms, and Places

1. a. **Describe** What was Yugoslavia? When did it break apart?
   b. **Explain** What role did the Balkan countries play in starting World War I?
2. a. **Identify** What are the four most common religions in the Balkans?
   b. **Analyze** Why are so many different languages spoken in the Balkans?
3. a. **Define** What is **ethnic cleansing**?
   b. **Elaborate** Why do you think other countries sent troops to Bosnia and Herzegovina? How has the country changed since the war ended?

Critical Thinking

4. **Summarizing** Draw a chart like this one. Use your notes to write a sentence about how each topic listed in the left column affected life in the Balkans after the breakup of Yugoslavia.

The Balkans Today

Soviet influence	
Ethnic diversity	
Religion	

FOCUS ON VIEWING

5. **Choosing a Country** Now that you have studied all of Eastern Europe, choose your topic. What information and pictures will you include?

The Breakup of Yugoslavia

Essential Elements

The World in Spatial Terms
Places and Regions
Physical Systems
Human Systems
Environment and Society
The Uses of Geography

Background A school playground has a limited amount of space. If many students want to use the playground at the same time, they have to work together and consider each other's feelings. Otherwise, conflict could break out.

Space on Earth is also limited. As a result, people are sometimes forced to live near people with whom they disagree. Like students on a playground, they must learn to work together to live in peace.

Yugoslavia The country of Yugoslavia was created after World War I. As a result, people from many ethnic groups—Serbs, Montenegrins, Bosnians, Croats, Slovenes, and Macedonians—lived together in one country. Each group had its own republic, or self-governed area, in the new country.

For decades, the republics of Yugoslavia worked together peacefully. People from various ethnic groups mixed within each republic. Then in 1991 Croatia, Macedonia, and Slovenia declared independence. The republic of Bosnia and Herzegovina did the same a year later. These republics were afraid Serbia wanted to take over Yugoslavia.

It appeared that they were right. Serbia's leader, Slobodan Milosevic (sloh-BOH-dahn mee-LOH-suh-vich), wanted to increase Serbia's power. He took land from other ethnic groups. He also called on Serbs who lived in other republics to vote to give Serbia more influence in the country.

Refugees Violence between ethnic groups led many people in Yugoslavia to leave their homes. The people in this photo are fleeing Bosnia to seek refuge in a safer area.

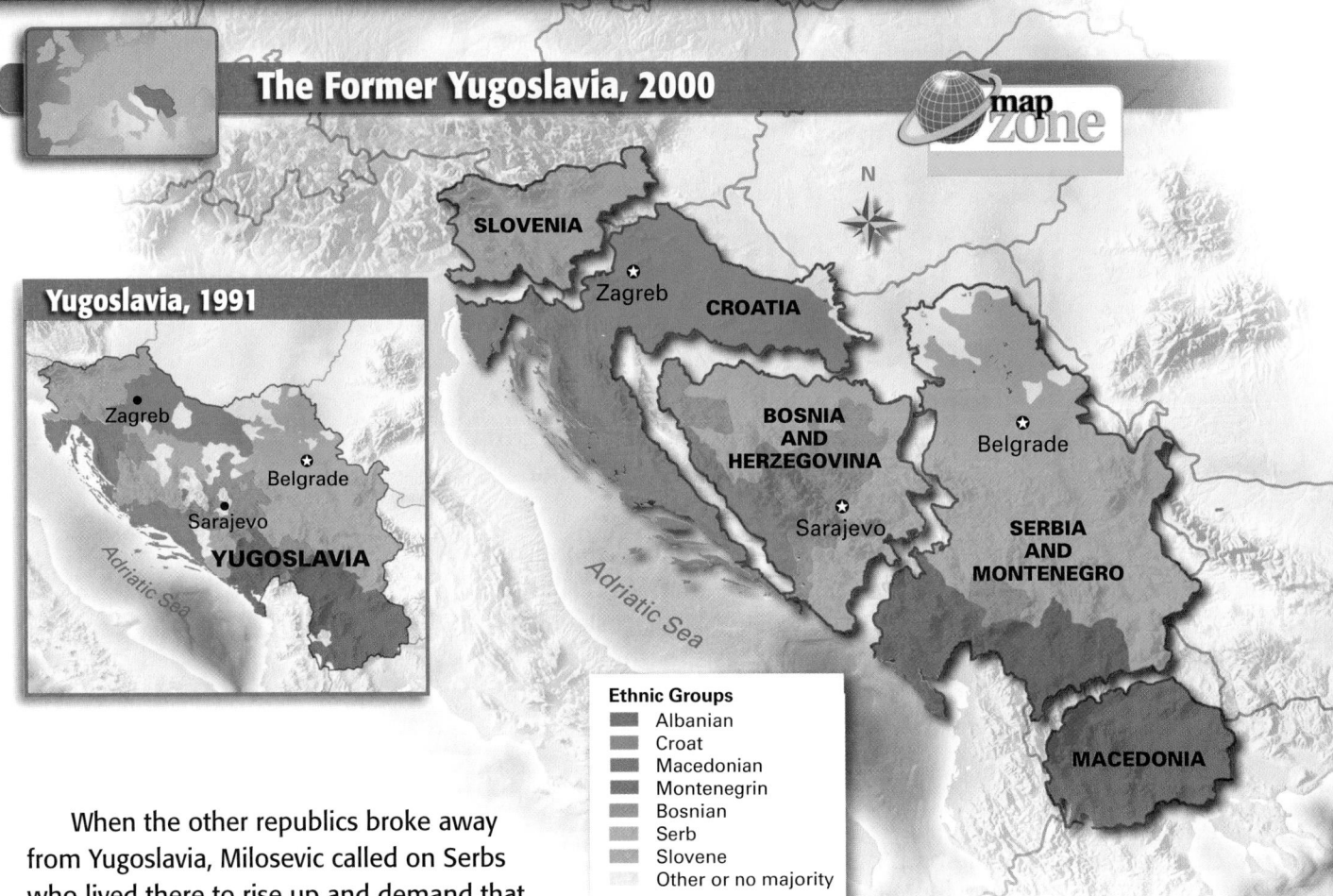

The Former Yugoslavia, 2000

map zone

Yugoslavia, 1991

Zagreb
Belgrade
Sarajevo
YUGOSLAVIA
Adriatic Sea

SLOVENIA
Zagreb
CROATIA
BOSNIA AND HERZEGOVINA
Belgrade
Sarajevo
SERBIA AND MONTENEGRO
Adriatic Sea
MACEDONIA

N

Ethnic Groups
- Albanian
- Croat
- Macedonian
- Montenegrin
- Bosnian
- Serb
- Slovene
- Other or no majority

When the other republics broke away from Yugoslavia, Milosevic called on Serbs who lived there to rise up and demand that they rejoin the country. He also provided aid to Serbian military groups in these republics. In Bosnia and Herzegovina, Serbian rebels fought for three years against the Bosnian army in a destructive civil war.

Milosevic's actions caused other ethnic groups in Yugoslavia to resent the Serbs. As a result, additional violence broke out. In Croatia, for example, the army violently expelled all Serbs from their country. War raged in the area until 1995, when a peace accord was signed. As a result of that accord, Yugoslavia was dissolved. In its place were five countries that had once been Yugoslav republics.

What It Means The violent breakup of Yugoslavia has taught other countries some valuable lessons. First, it reinforced the idea that national borders are not permanent. Borders can and do change.

More importantly, however, the struggles in Yugoslavia have made some countries more aware of their people's needs. People want to feel that they have some say in their lives. When they feel as though another group is trying to take that say from them, as many in Yugoslavia felt the Serbs were doing, then trouble will often follow.

Geography for Life Activity

1. What led to the breakup of Yugoslavia?

2. Look at the maps on this page. How did the pattern of ethnic groups in Yugoslavia change between 1991 and 2000? Why do you think this is so?

3. **Investigating Ethnic Relationships** Yugoslavia is not the only country in which multiple ethnic groups lived together. Research another country in which multiple groups live together, such as Switzerland or Indonesia. How do the groups who live there live together?

Social Studies Skills

Chart and Graph   Critical Thinking   Geography   Study

Analyzing Benefits and Costs

Learn

Decisions can be tough to make. A seemingly simple choice can have both positive effects, or benefits, and negative effects, or costs. Before you make a decision, it can be helpful to analyze all the possible benefits and costs that will result.

One way to analyze benefits and costs is to create a chart like the one below. On one side, list all the benefits that will result from your decision. On the other side, list the costs. Not all costs involve money. You must also consider opportunity costs, or the things that you might lose as a result of your decision. For example, going to a movie might mean that you have to miss a baseball game.

Practice

The chart to the right could have been written by an official considering whether to develop a tourism industry in Croatia. Decide whether each of the numbered items listed here should be added to the benefits column or the costs column. Once you have determined that, use the chart to decide whether the benefits of tourism outweigh the costs. Write a short paragraph to support your decision.

❶ Would mean that tourist areas were not available for farming or industry

❷ Would improve Croatia's image to people in other parts of the world

Tourism in Dalmatia, Croatia

Benefits	Costs
■ Would create much-needed income for towns in the region	■ Would require building of hotels, airports, and roads
■ Would not require much new investment, since tourists are drawn to region's beaches and climate	■ Increase in tourism could lead to damaging of local environments
■	■
■	■

Apply

Imagine that city leaders in your area are trying to decide whether to build a new school. They cannot make a decision and have asked you to help analyze the benefits and costs of building the school. Create a chart like the one above to list those benefits and costs. Then write a brief paragraph stating whether the benefits of the plan outweigh its costs.

Geography's Impact
video series
Review the video to answer the closing question:
How have the changing political borders in the Balkans affected people's lives?

Visual Summary

Use the visual summary below to help you review the main ideas of the chapter.

QUICK FACTS

Poland and the Baltics
The history of Poland and the Baltic Republics still shapes their culture, government, and economy.

Inland Eastern Europe
Once Communist, the countries of inland Eastern Europe have stable governments and strong economies.

The Balkans
Since the breakup of Yugoslavia, the Balkans have been faced with conflict and economic challenges.

Reviewing Vocabulary, Terms, and Places

Unscramble each group of letters below to spell a term that matches the given definition.

1. **arwswa**—the capital of Poland

2. **neicht glncaenis**—the effort to remove all members of a group from a country or region

3. **ebndua**—the major river that flows through Eastern Europe, one of the longest on the continent

4. **ageurp**—the capital and largest city of the Czech Republic

5. **ncimlaitpiso**—consequences

6. **laknab**—the peninsula on which much of Eastern Europe is located

7. **ufrnrtriuacste**—the set of resources, like roads and factories, that a country needs to support economic activities

8. **nrhatcapias**—a mountain range in Eastern Europe

Comprehension and Critical Thinking

SECTION 1 *(Pages 354–357)*

9. **a. Identify** Name two major bodies of water that border Eastern Europe.

b. Explain How do the Danube and other rivers affect life for people in Eastern Europe?

c. Evaluate If you could live in any region of Eastern Europe, where would it be? Why?

SECTION 2 *(Pages 358–361)*

10. **a. Identify** What are the three Baltic Republics? Why are they called that?

b. Compare and Contrast What are two cultural features that Poland and the Baltic Republics have in common? What are two features that are different in those countries?

c. Elaborate How did the collapse of the Soviet Union affect people in Poland and the Baltic Republics?

SECTION 3 *(Pages 362–365)*

11. a. Describe What is the government of Belarus like? What type of government do the other countries of inland Eastern Europe have?

b. Draw Conclusions Why do you think that some countries in inland Eastern Europe have stronger economies than others?

c. Elaborate How has its location influenced the culture of the Czech Republic?

SECTION 4 *(Pages 366–369)*

12. a. Identify What religions are common in the Balkan countries?

b. Explain Why did countries from around the world send troops to Kosovo?

c. Predict How do you think peace will affect life in the Balkans?

FOCUS ON READING AND VIEWING

13. Understanding Problems and Solutions Re-read the first paragraph under the heading The Region Today in Section 2. Then write a short paragraph that explains the main problem facing Poland and the Baltics today. End your paragraph by suggesting a solution their governments might use to address the problem.

14. Presenting and Viewing an Oral Report Write a brief report on the area of Eastern Europe that you have chosen. To help your audience follow along with your report, prepare a poster that illustrates your main ideas. Find pictures of major features of your chosen country and arrange them on a poster board. Write a short caption that explains what each picture is.

Present your report to the class. As you discuss each main idea, point out the pictures that illustrate it on your poster. Speak clearly and keep eye contact with your audience. Then, watch and listen as your peers present their reports and posters. Note whether they speak clearly and maintain eye contact with the audience. Do their posters illustrate the main ideas in their reports?

Using the Internet

go.hrw.com
KEYWORD: SG7 CH15

15. Activity: Writing a Report For centuries the Balkans have been an arena of conflict. Enter the activity keyword. Learn about the history and cultures of the Balkans and investigate recent conflicts there. Write a report on what you find.

Social Studies Skills

16. Analyzing Costs and Benefits Imagine that you are a government official in Ukraine. Your country cannot produce enough energy to meet its needs and has to buy energy from Russia. A company in Kiev has expressed interest in building nuclear power plants, but many people are leery of nuclear power since the Chernobyl incident. Make a list of the costs and benefits of nuclear power. Then write a statement that either supports or argues against the plan.

Map Activity ★Interactive

17. Eastern Europe On a separate sheet of paper, match the letters on the map with their correct labels.

Great Hungarian Plain	Kiev, Ukraine
Latvia	Warsaw, Poland
Albania	Danube River

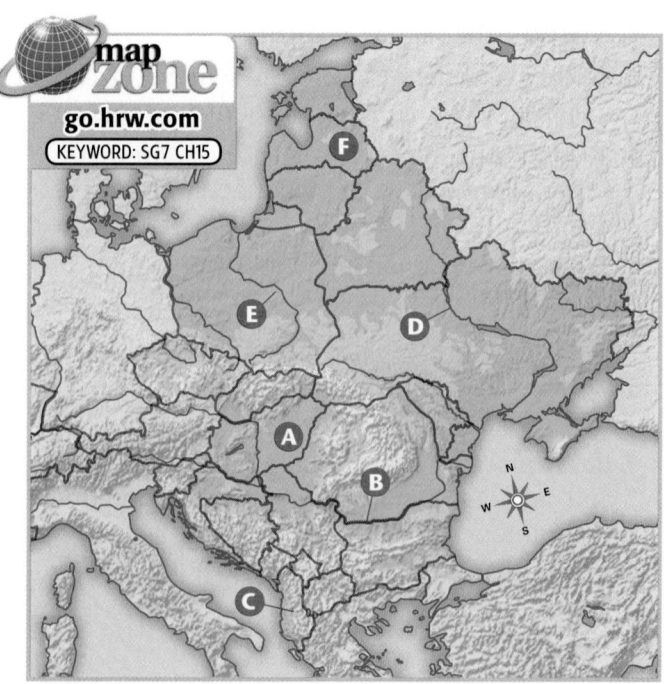

DIRECTIONS: Read questions 1 through 7 and write the letter of the best response. Then read question 8 and write your own well-constructed response.

1 The country *most* influential in Eastern Europe after World War II was

A the United States.

B the Soviet Union.

C France.

D Germany.

2 Which of the following countries violently broke apart in the 1990s?

A Poland

B Romania

C Czechoslovakia

D Yugoslavia

3 The major river of Eastern Europe is the

A Baltic River.

B Carpathian River.

C Danube River.

D Hungarian River.

4 Which of these countries is located on the Balkan Peninsula?

A Croatia

B Poland

C Belarus

D Estonia

5 Which of these statements about religion in Eastern Europe is correct?

A Nearly everyone in the region is Muslim.

B Nearly everyone in the region is Catholic.

C Nearly everyone in the region is Orthodox Christian.

D People in the region practice many different religions.

Hungary

For those in search of the heart and soul of Europe, there's nowhere better. Hungarians, who call themselves Magyars, speak a language and revel in a culture unlike any other. Away from the cosmopolitan charms of Budapest, life in the provinces is more redolent of times past—simpler, slower, often friendlier. There are endless opportunities for those with special interests—from horse riding and cycling to bird-watching and "taking the waters" at the country's many thermal spas.

–from *Lonely Planet World Guide Online*

6 Read the passage above from a travel guide to Hungary. According to this passage, what do people from Hungary call themselves?

A Hungarians

B Magyars

C Budapestians

D Europeans

7 Based on the above passage, which of the following statements is true?

A Hungarian culture is similar to many others in Europe.

B There are few things to do in Hungary.

C People outside of Budapest live simpler and slower lives than people in the city.

D Hungary is the largest country in Europe.

8 Extended Response Life in Eastern Europe is still influenced by the Soviet era, even though the Soviet Union collapsed many years ago. Consider what you have read in this chapter and write a paragraph in which you explain how Soviet influence is still felt in the region.

CHAPTER 16

Russia and the Caucasus

What You Will Learn...

In this chapter you will learn about the physical features, climate, and natural resources of Russia and the Caucasus. You will also study the histories and cultures of these countries. Finally, you will learn about life in each of the countries today.

FOCUS ON READING AND WRITING

Making Generalizations A generalization is a broad, general idea drawn from new information combined with what you already know. As you read this chapter, stop now and then to make a generalization. It will help you pull the pieces of information together and make sense of them. **See the lesson, Making Generalizations, on page R17.**

Creating a Real Estate Ad As you read this chapter, imagine you work for a real estate agency in Russia or the Caucasus. You are trying to sell a piece of property there. In order to sell the property, you must write an ad to be published in the newspaper and on the Internet. As you read, decide where your property would be located and what its characteristics would be.

Geography A volcano created Crater Bay in the Kuril Islands off the east coast of Russia. The islands have several active volcanoes.

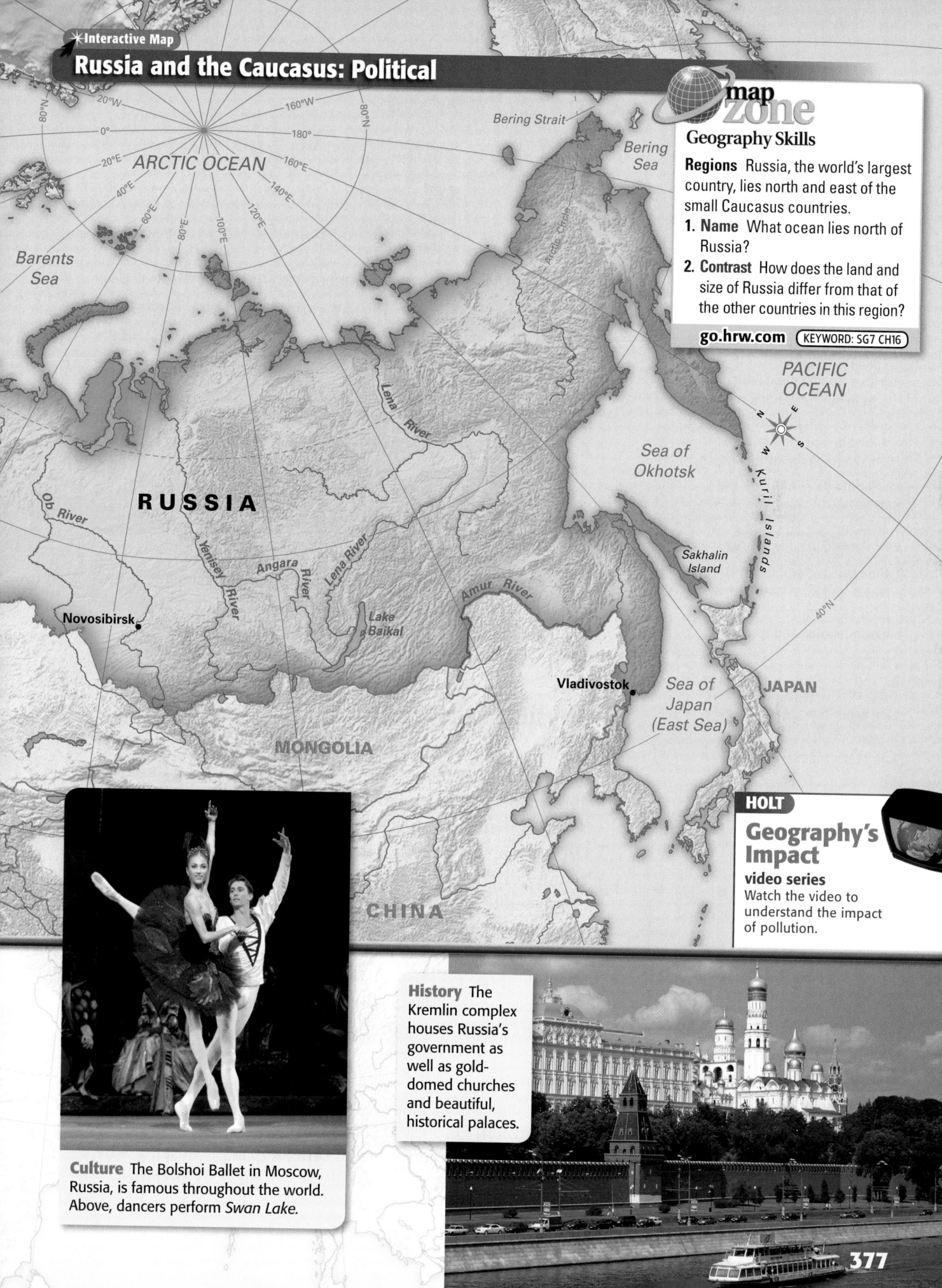

Russia and the Caucasus: Political

ARCTIC OCEAN

Barents
Sea

Bering Strait

Bering
Sea

Arctic Circle

Ob River

RUSSIA

Lena River

Yenisey River

Angara River

Lena River

Amur River

Novosibirsk

Lake
Baikal

Sea of
Okhotsk

Kuril Islands

Sakhalin
Island

Vladivostok

Sea of
Japan
(East Sea)

PACIFIC
OCEAN

JAPAN

MONGOLIA

CHINA

map zone
Geography Skills

Regions Russia, the world's largest country, lies north and east of the small Caucasus countries.

1. **Name** What ocean lies north of Russia?
2. **Contrast** How does the land and size of Russia differ from that of the other countries in this region?

go.hrw.com KEYWORD: SG7 CH16

HOLT
Geography's Impact
video series
Watch the video to understand the impact of pollution.

Culture The Bolshoi Ballet in Moscow, Russia, is famous throughout the world. Above, dancers perform *Swan Lake*.

History The Kremlin complex houses Russia's government as well as gold-domed churches and beautiful, historical palaces.

Physical Geography

If YOU lived there...

You are making a documentary about the Trans–Siberian Railroad, a famous train that crosses the vast country of Russia. The train travels more than 5,700 miles across plains and mountains and through thick forests. As the train leaves the city of Moscow, you look out the window and see wheat fields and white birch trees.

What scenes might you include in your film?

BUILDING BACKGROUND Look at a globe, and you will see that Russia extends nearly halfway around the world. Russia is the world's largest country. It is so vast that it spans 11 time zones. While huge, much of Russia consists of flat or rolling plains.

Physical Features

Have you ever stood on two continents at once? In Russia's **Ural** (YOOHR-uhl) **Mountains**, you can. There, the continents of Europe and Asia meet. Europe lies to the west; Asia to the east. Together, Europe and Asia form the large landmass of Eurasia. On the map, you can see that a large chunk of Eurasia is the country of Russia. In fact, Russia is the world's largest country. Compared to the United States, Russia is almost twice as big.

South of Russia are three much smaller countries—Georgia, Armenia (ahr-MEE-nee-uh), and Azerbaijan (a-zuhr-by-JAHN). They lie in the Caucasus (KAW-kuh-suhs), the area between the Black Sea and the **Caspian Sea**. This area, which includes part of southern Russia, is named for the **Caucasus Mountains**.

Landforms

As the map shows, Russia's landforms vary from west to east. The Northern European Plain stretches across western, or European, Russia. This fertile plain forms Russia's heartland, where most Russians live. **Moscow**, Russia's capital, is located there.

Russia and the Caucasus: Physical

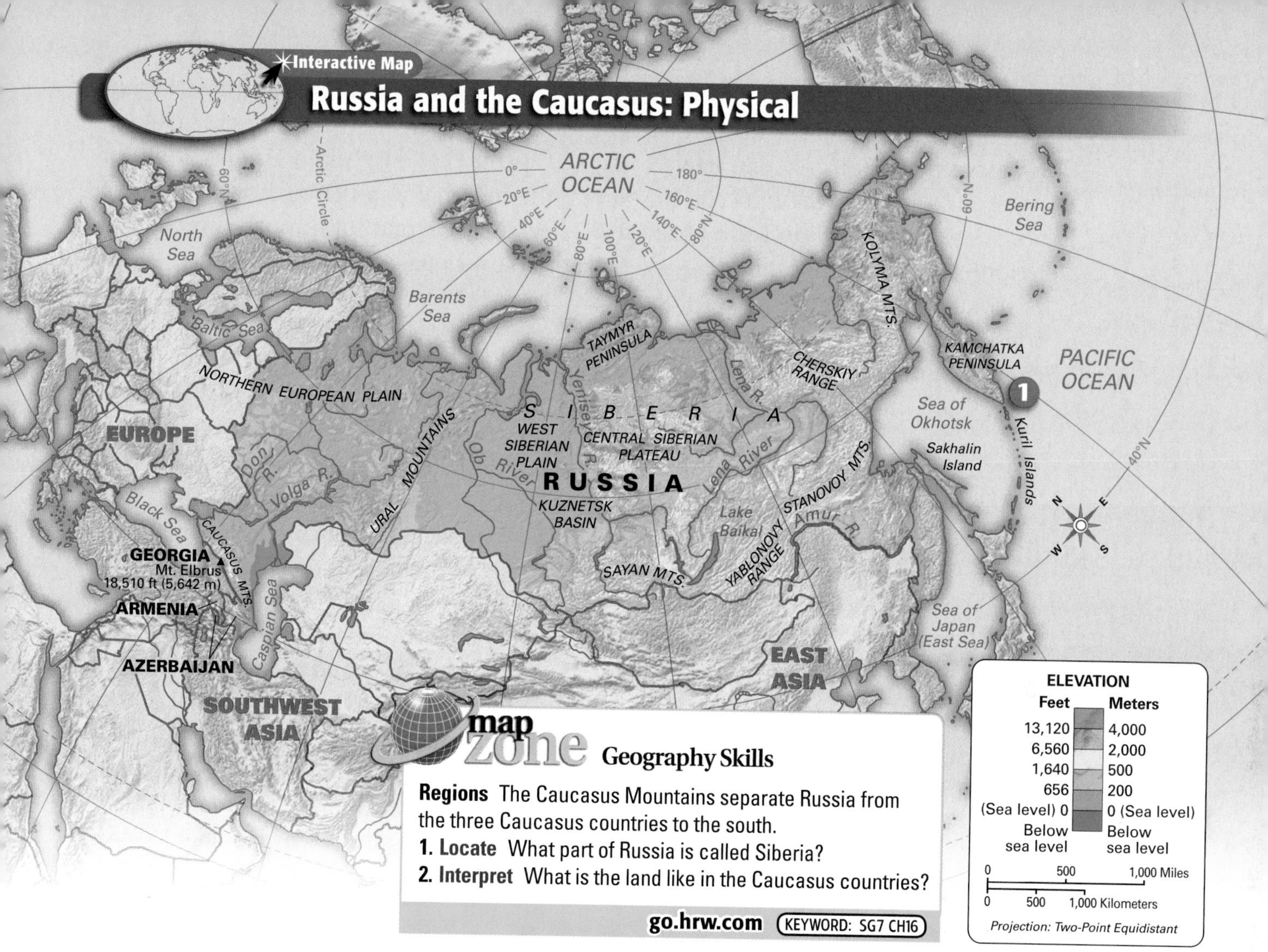

ARCTIC OCEAN

Bering Sea

North Sea

Barents Sea

Baltic Sea

NORTHERN EUROPEAN PLAIN

EUROPE

TAYMYR PENINSULA

KOLYMA MTS.

KAMCHATKA PENINSULA

PACIFIC OCEAN

CHERSKIY RANGE

SIBERIA

WEST SIBERIAN PLAIN

CENTRAL SIBERIAN PLATEAU

Lena R.

Sea of Okhotsk

Sakhalin Island

Kuril Islands

Don R.

URAL MOUNTAINS

Volga R.

Ob River

Yenisey River

RUSSIA

KUZNETSK BASIN

Lena River

STANOVOY MTS.

Amur R.

Black Sea

CAUCASUS MTS.

GEORGIA
Mt. Elbrus
18,510 ft (5,642 m)

ARMENIA

AZERBAIJAN

Caspian Sea

Lake Baikal

SAYAN MTS.

YABLONOVY RANGE

EAST ASIA

Sea of Japan (East Sea)

SOUTHWEST ASIA

Geography Skills

Regions The Caucasus Mountains separate Russia from the three Caucasus countries to the south.
1. **Locate** What part of Russia is called Siberia?
2. **Interpret** What is the land like in the Caucasus countries?

go.hrw.com (KEYWORD: SG7 CH16)

ELEVATION

Feet		Meters
13,120		4,000
6,560		2,000
1,640		500
656		200
(Sea level) 0		0 (Sea level)
Below sea level		Below sea level

0   500   1,000 Miles
0   500   1,000 Kilometers

Projection: Two-Point Equidistant

To the east, the plain rises to form the Ural Mountains. These low mountains are worn down and rounded from erosion.

The vast area between the Urals and the Pacific Ocean is **Siberia**. This area includes several landforms, shown on the map. The West Siberian Plain is a flat, marshy area. It is one of the largest plains in the world.

East of this plain is an upland called the Central Siberian Plateau. Mountain ranges run through southern and eastern Siberia.

Eastern Siberia is called the Russian Far East. This area includes the Kamchatka (kuhm-CHAHT-kuh) Peninsula and several islands. The Russian Far East is part of the Ring of Fire, the area circling the Pacific.

1 The Kamchatka Peninsula on Russia's east coast has many old and active volcanoes.

The Ring of Fire is known for its volcanoes and earthquakes, and the Russian Far East is no exception. It has several active volcanoes, and earthquakes can occur. In some areas, steam from within Earth breaks free to form geysers and hot springs.

South of Russia, the Caucasus countries consist largely of rugged uplands. The Caucasus Mountains cover much of Georgia and extend into Armenia and Azerbaijan.

These soaring mountains include Mount Elbrus (el-BROOS). At 18,510 feet (5,642 m), it is the highest peak in Europe. South of the mountains, a plateau covers much of Armenia. Gorges cut through this plateau, and earthquakes are common there. Lowlands lie along the Black and Caspian seas.

Bodies of Water

Some of the longest rivers in the world flow through the region of Russia and the Caucasus. One of the most important is the **Volga** (VAHL-guh) **River** in western Russia. The longest river in Europe, the Volga winds southward to the Caspian Sea. The Volga has long formed the core of Russia's river network. Canals link the Volga to the nearby Don River and to the Baltic Sea.

Even longer rivers than the Volga flow through Siberia in the Asian part of Russia. The Ob (AWB), Yenisey (yi-ni-SAY), and Lena rivers flow northward to the Arctic Ocean. Like many of Russia's rivers, they are frozen for much of the year. The ice often hinders shipping and trade and closes some of Russia's ports for part of the year.

In addition to its rivers, Russia has some 200,000 lakes. Lake Baikal (by-KAHL), in south-central Siberia, is the world's deepest lake. Although not that large in surface area, Lake Baikal is deep enough to hold all the water in all five of the Great Lakes. Because of its beauty, Lake Baikal is called the Jewel of Siberia. Logging and factories have polluted the water, but Russians are now working to clean up the lake.

In the southwest part of the region, the Black and Caspian Seas border Russia and the Caucasus. The Black Sea connects to the Mediterranean Sea and is important for trade. The Caspian Sea holds saltwater and is the world's largest inland sea.

READING CHECK **Summarizing** What are the major landforms in Russia and the Caucasus?

Russia's Climate and Plant Life

In the top photo, Russians bundled up in furs hurry through the snow and cold of Moscow, the capital. In the lower photo, evergreen forest called taiga blankets a Russian plain. In the distance, the low Ural Mountains mark the division between Europe and Asia.

Climate and Plant Life

Russians sometimes joke that winter lasts for 12 months and then summer begins. Russia is a cold country. The reason is its northern location partly within the Arctic Circle. In general, Russia has short summers and long, snowy winters. The climate is milder west of the Urals and grows colder and harsher as one goes north and east.

Russia's northern coast is tundra. Winters are dark and bitterly cold, and the brief summers are cool. Much of the ground is permafrost, or permanently frozen soil. Only small plants such as mosses grow.

South of the tundra is a vast forest of evergreen trees called **taiga** (TY-guh). This huge forest covers about half of Russia. In Siberia, snow covers the taiga much of the year. South of the taiga is a flat grassland called the steppe (STEP). With rich, black soil and a warmer climate, the steppe is Russia's most important farming area.

Farther south, the Caucasus countries are warmer than Russia in general. Climate in the Caucasus ranges from warm and wet along the Black Sea to cooler in the uplands to hot and dry in much of Azerbaijan.

READING CHECK **Finding Main Ideas** How does Russia's location affect its climate?

Natural Resources

Russia and the Caucasus have a wealth of resources. The Northern European Plain and the steppe provide fertile soil for farming. The taiga provides wood for building and paper products. Metals, such as copper and gold, and precious gems such as diamonds provide useful raw materials.

The region's main energy resources are coal, hydroelectricity, natural gas, and oil. Both Russia and Azerbaijan have large oil and gas fields. Oil also lies beneath the Caspian Sea.

The region's natural resources have been poorly managed, however. Until the early 1990s this region was part of the Soviet Union. The Soviet government put more importance on industry than on managing its resources. In Russia, many of the resources that were easy to access are gone. For example, most of the timber in western Russia has been cut down. Many remaining resources are in remote Siberia.

READING CHECK **Analyzing** Why are some of Russia's natural resources difficult to obtain?

SUMMARY AND PREVIEW Russia is big and cold, with vast plains and forests. The Caucasus countries are small, mountainous, and warmer. The region also has many natural resources. Next, you will read about Russia's history and culture.

FOCUS ON READING

What general idea can you draw from the text about natural resources? What facts or details support that idea?

Section 1 Assessment

go.hrw.com
Online Quiz
KEYWORD: SG7 HP16

Reviewing Ideas, Terms, and Places

1. a. **Describe** Why are the **Ural Mountains** significant?
   b. **Draw Conclusions** Why might the Russian Far East be a dangerous place to live?
2. a. **Describe** What are winters like in much of Russia?
   b. **Analyze** How does climate affect Russia's plant life?
3. a. **Recall** What valuable resource is in the **Caspian Sea**?
   b. **Make Inferences** Why might resources located in remote, cold areas be difficult to use?

Critical Thinking

4. **Generalizing** Draw a chart like the one here. Use your notes and enter one general idea for each topic in the chart.

Physical Features	
Climate and Plants	
Natural Resources	

FOCUS ON WRITING

5. **Describing the Physical Geography** Now that you know the physical geography of the region, make a list of possible locations for the house or land you are selling.

History and Culture of Russia

What You Will Learn...

Main Ideas

1. The Russian Empire grew under powerful leaders, but unrest and war led to its end.
2. The Soviet Union emerged as a Communist superpower with rigid government control.
3. Russia's history and diversity have influenced its culture.

The Big Idea

Strict rule, unrest, and ethnic diversity have shaped Russia's history and culture.

Key Terms and Places

Kiev, *p. 382*
Cyrillic, *p. 382*
czar, *p. 383*
Bolsheviks, *p. 383*
gulags, *p. 384*

TAKING NOTES As you read, use a concept web like the one here to take notes on Russia's history and culture.

If YOU lived there...

It is 1992, an exciting time in your home town of Moscow. At the end of 1991 the Soviet Union fell apart. Russia became independent. You watched on TV as people pulled down the red Soviet flag and knocked down statues of former leaders. Everyone is talking about new freedoms and a new kind of government.

What new freedoms do you hope to have?

BUILDING BACKGROUND The fall of the Soviet Union was not the first time Russia had experienced change. For centuries Russia was part of a great empire. Then in the early 1900s Communists overthrew the empire. The Soviet Union was born. Today it too is gone.

The Russian Empire

Russia's roots lie in the grassy, windswept plains of the steppe. For thousands of years, people from Asia moved across the steppe. These groups of people included the Slavs. As you read in the last chapter, the Slavs settled in Eastern Europe, including what is now Ukraine and western Russia.

Early History and Empire

The Slavs developed towns and began trading with people from other areas. In the AD 800s, Viking traders from Scandinavia invaded the Slavs. These Vikings were called Rus (ROOS), and the word *Russia* probably comes from their name. The Vikings shaped the first Russian state among the Slavs. This Russian state, called Kievan (KEE-e-fuhn) Rus, centered around the city of **Kiev**. This city is now the capital of Ukraine.

Over time, missionaries introduced the Orthodox Christian faith to Kiev. In addition, the missionaries introduced a form of the Greek alphabet called **Cyrillic** (suh-RI-lik). The Russians adopted this Cyrillic alphabet and still use it today.

History of Russian Expansion

Baltic republics: independent 1918–1940 and 1991

Finland: Russian territory 1809–1918

Poland: Russian territory 1815–1918

St. Petersburg

✪ Moscow

ARCTIC OCEAN

Bering Sea

Sea of Okhotsk

Sea of Japan (East Sea)

Black Sea

Caspian Sea

Baltic Sea

Arctic Circle

Russian territory 1871–1881

Legend:
- Russia, 1462–1533
- **Territory gained**
  - by 1689
  - by 1725
  - by 1801
  - by 1945
- Russian boundary, 1993

0 250 500 Miles
0 250 500 Kilometers

Projection: Two-Point Equidistant

map zone Geography Skills

Location The colors in the map show the growth of the Russian Empire and of the Soviet Union over time.
1. **Name** What city is located in territory gained by 1725?
2. **Interpret** When was the period of greatest expansion?

In the 1200s, fierce Mongol invaders called Tatars (TAH-ters) swept out of Central Asia and conquered Kiev. The Mongols allowed Russian princes to rule over local states. In time, Muscovy became the strongest state. Its main city was Moscow.

After about 200 years Muscovy's prince, Ivan III, seized control from the Mongols. In the 1540s his grandson, Ivan IV, crowned himself **czar** (ZAHR), or emperor. *Czar* is Russian for "caesar." As czar, Ivan IV had total power. A cruel and savage ruler, he became known as Ivan the Terrible.

In time, Muscovy developed into the country of Russia. Strong czars such as Peter the Great (1682–1725) and Catherine the Great (1762–1796) built Russia into a huge empire and a world power. This empire included many conquered peoples.

In spite of its growth, Russia remained largely a country of poor farmers, while the czars and nobles had most of the wealth. In the early 1900s Russians began demanding improvements. The czar agreed to some changes, but unrest continued to grow.

War and Revolution

In 1914 Russia entered World War I. The country suffered huge losses in the war. In addition, the Russian people experienced severe shortages of food. When the czar seemed to ignore the people's hardship, they rose up against him. He was forced to give up his throne in 1917.

Later that year the **Bolsheviks**, a radical Russian Communist group, seized power in the Russian Revolution. They then killed the czar and his family. In 1922 the Bolsheviks formed a new country, the Union of Soviet Socialist Republics (USSR), or the Soviet Union. It soon included 15 republics, the strongest of which was Russia. The first leader was Vladimir Lenin.

READING CHECK **Sequencing** What series of events led to the creation of the Soviet Union?

The Soviet Union

The Soviet Union, led by Lenin, became a Communist country. In this political system, the government owns all property and controls all aspects of life. In 1924 Lenin died. Joseph Stalin took power, ruling as a brutal and paranoid dictator.

The Soviet Union under Stalin

FOCUS ON READING
Based on the Soviet Union's economy, what generalization might you make about command economies?

Under Stalin, the Soviet Union set up a command economy. In this system, the government owns all businesses and farms and makes all decisions. People were told what to make and how much to charge. Without competition, though, efficiency and the quality of goods fell over time.

The Soviet Union strictly controlled its people as well as its economy. Stalin had anyone who spoke out against the government jailed, exiled, or killed. Millions of people were sent to **gulags**, harsh Soviet labor camps often located in Siberia.

Cold War and Collapse

During World War II, the Soviet Union fought with the Allies against Germany. Millions of Soviet citizens died in the war.

ACADEMIC VOCABULARY
reaction
a response to something

Stalin's **reaction** to the war was to build a buffer around the Soviet Union to protect it from invasion. To do so, he set up Communist governments in Eastern Europe.

The United States opposed communism and saw its spread as a threat to democracy. This opposition led to the Cold War, a period of tense rivalry between the Soviet Union and the United States. The two rival countries became superpowers as they competed to have superior weapons.

In part because of the high costs of weapons, the Soviet economy was near collapse by the 1980s. Mikhail Gorbachev (GAWR-buh-chawf), the Soviet leader, began making changes. He reduced government control and introduced some democracy.

Despite his actions, the Soviet republics began pushing for independence. In 1991 the Soviet Union collapsed. It broke apart into 15 independent countries, including Russia. The Soviet Union was no more.

READING CHECK **Analyzing** How did the Cold War help lead to the Soviet Union's collapse?

Culture

In the Soviet Union, the government had controlled culture just like everything else. Today, however, Russian culture is once again alive and vibrant.

People and Religion

Russia is big and diverse, with more than 140 million people. About 80 percent are ethnic Russians, or Slavs, but Russia also has many other ethnic groups. The largest are the Tatars and Ukrainians. Russia's many ethnic groups are once again taking great pride in their cultures.

Like ethnic culture, religious worship has seen a revival. The Soviet government opposed religion and closed many houses of worship. Today many have reopened, including historic Russian cathedrals with their onion-shaped domes. The main faith is Russian Orthodox Christian. Other religions include Islam, Buddhism, and other forms of Christianity.

Customs

Russian history has shaped its customs, such as holidays. Religious holidays, like Easter and Christmas, are popular. The main family holiday is New Year's Eve. To celebrate this holiday, families decorate a tree where, according to Russian folklore, Grandfather Frost and his helper the Snow Maiden leave gifts. A newer holiday is Russian Independence Day, which marks the end of the Soviet Union on June 12.

St. Basil's Cathedral

Colorful St. Basil's Cathedral, in Moscow's Red Square, has become a symbol of Russia. Czar Ivan IV had the cathedral built between 1555 and 1561 in honor of Russian military victories. According to legend, Ivan had the architects blinded so they could never design anything else as magnificent.

Steeply sloped towers, called tent roofs, and onion-shaped domes easily shed snow.

St. Basil's Cathedral houses nine small, separate chapels.

Onion-shaped domes, based on Byzantine designs, decorate many early Russian churches.

In 1588 a chapel was added for the tomb of St. Basil the Blessed, a popular saint in Russia. In time, his name became linked to the cathedral.

ANALYSIS SKILL **ANALYZING VISUALS**

Besides onion domes, what other shapes and patterns are visible on the cathedral?

Communist-era Poster

The Soviet Union used posters as propaganda. Propaganda is information designed to promote a specific cause or idea by influencing people's thoughts and beliefs. For example, Soviet posters often promoted the greatness and power of the Soviet state, its leaders, and their Communist policies.

The message of this 1924 poster reads, "Long live the Young Communist League! The young are taking over the older generation's torch!"

The color red in this poster symbolizes communism and the Russian Revolution.

ANALYSIS SKILL **ANALYZING PRIMARY SOURCES**

How do you think the poster's images and message influenced Soviet teens at the time?

The Arts and Sciences

Russia has made great contributions in the arts and sciences. In the performing arts, Russia's ballet companies are world famous for their skill. In music, Peter Tchaikovsky (chy-KAWF-skee) is Russia's most famous composer. His many works include *The Nutcracker* ballet and the *1812 Overture.*

In the material arts, Russia's Fabergé eggs are priceless. Gifts for the czars, these eggs are made of precious metals and covered with gems such as emeralds and rubies. Each egg opens to reveal a tiny surprise.

In the sciences, Russia has contributed to space research. In 1957 the Soviet Union launched Sputnik, the first artificial satellite in space. Russian scientists now help work on the International Space Station.

READING CHECK **Generalizing** How did the end of the Soviet Union affect Russian culture?

SUMMARY AND PREVIEW The history of Russia, from a great empire to a Communist superpower to a new nation, has shaped its rich culture. Next, you will read about life in Russia today.

go.hrw.com
Online Quiz
KEYWORD: SG7 HP16

Section 2 Assessment

Reviewing Ideas, Terms, and Places

1. **a. Define** Who were the **czars**?
   b. Analyze What role did the city of **Kiev** play in Russian history?
   c. Elaborate What problems and events caused the Russian Empire to decline?
2. **a. Identify** Why are Vladimir Lenin and Joseph Stalin significant in Russian history?
   b. Evaluate Do you think life in the Soviet Union was an improvement over life in the Russian empire? Why, or why not?
3. **a. Recall** What is the main religion in Russia?
   b. Summarize How has Russian culture changed since the collapse of the Soviet Union in 1991?

Critical Thinking

4. **Sequencing** Draw a chart like the one here. Use your notes to list the order of the major events leading up to the collapse of the Soviet Union.

   ◯ → ◯ → ◯ → ◯

FOCUS ON WRITING

5. **Considering Russia's History and Culture** Look at the locations you listed for Section 1. For the Russian locations, make notes about historical or cultural details you could include in your ad.

Interpreting a Population Map

Learn

Population maps give you a snapshot of the distribution of people in a region or country. Each color on a population map represents an average number of people living within a square mile or square kilometer. Sometimes symbols identify the cities with populations of a certain size. The map's legend identifies what the colors and symbols in the map mean.

Practice

1 Based on the map below, in which region of Russia do most of the country's people live?

2 Which two cities in Russia have the largest population?

3 How many Russian cities have more than 1 million people?

Russia: Population

Persons per square mile	Persons per square km
520	200
260	100
130	50
25	10
3	1
0	0

Major cities
- Over 2 million
- 1 to 2 million
- Under 1 million

Projection: Two-Point Equidistant

Apply

Use an atlas to locate a current population map of the United States. Using the map, identify where the most and the least populated regions of the United States are. Then identify the number of U.S. cities or metropolitan areas with more than 2 million people.

Russia Today

What You Will Learn...

Main Ideas

1. The Russian Federation is working to develop democracy and a market economy.
2. Russia's physical geography, cities, and economy define its many culture regions.
3. Russia faces a number of serious challenges.

The Big Idea

Russia is a federal republic with a growing market economy but faces tough challenges.

Key Terms and Places

dachas, *p. 389*
St. Petersburg, *p. 390*
smelters, *p. 391*
Trans-Siberian Railroad, *p. 391*
Chechnya, *p. 392*

TAKING NOTES As you read, use a chart like the one below to take notes on each of the topics listed.

Government & Economy	
Culture Regions	
Challenges	

If **YOU** lived there...

You live in St. Petersburg, a city of beautiful palaces and canals. You are looking forward to the end of school, when your family will go to their dacha, a cottage in the country. In midsummer, when the nights are long and the sun never really sets, you will go to concerts and other celebrations of the "White Nights" in your city.

What do you like about living in St. Petersburg?

BUILDING BACKGROUND Russians have always had a special feeling for the countryside, from the wheat fields and birch forests in the west to the endless grasslands of the steppe. But Russia's great cities are exciting, too, with many shops, museums, and events.

The Russian Federation

For decades, the Soviet Union reigned as a superpower, with Russia as its strongest republic. Then in 1991 the Soviet Union broke apart. Russia's leaders had to create a new government as they struggled to change from communism to democracy.

Government

The Russian Federation is a federal republic, a system in which power is divided between national and local governments. The voters elect a president to serve as the country's chief executive, Russia's most powerful official. The president appoints a prime minister to serve as the head of the government. A legislature, called the Federal Assembly, makes the country's laws.

Increased democracy has led to more freedom for Russians. Voters can choose from several political parties. Information flows more freely. The government no longer seeks to control every aspect of life. In addition, the move toward democracy has improved relations between Russia and Western nations.

Changing to a democratic system has been difficult, though. Problems such as government corruption, or dishonesty, have slowed the development of a free society in Russia. Time will tell whether Russia will continue to grow as a democracy.

Economy

With the move to democracy, Russia also began shifting to a market economy. This type of economy is based on free trade and competition. Today the Russian government has greatly reduced its control of the economy, and most businesses and farms are now privately owned. These changes have led to economic growth. At the same time, most of Russia's wealth is now in the hands of a small number of people.

Today Russia produces and exports oil, natural gas, timber, metals, and chemicals. Heavy industry, such as machinery, is still important. However, light industry, such as clothing and electronics, has grown. Furthermore, service industries now make up the largest part of Russia's economy.

In agriculture, Russia is now a major grower and exporter of grains. Other major crops are fruits, potatoes, and sugar beets.

City and Rural Life

The changes sweeping Russia are visible in its cities. More restaurants and shopping centers are available. Stores offer a wider range of consumer goods, such as TVs. Some Russians have become wealthy and can afford luxuries. In fact, in 2005 Russia had more billionaires than any other European country. Nevertheless, the average Russian's standard of living remains low.

About 75 percent of all Russians live in cities. Most of these people live in small apartments in high-rise buildings. In rural areas, more people live in houses.

Although most Russians live in cities, they still have access to nature. Cities often have large parks and wooded areas in and around them. Many richer Russians own **dachas**, or Russian country houses, where they can garden and enjoy the fresh air.

READING CHECK **Summarizing** How has Russia changed since it became independent?

CONNECTING TO Economics

Kaliningrad

The small region of Kaliningrad—only slightly bigger than Connecticut—is more than 200 miles (320 km) from the rest of Russia. So why would Russia want this area? The reason has to do with the country's cold climate. Kaliningrad is Russia's only Baltic seaport that is free of ice all year. This important port provides Russia with year-round access to profitable European markets and trade. Railroads connect the port to Russia's major cities, as the map below shows.

Drawing Conclusions How do you think Russia's economy benefits from a Baltic seaport that is free of ice all year?

Culture Regions

You have learned that Russia is vast and diverse. For this reason, we divide Russia into several culture regions, as the map on the next page shows. These regions differ in **features** such as population, natural resources, and economic activity.

The four western culture regions make up Russia's heartland. This area is home to the vast majority of Russia's people as well as to the country's capital and largest cities. In addition, the fertile plains of Russia's heartland are the country's most productive farming area.

ACADEMIC VOCABULARY
features
characteristics

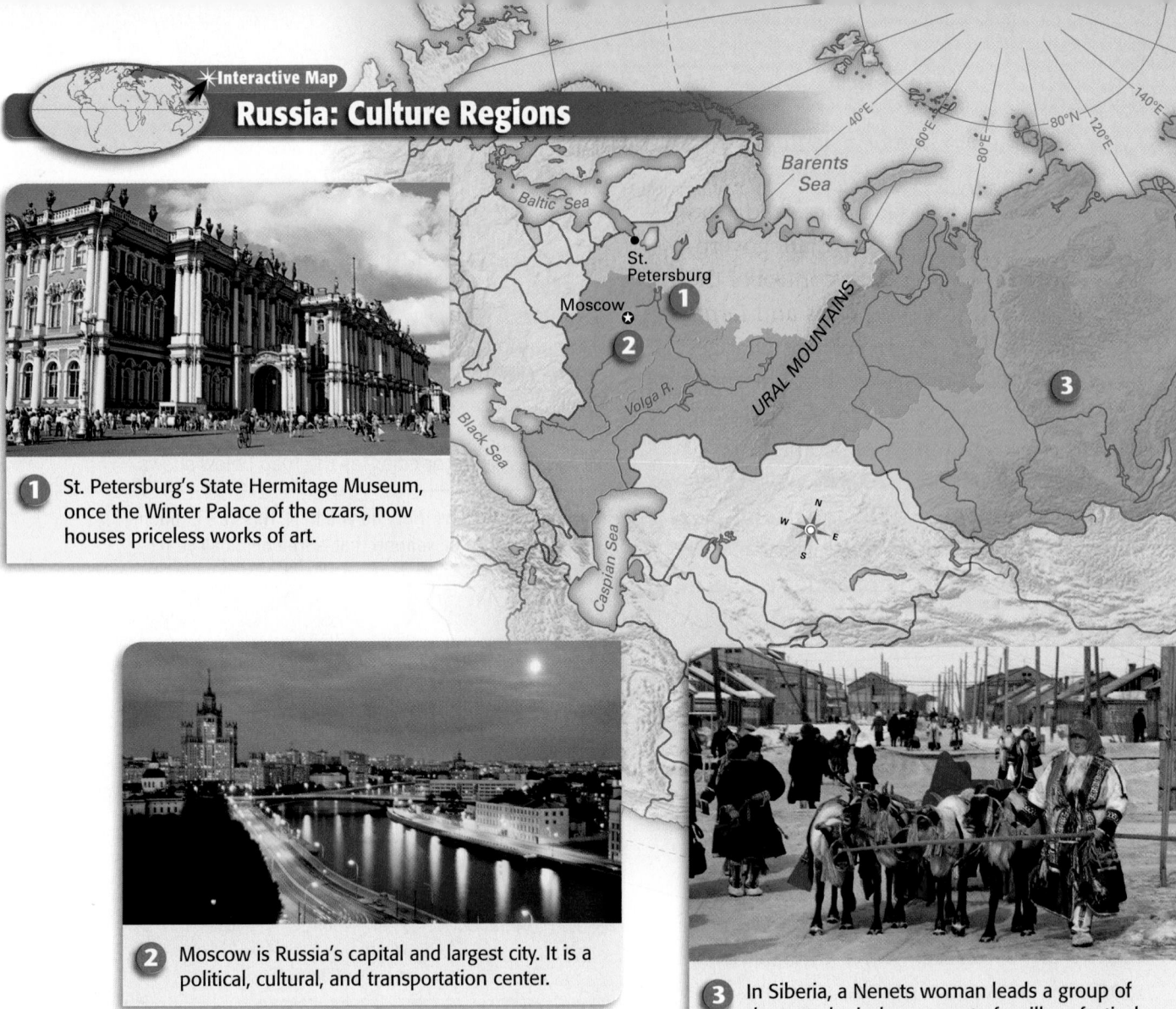

1 St. Petersburg's State Hermitage Museum, once the Winter Palace of the czars, now houses priceless works of art.

2 Moscow is Russia's capital and largest city. It is a political, cultural, and transportation center.

3 In Siberia, a Nenets woman leads a group of decorated reindeer as part of a village festival.

The Moscow Region

Moscow is Russia's capital and largest city. The sprawling, modern city has wide boulevards and large public squares. Its many cultural attractions include the world-famous Bolshoi Ballet and Moscow Circus.

At Moscow's heart is the Kremlin, the center of Russia's government. In Russian, *kremlin* means "fortress." The Kremlin consists of several buildings surrounded by a wall and towers. The buildings include not only government offices but also palaces, museums, and gold-domed churches.

Next to the Kremlin is Red Square, an immense plaza. It is lined by many famous landmarks, such as St. Basil's Cathedral.

The Moscow region is Russia's most important economic area, and its factories produce a wide range of goods. The city is also a transportation center and links by road, rail, and plane to all parts of Russia.

The St. Petersburg Region

St. Petersburg reflects Russians' desire for Western ways. Peter the Great founded the city and styled it after those of Western Europe. For some 200 years, St. Petersburg served as Russia's capital and home to the czars. It features wide avenues, grand palaces, and numerous canals. Theaters and museums enrich the city's cultural life.

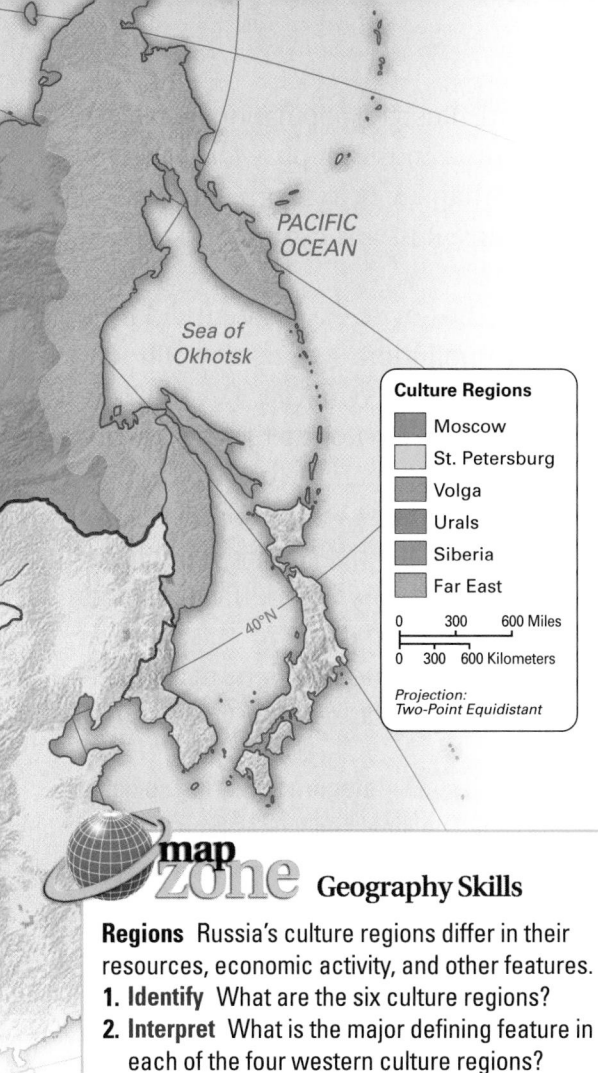

go.hrw.com (KEYWORD: SG7 CH16)

map zone Geography Skills

Regions Russia's culture regions differ in their resources, economic activity, and other features.
1. **Identify** What are the six culture regions?
2. **Interpret** What is the major defining feature in each of the four western culture regions?

St. Petersburg's location on the Gulf of Finland has made the city a major port and trade center. This northern location also produces "White Nights," a period during summer when it never gets totally dark.

The Volga and Urals Regions

The Volga River and Ural Mountains are the third and fourth culture regions. The broad Volga is a major shipping route. Dams along its course form lakes and provide hydroelectric power. Factories in the area process oil and gas. In addition, a site on the Caspian Sea provides fish called sturgeon. The eggs of this fish are called black caviar, which is a costly delicacy, or rare and valued food.

The Ural Mountains are an important mining region and produce nearly every major mineral. **Smelters**, factories that process metal ores, process copper and iron. The Urals region is also known for gems and semiprecious stones.

Siberia

East of the Urals lies the vast expanse of Siberia. In the Tatar language, *Siberia* means "Sleeping Land." Siberian winters are long and severe. As you have read, much of the land lies frozen or buried under snow for most or all of the year. The remote region has many valuable resources, but accessing them in the harsh climate is difficult.

Siberia's main industries are lumber, mining, and oil production. Large coal deposits are mined in southwest Siberia. Rivers produce hydroelectric power. The southern steppes, where the weather is warmer, are Siberia's main farmlands.

Because of Siberia's harsh climate, jobs there pay high wages. Even so, few people choose to live in Siberia. Most towns and cities are in the western and southern parts of the region. These cities tend to follow the **Trans-Siberian Railroad**. This rail line runs from Moscow to Vladivostok on the east coast, and is the longest single rail line in the world.

The Russian Far East

Russia has a long coastline on the Pacific Ocean. There, in the Russian Far East, much land remains heavily forested. In the few cities, factories process forest and mineral resources. Farming occurs in the Amur River valley. The city of Vladivostok is a naval base and the area's main seaport. Islands off the coast provide oil, minerals, and commercial fishing.

READING CHECK **Finding Main Ideas** What areas make up Russia's culture regions?

FOCUS ON READING
Based on settlement in Siberia, what generalization about human settlement can you make?

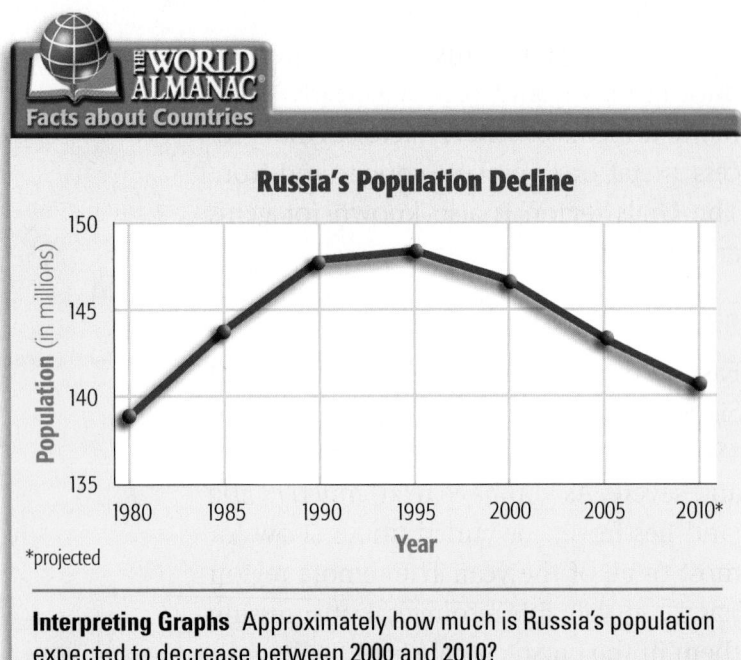

Russia's Population Decline

*projected

Interpreting Graphs Approximately how much is Russia's population expected to decrease between 2000 and 2010?

go.hrw.com KEYWORD: SG7 CH16

Russia's Challenges

Although Russia has made great progress since 1991, challenges remain. First, Russia's shift to a market economy has not been without problems. For example, prices and unemployment have risen, and the gap between rich and poor has widened.

Second, Russia's population is falling, as you can see in the graph. More Russians are dying than are being born. One reason is that many Russians cannot afford good health care.

Third, the Soviet government did little to prevent pollution. As a result pollution, such as industrial chemicals, has seriously harmed Russia's environment. The government must now repair the damage.

Last, Russia faces ethnic conflicts. One of the worst is in the Russian republic of **Chechnya** (CHECH-nyah) in the Caucasus Mountains. Some people in this Muslim area want independence. Fighting and terrorism there have caused many deaths.

READING CHECK **Categorizing** What social, economic, and political challenges face Russia?

SUMMARY AND PREVIEW As you have read, Russia is a federal republic working to build a market economy. The west is Russia's heartland, but Siberia has many valuable resources. In the next section, you will read about the Caucasus.

Section 3 Assessment

go.hrw.com
Online Quiz
KEYWORD: SG7 HP16

Reviewing Ideas, Terms, and Places

1. **a. Recall** What type of government does Russia now have?
   b. Explain How is Russia's economy changing?
2. **a. Recall** From west to east, what are Russia's major culture regions?
   b. Draw Conclusions Why do you think most Siberian towns and cities are located along the **Trans-Siberian Railroad**?
   c. Rate Which of Russia's culture regions would you most want to live in, and why?
3. **a. Identify** What are the main challenges that face Russia today?
   b. Elaborate What difficulties does **Chechnya** pose for Russia's leaders?

Critical Thinking

4. **Categorizing** Draw a concept web like the one shown. Use your notes to list facts about each Russian culture region.

FOCUS ON WRITING

5. **Collecting Details about Russia Today** Based on conditions in Russia today, what location would you choose for your property? Review your notes from Section 2 and this section. Then choose one location in Russia for the property you are selling.

from
The Endless Steppe

by Esther Hautzig

About the Reading *In* The Endless Steppe, *an autobiographical novel, Esther Hautzig writes about her own experiences as a teenage girl. In the novel, the girl Esther is from a wealthy Jewish family in Poland. In 1941 her family is deported to a labor camp in Siberia. In the excerpt below, Esther and her family are on the train to Siberia. She is dreading their destination.*

AS YOU READ Think about what Esther feels as she watches the passing landscape. What ideas does she already have about life in Siberia?

The flatness of this land was awesome. There wasn't a hill in sight; it was an enormous, unrippled sea of parched and lifeless grass.

"Tata, why is the earth so flat here?"

"These must be steppes, Esther."

"Steppes? But steppes are in Siberia."

"This is Siberia," he said quietly.

If I had been told that I had been transported to the moon, I could not have been more stunned.

"Siberia?" My voice trembled. "But Siberia is full of snow."

"It will be," my father said. ❶

Siberia! Siberia was the end of the world, a point of no return. Siberia was for criminals and political enemies, where the punishment was unbelievably cruel, and where people died like flies. ❷ Summer or no summer—and who had ever talked about hot Siberia?—Siberia was the tundra and mountainous drifts of snow. Siberia was *wolves*.

GUIDED READING

WORD HELP

deported forced to leave a country

parched very thirsty

Tata Polish word that means "daddy" or "papa"

steppes vast, grassy plains in southern Russia

tundra in subarctic climates, an almost treeless plain with permanently frozen subsoil

❶ At the time of the train journey, it is summer.

❷ The labor camps in Siberia, called gulags, were harsh places to live. Many people died at the camps.

Connecting Literature to Geography

1. **Analyzing** Russian soldiers took Esther's family from their home in Poland to work in Siberia. How do you think this fact affects Esther's feelings as she views the landscape of Siberia from the train?

2. **Drawing Inferences** Why do you think Siberia was chosen as a place of exile? What made it a punishment to live there?

The Caucasus

What You Will Learn...

Main Ideas

1. Many groups have ruled and influenced the Caucasus during its long history.
2. Today the Caucasus republics are working to improve their economies but struggle with ethnic unrest and conflict.

The Big Idea

In an area long ruled by outside groups, the Caucasus republics are struggling to strengthen their economies and to deal with ethnic unrest.

Key Places

Tbilisi, *p. 395*
Yerevan, *p. 395*
Baku, *p. 396*

TAKING NOTES As you read, use a chart like the one here to take notes on the three countries of the Caucasus. Include information about history and government.

Georgia	Armenia	Azerbaijan

If **YOU** lived there...

You live in Tbilisi, the capital of the country of Georgia. Several years ago, your sister and her college friends joined the Rose Revolution, a political protest that forced a corrupt president to resign. The protestors' symbol was a red rose. Since the protest, you have become more interested in politics.

What kind of government do you want?

BUILDING BACKGROUND Georgia is one of three republics in the area called the Caucasus. In 1991, when the Soviet Union ended, the Caucasus republics gained independence. Since then, the republics have struggled to become democracies with market economies.

History

The Caucasus lies in the rugged Caucasus Mountains between the Black and Caspian seas. Located where Europe blends into Asia, the Caucasus reflects a range of cultural influences. At one time or another, Persians, Greeks, Romans, Arabs, Turks, and Mongols have all ruled or invaded the area. The Russians took control of much of the Caucasus in the early 1800s.

Russian control in the Caucasus did not include what is now western Armenia. The Ottoman Turks held this area. Over time, the Turks grew to distrust the Armenians, however; and in the late 1800s began abusing and killing them. During World War I (1914–1918), the Turks forced all Armenians to leave. Hundreds of thousands of Armenians died during this ethnic cleansing, or attempt to remove an ethnic group. The Turks lost World War I, though, and had to give up western Armenia.

After World War I, Armenia, Azerbaijan, and Georgia gained independence—but not for long. By the early 1920s they were part of the vast Soviet Union. Finally in 1991, when the Soviet Union fell, the Caucasus republics achieved true independence.

READING CHECK **Finding Main Ideas** Why do the countries in the Caucasus reflect a range of cultural influences?

The snow-capped peaks of the Caucasus Mountains rise above a mountain village and the remains of a fortress built in the 900s.

Mount Elbrus
18,510 ft
(5,642 m)

National capital

Projection: Lambert Equal-Area

RUSSIA

CAUCASUS MOUNTAINS

Black Sea

GEORGIA

Tbilisi

Kur River

Baku

TURKEY

ARMENIA
Lake Sevan

AZERBAIJAN

40°N

Yerevan

Aras River

Caspian Sea

IRAN

map zone Geography Skills

Location South of western Russia, the Caucasus is located where Europe blends into Asia.
1. **Name** What two seas border the Caucasus?
2. **Contrast** Based on the map, how does Armenia differ from Azerbaijan and Georgia?

The Caucasus Today

The Caucasus may have a long history, but the Caucasus countries do not. Like other former Soviet republics, these young countries have had to create new governments and economies. Meanwhile, ethnic unrest and conflicts have slowed progress.

The Caucasus republics have similar governments. An elected president governs each nation, and an appointed prime minister runs each government. An elected parliament, or legislature, makes the laws.

Georgia

The country of Georgia lies in the Caucasus Mountains east of the Black Sea. **Tbilisi** is the capital. About 70 percent of the people are ethnic Georgians, and most belong to the Georgian Orthodox Church. The official language is Georgian, a unique language with its own alphabet. However, many other languages are also spoken.

Since 1991 Georgia has struggled with unrest and civil war. In 2003 Georgians forced out their president in the peaceful Rose Revolution. Meanwhile, ethnic groups in northern Georgia were fighting for independence. Because these groups now hold parts of northern Georgia, division and unrest continues.

Although unrest has hurt Georgia's economy, international aid is helping it improve. Georgia's economy is based on services and farming. Major crops include citrus fruits, grapes, and tea. In addition, Georgia produces steel and mines copper and manganese. Georgia is also famous for its wines. The Black Sea is a resort area, and tourism contributes to the economy, too.

Armenia

South of Georgia is the small, landlocked country of Armenia. The tiny country is slightly larger than the state of Maryland. **Yerevan** (yer-uh-VAHN) is the capital. Almost all the people are ethnic Armenian. Armenia prides itself as being the first country to adopt Christianity, and most people belong to the Armenian Orthodox Church.

Baku

Located on the Caspian Sea, the city of Baku is the capital and chief port of Azerbaijan.

FOCUS ON READING

What general statements can you make about the Caucasus as a whole?

In the early 1990s, Armenia fought a bitter war with its neighbor Azerbaijan. The war involved an area of Azerbaijan where most people are ethnic Armenian. Armenia wanted this area to become part of its country. Although a cease-fire stopped the fighting in 1994, Armenian armed forces still control the area. The issue remained unsettled as of the early 2000s.

This conflict has greatly hurt Armenia's economy. However, international aid is helping Armenia's economy recover and expand. For example, diamond processing is now a growing industry in Armenia.

Azerbaijan

East of Armenia is Azerbaijan. In contrast to the other Caucasus republics, Azerbaijan is largely Muslim. The Azeri (uh-ZE-ree) make up 90 percent of the population.

Azerbaijan's economy is based on oil, found along and under the Caspian Sea. **Baku**, the capital, is the center of a large oil-refining industry. This industry has led to strong economic growth. Corruption is high, though; and many people are poor. In addition, Azerbaijan has many refugees as a result of its conflict with Armenia.

READING CHECK **Summarizing** What challenges do the Caucasus republics face?

SUMMARY The Caucasus republics face challenges but are working to develop democracy and build their economies.

Section 4 Assessment

go.hrw.com
Online Quiz
KEYWORD: SG7 HP16

Reviewing Ideas, Terms, and Places

1. a. Identify Which country controlled much of the Caucasus for most of the 1800s?
   b. Identify Cause and Effect How did Turkish rule affect Armenians in the Ottoman Empire?
   c. Elaborate How has location affected the history and culture of the Caucasus area?
2. a. Recall How does **Baku** contribute to the economy of Azerbaijan?
   b. Compare and Contrast How is religion in Georgia and Armenia similar? How does religion in these countries differ from that in Azerbaijan?
   c. Elaborate How has the war that occurred between Armenia and Azerbaijan affected each country?

Critical Thinking

3. Comparing and Contrasting Draw a Venn diagram like the one here. Use your notes to identify the ways in which Georgia, Armenia, and Azerbaijan are similar and different.

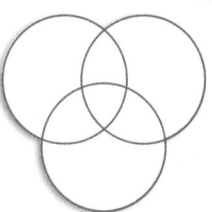

FOCUS ON WRITING

4. Collecting Details about the Caucasus You have narrowed Russian locations to one possibility. What features do the Caucasus countries have that might be attractive to potential buyers? Identify one Caucasus location you might use in your ad.

Geography's Impact
video series
Review the video to answer the closing question:
Why was the Soviet Union so determined to become a major industrial power?

Visual Summary

Use the visual summary below to help you review the main ideas of the chapter.

QUICK FACTS

Russia is an immense, cold country with plains, mountains, and forest. The Caucasus is a small, mountainous area.

With a long history and a rich culture, Russia ranges from large modern cities to the vast plains and forests of Siberia.

The three small Caucasus republics lie between the Black and Caspian seas, and face ethnic unrest and conflict.

Reviewing Vocabulary, Terms, and Places

For each statement below, write T if it is true and F if it is false. If the statement is false, replace the boldfaced term with one that makes the sentence a true statement.

1. The **Caucasus Mountains** separate European Russia from Asian Russia.

2. Russia's capital and largest city is **St. Petersburg**.

3. The Caucasus is bordered by the Black Sea to the west and **Lake Baikal** to the east.

4. Under the rule of the **Bolsheviks**, the Russian Empire expanded in size and power.

5. Much of the country of Georgia is located in the high, rugged **Ural Mountains**.

6. Many wealthier Russians have country houses, which are called **gulags**.

7. Russia's main government buildings are located in the **Kremlin** in Moscow.

8. Russia's culture regions differ in **features** such as cities, natural resources, and economic activity.

9. **Moscow** is a major port and was once home to Russia's czars.

10. The capital city of Armenia is **Yerevan**.

Comprehension and Critical Thinking

SECTION 1 *(Pages 378–381)*

11. **a. Recall** What is Russia's most important river, and to what major bodies of water does it link?

   b. Identify Cause and Effect How does Russia's location affect its climate?

   c. Elaborate Why might developing the many natural resources in Siberia be difficult?

SECTION 2 *(Pages 382–386)*

12. **a. Identify** Who was Joseph Stalin?

   b. Summarize How has Russia contributed to world culture?

   c. Elaborate How was the end of the Soviet Union similar to the end of the Russian Empire?

SECTION 3 (Pages 388–392)

13. a. Identify What four culture regions make up the Russian heartland?

b. Compare and Contrast How are Moscow and St. Petersburg similar and different?

c. Elaborate How might Siberia help make Russia an economic success?

SECTION 4 (Pages 394–396)

14. a. Recall What is the capital of each of the Caucasus republics?

b. Compare What do the three Caucasus countries have in common?

c. Elaborate What issues and challenges do the Caucasus countries need to address to improve their economies?

Using the Internet

15. Activity: Making a Map The Trans-Siberian Railroad is the longest single rail line in the world. Climb aboard in Moscow and travel all the way across Russia. Enter the activity keyword to start your journey. Research the people, places, and history along the railroad's route. Then create an illustrated map of your journey. On the map, show the train's route, indicate the places where you stopped, and include images and descriptions about what you saw.

Social Studies Skills

Interpreting a Population Map *Use a good atlas to find a population map of Europe. The map does not need to include Russia. Use the map to answer the following questions. Do not include the country of Russia when answering the questions.*

16. Not including the cities of Russia, how many cities or metropolitan areas in Europe have more than 2 million people?

17. Not including Russia, which regions of Europe are the most populated? Which regions of Europe are the least populated?

18. Making Generalizations Examine the information in Section 3 about the four culture regions that make up Russia's heartland. Based on the specific information about these regions, make two generalizations about western Russia.

19. Creating a Real Estate Ad Review your notes about locations in Russia and the Caucasus. Choose one location for the real estate you are selling. What are its best features? How would you describe the land and climate? What are the benefits of living there? If it is a building, what does it look like? What is nearby? Answer these questions in your real estate ad. Remember to include details that will make the property attractive to possible buyers.

Map Activity

20. Russia and the Caucasus On a separate sheet of paper, match the letters on the map with their correct labels.

Caucasus Mountains	Ural Mountains
Caspian Sea	Vladivostok, Russia
Kamchatka Peninsula	Volga River
Moscow, Russia	West Siberian Plain
St. Petersburg, Russia	

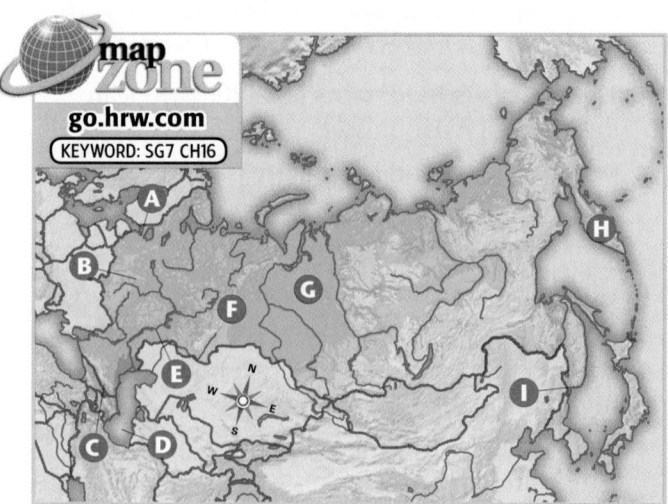

DIRECTIONS: Read questions 1 through 7 and write the letter of the best response. Then read question 8 and write your own well-constructed response.

1 Which word below *best* describes Russia's overall climate?

A Cold

B Dry

C Hot

D Wet

2 What is the name of the vast forest that covers much of Russia?

A Siberia

B Steppe

C Taiga

D Tundra

3 What was the name of the second Soviet leader, who ruled as a brutal dictator?

A Ivan III

B Ivan the Terrible

C Vladimir Lenin

D Joseph Stalin

4 The majority of Russians are descended from the

A Bolsheviks.

B Slavs.

C Tatars.

D Ukrainians.

5 What are the Caucasus countries?

A Armenia, Moscow, and St. Petersburg

B Azerbaijan, Georgia, and Russia

C Azerbaijan, Armenia, and Georgia

D Georgia, Moscow, and Russia

The Caucasus: Climate

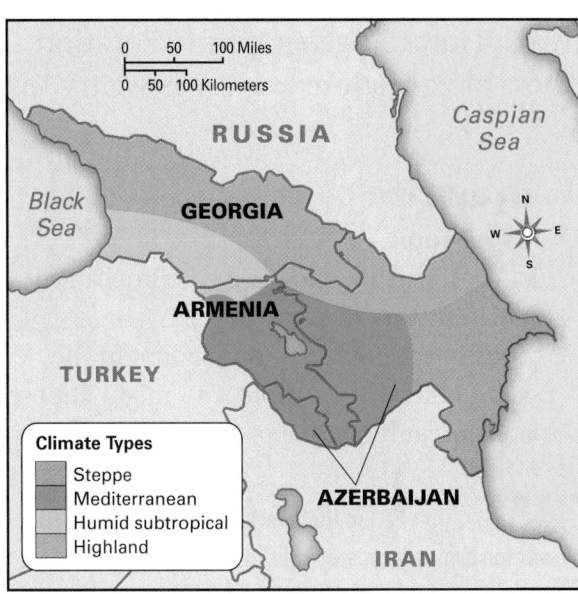

6 Based on the map above, which of the following climates is found along part of the coast of the Black Sea?

A Humid subtropical

B Mediterranean

C Steppe

D Tropical Savanna

7 What year did the Soviet Union collapse and break apart into 15 independent republics?

A 1990

B 1991

C 2000

D 2001

8 Extended Response Examine the Section 3 map of Russia's culture regions. Based on the map, describe how the physical geography in three of the culture regions contributes to the economic activity in those regions.

A Biographical Narrative

Peeople have shaped the world. Who are the important people in history? What were the critical events in their lives? How did geography or location affect those events? These are questions we ask as we try to understand our world.

Assignment

Write a biographical narrative about a significant event in the life of a historical figure such as Queen Isabella, Martin Luther, Napoleon, or Mikhail Gorbachev.

1. Prewrite

Choose a Topic

- Choose a person who affected European or Russian history in some way.
- Choose a specific event or incident in the person's life. For example, you might choose Napoleon at the Battle of Waterloo.

> **TIP** To choose the event, think about the person's importance or signficance. Choose an event that will help you make that point.

Gather and Organize Information

- Look for information about your topic in the library or on the Internet. Book-length biographies about the person are a good source.
- Identify the parts of the event. Organize them in chonological, or time, order. Note details about people, actions, and the location of the event.

2. Write

Use a Writer's Framework

A Writer's Framework

Introduction
- Introduce the person and the event.
- Identify the importance of the event.

Body
- Write at least one paragraph for each major part of the event. Include specific details.
- Use chronological, or time, order to organize the parts of the event.

Conclusion
- Summarize the importance of the person and event in the final paragraph.

3. Evaluate and Revise

Review and Improve Your Paper

- Read your first draft at least twice, and then use the questions below to evaluate your paper.
- Make the changes needed to improve your paper.

Evaluation Questions for a Biographical Narrative

1. Do you introduce the person and event and identify the importance of each?
2. Do you have one paragraph for each major part of the event?
3. Do you include specific details about people, actions, and location?
4. Do you use chronological order, the order in time, to organize the parts of the event?
5. Do you end the paper with a summary of the importance of the person and event?

4. Proofread and Publish

Give Your Explanation the Finishing Touch

- Make sure your transitional phrases—such as then, next, later, or finally—help clarify the order of the actions that took place.
- Make sure you capitalized all proper names.
- You can share your biographical narrative by reading it aloud in class or adding it to a class collection of biographies.

5. Practice and Apply

Use the steps and strategies outlined in this workshop to write your biographical narrative. Share your work with others, comparing and contrasting the importance of the people and events.

Southwest and Central Asia

The Caspian Sea

The vast Caspian Sea, which is the world's largest inland body of water, contains valuable resources like oil.

Great Mountains

In Central Asia, high mountain ranges such as the Tian Shan separate the region from other parts of Asia.

Huge Deserts

Southwest Asia is home to huge deserts such as the Rub' al-Khali, or "Empty Quarter," which is virtually uninhabited.

Southwest and Central Asia

Explore the Satellite Image
Vast deserts, high mountains, and large rivers stand out clearly on this satellite image of Southwest and Central Asia. How do you think these features influence life in the region?

The Satellite's Path

>44'56.08<

>>>>>>>>>665.00'87<

567.476.348   +355   +744   +999   +608

456.094.

Southwest and Central Asia: Physical

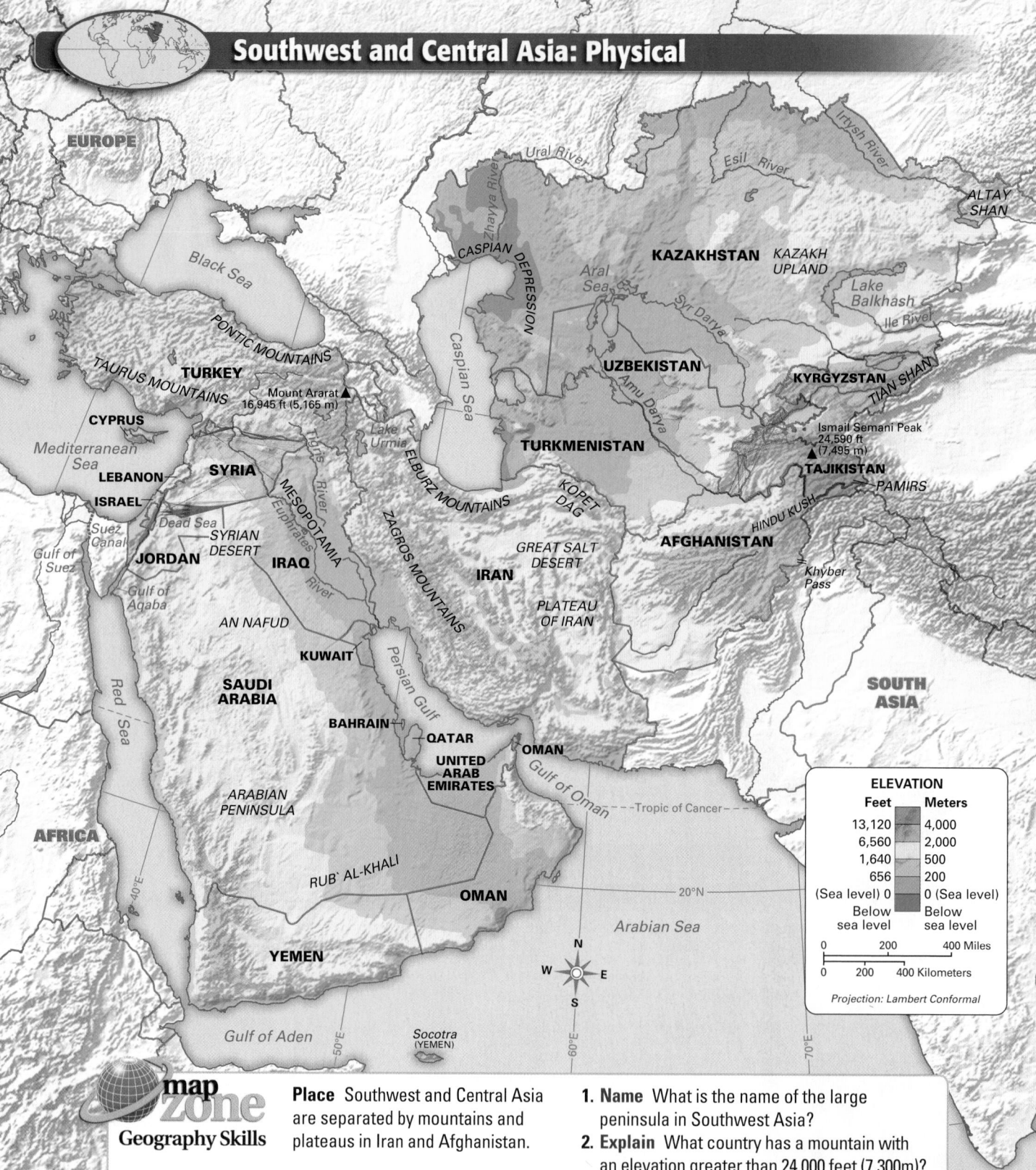

EUROPE

Black Sea

PONTIC MOUNTAINS

TAURUS MOUNTAINS

TURKEY

Mount Ararat ▲
16,945 ft (5,165 m)

CYPRUS

Mediterranean Sea

LEBANON

ISRAEL

SYRIA

MESOPOTAMIA

Tigris River

Euphrates River

Dead Sea

Suez Canal

Gulf of Suez

JORDAN

SYRIAN DESERT

Gulf of Aqaba

IRAQ

ZAGROS MOUNTAINS

AN NAFUD

KUWAIT

SAUDI ARABIA

Red Sea

BAHRAIN

QATAR

UNITED ARAB EMIRATES

Persian Gulf

ARABIAN PENINSULA

AFRICA

RUB' AL-KHALI

OMAN

OMAN

YEMEN

Gulf of Aden

Gulf of Oman

Arabian Sea

Socotra (YEMEN)

Tropic of Cancer

20°N

CASPIAN DEPRESSION

Zhayya River

Ural River

Esil River

Irtysh River

ALTAY SHAN

Caspian Sea

Aral Sea

KAZAKHSTAN

KAZAKH UPLAND

Lake Balkhash

Ile River

Syr Darya

UZBEKISTAN

Amu Darya

KYRGYZSTAN

TIAN SHAN

Lake Urmia

ELBURZ MOUNTAINS

TURKMENISTAN

KOPET DAG

GREAT SALT DESERT

IRAN

PLATEAU OF IRAN

Ismail Semani Peak
24,590 ft
(7,495 m) ▲

TAJIKISTAN

PAMIRS

HINDU KUSH

AFGHANISTAN

Khyber Pass

SOUTH ASIA

40°E

50°E

60°E

70°E

ELEVATION

Feet	Meters
13,120	4,000
6,560	2,000
1,640	500
656	200
(Sea level) 0	0 (Sea level)
Below sea level	Below sea level

0 — 200 — 400 Miles

0 — 200 — 400 Kilometers

Projection: Lambert Conformal

N W E S

map zone

Geography Skills

Place Southwest and Central Asia are separated by mountains and plateaus in Iran and Afghanistan.

1. **Name** What is the name of the large peninsula in Southwest Asia?

2. **Explain** What country has a mountain with an elevation greater than 24,000 feet (7,300m)?

Southwest and Central Asia

Facts about the World

Geographical Extremes: Southwest and Central Asia

Longest River	Euphrates River, Turkey/Syria/Iraq: 1,700 miles (2,735 km)
Highest Point	Qullai Ismoili Somoni, Tajikistan: 24,590 feet (7,495 m)
Lowest Point	Dead Sea, Israel/Jordan: 1,348 feet (411 m) below sea level
Highest Recorded Temperature	Tirat Tsvi, Israel: 129°F (53.9°C)
Driest Place	Aden, Yemen: 1.8 inches (4.6 cm) average precipitation per year
Largest Country	Kazakhstan: 1,049,155 square miles (2,717,311 square km)
Smallest Country	Bahrain: 257 square miles (666 square km)
Saltiest Lake	Dead Sea, Israel/Jordan: 33 percent salt content
Most Powerful Earthquake	Erzincan, Turkey, 1939: 8.0 magnitude

A high salt content keeps people afloat in the Dead Sea.

go.hrw.com   KEYWORD: SG7 UN4

Size Comparison: The United States and Southwest and Central Asia

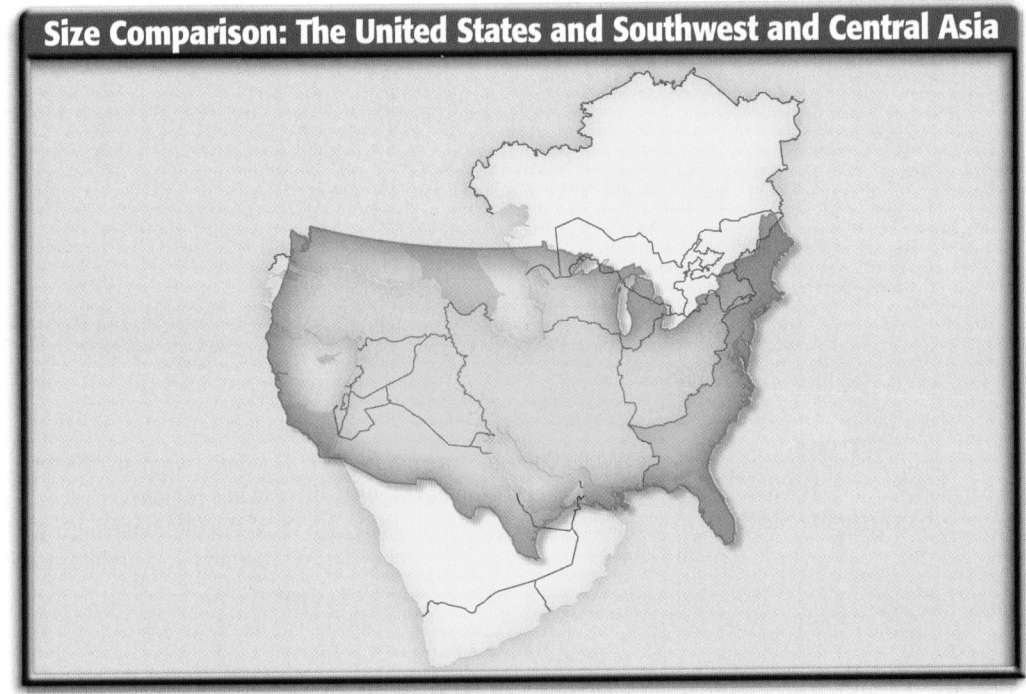

Southwest and Central Asia: Political

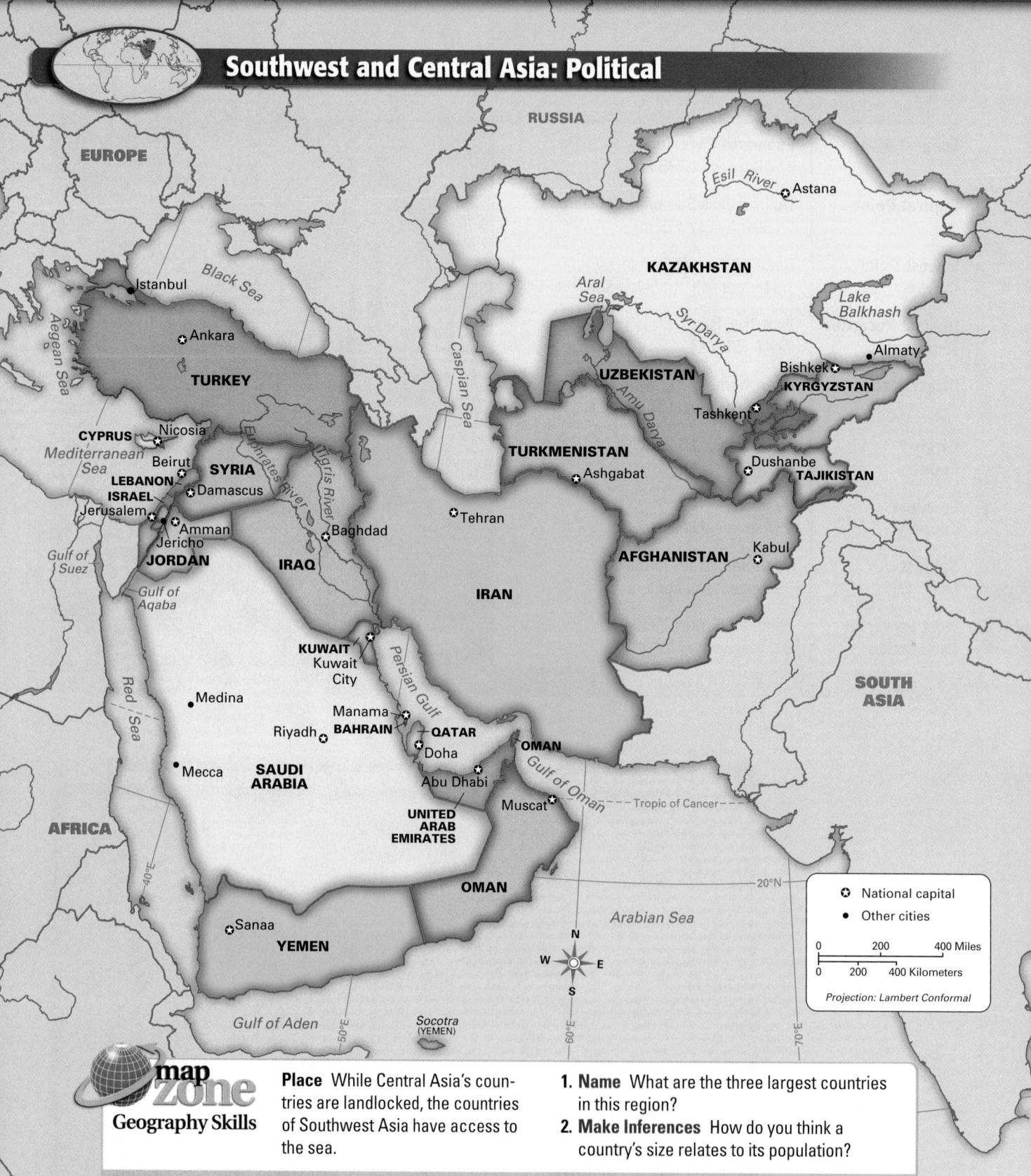

RUSSIA

EUROPE

Esil River • Astana

Black Sea

Istanbul

Aral Sea

KAZAKHSTAN

Lake Balkhash

Ankara

Syr Darya

Almaty

TURKEY

Caspian Sea

UZBEKISTAN

Bishkek

KYRGYZSTAN

Amu Darya

Tashkent

CYPRUS Nicosia

Mediterranean Sea

Beirut

SYRIA

TURKMENISTAN

Dushanbe

LEBANON Damascus

Euphrates River

Ashgabat

TAJIKISTAN

ISRAEL

Tigris River

Jerusalem

Amman Baghdad

Tehran

AFGHANISTAN

Kabul

Jericho

JORDAN

IRAQ

Gulf of Suez

IRAN

Gulf of Aqaba

KUWAIT

Kuwait City

Persian Gulf

SOUTH ASIA

Red Sea

Medina

Manama

Riyadh BAHRAIN

QATAR

Doha

OMAN

Mecca

SAUDI ARABIA

Abu Dhabi

Muscat

Gulf of Oman

Tropic of Cancer

AFRICA

UNITED ARAB EMIRATES

20°N

OMAN

Arabian Sea

N

Sanaa

W   E

YEMEN

S

Gulf of Aden

Socotra (YEMEN)

National capital

• Other cities

0   200   400 Miles

0   200   400 Kilometers

Projection: Lambert Conformal

Place While Central Asia's countries are landlocked, the countries of Southwest Asia have access to the sea.

1. **Name** What are the three largest countries in this region?

2. **Make Inferences** How do you think a country's size relates to its population?

map zone

Geography Skills

Southwest and Central Asia: Resources

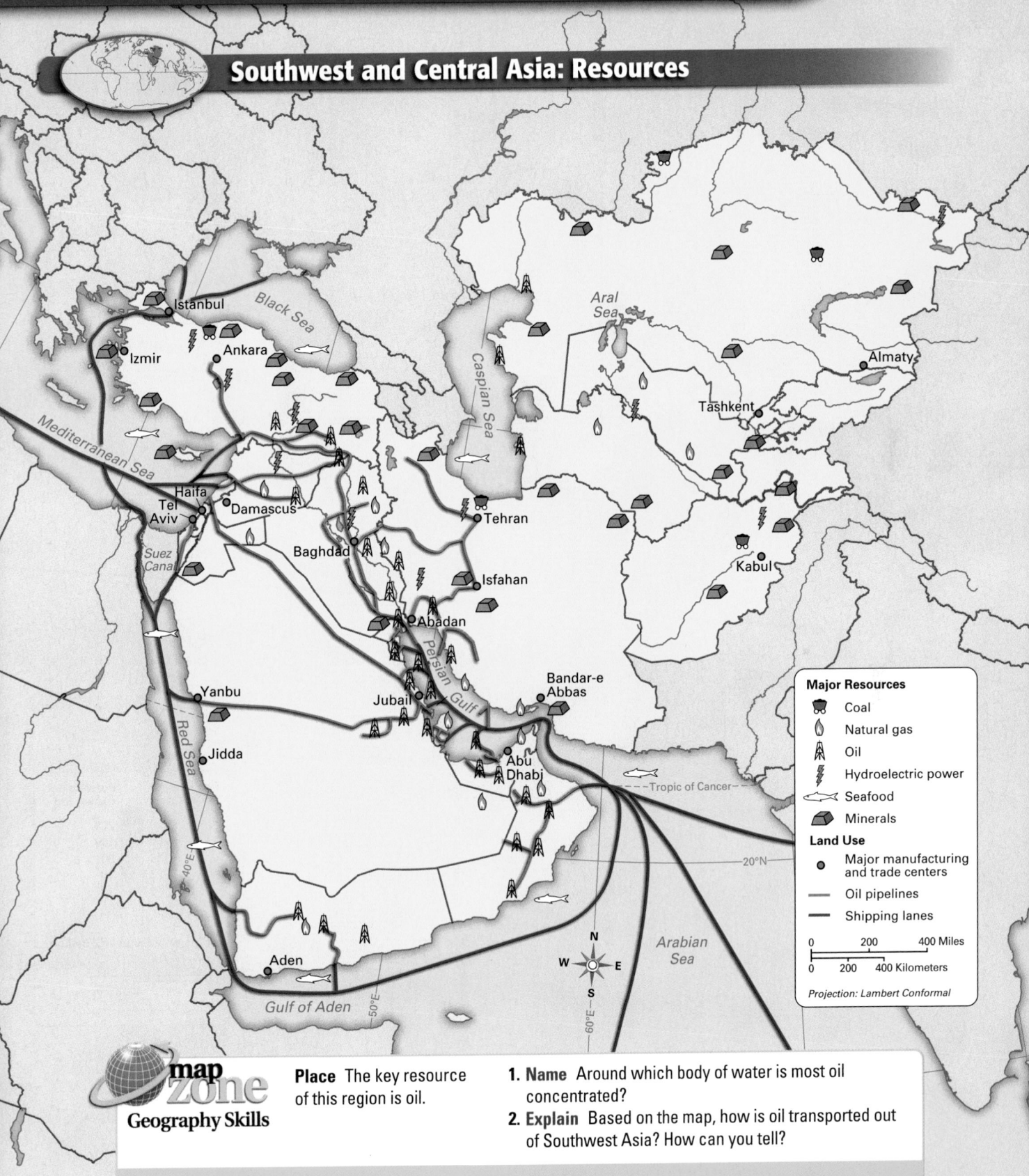

Major Resources

- Coal
- Natural gas
- Oil
- Hydroelectric power
- Seafood
- Minerals

Land Use

- ● Major manufacturing and trade centers
- ─── Oil pipelines
- ─── Shipping lanes

0   200   400 Miles

0   200   400 Kilometers

Projection: Lambert Conformal

map zone
Geography Skills

Place The key resource of this region is oil.

1. **Name** Around which body of water is most oil concentrated?

2. **Explain** Based on the map, how is oil transported out of Southwest Asia? How can you tell?

Southwest and Central Asia: Population

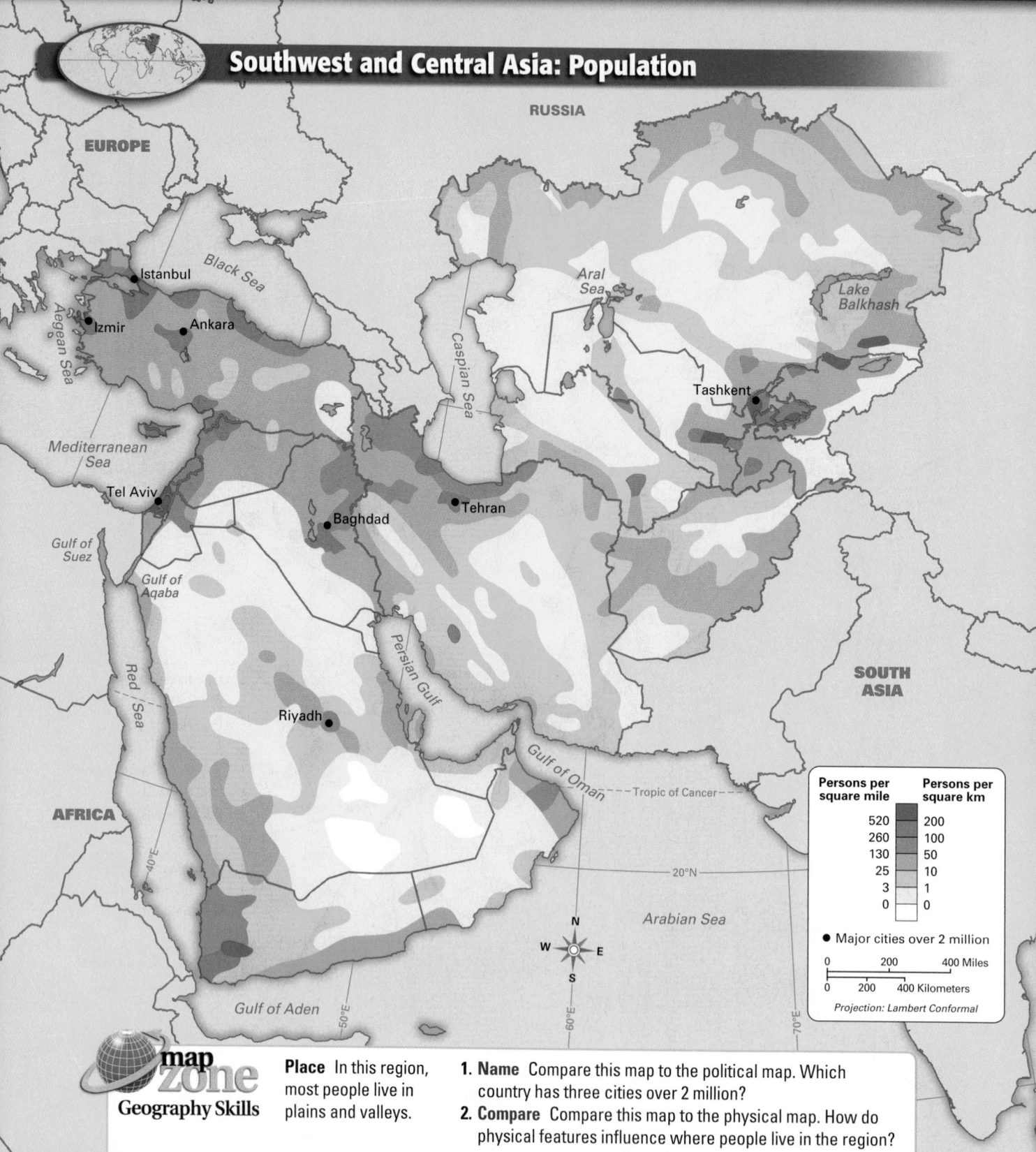

RUSSIA

EUROPE

Black Sea

Istanbul

Izmir

Ankara

Aegean Sea

Mediterranean Sea

Tel Aviv

Gulf of Suez

Gulf of Aqaba

Red Sea

40°E

AFRICA

Riyadh

Gulf of Aden

50°E

Caspian Sea

Aral Sea

Lake Balkhash

Tashkent

Tehran

Baghdad

Persian Gulf

Gulf of Oman

Tropic of Cancer

20°N

Arabian Sea

60°E

70°E

SOUTH ASIA

N
W E
S

Persons per square mile | **Persons per square km**
520 | 200
260 | 100
130 | 50
25 | 10
3 | 1
0 | 0

● Major cities over 2 million

0   200   400 Miles
0 200 400 Kilometers

Projection: Lambert Conformal

map zone
Geography Skills

Place In this region, most people live in plains and valleys.

1. **Name** Compare this map to the political map. Which country has three cities over 2 million?

2. **Compare** Compare this map to the physical map. How do physical features influence where people live in the region?

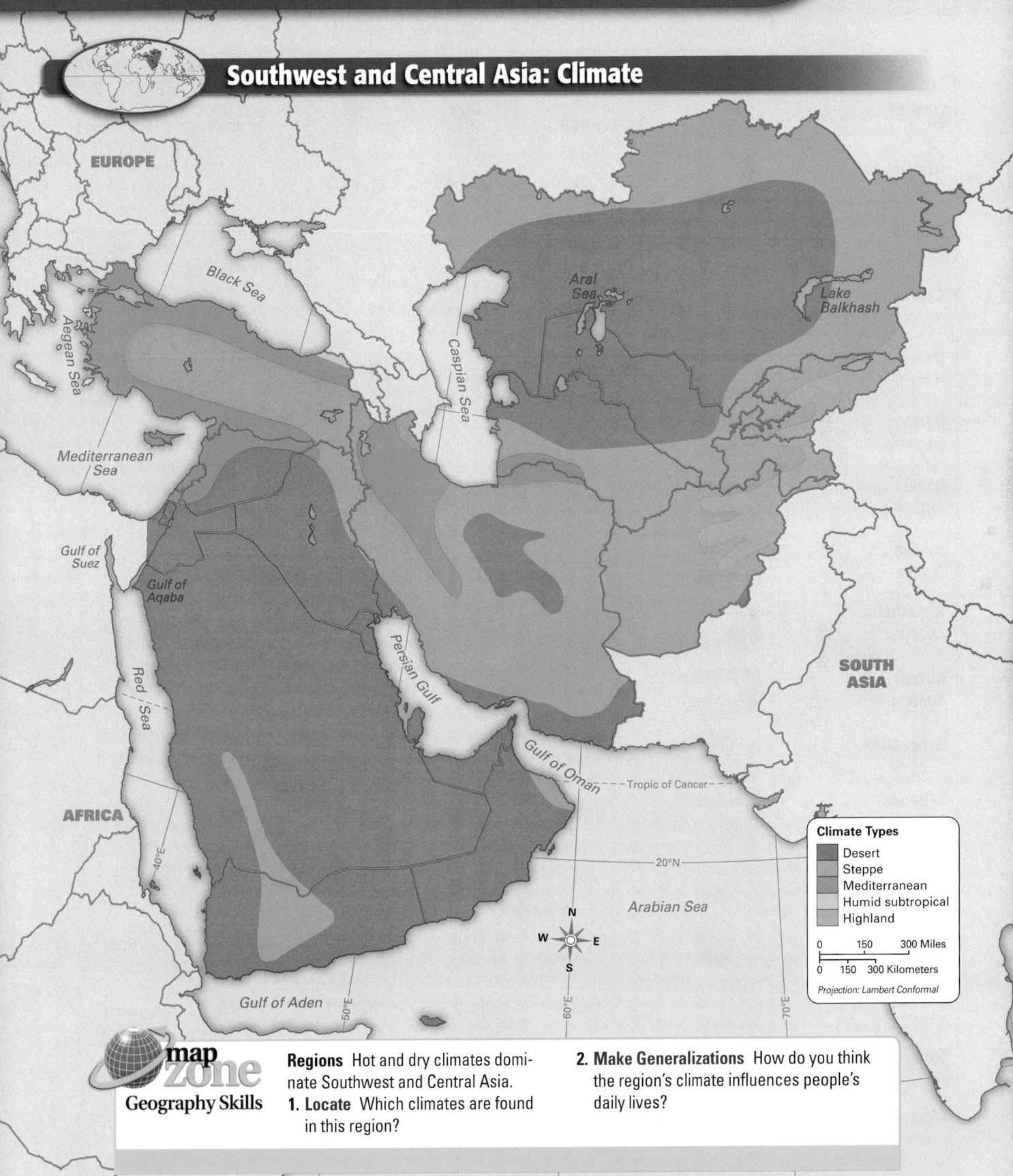

Southwest and Central Asia

EUROPE

Black Sea

Aral Sea

Lake Balkhash

Aegean Sea

Caspian Sea

Mediterranean Sea

Gulf of Suez

Gulf of Aqaba

Red Sea

Persian Gulf

SOUTH ASIA

Gulf of Oman

Tropic of Cancer

AFRICA

20°N

Arabian Sea

N
W   E
S

Gulf of Aden

Climate Types
- Desert
- Steppe
- Mediterranean
- Humid subtropical
- Highland

0   150   300 Miles

0   150   300 Kilometers

Projection: Lambert Conformal

map zone
Geography Skills

Regions Hot and dry climates dominate Southwest and Central Asia.

1. Locate Which climates are found in this region?

2. Make Generalizations How do you think the region's climate influences people's daily lives?

Facts about Countries

Southwest and Central Asia

COUNTRY Capital	FLAG	POPULATION	AREA (sq mi)	PER CAPITA GDP (U.S. $)	LIFE EXPECTANCY AT BIRTH	TVS PER 1,000 PEOPLE
Afghanistan Kabul		31.9 million	250,001	$800	43.8	14
Bahrain Manama		708,600	257	$25,300	74.7	446
Cyprus Nicosia		788,500	3,571	$22,700	78.0	154
Iran Tehran		65.3 million	636,296	$8,900	70.6	154
Iraq Baghdad		27.5 million	168,754	$2,900	69.3	82
Israel Jerusalem		6.4 million	8,019	$26,200	79.6	328
Jordan Amman		6.0 million	35,637	$4,900	78.6	83
Kazakhstan Astana		15.3 million	1,049,155	$9,100	67.2	240
Kuwait Kuwait City		2.5 million	6,880	$21,600	77.4	480
Kyrgyzstan Bishkek		5.3 million	76,641	$2,000	68.8	49
Lebanon Beirut		3.9 million	4,015	$5,500	73.1	355
Oman Muscat		3.2 million	82,031	$14,100	73.6	575
Qatar Doha		907,200	4,416	$29,400	74.1	866
Saudi Arabia Riyadh		27.6 million	756,985	$13,800	75.9	263
Syria Damascus		19.3 million	71,498	$4,000	70.6	68
United States Washington, D.C.		301.1 million	3,718,711	$43,500	78.0	844

COUNTRY Capital	FLAG	POPULATION	AREA (sq mi)	PER CAPITA GDP (U.S. $)	LIFE EXPECTANCY AT BIRTH	TVS PER 1,000 PEOPLE
Tajikistan Dushanbe		7.1 million	55,251	$1,300	64.6	328
Turkey Ankara		71.2 million	301,384	$8,900	72.9	328
Turkmenistan Ashgabat		5.1 million	188,456	$8,900	62.3	198
United Arab Emirates Abu Dhabi		4.4 million	32,000	$49,700	75.7	309
Uzbekistan Tashkent		27.8 million	172,742	$2,000	65.0	280
Yemen Sanaa		22.2 million	203,850	$900	62.5	286
United States Washington, D.C.		301.1 million	3,718,711	$43,500	78.0	844

ANALYSIS SKILL ANALYZING TABLES

1. How does the per capita GDP of countries in this region compare to the per capita GDP of the United States?
2. Based on the table, which countries seem to have the highest standard of living?

Oil Giants

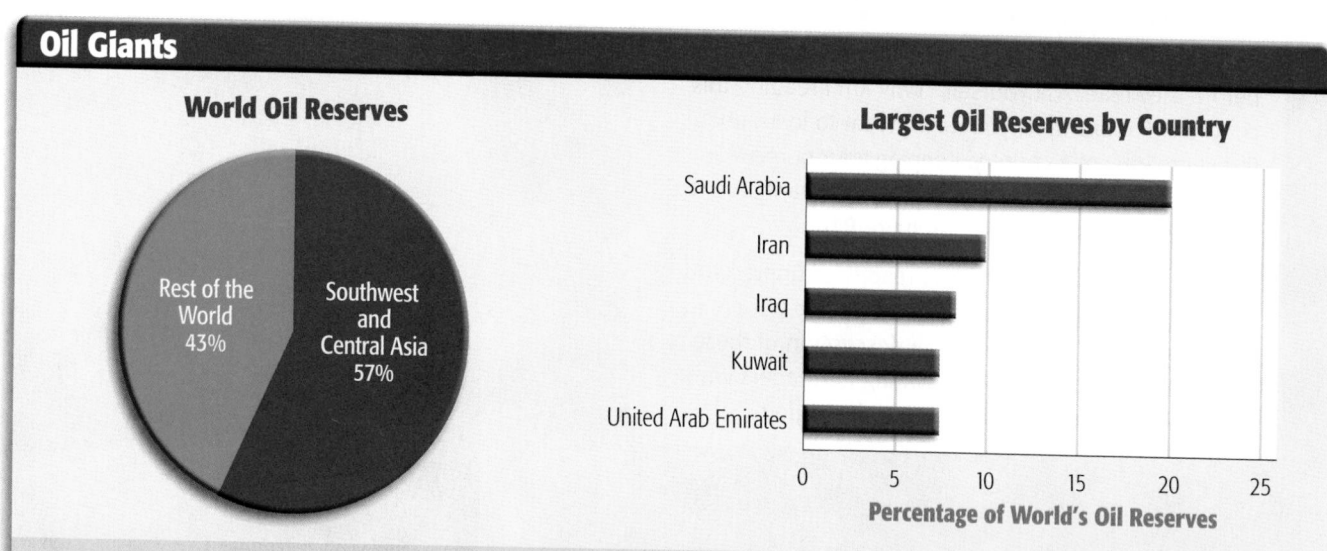

World Oil Reserves

Rest of the World 43%

Southwest and Central Asia 57%

Largest Oil Reserves by Country

Saudi Arabia
Iran
Iraq
Kuwait
United Arab Emirates

0   5   10   15   20   25
Percentage of World's Oil Reserves

The countries of Southwest and Central Asia contain nearly 60 percent of the world's oil. Saudi Arabia has by far the most oil, with about 20 percent of the world's total.

CHAPTER 17

The Eastern Mediterranean

What You Will Learn...

In this chapter you will learn about the countries of the Eastern Mediterranean region—Turkey, Israel, Syria, Lebanon, and Jordan. You will study their physical geography, history, government, economy, and culture.

FOCUS ON READING AND WRITING

Setting a Purpose Good readers often set a purpose before they read. Ask yourself, "Why am I reading this chapter?" For example, you might want to learn about the geography of a country. Keeping your purpose in mind will help you focus on what is important. **See the lesson, Setting a Purpose, on page R18.**

Writing a Description As your read this chapter, you will collect information about the lands and people in this region. Later you will write a description of these lands and people. You will be writing for readers who have not read the chapter or visited the region.

EUROPE

Istanbul

Sea of Marmara

40°N

Izmir

Gediz River

Menderes River

Aegean Sea

National capital

Other cities

Some areas controlled by the Palestinian Authority

0   50   100 Miles
0   50   100 Kilometers

Projection: Lambert Azimuthal Equal-Area

Mediterranean Sea

30°N

EGYPT

30°E

Geography The Jordan River valley in Israel provides fertile soils for farming.

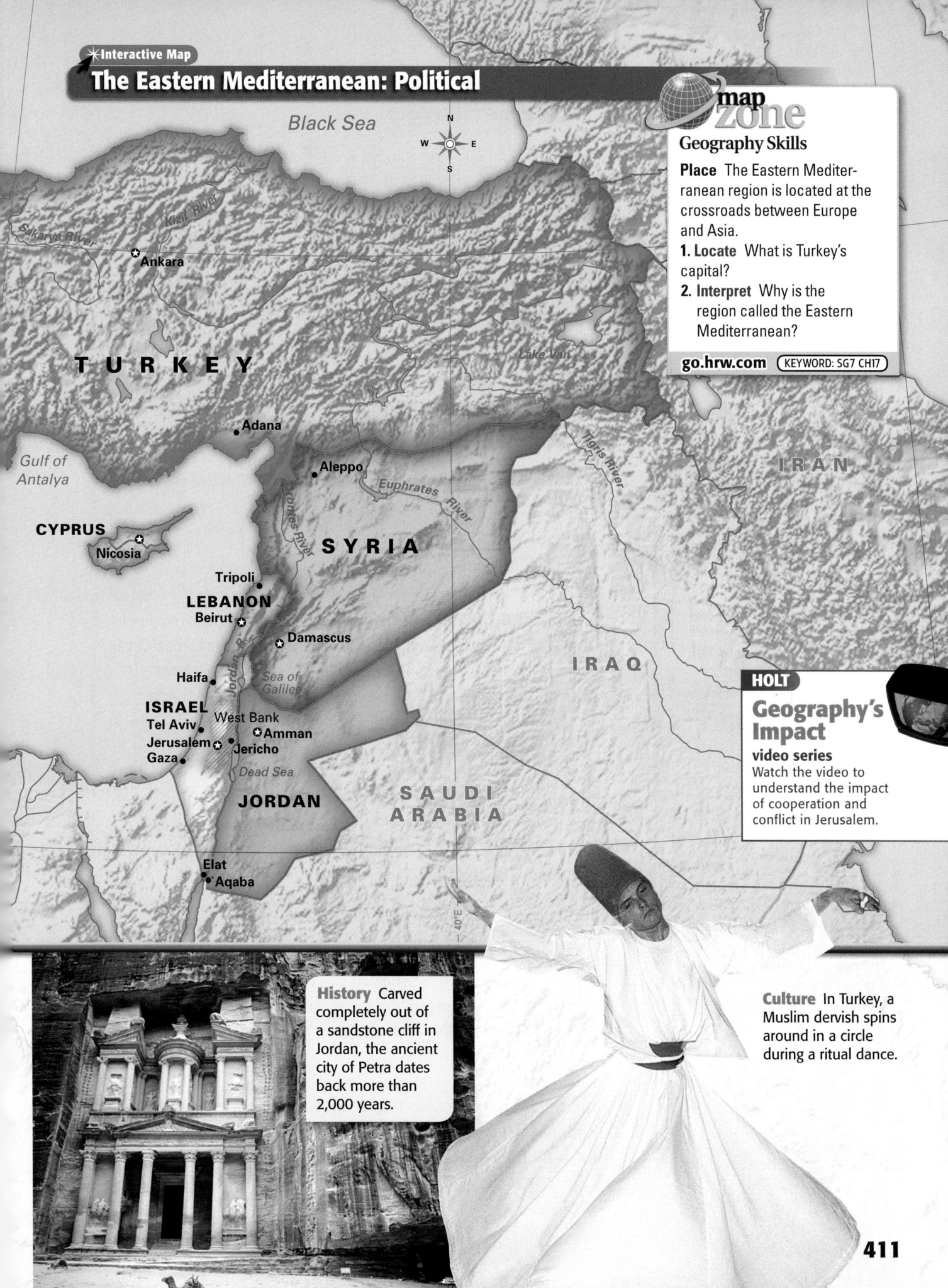

The Eastern Mediterranean: Political

Black Sea

map zone

Geography Skills

Place The Eastern Mediterranean region is located at the crossroads between Europe and Asia.

1. Locate What is Turkey's capital?

2. Interpret Why is the region called the Eastern Mediterranean?

go.hrw.com KEYWORD: SG7 CH17

Sakarya River

★ Ankara

Kızıl River

TURKEY

• Adana

Gulf of Antalya

Aleppo •

Euphrates River

Orontes River

SYRIA

Tigris River

IRAN

Lake Van

CYPRUS

★ Nicosia

Tripoli •

LEBANON

Beirut ★

• Damascus

Jordan R.

Haifa •

Sea of Galilee

ISRAEL

West Bank

Tel Aviv •

★ Amman

Jerusalem ★ • Jericho

Gaza •

Dead Sea

JORDAN

IRAQ

SAUDI ARABIA

Elat •
• Aqaba

40°E

HOLT

Geography's Impact

video series

Watch the video to understand the impact of cooperation and conflict in Jerusalem.

History Carved completely out of a sandstone cliff in Jordan, the ancient city of Petra dates back more than 2,000 years.

Culture In Turkey, a Muslim dervish spins around in a circle during a ritual dance.

Physical Geography

Main Ideas

1. The Eastern Mediterranean's physical features include the Bosporus, the Dead Sea, rivers, mountains, deserts, and plains.
2. The region's climate is mostly dry with little vegetation.
3. Important natural resources in the Eastern Mediterranean include valuable minerals and the availability of water.

The Big Idea

The Eastern Mediterranean, a region with a dry climate and valuable resources, sits in the middle of three continents.

Key Terms and Places

Dardanelles, *p. 412*
Bosporus, *p. 412*
Jordan River, *p. 413*
Dead Sea, *p. 413*
Syrian Desert, *p. 414*

TAKING NOTES As you read, take notes on the physical features, climate and vegetation, and natural resources of the region.

Physical Features	Climate and Vegetation	Natural Resources

If YOU lived there...

You live in Izmir, Turkey, on the Aegean Sea, but are traveling into the far eastern part of the country called eastern Anatolia. At home you are used to a warm, dry Mediterranean climate. You are surprised by the colder and wetter climate you're experiencing. Two mountain ranges come together here, and you notice that the peaks are covered with snow.

How does geography affect climate in these two places?

BUILDING BACKGROUND The Eastern Mediterranean region lies at the crossroads of Europe, Africa, and Asia. In ancient times, Greek colonists settled here, and it was later part of the Roman Empire. Geographically, however, it is almost entirely in Southwest Asia.

The countries of the Eastern Mediterranean make up part of a larger region called Southwest Asia. This region is sometimes referred to as the Middle East. Europeans first called the region the Middle East to distinguish it from the Far East, which included China and Japan.

Physical Features

As you can see on the physical map on the next page, a narrow waterway separates Europe from Asia. This waterway is made up of the **Dardanelles** (dahrd-uhn-ELZ), the **Bosporus** (BAHS-puh-ruhs), and the **Sea of Marmara** (MAHR-muh-ruh). Large ships travel through the waterway, which connects the Black Sea to the Mediterranean Sea. The Bosporus also splits the country of Turkey into two parts, a small part lies in Europe and the rest in Asia. The Asian part of Turkey includes the large peninsula called Anatolia (a-nuh-TOH-lee-uh).

The Eastern Mediterranean: Physical

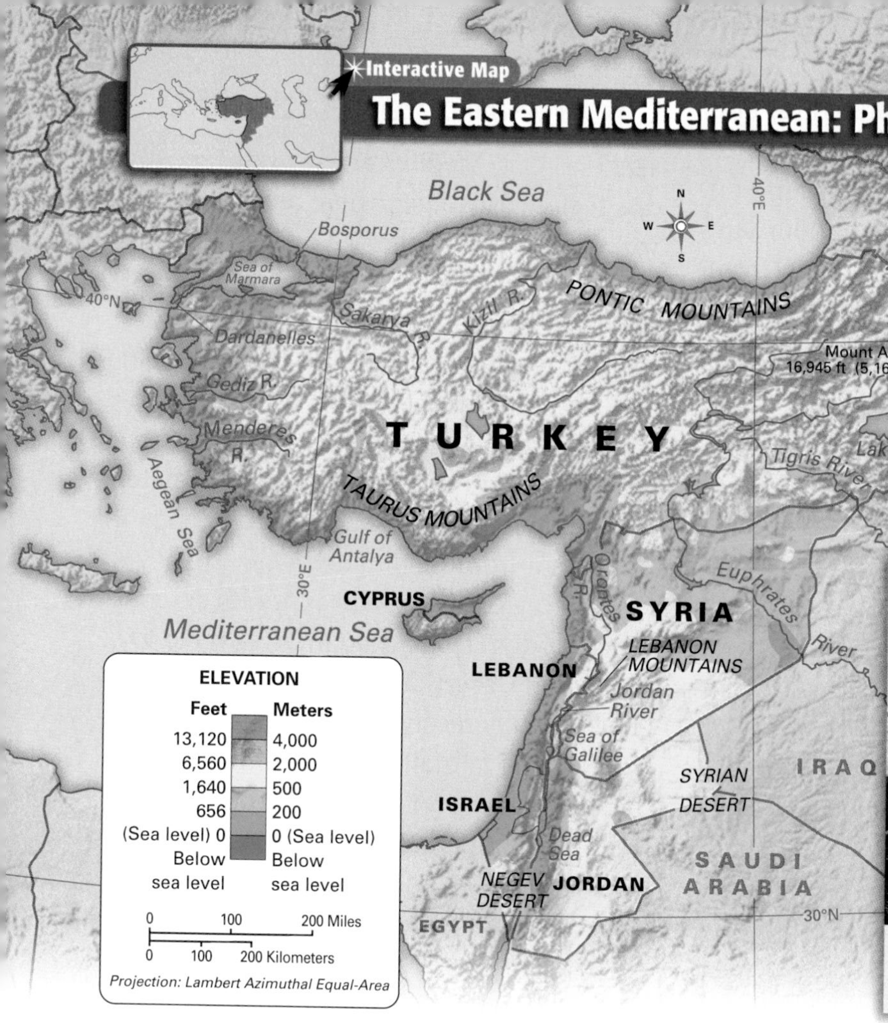

★Interactive Map

Black Sea
Bosporus
Sea of Marmara
Dardanelles
Gediz R.
Menderes R.
Aegean Sea
40°N
PONTIC MOUNTAINS
Sakarya
Kizil R.
Mount Ararat
16,945 ft (5,165 m)
T U R K E Y
TAURUS MOUNTAINS
Gulf of Antalya
Tigris River
Lake Van
40°E
Mediterranean Sea
CYPRUS
Orontes R.
S Y R I A
LEBANON MOUNTAINS
Euphrates River
LEBANON
Jordan River
Sea of Galilee
SYRIAN DESERT
I R A Q
ISRAEL
Dead Sea
NEGEV DESERT
JORDAN
S A U D I A R A B I A
EGYPT
30°N
30°E

ELEVATION

Feet	Meters
13,120	4,000
6,560	2,000
1,640	500
656	200
(Sea level) 0	0 (Sea level)
Below sea level	Below sea level

0   100   200 Miles
0   100   200 Kilometers
Projection: Lambert Azimuthal Equal-Area

map zone

Geography Skills

Place Turkey's elevation is higher than the rest of the region.
1. **Locate** Where is the Dead Sea located?
2. **Draw Conclusions** Notice the physical features in Jordan and Israel. What do you think the climate is like here?

go.hrw.com KEYWORD: SG7 CH17

Mount Ararat's snowcapped peak rises about 17,000 feet (5,180 m) in eastern Turkey.

Rivers and Lakes

The **Jordan River** begins in Syria and flows south through Israel and Jordan. The river finally empties into a large lake called the **Dead Sea**. As its name suggests, the Dead Sea contains little life. Only bacteria lives in the lake's extremely salty water. The world's saltiest lake, its surface is 1,312 feet (400 m) below sea level—the lowest point on any continent.

Mountains and Plains

As you can see on the map, two mountain systems stretch across Turkey. The Pontic Mountains run east–west along the northern edge. The Taurus Mountains run east–west along the southern edge.

Heading south from Turkey and into Syria lies a narrow plain. The Euphrates River flows southeast from Turkey through the plains to Syria and beyond.

Dead Sea

Because of its high salt content, swimmers do not sink in the Dead Sea.

ANALYZING VISUALS
What appears on the shore of the Dead Sea?

Farther inland lies plateaus, hills, and valleys. A rift valley that begins in Africa extends northward into Syria. Hills rise on both sides of the rift. Two main mountain ridges run north–south. One runs from southwestern Syria through western Jordan. The other, closer to the coast, runs through Lebanon and Israel.

READING CHECK **Summarizing** What are the region's main physical features?

Satellite View

The Bosporus is a strait that divides the city of Istanbul, Turkey.

Istanbul and the Bosporus

Throughout history, geography has almost always determined the location of a city. Istanbul, Turkey, which sits between Europe and Asia, is no exception. In this satellite image the city of Istanbul appears light brown and white. The body of water that cuts through the city is a strait called the Bosporus. It separates the Sea of Marmara in the south with the Black Sea in the north. Historically, the Bosporus has served as a prized area for empires that have controlled the city. Today, the strait is a major shipping route.

Drawing Conclusions Why do you think the Bosporus was seen as a strategic location?

Climate and Vegetation

The Eastern Mediterranean is a mostly dry region. However, there are important variations. As you can see on the map on the next page, Turkey's Black Sea coast and the Mediterranean coast all the way to northern Israel have a Mediterranean climate. Much of interior Turkey experiences a steppe climate. Central Syria and lands farther south have a desert climate. A small area of northeastern Turkey has a humid subtropical climate.

The region's driest areas are its deserts. Much of Syria and Jordan is covered by the **Syrian Desert**. This desert of rock and gravel usually receives less than five inches (12.7 cm) of rainfall a year. Another desert, the Negev (NE-gev), lies in southern Israel. Here the temperatures can reach as high as 114°F (46°C), and annual rainfall totals barely two inches.

In such dry conditions, only shrubs grow scattered throughout the region's deserts. However, in other areas vegetation is plentiful. In Israel, more than 2,800 species of plants thrive throughout the country's various environments.

READING CHECK **Generalizing** What are climates like in the Eastern Mediterranean?

Natural Resources

Because the Eastern Mediterranean is so dry, water is a valuable resource. The people of this region are mostly farmers. The region lacks oil resources, but does have valuable minerals.

Land and Water

In this dry region the limited availability of water limits how land is used. Commercial farms can only grow crops where rain or irrigation provides enough water.

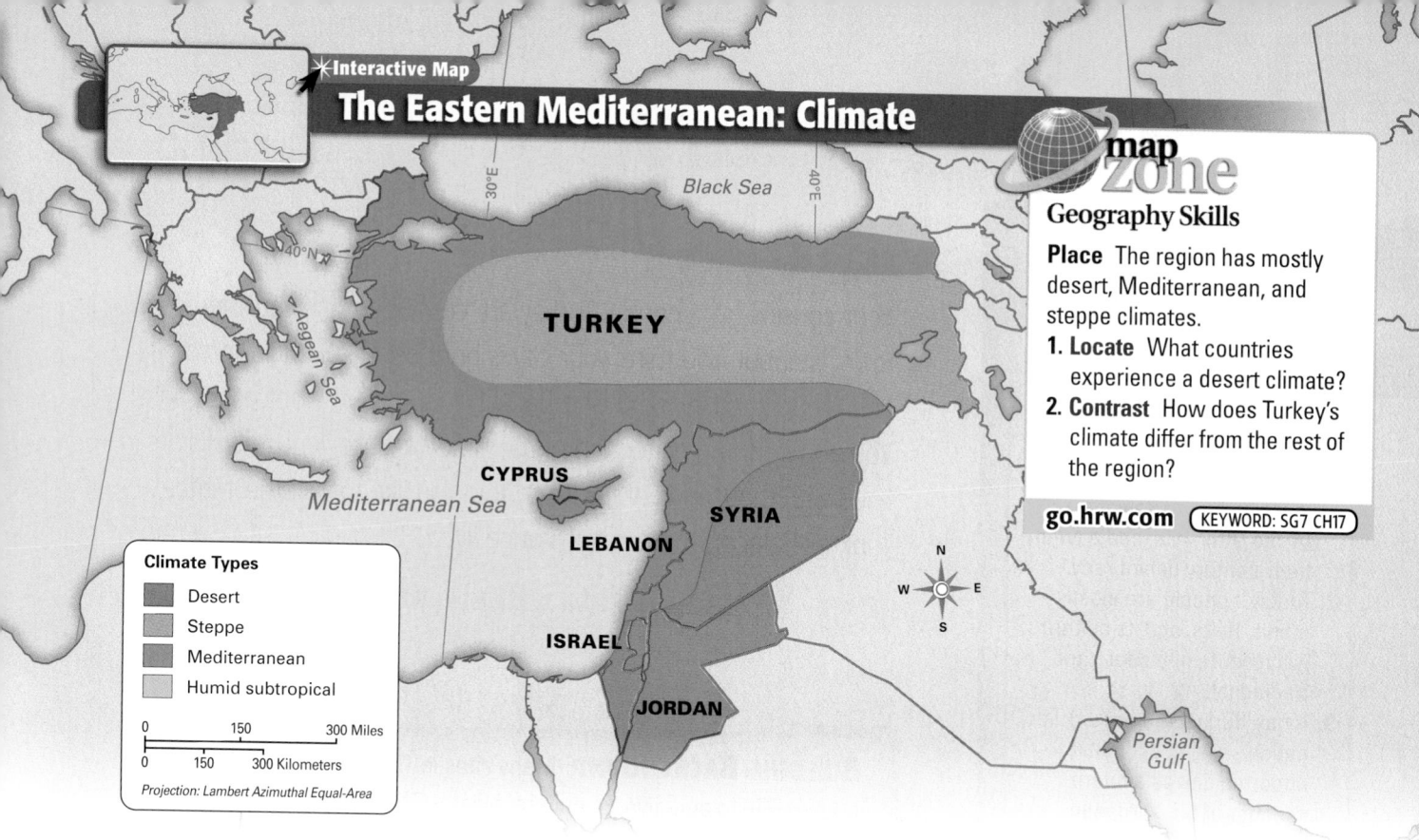

The Eastern Mediterranean: Climate

★Interactive Map

Black Sea

TURKEY

CYPRUS

Mediterranean Sea

SYRIA

LEBANON

ISRAEL

JORDAN

Aegean Sea

Persian Gulf

Climate Types

- Desert
- Steppe
- Mediterranean
- Humid subtropical

0   150   300 Miles
0   150   300 Kilometers
Projection: Lambert Azimuthal Equal-Area

map zone

Geography Skills

Place The region has mostly desert, Mediterranean, and steppe climates.
1. **Locate** What countries experience a desert climate?
2. **Contrast** How does Turkey's climate differ from the rest of the region?

go.hrw.com KEYWORD: SG7 CH17

In drier areas, subsistence farming and livestock herding are common. In the desert areas, available water supports a few nomadic herders, but no farming.

Mineral Resources

The region's resources include many minerals, including sulfur, mercury, and copper. Syria, Jordan, and Israel all produce phosphates—mineral salts that contain the element phosphorus. Phosphates are used to make fertilizers. This region also produces asphalt—the dark tarlike material used to pave streets.

READING CHECK Drawing Conclusions How do people use the region's mineral resources?

SUMMARY AND PREVIEW In this section you learned about the physical geography of the Eastern Mediterranean. Next, you will learn about Turkey.

Section 1 Assessment

Reviewing Ideas, Terms, and Places

1. **a. Describe** What makes the **Dead Sea** unusual?
   b. Explain What physical features separate Europe and Asia?
2. **a. Recall** What desert covers much of Syria and Jordan?
   b. Make Generalizations What is the climate of the Eastern Mediterranean like?
3. **a. Identify** What mineral resource is produced by Syria, Jordan, and Israel?
   b. Draw Conclusions Why must farmers in the region rely on irrigation?

Critical Thinking

4. **Summarizing** Using your notes, summarize the physical geography of Israel and Turkey. Use this chart to organize your notes.

Physical Features	
Turkey	Israel

FOCUS ON WRITING

5. **Describing the Physical Geography** What physical features would you include in your description? How would you describe the climate? Note your ideas.

Turkey

If **YOU** lived there...

Your cousins from central Turkey are coming to visit your home-town, Istanbul. You think your city is both beautiful and interesting. You like to stroll in the Grand Bazaar and smell the spices for sale. You admire the architecture of the Blue Mosque, whose walls are lined with thousands of tiny tiles. You also like to visit the elegant Topkapi Palace, where sultans once lived.

What sights will you show your cousins?

BUILDING BACKGROUND Many sites in Turkey reflect the country's long and diverse cultural history. Throughout the country you will find the ruins of ancient Greek temples and Roman palaces. You can also see magnificent early Christian buildings and art, as well as the palaces and mosques of Ottoman rulers.

What You Will Learn...

Main Ideas

1. Turkey's history includes invasion by the Romans, rule by the Ottomans, and a twentieth-century democracy.
2. Turkey's people are mostly ethnic Turks, and its culture is a mixture of modern and traditional.
3. Today, Turkey is a democratic nation seeking economic opportunities as a future member of the European Union.

The Big Idea

Although Turkey has historically been more Asian than European, its leaders are seeking to develop closer economic ties to Europe.

Key Terms and Places

Ankara, *p. 418*
Istanbul, *p. 419*
secular, *p. 419*

TAKING NOTES As you read, use a diagram like the one below to take notes on Turkey.

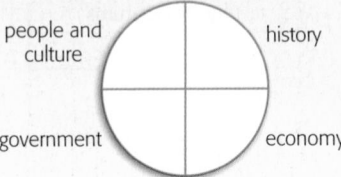

people and culture / history / government / economy

Close-up

Early Farming Village

The village of Çatal Hüyük in modern Turkey is one of the earliest farming villages discovered. Around 8,000 years ago, the village was home to about 5,000–6,000 people living in more than 1,000 houses. Villagers farmed, hunted and fished, traded with distant lands, and worshipped gods in special shrines.

Villagers used simple channels to move water to their fields.

Wheat, barley, and peas were some of the main crops grown outside the village.

History

Around 8,000 years ago the area that is now Turkey was home to one of the world's earliest farming villages. For centuries invasions from powerful empires shaped the region. By the 1920s Turkey was a democratic nation.

Invasions

When the Romans invaded the area, they captured the city of Byzantium and later renamed it Constantinople. Its location at the crossroads between Europe and Asia made Constantinople an important trading port. After the fall of Rome, Constantinople became the capital of the Byzantine Empire.

In the AD 1000s a nomadic people from central Asia called the Seljuk Turks invaded the area. In 1453 another Turkish people, the Ottoman Turks, captured the city of Constantinople and made it the capital of their Islamic empire.

The Ottoman Empire

During the 1500s and 1600s the Ottoman Empire was very powerful. The empire controlled territory in northern Africa, southwestern Asia, and southeastern Europe.

In World War I the Ottomans fought on the losing side. When the war ended, they lost most of their territory.

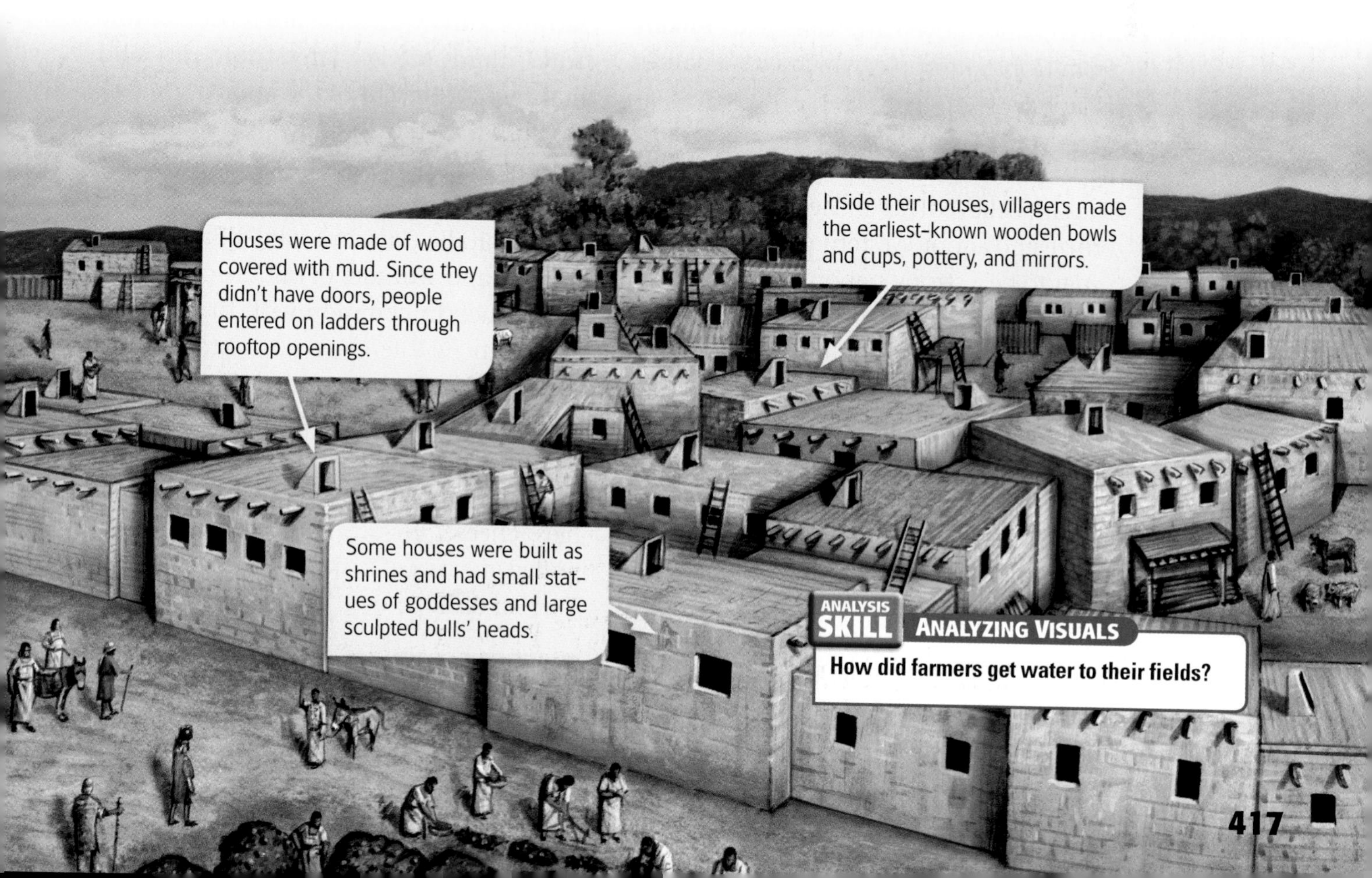

Houses were made of wood covered with mud. Since they didn't have doors, people entered on ladders through rooftop openings.

Inside their houses, villagers made the earliest-known wooden bowls and cups, pottery, and mirrors.

Some houses were built as shrines and had small statues of goddesses and large sculpted bulls' heads.

ANALYSIS SKILL **ANALYZING VISUALS**

How did farmers get water to their fields?

417

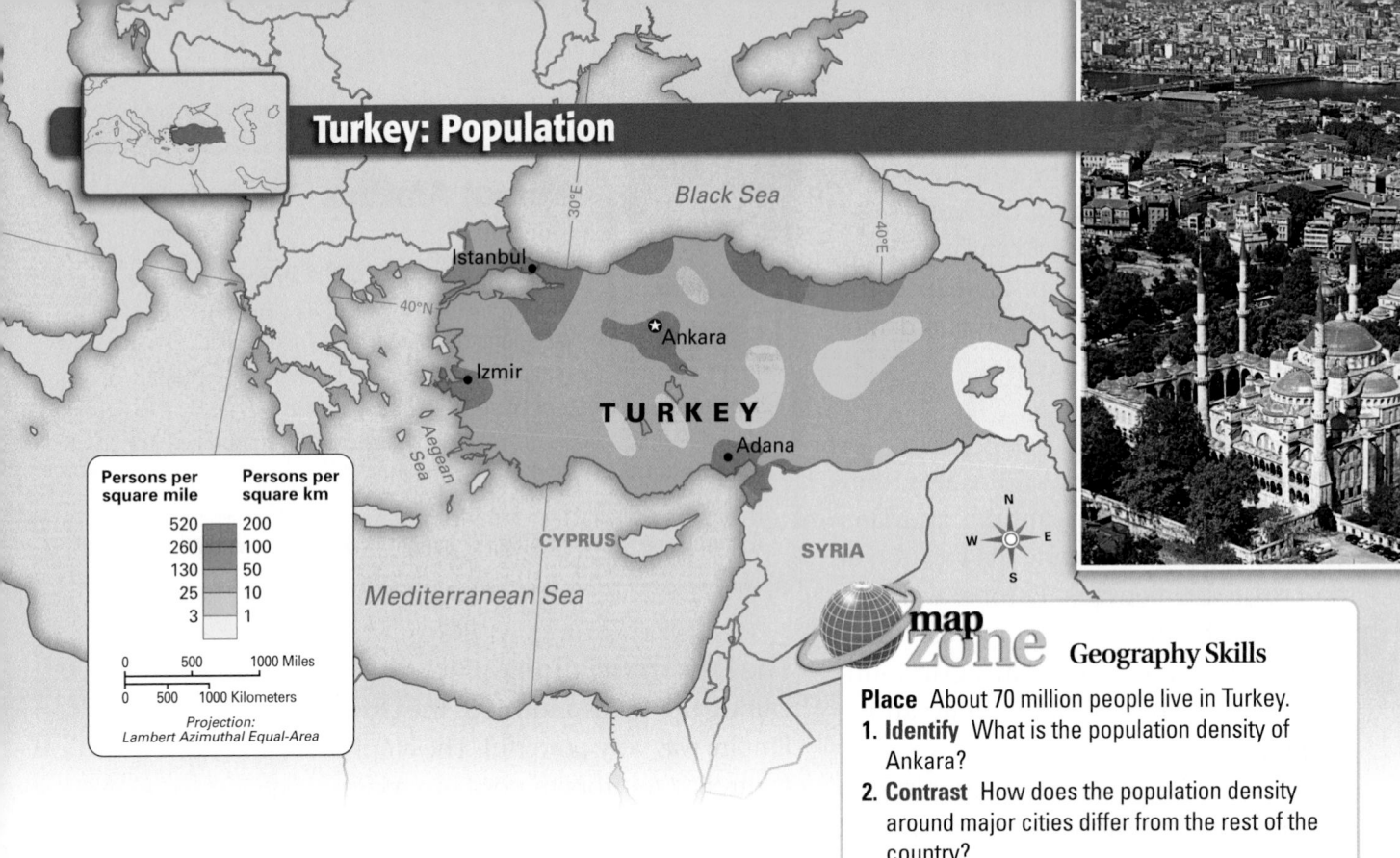

Turkey: Population

map zone Geography Skills

Persons per square mile	Persons per square km
520	200
260	100
130	50
25	10
3	1

0   500   1000 Miles
0   500   1000 Kilometers

Projection:
Lambert Azimuthal Equal-Area

Place About 70 million people live in Turkey.
1. **Identify** What is the population density of Ankara?
2. **Contrast** How does the population density around major cities differ from the rest of the country?

FOCUS ON READING

Set a purpose for reading by asking yourself what you want to learn about Turkey's people and culture.

Military officers then took over the government, led by a war hero, Mustafa Kemal. He later adopted the name Kemal Atatürk, which means Father of Turks. Atatürk created the democratic nation of Turkey and moved the capital to **Ankara** from Constantinople, which was renamed Istanbul.

Modern Turkey

ACADEMIC VOCABULARY

method a way of doing something

Atatürk believed Turkey needed to modernize and adopt Western **methods** in order to be a strong nation. For example, he banned the fez, the traditional hat of Turkish men, and required that they wear European-style hats. Reforms urged women to stop wearing traditional veils. Women were also encouraged to vote, work, and hold office. Other ways Atatürk modernized Turkey included replacing the Arabic alphabet with the Latin alphabet, and adopting the metric system.

READING CHECK Finding Main Ideas How did Atatürk modernize Turkey?

People and Culture

Most of Turkey's people are mostly ethnic Turks. Kurds are the largest minority and make up 20 percent of the population.

Turkey's culture today is a reflection of some of Kemal Atatürk's changes. He created a cultural split between Turkey's urban middle class and rural villagers. The lifestyle and attitudes of middle-class Turks have much in common with those of the European middle class. In contrast, most rural Turks are more traditional. Islam strongly influences their attitudes on matters such as the role of women.

Turkish cooking features olives, vegetables, cheese, yogurt, and bread. Kebabs—grilled meats on a skewer—are a favorite Turkish dish.

READING CHECK Contrasting How are urban Turks different from rural Turks?

With about 10 million people, Istanbul, shown here, is Turkey's largest city.

electronics. About 35 percent of Turkey's labor force works in agriculture. Grains, cotton, sugar beets, and hazelnuts are major crops.

Turkey is rich in natural resources, which include oil, coal, and iron ore. Water is also a valuable resource in the region. Turkey has spent billions of dollars building dams to increase its water supply. On one hand, these dams provide hydroelectricity. On the other hand, some of these dams have restricted the flow of river water into neighboring countries.

READING CHECK **Finding Main Ideas** What kind of government does Turkey have?

Turkey Today

Turkey's government meets in the capital of Ankara, but **Istanbul** is Turkey's largest city. Istanbul's location will serve as an economic bridge to Europe as Turkey plans to join the European Union.

Government

Turkey's legislature is called the National Assembly. A president and a prime minister share executive power.

Although most of its people are Muslim, Turkey is a secular state. **Secular** means that religion is kept separate from government. For example, the religion of Islam allows a man to have up to four wives. However, by Turkish law a man is permitted to have just one wife. In recent years Islamic political parties have attempted to increase Islam's role in Turkish society.

Economy and Resources

As a member of the European Union, Turkey's economy and people would benefit by increased trade with Europe. Turkey's economy includes modern factories as well as village farming and craft making.

Among the most important industries are textiles and clothing, cement, and

SUMMARY AND PREVIEW In this section you learned about Turkey's history, people, government, and economy. Next, you will learn about Israel.

go.hrw.com
Online Quiz
KEYWORD: SG7 HP17

Section 2 Assessment

Reviewing Ideas, Terms, and Places

1. **a. Recall** What city did both the Romans and Ottoman Turks capture?
   b. Explain In what ways did Atatürk try to modernize Turkey?
2. **a. Recall** What ethnic group makes up 20 percent of Turkey's population?
   b. Draw Conclusions What makes Turkey **secular**?
   c. Elaborate Why do you think Turkey wants to be a member of the European Union?

Critical Thinking

3. **Summarizing** Using the information in your notes, summarize Turkey's history and Turkey today.

Turkey's History	Turkey Today

FOCUS ON WRITING

4. **Describing Turkey** A description of Turkey might include details about its people, culture, government, and economy. Take notes on the details you think are important and interesting.

Israel

What You Will Learn...

Main Ideas

1. Israel's history includes the ancient Hebrews and the creation of the nation of Israel.
2. In Israel today, Jewish culture is a major part of daily life.
3. The Palestinian Territories are areas within Israel controlled partly by Palestinian Arabs.

The Big Idea

Israel and the Palestinian Territories are home to Jews and Arabs who continue to struggle over the region's land.

Key Terms and Places

Diaspora, *p. 420*
Jerusalem, *p. 420*
Zionism, *p. 421*
kosher, *p. 422*
kibbutz, *p. 422*
Gaza, *p. 423*
West Bank, *p. 423*

TAKING NOTES As you read, take notes on Israel and the Palestinian Territories. Use the chart below to organize your notes.

Israel	Palestinian Territories

If YOU lived there...

When you were only six years old, your family moved to Israel from Russia. You are learning Hebrew in school, but your parents and grandparents still speak Russian at home. When you first moved here, your parents worked in an office building, but you now live on a farm where you grow oranges and tomatoes.

What do you like about living in Israel?

BUILDING BACKGROUND Modern Israel was formed in 1948. Since then immigrants from many parts of the world have made the population of Israel very diverse. Many Jews emigrated to Israel from Russia, Europe, the Middle East, and the Americas.

History

Do you know that Israel is often referred to as the Holy Land? Some people call Israel the Holy Land because it is home to sacred sites for three major religions—Judaism, Christianity, and Islam. According to the Bible, many events in Jewish history and in the life of Jesus happened in Israel.

The Holy Land

The Hebrews (or Israelites), the ancestors of the Jews, first established the kingdom of Israel about 3,000 years ago. It covered roughly the same area as the modern state of Israel. In the 60s BC the Roman Empire conquered the region, which was called Judea. After several Jewish revolts, the Romans forced many Jews to leave the region and renamed it Palestine in AD 135. This scattering of the Jewish population is known as the **Diaspora**.

Muslims conquered Palestine in the mid-600s. However, from the late 1000s to the late 1200s, Christians from Europe launched a series of invasions of Palestine called the Crusades. The Crusaders captured the city of **Jerusalem** in 1099. In time the Crusaders were pushed out of the area. Palestine then became part of the Ottoman Empire. After World War I, it came under British control.

Creation of Israel

Zionism, a nationalist movement calling for Jews to establish a Jewish state in their ancient homeland, began in Europe in the late 1800s. Tens of thousands of Jews from around the world began moving to the region.

In 1947 the United Nations voted to divide Palestine, then under British control, into Jewish and Arab states. While Arab countries rejected this plan, the Jews accepted it, and a year later created the State of Israel. Arab armies then invaded Israel. In a very short war, the Israelis defeated the Arabs.

After Israel's victory, many Palestinians fled to neighboring Arab countries. Israel and Arab countries have fought each other in several wars since then. Disputes between the two sides continue today.

READING CHECK **Summarizing** What two groups played a large role in Israel's history?

Israel Today

Jews from all over the world, including many who fled from Arab lands, have settled in Israel hoping to find peace and stability. Yet, they have faced continual conflicts with neighboring countries. Despite these problems, Israelis have built a modern, democratic country.

HISTORIC DOCUMENT
The Dead Sea Scrolls

Written by Jews about 2,000 years ago, the Dead Sea Scrolls include prayers, commentaries, letters, and passages from the Hebrew Bible. Hidden in caves near the Dead Sea, these scrolls were not found until 1947. Here are two passages from a prayer written on one of the scrolls.

❝With knowledge shall I sing out my music, only for the glory of God, my harp, my lyre for His holiness established; the flute of my lips will I lift, His law its tuning fork.❞

❝When first I begin campaign or journey, His name shall I bless; when first I set out or turn to come back; when I sit down or rise up, when I spread my bed, then shall I rejoice in Him.❞

ANALYSIS SKILL **ANALYZING PRIMARY SOURCES**

What does this prayer from the Dead Sea Scrolls reveal about the people who wrote it?

Government and Economy

Israel has a prime minister and a parliament—the Knesset. There are several major political parties and many smaller ones.

Israel's government has built a strong military. At age 18 most Israeli men and women must serve at least one year.

FOCUS ON READING
What do you want to find out about Israel today?

Jerusalem

The city of Jerusalem is sacred to three world religions—Judaism, Islam, and Christianity.

Israel's economy is modern and diverse. Items like high-technology equipment and cut diamonds are important exports. Israel has increased food production by irrigating farmland. Israel's economy also benefits from the millions of visitors who come to Israel to see the country's historic sites.

Cities, Diversity, and Languages

Most of Israel's population lives in cities. With about 3 million people, Tel Aviv is Israel's largest city.

About 80 percent of Israel's population is Jewish. The rest of the country's people are mostly Arab. About three-fourths of Israeli Arabs are Muslim, but some are Christian. Israel's Jewish population includes Jews from all parts of the world. Many arrive not knowing Hebrew, one of Israel's official languages. To assist these new citizens, the government provides language classes. Israeli Arabs speak Arabic, Israel's other official language.

Culture and Rural Settlements

Israeli Jewish culture is rich in holidays and special foods. For Jews, the Sabbath, from sunset Friday until sundown Saturday, is a holy day. Yom Kippur, a very important Jewish holiday, is celebrated in the fall. Passover, in the spring, celebrates the Hebrews' escape from captivity in ancient Egypt.

Because Judaism is a way of life, religious laws address every aspect of daily life, including what Jews should eat. These laws are ancient and appear in the Hebrew Bible. **Kosher**, which means "proper" in Hebrew, is the term used to refer to Jewish dietary laws. Jews eating a kosher diet do not eat pork or shellfish. They also do not mix meat and milk products.

About 100,000 Israeli Jews live in rural settlements. Each settlement, or **kibbutz** (ki-BOOHTS), is a large farm where people share everything in common. Israeli Jews live in more than 250 kibbutzim.

READING CHECK **Generalizing** What is Jewish culture in Israel like?

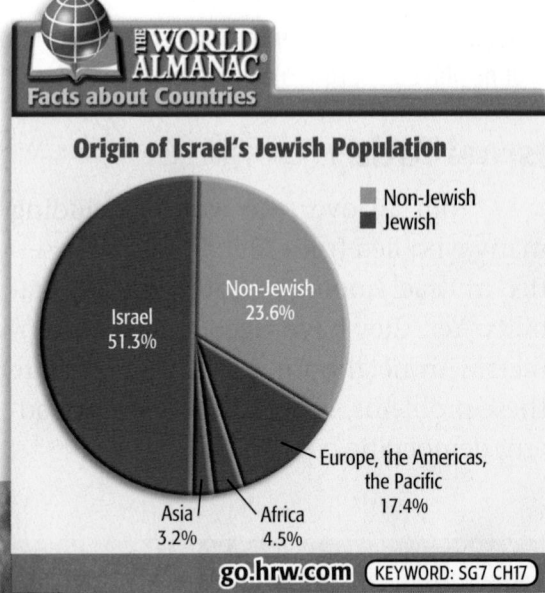

THE WORLD ALMANAC
Facts about Countries

Origin of Israel's Jewish Population

- Non-Jewish
- Jewish

Israel 51.3%

Non-Jewish 23.6%

Europe, the Americas, the Pacific 17.4%

Asia 3.2%

Africa 4.5%

go.hrw.com   KEYWORD: SG7 CH17

Jews from all over the world have settled in Israel. The graph above shows the percentages of Jews who migrated from different places. Non-Jews in Israel include Arabs, Christians, and Druze. This photo shows a Jewish teenager celebrating his bar mitzvah—a ceremony that acknowledges 13-year-old Jewish boys as adults in the Jewish community.

ANALYZING VISUALS According to the graph, what part of the world did the highest percentage of Israel's Jewish population emigrate from?

Israel's Population

The Palestinian Territories

In 1967 during the Six-Day War, Israel captured areas from Jordan and Egypt inhabited by Palestinian Arabs—Gaza, the West Bank, and East Jerusalem. Since then, Jews and Arabs have fought over the right to live in these areas.

Gaza

Gaza is a small, crowded piece of coastal land where more than a million Palestinians live. The area has almost no resources. However, citrus fruit is grown in irrigated fields. Unemployment is a problem for the Palestinians living in Gaza. Many travel to Israel each day to work.

West Bank

The **West Bank** is much larger than Gaza and has a population of about 2.4 million. It is mostly rural, but the territory has three large cities—Nablus, Hebron, and Ramallah. The West Bank's economy is mostly based on agriculture. Farmers rely on irrigation to grow their crops.

Since Israel took control of the West Bank, tens of thousands of Jews have moved into settlements there. However, the Palestinians consider the Jewish settlements an invasion of their land. This conflict over land causes the greatest tension and violence between Arabs and Israelis.

East Jerusalem

Other disputed land includes Israel's capital, Jerusalem. Control of Jerusalem is a difficult and often emotional issue for Jews, Muslims, and Christians. The city has sites that are holy to all three religions. Areas of the old city are divided into Jewish, Muslim, and Christian neighborhoods.

Palestinians claim East Jerusalem as their capital. However, Israel annexed East Jerusalem in 1980. Even before this,

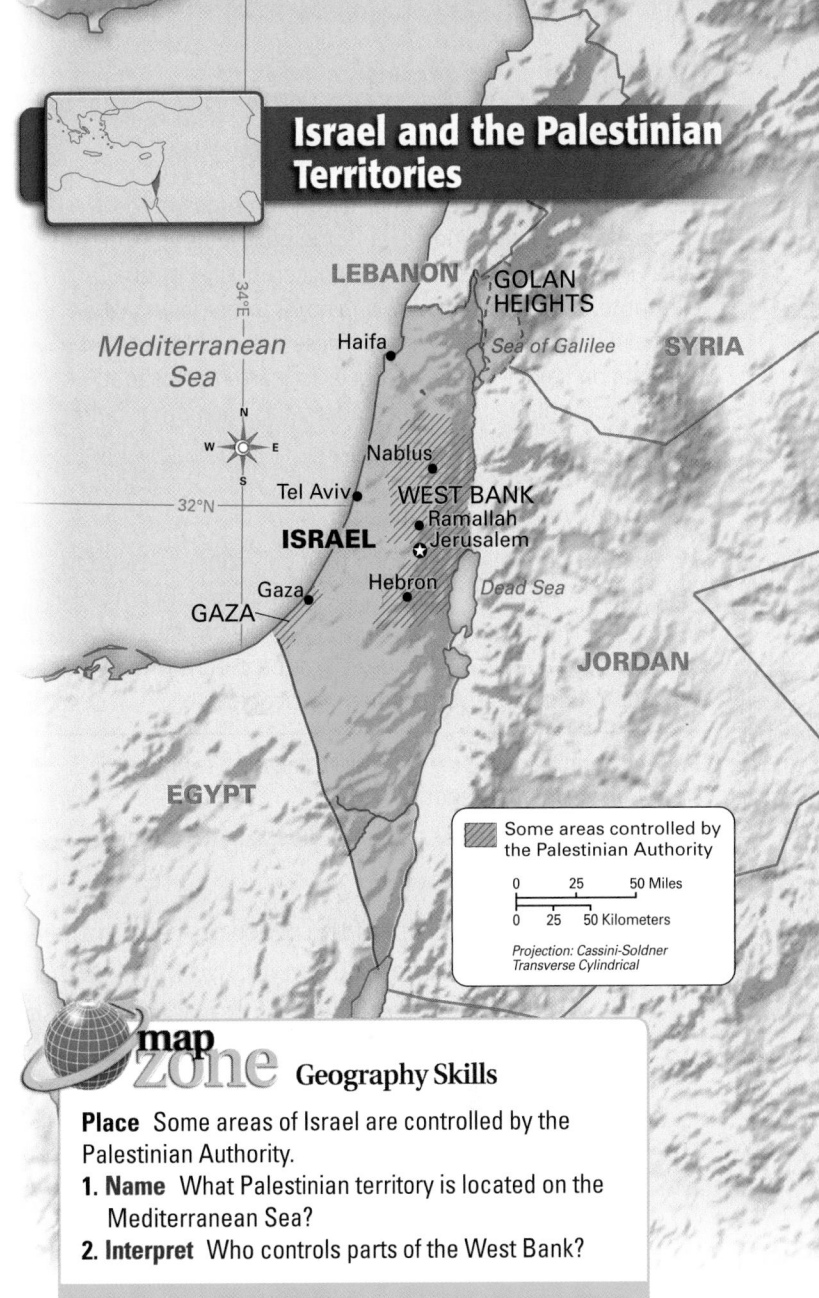

Israel and the Palestinian Territories

map zone Geography Skills

Place Some areas of Israel are controlled by the Palestinian Authority.
1. **Name** What Palestinian territory is located on the Mediterranean Sea?
2. **Interpret** Who controls parts of the West Bank?

the Israeli government had moved its capital to Jerusalem from Tel Aviv. Most foreign countries have chosen not to recognize this transfer.

The Future of the Territories

In the 1990s Israel agreed to turn over parts of the territories to the Palestinians. In return, the Palestinian Authority agreed to recognize Israel and renounce terrorism. In 2005 the Israelis transferred Gaza to the Palestinian Authority.

Israeli Teens for Peace

Peace between Israeli Jews and Palestinian Arabs has not been easy in the past. Moreover, some believe peace in the region might be impossible ever to accomplish. But don't tell that to a group of 200 Jewish and Arab teenagers who are making a difference in Israel. These teens belong to an organization called Seeds of Peace. To learn more about each other's cultures and thus understand each other better, these teens meet regularly. For example, Jews teach Arabs Hebrew and Arabs teach Jews Arabic. They also participate in community service projects.

By bridging the gap between their two cultures, these teens hope they can one day live peacefully together. A Palestinian boy in the group expressed his hope for the future. He explained, "I realize that peace is not a dream when you truly get to know who you are making peace with."

Drawing Conclusions How are Jewish and Arab teenagers in Israel working toward peace?

The future of the peace process is uncertain. Some Palestinian groups have continued to commit acts of terrorism. Jewish Israelis fear they would be open to attack if they withdrew from the territories.

READING CHECK **Analyzing** Why have the Palestinian Territories been a source of conflict?

SUMMARY AND PREVIEW In this section you learned about Israel's history, people, government and economy, and the future of the Palestinian Territories. In the next section you will learn about the history and culture of Israel's neighbors—Syria, Lebanon, and Jordan.

Section 3 Assessment

go.hrw.com
Online Quiz
KEYWORD: SG7 HP17

Reviewing Ideas, Terms, and Places

1. **a. Define** What is the **Diaspora**?
   b. Explain How did **Zionism** help create the nation of Israel?
2. **a. Recall** What are Jewish dietary laws called?
   b. Draw Conclusions Why have Israeli leaders built up a strong military?
   c. Elaborate Why do you think Jews from around the world migrate to Israel?
3. **a. Identify** Which territory is fully controlled by Palestinians and which is partly controlled?
   b. Make Inferences How might giving land to the Palestinians help or not help achieve peace in Israel?

Critical Thinking

4. **Categorizing** Use the chart below to separate your notes on Israel into categories.

Israel Today

Government	
Economy	
Diversity and Languages	
Jewish Culture	

FOCUS ON WRITING

5. **Describing Israel** What features make Israel unique? Take notes on how you might describe these features for your readers.

Analyzing a Cartogram

Learn

For statistical information like population figures, geographers sometimes create a special map called a cartogram. A cartogram displays information about countries by the size shown for each country. In contrast, a political map like the one on the right reflects countries' actual physical size. Here are some guidelines for reading and analyzing a cartogram.

- Read the title of the map to determine the subject area covered.

- Compare the political map to the cartogram. Notice how some countries are much different in size on the cartogram compared to the map.

- Read the cartogram's legend and think about what the information means.

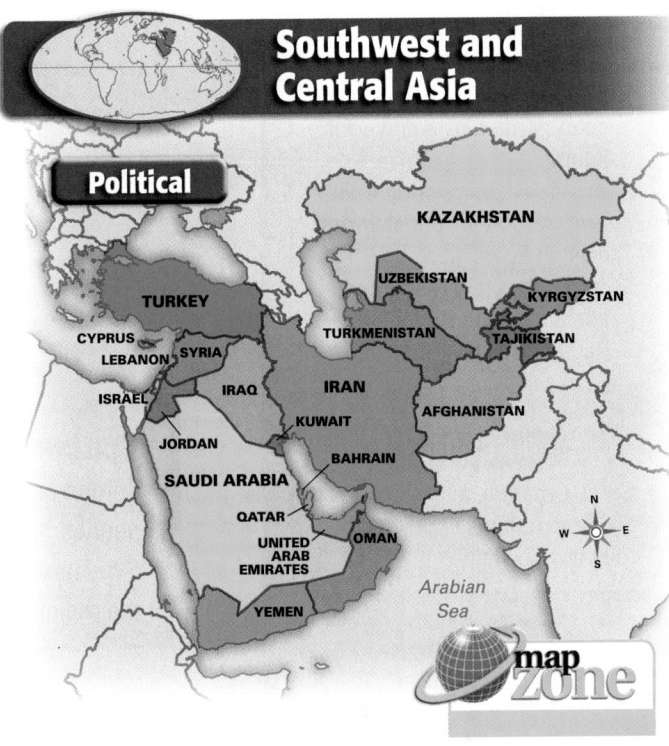

Southwest and Central Asia

Political

Practice

❶ Which country has the largest population?

❷ How is the size of Saudi Arabia's land area different from the size of its population?

❸ Using the cartogram legend, what is the approximate population of Lebanon?

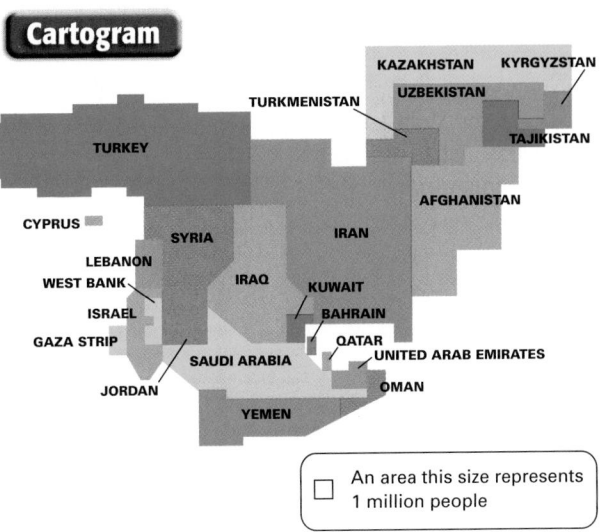

Cartogram

☐ An area this size represents 1 million people

Apply

Draw your own cartogram using the gross domestic product, or GDP, of each country in Southwest and Central Asia. Use a reference source or the Internet to find these statistics. Then determine the scale for sizing each country by GDP. For example, you might use one square unit of area per $10 billion or $100 billion. Countries with a high GDP should appear larger than countries with a low GDP.

Syria, Lebanon, and Jordan

What You Will Learn...

Main Ideas

1. Syria, once part of the Ottoman Empire, is an Arab country ruled by a powerful family.
2. Lebanon is recovering from civil war and its people are divided by religion.
3. Jordan has few resources and is home to Bedouins and Palestinian refugees.

The Big Idea

Syria, Lebanon, and Jordan are Arab nations coping with religious diversity.

Key Terms and Places

Damascus, *p. 426*
Beirut, *p. 428*
Bedouins, *p. 428*
Amman, *p. 429*

TAKING NOTES As you read, take notes on Syria, Lebanon, and Jordan. Use a chart like the one below to organize your notes.

Syria	
Lebanon	
Jordan	

If YOU lived there...

You live in Beirut, Lebanon. Your grandparents often tell you about the years before civil wars destroyed the heart of Beirut. The city then had wide boulevards, parks, and elegant shops. It was popular with tourists. Even though much of Beirut has been rebuilt, you find it hard to imagine what the city used to look like.

What hopes do you have for your country?

BUILDING BACKGROUND The histories of Lebanon, Syria, and Jordan have been tangled together since the countries gained independence in the 1940s. Syria is a large nation with a strong military. Syria has often dominated Lebanon's political life. Other conflicts in the region have also spilled over into Lebanon.

Look again at the map at the beginning of this chapter. Notice that Syria, Lebanon, and Jordan all border Israel. Because of their location near Israel, these countries have been involved in conflicts in the region. In addition, Syria, Lebanon, and Jordan also share a similar history, religion, and culture.

Syria

The capital of Syria, **Damascus**, is believed to be the oldest continuously inhabited city in the world. For centuries it was a leading regional trade center. Syria became part of the Ottoman Empire in the 1500s. After World War I, France controlled Syria. Syria finally became independent in the 1940s.

History and Government

From 1971 to 2000, the Syrian government was led by a dictator, Hafiz al-Assad. As president, Assad increased the size of Syria's military. He wanted to match Israel's military strength and protect his rule from his political enemies within Syria. After Assad's death in 2000, his son, Bashar, was elected president. Bashar al-Assad's goals during his seven-year term include improving Syria's economy.

Syria has a socialist government, which owns the country's oil refineries, larger electrical plants, railroads, and some factories. Syria's key manufactured goods are textiles, food products, and chemicals. Agriculture remains important. Syria has only small deposits of oil and natural gas. It is rich in iron ore, basalt, and phosphates.

Syria's People

Syria's population of more than 18 million is about 90 percent Arab. The other 10 percent includes Kurds and Armenians. About 74 percent of Syrians are Sunni Muslim. About 16 percent are Druze and Alawites, members of small religious groups related to Islam. About 10 percent of Syrians are Christian. There are also small Jewish communities in some cities.

READING CHECK **Analyzing** How is Syria's economy organized?

Lebanon

Lebanon is a small, mountainous country on the Mediterranean coast. It is home to several different groups of people. At times these different groups have fought.

Lebanon's History and People

During the Ottoman period, many religious and ethnic minority groups settled in Lebanon. After World War I, France controlled Lebanon and Syria. Lebanon finally gained independence in the 1940s. Even so, some aspects of French culture influenced Lebanese culture. For example, in addition to Arabic, many Lebanese also speak French.

Lebanon's people are overwhelmingly Arab, but they are divided by religion. Most Lebanese are either Muslim or Christian. Each of those groups is divided into several smaller groups. Muslims are divided into Sunni, Shia, and Druze.

The Maronites are the largest of the Christian groups in the country. Over time, however, Muslims have become Lebanon's majority religious group.

FOCUS ON READING

Look at the headings under Lebanon to set your purpose for reading these paragraphs.

Ancient Syria

In Syria today, ruins of an ancient Roman trading center still stand. The Romans called the city Palmyra, meaning "city of palm trees."

People of Syria, Lebanon, and Jordan

The people of Syria, Lebanon, and Jordan share many cultural traits. For example, most people living in this region are Arab and practice Islam.

ANALYZING VISUALS What can you see in these photos that tells you about daily life in the region?

Syria In Syria drinking tea is an important part of Arab culture. Many Syrians, like this carpet seller, drink tea every day with family and friends.

Conflict and Civil War

After independence, Christians and Muslims shared power in Lebanon. Certain government positions were held by different religious groups. For example, the president was always a Maronite. However, over time tensions between Christians and Muslims mounted.

In the 1970s civil war broke out. Lebanon's Muslims, including many Palestinian refugees, fought against Christians. Syria, Israel, and other countries became involved in the conflict. During the fighting, many people died and the capital, **Beirut**, was badly damaged. Warfare lasted until 1990.

After 1990, Syria continued to maintain a strong influence in Lebanon. In fact, Syrian troops stayed in Lebanon until they were pressured to leave in 2005. In 2006, cross border attacks by Lebanese guerrillas against Israel led to fighting between the two countries.

READING CHECK Drawing Conclusions
What has caused divisions in Lebanese society?

Jordan

Jordan's short history has been full of conflict. The country has few resources and several powerful neighbors.

Jordan's History and Government

The country of Jordan was created after World War I. The British controlled the area and named an Arab prince as the monarch of the new country. In the 1940s the country became fully independent.

At the time of its independence, Jordan's population was small. Most Jordanians lived a nomadic or semi-nomadic life. Hundreds of thousands of Palestinian Arab refugees fled Israel and came to live in Jordan. From 1952 to 1999 Jordan was ruled by King Hussein. The king enacted some democratic reforms in the 1990s.

Jordan's People and Resources

Many of Jordan's people are **Bedouins**, or Arabic-speaking nomads who mostly live in the deserts of Southwest Asia. Jordan produces phosphates, cement, and potash. Tourism and banking are becoming impor-

Lebanon After more than two decades of civil war, Lebanon's people are rebuilding their capital, Beirut. The city's people now enjoy a new public square.

Jordan Jordan's people value education and equal rights for women. Jordanian teenagers like these girls are required to attend school until age 15.

tant industries. Jordan depends on economic aid from the oil-rich Arab nations and the United States. **Amman**, the capital, is Jordan's largest city. Jordanian farmers grow fruits and vegetables and raise sheep and goats. A shortage of water is a crucial resource issue for Jordan.

READING CHECK **Summarizing** How did King Hussein affect Jordan's history?

SUMMARY AND PREVIEW In this section you learned about the history, government, and people of Syria, Lebanon, and Jordan. In the next chapter you will learn about Iraq and Iran and the countries of the Arabian Peninsula—Saudi Arabia, Kuwait, Bahrain, Qatar, the United Arab Emirates, Yemen, and Oman.

Section 4 Assessment

go.hrw.com
Online Quiz
KEYWORD: SG7 HP17

Reviewing Ideas, Terms, and Places

1. **a. Recall** What is the capital of Syria?
   b. Explain What does Syria's government own?
   c. Elaborate Why did Hafiz al-Assad want to increase the size of Syria's military?
2. **a. Identify** What European country ruled Lebanon after World War I?
   b. Analyze How was **Beirut** damaged?
   c. Elaborate What is the history of political divisions between religious groups in Lebanon's government?
3. **a. Define** Who are the **Bedouins**?
   b. Summarize Who provides economic aid to Jordan?

Critical Thinking

4. **Comparing and Contrasting** Use your notes to identify similarities and differences among the people in the three countries.

	Similarities	Differences
Syria		
Lebanon		
Jordan		

FOCUS ON WRITING

5. **Describing Syria, Lebanon, and Jordan** If you could only include two details about these countries, what would they be?

from
Red Brocade

by Naomi Shihab Nye

Drinking tea with guests is a traditional Arab custom.

GUIDED READING

WORD HELP

pine nuts a small sweet edible seed of some pine trees

brocade a heavy fabric of silk, cotton, or wool woven with a raised design, often using metallic threads

mint a plant with aromatic leaves that grows in northern temperate regions and is often used for flavoring

❶ Arabs are a cultural group that speak Arabic. They live mostly in Southwest Asia and North Africa.

❷ When entertaining, Arabs often sit on pillows on the floor.

About the Poem *In "Red Brocade," Arab-American writer Naomi Shihab Nye tells about an Arab custom. As a part of this custom, strangers are given a special welcome by those who meet them at the door. Since the poet is Arab-American, she is suggesting that we go "back to that" way of accepting new people.*

AS YOU READ Identify the special way that Arab people in Southwest Asia greet strangers at their door.

The Arabs ❶ used to say,
When a stranger appears at your
    door,
feed him for three days
before asking who he is,
where he's come from,
where he's headed.
That way, he'll have strength
enough to answer.
Or, by then you'll be
such good friends
you don't care.

Let's go back to that.
Rice? Pine nuts?

Here, take the red brocade
    pillow. ❷
My child will serve water
to your horse.

No, I was not busy when you
    came!
I was not preparing to be busy.
That's the armor everyone put
    on to pretend they had a purpose
in the world.

I refuse to be claimed.
Your plate is waiting.
We will snip fresh mint
into your tea.

Connecting Literature to Geography

1. Describing What details in the second verse show us that the Arab speaker is extending a warm welcome to the stranger?

2. Comparing and Contrasting Do you think this poem about greeting a stranger at the door would be different if it had taken place in another region of the world? Explain your answer.

Geography's Impact
video series
Review the video to answer the closing question:
Why do you think the conflict in Jerusalem today is difficult to solve?

Visual Summary

Use the visual summary below to help you review the main ideas of the chapter.

QUICK FACTS

The eastern Mediterranean is a dry region, and water is a key resource.

The region's history includes conflict between three major religions.

Most people living in the eastern Mediterranean are Arab Muslims.

Reviewing Vocabulary, Terms, and Places

Fill in the blanks with the correct term or place from this chapter.

1. The_____ is the lowest point on any continent and the world's saltiest body of water.

2. A desert located in southern Israel is called the_____.

3. A_____is a way of doing something.

4. Turkey's largest city is_____.

5. _____means that religion is kept separate from government.

6. The scattering of the Jewish population is known as_____.

7. A_____is a large farm where people share everything in common.

8. _____is Lebanon's capital that was badly damaged during the country's civil war.

Comprehension and Critical Thinking

SECTION 1 *(Pages 412–415)*

9. **a. Describe** How is the Eastern Mediterranean considered a part of the Middle East?

b. Draw Conclusions How would the region's dry climates affect where people lived?

c. Predict What would happen if the region's people did not have access to water?

SECTION 2 *(Pages 416–419)*

10. **a. Recall** How was control of Constantinople important?

b. Make Inferences How did modernization change Turkey?

c. Elaborate Why do you think Turkey wants to be a member of the European Union?

SECTION 3 *(Pages 420–424)*

11. **a. Define** What is Zionism?

SECTION 3 (continued)

b. Make Inferences Why does Israel need a strong military?

c. Elaborate How has Israel's history affected the country today?

SECTION 4 (Pages 426–429)

12. a. Identify What is the capital of Syria? Why is it historically significant?

b. Analyze Why did Lebanon have a civil war?

c. Evaluate How do you think Jordan survives with so few resources?

Using the Internet

go.hrw.com
KEYWORD: SG7 CH17

13. Creating an Exhibit Jerusalem is a city rich in tradition, history, and culture dating back thousands of years. Enter the activity keyword and travel back in time to historic Jerusalem. Explore its history, archaeology, buildings, daily life, food, and more. Then create a museum exhibit to highlight the artifacts, information, and stories you encounter in your journey through Jerusalem's past. Some things you may want to include are artifacts, models, time lines, maps, small placards providing information, and an exhibit guide for viewers.

Social Studies Skill

Analyzing a Cartogram *Use the cartogram and political map of Southwest and Central Asia on this chapter's Social Studies Skills page to answer the following questions.*

14. Why do you think Turkey's size on the political map is similar to its size on the cartogram?

15. How does the cartogram show the high population density of Israel and the Palestinian Territories?

16. From looking at the cartogram, is the population density of Kazakhstan, high or low? Explain your answer.

FOCUS ON READING AND WRITING

Setting a Purpose *Use the information in this chapter to answer the following questions.*

17. How does setting a purpose before you read help you become a better reader?

18. How is your purpose in reading this chapter different from your purpose when you read a newspaper comic strip?

19. How can looking at headings and main idea statements help you set a purpose for reading?

20. Writing a Description Look over your notes and choose one Eastern Mediterranean country to describe. Organize your notes by topic—physical features, people, culture and government. Then, write a one-to two-paragraph description of the country. Include information you think would be interesting to someone who knows nothing about the country. Add details that will help your readers picture the country.

Map Activity

21. The Eastern Mediterranean On a separate sheet of paper, match the letters on the map with their correct labels.

Bosporus   Negev

Jordan River   Euphrates River

Dead Sea

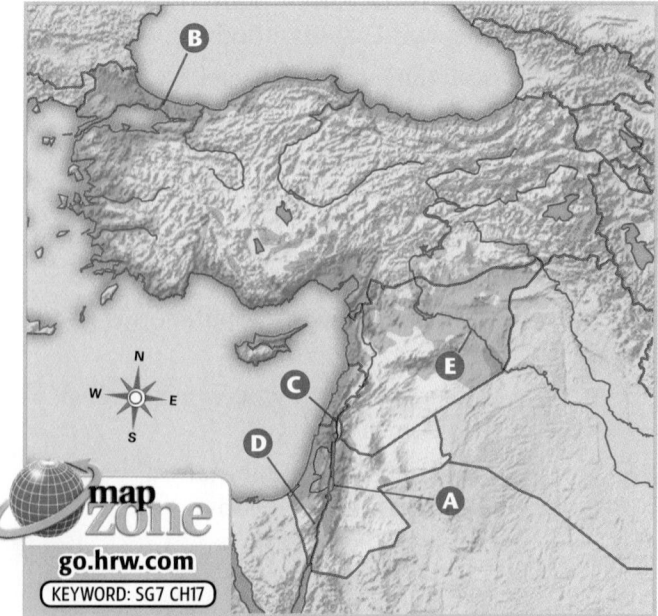

go.hrw.com
KEYWORD: SG7 CH17

DIRECTIONS: Read questions 1 through 7 and write the letter of the best response. Then read question 8 and write your own well-constructed response.

1 The climate of most of Israel, Jordan, and Syria is

A desert.

B steppe.

C humid subtropical.

D Mediterranean.

2 Turkey's government wants to be more like countries on what continent?

A Asia

B South America

C Australia

D Europe

3 Jews and Palestinian Arabs make up most of what country's population?

A Jordan

B Israel

C Turkey

D Lebanon

4 What city is sacred to Jews, Muslims, and Christians?

A Istanbul

B Tel Aviv

C Jerusalem

D Damascus

5 Most people living in Syria, Lebanon, and Jordan are

A Arabs.

B Jews.

C European.

D Christians.

Turkey: Physical Geography

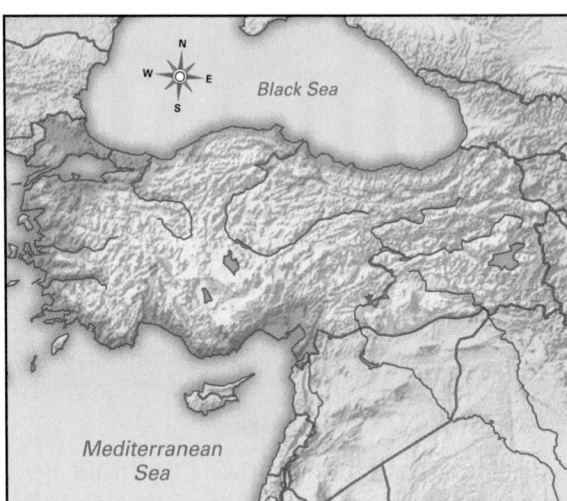

6 Based on the map above, what physical features surround most of Turkey?

A mountains

B seas

C plateaus

D lakes

7 Many of Jordan's people are

A Bedouins.

B Lebanese.

C Jewish.

D Turkish.

8 Extended Response Based on the map above and your knowledge of the region, write a brief essay explaining how Turkey's location has influenced its history and the country today.

The Arabian Peninsula, Iraq, and Iran

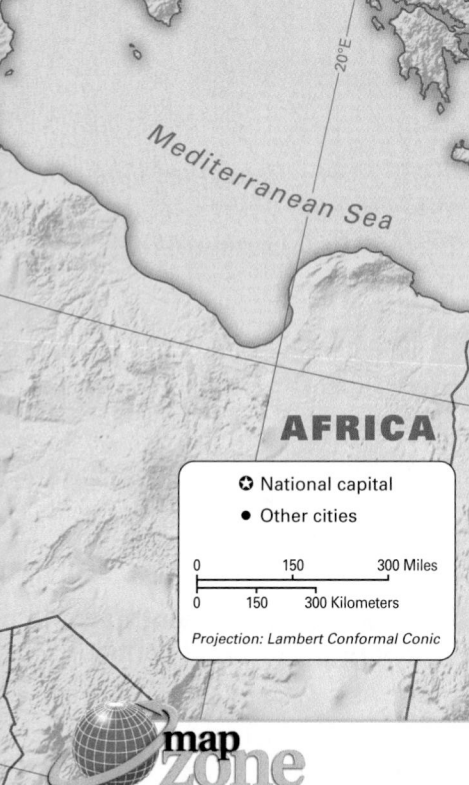

Mediterranean Sea

AFRICA

✪ National capital
● Other cities

0   150   300 Miles
0 150 300 Kilometers

Projection: Lambert Conformal Conic

What You Will Learn...

In this chapter you will learn about the Arabian Peninsula, which includes Saudi Arabia, Kuwait, Bahrain, Qatar, United Arab Emirates, Oman, and Yemen. You will also learn about the history and people of Iraq and Iran.

map zone
Geography Skills

Place The countries of the Arabian Peninsula, Iraq, and Iran are centered around the Persian Gulf.
1. **Locate** What is the capital of Saudi Arabia?
2. **Analyze** Approximately how many miles would you have to travel from Baghdad to Kuwait City?

go.hrw.com (KEYWORD: SG7 CH18)

FOCUS ON READING AND WRITING

Re-Reading Sometimes a single reading is not enough to fully understand a passage of text. If you feel like you do not fully understand something you have read, it may help to re-read the passage more slowly. **See the lesson, Re-Reading, on page R19.**

Creating a Geographer's Log You are a geographer taking a journey of discovery through the Arabian Peninsula, Iraq, and Iran. As you travel from place to place, create a geographer's log, a written record of what you see on your journey.

Culture Islam is a major part of the culture in every country in the region. These women pray at a mosque in Mecca, Saudi Arabia.

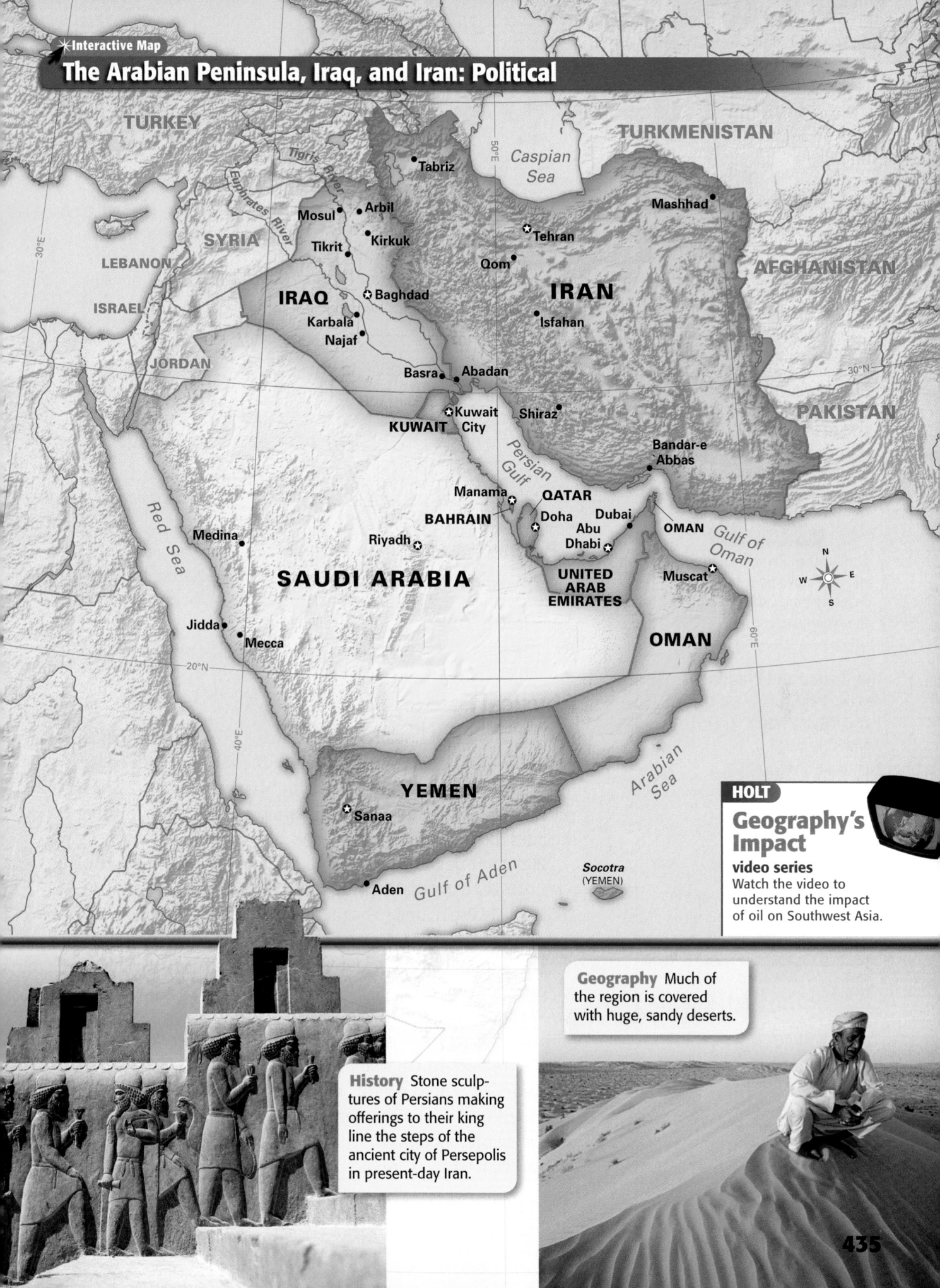

TURKEY

TURKMENISTAN

Tabriz

Caspian Sea

Mashhad

Tigris River

Euphrates River

Mosul

Arbil

SYRIA

Kirkuk

Tikrit

Tehran

Qom

IRAN

AFGHANISTAN

LEBANON

ISRAEL

IRAQ

Baghdad

Isfahan

JORDAN

Karbala

Najaf

30°N

PAKISTAN

Basra

Abadan

Shiraz

Kuwait City

Bandar-e Abbas

KUWAIT

Persian Gulf

Red Sea

Manama

QATAR

Doha

Dubai

Abu Dhabi

OMAN

Gulf of Oman

BAHRAIN

Medina

Riyadh

SAUDI ARABIA

UNITED ARAB EMIRATES

Muscat

N

W   E

S

Jidda

Mecca

20°N

OMAN

YEMEN

Arabian Sea

HOLT

Geography's Impact
video series
Watch the video to understand the impact of oil on Southwest Asia.

Sanaa

Aden

Gulf of Aden

Socotra (YEMEN)

Geography Much of the region is covered with huge, sandy deserts.

History Stone sculptures of Persians making offerings to their king line the steps of the ancient city of Persepolis in present-day Iran.

Physical Geography

What You Will Learn...

Main Ideas

1. Major physical features of the Arabian Peninsula, Iraq, and Iran are desert plains and mountains.
2. The region has a dry climate and little vegetation.
3. Most of the world is dependent on oil, a resource that is exported from this region.

The Big Idea

The Arabian Peninsula, Iraq, and Iran make up a mostly desert region with very valuable oil resources.

Key Terms and Places

Arabian Peninsula, *p. 436*
Persian Gulf, *p. 436*
Tigris River, *p. 436*
Euphrates River, *p. 436*
oasis, *p. 438*
wadis, *p. 439*
fossil water, *p. 439*

 **TAKING NOTES** As you read, use a chart like the one below to help organize your notes on the region's physical geography.

Physical Features	Climate and Vegetation	Resources

If **YOU** lived there...

You are in a plane flying over the vast desert areas of the Arabian Peninsula. As you look down, you see some tents of desert nomads around trees of an oasis. Sometimes you can see a truck or a line of camels crossing the dry, rocky terrain. A shiny oil pipeline stretches for miles in the distance.

What is life like for people in the desert?

BUILDING BACKGROUND Iran, Iraq, and the countries of the Arabian Peninsula are part of a region sometimes called the "Middle East." This region lies at the intersection of Africa, Asia, and Europe. Much of the region is dry and rugged.

Physical Features

Did you know that not all deserts are made of sand? The **Arabian Peninsula** has the largest sand desert in the world. But it also has huge expanses of desert covered with bare rock or gravel. These wide desert plains are a common landscape in the region that includes the Arabian Peninsula, Iraq, and Iran.

The countries of this region appear on the map in sort of a semicircle, with the **Persian Gulf** in the center. The Arabian Peninsula is also bounded by the Gulf of Oman, the Arabian Sea, and the Red Sea. The Caspian Sea borders Iran to the north.

The region contains four main landforms: rivers, plains, plateaus, and mountains. The **Tigris** (TY-gruhs) and **Euphrates** (yooh-FRAY-teez) rivers flow across a low, flat plain in Iraq. They join together before they reach the Persian Gulf. The Tigris and Euphrates are what are known as exotic rivers, or rivers that begin in humid regions and then flow through dry areas. The rivers create a narrow fertile area, which in ancient times was called Mesopotamia, or the "land between the rivers." The Arabian Peninsula has no permanent rivers.

The vast, dry expanse of the Arabian Peninsula is covered by plains in the east. The peninsula's desert plains are covered with sand in the south and volcanic rock in the north. As you can see on the map, the surface of the peninsula rises gradually from the Persian Gulf to the Red Sea. Near the Red Sea the landscape becomes one of plateaus and mountains, with almost no coastal plain. The highest point on the peninsula is in the mountains of Yemen.

Plateaus and mountains also cover most of Iran. In fact, Iran is one of the world's most mountainous countries. In the west, the land climbs sharply to form the Zagros Mountains. The Elburz Mountains and the Kopet-Dag lie in the north. Historically, this mountainous landscape has kept towns there isolated from each other.

FOCUS ON READING

After you read this paragraph, re-read it to make sure you understand Iran's landscape.

READING CHECK **Summarizing** What are the major physical features of this area?

Arabian Peninsula, Iraq, and Iran: Physical

✶Interactive Map

Geography Skills

Location This region lies at the intersection of Europe, Africa, and Asia.

1. **Locate** Where are the Elburz Mountains?
2. **Make Inferences** How might the region's location have affected its history?

go.hrw.com KEYWORD: SG7 CH18

ELEVATION

Feet	Meters
13,120	4,000
6,560	2,000
1,640	500
656	200
(Sea level) 0	0 (Sea level)
Below sea level	Below sea level

0   200   400 Miles
0   200   400 Kilometers

Projection: Lambert Conformal Conic

1 The Elburz Mountains in Iran are the highest land in the region.

2 The Euphrates River creates a narrow, fertile area in Iraq.

437

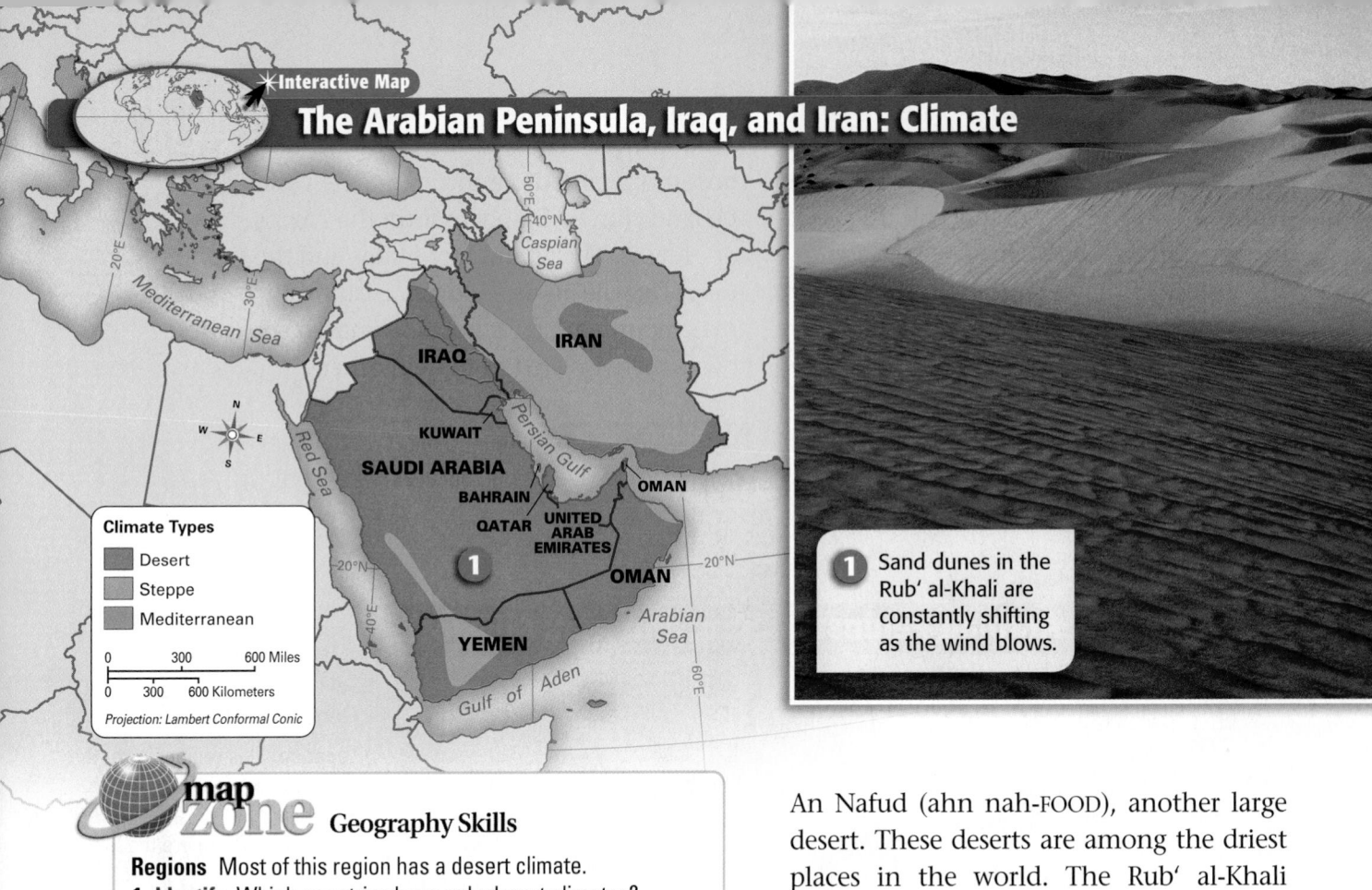

Climate Types
- Desert
- Steppe
- Mediterranean

0   300   600 Miles
0   300   600 Kilometers

Projection: Lambert Conformal Conic

1 Sand dunes in the Rub' al-Khali are constantly shifting as the wind blows.

map zone Geography Skills

Regions Most of this region has a desert climate.
1. **Identify** Which countries have only desert climates?
2. **Interpret** Look back at the physical map. How do landforms in the region influence climate?

go.hrw.com (KEYWORD: SG7 CH18)

Climate and Vegetation

As you have already read, most of this region has a desert climate. The desert can be both very hot and very cold. In the summer, afternoon temperatures regularly climb to over 100°F (38°C). During the night, however, the temperature may drop quickly. Nighttime temperatures in the winter sometimes dip below freezing.

The world's largest sand desert, the Rub' al-Khali (ROOB ahl-KAH-lee), covers much of southern Saudi Arabia. *Rub' al-Khali* means "Empty Quarter," a name given to the area because there is so little life there. Sand dunes in the desert can rise to 800 feet (245 m) high and stretch for nearly 200 miles! In northern Saudi Arabia is the

An Nafud (ahn nah-FOOD), another large desert. These deserts are among the driest places in the world. The Rub' al-Khali receives an average of less than 4 inches (10 cm) of rainfall each year.

Some plateau and mountain areas do get winter rains or snow. These higher areas generally have semiarid steppe climates. Some mountain peaks receive more than 50 inches (130 cm) of rain per year.

Rainfall supports vegetation in some parts of the region. Trees are common in mountain regions and in scattered desert oases. An **oasis** is a wet, fertile area in a desert that forms where underground water bubbles to the surface. Most desert plants have adapted to survive without much rain. For example, the shrubs and grasses that grow on the region's dry plains have roots that either grow deep or spread out far to capture as much water as possible. Still, some places in the region are too dry or too salty to support any vegetation.

READING CHECK Finding the Main Idea
What climate dominates this region?

Resources

Water is one of the region's two most valuable resources. However, this resource is very scarce. In some places in the desert, springs provide water. At other places, water can come from wells dug into dry streambeds called **wadis**. Modern wells can reach water deep underground, but the groundwater in these wells is often fossil water. **Fossil water** is water that is not being replaced by rainfall. Wells that pump fossil water will eventually run dry.

While water is scarce, the region's other important resource, oil, is plentiful. Oil exports bring great wealth to the countries that have oil fields. Most of the oil fields are located near the shores of the Persian Gulf. However, although oil is plentiful now, it cannot be replaced once it is taken from Earth. Too much drilling for oil now may cause problems in the future because most countries of the region are not rich in other resources. Iran is an exception with its many mineral deposits.

READING CHECK **Summarizing** What are the region's important resources?

Satellite View

Pivot-Irrigated Fields

This satellite image shows how fossil water has converted desert land into farmers' fields. Each circular plot of land has a water source at its center. An irrigation device extends out and pivots around the center.

Drawing Inferences Why are the fields circular?

SUMMARY AND PREVIEW The Arabian Peninsula, Iraq, and Iran form a desert region with significant oil resources. Next, you will learn more about the countries of the Arabian Peninsula.

Section 1 Assessment

go.hrw.com
Online Quiz
KEYWORD: SG7 HP18

Reviewing Ideas, Terms, and Places

1. **a. Describe** Where was Mesopotamia?
   b. Explain Where are the region's mountains?
   c. Elaborate Why do you think the **Tigris** and **Euphrates** rivers were so important in history?
2. **a. Recall** What parts of the region receive the most rainfall?
   b. Explain How have desert plants adapted to their environment?
3. **a. Define** What is **fossil water**?
   b. Make Inferences How do you think resources in the region influence where people live?
   c. Predict What might happen to the oil-rich countries if their oil was used up or if people found a new energy source to replace oil?

Critical Thinking

4. **Comparing and Contrasting** Using your notes and a graphic organizer like the one here, note physical characteristics unique to each area. Then list characteristics shared by all three areas.

Arabian Peninsula	Iraq	Iran
All		

FOCUS ON WRITING

5. **Describing Physical Geography** Take notes on the physical features, climate and vegetation, and resources that you could record in your log. What would you see and feel if you were in this region?

The Arabian Peninsula

Main Ideas

1. Islamic culture and an economy greatly based on oil influence life in Saudi Arabia.
2. Most other Arabian Peninsula countries are monarchies influenced by Islamic culture and oil resources.

The Big Idea

Most countries of the Arabian Peninsula share three main characteristics: Islamic religion and culture, monarchy as a form of government, and valuable oil resources.

Key Terms

Shia, *p. 440*
Sunni, *p. 440*
OPEC, *p. 441*

TAKING NOTES As you read, use a chart like the one here to take notes on the countries on the Arabian Peninsula.

Saudi Arabia	
Kuwait	
Bahrain	
Qatar	
United Arab Emirates	
Oman	
Yemen	

If YOU lived there...

You are a financial adviser to the ruler of Oman. Your country has been making quite a bit of money from oil exports. However, you worry that your economy is too dependent on oil. You think Oman's leaders should consider expanding the economy. Oman is a small country, but it has beautiful beaches, historic palaces and mosques, and colorful markets.

How would you suggest expanding the economy?

BUILDING BACKGROUND Oman and all the countries of the Arabian Peninsula have valuable oil resources. In addition to oil, these countries share two basic characteristics: Islamic religion and monarchy as a form of government. The largest country, and the one with the most influence in the region, is Saudi Arabia.

Saudi Arabia

Saudi Arabia is by far the largest of the countries of the Arabian Peninsula. It is also a major religious and cultural center and has one of the region's strongest economies.

People and Customs

Nearly all Saudis are Arabs and speak Arabic. Their culture is strongly influenced by Islam, a religion founded in Saudi Arabia by Muhammad. Islam is based on submitting to God and on messages Muslims believe God gave to Muhammad. These messages are writen in the Qur'an, the holy book of Islam.

Nearly all Saudis follow one of two main branches of Islam. **Shia** Muslims believe that true interpretation of Islamic teaching can only come from certain religious and political leaders called imams. **Sunni** Muslims believe in the ability of the majority of the community to interpret Islamic teachings. About 85 percent of Saudi Muslims are Sunni.

$$y = -2x(x^2 - 2x + 4) + 3x^3$$

Muslim Contributions to Math

During the early centuries of the Middle Ages, European art, literature, and science declined. However, during this same period, Muslim scholars made important advances in literature, art, medicine, and mathematics.

Our familiar system of numerals, which we call Arabic, was first created in India. However, it was Muslim thinkers who introduced that system to Europe. They also developed algebra and made advances in geometry. Muslims used math to advance the study of astronomy and physics. Muslim geographers calculated distances between cities, longitudes and latitudes, and the direction from one city to another. Muslim scientists even defined ratios and used mathematics to explain the appearance of rainbows.

Drawing Inferences Why do we need math to study geography?

$6 + x - 54 \div 102 = 9y \pm \div \pi\ 8 + x - 33 \times 157 + x - ab \div 102 = 8n \pm \div \pi\ 4 + x - 21 \times 76 \pm x - 637$

Islam influences Saudi Arabia's culture in many ways. For example, in part because Islam requires modesty, Saudi clothing keeps arms and legs covered. Men usually wear a long, loose shirt. They often wear a cotton headdress held in place with a cord. Saudi women traditionally wear a black cloak and veil in public, although some now wear Western-style clothing.

Saudi laws and customs limit women's activities. For example, a woman rarely appears in public without her husband or a male relative. Also, women are not allowed to drive cars. However, women can own and run businesses in Saudi Arabia.

Government and Economy

Saudi Arabia is a monarchy. Members of the Saud family have ruled Saudi Arabia since 1932. Most government officials are relatives of the king. The king may ask members of his family, Islamic scholars, and tribal leaders for advice on decisions.

The country has no elected legislature. Local officials are elected, but only men are allowed to vote.

Saudi Arabia's economy is based on oil. In fact, Saudi Arabia has the world's largest reserves, or supplies, of oil and is the world's leading exporter of oil. Because it controls so much oil, Saudi Arabia is an influential member of the Organization of Petroleum Exporting Countries, or OPEC. **OPEC** is an international organization whose members work to influence the price of oil on world markets by controlling the supply.

Oil has brought wealth to Saudi Arabia. The country has a sizable middle class, and the government provides free health care and education to its citizens. Even so, Saudi Arabia faces economic challenges. For example, it must import much of its food because freshwater needed for farming is scarce. The country uses desalination plants to remove salt from seawater, but this requires an extremely expensive **procedure**.

ACADEMIC VOCABULARY

procedure a series of steps taken to accomplish a task

FOCUS ON READING

After you read this paragraph, re-read it to make sure you understand Saudi Arabia's economic challenges.

Another economic challenge for Saudi Arabia is its high unemployment rate. One reason for the lack of jobs is the high population growth rate. More than 40 percent of Saudis are younger than 15. Another reason for unemployment is that many young Saudis choose to study religion instead of the technical subjects their economy requires.

READING CHECK **Finding Main Ideas** What religion influences Saudi Arabia's culture?

Other Countries of the Arabian Peninsula

Saudi Arabia shares the Arabian Peninsula with six smaller countries. Like Saudi Arabia, these countries are all influenced by Islam. Also like Saudi Arabia, most have monarchies and economies based on oil.

Kuwait

Oil was discovered in Kuwait in the 1930s. Since then it has made Kuwait very rich. In 1990 Iraq invaded Kuwait to try to control its oil, starting the Persian Gulf War. The United States and other countries defeated Iraq, but the war caused major destruction to Kuwait's oil fields.

Although Kuwait's government is dominated by a royal family, the country did elect a legislature in 1992. Only men from certain families—less than 15 percent of Kuwait's population—had the right to vote in these elections. However, Kuwait recently gave women the right to vote.

Bahrain and Qatar

Bahrain is a group of islands in the Persian Gulf. It is a monarchy with a legislature. Bahrain is a rich country. Most people there live well in big, modern cities. Oil made Bahrain wealthy, but in the 1990s the country began to run out of oil. Now banking and tourism are major industries.

Qatar occupies a small peninsula in the Persian Gulf. Like Bahrain, Qatar is ruled by a powerful monarch. In 2003 men and women in Qatar voted to approve a new constitution that would give more power to elected officials. Qatar is a wealthy country. Its economy relies on its oil and natural gas.

Oil Wealth

Big, modern cities such as Dubai, UAE, were built with money from oil exports. Many people in the region's cities can afford to buy luxury items.

ANALYZING VISUALS What kind of luxury items is this man selling?

The United Arab Emirates

The United Arab Emirates, or UAE, consists of seven tiny kingdoms. Profits from oil and natural gas have created a modern, comfortable lifestyle for the people of the UAE. Partly because it is so small, the UAE depends on foreign workers. In fact, it has more foreign workers than citizens.

Oman and Yemen

Oman covers most of the southeastern part of the Arabian Peninsula. Oman's economy is also based on oil. However, Oman does not have the great oil wealth of Kuwait or the UAE. Therefore, the government is attempting to develop new industries.

Yemen is located on the southwestern part of the Arabian Peninsula. The country has an elected government, but it has suffered from corruption. Oil was not discovered in Yemen until the 1980s. Oil and coffee generate much of the national income, but Yemen is still the poorest country on the Arabian Peninsula.

READING CHECK **Summarizing** How has oil affected the countries of the Arabian Peninsula?

Yemen
Yemen's architecture is an important part of its culture. These buildings are more than 2,000 years old.

SUMMARY AND PREVIEW Islam is a major influence on the people and culture of Saudi Arabia and the other countries of the Arabian Peninsula. The other major influence in the region is oil. Oil has brought wealth to most countries on the peninsula. In the next section you will learn about Iraq, a neighboring country with similar influences.

Section 2 Assessment

go.hrw.com
Online Quiz
KEYWORD: SG7 HP18

Reviewing Ideas, Terms, and Places

1. **a. Define** What is **OPEC**?
   b. Compare and Contrast How are **Sunni** and **Shia** Muslims similar, and how are they different from each other?
   c. Elaborate What do you think Saudi Arabia would be like if it did not have such huge oil reserves?
2. **a. Identify** What resource is the most important to the economies of countries on the Arabian Peninsula?
   b. Analyze How does its small size affect the United Arab Emirates?
   c. Predict How might Yemen change now that oil is a major part of its economy?

Critical Thinking

3. **Summarizing** Look at your notes on the countries of the Arabian Peninsula. Then copy the graphic organizer here and for each topic, write a one-sentence summary about the region.

	Summary
Culture	
Government	
Economy	

FOCUS ON WRITING

4. **Writing about the Arabian Peninsula** If you were traveling through these lands, what would you see or experience? Write some notes in your journal.

Oil in Saudi Arabia

Essential Elements

The World in Spatial Terms
Places and Regions
Physical Systems
Human Systems
Environment and Society
The Uses of Geography

Background Try to imagine your life without oil. You would probably walk or ride a horse to school. You would heat your home with coal or wood. You would never fly in a plane, walk in rubber-soled shoes, or even drink out of a plastic cup.

Our society depends on oil. However, oil is a nonrenewable resource. This means that supplies are limited, and we may one day run out of oil. In fact, the United States no longer produces enough oil to satisfy its own needs. We now depend on foreign countries, such as Saudi Arabia, for oil.

Oil Reserves in Saudi Arabia

Saudi Arabia has the world's largest supply of oil. This important resource, found naturally in the environment, has had a huge impact on Saudi Arabia's society.

Before the discovery of oil there in the 1930s, Saudi Arabia was a poor country. But income from oil exports has given the government money to invest in improvements such as new apartments, communications systems, airports, oil pipelines, and roads.

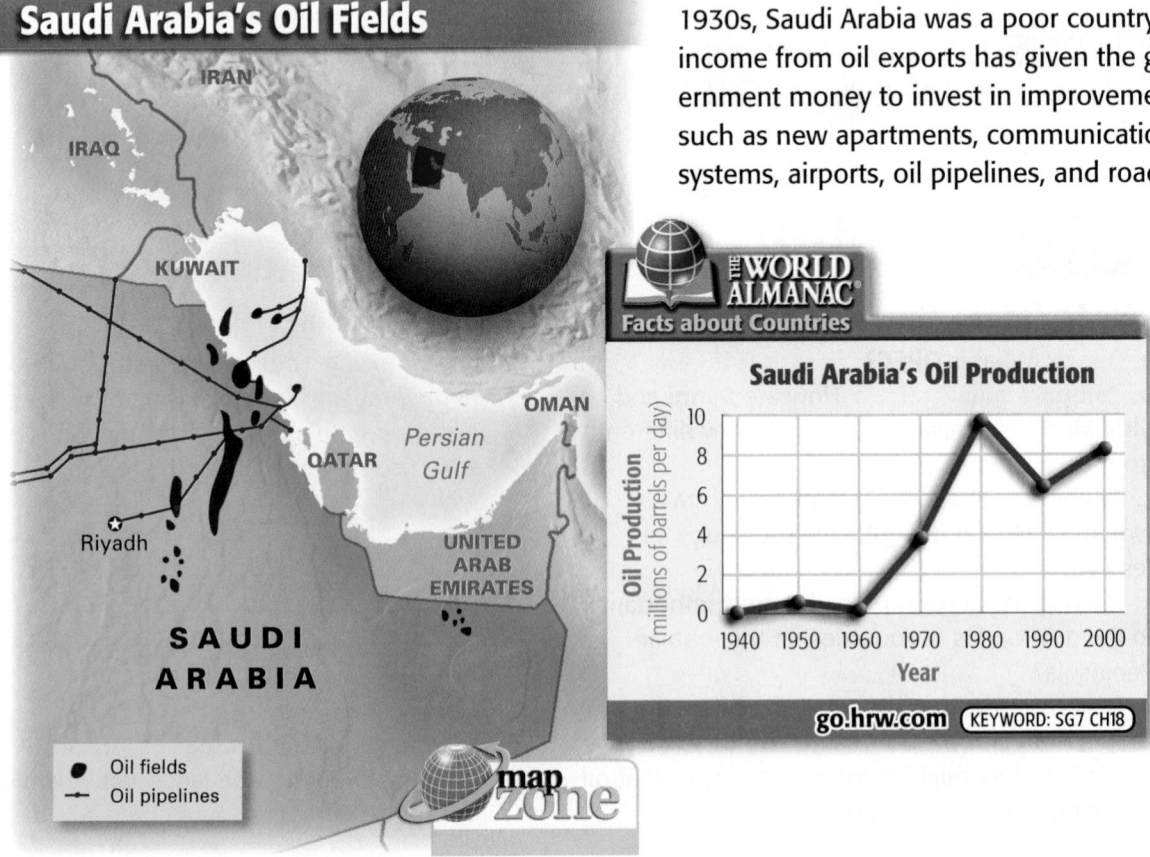

Saudi Arabia's Oil Fields

IRAN
IRAQ
KUWAIT
QATAR
Persian Gulf
OMAN
Riyadh
UNITED ARAB EMIRATES
SAUDI ARABIA

• Oil fields
⊷ Oil pipelines

THE WORLD ALMANAC®
Facts about Countries

Saudi Arabia's Oil Production

Oil Production (millions of barrels per day)

10
8
6
4
2
0

1940 1950 1960 1970 1980 1990 2000
Year

go.hrw.com KEYWORD: SG7 CH18

map zone

Saudi Arabia's oil is pumped through pipelines to tankers that ship the oil around the world. The oil industry has made Saudi Arabia a rich country.

THE WORLD ALMANAC
Facts about Countries

Saudi Arabia's Exports

Oil Products 91%

Other 9%

go.hrw.com KEYWORD: SG7 CH18

For example, in 1960 Saudi Arabia had only about 1,000 miles (1,600 km) of roads. By 2005 it had over 94,000 miles (152,000 km) of roads. These improvements have helped modernize Saudi Arabia's economy.

Oil exports have also affected Saudi society. Rising incomes have given many people there more money to spend on consumer goods. New stores and restaurants have opened, and new schools have been built throughout the country. Education is now available to all citizens. Increased education means the literacy rate has increased also—from about 3 percent when oil was discovered to about 79 percent today. Health care there has also improved.

The oil industry has also increased Saudi Arabia's importance in the world. Since it is a member of the Organization of Petroleum Exporting Countries (OPEC), Saudi Arabia influences the price of oil on the world market. Countries around the world want to have good relations with Saudi Arabia because of its vast oil reserves.

What It Means Today Saudi Arabia's government has a lot of money. This wealth has come almost entirely from the sale of oil. However, since the world's oil supplies are limited, Saudi Arabia's economy may be at risk in the future. Many countries are beginning to research other types of energy that can one day be used in place of oil. Until then, the many countries buying oil from Saudi Arabia will continue to pump wealth into Saudi society.

Geography for Life Activity

1. How has oil changed Saudi Arabia's society?

2. What are some advantages and disadvantages for a society that relies on oil?

3. **Other Types of Energy** Research other types of energy we can get from the environment. Based on your findings, do you think other types of energy will replace oil in the near future? Why or why not?

Iraq

What You Will Learn...

Main Ideas

1. Iraq's history includes rule by many conquerors and cultures, as well as recent wars.
2. Most of Iraq's people are Arabs, and Iraqi culture includes the religion of Islam.
3. Iraq today must rebuild its government and economy, which have suffered from years of conflict.

The Big Idea

Iraq, a country with a rich culture and natural resources, faces the challenge of rebuilding after years of conflict.

Key Terms and Places

embargo, *p. 447*
Baghdad, *p. 449*

TAKING NOTES Draw two boxes like the ones below. As you read, fill in the box on the left with your notes on Iraq's history. In the box on the right, take notes on Iraq today.

Iraq's History and Culture

Iraq Today

If YOU lived there...

You are a student in a school in Iraq's capital, Baghdad. During the war, your school and its library were badly damaged. Since then, you and your friends have had few books to read. Now your teachers and others are organizing a project to rebuild your library. They want to include books from all countries of the world as well as computers so students can use the Internet.

What would you like to have in the new library?

BUILDING BACKGROUND In spite of its generally harsh climate, the area that is now Iraq was one of the ancient cradles of civilization. Mesopotamia—the "land between the rivers"—was part of the "Fertile Crescent." Thousands of years ago, people there developed farming, domesticated animals, and organized governments.

History

Did you know that the world's first civilization was located in Iraq? Thousands of years ago people known as Sumerians settled in Mesopotamia—a region that is part of Iraq today. The country's recent history includes wars and a corrupt leader.

Early Civilization

Throughout Mesopotamia's history, different cultures and empires conquered the region. As you can see on the map on the next page, the Sumerians settled in southern Mesopotamia. By about 3000 BC, the Sumerians built the world's first known cities there. The Persians then conquered Mesopotamia in the 500s BC. By 331 BC Alexander the Great made it part of his empire. In the AD 600s Arabs conquered Mesopotamia, and the people gradually converted to Islam.

In the 1500s Mesopotamia became part of the Ottoman Empire. During World War I Great Britain took over the region. The British set up the kingdom of Iraq in 1932 and placed a pro-British ruler in power. In the 1950s a group of Iraqi army officers overthrew this government.

Saddam Takes Power

In 1968, after several more changes in Iraq's government, the Baath (BAHTH) Party took power. In 1979, a Baath leader named Saddam Hussein became Iraq's president. Saddam Hussein was a harsh ruler. He controlled Iraq's media, restricted personal freedoms, and killed an unknown number of political enemies.

Invasions of Iran and Kuwait

Under Saddam's leadership, Iraq invaded Iran in 1980. The Iranians fought back, and the Iran-Iraq War dragged on until 1988. Both countries' economies were seriously damaged and many people died.

In 1990 Iraq invaded Kuwait, Iraq's oil-rich neighbor to the south. This event shocked and worried many world leaders. They were concerned that Iraq might gain control of the region's oil. In addition, they worried about Iraq's supply of weapons of mass destruction, including chemical and biological weapons.

War and Its Effects

In 1991, an alliance of countries led by the United States forced the Iraqis out of Kuwait. This six week event was called the Persian Gulf War. Saddam, who remained in power after the war, would not accept all the United Nations' (UN) terms for peace. In response, the UN placed an **embargo**, or limit on trade, on Iraq. As a result, Iraq's economy suffered.

Soon after the fighting ended, Saddam faced two rebellions from Shia Muslims and Kurds. He brutally put down these uprisings. In response, the UN forced Iraq to end all military activity. The UN also required that Iraq allow inspectors into the country. They wanted to make sure that Saddam had destroyed the weapons of mass destruction. Iraq later refused to cooperate completely with the UN.

Ten years after the Persian Gulf War, the terrorist attacks of September 11, 2001, led to new tensions between the United States and Iraq. U.S. government officials believed that Iraq aided terrorists. In March 2003, President George W. Bush ordered U.S. forces to attack Iraqi targets. Within a few weeks the Iraqi army was defeated and Saddam's government was crushed. Saddam went into hiding, but U.S. soldiers later found Saddam hiding in an underground hole in rural Iraq. Saddam was arrested, tried, and executed for his crimes.

READING CHECK **Summarizing** What are some key events in Iraq's history?

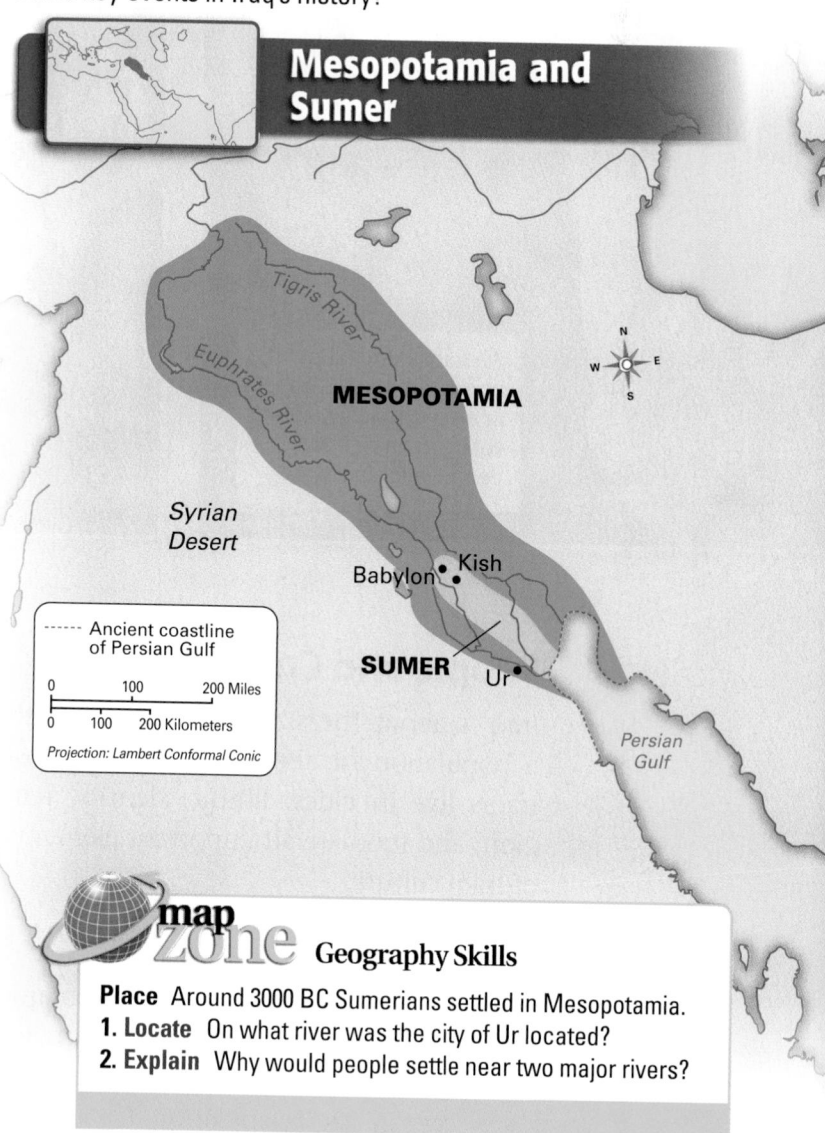

Mesopotamia and Sumer

----- Ancient coastline of Persian Gulf

0   100   200 Miles

0   100   200 Kilometers

Projection: Lambert Conformal Conic

Tigris River

Euphrates River

MESOPOTAMIA

Syrian Desert

Babylon · · Kish

SUMER   Ur ·

Persian Gulf

map zone Geography Skills

Place Around 3000 BC Sumerians settled in Mesopotamia.
1. **Locate** On what river was the city of Ur located?
2. **Explain** Why would people settle near two major rivers?

With the help of the United States, Iraqis are hopeful that they can rebuild their country.

ANALYZING VISUALS How is the United States helping Iraq's people today?

U.S. soldiers in Iraq search for suspected terrorists in 2007.

An Iraqi woman holds up her ink-stained finger in a sign of victory after voting in Iraq's first democratic elections.

A U.S. soldier passes out school supplies to Iraqi schoolchildren.

People and Culture

Iraq is about the size of California, with a population of about 27 million. Most Iraqis live in cities. Ethnic identity, religion, and food are all important elements of Iraqi culture.

Ethnic Groups

Most of Iraq's people belong to two major ethnic groups—Arabs and Kurds. Arabs are the largest group and make up more than 75 percent of Iraq's population. Iraqi Arabs speak the country's official language, Arabic. The smaller group, the Kurds, make up some 15 to 20 percent of the population. The Kurds are mostly farmers and live in a large region of northern Iraq. Most Iraqi Kurds speak Kurdish in addition to Arabic.

Religion

Like ethnic identity, religion plays a large role in the lives of most Iraqis. Nearly all Iraqis, both Arab and Kurdish, are Muslim. Within Iraq, the two different branches of Islam—Shia and Sunni—are practiced. About 60 percent of Iraqis are Shia and live in the south. Some 35 percent of Iraqis are Sunnis and live in the north.

READING CHECK **Summarizing** What ethnic groups do most Iraqis belong to?

Iraq Today

Despite years of war, Iraq is slowly rebuilding. However, the country faces many challenges, such as ongoing fighting.

Rebuilding Baghdad

Iraq's capital, **Baghdad**, was severely damaged in the overthrow of Saddam's government. For example, the city's 6 million people lost electricity and running water. To help the city's residents, U.S. military and private contractors worked with the Iraqis to restore electricity and water and to rebuild homes, businesses, and schools. However, violence in Baghdad continued, disrupting efforts to rebuild.

Government and Economy

In January 2005 Iraqis participated in democracy for the first time. Millions of Iraqis went to the polls to elect members to the National Assembly. One of the Assembly's first tasks was to create a new constitution. Deep divisions among Iraqis led to fierce internal fighting, however, and threatened the new government's stability.

Iraqis also began trying to rebuild their once strong economy. In the 1970s Iraq was the world's second-largest oil exporter. Time will tell if Iraq can again be a major oil producer.

Oil isn't Iraq's only resource. From earliest times, Iraq's wide plains and fertile soils have produced many food crops. Irrigation from the Tigris and Euphrates rivers allows farmers to grow barley, cotton, and rice.

After decades of a harsh government and wars, Iraq's future remains uncertain. Even with help from the United States, rebuilding may take years. Largely because of sectarian violence between Sunni and Shia groups, Iraq faces huge challenges in creating a free and prosperous society.

READING CHECK **Drawing Conclusions** What happened to Iraq's oil industry?

SUMMARY AND PREVIEW In this section, you have learned about Iraq's ancient history, rich culture, and efforts to rebuild. Next, you will learn about Iran, which also has an ancient history but is otherwise quite different from Iraq.

go.hrw.com
Online Quiz
KEYWORD: SG7 HP18

Section 3 Assessment

Reviewing Ideas, Terms, and Places

1. a. Recall Where was the world's first civilization located?
   b. Sequence What events led to the **embargo** on Iraq by the United Nations?
2. a. Identify What are two major ethnic groups in Iraq?
   b. Contrast What is one difference between Shia Muslims and Sunni Muslims?
3. a. Describe How was **Baghdad** damaged by war?
   b. Draw Conclusions What natural resource may help Iraq's economy recover?
   c. Predict What kind of country do you think Iraq will be in five years?

Critical Thinking

4. Summarizing Use your notes on Iraq today to fill in this table by summarizing what you have learned about Baghdad and Iraq's government and economy.

Baghdad	Government	Economy

FOCUS ON WRITING

5. Writing about Iraq Add details about Iraq's people, culture, and the country today to your notes. What sights have you seen that you might record in your log?

FOCUS ON READING
Do you understand everything you just read? If not, try re-reading the paragraphs that you do not understand.

Iran

If YOU lived there...

You are a student in Tehran, the capital of Iran. In school, you are taught that the way of life in the West—countries of Europe and the Americas—is bad. News reports and newspapers are filled with negative propaganda about Western countries. Yet you know that some of your friends secretly listen to Western popular music and watch American television programs that they catch using illegal satellite dishes at home. This makes you very curious about Western countries.

What would you like to know about life in other countries?

What You Will Learn...

Main Ideas

1. Iran's history includes great empires and an Islamic republic.
2. In Iran today, Islamic religious leaders restrict the rights of most Iranians.

The Big Idea

Islam is a huge influence on government and daily life in Iran.

Key Terms and Places

shah, *p. 451*
revolution, *p. 451*
Tehran, *p. 451*
theocracy, *p. 452*

TAKING NOTES As you read, take notes on Iran's history and life in the country today. Use the chart below to organize your notes.

Iran	
History	Today

BUILDING BACKGROUND Like Iraqis, Iranians have a proud and ancient history. While most people living in the Arabian Peninsula and Iraq are Arabs, the majority of Iranians are Persian. They have a distinct culture and language.

History

The early history of the country we now call Iran includes the Persian Empire and a series of Muslim empires. Iran's recent history includes an Islamic revolution. Today Iran is an Islamic republic, which limits the rights of many Iranians.

Persian Empire

Beginning in the 500s BC, the Persian Empire ruled the region around present-day Iran. For centuries Persia was a great center of art and learning. The Persian Empire was known for its spectacular paintings, carpets, metalwork, and architecture. In the empire's capital, Persepolis, walls and statues throughout the city glittered with gold, silver, and precious jewels.

The Persian Empire was later conquered by several Muslim empires. Muslims converted the Persians to Islam, but most people retained their Persian culture. They built beautiful mosques with colorful tiles and large domes.

The Shah and Islamic Revolution

In 1921 an Iranian military officer took power and encouraged change in Iran's government. He claimed the old Persian title of **shah**, or king. In 1941 the shah's son took control. This shah became an ally of the United States and Great Britain and tried to modernize Iran. His programs were unpopular with many Iranians.

In 1978 Iranians began a revolution. A **revolution** is a drastic change in a country's government and way of life. By 1979, Iranians overthrew the shah and set up an Islamic republic. This type of government follows strict Islamic law.

Soon after Iran's Islamic Revolution began, relations with the United States broke down. A mob of students attacked the U.S. Embassy in Iran's capital, **Tehran**. With the approval of Iran's government, the students took Americans working at the embassy hostage. More than 50 Americans were held by force for over a year.

READING CHECK Drawing Conclusions How did Iran's history lead to the Islamic Revolution?

Iran Today

Iranian culture differs from many other cultures of Southwest Asia. Unlike most of the Arab peoples living in the region, more than half of all Iranians are Persian. They speak Farsi, the Persian language.

People and Culture

With about 65 million people, Iran has one of the largest populations in Southwest Asia. Iran's population is very young. Over 35 million Iranians are younger than 25 years old. It is also ethnically diverse. Iranian ethnic groups other than the Persian majority include Azerbaijanis, Kurds, Arabs, and Turks.

Most Iranians belong to the Shia branch of Islam. Only about 10 percent are Sunni Muslim. The rest of Iran's people practice Christianity, Judaism, or other religions.

In addition to the Islamic holy days, Iranians celebrate Nowruz—the Persian New Year. Iranians tend to spend this holiday outdoors. As a part of this celebration, they display goldfish in their homes to symbolize life.

FOCUS ON READING
Re-read the paragraphs under The Shah and Islamic Revolution to better understand important parts of Iran's recent history.

Yazd, Iran

In the ancient city of Yazd, spectacular tilework covers the dome of an Islamic mausoleum built in the 1300s.

Iranian culture also includes close-knit families and respect for elders. Most family gatherings in Iran are centered around Persian food, which includes rice, bread, vegetables, fruits, lamb, and tea.

Economy and Government

Huge oil reserves, which are among the largest in the world, make Iran a wealthy country. In addition to oil, the production of beautiful woven carpets contributes to Iran's economy. The country's strong agricultural sector employs nearly one-third of the Iranian workforce.

The current government of Iran is a **theocracy**—a government ruled by religious leaders. These religious leaders, or *ayatollahs*, control Iran's government. The head of the *ayatollahs*, or supreme leader, has unlimited power. Even though religious leaders control Iran, its government has an elected president and parliament.

Life in Iran and the United States

Iran	United States
Daily Life	**Daily Life**
■ An Iranian woman has to cover her head and most of her body with clothing in public.	■ Americans are free to wear any type of clothing.
■ Iranians are forbidden to view most Western Web sites, and Internet use is monitored by the government.	■ Americans are free to surf the Internet and view most Web sites.
■ Boys and girls have separate schools, and they can not be alone with each other without adult supervision.	■ Boys and girls can attend the same school.
Government	**Government**
■ Iran is a theocracy.	■ The United States is a democracy.
■ A supreme religious leader rules Iran.	■ A president is the leader of our country.
■ Only candidates approved by the government can run for political office.	■ Any U.S. citizen can run for political office.
Basic Rights	**Basic Rights**
■ Freedom of speech, religion, and the press is limited.	■ Freedom of speech, religion, and the press is allowed.

Iranian teenagers can shop for computers, but a girl must wear clothing that covers most of her body.

Unlike Iranians, Americans are free to speak in public. Here a teenager speaks on the steps of the Texas State Capitol in Austin.

Contrasting In what ways does Iran's government differ from the U.S. government?

Iran's government has supported many hard-line policies. For example, it has called for the destruction of Israel. It has also supported terrorist groups in other countries. With a newly elected president in 1997, some signs indicated that Iran's government might adopt democratic reforms. This government attempted to improve Iran's economy and rights for women.

However, in 2005 Iranians moved away from democratic reforms by electing Mahmoud Ahmadinejad (mah-MOOD ah-mah-di-nee-ZHAHD) president. He wants Iranians to follow strict Islamic law. After the election, a reporter asked the new president if he had any plans for reforms. He responded, "We did not have a revolution in order to have a democracy."

More recently, international debate arose over Iran's expansion of its nuclear program. The United States and some of its allies feared that Iran was building nuclear weapons, which could threaten world security. Iran claimed it was using nuclear technology to create energy.

READING CHECK **Analyzing** What are Iran's government and people like?

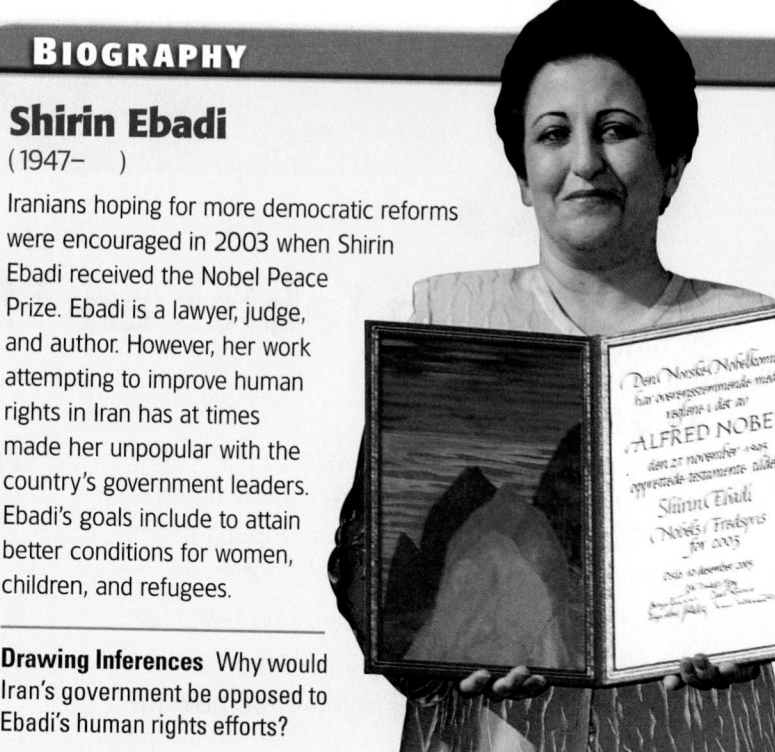

BIOGRAPHY

Shirin Ebadi
(1947–)

Iranians hoping for more democratic reforms were encouraged in 2003 when Shirin Ebadi received the Nobel Peace Prize. Ebadi is a lawyer, judge, and author. However, her work attempting to improve human rights in Iran has at times made her unpopular with the country's government leaders. Ebadi's goals include to attain better conditions for women, children, and refugees.

Drawing Inferences Why would Iran's government be opposed to Ebadi's human rights efforts?

SUMMARY AND PREVIEW In this section you learned about Iran's history, people, culture, economy, and government. In the next chapter, you will learn about the countries of Central Asia that lie to the north and east of Iran.

Section 4 Assessment

Reviewing Ideas, Terms, and Places

1. **a. Define** What is a **revolution**?
   b. Explain What was the Persian Empire known for?
   c. Elaborate What changes were made in Iran after the Islamic Revolution?
2. **a. Recall** What kind of leaders have authority over their people in a **theocracy**?
   b. Compare In what ways does Iran's culture differ from cultures in other countries of Southwest Asia?
   c. Predict How do you think the United States and other nations will deal with Iran's nuclear weapons program?

Critical Thinking

3. **Finding Main Ideas** Use your notes on Iran today to fill in this diagram with the main ideas of Iran's people, culture, economy, and government.

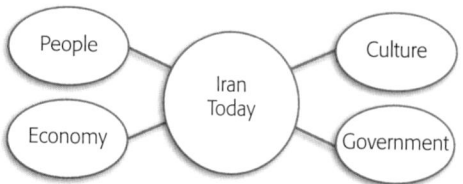

People — Iran Today — Culture
Economy — Iran Today — Government

FOCUS ON WRITING

4. **Writing about Iran** Record details about Iran in your log. What types of things would you see if you were traveling around Iran?

Analyzing Tables and Statistics

Learn

Tables provide an organized way of presenting statistics, or data. The data are usually listed side by side for easy reference and comparison. Use the following guidelines to analyze a table:

- Read the table's title to determine its subject.

- Note the headings and labels of the table's columns and rows. This will tell you how the data are organized.

- Locate statistics where rows and columns intersect by reading across rows and down columns.

- Use critical thinking skills to compare and contrast data, identify relationships, and note trends.

Literacy Rates in Southwest Asia			
	Literacy Rate (%)		
Country	Male	Female	Total
Iran	85.6	73.0	79.4
Iraq	55.9	24.4	40.4
Oman	83.1	76.2	75.8
Qatar	81.4	85.0	82.5
Saudi Arabia	84.7	70.8	78.8

Source: Central Intelligence Agency, *World Factbook 2005*

Practice

Use the table here to answer the following questions.

1. Which country has the highest total literacy rate? Which country has the lowest?

2. Which country has the largest difference between the literacy rate among men and the literacy rate among women?

3. What inference, or educated guess, can you make about education in these countries?

Apply

Using the Internet, an encyclopedia, or an almanac, locate information on the population density, birthrate, and death rate for each country listed in the table above. Then create your own table to show this information.

Chapter Review

Geography's Impact
video series
Review the video to answer the closing question:
Why is it important for countries to prepare for possible oil shortages?

Visual Summary

Use the visual summary below to help you review the main ideas of the chapter.

QUICK FACTS

Deserts cover much of the Arabian Peninsula. The region also has a lot of valuable oil reserves.

Many people in Iraq, such as this woman, enjoy more freedoms now that the country has a new government.

Iran is a theocracy. Islam is an important part of the country's government and culture.

Reviewing Vocabulary, Terms, and Places

Match the words in the columns with the correct definitions listed below.

1. wadis
2. revolution
3. embargo
4. procedure

5. fossil water
6. OPEC
7. shah
8. theocracy

a. the Persian title for a king

b. dry streambeds

c. a limit on trade

d. a series of steps taken to accomplish a task

e. water that is not being replaced by rainfall

f. an organization whose members try to influence the price of oil on world markets

g. a drastic change in a country's government

h. a government ruled by religious leaders

Comprehension and Critical Thinking

SECTION 1 *(Pages 436–439)*

9. a. Identify Through what country do the Tigris and Euphrates rivers flow?

b. Analyze Based on the landforms and climate, where do you think would be the best place in the region to live? Explain your answer.

c. Evaluate Do you think oil or water is a more important resource in the region? Explain your answer.

SECTION 2 *(Pages 440–443)*

10. a. Describe What kind of government does Saudi Arabia have?

b. Analyze In what ways does religion affect Saudi Arabia's culture and economy?

c. Elaborate What challenges might countries on the Arabian Peninsula face in attempting to create new industries in addition to oil?

SECTION 3 *(Pages 446–449)*

11. a. Recall What is the region of Mesopotamia known for?

b. Draw Conclusions Why did Iraq invade Kuwait in 1990?

c. Elaborate How did war damage Baghdad?

SECTION 4 *(Pages 450–453)*

12. a. Describe What occurred at the U.S. Embassy in Tehran after the Islamic Revolution?

b. Compare and Contrast How is Iran similar to or different from the United States?

c. Predict Do you think Iran's government will ever become more democratic? Why or why not?

FOCUS ON READING AND WRITING

13. Re-Reading Read the passage titled Resources in Section 1. After you read, write down the main ideas of the passage. Then go back and re-read the passage carefully. Identify at least one thing you learned from the passage when you re-read it and add the new information to your list of main ideas.

14. Creating a Geographer's Log Imagine that you began your journey in Saudi Arabia. Write the name of the country at the top of your log. Under the country's name, record details about what you saw as you traveled through the country. Then choose another country and do the same until you have created an entry in your log for each country. Look at your notes to help you remember what you saw. Be sure to include descriptions of the land and people.

Social Studies Skills

Analyzing Tables and Statistics *Use the Facts about Countries table at the beginning of the unit to answer the following questions.*

15. What is the population of Iraq?

16. What country is the smallest?

17. How many TVs per thousand people are there in Qatar?

Using the Internet

go.hrw.com
KEYWORD: SG7 CH18

18. Activity: Charting Democracy Some countries face challenges as they work to promote a more democratic form of government. Iraq, for example, has struggled as it has begun to develop its own form of democracy. How does democracy in Iraq, or elections in Saudi Arabia and Lebanon, affect the people of those countries? How do the media, literature, and arts in those areas reflect life in a democratic society? In what ways does democracy in Southwest Asia differ from democracy in the United States? Enter the activity keyword. Then create a chart or diagram that compares democratic life in the United States with democratic life in Iraq and other countries of Southwest Asia.

Map Activity

19. The Arabian Peninsula, Iraq, and Iran On a separate sheet of paper, match the letters on the map with their correct labels.

Rub' al-Khali

Persian Gulf

Tigris River

Tehran, Iran

Riyadh, Saudi Arabia

Euphrates River

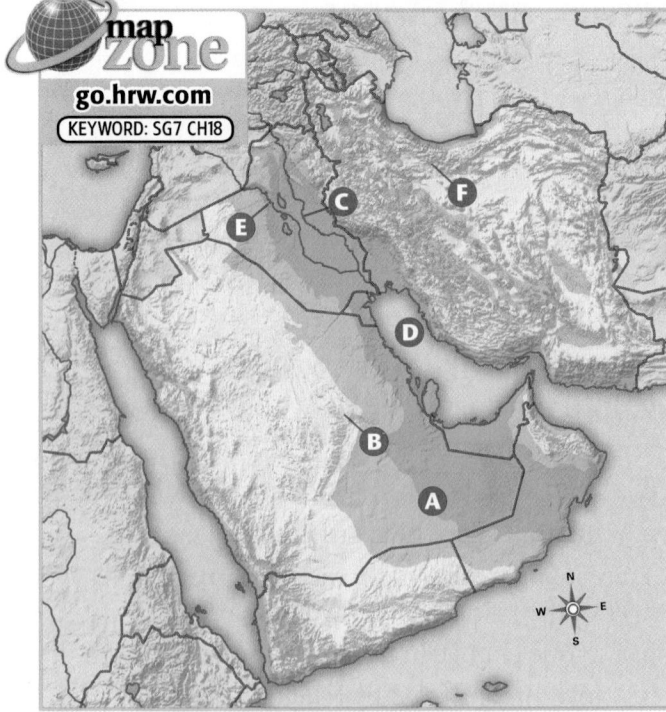

go.hrw.com
KEYWORD: SG7 CH18

DIRECTIONS: Read questions 1 through 7 and write the letter of the best response. Then read question 8 and write your own well-constructed response.

1 Dry streambeds in the desert are known as

A wadis.

B salty rivers.

C exotic rivers.

D disappearing rivers.

2 What kind of government does Saudi Arabia have?

A monarchy

B legislature

C democracy

D republic

3 Iraq's official language is

A Persian.

B Arabic.

C French.

D Kurdish.

4 Saddam Hussein is the former president of

A Saudi Arabia.

B Iraq.

C Oman.

D Iran.

5 Iran's government is a theocracy ruled by

A Islamic religious leaders.

B priests.

C Christian ministers.

D democratic leaders.

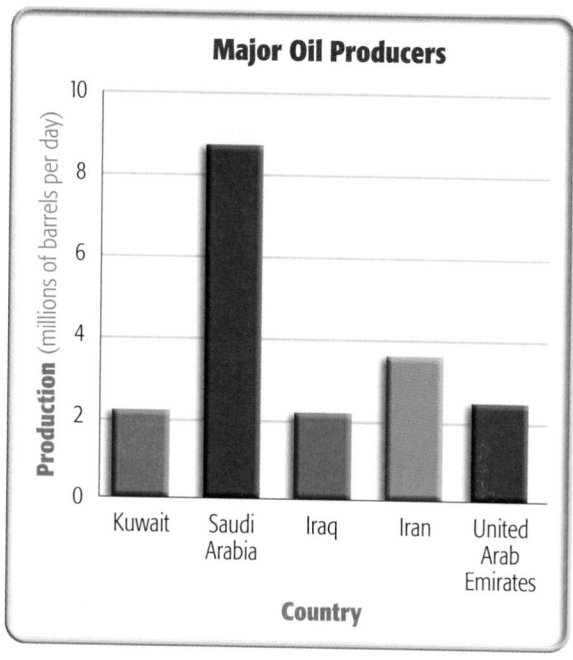

Major Oil Producers

Source: Central Intelligence Agency, *The World Factbook 2005*

6 Based on the graph above, about how many barrels of oil per day does Saudi Arabia produce?

A 9

B 9 thousand

C 9 million

D 9 billion

7 Based on the graph above, which country produces the second largest amount of oil in the region?

A United Arab Emirates

B Iran

C Iraq

D Kuwait

8 Extended Response Based on the graph above and your knowledge of the region, write a paragraph explaining the influence oil has on the region. Identify at least two ways in which oil affects the region.

Central Asia

What You Will Learn...

In this chapter you will learn about the rugged physical geography of Central Asia. This physical geography has affected the region's history. You will also learn about the many influences on Central Asia throughout history. Finally, you will see how these influences have affected the region's culture, governments, and economies today.

FOCUS ON READING AND VIEWING

Using Context Clues As you read, you may come across words in your textbook that you do not know. When this happens, look for context clues that restate the unknown word in other words that you know. **See the lesson, Using Context Clues, on page R20.**

Giving a Travel Presentation You work for a travel agency, and you are going to give a presentation encouraging people to visit Central Asia. Gather information from the chapter to help you prepare your presentation. Later you will view your classmates' presentations and provide feedback to them.

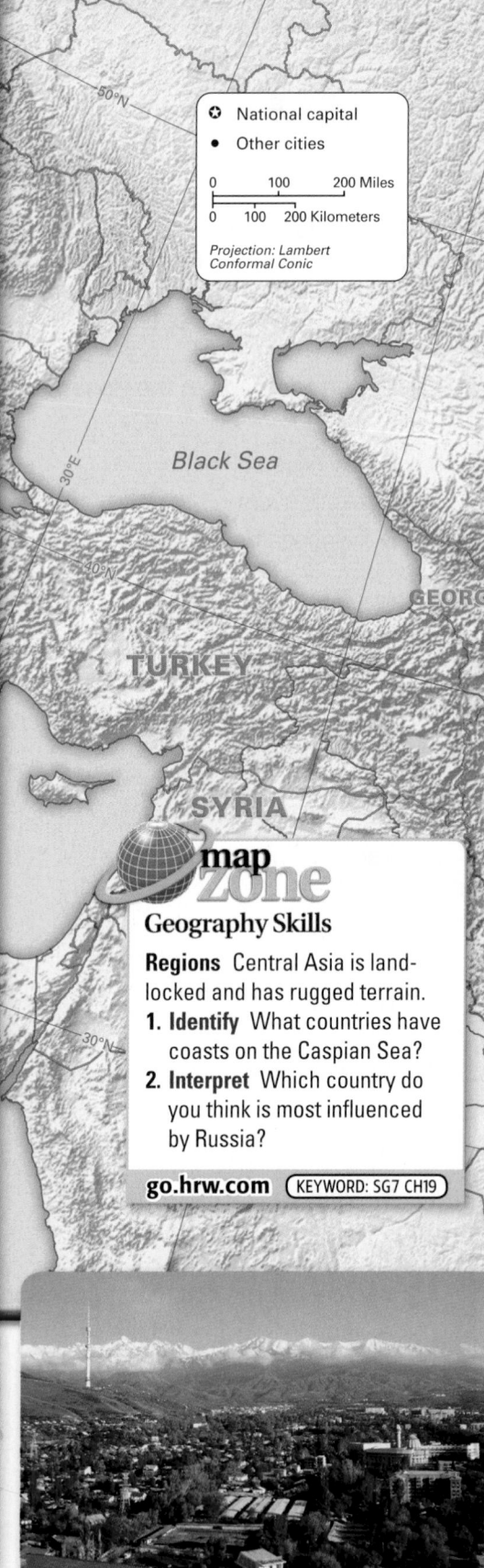

National capital
Other cities

0   100   200 Miles
0   100   200 Kilometers

Projection: Lambert Conformal Conic

Black Sea

GEORGIA

TURKEY

SYRIA

map Zone
Geography Skills

Regions Central Asia is landlocked and has rugged terrain.
1. **Identify** What countries have coasts on the Caspian Sea?
2. **Interpret** Which country do you think is most influenced by Russia?

go.hrw.com   KEYWORD: SG7 CH19

Geography Much of Central Asia's land is rugged. Here, mountains rise behind the city of Almaty, Kazakhstan.

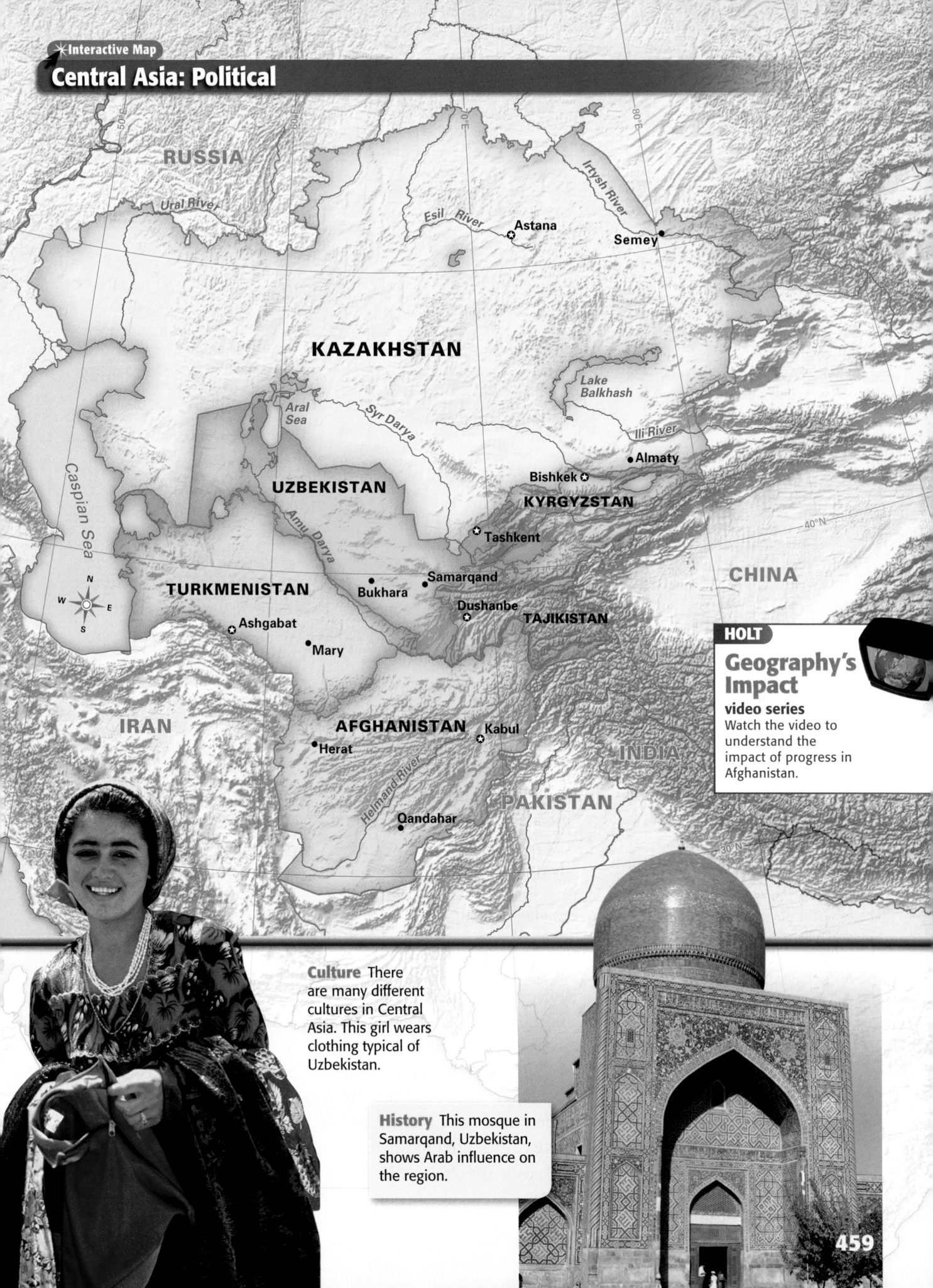

RUSSIA

Ural River

KAZAKHSTAN

Esil River

Astana

Semey

Irtysh River

Aral Sea

Syr Darya

Lake Balkhash

Ili River

UZBEKISTAN

Almaty

Bishkek

KYRGYZSTAN

Caspian Sea

Amu Darya

Tashkent

Samarqand

CHINA

TURKMENISTAN

Bukhara

Dushanbe

Ashgabat

TAJIKISTAN

N
W E
S

Mary

IRAN

AFGHANISTAN

Kabul

INDIA

Herat

Helmand River

PAKISTAN

Qandahar

40°N

30°N

HOLT

Geography's Impact
video series
Watch the video to understand the impact of progress in Afghanistan.

Culture There are many different cultures in Central Asia. This girl wears clothing typical of Uzbekistan.

History This mosque in Samarqand, Uzbekistan, shows Arab influence on the region.

459

Physical Geography

What You Will Learn...

Main Ideas

1. Key physical features of land-locked Central Asia include rugged mountains.
2. Central Asia has a harsh, dry climate that makes it difficult for vegetation to grow.
3. Key natural resources in Central Asia include water, oil and gas, and minerals.

The Big Idea

Central Asia, a dry, rugged, landlocked region, has oil and other valuable mineral resources.

Key Terms and Places

landlocked, *p. 460*
Pamirs, *p. 460*
Fergana Valley, *p. 461*
Kara-Kum, *p. 462*
Kyzyl Kum, *p. 462*
Aral Sea, *p. 463*

 **TAKING NOTES** As you read, use a chart like the one below to help you organize your notes on the physical geography of Central Asia.

Physical Features	
Climate and Vegetation	
Natural Resources	

If YOU lived there...

You are flying in a plane low over the mountains of Central Asia. You look down and notice that the area below you looks as if a giant hand has crumpled the land into steep mountains and narrow valleys. Icy glaciers fill some of the valleys. A few silvery rivers flow out of the mountains and across a green plain. This plain is the only green spot you can see in this rugged landscape.

How would this landscape affect people?

BUILDING BACKGROUND The physical geography of Central Asia affects the lives of the people who live there. This region has been shaped throughout its history by its isolated location, high mountains, dry plains, and limited resources.

Physical Features

As the name suggests, Central Asia lies in the middle of Asia. All of the countries in this region are landlocked. **Landlocked** means completely surrounded by land with no direct access to the ocean. This isolated location is just one challenge presented by the physical features of the region.

Mountains

Much of Central Asia has a rugged landscape. In the south, many high mountain ranges, such as the Hindu Kush, stretch through Afghanistan. Tajikistan and Kyrgyzstan are also very mountainous. Large glaciers are common in high mountains such as the **Pamirs**.

Like its landlocked location, Central Asia's rugged terrain presents a challenge for the region. Throughout history, the mountains have made travel and communication difficult and have contributed to the region's isolation. In addition, tectonic activity causes frequent earthquakes there.

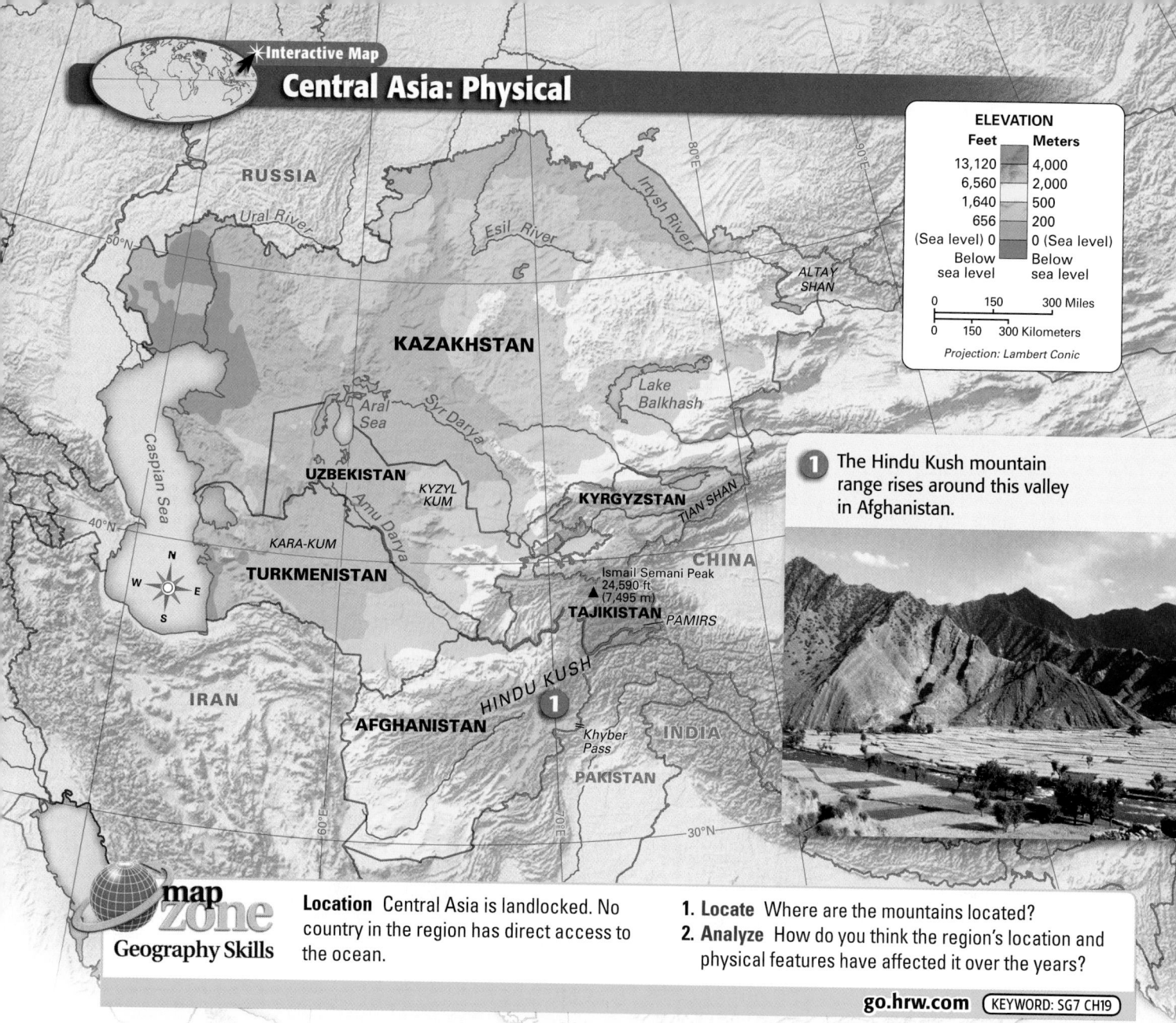

Central Asia: Physical

ELEVATION

Feet		Meters
13,120		4,000
6,560		2,000
1,640		500
656		200
(Sea level) 0		0 (Sea level)
Below sea level		Below sea level

0   150   300 Miles
0   150   300 Kilometers

Projection: Lambert Conic

RUSSIA

Ural River

Esil River

Irtysh River

ALTAY SHAN

KAZAKHSTAN

Lake Balkhash

Aral Sea

Syr Darya

1 The Hindu Kush mountain range rises around this valley in Afghanistan.

UZBEKISTAN

KYZYL KUM

KYRGYZSTAN

TIAN SHAN

Amu Darya

Caspian Sea

KARA-KUM

CHINA

TURKMENISTAN

Ismail Semani Peak
24,590 ft
(7,495 m) ▲

TAJIKISTAN — PAMIRS

IRAN

HINDU KUSH

AFGHANISTAN

1

Khyber Pass

INDIA

PAKISTAN

map Zone Geography Skills

Location Central Asia is landlocked. No country in the region has direct access to the ocean.

1. **Locate** Where are the mountains located?
2. **Analyze** How do you think the region's location and physical features have affected it over the years?

go.hrw.com   KEYWORD: SG7 CH19

Plains and Plateaus

From the mountains in the east, the land gradually slopes toward the west. There, near the Caspian Sea, the land is as low as 95 feet (29 m) below sea level. The central part of the region, between the mountains and the Caspian Sea, is covered with plains and low plateaus.

The plains region is the site of the fertile **Fergana Valley**. This large valley has been a major center of farming in the region for thousands of years.

Rivers and Lakes

The Fergana Valley is fertile because of two rivers that flow through it—the Syr Darya (sir duhr-YAH) and the Amu Darya (uh-MOO duhr-YAH). These rivers flow from eastern mountains into the Aral Sea, which is really a large lake. Another important lake, Lake Balkhash, has freshwater at one end and salty water at the other end.

READING CHECK **Generalizing** What challenges do the mountains present to this region?

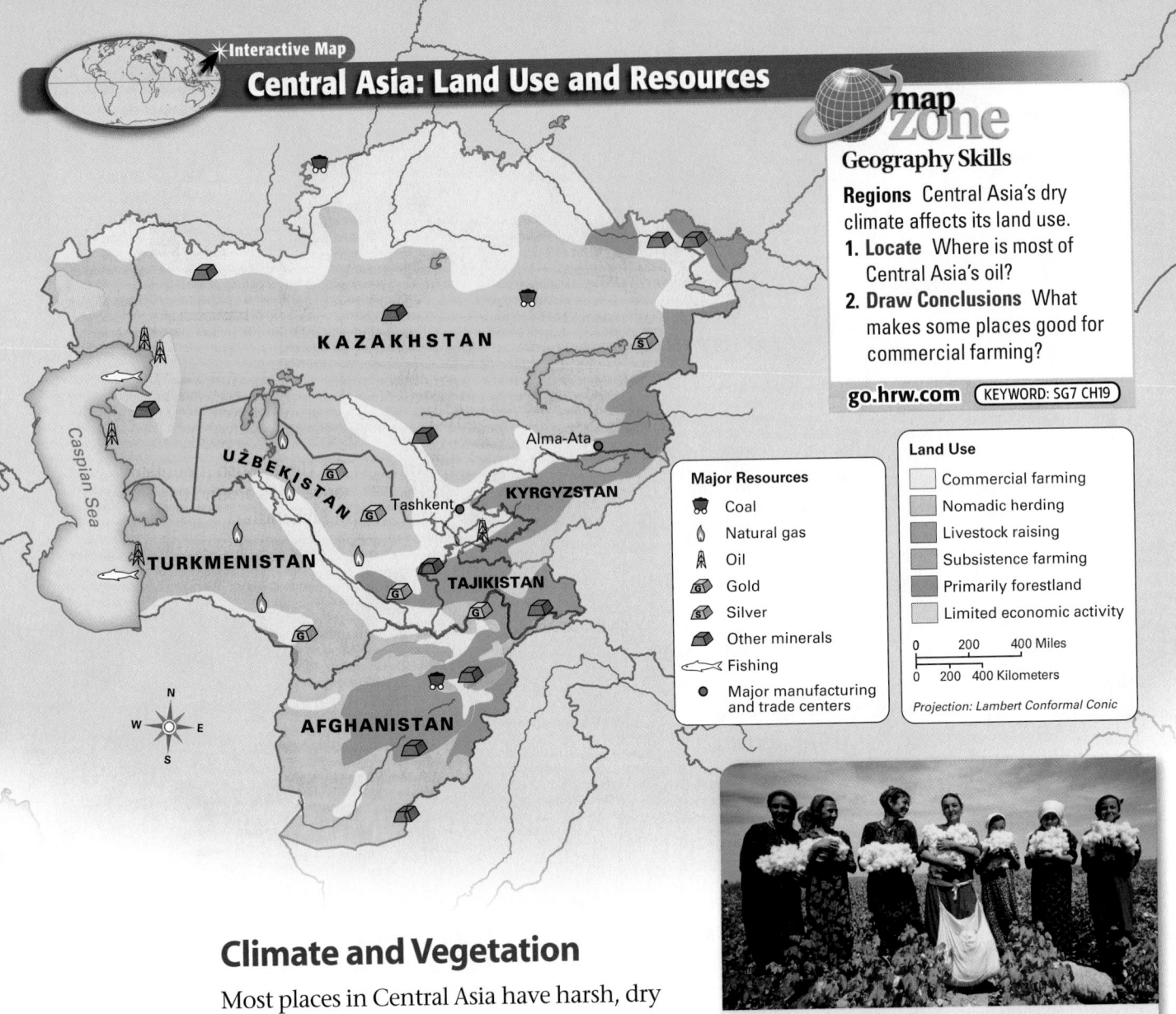

map zone

Geography Skills

Regions Central Asia's dry climate affects its land use.

1. **Locate** Where is most of Central Asia's oil?
2. **Draw Conclusions** What makes some places good for commercial farming?

go.hrw.com [KEYWORD: SG7 CH19]

KAZAKHSTAN

Caspian Sea

UZBEKISTAN

Alma-Ata

Tashkent

KYRGYZSTAN

TURKMENISTAN

TAJIKISTAN

AFGHANISTAN

N W E S

Major Resources

- Coal
- Natural gas
- Oil
- Gold
- Silver
- Other minerals
- Fishing
- Major manufacturing and trade centers

Land Use

- Commercial farming
- Nomadic herding
- Livestock raising
- Subsistence farming
- Primarily forestland
- Limited economic activity

0   200   400 Miles
0   200   400 Kilometers

Projection: Lambert Conformal Conic

Cotton is the main crop in Central Asia. Students often have to take time off from school to help harvest the cotton.

Climate and Vegetation

Most places in Central Asia have harsh, dry climates. Extreme temperature ranges and limited rainfall make it difficult for plants to grow there.

One area with harsh climates in the region is the mountain area in the east. The high peaks in this area are too cold, dry, and windy for vegetation.

West of the mountains and east of the Caspian Sea is another harsh region. Two deserts—the **Kara-Kum** (kahr-uh-KOOM) in Turkmenistan and the **Kyzyl Kum** (ki-ZIL KOOM) in Uzbekistan and Kazakhstan—have extremely high temperatures in the summer. Rainfall is limited, though both deserts contain several settlements. Rivers crossing this dry region make settlements possible, because they provide water for irrigation. Irrigation is a way of supplying water to an area of land.

The only part of Central Asia with a milder climate is the far north. There, temperature ranges are not so extreme and rainfall is heavy enough for grasses and trees to grow.

READING CHECK **Generalizing** Why is it hard for plants to grow in much of Central Asia?

Natural Resources

In this dry region, water is one of the most valuable resources. Although water is scarce, or limited, the countries of Central Asia do have oil and other resources.

Water

The main water sources in southern Central Asia are the Syr Darya and Amu Darya rivers. Since water is so scarce there, different ideas over how to use the water from these rivers have led to conflict between Uzbekistan and Turkmenistan.

Today farmers use river water mostly to irrigate cotton fields. Cotton grows well in Central Asia's sunny climate, but it requires a lot of water. Irrigation has taken so much water from the rivers that almost no water actually reaches the **Aral Sea** today. The effect of this irrigation has been devastating to the Aral Sea. It has lost more than 75 percent of its water since 1960. Large areas of seafloor are now exposed.

In addition to water for irrigation, Central Asia's rivers supply power. Some countries have built large dams on the rivers to generate hydroelectricity.

Oil and Other Resources

The resources that present the best economic opportunities for Central Asia are oil and gas. Uzbekistan, Kazakhstan, and Turkmenistan all have huge reserves of oil and natural gas.

However, these oil and gas reserves cannot benefit the countries of Central Asia unless they can be exported. Since no country in the region has an ocean port, the only way to transport the oil and gas efficiently is through pipelines. But the rugged mountains, along with economic and political turmoil in some surrounding countries, make building and maintaining pipelines difficult.

In addition to oil and gas, some parts of Central Asia are rich in other minerals. They have deposits of gold, silver, copper, zinc, uranium, and lead. Kazakhstan, in particular, has many mines with these minerals. It also has large amounts of coal.

FOCUS ON READING
What context clues give you a restatement of the term *scarce*?

READING CHECK Categorizing What are three types of natural resources in Central Asia?

SUMMARY AND PREVIEW In this section you learned about Central Asia's rugged terrain, dry climate, and limited resources. In the next section you will learn about the history and culture of Central Asia.

Section 1 Assessment

go.hrw.com
Online Quiz
KEYWORD: SG7 HP19

Reviewing Ideas, Terms, and Places

1. **a. Identify** What fertile area has been a center of farming in Central Asia for many years?
   b. Make Inferences How does Central Asia's terrain affect life there?
2. **a. Describe** Where do people find water in the deserts?
   b. Make Generalizations What is the climate like in most of Central Asia?
3. **a. Recall** What mineral resources does Central Asia have?
   b. Explain How have human activities affected the **Aral Sea**?
   c. Elaborate What kinds of situations would make it easier for countries of Central Asia to export oil and gas?

Critical Thinking

4. **Finding Main Ideas** Look at your notes on this section. Then, using a chart like the one here, write a main idea statement about each topic.

	Main Idea
Physical Features	
Climate and Vegetation	
Natural Resources	

FOCUS ON VIEWING

5. **Describing Physical Geography** Note information about physical features, climates, and resources of this region. Highlight information to include in your presentation.

History and Culture

If **YOU** lived there...

Your family has always farmed a small plot of land. Most days you go to school and work in the fields. One day you get news that invaders have taken over your country. They don't look like you and they speak a different language, but now they are in charge.

How do you think your life will change under the new rulers?

BUILDING BACKGROUND You may have noticed that the names of the countries in this region all end with *stan*. In the language of the region, *stan* means "land of." So, for example, Kazakhstan means "land of the Kazakhs." However, throughout history many different groups have ruled these lands.

History

Central Asia has been somewhat of a crossroads for traders and invaders for hundreds of years. As these different peoples have passed through Central Asia, they have each left their own unique and lasting influences on the region.

Trade

At one time, the best trade route between Europe and India ran through Afghanistan. The best route between Europe and China ran through the rest of Central Asia. Beginning in about 100 BC, merchants traveled along the China route to trade European gold and wool for Chinese spices and silk. As a result, this route came to be called the Silk Road. Cities along the road, such as **Samarqand** and Bukhara, grew rich from the trade.

By 1500 the situation in Central Asia had changed, however. When Europeans discovered they could sail to East Asia through the Indian Ocean, trade through Central Asia declined. The region became more isolated and poor.

Invasions

Because of its location on the Silk Road, many groups of people were interested in Central Asia. Group after group swarmed into the region. Among the first people to establish a lasting influence in the region were Turkic-speaking nomads who came from northern Asia in AD 500.

In the 700s Arab armies took over much of the region. They brought a new religion—Islam—to Central Asia. Many of the beautiful mosques in Central Asian cities date from the time of the Arabs.

Arabs, followed by other invaders, ruled Central Asia until the 1200s. Then, Mongol armies conquered Central Asia, destroying many cities with their violent attacks. Eventually, their empire crumbled. With the fall of the Mongols, various tribes of peoples, such as the Uzbeks, Kazakhs, and Turkmens moved into parts of the region.

Russian and Soviet Rule

In the mid-1800s the Russians became the next major group to conquer Central Asia. Although the Russians built railroads and expanded cotton and oil production, people began to resent their rule.

After the Russian Revolution in 1917, the new Soviet government wanted to weaken resistance to its rule. The new Soviet leaders did this by dividing the land into republics. The Soviets encouraged ethnic Russians to move to these areas and made other people settle on government-owned farms. The Soviets also built huge irrigation projects to improve cotton production.

The Soviet Union collapsed in 1991. As the Soviet government and economy fell apart, it could no longer control its huge territory. The Central Asian republics finally became independent countries.

READING CHECK **Generalizing** What groups of people influenced Central Asia?

Influences on Central Asia

The Arabs, Mongols, and Soviets all had a major influence on Central Asia.

Arab Influence

- The Arabs ruled Central Asia in the 700s and 800s.
- They introduced Islam and built beautiful mosques.
- They influenced styles of art and architecture in the region.

Mongol Influence

- The Mongols ruled from 1220 to the mid-1300s.
- They destroyed cities and irrigation systems.
- Eventually, they supported literature and the arts at Samarqand.

Soviet Influence

- The Soviet Union controlled Central Asia from 1917 to 1991.
- The Soviets separated ethnic groups and banned religious practices.
- They began growing cotton and constructed many useful but stark buildings.

Culture

The people who came through Central Asia influenced culture in the region. They brought new languages, religions, and ways of life that mixed with traditional ways of life in Central Asia.

Traditional Lives

For centuries, Central Asians have made a living by raising horses, cattle, sheep, and goats. Many herders live as **nomads**, people who move often from place to place. The nomads move their herds from mountain pastures in the summer to lowland pastures in the winter. Today most people in Central Asia live in more permanent settlements, but many others still live as nomads. The nomadic lifestyle is especially common in Kyrgyzstan.

Unique homes, called yurts, make moving with the herds possible. A **yurt** is a movable round house made of wool felt mats hung over a wood frame. Today the yurt is a symbol of the region's nomadic heritage. Even people who live in cities may put up yurts for special events such as weddings and funerals.

Close-up

Inside a Yurt

Historically, the nomadic life required that all possessions be portable—even houses. Nomads moved their yurts with them from place to place.

A hole at the top allows smoke from a fire to escape.

Nomads roll up part of the felt mat to create a door.

Traditional carpets provide decoration and warmth and are a yurt's main furniture.

ANALYSIS SKILL ANALYZING VISUALS

Why would a yurt be easier to move than another type of house?

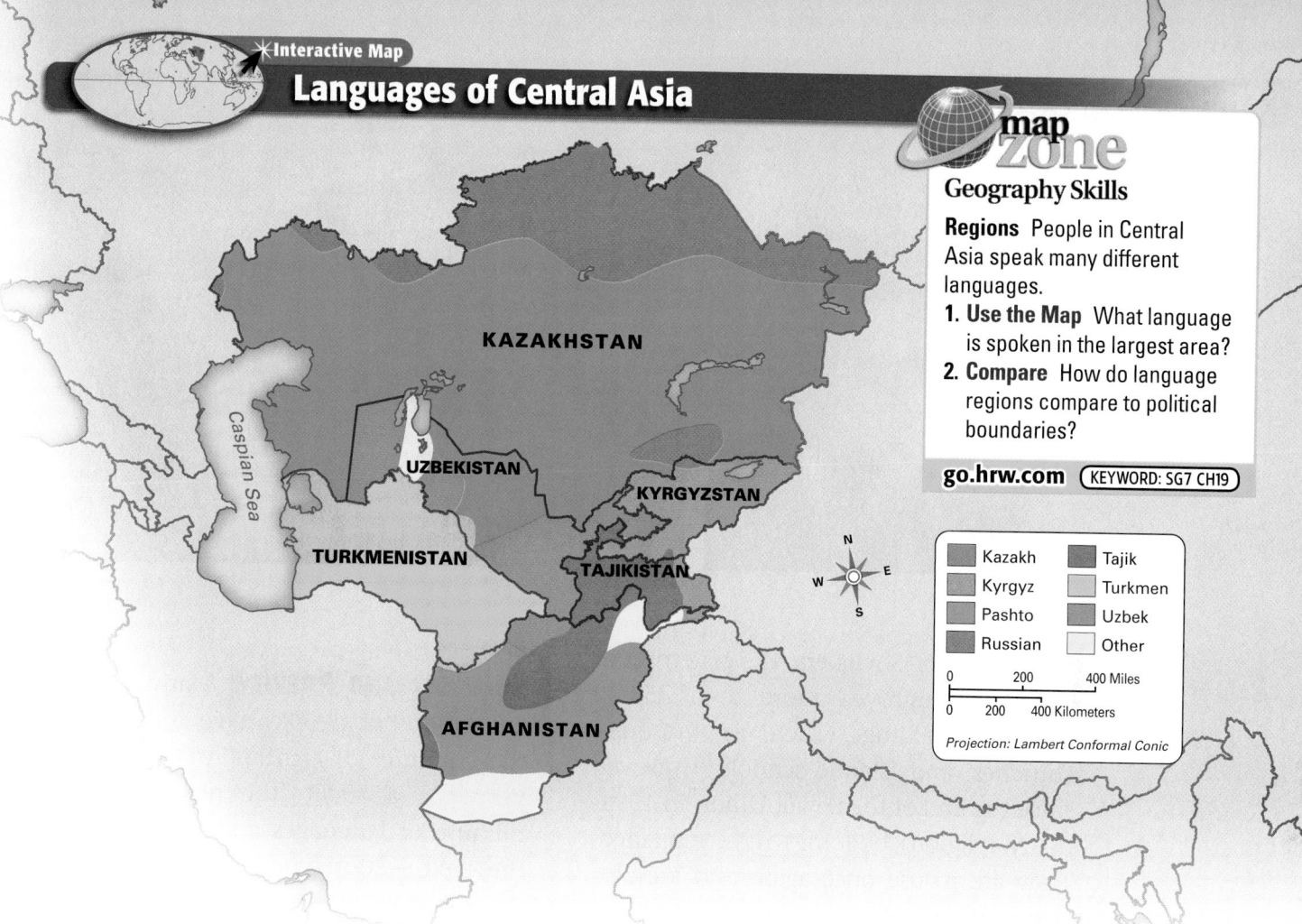

Interactive Map

Languages of Central Asia

map zone

Geography Skills

Regions People in Central Asia speak many different languages.

1. **Use the Map** What language is spoken in the largest area?
2. **Compare** How do language regions compare to political boundaries?

go.hrw.com KEYWORD: SG7 CH19

KAZAKHSTAN

Caspian Sea

UZBEKISTAN

KYRGYZSTAN

TURKMENISTAN

TAJIKISTAN

AFGHANISTAN

N W E S

Kazakh
Kyrgyz
Pashto
Russian
Tajik
Turkmen
Uzbek
Other

0   200   400 Miles
0   200   400 Kilometers

Projection: Lambert Conformal Conic

People, Languages, and Religion

Most people in Central Asia today belong to one of several ethnic groups that are part of a larger ethnic group called Turkic. Some of these ethnic groups are Kazakh (kuh-ZAHK), Kyrgyz (KIR-giz), Turkmen, and Uzbek (OOZ-bek). Another group, ethnic Russians, came to Central Asia when Russia conquered the region. They still live in every Central Asian country.

Each ethnic group speaks its own language. Look at the map above to see where a particular language is the primary language. In most countries in the region, more than one language is spoken.

When the Russians conquered Central Asia, they **established** their own language as the official language for business and government. It is still an official language in some Central Asian countries. The Russians also introduced the Cyrillic alphabet, the alphabet used to write the Russian language. Most countries in Central Asia now use the Latin alphabet, however, which is the one used to write English. Afghanistan also has its own alphabet. It is used for writing Pashto, one of that country's official languages.

Just as people in the region are of many ethnic groups and speak different languages, they also practice different religions. Traders and conquerors brought their religious beliefs and practices to the region. Islam, brought by the Arabs, is the main religion in Central Asia. Some people there also practice Christianity. Most of the region's Christians belong to the Russian Orthodox Church.

FOCUS ON READING

What context clues give a restatement of *Cyrillic alphabet*?

ACADEMIC VOCABULARY

establish to set up or create

Ethnic Groups of Central Asia

Uzbek

Kyrgyz

Traditional clothing, such as the hats men wear, distinguishes members of different ethnic groups in Central Asia.

ANALYZING VISUALS
Why do you think men wear different hats?

Turkmen

During the Soviet era, the government closed or destroyed more than 35,000 religious buildings, such as mosques, churches, and Islamic schools. However, since the end of the Soviet Union in 1991, many religious buildings have reopened. They are in use once again and are also beautiful symbols of the region's past.

READING CHECK **Summarizing** How did Russian and Soviet rule influence culture in Central Asia?

SUMMARY AND PREVIEW Many different groups of people have influenced the countries of Central Asia over the years. As a result, the region has a mixture of languages and religions. In the next section you will learn about the governments and economies of the countries of Central Asia today. You will also study some of the challenges these countries face.

Section 2 Assessment

go.hrw.com
Online Quiz
KEYWORD: SG7 HP19

Reviewing Ideas, Terms, and Places

1. a. Identify What people brought Islam to Central Asia?
b. Analyze What impact did the Silk Road have on Central Asia?
c. Elaborate How might Central Asia's history have been different without the influence of the Silk Road?
2. a. Define What is a **yurt**?
b. Analyze What are some of the benefits of nomadic life, and what are some of the challenges of this lifestyle?
c. Elaborate How might the mix of ethnic groups, languages, and religions in Central Asian countries affect life there today?

Critical Thinking

3. Sequencing Review your notes on the history of Central Asia. Then organize your information using a time line like the one below. You may add more dates if you need to.

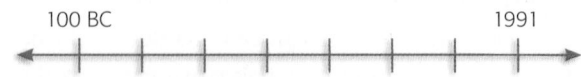

100 BC   1991

FOCUS ON VIEWING

4. Taking Notes on History and Culture What information about the history and culture of the region might encourage your listeners to visit Central Asia? What sites might they be interested in visiting? Jot down a few notes.

Central Asia Today

If YOU lived there...

Your country, Kyrgyzstan, has just had an election. You listen to the radio with your brother, anxiously awaiting the results of the election. When the radio announcer says that the same president has won again, your brother is very angry. He says the election was unfair, and he is going to protest outside the president's palace. He expects there to be a big crowd.

Will you join your brother? Why or why not?

BUILDING BACKGROUND Political protests have been fairly common in some Central Asian countries in recent years. Political instability is just one of the challenges facing Central Asia today as the region learns to deal with independence.

Central Asia Today

A history of invasions and foreign rule has made an impact on Central Asia. Because of years of fighting and changes in the region, today many countries of Central Asia face similar issues in building stable governments and strong economies.

Afghanistan

The situation in Afghanistan today is in many ways a result of a long war with the Soviet Union in the 1980s. The Soviets left in 1989. However, turmoil continued under an alliance of Afghan groups. In the mid-1990s a radical Muslim group known as the **Taliban** arose. The group's leaders took over most of the country, including the capital, **Kabul**.

The Taliban used a strict interpretation of Islamic teachings to rule Afghanistan. For example, the Taliban severely limited the role of women in society. They forced women to wear veils and to stop working outside the home. They also banned all music and dancing. Although most Muslims sharply disagreed with the Taliban's policies, the group remained in power for several years.

What You Will Learn...

Main Ideas

1. The countries of Central Asia are working to develop their economies and to improve political stability in the region.
2. The countries of Central Asia face issues and challenges related to the environment, the economy, and politics.

The Big Idea

Central Asian countries are mostly poor, but they are working to create stable governments and sound economies.

Key Terms and Places

Taliban, *p. 469*
Kabul, *p. 469*
dryland farming, *p. 471*
arable, *p. 471*

TAKING NOTES As you read, use a chart like the one below to help you take notes on governments, economies, and challenges in Central Asia today.

Afghanistan	
Kazakhstan	
Kyrgyzstan	
Tajikistan	
Turkmenistan	
Uzbekistan	

Reforms in Afghanistan

Some reforms have taken place in Afghanistan since the end of Taliban rule. However, the country still faces many challenges.

ANALYZING VISUALS What opportunities might education create for this girl?

Since the End of Taliban Rule . . .

- Afghanistan has a new constitution and an elected president.
- Many people are registered to vote.
- Afghanistan's rules are written and accessible to citizens for the first time.
- New clinics and trained doctors provide more people with access to health care.
- Women can work outside the home.
- Girls can attend school.

Eventually, the Taliban came into conflict with the United States. Investigation of the September 11, 2001, terrorist attacks on New York City and Washington, D.C., led to terrorist leader Osama bin Laden and his al Qaeda network, based in Afghanistan. U.S. and British forces attacked Taliban and al Qaeda targets and toppled Afghanistan's Taliban government.

Since the fall of the Taliban, Afghanistan's government has changed in many ways. The country has a new constitution. Also, all men and women age 18 and older can vote for the president and for the members of a national assembly. Some members of the assembly are appointed by the president, and the constitution requires that half of these appointees be women.

FOCUS ON READING

What is a restatement of *factions*?

Many Afghans hope their government will be stable. However, political factions, or opposing groups, disagree with some of the recent changes. These groups threaten violence, which may make Afghanistan's new government less stable.

Kazakhstan

Kazakhstan was the first part of Central Asia to be conquered by Russia. As a result, Russian influence remains strong in that country today. About one-third of Kazakhstan's people are ethnic Russians. Kazakh and Russian are both official languages. Many ethnic Kazakhs grow up speaking Russian at home and have to learn Kazakh in school.

Kazakhstan's economy was once tied to the former Soviet Union's. It was based on manufacturing. When the Soviet Union collapsed, the economy suffered. However, due to its valuable oil reserves and quick adaptation to the free market, Kazakhstan's economy is now growing steadily. The country is the richest in Central Asia.

Kazakhstan also has one of the more stable governments in Central Asia. The country is a democratic republic with an elected president and parliament. In 1998 Kazakhstan moved its capital from Almaty to Astana, which is closer to Russia.

Kyrgyzstan

The word *kyrgyz* means "forty clans." Throughout history, clan membership has been an important part of Kyrgyzstan's social, political, and economic life. Many people still follow nomadic traditions.

Many other people in Kyrgyzstan are farmers. Fertile soils there allow a mix of irrigated crops and **dryland farming**, or farming that relies on rainfall instead of irrigation. Farming is the most important industry in Kyrgyzstan. However, it does not provide much income for the country.

Although the standard of living in Kyrgyzstan is low, the economy shows signs of strengthening. Tourism might also help Kyrgyzstan's economy. The country has a Muslim pilgrimage site as well as the beautiful Lake Issyk-Kul.

Kyrgyzstan's government is changing. The country has been fairly stable for some years. However, protests in 2005 over what some people thought were unfair elections could signal that times are changing.

Tajikistan

Like other countries in Central Asia, Tajikistan is struggling to overcome its problems. In the mid-1990s the country's Communist government fought against a group of reformers. Some reformers demanded democracy. Others called for a government that ruled by Islamic law. The groups came together and signed a peace agreement in 1997. As a result, Tajikistan is now a republic with an elected president.

Years of civil war damaged Tajikistan's economy. Both industrial and agricultural production declined. Even with the decline in agricultural production, Tajikistan still relies on cotton farming for much of its income. However, only 5 to 6 percent of the country's land is **arable**, or suitable for growing crops. Lack of arable land makes progress there difficult.

Turkmenistan

Turkmenistan's president holds all power in the country. He was voted president for life by the country's parliament. He has used his power to name a month of the year after himself, and his face appears on almost everything in Turkmenistan.

The Turkmen government supports Islam and has ordered schools to teach Islamic principles. However, it also views Islam with caution. It does not want Islam to become a political movement.

Tajikistan's economy is based on oil, gas, and cotton. Although the country is a desert, about half of it is planted with cotton fields. Farming is possible because Turkmenistan has the longest irrigation channel in the world.

FOCUS ON CULTURE

Turkmen Carpets

Decorative carpets are an essential part of a nomad's home. They are also perhaps the most famous artistic craft of Turkmenistan. Carpet factories operate in cities all through Turkmenistan, but some women still weave carpets by hand. These weavers memorize hundreds of intricate designs so they can make rugs that look the same. Each of several different Turkmen tribes has its own rug design.

Analyzing Why are carpets good for a nomadic way of life?

Uzbekistan

Uzbekistan has the largest population of the Central Asian countries. It also has the largest cities in the region. Two cities—Bukhara and Samarqand—are famous for their mosques and monuments.

As in Turkmenistan, Uzbekistan's elected president holds all the political power. The United States has criticized the government for not allowing political freedom or respecting human rights.

The government also closely controls the economy. Uzbekistan's economy, based on oil, gold, and cotton, is fairly stable even though it is growing only very slowly.

READING CHECK Drawing Inferences How does physical geography affect the economies of Kyrgyzstan and Tajikistan?

Issues and Challenges

As you have read, the countries of Central Asia face similar issues and challenges. Their greatest challenges are in the areas of environment, economy, and politics.

Environment

One of the most serious environmental problems is the shrinking of the Aral Sea. Winds sweep the dry seafloor and blow dust, salt, and pesticides hundreds of miles. Also, towns that once relied on fishing are now dozens of miles from the shore.

Another problem is the damage caused by Soviet military practices. The Soviets tested nuclear bombs in Central Asia. Now people there suffer poor health because of radiation left over from the tests.

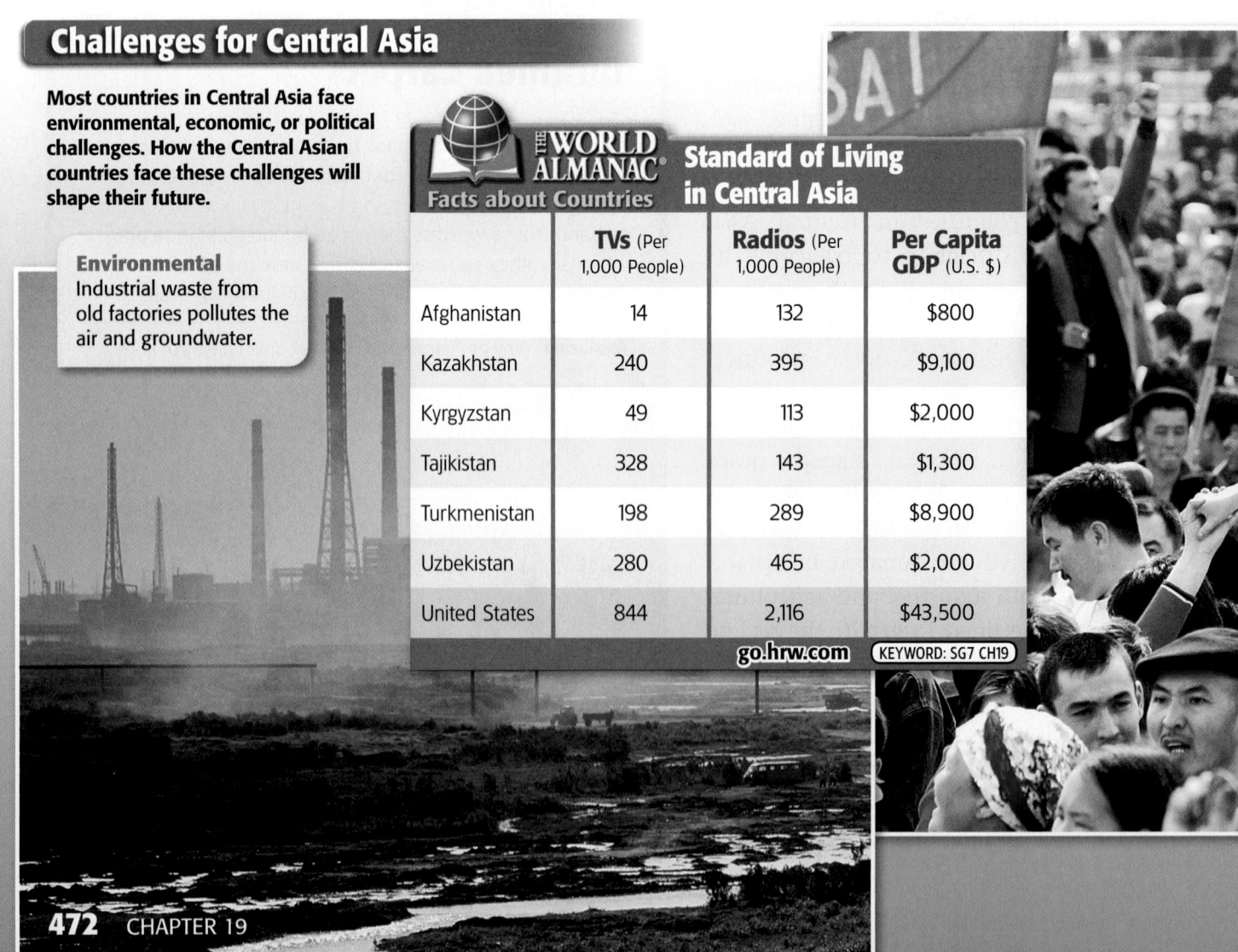

Challenges for Central Asia

Most countries in Central Asia face environmental, economic, or political challenges. How the Central Asian countries face these challenges will shape their future.

Environmental
Industrial waste from old factories pollutes the air and groundwater.

THE WORLD ALMANAC Facts about Countries — Standard of Living in Central Asia

	TVs (Per 1,000 People)	Radios (Per 1,000 People)	Per Capita GDP (U.S. $)
Afghanistan	14	132	$800
Kazakhstan	240	395	$9,100
Kyrgyzstan	49	113	$2,000
Tajikistan	328	143	$1,300
Turkmenistan	198	289	$8,900
Uzbekistan	280	465	$2,000
United States	844	2,116	$43,500

go.hrw.com KEYWORD: SG7 CH19

Another environmental problem has been caused by the overuse of chemicals to increase crop production. These chemicals have ended up ruining some farmlands. Instead of increasing crop production, the chemicals have hurt the economy.

Economy

Many of Central Asia's economic problems are due to reliance on one crop—cotton. Suitable farmland is limited, so employment in the cotton industry is limited. Also, the focus on cotton has not encouraged countries to develop manufacturing.

Some countries have oil and gas reserves that may someday make them rich. For now, though, outdated equipment, lack of funds, and poor transportation systems slow development in Central Asia.

Politics

The other main challenge in Central Asia today is lack of political stability. In some countries, such as Kyrgyzstan, people do not agree on the best kind of government. People who are dissatisfied with their government sometimes turn to violence. These countries today are often faced with terrorist threats from different political groups within their own countries.

READING CHECK **Summarizing** What environmental challenges does Central Asia face?

SUMMARY Central Asia is recovering from a history of foreign rule. The region is struggling to develop sound economies and stable governments.

Political Protesters show their opposition to the government in Kyrgyzstan.

ANALYSIS SKILL **ANALYZING VISUALS**

What do you think could be done to improve the environment in Central Asia?

Section 3 Assessment

Reviewing Ideas, Terms, and Places

1. a. **Describe** How did the **Taliban** affect Afghanistan?
   b. **Contrast** What are some major differences between Afghanistan and Kazakhstan?
   c. **Elaborate** What is one way a country might create more **arable** land?
2. a. **Identify** What three types of challenges does Central Asia face today?
   b. **Make Generalizations** Why does much of Central Asia face political instability?

Critical Thinking

3. **Categorizing** Using your notes and a chart like the one here, categorize your information on each Central Asian country. You will have to add more lines as needed.

	Government	Economy
Afghanistan		
Kazakhstan		

FOCUS ON VIEWING

4. **Describing Central Asia Today** Write notes about each country in Central Asia. Which countries will you suggest listeners visit? What details will encourage them?

Geography and History

The Aral Sea

In 1960 the Aral Sea was the world's fourth-largest lake. However, human activities over the years have caused the Aral Sea to shrink drastically. The lake's former seafloor is now a desert of sand and salt. Also, towns that once benefited from their lakeside location are now left without access to the water. Area governments have built dams to control the flow of water into the lake, but so far their efforts have been unsuccessful.

Cause
Farmers have taken water from the Amu Darya and the Syr Darya to irrigate cotton fields. Now, less water flows into the sea than evaporates from it.

Effect
Stranded boats are a reminder of the fishing industry once based near the Aral Sea. The fishing industry is dying with the sea.

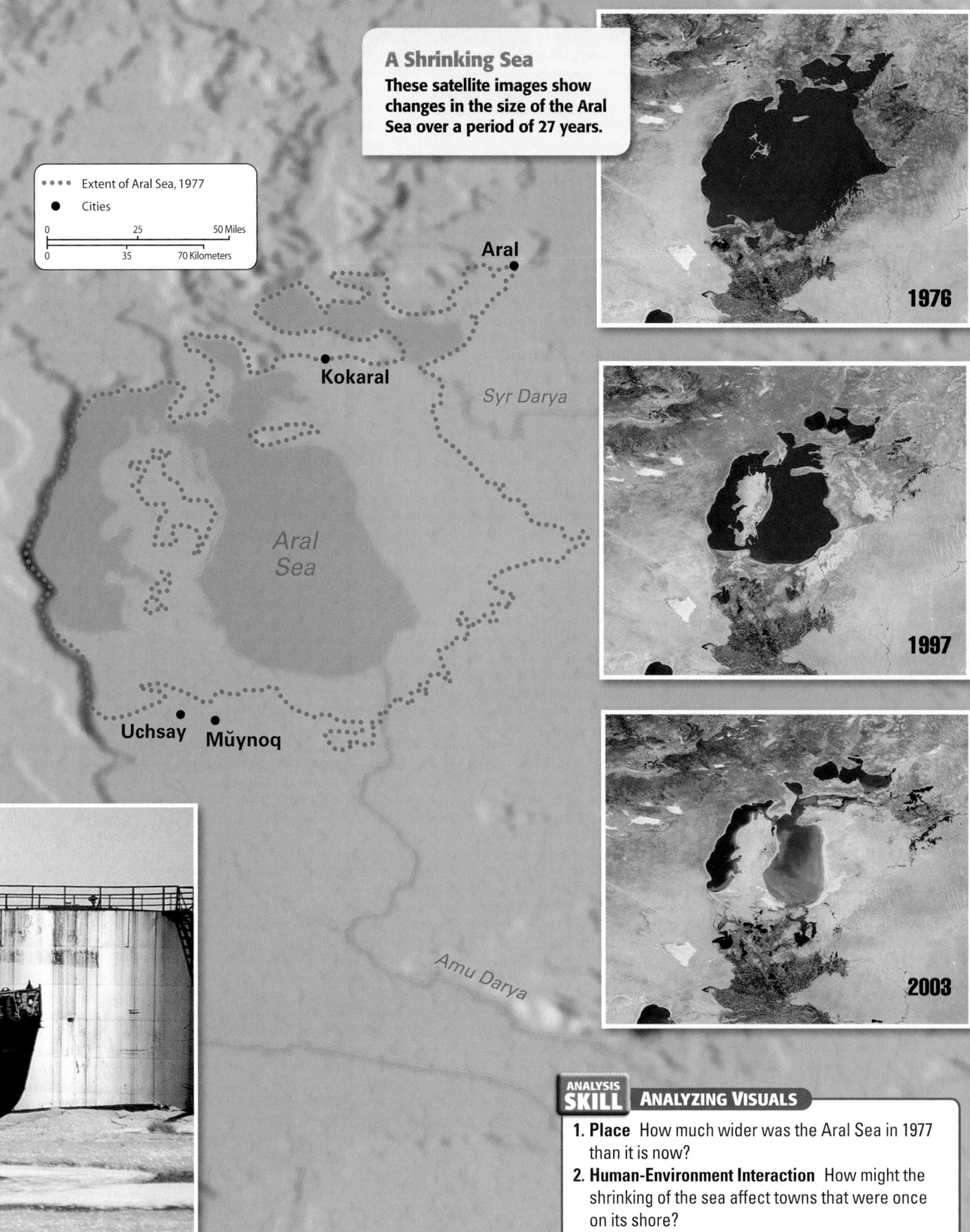

A Shrinking Sea
These satellite images show changes in the size of the Aral Sea over a period of 27 years.

····· Extent of Aral Sea, 1977
● Cities

0   25   50 Miles
0 35   70 Kilometers

Aral

Kokaral

Syr Darya

Aral Sea

Uchsay Mŭynoq

Amu Darya

1976

1997

2003

ANALYSIS SKILL **ANALYZING VISUALS**

1. **Place** How much wider was the Aral Sea in 1977 than it is now?
2. **Human-Environment Interaction** How might the shrinking of the sea affect towns that were once on its shore?

Social Studies Skills

Chart and Graph | Critical Thinking | Geography | Study

Using Scale

Learn

Mapmakers use scales to represent distances between points on a map. On each map legend in this book, you will notice some lines marked to measure miles and kilometers. These lines are the map's scale.

To find the distance between two points on a map, place a piece of paper so that the edge connects the two points. Mark the location of each point on the paper with a line or dot. Then compare the distance between the two dots with the map's scale.

Practice

Use the maps here to practice using scale and to answer the following questions.

1 Which map shows a larger region?

2 About how many miles does one inch represent on the map of Kyrgyzstan? on the map of Bishkek?

3 How far is it from Dubovy Park to Victory Square in Bishkek?

Apply

Use the map of Southwest Asia in the unit opener to answer the following questions.

1. How many miles does one inch represent? How many kilometers does one inch represent?

2. How long is the Caspian Sea from north to south?

3. How far is Turkmenistan from the Persian Gulf?

Bishkek

Kyrgyzstan

Chapter Review

Geography's Impact
video series
Review the video to answer the closing question:
What challenges do the people of Afghanistan face today?

Visual Summary

Use the visual summary below to help you review the main ideas of the chapter.

QUICK FACTS

Central Asia is a dry, rugged region. However, people use irrigation to grow cotton, the region's main crop.

Some people follow traditional ways of life. For example, nomads move their yurts from place to place.

Central Asia faces environmental, economic, and political challenges. One challenge is the Aral Sea's shrinking.

Reviewing Vocabulary, Terms, and Places

Unscramble each group of letters below to spell a term that matches the given definition.

1. **mnodsa**—people who move often from place to place

2. **yrddnal mrignaf**—farming that relies on rainfall, not irrigation

3. **tryu**—a moveable round house of wool felt mats hung over a wood frame

4. **ssblhieat**—to set up or create

5. **fgrenaa vlyela**—fertile region that has been a center of farming for thousands of years

6. **tlbania**—a radical Muslim group

7. **dknadclleo**—completely surrounded by land with no direct access to the ocean

8. **kluba**—the capital of Afghanistan

9. **aabler**—suitable for growing crops

10. **aalr sae**—body of water that is shrinking because of use of water for irrigation

Comprehension and Critical Thinking

SECTION 1 *(Pages 460–463)*

11. **a. Describe** How are farmers able to grow crops in Central Asia's dry landscapes?

    b. Analyze What factors make it difficult for the countries of Central Asia to export their oil and gas resources?

    c. Evaluate Do you think Central Asia's location or its mountains do more to keep the region isolated? Explain your answer.

SECTION 2 *(Pages 464–468)*

12. **a. Describe** How did life in Central Asia change under Russian and Soviet rule?

    b. Analyze In what ways do the people of Central Asia show their pride in their past and their culture?

    c. Evaluate Why do you think many former nomads now live in cities? Why do you think other people still choose to live as nomads?

13. a. Identify What are some reforms that have taken place in Afghanistan since the fall of the Taliban?

b. Analyze How does having a limited amount of arable land affect Tajikistan's economy?

c. Elaborate How do you think political and environmental challenges in Central Asia affect the region's economy?

Using the Internet

go.hrw.com
KEYWORD: SG7 CH19

14. Activity: Writing Home For thousands of years, nomads have traveled the lands of Central Asia. They move their herds to several different pasture areas as the seasons change. Enter the activity keyword and join a caravan of nomads. Find out what it is like to pack up your house, clothes, and all you own as you move from place to place. Then create a postcard to share your adventures with friends and family back home in the United States.

FOCUS ON READING AND VIEWING

15. Using Context Clues Look through your book for examples of restatement. Note one or two examples of restatement for each section of the chapter.

16. Giving a Travel Presentation Review your notes and select one country in Central Asia your audience might want to visit. Look for pictures of at least five locations in that country: buildings, monuments, or other interesting places. As you plan your presentation, create a brief introduction, a brief description of each location and its picture, and a conclusion. Hold up each picture and point out important features as you make your presentation.

As you watch your classmates' presentations, view and listen carefully. Make note of their eye contact with the audience, use of gestures to add interest, use of interesting pictures, and persuasiveness.

Social Studies Skills

Using Scale *Use the physical map of Central Asia in Section 1 to answer the following questions.*

17. How many miles does one inch represent?

18. How far is it from the shore of the Caspian Sea to Ismail Samani Peak?

19. How many kilometers long is the Amu Darya?

Map Activity  Interactive

20. Central Asia On a separate sheet of paper, match the letters on the map with their correct labels.

Aral Sea	Pamirs
Caspian Sea	Astana, Kazakhstan
Afghanistan	Tashkent, Uzbekistan

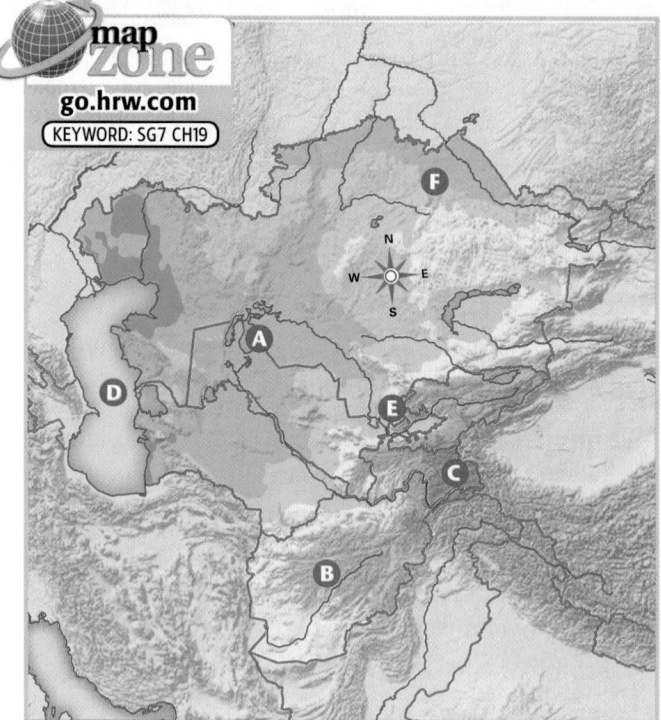

go.hrw.com
KEYWORD: SG7 CH19

DIRECTIONS: Read questions 1 through 7 and write the letter of the best response. Then read question 8 and write your own well-constructed response.

1 **What is the main crop grown in Central Asia?**

A wheat

B olives

C cotton

D corn

2 **Which of the following descriptions *best* describes the landscape of Central Asia?**

A dry and rugged

B dry and flat

C humid and landlocked

D humid and cold

3 **How did the Arabs influence Central Asia in the 700s and 800s?**

A separated ethnic groups

B destroyed cities and irrigation systems

C built railroads and expanded oil production

D introduced Islam

4 **Which of the following statements about the nomadic lifestyle is false?**

A Nomads move their herds depending on the season.

B Nomads decorate their yurts with carpets.

C It is a symbol of the region's heritage.

D Nomads often move from one dwelling to another.

5 **What country did the Taliban rule?**

A Kazakhstan

B Afghanistan

C Kyrgyzstan

D Uzbekistan

Farmland in Central Asia

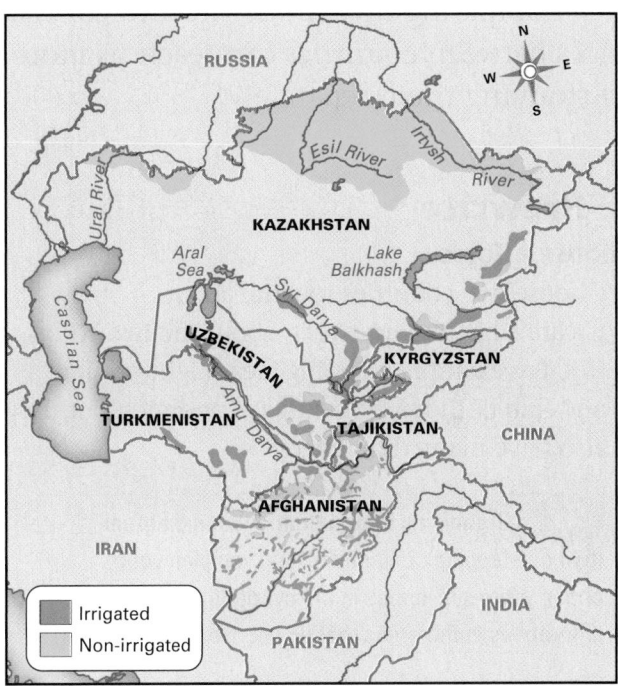

6 **Based on the map above, what country has the most non-irrigated farmland?**

A Kazakhstan

B Tajikistan

C Turkmenistan

D Uzbekistan

7 **Based on the map above and your knowledge of the physical geography of Central Asia, what is the main reason there is little farmland in eastern Kyrgyzstan and Tajikistan?**

A There are too many rivers.

B Most people live as nomads there.

C The area is too mountainous.

D The area is a desert.

8 **Extended Response** Using the map and your knowledge of Central Asia, write a brief essay explaining how irrigation has affected the region.

Compare and Contrast

Assignment
Write a paper comparing and contrasting two countries from this unit. Consider physical geography, government, and/or culture.

How are two countries alike? How are they different? Comparing the similarities and contrasting the differences between countries can teach us more than we can learn by studying them separately.

1. Prewrite

Choose a Topic

- Choose two countries to write about.
- Create a big idea, or thesis, about the two counries. For example, your big idea might be "Iran and Iraq both have oil-based economies, but they also have many differences."

> **TIP** **Organizing Information** A Venn diagram (two overlapping circles) can help you plan your paper. Write similarities in the overlapping area and differences in the areas that do not overlap.

Gather and Organize Information

- Identify at least three similarities or differences between the countries.
- Decide whether to write about each country one at a time or to discuss each point of similarity or difference one at a time.

2. Write

Use a Writer's Framework

> **A Writer's Framework**
>
> **Introduction**
> - Start with a fact or question relating to both countries.
> - Identify your big idea.
>
> **Body**
> - Write at least one paragraph for each country or each point of similarity or difference. Include facts and details to help explain each point.
> - Use block style or point-by-point style.
>
> **Conclusion**
> - Summarize the process in your final paragraph.

3. Evaluate And Revise

Review and Improve Your Paper

- Re-read your draft, then ask yourself the questions below to see if you have followed the framework.
- Make any changes needed to improve your comparison and conrast paper.

Evaluation Questions for a Compare and Contrast Paper

1. Do you begin with an interesting fact or question that relates to both countries?
2. Does your first paragraph clearly state your big idea and provide background information?
3. Do you discuss at least three similarities and differences between the countries?
4. Do you include facts and details to explain each similarity or difference?
5. Is your paper clearly organized by country or by similarities and differences?

4. Proofread And Publish

Give Your Explanation the Finishing Touch

- Make sure you have capitalized the names of countries and cities.
- Check for punctuation around transitional words and phrases like and, but, or similarly.
- Share your compare-and-contrast paper by reading it aloud in class or in small groups.

5. Practice And Apply

Use the steps outlined in this workshop to write a compare-and-contrast paper. Compare and contrast your paper to those of your classmates.

Africa

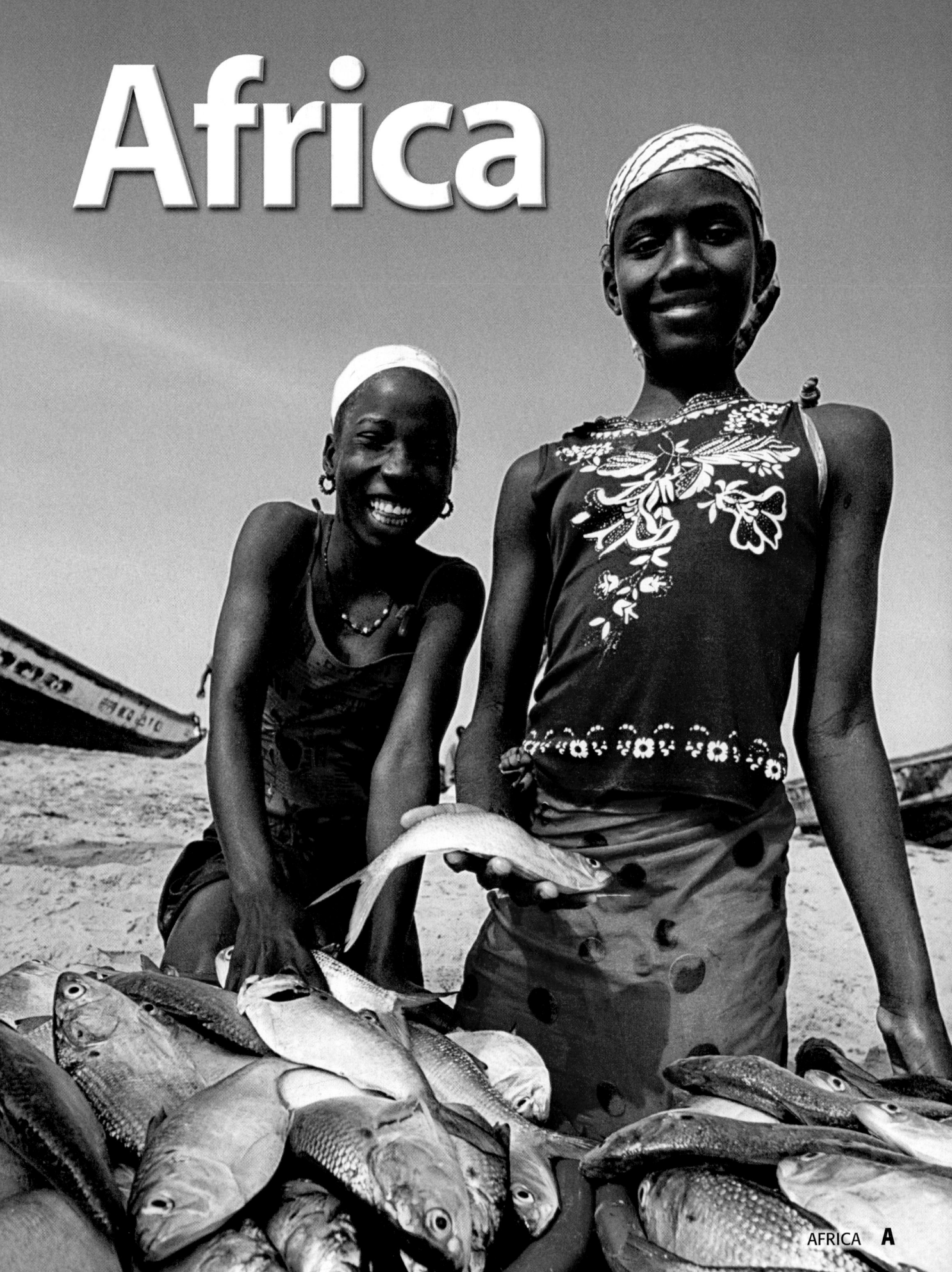

The world's largest desert, the Sahara, dominates land and life in North Africa.

Savannas

Grassy plains called savannas stretch across large parts of the continent and are home to much African wildlife.

Africa

Rift Valleys

In East Africa, Earth's crust is slowly being pulled apart. This causes hills, long lakes, and wide "rift valleys" to form.

Explore the Satellite Image
A huge continent, Africa is home to many different kinds of physical features. Based on this satellite image, how would you describe Africa's physical geography?

The Satellite's Path

>44'56.08<

>>>>>>>>>665.00'87<

567.476.348

456.094.

+803
+799

+966

+355

Africa: Physical

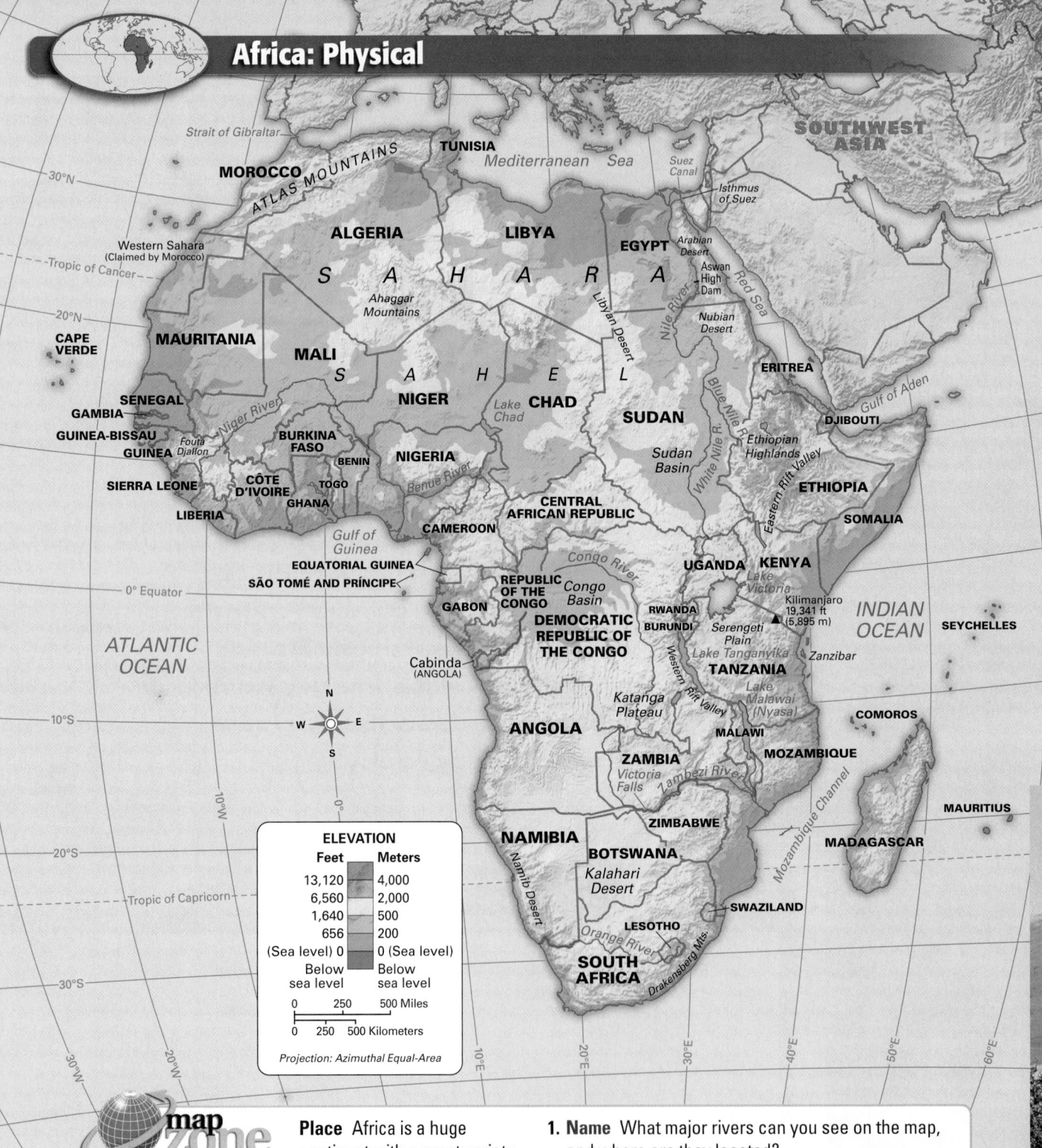

ELEVATION

Feet	Meters
13,120	4,000
6,560	2,000
1,640	500
656	200
(Sea level) 0	0 (Sea level)
Below sea level	Below sea level

0   250   500 Miles

0   250   500 Kilometers

Projection: Azimuthal Equal-Area

map zone

Geography Skills

Place Africa is a huge continent with a great variety of physical features.

1. **Name** What major rivers can you see on the map, and where are they located?

2. **Compare** How does the average elevation of southern Africa compare to that of northern Africa?

THE WORLD ALMANAC®
Facts about the World — Geographical Extremes: Africa

Longest River	Nile River, Egypt: 4,160 miles (6,693 km)	**Driest Place**	Wadi Halfa, Sudan: .1 inches (.3 cm) average precipitation per year
Highest Point	Mount Kilimanjaro, Tanzania: 19,340 feet (5,895 m)	**Largest Country**	Sudan: 967,498 square miles (2,505,820 square km)
Lowest Point	Lake Assal, Djibouti: 512 feet (156 m) below sea level	**Smallest Country**	Seychelles: 176 square miles (456 square km)
Highest Recorded Temperature	El Azizia, Libya: 136°F (57.8°C)	**Largest Desert**	Sahara: 3,500,000 square miles (9,065,000 square km)
Lowest Recorded Temperature	Ifrane, Morocco: -11°F (-23.9°C)	**Largest Island**	Madagascar: 226,658 square miles (587,044 square km)
Wettest Place	Debundscha, Cameroon: 405 inches (1,028.7 cm) average precipitation per year	**Highest Waterfall**	Tugela, South Africa: 2,014 feet (614 m)

go.hrw.com **KEYWORD: SG7 UN5**

Size Comparison: The United States and Africa

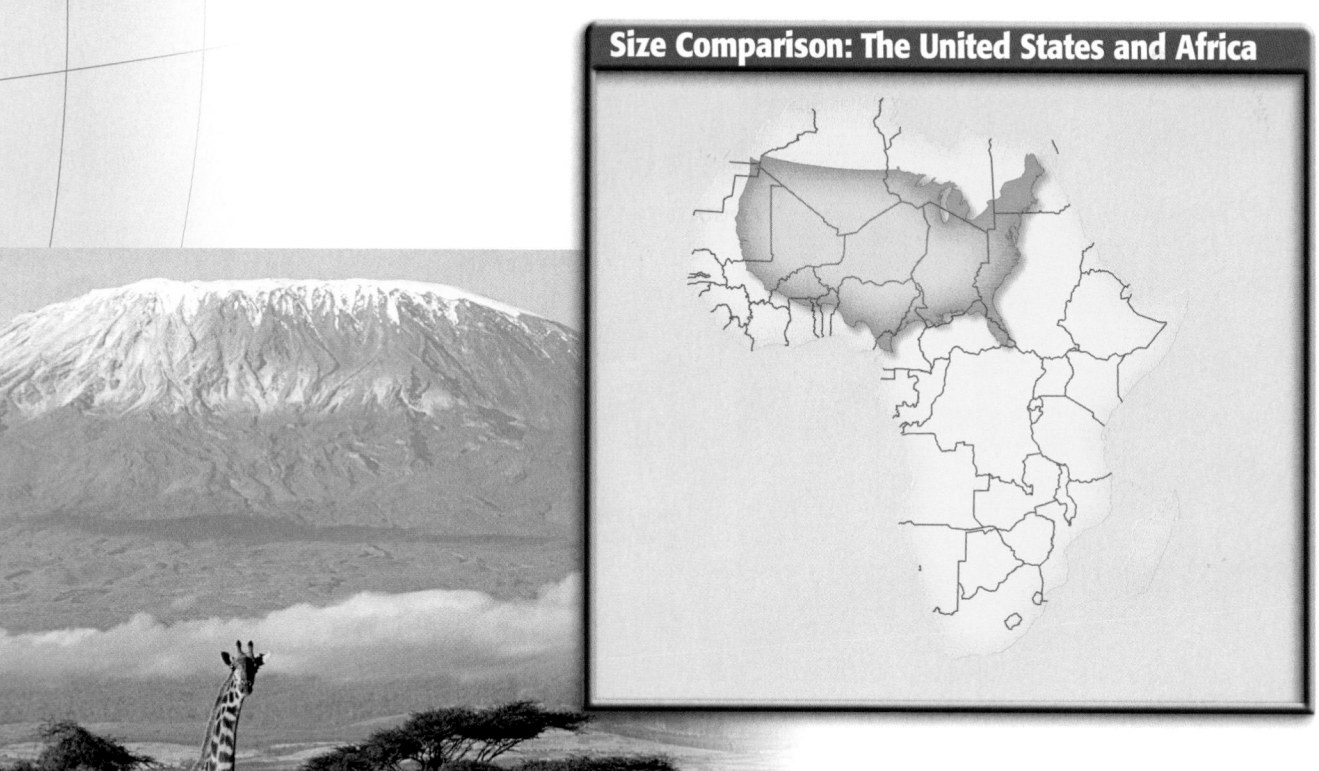

Mount Kilimanjaro, Tanzania

Africa: Political

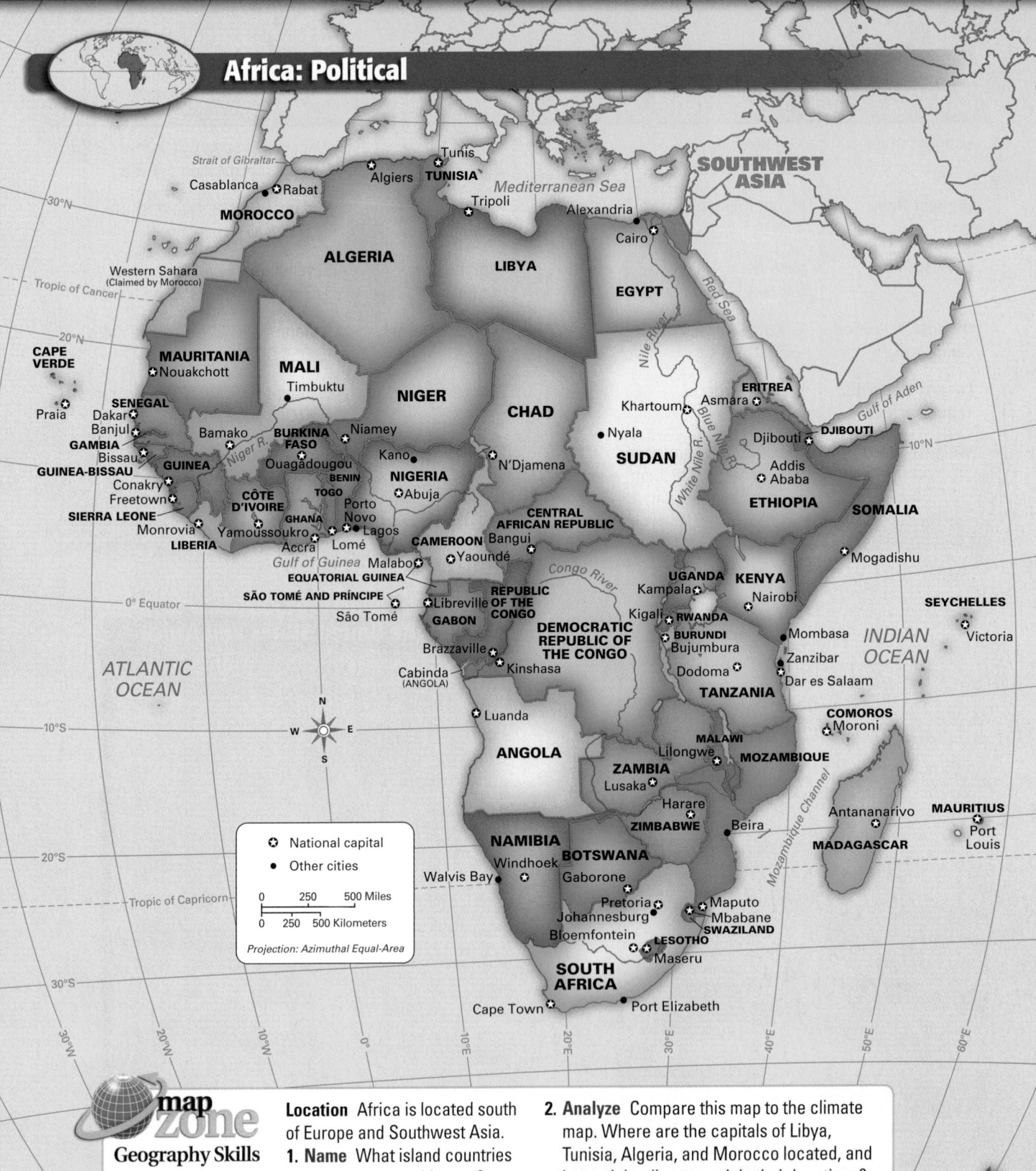

Strait of Gibraltar

Casablanca ◉Rabat

MOROCCO

Tunis
Algiers ◉TUNISIA
Tripoli

Mediterranean Sea

Alexandria
◉Cairo

SOUTHWEST ASIA

30°N

ALGERIA

LIBYA

EGYPT

Western Sahara
(Claimed by Morocco)

Tropic of Cancer

20°N

Red Sea

CAPE
VERDE

MAURITANIA
◉Nouakchott

MALI

Timbuktu

NIGER

CHAD

Nile River

Khartoum◉

SUDAN

ERITREA

Asmara◉

Blue Nile R.

Gulf of Aden

DJIBOUTI
Djibouti ◉DJIBOUTI

10°N

Praia ◉

SENEGAL
Dakar◉
Banjul◉

Bamako

Niamey

Kano

N'Djamena

●Nyala

White Nile R.

Addis
◉Ababa

SOMALIA

GAMBIA

Niger R.

BURKINA
FASO
Ouagadougou

NIGERIA

ETHIOPIA

Bissau
GUINEA-BISSAU

GUINEA

BENIN

Abuja◉

CENTRAL
AFRICAN REPUBLIC

Conakry◉
Freetown◉

TOGO

Porto
Novo

Bangui◉

UGANDA

KENYA

Mogadishu

SEYCHELLES

SIERRA LEONE
Monrovia◉

CÔTE
D'IVOIRE
Yamoussoukro◉

GHANA
Accra◉
Lomé

Lagos

CAMEROON

Kampala◉

Nairobi◉

LIBERIA

Gulf of Guinea

Malabo◉

Yaoundé◉

Congo River

Kigali◉RWANDA

Mombasa

Victoria◉

EQUATORIAL GUINEA

SÃO TOMÉ AND PRÍNCIPE

0° Equator

São Tomé

Libreville◉

REPUBLIC
OF THE
CONGO

BURUNDI
Bujumbura◉

Zanzibar

INDIAN
OCEAN

GABON

DEMOCRATIC
REPUBLIC OF
THE CONGO

Dodoma◉

Dar es Salaam

ATLANTIC
OCEAN

Brazzaville◉

Cabinda
(ANGOLA)

Kinshasa◉

TANZANIA

COMOROS
◉Moroni

10°S

●Luanda

MALAWI

Lilongwe◉

Antananarivo◉

MAURITIUS

ANGOLA

ZAMBIA

MOZAMBIQUE

◉Port
Louis

Lusaka◉

MADAGASCAR

Harare◉

Beira

◉ National capital

● Other cities

ZIMBABWE

20°S

NAMIBIA

BOTSWANA

0   250   500 Miles

Walvis Bay●

Windhoek◉

0   250   500 Kilometers

Gaborone◉

Projection: Azimuthal Equal-Area

Tropic of Capricorn

Pretoria◉
Johannesburg●
Bloemfontein◉

◉Maputo
Mbabane◉
SWAZILAND

LESOTHO
◉Maseru

30°S

SOUTH
AFRICA

Cape Town◉

●Port Elizabeth

30°W   20°W   10°W   0°   10°E   20°E   30°E   40°E   50°E   60°E

map zone
Geography Skills

Location Africa is located south of Europe and Southwest Asia.

1. Name What island countries can you see on this map?

2. Analyze Compare this map to the climate map. Where are the capitals of Libya, Tunisia, Algeria, and Morocco located, and how might climate explain their locations?

Africa: Resources

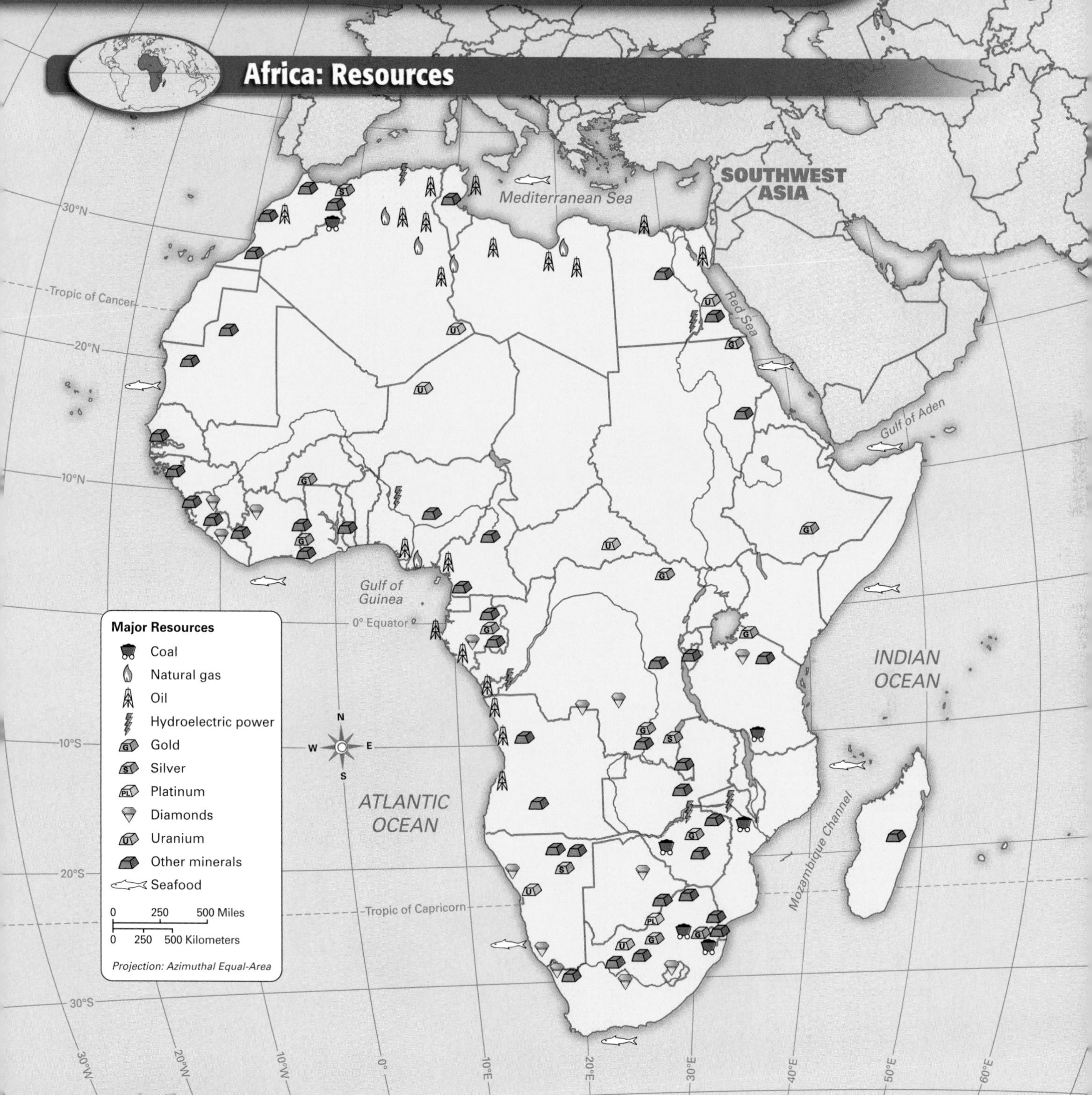

SOUTHWEST ASIA

Mediterranean Sea

Red Sea

Gulf of Aden

Tropic of Cancer

30°N

20°N

10°N

Gulf of Guinea

0° Equator

INDIAN OCEAN

ATLANTIC OCEAN

10°S

Mozambique Channel

20°S

Tropic of Capricorn

30°S

Major Resources

- Coal
- Natural gas
- Oil
- Hydroelectric power
- Gold
- Silver
- Platinum
- Diamonds
- Uranium
- Other minerals
- Seafood

0   250   500 Miles

0   250   500 Kilometers

Projection: Azimuthal Equal-Area

30°W 20°W 10°W 0° 10°E 20°E 30°E 40°E 50°E 60°E

map zone
Geography Skills

Place The African continent is rich in resources.

1. Identify What are some of the key resources in southern Africa?

2. Make Generalizations Where in Africa are oil resources found? How do you think oil affects the economies of these regions?

Africa: Population

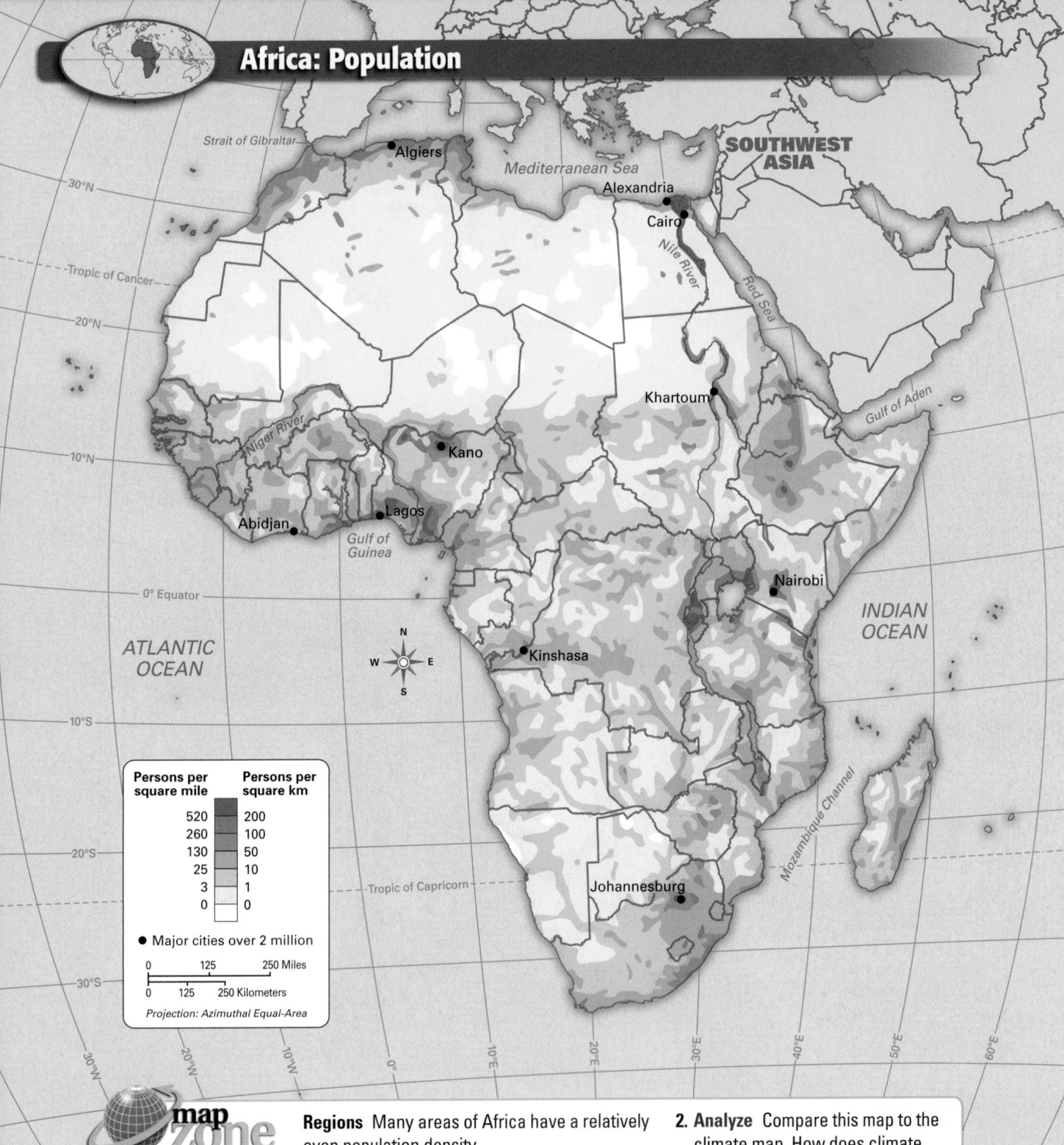

Strait of Gibraltar

Algiers

Mediterranean Sea

SOUTHWEST ASIA

30°N

Alexandria

Cairo

Tropic of Cancer

Nile River

Red Sea

20°N

Khartoum

Gulf of Aden

Niger River

10°N

Kano

Lagos

Abidjan

Gulf of Guinea

0° Equator

Nairobi

INDIAN OCEAN

ATLANTIC OCEAN

N
W E
S

Kinshasa

10°S

Mozambique Channel

20°S

Tropic of Capricorn

Johannesburg

30°S

Persons per square mile	**Persons per square km**
520	200
260	100
130	50
25	10
3	1
0	0

● Major cities over 2 million

0   125   250 Miles
0   125   250 Kilometers

Projection: Azimuthal Equal-Area

30°W   20°W   10°W   0°   10°E   20°E   30°E   40°E   50°E   60°E

map zone
Geography Skills

Regions Many areas of Africa have a relatively even population density.

1. Name What river in North Africa has a very high population density along its course?

2. Analyze Compare this map to the climate map. How does climate seem to influence population patterns in Africa?

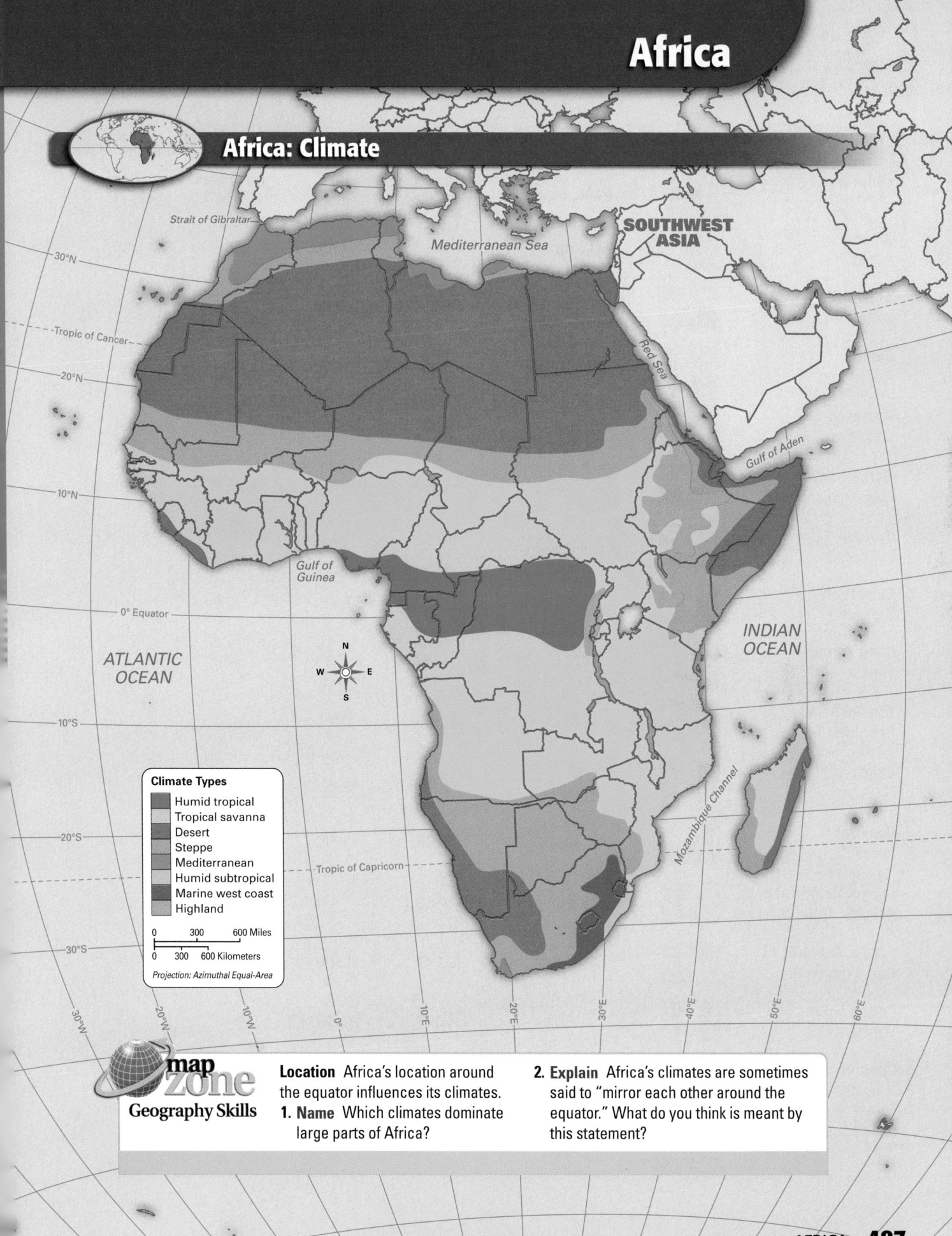

Africa: Climate

Climate Types
- Humid tropical
- Tropical savanna
- Desert
- Steppe
- Mediterranean
- Humid subtropical
- Marine west coast
- Highland

0   300   600 Miles
0   300   600 Kilometers

Projection: Azimuthal Equal-Area

map zone
Geography Skills

Location Africa's location around the equator influences its climates.
1. Name Which climates dominate large parts of Africa?

2. Explain Africa's climates are sometimes said to "mirror each other around the equator." What do you think is meant by this statement?

Africa

COUNTRY Capital	FLAG	POPULATION	AREA (sq mi)	PER CAPITA GDP (U.S. $)	LIFE EXPECTANCY AT BIRTH	TVS PER 1,000 PEOPLE
Algeria Algiers		33.3 million	919,595	$7,700	73.5	107
Angola Luanda		12.2 million	481,354	$4,300	37.6	15
Benin Porto-Novo		8.1 million	43,483	$1,100	53.4	44
Botswana Gaborone		1.8 million	231,804	$11,400	33.7	21
Burkina Faso Ouagadougou		14.3 million	105,869	$1,300	49.2	11
Burundi Bujumbura		8.4 million	10,745	$700	51.3	15
Cameroon Yaoundé		18.1 million	183,568	$2,400	52.9	34
Cape Verde Praia		423,600	1,557	$6,000	71.0	5
Central African Republic; Bangui		4.4 million	240,535	$1,100	43.7	6
Chad N'Djamena		9.9 million	495,755	$1,500	47.9	1
Comoros Moroni		711,400	838	$600	62.7	4
Congo, Democratic Republic of the; Kinshasa		65.8 million	905,568	$700	51.9	2
Congo, Republic of the; Brazzaville		3.8 million	132,047	$1,300	53.3	13
Côte d'Ivoire Yamoussoukro		18 million	124,503	$1,600	49.0	65
Djibouti Djibouti		496,400	8,880	$1,000	43.3	48
United States Washington, D.C.		301.1 million	3,718,711	$43,500	78.0	844

COUNTRY Capital	FLAG	POPULATION	AREA (sq mi)	PER CAPITA GDP (U.S. $)	LIFE EXPECTANCY AT BIRTH	TVS PER 1,000 PEOPLE
Egypt Cairo		80.3 million	386,662	$4,200	71.6	170
Equatorial Guinea Malabo		551,200	10,831	$50,200	49.5	116
Eritrea Asmara		4.9 million	46,842	$1,000	59.6	16
Ethiopia Addis Ababa		76.5 million	435,186	$1,000	49.2	5
Gabon Libreville		1.5 million	103,347	$7,200	54.0	251
Gambia Banjul		1.7 million	4,363	$2,000	54.5	3
Ghana Accra		22.9 million	92,456	$2,600	59.1	115
Guinea Conakry		9.9 million	94,926	$2,000	49.7	47
Guinea-Bissau Bissau		1.5 million	13,946	$900	47.2	43
Kenya Nairobi		36.9 million	224,962	$1,200	55.3	22
Lesotho Maseru		2.1 million	11,720	$2,600	34.5	16
Liberia Monrovia		3.2 million	43,000	$1,000	40.4	26
Libya Tripoli		6 million	679,362	$12,700	76.9	139
Madagascar Antananarivo		19.4 million	226,657	$900	62.1	23
Malawi Lilongwe		13.6 million	45,745	$600	43.0	3
United States Washington, D.C.		301.1 million	3,718,711	$43,500	78.0	844

THE WORLD ALMANAC® Facts about Countries

COUNTRY Capital	FLAG	POPULATION	AREA (sq mi)	PER CAPITA GDP (U.S. $)	LIFE EXPECTANCY AT BIRTH	TVS PER 1,000 PEOPLE
Mali Bamako		11.9 million	478,767	$1,200	49.5	13
Mauritania Nouakchott		3.3 million	397,955	$2,600	53.5	95
Mauritius Port Louis		1.3 million	788	$13,500	72.9	248
Morocco Rabat		33.8 million	172,414	$4,400	71.2	165
Mozambique Maputo		20.9 million	309,496	$1,500	40.9	5
Namibia Windhoek		2.1 million	318,696	$7,400	43.1	38
Niger Niamey		13 million	489,191	$1,000	44.0	15
Nigeria Abuja		135 million	356,669	$1,400	47.4	69
Rwanda Kigali		9.9 million	10,169	$1,600	49.0	0.09
São Tomé and Príncipe; São Tomé		199,600	386	$1,200	67.6	229
Senegal Dakar		12.5 million	75,749	$1,800	56.7	41
Seychelles Victoria		81,900	176	$7,800	72.3	214
Sierra Leone Freetown		6.1 million	27,699	$900	40.6	13
Somalia Mogadishu		9.1 million	246,201	$600	48.8	14
United States Washington, D.C.		301.1 million	3,718,711	$43,500	78.0	844

COUNTRY Capital	FLAG	POPULATION	AREA (sq mi)	PER CAPITA GDP (U.S. $)	LIFE EXPECTANCY AT BIRTH	TVS PER 1,000 PEOPLE
South Africa; Pretoria, Cape Town, Bloemfontein		44 million	471,010	$13,000	42.5	138
Sudan Khartoum		39.4 million	967,498	$2,300	59.3	173
Swaziland Mbabane		1.2 million	6,704	$5,500	32.2	112
Tanzania Dar es Salaam, Dodoma		39.4 million	364,900	$800	46.1	21
Togo Lomé		5.7 million	21,925	$1,700	57.9	22
Tunisia Tunis		10.3 million	63,170	$8,600	75.3	190
Uganda Kampala		30.3 million	91,136	$1,800	51.8	28
Zambia Lusaka		11.5 million	290,586	$1,000	38.4	145
Zimbabwe Harare		12.3 million	150,804	$2,000	39.5	35
United States Washington, D.C.		301.1 million	3,718,711	$43,500	78.0	844

Africa's Growing Population

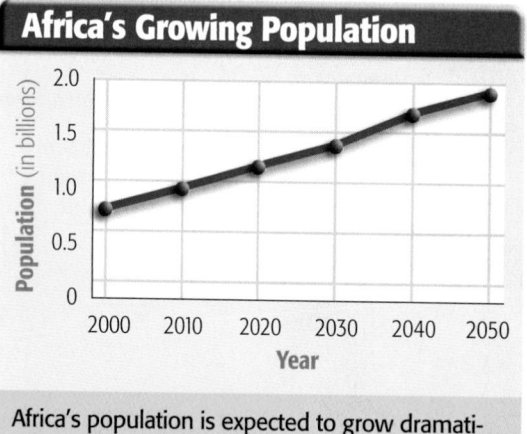

Africa's population is expected to grow dramatically in the next 50 years.

Africa and the World

	Average Age	Life Expectancy at Birth	Per Capita GDP (in U.S. $)
Africa	19.3 years	51.9	$2,800
Rest of the World	28.0 years	65.7	$10,000

Compared to the rest of the world, Africa's population is younger, has a shorter life expectancy, and has less money.

ANALYSIS SKILL ANALYZING INFORMATION

1. Based on the information above, what do you think are some key challenges in Africa today?

North Africa

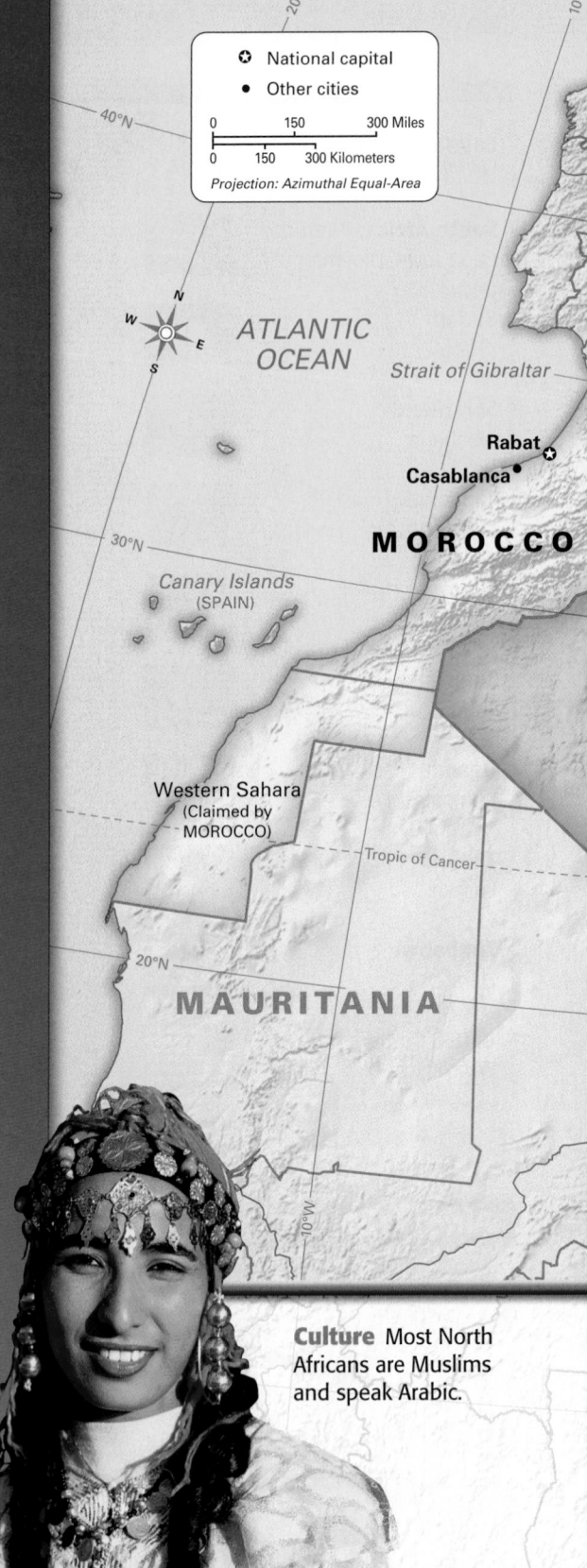

What You Will Learn...

In this chapter you will learn about five countries located in the region of North Africa—Egypt, Libya, Tunisia, Algeria, and Morocco. You will learn about the importance of water in this dry region. You will also study the histories of these countries, which include ancient Egyptian civilization. In addition, you will learn about North Africa's cultures, economies, and governments.

FOCUS ON READING AND WRITING

Summarizing To better understand what you read, it is sometimes helpful to stop and summarize the information you have read. A summary is a short restatement of important events or main ideas. As you read this chapter, stop now and then to summarize what you have read. **See the lesson, Summarizing, on page R21.**

Writing a Myth Ancient people created stories called myths to explain things about the world. For example, they created myths to explain the seasons and to explain the powers of their gods. As you read this chapter, look for information that might have seemed mysterious to ancient peoples. Later you will write your own myth to explain something about North Africa.

Culture Most North Africans are Muslims and speak Arabic.

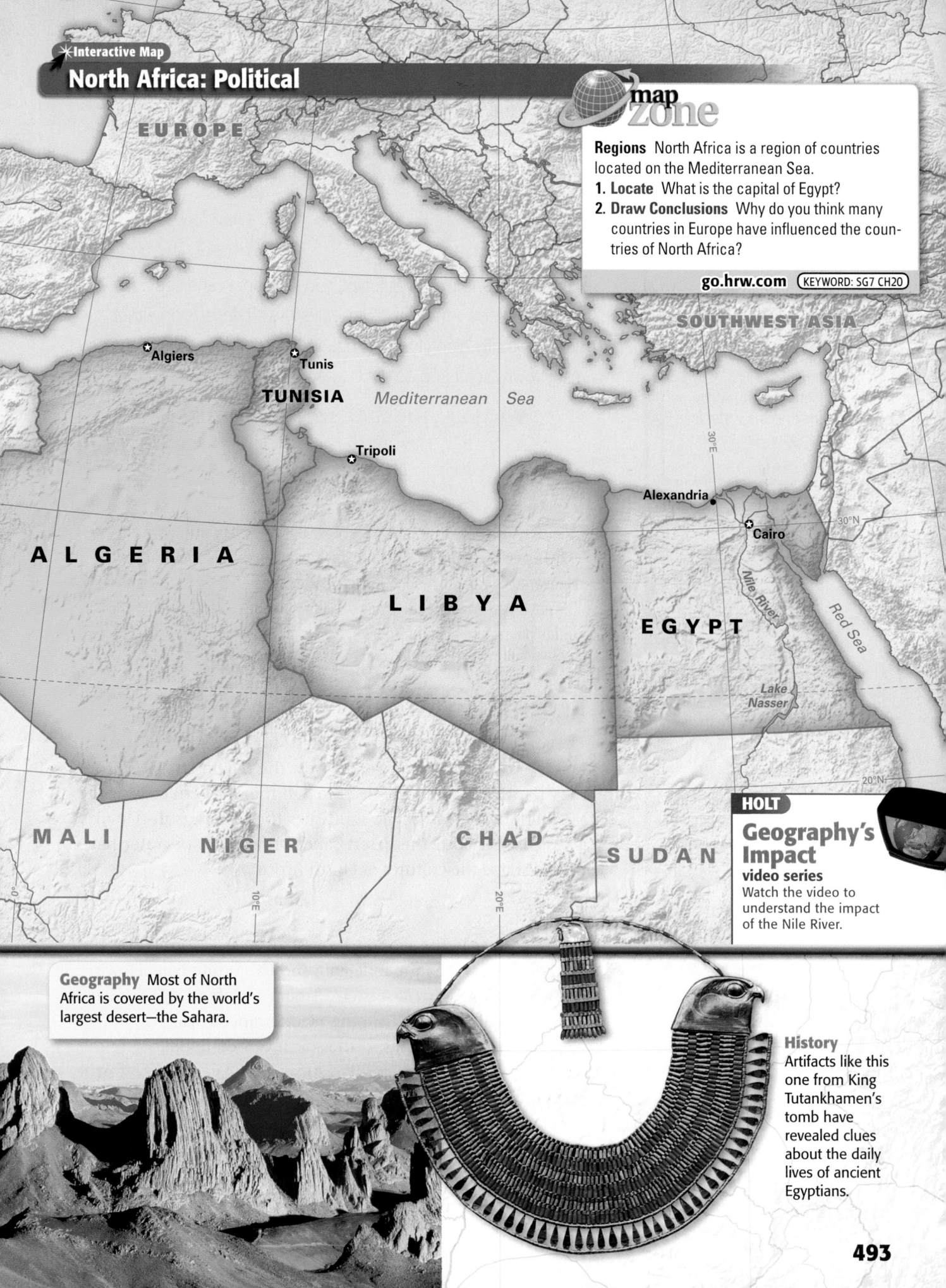

map zone

Regions North Africa is a region of countries located on the Mediterranean Sea.
1. **Locate** What is the capital of Egypt?
2. **Draw Conclusions** Why do you think many countries in Europe have influenced the countries of North Africa?

go.**hrw**.com   KEYWORD: SG7 CH20

EUROPE

SOUTHWEST ASIA

Algiers

Tunis

TUNISIA   *Mediterranean Sea*

Tripoli

Alexandria

30°E

Cairo

30°N

ALGERIA

LIBYA

EGYPT

Nile River

Red Sea

Lake Nasser

20°N

MALI   NIGER   CHAD   SUDAN

10°E   20°E

HOLT

Geography's Impact
video series
Watch the video to understand the impact of the Nile River.

Geography Most of North Africa is covered by the world's largest desert—the Sahara.

History
Artifacts like this one from King Tutankhamen's tomb have revealed clues about the daily lives of ancient Egyptians.

Physical Geography

If YOU lived there...

As your airplane flies over Egypt, you look down and see a narrow ribbon of green—the Nile River Valley—with deserts on either side. As you fly along North Africa's Mediterranean coast, you see many towns scattered across rugged mountains and green valleys.

What are the challenges of living in a mainly desert region?

BUILDING BACKGROUND Even though much of North Africa is covered by rugged mountains and huge areas of deserts, the region is not a bare wasteland. Areas of water include wet, fertile land with date palms and almond trees.

Physical Features

The region of North Africa includes Morocco, Algeria, Tunisia, Libya, and Egypt. From east to west the region stretches from the Atlantic Ocean to the Red Sea. Off the northern coast is the Mediterranean Sea. In the south lies the **Sahara** (suh-HAR-uh), a vast desert. Both the desert sands and bodies of water have helped shape the cultures of North Africa.

The Nile

The **Nile River** is the world's longest river. It is formed by the union of two rivers, the Blue Nile and the White Nile. Flowing northward through the eastern Sahara for about 4,000 miles, the Nile finally empties into the Mediterranean Sea.

For centuries, rain far to the south caused floods along the northern Nile, leaving rich silt in surrounding fields. **Silt** is finely ground fertile soil that is good for growing crops.

The Nile River valley is like a long oasis in the desert. Farmers use water from the Nile to irrigate their fields. The Nile fans out near the Mediterranean Sea, forming a large delta. A delta

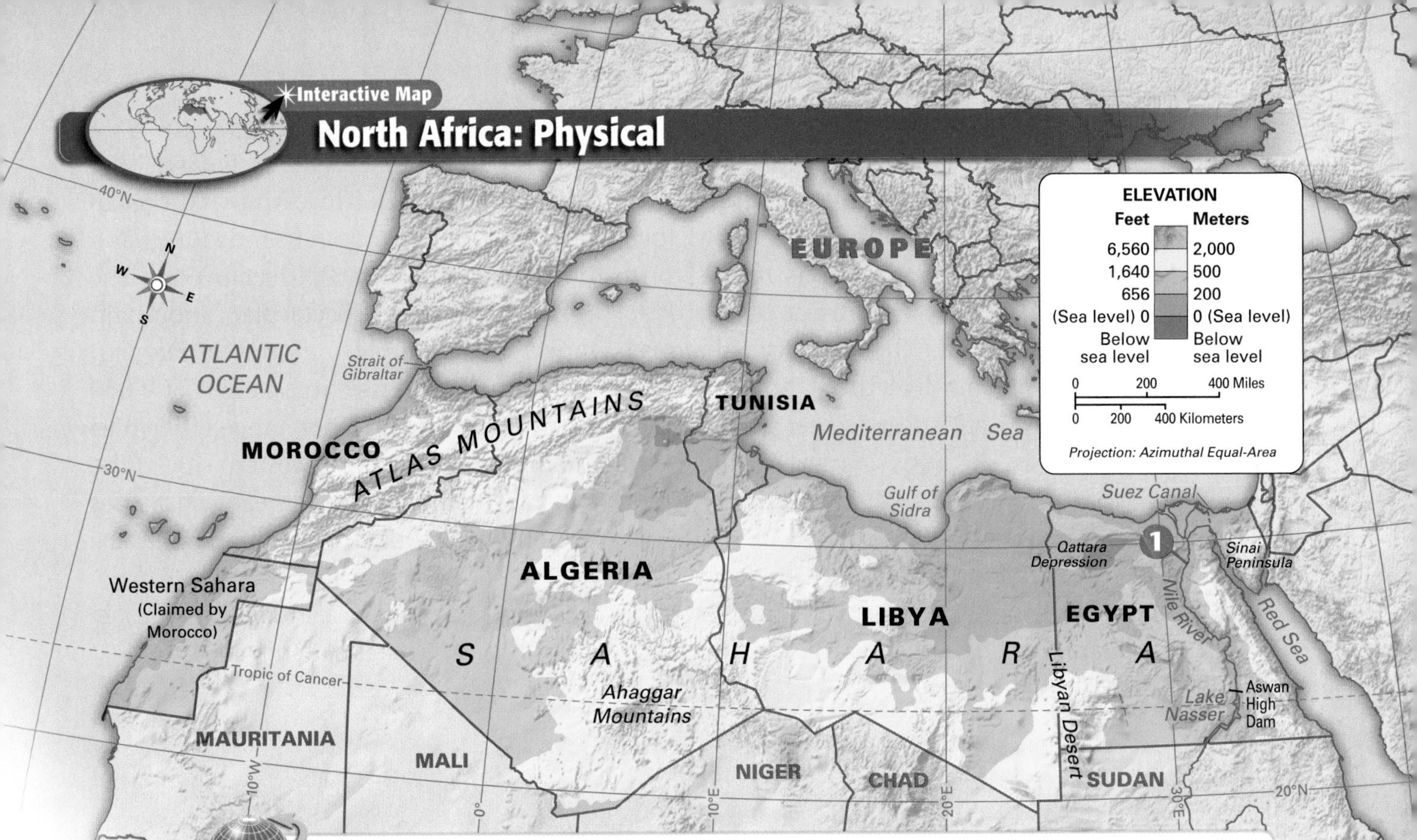

North Africa: Physical

EUROPE

ATLANTIC OCEAN

40°N

Strait of Gibraltar

MOROCCO

ATLAS MOUNTAINS

TUNISIA

Mediterranean Sea

Gulf of Sidra

30°N

Western Sahara (Claimed by Morocco)

ALGERIA

S A H A R A

LIBYA

EGYPT

Qattara Depression

Suez Canal

Sinai Peninsula

Red Sea

Nile River

Tropic of Cancer

Ahaggar Mountains

Libyan Desert

Lake Nasser

Aswan High Dam

MAURITANIA

MALI

NIGER

CHAD

SUDAN

20°N

0°

10°E

20°E

30°E

ELEVATION

Feet	Meters
6,560	2,000
1,640	500
656	200
(Sea level) 0	0 (Sea level)
Below sea level	Below sea level

0   200   400 Miles

0   200   400 Kilometers

Projection: Azimuthal Equal-Area

map zone
Geography Skills

Place The Sahara and the Mediterranean Sea are major physical features of the region of North Africa.

1. **Identify** In which country is the highest elevation located?
2. **Contrast** How does the physical geography of Egypt differ from the physical geography of Tunisia?

go.hrw.com (KEYWORD: SG7 CH20)

is a landform at the mouth of a river that is created by the deposit of sediment. The sediment in the Nile delta makes the area extremely fertile.

The Aswan High Dam controls flooding along the Nile. However, the dam also traps silt, preventing it from being carried downriver. Today some of Egypt's farmers must use fertilizers to enrich the soil.

The Sinai and the Suez Canal

East of the Nile is the triangular Sinai Peninsula. Barren, rocky mountains and desert cover the Sinai. Between the Sinai and the rest of Egypt is the **Suez Canal**. The French built the canal in the 1860s. It is a narrow waterway that connects the Mediterranean Sea with the Red Sea. Large cargo ships carry oil and goods through the canal.

1 Flowing for 4,132 miles, the Nile is the longest river in the world.

495

The Sahara

ACADEMIC VOCABULARY

impact effect, result

The Sahara, the largest desert in the world, covers most of North Africa. The name Sahara comes from the Arabic word for "desert." It has an enormous **impact** on the landscapes of North Africa.

One impact of the very dry Sahara is that few people live there. Small settlements are located near a water source such as an oasis. An **oasis** is a wet, fertile area in a desert where a natural spring or well provides water.

In addition to broad, windswept gravel plains, sand dunes cover much of the Sahara. Dry streambeds are also common.

Mountains

Do you think of deserts as flat regions? You may be surprised to learn that the Sahara is far from flat. Some sand dunes and ridges rise as high as 1,000 feet (305 m). The Sahara also has spectacular mountain ranges. For example, a mountain range in southern Algeria rises to a height of 9,800 feet (3,000 m). Another range, the **Atlas Mountains** on the northwestern side of the Sahara near the Mediterranean coast, rises even higher, to 13,600 feet (4,160 m).

READING CHECK **Summarizing** What are the major physical features of North Africa?

Close-up

A Sahara Oasis

The largest desert in the world, the Sahara, spans almost 4 million square miles across North Africa. From ancient times to today, traders crossing the Sahara have relied on the desert's oases. These oases provide water and shade.

Date palms thrive on the banks of this natural spring, which provides water to travelers and irrigated fields.

By carrying supplies, camels help the nomadic Tuareg people travel from oasis to oasis.

Climate and Resources

North Africa is very dry. However, rare storms can cause flooding. In some areas these floods as well as high winds have carved bare rock surfaces out of the land.

North Africa has three main climates. A desert climate covers most of the region. Temperatures range from mild to very hot. How hot can it get? Temperatures as high as 136°F (58°C) have been recorded in Libya. However, the humidity is very low. As a result, temperatures can drop quickly after sunset. In winter temperatures can fall below freezing at night.

The second climate type in the region is a Mediterranean climate. Much of the northern coast west of Egypt has this type of climate. Winters there are mild and moist. Summers are hot and dry. Areas between the coast and the Sahara have a steppe climate.

Oil and gas are important resources, particularly for Libya, Algeria, and Egypt. Morocco mines iron ore and minerals used to make fertilizers. The Sahara has natural resources such as coal, oil, and natural gas.

READING CHECK **Generalizing** What are North Africa's major resources?

FOCUS ON READING

Summarize the details of what you just read about North Africa's climate.

SUMMARY AND PREVIEW In this section, you learned about the physical geography of North Africa. Next, you will learn about the history and cultures of the countries of North Africa.

Shelters like this one provide a place for travelers to rest.

ANALYSIS SKILL **ANALYZING VISUALS**

Why do you think an oasis would be important to people traveling through the Sahara?

Section 1 Assessment

go.hrw.com
Online Quiz
KEYWORD: SG7 HP20

Reviewing Ideas, Terms, and Places

1. **a. Define** What is an **oasis**?
   b. Explain Why is the **Suez Canal** an important waterway?
   c. Elaborate Would it be possible to farm in Egypt if the **Nile River** did not exist? Explain your answer.
2. **a. Recall** What is the climate of most of North Africa?
   b. Draw Conclusions What resources of North Africa are the most valuable?

Critical Thinking

3. **Categorizing** Draw a diagram like the one shown here. Use your notes to list two facts about each physical feature of North Africa.

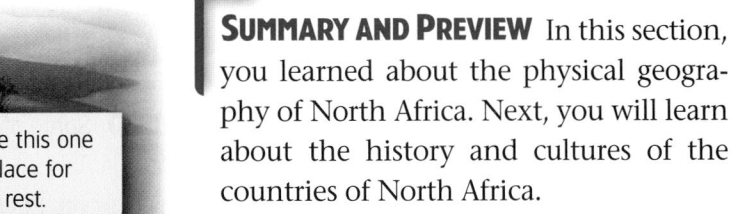

FOCUS ON WRITING

4. **Writing about Physical Geography** What physical feature will you choose as the subject of your myth? How will you describe this feature? Note your ideas.

History and Culture

What You Will Learn...

Main Ideas

1. North Africa's history includes ancient Egyptian civilization.
2. Islam influences the cultures of North Africa and most people speak Arabic.

The Big Idea

North Africa is rich in history and Islamic culture.

Key Terms and Places

Alexandria, *p. 499*
Berbers, *p. 501*

TAKING NOTES Draw two boxes like the ones below. As you read, take notes on the history and culture of North Africa.

North Africa	
History	Culture

If YOU lived there...

You live in a village in ancient Egypt in about 800 BC. Your family grows wheat and date palms along the banks of the Nile River, which brings water for your crops. You and your friends like to explore the marshy areas along the banks of the river, where many kinds of birds live in the tall reeds.

How is the Nile River important in your life?

BUILDING BACKGROUND Some of the world's earliest civilizations began in river valleys in Asia and Africa. One of these civilizations was the Nile Valley in Egypt. Egypt was called the "gift of the Nile," because the river's floods brought rich soil to the valley. The soil built up a fertile delta where the Nile emptied into the sea.

Egypt's Nile River Valley was home to some of the world's oldest civilizations. These ancient Egyptians built large monuments, participated in trade, and developed a writing system.

The Great Sphinx at Giza is one of the many monuments built by the ancient Egyptians.

North Africa's History

Sometime after 3200 BC people along the northern Nile united into one Egyptian kingdom. The ancient Egyptians built large stone monuments and developed a written system. Later Greeks and Arabs, who wanted to expand their empires, invaded North Africa.

The Ancient Egyptians

What is the first thing that comes to mind when we think of the ancient Egyptians? Most of us think of the great stone pyramids. The Egyptians built these huge monuments as tombs, or burial places, for pharaohs, or kings.

How did the Egyptians build these huge monuments? Scholars believe thousands of workers cut large blocks of stone far away and rolled them on logs to the Nile. From there the blocks were moved on barges. At the building site, the Egyptians finished carving the blocks. They built dirt and brick ramps alongside the pyramids. Then they hauled the blocks up the ramps.

One of the largest pyramids, the Great Pyramid, contains 2.3 million blocks of stone. Each stone averages 2.5 tons (2.25 metric tons) in weight. Building the Great Pyramid probably required from 10,000 to 30,000 workers. They finished the job in about 20 years, and the pyramid still stands thousands of years later.

Egyptian Writing

The ancient Egyptians developed a sophisticated writing system, or hieroglyphics (hy-ruh-GLIH-fiks). This writing system used pictures and symbols that stood for ideas or words. Each symbol represented one or more sounds in the Egyptian language. The Egyptians carved hieroglyphics on their temples and stone monuments. Many of these writings recorded the words and achievements of the pharaohs.

Greek and Arab Civilizations

Because of North Africa's long Mediterranean coastline, the region was open to invaders over the centuries. Those invaders included people from the eastern Mediterranean, Greeks, and Romans. For example, one invader was the Macedonian king Alexander the Great. Alexander founded the city of **Alexandria** in Egypt in 332 BC.

FOCUS ON READING

What details would you use to summarize the ancient Egyptians and their writing?

Ancient Egypt's King Tut

More than 3,300 years ago a 19-year-old named King Tutankhamen ruled ancient Egypt. Since the discovery of Tut's mummy in 1922, many have wondered how he died. In 2005, scientists used modern technology to help find possible clues to King Tut's cause of death.

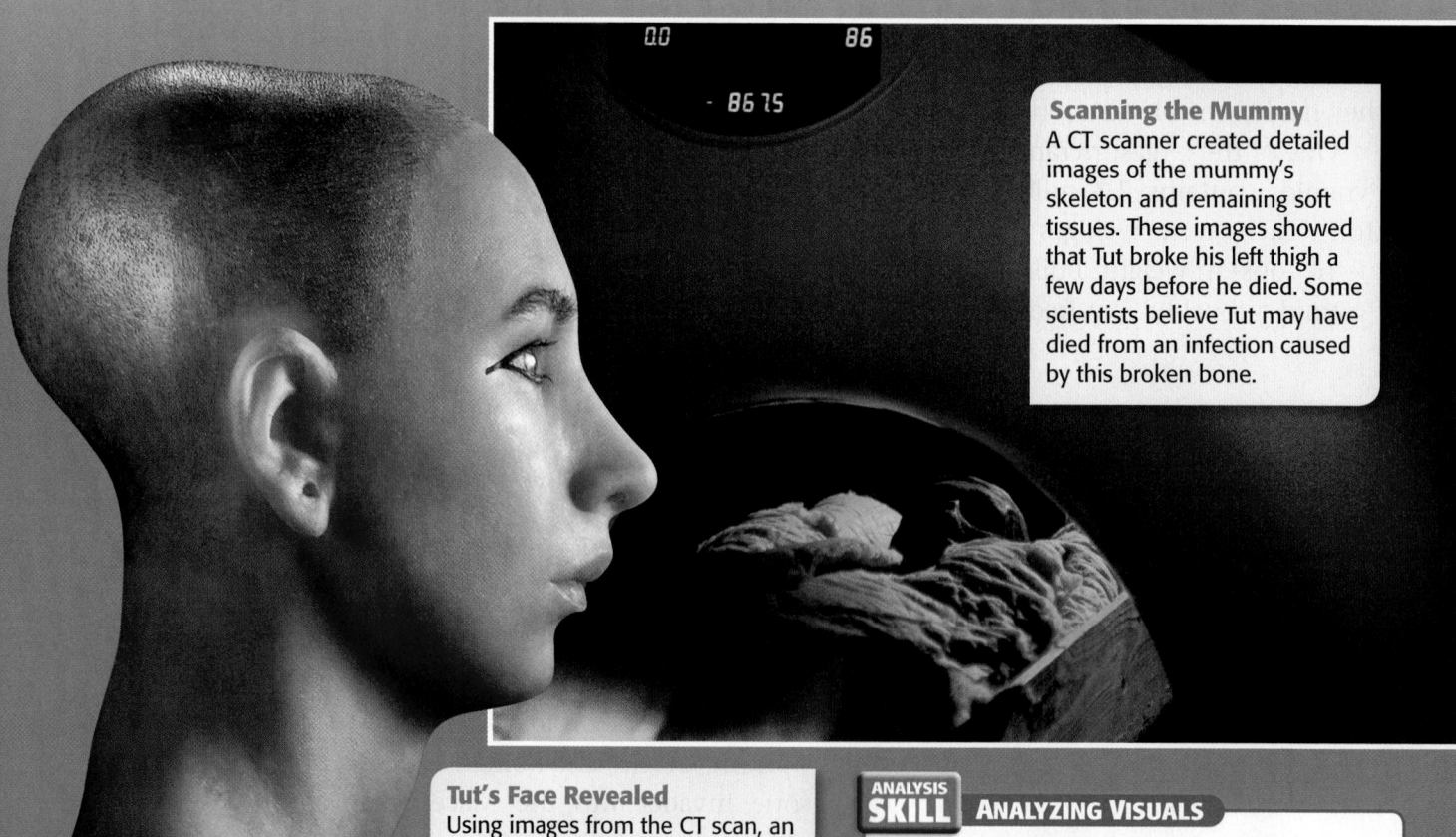

Mummy Unveiled
Inside King Tut's burial chamber, Egyptian archaeologist Zahi Hawass sees the mummy's face for the first time.

Scanning the Mummy
A CT scanner created detailed images of the mummy's skeleton and remaining soft tissues. These images showed that Tut broke his left thigh a few days before he died. Some scientists believe Tut may have died from an infection caused by this broken bone.

Tut's Face Revealed
Using images from the CT scan, an artist reconstructed the mummy's face with clay and plastic.

ANALYSIS SKILL ANALYZING VISUALS

By looking at King Tut's burial chamber, how can you tell that King Tut was an important person?

Alexandria became an important seaport and trading center. The city was also a great center of learning.

Beginning in the AD 600s, Arab armies from Southwest Asia swept across North Africa. They brought the Arabic language and Islam to the region. Under Muslim rule, North African cities became major centers of learning, trade, and craft making. These cities included Cairo in Egypt and Fès in Morocco.

European Influence

In the 1800s European countries began to take over the region. By 1912 they had authority over all of North Africa. In that year Italy captured Libya. Spain already controlled northern Morocco. France ruled the rest of Morocco as well as Tunisia and Algeria. The British controlled Egypt.

The countries of North Africa gradually gained independence. Egypt gained limited independence in 1922. The British kept military bases there and maintained control of the Suez Canal until 1956. During World War II the region was a major battleground. Libya, Morocco, and Tunisia each won independence in the 1950s.

Algeria was the last North African country to win independence. Many French citizens had moved to the country, and they considered Algeria part of France. Algeria finally won independence in 1962.

Modern North Africa

Since independence, the countries of North Africa have tried to build stronger ties with other Arab countries. Before signing a peace treaty in 1979, Egypt led other Arab countries in several wars against Israel. In 1976 Morocco took over the former Spanish colony of Western Sahara.

READING CHECK **Evaluating** What was one significant event in North Africa's history?

Cultures of North Africa

As you have just read, many of the countries of North Africa share a common history. Likewise, the people of North Africa share many aspects of culture—language, religion, foods, holidays, customs, and arts and literature.

People and Language

Egyptians, Berbers, and Bedouins make up nearly all of Egypt's population. Bedouins are nomadic herders who travel throughout the deserts of Egypt.

Most people in the other countries of North Africa are of mixed Arab and Berber ancestry. The **Berbers** are an ethnic group who are native to North Africa and speak Berber languages. The majority of North Africans speak Arabic.

Most ethnic Europeans left North Africa after the region's countries became independent. However, because of the European influence in the region, some North Africans also speak French, Italian, and English.

Religion

Most North Africans are Muslims who practice the religion of Islam. Islam plays a major role in North African life. For example, North African Muslims stop to pray five times a day. In addition, Fridays are special days when Muslims meet in mosques for prayer. About 6 percent of Egyptians are Christians or practice other religions.

Foods

What kinds of food would you eat on a trip to North Africa? Grains, vegetables, fruits, and nuts are common foods.

You would also notice that most meals in North Africa include couscous (KOOS-koos). This dish is made from wheat and looks like small pellets of pasta.

Couscous is usually steamed over boiling water or soup. Often it is served with vegetables or meat, butter, and olive oil.

Egyptians also enjoy a dish called *fuul*. It is made with fava beans mashed with olive oil, salt, pepper, garlic, and lemons. It is often served with hard-boiled eggs and bread. Many Egyptians eat these foods on holidays and at family gatherings.

FOCUS ON CULTURE

The Berbers

Before the AD 600s when Arabs settled in North Africa, a people called the Berbers lived in the region. The descendants of these ancient peoples live throughout North Africa today—mostly in Morocco and Algeria. Some Berbers are nomadic and live in goat-hair tents. Other Berbers farm crops that include wheat, barley, fruits, and olives. Some also raise cattle, sheep, or goats.

Berber culture is centered on a community made up of different tribes. Once a year, Berber tribes gather at large festivals. At these gatherings Berbers trade goods, and many couples get married in elaborate ceremonies.

Drawing Conclusions How have Berbers kept their culture alive?

Holidays and Customs

Important holidays in North Africa include the birthday of Muhammad, the prophet of Islam. This holiday is marked with lights, parades, and special sweets of honey, nuts, and sugar. During the holy month of Ramadan, Muslims abstain from food and drink during the day.

Gathering at cafes is a custom practiced by many men in North Africa. The cafes are a place where they go to play chess or dominoes. Most women in North Africa socialize only in their homes.

A certain way of greeting each other on the street is another North African custom. People greet each other by shaking hands and then touching their hand to their heart. If they are family or friends, they will kiss each other on the cheek. The number of kisses varies from country to country.

Many North Africans wear traditional clothes, which are long and loosely fitted. Such styles are ideal for the region's hot climate. Many North African women dress according to Muslim tradition. Their clothing covers all of the body except the face and hands.

The Arts and Literature

North Africa has a rich and varied tradition in the arts and literature. Traditional arts include wood carving and weaving. The region is famous for beautiful hand-woven carpets. The women who weave these carpets use bright colors to create complex geometric patterns. Beautifully detailed handpainted tilework is also a major art form in the region.

Other arts in Egypt include its growing movie industry. Egyptian films in Arabic have become popular throughout Southwest Asia and North Africa.

Many North Africans also enjoy popular music based on singing and poetry. The musical scale there has many more notes

Fès, Morocco

At a tannery in the city of Fès, men dye sheepskins in large vats of dyes. The city's craftspeople use yellow-dyed leather to make distinctive leather shoes.

ANALYZING VISUALS What other colors are the sheepskins dyed?

Vats of different colored dyes

Yellow-dyed sheepskins are laid out to dry.

than are common in Western music. As a result of this difference, North African tunes seem to wail or waver. Musicians in Morocco often use instruments such as the three-stringed sintir.

The region has also produced important writers and artists. For example, Egyptian poetry and other writing date back thousands of years. One of Egypt's most famous writers is Naguib Mahfouz. In 1988 he became the first Arab writer to win the Nobel Prize for Literature.

READING CHECK Analyzing What are some important facts about the people and culture of North Africa?

SUMMARY AND PREVIEW In this section you learned about the history and culture of North Africa. Next, you will learn about the region today.

go.hrw.com
Online Quiz
KEYWORD: SG7 HP20

Section 2 Assessment

Reviewing Ideas, Terms, and Places

1. **a. Define** What are hieroglyphics?
   b. Make Inferences What made the city of **Alexandria** important?
   c. Evaluate Why do you think European countries wanted to take over countries in North Africa?
2. **a. Recall** What language do most North Africans speak?
   b. Summarize What is one custom practiced in North Africa?
   c. Elaborate How is Islam a major part of the daily lives of many North Africans?

Critical Thinking

3. **Summarizing** Use your notes to summarize what you learned about the culture of North Africa.

Language	
Religion	
Food	
The Arts	
Literature	

FOCUS ON WRITING

4. **Choosing Details** Which details about North Africa's history and culture will you include in your myth? Write a sentence or two about each detail.

Analyzing a Diagram

Learn

Diagrams are drawings that use lines and labels to explain or illustrate something. Pictorial diagrams show an object in simple form, much like it would look if you were viewing it. Cutaway diagrams, like the one of an Egyptian pyramid below, show the "insides" of an object. These diagrams usually have labels that identify important areas of the diagram.

Practice

Analyze the diagram below, and answer the following questions.

① What type of diagram is this?

② What labels in the diagram suggest what this pyramid was used for?

③ Of what materials was the pyramid made?

An Egyptian Pyramid

King's burial chamber

Air shaft

Grand gallery

Tunnel

Apply

Draw a cutaway diagram of your school. Label classrooms, hallways, the cafeteria, and other areas. Use your diagram to answer the following questions.

1. How many stories are in your school?

2. Where is the closest exit located from the classroom you are sitting in now?

3. What are some of the materials your school is made of?

North Africa Today

If YOU lived there...

You live in the colorful city of Marrakesh, Morocco. This is the week of carnival, an exotic celebration where you can stroll among the crowds and see storytellers, musicians, and snake charmers. You may stop at a food stall for a snack and a cup of mint tea. But even in an ordinary week, you can explore the markets and see palaces and gardens with fountains.

Why is Marrakesh an exciting place to live?

BUILDING BACKGROUND Several countries and cultures have influenced modern North Africa. Some countries in North Africa were once colonies of France or Italy. As a result, the region is still linked with events in Europe.

Egypt

With a population of more than 78 million, Egypt is North Africa's most populous country. Egypt's government faces many challenges today. Most Egyptians are poor farmers because Egypt has limited resources and jobs.

Government and Society

Even though Egypt is a republic, its government is heavily influenced by Islamic law. Egypt's government has a constitution and Egyptians elect their government officials. Power is shared between Egypt's president and the prime minister.

Many Egyptians debate over the role of Islam in the country. Some Egyptian Muslims believe Egypt's government, laws, and society should be based on Islamic law. However, some Egyptians worry that such a change in government would mean fewer personal freedoms.

Egyptians are divided over their country's role in the world. Some Egyptians want their government to remain a leader among Arab countries. However, others want their government to focus more on improving their daily life.

What You Will Learn...

Main Ideas

1. Many of Egypt's people are farmers and live along the Nile River.
2. People in the other countries of North Africa are mostly pastoral nomads or farmers, and oil is an important resource in the region.

The Big Idea

Many people of North Africa are farmers, and oil is an important resource.

Key Terms and Places

Cairo, *p. 507*
Maghreb, *p. 508*
souks, *p. 509*
free port, *p. 509*
dictator, *p. 509*

TAKING NOTES Using the chart below, take notes on the governments, economies, and cities in Egypt and the other countries of North Africa.

	Egypt	Other Countries of North Africa
Government		
Economy		
Cities		

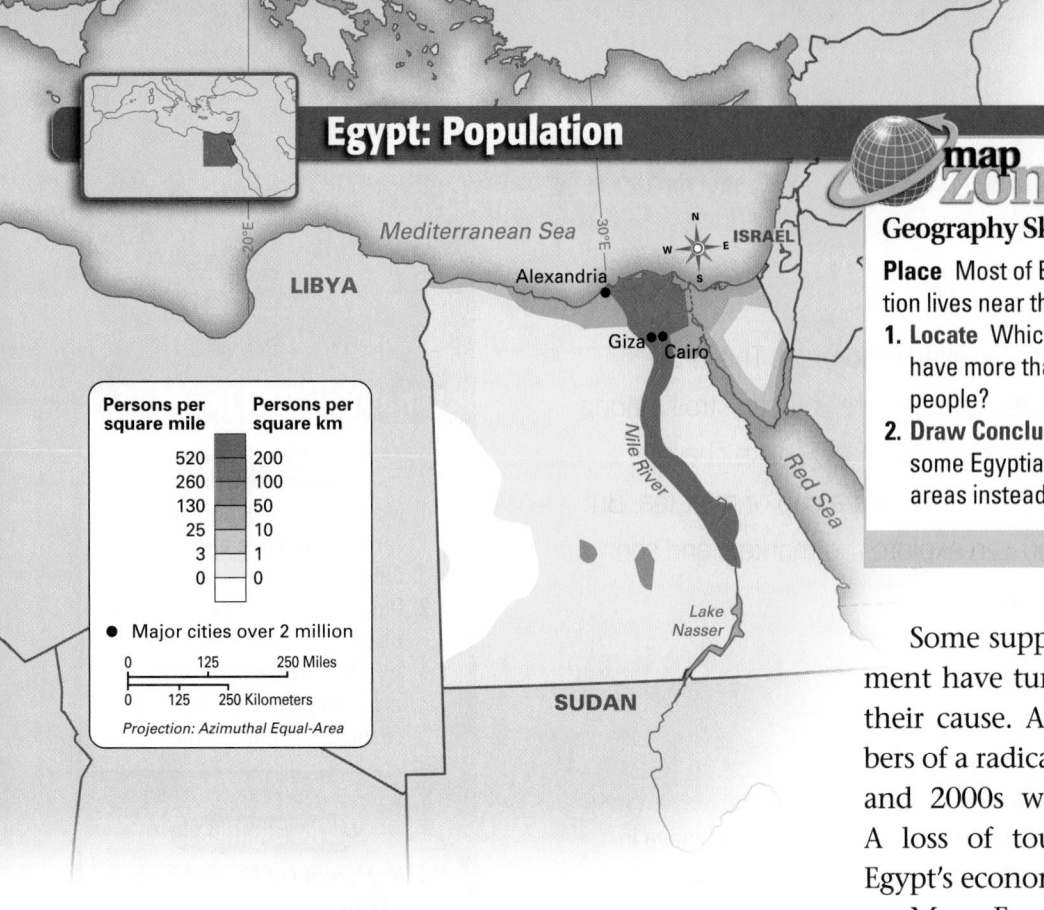

Egypt: Population

Mediterranean Sea

LIBYA

Alexandria

Giza● ●Cairo

ISRAEL

Nile River

Red Sea

Lake Nasser

SUDAN

Persons per square mile	Persons per square km
520	200
260	100
130	50
25	10
3	1
0	0

● Major cities over 2 million

0   125   250 Miles
0   125   250 Kilometers
Projection: Azimuthal Equal-Area

Geography Skills

Place Most of Egypt's population lives near the Nile River.
1. **Locate** Which cities have more than 2 million people?
2. **Draw Conclusions** Why do some Egyptians live in rural areas instead of cities?

Some supporters of an Islamic government have turned to violence to advance their cause. Attacks on tourists by members of a radical Islamic group in the 1990s and 2000s were particularly worrisome. A loss of tourism would severely hurt Egypt's economy.

Many Egyptians live in severe poverty. Many do not have clean water for cooking or washing. The spread of disease in crowded cities is also a problem. In addition, about half of Egyptians cannot read and write. Still, Egypt's government has made progress. Today Egyptians live longer and are much healthier than they were 50 years ago.

Resources and Economy

Egypt is challenged by its limited resources. For example, the country's only farmland is located in the Nile River Valley and Delta. To keep the land productive, farmers must use more and more fertilizer. In addition, salt water drifting up the Nile from the Mediterranean has brought salts to the surface that are harmful to crops. These problems and a rapidly growing population have forced Egypt to import much of its food.

About 32 percent of Egyptians are farmers, but less than 3 percent of the land is used for farming. Most farming is located

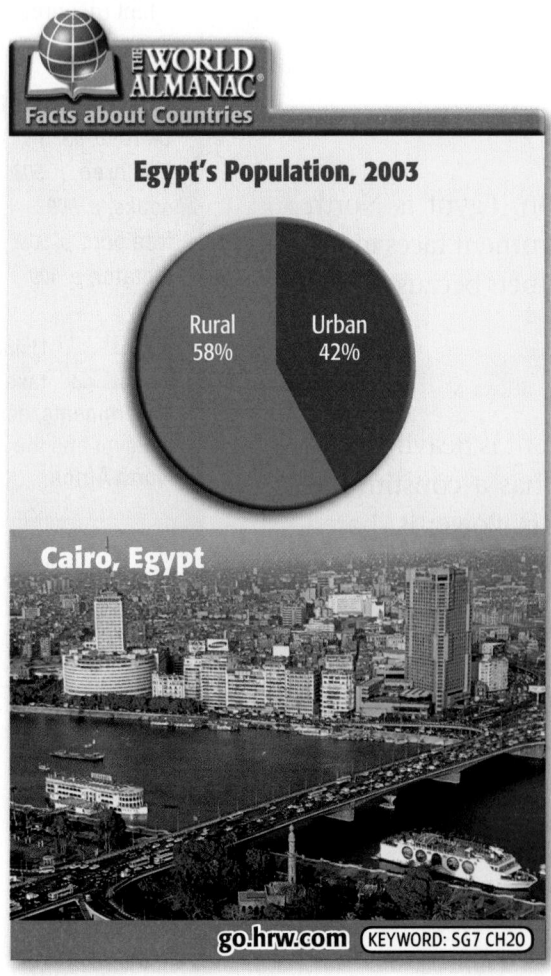

THE WORLD ALMANAC
Facts about Countries

Egypt's Population, 2003

Rural 58%

Urban 42%

Cairo, Egypt

go.hrw.com KEYWORD: SG7 CH20

along the Nile Delta, which is extremely fertile. A warm, sunny climate and water for irrigation make the delta ideal for growing cotton. Farmlands along the Nile River are used for growing vegetables, grain, and fruit.

The Suez Canal is an important part of Egypt's economy. The canal makes about $3 billion a year by requiring tolls from ships that pass through the canal. Thousands of ships use the canal each year to avoid making long trips around Southern Africa. This heavy traffic makes the canal one of the world's busiest waterways.

Egypt's economy depends mostly on agriculture, petroleum exports, and tourism. To provide for its growing population, Egypt is working to expand its industries. Recently, the government has invested in the country's communications and natural gas industries.

Many Egyptians also depend on money sent home by family members working in other countries. Some Egyptians work in other countries because there are not enough jobs in Egypt. Many Egyptians work in Europe or oil-rich countries in Southwest Asia.

Cities and Rural Life

Most North Africans live in cities along the Mediterranean coast or in villages in the foothills of the Atlas Mountains. Although, in Egypt 99 percent of the population lives in the Nile Valley and Delta. Egypt's capital, **Cairo**, is located in the Nile Delta.

With more than 10 million people, Cairo is the largest urban area in North Africa. The city is crowded, poor, and polluted. Cairo continues to grow as people move into the city from Egypt's rural areas in search of work. For centuries, Cairo's location at the southern end of the Nile Delta helped the city grow. The city also lies along old trading routes.

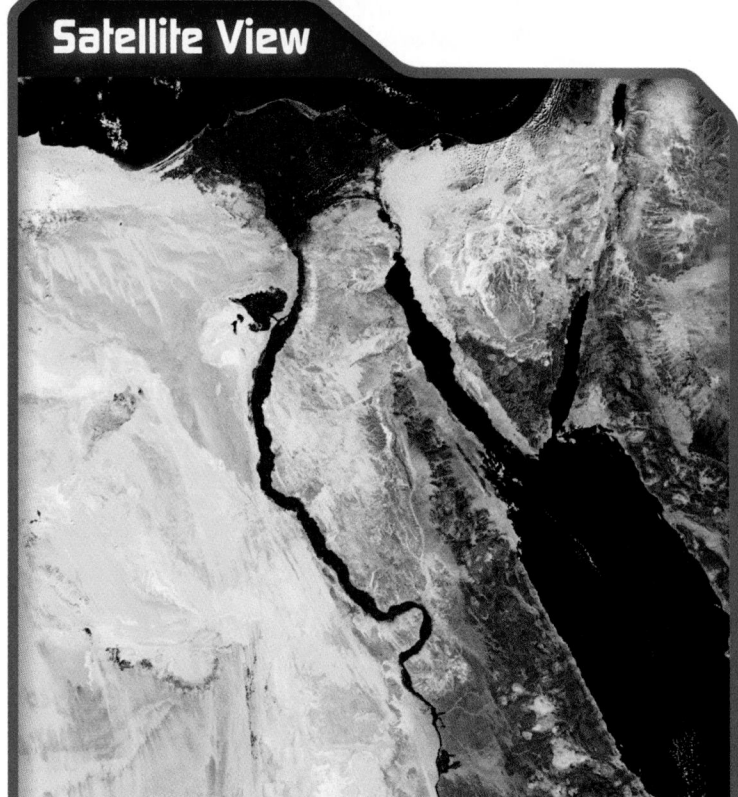

Satellite View

The Nile River

From space, the Nile looks like a river of green. Actually, the areas that appear green in this satellite image are thousands of irrigated fields that line the banks of the river. The river deposits silt along its banks, which makes the land extremely fertile. Farmers also depend on the Nile's waters to irrigate their crops. Without water, they could not farm in the desert.

Notice how the river appears smaller at the bottom of this image. The Aswan High Dam controls the river's flow here, which prevents flooding and provides electricity.

Drawing Conclusions How is the Nile important to Egypt's people?

Today the landscape of Cairo is a mixture of modern buildings, historic mosques, and small, mud-brick houses. However, there is not enough housing in Cairo for its growing population. Many people live in makeshift housing in the slums or boats along the Nile. Communities have even developed in cemeteries, where people convert tombs into bedrooms and kitchens.

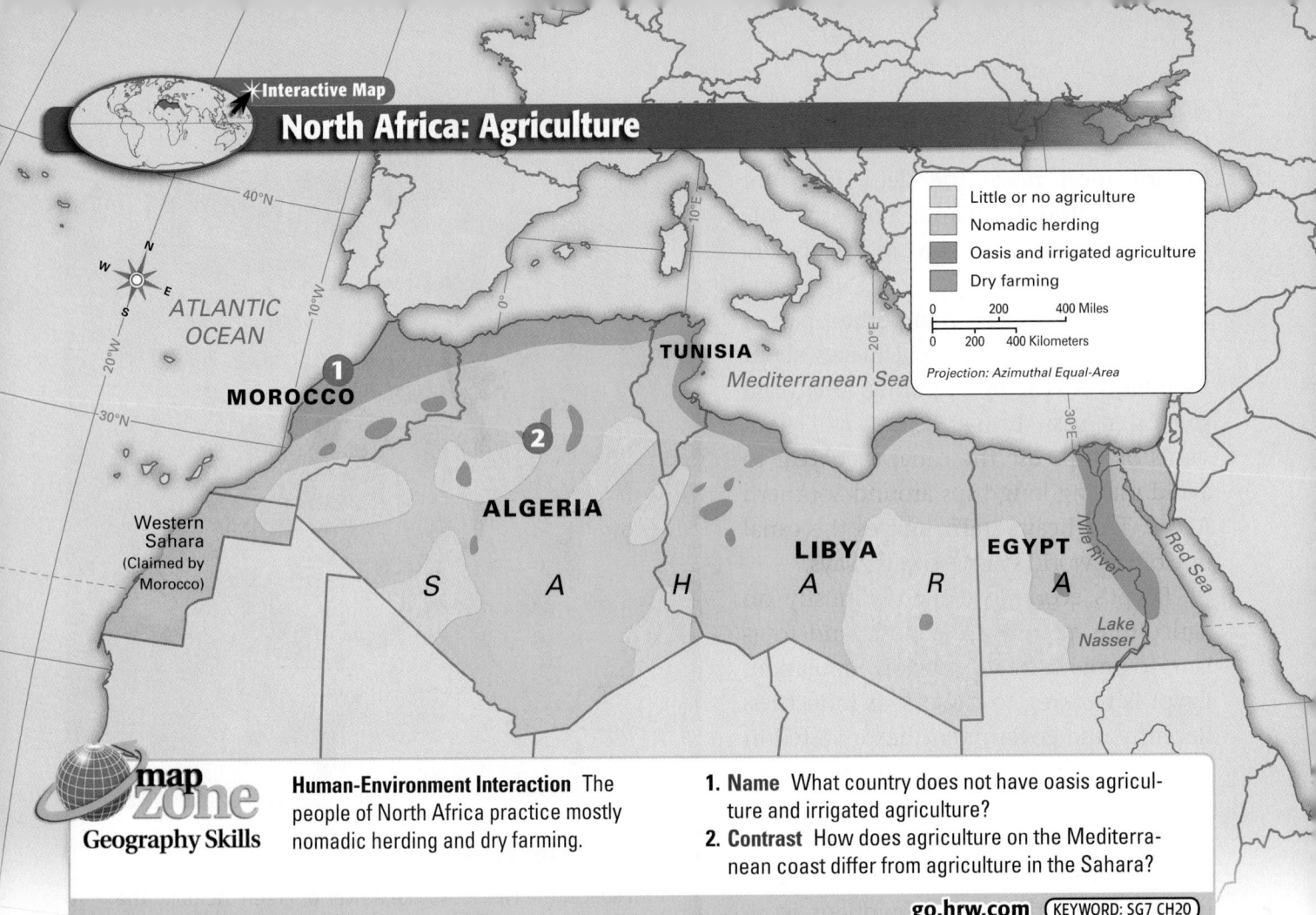

Little or no agriculture
Nomadic herding
Oasis and irrigated agriculture
Dry farming

0   200   400 Miles
0   200   400 Kilometers

Projection: Azimuthal Equal-Area

ATLANTIC OCEAN

① MOROCCO

TUNISIA

Mediterranean Sea

② ALGERIA

Western Sahara (Claimed by Morocco)

S   A   H   A   R   A

LIBYA

EGYPT

Nile River

Red Sea

Lake Nasser

map zone
Geography Skills

Human-Environment Interaction The people of North Africa practice mostly nomadic herding and dry farming.

1. **Name** What country does not have oasis agriculture and irrigated agriculture?
2. **Contrast** How does agriculture on the Mediterranean coast differ from agriculture in the Sahara?

go.hrw.com (KEYWORD: SG7 CH20)

FOCUS ON READING

Think about what details are important in a summary of Egypt's government, economy, and cities.

Alexandria is Egypt's second-largest city. The city was founded by Alexander the Great. Known in ancient times for its spectacular library, it is now the home to a large university and many industries. Its location on the Mediterranean Sea has made it a major seaport. The home of some 4 million people, Alexandria is as poor and crowded as Cairo.

More than half of all Egyptians live in small villages and other rural areas. Most rural Egyptians are farmers called fellahin (fel-uh-HEEN). These farmers own very small plots of land along the Nile River. Some fellahin also work large farms owned by powerful families.

READING CHECK **Finding Main Ideas** What are some of the challenges Cairo faces today?

Other Countries of North Africa

Western Libya, Tunisia, Algeria, and Morocco are often called the **Maghreb** (MUH-gruhb). This Arabic word means "west" or "the direction of the setting sun." Since most of the Maghreb is covered by the Sahara, cities and farmland are located in narrow bands along the coast.

Government and Economy

A major challenge in North Africa is the conflict over the role of Islam in society. For example, in Algeria some groups want a government based on Islamic principles and laws. In 1992 the government canceled elections that many believed would be won by Islamic groups.

1 **Dry farming** In Morocco, hungry goats climb an argan nut tree. These trees and other hardy crops thrive without much water.

2 **Oasis agriculture** In Algeria, oases in the desert provide enough water to irrigate crops and date palms.

Oil, mining, and tourism are important industries for the countries of North Africa. Oil is the most important resource, particularly in Libya and Algeria. Money from oil pays for schools, health care, food, social programs, and military equipment. The region's countries also have large deposits of natural gas, iron ore, and lead. The largest trade partners of Algeria, Libya, and Morocco are European Union members.

Agriculture is a major economic activity in North Africa. About one in six workers in Libya, Tunisia, and Algeria is a farmer. In Morocco, farmers make up about 40 percent of the labor force. North Africa's farmers grow and export wheat, olives, fruits, and nuts. Tourism is also an important economic activity in the region, especially in Morocco and Tunisia.

Cities

Many North African cities have large marketplaces, or **souks**. The souks are located in the old district of a city called the Casbah. These souks sell various goods such as spices, carpets, and copper teapots. The Casbah in Algeria's capital, Algiers, is a maze of winding alleys and tall walls.

Libya and Tunisia's cities and most of its population are found in the coastal areas. Libya is the most urbanized country in the region. More than 86 percent of Libya's roughly 6 million people live in cities. The largest cities are Benghazi and the capital, Tripoli. Tunisia's capital and largest city, Tunis, lies on the Mediterranean coast.

Morocco's largest city, Casablanca, has about 3.3 million people. Another Moroccan city, Tangier, overlooks the Strait of Gibraltar. This beautiful city was once a Spanish territory. Today tourists can take a quick ferry ride from Spain across the strait to Tangier, a free port. A **free port** is a city in which almost no taxes are placed on goods sold there.

The Countries Today

In addition to sharing similar economies, the countries of North Africa also share similar challenges. Some countries are dealing with violence, while others are strengthening their trading relationships with the United States and Europe.

Libya Since 1969 Libya has been ruled by a dictator, General Mu'ammar al-Gadhafi. A **dictator** is someone who rules a country with complete power. Gadhafi has supported acts of violence against Israel and its neighbors. As a result, many countries limited their economic relationship with Libya. However, Libya's relations with the West have recently improved after the Libyan government spoke out against terrorism and gave up many weapons programs.

Algiers, Algeria

Algeria's capital and major port, Algiers, sits on the Mediterranean Sea.

Algeria Violence between Algeria's government and some Islamic groups claimed thousands of lives in the 1990s. Today, Algeria is trying to recover from the violence and strengthen the country's economy with exports to Europe.

Tunisia Tunisia's government has granted Tunisian women more rights than women in any other North African country. Tunisia has close economic relationships with European countries. Today about two-thirds of Tunisia's imported goods are from European Union countries.

Morocco Morocco is the only North African country with little oil. Today, the country is an important producer and exporter of fertilizer.

READING CHECK **Summarizing** What are some of the challenges these countries face?

SUMMARY AND PREVIEW In this section you learned about North Africa today. In the next chapter you will learn about the region of West Africa.

Section 3 Assessment

Reviewing Ideas, Terms, and Places

1. **a. Define** What is a **souk**?
   b. Draw Conclusions Why is housing scarce in **Cairo**?
   c. Predict In what ways do you think Egypt's government can help solve the country's poverty?
2. **a. Recall** What countries in North Africa make up the **Maghreb**?
   b. Compare and Contrast How is Libya similar to and different from Morocco?
   c. Evaluate How do you think the countries of North Africa can improve their economies?

Critical Thinking

3. **Comparing** Use your notes to compare Egypt with the other countries of North Africa.

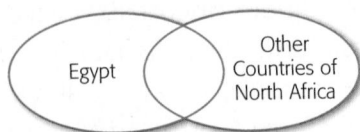

FOCUS ON WRITING

4. **Taking Notes on North Africa** Are there any characteristics of North Africa today that you might feature in your myth? Write down your ideas.

Chapter Review

Geography's Impact
video series
Review the video to answer the closing question:
What are two benefits and two consequences of the Aswan High Dam?

Visual Summary

Use the visual summary below to help you review the main ideas of the chapter.

QUICK FACTS

The Sahara is a major physical feature of North Africa.

One of the world's earliest civilizations thrived on the Nile River in ancient Egypt.

Most major cities in North Africa are located on the Mediterranean Sea.

Reviewing Vocabulary, Terms, and Places

Unscramble each group of letters below to spell a term or place that matches the given definition.

1. **sasoi**—wet, fertile area in a desert where a spring or well provides water

2. **ashraa**—the largest desert in the world that covers most of North Africa

3. **ipmtac**—effect, result

4. **enli virer**—the world's longest river that empties into the Mediterranean Sea in Egypt

5. **oicar**—a city founded more than 1,000 years ago on the Nile and is the capital of Egypt today

6. **uahtroyti**—power; right to rule

7. **tidrotca**—someone who rules a country with complete power

8. **ksuos**—marketplaces

9. **efer tpro**—a city in which almost no taxes are placed on goods sold there

Comprehension and Critical Thinking

SECTION 1 *(Pages 494–497)*

10. **a. Describe** What is the Nile River Valley like? Describe the river and the landscape.

    b. Draw Conclusions How important are oases to people traveling through the Sahara?

    c. Elaborate Why do you think few people live in the Sahara? What role does climate play in where people live? Explain your answer.

SECTION 2 *(Pages 498–503)*

11. **a. Recall** What types of monuments did the ancient Egyptians build?

    b. Make Inferences Why did European countries want to control most of North Africa?

    c. Elaborate Why do you think some groups living in North Africa are nomadic people?

SECTION 3 *(Pages 505–510)*

12. a. Define What is the Maghreb? What physical feature covers this region?

b. Contrast How does Egypt's economy differ from the economies of the other countries of North Africa?

c. Predict In what ways do you think Egypt could improve the lives of its people, who are mostly poor? Explain your answer.

Using the Internet

go.hrw.com
KEYWORD: SG7 CH20

13. Activity: Exploring the Sahara The Sahara is the largest desert in the world and is covered by great seas of sand dunes. One of the most inhospitable, hostile places on Earth, few people live in the Sahara, and few people even travel through it. Enter the activity keyword to begin your journey through the Sahara. See pictures of the Sahara and learn more about its history and geography. Imagine what it would be like to cross the desert. Then create a PowerPoint presentation or a visual display that summarizes your adventures across the great Sahara.

Social Studies Skills

Analyzing a Diagram Use the diagram of an Egyptian pyramid on this chapter's Social Studies Skills page to answer the following questions.

14. From looking at the title of the diagram, who built this pyramid?

15. How did the pyramid builders get to the king's burial chamber?

16. In what kind of climate is the pyramid located?

17. Summarizing Re-read the paragraphs under Physical Features in Section 1. Create a short summary of each paragraph. Then combine these paragraph summaries into a summary of the whole passage.

18. Writing a Myth Choose one physical feature of North Africa to be the subject of your myth. Then, write two to three paragraphs describing some characteristics of the physical feature. Use your imagination! You might describe the characteristics of the physical feature and how you think ancient peoples would find it mysterious. For example, you might explain why it rarely rains in the Sahara or why the Nile flows to the Mediterranean Sea.

Map Activity

19. North Africa On a separate sheet of paper, match the letters on the map with their correct labels.

Nile River   Tripoli

Atlas Mountains   Strait of Gibraltar

Cairo

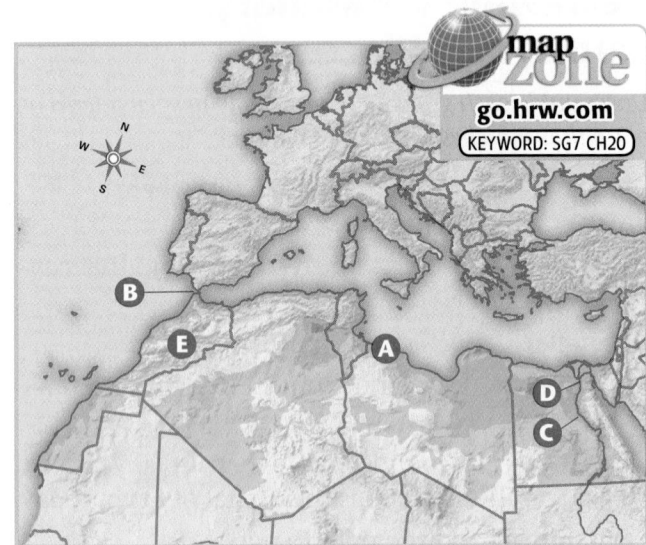

go.hrw.com
KEYWORD: SG7 CH20

DIRECTIONS: Read questions 1 through 7 and write the letter of the best response. Question 8 will require a brief essay.

1 **What physical feature covers most of North Africa?**

A the Nile

B the Sahara

C Sinai Peninsula

D Atlas Mountains

2 **The Nile flows through Egypt and empties into the**

A Red Sea.

B Atlantic Ocean.

C Mediterranean Sea.

D Sahara.

3 **The ancient Egyptians built pyramids to bury their**

A relatives.

B pharaohs.

C pets.

D valuable goods.

4 **What language do the majority of North Africans speak?**

A English

B French

C Italian

D Arabic

5 **Most North Africans are**

A Christians.

B Buddhists.

C Muslims.

D Hindus.

North Africa

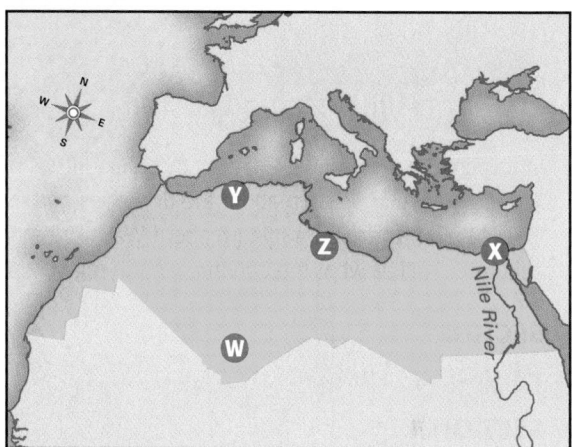

6 **Use the map to answer the following question. Ancient Egyptian civilization thrived in North Africa at the location marked on the map by the letter**

A W.

B Z.

C X.

D Y.

7 **What do ships use to avoid sailing around Southern Africa?**

A the Nile

B the Suez Canal

C the Aswan High Dam

D the Strait of Gibraltar

8 **Extended Response** Look at the physical map in Section 1. Write a short essay describing the physical features of North Africa. Explain why people live only in certain areas of the region.

CHAPTER 21

West Africa

What You Will Learn...

In this chapter you will learn about the 17 countries of West Africa. First, you will learn about the dry plains and major rivers in the region. Then you will learn about West Africa's history and culture as well as what the countries in the region are like today.

FOCUS ON READING AND SPEAKING

Understanding Comparison-Contrast Comparing and contrasting, or looking for similarities and differences, can help you more fully understand the subject you are studying. As you read, look for ways to compare and contrast the information in your text. **See the lesson, Understanding Comparison-Contrast, on page R22.**

Giving an Oral Description Storytelling is an important part of West Africa's history and culture. Storytellers pass along information to the community about events, places, and people. As you read this chapter, imagine that you are a storyteller. You are going to pass on some information about a person who lives, or has lived, in this region.

History People such as the Dogon cliff dwellers have been living in Mali for hundreds of years.

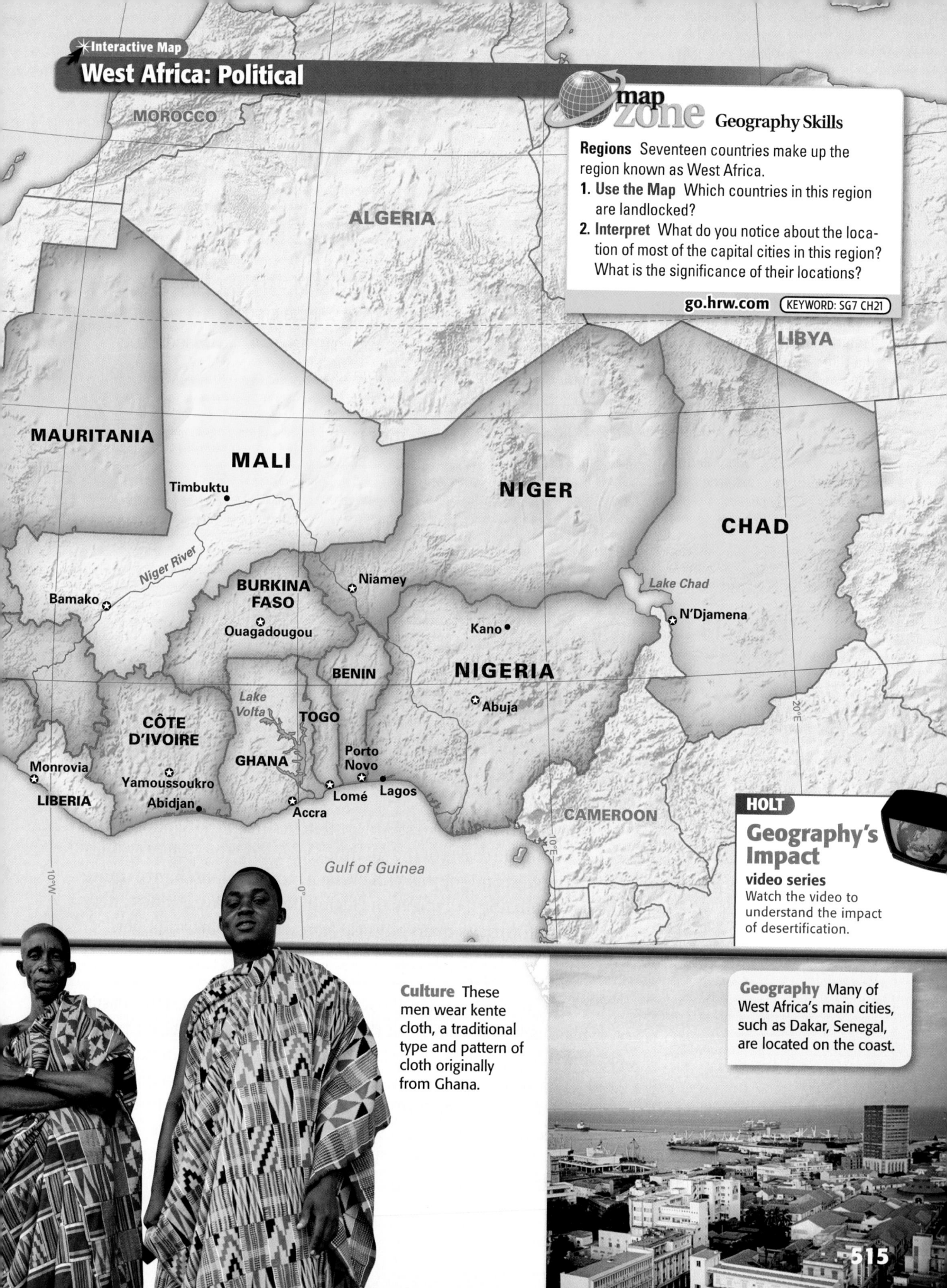

MOROCCO

ALGERIA

LIBYA

MAURITANIA

MALI

NIGER

CHAD

Timbuktu

Niger River

BURKINA
FASO

Niamey

Lake Chad

Bamako

Ouagadougou

Kano

N'Djamena

BENIN

NIGERIA

Lake
Volta

TOGO

Abuja

CÔTE
D'IVOIRE

Monrovia

GHANA

Porto
Novo

Yamoussoukro

Lomé

Lagos

LIBERIA

Abidjan

Accra

CAMEROON

Gulf of Guinea

10°W

0°

10°E

20°E

map zone Geography Skills

Regions Seventeen countries make up the region known as West Africa.
1. **Use the Map** Which countries in this region are landlocked?
2. **Interpret** What do you notice about the location of most of the capital cities in this region? What is the significance of their locations?

go.hrw.com KEYWORD: SG7 CH21

HOLT

Geography's Impact
video series
Watch the video to understand the impact of desertification.

Culture These men wear kente cloth, a traditional type and pattern of cloth originally from Ghana.

Geography Many of West Africa's main cities, such as Dakar, Senegal, are located on the coast.

Physical Geography

What You Will Learn...

Main Ideas

1. West Africa's key physical features include plains and the Niger River.
2. West Africa has distinct climate and vegetation zones that go from arid in the north to tropical in the south.
3. West Africa has good agricultural and mineral resources that may one day help the economies in the region.

The Big Idea

West Africa, which is mostly a region of plains, has climates ranging from arid to tropical and has important resources.

Key Terms and Places

Niger River, *p. 517*
zonal, *p. 518*
Sahel, *p. 518*
desertification, *p. 518*
savanna, *p. 518*

TAKING NOTES As you read, use a chart like the one below to help you organize your notes on the physical geography of West Africa.

Physical features	
Climate and vegetation	
Resources	

If YOU lived there...

Your family grows crops on the banks of the Niger River. Last year, your father let you go with him to sell the crops in a city down the river. This year you get to go with him again. As you paddle your boat, everything looks the same as last year—until suddenly the river appears to grow! It looks as big as the sea, and there are many islands all around. The river wasn't like this last year.

What do you think caused the change in the river?

BUILDING BACKGROUND The Niger River is one of West Africa's most important physical features. It brings precious water to the region's dry plains. Much of the interior of West Africa experiences desertlike conditions, but the region's rivers and lakes help to support life there.

Physical Features

The region we call West Africa stretches from the Sahara in the north to the coasts of the Atlantic Ocean and the Gulf of Guinea in the west and south. While West Africa's climate changes quite a bit from north to south, the region does not have a wide variety of landforms. Its main physical features are plains and rivers.

Plains and Highlands

Plains, flat areas of land, cover most of West Africa. The coastal plain is home to most of the region's cities. The interior plains provide land where people can raise a few crops or animals.

West Africa's plains are vast, interrupted only by a few highland areas. One area in the southwest has plateaus and cliffs. People have built houses directly into the sides of these cliffs for many hundreds of years. The region's only high mountains are the Tibesti Mountains in the northeast.

The Niger River

As you can see on the map below, many rivers flow across West Africa's plains. The most important river is the Niger (NY-juhr). The **Niger River** starts in some low mountains not too far from the Atlantic Ocean. From there, it flows 2,600 miles (4,185 km) into the interior of the region before emptying into the Gulf of Guinea.

The Niger brings life-giving water to West Africa. Many people farm along its banks or fish in its waters. It is also an important transportation route, especially during the rainy season. At that time, the river floods and water flows smoothly over its rapids.

Part of the way along its route the river divides into a network of channels, swamps, and lakes. This watery network is called the inland delta. Although it looks much like the delta where a river flows into the sea, this one is actually hundreds of miles from the coast in Mali.

FOCUS ON READING

The word *although* signals contrast in this paragraph. What is being contrasted?

READING CHECK **Summarizing** Why is the Niger River important to West Africa?

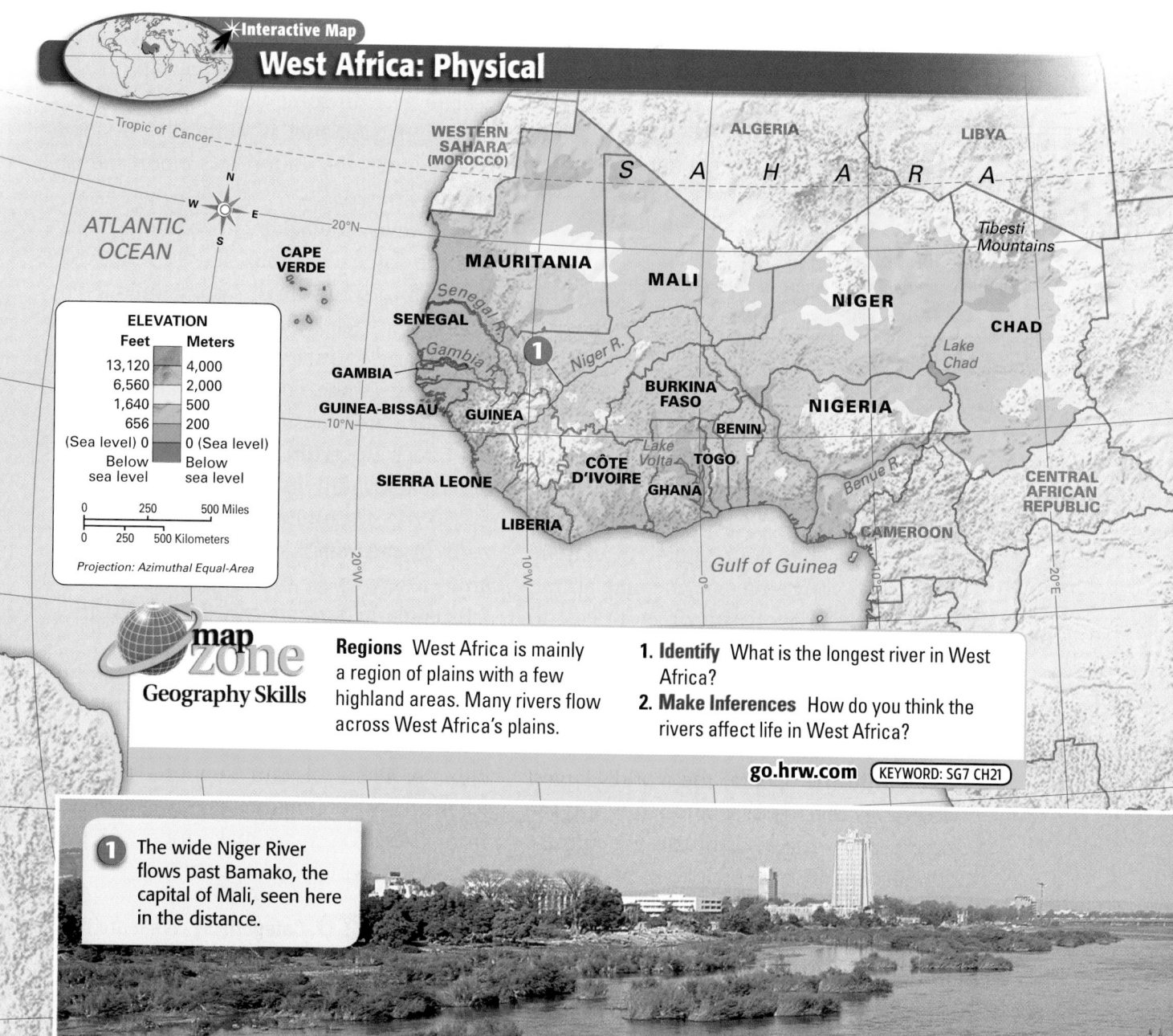

Interactive Map

West Africa: Physical

ELEVATION

Feet	Meters
13,120	4,000
6,560	2,000
1,640	500
656	200
(Sea level) 0	0 (Sea level)
Below sea level	Below sea level

0   250   500 Miles
0   250   500 Kilometers

Projection: Azimuthal Equal-Area

map zone
Geography Skills

Regions West Africa is mainly a region of plains with a few highland areas. Many rivers flow across West Africa's plains.

1. **Identify** What is the longest river in West Africa?
2. **Make Inferences** How do you think the rivers affect life in West Africa?

go.hrw.com   KEYWORD: SG7 CH21

1 The wide Niger River flows past Bamako, the capital of Mali, seen here in the distance.

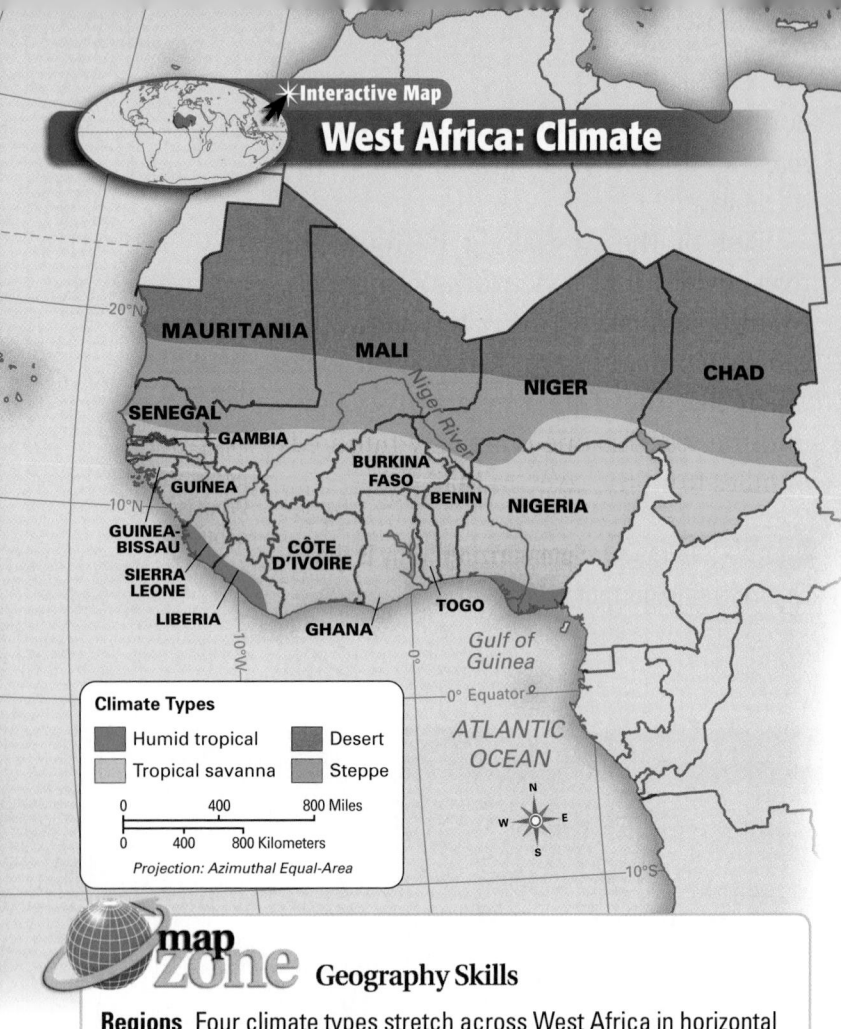

West Africa: Climate

Interactive Map

Climate Types

- Humid tropical
- Tropical savanna
- Desert
- Steppe

0   400   800 Miles
0 400 800 Kilometers
Projection: Azimuthal Equal-Area

map zone Geography Skills

Regions Four climate types stretch across West Africa in horizontal bands.
1. **Identify** What countries have desert climates?
2. **Make Inferences** What areas do you think get the most rainfall?

go.hrw.com   (KEYWORD: SG7 CH21)

Sahel Vegetation in the semiarid Sahel is limited, but it does support some grazing animals.

Climate and Vegetation

West Africa has four different climate regions. As you can see on the map above, these climate regions stretch from east to west in bands or zones. Because of this, geographers say the region's climates are **zonal**, which means "organized by zone."

The northernmost zone of the region lies within the Sahara, the world's largest desert. Hardly any vegetation grows in the desert, and large areas of this dry climate zone have few or no people.

South of the Sahara is the semiarid **Sahel** (SAH-hel), a strip of land that divides the desert from wetter areas. It has a steppe climate. Rainfall there varies greatly from year to year. In some years it never rains. Although the Sahel is quite dry, it does have enough vegetation to support hardy grazing animals.

However, the Sahel is becoming more like the Sahara. Animals have overgrazed the land in some areas. Also, people have cut down trees for firewood. Without these plants to anchor the soil, wind blows soil away. These conditions, along with drought, are causing desertification in the Sahel. **Desertification** is the spread of desertlike conditions.

To the south of the Sahel is a savanna zone. A **savanna** is an area of tall grasses and scattered trees and shrubs. When rains fall regularly, farmers can do well in this region of West Africa.

The fourth climate zone lies along the coasts of the Atlantic and the Gulf of Guinea. This zone has a humid tropical climate. Plentiful rain supports tropical forests. However, many trees have been cut from these forests to make room for the region's growing populations.

READING CHECK **Categorizing** What are the region's four climate zones?

Savanna Grasses and scattered trees grow on the savanna. This region can be good for farming.

Tropical Forest Thick forests are found along the coasts of West Africa. The tall trees provide homes for many animals.

Resources

West Africa has a variety of resources. These resources include agricultural products, oil, and minerals.

The climate in parts of West Africa is good for agriculture. For example, Ghana is the world's leading producer of cacao, which is used to make chocolate. Coffee, coconuts, and peanuts are also among the region's main exports.

Oil, which is found off the coast of Nigeria, is the region's most valuable resource. Nigeria is a major exporter of oil. West Africa also has mineral riches, such as diamonds, gold, iron ore, and bauxite. Bauxite is the main source of aluminum.

READING CHECK **Summarizing** What are some of the region's resources?

SUMMARY AND PREVIEW West Africa is mostly covered with plains. Across these plains stretch four different climate zones, most of which are dry. In spite of the harsh climate, West Africa has some valuable resources. Next, you will learn about West Africa's history and culture.

---

go.hrw.com

Section 1 Assessment

Online Quiz
KEYWORD: SG7 HP21

Reviewing Ideas, Terms, and Places

1. **a. Describe** What is the inland delta on the **Niger River** like?
   b. Summarize What is the physical geography of West Africa like?
   c. Elaborate Why do you think most of West Africa's cities are located on the coastal plain?
2. **a. Recall** Why do geographers say West Africa's climates are **zonal**?
   b. Compare and Contrast What is one similarity and one difference between the **Sahel** and the **savanna**?
   c. Evaluate How do you think **desertification** affects people's lives in West Africa?
3. **a. Identify** What is the most valuable resource in West Africa?
   b. Make Inferences Where do you think most of the crops in West Africa are grown?

Critical Thinking

4. **Identifying Cause and Effect**
   Review your notes on climate. Using a graphic organizer like the one here, identify the causes and effects of desertification.

   | Causes | → | Desertification | → | Effects |

FOCUS ON SPEAKING

5. **Describing the Physical Geography** The person you will describe will live or have lived in this region. How might the physical geography have affected his or her life?

History and Culture

What You Will Learn...

Main Ideas

1. In West Africa's history, trade made great kingdoms rich, but this greatness declined as Europeans began to control trade routes.
2. The culture of West Africa includes many different ethnic groups, languages, religions, and housing styles.

The Big Idea

Powerful early kingdoms, European slave trade and colonization, and traditions from a mix of ethnic groups have all influenced West African culture.

Key Terms and Places

Timbuktu, *p. 521*
animism, *p. 522*
extended family, *p. 523*

TAKING NOTES As you read, use a graphic organizer like the one below to take notes on West Africa's history and culture.

History	Culture

If YOU lived there...

When you were a small child, your family moved to Lagos, the largest city in Nigeria. You live in a city apartment now, but you still visit your aunts and uncles and cousins in your home village. There are more types of activities in the city, but you also remember that it was fun to have all your family members around.

Do you want to stay in the city or move back to your village? Why?

BUILDING BACKGROUND West African societies are changing as people like this family move to cities where they meet people whose habits and language are strange to them. West Africa has been home to many different ethnic groups throughout its history.

History

Much of what we know about West Africa's early history is based on archaeology. Archaeology is the study of the past based on what people left behind. Oral history—a spoken record of past events—offers other clues.

Merchants from North Africa crossed the Sahara to trade for West African gold and salt.

Great Kingdoms

Ancient artifacts suggest that early trading centers developed into great kingdoms in West Africa. One of the earliest kingdoms was Ghana (GAH-nuh). By controlling the Sahara trade in gold and salt, Ghana became rich and powerful by about 800.

According to legend, Ghana fell to a mighty warrior from a neighboring kingdom in about 1300. Under this leader, the empire of Mali (MAH-lee) replaced Ghana. Mali gained control of the Sahara trade routes. Mali's most famous king, Mansa Musa, used wealth from trade to support artists and scholars. However, invasions caused the decline of Mali by the 1500s.

As Mali declined, the kingdom of Songhai (SAWNG-hy) came to power. With a university, mosques, and more than 100 schools, the Songhai city of **Timbuktu** was a cultural center. By about 1600, however, invasions had weakened this kingdom.

The great West African trade cities also faded when the Sahara trade decreased. Trade decreased partly because Europeans began sailing along the west coast of Africa. They could trade for gold on the coast rather than with the North African traders who carried it through the desert.

The Slave Trade

For a while, both Europeans and Africans profited from trade with each other. However, in the 1500s the demand for labor in Europe's American colonies changed this relationship. European traders met the demand for labor by selling enslaved Africans to colonists.

The slave trade was profitable for these traders, but it devastated West Africa. Many families were broken up when members were kidnapped and enslaved. Africans often died on the voyage to the Americas. By the end of the slave trade in the 1800s, millions of Africans had been enslaved.

Primary Source

BOOK
I Speak of Freedom

As European colonizers left West Africa, some people believed that Africa should not be divided into independent countries. Kwame Nkrumah, a future leader of Ghana, explained in 1961 why he thought Africans should unite.

❝It is clear that we must find an African solution to our problems, and that this can only be found in African unity. Divided we are weak; united, Africa could become one of the greatest forces for good in the world.**❞**

—Kwame Nkrumah, from *I Speak of Freedom: A Statement of African Ideology*

ANALYSIS SKILL **ANALYZING PRIMARY SOURCES**

Why did Kwame Nkrumah think Africa would be better off united than divided?

Colonial Era and Independence

Even with the end of the slave trade, Europeans wanted access to West Africa's resources. To ensure that access, France, Britain, Germany, and Portugal all claimed colonies in the region in the 1800s.

Some Europeans moved to West Africa to run the colonies. They built schools, roads, and railroads. However, they also created new and difficult problems for the people of West Africa. For example, many West Africans gave up farming and instead earned only low wages working in the new commercial economy.

After World War II, Africans worked for independence. Most of the colonies became independent during the 1950s and 1960s. All were independent by 1974.

FOCUS ON READING

What words in the discussion of the slave trade signal comparison or contrast?

READING CHECK **Summarizing** What impact did Europeans have on West Africa?

Culture

West African societies are very diverse. Their culture reflects three main influences—traditional African cultures, European culture, and Islam.

People and Languages

West Africa's people belong to hundreds of different ethnic groups. In fact, Nigeria alone is made up of more than 250 ethnic groups. The biggest ethnic groups there are Hausa and Fulani, Yoruba, and Igbo. Members of some ethnic groups in West Africa still live in their traditional villages. Other ethnic groups mix with each other in the region's cities.

Because of the way the European colonizers drew political boundaries, country borders sometimes separated members of the same ethnic group. Other borders grouped together peoples that did not get along. As a result, many West Africans are more loyal to their own ethnic groups than they are to their countries.

Because of the huge number of ethnic groups, hundreds of different languages are spoken in West Africa. In some areas, using the colonial languages of French, English, or Portuguese helps people from different groups communicate with each other. Also, West African languages that many people share, such as Fula and Hausa, help with communication in the region.

Religion

Like peoples and languages, many forms of religion exist in West Africa. Traditional religions of West Africa have often been forms of animism. **Animism** is the belief that bodies of water, animals, trees, and other natural objects have spirits. Animists also honor the memories of ancestors.

The two most common religions came from outside the region. They are Islam and Christianity. North African traders brought Islam to West Africa. Europeans introduced Christianity. Today most West Africans of the Sahel practice Islam. Many towns there have mosques built of mud. Christianity is the most common religion south of the Sahel.

Clothing, Families, and Homes

West Africans wear a mix of traditional and modern clothing styles. Some West Africans, particularly in the cities, wear Western-style clothing. Traditional robes, pants, blouses, and skirts are made from colorful cotton fabrics. Women often wear beautiful wrapped headdresses. Because of the warm climate, most clothing is loose.

CONNECTING TO the Arts

Masks

Masks are one of the best-known West African arts. They are traditionally carved out of wood only by skilled and respected men. The colors and shape of a mask have specific meanings. For example, the color white represents the spirit world.

Masks are used in ceremonies to call spirits or to prepare boys and girls for adulthood. Ceremony participants often wear a mask as part of a costume that completely hides the body. The wearer is believed to become what the mask represents.

Drawing Inferences Why would someone want to wear a mask?

A West African Village

These homes are in Burkina Faso. Trees are scarce in the Sahel and savanna so there is little wood for construction.

Women are responsible for painting and decorating the walls of the homes.

These homes are made of a mixture of mud, water, and cow dung.

Rural homes are small and simple. Many homes in the Sahel and savanna zones are circular. Straw or tin roofs sit atop mud, mud-brick, or straw huts. Large extended families often live close together in the same village. An **extended family** includes the father, mother, children, and close relatives in one household.

In urban areas also, members of an extended family may all live together. However, in West Africa's cities you will find modern buildings. People may live in houses or high-rise apartments.

READING CHECK **Generalizing** What are some features of West African culture?

SUMMARY AND PREVIEW Great kingdoms and European colonists once ruled West Africa. These historical influences still affect West Africa's diverse cultures. Next, you will learn about the countries of West Africa today.

go.hrw.com
Online Quiz
KEYWORD: SG7 HP21

Section 2 Assessment

Reviewing Ideas, Terms, and Places

1. **a. Identify** What was the significance of **Timbuktu**?
   b. Explain How did the slave trade affect West Africa?
   c. Evaluate Do you think West Africans mostly appreciated or disliked the European colonizers? Explain your answer.
2. **a. Recall** What do people who believe in **animism** think about natural objects?
   b. Analyze How did European colonizers affect tension between ethnic groups?

Critical Thinking

3. **Sequencing** Look over your notes on the history of West Africa. Then, using a diagram like the one here, put major events in chronological order.

FOCUS ON SPEAKING

4. **Describing History and Culture** What details about West Africa's history might affect the daily life of someone in the area? Many aspects of culture in the region would affect someone in West Africa. What religion would this person practice? How would he or she dress? List some ideas for your description.

Geography and History

The Atlantic Slave Trade

Between 1500 and 1870, British, French, Dutch, Portuguese, and Spanish traders sent millions of enslaved Africans to colonies in the Americas. The highest number of slaves went to British and French colonies in the West Indies. The climate in the colonies was good for growing crops like cotton, tobacco, and sugarcane. These crops required a great deal of labor to grow and process. The colonists relied on enslaved Africans to meet this demand for labor.

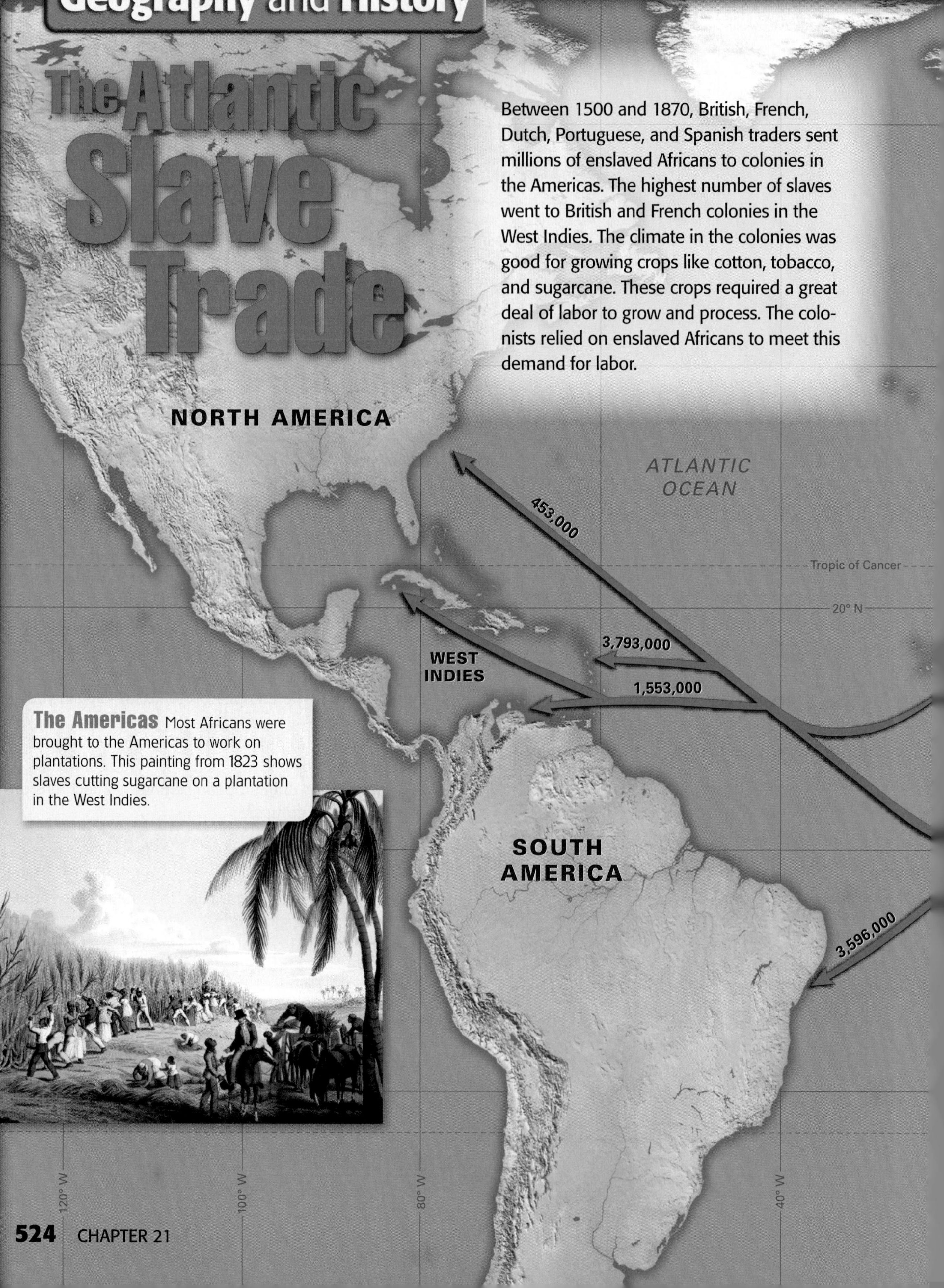

NORTH AMERICA

ATLANTIC OCEAN

453,000

Tropic of Cancer

20° N

3,793,000

1,553,000

WEST INDIES

The Americas Most Africans were brought to the Americas to work on plantations. This painting from 1823 shows slaves cutting sugarcane on a plantation in the West Indies.

SOUTH AMERICA

3,596,000

120° W

100° W

80° W

40° W

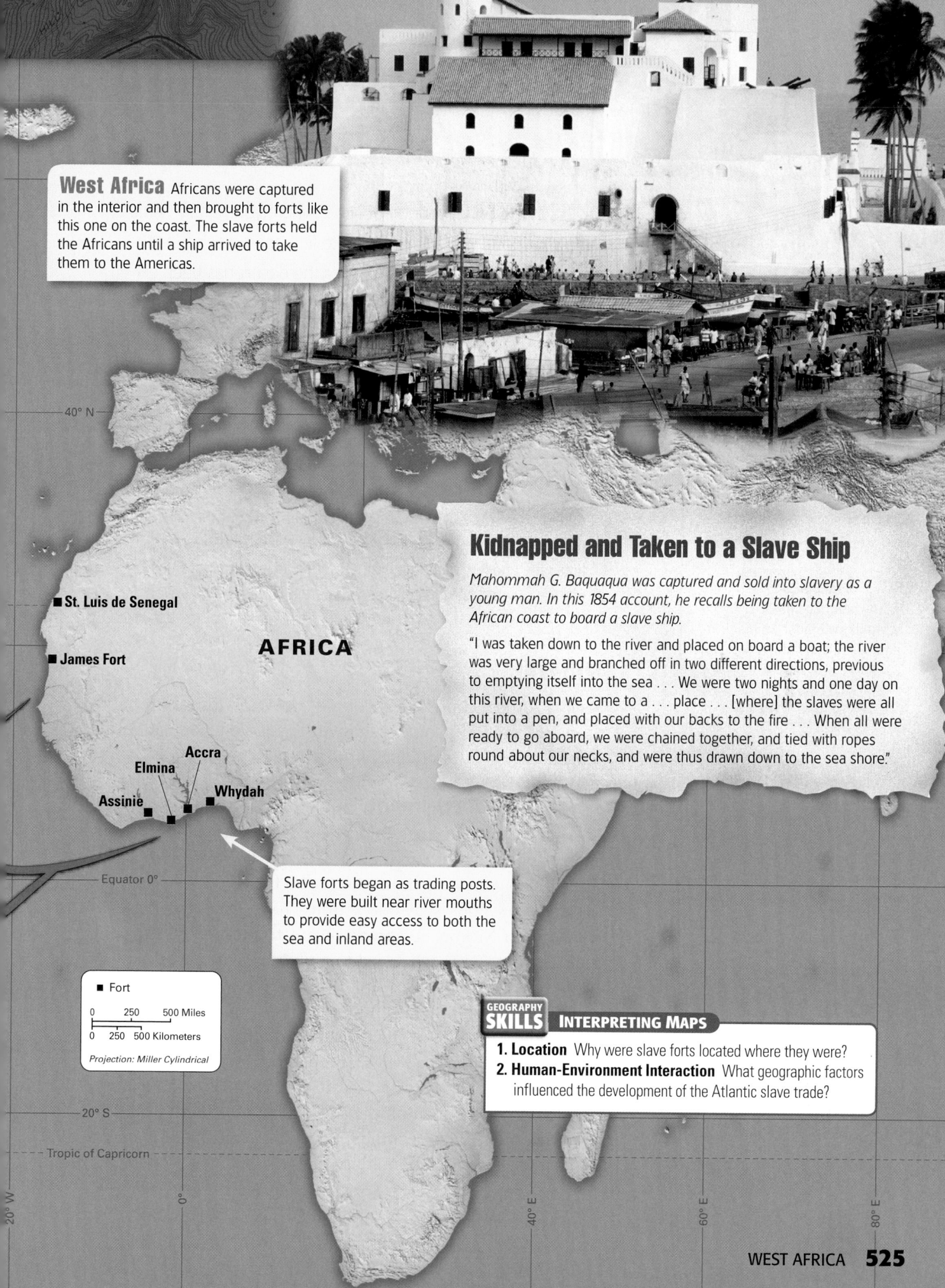

West Africa Africans were captured in the interior and then brought to forts like this one on the coast. The slave forts held the Africans until a ship arrived to take them to the Americas.

AFRICA

- St. Luis de Senegal
- James Fort
- Assinie
- Elmina
- Accra
- Whydah

Equator 0°

40° N

20° S

Tropic of Capricorn

- Fort

0   250   500 Miles

0   250   500 Kilometers

Projection: Miller Cylindrical

20° W   0°   40° E   60° E   80° E

Slave forts began as trading posts. They were built near river mouths to provide easy access to both the sea and inland areas.

Kidnapped and Taken to a Slave Ship

Mahommah G. Baquaqua was captured and sold into slavery as a young man. In this 1854 account, he recalls being taken to the African coast to board a slave ship.

"I was taken down to the river and placed on board a boat; the river was very large and branched off in two different directions, previous to emptying itself into the sea . . . We were two nights and one day on this river, when we came to a . . . place . . . [where] the slaves were all put into a pen, and placed with our backs to the fire . . . When all were ready to go aboard, we were chained together, and tied with ropes round about our necks, and were thus drawn down to the sea shore."

GEOGRAPHY SKILLS INTERPRETING MAPS

1. **Location** Why were slave forts located where they were?
2. **Human-Environment Interaction** What geographic factors influenced the development of the Atlantic slave trade?

West Africa Today

What You Will Learn...

Main Ideas

1. Nigeria has many different ethnic groups, an oil-based economy, and one of the world's largest cities.
2. Most coastal countries of West Africa have struggling economies and weak or unstable governments.
3. Lack of resources in the Sahel countries is a main challenge to economic development.

The Big Idea

Many countries in West Africa struggle with poor economies and political instability.

Key Terms and Places

secede, p. 526
Lagos, p. 527
famine, p. 529

TAKING NOTES As you read, use a graphic organizer like the one below to take notes on the governments and economies of the different regions of West Africa.

	Government	Economy
Nigeria		
Other Coastal Countries		
Sahel Countries		

If YOU lived there...

You live in the Sahel country of Niger, where your family herds cattle. You travel with your animals to find good grazing land for them. In the past few years, however, the desert has been expanding. It is getting harder and harder to find good grass and water for your cattle. You worry about the coming years.

How does this environment affect your life and your future?

BUILDING BACKGROUND The countries of West Africa are very different from one another. Some, such as Niger, have poor soils, little rain, and few resources. Others, such as Nigeria, have good natural resources. None of these countries is wealthy, however.

Nigeria

Nigeria is the second largest country in West Africa. With more than 130 million people, it has Africa's largest population, its second largest city, and one of the strongest economies.

People and Government

Like many other former colonies, Nigeria has many different ethnic groups within its borders. Conflicts have often taken place among those ethnic groups. In the 1960s one conflict became so serious that one ethnic group, the Igbo, tried to secede from Nigeria. To **secede** means to break away from the main country. This action led to a bloody civil war, which the Igbo eventually lost.

Ethnic and regional conflicts have continued to be an issue in Nigeria. Avoiding conflict was important in choosing a site for a new capital in the 1990s. Leaders chose Abuja (ah-BOO-jah) because it was centrally located in an area of low population density. A low population density meant that there would be fewer people to cause conflicts. Nigeria's government is now a democracy after years of military rule.

Crowding in Lagos

Lagos is a busy seaport and industrial center. Overcrowding leads to problems common in big cities such as traffic jams and poor housing.

ANALYZING VISUALS What activities are these people participating in?

THE WORLD ALMANAC
Facts about the World

Africa's Largest Cities

Population (in millions) vs Cities: Cairo, Lagos, Kinshasa, Khartoum

go.hrw.com (KEYWORD: SG7 CH21)

Economy

Nigeria has some of Africa's richest natural resources. Major oil fields, the country's most important resource, are located in the Niger River delta and just off the coast. Oil accounts for about 95 percent of the country's export earnings. Income from oil exports has allowed Nigeria to build good roads and railroads for transporting oil. The oil industry is centered around **Lagos** (LAY-gahs). Also the former capital, Lagos is the most populous city in West Africa.

Although Nigeria is rich in resources, many Nigerians are poor. One cause of the poverty there is a high birthrate. Nigeria cannot produce enough food for its growing population. Another cause of Nigeria's poverty is a history of bad government. Corrupt government officials have used their positions to enrich themselves.

READING CHECK **Drawing Inferences** What are some obstacles to progress in Nigeria?

Other Coastal Countries

Several West African countries lie along the Atlantic Ocean and the Gulf of Guinea. Many of these countries have struggling economies and unstable governments.

Senegal and Gambia

Senegal wraps around Gambia. The odd border was created by French and British diplomats during the colonial era. Senegal is larger and richer than Gambia, but the two countries do have many similarities. For example, peanuts are their major crops. Also, tourism is becoming more important in both countries.

FOCUS ON READING

How are Senegal and Gambia similar?

Many people in Senegal and Gambia speak a language called Wolof (WOH-lawf). Griots (GREE-ohz), or storytellers, are important to the Wolof speakers there and to other West Africans.

Guinea, Guinea-Bissau, and Cape Verde

Guinea and its small neighbor, Guinea-Bissau (GI-nee bi-SOW), are poor countries. Guinea's main natural resource is bauxite, which is used to make aluminum. Guinea-Bissau has undeveloped mineral resources.

Cape Verde (VUHRD) is a group of volcanic islands in the Atlantic. It is West Africa's only island country. Once a Portuguese colony, Cape Verde now has one of the most stable democratic governments in Africa. Services such as tourism form the main part of the country's economy.

Liberia and Sierra Leone

Liberia is Africa's oldest republic. Americans founded it in the 1820s as a home for freed slaves. The freed slaves who settled in Liberia and their descendants lived in towns on the coast. They often clashed with Africans already living there. Those Africans were usually poorer and lived in rural areas. In the 1980s these conflicts led to a civil war, which ended in 2003.

Sierra Leone (lee-OHN) also experienced violent civil war, from 1991 to 2002. The fighting wrecked the country's economy, killed thousands of people, and forced millions from their homes.

Now, both Liberia and Sierra Leone are trying to rebuild. They do have natural resources on which to build stronger economies. Liberia exports rubber and iron ore while Sierra Leone exports diamonds.

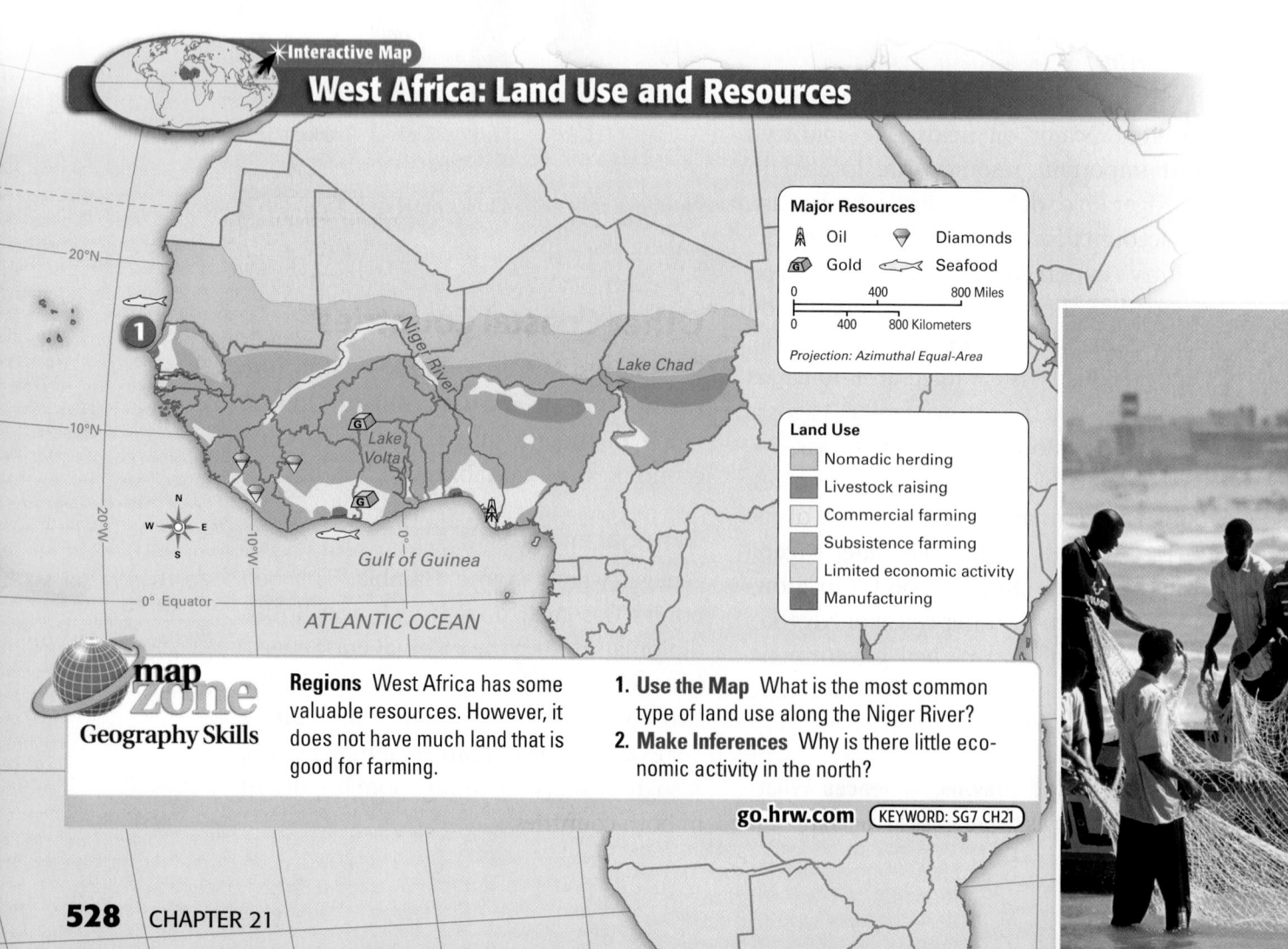

Interactive Map

West Africa: Land Use and Resources

Major Resources

- Oil
- Gold
- Diamonds
- Seafood

0   400   800 Miles
0   400   800 Kilometers

Projection: Azimuthal Equal-Area

Land Use

- Nomadic herding
- Livestock raising
- Commercial farming
- Subsistence farming
- Limited economic activity
- Manufacturing

Lake Chad

Niger River

Lake Volta

Gulf of Guinea

ATLANTIC OCEAN

0° Equator

20°N

10°N

map zone Geography Skills

Regions West Africa has some valuable resources. However, it does not have much land that is good for farming.

1. **Use the Map** What is the most common type of land use along the Niger River?
2. **Make Inferences** Why is there little economic activity in the north?

go.hrw.com   KEYWORD: SG7 CH21

Ghana and Côte d'Ivoire

Ghana is named for an ancient kingdom. Côte d'Ivoire (koht-dee-VWAHR) is a former French colony whose name means "Ivory Coast" in English. Côte d'Ivoire boasts Africa's largest Christian church building.

These two countries have rich natural resources. Gold, timber, and cacao (kuh-KOW) are major products of Ghana. Côte d'Ivoire is a world leader in export of cacao and coffee. However, civil war there has hurt the economy.

Togo and Benin

Unstable governments have troubled Togo and Benin (buh-NEEN) since independence. These two countries have experienced periods of military rule. Their fragile economies have contributed to their unstable and sometimes violent politics.

Both Togo and Benin are poor. The people depend on farming and herding for income. Palm products, cacao, and coffee are the main crops in both countries.

READING CHECK **Generalizing** What are the economies of the coastal countries like?

1 Fishing is an important industry in the coastal countries of West Africa.

Sahel Countries

The Sahel region of West Africa includes some of the poorest and least developed countries in the world. Drought and the expanding desert make feeding the people in these countries difficult.

Mauritania, Niger, and Chad

Most Mauritanians were once nomadic herders. Today the expanding Sahara has driven more than half of the nomads into cities. People in these cities, as well as the rest of the country, are very poor. Only in the far south, near the Senegal River, can people farm. Near the Atlantic Ocean, people fish for a living. Corrupt governments and ethnic tensions between blacks and Arabs add to Mauritania's troubles.

In Niger, only about 3 percent of the land is good for farming. The country's only farmland lies along the Niger River and near the Nigerian border. Farmers there grow staple, or main, food crops, such as millet and sorghum. These grains are cooked like oatmeal.

In the early 2000s, locusts and drought destroyed Niger's crops. The loss of crops caused widespread **famine**, or an extreme shortage of food. International groups provided some aid, but it was impossible to **distribute** food to all who needed it.

Chad has more land for farming than Mauritania or Niger, and conditions there are somewhat better than in the other two countries. In addition to farming, Lake Chad once had a healthy fishing industry and supplied water to several countries. However, drought has evaporated much of the lake's water in the past several years.

The future may hold more promise for Chad. A long civil war finally ended in the 1990s. Also, oil was recently discovered there, and Chad began to export this valuable resource in 2004.

ACADEMIC VOCABULARY
distribute to divide among a group of people

Water well

Dry Croplands

This aerial view shows how, with just a little water, people can farm in the dry Sahel.

Mali and Burkina Faso

The Sahara covers about 40 percent of the land in Mali. The scarce amount of land available for farming makes Mali among the world's poorest countries. The available farmland lies in the southwest, along the Niger River. Most people in Mali fish or farm in this small area along the river. Cotton and gold are Mali's main exports.

Mali's economy does have some bright spots, however. A fairly stable democratic government has begun economic reforms. Also, the ancient cities of Timbuktu and Gao (GOW) continue to attract tourists.

Burkina Faso is also a poor country. It has thin soil and few mineral resources. Few trees remain in or near the capital, Ouagadougou (wah-gah-DOO-goo), because they have been cut for firewood and building material. Jobs in the city are also scarce. To support their families many men try to find work in other countries. Thus, when unrest disrupts work opportunities in other countries, Burkina Faso's economy suffers.

READING CHECK **Summarizing** What are the challenges facing Chad and Burkina Faso?

SUMMARY AND PREVIEW Countries in West Africa struggle with poor economies. In addition, many have faced political instability since independence. In the next chapter, you will learn about how the countries in East Africa face some similar issues.

Section 3 Assessment

Reviewing Ideas, Terms, and Places

1. **a. Recall** Why did the Igbo try to **secede**?
   b. Evaluate What do you think were some benefits and drawbacks to Nigeria's leaders moving the capital from **Lagos** to Abuja?

2. **a. Identify** What is West Africa's only island country?
   b. Compare What are some similarities between Togo and Benin?
   c. Elaborate Why do you think countries with poor economies often have unstable governments?

3. **a. Describe** What caused **famine** in Niger?
   b. Evaluate What do you think is the biggest problem facing the Sahel countries? Explain.

Critical Thinking

4. **Compare and Contrast** Review your notes on the coastal countries and the Sahel countries. Then use a diagram like the one here to compare and contrast the two regions.

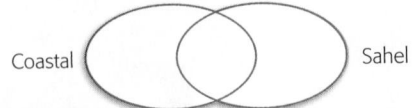

Coastal   Sahel

FOCUS ON SPEAKING

5. **Describing Countries of West Africa** Think about the countries of West Africa. Which one might be a good location for the person you are going to describe? Take some notes about that place.

from
AKÉ: The Years of Childhood

by Wole Soyinka

Merchants from North Africa sometimes traded brass objects in West Africa.

About the Reading *In this excerpt from* Aké: The Years of Childhood, *Nigerian-born Wole Soyinka describes some traders who came to his childhood home in Aké. As a young boy, he was fascinated with the appearance of the exotic goods.*

AS YOU READ Notice the variety of goods the traders brought to the author's house.

It was a strange procedure, one which made little sense to me. ❶ They spread their wares in front of the house and I had to be prised off them. There were brass figures, horses, camels, trays, bowls, ornaments. Human figures spun on a podium, balanced by weights at the end of curved light metal rods. We spun them round and round, yet they never fell off their narrow perch. The smell of fresh leather filled the house as pouffs, handbags, slippers and worked scabbards were unpacked. There were bottles encased in leather, with leather stoppers, . . . scrolls, glass beads, bottles of scent with exotic names—I never forgot, from the first moment I read it on the label—Bint el Sudan, with its picture of a turbanned warrior by a kneeling camel. A veiled maiden offered him a bowl of fruits. They looked unlike anything in the orchard and Essay said they were called dates. ❷ I did not believe him; dates were figures which appeared on a calendar on the wall, so I took it as one of his jokes.

GUIDED READING

WORD HELP

wares goods
prised taken by force
pouff fluffy clothing or accessory
scabbard a case to hold a knife
turbanned wearing a turban, or wrapped cloth, on the head

❶ The author is describing a visit by the Hausa traders who came from northwestern Africa.

❷ Essay is the author's father.

Connecting Literature to Geography

1. **Drawing Inferences** The author describes many unusual things. What descriptions or comments lead you to believe that the trader traveled to Aké from far away?

2. **Analyzing** Think about the way the author described the goods. What senses did the author use as a child to discover the goods the traders brought?

Social Studies Skills

Analyzing a Precipitation Map

Learn

A precipitation map shows how much rain or snow typically falls in a certain area over a year. Studying a precipitation map can help you understand a region's climate.

To read a precipitation map, first look at the legend to see what the different colors mean. Compare the legend to the map to see how much precipitation different areas get.

Practice

Use the map on this page to answer the following questions.

❶ What countries have areas that get over 80 inches of rain every year?

❷ In what part of the region does the least amount of rain fall?

❸ What do you think vegetation is like in the north? in the south?

❹ Compare this map to the climate map in Section 1. How are the two maps similar?

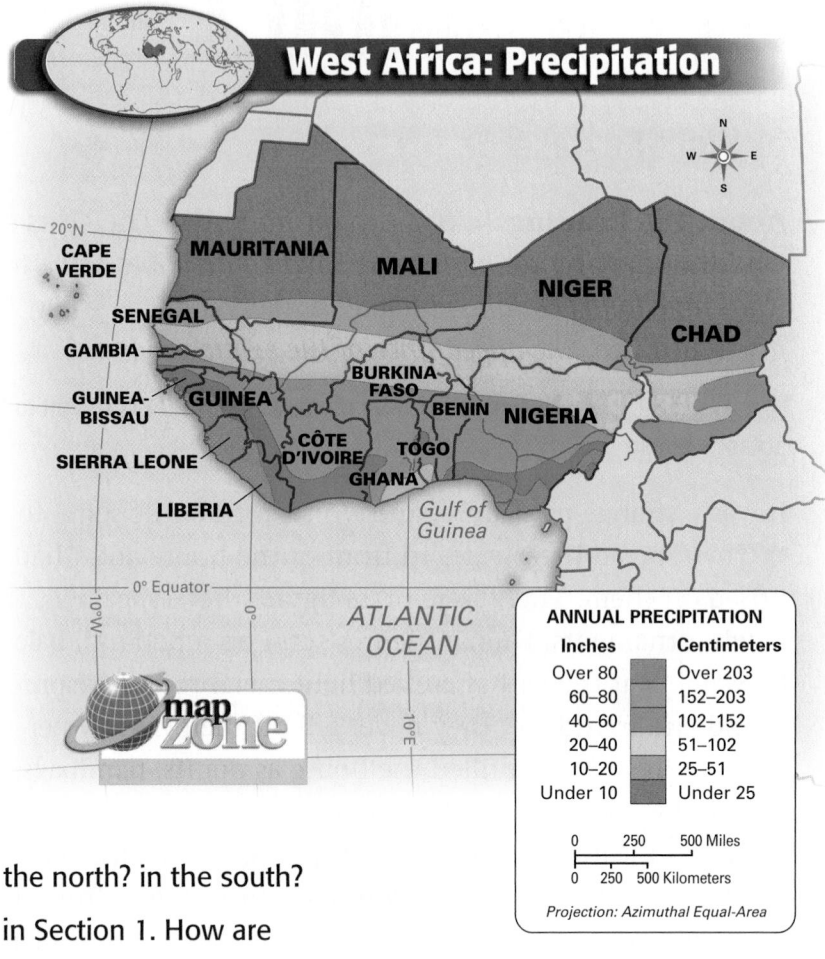

West Africa: Precipitation

ANNUAL PRECIPITATION

Inches		Centimeters
Over 80		Over 203
60–80		152–203
40–60		102–152
20–40		51–102
10–20		25–51
Under 10		Under 25

0   250   500 Miles
0   250   500 Kilometers

Projection: Azimuthal Equal-Area

Apply

Using an atlas or the Internet, find a precipitation map of the United States. Use that map to answer the following questions.

1. What area of the country gets the most precipitation?

2. What area of the country gets the least precipitation?

3. How much annual precipitation does Hawaii get?

Geography's Impact
video series
Review the video to answer the closing question:
What are some of the ways desertification can be slowed, stopped, or even reversed?

Visual Summary

Use the visual summary below to help you review the main ideas of the chapter.

QUICK FACTS

West Africa has four distinct climate zones. In the dry Sahel, people try to farm or herd cattle.

Masks are just one example of traditional African culture that can be seen in West Africa today.

Most West African countries are poor. Fishing is important to the economy along rivers and in coastal areas.

Reviewing Vocabulary, Terms, and Places

For each statement below, write T if it is true and F if it is false. If the statement is false, write the correct term that would make the sentence a true statement.

1. West Africa's climate is described as <u>savanna</u> because it is organized by zone.

2. <u>Animism</u>, a belief that natural objects have spirits, is a traditional religion in West Africa.

3. An <u>extended family</u> is one that includes a mother, father, children, and close relatives in one household.

4. International aid agencies have tried to <u>distribute</u> food in Niger.

5. <u>Timbuktu</u> is the largest city in Nigeria.

6. The <u>Niger River</u> flows through many countries in West Africa and empties into the Gulf of Guinea.

7. The spread of desertlike conditions is <u>famine</u>.

8. Some animals can graze in the <u>Sahel</u>.

Comprehension and Critical Thinking

SECTION 1 *(Pages 516–519)*

9. **a. Identify** What are the four climate zones of West Africa?

   b. Make Inferences What are some problems caused by desertification?

   c. Elaborate West Africa has valuable resources such as gold and diamonds. Why do you think these resources have not made West Africa a rich region?

SECTION 2 *(Pages 520–523)*

10. **a. Recall** What religion do most people in the Sahel practice?

    b. Analyze What role did trade play in the early West African kingdoms and later in West Africa's history?

    c. Elaborate What might be some advantages of living with an extended family?

SECTION 3 *(Pages 526–530)*

11. a. Identify Which country in West Africa has an economy based nearly entirely on oil?

   b. Compare and Contrast What is one similarity and one difference between the cause of civil war in Nigeria and its cause in Liberia?

   c. Predict How might the recent discovery of oil in Chad affect that country in the future?

Using the Internet

12. Activity: Creating a Postcard Come and learn about the mighty baobab tree. This unique tree looks as if it has been plucked from the ground and turned upside down. These trees are known not only for their unique look but also for their great size. Some are so big that a chain of 30 people is needed to surround one tree trunk! Enter the activity keyword to visit Web sites about baobab trees in West Africa. Then create a postcard about this strange wonder of nature.

FOCUS ON READING AND SPEAKING

Understanding Comparison-Contrast *Look over your notes or re-read Section 1. Use the information on climate and vegetation to answer the following questions.*

13. How are the Sahara and the Sahel similar?

14. How are the Sahara and the Sahel different?

15. Compare the Sahel and the savanna zone. How are they similar?

16. Contrast the savanna region and the humid tropical region along the coast. How are these areas different?

17. Giving an Oral Description Read over your notes. Then prepare a brief oral presentation about a day in the life of someone from West Africa. Tell about the land, climate, and vegetation. Describe the culture, including family life. Tell what this person does for a living. Practice your presentation several times before you give it so you can make frequent eye contact with your audience. During your presentation, remember to speak loudly and clearly. Use good descriptive language to interest your audience in your topic.

Social Studies Skills

Analyzing a Precipitation Map *Use the precipitation map in the Social Studies Skills lesson to answer the following questions.*

18. What countries have areas that receive under 10 inches of rain every year?

19. Where in West Africa does the most rain typically fall?

20. How would you describe annual precipitation in Chad?

21. How would you describe annual precipitation in Benin?

Map Activity

22. West Africa On a separate sheet of paper, match the letters on the map with their correct labels.

Niger River	Senegal River
Lagos, Nigeria	Mali
Gulf of Guinea	

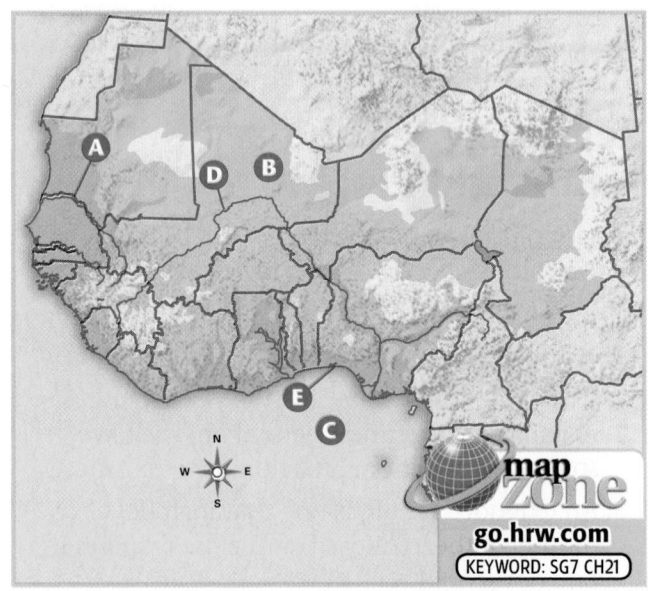

DIRECTIONS: Read questions 1 through 6 and write the letter of the best response. Then read question 7 and write your own well-constructed response.

1 The climate zone just south of the Sahara is called the

A desert.

B savanna.

C Sahel.

D tropical forest.

2 Which West African country was named for an ancient kingdom in the region?

A Liberia

B Nigeria

C Chad

D Ghana

3 Which of the following statements about the slave trade is false?

A European slave traders built schools and railroads in West Africa.

B European slave traders profited from it.

C It broke up families in West Africa.

D Enslaved Africans were sent to the Americas to meet the increased demand for labor there.

4 Which country in West Africa has an economy based on oil?

A Niger

B Nigeria

C Mauritania

D Mali

5 Which country has one of the most stable democratic governments in Africa?

A Nigeria

B Liberia

C Cape Verde

D Sierra Leone

West Africa: Population

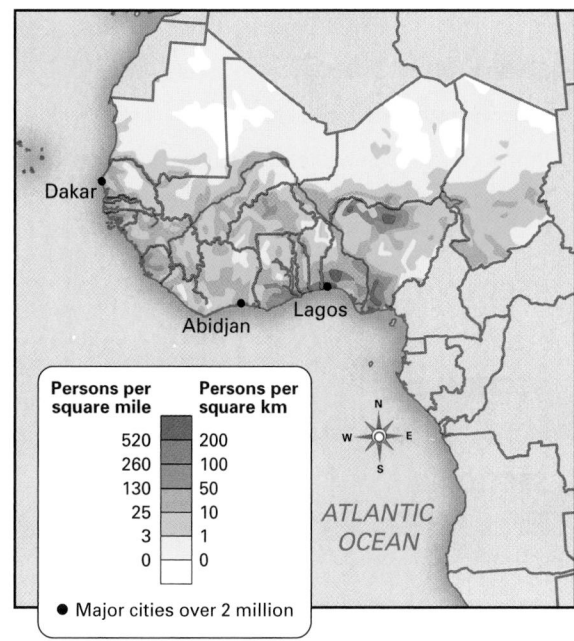

6 Based on the map above, which of the following sentences is true?

A West Africa has only one city with a population over 2 million.

B West Africa's highest population density is in the Sahel countries.

C Most of the region's population is in the south.

D The region around Dakar has a population density of over 520 people per square mile.

7 Extended Response Compare the map above to the climate map in Section 1. Then write a brief essay explaining factors that affect human settlement in West Africa. One paragraph should explain how the two maps are related. Another paragraph should describe physical factors that influence settlement.

East Africa

What You Will Learn...

In this chapter you will learn about the physical geography of East Africa. You will also learn about the region's rich history and culture. Finally, you will study the countries of East Africa today.

FOCUS ON READING AND WRITING

Identifying Supporting Details Supporting details are the facts and examples that provide information to support the main ideas of a chapter, section, or paragraph. At the beginning of each section in this book, there is a list of main ideas. As you read this chapter, look for the details that support each section's main ideas. **See the lesson, Identifying Supporting Details, on page R23**.

Writing a Letter Home Imagine that you are spending your summer vacation visiting the countries of East Africa. You want to write a letter home to a friend in the United States describing the land and its people. As you read this chapter, you will gather information that you can include in your letter.

History This gold artifact is from the early Nubian civilization of northern Sudan.

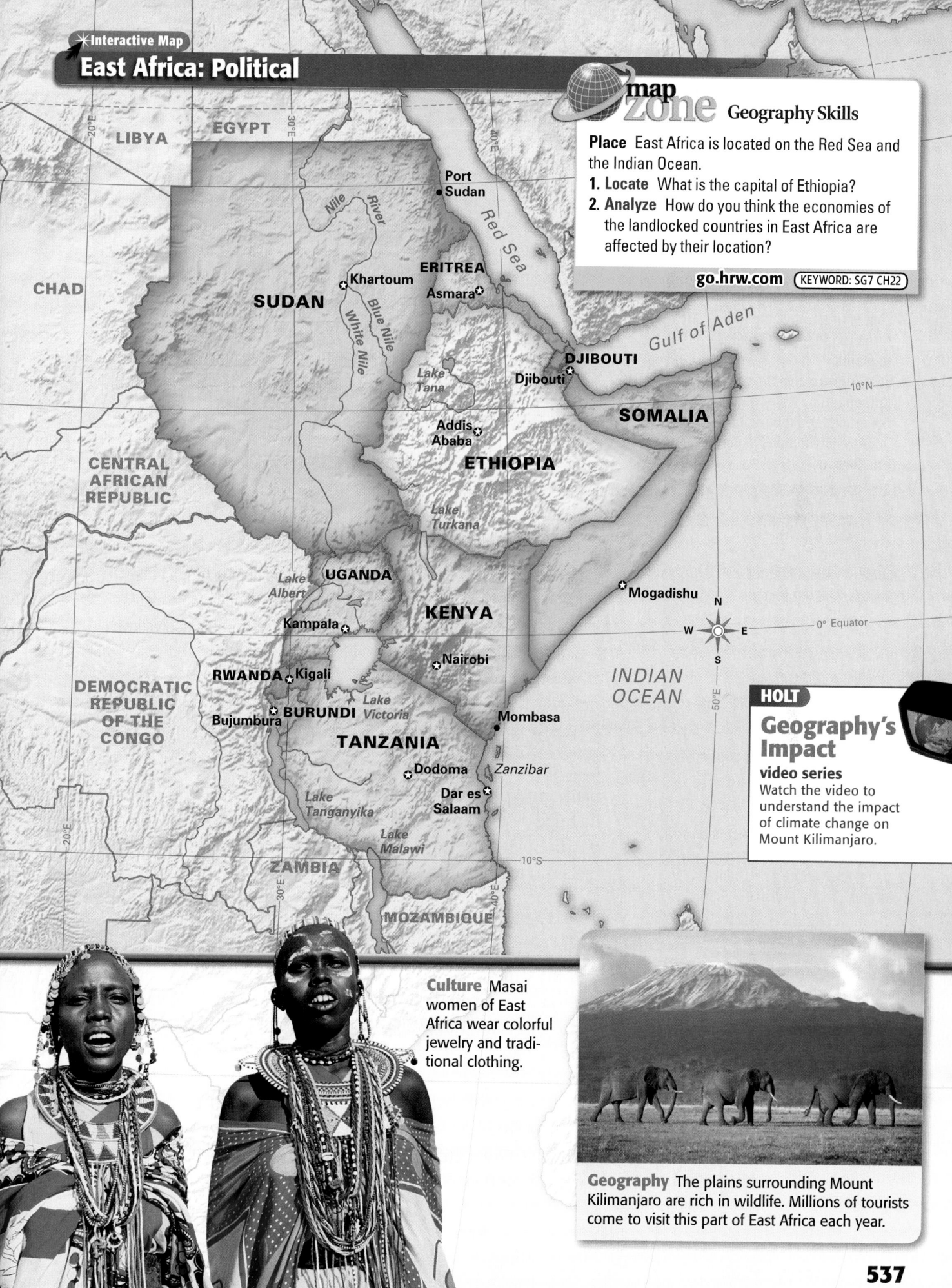

map zone Geography Skills

Place East Africa is located on the Red Sea and the Indian Ocean.
1. **Locate** What is the capital of Ethiopia?
2. **Analyze** How do you think the economies of the landlocked countries in East Africa are affected by their location?

go.hrw.com **KEYWORD: SG7 CH22**

LIBYA

EGYPT

20°E

30°E

Nile River

Port Sudan

Red Sea

40°E

CHAD

SUDAN

Khartoum

White Nile

Blue Nile

ERITREA

Asmara

Gulf of Aden

CENTRAL AFRICAN REPUBLIC

Lake Tana

DJIBOUTI

Djibouti

SOMALIA

10°N

Addis Ababa

ETHIOPIA

Lake Turkana

UGANDA

Lake Albert

Kampala

KENYA

Mogadishu

N

DEMOCRATIC REPUBLIC OF THE CONGO

RWANDA Kigali

Nairobi

W   E

S

0° Equator

BURUNDI

Bujumbura

Lake Victoria

Mombasa

INDIAN OCEAN

50°E

HOLT

Geography's Impact
video series
Watch the video to understand the impact of climate change on Mount Kilimanjaro.

TANZANIA

Dodoma

Zanzibar

Lake Tanganyika

Dar es Salaam

Lake Malawi

20°E

30°E

10°S

40°E

ZAMBIA

MOZAMBIQUE

Culture Masai women of East Africa wear colorful jewelry and traditional clothing.

Geography The plains surrounding Mount Kilimanjaro are rich in wildlife. Millions of tourists come to visit this part of East Africa each year.

537

Physical Geography

If YOU lived there...

You and your friends are planning to hike up Mount Kilimanjaro, near the equator in Tanzania. It is hot in your camp at the base of the mountain. You're wearing shorts and a T-shirt, but your guide tells you to pack a fleece jacket and jeans. You start your climb, and soon you understand this advice. The air is much colder, and there's snow on the nearby peaks.

Why is it cold at the top of the mountain?

BUILDING BACKGROUND The landscapes of East Africa have been shaped by powerful forces. The movement of tectonic plates has stretched the Earth's surface here, creating steep-sided valleys and huge lakes.

Physical Features

East Africa is a region of spectacular landscapes and wildlife. Vast plains and plateaus stretch throughout the region. In the north lie huge deserts and dry grasslands. In the southwest, large lakes dot the plateaus. In the east, sandy beaches and colorful coral reefs run along the coast.

The Rift Valleys

Look at the map on the next page. As you can see, East Africa's rift valleys cut from north to south across the region. **Rift valleys** are places on Earth's surface where the crust stretches until it breaks. Rift valleys form when Earth's tectonic plates move away from each other. This movement causes the land to arch and split along the rift valleys. As the land splits open, volcanoes erupt and deposit layers of rock in the region.

Seen from the air, the **Great Rift Valley** looks like a giant scar. The Great Rift Valley is the largest rift on Earth and is made up of two rifts—the eastern rift and the western rift.

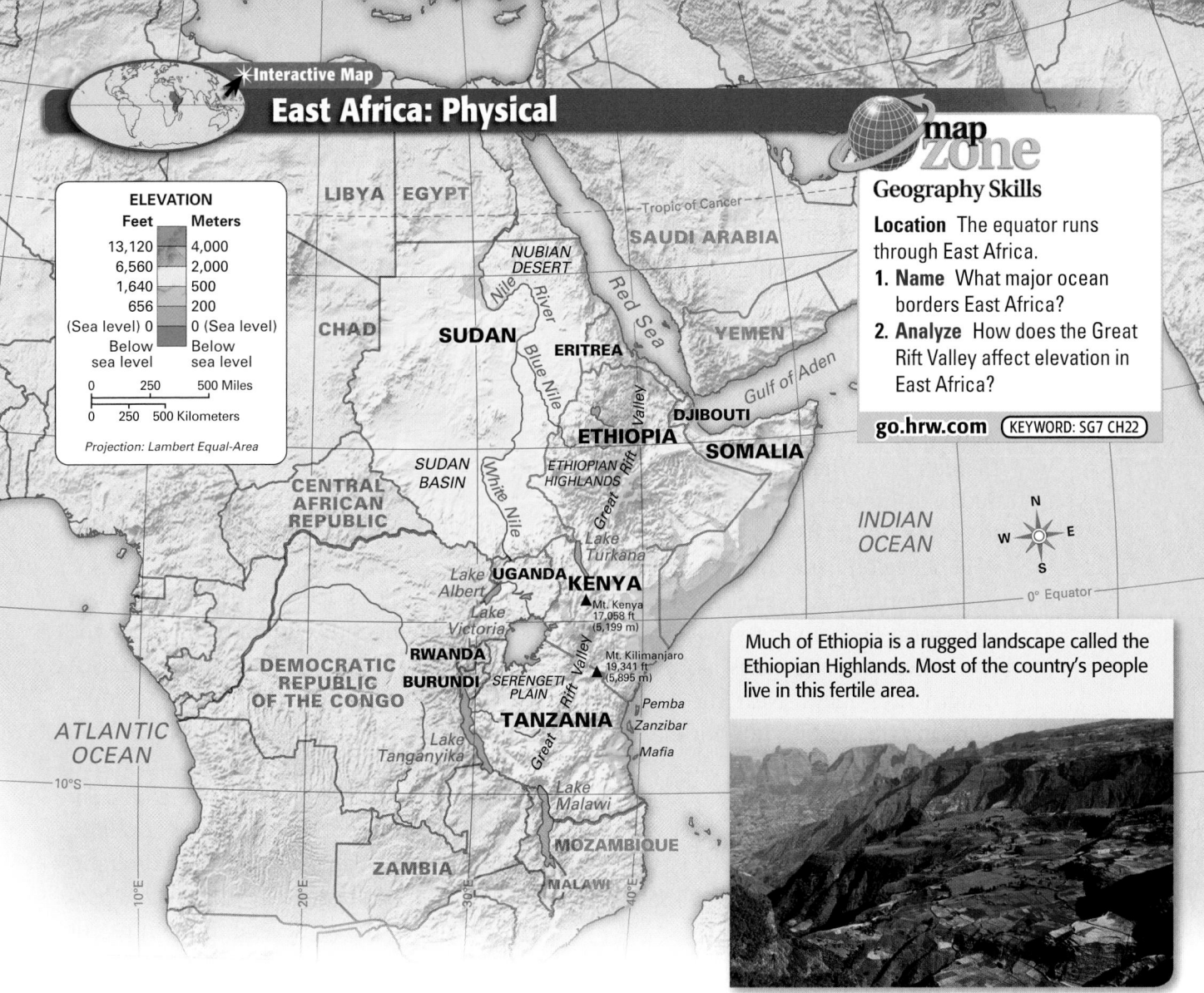

East Africa: Physical

map zone

ELEVATION

Feet	Meters
13,120	4,000
6,560	2,000
1,640	500
656	200
(Sea level) 0	0 (Sea level)
Below sea level	Below sea level

0   250   500 Miles

0   250   500 Kilometers

Projection: Lambert Equal-Area

Geography Skills

Location The equator runs through East Africa.
1. **Name** What major ocean borders East Africa?
2. **Analyze** How does the Great Rift Valley affect elevation in East Africa?

go.hrw.com   **KEYWORD: SG7 CH22**

LIBYA   EGYPT

Tropic of Cancer

SAUDI ARABIA

NUBIAN DESERT

Nile

River

Red Sea

CHAD   SUDAN   ERITREA   YEMEN

Blue Nile

Gulf of Aden

DJIBOUTI

ETHIOPIA   SOMALIA

CENTRAL AFRICAN REPUBLIC

SUDAN BASIN

ETHIOPIAN HIGHLANDS

Great Rift Valley

White Nile

Lake Turkana

INDIAN OCEAN

N W E S

0° Equator

Lake Albert   UGANDA   KENYA

▲ Mt. Kenya 17,058 ft (5,199 m)

Lake Victoria

RWANDA   Mt. Kilimanjaro 19,341 ft (5,895 m) ▲

DEMOCRATIC REPUBLIC OF THE CONGO

BURUNDI   SERENGETI PLAIN

Great Rift Valley

TANZANIA   Pemba Zanzibar

Mafia

ATLANTIC OCEAN

10°S

Lake Tanganyika

Lake Malawi

ZAMBIA   MOZAMBIQUE

MALAWI

Much of Ethiopia is a rugged landscape called the Ethiopian Highlands. Most of the country's people live in this fertile area.

The rift walls are usually a series of steep cliffs. These cliffs rise as much as 6,000 feet (2,000 m).

Mountains and Highlands

The landscape of East Africa has many high volcanic mountains. The highest mountain in Africa, **Mount Kilimanjaro** (ki-luh-muhn-JAHR-oh), rises to 19,340 feet (5,895 m). Despite Kilimanjaro's location near the equator, the mountain's peak has long been covered in snow. This much colder climate is caused by Kilimanjaro's high elevation.

Other areas of high elevation in East Africa include the Ethiopian Highlands.

These highlands, which lie mostly in Ethiopia, are very rugged. Deep river valleys cut through this landscape.

Plains

Even though much of East Africa lies at high elevations, some areas are flat. For example, plains stretch as far as the eye can see along the eastern rift in Tanzania and Kenya. Tanzania's **Serengeti Plain** is one of the largest plains. It is here that an abundance of wildlife thrives. The plain's grasses, trees, and water provide nutrition for wildlife that includes elephants, giraffes, lions, and zebras. To protect this wildlife, Tanzania established a national park.

Rivers and Lakes

FOCUS ON READING
What details in this paragraph support this section's second main idea?

East Africa also has a number of rivers and large lakes. The world's longest river, the Nile, begins in East Africa and flows north to the Mediterranean Sea. The Nile is formed by the meeting of the Blue Nile and the White Nile at Khartoum, Sudan. The White Nile is formed by the water that flows into Africa's largest lake, **Lake Victoria**. The Blue Nile is formed from waters that run down from Ethiopia's highlands. As the Nile meanders through Sudan, it provides a narrow, fertile lifeline to farmers in the desert.

The region has a number of great lakes in addition to Lake Victoria. One group of lakes forms a chain in the western rift valleys. There are also lakes along the drier eastern rift valleys. Near the eastern rift, heat from the Earth's interior makes some lakes so hot that no human can swim in them. In addition, some lakes are extremely salty. However, some of these rift lakes provide algae for the region's flamingos.

READING CHECK **Evaluating** What river is the most important in this region? Why?

Climate and Vegetation

When you think of Africa, do you think of it as being a hot or cold place? Most people usually think all of Africa is hot. However, they are mistaken. Some areas of East Africa have a cool climate.

East Africa's location on the equator and differences in elevation influence the climates and types of vegetation in East Africa. For example, areas near the equator receive the greatest amount of rainfall. Areas farther from the equator are much drier and seasonal droughts are common. **Droughts** are periods when little rain falls, and crops are damaged. During a drought, crops and the grasses for cattle die and people begin to starve. Several times in recent decades droughts have affected the people of East Africa.

Further south of the equator the climate changes to tropical savanna. Tall grasses and scattered trees make up the savanna landscape. Here the greatest climate changes occur along the sides of the rift valleys. The rift floors are dry with grasslands and thorn shrubs.

North of the equator, areas of plateaus and mountains have a highland climate and dense forests. Temperatures in the highlands are much cooler than temperatures on the savanna. The highlands experience heavy rainfall because of its high elevation, but the valleys are drier. This mild climate makes farming possible. As a result, most of the region's population lives in the highlands.

Satellite View

Great Rift Valley

This satellite image of part of the Great Rift Valley in Ethiopia was created by using both infrared light and true color. The bright blue dots are some of the smaller lakes that were created by the rifts. Once active volcanoes, some of these lakes are very deep. Vegetation appears as areas of green. Bare, rocky land appears pink and gray.

Analyzing How were the lakes in the Great Rift Valley created?

Ancient volcanoes surround Uganda's Lake Mutanda. Here villagers rely on the lake's plentiful supply of fish.

Areas east of the highlands and on the Indian Ocean coast are at a much lower elevation. These areas have desert and steppe climates. Vegetation is limited to shrubs and hardy grasses that are adapted to water shortages.

READING CHECK **Categorizing** What are some of East Africa's climate types?

SUMMARY AND PREVIEW In this section you learned about East Africa's rift valleys, mountains, highlands, plains, rivers, and lakes. You also learned that the region's location and elevation affect its climate and vegetation. In the next section you will learn about East Africa's history and culture.

Section 1 Assessment

go.hrw.com
Online Quiz
KEYWORD: SG7 HP22

Reviewing Ideas, Terms, and Places

1. **a. Define** What are **rift valleys**?
   b. Explain Why is there snow on **Mount Kilimanjaro**?
   c. Elaborate What are some unusual characteristics of the lakes in the **Great Rift Valley**?
2. **a. Recall** What is the climate of the highlands in East Africa like?
   b. Draw Conclusions What are some effects of **drought** in the region?
   c. Develop How are the climates of some areas of East Africa affected by elevation?

Critical Thinking

3. **Categorizing** Using your notes and this chart, place details about East Africa's physical features into different categories.

Physical Features			
Rift Valleys	Mountains and Highlands	Plains	Rivers and Lakes

FOCUS ON WRITING

4. **Describing the Physical Geography** Note the physical features of East Africa that you can describe in your letter. How do these features compare to the features where you live?

History and Culture

What You Will Learn...

Main Ideas

1. The history of East Africa is one of religion, trade, and European influence.
2. East Africans speak many different languages and practice several different religions.

The Big Idea

East Africa is a region with a rich history and diverse cultures.

Key Terms and Places

Nubia, *p. 542*
Zanzibar, *p. 543*
imperialism, *p. 543*

TAKING NOTES As you read, use this diagram to take notes on East Africa's history and culture.

History

Culture

If **YOU** lived there...

You live on the island of Zanzibar, part of the country of Tanzania. Your hometown has beautiful beaches, historic palaces, and sites associated with the East African slave trade. Although you and your friends learn English in school, you speak the African language of Swahili to each other.

How has your country's history affected your life today?

BUILDING BACKGROUND For almost a century, nearly all the countries of East Africa were controlled by European countries. Before that, however, the region's people had close trade ties with Arabs from Southwest Asia. This Arab influence blended with native African cultures to form a new culture and language.

History

Early civilizations in East Africa were highly developed. Later, Christianity and Islam influenced the lives of many East Africans. Other influences included trade, the arrival of Europeans, ethnic conflict, and independence.

Christianity and Islam

Christian missionaries from Egypt first introduced Christianity to Ethiopia as early as the AD 300s. About 200 years later Christianity spread into **Nubia**, an area of Egypt and Sudan today.

In the early 1200s, a powerful Christian emperor named Lalibela ruled Ethiopia. Lalibela is best known for the 11 rock churches he built during his reign. He claimed that God told him to carve the churches out of the rocky ground. Today, the town where the churches are located is called Lalibela.

By about AD 700, Islam was a major religion in Egypt and other parts of North Africa. Gradually, Muslim Arabs from Egypt

Lalibela, Ethiopia

In the 1200s, highly skilled Ethiopian architects and craftspeople built this Christian church at Lalibela.

ANALYZING VISUALS What Christian symbol does the church resemble?

Workers dug deep trenches to carve out the church.

Craftspeople used special tools to carve windows and doors out of solid rock.

spread into northern Sudan and brought their Islamic faith with them. At the same time, Islam spread to the Indian Ocean coast of what is now Somalia. City-states such as Mogadishu and Mombasa became major Islamic centers and controlled trade on the coast.

The Slave Trade

The slave trade along the Indian Ocean coast dates back more than 1,000 years. East Africans, Arabs, and Europeans all participated in the slave trade in East Africa. They kidnapped Africans, enslaved them, and shipped them to ports throughout Africa and Southwest Asia. Most of these slaves went to Islamic countries. By the early 1500s the Portuguese had begun setting up forts and settlements on the East African coast to support the slave trade.

In the late 1700s the East African island of **Zanzibar** became an international slave-trading center. Later, large plantations with slave labor were set up by Europeans in the interior. They grew crops of cloves and sugarcane.

European Influence and Conflict

Most European nations ended slavery in the early 1800s. They focused instead on trading products such as gold, ivory, and rubber. To get these goods, Europeans believed they needed to dominate regions of Africa rich in these natural resources. Europeans also wanted to expand their empires by establishing more colonies. The British were the most aggressive, and they gained control over much of East Africa.

In the 1880s Britain and other European powers divided up most of Africa. They drew boundaries that separated some ethnic groups. To maintain power over their colonies, Europeans used **imperialism**, a practice that tries to dominate other countries' government, trade, and culture.

Within East Africa, just Kenya was settled by large numbers of Europeans. Under imperialism, colonial rulers usually controlled their countries through African deputies. Many of the deputies were traditional chiefs. These chiefs were loyal to their own peoples, which tended to strengthen ethnic rivalries. Today governments are trying to influence feelings of national identity, but ethnic conflict is still strong in many countries.

FOCUS ON READING

In the second paragraph under Languages, find at least two details to support the main idea in the first sentence.

In the early 1960s, most East African countries gained independence from European colonizers. Ethiopia was never colonized. Its mountains provided natural protection, and its peoples resisted European colonization.

Independence, however, did not solve all of the problems of the former colonies. In addition, new challenges faced the newly independent countries. For example, some countries experienced ethnic conflicts.

READING CHECK **Evaluating** Why was Ethiopia never a European colony?

Culture

Over thousands of years of human settlement, East Africa developed a great diversity of people and ways of life. As a result, East Africans speak many different languages and practice several religions.

Language

East Africa's history of European imperialism influenced language in many countries in the region. For example, French is an official language in Rwanda, Burundi, and Djibouti today. English is the primary language of millions of people in Uganda, Kenya, and Tanzania.

In addition to European languages, many East Africans also speak African languages. Swahili is the most widely spoken African language in the region. As East Africans traded with Arabic speakers from Southwest Asia, Swahili developed. In fact, Swahili comes from the Arabic word meaning "on the coast." Today about 80 million people speak Swahili. Ethiopians speak Amharic, and Somalians speak Somali.

FOCUS ON CULTURE

The Swahili

For more than 1,000 years, a culture unlike any other has thrived along the coast of modern-day Kenya and Tanzania. In the AD 700s, trade contacts between East Africans and Arab traders began. Over time these interactions led to the creation of a unique language and culture known as Swahili.

The Swahili adopted some cultural traits from Arab traders. For example, many East Africans converted to the religion of the Arab traders—Islam. African languages blended with Arabic to form the Swahili language.

Generalizing What effects did Arab traders have on Swahili culture?

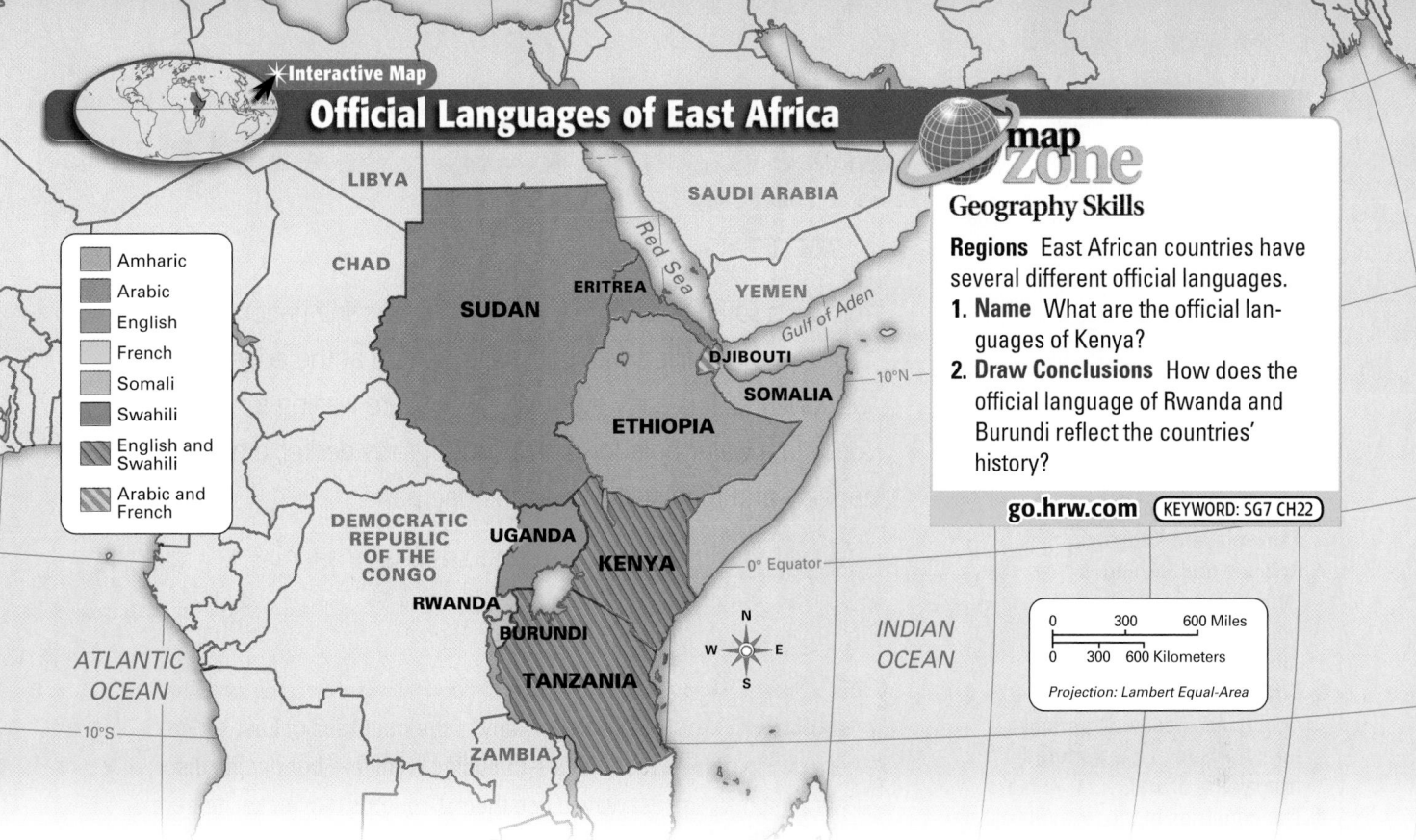

Official Languages of East Africa

Interactive Map

Legend:
- Amharic
- Arabic
- English
- French
- Somali
- Swahili
- English and Swahili
- Arabic and French

map zone

Geography Skills

Regions East African countries have several different official languages.
1. **Name** What are the official languages of Kenya?
2. **Draw Conclusions** How does the official language of Rwanda and Burundi reflect the countries' history?

go.hrw.com KEYWORD: SG7 CH22

Religion

Religion is an important aspect of culture for many East Africans. While the religions in East Africa vary greatly, most of them place emphasis on honoring ancestors.

Many East Africans are followers of animist religions. Animists believe the natural world contains spirits. Some people also combine animist worship with religions such as Christianity. Most Christians in East Africa live in Ethiopia. Islam is also practiced in the region. Sudan and Somalia are predominantly Muslim.

READING CHECK **Analyzing** Why might people in East Africa speak a European language?

SUMMARY AND PREVIEW In this section you learned about the history and culture of East Africa. Next, you will learn about the countries of East Africa today.

---

go.hrw.com
Online Quiz
KEYWORD: SG7 HP22

Section 2 Assessment

Reviewing Ideas, Terms, and Places

1. **a. Define** What is **imperialism**?
   b. Explain What did the emperor Lalibela have architects build in Ethiopia?
   c. Evaluate Why do you think Europeans wanted colonies in East Africa?
2. **a. Identify** What language do most people in Uganda speak?
   b. Explain What do animists believe?
   c. Elaborate How have languages and religion influenced culture in East Africa?

Critical Thinking

3. **Summarizing** Using your notes and this chart, write two sentences that summarize what you learned about the region's languages and religions.

Language	
Religion	

FOCUS ON WRITING

4. **Writing about History and Culture** What aspects of the history and culture of East Africa might interest your friend? Note ideas for your letter.

East Africa Today

If YOU lived there...

You are a safari guide in one of Kenya's amazing national parks. Your safari van, filled with tourists, is parked at the edge of the vast savanna. It is early evening, and you are waiting for animals to come to a water hole for a drink. As it grows darker, a huge lion appears and then stalks away on huge paws.

What benefits do tourists bring to your country?

BUILDING BACKGROUND Many of the countries of East Africa are rich in natural resources—including wildlife—but people disagree about the best way to use them. Droughts can make life here difficult. In addition, political and ethnic conflicts have led to unrest and violence in some areas of the region.

What You Will Learn...

Main Ideas

1. National parks are a major source of income for Tanzania and Kenya.
2. Rwanda and Burundi are densely populated rural countries with a history of ethnic conflict.
3. Both Sudan and Uganda have economies based on agriculture, but Sudan has suffered from years of war.
4. The countries of the Horn of Africa are among the poorest in the world.

The Big Idea

East Africa has abundant national parks, but most of the region's countries are poor and recovering from conflicts.

Key Terms and Places

safari, *p. 547*
geothermal energy, *p. 547*
genocide, *p. 549*
Darfur, *p. 549*
Mogadishu, *p. 551*

TAKING NOTES As you read, take notes on East Africa's people and economies. Use a chart like the one below to organize your notes.

	People	Economy
Tanzania and Kenya		
Rwanda and Burundi		
Sudan and Uganda		
Horn of Africa		

Close-up

Serengeti National Park

The Serengeti Plain is home to one of the world's greatest concentrations of wildlife. In Tanzania, part of the plain is a national park. About 100,000 tourists visit the Serengeti each year to view its diverse wildlife.

Huge herds of wildebeest migrate across the Serengeti each year.

ANALYSIS SKILL **ANALYZING VISUALS**

How would you describe the Serengeti landscape?

Tanzania and Kenya Today

The economies of both Tanzania and Kenya rely heavily on tourism and agriculture. However, both countries are among the poorest in the world.

Economy and Resources

Tanzania and Kenya are popular tourist destinations. With about 2 million tourists visiting each year, tourism is a major source of income for both countries. Today many tourists visit Tanzania and Kenya to go on a safari in the countries' numerous national parks. A **safari** is an overland journey to view African wildlife.

In addition to tourism, Tanzania is particularly rich in gold and diamonds. However, it is still a poor country of mainly subsistence farmers. Poor soils and limited technology have restricted productivity.

In Kenya, much of the land has been set aside as national parkland. Many people would like to farm these lands, but farming would endanger African wildlife. Kenya's economy and tourism industry would likely be **affected** as well.

Kenya's economy relies mostly on agriculture. Mount Kilimanjaro's southern slopes are a rich agricultural region. The rich soils here provide crops of coffee and tea for exports.

Kenya's economy also benefits from another natural resource—geothermal energy. **Geothermal energy** is energy produced from the heat of Earth's interior. This heat—in the form of extremely hot steam—comes up to the surface through cracks in the rift valleys.

ACADEMIC VOCABULARY

affect to change or influence

READING CHECK **Finding Main Ideas** What activity supports the economies of both Tanzania and Kenya?

Tanzanian guides take visitors on a safari to view Serengeti's wildlife.

Watering holes attract wildlife, which includes flamingos, hippos, and giraffes.

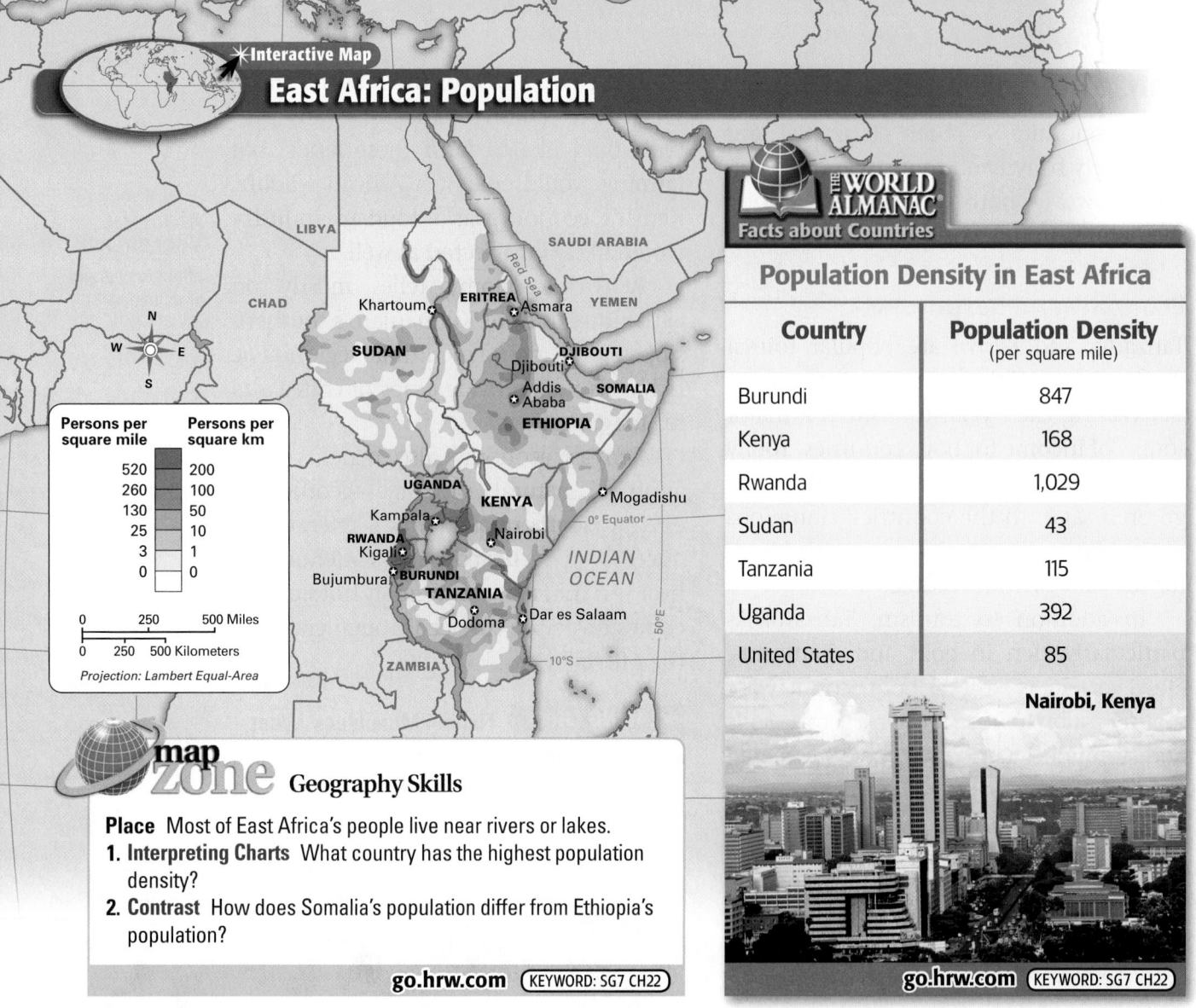

THE WORLD ALMANAC
Facts about Countries

Population Density in East Africa

Country	Population Density (per square mile)
Burundi	847
Kenya	168
Rwanda	1,029
Sudan	43
Tanzania	115
Uganda	392
United States	85

Nairobi, Kenya

go.hrw.com **KEYWORD: SG7 CH22**

Persons per square mile / Persons per square km

Persons per square mile	Persons per square km
520	200
260	100
130	50
25	10
3	1
0	0

0   250   500 Miles
0   250   500 Kilometers
Projection: Lambert Equal-Area

map zone Geography Skills

Place Most of East Africa's people live near rivers or lakes.
1. **Interpreting Charts** What country has the highest population density?
2. **Contrast** How does Somalia's population differ from Ethiopia's population?

go.hrw.com **KEYWORD: SG7 CH22**

Cities

Imagine a large city with businesspeople hurrying to work, colorful outdoor markets, soaring skyscrapers, and beautiful parks. The capitals of Tanzania and Kenya both fit this description of a vibrant, modern African city.

Tanzania's official capital is Dodoma. The Tanzanian government began moving its capital from Dar es Salaam to Dodoma in the mid-1970s. Dar es Salaam, a port city with about 3 million people, is located on the Indian Ocean and is Tanzania's business center.

Kenya's capital, Nairobi, also serves as the country's industrial center. In addition, Nairobi is well connected with the rest of East Africa by a network of railways. By rail, Kenya transports tea and other major crops to the major port of Mombasa.

Even though Kenya and Tanzania are peaceful countries, Dar es Salaam and Nairobi have both endured terrorist attacks. In 1998 members of the al Qaeda terrorist group bombed the U.S. embassies in Dar es Salaam and Nairobi. Most of the more than 250 people killed and the thousands injured were Africans.

READING CHECK **Draw Conclusions** Why do you think it would be important for the railroad to link Kenya's cities?

Rwanda and Burundi Today

Rwanda and Burundi are mostly populated by two ethnic groups—the Tutsi and the Hutu. Since gaining independence from Germany, differences between the Tutsi and Hutu ethnic groups have led to conflict in Rwanda and Burundi. These conflicts have roots in the region's history. The colonial borders of Rwanda and Burundi drawn by Europeans often lumped different ethnic groups into one country.

In Rwanda in the 1990s, hatred between the Hutu and the Tutsi led to genocide. A **genocide** is the intentional destruction of a people. The Hutu tried to completely wipe out the Tutsi. Armed bands of Hutu killed hundreds of thousands of Tutsi.

Rwanda and Burundi are two of the most densely populated countries in all of Africa. These two countries are located in fertile highlands and share a history as German colonies. Both countries lack resources and rely on coffee and tea exports for economic earnings.

READING CHECK **Analyzing** What contributed to the region's ethnic conflict?

Sudan and Uganda Today

Sudan is Africa's largest country. It is a mainly agricultural country with few mineral resources. Arab Muslims make up about 40 percent of Sudan's population and have political power. They dominate northern Sudan and the capital, Khartoum.

For decades, Sudan has suffered from religious and ethnic conflict. Muslims and Christians fought a civil war for many years. More recently, a genocide occurred in a region of Sudan called **Darfur**. Ethnic conflict there resulted in tens of thousands of black Sudanese being killed by an Arab militia group. Millions more have fled Darfur and are scattered throughout the region as refugees.

Today Uganda is still recovering from several decades of a military dictatorship. Since 1986 Uganda has become more democratic, but economic progress has been slow. About 80 percent of Uganda's workforce is employed in agriculture, with coffee as the country's major export.

READING CHECK **Summarizing** What ethnic group dominates northern Sudan?

FOCUS ON READING

In the paragraphs under Rwanda and Burundi, what details support the main idea that these countries have a history of ethnic conflict?

Refugees in Sudan

People from Sudan who fled the country's Darfur region receive food and aid at a refugee camp.

People of the Horn of Africa

More than half of Eritrea's population are Christian and belong to the Ethiopian Orthodox Church.

In Ethiopia, boys help their families herd sheep.

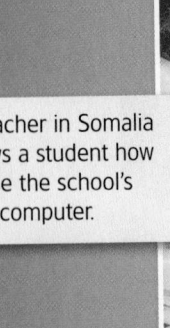

A teacher in Somalia shows a student how to use the school's new computer.

The Horn of Africa

Four East African countries located on the Red Sea and the Indian Ocean are called the Horn of Africa. This area is called the Horn because it resembles the horn of a rhinoceros. The Horn's people, economies, and resources vary by country.

Ethiopia

Unlike the other countries of the Horn of Africa, Ethiopia has never been under foreign rule. The country's mountains have protected the country from invasion.

In addition to providing a natural defense barrier, Ethiopia's rugged mountain slopes and highlands have rich volcanic soil. As a result, agriculture is Ethiopia's chief economic activity. Ethiopia's economy benefits from exports of coffee, livestock, and oilseeds. Many people also herd sheep and cattle.

During the last 30 years Ethiopia has experienced serious droughts. In the 1980s, drought caused the loss of crops and the starvation of several million people. In contrast, Ethiopia has experienced plenty of rainfall in recent years. Farmers are now able to grow their crops.

Most Ethiopians living in the highlands are Christian, while most of the lowland people are Muslim. Many Ethiopians speak Amharic, the country's official language.

Eritrea

In the late 1800s the Italians made present-day Eritrea a colony. In the 1960s it became an Ethiopian province.

After years of war with Ethiopia, Eritrea broke away from Ethiopia in 1993. Since then the economy has slowly improved. The country's Red Sea coastline is lined with spectacular coral reefs, which attract tourists to the country. Most Eritreans are farmers or herders. The country's economy relies largely on cotton exports.

Somalia

Somalia is a country of deserts and dry savannas. Because Somalia is so dry, much of the land is not suitable for farming. As a result, Somalis are nomadic herders. Livestock is the country's main export.

Somalia is less diverse than most other African countries. Most people in the country are members of a single ethnic group, the Somali. In addition, most Somalis are Muslims and speak the same African language, also called Somali.

Somalia has been troubled by violence in the past. In addition, the country has often had no central government of any kind. Different clans have fought over grazing rights and control over port cities such as **Mogadishu**.

In the 1990s Somalis experienced widespread starvation caused by a civil war and a severe drought. The United Nations sent aid and troops to the country. U.S. troops also assisted with this operation.

Djibouti

Djibouti (ji-BOO-tee) is a small, desert country. It lies on the Bab al-Mandab, which is the narrow strait that connects the Red Sea and the Indian Ocean. The strait lies along a major shipping route.

In the 1860s the French took control of Djibouti. It did not gain independence from France until 1977. The French government still contributes economic and military support to the country. As a result, French is one of Djibouti's two official languages. The other is Arabic.

The country's capital and major port is also called Djibouti. The capital serves as a port for landlocked Ethiopia. Since Djibouti has very few resources, the port is a major source of the country's income.

The people of Djibouti include two major ethnic groups—the Issa and the Afar. The Issa are closely related to the people of Somalia. The Afar are related to the people of Ethiopia. Members of both groups are Muslim. In the early 1990s, a civil war between the Afar and Issa broke out. In 2001 the two groups signed a peace treaty, which ended the fighting.

READING CHECK **Generalizing** What do the people of Djibouti have in common with people from other countries in East Africa?

SUMMARY AND PREVIEW The countries of East Africa are poor, but rich in wildlife and resources. Next, you will learn about the region of Central Africa.

go.hrw.com
Online Quiz
KEYWORD: SG7 HP22

Section 3 Assessment

Reviewing Ideas, Terms, and Places

1. a. **Define** What is **geothermal energy**?
   b. **Make Generalizations** Why are Kenyans not allowed to farm in national parks?
2. a. **Define** What is **genocide**?
   b. **Explain** What are the two ethnic groups that make up the population of Rwanda and Burundi?
3. a. **Identify** What is the largest country in Africa?
   b. **Analyze** Why are millions of Sudanese refugees?
4. a. **Recall** What two major world religions are practiced in Ethiopia?
   b. **Analyze** How do you think Djibouti's location has helped its economy?

Critical Thinking

5. **Summarize** Draw a chart like this one. Using your notes, summarize in at least two sentences what you learned about each country.

Ethiopia	→
Eritrea	→
Somalia	→
Djibouti	→

FOCUS ON WRITING

6. **Writing about East Africa Today** Think about what it would be like to travel through the East African countries. What would you want to tell your friend about their people, their governments, their economies? Make a list of the details you would share.

Social Studies Skills

Chart and Graph	Critical Thinking	Geography	Study

Doing Fieldwork and Using Questionnaires

Learn

To a geographer, fieldwork means visiting a place to learn more about it. While there, the geographer might visit major sites or talk to people to learn about their lives. He or she might also distribute a questionnaire.

A questionnaire is a document that asks people to provide information. Geographers use them to find out specific details about the people in an area, such as what languages they speak. Governments and other groups also use questionnaires to learn more about the people they serve.

Practice

The questionnaire to the right is one that might have been created by the government of Kenya. Study it to answer the questions below.

1 What details does the questionnaire ask about people living in the household?

2 How are the questions organized? Why do you think that is?

3 Why would asking for the person's age be an important question?

Republic of Kenya Population and Housing Census Form A: Information Regarding All Persons

Name
What are the names of all persons who live in this household?

_____

Relationship
What is your relationship to the head of the household? (circle one)

  1 Head
  2 Spouse
  3 Son
  4 Daughter
  5 Brother/Sister
  6 Father/Mother
  7 Other relative
  8 Non-relative

Age
How old are you?

Tribe Nationality
What is your tribe or nationality?

Religion
What is your religion? (circle one)

  1 Catholic
  2 Protestant
  3 Other Christian
  4 Muslim
  5 Traditionalist
  6 Other Religion
  7 No Religion

Birthplace
Where were you born?

_____

Apply

Work with a group of classmates to create a questionnaire about popular music. Think of five questions about popular music that you could ask your fellow students. Try to ask only multiple-choice and yes-or-no questions. These types of questions are easier to study than other questions are. Once you have completed your questionnaire, write a short explanation of what you hope to learn from each question.

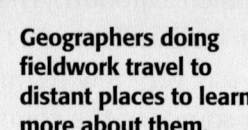

Geographers doing fieldwork travel to distant places to learn more about them.

Geography's Impact
video series
Review the video to answer the closing question:
How might the loss of Mount Kilimanjaro's glaciers affect people living in the area?

Visual Summary

Use the visual summary below to help you review the main ideas of the chapter.

QUICK FACTS

East Africa is a land of spectacular mountains, highlands, and lakes.

East Africa's history includes European imperialism and independence.

Even though many countries in East Africa are very poor, they are trying to improve educational opportunities.

Reviewing Vocabulary, Terms, and Places

Choose one word from each word pair to correctly complete each sentence below.

1. A_____(rift valley/plain) is a place on Earth's surface where the crust stretches until it breaks.

2. The tallest mountain in Africa is_____. (Mount Kilimanjaro/Mount Kenya)

3. _____means to change or influence. (geothermal energy/affect)

4. A_____is an overland journey that is taken to view African wildlife. (drought/safari)

5. _____has experienced serious droughts over the past 30 years. (Ethiopia/Kenya)

6. _____are periods when little rain falls and crops are damaged. (flood/drought)

7. The intentional destruction of a people is called_____. (murder/genocide)

8. _____is a practice which tries to dominate other countries' government, trade, and culture. (imperialism/influence)

9. A genocide committed by an Arab militia occured in the region of Sudan known as _____. (Darfur/Khartoum)

10. _____is an East African island that was an international slave-trading center in the late 1700s. (Madagascar/Zanzibar)

Comprehension and Critical Thinking

SECTION 1 *(Pages 538–541)*

11. **a. Identify** What is the Great Rift Valley? What is it made of?

 b. Draw Conclusions How is the Nile necessary for farming in the desert?

 c. Predict How do you think the effects of drought can be avoided in the future?

SECTION 2 *(Pages 542–545)*

12. **a. Recall** In which East African country did an emperor build 11 rock churches?

   b. Contrast How does the major religion practiced in Ethiopia differ from other religions practiced in East Africa?

   c. Elaborate How did the African language of Swahili develop?

SECTION 3 *(Pages 546–551)*

13. **a. Define** What is a safari?

   b. Draw Conclusions What economic activity do both Kenya and Tanzania rely on?

   c. Evaluate Why do you think the al Qaeda terrorist group bombed U.S. embassies in Dar es Salaam and Nairobi?

Using the Internet

go.hrw.com
KEYWORD: SG7 CH22

14. **Activity: Understanding Cultures** In the East African countries you read about in this chapter, there are hundreds of different ethnic groups. Enter the activity keyword. Discover some ethnic groups of East Africa as you visit Web sites about their culture. Then create a graphic organizer or chart that compares East African ethnic groups. It might include comparisons of language, beliefs, traditions, foods, and more.

Social Studies Skills

15. **Doing Fieldwork and Using Questionnaires** As in Kenya, the United States conducts a census of its population. Research what kinds of questions the U.S. Census asks Americans every 10 years. Go to the official U.S. Census Bureau's Web site at www.census.gov. There you will find examples of the questionnaires used in the 2000 Census. How do you think the questionnaires on the next U.S. Census in 2010 will be the same or different than the questions that were asked on the 2000 Census?

16. **Identifying Supporting Details** Look back over the paragraphs under the Culture heading in Section 2. Then make a list of details you find to support the section's main ideas. Make sure you include details about the different languages spoken in East Africa today.

17. **Writing a Letter** Now that you have information about East Africa, you need to organize it. Think about your audience, a friend at home, and what would feel natural if you had been traveling. Would you organize by topics like physical geography and culture? Or would you organize by country? After you organize your information, write a one-page letter.

Map Activity  Interactive

18. **East Africa** On a separate sheet of paper, match the letters on the map with their correct labels.

   Great Rift Valley   Mount Kilimanjaro

   Lake Victoria   Nile River

   Indian Ocean

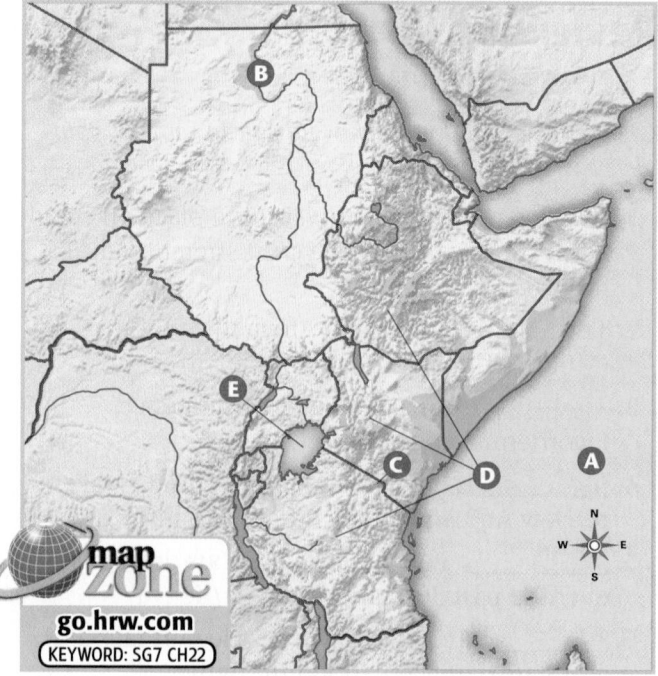

map zone
go.hrw.com
KEYWORD: SG7 CH22

Standardized Test Practice

DIRECTIONS: Read questions 1 through 7 and write the letter of the best response. Then read question 8 and write your own well-constructed response.

1 **What physical feature of East Africa is usually covered with snow and ice?**

A Serengeti Plain

B Mount Kilimanjaro

C Great Rift Valley

D Mount Kenya

2 **What is one cause of the cool climate in some areas of East Africa?**

A elevation

B drought

C Indian Ocean

D Great Rift Valley

3 **The Swahili language developed through trade contacts between East Africans and**

A the Chinese.

B Europeans.

C Arabs.

D West Africans.

4 **Tourism is a large part of the economy in**

A Tanzania and Kenya.

B Sudan and Uganda.

C Ethiopia and Eritrea.

D Rwanda and Burundi.

5 **Which East African country used to be a province of Ethiopia?**

A Djibouti

B Somalia

C Eritrea

D Kenya

> *"*Then they were over the first hills and the wildebeeste were trailing up them, and then they were over the mountains with sudden depths of green-rising forest and solid bamboo slopes, and then the heavy forest again, sculptured into peaks and hollows until they crossed, and hills sloped down and then another plain, hot now, and purple brown, bumpy with heat...*"*
>
> —Ernest Hemingway, "The Snows of Kilimanjaro"

6 **In the passage above, Hemingway describes the view of the Mount Kilimanjaro landscape from a plane. The landscape he describes is filled with**

A rivers.

B lakes.

C deserts.

D forests.

7 **In the passage above, the climate of the plain is described as**

A hot.

B dry.

C wet.

D cold.

8 **Extended Response** Look at the table and map of East Africa's population density in Section 3. Write a paragraph explaining why you think some areas of East Africa are more populated than other areas. Identify at least two reasons.

CHAPTER 23

Central Africa

What You Will Learn...

In this chapter you will learn about the rivers, forests, and resources of Central Africa. This region has been influenced by native traditions and Europeans, and you will read about how these influences have affected Central Africa's culture. Finally, you will learn about the different countries in Central Africa and some of the challenges these countries face.

FOCUS ON READING AND WRITING

Using Word Parts Many English words have little word parts at the beginning (prefixes) or the end (suffixes) of the word. When you come to an unfamiliar word in your reading, see if you can recognize a prefix or suffix to help you figure out the meaning of the word. **See the lesson, Using Word Parts, on page R24.**

Writing an Acrostic An acrostic is a type of poem in which the first letters of each line spell a word. The lines of the poem describe that word. As you read the chapter, think of a word—maybe a country name or a physical feature—that you would like to describe in your acrostic.

ATLANTIC OCEAN

0° Equator

- ⊛ National capital
- • Other cities

0   200   400 Miles
0   200   400 Kilometers

Projection: Lambert Azimuthal Equal-Area

10°S

Culture Drums and horns are used in traditional music from Central Africa. These musicians are from Cameroon.

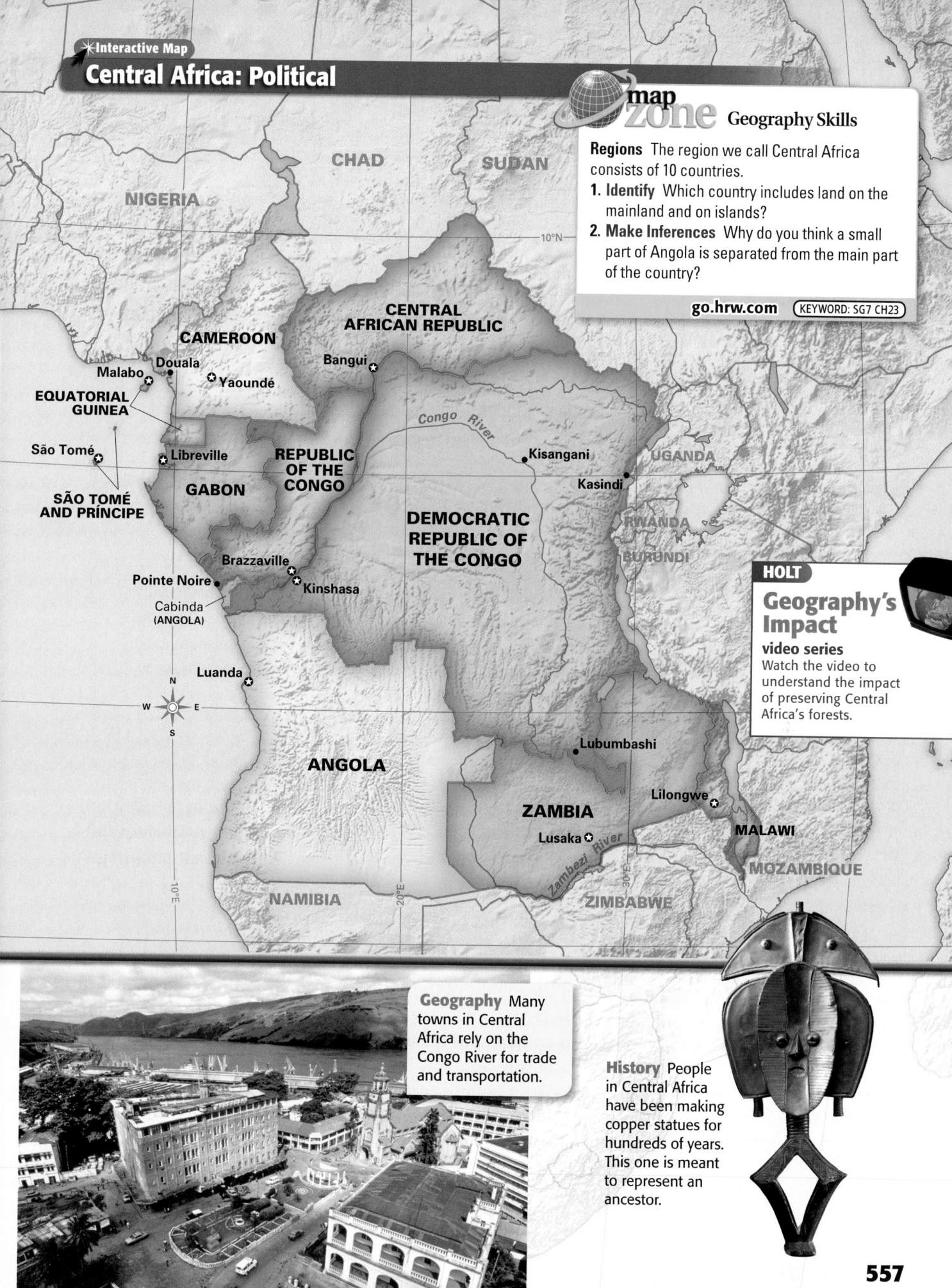

map zone Geography Skills

Regions The region we call Central Africa consists of 10 countries.
1. **Identify** Which country includes land on the mainland and on islands?
2. **Make Inferences** Why do you think a small part of Angola is separated from the main part of the country?

go.hrw.com KEYWORD: SG7 CH23

NIGERIA

CHAD

SUDAN

10°N

CENTRAL AFRICAN REPUBLIC

CAMEROON

Malabo

Douala

Yaoundé

Bangui

EQUATORIAL GUINEA

Congo River

Kisangani

São Tomé

Libreville

UGANDA

SÃO TOMÉ AND PRÍNCIPE

REPUBLIC OF THE CONGO

GABON

Kasindi

RWANDA

BURUNDI

DEMOCRATIC REPUBLIC OF THE CONGO

Brazzaville

Pointe Noire

Kinshasa

Cabinda (ANGOLA)

Luanda

Lubumbashi

N W E S

ANGOLA

Lilongwe

ZAMBIA

MALAWI

Lusaka

Zambezi River

MOZAMBIQUE

10°E

20°E

30°E

NAMIBIA

ZIMBABWE

HOLT

Geography's Impact

video series
Watch the video to understand the impact of preserving Central Africa's forests.

Geography Many towns in Central Africa rely on the Congo River for trade and transportation.

History People in Central Africa have been making copper statues for hundreds of years. This one is meant to represent an ancestor.

557

Physical Geography

Main Ideas

1. Central Africa's major physical features include the Congo Basin and plateaus surrounding the basin.
2. Central Africa has a humid tropical climate and dense forest vegetation.
3. Central Africa's resources include forest products and valuable minerals such as diamonds and copper.

The Big Idea

The Congo River, tropical forests, and mineral resources are important features of Central Africa's physical geography.

Key Terms and Places

Congo Basin, *p. 558*
basin, *p. 558*
Congo River, *p. 559*
Zambezi River, *p. 559*
periodic market, *p. 561*
copper belt, *p. 561*

 **TAKING NOTES** As you read, use a chart like the one here to note characteristics of Central Africa's physical geography.

Physical features	
Climate and vegetation	
Resources	

If **YOU** lived there...

You are on a nature hike with a guide through the forests of the Congo Basin. It has been several hours since you have seen any other people. Sometimes your guide has to cut a path through the thick vegetation, but mostly you try not to disturb any plants or animals. Suddenly, you reach a clearing and see a group of men working hard to load huge tree trunks onto big trucks.

How do you feel about what you see?

BUILDING BACKGROUND Much of Central Africa, particularly in the Congo Basin, is covered with thick, tropical forests. The forests provide valuable resources, but people have different ideas about how the forests should be used. Forests are just one of the many types of landscapes in Central Africa.

Physical Features

Central Africa is bordered by the Atlantic Ocean in the west. In the east, it is bordered by a huge valley called the Western Rift Valley. The land in between has some of the highest mountains and biggest rivers in Africa.

Landforms

You can think of the region as a big soup bowl with a wide rim. Near the middle of the bowl is the **Congo Basin**. In geography, a **basin** is a generally flat region surrounded by higher land such as mountains and plateaus.

Plateaus and low hills surround the Congo Basin. The highest mountains in Central Africa lie farther away from the basin, along the Western Rift Valley. Some of these snowcapped mountains rise to more than 16,700 feet (5,090 m). Two lakes also lie along the rift—Lake Nyasa and Lake Tanganyika (tan-guhn-YEE-kuh). Lake Nyasa is also called Lake Malawi.

Rivers

The huge **Congo River** is fed by hundreds of smaller rivers. They drain the swampy Congo Basin and flow into the river as it runs toward the Atlantic. Many rapids and waterfalls lie along its route, especially near its mouth. These obstacles make it impossible for ships to travel from the interior of Central Africa all the way to the Atlantic. The Congo provides an important transportation route in the interior, however.

In the southern part of the region, the **Zambezi** (zam-BEE-zee) **River** flows eastward toward the Indian Ocean. Many rivers in Angola and Zambia, as well as water from Lake Nyasa, flow into the Zambezi. The Zambezi also has many waterfalls along its route, the most famous of which are the spectacular Victoria Falls.

READING CHECK **Finding Main Ideas** Where is the highest land in Central Africa?

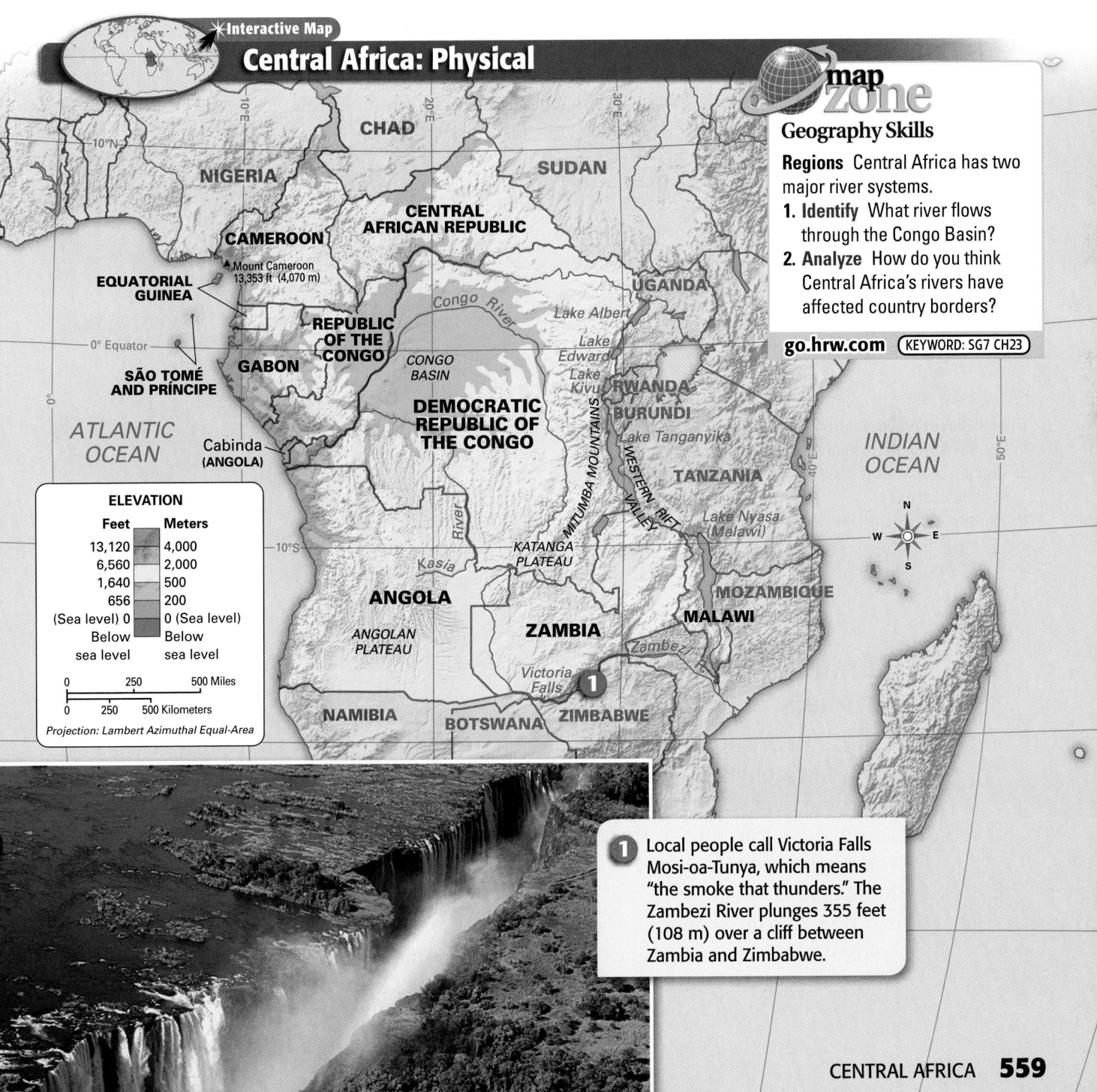

Interactive Map

Central Africa: Physical

map zone

Geography Skills

Regions Central Africa has two major river systems.

1. **Identify** What river flows through the Congo Basin?
2. **Analyze** How do you think Central Africa's rivers have affected country borders?

go.hrw.com (KEYWORD: SG7 CH23)

ELEVATION

Feet	Meters
13,120	4,000
6,560	2,000
1,640	500
656	200
(Sea level) 0	0 (Sea level)
Below sea level	Below sea level

0   250   500 Miles
0   250   500 Kilometers

Projection: Lambert Azimuthal Equal-Area

CHAD
NIGERIA
SUDAN
CAMEROON
CENTRAL AFRICAN REPUBLIC
Mount Cameroon 13,353 ft (4,070 m)
EQUATORIAL GUINEA
UGANDA
Congo River
Lake Albert
0° Equator
REPUBLIC OF THE CONGO
CONGO BASIN
Lake Edward
GABON
SÃO TOMÉ AND PRÍNCIPE
Lake Kivu
RWANDA
BURUNDI
ATLANTIC OCEAN
DEMOCRATIC REPUBLIC OF THE CONGO
Lake Tanganyika
Cabinda (ANGOLA)
MITUMBA MOUNTAINS
WESTERN RIFT VALLEY
TANZANIA
INDIAN OCEAN
River
Kasia
KATANGA PLATEAU
Lake Nyasa (Malawi)
ANGOLA
MOZAMBIQUE
MALAWI
ANGOLAN PLATEAU
ZAMBIA
Zambezi
Victoria Falls
1
NAMIBIA
BOTSWANA
ZIMBABWE

1 Local people call Victoria Falls Mosi-oa-Tunya, which means "the smoke that thunders." The Zambezi River plunges 355 feet (108 m) over a cliff between Zambia and Zimbabwe.

National parks in Central Africa protect the habitat of gorillas (above), which are endangered, and okapis (below).

National park areas

0	400	800 Miles
0	400	800 Kilometers

Projection: Lambert Azimuthal Equal-Area

map zone Geography Skills

Human-Environment Interaction People have created national parks in Central Africa to try to protect the region's landscapes and animals.
1. **Use the Map** What Central African countries have national parks in coastal areas?
2. **Explain** Why do people want to protect natural environments?

Climate, Vegetation, and Animals

Central Africa lies along the equator and in the low latitudes. Therefore, the Congo Basin and much of the Atlantic coast have a humid tropical climate. These areas have warm temperatures all year and receive a lot of rainfall.

This climate supports a large, dense tropical forest. The many kinds of tall trees in the forest form a complete canopy. The canopy is the uppermost layer of the trees where the limbs spread out. Canopy leaves block sunlight to the ground below.

Such animals as gorillas, elephants, wild boars, and okapis live in the forest. The okapi is a short-necked relative of the giraffe. However, since little sunlight shines through the canopy, only a few animals live on the forest floor. Some animals, such as birds, monkeys, bats, and snakes, live in the trees. Many insects also live in Central Africa's forest.

The animals in Central Africa's tropical forests, as well as the forests themselves, are in danger. Large areas of forest are being cleared rapidly for farming and logging. Also, people hunt the large animals in the forests to get food. To <u>promote</u> protection of forests and other natural environments, governments have set up national park areas in their countries.

North and south of the Congo Basin are large areas with a tropical savanna climate. Those areas are warm all year, but they have distinct dry and wet seasons. There are grasslands, scattered trees, and shrubs. The high mountains in the east have a highland climate. Dry steppe and even desert climates are found in the far southern part of the region.

READING CHECK **Summarizing** What are the climate and vegetation like in the Congo Basin?

Resources

The tropical environment of Central Africa is good for growing crops. Most people in the region are subsistence farmers. However, many farmers are now beginning to grow crops for sale. Common crops are coffee, bananas, and corn. In rural areas, people trade agricultural and other products in periodic markets. A **periodic market** is an open-air trading market that is set up once or twice a week.

Central Africa is rich in other natural resources as well. The large tropical forest provides timber, while the rivers provide a way to travel and to trade. Dams on the rivers produce hydroelectricity, an important energy resource. Other energy resources in the region include oil, natural gas, and coal.

Central Africa also has many valuable minerals, including copper, uranium, tin, zinc, diamonds, gold, and cobalt. Of these, copper is the most important. Most of

Africa's copper is found in an area called the **copper belt**. The copper belt stretches through northern Zambia and southern Democratic Republic of the Congo. However, poor transportation systems and political problems have kept the region's resources from being fully developed.

READING CHECK **Analyzing** Why are Central Africa's rivers an important natural resource?

FOCUS ON READING

What prefix do you recognize in *promote*?

SUMMARY AND PREVIEW Mighty rivers, the tropical forest of the Congo Basin, and mineral resources characterize the physical geography of Central Africa. These landscapes have influenced the region's history. Next, you will read about Central Africa's history and culture.

Section 1 Assessment

go.hrw.com
Online Quiz
KEYWORD: SG7 HP23

Reviewing Ideas, Terms, and Places

1. **a. Describe** What is the **Congo Basin**?
   b. Elaborate How do you think the **Congo River**'s rapids and waterfalls affect the economy of the region?
2. **a. Recall** What part of Central Africa has a highland climate?
   b. Explain Why have governments in the region set up national parks?
   c. Evaluate Is it more important to use the forest's resources or to protect the natural environment? Why?
3. **a. Define** What is a **periodic market**?
   b. Elaborate What kinds of political problems might keep mineral resources from being fully developed?

Critical Thinking

4. **Contrasting** Use your notes and a graphic organizer like this one to list differences between the Congo Basin and the areas surrounding it in Central Africa.

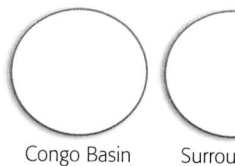

Congo Basin   Surrounding Areas

FOCUS ON WRITING

5. **Describing Physical Geography** What topics in this section might work well in your acrostic? Jot down notes on one or two topics you could feature in your poem.

Mapping Central Africa's Forests

Essential Elements

The World in Spatial Terms
Places and Regions
Physical Systems
Human Systems
Environment and Society
The Uses of Geography

Background Imagine taking a walk along a street in your neighborhood. Your purpose is to see the street in spatial terms and gather information to help you make a map. While you walk, you ask the kinds of questions geographers ask. How many houses, apartment buildings, or businesses are on the street? What kinds of animals or trees do you see? Your walk ends, and you organize your data. Now imagine that you are going to gather data on another walk. This walk will be 2,000 miles long.

A 2,000-Mile Walk In September 1999, an American scientist named Michael Fay began a 465-day, 2,000-mile walk through Central Africa's forests. He and his team followed elephant trails through thick vegetation. They waded through creeks and mucky swamps.

On the walk, Fay gathered data on the number and kinds of animals he saw. He counted elephant dung, chimpanzee nests, leopard tracks, and gorillas. He counted the types of trees and other plants along his

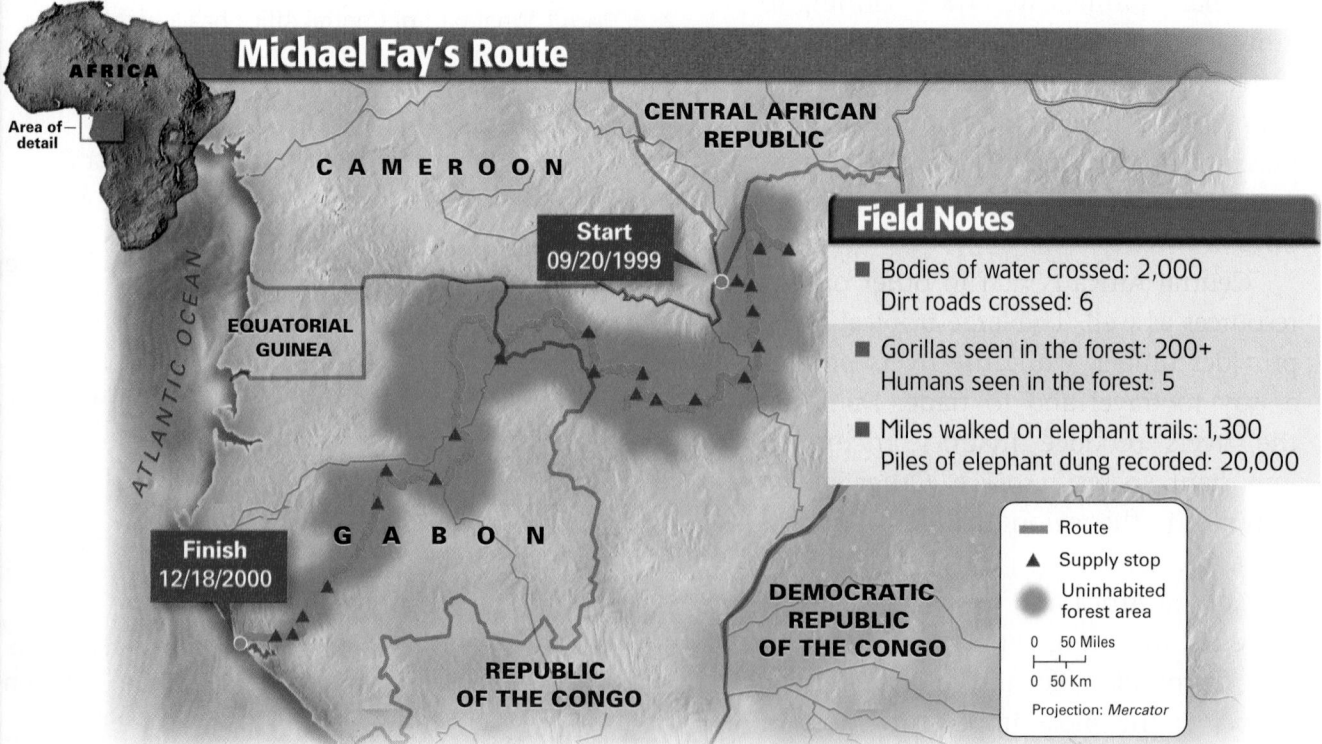

Michael Fay's Route

AFRICA

Area of detail

CENTRAL AFRICAN REPUBLIC

CAMEROON

ATLANTIC OCEAN

EQUATORIAL GUINEA

Start 09/20/1999

Finish 12/18/2000

GABON

REPUBLIC OF THE CONGO

DEMOCRATIC REPUBLIC OF THE CONGO

Field Notes

- Bodies of water crossed: 2,000
  Dirt roads crossed: 6

- Gorillas seen in the forest: 200+
  Humans seen in the forest: 5

- Miles walked on elephant trails: 1,300
  Piles of elephant dung recorded: 20,000

- Route
- ▲ Supply stop
- Uninhabited forest area

0   50 Miles
0   50 Km

Projection: *Mercator*

Michael Fay (above) and his team had to chop their way through thick forest vegetation. In a clearing, they spotted this group of elephants.

route. He also counted human settlements and determined the effect of human activities on the environment.

Fay used a variety of tools to record the data he gathered on his walk. He wrote down what he observed in waterproof notebooks. He shot events and scenes with video and still cameras. To measure the distance he and his team walked each day, he used a tool called a Fieldranger. He also kept track of his exact position in the forest by using a GPS, or global positioning system.

What It Means Michael Fay explained the purpose of his long walk. "The whole idea behind this is to be able to use the data we've collected as a tool." Other geographers can compare Fay's data with their own. Their comparison may help them create more accurate maps. These maps will show where plants, animals, and humans are located in Central Africa's forests.

Fay's data can also help scientists plan the future use of land or resources in a region. For example, Fay has used his data to convince government officials in Gabon to set aside 10 percent of its land to create 13 national parks. The parks will be protected from future logging and farming. They also will preserve many of the plants and animals that Fay and his team observed on their long walk.

Geography for Life Activity

1. Why did Michael Fay walk 2,000 miles?

2. In what practical way has Michael Fay used his data?

3. **Read More about Fay's Walk** Read the three-part article on Michael Fay's walk in *National Geographic* October 2000, March 2001, and August 2001. After you read the article, explain why Fay called his walk a "megatransect."

History and Culture

What You Will Learn...

Main Ideas

1. Great African kingdoms and European colonizers have influenced the history of Central Africa.
2. The culture of Central Africa includes many ethnic groups and languages, but it has also been influenced by European colonization.

The Big Idea

Central Africa's history and culture have been influenced by native traditions and European colonizers.

Key Terms and Places

Kongo Kingdom, *p. 564*
dialects, *p. 566*

TAKING NOTES As you read, use a graphic organizer like the one here to take notes on Central Africa's history and culture.

History	
Culture	

If **YOU** lived there...

You live in Central Africa in the 1300s. Over the past year, many new people have moved to your village. They speak a different language—one that you don't understand. They also have some customs that seem strange to you. But they have begun bringing fancy items such as animal skins and shells to your village. Now your village seems very rich.

How do you feel about these new people?

BUILDING BACKGROUND Different groups of people have influenced Central Africa throughout its history. Whether they came from near or far, and whether they stayed in Central Africa only decades or for more than hundred years, these groups brought their own cultures and customs to the region.

History

Early humans lived in Central Africa many thousands of years ago. However, the descendants of these people have had less impact on the region's history than people from the outside. Tribes from West Africa, and later European colonists, brought their customs to the region and changed the way people lived.

Early History

About 2,000 years ago new peoples began to migrate to Central Africa from West Africa. They eventually formed several kingdoms in Central Africa. Among the most important was the **Kongo Kingdom**. Founded in the 1300s, it was located near the mouth of the Congo River.

The Kongo people established trade routes to western and eastern Africa. Their kingdom grew rich from the trade of animal skins, shells, slaves, and ivory. Ivory is a cream-colored material that comes from elephant tusks.

Ivory Trade

Ivory traders collected elephant tusks for export to Europe.

ANALYZING VISUALS Who was involved in the ivory trade?

In the late 1400s, Europeans came to the region. They wanted the region's forest products and other resources such as ivory. They used ivory for fine furniture, jewelry, statues, and piano keys. Europeans also began to trade with some Central African kingdoms for slaves. Over a span of about 300 years, the Europeans took millions of enslaved Africans to their colonies in the Americas.

Some African kingdoms became richer by trading with Europeans. However, all were gradually changed and weakened by European influence. In the late 1800s, European countries divided all of Central Africa into colonies. The colonial powers were France, Belgium, Germany, Spain, the United Kingdom, and Portugal.

These European powers drew colonial borders that ignored the homelands of different ethnic groups. Many different ethnic groups were lumped together in colonies where they had to interact. These groups spoke different languages and had different customs. Their differences caused conflicts, especially after the colonies won independence.

Modern Central Africa

Central African colonies gained their independence from European powers after World War II. Some of the colonies fought bloody wars to win their independence. The last country to become independent was Angola. It won freedom from Portugal in 1975.

Independence did not bring peace to Central Africa, however. Ethnic groups continued to fight one another within the borders of the new countries. Also, the United States and the Soviet Union used Central Africa as a battleground in the Cold War. They supported different allies in small wars throughout Africa. The wars in the region killed many people and caused great damage.

FOCUS ON READING
What prefix do you recognize in *interact*?

READING CHECK **Summarizing** What role did Europeans play in Central Africa's history?

Culture

Today about 100 million people live in Central Africa. These people belong to many different ethnic groups and have different customs.

People and Language

The people of Central Africa speak hundreds of different languages. They also speak different **dialects**, regional varieties of a language. For example, although many Central Africans speak Bantu languages, those languages can be quite different from one another.

The main reason for this variety is the number of ethnic groups. Most ethnic groups have their own language or dialect. Most people in the region speak traditional African languages in their daily lives. However, the official languages of the region are European because of the influence of the colonial powers. For example, French is the official language of the Democratic Republic of the Congo. Portuguese is the language of Angola. English is an official language in Zambia and Malawi.

Religion

Central Africa's colonial history has also influenced religion. Europeans introduced Christianity to the region. Now many people in the former French, Spanish, and Portuguese colonies are Roman Catholic. Protestant Christianity is most common in former British colonies.

Two other religions came to parts of Central Africa from other regions. Influenced by the Muslim countries of the Sahel, the northern part of Central Africa has many Muslims. Zambia is the home of Muslims as well as Hindus.

The Arts

Central Africa's traditional cultures influence the arts of the region. The region is famous for sculpture, carved wooden masks, and beautiful cotton gowns dyed in bright colors.

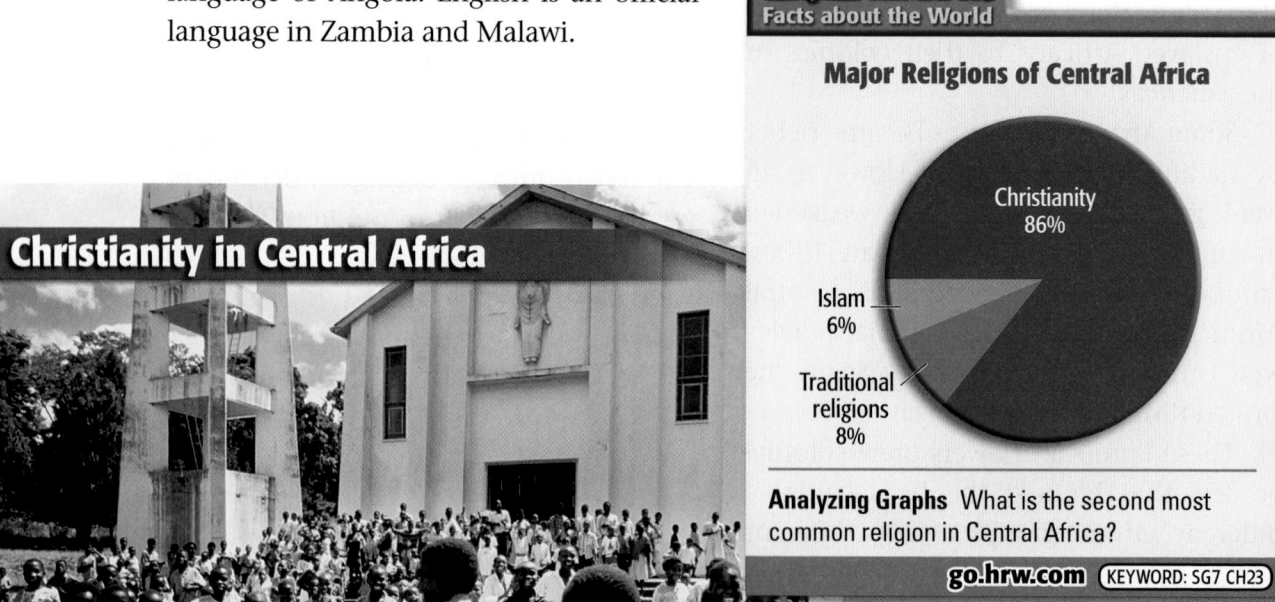

Christianity in Central Africa

THE WORLD ALMANAC®
Facts about the World

Major Religions of Central Africa

- Christianity 86%
- Islam 6%
- Traditional religions 8%

Analyzing Graphs What is the second most common religion in Central Africa?

go.hrw.com (KEYWORD: SG7 CH23)

Christian missionaries established churches and schools throughout Central Africa. These students attend a Catholic school in Malawi.

Bantu Languages

About 2,000 years ago people who spoke Bantu languages migrated out of West Africa. They moved to Central Africa as well as eastern and southern Africa. The Bantu speakers mixed with peoples who already lived in these lands.

The migration of Bantu speakers had important effects on African life. They brought new ways for growing food. They used tools made of iron, which others also began to use. The Bantu speakers also brought their languages. Today many Central Africans speak one or more of the some 500 Bantu languages such as Rundi, Bemba, or Luba.

Drawing Inferences How do you think the number of languages affects communication in the region?

Central Africa also has popular styles of music. The *likembe*, or thumb piano, was invented in the Congo region. Also, a type of dance music called *makossa* originated in Cameroon and has become popular throughout Africa. It can be played with guitars and electric keyboards.

READING CHECK **Generalizing** What are characteristics of culture in Central Africa?

SUMMARY AND PREVIEW Central Africa's history was influenced by great kingdoms that controlled trade and by Europeans, who originally came to the region looking for trade goods. European and traditional African influences have shaped the region's culture. Next, you will learn about the countries of Central Africa and what life is like there today.

Section 2 Assessment

go.hrw.com
Online Quiz
KEYWORD: SG7 HP23

Reviewing Ideas, Terms, and Places

1. a. Recall What Central African resource did Europeans value for making jewelry and crafts?
b. Explain How did the **Kongo Kingdom** become important?
c. Elaborate How do you think the colonial borders affected Central African countries' fights for independence?
2. a. Define What is a **dialect**?
b. Summarize How did the colonial era affect Central Africa's culture?
c. Elaborate How might Central Africa's culture be different today if the region had not been colonized by Europeans?

Critical Thinking

3. Sequencing Review your notes on Central Africa's history. Using a graphic organizer like this one, put major events in chronological order.

FOCUS ON WRITING

4. Taking Notes on History and Culture Your acrostic could describe the region's history and culture as well as physical geography. Take notes on interesting information you might include in your poem.

Central Africa Today

What You Will Learn...

Main Ideas

1. The countries of Central Africa are mostly poor, and many are trying to recover from years of civil war.
2. Challenges to peace, health, and the environment slow economic development in Central Africa.

The Big Idea

War, disease, and environmental problems have made it difficult for the countries of Central Africa to develop stable governments and economies.

Key Terms and Places

Kinshasa, *p. 569*
inflation, *p. 571*
malaria, *p. 572*
malnutrition, *p. 573*

TAKING NOTES As you read, use a graphic organizer like the one here to organize your notes on the countries of Central Africa and the challenges facing those countries.

Countries	Challenges

If YOU lived there...

You are an economic adviser in Zambia. Your country is poor, and most people are farmers. But scientists say Zambia has a lot of copper under ground. With a new copper mine, you could sell valuable copper to other countries. However, the mine would destroy a lot of farmland.

Do you support building the mine? Why or why not?

BUILDING BACKGROUND You have already read about Central Africa's great resources. Many countries in the region have the potential for great wealth. However, several factors throughout history have made it difficult for Central African countries to develop their resources.

Countries of Central Africa

Most of the countries in Central Africa are very poor. After years of colonial rule and then civil war, they are struggling to build stable governments and strong economies.

Democratic Republic of the Congo

The Democratic Republic of the Congo was a Belgian colony until 1960. When the country gained independence, many Belgians left. Few teachers, doctors, and other professionals remained in the former colony. In addition, various ethnic groups fought each other for power. These problems were partly to blame for keeping the new country poor.

A military leader named Joseph Mobutu came to power in 1965. He ruled as a dictator. One way Mobutu used his power was to change the name of the country to Zaire—a name that was traditionally African rather than European. He also changed his own name to Mobutu Sese Seko.

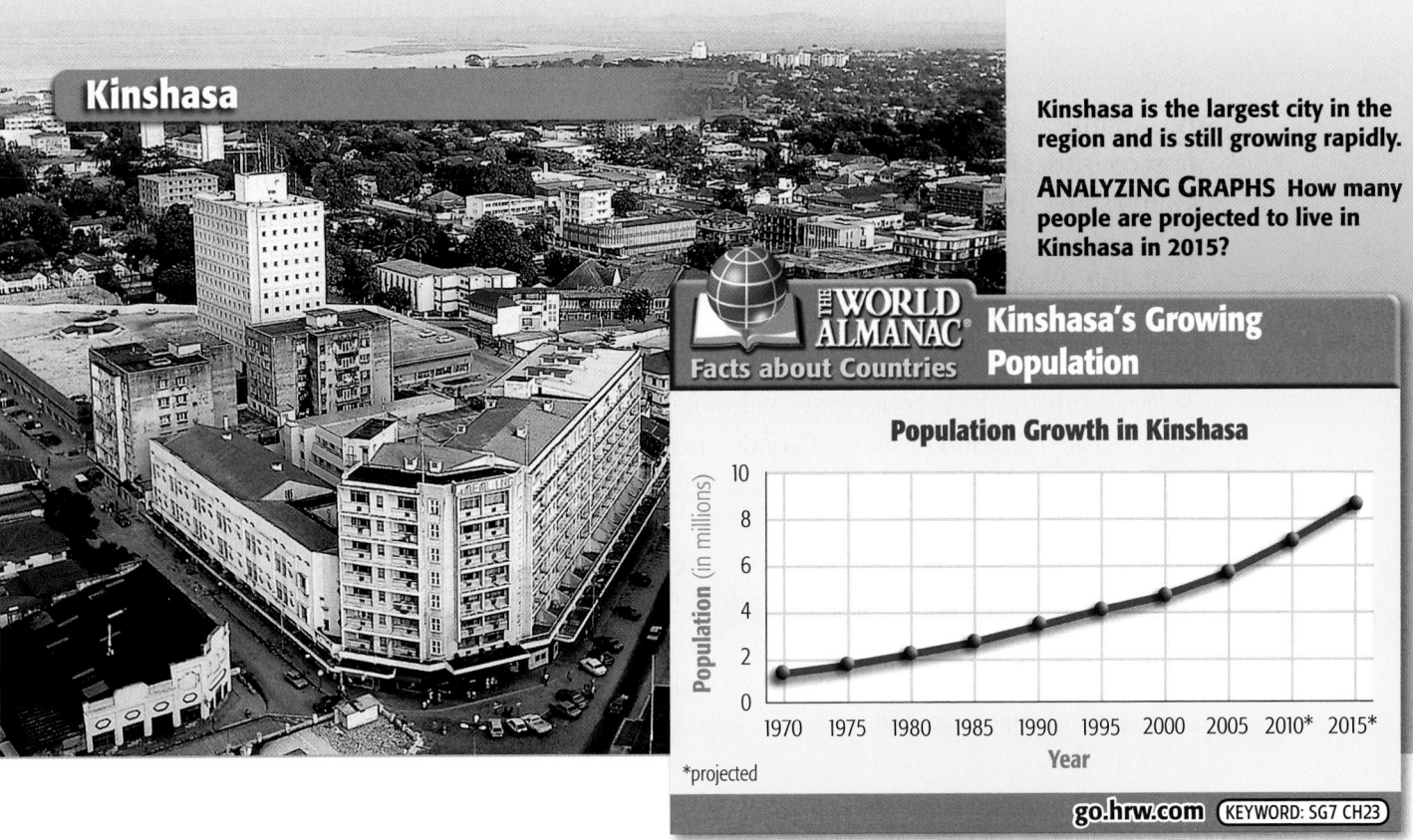

Kinshasa

Kinshasa is the largest city in the region and is still growing rapidly.

ANALYZING GRAPHS How many people are projected to live in Kinshasa in 2015?

THE WORLD ALMANAC® Facts about Countries — **Kinshasa's Growing Population**

Population Growth in Kinshasa

Population (in millions) vs. Year (1970, 1975, 1980, 1985, 1990, 1995, 2000, 2005, 2010*, 2015*)

*projected

go.hrw.com KEYWORD: SG7 CH23

During his rule, the government took over foreign-owned industries. It borrowed money from foreign countries to try to expand industry. However, most farmers suffered, and government and business leaders were corrupt. While the economy collapsed, Mobutu became one of the richest people in the world and used violence against people who challenged him.

In 1997, after a civil war, a new government took over. The new government renamed the country the Democratic Republic of the Congo.

The Democratic Republic of the Congo is a treasure chest of minerals that could bring wealth to the country. The south is part of Central Africa's rich copper belt. The country also has gold, diamonds, and cobalt. In addition, the tropical forest provides wood, food, and rubber. However, civil war, bad government, and crime have scared many foreign businesses away. As a result, the country's resources have helped few of its people.

Most people in the Democratic Republic of the Congo are poor. They usually live in rural areas where they must farm and trade for food. Many people are moving to the capital, **Kinshasa**. This crowded city has some modern buildings, but most of the city consists of poor slums.

Central African Republic and Cameroon

North of the Democratic Republic of the Congo is the landlocked country of Central African Republic. Since independence, this country has struggled with military coups, corrupt leaders, and improper elections.

In addition to political instability, the country suffers from a weak economy. Most people there are farmers. Although the country has diamonds and gold, it does not have railroads or ports needed to transport the resources for export. Central African Republic receives some aid from foreign countries, but this is not enough to meet the needs of its people.

FOCUS ON READING

If *–al* means "relating to," what does *political* mean?

Between Central African Republic and the Atlantic Ocean is Cameroon. Unlike most countries in Central Africa, Cameroon is fairly stable. It is a republic. The president is elected and holds most of the power.

Political stability has made economic growth possible. The country has oil reserves and good conditions for farming. Cacao, cotton, and coffee are valuable export crops. A good system of roads and railways helps people transport these goods for export to other countries.

Because of the steady economy, the people of Cameroon have a high standard of living for the region. For example, more people in Cameroon are enrolled in school than in most places in Africa.

Equatorial Guinea and São Tomé and Príncipe

Tiny Equatorial Guinea is divided between the mainland and five islands. The country is a republic. It has held elections, but many have seen the elections as being flawed. These elections have kept the same president ruling the country for more than 25 years. Although the recent discovery of oil has produced economic growth, living conditions for most people are still poor.

The island country of São Tomé and Príncipe has struggled with political instability. In addition, it is a poor country with few resources. It produces much cacao but has to import food. The recent discovery of oil in its waters may help the economy.

Village Architecture

Although Central Africa has several big cities, many people still live in rural villages. Different groups of people have different styles of architecture for their villages. Building materials vary depending on the resources available in the geographic setting.

An extended family lives together in these adobe homes in the mountains of Cameroon.

The strong tropical sun provides power for this hut in Angola.

Gabon and Republic of the Congo

Gabon has had only one president since 1967. For many years, Gabon held no multi-party elections. Gabon's economy provides the highest standard of living in the region. More than half the country's income comes from oil.

Like Gabon, the Republic of the Congo receives much of its income from oil. It also receives income from forest products. Despite these resources, a civil war in the late 1990s hurt the economy.

The Republic of the Congo is mostly urban and growing more so. Many people are moving from villages to cities. The biggest city is the capital, Brazzaville.

Angola

Angola won independence from Portugal in 1975. The country then plunged into a long civil war. Fighting finally ended in 2002, and the country has been more stable since then. Angola is now a republic with an elected president.

Even with peace, Angola's economy is struggling. For about 85 percent of the population, subsistence farming is the only source of income. Even worse, land mines left over from the civil war endanger the farmers. A high rate of **inflation**, the rise in prices that occurs when currency loses its buying power, has also weakened the economy. Finally, corrupt officials have taken large amounts of money meant for public projects.

Angola does have potential, however. The country has diamonds and oil. The oil is found offshore and in Cabinda. Cabinda is a part of Angola that is separated from the rest of the country by the Democratic Republic of the Congo.

Zambia and Malawi

The southernmost countries in Central Africa are Zambia and Malawi. About 85 percent of Zambia's workers are farmers. Though rich with copper mines, Zambia's economy is growing very slowly. It is hurt by high levels of debt and inflation.

Nearly all of Malawi's people farm for a living. About 75 percent of the people live in villages in rural areas. Aid from foreign countries and religious groups has been important to the economy. However, the country has been slow to build factories and industries. In the future, Malawi will probably have to develop its own industries rather than rely on aid from foreign countries.

A family sits outside their home in Zambia.

ANALYSIS SKILL **ANALYZING VISUALS**

How does the construction of the huts help you recognize different climates in Central Africa?

READING CHECK **Generalizing** What are the economies like in Central African countries?

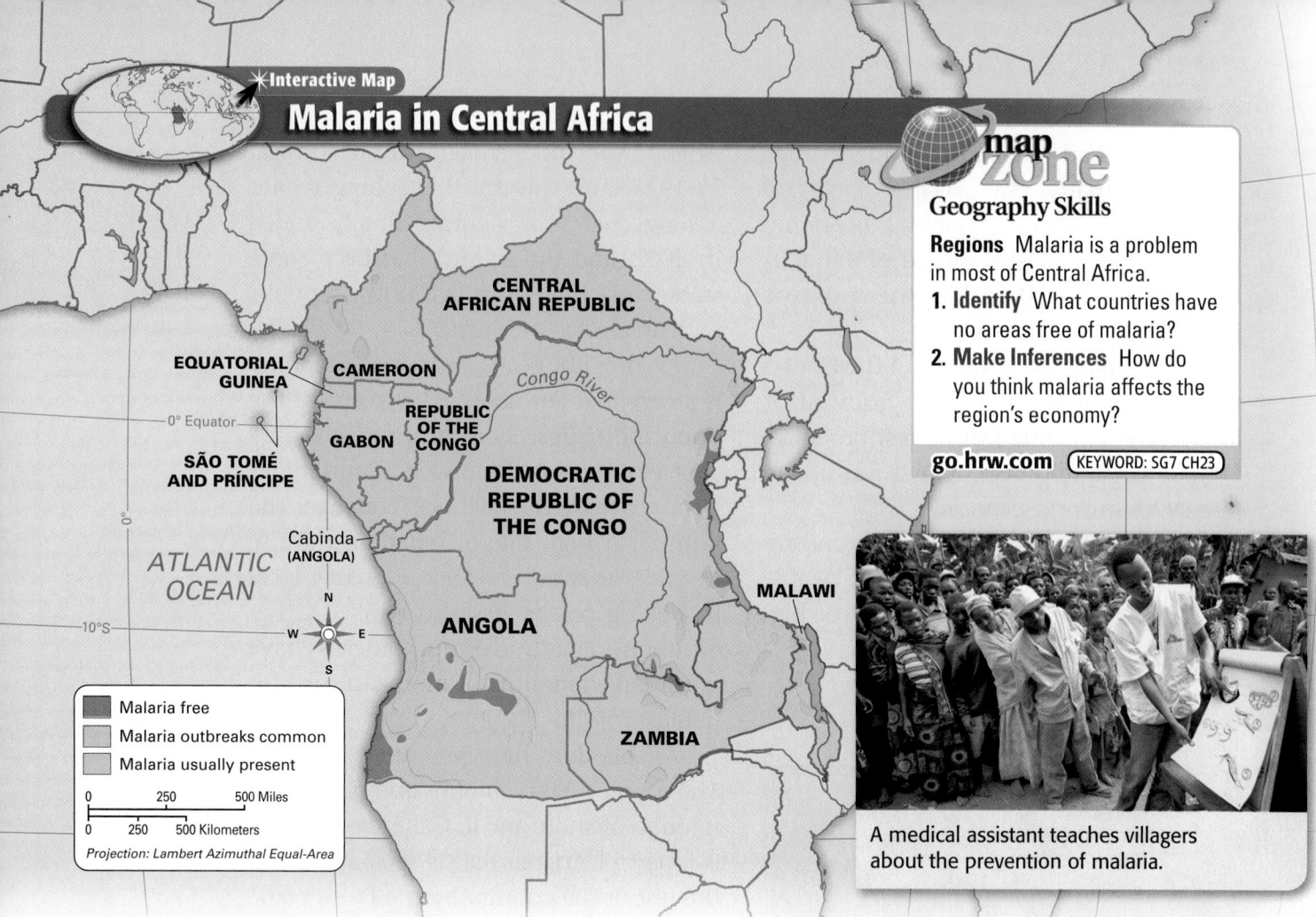

CENTRAL AFRICAN REPUBLIC

EQUATORIAL GUINEA

CAMEROON

Congo River

REPUBLIC OF THE CONGO

GABON

0° Equator

SÃO TOMÉ AND PRÍNCIPE

Cabinda (ANGOLA)

ATLANTIC OCEAN

DEMOCRATIC REPUBLIC OF THE CONGO

MALAWI

ANGOLA

ZAMBIA

N
W E
S

Malaria free
Malaria outbreaks common
Malaria usually present

| 0 | 250 | 500 Miles |
| 0 | 250 | 500 Kilometers |

Projection: Lambert Azimuthal Equal-Area

map zone

Geography Skills

Regions Malaria is a problem in most of Central Africa.
1. **Identify** What countries have no areas free of malaria?
2. **Make Inferences** How do you think malaria affects the region's economy?

go.hrw.com [KEYWORD: SG7 CH23]

A medical assistant teaches villagers about the prevention of malaria.

Issues and Challenges

As you have read, many of the countries in Central Africa have unstable governments and poor economies. These circumstances have been either the cause or effect of other issues and challenges in the region today.

Ethnic and Regional Conflict

A mix of ethnic groups and competing desires for power has led to civil war in many of the region's countries. Thousands of people have been killed in these wars over the past several years.

Wars have also contributed to poor economies in the region. The people killed or injured in the fighting can no longer work. In addition, the fighting destroys land and other resources that could be used in more productive ways.

ACADEMIC VOCABULARY
implement to put in place

Health

Like war, disease kills many people in the region. **Malaria** is a disease spread by mosquitoes that causes fever and pain. Without treatment it can lead to death. In fact, malaria is by far the most common cause of death in Central Africa. A child there dies from malaria every 30 seconds. On the map above, you can see that this disease is a problem almost everywhere.

International health organizations and some national governments have begun to **implement** strategies to control malaria. These strategies include educating people about the disease and passing out nets treated with insecticide. The nets and medicine are expensive, and not everyone can afford them. However, people who sleep under these nets will be protected from mosquitoes and malaria.

While some countries are beginning to control malaria, another disease is spreading rapidly. HIV, the virus that causes AIDS, is very common in Central Africa. Hundreds of thousands of people die of AIDS each year in Central Africa. There is no cure for HIV infection, and medicines to control it are very expensive. International groups are working hard to find a cure for HIV and to slow the spread of the disease.

Partly because so many people die of disease, Central Africa has a very young population. Almost 50 percent of people living in Central Africa are under age 15. For comparison, only about 20 percent of the people in the United States are under age 15. Although many young people in Central Africa work, they do not contribute to the economy as much as older, more experienced workers do.

Resources and Environment

To help their economies and their people, the countries of Central Africa must begin to develop their natural resources more effectively. Agricultural land is one resource that must be managed more effectively. In some places, partly because of war, food production has actually declined. Also, food production cannot keep up with the demands of the growing population. The results are food shortages and malnutrition. **Malnutrition** is the condition of not getting enough nutrients from food.

The environment is another important resource that must be managed. Some of Central Africa's most important industries are destroying the environment. Lumber companies cut down trees in the tropical forest, threatening the wildlife that lives there. Mining is also harming the environment. Diamonds and copper are mined in huge open pits. This mining process removes large areas of land and destroys the landscape.

Many people in Central Africa and around the world are working hard and spending billions of dollars to improve conditions in the region. National parks have been set up to protect the environment. Projects to provide irrigation and prevent erosion are helping people plant more crops. Central Africa's land and people hold great potential for the future.

READING CHECK Summarizing What are some threats to Central Africa's environment?

SUMMARY AND PREVIEW Countries in Central Africa are trying to build stable governments and strong economies after years of civil war, but challenges slow economic development. Next, you will learn about the places and people of Southern Africa.

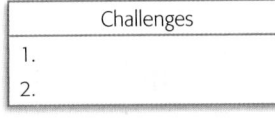
go.hrw.com
Online Quiz
KEYWORD: SG7 HP23

Section 3 Assessment

Reviewing Ideas, Terms, and Places

1. a. **Define** What is **inflation**?
   b. **Summarize** What effect did Mobutu Sese Seko's rule have on the Democratic Republic of the Congo?
   c. **Evaluate** Do you think Central African countries would benefit more from a stable government or from a strong economy? Explain your answer.
2. a. **Identify** What causes **malaria**?
   b. **Explain** How are some countries coping with environmental challenges?

Critical Thinking

3. **Evaluating** Look over your notes on Central Africa. Using a graphic organizer like the one here, rank the challenges facing Central Africa. Put the one you see as the biggest challenge first.

Challenges
1.
2.

FOCUS ON WRITING

4. **Describing Countries** You can focus on one country or on the whole region in your acrostic. Review your notes, and then decide whether to select one to write about.

Social Studies Skills

Chart and Graph

Critical Thinking

Geography

Study

Interpreting a Population Pyramid

Learn

A population pyramid shows the percentages of males and females by age group in a country's population. The pyramids are split into two sides. Each bar on the left shows the percentage of a country's population that is male and of a certain age. The bars on the right show the same information for females.

Population pyramids help us understand population trends in countries. Countries that have large percentages of young people have populations that are growing rapidly. Countries with more older people are growing slowly or not at all.

Practice

Use the population pyramid of Angola to answer the following questions.

❶ What age group is the largest?

❷ What percent of Angola's population is made up of 15- to 19-year-old males?

❸ What does this population pyramid tell you about the population trend in Angola?

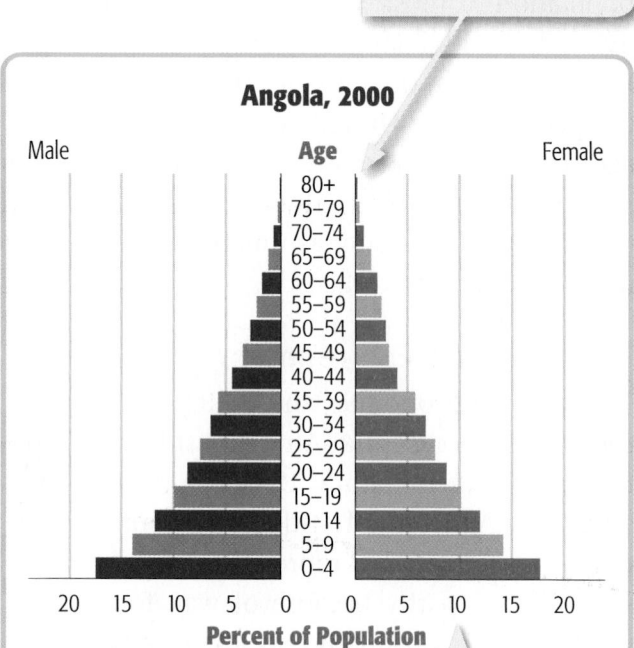

Ages are listed down the middle of the diagram.

Source: U.S. Census Bureau, International Data Base

Percentages are labeled across the bottom of the diagram.

Apply

Do research at the library or on the Internet to find age and population data for the United States. Use that information to answer the following questions.

1. What age group is the largest?

2. Are there more males or females over age 80?

3. How would you describe the shape of the population pyramid?

Geography's Impact
video series
Review the video to answer the closing question:
Why do you think the president of Gabon passed a law establishing new national parks?

Visual Summary

Use the visual summary below to help you review the main ideas of the chapter.

QUICK FACTS

The forests of Central Africa's Congo Basin are home to gorillas and many other kinds of animals.

Ivory attracted Europeans to Central Africa. They left their influence on the region's history and culture.

Countries of Central Africa are looking for ways to solve many of their challenges, such as preventing disease.

Reviewing Vocabulary, Terms, and Places

Using your own paper, complete the sentences below by providing the correct term for each blank.

1. The _____ is a low area near the middle of Central Africa.

2. _____ is a disease spread by mosquitoes that causes fever and aching.

3. People who do not get enough nutrients from their food suffer from _____.

4. To _____ a system is to put it in place.

5. _____ is the rise in prices that occurs when currency loses its buying power.

6. A _____ is a regional variety of a language.

7. The river that flows through Central Africa and into the Atlantic Ocean is the _____.

8. A _____ is an open-air market set up once or twice a week.

9. Much of the copper in Central Africa comes from a region known as the _____.

Comprehension and Critical Thinking

SECTION 1 *(Pages 558–561)*

10. **a. Describe** What are the main landforms in Central Africa?

   b. Make Inferences Why would people in rural areas be more likely to shop at periodic markets than at grocery stores?

   c. Elaborate How does the development of national parks affect people in the region? How does it affect people around the world?

SECTION 2 *(Pages 564–567)*

11. **a. Recall** When did European countries divide Central Africa into colonies?

   b. Analyze What factors besides European colonization influenced where different religions are most common in Central Africa today?

   c. Evaluate What do you think was the most significant influence or effect the Europeans had on Central Africa? Explain your answer.

SECTION 3 *(Pages 568–573)*

12. a. Identify What are the diseases that affect many people in Central Africa?

b. Analyze What factors have allowed certain countries like Cameroon and Gabon to have stronger economies than other countries in the region?

c. Evaluate What are the benefits of foreign aid to Central Africa? What might be some possible drawbacks?

FOCUS ON READING AND WRITING

Using Word Parts *Look at the list of prefixes and suffixes and their meanings below. Then answer the questions that follow.*

mal- (bad)	*-ous* (characterized by)
in- (not)	*-ment* (result, action)
re- (again)	*-ion* (action, condition)

13. Which of the following words means "getting only poor nutrients"?

a. nutriment   **c.** renutrition

b. malnutrition   **d.** nutrious

14. Which of the following words means "the condition of being protected"?

a. reprotect   **c.** protection

b. protectment   **d.** protectous

15. Writing Your Acrostic Your poem will describe Central Africa or a part of it. Choose the place you want to describe and write the letters of that word vertically, with one letter on each line of your paper. For each letter, use your notes to write a descriptive word or phrase that tells about your subject. Make a final copy of your acrostic to share with classmates.

Social Studies Skills

Interpreting a Population Pyramid *Use the population pyramid in the Social Studies Skills lesson to answer the following questions.*

16. What age group is the smallest?

17. How would you describe the current population in Angola?

Using the Internet

18. Activity: Making a Scrapbook Central Africa is home to many different ethnic groups. Although there are similarities among them, they each have unique characteristics as well. Enter the activity keyword and take a journey to Central Africa. Research some of the many groups that live there. Then create an illustrated scrapbook that documents some of the groups that you have met in your travels. Include information on their towns, ways of life, and environments. You may also want to include maps, souvenirs, and pictures from your journey.

Map Activity

19. Central Africa On a separate sheet of paper, match the letters on the map with their correct labels.

Congo River	Congo Basin
Zambezi River	Lake Nyasa
Angola	

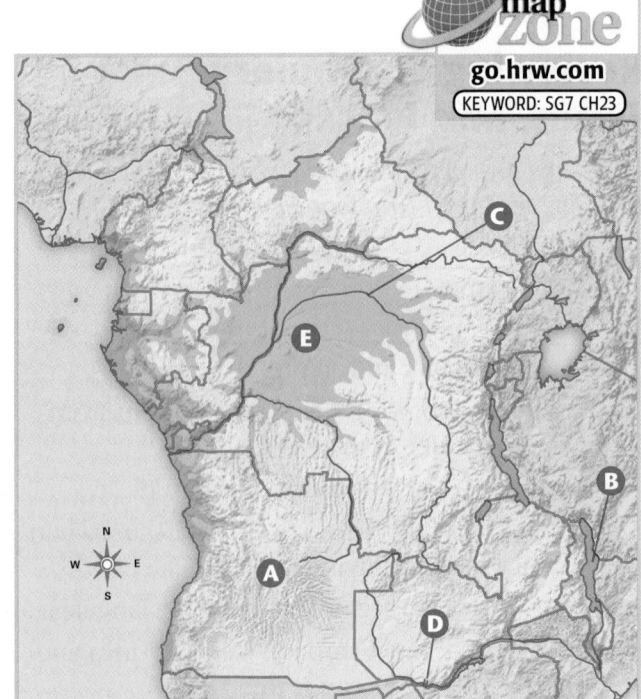

DIRECTIONS: *Read questions 1 through 6 and write the letter of the best response. Then read question 7 and write your own well-constructed response.*

1 What major river flows through Central Africa and into the Atlantic Ocean?

A Zambezi River

B Congo Basin

C Niger River

D Congo River

2 In rural areas, people are most likely to trade goods at a

A copper belt.

B periodic market.

C supermarket.

D dialect.

3 Why did Europeans become interested in Central Africa?

A They wanted resources and trade goods.

B They wanted to teach people European languages.

C They wanted to divide up ethnic groups.

D They wanted to destroy African kingdoms.

4 What disease is spread by mosquitoes and is very common in Central Africa?

A malnutrition

B HIV

C malaria

D inflation

5 Most people in Zambia and Malawi work in

A copper mines.

B the oil industry.

C cities.

D farming.

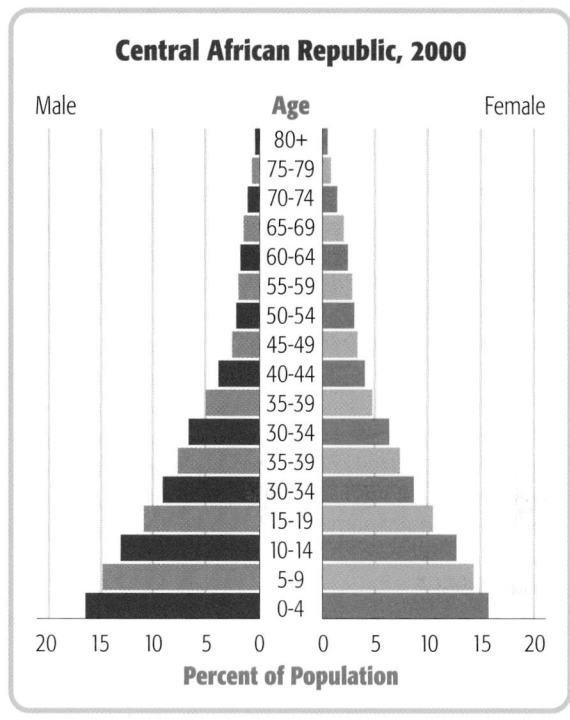

Central African Republic, 2000

Male — Age — Female

80+
75-79
70-74
65-69
60-64
55-59
50-54
45-49
40-44
35-39
30-34
35-39
30-34
15-19
10-14
5-9
0-4

20 15 10 5 0   0 5 10 15 20

Percent of Population

Source: U.S. Census Bureau, International Data Base

6 Based on the graph above, which of the following statements is false?

A Females ages 15–19 make up about 10 percent of the population.

B Males and females ages 0–4 each make up over 15 percent of the population.

C The population of Central African Republic is growing at a very slow rate.

D There are more males ages 5–9 than there are females.

7 Extended Response Using the graph above and the graph of Population Growth in Kinshasa in Section 3, write a paragraph explaining how Central Africa's population and people's lives in the region are changing.

CHAPTER 24

Southern Africa

What You Will Learn...

In this chapter you will learn about nine countries that are located in the region of Southern Africa—South Africa, Lesotho, Swaziland, Namibia, Botswana, Zimbabwe, Mozambique, Madagascar, and Comoros. You will learn about the region's history, cultures, and economies.

FOCUS ON READING AND VIEWING

Making Generalizations A generalization is a broad, general conclusion drawn from examples, facts, or other information. As you read this chapter, try to make generalizations about the facts and information in the text. Making generalizations will help you understand the meaning of what you are reading. **See the lesson, Making Generalizations, on page R25.**

Viewing a TV News Report You are a journalist covering world news. Your assignment is to create a brief TV news report on something about Southern Africa. As you read this chapter, you will collect information about the region and plan your report. Later you and your classmates will give your TV news reports and evaluate one another's reports.

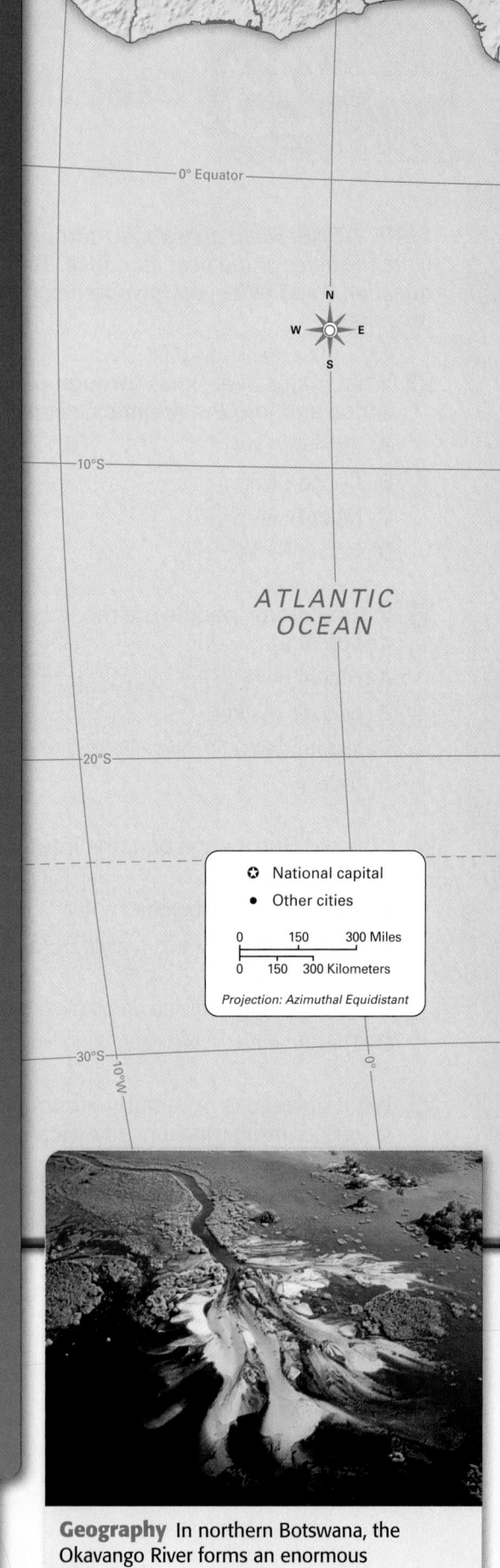

Geography In northern Botswana, the Okavango River forms an enormous inland delta.

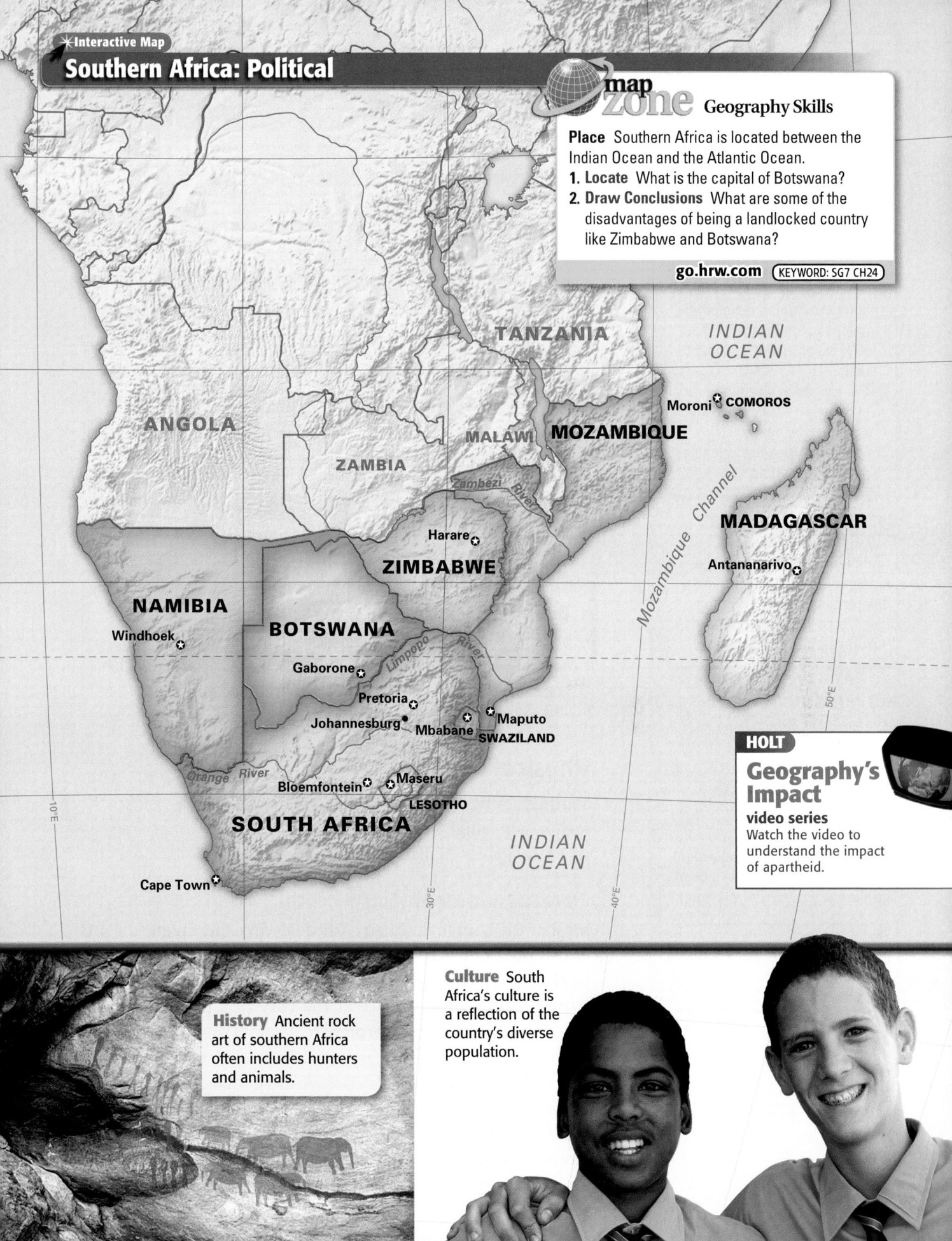

map zone
Geography Skills

Place Southern Africa is located between the Indian Ocean and the Atlantic Ocean.
1. **Locate** What is the capital of Botswana?
2. **Draw Conclusions** What are some of the disadvantages of being a landlocked country like Zimbabwe and Botswana?

go.hrw.com KEYWORD: SG7 CH24

TANZANIA

INDIAN OCEAN

Moroni • COMOROS

ANGOLA

ZAMBIA

MALAWI

MOZAMBIQUE

Zambezi River

MADAGASCAR

Harare •

ZIMBABWE

Antananarivo •

Mozambique Channel

NAMIBIA

Windhoek •

BOTSWANA

Gaborone •

Limpopo River

Pretoria •
Johannesburg •
Mbabane •
Maputo •
SWAZILAND

Orange River

Bloemfontein • • Maseru

LESOTHO

SOUTH AFRICA

INDIAN OCEAN

Cape Town •

HOLT
Geography's Impact
video series
Watch the video to understand the impact of apartheid.

History Ancient rock art of southern Africa often includes hunters and animals.

Culture South Africa's culture is a reflection of the country's diverse population.

579

Physical Geography

What You Will Learn...

Main Ideas

1. Southern Africa's main physical feature is a large plateau with plains, rivers, and mountains.
2. The climate and vegetation of Southern Africa is mostly savanna and desert.
3. Southern Africa has valuable mineral resources.

The Big Idea

Southern Africa's physical geography includes a high, mostly dry plateau, grassy plains and rivers, and valuable mineral resources.

Key Terms and Places

escarpment, *p. 580*
veld, *p. 582*
Namib Desert, *p. 582*
pans, *p. 582*

TAKING NOTES As you read, take notes on the physical geography of Southern Africa. Use a chart like this one to organize your notes.

Physical Features	
Climate and Vegetation	
Resources	

If YOU lived there...

You are a member of the San, a people who live in the Kalahari Desert. Your family lives with several others in a group of circular grass huts. You are friends with the other children. Sometimes you help your mom look for eggs or plants to use for carrying water. Your water containers, clothes, carrying bags, and weapons all come from the resources you find in the desert. Next year you will move away to attend school in a town.

How will your life change next year?

BUILDING BACKGROUND Parts of Southern Africa have a desert climate. Little vegetation grows in these areas, but some people do live there. Most of Southern Africa's people live in cooler and wetter areas, such as on the high, grassy plains in the south and east.

Physical Features

Southern Africa has some amazing scenery. On a visit to the region, you might see grassy plains, steamy swamps, mighty rivers, rocky waterfalls, and steep mountains and plateaus.

Plateaus and Mountains

Most of the land in Southern Africa lies on a large plateau. Parts of this plateau reach more than 4,000 feet (1,220 m) above sea level. To form the plateau, the land rises sharply from a narrow coastal plain. The steep face at the edge of a plateau or other raised area is called an **escarpment**.

In eastern South Africa, part of the escarpment is made up of a mountain range called the Drakensberg (DRAH-kuhnz-buhrk). The steep peaks rise as high as 11,425 feet (3,482 m). Farther north, another mountain range, the Inyanga (in-YANG-guh) Mountains, separates Zimbabwe and Mozambique. Southern Africa also has mountains along its western coast.

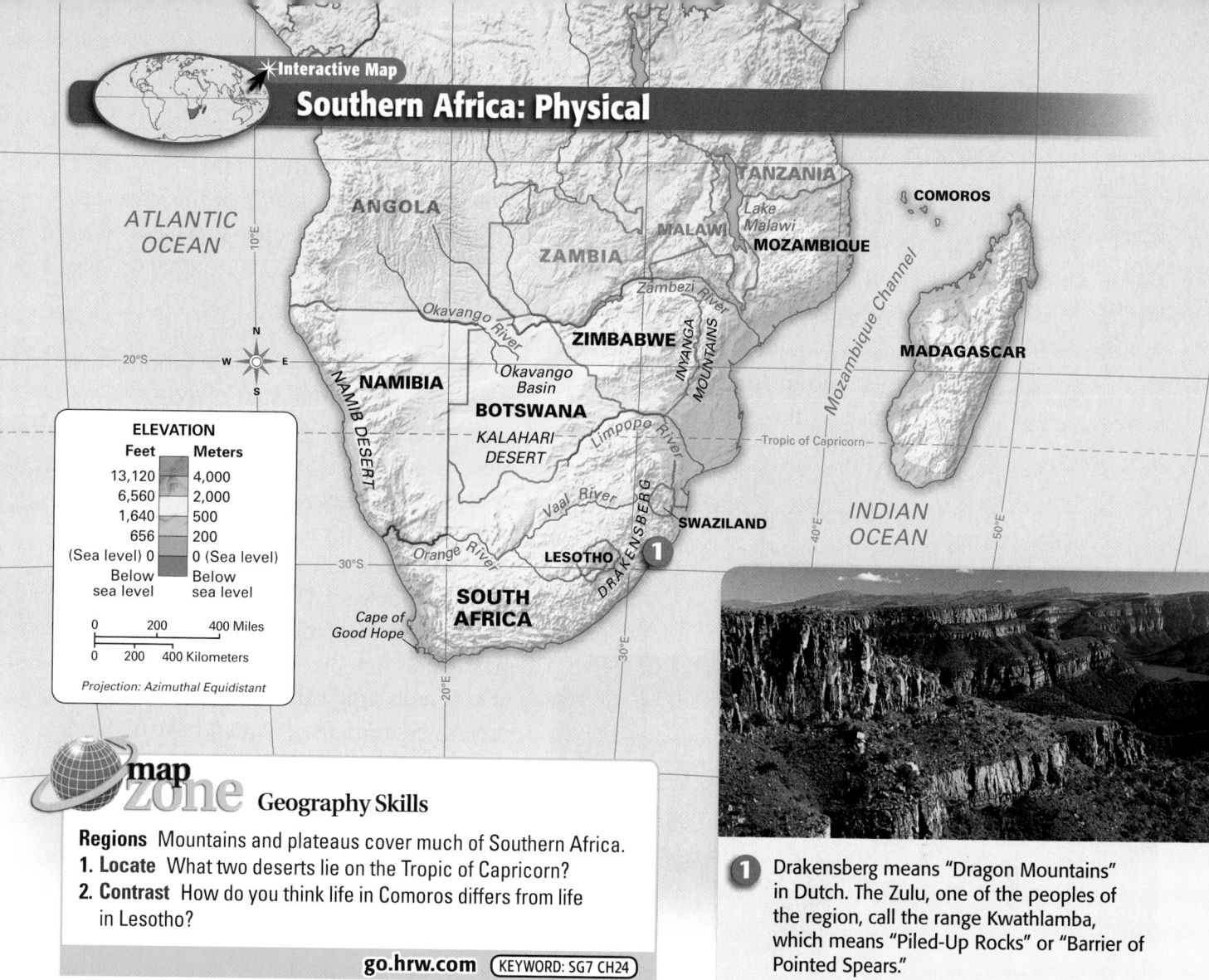

Southern Africa: Physical

ATLANTIC OCEAN

ANGOLA

ZAMBIA

TANZANIA

Lake Malawi

MALAWI

MOZAMBIQUE

COMOROS

Zambezi River

ZIMBABWE

INYANGA MOUNTAINS

MADAGASCAR

Mozambique Channel

Okavango River

NAMIBIA

Okavango Basin

BOTSWANA

KALAHARI DESERT

Limpopo River

Tropic of Capricorn

NAMIB DESERT

Vaal River

DRAKENSBERG

SWAZILAND

INDIAN OCEAN

Orange River

LESOTHO

SOUTH AFRICA

Cape of Good Hope

ELEVATION

Feet	Meters
13,120	4,000
6,560	2,000
1,640	500
656	200
(Sea level) 0	0 (Sea level)
Below sea level	Below sea level

0   200   400 Miles

0   200   400 Kilometers

Projection: Azimuthal Equidistant

map zone Geography Skills

Regions Mountains and plateaus cover much of Southern Africa.
1. **Locate** What two deserts lie on the Tropic of Capricorn?
2. **Contrast** How do you think life in Comoros differs from life in Lesotho?

go.hrw.com (KEYWORD: SG7 CH24)

1 Drakensberg means "Dragon Mountains" in Dutch. The Zulu, one of the peoples of the region, call the range Kwathlamba, which means "Piled-Up Rocks" or "Barrier of Pointed Spears."

Plains and Rivers

Southern Africa's narrow coastal plain and the wide plateau are covered with grassy plains. These flat plains are home to animals such as lions, leopards, elephants, baboons, and antelope.

Several large rivers cross Southern Africa's plains. The Okavango River flows from Angola into a huge basin in Botswana. This river's water never reaches the ocean. Instead it forms a swampy inland delta that is home to crocodiles, zebras, hippos, and other animals. Many tourists travel to Botswana to see these wild animals in their natural habitat.

The Orange River passes through the rocky Augrabies (oh-KRAH-bees) Falls as it flows to the Atlantic Ocean. When the water in the river is at its highest, the falls are several miles wide. The water tumbles down 19 separate waterfalls. The Limpopo River is another of the region's major rivers. It flows into the Indian Ocean. **Features** such as waterfalls and other obstacles block ships from sailing up these rivers. However, the rivers do allow irrigation for farmland in an otherwise dry area.

ACADEMIC VOCABULARY

features characteristics

READING CHECK **Generalizing** What are Southern Africa's main physical features?

Climate and Vegetation

FOCUS ON READING

What generalization can you make about Southern Africa's climate?

Southern Africa's climates vary from east to west. The wettest place in the region is the east coast of the island of Madagascar. On the mainland, winds carrying moisture blow in from the Indian Ocean. Because the Drakensberg's high elevation causes these winds to blow upward, the eastern slopes of these mountains are rainy.

In contrast to the eastern part of the continent, the west is very dry. From the Atlantic coast, deserts give way to plains with semiarid and steppe climates.

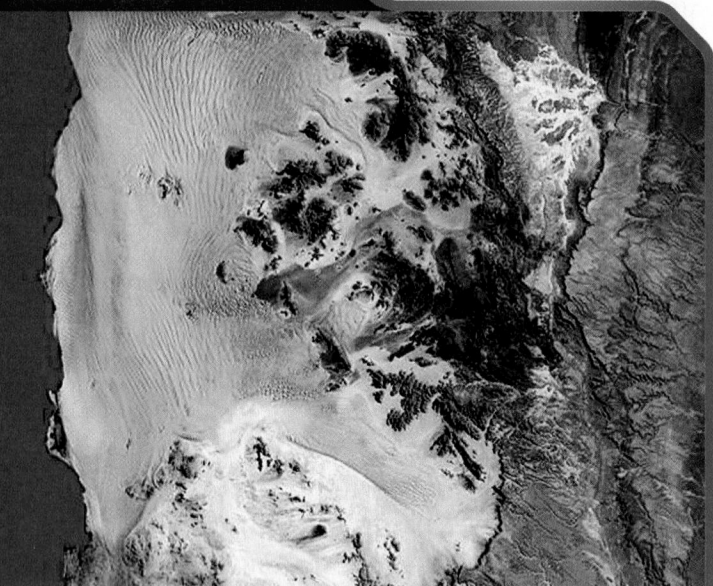

Satellite View

Namib Desert

One of the world's most unusual deserts, the Namib lies on the Atlantic coast in Namibia. As this satellite image shows, the land there is extremely dry. Some of the world's highest sand dunes stretch for miles along the coast.

In spite of its harsh conditions, some insects have adapted to life in the desert. They can survive there because at night a fog rolls in from the ocean. The insects use the fog as a source of water.

Drawing Conclusions How have some insects adapted to living in the Namib Desert?

Savanna and Deserts

A large savanna region covers much of Southern Africa. Shrubs and short trees grow on the grassy plains of the savanna. In South Africa, these open grassland areas are known as the **veld** (VELT). As you can see on the map on the next page, vegetation gets more sparse in the south and west.

The driest place in the region is the **Namib Desert** on the Atlantic coast. Some parts of the Namib get as little as a half an inch (13 mm) of rainfall per year. In this dry area, plants get water from dew and fog rather than from rain.

Another desert, the Kalahari, occupies most of Botswana. Although this desert gets enough rain in the north to support grasses and trees, its sandy plains are mostly covered with scattered shrubs. Ancient streams crossing the Kalahari have drained into low, flat areas, or **pans**. On these flat areas, minerals left behind when the water evaporated form a glittering white layer.

Tropical Forests

Unlike the mainland, Madagascar has lush vegetation and tropical forests. It also has many animals found nowhere else. For example, some 50 species of lemurs, relatives of apes, live only on this island. However, the destruction of Madagascar's forests has endangered many of the island's animals.

READING CHECK Summarizing What is the climate and vegetation like in Southern Africa?

Resources

Southern Africa is rich in natural resources. Madagascar's forests provide timber. The region's rivers supply hydroelectricity and water for irrigation. Where rain is plentiful or irrigation is possible, farmers can grow a wide range of crops.

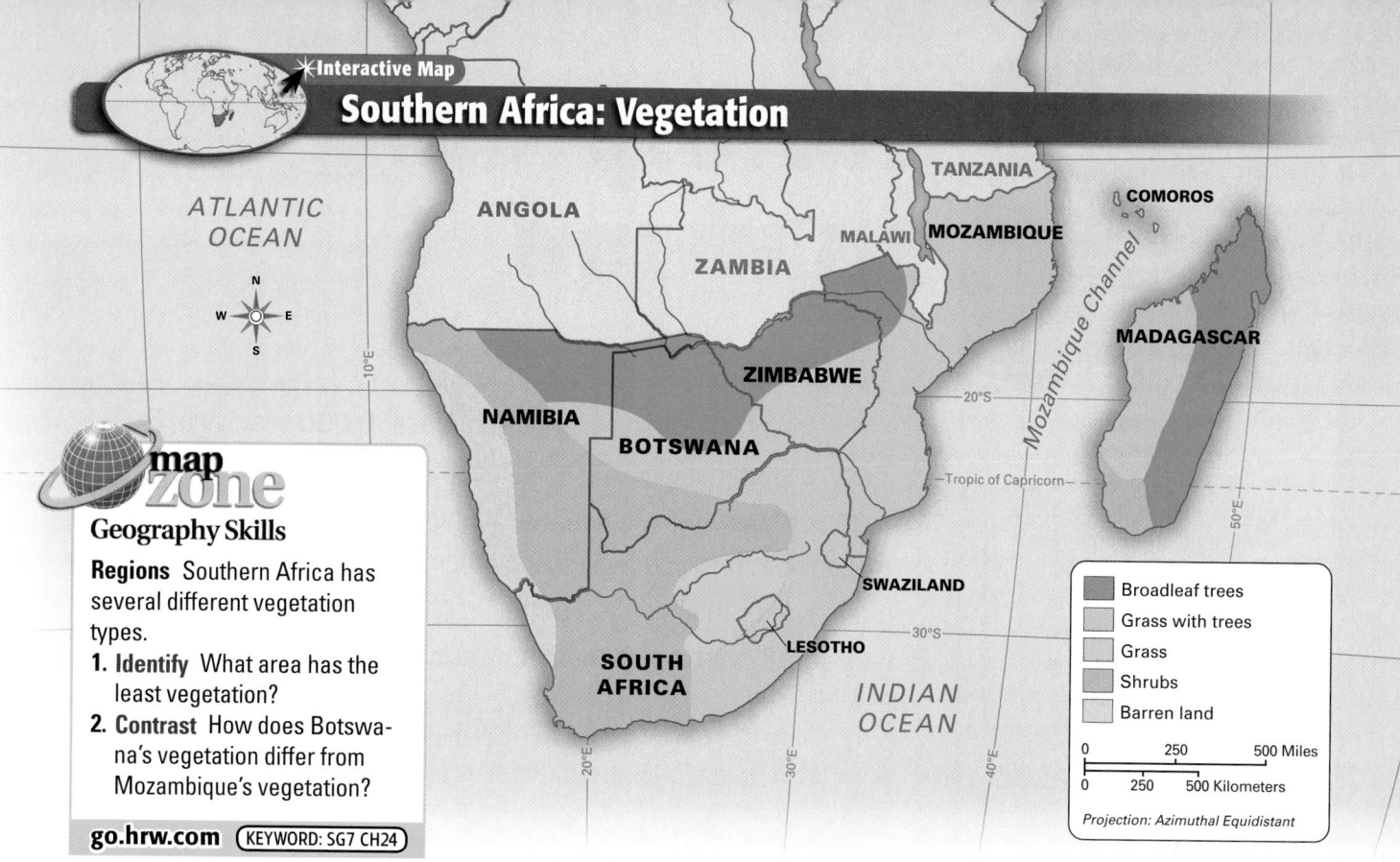

Southern Africa: Vegetation

Interactive Map

ATLANTIC OCEAN

ANGOLA

ZAMBIA

TANZANIA

MALAWI MOZAMBIQUE

COMOROS

Mozambique Channel

MADAGASCAR

ZIMBABWE

NAMIBIA

BOTSWANA

Tropic of Capricorn

SWAZILAND

LESOTHO

SOUTH AFRICA

INDIAN OCEAN

map zone

Geography Skills

Regions Southern Africa has several different vegetation types.
1. **Identify** What area has the least vegetation?
2. **Contrast** How does Botswana's vegetation differ from Mozambique's vegetation?

go.hrw.com (KEYWORD: SG7 CH24)

Legend:
- Broadleaf trees
- Grass with trees
- Grass
- Shrubs
- Barren land

0   250   500 Miles
0   250   500 Kilometers

Projection: Azimuthal Equidistant

The region's most valuable resources, however, are minerals. Mines in South Africa produce most of the world's gold. In addition, South Africa, Botswana, and Namibia have productive diamond mines. Other mineral resources in Southern Africa include coal, platinum, copper, uranium, and iron ore. Although mining is very important to the economy of the region, the mines can have damaging effects on the surrounding natural environments.

READING CHECK **Finding Main Ideas** What are the main resources of Southern Africa?

SUMMARY AND PREVIEW Southern Africa is mainly covered with grassy plains and deserts atop a large plateau. Minerals are among the region's main resources. In the next section, you will learn about Southern Africa's history and culture.

Section 1 Assessment

go.hrw.com **Online Quiz** KEYWORD: SG7 HP24

Reviewing Ideas, Terms, and Places

1. **a. Define** What is an **escarpment**?
   b. Elaborate How is the Okavango River different from most other rivers you have studied?
2. **a. Recall** Where in Southern Africa is the driest climate?
   b. Explain What caused minerals to collect in **pans** in the Kalahari Desert?
3. **a. Identify** What are Southern Africa's most valuable resources?
   b. Elaborate How do you think the gold and diamond mines have affected South Africa's economy?

Critical Thinking

4. **Categorizing** Review your notes and use a graphic organizer like this one to sort characteristics by location.

	East	West
Physical Features		
Climate and Vegetation		

FOCUS ON VIEWING

5. **Telling about the Physical Geography** Your TV news report might focus on some part of the geography of Southern Africa. Could you focus on the destruction of the rain forest or life in the desert?

History and Culture

What You Will Learn...

Main Ideas

1. Southern Africa's history began with hunter-gatherers, followed by great empires and European settlements.
2. The cultures of Southern Africa are rich in different languages, religions, customs, and art.

The Big Idea

Native African ethnic groups and European settlements influenced the history and culture of Southern Africa.

Key Terms and Places

Great Zimbabwe, *p. 585*
Cape of Good Hope, *p. 585*
Afrikaners, *p. 586*
Boers, *p. 586*
apartheid, *p. 586*
township, *p. 587*

TAKING NOTES As you read, take notes on the history and culture of Southern Africa. Use the chart below to organize your notes.

History	Culture

If YOU lived there...

You are a hunter living in Southern Africa 10,000 years ago. The animals you hunt include antelope, rhinoceros, and ostrich. A spear is your only weapon. You spend several days following herds of animals until you and several other people are able to surround them. After the hunt, you decide to paint your hunting experience on a rock overhang near where you live.

Why do you paint these images of animals?

BUILDING BACKGROUND Southern Africa's fertile land and its abundance of wildlife have supported different peoples for tens of thousands of years. Hunter-gatherers were the first peoples to thrive in the region. Much later, peoples from West Africa migrated to the region, and then eventually Europeans.

History

As you learned in the previous chapter, Bantu farmers migrated from West Africa to Central Africa as early as 2,000 years ago. These peoples also migrated to Southern Africa at about the same time. Much later, in the 1700s, Europeans arrived on the coast of Southern Africa and forever changed the landscape and ways of life of the people in the region.

Early History

For many centuries the Khoisan peoples lived in Southern Africa. Divided into several ethnic groups, the Khoisan were hunter-gatherers and herders. When the early Bantu peoples migrated from West and Central Africa, they brought new languages and iron tools.

One Bantu group, the Shona, built an empire that reached its height in the 1400s. The Shona Empire included much of what is now the countries of Zimbabwe and Mozambique.

The Shona farmed, raised cattle, and traded gold with other groups on the coast.

The Shona are best known for **Great Zimbabwe**, their stone-walled capital. In fact, the name Zimbabwe is the Shona word for stone-walled towns. The builders of Great Zimbabwe used huge granite boulders and rectangular blocks of stone to build the capital's walls.

Founded in the late 1000s, Great Zimbabwe was a small trading and herding center. In the 1100s, the population grew, and both gold mining and farming grew in importance. Great Zimbabwe may have had 10,000 to 20,000 residents. With these resources, the city eventually became the center of a large trading network.

Trade made Great Zimbabwe's rulers wealthy and powerful. However, in the 1400s the gold trade declined. Deprived of its main source of wealth, Great Zimbabwe weakened. By 1500 it was no longer a capital and trading center.

Archaeologists have found Chinese porcelain and other artifacts from Asia at Great Zimbabwe. These artifacts suggest that the Shona traded widely. In addition to trading with peoples of Asia, the Shona apparently traded with the Swahili. The Swahili were Muslim Africans living along the East Africa coast. In effect, all of these peoples were once connected by an Indian Ocean trade network.

Europeans in Southern Africa

In the late 1400s traders from Portugal explored the Southern African coast on their way to Asia to trade for spices. To get to Asia from Portugal, they had to sail around the southern tip of Africa and then cross the Indian Ocean. The trip was long and difficult, so they set up bases on the Southern African coast. These bases provided the ships with supplies.

The Dutch Other Europeans arrived in Southern Africa after the Portuguese. People from the Netherlands, or the Dutch, were the first Europeans to settle in the region. In 1652 the Dutch set up a trade station at a natural harbor near the **Cape of Good Hope**.

Great Zimbabwe

Highly skilled craftspeople built several stone walls that surrounded the Shona capital of Great Zimbabwe. Today the ruins are a World Heritage Site.

ANALYZING VISUALS Why do you think Great Zimbabwe was made of stone?

The Cape sits at the tip of Africa. The land around the Cape lacked the gold and copper of the interior. However, it had a mild climate, similar to the climate the Dutch were used to back home.

This small colony on the Cape provided supplies to Dutch ships sailing between Dutch colonies in the East Indies and the Netherlands. The Dutch eventually brought in slaves from the region and Southeast Asia to work in the colony.

The Afrikaners and the Boers The people of the colony were very diverse. In addition to the Dutch, other Europeans also settled on the Cape. Dutch, French, and German settlers and their descendants in South Africa were called **Afrikaners**. Over time, a new language called Afrikaans emerged in the Cape colony. This language combined Dutch with Khoisan and Bantu words. German, French, and English also influenced the language's development.

Dutch Settlers

This painting shows a meeting between a Dutch governor and a Khoisan chief.

In the early 1800s, Great Britain took over the area of the Cape. The **Boers**, Afrikaner frontier farmers who had spread out from the original Cape colony, resisted the British. Many Boers packed all their belongings into wagons and soon moved farther east and north.

The Zulu and the British At about the same time, a Bantu-speaking group, the Zulu, became a powerful fighting force in the region. They conquered the surrounding African peoples, creating their own empire. When the Boers moved north of the Cape, they entered Zulu territory. The two sides clashed over control of the land. Eventually the British also wanted Zulu land. After a series of battles, the British defeated the Zulu.

The ending of slavery in the British Empire in the 1830s brought changes to the economy of colonial settlements in the region. Instead of slaves, people traded ivory—the tusks of elephants. Over time, however, hunters wiped out the entire elephant population in some parts of Southern Africa. With ivory in short supply, trade shifted to diamonds and gold, which were discovered in South Africa in the 1860s.

Apartheid

In the early 1900s South Africa's government, which was dominated by white Afrikaners, became increasingly racist. As a result, black South Africans opposed the government. To defend their rights, they formed the African National Congress (ANC) in 1912.

However, the trend toward racial division and inequality continued. South Africa's government set up a policy of separation of races, or **apartheid**, which means "apartness." This policy divided people into four groups: whites, blacks, Coloureds, and Asians.

Music of South Africa

Stomping. Spinning. Swaying. This is the kind of dancing you might see at a performance of South African music. In addition, musicians playing drums, guitars, and traditional flutes provide a rhythmic beat that makes it impossible to stand still.

One of the groups that does it the best are the Mahotella Queens. They are grandmothers who have been singing together for over 40 years. Their songs mix gospel with traditional African music. Performing all over the world, the Queens give unforgettable performances of nonstop singing and dancing.

Drawing Conclusions Why do you think South African music is popular around the world?

Coloureds and Asians were only allowed to live in certain areas. Each African tribe or group was given its own rural "homeland." These homelands generally did not include good farmland, mines, and other natural resources. Those resources were owned by the whites, and blacks had no rights in white areas.

Housing, health care, and schools for blacks were poor compared to those for whites. Schools for Coloureds were poor, but slightly better than the black schools.

During apartheid, many blacks found work in white-owned industries, mines, shops, and farms. Blacks had to live in separate areas called **townships**, which were often crowded clusters of tiny homes. The townships were far from the jobs in the cities and mines.

Independence

Beginning in the 1960s, many colonies gained independence from the European countries that had once colonized them. Some gained independence rather peacefully, but others struggled. For example, the British colonists in Rhodesia fought native Africans for years. Fighting broke out after the colonists declared their own white-dominated republic in 1970. Finally, in 1980, the Africans won independence and renamed their country Zimbabwe.

Independence also did not come easy for other countries. Despite violent resistance, Namibia continued to be ruled by South Africa until 1990. Mozambique was granted independence in 1975 after 10 years of war against Portuguese rule.

READING CHECK **Generalizing** Why did Europeans settle Southern Africa?

Culture

Over time, many groups of people created a diverse culture in Southern Africa. As a result, the region's culture reflects both European and African influence.

Ndebele Village

The Ndebele are one of many ethnic groups in South Africa who have kept their traditional culture alive. Many live in villages of brightly painted houses and courtyards.

ANALYSIS SKILL | ANALYZING VISUALS

What aspect of Ndebele culture do you see in these two photographs?

People

The people of Southern Africa belong to hundreds of different ethnic groups. Some groups are very large. For example, about 9 million people in South Africa are Zulu. More than 1.2 million of Botswana's 1.6 million people belong to a single ethnic group, the Tswana.

Other ethnic groups are small and usually not native to Africa. For example, about 6 percent of Namibia's population is of German descent. In Madagascar people are a mix of 18 small ethnic groups. These Malagasy groups descended from people who migrated across the Indian Ocean from Indonesia.

Languages

FOCUS ON READING

What generalization can you make about the languages spoken in Southern Africa?

Because people in Southern Africa belong to hundreds of different ethnic groups, they speak many languages. Most of the African languages spoken in Southern Africa are related to one of two language families—Khoisan or Bantu.

The early peoples of Southern Africa spoke different Khoisan languages. Khoisan speakers are known for the "click" sounds they make when they speak. Today, the majority of Khoisan speakers belong to the San ethnic group and live in remote areas of Botswana and Namibia.

Most people in Southern Africa speak one of the more than 200 Bantu languages. For example, most of South Africa's 11 official languages are Bantu.

In countries with European influence, European languages are also spoken. For example, English is the official language of Namibia and Zimbabwe. The official language of Mozambique is Portuguese.

Religion

In addition to language, Europeans brought the religion of Christianity to Southern Africa. As a result, millions of people in Southern Africa are Christians. In Namibia and South Africa the majority of the population is Christian.

Painting houses is traditionally the role of Ndebele women. They use colorful geometric patterns.

Artists in Zimbabwe are known for their beautiful stone sculptures of birds and other animals. Traditional crafts of Botswana include ostrich-eggshell beadwork and woven baskets with complex designs. People there also produce colorful wool rugs.

READING CHECK **Analyzing** Why do you think the people of Southern Africa speak several different languages?

SUMMARY AND PREVIEW Southern Africa's ancient history and later European settlement greatly influenced the region's culture. Next, you will learn about the governments and economies of the region's countries today.

Many people in Southern Africa who are not Christian practice traditional African religions. Some of these people believe that ancestors and the spirits of the dead have divine powers. In Zimbabwe, traditional beliefs and Christianity have been mixed together. About half of the people in Zimbabwe practice a combination of traditional beliefs and Christianity.

Celebrations and Art

Southern Africans celebrate many holidays. On Heritage Day, South Africans celebrate their country's diverse population. Most countries in Southern Africa celebrate their countries' independence day. Many Christian holidays such as Christmas Day are also celebrated throughout the region.

Southern Africa's art reflects its many cultures. For example, South African artists make traditional ethnic designs for items such as clothing, lamps, linens, and other products. Artists in Lesotho are famous for their woven tapestries of daily life.

Section 2 Assessment

Reviewing Ideas, Terms, and Places
1. **a. Define** What was **apartheid**?
   b. Draw Conclusions Why did the Shona capital of **Great Zimbabwe** decline as a trading center?
   c. Elaborate Why do you think the language of Afrikaans developed among the European colonists?
2. **a. Recall** What ethnic group in Southern Africa speaks languages that use click sounds?
   b. Draw Conclusions How do the religions practiced in Southern Africa reflect the region's history?
   c. Evaluate Why do you think Heritage Day is a national holiday in South Africa?

Critical Thinking
3. **Sequencing** Review your notes on the history of Southern Africa. Then organize your information using a time line like the one below. You may add more dates if you need to.

AD 1000   1990

FOCUS ON VIEWING
4. **Discussing History and Culture** Which information about the history and culture of Southern Africa might make a good TV news report? What visuals would be interesting?

Southern Africa Today

Main Ideas

1. South Africa ended apartheid and now has a stable government and strong economy.
2. Some countries of Southern Africa have good resources and economies, but several are still struggling.
3. Southern African governments are responding to issues and challenges such as drought, disease, and environmental destruction.

The Big Idea

Countries of Southern Africa today are trying to use their governments and resources to improve their economies and deal with challenges.

Key Terms and Places

sanctions, *p. 590*
Cape Town, *p. 592*
enclave, *p. 592*

TAKING NOTES As you read, take notes on the countries of Southern Africa today and the challenges they face. Use this chart to organize your notes.

South Africa	
Other Countries	
Challenges	

If YOU lived there...

You are an economic adviser in Botswana. In recent years your country has made progress toward improving people's lives, but you think there is room for improvement. One way you plan to help the economy is by promoting tourism. Botswana already has amazing natural landscapes and fascinating animals.

What could your country do to attract more tourists?

BUILDING BACKGROUND Some of the countries in Southern Africa are relatively well off, with plentiful resources and good jobs and transportation systems. Others lack these positive conditions. One of the most successful countries in the region is South Africa.

South Africa

Today South Africa has a stable government and the strongest economy in the region. In addition, many South Africans are enjoying new rights and freedoms. The country has made great progress in resolving the problems of its past, but it still faces many challenges.

End of Apartheid

Ending apartheid, the separation of races, has probably been South Africa's biggest challenge in recent years. Many people around the world objected to the country's apartheid laws. For that reason, they put **sanctions**—economic or political penalties imposed by one country on another to force a change in policy—on South Africa. Some countries banned trade with South Africa. Several companies in the United States and Europe refused to invest their money in South Africa. In addition, many international scientific and sports organizations refused to include South Africans in meetings or competitions.

Celebrating Mandela's Freedom

South Africans in Soweto warmly welcomed Nelson Mandela after he was released from prison in 1990.

BIOGRAPHY

Nelson Mandela
(1918–   )

Because he protested against apartheid, Nelson Mandela was imprisoned for 26 years. In 1990, however, South Africa's President de Klerk released Mandela from prison. Mandela and de Klerk shared the Nobel Peace Prize in 1993. One year later, Mandela became South Africa's first black president. He wrote a new constitution and worked to improve the living conditions of black South Africans.

Summarizing What did Nelson Mandela accomplish when he was South Africa's president?

The sanctions isolated South Africa. As other countries in Southern Africa gained independence, South Africa became even more isolated. Protest within the country increased. In response, the government outlawed the African National Congress (ANC). This group had been formed to protect the rights of black South Africans. Many ANC members were jailed or forced to leave the country.

The antiapartheid protests continued, however. Finally, in the late 1980s South Africa began to move away from the apartheid system. In 1990 the government released its political prisoners, including Nelson Mandela. Mandela was elected president in 1994 after South Africans of all races were given the right to vote.

Today all races have equal rights in South Africa. The country's public schools and universities are open to all people, as are hospitals and transportation. However, economic equality has come more slowly. White South Africans are still wealthier than the vast majority of black South Africans. Still, South Africans now have opportunities for a better future.

Government and Economy

South Africa's government and economy are well positioned to create a better future for the country. South Africa's new government is a republic with an elected president. The country's constitution emphasizes equality and human rights.

In working toward equality, the government is trying to create jobs and better conditions for black workers and farmers. Currently, most of South Africa's wealth and industries are still controlled by whites. However, even some officials who favor reform are afraid to **execute** new policies. They fear that rapid change will weaken the economy. They are also concerned that it might cause educated and wealthy whites to leave the country.

ACADEMIC VOCABULARY

execute to perform, to carry out

South Africa's strong economy may help bring economic opportunities to the entire population. The country has more resources and industry than most African countries. For example, South Africa is the world's largest producer of several valuable minerals—gold, platinum, and chromium. The country is also a major exporter of gold and diamonds.

Large cities in South Africa also contribute to the country's economy. Africa's largest industrial area is located in Johannesburg. In addition, beautiful cities such as **Cape Town** attract many tourists.

READING CHECK **Analyzing** Why and how did South Africa do away with apartheid?

Other Countries of Southern Africa

The eight other countries in the region share some characteristics with South Africa. Some, but not all, have strong economies and stable governments.

Lesotho and Swaziland

These two countries are particularly influenced by South Africa. Lesotho and Swaziland are both enclaves. An **enclave** is a small territory surrounded by foreign territory. Lesotho and Swaziland are both located completely, or almost completely, within South Africa. Swaziland shares part of its border with Mozambique.

Close-up

Cape Town

Founded by the Dutch in 1652, Cape Town is a bustling international port city today. It lies on the South Atlantic Ocean and is home to about 3 million people.

Hiking trails lead to the top of Lion's Head for an amazing view of the city.

ANALYSIS SKILL **ANALYZING VISUALS**

What can you see in this photograph that might reveal why Cape Town is popular with tourists?

Because it is so small, Lesotho has few resources or agricultural land. As a result, it is a poor country. Many of its people work in nearby South Africa. In spite of its poverty, Lesotho has the highest female literacy rate in Africa. Most children, including females, get at least a primary education in free schools run by Christian churches.

Swaziland has some important mineral deposits and industry. Cattle raising and farming are also common there. A good transportation system helps Swaziland to participate in foreign trade.

Lesotho and Swaziland are both kingdoms. Although each country has a king as head of state, each is governed by an elected prime minister and a parliament.

The city's buildings are a mix of modern and Dutch colonial architecture.

People jog, bike, and rollerblade on this trail along the ocean.

Namibia

Namibia gained its independence from South Africa as recently as 1990. Now it is a republic with an elected president and legislature. Its capital, Windhoek, is located in the central highlands.

Very few people live in Namibia's deserts in the east and the west, but these areas are the sites of some of the richest mineral deposits in Africa. Most of the country's income comes from the mining of diamonds, copper, uranium, lead, and zinc. Fishing in the Atlantic Ocean and sheep ranching are also important sources of income. In spite of this strong economy, however, most people are still poor.

Botswana

Botswana is one of Africa's success stories, thanks to mineral resources and a stable democratic government. The main economic activities in Botswana are cattle ranching and diamond mining. Recently, international companies have built factories there, and tourism is increasing. Although unemployment is high, the country has had one of the world's highest rates of economic growth since the 1960s.

FOCUS ON READING

In general, what is Botswana's economy like?

Zimbabwe

Zimbabwe has suffered from a poor economy and political instability. Zimbabwe does not lack resources. It has gold and copper mines as well as productive agriculture and manufacturing. However, high inflation, debts, and war have hurt the economy.

In addition, there is much inequality. Although white residents made up less than 1 percent of the population, they owned most of the large farms and ranches. In 2000 the president began a program to take farmland from white farmers and give the land to black residents. This action led many white farmers to leave the country and caused food shortages.

Tourism in Southern Africa

Tourism is a rapidly growing industry in a number of countries in Southern Africa. The region's wildlife is its main attraction. People come from all over the world to see lions, elephants, zebras, and giraffes in their natural habitats. Many countries have established huge parks to protect these habitats.

Analyzing How do you think tourism affects a country?

THE WORLD ALMANAC
Facts about Countries

Tourism in Southern Africa

	Country	Numbers of Visitors in 2003
1	South Africa	6.6 million
2	Zimbabwe	2.3 million
3	Botswana	975,000
4	Mozambique	726,000
5	Namibia	695,000

Interpreting Tables How many people visited Zimbabwe?

go.hrw.com KEYWORD: SG7 CH24

The attempt at land reform, the poor economy, and violent acts against political opponents have made people in Zimbabwe unhappy with the president. Although he was re-elected in 2002, most people think the election was flawed.

Mozambique

Mozambique is one of the world's poorest countries. The economy has been badly damaged by civil war, but it is improving. Mozambique's ports ship many products from the interior of Africa. Taxes collected on these shipments are an important source of income. Also, plantations grow cashews, cotton, and sugar for export. The country must import more than it exports, however, and it relies on foreign aid.

Madagascar and Comoros

Madagascar was ruled for more than 20 years by a socialist dictator. Today the elected president is working to improve the struggling economy. Most of the country's income comes from exports of coffee, vanilla, sugar, and cloves. Madagascar also has some manufacturing, and the country is popular with tourists who come to see the unique plants and animals.

Comoros is a country made up of four tiny islands. It suffers from a lack of resources and political instability. The government of Comoros is struggling to improve education and promote tourism.

READING CHECK **Contrasting** In what ways are Botswana and Zimbabwe different?

Issues and Challenges

Although conditions in many countries of Southern Africa are better than they are on much of the continent, the region has its own challenges. One of the most serious problems facing Southern Africa is poverty. Terrible droughts often destroy food crops. In addition, many of Southern Africa's people are unemployed.

Disease is another problem. Southern Africa has high numbers of people infected with HIV. The region's governments are trying to educate people to slow the spread of disease.

Another challenge is environmental destruction. For example, in Madagascar, deforestation leads to erosion. There is hope for the future, though. Namibia was the first country in the world to put environmental protection in its constitution. Also, the African Union (AU) works to promote cooperation among African countries. The AU tries to solve problems across the continent.

READING CHECK **Generalizing** What main challenges does Southern Africa face?

Baobab trees line a street in Madagascar.

SUMMARY Southern Africa has valuable mineral resources and landscapes popular with tourists. Some countries have more stable governments and economies than much of Africa. However, the region still faces many challenges.

Section 3 Assessment

Reviewing Ideas, Terms, and Places

1. **a. Describe** What effect did **sanctions** have on South Africa?
   b. Interpret What have been two effects of the end of apartheid?
2. **a. Recall** Which country's president began a program to take farmland from white farmers?
   b. Make Inferences Why might being an **enclave** affect a country's economy?
   c. Rank Besides South Africa, which two countries in the region seem to have the best economies?
3. **a. Describe** How does terrible drought lead to poverty?
   b. Explain How are people in Southern Africa addressing the challenges in the region?

Critical Thinking

4. **Summarizing** Review your notes on South Africa. Then using a graphic organizer like this one, describe what the country has been like at each different period.

Before the 1990s	The 1990s	Today

FOCUS ON VIEWING

5. **Telling about Southern Africa Today** Would you try to include information about all of Southern Africa in your report? Or would you just focus on one country? Take notes on your ideas.

SOUTHERN AFRICA **595**

Evaluating a Web Site

Learn

The Internet is one of the most valuable tools available for research today. However, not everything that you find on the Internet is useful or accurate. You have to be careful and analyze the sites you use.

A good Web site should be accurate and up-to-date. Before you use a site for research, find out who produced it. The author should be qualified and unbiased. Also, check to see when the site was last updated. If it has not been updated recently, the information it contains may no longer be accurate.

Practice

Study this page taken from a Web site and then answer these questions.

1 Who do you think produced this Web site? How can you tell?

2 What kinds of information can you find on this site?

3 Do you think this would be a good site for research? Why or why not?

A country's official Web site is usually a good source for information.

Check to see how current the articles on the Web site are. Have they been updated regularly?

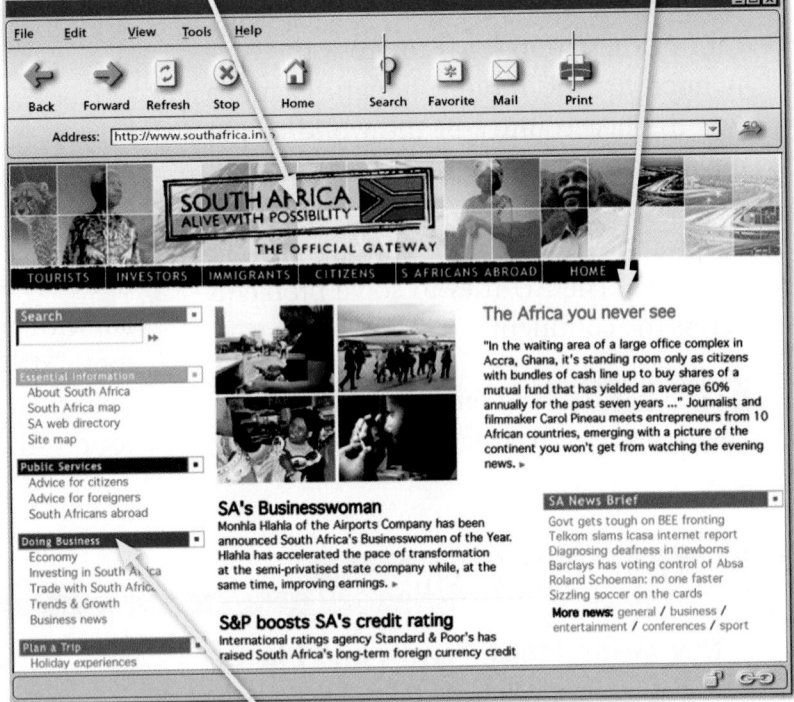

Notice what type of information is present on the Web site. Is the site biased or unbalanced?

Apply

Search the Internet to find a Web page about one of the countries of Southern Africa. Analyze the site and determine whether you think it would be a good site for research. Write a paragraph to explain your decision. Make sure to include the site's URL and the date on which you visited it in your report.

Geography's Impact
video series
Review the video to answer the
closing question:
*What are some ways South
Africans could continue working together?*

Visual Summary

*Use the visual summary below to help you review
the main ideas of the chapter.*

QUICK
FACTS

The Drakensberg rises to meet a high
plateau that dominates the physical
geography of Southern Africa.

Traditional African and European cultures mix in Southern Africa. Music and
dance are very important.

Countries such as South Africa have
strong economies and modern cities.
Other countries struggle with poverty.

Reviewing Vocabulary, Terms, and Places

Match the words with their definitions.

1. Great Zimbabwe   **5.** sanctions

2. features   **6.** townships

3. Boers   **7.** escarpment

4. apartheid   **8.** enclave

a. the steep face at the edge of a plateau or other raised area

b. economic or political penalties imposed by one country on another to force a change in policy

c. a large, stone-walled town built by the Shona

d. Afrikaner frontier farmers in South Africa

e. a small territory surrounded by foreign territory

f. characteristics

g. South Africa's policy of separation of races

h. separate areas with clusters of tiny homes for black South Africans

Comprehension and Critical Thinking

SECTION 1 *(Pages 580–583)*

9. a. Identify What are the two main deserts in Southern Africa?

b. Contrast How is the eastern part of Southern Africa different from the western part?

c. Elaborate How do you think the geography of Southern Africa has affected settlement patterns in the region?

SECTION 2 *(Pages 584–589)*

10. a. Define Who are the Afrikaners? What country do they live in?

b. Contrast How does the origin of Khoisan languages differ from Bantu languages? What is unusual about Khoisan languages?

c. Elaborate What was life like for non-whites under the policy of apartheid? What rights were blacks, Coloureds, and Asians denied?

SECTION 3 (Pages 590–595)

11. a. Identify Which countries are enclaves?

b. Analyze In what ways has South Africa changed with the end of apartheid? In what ways has it stayed the same?

c. Evaluate Poverty is the most serious challenge facing Southern Africa. Do you agree or disagree with this statement? Explain your answer.

Using the Internet

go.hrw.com
KEYWORD: SG7 CH24

12. Activity: Researching Apartheid From 1948 until 1994, many people in South Africa were legally discriminated against under the policy known as apartheid. Enter the activity keyword. Imagine that you are a reporter writing an article on the history of apartheid. Using both primary and secondary sources, research who started apartheid, how people struggled against it, and when it finally came to an end. Using that information, create an outline for your article. Be sure to include details from your research that support the main ideas.

FOCUS ON READING AND VIEWING

13. Making Generalizations Re-read the information about South Africa today in Section 3. Based on the specific information you read, make one generalization about the country's economy and one about its resources.

14. Presenting a TV News Report Review your notes and decide on a topic for your report. Next, identify the point you want to make about your topic—your purpose. Your purpose may be to share interesting information—a recently celebrated holiday, for example. Or your purpose may be more serious—perhaps the need to reduce poverty. Decide what images you will show and what you will say to make your point.

Create a script identifying visuals and voice over. Present your report to the class using visuals, just as though you were on the TV news. Listen and watch your classmates' reports. Evaluate their reports based on accuracy of content and visual interest.

Social Studies Skills

15. Analyzing a Web Site Search the Internet to find two Web sites about topics in Southern Africa. One Web site should be one you would consider good to use for research. The other site should be one you do not consider to be a good source of information for research. Write a paragraph comparing and contrasting the two sites. Be sure to explain why one site seems more useful and accurate than the other.

Map Activity

16. Southern Africa On a separate sheet of paper, match the letters on the map with their correct labels.

Cape of Good Hope   Namib Desert

Okavango Basin   Drakensberg

Orange River

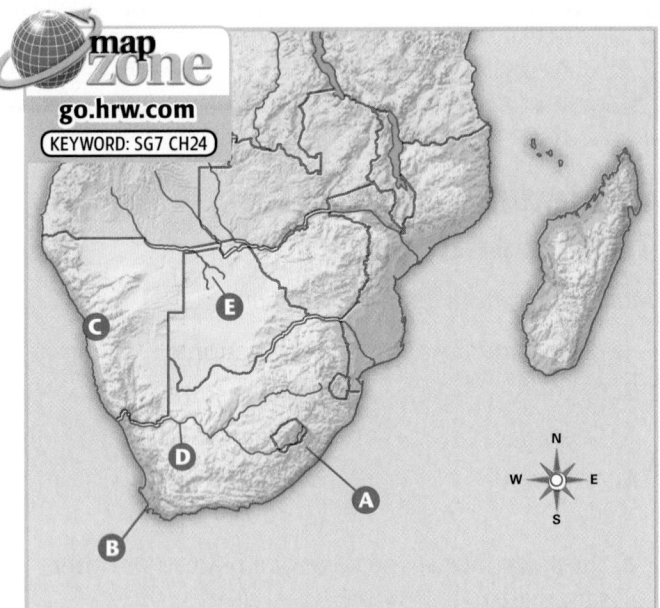

go.hrw.com
KEYWORD: SG7 CH24

DIRECTIONS: Read questions 1 through 7 and write the letter of the best response. Then read question 8 and write your own well-constructed response.

1 Most of the land in Southern Africa lies on a

A mountain range.

B coastal plain.

C plateau.

D delta.

2 The Dutch first settled in Southern Africa in 1652 near the

A Inyanga Mountains.

B Cape of Good Hope.

C Okavango Basin.

D Namib Desert.

3 Who were the first Europeans to explore the southern coast of Africa?

A Portuguese

B Dutch

C French

D German

4 Which country had a policy called apartheid to separate different races?

A Zimbabwe

B Madagascar

C Namibia

D South Africa

5 Which of the following statements about the end of apartheid is false?

A Sanctions helped bring the end of apartheid.

B Black people and white people now have economic equality.

C Both black people and white people can vote.

D Public schools and universities are open to all people.

Madagascar: Climate

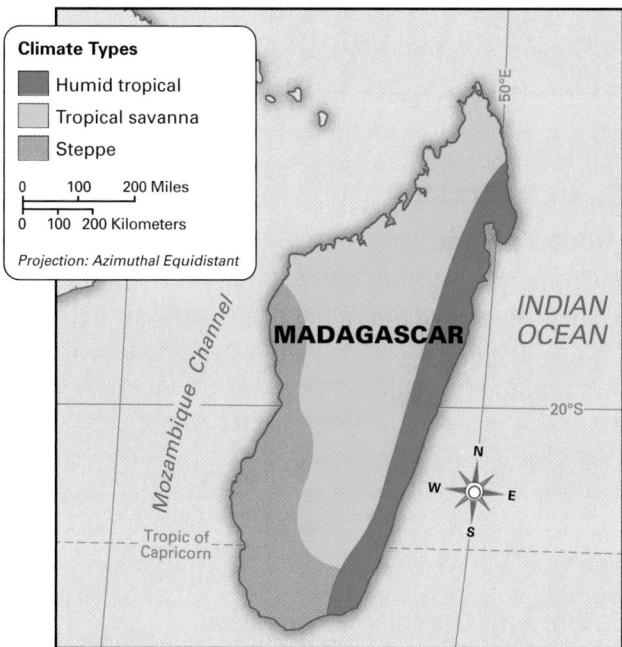

6 Based on the map above, where would Madagascar's tropical forests likely be located?

A in the east

B in the west

C on the savanna

D in the north

7 Which two countries are enclaves?

A South Africa and Lesotho

B Madagascar and Comoros

C Lesotho and Swaziland

D Zimbabwe and Mozambique

8 Extended Response Choose two countries from the table in Section 3 on Tourism in Southern Africa. Think about the information in this chart and what you know about the resources in these two countries. Write a paragraph explaining reasons for the differences and similarities in the number of tourists who visit each country.

Explaining Cause or Effect

"Why did it happen?" "What were the results?" Questions like these help us identify causes and effects. This, in turn, helps us understand the relationships among physical geography, history, and culture.

Assignment

Write a paper about one of these topics:

- causes of economic problems in West Africa
- effects of European colonization in Southern Africa

1. Prewrite

Choose a Topic

- Choose one of the topics above to write about.
- Turn that topic into a big idea, or thesis. For example, "Three main factors cause most of the economic problems in West Africa."

> **TIP** **What Relationships?** Transitional words like *as a result, because, since,* and *so* can help make connections between causes and effects.

Gather and Organize Information

- Depending on the topic you have chosen, identify at least three causes or three effects. Use your textbook, the library, or the Internet.
- Organize causes or effects in their order of importance. To have the most impact on your readers, put the most important cause or effect last.

2. Write

Use a Writer's Framework

A Writer's Framework

Introduction
- Start with an interesting fact or question related to your big idea, or thesis.
- State your big idea and provide background information.

Body
- Write at least one paragraph, including supporting facts and examples, for each cause or effect.
- Organize your causes or effects by order of importance.

Conclusion
- Summarize the causes or effects.
- Restate your big idea.

3. Evaluate and Revise

Review and Improve Your Paper

- Re-read your paper and use the questions below to determine how to make your paper better.
- Make changes to improve your paper.

Evaluation Questions for a Cause and Effect Explanation

1. Do you begin with a fact or question related to your big idea, or thesis?
2. Does your introduction identify your big idea and provide any needed background?
3. Do you have at least one paragraph for each cause or effect?
4. Do you include facts and details to support the connections between causes and effects?
5. Do you explain the causes or effects in order of importance?
6. Do you summarize the causes or effects and restate your big idea?

4. Proofread and Publish

Give Your Explanation the Finishing Touch

- Make sure transitional words and phrases connect causes and effects as clearly as possible.
- Check for capitalization of proper nouns, such as the names of countries and regions.
- Have someone else read your paper.

5. Practice and Apply

Use the steps and strategies outlined in this workshop to write your cause-and-effect paper. Share your paper with other students who wrote on the same topic. Compare your lists of causes or effects.

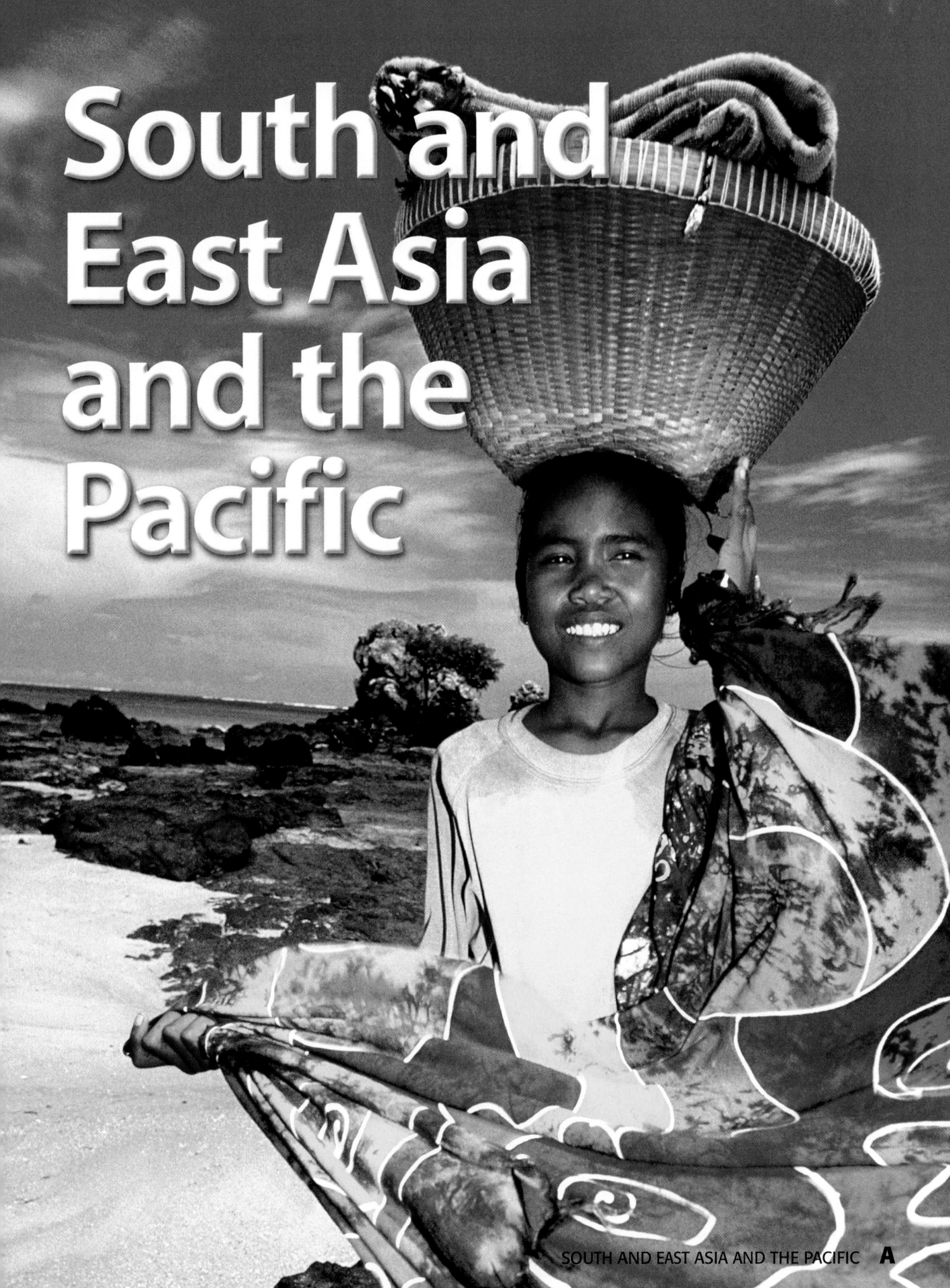

South and East Asia and the Pacific

Himalayas

The highest mountain range in the world, the Himalayas, separates the Indian Subcontinent from the rest of Asia.

The Outback

About 75 to 80 percent of Australia is covered by the Outback, a dry interior region of ancient rocks and plains.

South and East Asia and the Pacific

Rain Forest

The rich green color of Southeast Asia is caused by tropical rain forests. They are home to rare animals like the orangutan, found only in this region.

Explore the Satellite Image Towering mountains, dense rain forests, and dry plains are all features of this large region in Asia and the Pacific. What other physical features can you see in this satellite image?

The Satellite's Path

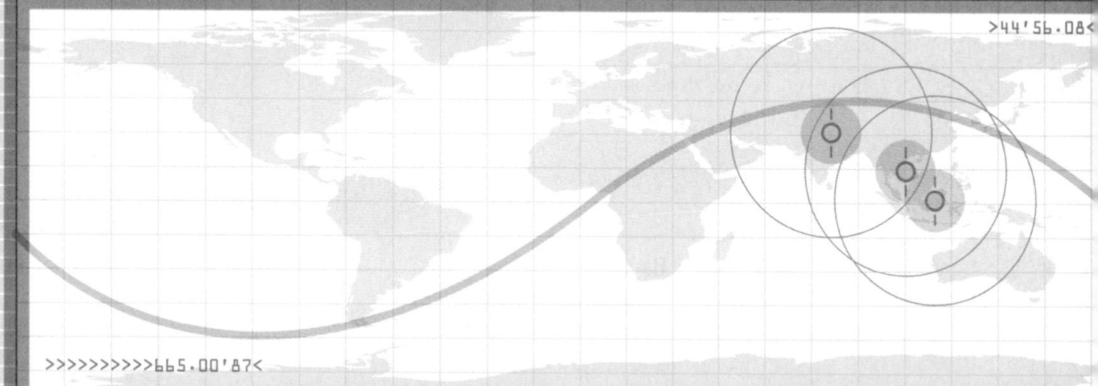

>44'56.08<

>>>>>>>>>>665.00'87<

+355

567.476.348

456.094.

+799

+803

+996

South and East Asia: Physical

ELEVATION

Feet	Meters
13,120	4,000
6,560	2,000
1,640	500
656	200
(Sea level) 0	0 (Sea level)
Below sea level	Below sea level

0   250   500   750 Miles

0   250   500   750 Kilometers

Projection: Two-Point Equidistant

map zone

Geography Skills

Regions South and East Asia includes many major rivers, long coastal plains, and large islands.

1. **Identify** What major rivers can you see in China and India?

2. **Make Inferences** How do you think rivers influence where people live in this region?

THE WORLD ALMANAC®
Facts about the World

Geographical Extremes: South and East Asia

Longest River	Chang Jiang (Yangzi River), China: 3,964 miles (6,378 km)
Highest Point	Mount Everest, Nepal/China: 29,035 feet (8,850 m)
Lowest Point	Turpan Depression, China: 505 feet (154 m) below sea level
Highest Recorded Temperature	Tuguegarao, Philippines: 108°F (42°C)
Wettest Place	Mawsynram, India: 467.4 inches (1,187.2 cm) average precipitation per year
Largest Country	China: 3,705,405 square miles (9,596,999 square km)
Smallest Country	Maldives: 116 square miles (300 square km)
Largest Rain Forest	Indonesia: 386,000 square miles (999,740 square km)
Strongest Earthquake	Off the coast of Sumatra, Indonesia, on December 26, 2004: Magnitude 9.0

Mount Everest

go.hrw.com KEYWORD: SG7 UN6

Size Comparison: The United States and South and East Asia

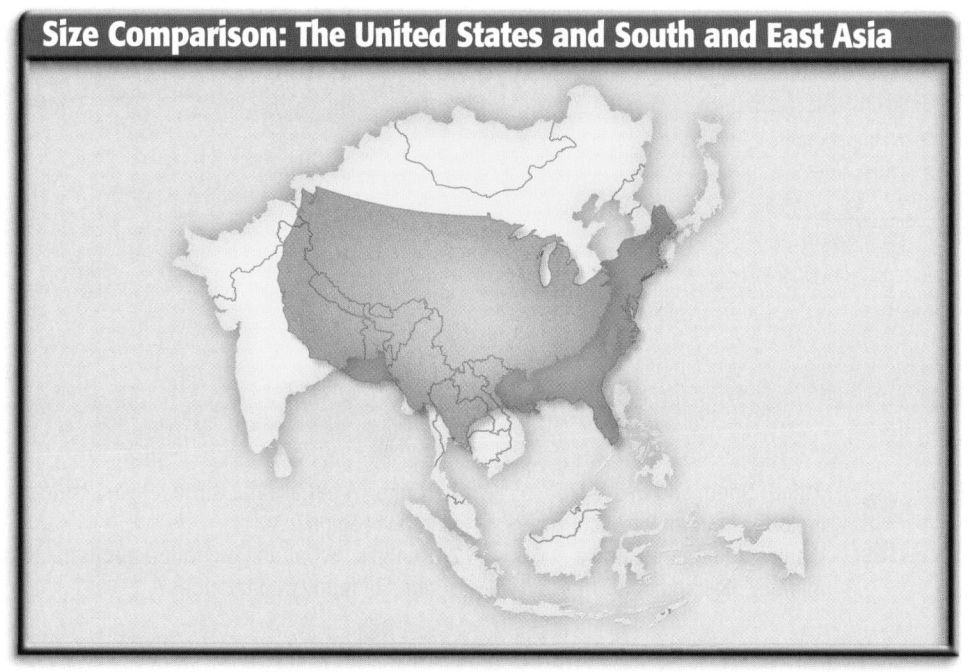

South and East Asia: Political

RUSSIA

CENTRAL ASIA

MONGOLIA

Ulaanbaatar ✪

NORTH KOREA

Pyongyang ✪

Seoul ✪

SOUTH KOREA

Sea of Japan (East Sea)

Tokyo ✪

JAPAN

PACIFIC OCEAN

Beijing ✪

Yellow Sea

Huang He (Yellow River)

CHINA

Shanghai ●

East China Sea

Tropic of Cancer

Islamabad ✪

KASHMIR

Indus River

PAKISTAN

Karachi ●

New Delhi ✪

NEPAL

Kathmandu ✪

BHUTAN

Thimphu ✪

Ganges River

Chongqing ●

Chang Jiang (Yangzi River)

Taipei ●

TAIWAN

Kolkata (Calcutta) ●

Dhaka ✪

MYANMAR (BURMA)

INDIA

Hong Kong

Mumbai (Bombay) ●

BANGLADESH

Hyderabad ●

Naypyidaw ✪

LAOS

Vientiane ✪

Hanoi ✪

Manila ✪

PHILIPPINES

Bay of Bengal

Yangon (Rangoon) ●

THAILAND

VIETNAM

South China Sea

Bangalore ●

Chennai (Madras) ●

Bangkok ✪

CAMBODIA

Phnom Penh ✪

MALDIVES

Colombo ✪

SRI LANKA

BRUNEI

Bandar Seri Begawan ✪

Male ✪

Kuala Lumpur ✪

MALAYSIA

Singapore ● SINGAPORE ✪

INDONESIA

Dili ✪

EAST TIMOR

0° Equator

INDIAN OCEAN

Jakarta ●

AUSTRALIA

Legend:
- ✪ National capital
- ● Other cities

0   250   500   750 Miles

0   250   500   750 Kilometers

Projection: Two-Point Equidistant

map zone
Geography Skills

Place South and East Asia includes several large countries, many smaller ones, and a number of island countries.

1. **Name** What are the three largest countries in this region?
2. **Analyze** What do you notice about the locations of many capital cities?

South and East Asia and the Pacific

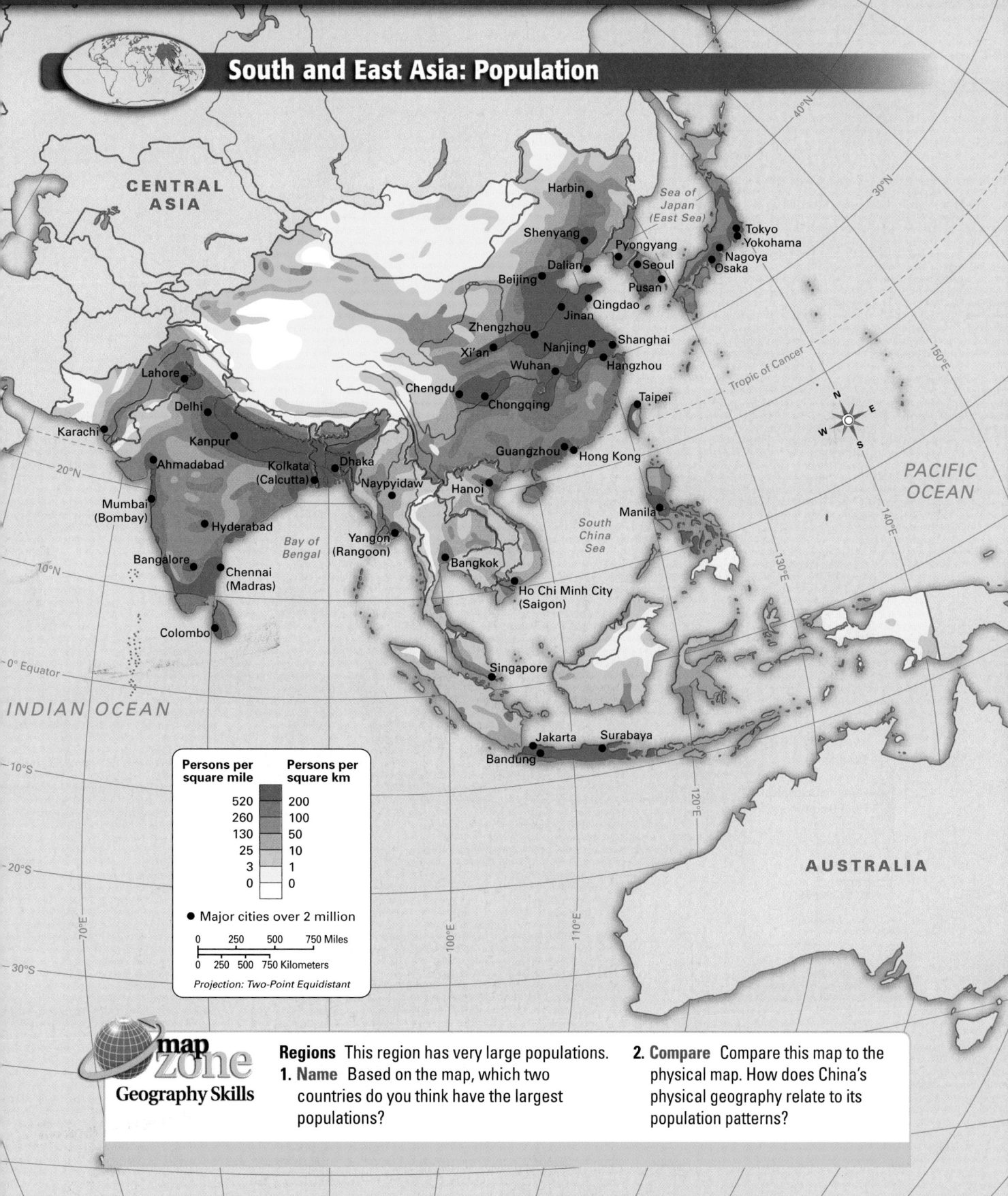

South and East Asia: Population

CENTRAL ASIA

Harbin
Shenyang
Pyongyang
Dalian
Beijing
Seoul
Pusan
Jinan
Qingdao
Zhengzhou
Nanjing
Shanghai
Xi'an
Wuhan
Hangzhou
Chengdu
Chongqing
Taipei
Guangzhou
Hong Kong

Sea of Japan (East Sea)

Tokyo
Yokohama
Nagoya
Osaka

Tropic of Cancer

PACIFIC OCEAN

Lahore
Delhi
Karachi
Kanpur
Ahmadabad
Kolkata (Calcutta)
Dhaka
Mumbai (Bombay)
Hyderabad
Naypyidaw
Hanoi
Bangalore
Chennai (Madras)
Yangon (Rangoon)
Bangkok
Manila
Colombo
Ho Chi Minh City (Saigon)
Singapore

Bay of Bengal

South China Sea

INDIAN OCEAN

Jakarta
Surabaya
Bandung

AUSTRALIA

Persons per square mile / Persons per square km

Persons per square mile	Persons per square km
520	200
260	100
130	50
25	10
3	1
0	0

● Major cities over 2 million

0   250   500   750 Miles
0   250 500 750 Kilometers

Projection: Two-Point Equidistant

map zone
Geography Skills

Regions This region has very large populations.
1. Name Based on the map, which two countries do you think have the largest populations?

2. Compare Compare this map to the physical map. How does China's physical geography relate to its population patterns?

South and East Asia: Climate

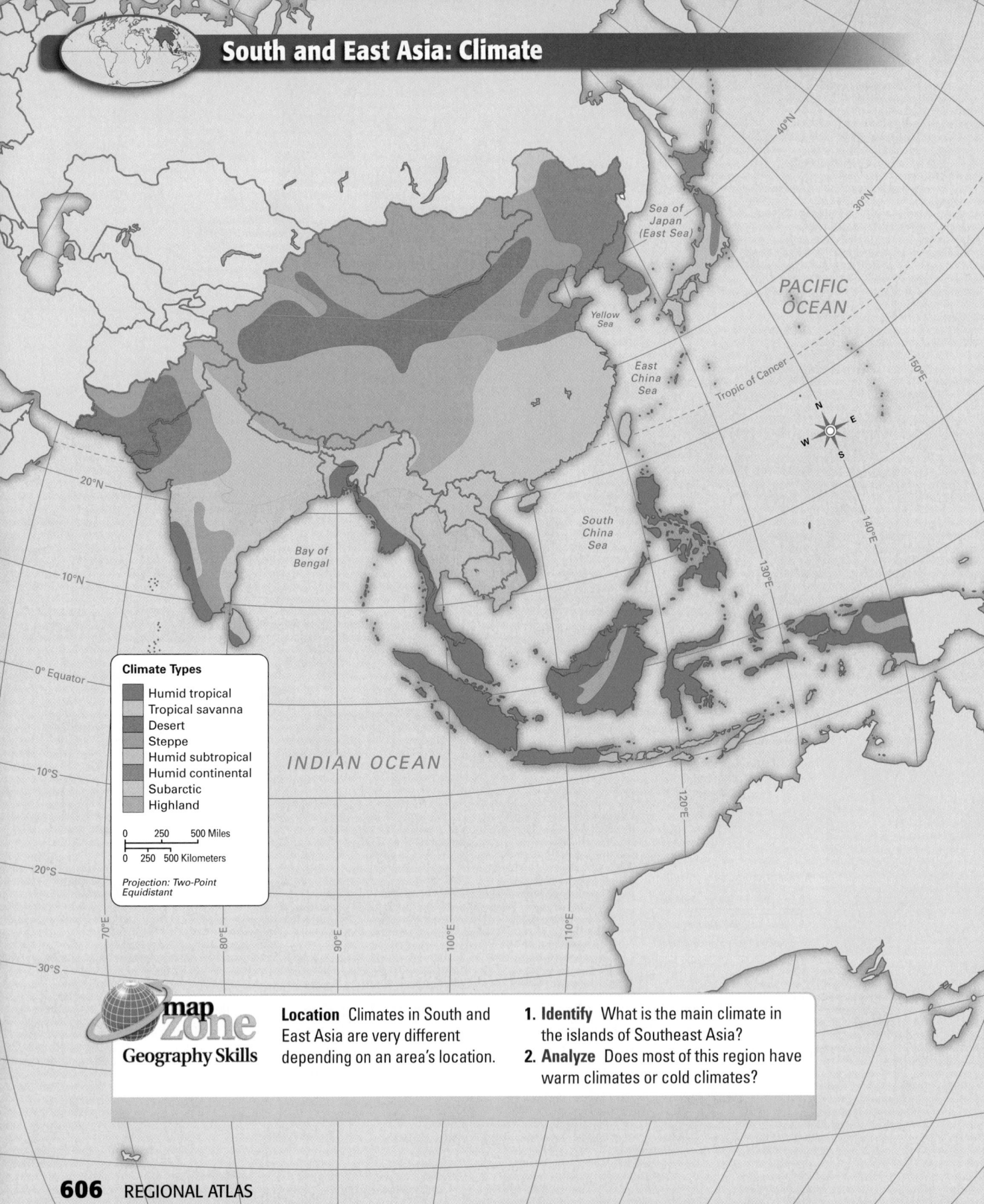

Climate Types

- Humid tropical
- Tropical savanna
- Desert
- Steppe
- Humid subtropical
- Humid continental
- Subarctic
- Highland

0   250   500 Miles

0   250   500 Kilometers

Projection: Two-Point Equidistant

Sea of Japan (East Sea)

PACIFIC OCEAN

Yellow Sea

East China Sea

Tropic of Cancer

South China Sea

Bay of Bengal

INDIAN OCEAN

map zone
Geography Skills

Location Climates in South and East Asia are very different depending on an area's location.

1. **Identify** What is the main climate in the islands of Southeast Asia?

2. **Analyze** Does most of this region have warm climates or cold climates?

South and East Asia and the Pacific

South and East Asia: Land Use and Resources

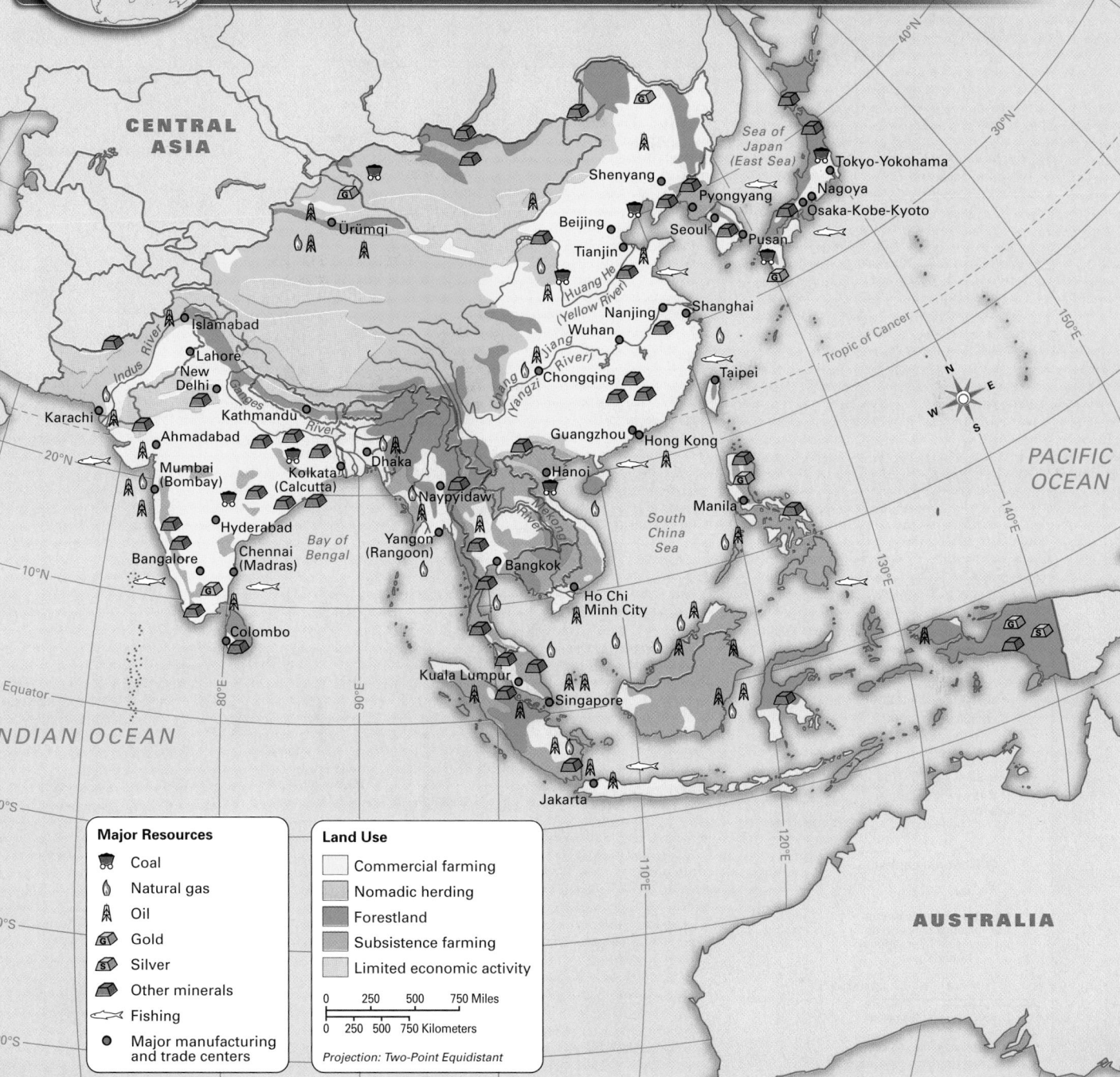

Major Resources

- 🪨 Coal
- 💧 Natural gas
- Oil
- 🥇 Gold
- 🥈 Silver
- Other minerals
- Fishing
- ● Major manufacturing and trade centers

Land Use

- Commercial farming
- Nomadic herding
- Forestland
- Subsistence farming
- Limited economic activity

```
0    250    500    750 Miles
0  250  500  750 Kilometers
```

Projection: Two-Point Equidistant

Geography Skills

Human-Environment Interaction
People have converted much of this region to farmland. South and East Asia is also rich in resources.

1. **Locate** In which part of China is commercial farming found?
2. **Explain** Why do you think interior parts of Asia have only limited economic activity?

The Pacific World: Physical

PACIFIC OCEAN

International Date Line

South China Sea

Philippine Sea

Northern Mariana Islands (U.S.)
Saipan

Wake Island (U.S.)

Guam (U.S.)

MARSHALL ISLANDS

SOUTHEAST ASIA

Koror
PALAU

MICRONESIA

Caroline Islands

Palikir

FEDERATED STATES OF MICRONESIA

Majuro

Howla Isla (U.

Tarawa

Bake (U.

0° Equator

New Ireland

NAURU

New Guinea

PAPUA NEW GUINEA

Bougainville I.

SOLOMON ISLANDS

TUVALU

INDIAN OCEAN

Darwin

Port Moresby

Honiara

Funafuti

Wallis Futuna

Cape York Peninsula

Coral Sea

VANUATU

Port-Vila

FIJI

Suva

20°S

AUSTRALIA

Great Barrier Reef

New Caledonia (FRANCE)

Noumea

Loyalty Islands (FRANCE)

Tropic of Capricorn

OUTBACK

WESTERN PLATEAU

MACDONNELL RANGES

Uluru (Ayers Rock) 2,845 ft (867 m)

Lake Eyre

Great Artesian Basin

GREAT DIVIDING RANGE

Brisbane

Norfolk Island (AUSTRALIA)

Kermadec Islands (N.Z.)

ELEVATION

Feet	Meters
13,120	4,000
6,560	2,000
1,640	500
656	200
(Sea level) 0	0 (Sea level)
Below sea level	Below sea level

Ice cap

✪ National capital

● City

Island boundaries are for convenience only and do not represent international boundaries.

Perth

NULLARBOR PLAIN

Darling R.

Lachlan R.

Sydney

Canberra

Mount Kosciusko 7,310 ft (2,228 m)

North Island

Auckland

Adelaide

Murray River

NEW ZEALAND

Wellington

Melbourne

Tasman Sea

Mount Cook 12,349 ft (3,764 m)

Christchurch

0   500   1,000 Miles

0   500   1,000 Kilometers

Projection: Mercator

Tasmania

Hobart

South Island

Chatha Islan (N

Stewart Island

N
W   E
S

Auckland Islands (NEW ZEALAND)

map zone
Geography Skills

Place The continent of Australia dominates the geography of the Pacific World.

1. **Name** What large island country is located southeast of Australia?

2. **Make Inferences** How do you think this region's island geography influences travel and trade?

100°E   120°E   140°E   160°E   180°

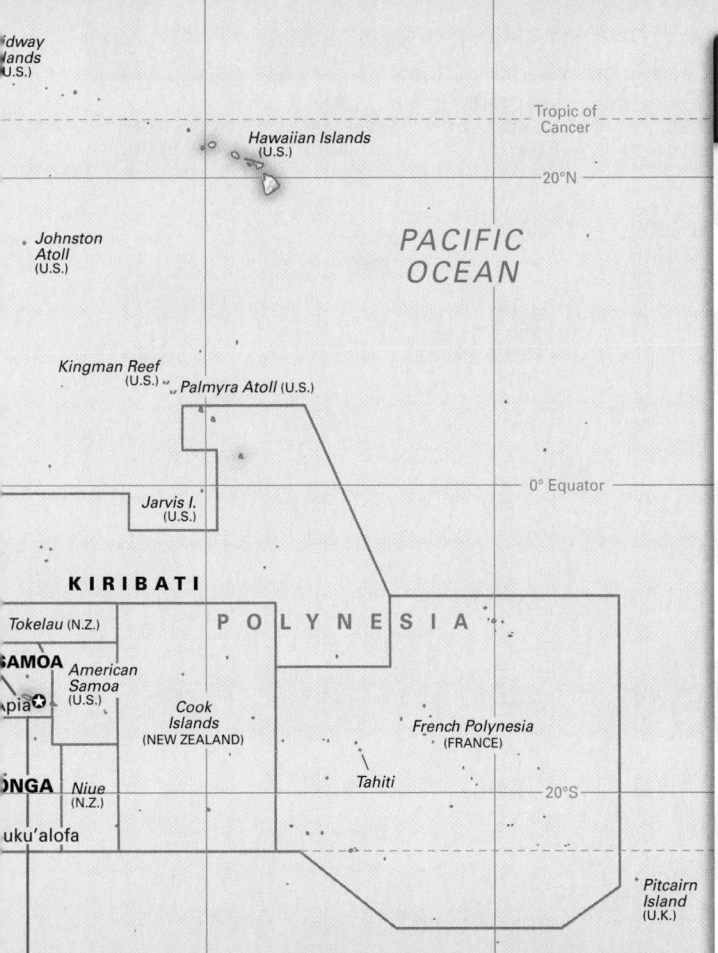

Hawaiian Islands (U.S.)

Tropic of Cancer

20°N

PACIFIC OCEAN

Johnston Atoll (U.S.)

Midway Islands (U.S.)

Kingman Reef (U.S.)

Palmyra Atoll (U.S.)

0° Equator

Jarvis I. (U.S.)

KIRIBATI

POLYNESIA

Tokelau (N.Z.)

SAMOA

American Samoa (U.S.)

Apia

Cook Islands (NEW ZEALAND)

French Polynesia (FRANCE)

Tahiti

TONGA

Niue (N.Z.)

20°S

Nuku'alofa

Pitcairn Island (U.K.)

THE WORLD ALMANAC
Facts about the World
Geographical Extremes: The Pacific World

Highest Point	Mount Wilhelm, Papua New Guinea: 14,793 feet (4,509 m)
Lowest Point	Lake Eyre, Australia: 52 feet (16 m) below sea level
Highest Recorded Temperature	Cloncurry, Australia: 128˚F (53˚C)
Lowest Recorded Temperature	Charlotte Pass, Australia: –9˚F (–22˚C)
Wettest Place	Bellenden Ker, Australia: 340 inches (863.6 cm) average precipitation per year
Driest Place	Mulka, Australia: 4.1 inches (10.4 cm) average precipitation per year
Largest Country	Australia: 2,967,908 square miles (7,686,882 square km)
Smallest Country	Nauru: 8 square miles (20.7 square km)
Largest Rain Forest	Papua New Guinea: 130,000 square miles (336,700 square km)
Longest Coral Reef	Great Barrier Reef, Australia: 1,250 miles (2,011 km)

Australia's Great Barrier Reef

go.hrw.com KEYWORD: SG7 UN6

Antarctica

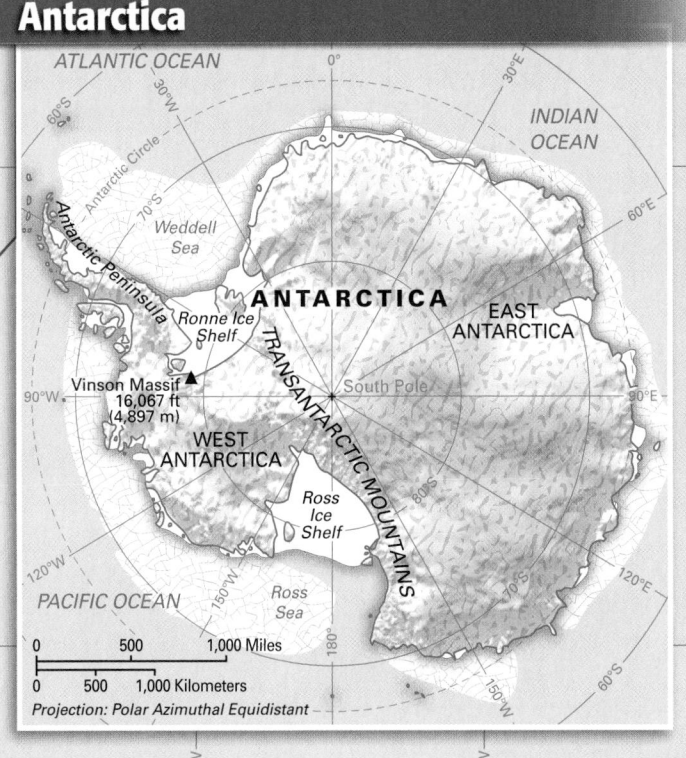

ATLANTIC OCEAN

0°

30°E

30°W

INDIAN OCEAN

60°S

Antarctic Circle

70°S

60°E

Weddell Sea

Antarctic Peninsula

ANTARCTICA

EAST ANTARCTICA

Ronne Ice Shelf

TRANSANTARCTIC MOUNTAINS

South Pole

90°W

90°E

Vinson Massif 16,067 ft (4,897 m)

WEST ANTARCTICA

Ross Ice Shelf

120°W

80°S

120°E

70°S

PACIFIC OCEAN

Ross Sea

0   500   1,000 Miles
0   500   1,000 Kilometers
Projection: Polar Azimuthal Equidistant

150°W

180

150°E

160°W

140°W

120°W

60°E

South and East Asia and the Pacific

COUNTRY Capital	FLAG	POPULATION	AREA (sq mi)	PER CAPITA GDP (U.S. $)	LIFE EXPECTANCY AT BIRTH	TVS PER 1,000 PEOPLE
Australia Canberra		20.4 million	2,967,909	$32,900	80.6	716
Bangladesh Dhaka		150.4 million	55,599	$2,200	62.8	7
Bhutan Thimphu		2.3 million	18,147	$1,400	55.2	6
Brunei Bandar Seri Begawan		374,600	2,228	$25,600	75.2	637
Cambodia Phnom Penh		14 million	69,900	$2,600	59.7	9
China Beijing		1,322 million	3,705,407	$7,600	72.9	291
East Timor Dili		1.1 million	5,794	$800	66.6	NA
Fiji Suva		918,700	7,054	$6,100	70.1	110
India New Delhi		1,129.8 million	1,269,346	$3,700	68.6	75
Indonesia Jakarta		234.7 million	741,100	$3,800	70.2	143
Japan Tokyo		127.4 million	145,883	$33,100	81.4	719
Kiribati Tarawa		107,800	313	$2,700	62.5	23
Laos Vientiane		6.5 million	91,429	$2,100	55.9	10
Malaysia Kuala Lumpur		24.8 million	127,317	$12,700	72.8	174
Maldives Male		369,000	116	$3,900	64.8	38
United States Washington, D.C.		301.1 million	3,718,711	$43,500	78.0	844

COUNTRY Capital	FLAG	POPULATION	AREA (sq mi)	PER CAPITA GDP (U.S. $)	LIFE EXPECTANCY AT BIRTH	TVS PER 1,000 PEOPLE
Marshall Islands Majuro		61,800	70	$2,900	70.6	NA
Micronesia, Federated States of Palikir		107,800	271	$2,300	70.4	20
Mongolia Ulaanbaatar		2.9 million	603,909	$2,000	65.3	58
Myanmar (Burma); Yangon (Rangoon), Naypyidaw		47.4 million	261,970	$1,800	62.5	7
Nauru No official capital		13,500	8	$5,000	63.4	1
Nepal Kathmandu		28.9 million	54,363	$1,500	60.6	6
New Zealand Wellington		4.1 million	103,738	$26,000	79.0	516
North Korea Pyongyang		23.3 million	46,541	$1,800	71.9	55
Pakistan Islamabad		164.7 million	310,403	$2,600	63.8	105
Palau Koror		20,800	177	$7,600	70.7	98
Papua New Guinea Port Moresby		5.8 million	178,704	$2,700	65.6	13
Philippines Manila		91.1 million	115,831	$5,000	70.5	110
Samoa Apia		214,300	1,137	$2,100	71.3	56
Singapore Singapore		4.6 million	268	$30,900	81.8	341
Solomon Islands Honiara		566,800	10,985	$600	73.2	16
United States Washington, D.C.		301.1 million	3,718,711	$43,500	78.0	844

COUNTRY Capital	FLAG	POPULATION	AREA (sq mi)	PER CAPITA GDP (U.S. $)	LIFE EXPECTANCY AT BIRTH	TVS PER 1,000 PEOPLE
South Korea Seoul		49 million	38,023	$24,200	77.2	364
Sri Lanka Colombo		20.9 million	25,332	$4,600	74.8	102
Taiwan Taipei		22.8 million	13,892	$29,000	77.6	327
Thailand Bangkok		65.1 million	198,457	$9,100	72.6	274
Tonga Nuku'alofa		116,900	289	$2,200	70.1	61
Tuvalu Funafuti		12,000	10	$1,600	68.6	9
Vanuatu Port-Vila		212,000	4,710	$2,900	63.2	12
Vietnam Hanoi		85.3 million	127,244	$3,100	71.1	184
United States Washington, D.C.		301.1 million	3,718,711	$43,500	78.0	844

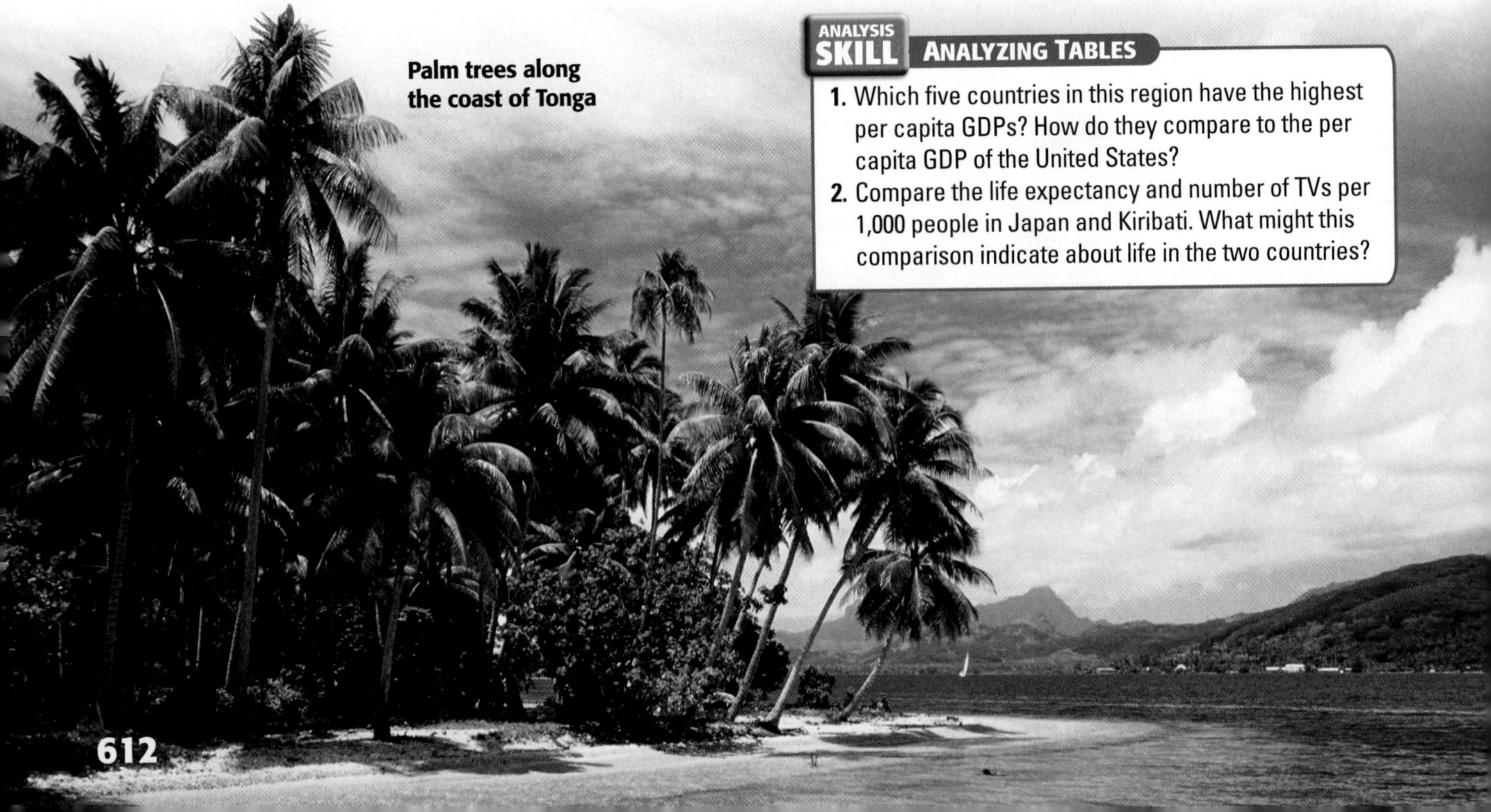

Palm trees along the coast of Tonga

ANALYSIS SKILL **ANALYZING TABLES**

1. Which five countries in this region have the highest per capita GDPs? How do they compare to the per capita GDP of the United States?
2. Compare the life expectancy and number of TVs per 1,000 people in Japan and Kiribati. What might this comparison indicate about life in the two countries?

Population Giants

World's Largest Populations

Country	Population
China	1.3 billion
India	1.1 billion
United States	301.1 million
Indonesia	234.7 million
Brazil	190.0 million
Pakistan	164.7 million
Bangladesh	150.4 million
Russia	141.4 million
Nigeria	135.0 million
Japan	127.4 million

■ Asian Countries
■ Other Countries

Of the ten countries with the largest populations, six are located in South and East Asia.

Percent of World Population

China 20%
India 17%
Rest of Asia 24%
Rest of the world 39%

The large populations of China and India help make Asia home to more than 60 percent of the world's people.

Economic Powers

Japan

- World's third-largest economy
- $590.3 billion in exports
- Per capita GDP of $33,100
- Major exports: transportation equipment, cars, semiconductors, electronics

Japan is one of the most technologically advanced countries and is a leading producer of hi-tech goods.

China

- World's second-largest economy
- $974 billion in exports
- GDP growth rate of 10.5%
- Major exports: machinery and electronics, clothing, plastics, furniture, toys

China is an emerging economic powerhouse with a huge population and a fast growing economy.

ANALYSIS SKILL **ANALYZING VISUALS**

1. Which two countries have the largest populations?
2. What kinds of exports help make Japan and China economic powers?

CHAPTER 25

The Indian Subcontinent

What You Will Learn...

In this chapter you will learn about the physical geography of the Indian Subcontinent. You will also discover the history and culture of the region. Finally, you will learn about the countries of the Indian Subcontinent today.

FOCUS ON READING AND VIEWING

Visualizing As you read, try to visualize the people, places, or events that the text describes. Visualizing, or creating mental images, helps you to better understand and remember the information that is presented. Use your senses to imagine how things look, sound, smell, and feel. **See the lesson, Visualizing, on page R26.**

Presenting and Viewing a Travelogue You are journeying through the Indian Subcontinent, noting the sights and sounds of this beautiful and bustling region of the world. As you read this chapter you will gather details about this region. Then you will create an oral presentation of a travelogue, or traveler's journal. After you present your travelogue, you will watch and listen as your classmates present their travelogues.

IRAQ

IRAN

○ National capital
● Major city
--- Disputed boundary

0   150   300 Miles
0   150   300 Kilometers

Projection: Albers Equal-Area

30°N

SAUDI ARABIA

20°N

OMAN

YEMEN

50°E

map zone

Geography Skills

Place The Indian Subcontinent is a large landmass in South Asia.
1. **Locate** What bodies of water border the Indian Subcontinent?
2. **Analyze** What separates the Indian Subcontinent from the rest of Asia?

go.hrw.com (KEYWORD: SG7 CH25)

Culture The people of the subcontinent represent the many cultures and religions of the region.

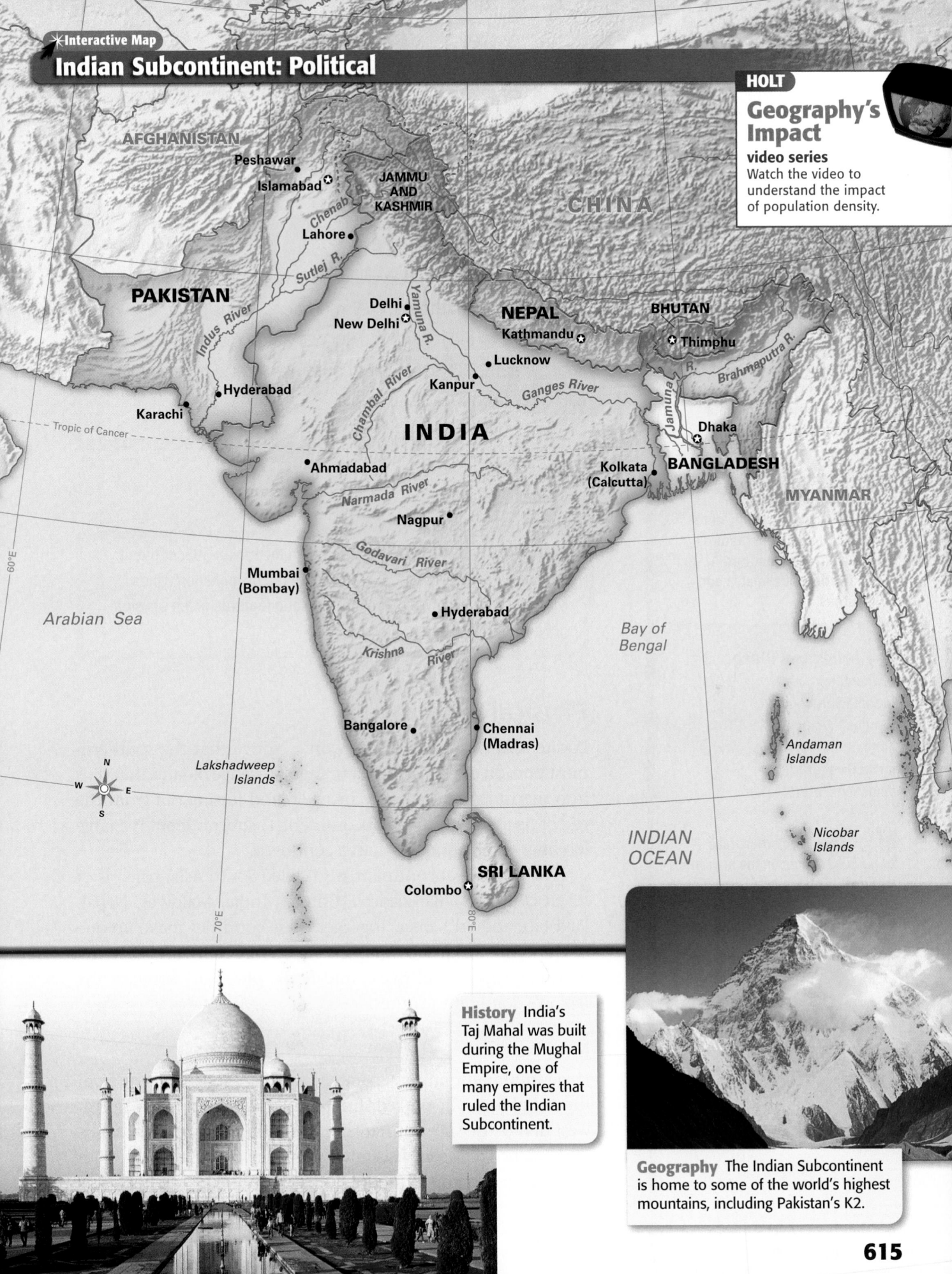

AFGHANISTAN

Peshawar
Islamabad ✪

JAMMU
AND
KASHMIR

CHINA

Chenab

Lahore

Sutlej R.

PAKISTAN

Indus River

Delhi
New Delhi ✪

Yamuna R.

NEPAL

Kathmandu ✪

BHUTAN

✪ Thimphu

Brahmaputra R.

Lucknow

Hyderabad

Kanpur

Chambal River

Ganges River

Jamuna R.

Karachi

Tropic of Cancer

INDIA

Dhaka

Kolkata
(Calcutta)

BANGLADESH

MYANMAR

Ahmadabad

Narmada River

Nagpur

Godavari River

Mumbai
(Bombay)

Hyderabad

Arabian Sea

Krishna   River

Bay of
Bengal

Andaman
Islands

Bangalore

Chennai
(Madras)

Lakshadweep
Islands

N
W ✦ E
S

INDIAN
OCEAN

Nicobar
Islands

SRI LANKA

Colombo ✪

60°E

70°E

80°E

HOLT

Geography's Impact
video series
Watch the video to
understand the impact
of population density.

History India's
Taj Mahal was built
during the Mughal
Empire, one of
many empires that
ruled the Indian
Subcontinent.

Geography The Indian Subcontinent
is home to some of the world's highest
mountains, including Pakistan's K2.

Physical Geography

What You Will Learn...

Main Ideas

1. Towering mountains, large rivers, and broad plains are the key physical features of the Indian Subcontinent.
2. The Indian Subcontinent has a great variety of climate regions and resources.

The Big Idea

The physical geography of the Indian Subcontinent features unique physical features and a variety of climates and resources.

Key Terms and Places

subcontinent, *p. 616*
Mount Everest, *p. 617*
Ganges River, *p. 617*
delta, *p. 617*
Indus River, *p. 618*
monsoons, *p. 619*

TAKING NOTES As you read, take notes on the physical features, climates, and resources of the Indian Subcontinent. Use a diagram like the one below to organize your notes.

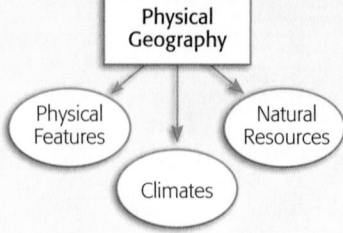

If YOU lived there...

You live in a small farming village in central India. Every year your father talks about the summer monsoons, winds that can bring heavy rains to the region. You know that too much rain can cause floods that may threaten your house and family. Too little rain could cause your crops to fail.

How do you feel about the monsoons?

BUILDING BACKGROUND Weather in the Indian Subcontinent, a region in southern Asia, is greatly affected by monsoon winds. Monsoons are just one of the many unique features of the physical geography of the Indian Subcontinent.

Physical Features

Locate Asia on a map of the world. Notice that the southernmost portion of Asia creates a triangular wedge of land that dips into the Indian Ocean. The piece of land jutting out from the rest of Asia is the Indian Subcontinent. A **subcontinent** is a large landmass that is smaller than a continent.

The Indian Subcontinent, also called South Asia, consists of seven countries—Bangladesh, Bhutan, India, Maldives, Nepal, Pakistan, and Sri Lanka. Together these countries make up one of the most unique geographic regions in the world. Soaring mountains, powerful rivers, and fertile plains are some of the region's dominant features.

Mountains

Huge mountain ranges separate the Indian Subcontinent from the rest of Asia. The rugged Hindu Kush mountains in the northwest divide the subcontinent from Central Asia. For thousands of years, peoples from Asia and Europe have entered the Indian Subcontinent through mountain passes in the Hindu Kush.

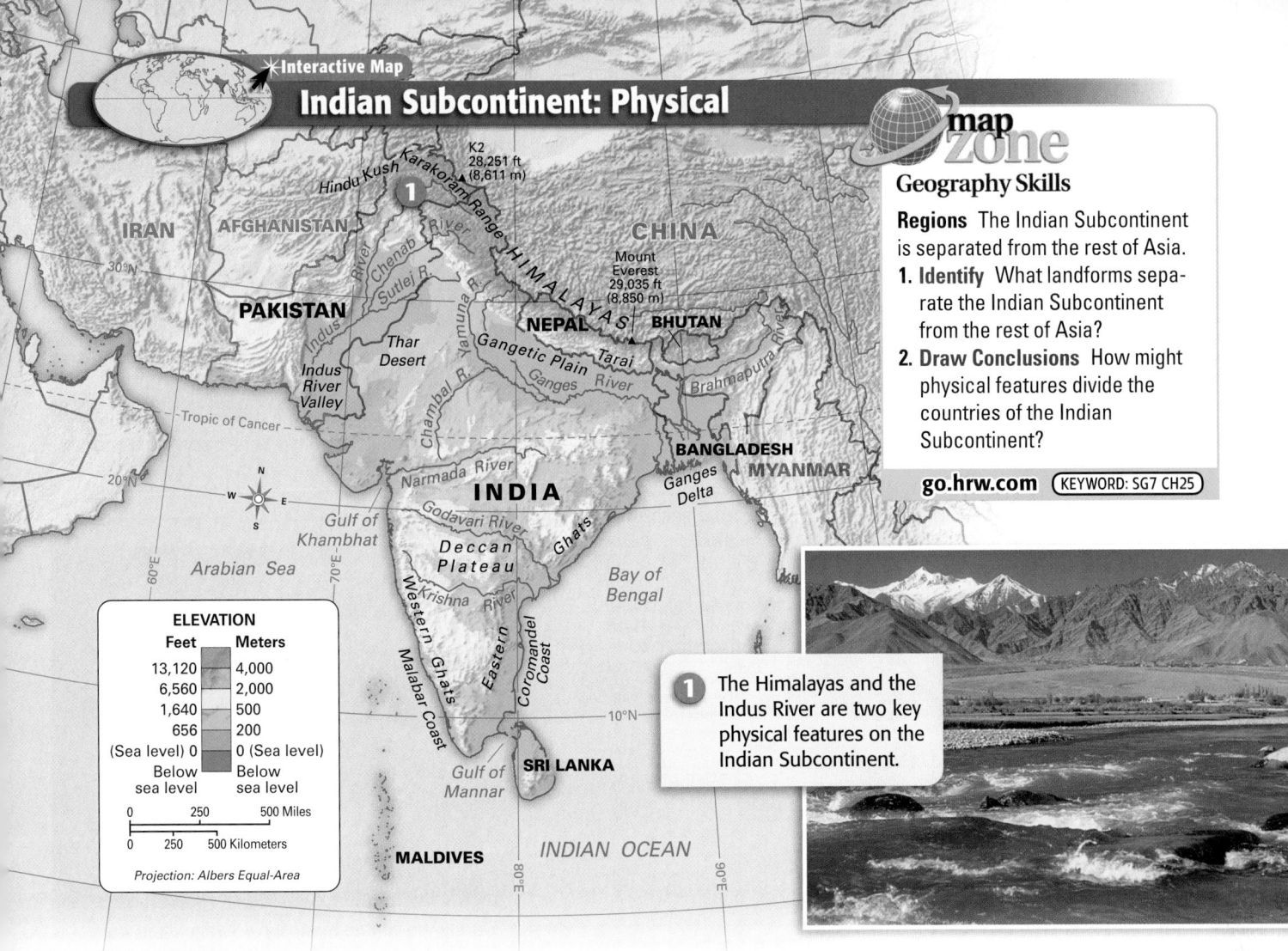

Indian Subcontinent: Physical

map zone

Geography Skills

Regions The Indian Subcontinent is separated from the rest of Asia.

1. **Identify** What landforms separate the Indian Subcontinent from the rest of Asia?
2. **Draw Conclusions** How might physical features divide the countries of the Indian Subcontinent?

go.hrw.com KEYWORD: SG7 CH25

ELEVATION

Feet	Meters
13,120	4,000
6,560	2,000
1,640	500
656	200
(Sea level) 0	0 (Sea level)
Below sea level	Below sea level

0   250   500 Miles
0   250   500 Kilometers

Projection: Albers Equal-Area

1 The Himalayas and the Indus River are two key physical features on the Indian Subcontinent.

Two smaller mountain ranges stretch down India's coasts. The Eastern and Western Ghats (GAWTS) are low mountains that separate India's east and west coasts from the country's interior.

Perhaps the most impressive physical features in the subcontinent, however, are the Himalayas. These enormous mountains stretch about 1,500 miles (2,415 km) along the northern border of the Indian Subcontinent. Formed by the collision of two massive tectonic plates, the Himalayas are home to the world's highest mountains. On the border between Nepal and China is **Mount Everest**, the highest mountain on the planet. It measures some 29,035 feet (8,850 m). K2 in northern Pakistan is the world's second highest peak.

Rivers and Plains

Deep in the Himalayas are the sources of some of Asia's mightiest rivers. Two major river systems—the Ganges (GAN-jeez) and the Indus—originate in the Himalayas. Each carries massive amounts of water from the mountains' melting snow and glaciers. For thousands of years, these rivers have flooded the surrounding land, leaving rich soil deposits and fertile plains.

India's most important river is the Ganges. The **Ganges River** flows across northern India and into Bangladesh. There, the Ganges joins with other rivers and creates a huge delta. A **delta** is a landform at the mouth of a river created by sediment deposits. Along the length of the Ganges is a vast area of rich soil and fertile farmland.

FOCUS ON READING

What words in this paragraph help you to visualize the information?

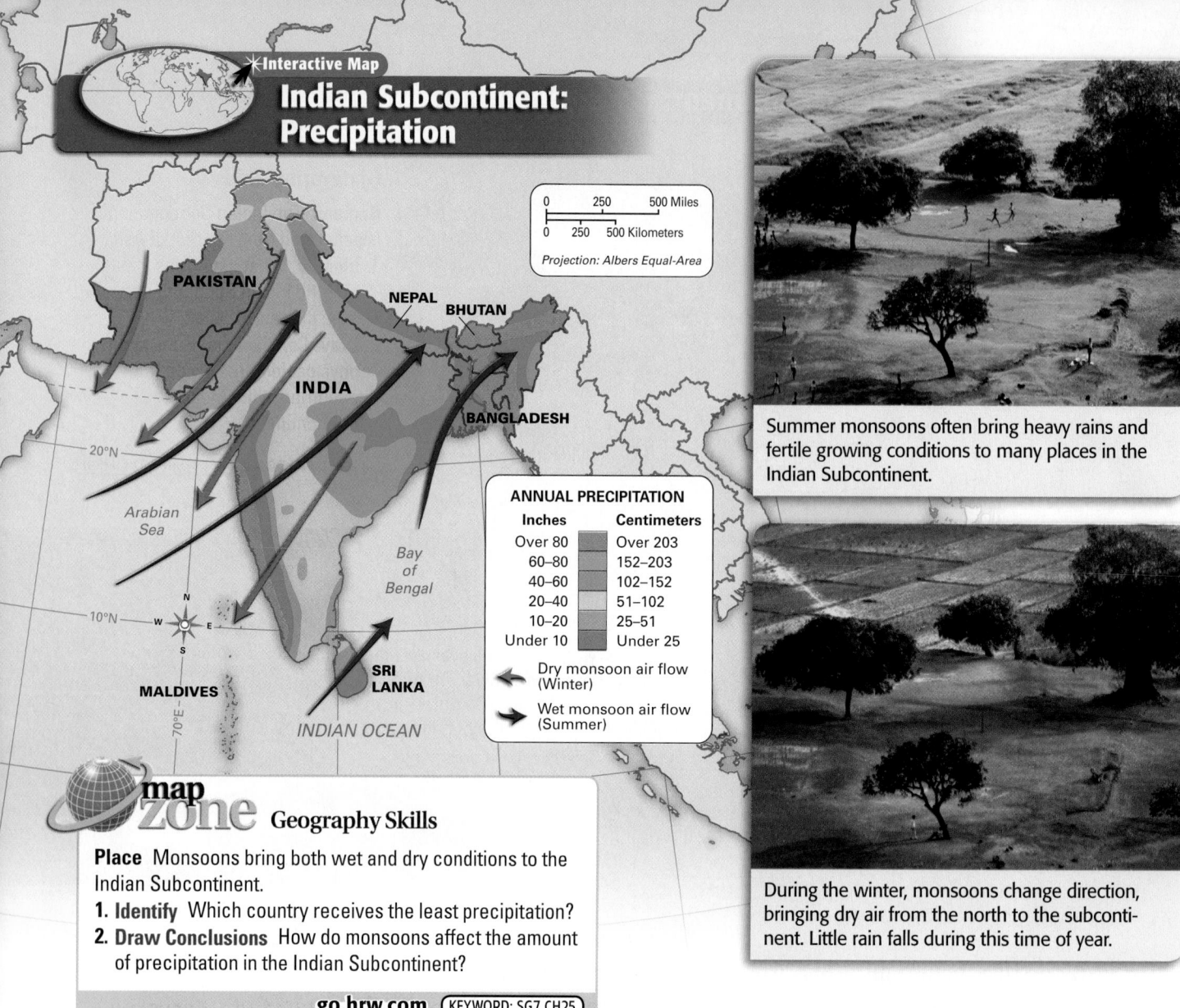

Indian Subcontinent: Precipitation

0   250   500 Miles
0   250   500 Kilometers
Projection: Albers Equal-Area

PAKISTAN

NEPAL   BHUTAN

INDIA

BANGLADESH

20°N

Arabian
Sea

Bay
of
Bengal

10°N

MALDIVES

SRI
LANKA

INDIAN OCEAN

ANNUAL PRECIPITATION

Inches		Centimeters
Over 80		Over 203
60–80		152–203
40–60		102–152
20–40		51–102
10–20		25–51
Under 10		Under 25

⬅ Dry monsoon air flow (Winter)

➡ Wet monsoon air flow (Summer)

Summer monsoons often bring heavy rains and fertile growing conditions to many places in the Indian Subcontinent.

During the winter, monsoons change direction, bringing dry air from the north to the subcontinent. Little rain falls during this time of year.

map zone Geography Skills

Place Monsoons bring both wet and dry conditions to the Indian Subcontinent.
1. **Identify** Which country receives the least precipitation?
2. **Draw Conclusions** How do monsoons affect the amount of precipitation in the Indian Subcontinent?

go.hrw.com   KEYWORD: SG7 CH25

Known as the Ganges Plain, this region is India's farming heartland.

Likewise, Pakistan's **Indus River** also creates a fertile plain known as the Indus River Valley. This valley was once home to the earliest Indian civilizations. Today, it is Pakistan's most densely populated region.

Other Features

Other geographic features are scattered throughout the subcontinent. South of the Ganges Plain, for example, is a large, hilly plateau called the Deccan. East of the Indus Valley is the Thar (TAHR), or Great Indian Desert. Marked by rolling sand dunes, parts of this desert receive as little as 4 inches (100 mm) of rain per year. Still another geographic region is the Tarai (tuh-RY) in southern Nepal. It has fertile farmland and tropical jungles.

READING CHECK **Summarizing** What are the physical features of the Indian Subcontinent?

Climates and Resources

Just as the physical features of the Indian Subcontinent differ, so do its climates and resources. A variety of climates and natural resources exist throughout the region.

Climate Regions

From the Himalayas' snow-covered peaks to the dry Thar Desert, the climates of the Indian Subcontinent differ widely. In the Himalayas, a highland climate brings cool temperatures to much of Nepal and Bhutan. The plains south of the Himalayas have a humid subtropical climate. Hot, humid summers with plenty of rainfall are common in this important farming region.

Tropical climates dominate much of the subcontinent. The tropical savanna climate in central India and Sri Lanka keeps temperatures there warm all year long. This region experiences wet and dry seasons during the year. A humid tropical climate brings warm temperatures and heavy rains to parts of southwest India, Sri Lanka, Maldives, and Bangladesh.

The remainder of the subcontinent has dry climates. Desert and steppe climates extend throughout southern and western India and most of Pakistan.

Monsoons have a huge influence on the weather and climates in the subcontinent. **Monsoons** are seasonal winds that bring either moist or dry air to an area. From June to October, summer monsoons bring moist air up from the Indian Ocean, causing heavy rains. Flooding often accompanies these summer monsoons. In 2005, for example, the city of Mumbai (Bombay), India received some 37 inches (94 cm) of rain in just 24 hours. However, in winter the monsoons change direction, bringing dry air from the north. Because of this, little rain falls from November to January.

Natural Resources

A wide variety of resources are found on the Indian Subcontinent. Agricultural and mineral resources are the most plentiful.

Perhaps the most important resource is the region's fertile soil. Farms produce many different crops, such as tea, rice, nuts, and jute, a plant used for making rope. Timber and livestock are also key resources in the subcontinent, particularly in Nepal and Bhutan.

The Indian Subcontinent also has an abundance of mineral resources. Large deposits of iron ore and coal are found in India. Pakistan has natural gas reserves, while Sri Lankans mine many gemstones.

READING CHECK **Summarizing** What climates and resources are located in this region?

SUMMARY AND PREVIEW In this section you learned about the wide variety of physical features, climates, and resources in the Indian Subcontinent. Next, you will learn about the rich history and culture of this unique region.

go.hrw.com

Section 1 Assessment

Online Quiz
KEYWORD: SG7 HP25

Reviewing Ideas, Terms, and Places

1. **a. Define** What is a **subcontinent**?
   b. Make Inferences Why do you think the **Indus River** Valley is so heavily populated?
   c. Rank Which physical features in the Indian Subcontinent would you most want to visit? Why?
2. **a. Identify** What natural resources are found in the Indian Subcontinent?
   b. Analyze What are some of the benefits and drawbacks of **monsoons**?

Critical Thinking

3. **Drawing Inferences** Draw a chart like the one shown here. Using your notes, write a sentence explaining how each aspect affects life on the Indian Subcontinent.

	Effect on Life
Physical Features	
Climates	
Natural Resources	

FOCUS ON VIEWING

4. **Telling about Physical Geography** What information and images of the region's physical geography might you include in your travelogue? Jot down some ideas.

History and Culture of India

What You Will Learn...

Main Ideas

1. Advanced civilizations and powerful empires shaped the early history of India.
2. Powerful empires controlled India for hundreds of years.
3. Independence from Great Britain led to the division of India into several countries.
4. Religion and the caste system are two important parts of Indian culture.

The Big Idea

Ancient civilizations and powerful empires have shaped the history and culture of India.

Key Terms and Places

Delhi, *p. 622*
colony, *p. 622*
partition, *p. 623*
Hinduism, *p. 624*
Buddhism, *p. 624*
caste system, *p. 624*

TAKING NOTES As you read, take notes on the history and culture of India. Use a diagram like this one to organize your notes.

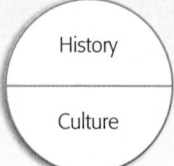

History

Culture

If YOU lived there...

You live in New Delhi, India's capital city. Museums in your city display artifacts from some of India's oldest civilizations. People can visit beautiful buildings built by powerful empires. Statues and parades celebrate your country's independence.

How does your city celebrate India's history?

BUILDING BACKGROUND The Indian Subcontinent has a rich and interesting history. Ancient civilizations, powerful empires, rule by foreigners, and the struggle for independence have shaped not only the history, but also the culture of India and its neighbors.

Early Civilizations and Empires

India, the largest country on the Indian Subcontinent, is one of the world's oldest civilizations. Early civilizations and empires greatly influenced the history of the Indian Subcontinent.

India's History

Ancient Civilizations

- Around 2300 BC the Harappan civilization begins in the Indus River Valley.
- The Aryans, invaders from Central Asia, enter India around 1500 BC.
- Aryan culture helps shape the languages, religion, and caste system of India.

Harappan artifact

Early Empires

- By 233 BC the Mauryan Empire controls most of the Indian Subcontinent.
- Emperor Asoka helps spread Buddhism in India.
- Indian trade and culture flourish during the Gupta Empire.

Mauryan troops atop a war elephant

Ancient Civilizations

The first urban civilization in the Indian Subcontinent was centered around the Indus River Valley in present-day Pakistan. We call this ancient Indian civilization the Harappan (huh-RA-puhn) civilization after one of its main cities. Historians believe that the Harappan civilization flourished between 2300 and 1700 BC. By about 1700 BC, however, this civilization began to decline. No one is certain what led to its decline. Perhaps invaders or natural disasters destroyed the Harappan civilization.

Not long after the Harappan civilization ended, a new group rose to power. Around 1500 BC the Aryans (AIR-ee-uhnz), a group of people from Central Asia, entered the Indian Subcontinent. Powerful warriors, the Aryans eventually conquered and settled the fertile plains along the Indus and Ganges rivers.

The Aryans greatly **influenced** Indian culture. Their language, called Sanskrit, served as the basis for several languages in South Asia. For example, Hindi, the official language of India, is related to Sanskrit. As the Aryans settled in India, they mixed with Indian groups already living there. Their religious beliefs and customs mixed as well, forming the beginnings of India's social system and Hindu religion.

Early Empires

Over time, powerful kingdoms began to emerge in northern India. One kingdom, the Mauryan Empire, dominated the region by about 320 BC. Strong Mauryan rulers raised huge armies and conquered almost the entire subcontinent. Asoka (uh-SOH-kuh), one of the greatest Mauryan emperors, helped expand the empire and improve trade. Asoka also encouraged the acceptance of other religions. After his death, however, the empire slowly crumbled. Power struggles and invasions destroyed the Mauryan Empire.

After the fall of the Mauryan Empire, India split into many small kingdoms. Eventually, however, a strong new empire rose to power. In the AD 300s, the Gupta (GOOP-tuh) Empire united much of northern India. Under Gupta rulers, trade and culture thrived. Scholars made important advances in math, medicine, and astronomy. Indian mathematicians, for example, first introduced the concept of zero.

Gradually, the Gupta Empire also declined. Attacks by invaders from Asia weakened the empire. By about 550, India was once again divided.

READING CHECK **Summarizing** How did early civilizations and empires influence India?

The Mughal Empire

- Babur establishes the Mughal Empire in northern India in 1526.

- Indian trade, culture, and religion thrive under the rule of Akbar the Great.

- By 1700 the Mughal Empire rules almost all of the Indian Subcontinent.

The first Mughal emperor, Babur

The British Empire

- The British East India Company establishes trade in northern India in the early 1600s.

- Indian troops trigger a massive revolt against the East India Company.

- The British government takes direct control of India in 1858.

- India and Pakistan gain independence in 1947.

Indian troop in the British Army

Powerful Empires

Powerful empires controlled India for much of its history. First the Mughal Empire and then the British Empire ruled India for hundreds of years.

The Mughal Empire

In the late 600s Muslim armies began launching raids into India. Some Muslims tried to take over Indian kingdoms. Turkish Muslims, for example, established a powerful kingdom at **Delhi** in northern India. In the 1500s a new group of Muslim invaders swept into the subcontinent. Led by the great warrior Babur (BAH-boohr), they conquered much of India. In 1526 Babur established the Mughal (MOO-guhl) Empire.

Babur's grandson, Akbar, was one of India's greatest rulers. Under Akbar's rule, trade flourished. Demand for Indian goods like spices and tea grew. The Mughal Empire grew rich from trade.

Akbar and other Mughal rulers also promoted culture. Although the Mughals were Muslim, most Indians continued to practice Hinduism. Akbar's policy of religious tolerance, or acceptance, encouraged peace throughout his empire. Architecture also thrived in the Mughal Empire. One of India's most spectacular buildings, the Taj Mahal, was built during Mughal rule.

The British Empire

The Mughals were not the only powerful empire in India. As early as the 1500s Europeans had tried to control parts of India. One European country, England, rose to power as the Mughal Empire declined.

The English presence in India began in the 1600s. At the time, European demand for Indian goods, such as cotton and sugar, was very high. Mughal rulers granted the East India Company, a British trading company, valuable trading rights.

At first, the East India Company controlled small trading posts. However, the British presence in India gradually grew. The East India Company expanded its territory and its power. By the mid-1800s the company controlled more than half of the Indian Subcontinent. India had become a British **colony**, a territory inhabited and controlled by people from a foreign land.

British rule angered and frightened many Indians. The East India Company controlled India with the help of an army made up mostly of Indian troops commanded by British officers. In 1857 Indian troops revolted, triggering violence all across India. The British government crushed the rebellion and took control of India away from the East India Company. With that, the British government began to rule India directly.

READING CHECK **Analyzing** How did powerful empires affect Indian history?

Independence and Division

By the late 1800s many Indians had begun to question British rule. Upset by their position as second-class citizens, a group of Indians created the Indian National Congress. Their goal was to gain more rights and opportunities.

As more and more Indians became dissatisfied with British rule, they began to demand independence. Mohandas Gandhi was the most important leader of this Indian independence movement. During the 1920s and 1930s his strategy of nonviolent protest convinced millions of Indians to support independence.

Finally, Great Britain agreed to make India independent. However, tensions between the Hindu and Muslim communities caused a crisis. Fearing they would have little say in the new government, India's Muslims called for a separate nation.

To avoid a civil war, the British government agreed to the **partition**, or division, of India. In 1947 two independent countries were formed. India was mostly Hindu. Pakistan, which included the area that is now Bangladesh, was mostly Muslim. As a result, some 10 million people rushed to cross the border. Muslims and Hindus wanted to live in the country where their religion held a majority.

Soon after India and Pakistan won their independence, other countries in the region gradually did too. Sri Lanka and Maldives gained their independence from Great Britain. In 1971, after a bloody civil war that killed almost 1 million people, East Pakistan broke away to form the country of Bangladesh.

READING CHECK Identifying Cause and Effect
What were the effects of Indian independence from Great Britain?

FOCUS ON READING
As you read this paragraph, visualize the events described. Draw a rough sketch to depict what you imagine.

The Partition of India

A massive wave of migration took place after the partition of India and Pakistan. Millions of Hindus and Muslims crowded onto trains that would take them to their new homelands in India and Pakistan.

Indian Culture

As you might imagine, the rich and unique history of the Indian Subcontinent has created an equally unique culture. Two aspects of that culture are religion and a strict social class system.

Religion

Religion has played a very important role in Indian history. In fact, India is the birthplace of several major religions, including Hinduism and Buddhism.

Hinduism One of the world's oldest religions is **Hinduism**, the dominant religion of India. According to Hindu beliefs, everything in the universe is part of a single spirit called Brahman. Hindus believe that their ultimate goal is to reunite their souls with that spirit. Hinduism teaches that souls are reincarnated, or reborn, many times before they join with Brahman.

Buddhism Another Indian religion is Buddhism, which began in northern India in the late 500s BC. **Buddhism** is a religion based on the teachings of Siddhartha Gautama—the Buddha. According to the Buddha's teachings, people can rise above their desire for material goods and reach nirvana. Nirvana is a state of perfect peace in which suffering and reincarnation end.

Caste System

Thousands of years ago, the Aryans organized Indian society into a unique social class system known as the caste system. The **caste system** divided Indian society into groups based on a person's birth or occupation.

The caste system features four main classes, or castes, originally based on occupations. Below these four castes are the Dalits, members of India's lowest class. Many rules guided interaction between the classes. For example, people from different castes were not allowed to eat together.

READING CHECK **Analyzing** How do religion and the caste system influence Indian culture?

SUMMARY AND PREVIEW In this section you learned about the rich history and culture of the Indian Subcontinent. Next, you will learn about important issues that affect India today.

Section 2 Assessment

Reviewing Ideas, Terms, and Places

1. **a. Identify** What different peoples ruled India?
   b. Analyze How did these early civilizations and empires influence Indian culture?
2. **a. Describe** What were some accomplishments of the Mughal Empire?
   b. Predict How might Indian history have been different if the British had not ruled India?
3. **a. Recall** Who was the leader of India's independence movement?
   b. Explain What led to the **partition** of India?
4. **a. Define** What is the **caste system**?
   b. Elaborate Why do you think India is home to some of the world's oldest religions?

Critical Thinking

5. **Summarizing** Use your notes and a diagram like the one here to write a sentence summarizing each aspect of Indian history and culture.

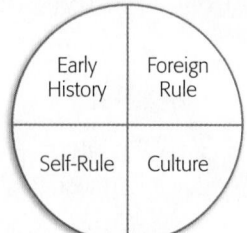

Early History | Foreign Rule
Self-Rule | Culture

FOCUS ON VIEWING

6. **Discussing History and Culture** Which details about India's history and culture will you use? How will you explain and illustrate them?

Analyzing a Line Graph

Learn

Line graphs are drawings that display information in a clear, visual form. People often use line graphs to track changes over time. For example, you may want to see how clothing prices change from year to year. Line graphs also provide an easy way to see patterns, like increases or decreases, that emerge over time. Use the following guidelines to analyze a line graph.

- Read the title. The title will tell you about the subject of the line graph.
- Examine the labels. Note the type of information in the graph, the time period, and the units of measure.
- Analyze the information. Be sure to look for patterns that emerge over time.

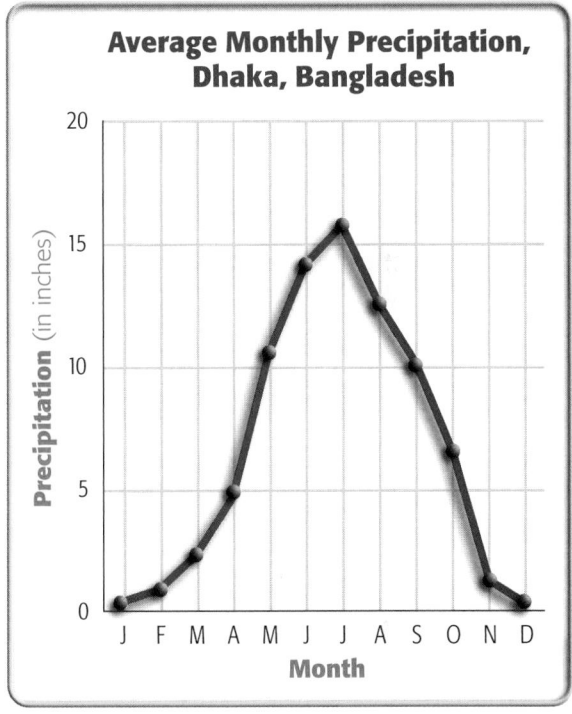

Average Monthly Precipitation, Dhaka, Bangladesh

Source: *National Geographic Atlas of the World, Seventh Edition*

Practice

Examine the line graph carefully, then answer the questions below.

1. What is the subject of this line graph?

2. What units of measure are used? What period of time does the line graph reflect?

3. What pattern does the line graph indicate? How can you tell?

Apply

Create a line graph that tracks your grades in a particular class. Start by organizing your grades by the date of the assignment. Then plot your grades on a line graph. Be sure to use labels and a title to identify the subject and information presented in your line graph. Finally, identify any patterns that you see in the line graph.

India Today

If YOU lived there...

You live in Mumbai, India's largest city. A major port, Mumbai is home to many industries, such as textiles and electronics. Museums and theaters offer entertainment. Every year, thousands of people flock to Mumbai in search of jobs or to enroll in its universities. The streets are crowded, and pollution is often heavy.

Do you enjoy living in Mumbai? Why or why not?

BUILDING BACKGROUND India has undergone many changes since gaining its independence from Great Britain. Cities have grown dramatically, new businesses and industries have developed, and the population has exploded. India today faces many challenges.

Daily Life in India

More than 1 billion people live in India today. This huge population represents modern India's many different ethnic groups, religions, and lifestyles. Despite these many differences, city life, village life, and religion all help unite the people of India.

Cities

Millions of Indians live in large, bustling cities. In fact, India's two largest cities, **Mumbai (Bombay)** and **Kolkata (Calcutta)**, are among the world's most populous cities. Many people in Indian cities work in factories and offices. Some cities, like Bangalore and Mumbai, are home to universities, research centers, and high-tech businesses. Most city-dwellers, however, struggle to earn a living. Many people live in shacks made of scraps of wood or metal. They often have no plumbing and little clean water.

Villages

Most Indians still live in rural areas. Hundreds of thousands of villages are home to more than 70 percent of India's population. Most villagers work as farmers and live with an extended family in simple homes. Only recently have paved roads and electricity reached many Indian villages.

Religion

In both cities and villages, religion plays a key role in Indian daily life. While most Indians practice Hinduism, many people follow several other religions such as Islam, Buddhism, and traditional religions. In addition, millions of Indians practice two native religions, Sikhism and Jainism.

Religious celebrations are an important part of Indian life today. One of India's most popular festivals is Diwali, the festival of lights. Diwali celebrates Hindu, Sikh, and Jain beliefs.

READING CHECK **Contrasting** How does life in Indian cities and villages differ?

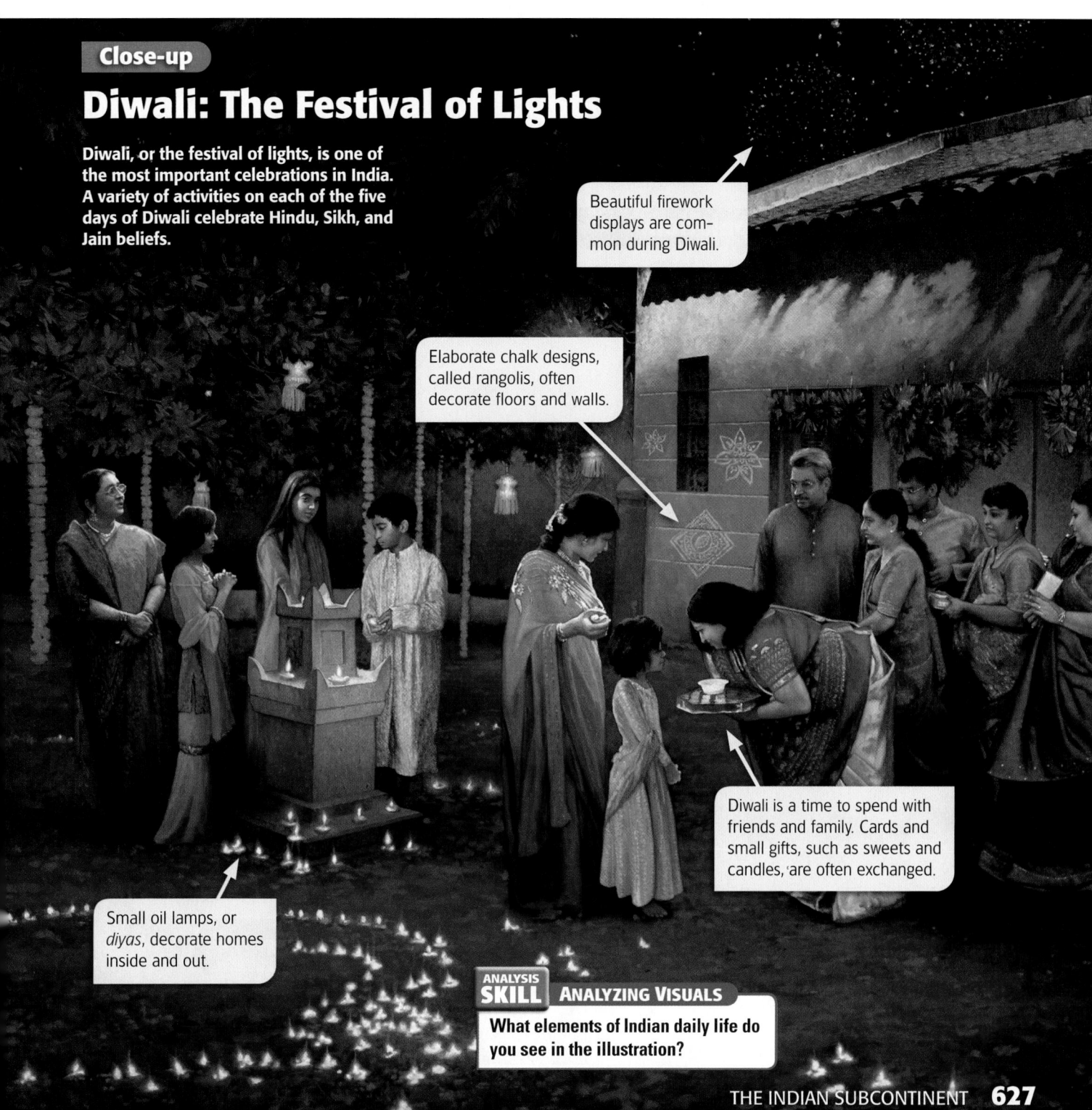

Close-up

Diwali: The Festival of Lights

Diwali, or the festival of lights, is one of the most important celebrations in India. A variety of activities on each of the five days of Diwali celebrate Hindu, Sikh, and Jain beliefs.

Beautiful firework displays are common during Diwali.

Elaborate chalk designs, called rangolis, often decorate floors and walls.

Diwali is a time to spend with friends and family. Cards and small gifts, such as sweets and candles, are often exchanged.

Small oil lamps, or *diyas*, decorate homes inside and out.

ANALYSIS SKILL **ANALYZING VISUALS**

What elements of Indian daily life do you see in the illustration?

India's Challenges

India has undergone drastic changes since gaining independence. Today the country faces several challenges, such as dealing with a growing population and managing its economic development.

Population

Its more than 1 billion people make India the world's second most populous country. Only China has a larger population. India's population has grown rapidly, doubling since 1947. This huge population growth places a strain on India's environment and many of its resources, including food, housing, and schools.

India's cities are particularly affected by the growing population. As the country's population has grown, urbanization has taken place. **Urbanization** is the increase in the percentage of people who live in cities. Many millions of people have moved to India's cities in search of jobs.

Government and Economy

Since India gained independence, its leaders have strengthened the government and economy. Today India is the world's

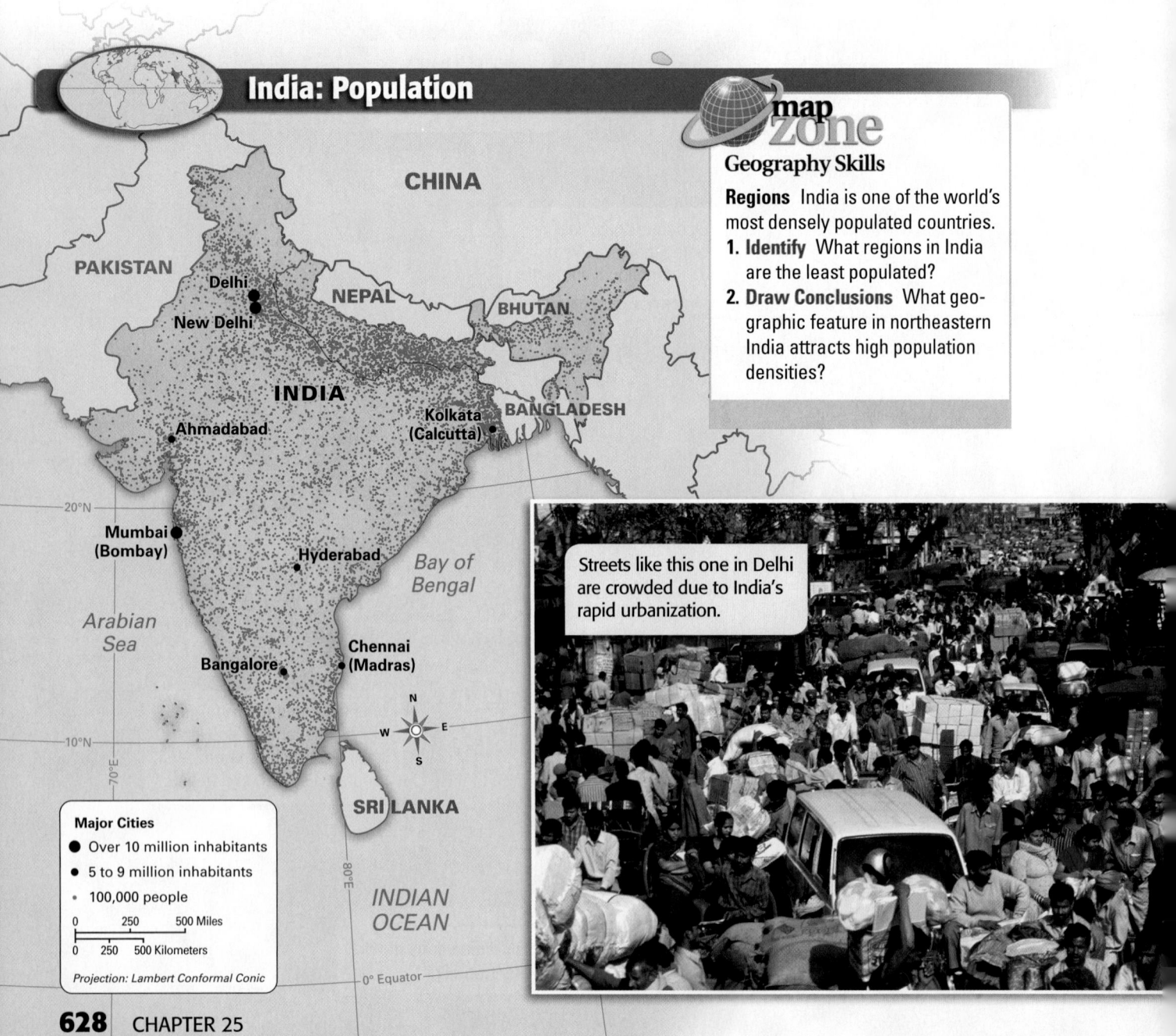

India: Population

CHINA

PAKISTAN

Delhi
New Delhi

NEPAL

BHUTAN

INDIA

Ahmadabad

Kolkata (Calcutta)

BANGLADESH

20°N

Mumbai (Bombay)

Hyderabad

Bay of Bengal

Arabian Sea

Chennai (Madras)

Bangalore

10°N

70°E

SRI LANKA

80°E

INDIAN OCEAN

0° Equator

Major Cities
- Over 10 million inhabitants
- 5 to 9 million inhabitants
- 100,000 people

0   250   500 Miles
0   250   500 Kilometers

Projection: Lambert Conformal Conic

map zone

Geography Skills

Regions India is one of the world's most densely populated countries.
1. **Identify** What regions in India are the least populated?
2. **Draw Conclusions** What geographic feature in northeastern India attracts high population densities?

Streets like this one in Delhi are crowded due to India's rapid urbanization.

largest democracy and one of the strongest nations in Asia. The greatest challenges facing India's government are providing for a growing population and resolving conflicts with its neighbor, Pakistan. Both India and Pakistan have nuclear weapons.

India's gross domestic product (GDP) places it among the world's top 5 industrial countries. However, its per capita, or per person, GDP is only $3,700. As a result, millions of Indians live in poverty.

India's government has taken steps to reduce poverty. In the 1960s and 1970s the **green revolution**, a program that encouraged farmers to adopt modern agricultural methods, helped farmers produce more food. Recently, the government has succeeded in attracting many high-tech businesses to India.

READING CHECK **Finding Main Ideas** What are India's government and economy like?

SUMMARY AND PREVIEW India today faces many challenges as it continues to modernize. Next, you will learn about India's neighbors on the subcontinent.

CONNECTING TO Economics

Bollywood

One of India's largest industries is its moviemaking industry. Much of India's film industry is located in Mumbai (Bombay). Many people refer to the industry as Bollywood—a combination of Bombay and Hollywood. Bollywood produces more films every year than any other country. In 2003, for example, India produced 1,100 films—almost twice the number of films produced in the United States. In recent years, Bollywood films have become increasingly popular outside of India—particularly in the United Kingdom and the United States.

Drawing Conclusions How might the film industry affect India's economy?

Section 3 Assessment

go.hrw.com
Online Quiz
KEYWORD: SG7 HP25

Reviewing Ideas, Terms, and Places

1. **a. Identify** What different religions are practiced in India today?
   b. Compare and Contrast In what ways are Indian cities similar to cities in the United States? How are they different from U.S. cities?
   c. Elaborate Why do you think that a majority of Indians live in villages?
2. **a. Recall** What is **urbanization**? What is one cause of urbanization?
   b. Make Inferences How did the **green revolution** affect India's economy?
   c. Predict What effects might India's growing population have on its resources and environment in the future?

Critical Thinking

3. **Finding Main Ideas** Using your notes and the web diagram, write the main idea for each element of India today.

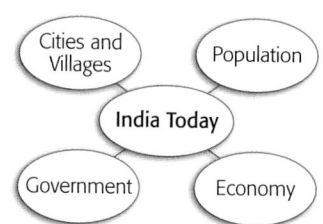

Cities and Villages — Population — India Today — Government — Economy

FOCUS ON VIEWING

4. **Telling about India Today** You will need some images, or pictures, for your travelogue. What images can you use to tell about India today?

India's Neighbors

If YOU lived there...

You live in the mountainous country of Bhutan. For many years Bhutan's leaders kept the country isolated from outsiders. Recently, they have begun to allow more tourists to enter the country. Some of your neighbors believe that tourism will greatly benefit the country. Others think it could harm the environment.

How do you feel about tourism in Bhutan?

BUILDING BACKGROUND After years of isolation or control by Great Britain, the 1900s brought great changes to the countries on the Indian Subcontinent. Today these countries face rapid population growth and economic and environmental concerns.

Culture

Five countries—Pakistan, Bangladesh, Nepal, Bhutan, and Sri Lanka—share the subcontinent with India. Though they are neighbors, these countries have significantly different cultures.

People The cultures of the countries that border India reflect the customs of many ethnic groups. For example, the **Sherpas**, an ethnic group from the mountains of Nepal, often serve as guides through the Himalayas. Members of Bhutan's largest ethnic group originally came from Tibet, a region in southern China. Many of Sri Lanka's Tamil (TA-muhl) people came from India to work the country's huge plantations.

Religion As you can see on the map on the next page, a variety of religions exist on the Indian Subcontinent. Most countries, like India, have one major religion. In Pakistan and Bangladesh, for example, most people practice Islam and small portions of the population follow Hinduism, Christianity, and tribal religions. In Nepal, the dominant religion is Hinduism, although Buddhism is practiced in some parts of the country. Buddhism dominates both Bhutan and Sri Lanka.

READING CHECK **Contrasting** In what ways are the cultures of this region different?

What You Will Learn...

Main Ideas

1. Many different ethnic groups and religions influence the culture of India's neighbors.
2. Rapid population growth, ethnic conflicts, and environmental threats are major challenges to the region today.

The Big Idea

Despite cultural differences, the countries that border India share similar challenges.

Key Terms and Places

Sherpas, *p. 630*
Kashmir, *p. 631*
Dhaka, *p. 632*
Kathmandu, *p. 632*

TAKING NOTES As you read, take notes on the culture and issues in the countries that border India. Organize your notes in a diagram like the one below.

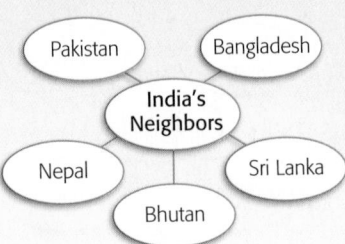

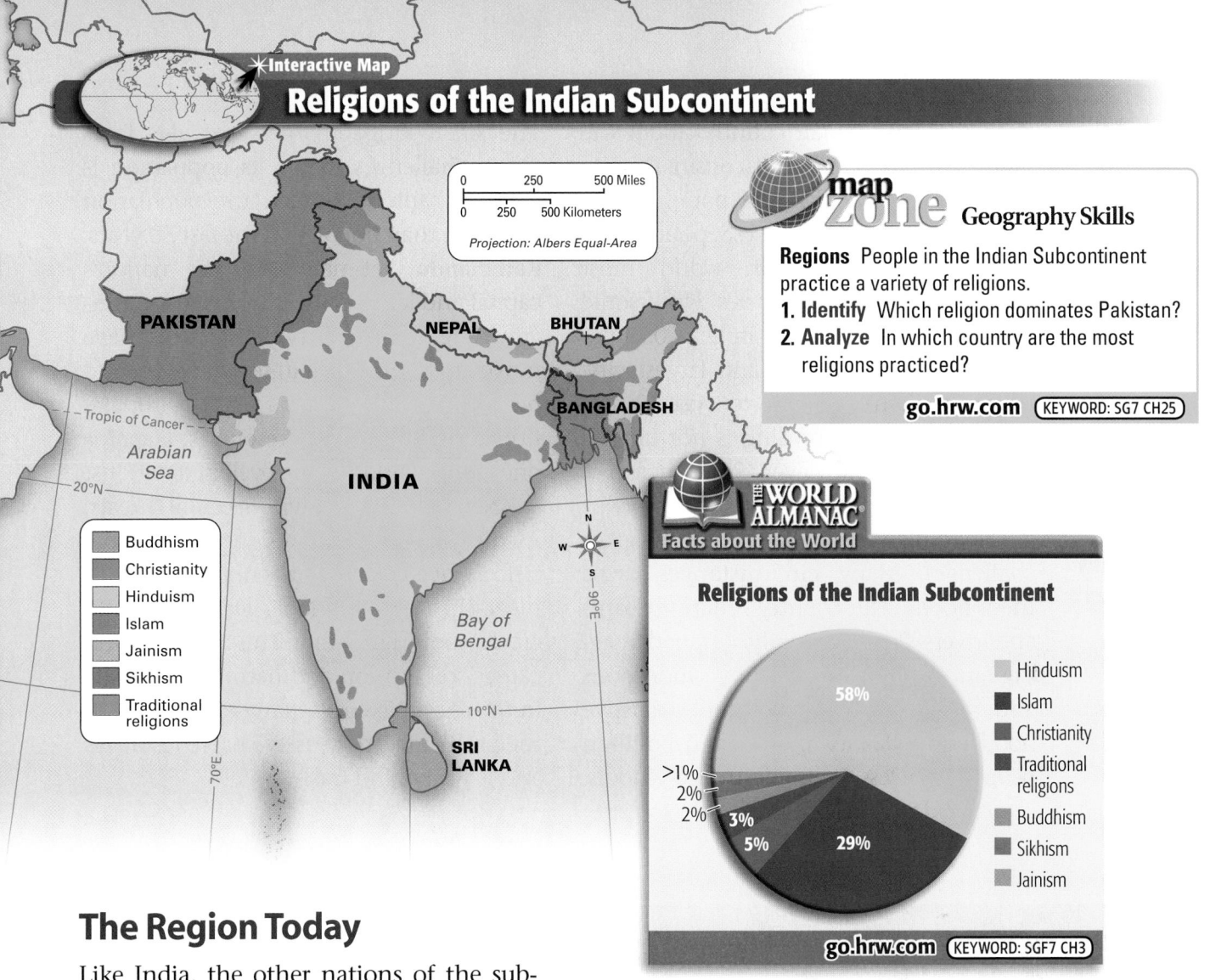

Interactive Map
Religions of the Indian Subcontinent

0   250   500 Miles

0   250   500 Kilometers

Projection: Albers Equal-Area

map zone Geography Skills

Regions People in the Indian Subcontinent practice a variety of religions.
1. **Identify** Which religion dominates Pakistan?
2. **Analyze** In which country are the most religions practiced?

go.hrw.com KEYWORD: SG7 CH25

PAKISTAN

NEPAL   BHUTAN

BANGLADESH

Tropic of Cancer

Arabian Sea

20°N

INDIA

- Buddhism
- Christianity
- Hinduism
- Islam
- Jainism
- Sikhism
- Traditional religions

Bay of Bengal

10°N

SRI LANKA

70°E

90°E

THE WORLD ALMANAC
Facts about the World

Religions of the Indian Subcontinent

58%

>1%
2%
2%
3%
5%
29%

- Hinduism
- Islam
- Christianity
- Traditional religions
- Buddhism
- Sikhism
- Jainism

go.hrw.com KEYWORD: SGF7 CH3

The Region Today

Like India, the other nations of the subcontinent face a variety of challenges. Two of the greatest challenges are population growth and poverty.

Pakistan

One of the greatest challenges Pakistan faces is the lack of government stability. Since its creation in 1947, Pakistan has suffered from rebellions and assassinations of government leaders. In 2001, General Pervez Musharraf came to power in a military coup.

Another challenge in Pakistan is rapid population growth. The country's government struggles to manage resources and to reduce poverty. Some people fear that Pakistan's large population and high levels of poverty could cause even more instability.

Relations with India are another important issue in Pakistan today. Since the partition in 1947, the two countries have clashed over the territory of **Kashmir**. Both India and Pakistan claim control of the region. Today Pakistan controls western Kashmir while India controls the east. Armed troops from both countries guard a "line of control" that divides Kashmir.

Since 2001 Pakistan has aided the United States in its war on terrorism. Pakistan's military has arrested hundreds of terrorists and provided information about suspected terrorists. Despite this crackdown, however, many people believe that there are still terrorists within Pakistan's borders.

FOCUS ON READING
Visualize the information described in this paragraph. Describe what mental images you see.

THE INDIAN SUBCONTINENT **631**

Bangladesh

Bangladesh is a small country about the same size as the state of Wisconsin. Despite its small size, Bangladesh's population is almost half the size of the U.S. population. As a result, it is one of the world's most densely populated countries with some 2,850 people per square mile (1,055 per square km). The capital and largest city, **Dhaka** (DA-kuh), is home to over 12 million people. Overcrowding is not limited to urban areas, however. Rural areas are also densely populated.

Flooding is one of Bangladesh's biggest challenges. Many <u>circumstances</u> cause these floods. The country's many streams and rivers flood annually, often damaging farms and homes. Summer monsoons also cause flooding. For example, massive flooding in 2004 left more than 25 million people homeless. It also destroyed schools, farms, and roads throughout the country.

ACADEMIC VOCABULARY

circumstances conditions that influence an event or activity

Nepal

The small kingdom of Nepal also faces many challenges today. Its population is growing rapidly. In fact, the population has more than doubled in the last 30 years. **Kathmandu** (kat-man-DOO), the nation's capital and largest city, is troubled by overcrowding and poverty. Thousands have moved to Kathmandu in search of jobs and better opportunities. As a result of population growth and poor resources, Nepal is one of the world's least-developed nations.

Nepal also faces environmental threats. As the population grows, more and more land is needed to grow enough food. To meet this need, farmers clear forests to create more farmland. This deforestation causes soil erosion and harms the wildlife in the region. Nepal's many tourists add to the problem as they use valuable resources and leave behind trash.

Bhutan

Bhutan is a small mountain kingdom that lies in the Himalayas between India and China. Because of the rugged mountains, Bhutan has been isolated throughout much of its history. This isolation limited outside influences until the 1900s, when Bhutan's king established ties first with Great Britain and later with India. By the mid-1900s Bhutan had ended its long isolation. Efforts to modernize Bhutan resulted in the construction of new roads, schools, and hospitals.

Today Bhutan continues to develop economically. Most Bhutanese earn a living as farmers, growing rice, potatoes, and

Nepal

Many of Nepal's people live in the rugged Himalayas and earn a living herding animals.

corn. Some raise livestock like yaks, pigs, and horses. Another important industry is tourism. The government, however, limits the number of visitors to Bhutan to protect Bhutan's environment and way of life.

Sri Lanka

Sri Lanka is a large island country located some 20 miles (32 km) off India's southeast coast. As a result of its close location, India has greatly influenced Sri Lanka. In fact, Sri Lanka's two largest ethnic groups—the Tamil and the Sinhalese (sing-guh-LEEZ)—are descended from Indian settlers.

Conflicts between the Sinhalese and the Tamil divide Sri Lanka today. The Tamil minority has fought for years to create a separate state. Despite a 2002 cease-fire, violence between the two sides continues to disrupt the island nation.

Parts of Sri Lanka were devastated by the 2004 tsunami in the Indian Ocean. Thousands of Sri Lankans were killed, and more than 500,000 people were left homeless. The tsunami also damaged Sri Lanka's fishing and agricultural industries, which are still struggling to rebuild.

Sri Lanka

These women are picking tea on one of Sri Lanka's many tea plantations.

SUMMARY AND PREVIEW You have learned about the important challenges that face India's neighbors on the subcontinent. In the next chapter, you will learn about the physical geography, history, and culture of China, Mongolia, and Taiwan.

READING CHECK **Summarizing** What key issues affect India's neighbors today?

Section 4 Assessment

go.hrw.com
Online Quiz
KEYWORD: SG7 HP25

Reviewing Ideas, Terms, and Places

1. **a. Identify** What are the major religions of the Indian Subcontinent?
   b. Summarize What cultural differences exist among India's neighbors?
   c. Elaborate Why do you think there are so many different religions in this region?
2. **a. Identify** What is the capital of Nepal?
   b. Compare and Contrast In what ways are the countries of this region similar and different?
   c. Predict How might conflict over **Kashmir** cause problems in the future?

Critical Thinking

3. **Solving Problems** Using your notes and a chart like the one here, identify one challenge facing each of India's neighbors. Then develop a solution for each challenge.

Challenges	Solutions

FOCUS ON VIEWING

4. **Telling about India's Neighbors** Your travels include voyages to India's neighbors. Include important or intriguing details and images in your travelogue.

from
Shabanu:
Daughter of the Wind

by Suzanne Fisher Staples

A Pakistani bride on her wedding day

GUIDED READING

WORD HELP

chadrs cloths worn by women as a head cover

henna a reddish dye made from a shrub; often used to decorate the hands and feet

cacophony a combination of loud sounds

curry a dish prepared in a highly spiced sauce

lapis a stone with a rich, deep blue color

❶ At a *mahendi* celebration women gather to prepare the bride for her wedding day.

❷ To line the eyes means to darken the rims of the eyelids with black kohl, an eyeliner.

About the Reading *In* Shabanu, *writer Suzanne Fisher Staples writes about the life of Shabanu, a young girl who is part of a nomadic desert culture in Pakistan. In this passage, Shabanu and her family prepare for the wedding of her older sister.*

AS YOU READ Look for details about the customs and traditions of Shabanu and her people.

Two days before the wedding, Bibi Lal . . . heads a procession of women to our house for the *mahendi* celebration ❶ . . . Bibi Lal looks like a giant white lily among her cousins and nieces, who carry baskets of sweets atop their flower-colored *chadrs*. They sing and dance through the fields, across the canal, to our settlement at the edge of the desert.

Sakina carries a wooden box containing henna. The *mahendi* women, Hindus from a village deep in the desert who will paint our hands and feet, walk behind her. Musicians and a happy cacophony of horns, pipes, and cymbals drift around them.

Mama, the servant girl, and I have prepared a curry of chicken, dishes of spiced vegetables, sweet rice, and several kinds of bread to add to the food that the women of Murad's family bring . . . Sharma has washed and brushed my hair. I wear a new pink tunic. She lines my eyes and rubs the brilliant lapis powder into my lids. ❷

Connecting Literature to Geography

1. Describing How did the women prepare for the upcoming wedding? What was the *mahendi* celebration like?

2. Interpreting Women come to Shabanu's house from a distant village to paint the girls' hands and feet with henna. Why do you think this custom is important to the women and girls? What might it symbolize?

Geography's Impact
video series
Review the video to answer the closing question:
How might population density affect a country?

Visual Summary

Use the visual summary below to help you review the main ideas of the chapter.

QUICK FACTS

Towering mountains and powerful monsoons characterize the physical geography of the Indian Subcontinent.

India's Taj Mahal represents the subcontinent's rich history and culture.

The nations that border India face many economic, political, and environmental challenges today.

Reviewing Vocabulary, Terms, and Places

Choose one word from each word pair to correctly complete each sentence below.

1. _____ often bring heavy rains to the Indian Subcontinent in summer. **(Monsoons/Ghats)**

2. The most popular religion in India today is _____. **(Buddhism/Hinduism/Islam)**

3. A _____ is a condition that influences an event or activity. **(feature/circumstance)**

4. _____ are an ethnic group from the mountains of Nepal. **(Tamil/Sherpas)**

5. The highest peak in the Indian Subcontinent and the world is _____. **(Mount Everest/K2)**

6. India's _____ system divides society based on a person's birth, wealth, and job. **(caste/colonial)**

7. Pakistan is located on the Indian _____, a large landmass. **(Peninsula/Subcontinent)**

Comprehension and Critical Thinking

SECTION 1 *(Pages 616–619)*

8. **a. Recall** What is a delta?

   b. Draw Conclusions Why are rivers important to the people of the Indian Subcontinent?

   c. Evaluate Do you think monsoons have a positive or negative effect on India? Why?

SECTION 2 *(Pages 620–624)*

9. **a. Describe** What was the partition of India? When and why did it take place?

   b. Compare and Contrast In what ways were Mughal and British rule of India similar and different?

   c. Evaluate In your opinion, was partitioning India a good decision? Why or why not?

SECTION 3 *(Pages 626–629)*

10. **a. Identify** What program introduced modern agricultural methods to India?

SECTION 3 (continued)

b. Analyze How has population growth affected India's economy?

c. Elaborate If you lived in India, would you prefer to live in a city or a village? Why?

SECTION 4 (Pages 630–633)

11. a. Identify What countries share the subcontinent with India?

b. Analyze How was Sri Lanka affected by the 2004 tsunami?

c. Predict How might conflict between India and Pakistan lead to problems in the future?

Social Studies Skills

Analyzing Line Graphs *Use the line graph to help you answer the questions that follow.*

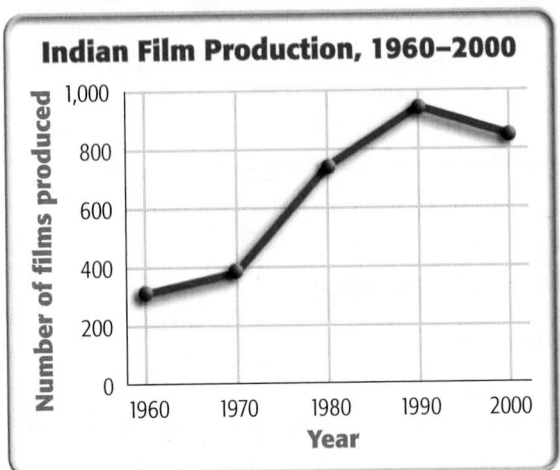

Indian Film Production, 1960–2000

Source: *Bollywood, India's Film Industry*

12. What is the subject of the line graph?

13. What general pattern or trend does the line graph indicate?

Using the Internet

go.hrw.com
KEYWORD: SG7 CH25

14. Touring India Pack your bags and experience India! It's a country where you can climb towering mountains, journey across vast deserts, and even hike through rain forests. Enter the activity keyword and discover the regions of India. Then make an illustrated travel brochure that features some of the regions you have explored.

FOCUS ON READING AND VIEWING

15. Visualizing Read the literature selection *Shabanu: Daughter of the Wind*. As you read, visualize the scenes the author describes. Then make a list of words from the passage that help you create a mental image of the events. Lastly, draw a rough sketch of your mental image of the *mahendi* celebration.

16. Creating and Viewing a Travelogue Use your notes to create a one- to two-minute script describing your travels in the Indian Subcontinent. Identify and collect the images you need to illustrate your talk. Present your oral travelogue to the class, giving an exciting view of the region. Observe as others present their travelogues. How is each travelogue unique? How are they similar?

Map Activity

17. The Indian Subcontinent On a separate sheet of paper, match the letters on the map with their correct labels.

Deccan	Mount Everest
Himalayas	Mumbai (Bombay)
Indus River	New Delhi
Kashmir	Sri Lanka

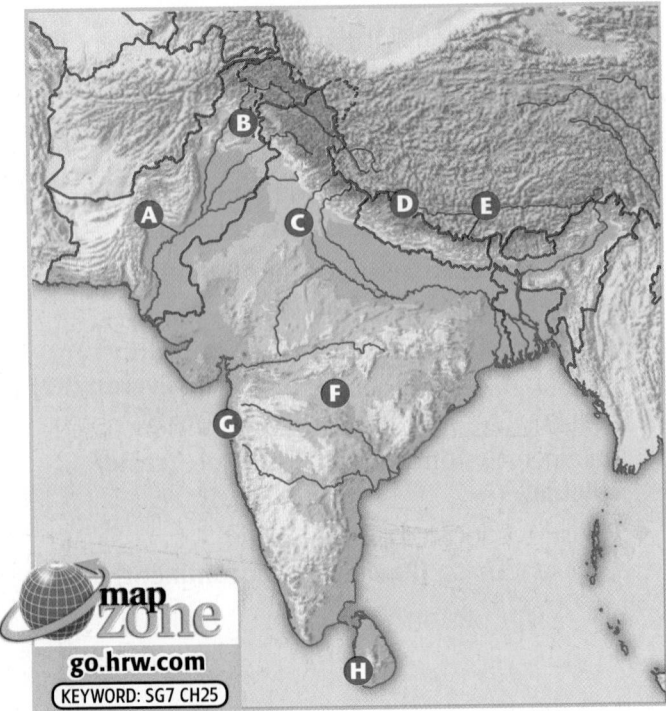

map zone
go.hrw.com
KEYWORD: SG7 CH25

DIRECTIONS: *Read questions 1 through 7 and write the letter of the best response. Then read question 8 and write your own well-constructed response.*

1 Which of the following is the *oldest* Indian civilization?

A Aryan

B Harappan

C Mughal

D Pakistani

2 Which of the following is a cause of India's rapid urbanization?

A People have moved away from cities to escape overcrowding and poverty.

B People have left villages to avoid rural warfare.

C People have left India in search of land.

D People have moved to cities in search of jobs.

3 Isolationism, Buddhism, and monarchy are all associated with which country?

A Bhutan

B India

C Nepal

D Sri Lanka

4 The majority of Indians today live

A in the Indus River Valley.

B on the coast.

C in cities.

D in villages.

5 The division of Indian society is known as

A the caste system.

B Diwali.

C Hinduism.

D the partition of India.

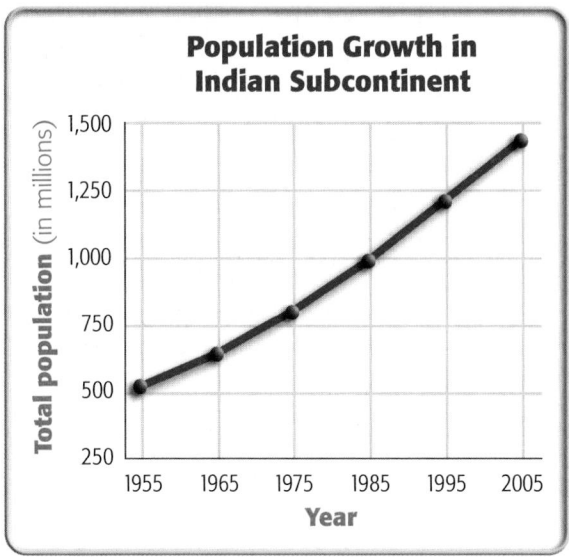

Population Growth in Indian Subcontinent

Source: United Nations Population Division

6 Based on the line graph above, what was the approximate population of South Asia in 1985?

A 500,000,000

B 760,000,000

C 1,000,000,000

D 1,400,000,000

7 These seasonal winds bring both wet and dry conditions to much of the Indian Subcontinent.

A hurricanes

B monsoons

C tsunamis

D typhoons

8 Extended Response Using information from the map in Section 3 titled India: Population, write a paragraph describing the settlement patterns in India today.

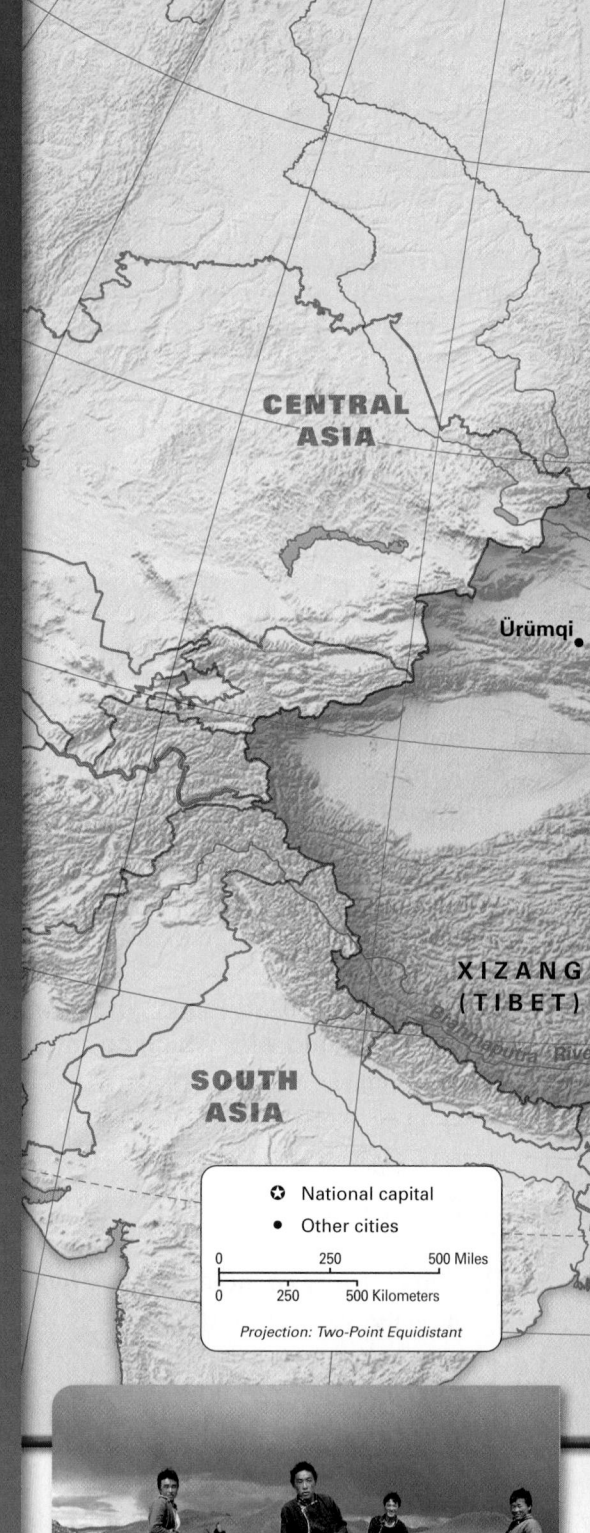

CHAPTER 26
China, Mongolia, and Taiwan

What You Will Learn...

In this chapter you will learn about the physical features, climate, and resources of China, Mongolia, and Taiwan. You will also study the histories of these countries, how different influences have shaped their cultures, and what life is like in these regions today.

FOCUS ON READING AND WRITING

Identifying Implied Main Ideas The main idea in a piece of writing is sometimes stated directly. Other times, you must figure out the main idea. As you read, look for key details or ideas to help you identify the implied main ideas. **See the lesson, Identifying Implied Main Ideas, on page R27.**

Writing a Legend Since ancient times, people have passed along legends. These stories often tell about supernatural people or events from the past. Read the chapter. Then write your own legend describing the supernatural creation of a physical feature in this region.

Geography Horses play an important role in Mongolian life and culture. Many Mongolians are nomads and use horses to travel across the country's large plains.

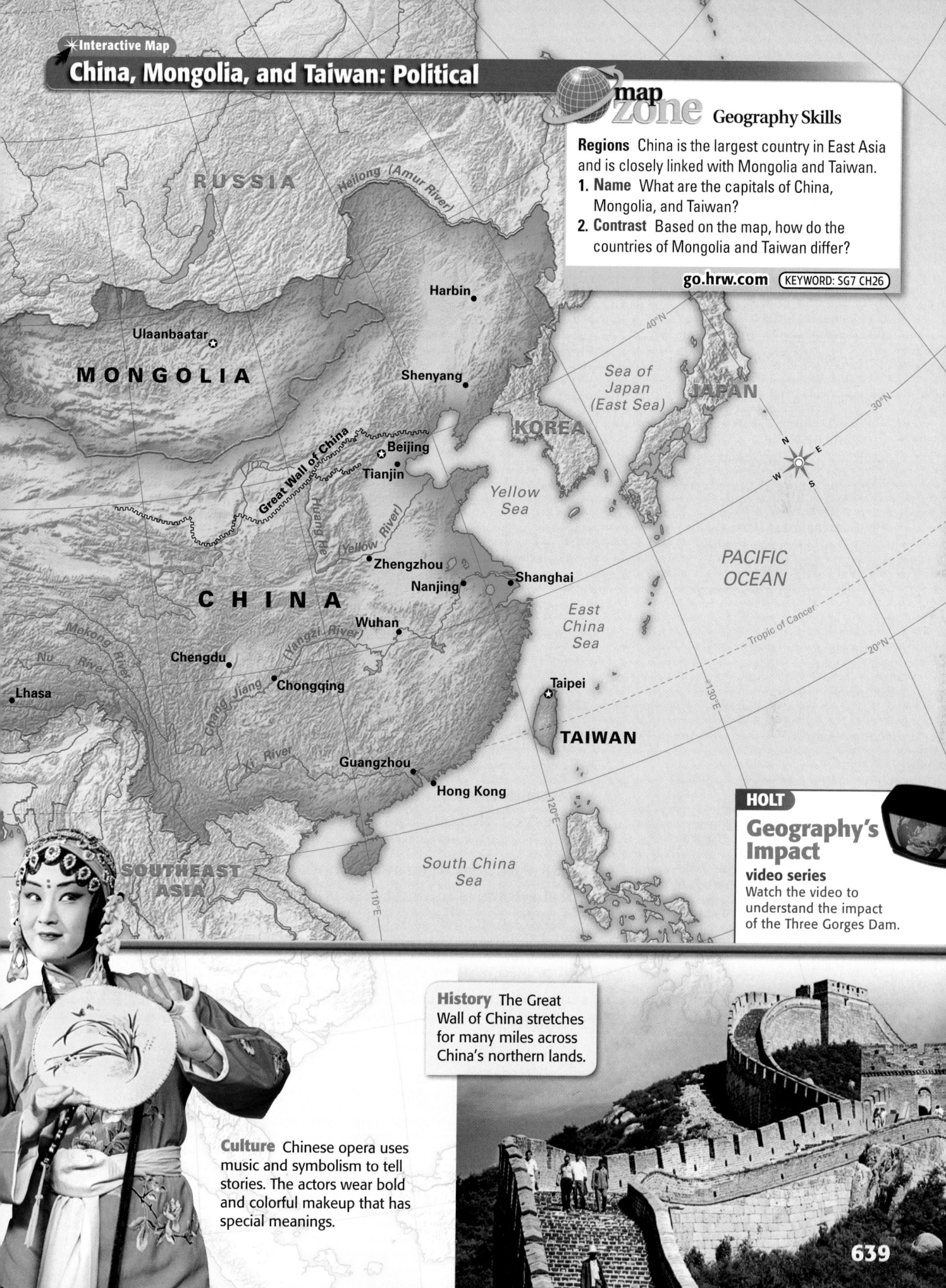

map zone Geography Skills

Regions China is the largest country in East Asia and is closely linked with Mongolia and Taiwan.
1. **Name** What are the capitals of China, Mongolia, and Taiwan?
2. **Contrast** Based on the map, how do the countries of Mongolia and Taiwan differ?

go.hrw.com   KEYWORD: SG7 CH26

RUSSIA

Heilong (Amur River)

Harbin

Ulaanbaatar

MONGOLIA

Shenyang

Sea of Japan (East Sea)

JAPAN

KOREA

Great Wall of China

Beijing

Tianjin

Huang He

Yellow River

Yellow Sea

Zhengzhou

Nanjing

Shanghai

East China Sea

PACIFIC OCEAN

CHINA

Wuhan

Chengdu

Chang Jiang (Yangzi River)

Chongqing

Mekong River

Nu River

Lhasa

Tropic of Cancer

Taipei

TAIWAN

Xi River

Guangzhou

Hong Kong

SOUTHEAST ASIA

South China Sea

40°N

30°N

20°N

130°E

120°E

110°E

HOLT

Geography's Impact

video series
Watch the video to understand the impact of the Three Gorges Dam.

History The Great Wall of China stretches for many miles across China's northern lands.

Culture Chinese opera uses music and symbolism to tell stories. The actors wear bold and colorful makeup that has special meanings.

Physical Geography

What You Will Learn...

Main Ideas

1. Physical features of China, Mongolia, and Taiwan include mountains, plateaus and basins, plains, and rivers.
2. China, Mongolia, and Taiwan have a range of climates and natural resources.

The Big Idea

Physical features, climate, and resources vary across China, Mongolia, and Taiwan.

Key Terms and Places

Himalayas, *p. 640*
Plateau of Tibet, *p. 641*
Gobi, *p. 641*
North China Plain, *p. 642*
Huang He, *p. 642*
loess, *p. 642*
Chang Jiang, *p. 642*

TAKING NOTES As you read, use a chart like the one below to take notes on the physical features, climate, and resources of China, Mongolia, and Taiwan.

Mountains	
Other Landforms	
Rivers	
Climate and Resources	

If **YOU** lived there...

You are a young filmmaker who lives in Guangzhou, a port city in southern China. You are preparing to make a documentary film about the Huang He, one of China's great rivers. To make your film, you will follow the river across northern China. Your journey will take you from the Himalayas to the coast of the Yellow Sea.

What do you expect to see on your travels?

BUILDING BACKGROUND China, Mongolia, and Taiwan make up a large part of East Asia. They include a range of physical features and climates—dry plateaus, rugged mountains, fertile plains. This physical geography has greatly influenced life in each country.

Physical Features

Have you seen the view from the top of the world? At 29,035 feet (8,850 m), Mount Everest in the **Himalayas** is the world's highest mountain. From atop Everest, look east. Through misty clouds, icy peaks stretch out before you, fading to land far below. This is China. About the size of the United States, China has a range of physical features. They include not only the world's tallest peaks but also some of its driest deserts and longest rivers.

Two other areas are closely linked to China. To the north lies Mongolia (mahn-GOHL-yuh). This landlocked country is dry and rugged, with vast grasslands and desert. In contrast, Taiwan (TY-WAHN), off the coast of mainland China, is a green tropical island. Look at the map to see the whole region's landforms.

Mountains

Much of the large region, including Taiwan, is mountainous. In southwest China, the Himalayas run along the border. They are Earth's tallest mountain range. Locate on the map the region's other ranges. As a tip, the Chinese word *shan* means "mountain."

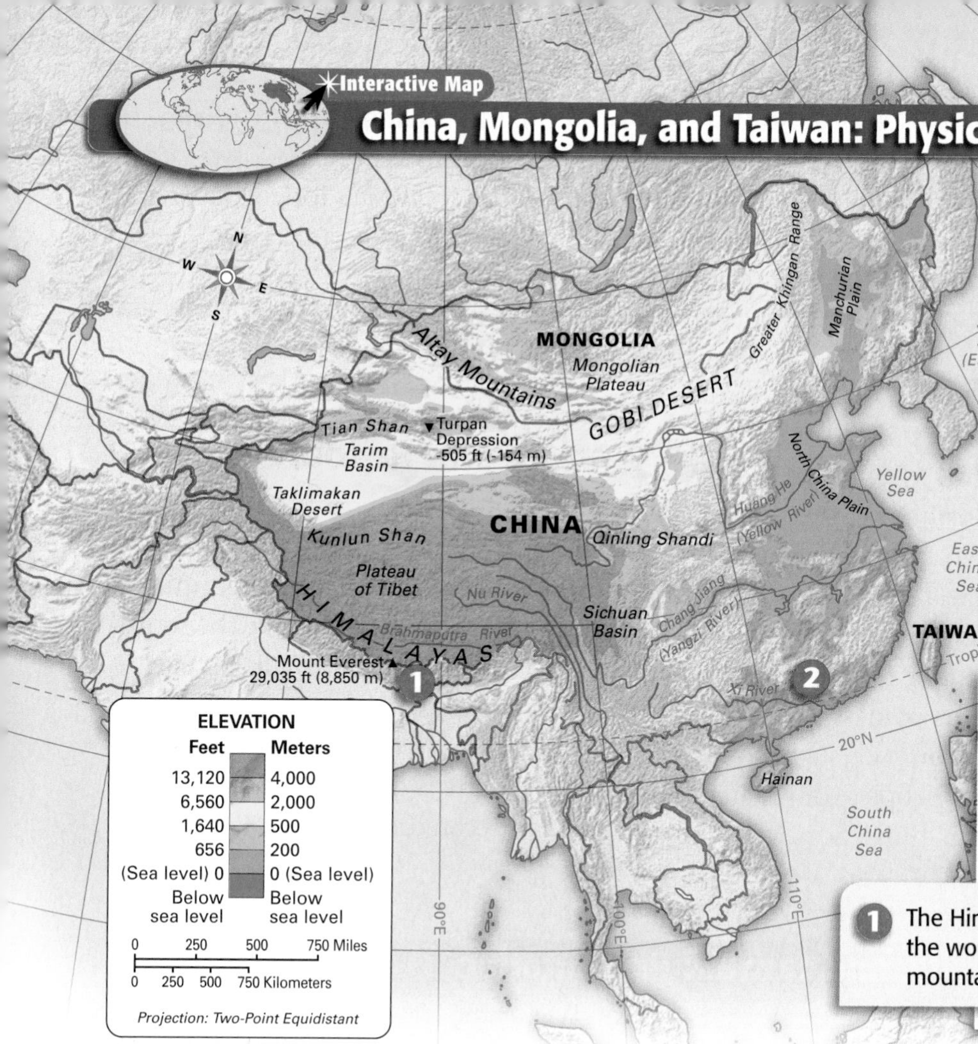

China, Mongolia, and Taiwan: Physical

MONGOLIA
Mongolian Plateau
Altay Mountains
GOBI DESERT
Greater Khingan Range
Manchurian Plain
Sea of Japan (East Sea)
Tian Shan
Turpan Depression -505 ft (-154 m)
Tarim Basin
Taklimakan Desert
Kunlun Shan
CHINA
Qinling Shandi
Huáng He
Yellow River
Yellow Sea
North China Plain
Plateau of Tibet
Nu River
East China Sea
H I M A L A Y A S
Brahmaputra River
Sichuan Basin
Chang Jiang (Yangzi River)
TAIWAN
Tropic of Cancer
PACIFIC OCEAN
Mount Everest 29,035 ft (8,850 m)
Xi River
Hainan
South China Sea
40°N
30°N
130°E
20°N
90°E
100°E
110°E
140°E

ELEVATION

Feet		Meters
13,120		4,000
6,560		2,000
1,640		500
656		200
(Sea level) 0		0 (Sea level)
Below sea level		Below sea level

0   250   500   750 Miles
0   250   500   750 Kilometers

Projection: Two-Point Equidistant

map zone

Geography Skills

Place Physical features vary across the region.
1. **Identify** What major rivers begin in the Plateau of Tibet?
2. **Make Generalizations** In general, how does China's elevation differ from west to east?

go.hrw.com   KEYWORD: SG7 CH26

1 The Himalayas are the world's highest mountain range.

Other Landforms

Many of the mountain ranges are separated by plateaus, basins, and deserts. In southwest China, the **Plateau of Tibet** lies north of the Himalayas. The world's highest plateau, it is called the Roof of the World.

Moving north, we find a low, dry area. A large part of this area is the Taklimakan (tah-kluh-muh-KAHN) Desert, a barren land of sand dunes and blinding sandstorms.

In fact, sandstorms are so common that the desert's Turkish name, Taklimakan, has come to mean "Enter and you will not come out." To the northeast, the Turpan (toohr-PAHN) Depression is China's lowest point, at 505 feet (154 m) below sea level.

Continuing northeast, in Mongolia we find the **Gobi**. This harsh area of gravel and rock is the world's coldest desert. Temperatures can drop to below –40°F (–40°C).

2 Hills that are called karst towers line the Li River in southeast China. These dramatic hills formed over time as rainwater eroded limestone.

In east China, the land levels out into low plains and river valleys. These fertile plains, such as the **North China Plain**, are China's main population centers and farmlands. On Taiwan, a plain on the west coast is the island's main population center.

Rivers

FOCUS ON READING
Which details help you identify the main idea of the paragraph to the right?

In China, two great rivers run west to east. The **Huang He** (HWAHNG HEE), or the Yellow River, flows across northern China. Along its course, this river picks up large amounts of **loess** (LES), or fertile, yellowish soil. The soil colors the river and gives it its name.

In summer, the Huang He often floods. The floods spread layers of loess, enriching the soil for farming. However, such floods have killed millions of people. For this reason, the river is called China's Sorrow.

The mighty **Chang** (CHAHNG) **Jiang**, or the Yangzi (YAHNG-zee) River, flows across central China. It is Asia's longest river and a major transportation route.

READING CHECK **Summarizing** What are the main physical features found in this region?

Climate and Resources

Climate varies widely across the region. The tropical southeast is warm to hot, and monsoons bring heavy rains in summer. In addition, typhoons can strike the southeast coast in summer and fall. Similar to hurricanes, these violent storms bring high winds and rain. As we move to the northeast, the climate is drier and colder. Winter temperatures can drop below 0°F (–18°C).

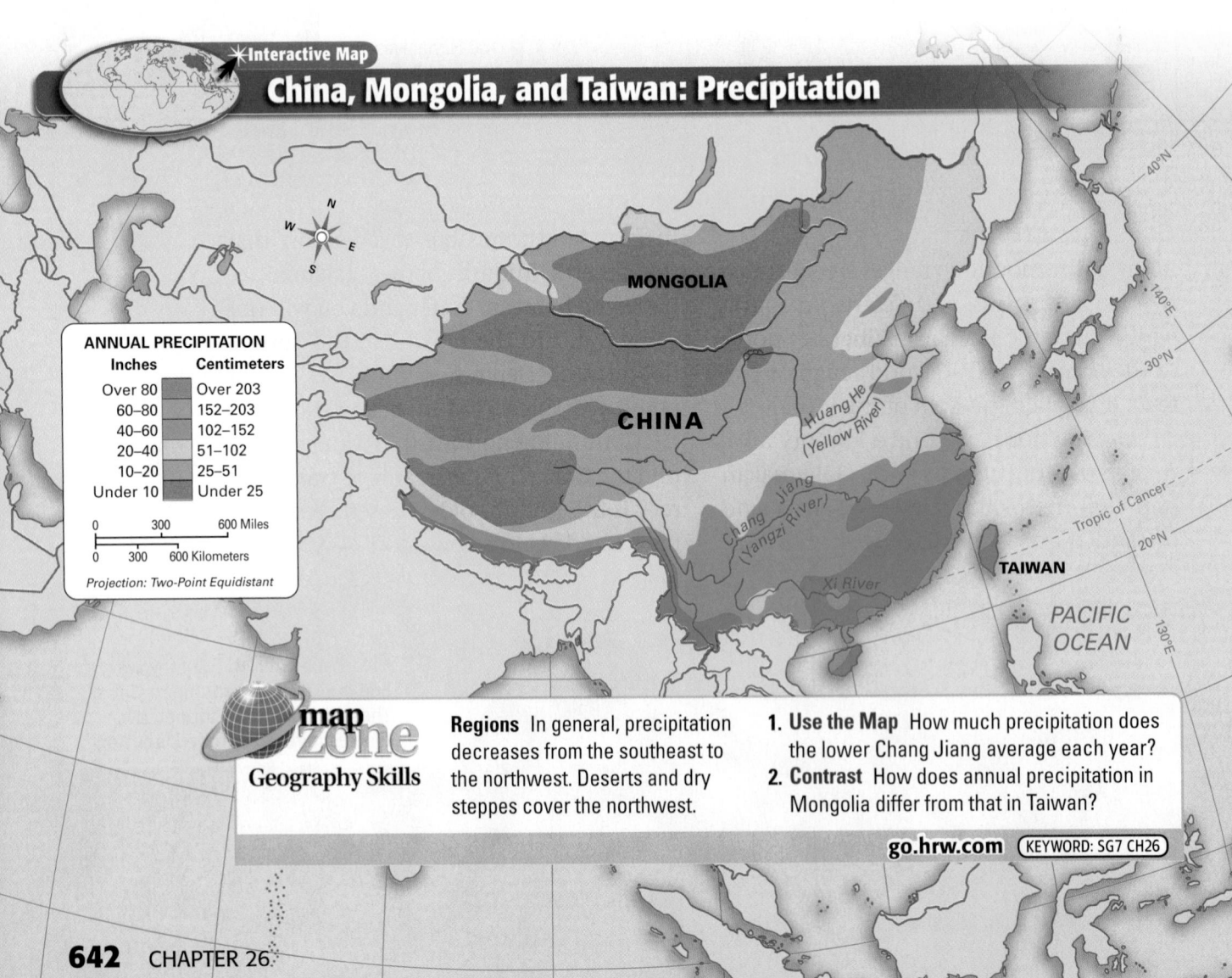

Interactive Map

China, Mongolia, and Taiwan: Precipitation

ANNUAL PRECIPITATION	
Inches	Centimeters
Over 80	Over 203
60–80	152–203
40–60	102–152
20–40	51–102
10–20	25–51
Under 10	Under 25

0   300   600 Miles
0   300   600 Kilometers
Projection: Two-Point Equidistant

MONGOLIA

CHINA

Huang He (Yellow River)

Chang Jiang (Yangzi River)

Xi River

TAIWAN

PACIFIC OCEAN

Tropic of Cancer

map zone Geography Skills

Regions In general, precipitation decreases from the southeast to the northwest. Deserts and dry steppes cover the northwest.

1. **Use the Map** How much precipitation does the lower Chang Jiang average each year?
2. **Contrast** How does annual precipitation in Mongolia differ from that in Taiwan?

go.**hrw**.com KEYWORD: SG7 CH26

Flooding in China

China's rivers and lakes often flood during the summer rainy season. The satellite images here show Lake Dongting Hu in southern China. The lake appears blue, and the land appears red. Soon after the Before image was taken, heavy rains led to flooding. The After image shows the results. Compare the two images to see the extent of the flood, which killed more than 3,000 people and destroyed some 5 million homes.

Before

After

For comparison, these arrows are pointing to the same place in each image.

Drawing Inferences Why might people continue to live in areas that often flood?

In the north and west, the climate is mainly dry. Temperatures vary across the area and can get both very hot and cold.

Like the climate, the region's natural resources cover a wide range. China has a wealth of natural resources. The country is rich in mineral resources and is a leading producer of coal, lead, tin, and tungsten. China produces many other minerals and metals as well. China's forestland and farmland are also valuable resources.

Mongolia's natural resources include minerals such as coal, iron, and tin as well as livestock. Taiwan's major natural resource is its farmland. Important crops include sugarcane, tea, and bananas.

READING CHECK **Contrasting** Which of these three countries has the most natural resources?

SUMMARY AND PREVIEW As you have read, China, Mongolia, and Taiwan have a range of physical features, climate, and resources. Next, you will read about the history and culture of China.

Section 1 Assessment

go.hrw.com
Online Quiz
KEYWORD: SG7 HP26

Reviewing Ideas, Terms, and Places

1. **a. Identify** What two major rivers run through China?
   b. Explain How does the **Huang He** both benefit and hurt China's people?
   c. Elaborate Why do you think many people in China live on the **North China Plain**?
2. **a. Define** What is a typhoon?
   b. Contrast What are some differences between the climates of southeast and northwest China?
   c. Rate Based on the different climates in this region, which part of the region would you prefer to live in? Why?

Critical Thinking

3. **Categorizing** Look back over your notes for this section. Then use a chart like the one shown here to organize, identify, and describe the main physical features of China, Mongolia, and Taiwan.

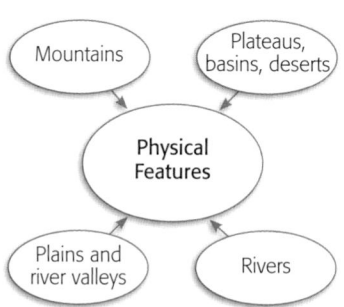

Mountains → Physical Features ← Plateaus, basins, deserts

Plains and river valleys → Physical Features ← Rivers

FOCUS ON WRITING

4. **Writing about Physical Geography** Note the main physical features of this region. Consider which feature you might want to explain in your legend. Features to consider include mountains, plateaus, and deserts.

History and Culture of China

What You Will Learn...

Main Ideas

1. Family lines of emperors ruled China for most of its early history.
2. In China's modern history, revolution and civil war led to a Communist government.
3. China has the world's most people and a rich culture shaped by ancient traditions.

The Big Idea

Ruled by dynasties in its early history, China is a Communist country with an enormous population and ancient traditions.

Key Terms

dynasty, *p. 645*
dialect, *p. 647*
Daoism, *p. 648*
Confucianism, *p. 648*
pagodas, *p. 649*

TAKING NOTES As you read, use a chart like the one below to take notes on China's history, people, and culture.

China		
History	People	Culture

If YOU lived there...

Your parents own a small farm in the Chinese countryside in the mid-1950s. China's new leaders are making changes, however. They are taking people's farms and combining them to create large government-run farms. Your family and neighbors will now work a large farm together. China's leaders will tell you what to grow and pay you based on how much the farm produces.

How do you feel about these changes?

BUILDING BACKGROUND In 1949 China established a strong central government. This new government changed many familiar patterns of life. For much of its history, though, China had been ruled by family lines of emperors. During this period, China developed one of the world's most advanced civilizations.

China's Early Dynasties

Dynasties ruled China for some 3,500 years. The major achievements of the early dynasties are shown here.

Shang, c. 1500–1050 BC

- First recorded Chinese dynasty
- Strongest in the Huang He valley
- Developed China's first writing system, a calendar, and chopsticks
- Skilled at bronze casting

Shang bronze tigress container

Zhou, c. 1050–400 BC

- Longest-lasting Chinese dynasty
- Expanded China but declined into a period of disorder
- Influenced by the new teachings of Confucianism, Daoism, and Legalism
- Began using iron tools and plows

Confucius, a Zhou thinker

China's Early History

When we enjoy the colorful fireworks on the Fourth of July, we can thank the early Chinese people. They invented fireworks. China's early civilization was one of the most advanced in the world. Its many achievements include the magnetic compass, gunpowder, paper, printing, and silk.

Today China can boast a civilization some 4,000 years old, older than any other. Understanding this long history is central to understanding China and its people.

China's Dynasties

For much of its history, China was ruled by dynasties. A **dynasty** is a series of rulers from the same family line. The rulers of China's dynasties were called emperors. Over time, many dynasties rose and fell in China. Between some dynasties, periods of chaos occurred as kingdoms or warlords fought for power. At other times, invaders came in and took control. Through it all, Chinese culture endured and evolved.

One of the most important dynasties is the Qin (CHIN), or Ch'in. It was the first dynasty to unite China under one empire. The greatest Qin ruler was Shi Huangdi (SHEE hwahng-dee). He ordered the building of much of the Great Wall of China.

Made to keep out invaders, the wall linked many older walls in northern China. In addition, Shi Huangdi had thousands of terra-cotta, or clay, warriors made to guard his tomb. These life-size warriors, each of which is unique, are skillful works of art.

The last dynasty in China was the Qing (CHING). Invaders called the Manchu ruled this dynasty starting in 1644. In time, outside influences would help lead to its end.

Outside Influences in China

Throughout history, China often limited contact with the outside world. The Chinese saw their culture as superior and had little use for foreigners. The tall mountains, deserts, and seas around China further limited contact and isolated the region.

Yet, other people increasingly wanted Chinese goods such as silk and tea. To gain access to the goods, some European powers forced China to open up trade in the 1800s. Europeans took control of parts of the country as well. These actions angered many Chinese, some of whom blamed the emperor. At the same time, increased contact with the West exposed the Chinese to new ideas.

READING CHECK **Drawing Conclusions** How did geography affect China's early history?

Qin, c. 221–206 BC

- First unified Chinese empire
- Strong central government with strict laws
- Created standardized money and writing systems
- Built a network of roads and canals and much of the Great Wall

Qin life-size terra-cotta warrior

Han, c. 206 BC–AD 220

- Based government on Confucianism
- Began trading over Silk Road
- Spread of Buddhism from India
- Invented paper, sundial, and acupuncture

Han bronze oil lamp

China's Modern History

As foreign influences increased, China's people grew unhappy with imperial rule. This unhappiness sparked a revolution.

Revolution and Civil War

In 1911, rebels forced out China's last emperor. They then formed a republic, a political system in which voters elect their leaders. Power struggles continued, however. In time, two rival groups emerged—the Nationalists, led by Chiang Kai-shek (chang ky-SHEK), and the Communists, led by Mao Zedong (MOW ZUH-DOOHNG).

The two groups fought a violent civil war. That war ended in October 1949 with the Communists as victors. They founded a new government, the People's Republic of China. The Nationalists fled to Taiwan, where they founded the Republic of China.

FOCUS ON READING

What is the main idea of the second paragraph under Population and Settlement on the next page?

Communist China under Mao

Mao, the Communists' leader, became the head of China's new government. In a Communist system, the government owns most businesses and land and controls all areas of life. China's new Communist government began by taking over control of the economy. The government seized all private farms and organized them into large, state-run farms. It also took over all businesses and factories.

While some changes improved life, others did not. On one hand, women gained more rights and were able to work. On the other hand, the government limited freedoms and imprisoned people who criticized it. In addition, many economic programs were unsuccessful, and some were outright disasters. In the early 1960s, for example, poor planning and drought led to a famine that killed millions.

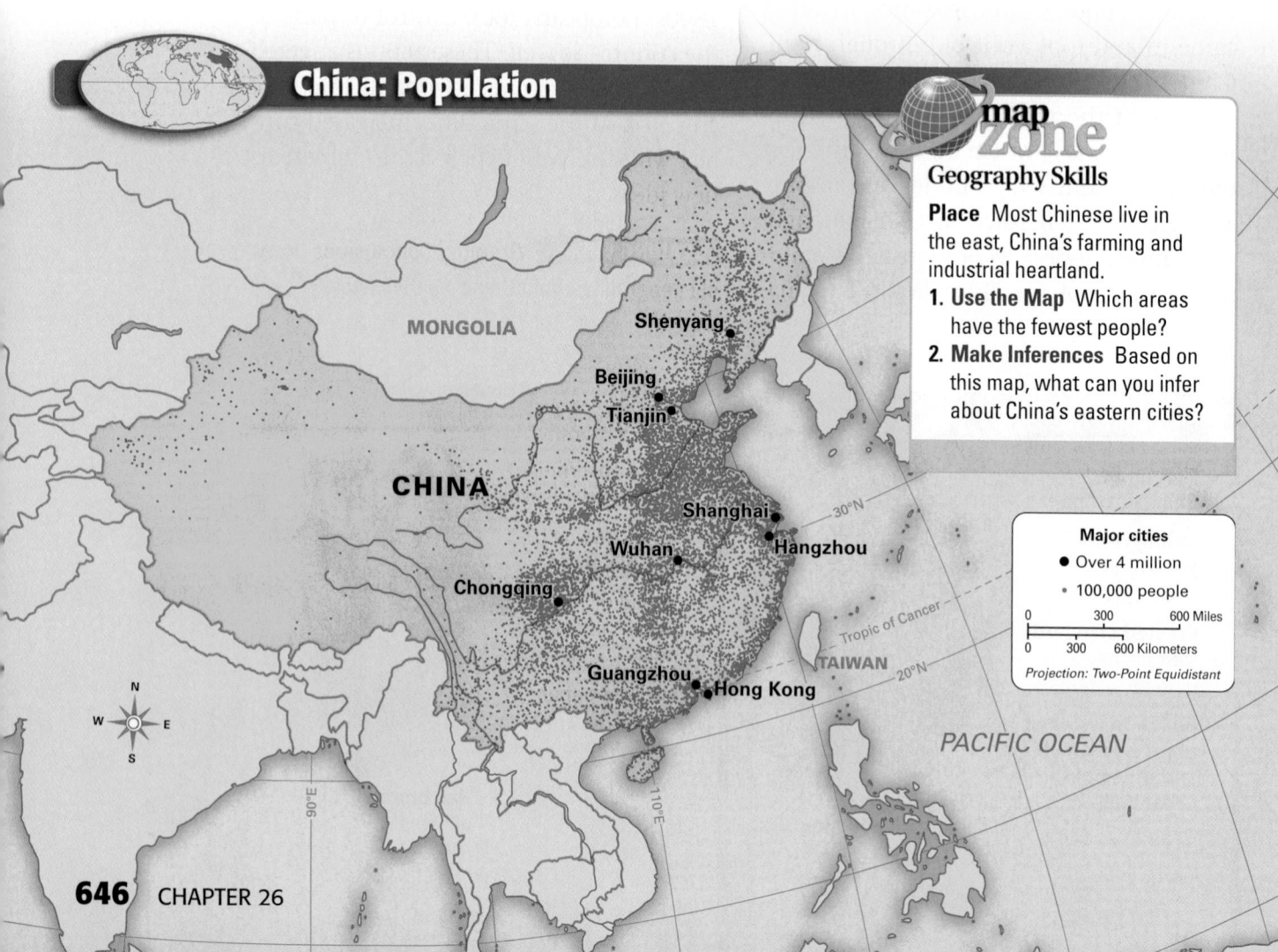

China: Population

map zone

Geography Skills

Place Most Chinese live in the east, China's farming and industrial heartland.

1. **Use the Map** Which areas have the fewest people?
2. **Make Inferences** Based on this map, what can you infer about China's eastern cities?

MONGOLIA
Shenyang
Beijing
Tianjin
CHINA
Shanghai
Wuhan
Hangzhou
Chongqing
Guangzhou
Hong Kong
TAIWAN
PACIFIC OCEAN

Tropic of Cancer
30°N
20°N

Major cities
● Over 4 million
· 100,000 people

| 0 | 300 | 600 Miles |
| 0 | 300 | 600 Kilometers |

Projection: Two-Point Equidistant

Communist China Since Mao

Mao died in 1976, and Deng Xiaoping (DUHNG SHOW-PING) soon rose to power. Deng admitted the government had made mistakes. He then worked to modernize and improve China's economy. He allowed some private businesses and encouraged countries to invest in China. As a result, the economy began growing rapidly. Leaders after Deng continued economic reforms.

READING CHECK **Summarizing** How did communism change life in China?

China's People and Culture

One of China's best known features is its people—all 1.3 billion of them. China has the world's largest population. More people live there than in all of Europe, Russia, and the United States combined.

Population and Settlement

As the map shows, this huge population is not evenly spread out. Only 10 percent of the people live in the west, while the rest are jam-packed into the east. In fact, more people live in the Manchurian and North China Plains than in the United States!

Meanwhile, China's population continues to grow—by about 7.5 million each year. China's officials have worked to slow this growth. Officials have urged people to delay having children and have tried to limit each couple to one child. These actions have succeeded in slowing China's population growth.

Ethnic Groups and Language

Of China's millions of people, 92 percent identify their ancestry as Han Chinese. These people share the same culture and traditions. Many Han speak Mandarin, China's official language. Others speak a **dialect**, a regional version of a language.

Ethnic Groups

The majority of Chinese are Han. However, China includes 55 other ethnic groups. Most of these people live in western and southern China.

Han This woman and other Han make up about 92 percent of China's population. They share the same culture and traditions.

Hui This Hui man is from Gansu province, in central China. Most Hui are Sunni Muslims.

Zhuang This Zhuang man is from Guizhou, in southern China. The Zhuang are China's largest minority group.

Some 55 other ethnic groups make up the remaining 8 percent of China's population. Most of these minority groups live in western and southern China, where they have their own distinct cultures.

Religion, Values, and Beliefs

Ancient religions, **values**, and beliefs shape life for China's many people, even though the Communist government discourages the practice of religion. China's two main belief systems are Daoism (DOW-i-zuhm) and Buddhism. **Daoism** stresses living simply and in harmony with nature. It takes its name from the word *Dao,* which means "the way."

Buddhism came to China from India about AD 100. This religion is based on the teachings of Siddhartha Gautama—the Buddha, who lived from 563 to 483 BC. Buddhists believe moral behavior, kindness, and meditation can lead to peace.

Many Chinese blend **elements** of Daoism and Buddhism with **Confucianism**, a philosophy based on the ideas and teachings of Confucius. This philosophy stresses the importance of family, moral values, and respect for one's elders.

Other major religions in China include Christianity and Islam. Ancestor worship and fortune-telling are popular among the Chinese as well.

Close-up

Beijing's National Day

China celebrates National Day on October 1 with huge parades in Tiananmen Square. This square is one of the world's largest public gathering places. The space is needed because parades can include more than 500,000 participants.

Beijing

CHINA

PACIFIC OCEAN

The Gate of Heavenly Peace displays Mao Zedong's portrait above the entrance.

The parades include couples married on National Day, a popular time to wed.

A military parade of soldiers, tanks, and other equipment shows China's power.

中华人民共和国万岁

The Arts and Popular Culture

China has a rich artistic tradition. Chinese crafts include items made of bronze, jade, ivory, silk, or wood. Chinese porcelain, which the ancient Chinese developed, is highly prized for its quality and beauty.

Traditional Chinese painting is done on silk or fine paper and reflects a focus on balance and harmony with nature. Popular subjects are landscapes, such as scenes of rugged mountains, trees, and lakes.

Chinese art often includes calligraphy, or decorative writing. Chinese writing uses symbols, or characters, instead of letters. This writing makes beautiful art, and some paintings feature just Chinese calligraphy.

In literature, the Chinese are known for their beautiful poetry. The Chinese highly value poetry, and poems appear on paintings and in novels and plays.

In theater, traditional Chinese opera is popular. These operas tell stories through spoken words, music, and dance. Actors wear elaborate costumes and makeup that have special meanings.

Traditional Chinese architecture features wooden buildings on stone bases. Large tiled roofs curve upward at the edge. Also common are **pagodas**, Buddhist temples that have multi-storied towers with an upward curving roof at each floor. Many cities are a mix of traditional and modern.

ANALYSIS
SKILL **ANALYZING VISUALS**

Why might China's government include so many different groups in the National Day parades?

The Chinese believe dragon dances bring good fortune to important events.

世界人民大团结万岁

Lion dances are performed to spread good blessings to the community.

Chinese Martial Arts

Can you imagine getting up each day at 5 AM and exercising for 12 hours or more? Chinese teenagers who attend martial arts schools do just that. Many of the schools' instructors are Buddhist monks trained in the Chinese martial art of kung fu. These instructors teach their students self-defense techniques as well as the importance of hard work, discipline, and respect for one's elders. These values are important in Chinese culture and religion.

Starting as early as age 6, students memorize up to several hundred martial arts movements. These movements include different kicks, jumps, and punches. Some students dream of one day using their martial arts skills to star in a Chinese or American action movie.

Drawing Conclusions Why do you think discipline, hard work, and respect might be important for learning martial arts?

Popular culture includes many activities. Popular sports are martial arts and table tennis. A popular game is mah-jongg, played with small tiles. People also enjoy karaoke clubs, where they sing to music.

READING CHECK **Evaluating** Which aspect of Chinese culture most interests you? Why?

SUMMARY AND PREVIEW After centuries of imperial rule under dynasties, China became a Communist country. China has a rich and ancient culture and is the world's most populous country. In the next section you will read about China's economy, government, and cities.

Section 2 Assessment

Reviewing Ideas, Terms, and Places

1. **a. Define** What is a **dynasty**?
   b. Summarize How did outside influences affect China's early history?
2. **a. Recall** Which two groups fought for power during China's civil war, and which group won?
   b. Contrast How did China's economy under Mao differ from China's economy since his death?
3. **a. Recall** What are some popular pastimes in China today?
   b. Explain What are China's population problems, and how is China addressing them?
   c. Elaborate How are Buddhism, **Confucianism**, and **Daoism** important in Chinese culture?

Critical Thinking

4. **Sequencing** Look back over your notes and then create a chart like this one. List the main events in China's history in the order in which they occurred. Add or remove boxes as necessary.

FOCUS ON WRITING

5. **Collecting Information about China's History and Culture** Note historical or cultural details that you might want to include in your legend. For example, you might include some aspect of Chinese beliefs or artistic traditions in your legend.

China Today

If YOU lived there...

For many years your parents have been farmers, growing tea plants. Since the government began allowing private businesses, your parents have been selling tea in the market as well. With the money they have made, they are considering opening a tea shop.

What do you think your parents should do?

> **BUILDING BACKGROUND** When a Communist government took over China in 1949, it began strictly controlling all areas of life. Over time, China's government has loosened control of the economy. Control over politics and other areas of life remains strict, however.

China's Economy

Think ahead to the day you start working. Would you rather choose your career or have the government choose it for you? The first situation describes a market economy, which we have in the United States. In this type of economy, people can choose their careers, decide what to make or sell, and keep the profits they earn. The second situation describes a **command economy**, an economic system in which the government owns all the businesses and makes all decisions, such as where people work. Communist China used to have a command economy. Then in the 1970s, China began allowing aspects of a market economy.

What You Will Learn...

Main Ideas

1. China's booming economy is based on agriculture, but industry is growing rapidly.
2. China's government controls many aspects of life and limits political freedom.
3. China is mainly rural, but urban areas are growing.
4. China's environment faces a number of serious problems.

The Big Idea

China's economy and cities are growing rapidly, but the Chinese have little political freedom and many environmental problems.

Key Terms and Places

command economy, *p. 651*
Beijing, *p. 652*
Tibet, *p. 653*
Shanghai, *p. 654*
Hong Kong, *p. 654*

TAKING NOTES As you read, use a chart like the one below to take notes on China today.

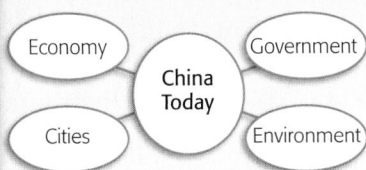

Economy — China Today — Government
Cities — Environment

Farmers near Yunnan, in southern China, use traditional methods to work rice paddies.

China developed a mixed economy because it had major economic problems. For example, the production of goods had fallen. In response, the government closed many state-run factories and began allowing privately owned businesses. In addition, the government created special economic zones where foreign business-people could own companies. A mixed economic approach has helped China's economy boom. Today China has the world's second largest economy.

Agriculture and Industry

More Chinese work in farming than in any other economic activity. The country is a leading producer of several crops, such as rice, wheat, corn, and potatoes. China's main farmlands are in the eastern plains and river valleys. To the north, wheat is the main crop. To the south, rice is.

Only about 10 percent of China's land is good for farming. So how does China produce so much food? More than half of all Chinese workers are farmers. This large labor force can work the land at high lev-els. In addition, farmers cut terraces into hillsides to make the most use of the land.

Although China is mainly agricultural, industry is growing rapidly. Today China produces everything from satellites and chemicals to clothing and toys. Moreover, industry and manufacturing are now the most profitable part of China's economy.

Results of Economic Growth

Economic growth has improved wages and living standards in China. Almost all homes now have electricity, even in rural areas. More and more Chinese can afford goods such as TVs, computers, and even cars. At the same time, many rural Chinese remain poor, and unemployment is high.

READING CHECK **Summarizing** How has China changed its economy in recent times?

China's Government

More economic freedom in China has not led to more political freedom. The Com-munist government tightly controls most areas of life. For example, the government controls newspapers and Internet access, which helps to restrict the flow of informa-tion and ideas.

In addition, China harshly punishes people who oppose the government. In 1989 more than 100,000 pro-democracy protestors gathered in Tiananmen Square in **Beijing**, China's capital. The protestors were demanding more political rights and freedoms. The Chinese government tried to get the protestors to leave the square. When they refused, the government used troops and tanks to make them leave. Hun-dreds of protestors were killed, and many more were injured or imprisoned.

China's Urban Growth

China has taken harsh actions against ethnic rebellions as well. As an example, since 1950 China has controlled the Buddhist region of **Tibet**, in southwest China. When the Tibetans rebelled in 1959, the Chinese quickly crushed the revolt. The Dalai Lama (dah-ly LAH-muh), Tibet's Buddhist leader, had to flee to India. China then cracked down on Tibetans' rights.

Because of actions such as these, many other countries have accused China of not respecting human rights. Some of these countries have considered limiting or stopping trade with China. For example, some U.S. politicians want our government to limit trade with China until it shows more respect for human rights.

READING CHECK **Analyzing** What adjectives might you use to describe China's government?

Rural and Urban China

China is a land in the midst of change. Although its countryside remains set in the past, China's cities are growing rapidly and rushing headlong toward the future.

Rural China

Most of China's people live in small, rural villages. Farmers work the fields using the same methods they have used for decades. In small shops and along the streets, sellers cook food and offer goods. Although some villagers' standards of living are improving, the modern world often seems far away.

Urban China

Many people are leaving China's villages for its booming cities, however. The graph below shows how China's urban population is expected to rise in the future.

FOCUS ON READING
What is the implied main idea of the text under Rural China?

THE WORLD ALMANAC
Facts about Countries

China's Projected Urban Population

go.hrw.com KEYWORD: SG7 CH26

Many of China's rapidly growing cities are severely crowded, as can be seen in this Shanghai shopping area. Overcrowding is expected to worsen as China's cities continue to grow.

INTERPRETING GRAPHS About when is China's urban population expected to be larger than its rural population?

CHINA, MONGOLIA, AND TAIWAN **653**

China's Environmental Challenges

Legend:
- Forest areas
- Forest destroyed
- Desertification
- Soil erosion
- High risk of flooding
- Poor urban air quality

0   250   500   750 Miles
0   250 500 750 Kilometers

Projection: Two-Point Equidistant

CHINA

Shenyang
Baotou
Beijing
Lanzhou
Xi'an
Huang He (Yellow River)
Huai He
Shanghai
Min Jiang
Nu River
Chang Jiang (Yangzi River)
Brahmaputra River
Xi River
Guangzhou
Mekong River
Liao He

PACIFIC OCEAN
Tropic of Cancer

map zone Geography Skills

Human-Environment Interaction China faces a number of serious environmental challenges.
1. **Identify** Which rivers does the map show as having a high risk of flooding?
2. **Interpret** Which environmental problem has had the most impact on southern China?

China's growing economy has led to its rapid city growth. Look at the population map in Section 2 and find the cities with more than 4 million people. Most are on the coast or along major rivers. These areas have benefited from growing industry and trade. Places that were rice fields not long ago are now bustling urban centers with skyscrapers, factories, and highways.

China's largest city is **Shanghai**, with some 14 million people. Located where the Chang Jiang meets the East China Sea, it is China's leading seaport and an industrial and commercial center. The city is also known for its European feel and nightlife.

China's second-largest city is its capital, Beijing. Also known as Peking, this historic city has many beautiful palaces and temples. A mix of the old and new, Beijing is China's political and cultural center.

In central Beijing, large walls hide the golden-roofed palaces of the Forbidden City, former home of China's emperors. Once off-limits to all but the emperor's household, the city is now a museum open to the public. Nearby, Tiananmen Square is the site of many parades and other public events. Government buildings and museums line this immense square.

In southern China, **Hong Kong** and Macao (muh-KOW) are major port cities and centers of trade and tourism. Both cities were European colonies until recently. The United Kingdom returned Hong Kong to China in 1997, and Portugal returned Macao in 1999. The two modern, crowded cities provide a mix of cultures.

READING CHECK **Contrasting** In what ways might rural life differ from city life in China?

1 Residents of Baotou, in north-central China, wear masks to keep from inhaling harmful particles in the city's polluted air.

2 These children are planting trees to help create new forestland north of Beijing.

China's Environment

China's economic and urban growth has created serious environmental problems. A major problem is pollution. The country's rising number of cars and factories pollute the air and water. At the same time, China burns coal for much of its electricity, which further pollutes the air.

Another serious problem is the loss of forestland and farmland. For centuries the Chinese cut down trees without replanting more. In addition, many of China's expanding cities are in its best farmlands.

The Chinese are working to address such problems. For example, China hopes to lessen pollution by using more hydroelectric power, electricity produced from dams. China is currently building the Three Gorges Dam on the Chang Jiang.

This dam is set to be finished in 2009. When completed, it will be the world's largest dam and generate as much power as 15 coal-burning power plants. On the other hand, the dam will drown hundreds of towns and huge amounts of farmland. Millions of people will have to move, and plant and animal habitats will be harmed.

READING CHECK **Finding Main Ideas** What are some of China's environmental problems?

SUMMARY AND PREVIEW China's economy and cities are growing rapidly, but its government restricts political freedom and faces environmental problems. In the next section you will learn about Mongolia and Taiwan.

Section 3 Assessment

Reviewing Ideas, Terms, and Places

1. **a. Define** What is a **command economy**?
   b. Identify Cause and Effect What changes have helped lead to China's rapid economic growth?
2. **a. Describe** In what ways does China's government restrict freedom?
   b. Evaluate What is your opinion of China's handling of the 1989 demonstration at Tiananmen Square?
3. **a. Identify** What is China's largest city and leading port?
   b. Compare How are **Hong Kong** and Macao similar?
4. **a. Recall** What are China's environmental problems?
   b. Evaluate Do you think China should build the Three Gorges Dam? Why or why not?

Critical Thinking

5. **Categorizing** Create a table like the one shown to organize the challenges that China faces today.

Challenges Facing China		
Economic	Political	Environmental

FOCUS ON WRITING

6. **Collecting Information about China Today** Note any details about China's current economy, government, cities, or environment that you might include in your legend.

Mongolia and Taiwan

Main Ideas

1. Mongolia is a sparsely populated country where many people live as nomads.
2. Taiwan is a small island with a dense population and a highly industrialized economy.

The Big Idea

Mongolia is a rugged land with a nomadic way of life and growing cities, while Taiwan is a densely settled and industrialized island.

Key Terms and Places

gers, *p. 657*
Ulaanbaatar, *p. 657*
Taipei, *p. 658*
Kao-hsiung, *p. 658*

TAKING NOTES As you read, use a chart like the one below to take notes on the history, culture, and region today of Mongolia and Taiwan.

	Mongolia	Taiwan
History		
Culture		
Region Today		

If **YOU** lived there...

Like many Mongolians, you have loved horses since you were a small child. You live in an apartment in the city of Ulaanbaatar, however. Some of your family are talking about leaving the city and becoming nomadic herders like your ancestors were. You think you might like being able to ride horses more. You're not sure you would like living in a tent, though, especially in winter.

Do you want to move back to the land?

BUILDING BACKGROUND While Mongolia is a rugged land where some people still live as nomads, Taiwan is a modern and highly industrialized island. The two regions do have a few things in common, however. Mongolia and Taiwan are both neighbors of China, both are becoming more urban, and both are democracies.

Mongolia

A wild and rugged land, Mongolia is home to the Mongol people. They have a proud and fascinating history. This history includes conquests and empires and a culture that prizes horses.

Mongolia's History

Today when people discuss the world's leading countries, they do not mention Mongolia. However, 700 years ago Mongolia was perhaps the greatest power in the world. Led by the ruler Genghis Khan, the Mongols conquered much of Asia, including China. Later Mongol leaders continued the conquests. They built the greatest empire the world had seen at the time.

The Mongol Empire reached its height in the late 1200s. During that time, the empire stretched from Europe's Danube River in the west to the Pacific Ocean in the east. As time passed, however, the Mongol Empire declined. In the late 1600s China conquered Mongolia and ruled it for more than 200 years.

Nomadic Life in Mongolia

Some Mongolians are nomads, who live in tents called gers. Inside, gers are furnished mainly with rugs. Different areas of the gers are used for specific purposes. For example, the back is used for an altar.

ANALYZING VISUALS What do you think it is like to live in a ger?

Gers have wooden, painted doors. The doors always face south because the wind usually blows from the northeast.

With Russia's help, Mongolia declared independence from China in 1911. Soon Communists gained control and in 1924 formed the Mongolian People's Republic. Meanwhile, Russia had become part of the Soviet Union, a large Communist country north of Mongolia. The Soviet Union strongly influenced Mongolia and gave it large amounts of economic aid. This aid ended, however, after the Soviet Union collapsed in 1991. Since then, Mongolians have struggled to build a democratic government and a free-market economy.

Mongolia's Culture

In spite of years of Communist rule, the Mongolian way of life remains fairly traditional. Nearly half of Mongolia's people live as nomads. They herd livestock across Mongolia's vast grasslands and make their homes in **gers** (GUHRZ). These are large, circular, felt tents that are easy to put up, take down, and move.

Since many Mongols live as herders, horses play a major **role** in Mongolian life. As a result, Mongolian culture highly prizes horse skills, and Mongolian children often learn to ride when they are quite young.

Mongolia Today

Mongolia is sparsely populated. Slightly larger than Alaska, it has about 3 million people. More than a quarter of them live in **Ulaanbaatar** (oo-lahn-BAH-tawr), the capital and only large city. Mongolia's other cities are quite small. However, Mongolia's urban population is slowly growing.

The country's main industries include textiles, carpets, coal, copper, and oil. The city of Ulaanbaatar is the main industrial and commercial center. Mongolia produces little food other than from livestock, however, and faces food and water shortages.

READING CHECK Summarizing What are some features of Mongolian culture?

ACADEMIC VOCABULARY
role part or function

FOCUS ON READING
Read the second paragraph under Mongolia Today. Determine the topic of each sentence. What is the implied main idea?

Taiwan

When Portuguese sailors visited the island of Taiwan in the late 1500s, they called it *Ilha Formosa*, or "beautiful island." For many years, Westerners called Taiwan by the name Formosa. Today the loveliness of Taiwan's green mountains and waterfalls competes with its modern, crowded cities.

Taiwan's History

The Chinese began settling Taiwan in the 600s. At different times in history, both China and Japan have controlled Taiwan. In 1949, though, the Chinese Nationalists took over Taiwan. Led by Chiang Kai-shek, the Nationalists were fleeing the Communists, who had taken control of China's mainland. The Chinese Nationalist Party ruled Taiwan under martial law, or military rule, for 38 years. Today Taiwan's government is a multiparty democracy.

As the chart below explains, tensions remain between China and Taiwan. The Chinese government claims that Taiwan is a rebel part of China. In contrast, Taiwan's government claims to be the true government of China. For all practical purposes, though, Taiwan functions as an independent country.

Taiwan's Culture

Taiwan's history is reflected in its culture. Its population is about 85 percent native Taiwanese. These people are descendants of Chinese people who migrated to Taiwan largely in the 1700s and 1800s. As a result, Chinese ways dominate Taiwan's culture.

Other influences have shaped Taiwan's culture as well. Because Japan once ruled Taiwan, Japanese culture can be seen in some Taiwanese buildings and foods. More recently, European and American practices and customs are becoming noticeable in Taiwan, particularly in larger cities.

Taiwan Today

Taiwan is a modern country with a population of about 23 million. These people live on an island about the size of Delaware and Maryland combined. Because much of Taiwan is mountainous, most people live on the island's western coastal plain. This region is home to Taiwan's main cities.

The two largest cities are **Taipei** (TY-PAY) and **Kao-hsiung** (KOW-SHYOOHNG). Taipei, the capital, is Taiwan's main financial center. Because it has grown so quickly, it faces serious overcrowding and environmental problems. Kao-hsiung is a center of heavy industry and Taiwan's main seaport.

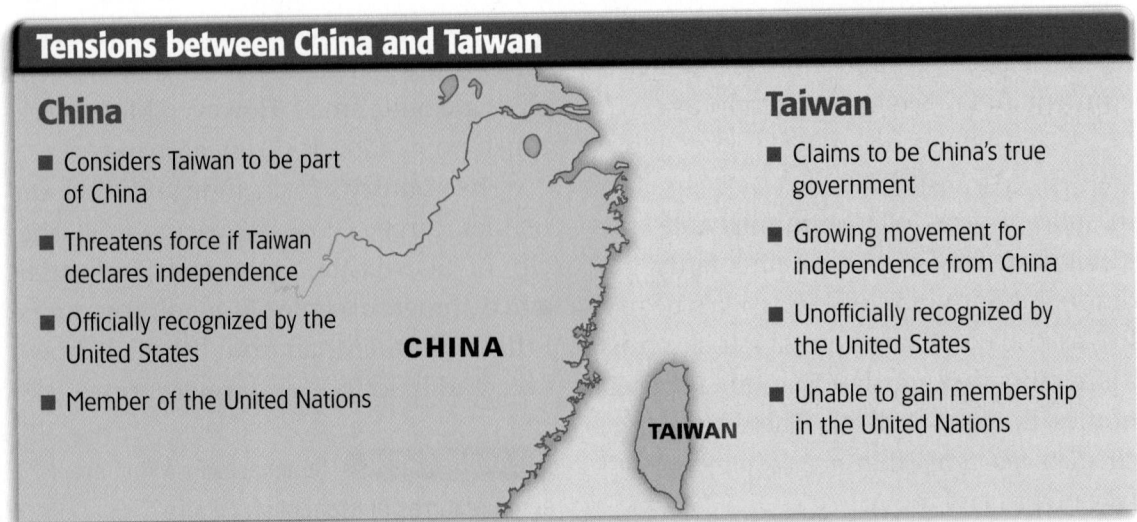

Tensions between China and Taiwan

China
- Considers Taiwan to be part of China
- Threatens force if Taiwan declares independence
- Officially recognized by the United States
- Member of the United Nations

Taiwan
- Claims to be China's true government
- Growing movement for independence from China
- Unofficially recognized by the United States
- Unable to gain membership in the United Nations

CHINA

TAIWAN

Taipei

Taipei, Taiwan's capital, is a bustling city of more than 2 million people. The tall tower in the photo is the Taipei 101, which is 101 stories tall.

Taiwan is one of Asia's richest and most industrialized countries. It is a leader in the production and export of computers and sports equipment. Taiwan's farmers grow many crops as well, such as sugarcane.

READING CHECK **Contrasting** How does Taiwan's economy differ from Mongolia's?

SUMMARY AND PREVIEW Mongolia and Taiwan are smaller countries bordering China. Mongolia is a wild land with a nomadic people who prize horses. In contrast, Taiwan is a modern and industrialized island. In the next chapter, you will learn about Japan and the Koreas.

Section 4 Assessment

go.hrw.com
Online Quiz
KEYWORD: SG7 HP26

Reviewing Ideas, Terms, and Places

1. **a. Define** What are **gers**, and what are their roles in Mongolia's culture?
   b. Make Inferences Why might many Mongolians be proud of their country's history?
   c. Elaborate Why does Mongolia's culture prize horses?
2. **a. Recall** Why is **Taipei** an important Taiwanese city, and what problems does the city face?
   b. Summarize What is the significance of Chiang Kai-shek in Taiwan's history?
   c. Evaluate Would you rather live in Taiwan or Mongolia? Provide information about each place to explain your answer.

Critical Thinking

3. **Comparing and Contrasting** Create a Venn diagram like the one shown. Use your notes and compare and contrast the histories, cultures, and societies of Mongolia and Taiwan.

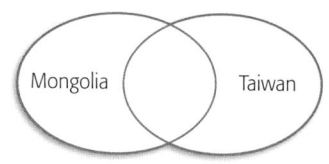

Mongolia   Taiwan

FOCUS ON WRITING

4. **Collecting Information about Mongolia and Taiwan** Consider Mongolia and Taiwan as settings for your legend. For example, your legend might explain the creation of the Gobi, a large desert located partly in Mongolia.

CHINA, MONGOLIA, AND TAIWAN **659**

Social Studies Skills

Analyzing Points of View

Learn

Geography involves issues, situations where people disagree. The way people look at an issue is their point of view. To analyze points of view, use these tips:

- Consider a person's background. Think about where the person lives, what the person does, and what his or her beliefs and attitudes are.

- Look for emotional language, such as name calling or biased terms. Emotional language often reveals a person's point of view.

- Look at the evidence, or facts and statistics, to see what point of view they support.

- Put it all together to identify the point of view.

Practice

Read the passage below about a law forbidding any part of China to declare independence. Then answer the questions that follow.

❶ What is China's point of view about Taiwan?

❷ What is Taiwan's point of view about China?

New Law Angers Taiwan

Taiwan's government has warned that China's new anti-secession [anti-independence] law . . . will have a "serious impact" on security in the region. . .

Taiwan officials were quick to call the measure a "war bill," coming as China boosts its military spending by 13 percent to $30 billion. . .

But Chinese Premier Wen Jiabao said the new legislation [law] was not a "war bill" and warned outsiders not to get involved . . . "It is not targeted at the people of Taiwan, nor is it a war bill," Wen said at a news conference.

Source: *CNN International*, March 14, 2005

Consider background—China considers Taiwan a rebel province. Taiwan has a growing movement for independence.

Look for emotional language—The phrase "war bill" appeals to the emotions. People have strong feelings about war.

Look at the evidence—The information about military spending is evidence supporting one point of view.

Put it all together to identify each point of view.

Apply

1. In the passage above, how does each side's background affect its point of view?

2. Which point of view does the evidence about China's military spending support?

Chapter Review

Geography's Impact
video series
Review the video to answer the closing question:
If you were involved in the decision to build the Three Gorges Dam, would you support it or vote against it? Why?

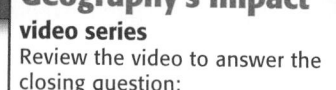

Visual Summary

Use the visual summary below to help you review the main ideas of the chapter.

QUICK FACTS

China is a large Communist country with a rich culture. Both its economy and population are growing rapidly.

Mongolia lies to the north of China. It is a harsh, wild land. Many Mongolians are nomads who herd livestock.

Taiwan is an island off the southern coast of China. It is a modern and industrialized region.

Reviewing Vocabulary, Terms, and Places

Match the words or places below with their definitions or descriptions.

1. command economy
2. North China Plain
3. pagodas
4. gers
5. Tibet
6. dialect
7. Himalayas
8. Taipei

a. Buddhist region in southwest China

b. world's highest mountain range

c. regional version of a language

d. capital city of Taiwan

e. system in which the government owns most businesses and makes most economic decisions

f. fertile and highly populated region in eastern China

g. circular, felt tents in which Mongol nomads live

h. Buddhist temples with multiple stories

Comprehension and Critical Thinking

SECTION 1 *(Pages 640–643)*

9. **a. Recall** What physical features separate many of the mountain ranges in this region?

   b. Explain What is the Huang He called in English, and how did the river get its name?

   c. Elaborate What major physical features might a traveler see during a trip from the Himalayas, in southwestern China, to Beijing, in northeastern China?

SECTION 2 *(Pages 644–650)*

10. **a. Identify** Who is Mao Zedong, and why is he significant in China's history?

    b. Summarize What are some of China's artistic traditions, and how have they contributed to world culture?

    c. Predict What future challenges do you think China might face if its population continues to grow at its current rate?

SECTION 3 *(Pages 651–655)*

11. a. Recall What do more than half of China's workers do for a living?

   b. Summarize What elements of free enterprise does China's command economy now include?

   c. Evaluate What is your opinion about China's treatment of Tibet?

SECTION 4 *(Pages 656–659)*

12. a. Identify What is the capital of Mongolia?

   b. Analyze How is Taiwan's history reflected in the island's culture today?

   c. Predict Do you think China and Taiwan can resolve their disagreements? Why or why not?

Using the Internet

go.hrw.com
KEYWORD: SG7 CH26

13. Activity: Touring China's Great Wall The construction of the Great Wall of China began more than 2,000 years ago. The wall was built over time to keep out invaders and to protect China's people. Enter the activity keyword to explore this wonder of the world. Take notes on the wall's history, myths and legends, and other interesting facts. Then make a brochure about your virtual visit to the Great Wall of China.

Social Studies Skills

Analyzing Points of View *Read the following passage from this chapter. Then answer the questions below.*

> "In 1989 more than 100,000 pro-democracy protestors gathered in Tiananmen Square in Beijing, China's capital. The protestors were demanding more political rights and freedoms. The Chinese government tried to get the protestors to leave the square. When they refused, the government used troops and tanks to make them leave. Hundreds of protestors were injured or killed."

14. What was the point of view of the protestors toward China's government?

15. What was the point of view of China's government toward the protestors?

---

16. Identifying Implied Main Ideas Read the first paragraph under the heading Revolution and Civil War in Section 2. What is the implied main idea of this paragraph? What words and phrases help signal the implied main idea?

17. Writing a Legend Choose one physical feature and decide how you will explain its creation. Then review your notes and choose characters, events, and settings for your legend. Your legend should be two to three paragraphs. It should include (a) a beginning; (b) a middle that includes a climax, or high point of the story; and (c) a conclusion, or end. Remember, legends tell about extraordinary events, so you should use your imagination and creativity.

Map Activity

18. China, Mongolia, and Taiwan On a separate sheet of paper, match the letters on the map with their correct labels below.

Beijing, China	Hong Kong, China
Chang Jiang	Huang He
Great Wall of China	Taipei, Taiwan
Himalayas	Ulaanbaatar, Mongolia

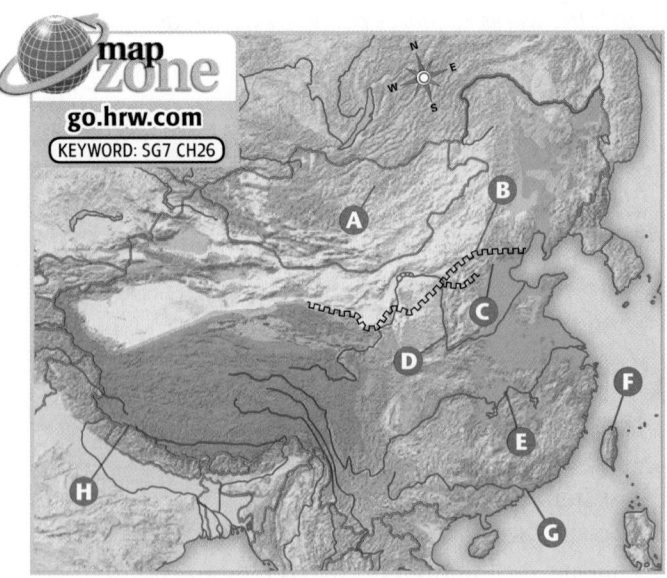

map zone
go.hrw.com
KEYWORD: SG7 CH26

DIRECTIONS: Read questions 1 through 7 and write the letter of the best response. Then read question 8 and write your own well-constructed response.

1 **What is the world's highest mountain range?**

A Himalayas

B Kunlun Shan

C Tian Shan

D Qinling Shandi

2 **Why is China's Qin dynasty significant?**

A first recorded dynasty in China

B longest-lasting dynasty in China

C first dynasty to unify China

D first dynasty to practice Buddhism

3 **In which area do most people in China live?**

A west

B east

C south

D north

4 **Which of these challenges faces China?**

A slow population growth

B a weak economy

C lack of urban growth

D air and water pollution

5 **Which phrase *best* describes Taiwan?**

A a nomadic culture that prizes horses

B modern and industrialized cities

C strict government and few political freedoms

D mainly rural and agricultural

6 **Who was a great ruler in Mongolian history?**

A Genghis Khan

B Chiang Kai-shek

C Mao Zedong

D Shi Huangdi

China, Mongolia, and Taiwan: Precipitation

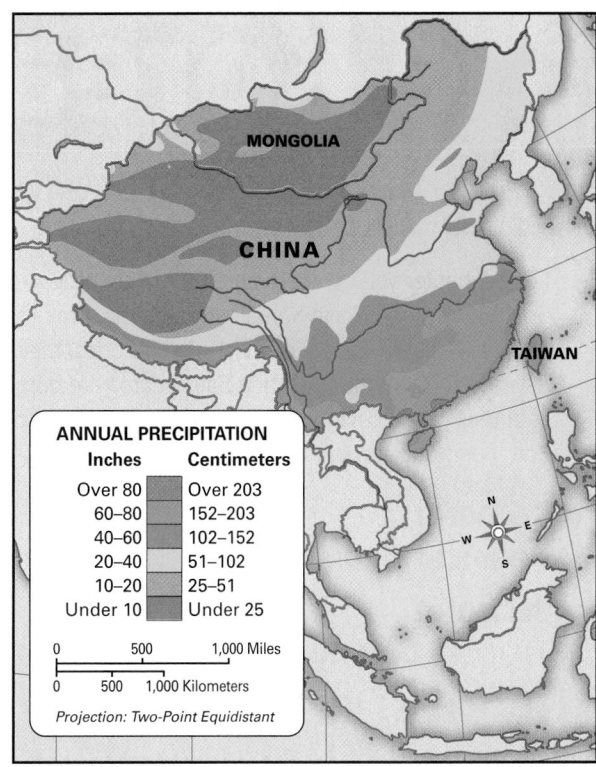

7 **Based on the map, which statement best describes precipitation across this region?**

A increases from east to west

B decreases from north to south

C decreases from the southeast to the northwest

D increases from the southeast to the northwest

8 **Extended Response** Look at the map titled China's Environmental Challenges in Section 3. Write two to three paragraphs explaining why the Chinese government should take action to address environmental problems. Make certain to include a description of the ways in which each problem affects China.

CHAPTER 27

Japan and the Koreas

What You Will Learn...

In this chapter you will learn about three countries—Japan, South Korea, and North Korea. Although the three share some physical features and have intertwined histories, they are all very different today. Both Japan and South Korea are democratic countries with prosperous economies, while North Korea is a Communist dictatorship faced with economic hardships.

FOCUS ON READING AND WRITING

Understanding Fact and Opinion A fact is a statement that can be proved true. An opinion is someone's belief about something. When you read a textbook, you need to recognize the difference between facts and opinions. **See the lesson, Understanding Fact and Opinion, on page R28.**

Composing a Five-Line Poem For centuries, Japanese poets have written five-line poems called tankas. Most tanka poems describe a single image or emotion in very few words. After you read this chapter, you will choose one image of Japan or the Koreas to use as the subject of your own five-line poem.

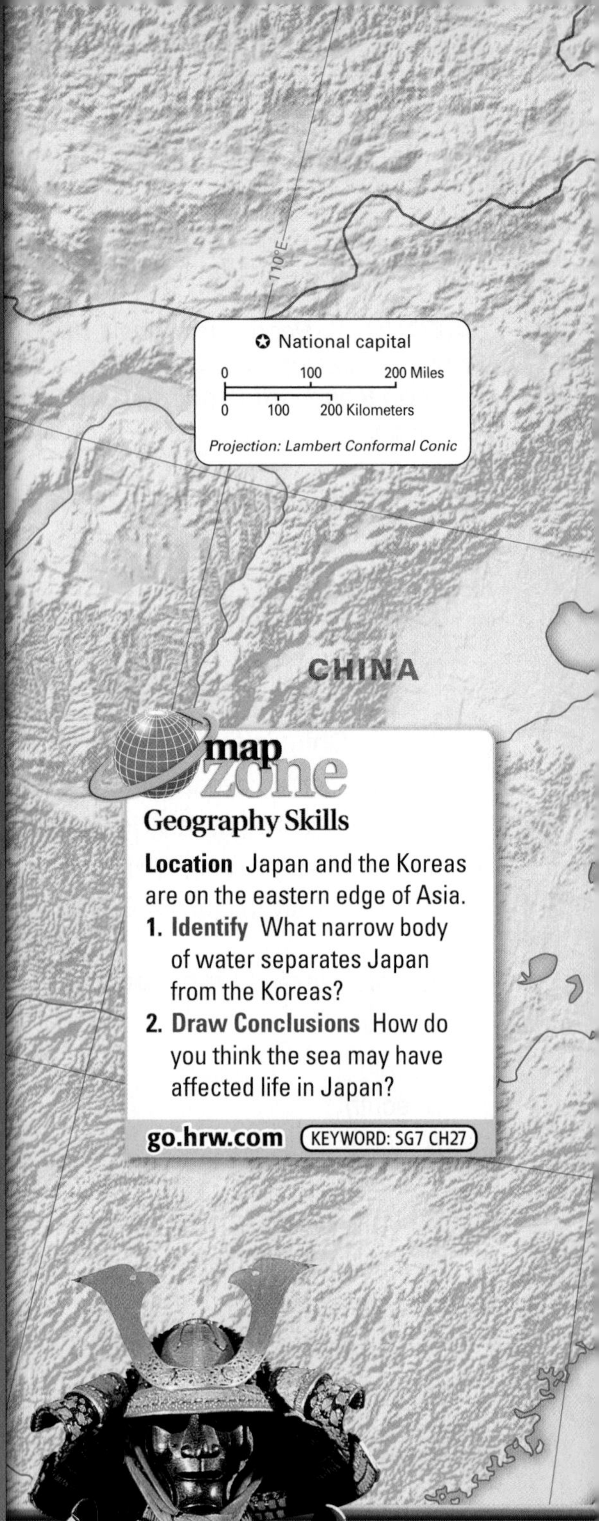

◆ National capital

| 0 | 100 | 200 Miles |

| 0 | 100 | 200 Kilometers |

Projection: Lambert Conformal Conic

CHINA

map zone

Geography Skills

Location Japan and the Koreas are on the eastern edge of Asia.
1. **Identify** What narrow body of water separates Japan from the Koreas?
2. **Draw Conclusions** How do you think the sea may have affected life in Japan?

go.hrw.com **KEYWORD: SG7 CH27**

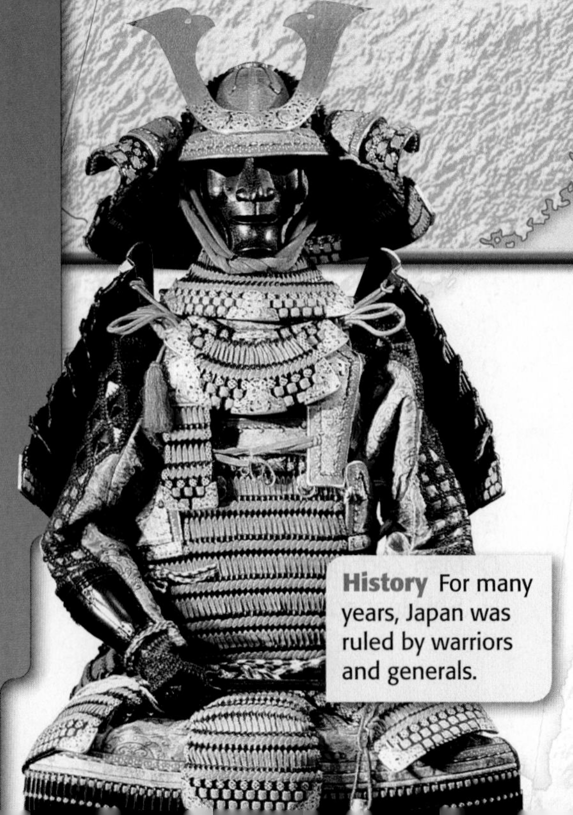

History For many years, Japan was ruled by warriors and generals.

Japan and the Koreas: Political

RUSSIA

Sea of
Okhotsk

Sapporo

**NORTH
KOREA**

Pyongyang ✪
Nampo ●

Tumen

Yalu River

Sea of Japan
(East Sea)

Inchon ●
Seoul ✪

Yellow
Sea

**SOUTH
KOREA**

Taegu ●

Pusan ●

Korea Strait

Hiroshima ●

Kyoto ●
Osaka ●

JAPAN

Tokyo ✪
Nagoya ●
Yokohama ●

PACIFIC
OCEAN

Nagasaki ●

East
China
Sea

30°N

N
W ✦ E
S

Philippine Sea

HOLT

Geography's Impact
video series
Watch the video to
understand the impact
of natural hazards.

Geography Mount Fuji, a
common symbol of Japan,
is one of the thousands of
mountains found in the region.

Culture Under Kim Il Sung, North Korea
became a Communist country.

665

Physical Geography

What You Will Learn...

Main Ideas

1. The main physical features of Japan and the Koreas are rugged mountains.
2. The climates and resources of Japan and the Koreas vary from north to south.

The Big Idea

Japan and Korea are both rugged, mountainous areas surrounded by water.

Key Terms and Places

Fuji, *p. 667*
Korean Peninsula, *p. 667*
tsunamis, *p. 668*
fishery, *p. 669*

TAKING NOTES Draw a table like the one below. As you read, take notes about the physical geography of Japan in one column and about the Korean Peninsula in the other column.

Physical Geography	
Japan	Korean Peninsula

If YOU lived there...

You are a passenger on a very fast train zipping its way across the countryside. If you look out the window to your right, you can see the distant sparkle of sunlight on the ocean. If you look to the left, you see rocky, rugged mountains. Suddenly the train leaves the mountains, and you see hundreds of trees covered in delicate pink flowers. Rising above the trees is a single snowcapped volcano.

How does this scenery make you feel?

BUILDING BACKGROUND The train described above is one of the many that cross the islands of Japan every day. Japan's mountains, trees, and water features give the islands a unique character. Not far away, the Korean Peninsula also has a distinctive landscape.

Physical Features

Japan, North Korea, and South Korea are on the eastern edge of the Asian continent, just east of China. Separated from each other only by a narrow strait, Japan and the Koreas share many common landscape features.

Physical Features of Japan

Japan is an island country. It is made up of four large islands and more than 3,000 smaller islands. These islands are arranged in a long chain more than 1,500 miles (2,400 km) long. This is about the same length as the eastern coast of the United States, from southern Florida to northern Maine. All together, however, Japan's land area is slightly smaller than the state of California.

About 95 percent of Japan's land area is made up of four large islands. From north to south, these major islands are Hokkaido (hoh-KY-doh), Honshu (HAWN-shoo), Shikoku (shee-KOH-koo), and Kyushu (KYOO-shoo). Together they are called the home islands. Most of Japan's people live there.

Rugged, tree-covered mountains are a common sight in Japan. In fact, mountains cover some 75 percent of the country. For the most part, Japan's mountains are very steep and rocky. As a result, the country's largest mountain range, the Japanese Alps, is popular with climbers and skiers.

Japan's highest mountain, **Fuji**, is not part of the Alps. In fact, it is not part of any mountain range. A volcano, Mount Fuji rises high above a relatively flat area in eastern Honshu. The mountain's cone-shaped peak has become a symbol of Japan. In addition, many Japanese consider Fuji a sacred place. As a result, many shrines have been built at its foot and summit.

Physical Features of Korea

Jutting south from the Asian mainland, the **Korean Peninsula** includes both North Korea and South Korea. Like the islands of Japan, much of the peninsula is covered with rugged mountains. These mountains form long ranges that run along Korea's eastern coast. The peninsula's highest mountains are in the north.

Unlike Japan, Korea also has some large plains. These plains are found mainly along the peninsula's western coast and in river valleys. Korea also has more rivers than Japan does. Most of these rivers flow westward across the peninsula and pour into the Yellow Sea.

FOCUS ON READING

Are these sentences facts or opinions? How can you tell?

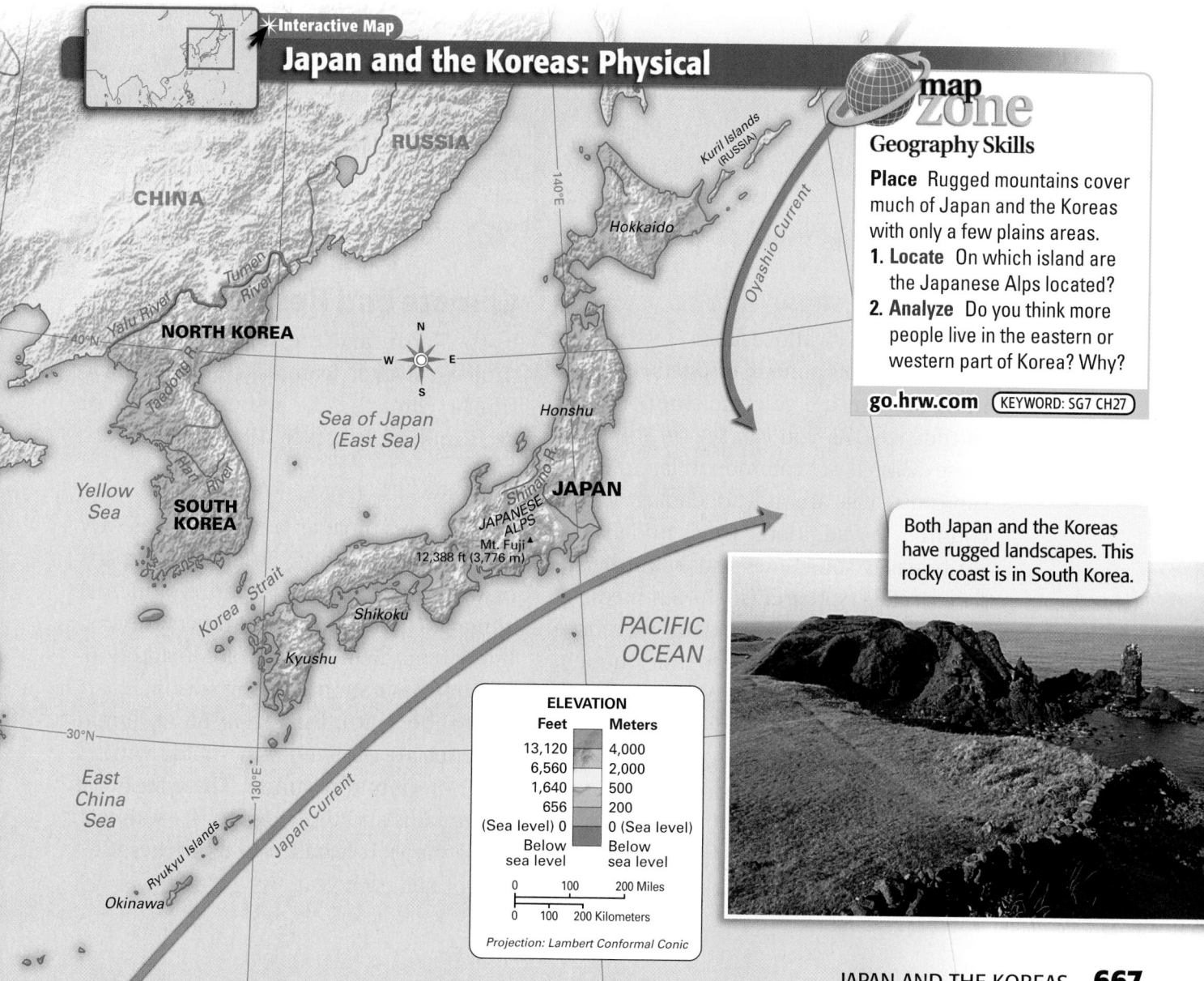

Japan and the Koreas: Physical

map zone

Geography Skills

Place Rugged mountains cover much of Japan and the Koreas with only a few plains areas.

1. **Locate** On which island are the Japanese Alps located?
2. **Analyze** Do you think more people live in the eastern or western part of Korea? Why?

go.hrw.com (KEYWORD: SG7 CH27)

Both Japan and the Koreas have rugged landscapes. This rocky coast is in South Korea.

ELEVATION

Feet		Meters
13,120		4,000
6,560		2,000
1,640		500
656		200
(Sea level) 0		0 (Sea level)
Below sea level		Below sea level

0   100   200 Miles

0   100   200 Kilometers

Projection: Lambert Conformal Conic

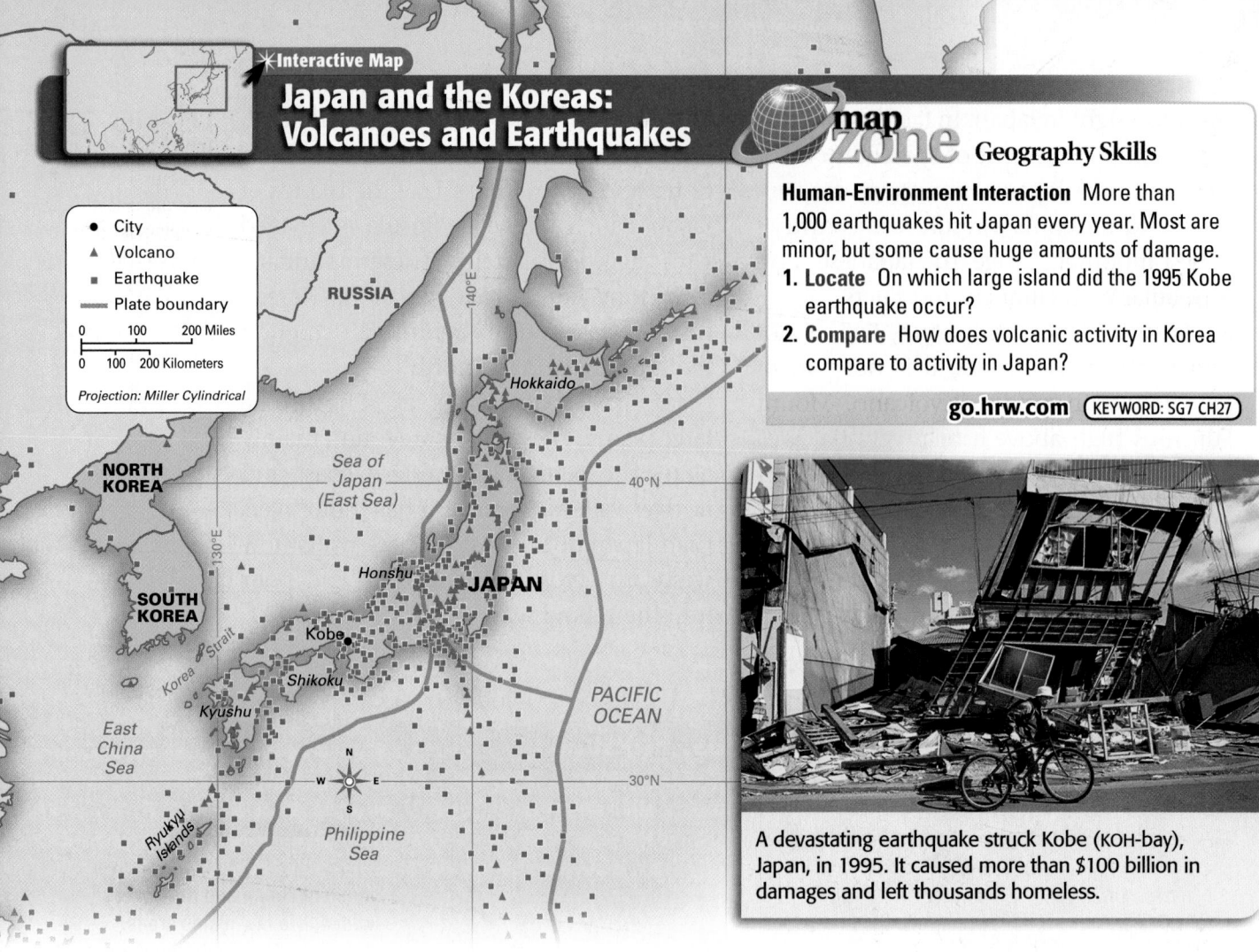

Japan and the Koreas: Volcanoes and Earthquakes

map zone Geography Skills

Human-Environment Interaction More than 1,000 earthquakes hit Japan every year. Most are minor, but some cause huge amounts of damage.

1. **Locate** On which large island did the 1995 Kobe earthquake occur?
2. **Compare** How does volcanic activity in Korea compare to activity in Japan?

go.hrw.com KEYWORD: SG7 CH27

- ● City
- ▲ Volcano
- ■ Earthquake
- ⚊⚊ Plate boundary

0 100 200 Miles
0 100 200 Kilometers

Projection: Miller Cylindrical

RUSSIA

140°E

Hokkaido

NORTH KOREA

Sea of Japan (East Sea)

40°N

130°E

Honshu

JAPAN

SOUTH KOREA

Kobe

Shikoku

PACIFIC OCEAN

Kyushu

East China Sea

30°N

Ryukyu Islands

Philippine Sea

A devastating earthquake struck Kobe (KOH-bay), Japan, in 1995. It caused more than $100 billion in damages and left thousands homeless.

Natural Disasters

Because of its location, Japan is subject to many sorts of natural disasters. Among these disasters are volcanic eruptions and earthquakes. As you can see on the map, these disasters are common in Japan. They can cause huge amounts of damage in the country. In addition, large underwater earthquakes sometimes cause destructive waves called **tsunamis** (sooh-NAH-mees).

Korea does not have many volcanoes or earthquakes. From time to time, though, huge storms called typhoons sweep over the peninsula from the Pacific. These storms cause great damage in both the Korean Peninsula and Japan.

READING CHECK **Contrasting** How are the physical features of Japan and Korea different?

Climate and Resources

Just as Japan and the Koreas have many similar physical features, they also have similar climates. The resources found in each country, however, differ greatly.

Climate

The climates of Japan and the Koreas vary from north to south. The northern parts of the region have a humid continental climate. This means that summers are cool, but winters are long and cold. In addition, the area has a short growing season.

To the south, the region has a humid subtropical climate with mild winters and hot, humid summers. These areas see heavy rains and typhoons in the summer. Some places receive up to 80 inches (200 cm) of rain each year.

Resources

Resources are not evenly distributed among Japan and the Koreas. Neither Japan nor South Korea, for example, is very rich in mineral resources. North Korea, on the other hand, has large deposits of coal, iron, and other minerals.

Although most of the region does not have many mineral resources, it does have other resources. For example, the people of the Koreas have used their land's features to generate electricity. The peninsula's rocky terrain and rapidly flowing rivers make it an excellent location for creating hydroelectric power.

In addition, Japan has one of the world's strongest fishing economies. The islands lie near one of the world's most productive fisheries. A **fishery** is a place where lots of fish and other seafood can be caught. Swift ocean currents near Japan carry countless fish to the islands. Fishers then use huge nets to catch the fish and bring them to Japan's many bustling fish markets. These fish markets are among the busiest in the world.

READING CHECK **Analyzing** What are some resources found in Japan and the Koreas?

This fish market in Tokyo, Japan, is the busiest in the world. People gather here every morning to buy freshly caught fish.

SUMMARY AND PREVIEW The islands of Japan and the Korean Peninsula share many common features. In the next section, you will see how the people of Japan and Korea also share some similar customs and how their histories have been intertwined for centuries.

Section 1 Assessment

go.hrw.com
Online Quiz
KEYWORD: SG7 HP27

Reviewing Ideas, Terms, and Places

1. **a. Identify** What types of landforms cover Japan and the **Korean Peninsula**?

    b. Compare and Contrast How are the physical features of Japan and Korea similar? How are they different?

    c. Predict How do you think natural disasters affect life in Japan and Korea?

2. **a. Describe** What kind of climate is found in the northern parts of the region? What kind of climate is found in the southern parts?

    b. Draw Conclusions Why are **fisheries** important to Japan's economy?

Critical Thinking

3. **Categorizing** Draw a chart like this one. In each row, describe the region's landforms, climate, and resources.

	Japan	Korean Peninsula
Landforms		
Climate		
Resources		

FOCUS ON WRITING

4. **Thinking about Nature** Many Japanese poems deal with nature—the beauty of a flower, for example. What could you write about the region's physical environment in your poem?

Social Studies Skills

Chart and Graph	Critical Thinking	Geography	Study

Using a Topographic Map

Learn

Topographic maps show elevation, or the height of land above sea level. They do so with contour lines, lines that connect points on the map that have equal elevation. Every point on a contour line has the same elevation. In most cases, everything inside that line has a higher elevation. Everything outside the line is lower. Each contour line is labeled to show the elevation it indicates.

An area that has lots of contour lines is more rugged than an area with few contour lines. The distance between contour lines shows how steep an area is. If the lines are very close together, then the area has a steep slope. If the lines are farther apart, then the area has a much gentler incline. Other symbols on the map show features such as rivers and roads.

Practice

Use the topographic map on this page to answer the following questions.

1. Is Awaji Island more rugged in the south or the north? How can you tell?

2. Does the land get higher or lower as you travel west from Yura?

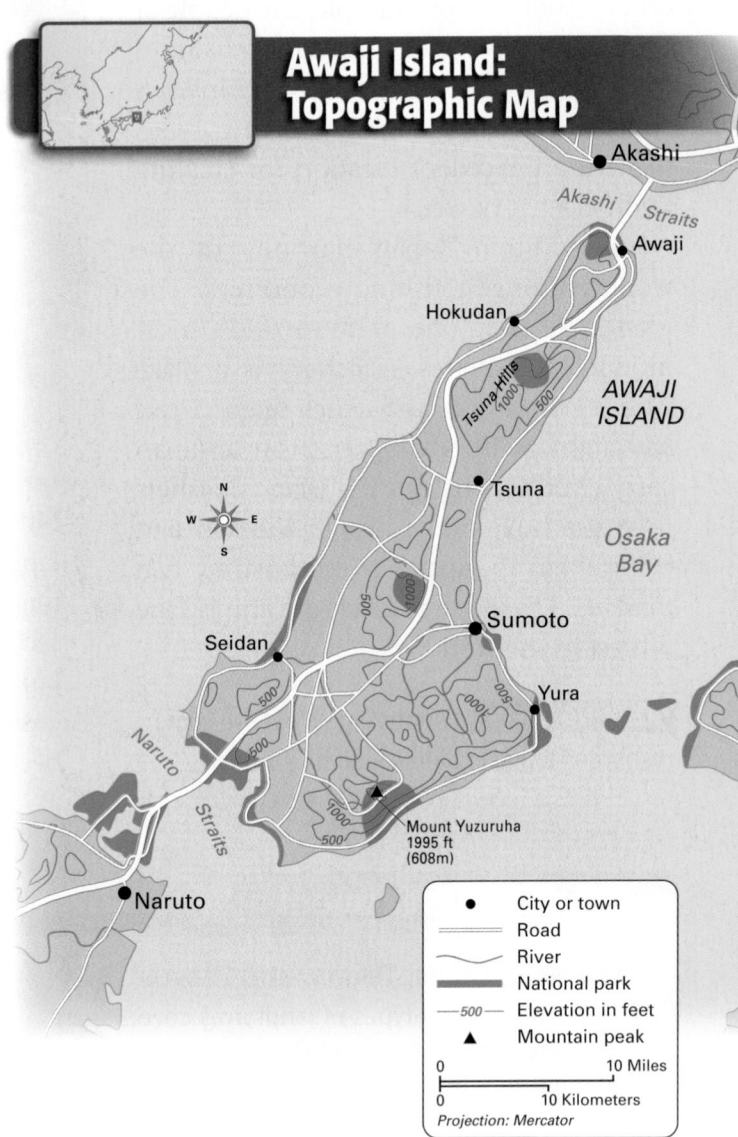

Awaji Island: Topographic Map

- • City or town
- ═══ Road
- ∼ River
- ▬ National park
- —500— Elevation in feet
- ▲ Mountain peak

0 — 10 Miles
0 — 10 Kilometers
Projection: Mercator

Apply

Search the Internet or look in a local library to find a topographic map of your area. Study the map to find three major landmarks and write down their elevations. Then write two statements about the information you can see on the map.

History and Culture

If YOU lived there...

You live in Kyoto, one of the most beautiful cities in Japan. Your class is visiting a museum to see an amazing demonstration by a sword maker. You all stare in amazement as he hammers red-hot metal into a curved sword, then plunges it into cold water. He tells you that his family has been making swords for 300 years.

What kind of craft would you like to know?

BUILDING BACKGROUND Even though Japan is an industrial nation, the Japanese still respect and admire traditional arts and crafts and the people who make them, such as this sword maker. In fact, traditions continue to shape life in Japan and the Koreas today.

History

Both Japan and the Koreas have very long histories. Early in these histories, their cultures were intertwined. As time passed, though, Japan and the Koreas developed very differently.

Early History

Early in their histories, both Japan and the Koreas were influenced by China. Since the Korean Peninsula borders China, and Japan lies just across the sea, elements of Chinese culture seeped into both places.

Among the elements of Chinese culture that influenced Japan and Korea was Buddhism. Scholars and missionaries first brought Buddhism into Korea. From there, visitors carried it to Japan. Before long, Buddhism was the main religion in both countries.

What You Will Learn...

Main Ideas

1. The early histories of Japan and Korea were closely linked, but the countries developed very differently.
2. Japanese culture blends traditional customs with modern innovations.
3. Though they share a common culture, life is very different in North and South Korea.

The Big Idea

History and tradition are very important to the people of Japan and the Koreas.

Key Terms and Places

Kyoto, *p. 672*
shoguns, *p. 672*
samurai, *p. 672*
kimonos, *p. 674*
kimchi, *p. 675*

TAKING NOTES Draw two boxes like the ones shown here. In one box, take notes about the history and culture of Japan. In the other, take notes about the history and culture of the Koreas.

History and Culture	
Japan	The Koreas

Japanese Buddha statue

FOCUS ON
READING
Where could you
look to find out
whether these
facts are true?

Emperors, Shoguns, and Samurai

The first central government in Japan was based on China's government. For many centuries, emperors ruled in Japan just as they did in China. The imperial capital at Heian, now called **Kyoto**, was a center of art, literature, and learning. At times, some of Japan's emperors were more concerned with art than with running the country. Eventually, their power slipped away.

As the emperors' power faded, Japan fell under the control of military leaders called **shoguns**. Powerful generals, the shoguns ruled Japan in the emperor's name. Only one shogun could hold power at a time.

Serving under the shogun were armies of **samurai**, or highly trained warriors. They were fierce in battle and devoted to their leaders. As a result, the samurai were very respected in Japanese society. With their support, the shoguns continued to rule Japan well into the 1800s.

BIOGRAPHY

Hirohito
(1901–1989)

Hirohito was Japan's emperor for most of the 1900s. As such, he led the country through periods of great crisis and change. He was emperor when Japan launched wars against China and Russia in the 1930s. He was also in power in 1945 when the United States bombed Hiroshima and Naga-saki. After World War II ended, Hirohito led Japan through changes in its government and economy. Many of these changes affected Hirohito personally. For example, he gave up much of the power he had once held as emperor in favor of a democratic government.

Drawing Conclusions Why might a ruler give up much of his power?

Later Japan

Not everyone was happy with the rule of the shoguns. In 1868 a group of samurai overthrew the shogun and gave power back to the emperor.

When World War II began, Japan allied itself with Germany and Italy. It wanted to build an empire in Southeast Asia and the Pacific. The Japanese drew the United States into the war in 1941 when they bombed the naval base at Pearl Harbor, Hawaii. After many years of fighting, the Americans took drastic measures to end the war. They dropped devastating atomic bombs on two Japanese cities, Hiroshima and Nagasaki. Shocked by these terrible weapons, the Japanese surrendered.

Korea

Like Japan, the Korean Peninsula has long been influenced by China. Although Korea remained independent, it was considered part of China's empire. Later, the Japanese invaded the Korean Peninsula. They were harsh rulers, and the Korean people grew to resent the Japanese.

After World War II, Korea was taken away from Japan and once again made independent. Rather than forming one country, though, the Koreans formed two. Aided by the Soviet Union, North Korea created a Communist government. In South Korea, the United States helped build a democratic government.

In 1950 North Korea invaded South Korea, starting the Korean War. The North Koreans wanted to unify all of Korea under a Communist government. With the aid of many other countries, including the United States, the South Koreans drove the invaders back. The Korean War was costly, and its effects linger in the Koreas today.

READING CHECK **Analyzing** How did the Koreas change after the Korean War?

A Buddhist Temple

Buddhism has been a major religion in Japan for centuries. This temple in Nara was built around the year 600.

Japanese Culture

Japan's culture reflects the country's long and varied history. For example, some elements of the culture reflect the influence of the Chinese, while others are native to Japan. Since World War II, Western ideas and innovations have also helped shape Japanese life.

Language

Nearly everyone in Japan speaks Japanese. The Japanese language is complicated and can be difficult for other people to learn. This difficulty stems in large part from the Japanese writing system. Japanese writing uses two different types of characters. Some characters, called kanji, represent whole words. There are about 2,000 kanji characters in common use today. Other characters, called kana, stand for parts of words. Most texts written in Japanese use both kanji and kana characters.

Religion

Religion can also be complicated in Japan. Most people who live there blend elements of two religions—Shinto and Buddhism.

Unlike Buddhism, which was brought to Japan from Korea, Shinto is native to the islands. According to Shinto teachings, nature spirits called *kami* (KAH-mee) live in the world. Shintoists believe everything in nature—the sun, the moon, trees, rocks, waterfalls, and animals—has *kami*. They also believe that some *kami* help people live and keep them from harm. As a result, they build shrines to the *kami* and perform ceremonies to ask for their blessings.

Buddhists have also built shrines and temples all over Japan. Some temples, like the one pictured above, are very old. They date back to the earliest days of Buddhism in Japan. People visit these temples to seek peace and enlightenment. The search for enlightenment is Buddhists' main goal.

Traditional Dress

These Korean dancers are wearing traditional costumes to perform a fan dance. Most of the time, people in both South Korea and North Korea wear Western-style clothes.

Customs and Traditions

Japan's history lives on in its customs and traditions. For example, many Japanese wear traditional robes called **kimonos** on special occasions, just as samurai did long ago. Most of the time, though, people in Japan wear Western-style clothing.

Traditional forms of art are also still popular in Japan. Among these art forms are two types of drama, Noh and Kabuki. Noh plays use music and dance to tell a story. Actors do not move much and wear masks, using their gestures to convey their tale. Kabuki actors, on the other hand, are much more active. Kabuki plays tell stories, but they often teach lessons about duty and other **abstract** ideas as well.

ACADEMIC VOCABULARY

abstract expressing a quality or idea without reference to an actual thing

READING CHECK **Summarizing** How did Japan's history affect its culture today?

Korean Culture

Like Japan's, Korea's culture reflects the peninsula's long history. Traditional ways of life influence how people act and think.

Language and Religion

People in both North Korea and South Korea speak Korean. Unlike Japanese, Korean is written with an alphabet. People combine letters to form words, rather than using symbols to represent entire words or syllables as in Japanese.

In the past, most people in Korea were Buddhists and Confucianists. Recently, though, Christianity has also become widespread. About one-fourth of South Korea's people are Christian. North Korea, like many Communist countries, discourages people from practicing any religion.

Kimonos are the traditional clothing style in Japan. Both men and women wear kimonos for special occasions, such as weddings.

In South Korea, urbanization and the spread of modern lifestyles have led to a decline in some traditional customs. Rural areas are still very traditional, but people in urban areas have adopted new ways of life. Many of these ways are combinations of old and new ideas. For example, Korean art today combines traditional themes such as nature with modern forms, like film.

READING CHECK **Contrasting** How are North and South Korea's cultures different?

SUMMARY AND PREVIEW In this section, you learned that the cultures of Japan and the Koreas have been shaped by the countries' histories. In the next section you will see how traditional cultures continue to influnce life in Japan today.

Customs and Traditions

Like the Japanese, the people of Korea have kept many ancient traditions alive. Many Korean foods, for example, have been part of the Korean diet for centuries.

One example of a long-lasting Korean food is **kimchi**, a dish made from pickled cabbage and various spices. First created in the 1100s, kimchi is still served at many Korean meals. In fact, many people think of it as Korea's national dish.

Traditional art forms have also remained popular in parts of the Koreas. This is true especially in North Korea. Since World War II, the Communist government of North Korea has encouraged people to retain many of their old customs and traditions. The Communists think that Korean culture is the best in the world and do everything they can to preserve it.

go.hrw.com
Online Quiz
KEYWORD: SG7 HP27

Section 2 Assessment

Reviewing Ideas, Terms, and Places

1. **a. Define** Who were **shoguns**?
   b. Elaborate How did World War II affect life in Japan?
2. **a. Identify** What is one traditional style of clothing in Japan? What do people wear most of the time?
   b. Elaborate How does Japan's religion reflect its history?
3. **a. Recall** What is **kimchi**? Why is it important in Korea?
   b. Explain What has led to many of the differences between modern culture in North and South Korea?

Critical Thinking

4. **Analyzing** Draw a diagram like this one. Using your notes, list two features of Japanese culture in the left box and of Korean culture in the right box. Below each box, write a sentence about how each country's culture reflects its history.

Japanese Culture	Korean Culture

FOCUS ON WRITING

5. **Analyzing Cultures** Traditions and customs are central to life in Japan and the Koreas. How can you reflect this importance in your poem?

Japan Today

What You Will Learn...

Main Ideas

1. Since World War II, Japan has developed a democratic government and one of the world's strongest economies.
2. A shortage of open space shapes daily life in Japan.
3. Crowding, competition, and pollution are among Japan's main issues and challenges.

The Big Idea

Japan has overcome many challenges to become one of the most highly developed countries in Asia.

Key Terms and Places

Diet, *p. 676*
Tokyo, *p. 676*
work ethic, *p. 677*
trade surplus, *p. 677*
tariff, *p. 677*
Osaka, *p. 680*

TAKING NOTES Draw a diagram like the one below. As you read, take notes about Japan's government, economy, and daily life in the appropriate ovals.

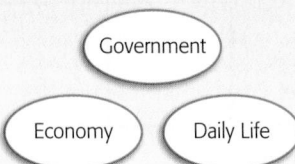

Government
Economy   Daily Life

If YOU lived there...

You and your family live in a small apartment in the crowded city of Tokyo. Every day you and your friends crowd into jammed subway trains to travel to school. Since your work in school is very hard and demanding, you really look forward to weekends. You especially like to visit mountain parks where there are flowering trees, quiet gardens, and ancient shrines.

Do you like your life in Tokyo? Why or why not?

BUILDING BACKGROUND Although Japan has become an economic powerhouse, it is still a small country in area. Its cities have become more and more crowded with high-rise office and apartment buildings. Most people live in these cities today, though many feel a special fondness for natural areas like mountains and lakes.

Government and Economy

Do you own any products made by Sony? Have you seen ads for vehicles made by Honda, Toyota, or Mitsubishi? Chances are good that you have. These companies are some of the most successful in the world, and all of them are Japanese.

Since World War II, Japan's government and economy have changed dramatically. Japan was once an imperial state that was shut off from the rest of the world. Today Japan is a democracy with one of the world's strongest economies.

Government

Since the end of World War II, Japan's government has been a constitutional monarchy headed by an emperor. Although the emperor is officially the head of state, he has little power. His main role is to act as a symbol of Japan and of the Japanese people. In his place, power rests in an elected legislature called the **Diet** and in an elected prime minister. From the capital city of **Tokyo**, the Diet and the prime minister make the laws that govern life in Japan today.

Economy

Today Japan is an economic powerhouse. However, this was not always the case. Until the 1950s, Japan's economy was not that strong. Within a few decades, though, the economy grew tremendously.

The most successful area of Japan's economy is manufacturing. Japanese companies are known for making high-quality products, especially cars and electronics. Japanese companies are among the world's leading manufacturers of televisions, DVD players, CD players, and other electronic items. The methods that companies use to make these products are also celebrated. Many Japanese companies are leaders in new technology and ideas.

Reasons for Success Many factors have contributed to Japan's economic success. One factor is the government. It works closely with business leaders to control production and plan for the future.

Japan's workforce also contributed to its success. Japan has well-educated, highly trained workers. As a result, its companies tend to be both efficient and productive. Most workers in Japan also have a strong work ethic. A **work ethic** is the belief that work in itself is worthwhile. Because of their work ethic, most Japanese work hard and are loyal to their companies. As a result, the companies are successful.

Trade Japan's economy depends on trade. In fact, many products manufactured in the country are intended to be sold outside of Japan. Many of these goods are sent to China and the United States. The United States is Japan's major trading partner.

Japan's trade has been so successful that it has built up a huge trade surplus. A **trade surplus** exists when a country exports more goods than it imports. Because of this surplus, many Japanese companies have become very wealthy.

CONNECTING TO Technology

Building Small

The Japanese are known as masters of technology. Companies use this technology in many ways to create new products and improve existing ones. One way many Japanese companies have sought to improve their products—especially personal electronics products—is by making them smaller.

Since Sony released the first personal stereo system in the late 1970s, making small products has been a major business in Japan. Now shoppers can buy tiny radios, video games, cell phones, and cameras. Some of these products are smaller than the palm of your hand.

Generalizing Why might people want to buy small versions of products?

Japan is able to export more than it imports in part because of high tariffs. A **tariff** is a fee that a country charges on imports or exports. For many years, Japan's government has placed high tariffs on goods brought into the country. This makes imported goods more expensive, and so people buy Japanese goods rather than imported ones.

Resources Although its economy is based on manufacturing, Japan has few natural resources. As a result, the country must import raw materials. In addition, Japan has little arable land. Farms cannot grow enough food for the country's growing population. Instead, the Japanese have to buy food from other countries, including China and the United States.

READING CHECK Summarizing What have the Japanese done to build their economy?

Daily Life

Japan is a densely populated country. Slightly smaller than California, it has nearly four times as many people! Most of these people live in crowded cities such as the capital, Tokyo.

Life in Tokyo

Besides serving as the national capital, Tokyo is the center of Japan's banking and communication industries. As a result, the city is busy, noisy, and very crowded. More than 35 million people live in a relatively small area. Because Tokyo is so densely populated, land is scarce. As a result, Tokyo's real estate prices are among the highest in the world. Some people save up for years to buy homes in Tokyo. They earn money by putting money in savings accounts or by investing in stocks and bonds.

Because space is so limited in Tokyo, people have found creative ways to adapt. Buildings tend to be fairly tall and narrow so that they take less land area. People also use space under ground. For example, shops and restaurants can be found below the streets in subway stations. Another way the Japanese have found to save space is the capsule hotel. Guests in these hotels—mostly traveling businesspeople—crawl into tiny sleeping chambers rather than having rooms with beds.

Many people work in Tokyo but live outside the city. So many people commute to and from Tokyo that trains are very crowded. During peak travel times, commuters are crammed into train cars.

Tokyo is not all about work, though. During their leisure time, people can visit Tokyo's many parks, museums, and stores. They can also take short trips to local amusement parks, baseball stadiums, or other attractions. Among these attractions are a huge indoor beach and a ski resort filled with artificial snow.

Close-up

Life in Tokyo

映画館

Home to some 30 million people, Tokyo is one of the world's busiest cities. This illustration shows what a typical day in Tokyo is like.

Small Shinto shrines can be found even in the heart of busy Tokyo.

During peak travel times, Tokyo's trains are so crowded that people need to be pushed aboard.

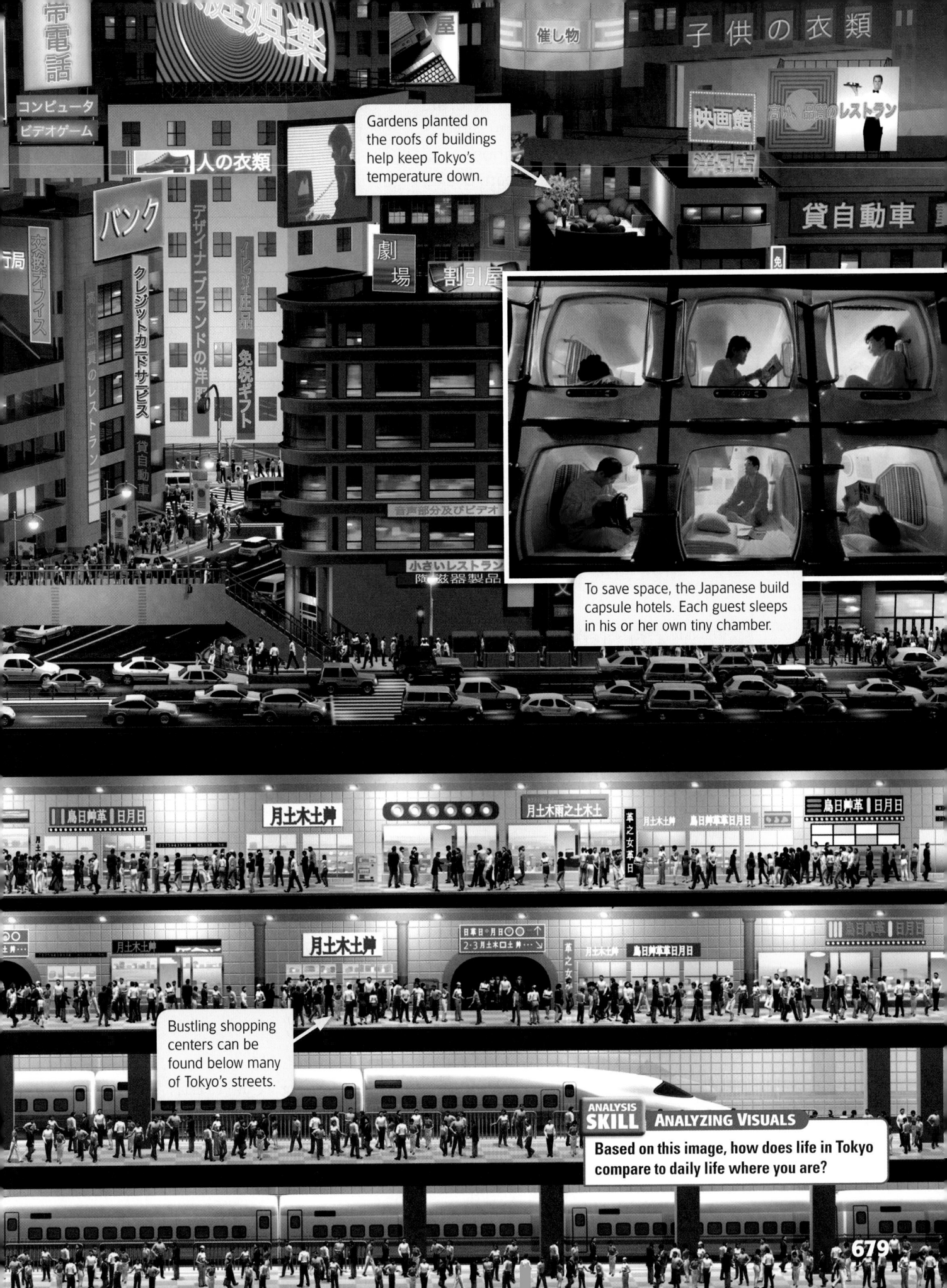

Gardens planted on the roofs of buildings help keep Tokyo's temperature down.

To save space, the Japanese build capsule hotels. Each guest sleeps in his or her own tiny chamber.

Bustling shopping centers can be found below many of Tokyo's streets.

ANALYSIS SKILL **ANALYZING VISUALS**

Based on this image, how does life in Tokyo compare to daily life where you are?

Life in Other Cities

Most of Japan's other cities, like Tokyo, are crowded and busy. Many of them serve as centers of industry or transportation.

The second largest city in Japan, **Osaka**, is located in western Honshu. In Osaka—as in Tokyo and other cities—tall, modern sky-scrapers stand next to tiny Shinto temples. Another major city is Kyoto. Once Japan's capital, Kyoto is full of historic buildings.

Transportation between Cities

To connect cities that lie far apart, the Japanese have built a network of rail lines. Some of these lines carry very fast trains called *Shinkansen*, or bullet trains. They can reach speeds of more than 160 miles per hour (250 kph). Japan's train system is very **efficient**. Trains nearly always leave on time and are almost never late.

ACADEMIC VOCABULARY

efficient
productive and not wasteful

Rural Life

Not everyone in Japan lives in cities. Some people live in the country in small villages. The people in these villages own or work on farms.

Relatively little of Japan's land is arable, or suitable for farming. Much of the land is too rocky or steep to grow crops on. As a result, most farms are small. The average Japanese farm is only about 2.5 acres (1 hectare). In contrast, the average farm in the United States is 175 times that size.

Because their farms are so small and Japan imports so much of its food, many farmers cannot make a living from their crops. As a result, many people have left rural areas to find jobs in cities.

READING CHECK **Finding Main Ideas** What are Japanese cities like?

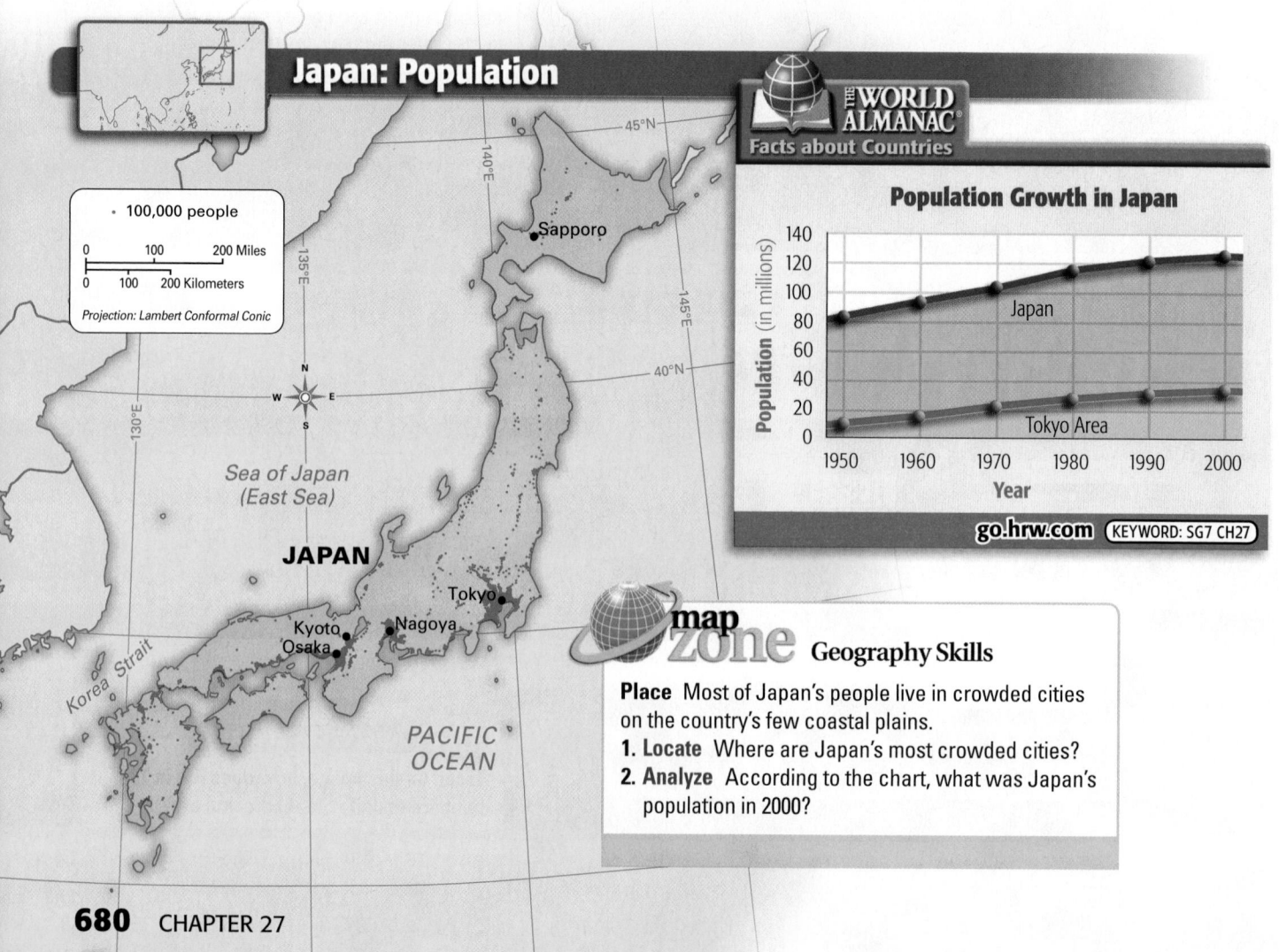

Japan: Population

• 100,000 people

0   100   200 Miles
0   100   200 Kilometers

Projection: Lambert Conformal Conic

Sapporo

Sea of Japan
(East Sea)

JAPAN

Tokyo
Kyoto   Nagoya
Osaka

Korea Strait

PACIFIC
OCEAN

THE **WORLD ALMANAC**
Facts about Countries

Population Growth in Japan

Japan

Tokyo Area

go.hrw.com   KEYWORD: SG7 CH27

map zone **Geography Skills**

Place Most of Japan's people live in crowded cities on the country's few coastal plains.
1. **Locate** Where are Japan's most crowded cities?
2. **Analyze** According to the chart, what was Japan's population in 2000?

Issues and Challenges

Many people consider Japan one of the world's most successful countries. In recent years, however, a few issues have arisen that present challenges for Japan's future.

One of these issues is Japan's lack of space. As cities grow, crowding has become a serious issue. To make space, some people have begun to construct taller buildings. Such buildings have to be carefully planned, though, to withstand earthquakes.

Japan also faces economic challenges. For many years, it had the only strong economy in East Asia. Recently, however, other countries have challenged Japan's economic dominance. Competition from China and South Korea has begun taking business from some Japanese companies.

Pollution has also become a problem in Japan. In 1997 officials from more than 150 countries met in Japan to discuss the pollution problem. They signed the Kyoto Protocol, an agreement to cut down on pollution and improve air quality.

READING CHECK **Finding Main Ideas** What are three issues facing Japan?

Technology

Advanced technology has helped Japan keep its economic edge over other countries. In this photo, workers use robots to assemble a car.

SUMMARY AND PREVIEW Since World War II, Japan has created a democratic government and a strong, highly technological economy. In the next section, you will learn about changes that have occurred in South Korea and North Korea in the same time period.

Section 3 Assessment

Reviewing Ideas, Terms, and Places

1. **a. Identify** What are some goods made in Japan?
   b. Explain How has Japan's government changed since World War II?
   c. Elaborate Why do you think **work ethic** is so important to the Japanese economy?
2. **a. Describe** How have people tried to save space in Japanese cities?
   b. Evaluate Do you think you would like living in **Tokyo**? Why or why not?
3. **a. Identify** What is one issue that crowding has caused for Japan?
   b. Analyze How are other countries presenting challenges to Japan's economy?

Critical Thinking

4. **Analyzing** Draw a graphic organizer like the one shown here. In one circle, write two sentences about city life in Japan. In another, write two sentences about rural life. In the third, write two sentences about issues facing the Japanese.

   (City Life)   (Rural Life)   (Issues)

FOCUS ON WRITING

5. **Thinking about Japan** What image, or picture, of life in Japan could you write about in your poem? List two or three ideas. Then decide which is the most promising idea for your poem.

The Koreas Today

What You Will Learn...

Main Ideas

1. The people of South Korea today have freedom and economic opportunities.
2. The people of North Korea today have little freedom or economic opportunity.
3. Some people in both South and North Korea support the idea of Korean reunification.

The Big Idea

Though they share a common history and culture, the two Koreas have very different governments and economies.

Key Terms and Places

Seoul, *p. 683*
demilitarized zone, *p. 683*
Pyongyang, *p. 685*

TAKING NOTES In your notebook, draw two boxes like the ones shown here. As you read, take notes about South Korea in the left box and notes about North Korea in the right. Note similarities between the countries below the boxes.

South Korea	North Korea

If YOU lived there...

You live in Inchon, one of South Korea's largest cities. Sometimes your grandparents tell you about the other family members who still live in North Korea. You have never met them, of course, and your grandparents have not seen them since they were children, more than 50 years ago. After hearing stories about these family members, you are curious about their lives.

Would you like to visit North Korea?

BUILDING BACKGROUND A truce ended the Korean War in 1953, but it left the Korean Peninsula divided into two very different countries. The conflict separated families from their relatives on the other side of the zone that divides South Korea from North Korea. Since then, the countries have developed in very different ways.

South Korea Today

Japan's closest neighbor is both a major economic rival and a key trading partner. That neighbor is South Korea. Like Japan, South Korea is a democratic country with a strong economy. Unlike Japan, South Korea shares a border with a hostile neighbor—North Korea.

Government and Economy

The official name of South Korea is the Republic of Korea. As the name suggests, South Korea's government is a republic. It is headed by a president and an assembly elected by the people, much like the United States is. In fact, the United States helped create South Korea's government after World War II.

The United States also helped make South Korea's economy one of the strongest in East Asia. In addition, Korean business leaders and government officials have worked together to ensure that the economy stays strong. In recent years, South Korea has become a major manufacturing country, exporting goods to places all around the world.

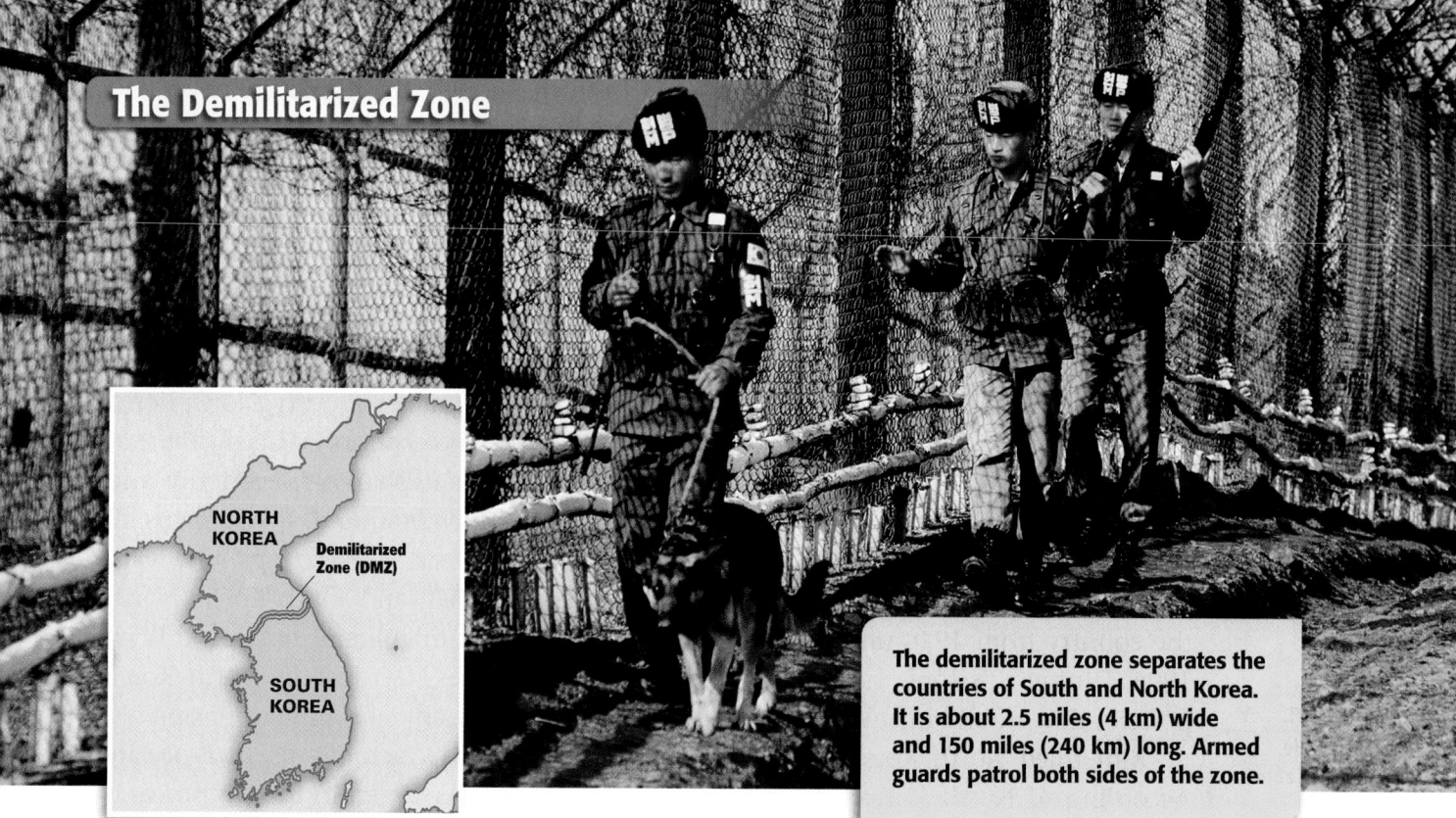

The Demilitarized Zone

NORTH KOREA

Demilitarized Zone (DMZ)

SOUTH KOREA

The demilitarized zone separates the countries of South and North Korea. It is about 2.5 miles (4 km) wide and 150 miles (240 km) long. Armed guards patrol both sides of the zone.

Daily Life

Like Japan, South Korea is very densely populated. The capital city, **Seoul** (SOHL), is one of the most densely populated cities in the world. It has more than 40,000 people per square mile (15,000/sq km).

Although parts of South Korea are densely populated, very few people live in the mountainous interior. Most people live near the coast. A coastal plain in western South Korea is the most crowded part of the country.

In South Korea's cities, most people live in small apartments. Because space is scarce, housing is expensive. Also, cities sometimes suffer from pollution from the many factories, cars, and coal-fired heating systems found there. In some cities, industrial waste has also polluted the water.

Outside the cities, many South Koreans still follow traditional ways of life. Most of them are farmers who grow rice, beans, and cabbage they can use to make kimchi. They usually live on small farms.

Issues and Challenges

Government policies and international politics have led to some challenges for South Korea. Although South Korea has a successful economy, some people feel that its government is corrupt. For many years, four families have controlled much of the country's industry. As a result, wealth and power became concentrated in the hands of big business. This led to corruption of government officials, but efforts are being made to reform business practices.

A bigger challenge to South Korea is its relationship with North Korea. Since the end of the Korean War in the 1950s, the two countries have been separated. Between them is a **demilitarized zone**, an empty buffer zone created to keep the two countries from fighting. Although troops are not allowed in the demilitarized zone, guards patrol both sides.

READING CHECK **Summarizing** What issues face South Korea today?

North Korea Today

The official name of North Korea is the Democratic People's Republic of Korea. Its name, however, is misleading. North Korea is neither a democracy nor a republic. It is a totalitarian state, and the Communist Party controls both the government and the economy.

Government and Economy

The Communist government of North Korea was created soon after World War II. Its first leader was Kim Il Sung. He ruled the country from 1948 until his death in 1994. During this time, he created many **policies** that are still in effect today.

Kim ruled North Korea as a dictator. According to North Korea's constitution, most power rests in an elected legislature.

In truth, though, the legislature never had much power. Advised by members of the Communist Party, Kim ruled alone.

When Kim Il Sung died in 1994, his son Kim Jong Il took over. Like his father, the younger Kim rules as a dictator. He was elected by the North Korean legislature. The people had no say in his election.

As a Communist country, North Korea has a command economy. This means that the government plans the economy and decides what is produced. It also owns all land and controls access to jobs.

Unlike Japan and South Korea, North Korea is rich in mineral resources. With these resources, factories in North Korea make machinery and military supplies. However, most factories use out-of-date technology. As a result, North Korea is much poorer than Japan and South Korea.

ACADEMIC VOCABULARY
policy rule, course of action

Life in Korea

Because it is so rocky, very little of North Korea's land can be farmed. The farmland that does exist is owned by the government. It is farmed by cooperatives—large groups of farmers who work the land together. These cooperatives are not able to grow enough food for the country. As a result, the government has to import food. This can be a difficult task because North Korea's relations with most other countries are strained.

Daily Life

Like Japan and South Korea, North Korea is largely an urban society. Most people live in cities. The largest city is the capital, **Pyongyang** (PYUHNG-YAHNG), in the west. Pyongyang is a crowded urban area. More than 3 million people live in the city.

The differences between life in South Korea and North Korea can be seen in their capitals. Seoul, South Korea (shown to the left), is a busy, modern city and a major commercial center. In comparison, North Korea's capital, Pyongyang (shown above), has little traffic or commercial development.

ANALYZING VISUALS What do these photos suggest about life in Seoul and Pyongyang?

Life in Pyongyang is very different from life in Tokyo or Seoul. For example, few people in Pyongyang own private cars. The North Korean government allows only top Communist officials to own cars. Most residents have to use buses or the subway to get around. At night, many streets are dark because of electricity shortages.

The people of North Korea have fewer rights than the people of Japan or South Korea. For example, the government controls individual speech as well as the press. Because the government feels that religion conflicts with many Communist ideas, it also discourages people from practicing any religions.

Issues and Challenges

Why does North Korea, which is rich in resources, have shortages of electricity and food? These problems are due in part to choices the government has made. For years, North Korea had ties mostly with other Communist countries. Since the breakup of the Soviet Union, North Korea has been largely isolated from the rest of the world. It has closed its markets to foreign goods, which means that other countries cannot sell their goods there. At the same time, North Korea lacks the technology to take advantage of its resources. As a result, many people suffer and resources go unused.

In addition, many countries worry about North Korea's ability to make and use nuclear weapons. In 2002 North Korea announced that it had enough materials to build six nuclear bombs. Then in 2006 it conducted a nuclear weapons test. These developments worried countries in Asia and around the world.

READING CHECK **Generalizing** What is North Korea's relationship with the world?

Young people at a political rally express support for reunification. The flag in the background shows a united Korea.

The governments of both South Korea and North Korea have also expressed their support for reunification. Leaders from the two countries met in 2000 for the first time since the Korean War. As part of their meeting, they discussed ways to improve relations and communication between the two countries. For example, they agreed to build a road through the demilitarized zone to connect the two Koreas.

The chief obstacle to the reunification of Korea is the question of government. South Koreans want a unified Korea to be a democracy. North Korean leaders, on the other hand, have insisted that Korea should be Communist. Until this issue is resolved, the countries will remain separate.

READING CHECK **Summarizing** What issues stand in the way of Korean reunification?

Korean Reunification

FOCUS ON READING

What opinion do many Koreans hold toward reunification?

For years, people from both South and North Korea have called for their countries to be reunited. Because the two Koreas share a common history and culture, these people believe they should be one country. As time has passed, more and more people have voiced support for reunification.

SUMMARY AND PREVIEW In this chapter you learned about the history, cultures, and people of Japan and the Koreas. In the next chapter, you will examine a region that lies farther south, a region called Southeast Asia.

go.hrw.com
Online Quiz
KEYWORD: SG7 HP27

Section 4 Assessment

Reviewing Ideas, Terms, and Places

1. **a. Define** What is the **demilitarized zone**? Why does it exist?
   b. Summarize What factors have helped South Korea develop a strong economy?
2. **a. Identify** What is the capital of North Korea? What is life like there?
   b. Contrast How is North Korea's government different from South Korea's?
3. **a. Recall** Why do many Koreans support the idea of reunification?
   b. Evaluate If you lived in North or South Korea, do you think you would support the reunification of the countries? Why or why not?

Critical Thinking

4. **Analyze** Draw a diagram like the one below. In the left box, write three statements about South Korea. In the right box, write three statements about North Korea. In the oval, list one factor that supports reunification and one that hinders it.

   | South Korea | Reunification | North Korea |

FOCUS ON WRITING

5. **Considering Korea** As you read about the Koreas, did you think of an image, or picture, that would work in a poem? List your ideas.

Geography's Impact
video series
Review the video to answer the closing question:
How has Japan's location on the Ring of Fire made it so prone to natural hazards?

Visual Summary

Use the visual summary below to help you review the main ideas of the chapter.

QUICK FACTS

Japan and the Korean Peninsula have rugged landscapes that are largely covered by mountains.

Japan has one of the world's strongest economies, due in large part to its superior technology.

Since World War II, life in democratic South Korea has been very different from life in Communist North Korea.

Reviewing Vocabulary, Terms, and Places

Imagine these terms from the chapter are correct answers to items in a crossword puzzle. Write the clues for the answers.

1. Tokyo
2. abstract
3. trade surplus
4. tariff
5. kimono
6. efficient
7. work ethic
8. Seoul
9. fishery
10. Pyongyang
11. kimchi
12. policy

Comprehension and Critical Thinking

SECTION 1 *(Pages 666–669)*

13. **a. Identify** What physical feature covers most of Japan and the Korean Peninsula? What is one famous example of this landform?

b. Draw Conclusions Fish and seafood are very important in the Japanese diet. Why do you think this is so?

c. Predict How do you think earthquakes and typhoons would affect your life if you lived in Japan?

SECTION 2 *(Pages 671–675)*

14. **a. Identify** Who were the shoguns? What role did they play in Japanese history?

b. Explain What caused the Korean War? What happened as a result of the war?

c. Elaborate How have the histories of Japan and Korea affected their cultures?

SECTION 3 *(Pages 676–681)*

15. **a. Recall** What is the most important aspect of Japan's economy?

b. Make Inferences Why is Tokyo such a busy and crowded city?

c. Develop How might Japan try to address the problem of crowding in its cities?

SECTION 4 *(Pages 682–686)*

16. a. Recall What type of government does South Korea have? What type of government does North Korea have?

b. Contrast How is South Korea's economy different from North Korea's? Which has been more successful?

c. Predict Do you think the reunification of the Koreas will happen in the near future? Why or why not?

Social Studies Skills

Using a Topographic Map *Use the topographic map in this chapter's Social Studies Skills lesson to answer the following questions.*

17. What elevations do the contour lines on this map show?

18. Where are the highest points on Awaji Island located? How can you tell?

19. Is the city of Sumoto located more or less than 500 feet above sea level?

FOCUS ON READING AND WRITING

Understanding Fact and Opinion *Decide whether each of the following statements is a fact or an opinion.*

20. Japan would be a great place to live.

21. Japan is an island country.

22. North Korea should give up Communism.

23. The Koreas should reunify.

Writing Your Five-Line Poem *Use your notes and the instructions below to create your poem.*

24. Review your notes and decide on a topic to write about. Remember that your poem should describe one image or picture—an object, a place, etc.—from Japanese or Korean culture.

The first three lines of your poem should describe the object or place you have chosen. The last two should express how it makes you feel. Try to use the traditional Tanka syllable count in your poem: five syllables in lines 1 and 3; seven syllables in lines 2, 4, and 5. Remember that your poem does not have to rhyme.

Using the Internet

go.hrw.com
KEYWORD: SG7 CH27

25. Activity: Comparing Schools Have you ever wondered what it would be like to live in Japan? How would your life be different if you lived there? What would you learn about in school? What would you eat for lunch? Enter the activity keyword. Learn about Japan and about Japanese culture by exploring the Web links provided. Look for ways that your life would be the same and different if you grew up in Japan. Then record what you learned in a chart or a graphic organizer.

Map Activity ✴Interactive

26. Japan and the Koreas On a separate sheet of paper, match the letters on the map with their correct labels.

North Korea   Tokyo, Japan

South Korea   Hokkaido

Korea Strait   Sea of Japan (East Sea)

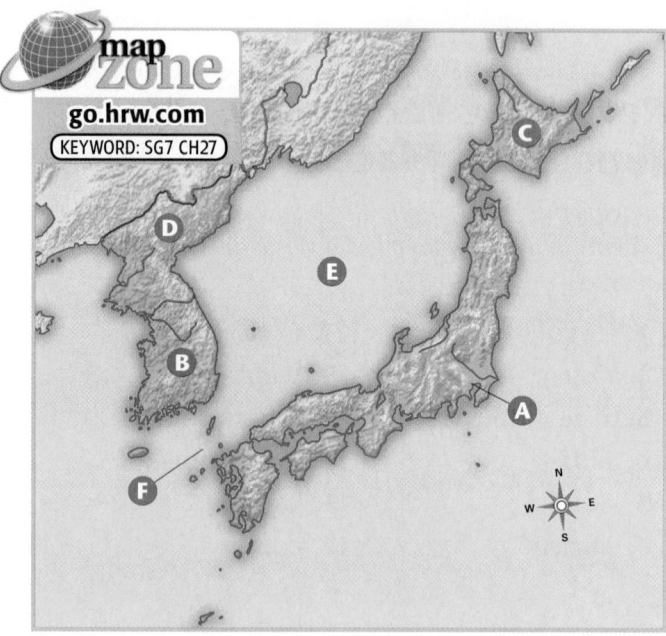

DIRECTIONS: Read questions 1 through 7 and write the letter of the best response. Then read question 8 and write your own well-constructed response.

1 Tokyo, Osaka, and Kyoto are all cities in which country?

A South Korea.

B North Korea.

C Japan.

D Honshu.

2 North Korea and South Korea are separated by the

A Korea Strait.

B demilitarized zone.

C Sea of Japan.

D Japanese Alps.

3 Kim Il Sung and Kim Jong Il are famous leaders from which country?

A South Korea

B North Korea

C Japan

D Honshu

4 The country that had the strongest influence on early Korea and Japan was

A Russia.

B India.

C China.

D the United States.

5 What is one reason that many people in Korea support reunification?

A They want a socialist government.

B They want to have the largest country in the world.

C They are afraid of an attack from Japan.

D They believe that all Koreans share a common history and culture.

Japan and the Koreas

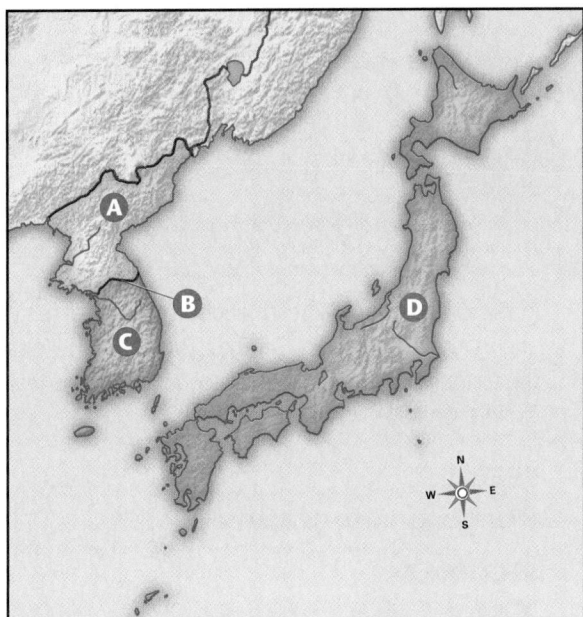

6 On the map above, which letter appears in an area led by a Communist government?

A A

B B

C C

D D

7 Which country has the strongest economy in the region?

A South Korea

B North Korea

C Japan

D Honshu

8 **Extended Response** Write a brief paragraph explaining why the coastal plains of Japan and Korea are so crowded. You may wish to refer to the map above as you prepare your answer.

CHAPTER 28

Southeast Asia

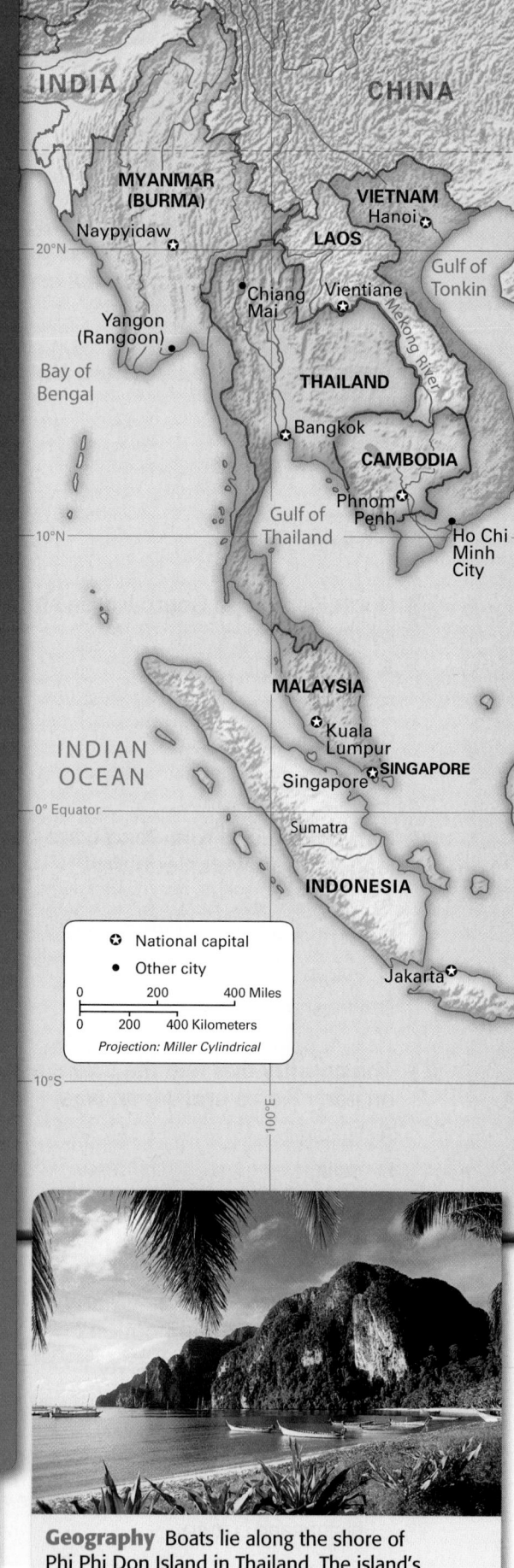

What You Will Learn...

In this chapter you will learn about the physical features, climate, and natural resources of Southeast Asia. You will also examine the histories and cultures of the countries in this region and explore what life is like there today.

FOCUS ON READING AND SPEAKING

Using Context Clues—Definitions As you read, you may run across words you do not know. You can often figure out the meaning of an unknown word by using context clues. One type of context clue is a definition of a word, or a restatement of its meaning. To use these clues, look at the words and sentences around the unknown word—its context. **See the lesson, Using Context Clues—Definitions, on page R29.**

Presenting an Interview With a partner, you will role-play a journalist interviewing a regional expert on Southeast Asia. First, read about the region. Then with your partner create a question-and-answer interview script about the region to present to your classmates.

Geography Boats lie along the shore of Phi Phi Don Island in Thailand. The island's beauty makes it a popular vacation spot.

Tropic of Cancer

N
W · E
S

Luzon
Quezon City
Manila
PHILIPPINES

Philippine Sea

South China Sea

Palawan

Mindanao

BRUNEI
Bandar Seri Begawan

MALAYSIA

Celebes Sea

Sulawesi (Celebes)

Borneo

I N D O N E S I A

Moluccas

Java Sea

IRIAN JAYA

New Guinea

PACIFIC OCEAN

Java   Bali

EAST TIMOR

Dili

Lesser Sunda Islands

Timor

120°E   130°E   140°E   150°E

map zone Geography Skills

Regions The region of Southeast Asia includes 11 countries—some quite small.
1. **Name** What are the names of the 11 countries located in Southeast Asia?
2. **Make Inferences** The countries of Indonesia and the Philippines consist of many islands. How do you think this fact affects life there?

go.hrw.com   KEYWORD: SG7 CH28

HOLT

Geography's Impact
video series
Watch the video to understand the impact of biodiversity.

Culture Traditional dances remain an important part of the culture of Bali. *Barong* dancers use their hands, arms, and eyes to tell a traditional story.

History The golden Shwedagon Pagoda is a Buddhist shrine in Yangon, Myanmar. Pagodas have been on this site since the 500s BC.

Physical Geography

Main Ideas

1. Southeast Asia's physical features include peninsulas, islands, rivers, and many seas, straits, and gulfs.
2. The tropical climate of Southeast Asia supports a wide range of plants and animals.
3. Southeast Asia is rich in natural resources such as wood, rubber, and fossil fuels.

The Big Idea

Southeast Asia is a tropical region of peninsulas, islands, and waterways with diverse plants, animals, and resources.

Key Terms and Places

Indochina Peninsula, *p. 692*
Malay Peninsula, *p. 692*
Malay Archipelago, *p. 692*
archipelago, *p. 692*
New Guinea, *p. 693*
Borneo, *p. 693*
Mekong River, *p. 693*

TAKING NOTES As you read, use a chart like this one to help you take notes on the physical geography of Southeast Asia.

Physical Features	
Climate, Plants, Animals	
Natural Resources	

If YOU lived there...

Your family lives on a houseboat on a branch of the great Mekong River in Cambodia. You catch fish in cages under the boat. Your home is part of a floating village of houseboats and houses built on stilts in the water. Boats loaded with fruits and vegetables travel from house to house. Even your school is on a nearby boat.

How does water shape life in your village?

BUILDING BACKGROUND Waterways, such as rivers, canals, seas, and oceans, are important to life in Southeast Asia. Waterways are both "highways" and sources of food. Where rivers empty into the sea, they form deltas, areas of rich soil good for farming.

Physical Features

Where can you find a flower that grows up to 3 feet across and smells like rotting garbage? How about a lizard that can grow up to 10 feet long and weigh up to 300 pounds? These amazing sights as well as some of the world's most beautiful tropical paradises are all in Southeast Asia.

The region of Southeast Asia is made up of two peninsulas and two large island groups. The **Indochina Peninsula** and the **Malay** (muh-LAY) **Peninsula** extend from the Asian mainland. We call this part of the region Mainland Southeast Asia. The two island groups are the Philippines and the **Malay Archipelago**. An **archipelago** (ahr-kuh-PE-luh-goh) is a large group of islands. We call this part of the region Island Southeast Asia.

Landforms

In Mainland Southeast Asia, rugged mountains fan out across the countries of Myanmar (MYAHN-mahr), Thailand (TY-land), Laos (LOWS), and Vietnam (vee-ET-NAHM). Between these mountains are low plateaus and river floodplains.

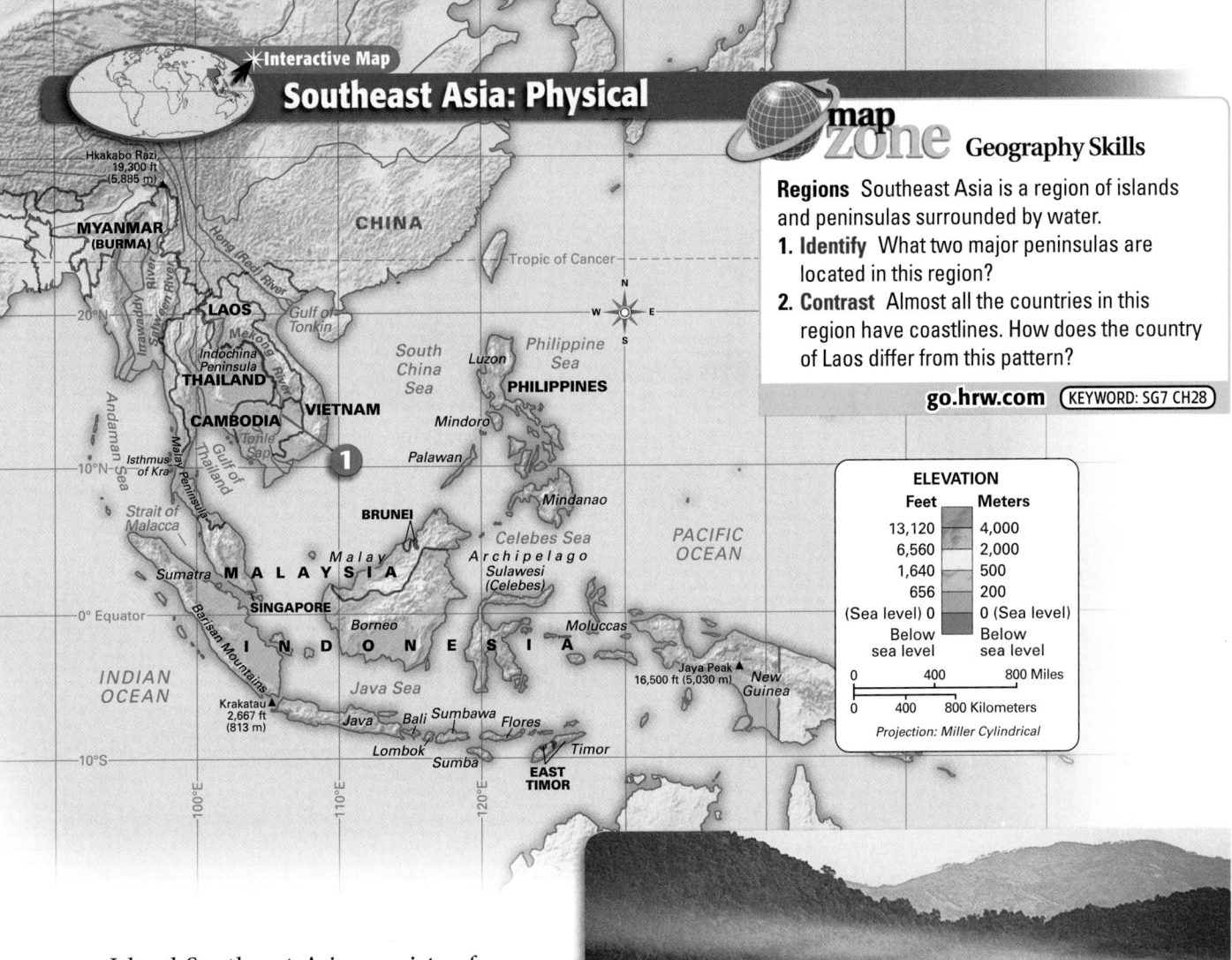

Southeast Asia: Physical

Interactive Map

Hkakabo Razi
19,300 ft
(5,885 m)

MYANMAR
(BURMA)

CHINA

Tropic of Cancer

LAOS

Gulf of
Tonkin

Indochina
Peninsula
THAILAND

South
China
Sea

Philippine
Sea

Luzon

PHILIPPINES

CAMBODIA

VIETNAM

Mindoro

Andaman
Sea

Tonle
Sap

Palawan

Isthmus
of Kra

Gulf of
Thailand

Mindanao

PACIFIC
OCEAN

Strait of
Malacca

BRUNEI

Celebes Sea

Malay Archipelago

Sumatra

MALAYSIA

Sulawesi
(Celebes)

SINGAPORE

Borneo

Moluccas

INDIAN
OCEAN

INDONESIA

Jaya Peak
16,500 ft (5,030 m)

New
Guinea

Java Sea

Krakatau
2,667 ft
(813 m)

Java

Bali

Sumbawa

Flores

Lombok

Sumba

Timor

EAST
TIMOR

map zone Geography Skills

Regions Southeast Asia is a region of islands and peninsulas surrounded by water.

1. **Identify** What two major peninsulas are located in this region?
2. **Contrast** Almost all the countries in this region have coastlines. How does the country of Laos differ from this pattern?

go.hrw.com (KEYWORD: SG7 CH28)

ELEVATION

Feet	Meters
13,120	4,000
6,560	2,000
1,640	500
656	200
(Sea level) 0	0 (Sea level)
Below sea level	Below sea level

0   400   800 Miles

0   400   800 Kilometers

Projection: Miller Cylindrical

Island Southeast Asia consists of more than 20,000 islands, some of them among the world's largest. **New Guinea** is Earth's second largest island, and **Borneo** its third largest. Many of the area's larger islands have high mountains. A few peaks are high enough to have snow and glaciers.

Island Southeast Asia is a part of the Ring of Fire as well. As a result, earthquakes and volcanic eruptions often rock the area. When such events occur underwater, they can cause tsunamis, or giant series of waves. In 2004 a tsunami in the Indian Ocean killed hundreds of thousands of people, many in Southeast Asia.

Bodies of Water

Water is a central part of Southeast Asia. Look at the map to identify the many seas, straits, and gulfs in this region.

① Mist hovers over the Mekong River as it flows through the forested mountains of northern Thailand.

In addition, several major rivers drain the mainland's peninsulas. Of these rivers, the mighty **Mekong** (MAY-KAWNG) **River** is the most important. The mainland's fertile river valleys and deltas support farming and are home to many people.

READING CHECK **Finding Main Ideas** What are Southeast Asia's major physical features?

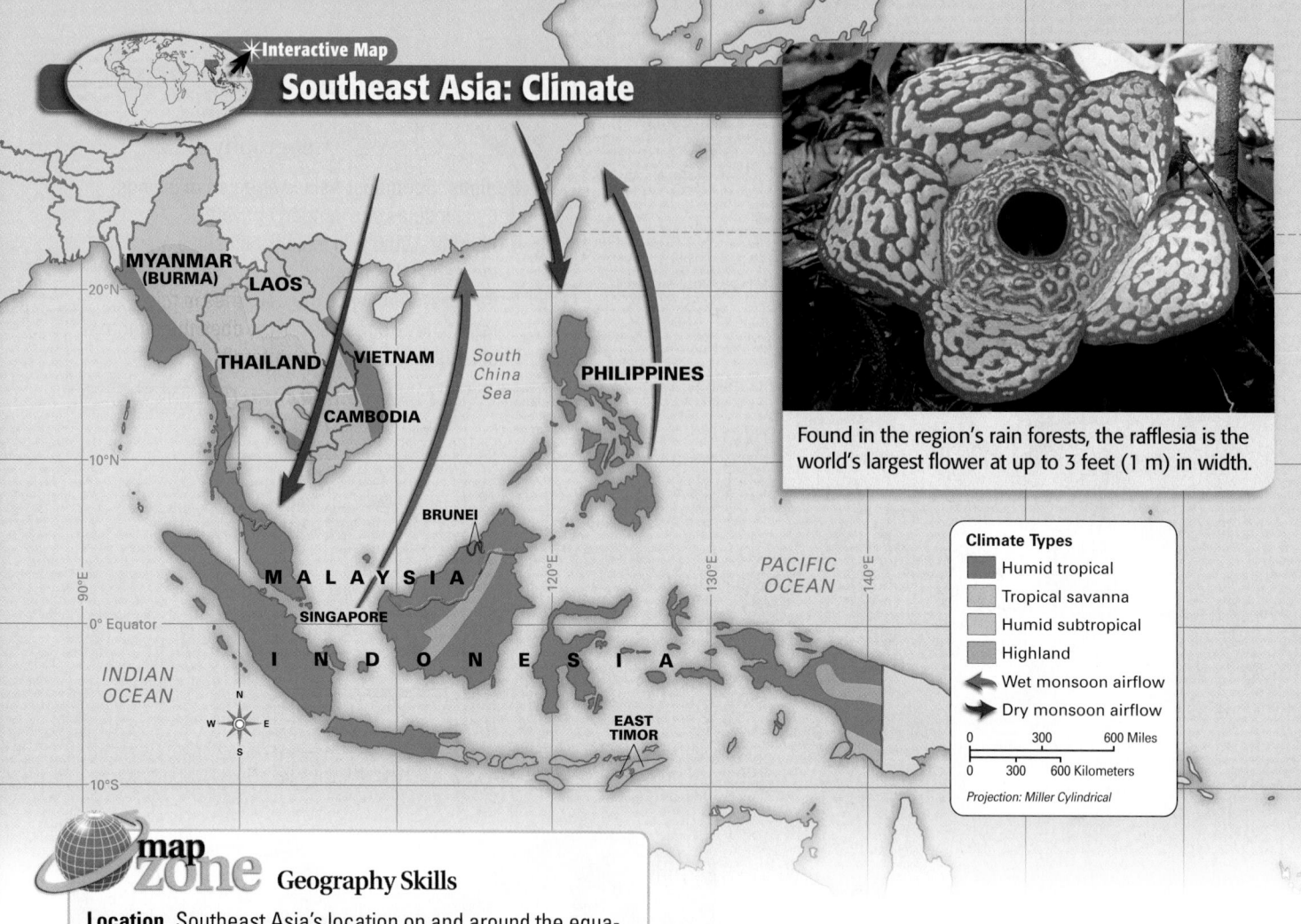

Southeast Asia: Climate

Found in the region's rain forests, the rafflesia is the world's largest flower at up to 3 feet (1 m) in width.

Climate Types
- Humid tropical
- Tropical savanna
- Humid subtropical
- Highland
- ← Wet monsoon airflow
- → Dry monsoon airflow

| 0 | 300 | 600 Miles |
| 0 | 300 | 600 Kilometers |

Projection: Miller Cylindrical

map zone Geography Skills

Location Southeast Asia's location on and around the equator affects the region's climate.
1. **Identify** What is the main climate found in Indonesia, Malaysia, and the Philippines?
2. **Interpret** Based on the map, how do monsoons affect the climate of this region?

go.hrw.com (KEYWORD: SG7 CH28)

Climate, Plants, and Animals

Southeast Asia lies in the tropics, the area on and around the equator. Temperatures are warm to hot year-round, but become cooler to the north and in the mountains.

Much of the mainland has a tropical savanna climate. Seasonal <u>monsoon</u> winds from the oceans bring heavy rain in summer and drier weather in winter. Severe flooding is common during wet seasons. This climate supports savannas—areas of tall grasses and scattered trees and shrubs.

The islands and the Malay Peninsula mainly have a humid tropical climate. This climate is hot, muggy, and rainy all year. Showers or storms occur almost daily. In addition, huge storms called typhoons can bring heavy rains and powerful winds.

The humid tropical climate's heat and heavy rainfall support tropical rain forests. These lush forests are home to a huge number of different plants and animals. About 40,000 kinds of flowering plants grow in Indonesia alone. These plants include the rafflesia, the world's largest flower. Measuring up to 3 feet (1 m) across, this flower produces a horrible, rotting stink.

Rain forest animals include elephants, monkeys, tigers, and many types of birds. Some species are found nowhere else. They include orangutans and Komodo dragons, lizards that can grow 10 feet (3 m) long.

FOCUS ON READING

What context clues help you figure out the definition of *monsoon*?

Orangutans live in the rain forests of Borneo and Sumatra. Deforestation has seriously reduced their habitat.

Natural Resources

Southeast Asia has a number of valuable natural resources. The region's hot, wet climate and rich soils make farming highly productive. Rice is a major crop, and others include coconuts, coffee, sugarcane, palm oil, and spices. Some countries, such as Indonesia and Malaysia (muh-LAY-zhuh), also have large rubber tree plantations.

The region's seas provide fisheries, and its tropical rain forests provide valuable hardwoods and medicines. The region also has many minerals and fossil fuels, including tin, iron ore, natural gas, and oil. For example, the island of Borneo sits atop an oil field.

READING CHECK **Summarizing** What are the region's major natural resources?

Many of these plants and animals are endangered because of loss of habitat. People are clearing the tropical rain forests for farming, wood, and mining. These actions threaten the area's future diversity.

READING CHECK **Analyzing** How does climate contribute to the region's diversity of life?

SUMMARY AND PREVIEW Southeast Asia is a tropical region of peninsulas, islands, and waterways with diverse life and rich resources. Next, you will read about the region's history and culture.

---

go.hrw.com
Online Quiz
KEYWORD: SG7 HP28

Section 1 Assessment

Reviewing Ideas, Terms, and Places

1. **a. Define** What is an **archipelago**?
   b. Compare and Contrast How do the physical features of Mainland Southeast Asia compare and contrast to those of Island Southeast Asia?
2. **a. Recall** What type of forest occurs in the region?
   b. Summarize What is the climate like across much of Southeast Asia?
   c. Predict What do you think might happen to the region's wildlife if the tropical rain forests continue to be destroyed?
3. **a. Identify** Which countries in the region are major producers of rubber?
   b. Analyze How does the region's climate contribute to its natural resources?

Critical Thinking

4. **Summarizing** Draw a chart like this one. Use your notes to provide information about the climate, plants, and animals in Southeast Asia. In the left-hand box, also note how climate shapes life in the region.

Climate of Southeast Asia → Plants
Climate of Southeast Asia → Animals

FOCUS ON SPEAKING

5. **Writing Questions about the Region's Physical Geography** Note information about the region's physical features, climate, plants, animals, and natural resources. Write two questions and answers for your interview. For example, you might ask a question about the region's tropical rain forests.

Tsunami!

Essential Elements

The World in Spatial Terms
Places and Regions
Physical Systems
Human Systems
Environment and Society
The Uses of Geography

Background "Huge Waves Hit Japan." This event is a tsunami (soo-NAH-mee), a series of giant sea waves. Records of deadly tsunamis go back 3,000 years. Some places, such as Japan, have been hit time and again.

Tsunamis occur when an earthquake, volcanic eruption, or other event causes seawater to move in huge waves. The majority of tsunamis occur in the Pacific Ocean because of the region's many earthquakes.

Warning systems help alert people to tsunamis. The Pacific Tsunami Warning Center monitors tsunamis in the Pacific Ocean. Sensors on the ocean floor and buoys on the water's surface help detect earthquakes and measure waves. When a tsunami threatens, radio, TV, and sirens alert the public.

Indian Ocean Catastrophe

On December 26, 2004, a massive earthquake erupted below the Indian Ocean. The earthquake launched a monster tsunami. Within half an hour, walls of water up to 65 feet high came barreling ashore in Indonesia. The water swept away boats, buildings, and people. Meanwhile, the tsunami kept traveling in ever-widening rings across the ocean. The waves eventually wiped out coastal communities in a dozen countries. Some 200,000 people eventually died.

At the time, the Indian Ocean did not have a tsunami warning system. Tsunamis are rare in that part of the world. As a result, many countries there had been unwilling to invest in a warning system.

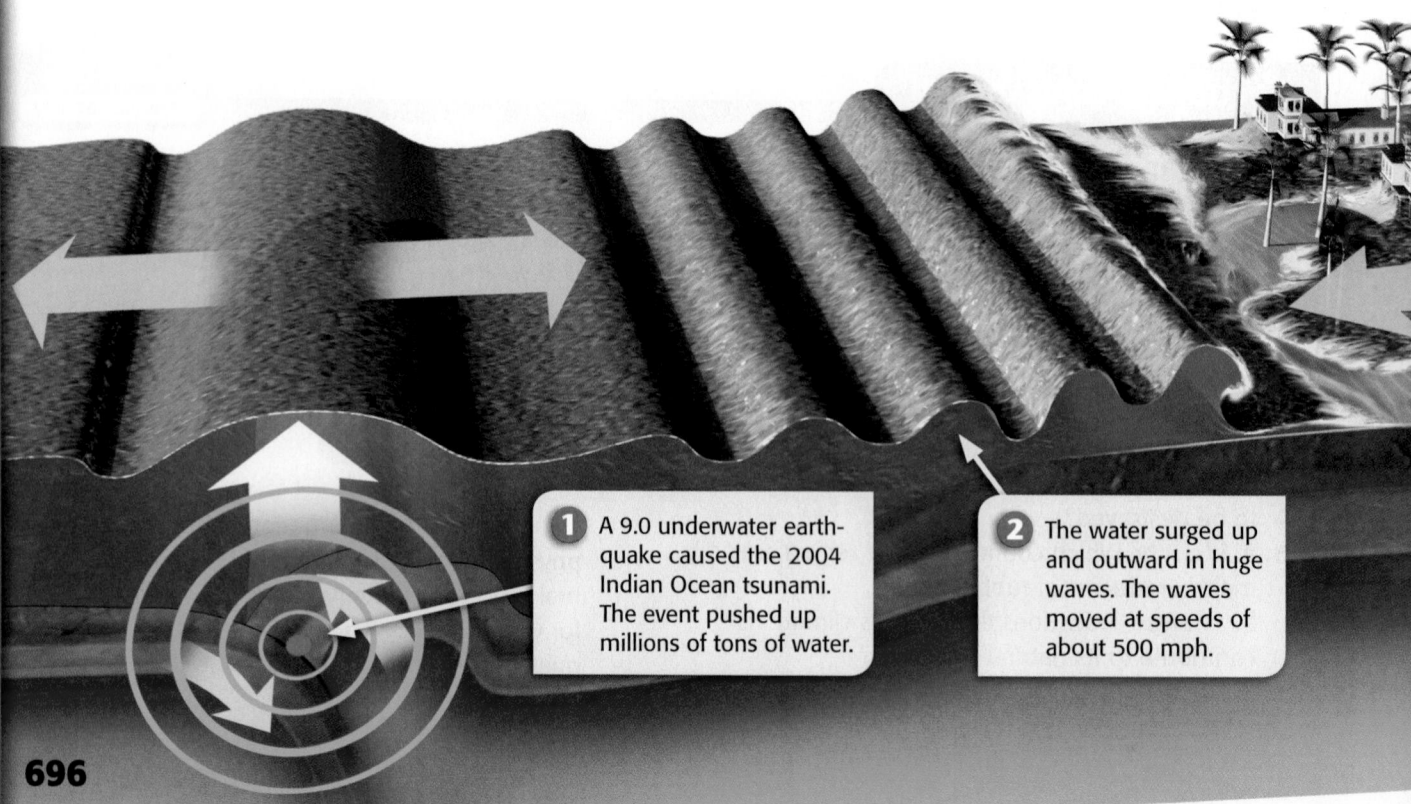

1 A 9.0 underwater earthquake caused the 2004 Indian Ocean tsunami. The event pushed up millions of tons of water.

2 The water surged up and outward in huge waves. The waves moved at speeds of about 500 mph.

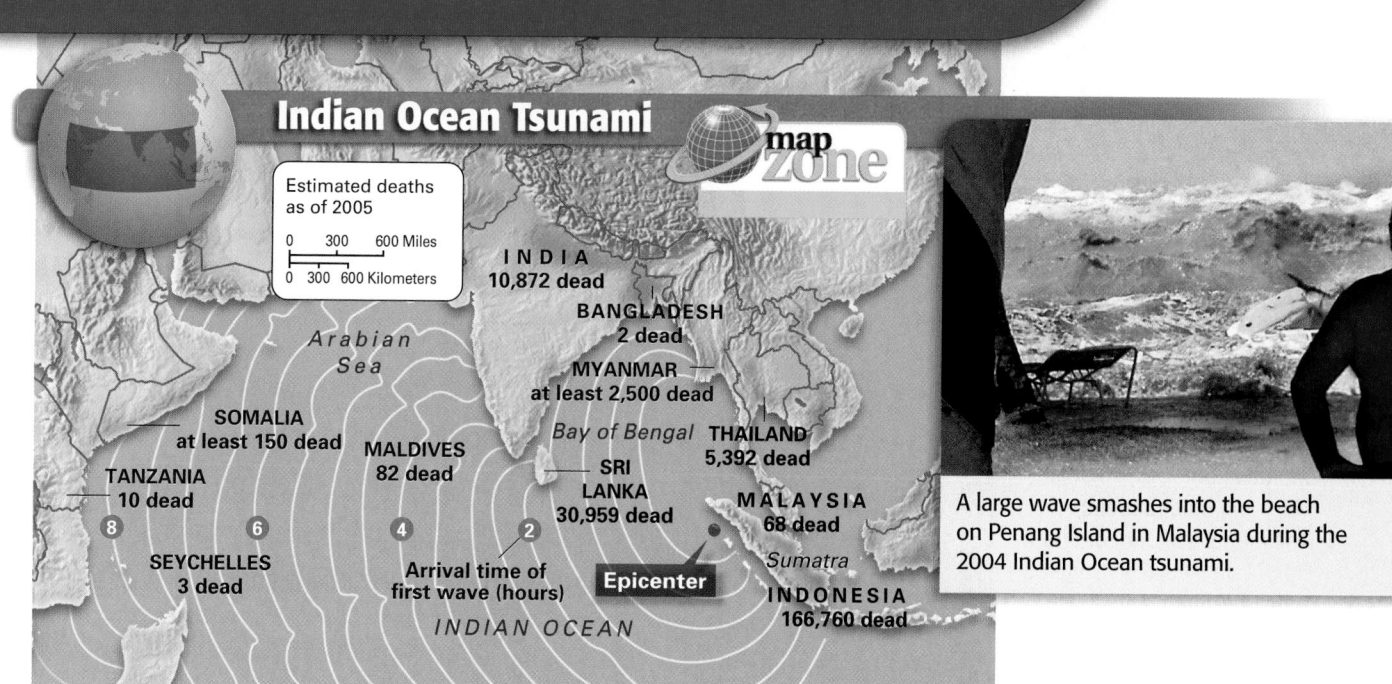

Indian Ocean Tsunami

map zone

Estimated deaths as of 2005

0   300   600 Miles
0   300   600 Kilometers

Arabian Sea

INDIA 10,872 dead

BANGLADESH 2 dead

MYANMAR at least 2,500 dead

Bay of Bengal

THAILAND 5,392 dead

SOMALIA at least 150 dead

MALDIVES 82 dead

SRI LANKA 30,959 dead

MALAYSIA 68 dead

TANZANIA 10 dead

⑧   ⑥   ④   ②

SEYCHELLES 3 dead

Arrival time of first wave (hours)

Epicenter

Sumatra

INDONESIA 166,760 dead

INDIAN OCEAN

A large wave smashes into the beach on Penang Island in Malaysia during the 2004 Indian Ocean tsunami.

In 2004 these countries paid a terrible price for their decision. As the map shows, the 2004 tsunami hit countries from South Asia to East Africa. Most people had no warning of the tsunami. In addition, many people did not know how to protect themselves. Instead of heading to high ground, some people went to the beach for a closer look. Many died when later waves hit.

Tilly Smith, a 10-year-old on vacation in Thailand, was one of the few who understood the danger. Two weeks earlier, her geography teacher had discussed tsunamis. As the water began surging, Smith warned her family and other tourists to flee. Her geographic knowledge saved their lives.

What It Means No one can prevent tsunamis. Yet, by studying geography, we can prepare for these disasters and help protect lives and property. The United Nations is now working to create a global tsunami warning system. People are also trying to plant more mangroves along coastlines. These bushy swamp trees provide a natural barrier against high waves.

③ When they strike, tsunamis often look like a rapidly rising tide or swell of water. The water then rushes far inland and back out.

Geography for Life Activity

1. What steps are being taken to avoid another disaster such as the Indian Ocean tsunami in 2004?

2. About 75 percent of tsunami warnings since 1948 were false alarms. What might be the risks and benefits of early warnings to move people out of harm's way?

3. **Creating a Survival Guide** Create a tsunami survival guide. List the dos and don'ts for this emergency.

History and Culture

What You Will Learn...

Main Ideas

1. Southeast Asia's early history includes empires, colonial rule, and independence.
2. The modern history of Southeast Asia involves struggles with war and communism.
3. Southeast Asia's culture reflects its Chinese, Indian, and European heritage.

The Big Idea

People, ideas, and traditions from China, India, Europe, and elsewhere have shaped Southeast Asia's history and culture.

Key Terms and Places

Timor, *p. 699*
domino theory, *p. 700*
wats, *p. 700*

TAKING NOTES As you read, use a chart like the one here to help you take notes on the history and culture of Southeast Asia.

History	Culture

If YOU lived there...

You and your friends are strolling through the market in Jakarta, Indonesia, looking for a snack. You have many choices—tents along the street, carts called gerobak, and vendors on bicycles all sell food. You might choose satay, strips of chicken or lamb grilled on a stick. Or you might pick one of many rice dishes. For dessert, you can buy fruit or order an ice cream cone.

What do you like about living in Jakarta?

BUILDING BACKGROUND Colonial rule helped shape Southeast Asia's history and culture—including foods. Throughout the region you can see not only a blend of different Asian influences but also a blend of American, Dutch, French, and Spanish influences.

Early History

Southeast Asia lies south of China and east of India, and both countries have played a strong role in the region's history. Over time, many people from China and India settled in Southeast Asia. As settlements grew, trade developed with China and India.

Early Civilization

The region's most advanced early civilization was the Khmer (kuh-MER). From the AD 800s to the mid-1200s the Khmer controlled a large empire in what is now Cambodia. The remains of Angkor Wat, a huge temple complex the Khmer built in the 1100s, reflect their advanced civilization and Hindu religion.

In the 1200s the Thai (TY) from southern China settled in the Khmer area. Around the same time, Buddhism, introduced earlier from India and Sri Lanka, began replacing Hinduism in the region.

Colonial Rule and Independence

As in many parts of the world, European powers started colonizing Southeast Asia during the 1500s. Led by Portugal, European powers came to the region in search of spices and other trade goods.

In 1521 explorer Ferdinand Magellan reached the Philippines and claimed the islands for Spain. The Spaniards who followed came to colonize, trade, and spread Roman Catholicism. This religion remains the main faith in the Philippines today.

In the 1600s and 1700s Dutch traders drove the Portuguese out of much of the region. Portugal kept only the small island of **Timor**. The Dutch gained control of the tea and spice trade on what became the Dutch East Indies, now Indonesia.

In the 1800s the British and French set up colonies with plantations, railroads, and mines. Many people from China and India came to work in the colonies. The British and French spread Christianity as well.

In 1898 the United States entered the region when it won the Philippines from Spain after the Spanish-American War. By the early 1900s, colonial powers ruled most of the region, as the map on the next page shows. Only Siam (sy-AM), now Thailand, was never colonized, although it lost land.

In World War II (1939–1945), Japan invaded and occupied most of Southeast Asia. After Japan lost the war, the United States gave the Philippines independence. Soon, other people in the region began to fight for their independence.

One of the bloodiest wars for independence was in French Indochina. In 1954 the French left. Indochina then split into the independent countries of Cambodia, Laos, and Vietnam. By 1970, most of Southeast Asia had thrown off colonial rule.

READING CHECK **Identifying Cause and Effect** What reasons led other countries to set up colonies across most of Southeast Asia?

Angkor Wat

The stone towers of Angkor Wat rise from the rain forest in what is now Cambodia. To the Khmer, Angkor Wat symbolized the center of the universe.

ANALYZING VISUALS
What conclusions can you draw about the Khmer based on Angkor Wat?

The towers represent the peaks of Mount Meru, the home of the gods in Hindu mythology.

The pathway represents the rainbow bridge, the link between the gods and people in Hindu mythology.

Angkor Wat was built in the mid-1100s as a Hindu temple. It later became a Buddhist temple.

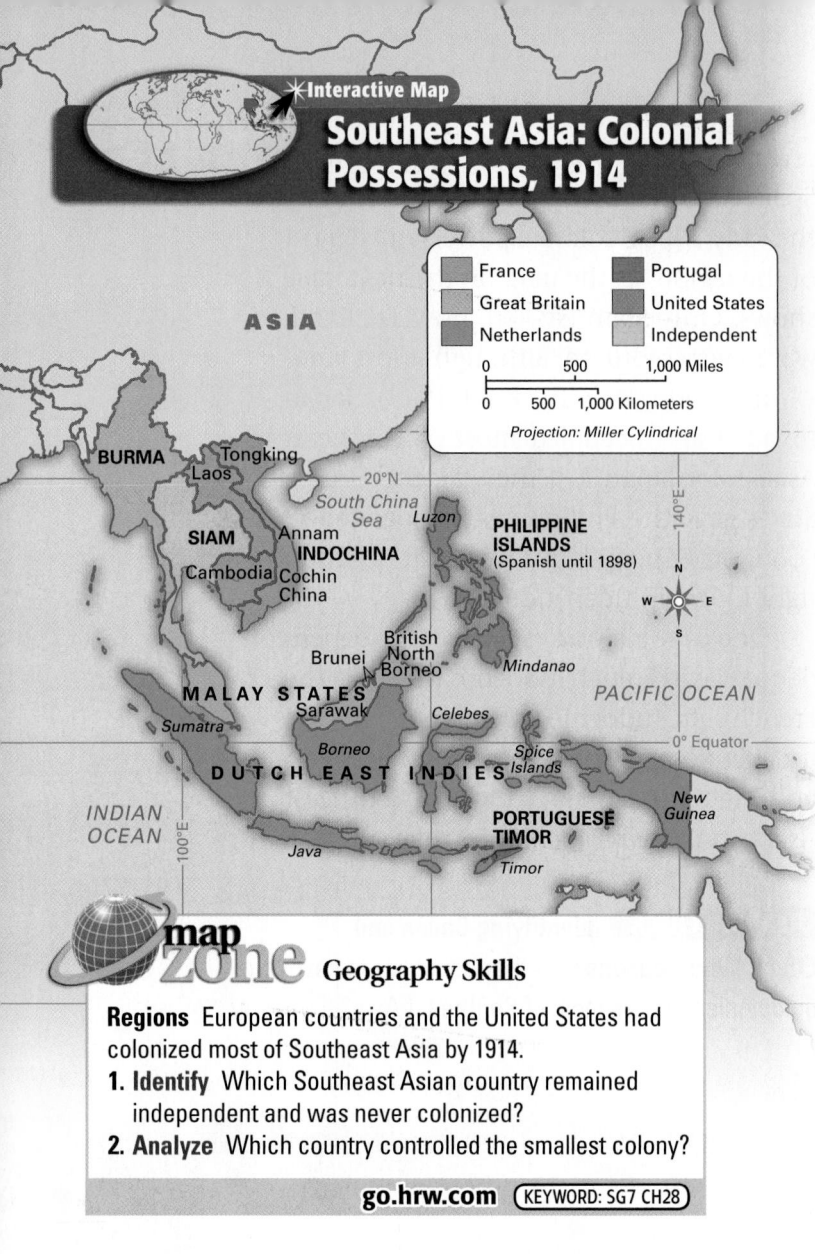

Southeast Asia: Colonial Possessions, 1914

Interactive Map

Legend:
- France
- Great Britain
- Netherlands
- Portugal
- United States
- Independent

0   500   1,000 Miles
0   500   1,000 Kilometers
Projection: Miller Cylindrical

ASIA

BURMA
Tongking
Laos
20°N
South China Sea
SIAM
Annam
INDOCHINA
Cambodia Cochin China
Luzon
PHILIPPINE ISLANDS
(Spanish until 1898)
Brunei
British North Borneo
Mindanao
MALAY STATES
Sarawak
Sumatra
Celebes
Borneo
DUTCH EAST INDIES
Spice Islands
0° Equator
140°E
PACIFIC OCEAN
New Guinea
PORTUGUESE TIMOR
INDIAN OCEAN
100°E
Java
Timor

map zone Geography Skills

Regions European countries and the United States had colonized most of Southeast Asia by 1914.

1. **Identify** Which Southeast Asian country remained independent and was never colonized?
2. **Analyze** Which country controlled the smallest colony?

go.hrw.com   KEYWORD: SG7 CH28

Modern History

FOCUS ON READING

How does the context help explain the meaning of the term *oust* in the paragraph to the right?

The move toward independence was not easy. In Vietnam, the fighting to <u>oust</u> the French left the country divided into North and South Vietnam. A civil war then broke out in the South. To defend South Vietnam from Communist forces in that war, the United States sent in troops in the 1960s.

The United States based its decision to send troops on one **criterion**—the potential spread of communism. According to the **domino theory**, if one country fell to communism, other countries nearby would follow like falling dominoes.

ACADEMIC VOCABULARY

criterion rule or standard for defining

Years of war caused millions of deaths and terrible destruction. In the end, North and South Vietnam reunited as one Communist country. As the Communists took over, about 1 million refugees fled South Vietnam. Many went to the United States.

Civil wars also raged in Cambodia and Laos. In 1975 Communist forces took over both countries. The government in Cambodia was brutal, causing the deaths of more than 1 million people there. Then in 1978 Vietnam helped to overthrow Cambodia's government. This event sparked further fighting, which continued off and on until the mid-1990s. The United Nations then helped Cambodia achieve peace.

READING CHECK **Summarizing** What are some key events in the region's modern history?

Culture

The many groups that influenced Southeast Asia's history also shaped its culture. This diverse culture blends native, Chinese, Indian, and European ways of life.

People and Languages

The countries in Southeast Asia have many ethnic groups. As an example, Indonesia has more than 300 ethnic groups. Most of the countries have one main ethnic group plus many smaller ethnic groups.

Not surprisingly, many languages are spoken in Southeast Asia. These languages include native languages and dialects as well as Chinese and European languages.

Religions

The main religions in Southeast Asia are Buddhism, Christianity, Hinduism, and Islam. Buddhism is the main faith on the mainland. This area features many beautiful **wats**, Buddhist temples that also serve as monasteries.

Islam is the main religion in Malaysia, Brunei, and Indonesia. In fact, Indonesia has more Muslims than any other country. In the Philippines, most people are Roman Catholic. Hinduism is practiced in Indian communities and on the island of Bali.

Customs

Customs differ widely across the region, but some similarities exist. For example, religion often shapes life, and people celebrate many religious festivals. Some people continue to practice traditional customs, such as dances and music. These customs are especially popular in rural areas. In addition, many people wear traditional clothing, such as sarongs, strips of cloth worn wrapped around the body.

READING CHECK Generalizing How has Southeast Asia's history influenced its culture?

SUMMARY AND PREVIEW Southeast Asia has a long history that has helped shape its diverse culture. Next, you will read about Mainland Southeast Asia.

FOCUS ON CULTURE

Thai Teenage Buddhist Monks

Would you be willing to serve as a monk for a few months? In Thailand, many Buddhist boys and young men serve as monks for a short period. This period might last from one week to a few months. These temporary monks follow the lifestyle of actual Buddhist monks, shaving their heads, wearing robes, and maintaining a life of simplicity. During their stay, the teenage monks learn about Buddhism and practice meditation. Some Thai teens decide to become Buddhist monks permanently. This decision is considered a great honor for their families.

Summarizing What are some of the things that Thai boys and young men do while serving as Buddhist monks?

Section 2 Assessment

go.hrw.com
Online Quiz
KEYWORD: SG7 HP28

Reviewing Ideas, Terms, and Places

1. **a. Describe** What was the significance of the Khmer Empire?
   b. Identify Cause and Effect What was the result of the war for independence in French Indochina?
   c. Elaborate How did European colonization shape Southeast Asia's history?
2. **a. Define** What was the **domino theory**?
   b. Summarize What role has communism played in Southeast Asia's modern history?
3. **a. Define** What is a **wat**?
   b. Contrast How does religion in the mainland and island countries differ?
   c. Elaborate How has the history of Southeast Asia shaped the region's culture?

Critical Thinking

4. **Sequencing** Copy the time line shown below. Using your notes, identify on the time line the important people, periods, events, and years in Southeast Asia's history.

   800s   2000

   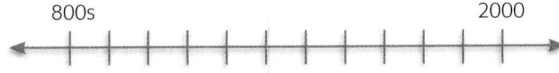

FOCUS ON SPEAKING

5. **Writing Questions about History and Culture** What interesting questions could you ask about the history and culture of Southeast Asia? Write two questions and their answers to add to your notes.

Social Studies Skills

| Chart and Graph | Critical Thinking | Geography | Study |

Analyzing Visuals

Learn

Geographers get information from many sources. These sources include not only text and data but also visuals, such as diagrams and photographs. Use these tips to analyze visuals:

- **Identify the subject.** Read the title and caption, if available. If not, look at the content of the image. What does it show? Where is it located?

- **Analyze the content.** What is the purpose of the image? What information is in the image? What conclusions can you draw from this information? Write your conclusions in your notes.

- **Summarize your analysis.** Write a summary of the information in the visual and of the conclusions you can draw from it.

Practice

Analyze the photograph at right. Then answer the following questions.

❶ What is the title of the photograph?

❷ Where is this scene, and what is happening?

❸ What conclusions can you draw from the information in the photograph?

City Life in Southeast Asia

The title tells you that the photo's purpose is to show life in the region's cities.

The photo shows forms of travel, numbers of people, and air quality in Hanoi.

Southeast Asia's cities are growing rapidly. In Hanoi, Vietnam, vehicles and people crowd the streets.

Apply

Analyze the images of the rubber tree plantation in Section 4. Then answer the following questions.

1. What is the purpose of the two photos?

2. What do the photos show about rubber tree farming?

3. Based on the information in the photos, what conclusions can you draw about rubber tree farming in particular and about agriculture in Island Southeast Asia in general?

Mainland Southeast Asia Today

If YOU lived there...

You live in Vietnam, where your family works on a collective state-run farm. On the side, your family also sells vegetables. Now your older brother wants to start his own business—a bicycle repair shop. The Communist government allows this, but your parents think it is safer for him to keep working on the farm.

What do you think your brother should do?

BUILDING BACKGROUND After decades of war and hardship, most countries in Mainland Southeast Asia are moving forward. Even those countries with Communist governments, such as Vietnam and Laos, are working to develop freer and stronger economies.

The Area Today

Look at the map at the start of the chapter and identify the countries of Mainland Southeast Asia. These countries include Myanmar, Thailand, Cambodia, Laos, and Vietnam.

War, harsh governments, and other problems have slowed progress in most of Mainland Southeast Asia. However, the area's countries have rich resources and are working to improve their futures. For example, as of 2005 all the countries of Southeast Asia except East Timor had joined the Association of Southeast Asian Nations (ASEAN). This organization promotes political, economic, and social cooperation throughout the region.

Rural Life

Mainland Southeast Asia is largely rural. Most people are farmers who live in small villages and work long hours in the fields. Most farm work is done by hand or using traditional methods. Farmers grow rice, the region's main crop, on fertile slopes along rivers and on terraced shelves of land. The wet, tropical climate enables farmers to grow two or three crops each year.

What You Will Learn...

Main Ideas

1. The area today is largely rural and agricultural, but cities are growing rapidly.
2. Myanmar is poor with a harsh military government, while Thailand is a democracy with a strong economy.
3. The countries of Indochina are poor and struggling to rebuild after years of war.

The Big Idea

Many of the farming countries in Mainland Southeast Asia are poor but are working to improve their economies.

Key Terms and Places

Yangon, *p. 704*
human rights, *p. 704*
Bangkok, *p. 704*
klongs, *p. 704*
Phnom Penh, *p. 707*
Hanoi, *p. 707*

TAKING NOTES As you read, use a chart like this one to take notes on each country in Mainland Southeast Asia. Add a row for each country.

Country	→	Description

Most rural people live in the area's fertile river valleys and deltas, which have the best farmland. A delta is an area of fertile land around the mouth of a river. A few people live in remote villages in the rugged, forested mountains. These areas have poor soils that make farming difficult. Many of the people who live there belong to small ethnic groups known as hill peoples.

Urban Life

FOCUS ON READING
What words in the paragraph to the right tell you the definition of *pedicabs*?

Although most people live in rural areas, Mainland Southeast Asia has several large cities. Most are growing rapidly as people move to them for work. Rapid growth has led to crowding and pollution. People, bicycles, scooters, cars, and buses clog city streets. Smog hangs in the still air. Growing cities also mix the old and new. Skyscrapers tower over huts, and cars zip past pedicabs, taxicabs that are pedaled like bikes.

READING CHECK **Finding Main Ideas** Where do most people in Mainland Southeast Asia live?

BIOGRAPHY

Aung San Suu Kyi
(1945–   )

Aung San Suu Kyi has dedicated herself to making life better in her native Myanmar. Suu Kyi is the best-known opponent of the country's harsh military government. Her party, the National League for Democracy (NLD), won control of the country's parliament in 1990. The military government refused to give up power, however. The government then placed Aung San Suu Kyi and other NLD members under house arrest. For her efforts to bring democracy to Myanmar, Suu Kyi received the Nobel Peace Prize in 1991. Even though she remains under house arrest, Suu Kyi continues to fight for democratic reform and free elections in Myanmar. Her efforts have led the United States and some Asian countries to press Myanmar's government to change.

Identifying Points of View What does Aung San Suu Kyi hope to achieve through her efforts in Myanmar?

Myanmar and Thailand

Myanmar and Thailand form the northwestern part of Mainland Southeast Asia. While Myanmar is poor, Thailand boasts the area's strongest economy.

Myanmar

Myanmar lies south of China on the Bay of Bengal. Also known as Burma, the country gained independence from Great Britain in 1948. The capital is **Yangon**, or Rangoon, and the administrative capital is Naypyidaw.

Most of the people in Myanmar are Burmese. Many live in small farming villages in houses built on stilts. Buddhism is the main religion, and village life often centers around a local Buddhist monastery.

Life is difficult in Myanmar because a harsh military government rules the country. The government abuses **human rights**, rights that all people deserve such as rights to equality and justice. A Burmese woman, Aung San Suu Kyi (awng sahn soo chee), has led a movement for more democracy and rights. She and others have been jailed and harassed for their actions.

Myanmar's poor human-rights record has isolated the country and hurt its economy. Some countries, such as the United States, will no longer trade with Myanmar. Despite rich natural resources—such as oil, timber, metals, jade, and gems—Myanmar and most of its people remain poor.

Thailand

To the southwest of Malaysia is Thailand, once known as Siam. The capital and largest city is **Bangkok**. Modern and crowded, it lies near the mouth of the Chao Phraya (chow PRY-uh) River. Bangkok is known for its many spectacular palaces and Buddhist wats. The city is also famous for its **klongs**, or canals. Klongs are used for transportation and trade, and to drain floodwater.

A Bangkok Canal

Sick of crowded roads? In Bangkok, you can use a network of canals, called klongs, to travel through parts of the city. Water taxis and boats transport people and goods. At floating markets, vendors sell fish, fruit, and other foods to locals and tourists.

To move around the klongs, people use narrow, shallow boats and poles.

ประกาศ
ห้ามเรือทุกชนิดใช้เครื่องยนต์
ตั้งแต่เวลา 08.00-12.00 น.
ฝ่าฝืนมีโทษปรับไม่เกิน 1,000 บาท
สภ.อ.ดำเนินสะดวก

Many sellers wear bamboo hats with wide brims to block the sun and rain.

Vendors sell both cooked food and raw produce, such as the pomelos shown here.

Small bananas, called finger bananas, are displayed on green banana leaves.

ANALYSIS SKILL | **ANALYZING VISUALS**

What advantages do you think klongs provide to both travelers and people selling goods?

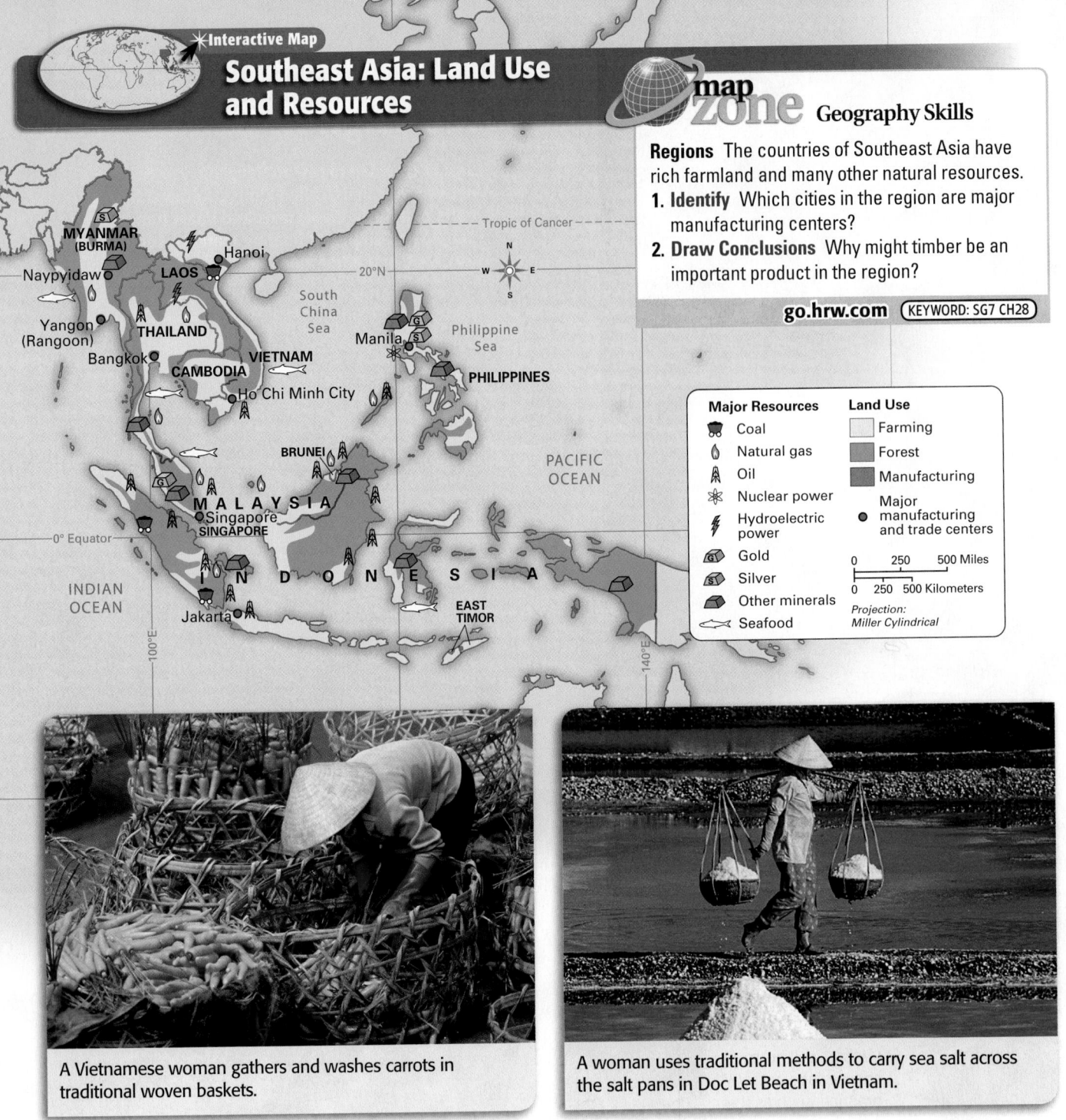

Southeast Asia: Land Use and Resources

Interactive Map

map Zone — Geography Skills

Regions The countries of Southeast Asia have rich farmland and many other natural resources.
1. **Identify** Which cities in the region are major manufacturing centers?
2. **Draw Conclusions** Why might timber be an important product in the region?

go.hrw.com [KEYWORD: SG7 CH28]

Major Resources
- Coal
- Natural gas
- Oil
- Nuclear power
- Hydroelectric power
- Gold
- Silver
- Other minerals
- Seafood

Land Use
- Farming
- Forest
- Manufacturing
- Major manufacturing and trade centers

0 250 500 Miles
0 250 500 Kilometers
Projection: Miller Cylindrical

A Vietnamese woman gathers and washes carrots in traditional woven baskets.

A woman uses traditional methods to carry sea salt across the salt pans in Doc Let Beach in Vietnam.

Thailand is a constitutional monarchy. A monarch, or king, serves as a ceremonial head of state. A prime minister and elected legislature hold the real power, however.

A democratically elected government and rich resources have helped Thailand's economy to grow. Industry, farming, fishing, mining, and tourism fuel this growth. Farms produce rice, pineapples, and rubber. Factories produce computers, textiles, and electronics. Magnificent Buddhist wats and unspoiled beaches draw tourists.

READING CHECK **Comparing and Contrasting**
What are some similarities and differences between Myanmar and Thailand?

The Countries of Indochina

The former countries of French Indochina lie to the east and south of Thailand. They are struggling to overcome decades of war.

Cambodia

Cambodia lies to the northeast of the Gulf of Thailand. **Phnom Penh** (puh-NAWM pen) is the capital and chief city. Located in the Mekong River valley, it is a center of trade.

Some 20 years of war, terror, and devastation in Cambodia finally ended in the early 1990s. Today the country has a stable, elected government similar to Thailand's. Years of conflict left their mark, however. Although farming has improved, the country has little industry. In addition, many land mines remain hidden in the land.

Laos

Laos is landlocked with rugged mountains. Poor and undeveloped, it has few roads, no railroads, and limited electricity.

The Communist government of Laos has been increasing economic freedom in hopes of improving the economy. Even so, Laos remains the area's poorest country.

The economy is based on farming, but good farmland is limited. Most people are subsistence farmers, meaning they grow just enough food for their families.

Vietnam

Like Laos, Vietnam is rugged and mountainous. The capital, **Hanoi**, is located in the north in the Hong (Red) River delta. The largest city, Ho Chi Minh City, is in the south in the Mekong delta.

Vietnam's Communist government has been allowing more economic freedom and private business. The changes have helped the economy grow. Most people still farm, but industry and services are expanding. Fishing and mining are also important.

READING CHECK **Evaluating** How would you rate the economies of these three countries?

SUMMARY AND PREVIEW The mainland countries are rural and agricultural with fast-growing cities. Most of the countries are poor despite rich resources. Next, you will read about Island Southeast Asia.

Section 3 Assessment

Reviewing Ideas, Terms, and Places

1. **a. Recall** In what areas do most people in Mainland Southeast Asia live?
   b. Identify Cause and Effect How has rapid growth affected the area's cities?
2. **a. Define** What are **klongs**, and in what ways are they used?
   b. Contrast How does Thailand's economy differ from Myanmar's economy?
   c. Predict How might Myanmar's economy change if the country had a government that respected **human rights**? Explain your answer.
3. **a. Identify** What is the area's poorest country?
   b. Summarize What issues and challenges face Cambodia, Laos, and Vietnam?

Critical Thinking

4. **Categorizing** Draw a chart like the one shown. Use your notes to provide information for each category in the chart.

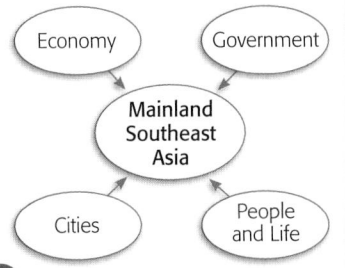

FOCUS ON SPEAKING

5. **Writing Questions about Mainland Southeast Asia Today** Write one question about each country covered in this section. Your questions might highlight differences among the countries or focus on similarities across the area.

Island Southeast Asia Today

What You Will Learn...

Main Ideas

1. The area today has rich resources and growing cities but faces challenges.
2. Malaysia and its neighbors have strong economies but differ in many ways.
3. Indonesia is big and diverse with a growing economy, and East Timor is small and poor.
4. The Philippines has less ethnic diversity, and its economy is improving.

The Big Idea

The countries of Island Southeast Asia range from wealthy and urban to poor and rural.

Key Terms and Places

kampong, *p. 709*
Jakarta, *p. 709*
Kuala Lumpur, *p. 709*
free ports, *p. 710*
sultan, *p. 711*
Java, *p. 711*
Manila, *p. 712*

TAKING NOTES As you read, use a chart like this one to take notes on each country in Island Southeast Asia. Add a row for each country.

If YOU lived there...

You live in Canada but are visiting your cousins in Singapore. You start to cross the street in the middle of a block, but your cousin quickly stops you. "You have to pay a big fine if you do that!" he says. Singapore has many strict laws and strong punishments, he explains. These laws are meant to make the city safe.

What do you think about Singapore's laws?

BUILDING BACKGROUND Singapore and the other countries of Island Southeast Asia present many contrasts. You can quickly go from skyscrapers to rice paddies to tropical rain forests. Many ethnic groups may live in one country, which can lead to unrest.

The Area Today

Island Southeast Asia lies at a crossroads between major oceans and continents. The area's six countries are Malaysia, Singapore, Brunei (brooh-NY), Indonesia, East Timor, and the Philippines.

The future for these countries could be bright. They have the potential for wealth and good standards of living, such as rich resources and a large, skilled labor force. In addition, most of the countries have growing economies and belong to ASEAN. This organization promotes cooperation in Southeast Asia.

Island Southeast Asia faces challenges, however. First, violent ethnic conflicts have hurt progress in some countries. Second, many people live in poverty, while a few leaders and business-people control much of the money. Third, the area has many environmental problems, such as pollution.

Rural and Urban Life

Many people in Island Southeast Asia live in rural areas, where they farm or fish. As on the mainland, rice is the main crop. Others include coffee, spices, sugarcane, tea, and tropical fruit.

Rubber is a major crop as well, and Indonesia and Malaysia are the world's largest producers of natural rubber. Seafood is the area's main source of protein.

As on the mainland, many people in Island Southeast Asia are leaving rural villages to move to cities for work. The largest cities, the major capitals, are modern and crowded. Common problems in these cities include smog and heavy traffic. Some cities also have large slums.

In Malaysia, Indonesia, and other parts of the area, many people live in kampongs. A **kampong** is a village or city district with traditional houses built on stilts. The stilts protect the houses from flooding, which is common in the area. The term *kampong* also refers to the slums around the area's cities such as **Jakarta**, Indonesia's capital.

READING CHECK **Summarizing** Why could the future be bright for Island Southeast Asia?

Malaysia and Its Neighbors

Malaysia and its much smaller neighbors, Singapore and Brunei, were all once British colonies. Today all three countries are independent and differ in many ways.

Malaysia

Malaysia consists of two parts. One is on the southern end of the Malay Peninsula. The other is on northern Borneo. Most of the country's people live on the peninsula. **Kuala Lumpur** (KWAH-luh LOOHM-poohr), Malaysia's capital, is there as well. The capital is a cultural and economic center.

Malaysia is ethnically diverse. The Malays are the main ethnic group, but many Chinese and other groups live in Malaysia as well. As a result, the country has many languages and religions. Bahasa Malay is the main language, and Islam and Buddhism are the main religions.

Rubber Tree Plantations

Southeast Asia's tropical climate is well suited to rubber trees. At left, a man taps, or cuts, a rubber tree at a Malaysia plantation. A milky liquid drains from the cut into a cup, as shown above. The liquid dries to form a rubbery material.

ANALYZING VISUALS What do you think it is like to work on a rubber tree plantation?

Singapore

Primary Source

INTERVIEW
Lee Kuan Yew on Singapore

Lee Kuan Yew was Singapore's prime minister from 1959 to 1990. He remade the tiny country into an economic power. In a 1994 interview, Lee discussed Singapore's strict laws.

" *The expansion of the right of the individual to behave or misbehave as he pleases has come at the expense of orderly society. In the East the main object is to have a well-ordered society so that everybody can have maximum enjoyment of his freedoms. This freedom can exist only in an ordered state.*"

—from "A Conversation with Lee Kuan Yew"

ANALYSIS SKILL ANALYZING PRIMARY SOURCES

Do you agree with Lee that freedom for all can exist only in a society with strict order? Why or why not?

Singapore

A populous country, Singapore is squeezed onto a tiny island at the tip of the Malay Peninsula. The island lies on a major shipping route. This location has helped make Singapore a rich country.

Today Singapore is one of the world's busiest **free ports,** ports that place few if any taxes on goods. It is also an industrial center, and many foreign banks and high-tech firms have located offices there.

Singapore sparkles as the gem of Southeast Asia. The country is modern, wealthy, orderly, and clean. Crime rates are low.

How has Singapore achieved such success? The government has worked hard to clean up slums and improve housing. In addition, laws are extremely strict. To provide **concrete** examples, fines for littering are stiff, and people caught with illegal drugs can be executed. Moreover, the government strictly controls politics and the media. Certain movies are banned, as are satellite dishes. Recently, however, Singapore has loosened up some restrictions.

Malaysia is a constitutional monarchy. The king's duties are largely ceremonial, and local rulers take turns being king. A prime minister and elected legislature hold the real power.

Malaysia's economy is one of the stronger in the area. Well-educated workers and rich resources help drive this economy. The country produces and exports natural rubber, palm oil, electronics, oil, and timber.

ACADEMIC VOCABULARY
concrete
specific, real

Brunei

The tiny country of Brunei is on the island of Borneo, which it shares with Malaysia and Indonesia. A **sultan**, the supreme ruler of a Muslim country, governs Brunei.

The country has grown wealthy from large oil and gas deposits. Because of this wealth, Brunei's citizens do not pay income tax and receive free health care and other benefits. Brunei's oil will run out around 2020, however. As a result, the government is developing other areas of the economy.

READING CHECK **Contrasting** How do Malaysia, Singapore, and Brunei differ?

Indonesia and East Timor

Indonesia is the largest of the island countries. East Timor, once part of Indonesia, is one of the area's smallest countries.

Indonesia

Indonesia has several claims to fame. It is the world's largest archipelago, with some 13,500 islands. It has the fourth-largest population of any country as well as the largest Muslim population. Indonesia is extremely diverse as well, as you have read. It has more than 300 ethnic groups who speak more than 250 languages.

Indonesia's main island is **Java**. The capital, Jakarta, is there, as are more than half of Indonesia's people. For this reason, Java is extremely crowded. To reduce the crowding, the government has been moving people to less-populated islands. Many people on those islands dislike that policy.

Indonesia's rich resources have helped its economy to grow. The main resources include rubber, oil and gas, and timber. The country also has good farmland for rice and other crops. Factories turn out clothing and electronics. Islands such as Bali draw thousands of tourists each year.

At the same time, problems have hurt Indonesia's economy. Many of the people are poor, and unemployment is high. In some areas, ethnic and religious conflicts have led to fighting and terrorism.

East Timor

East Timor is located on the small island of Timor. In 1999 East Timor declared independence from Indonesia. The island then plunged into violence. East Timor only gained its independence after the United Nations sent in troops to restore peace. Years of fighting have left East Timor one of the region's poorest countries. Most people farm, and coffee is the main export.

READING CHECK **Generalizing** How has violence affected Indonesia and East Timor?

FOCUS ON READING
How does the highlighted text help you understand the meaning of *sultan?*

Rice Farming

Terraced rice paddies, such as these in Quezon in the Philippines, are common throughout Southeast Asia.

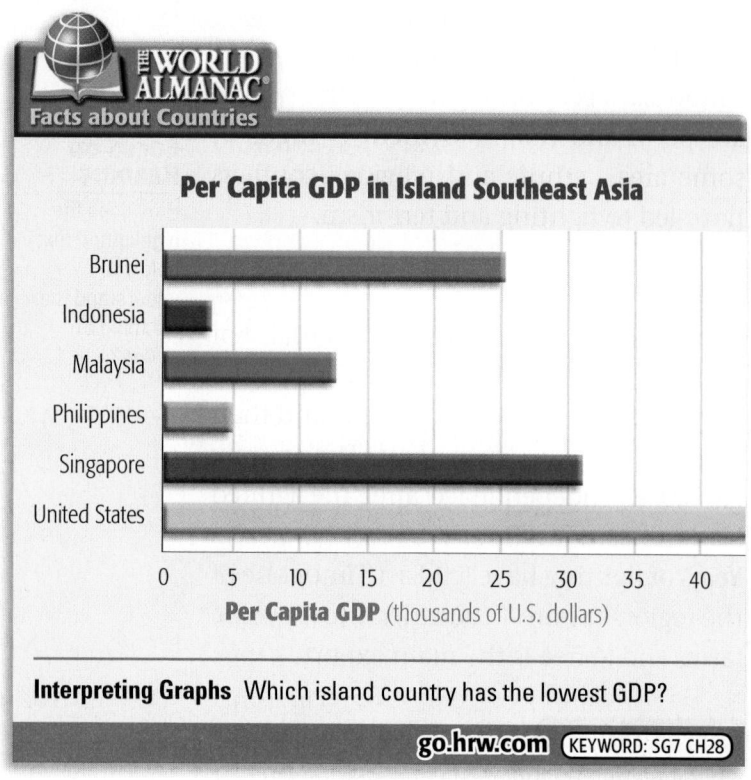

Per Capita GDP in Island Southeast Asia

Per Capita GDP (thousands of U.S. dollars)

Interpreting Graphs Which island country has the lowest GDP?

go.hrw.com (KEYWORD: SG7 CH28)

The Philippines has many resources to fuel economic growth. Natural resources include copper and other metals, oil, and tropical wood. Farmers grow coconuts, sugarcane, rice, and corn. Factories produce and export clothing and electronics.

Although the economy of the Philippines has improved in recent years, a wide gap still exists between the rich and the poor. A few Filipinos are wealthy. Most, however, are poor farmers who do not own the land they work.

The Philippines has experienced religious conflict as well. Although the country is mainly Roman Catholic, some areas are largely Muslim and want independence.

READING CHECK **Contrasting** How does the Philippines differ from much of the area?

The Philippines

The Philippines includes more than 7,000 islands. The largest and most populated is Luzon, which includes the capital, **Manila**. The Philippines has less ethnic diversity than the other island countries. Almost all Filipinos are ethnic Malays.

SUMMARY AND PREVIEW You have read that Island Southeast Asia has many contrasts. While some countries are wealthy, others are poor. While some countries are modern and urban, others are more traditional and rural. In the next chapter you will read about the Pacific World.

Section 4 Assessment

go.hrw.com
Online Quiz
KEYWORD: SG7 HP28

Reviewing Ideas, Terms, and Places

1. **a. Identify** What problems does the area face?
   b. Compare How does urban life compare between the island and mainland countries?
2. **a. Define** What is a **sultan**?
   b. Explain How have Singapore and Brunei become rich countries?
3. **a. Recall** What island is **Jakarta** located on?
   b. Sequence What series of events led to East Timor's independence?
4. **a. Identify** What are the capital city and the main island in the Philippines?
   b. Analyze Why is the Philippines' economic improvement not benefiting many of its people?

Critical Thinking

5. **Categorizing** Draw a chart like the one shown. Use your notes to provide information for each category in the chart.

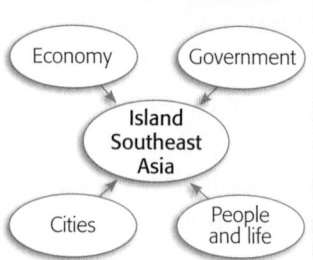

FOCUS ON SPEAKING

6. **Writing Questions about Island Southeast Asia Today** Write one question about each country covered in this section. Your questions might highlight differences among the countries or focus on similarities across the area.

Chapter Review

Geography's Impact
video series
Review the video to answer the closing question:
Why do you think it is important to preserve the environment of the Malay Archipelago?

Visual Summary

Use the visual summary below to help you review the main ideas of the chapter.

QUICK FACTS

Southeast Asia is a tropical region of peninsulas, islands, and water. Its history includes empires and colonization.

Mainland Southeast Asia is rural with growing cities. Many of the countries are poor but have rich resources.

Island Southeast Asia is more urban, and some countries are wealthy. Many of the area's people are poor, though.

Reviewing Vocabulary, Terms, and Places

For each group of terms below, write a sentence that shows how all the terms in the group are related.

1. archipelagos
   Indonesia
   Philippines

2. Aung San Suu Kyi
   human rights
   Myanmar

3. Bangkok
   klongs

4. Indochina
   domino theory

5. Jakarta
   kampongs

6. Singapore
   free port

7. Brunei
   sultan

Comprehension and Critical Thinking

SECTION 1 *(Pages 692–695)*

8. **a. Identify** What are the two peninsulas and the two archipelagos that make up the region of Southeast Asia?

   b. Compare and Contrast In what ways are the main climate of Mainland Southeast Asia and of Island Southeast Asia similar and different?

   c. Develop What different needs should people weigh when considering how best to protect the region's tropical rain forests?

SECTION 2 *(Pages 698–701)*

9. **a. Recall** What theory led the U.S. military to become involved in Southeast Asia?

   b. Identify Cause and Effect Why are so many languages spoken in Southeast Asia?

   c. Predict How do you think Southeast Asia might be different today if Europeans had never explored and colonized the area?

SECTION 3 *(Pages 703–707)*

10. a. Describe Where do most people live and work in Mainland Southeast Asia?

b. Summarize What factors have slowed economic progress in Mainland Southeast Asia?

c. Develop What actions might Myanmar take to try to improve its economy?

SECTION 4 *(Pages 708–712)*

11. a. Identify Which two countries in Island Southeast Asia have wealthy economies?

b. Compare What are some ways in which Indonesia and the Philippines are similar?

c. Elaborate How has ethnic diversity affected the countries of Island Southeast Asia?

Using the Internet

go.hrw.com
KEYWORD: SG7 CH28

12. Activity: Writing a Report on Rain Forests The tropical rain forests of Indonesia are home to a rich diversity of life. Enter the activity keyword to research these rain forests. Then write a short report that summarizes the threats they face.

FOCUS ON READING AND SPEAKING

Using Context Clues—Definitions *Add a phrase or sentence to provide a definition for the underlined word.*

13. In Thailand, many young men serve for short periods in Buddhist <u>monasteries</u>.

14. Much of the <u>cultivated</u> land in Southeast Asia is used to grow rice.

Presenting an Interview *Use your interview notes to complete the activity below.*

15. Working with your partner, choose the five best questions and answers for your interview. Write a brief introduction and conclusion for the journalist to present at the start and end of the interview. Decide who will play the journalist and who will play the expert. Practice the interview until it sounds natural and then present it to your class.

Social Studies Skills

Analyzing Visuals *Turn to Section 3 and analyze the large photograph of a Bangkok canal. Then answer the following questions about the photograph.*

16. What are the title and location of the photo?

17. How do the captions help you understand the information in the photograph?

18. What types of activities are taking place in the photograph?

19. Based on the information in the photo, what conclusions can you draw about the use of canals in the city of Bangkok?

Map Activity ✴Interactive

20. Southeast Asia On a separate sheet of paper, match the letters on the map with their correct labels below.

Bangkok, Thailand	Jakarta, Indonesia
Borneo	Malay Peninsula
Hanoi, Vietnam	Manila, Philippines
Indochina Peninsula	Singapore

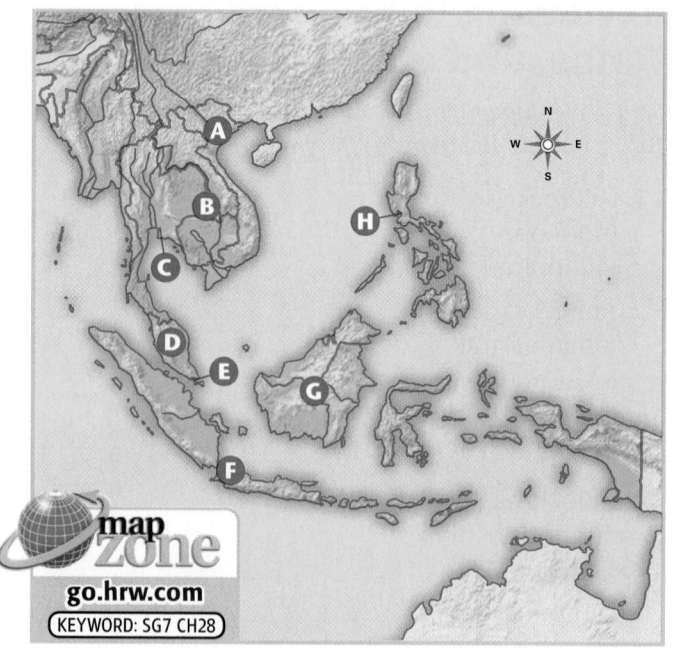

map
zone
go.hrw.com
KEYWORD: SG7 CH28

DIRECTIONS: Read questions 1 through 7 and write the letter of the best response. Then read question 8 and write your own well-constructed response.

1 The two peninsulas in Southeast Asia are the Indochina Peninsula and the

A Burma Peninsula.

B Malay Peninsula.

C Philippine Peninsula.

D Thai Peninsula.

2 What is the largest island in this region?

A Bali

B Borneo

C Java

D New Guinea

3 Which early advanced society in Southeast Asia was located in what is now Cambodia?

A Burmese

B Khmer

C Malays

D Thais

4 Which country in Mainland Southeast Asia has a harsh military government?

A Cambodia

B Laos

C Myanmar

D Thailand

5 What interesting feature of Bangkok helps people get around the city?

A kampongs

B klongs

C sultans

D wats

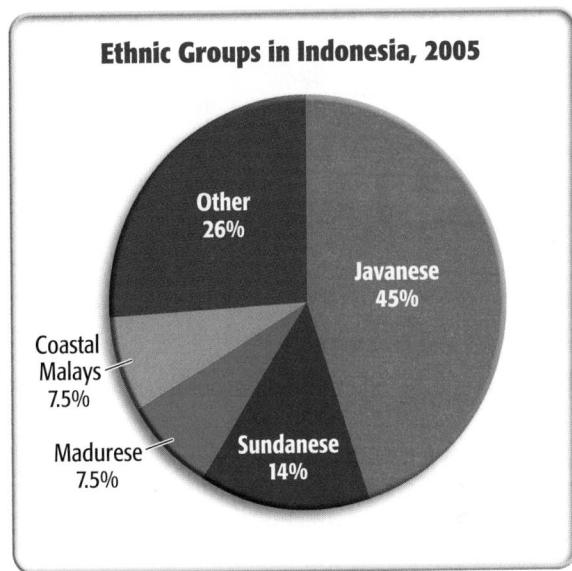

Ethnic Groups in Indonesia, 2005

Other 26%
Javanese 45%
Coastal Malays 7.5%
Madurese 7.5%
Sundanese 14%

Source: Central Intelligence Agency, *The World Factbook 2005*

6 Based on the circle graph above, which of the following was the largest ethnic group in Indonesia in 2005?

A Coastal Malays

B Javanese

C Madurese

D Sundanese

7 Which small country in Island Southeast Asia has become wealthy from oil?

A Brunei

B East Timor

C Indonesia

D Philippines

8 Extended Response Examine the Section 1 map titled Southeast Asia: Climate. Based on the information in the map and in the text, write two or three paragraphs explaining how climate affects life in Southeast Asia. Consider plant life, animal life, and how people live and work.

CHAPTER 29

The Pacific World

What You Will Learn...

In this chapter you will learn about the vast world located in the Pacific Ocean. You will study the geography, history, and culture of Australia and New Zealand. You will also discover one of the most unique places in the world—the Pacific Islands. Finally, you will examine the immense and isolated continent of Antarctica.

FOCUS ON READING AND WRITING

Drawing Conclusions When you read, you discover new information. However, to find out what that information means, you have to draw conclusions. Conclusions are judgments we make as we combine new information with what we already know. As you read about the Pacific world, draw conclusions about the information you come across. **See the lesson, Drawing Conclusions, on page R30.**

Creating a Brochure You work for an advertising agency, and your assignment is to create a brochure about the natural resources in the Pacific world. Your goal is to encourage people to invest money in developing the local economies. As you read this chapter, collect information to use in your brochure.

Geography From Uluru in the dry Australian Outback to freezing Antarctica, the Pacific world is a land of great geographic variety.

Interactive Map

The Pacific World: Political

Midway Islands
Hawaiian Islands (U.S.)
Wake Island
Johnston Atoll
MARSHALL ISLANDS
Kingman Reef
Palmyra Atoll
PACIFIC OCEAN
Howland Island
Gilbert Islands
0° Equator
NAURU
Bougainville
Line Islands
KIRIBATI
SOLOMON ISLANDS
TUVALU
Marquesas Islands
Wallis and Futuna (FRANCE)
SAMOA
American Samoa (U.S.)
French Polynesia (FRANCE)
VANUATU
Cook Islands (NEW ZEALAND)
Tahiti
New Caledonia (FRANCE)
FIJI
TONGA
Loyalty Islands
Niue
20°S
Pitcairn Islands
Easter Island
N
W
E
S
Tasman Sea
Auckland
NEW ZEALAND
Wellington
Chatham Islands
Auckland Islands
National capital
Other cities
Island boundaries are for convenience only and do not represent international boundaries.
0 300 600 Miles
0 300 600 Kilometers
Projection: Miller Cylindrical
160°E
180°
160°W
140°W
ATLANTIC OCEAN
Antarctic Circle
30°W
0°
30°E
Weddell Sea
Antarctic Peninsula
Ronne Ice Shelf
ANTARCTICA
60°E
90°W
South Pole
90°E
Transantarctic Mountains
Ross Ice Shelf
120°W
120°E
Ross Sea
PACIFIC OCEAN
INDIAN OCEAN
150°W
180°
150°E

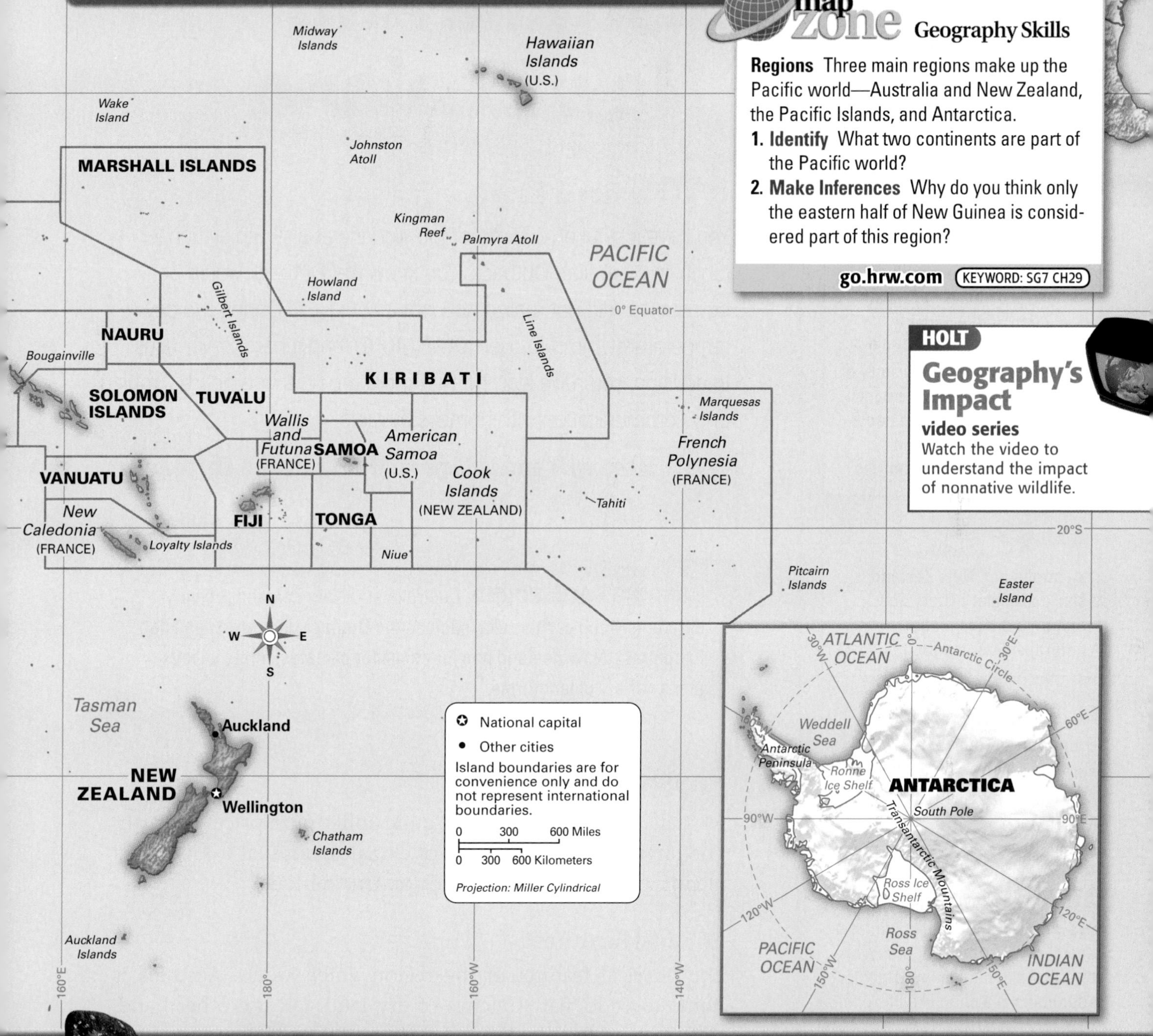

map zone Geography Skills

Regions Three main regions make up the Pacific world—Australia and New Zealand, the Pacific Islands, and Antarctica.

1. **Identify** What two continents are part of the Pacific world?
2. **Make Inferences** Why do you think only the eastern half of New Guinea is considered part of this region?

go.hrw.com (KEYWORD: SG7 CH29)

HOLT

Geography's Impact

video series

Watch the video to understand the impact of nonnative wildlife.

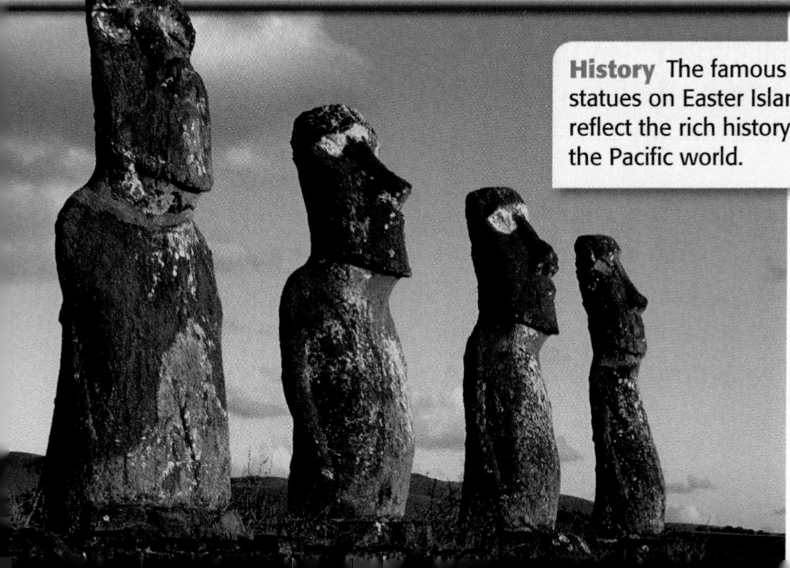

History The famous *moai* statues on Easter Island reflect the rich history of the Pacific world.

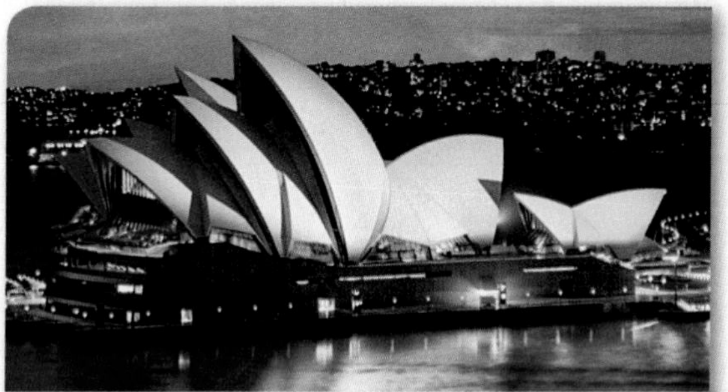

Culture Sydney's Opera House is one example of the vibrant culture that exists throughout the Pacific world.

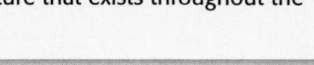

Australia and New Zealand

What You Will Learn...

Main Ideas

1. The physical geography of Australia and New Zealand is diverse and unusual.
2. Native peoples and British settlers shaped the history of Australia and New Zealand.
3. Australia and New Zealand today are wealthy and culturally diverse countries.

The Big Idea

Australia and New Zealand share a similar history and culture but have unique natural environments.

Key Terms and Places

Great Barrier Reef, *p. 719*
coral reef, *p. 719*
Aborigines, *p. 721*
Maori, *p. 721*
Outback, *p. 722*

TAKING NOTES As you read, take notes on Australia and New Zealand's physical geography, history, and situation today. Organize your notes in a chart like this one.

	Australia	New Zealand
Physical Geography		
History		
The Region Today		

If YOU lived there...

You have just taken a summer job working at a sheep station, or ranch, in Australia's Outback. You knew the Outback would be hot, but you did not realize how hot it could get! During the day, temperatures climb to over 100°F (40°C), and it hardly ever rains. In addition, you have learned that there are no towns nearby. Your only communication with home is by radio.

How will you adapt to living in the Outback?

BUILDING BACKGROUND Australia and New Zealand are very different. Much of Australia, such as the Outback, is hot, dry, and flat. In contrast, New Zealand has much milder climates, fertile valleys, and a variety of landforms.

Physical Geography

Australia and New Zealand are quite unlike most places on Earth. The physical features, variety of climates, unusual wildlife, and plentiful resources make the region truly unique.

Physical Features

The physical features of the region differ widely. Australia is home to wide, flat stretches of dry land. On the other hand, New Zealand features beautiful green hills and tall mountains.

Australia Similar to an island, Australia is surrounded by water. However, due to its immense size—almost 3 million square miles (7.7 million square km)—geographers consider Australia a continent.

A huge plateau covers the western half of Australia. Mostly flat and dry, this plateau is home to Uluru, a rock formation also known as Ayers Rock. Uluru is one of Australia's best-known landforms. Low mountains, valleys, and a major river system cover much of Eastern Australia. Fertile plains lie along the

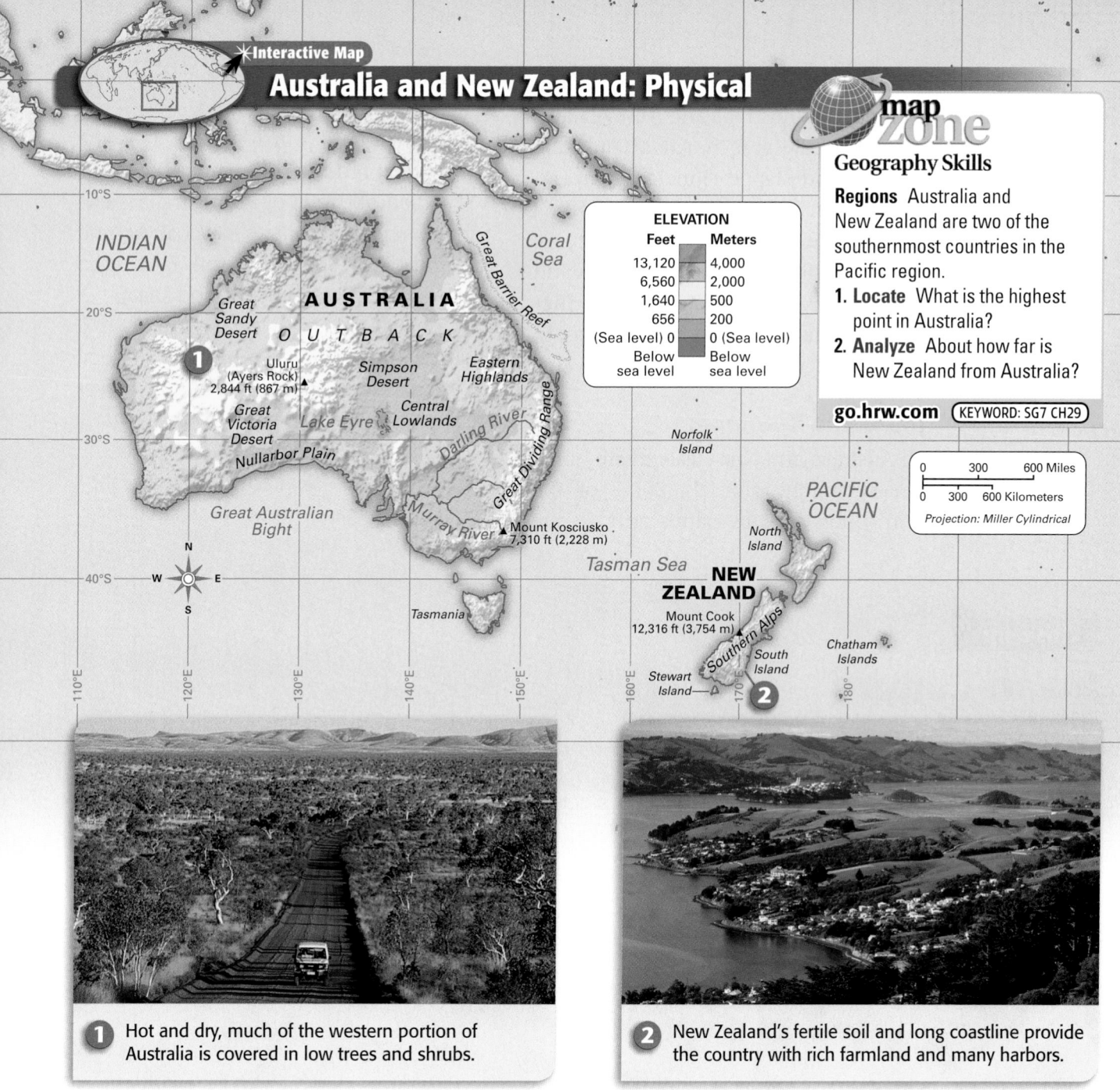

map Zone

Geography Skills

Regions Australia and New Zealand are two of the southernmost countries in the Pacific region.
1. **Locate** What is the highest point in Australia?
2. **Analyze** About how far is New Zealand from Australia?

go.hrw.com   KEYWORD: SG7 CH29

INDIAN OCEAN

Coral Sea

Great Barrier Reef

AUSTRALIA

O U T B A C K

Great Sandy Desert

Uluru (Ayers Rock) ▲ 2,844 ft (867 m)

Simpson Desert

Eastern Highlands

Great Victoria Desert

Central Lowlands

Lake Eyre

Darling River

Nullarbor Plain

Great Australian Bight

Murray River

Great Dividing Range

▲ Mount Kosciusko 7,310 ft (2,228 m)

Tasmania

Tasman Sea

Norfolk Island

PACIFIC OCEAN

North Island

NEW ZEALAND

Mount Cook 12,316 ft (3,754 m)

Southern Alps

South Island

Chatham Islands

Stewart Island

ELEVATION

Feet	Meters
13,120	4,000
6,560	2,000
1,640	500
656	200
(Sea level) 0	0 (Sea level)
Below sea level	Below sea level

0   300   600 Miles
0   300   600 Kilometers
Projection: Miller Cylindrical

① Hot and dry, much of the western portion of Australia is covered in low trees and shrubs.

② New Zealand's fertile soil and long coastline provide the country with rich farmland and many harbors.

coasts. Off Australia's northeastern coast is the **Great Barrier Reef**, the world's largest coral reef. A **coral reef** is a collection of rocky material found in shallow, tropical waters. The Great Barrier Reef is home to an incredible variety of marine animals.

New Zealand New Zealand, located some 1,000 miles southeast of Australia, includes two main islands, North Island and South Island. North Island is covered by hills and coastal plains. It is also home to volcanoes, geysers, and hot springs. One of the key features on South Island is a large mountain range called the Southern Alps. Thick forests, deep lakes, and even glaciers are found in the Southern Alps. The rest of the island is covered by fertile hills and rich plains. Fjords, or narrow inlets of the sea, create many natural harbors along the coasts of both islands.

Climates

The climates of Australia and New Zealand differ greatly. Because much of Australia has desert and steppe climates, temperatures are warm and rainfall is limited. However, along the coasts the climate is more temperate. Unlike Australia, New Zealand is mild and wet. A marine climate brings plentiful rainfall and mild temperatures to much of the country.

Wildlife and Resources

Both Australia and New Zealand are home to many unique animals. Some of the region's most famous native animals are Australia's kangaroo and koala and New Zealand's kiwi, a flightless bird.

Australia is rich in resources. It is the world's top producer of bauxite and lead as well as diamonds and opals. Australia is also home to energy resources like coal, natural gas, and oil. Despite poor soil, farms and ranches raise wheat, cotton, and sheep.

Unlike Australia, New Zealand has a great deal of fertile land but few mineral resources. New Zealand's main resources are wool, timber, and gold.

READING CHECK **Contrasting** How does the physical geography of the two countries differ?

Maori Culture

The Maori, the descendants of New Zealand's earliest settlers, lived in small settlements throughout the islands. Their rich culture and traditions are still alive in New Zealand today.

Beautifully decorated store-houses served as a sign of a village's wealth and power. They often held weapons, tools, and foods.

The *moko*, or tattoos, of Maori warriors were symbols of a warrior's bravery. They also helped intimidate the enemy during battle.

The Maori used elaborately carved war canoes to launch attacks on their enemies.

History

Despite their many geographic differences, Australia and New Zealand share a similar history. Both countries were originally inhabited by settlers from other parts of the Pacific. Later, both Australia and New Zealand were colonized by the British.

Early Settlers

The first settlers in Australia likely migrated there from Southeast Asia at least 40,000 years ago. These settlers, the **Aborigines** (a-buh-RIJ-uh-nees), were the first humans to live in Australia. Early Aborigines were nomads who gathered various plants and hunted animals with boomerangs and spears. Nature played an important role in the religion of the early Aborigines, who believed that it was their duty to preserve the land.

New Zealand's first settlers came from other Pacific islands more recently, about 1,200 years ago. The descendants of these early settlers, the **Maori** (MOWR-ee), settled throughout New Zealand. Like Australia's Aborigines, the Maori were fishers and hunters. Unlike the Aborigines, however, the Maori also used farming to survive.

The Arrival of Europeans

European explorers first sighted Australia and New Zealand in the 1600s. It wasn't until later, however, that Europeans began to explore the region. In 1769 British explorer James Cook explored the main islands of New Zealand. The following year, Cook landed on the east coast of Australia and claimed the land for Britain.

Within 20 years of Cook's claim, the British began settling in Australia. Many of the first to arrive were British prisoners, but other settlers came, too. As the settlers built farms and ranches, they took over the Aborigines' lands. Many Aborigines died of diseases introduced by the Europeans.

In New Zealand, large numbers of British settlers started to arrive in the early 1800s. After the British signed a treaty with the Maori in 1840, New Zealand became a part of the British Empire. However, tensions between the Maori and British settlers led to a series of wars over land.

Australia and New Zealand both gained their independence in the early 1900s. Today the two countries are members of the British Commonwealth of Nations and are close allies of the United Kingdom.

READING CHECK **Finding Main Ideas** How did early settlers influence the region?

Maori life centered around a village meetinghouse, where important gatherings like weddings and funerals were held.

ANALYSIS SKILL **ANALYZING VISUALS**

Based on the illustration, what elements were important in Maori culture?

FOCUS ON READING

What conclusions can you draw about why European settlers were attracted to Australia?

Australian Sports

Outdoor sports are tremendously popular in sunny Australia. Some of Australia's most popular activities include water sports, such as swimming, surfing, and water polo. In recent years, many Australians have dominated the swimming competition at the summer Olympic Games.

Australia's national sport is cricket, a game played with a bat and ball. Cricket was first introduced to Australia by British settlers. Other popular sports with British roots are rugby and Australian Rules football. These two sports allow players to kick, carry, or pass the ball with their hands or feet. Every year hundreds of thousands of Australians attend professional rugby matches like the one in the photo below.

Drawing Conclusions Why do you think outdoor sports are so popular in Australia?

Australia and New Zealand Today

Despite their isolation from other nations, Australia and New Zealand today are rich and well-developed. Their governments, economies, and people make them among the world's most successful countries.

Government

As former British colonies, the British style of government has influenced both Australia and New Zealand. As a result, both countries have similar governments.

For example, the British monarch is the head of state in both Australia and New Zealand. Both countries are parliamentary democracies, a type of government in which citizens elect members to represent them in a parliament. Each country has a prime minister. The prime minister, along with Parliament, runs the government.

The governments of Australia and New Zealand have many features in common with the U.S. government. For example, Australia has a federal system like that of the United States. In this system, a central government shares power with the states. Australia's Parliament, similar to the U.S. Congress, consists of two houses—a House of Representatives and a Senate. A Bill of Rights also protects the individual rights of New Zealand's citizens.

Economy

Australia and New Zealand are both rich, economically developed countries. Agriculture is a major part of their economies. The two countries are among the world's top producers of wool. In fact, Australia regularly supplies about one-quarter of the wool used in clothing. Both countries also export meat and dairy products.

Australia and New Zealand also have other important industries. Mining is one of Australia's main industries. Companies mine bauxite, gold, and uranium throughout the **Outback**, Australia's interior. Other industries include steel, heavy machines, and computers. New Zealand has also become more industrialized in recent years. Factories turn out processed food, clothing, and paper products. Banking, insurance, and tourism are also important industries.

People

Today Australia and New Zealand have diverse populations. Most Australians and New Zealanders are of British ancestry. In recent years, however, peoples from around the world have migrated to the region. For example, since the 1970s Asians and Pacific Islanders have settled in Australia and New Zealand in growing numbers.

Native Maori and Aborigines make up only a small percentage of New Zealand's and Australia's populations. One challenge facing both countries today is improving the economic and political status of the those populations. Many of the region's Maori and Aborigines trail the rest of the population in terms of education, land ownership, and employment.

Most Australians and New Zealanders live in urban areas. About 90 percent of Australia's population lives in large cities along the coasts. Sydney and Melbourne, Australia's two largest cities, are home to almost 8 million people. Rural areas like the Outback, on the other hand, have less than 10 percent of the population. In New Zealand, a majority of the population lives on the North Island. There, large cities like Auckland are common.

READING CHECK Summarizing What are the economic strengths of these countries?

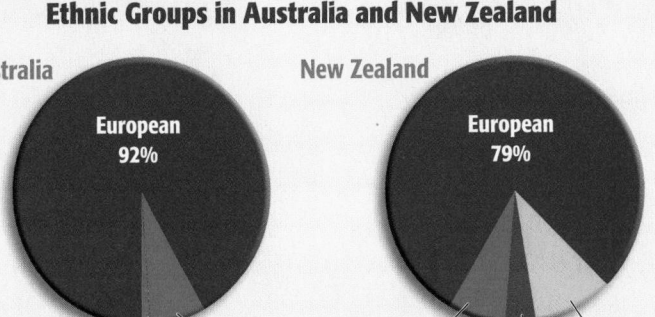

Ethnic Groups in Australia and New Zealand

Australia

European 92%

Aboriginal and other 1%   Asian 7%

New Zealand

European 79%

Asian and other 7%   Pacific Islander 4%   Maori 10%

Comparing and Contrasting In what ways are the ethnic populations of Australia and New Zealand similar and different?

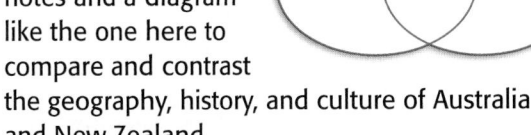
go.hrw.com KEYWORD: SG7 CH29

SUMMARY AND PREVIEW Despite their geographical differences, Australia and New Zealand have much in common. The two countries share a similar history, culture, and economy. In the next section you will learn about another region in the Pacific world—the Pacific Islands.

Section 1 Assessment

go.hrw.com
Online Quiz
KEYWORD: SG7 HP29

Reviewing Ideas, Terms, and Places

1. **a. Identify** What is the **Great Barrier Reef**? Where is it located?
   b. Elaborate Given its harsh climate, why do you think so many people have settled in Australia?
2. **a. Describe** Who are the **Maori**? From where did they originate?
   b. Draw Conclusions How might the **Aborigines'** relationship with nature have differed from that of other peoples?
3. **a. Recall** Where do most Australians and New Zealanders live?
   b. Compare and Contrast How are the governments of Australia and New Zealand similar to and different from that of the United States?

Critical Thinking

4. **Comparing and Contrasting** Use your notes and a diagram like the one here to compare and contrast the geography, history, and culture of Australia and New Zealand.

Australia   Both   New Zealand

FOCUS ON WRITING

5. **Describing Australia and New Zealand** What natural resources do these two countries produce? Make a list of the ones people might want to invest in. What illustrations could you include?

Settling the Pacific

For years scholars have puzzled over a mystery in the Pacific. How exactly did humans reach the thousands of islands scattered throughout the Pacific world? While we don't know all the details, evidence suggests that people from Southeast Asia originally settled the Pacific Islands. Over tens of thousands of years these people and their descendants slowly migrated throughout the Pacific. Thanks to expert canoe-building and navigational skills, these settlers reached islands many thousands of miles apart.

Many long-distance voyages were likely made on double canoes built with two hulls carved from huge logs.

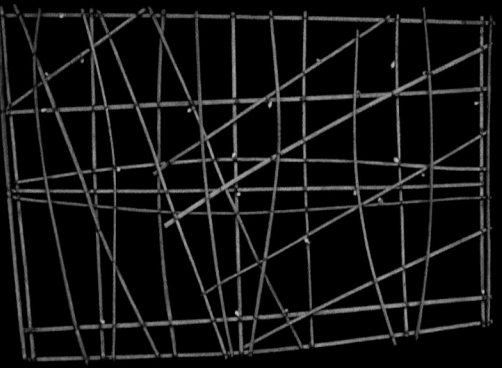

Stick Charts Stick charts like this one from the Marshall Islands were probably used to navigate from island to island. The sticks show the direction of waves and ocean currents. Shells indicate the location of islands and other landmarks.

Settling the Pacific

map zone

Pacific Ocean

Hawaiian Islands

PHILIPPINES

Mariana Islands

MICRONESIA

Marshall Islands

MELANESIA

INDONESIA

NEW GUINEA

Solomon Islands

POLYNESIA

Samoa

Coral Sea

Fiji   Tonga

Tahiti

AUSTRALIA

Easter Island

NEW ZEALAND

c. 50,000 BC–25,000 BC
c. 1500 BC–AD 1
c. AD 1–1000

Double canoes used one or two sails and could reach speeds of up to 25 miles per hour (41 km per hour).

Double-hulled canoes likely included a shelter to store food, seeds, and other essentials.

Settlers took along food items, such as dried bananas, and animals such as pigs and chickens.

Three Waves The Pacific world was settled in three main waves. People from Southeast Asia migrated first to Australia and New Guinea. Over thousands of years migrations took place from Southeast Asia and New Guinea to the islands of Micronesia and western Polynesia. In the last great wave of migration, Polynesians settled New Zealand, Hawaii, and Easter Island.

ANALYSIS SKILL **ANALYZING VISUALS**

1. What were the last Pacific islands to be settled?
2. Why might the settlers have taken seeds and animals on their journey?

725

Locating Information

Learn

Your teacher has asked you to find information about New Zealand's Maori. Where should you go? What should you do? The best place to start your search for information is in the library. The chart at right includes some library resources you may find helpful.

Practice

Determine which of the sources described here you would most likely use to locate the information in the questions that follow.

❶ Which different sources could you use to find information about Maori culture?

❷ In which source would you most likely find maps of Maori migration routes to New Zealand?

❸ Where might you look to find videos about Maori art and music?

❹ Which resource would be best for locating information about the current population of Maori in New Zealand?

Library Resources	
almanac	a collection of current statistics and general information usually published annually
atlas	a collection of maps and charts
electronic database	a collection of information you can access and search by computer
encyclopedias	books or computer software with short articles on a variety of subjects, usually arranged in alphabetical order
magazine and newspaper indexes	listings of recent and past articles from newspapers and magazines
online catalog	a computerized listing of books, videos, and other library resources; you search for resources by title, author, keyword, or subject
World Wide Web	a collection of information on the Internet; if you use a Web site, be sure to carefully examine its reliability, or trustworthiness

Apply

Use resources from a local library to answer the questions below.

1. About when did the Maori first settle in New Zealand?

2. What different subtopics can you find on the Maori in the library catalog?

3. Write a list of important facts about the Maori.

The Pacific Islands

If **YOU** lived there...

You live on a small island in the South Pacific. For many years, the people on your island have made their living by fishing. Now, however, a European company has expressed interest in building an airport and a luxury hotel on your island. It hopes that tourists will be drawn by the island's dazzling beaches and tropical climate. The company's leaders want your permission before they build.

Will you give them permission? Why or why not?

BUILDING BACKGROUND Thousands of islands are scattered across the Pacific Ocean. Many of these islands are tiny and have few mineral resources. Among the resources they do have are pleasant climates and scenic landscapes. As a result, many Pacific islands have become popular tourist destinations.

Physical Geography

The Pacific Ocean covers more than one-third of Earth's surface. Scattered throughout this ocean are thousands of islands with similar physical features, climates, and resources.

Island Regions

We divide the Pacific Islands into three regions—Micronesia, Melanesia, and Polynesia—based on their culture and geography. **Micronesia**, which means "tiny islands," is located just east of the Philippines. Some 2,000 small islands make up this region. South of Micronesia is **Melanesia**, which stretches from New Guinea in the west to Fiji in the east. Melanesia is the most heavily populated Pacific Island region. The largest region is **Polynesia**, which means "many islands." Among Polynesia's many islands are Tonga, Samoa, and the Hawaiian Islands.

Physical Features

The Pacific Islands differ greatly. Some islands, like New Guinea (GI-nee), cover thousands of square miles. Other islands are tiny. For example, Nauru covers only 8 square miles (21 square km).

What You Will Learn...

Main Ideas

1. Unique physical features, tropical climates, and limited resources shape the physical geography of the Pacific Islands.
2. Native customs and contact with the western world have influenced the history and culture of the Pacific Islands.
3. Pacific Islanders today are working to improve their economies and protect the environment.

The Big Idea

The Pacific islands have tropical climates, rich cultures, and unique challenges.

Key Terms and Places

Micronesia, *p. 727*
Melanesia, *p. 727*
Polynesia, *p. 727*
atoll, *p. 728*
territory, *p. 729*

TAKING NOTES As you read, use a diagram like this one to take notes on the Pacific Islands.

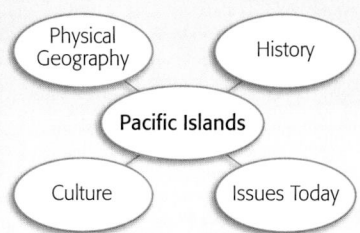

Geographers classify the islands of the Pacific as either high islands or low islands. High islands tend to be mountainous and rocky. Most high islands are volcanic islands. They were formed when volcanic mountains grew from the ocean floor and reached the surface. The islands of Tahiti and Hawaii in Polynesia are examples of high islands. Other high islands, such as New Guinea, are formed from continental rock rather than volcanoes. For example, the country of Papua (PA-pyooh-wuh) New Guinea, located on the eastern half of the island of New Guinea, has rocky mountains that rise above 13,000 feet (3,960 m).

Low islands are typically much smaller than high islands. Most barely rise above sea level. Many low islands are atolls. An **atoll** is a small, ring-shaped coral island that surrounds a lagoon. Wake Island, west of the Hawaiian Islands, is an example of an atoll. Wake Island rises only 21 feet (6.4 m) above sea level and covers only 2.5 square miles (6.5 square km).

High and Low Islands

Many high islands, like the island of Hawaii, often have mountainous terrain, rich soils, and dense rain forests. Many low islands, like this small island in the Society Islands chain, are formed from coral reefs. Because most low islands have poor soils, agriculture is limited.

Climate and Resources

All but two of the Pacific Island countries lie in the tropics. As a result, most islands have a humid tropical climate. Rain falls all year and temperatures are warm. Tropical savanna climates with rainy and dry seasons exist in a few places, such as New Caledonia. The mountains of New Guinea are home to a cool highland climate.

Resources in the Pacific Islands vary widely. Most low islands have thin soils and little vegetation. They have few trees other than the coconut palm. In addition, low islands have few mineral or energy resources. Partly because of these conditions, low islands have small populations.

In contrast to low islands, the Pacific's high islands have many natural resources. Volcanic soils provide fertile farmland and dense forests. Farms produce crops such as coffee, cocoa, bananas, and sugarcane. Some high islands also have many mineral resources. Papua New Guinea, for example, exports gold, copper, and oil.

READING CHECK **Contrasting** How do the Pacific's low islands differ from high islands?

The Formation of an Atoll

The Pacific Islands are home to many atolls, or small coral islands that surround shallow lagoons. Coral reefs are formed from the skeletons of many tiny sea animals. When a coral reef forms on the edges of a volcanic island, it often forms a barrier reef around the island.

As the volcanic island sinks, the coral remains. Sand and other debris gradually collects on the reef's surface, raising the land above sea level. Eventually, all that remains is an atoll.

Sequencing Describe the process in which atolls form.

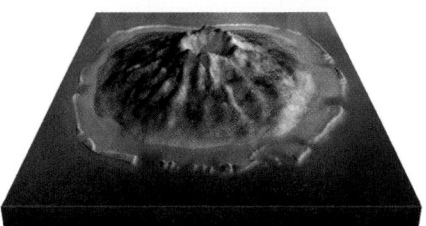

Coral reefs will sometimes form along the edges of a volcanic island, creating a ring around the island.

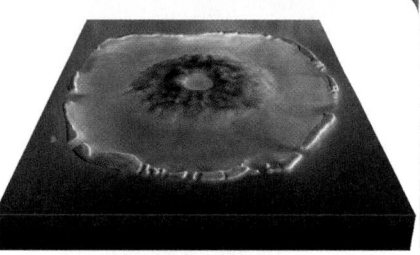

As the island sinks into the ocean floor, the coral reef grows upward and forms an offshore barrier reef.

Over time, sand collects on the surface of the reef, allowing grasses and shrubs to grow. When the island is submerged, the reef forms an atoll, or a ring of coral islands surrounding a lagoon.

History and Culture

The Pacific Islands were one of the last places settled by humans. Because of their isolation from other civilizations, the islands have a unique history and culture.

Early History

Scholars believe that people began settling the Pacific Islands at least 35,000 years ago. The large islands of Melanesia were the first to be settled. Over time, people spread to the islands of Micronesia and Polynesia.

Europeans first encountered the Pacific Islands in the 1500s. Two centuries later, British captain James Cook explored all the main Pacific Island regions. By the late 1800s European powers such as Spain, Great Britain, and France controlled most of the Pacific Islands.

Modern History

By the early 1900s, other countries were entering the Pacific as well. In 1898 the United States defeated Spain in the Spanish-American War. As a result, Guam became a U.S. territory. A **territory** is an area that is under the authority of another government. Japan also expanded its empire into the Pacific Ocean in the early 1900s. In World War II, the Pacific Islands were the scene of many tough battles between Allied and Japanese forces. After Japan's defeat in 1945, the United Nations placed some islands under the control of the United States and other Allies.

In the last half of the 1900s many Pacific Islands gained their independence. However, several countries—including the United States, France, and New Zealand—still have territories in the Pacific Islands.

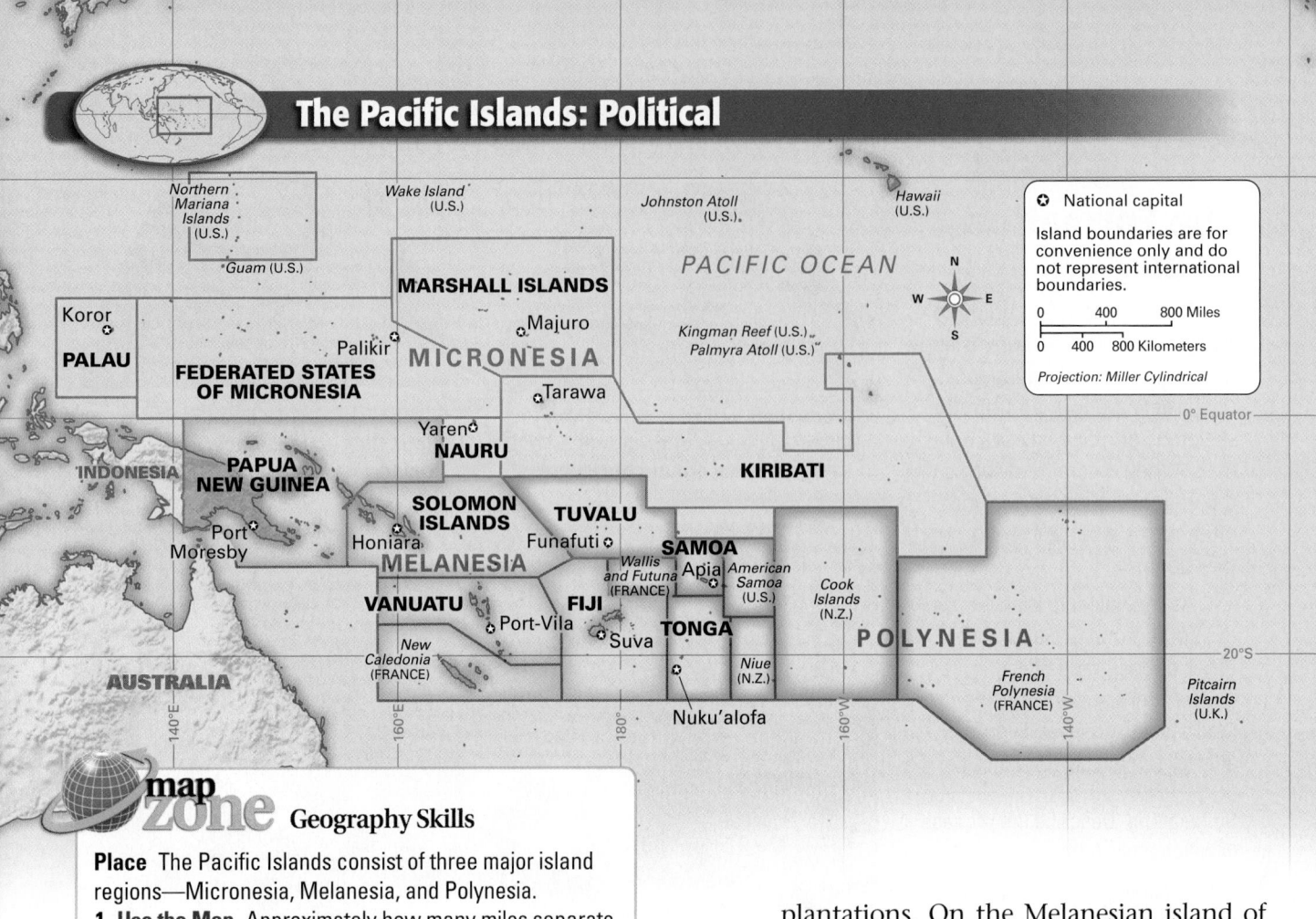

National capital

Island boundaries are for convenience only and do not represent international boundaries.

0   400   800 Miles

0   400   800 Kilometers

Projection: Miller Cylindrical

PACIFIC OCEAN

0° Equator

20°S

map zone Geography Skills

Place The Pacific Islands consist of three major island regions—Micronesia, Melanesia, and Polynesia.
1. **Use the Map** Approximately how many miles separate the islands of Palau and French Polynesia?
2. **Contrast** Based on the map, how do the Melanesian islands differ from those of French Polynesia?

Culture

A variety of cultures thrive throughout the Pacific Islands. Some culture traits, such as fishing, are common throughout the entire region. Others are only found on a specific island or island chain.

FOCUS ON READING

What can you conclude about the influence other cultures have had on the Pacific Islands?

People Close to 9 million people live in the Pacific Islands today. Most Pacific Islanders are descendants of the region's original settlers. However, the population of the Pacific Islands also includes large numbers of ethnic Europeans and Asians, particularly Indians and Chinese. Many ethnic Asians are descended from people brought to the islands to work on colonial plantations. On the Melanesian island of Fiji, for example, Indians make up nearly half of the population.

Before the arrival of Europeans, the people of the Pacific Islands practiced hundreds of different religions. Today most Pacific Islanders are Christian. In Melanesia, however, some people continue to practice traditional local religions.

Traditions Although modern culture exists throughout the Pacific Islands, many people continue to practice traditional customs. In parts of Polynesia, for example, people still construct their homes from bamboo and palm leaves. Many Pacific Islanders today continue to live in ancient villages, practice customary art styles, and hold ceremonies that feature traditional costumes and dances.

READING CHECK Making Inferences In what ways have the Pacific Islands been influenced by contact with westerners?

The Pacific Islands Today

Many people imagine sunny beaches and tourists when they think of the Pacific Islands today. Despite the region's healthy tourism industry, however, Pacific Island countries face important challenges.

The countries of the Pacific Islands have developing economies. Fishing, tourism, and agriculture are key industries. Some countries, particularly Papua New Guinea, export minerals and timber. The region's isolation from other countries, however, hinders its ability to trade.

The environment is an important concern in the Pacific Islands. The Pacific Islands were used for nuclear testing grounds from the 1940s to the 1990s. Many people fear that one **effect** of these tests may be health problems for people in the region. Global warming also concerns Pacific Islanders. Some researchers believe that rising temperatures may cause polar ice to melt. The rise in ocean levels would threaten low-lying Pacific Islands.

READING CHECK **Summarizing** What are some challenges Pacific Islanders face today?

Villagers on Tanna Island in Vanuatu perform a traditional dance.

SUMMARY AND PREVIEW The Pacific Islands are one of the most isolated regions in the world. As a result, unique cultures and challenges exist in the region. In the next section you will learn about another isolated part of the globe—Antarctica.

ACADEMIC VOCABULARY

effect the results of an action or decision

Section 2 Assessment

go.hrw.com
Online Quiz
KEYWORD: SG7 HP29

Reviewing Ideas, Terms, and Places

1. a. Describe Into what regions are the Pacific Islands divided?
b. Draw Conclusions Why might high islands have larger populations than low islands?
2. a. Define What is a **territory**?
b. Make Inferences Why did other countries seek to control the Pacific Islands?
c. Elaborate Why do you think that many Pacific Islanders continue to practice traditional customs?
3. a. Recall What economic resources are available to the Pacific Islands?
b. Predict How might the Pacific Islands be affected by global warming in the future?

Critical Thinking

4. Finding Main Ideas Draw a chart like the one shown. Using your notes, identify the main idea of each topic and write a sentence for each.

Physical Geography	History	Culture	Issues Today

FOCUS ON WRITING

5. Telling about the Resources of the Pacific Add to your list by noting the natural resources of the Pacific Islands. Which resources will you describe in your brochure? How might you describe them?

Antarctica

If YOU lived there...

You are a scientist working at a research laboratory in Antarctica. One day you receive an e-mail message from a friend. She wants to open a company that will lead public tours through Antarctica so people can see its spectacular icy landscapes and wildlife. Some of your fellow scientists think that tours are a good idea, while others think that they could ruin the local environment.

What will you tell your friend?

What You Will Learn...

Main Ideas

1. Freezing temperatures, ice, and snow dominate Antarctica's physical geography.
2. Explorations in the 1800s and 1900s led to Antarctica's use for scientific research.
3. Research and protecting the environment are key issues in Antarctica today.

The Big Idea

Antarctica's unique environment has made it an important site for research.

Key Terms and Places

ice shelf, *p. 733*
icebergs, *p. 733*
Antarctic Peninsula, *p. 733*
polar desert, *p. 733*
ozone layer, *p. 734*

TAKING NOTES As you read, take notes on Antarctica's physical geography, early exploration, and issues today. Record your notes in a graphic organizer like the one below.

Physical Geography	Early Explorers	Antarctica Today

BUILDING BACKGROUND Antarctica, the continent surrounding the South Pole, has no permanent residents. The only people there are scientists who research the frozen land. For many years, people around the world have debated the best way to use this frozen land.

Physical Geography

In the southernmost part of the world is the continent of Antarctica. This frozen land is very different from any other place on Earth.

The Land

Ice covers about 98 percent of Antarctica's 5.4 million square miles (14 million square km). This ice sheet contains more than 90 percent of the world's ice. On average the ice sheet is more than 1 mile (1.6 km) thick.

Penguins live in the icy waters around Antarctica, a continent almost completely covered in ice.

The weight of Antarctica's ice sheet causes ice to flow slowly off the continent. As the ice reaches the coast, it forms a ledge over the surrounding seas. This ledge of ice that extends over the water is called an **ice shelf**. Antarctica's ice shelves are huge. In fact, the Ross Ice Shelf, Antarctica's largest, is about the size of France.

Sometimes parts of the ice shelf break off into the surrounding water. Floating masses of ice that have broken off a glacier are **icebergs**. When one iceberg recently formed, it was approximately the size of the country of Luxembourg.

In western Antarctica, the **Antarctic Peninsula** extends north of the Antarctic Circle. As a result, temperatures there are often warmer than in other parts of the continent.

Climate and Resources

Most of Antarctica's interior is dominated by a freezing ice-cap climate. Temperatures can drop below –120°F (–84°C), and very little precipitation falls. As a result, much of Antarctica is considered a **polar desert**, a high-latitude region that receives very little precipitation. The precipitation that does fall does not melt due to the cold temperatures. Instead, it remains as ice.

Because of Antarctica's high latitude, the continent is in almost total darkness during winter months. Seas clog with ice as a result of the extreme temperatures.

In the summer, the sun shines around the clock and temperatures rise to near freezing.

Plant life only survives in the ice-free tundra areas. Insects are the frozen land's only land animals. Penguins, seals, and whales live in Antarctica's waters. Antarctica has many mineral resources, including iron ore, gold, copper, and coal.

READING CHECK **Summarizing** What are the physical features and resources of Antarctica?

Primary Source

BOOK
Crossing Antarctica

In 1989 a six-person team set off to cross Antarctica on foot. The 3,700-mile journey took seven months to complete. Team member Will Steger describes his first view of the continent.

> Now, flying over the iceberg-laden Weddell Sea, the biggest adventure of my life was about to begin . . .
>
> To the south I could barely pick out the peaks of mountains, mountains I knew jutted three thousand feet into the air. They lined the peninsula's coast for hundreds of miles. Leading up to them was a two-mile-wide sheet of snow and ice, preceded by the blue of the sea. It was a picture of purity, similar to many I had seen in the picture books . . .

—from *Crossing Antarctica*, by Will Steger and John Bowermaster

ANALYSIS SKILL **ANALYZING PRIMARY SOURCES**

What physical features does the author notice on his trip over Antarctica?

Sir Ernest Shackleton
(1874–1922)

Irish-born Ernest Shackleton was one of several early explorers of Antarctica. Shackleton led a British expedition in 1907–1909 that climbed Mt. Erebus, an active volcano, discovered the Beardmore Glacier, and came within 97 miles of the South Pole—the farthest south anyone had ever been.

In the early 1900s several expeditions set out to find the South Pole. The first to reach the pole were members of a Norwegian expedition led by Roald Amundsen. In this photo a member of the Norwegian expedition poses with his team of dogs near the flag that marks the South Pole.

Early Explorations

The discovery of Antarctica is a fairly recent one. Although explorers long believed there was a southern continent, it was not until 1775 that James Cook first sighted the Antarctic Peninsula. In the 1800s explorers first investigated Antarctica. One **motive** of many explorers was to discover the South Pole and other new lands. In 1911 a team of Norwegian explorers became the first people to reach the South Pole.

Since then, several countries—including the United States, Australia, and Chile—have claimed parts of Antarctica. In 1959 the international Antarctic Treaty was signed to preserve the continent "for science and peace." This treaty banned military activity in Antarctica and set aside the entire continent for research.

READING CHECK **Making Inferences** Why do you think Antarctica is set aside for research?

ACADEMIC VOCABULARY

motive
a reason for doing something

FOCUS ON READING

What conclusions can you draw about why some countries wanted to preserve Antarctica for research?

Antarctica Today

Today Antarctica is the only continent without a permanent human population. Scientists use the continent to conduct research and to monitor the environment.

Scientific Research

While they are conducting research in Antarctica, researchers live in bases, or stations. Several countries, including the United States, the United Kingdom, and Russia, have bases in Antarctica.

Antarctic research covers a wide range of topics. Some scientists concentrate on the continent's plant and animal life. Others examine weather conditions. One group of researchers is studying Earth's ozone layer. The **ozone layer** is a layer of Earth's atmosphere that protects living things from the harmful effects of the sun's ultraviolet rays. Scientists have found a thinning in the ozone layer above Antarctica.

Environmental Threats

Many people today are concerned about Antarctica's environment. Over the years, researchers and tourists have left behind trash and sewage, polluting the environment. Oil spills have damaged surrounding seas. In addition, companies have hoped to exploit Antarctica's valuable resources.

Some people fear that any mining of the resources in Antarctica will result in more environmental problems. To prevent this, a new international agreement was reached in 1991. This agreement forbids most activities that do not have a scientific purpose. It bans mining and drilling and limits tourism.

READING CHECK **Finding Main Ideas** What are some issues that affect Antarctica today?

SUMMARY In this section, you have learned about Antarctica's unusual physical geography and harsh climates. Despite the difficulty of living in such harsh conditions, Antarctica remains an important place for scientific research.

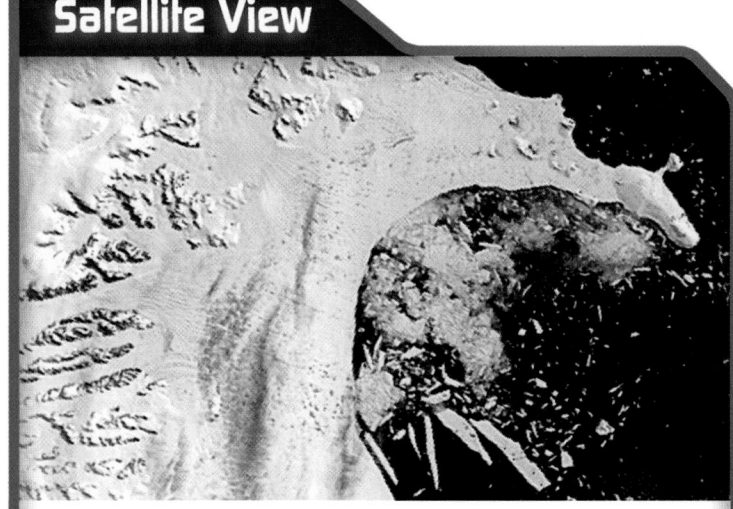

Satellite View

Antarctica's Ice Shelves

Antarctica is home to many large ice shelves. An ice shelf is a piece of a glacier that extends over the surrounding seas. In recent years, scientists have become concerned that rising temperatures on the planet are causing the rapid disintegration of some of Antarctica's ice shelves. This satellite image from 2002 shows the breakup of a huge portion of Antarctica's Larsen B Ice Shelf, located on the Antarctic Peninsula. The breakup of this ice shelf released some 720 billion tons of ice into the Weddell Sea.

Identifying Cause and Effect What do scientists believe has led to growing disintegration of Antarctica's ice shelves?

Section 3 Assessment

go.hrw.com
Online Quiz
KEYWORD: SG7 HP29

Reviewing Ideas, Terms, and Places

1. **a. Define** What are **ice shelves** and **icebergs**?
   b. Contrast How does Antarctica differ from most other continents?
   c. Elaborate What aspects of Antarctica's physical geography would you most like to see? Why?
2. **a. Identify** What was the Antarctic Treaty of 1959?
   b. Predict What might have happened if countries had not agreed to preserve Antarctica for research?
3. **a. Recall** What is Antarctica used for today?
   b. Analyze How has Antarctic research benefited science?
   c. Elaborate Do you agree with bans on tourism and mining in Antarctica? Why or why not?

Critical Thinking

4. **Summarizing** Draw a diagram like the one here. Use your notes to list three facts about each aspect of Antarctica's physical geography.

Physical Geography	→	
Early Explorers	→	
Antarctica Today	→	

FOCUS ON WRITING

5. **Describing Antarctica** In your notebook, describe the natural resources of Antarctica. Decide which to include in your brochure. What illustrations might you include?

from
Antarctic Journal:
Four Months at the Bottom of the World

by Jennifer Owings Dewey

Adelie penguins jump off an iceberg near Antarctica.

GUIDED READING

WORD HELP

rampart an embankment made of earth used for protection

❶ The Weddell Sea is a part of the Southern Ocean, which borders the western part of Antarctica.

About the Reading *In her book,* Antarctic Journal: Four Months at the Bottom of the World, *writer and artist Jennifer Owings Dewey describes her four-month visit to Antarctica as a visiting researcher at Palmer research station.*

AS YOU READ Identify what the icebergs mean to the author.

Coming back we see icebergs drifting south out of the Weddell Sea. ❶ The bergs originate hundreds of miles away and ride ocean currents.

We sail close, but not too close, for beneath the waves is where the bulk of an iceberg is.

Seawater splashes up on iceberg shores shaped by years of wave action. Sunlight strikes gleaming ramparts that shine with rainbow colors. Erosion works at the ice, creating caves and hollows, coves and inlets.

Penguins and seals hitch rides on icebergs. Gulls and other seabirds rest on high points.

One iceberg collides in slow motion with another. The smaller one topples, rolls, and heaves like a dying rhinoceros, emerald seawater mixed with spray drenching its surfaces.

I yearn to ride an iceberg like a penguin or a gull, touching its frozen sides, drifting slowly on the waves. I draw them, but I can't capture their splendour.

Connecting Literature to Geography

1. **Describe** What details in the passage tell you that the icebergs are in motion?
2. **Compare and Contrast** The author was clearly moved by the beauty of the place she was observing. Think of a place you have seen in your community that made a lasting impression on your senses. Tell how the author's description of icebergs is like your own experience. Then explain how the two experiences are different.

Geography's Impact
video series
Review the video to answer the closing question:
What are some ways to help prevent or limit the spread of nonnative species?

Visual Summary

Use the visual summary below to help you review the main ideas of the chapter.

QUICK FACTS

Australia and New Zealand
Despite different physical features, Australia and New Zealand have much in common.

The Pacific Islands
The Pacific Islands are home to tropical climates and beautiful beaches.

Antarctica
Antarctica's unique environment makes it an important site for scientific research.

Reviewing Vocabulary, Terms, and Places

Choose the letter of the answer that best completes each statement below.

1. The original inhabitants of Australia are the
   a. Aborigines **c.** Papuans
   b. Maori **d.** Polynesians

2. A floating mass of ice that has broken off a glacier is a(n)
   a. atoll **c.** iceberg
   b. coral reef **d.** polar desert

3. Located off the northeast coast of Australia, this is the world's largest coral reef
   a. Australian Reef **c.** Kiwi Reef
   b. Great Barrier Reef **d.** Reef of the Coral Sea

4. The result of an action or decision is a(n)
   a. agreement **c.** motive
   b. effect **d.** purpose

Comprehension and Critical Thinking

SECTION 1 *(Pages 718–723)*

5. **a. Describe** What is the physical geography of Australia like?

   b. Compare and Contrast In what ways are the countries of Australia and New Zealand similar and different?

   c. Elaborate Why do you think the economies of Australia and New Zealand are so strong?

SECTION 2 *(Pages 727–731)*

6. **a. Identify** What two types of islands are commonly found in the Pacific Ocean? How are they different?

   b. Analyze How were the islands of the Pacific Ocean originally settled?

   c. Elaborate Many Pacific Islands are very isolated from other societies. Would you want to live in these isolated communities? Why or why not?

SECTION 3 *(Pages 732–735)*

7. a. Describe What types of wildlife are found in and around Antarctica?

b. Draw Conclusions Why do you think many of the world's countries supported setting aside Antarctica for scientific research?

c. Predict What effects might the thinning of the ozone layer have on Antarctica?

Social Studies Skills

Locating Information *Use your knowledge about locating information to answer the questions below.*

8. Where might you look to find information about recent weather statistics in Antarctica?

9. What types of sources might you use to find books about early explorations of Antarctica?

10. What sources could you use to find electronic resources about Antarctica?

FOCUS ON READING AND WRITING

Drawing Conclusions *Read the paragraph below, then answer the questions that follow.*

> Getting an education can be a challenge in the Outback, where students are spread across vast distances. Basic education comes from the School of the Air, which broadcasts classes via radio. Other lessons are conducted by videotape or mail. The use of the Internet, e-mail, and videoconferencing has been used in recent years.

11. What did you know about education and Australia before you read this paragraph?

12. What conclusion(s) can you draw about education in Australia's Outback?

Writing a Brochure *Use your notes and the directions below to create a brochure.*

13. Divide your brochure into sections—one on Australia and New Zealand, one on the Pacific Islands, and one on Antarctica. In each section, identify the important resources and try to convince the reader to invest in them. Use illustrations to support the points you want to make. Finally, design a cover page for your brochure.

Using the Internet

go.hrw.com
KEYWORD: SG7 CH29

14. Activity: Creating a Display The original people of Australia, the Aborigines, came from Southeast Asia at least 40,000 years ago. Today many Aborigines work to keep their languages, religion, and customs alive. Enter the activity keyword. Take notes about Aborigine culture as you view the Web sites. Then create a visual display or multimedia presentation featuring the interesting things you discover about their dreamtime, art, music, and more.

Map Activity ✳Interactive

15. The Pacific World On a separate sheet of paper, match the letters on the map with their correct labels.

Great Barrier Reef	Pacific Ocean
Melbourne	Papua New Guinea
North Island	Perth
Outback	Sydney

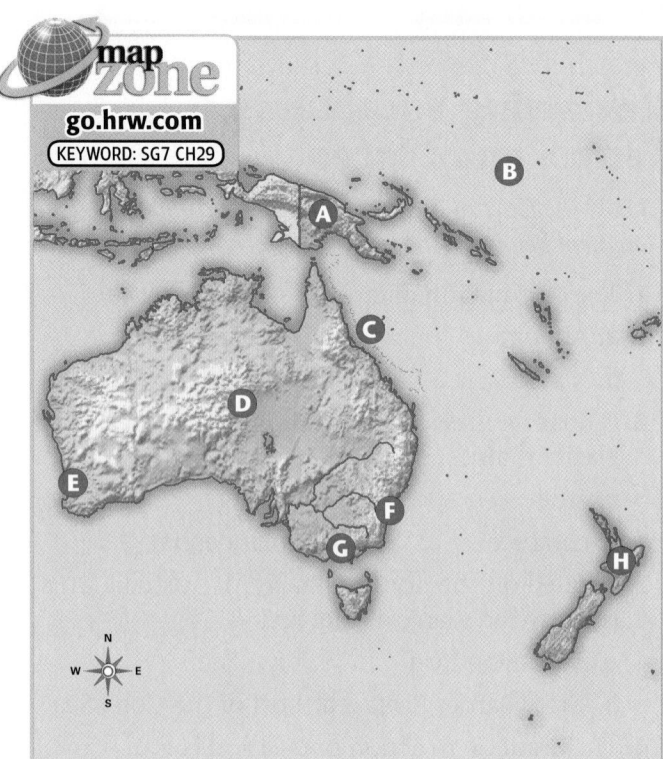

map zone
go.hrw.com
KEYWORD: SG7 CH29

DIRECTIONS: *Read questions 1 through 7 and write the letter of the best response. Then read question 8 and write your own well-constructed response.*

1 **What is the world's only country that is also a continent?**

A Australia

B Micronesia

C New Zealand

D Polynesia

2 **What physical feature lies off Australia's northeastern coast?**

A Nullarbor Plain

B Central Lowlands

C Great Barrier Reef

D Outback

3 **The descendants of the first people to live in New Zealand are called the**

A Aborigines.

B Maori.

C goa.

D kiwi.

4 **A ring-shaped island surrounding a lagoon is called**

A a high island.

B a low island.

C an atoll.

D a territory.

5 **The only people who live in Antarctica are**

A scientists.

B tourists.

C miners.

D government officials.

Australia and New Zealand: Climate

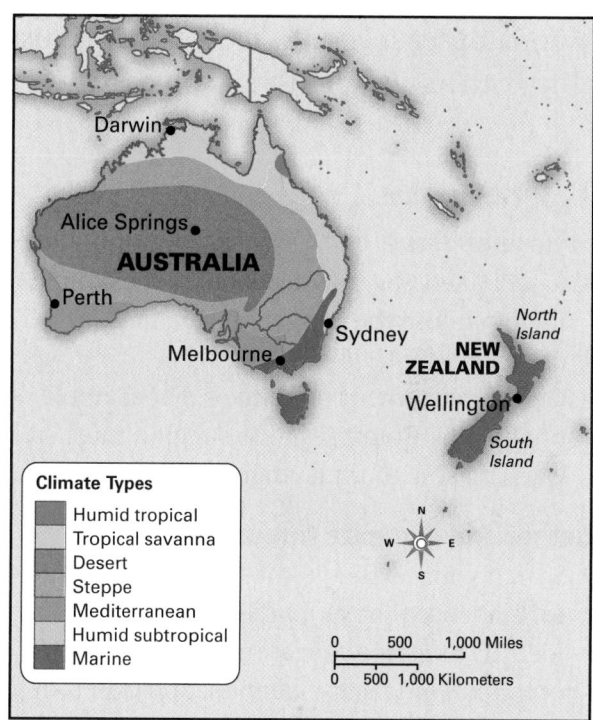

6 **According to the map above, what city has a desert climate?**

A Alice Springs

B Melbourne

C Perth

D Wellington

7 **According to the map, New Zealand has what kind of climate?**

A humid tropical

B steppe

C tropical savanna

D marine

8 **Extended Response** The vast majority of Australia's population lives along the coast, especially the east and southeast coasts. Study the map above. Then write a brief paragraph explaining why you think this is true.

Persuasion

Persuasion is about convincing others to act or believe in a certain way. Just as you use persuasion to convince your friends to see a certain movie, people use persuasion to convince others to help them solve the world's problems.

Assignment

Write a persuasive paper about an issue faced by the people of Asia and the Pacific. Choose an issue related to the natural environment or culture of the area.

1. Prewrite

Choose an Issue

- Choose an issue to write about. For example, you might choose the danger of tsunamis or the role of governments.
- Create a statement of opinion. For example, you might say, "Countries in this region must create a warning system for tsunamis."

Gather and Organize Information

- Search your textbook, the library, or the Internet for evidence that supports your opinion.
- Identify at least two reasons to support your opinion. Find facts, examples, and expert opinions to support each reason.

> **TIP** **That's a Reason** Convince your readers by presenting reasons to support your opinion. For example, one reason to create a warning system for tsunamis is to save lives.

2. Write

Use a Writer's Framework

A Writer's Framework

Introduction
- Start with a fact or question related to the issue you will discuss.
- Clearly state your opinion in a sentence.

Body
- Write one paragraph for each reason. Begin with the least important reason and end with the most important.
- Include facts, examples and expert opinions as support.

Conclusion
- Restate your opinion and summarize your reasons.

3. Evaluate and Revise

Review and Improve Your Paper

- As you review your paper, use the questions below to evaluate it.
- Make changes to improve your paper.

Evaluation Questions for a Persuasive Essay

1. Do you begin with an interesting fact or question related to the issue?
2. Does your introduction clearly state your opinion and provide any necessary background information?
3. Do you discuss your reasons from least to most important?
4. Do you provide facts, examples, or expert opinions to support each of your reasons?
5. Does your conclusion restate your opinion and summarize your reasons?

4. Proofread and Publish

Give Your Paper the Finishing Touch

- Make sure you have correctly spelled and capitalized all names of people or places.
- Check for correct comma usage when presenting a list of reasons or evidence.
- Decide how to share your paper. For example, could you publish it in a school paper or in a classroom collection of essays?

5. Practice and Apply

Use the steps and strategies outlined in this workshop to write your persuasive essay. Share your opinion with others to see whether they find your opinion convincing.

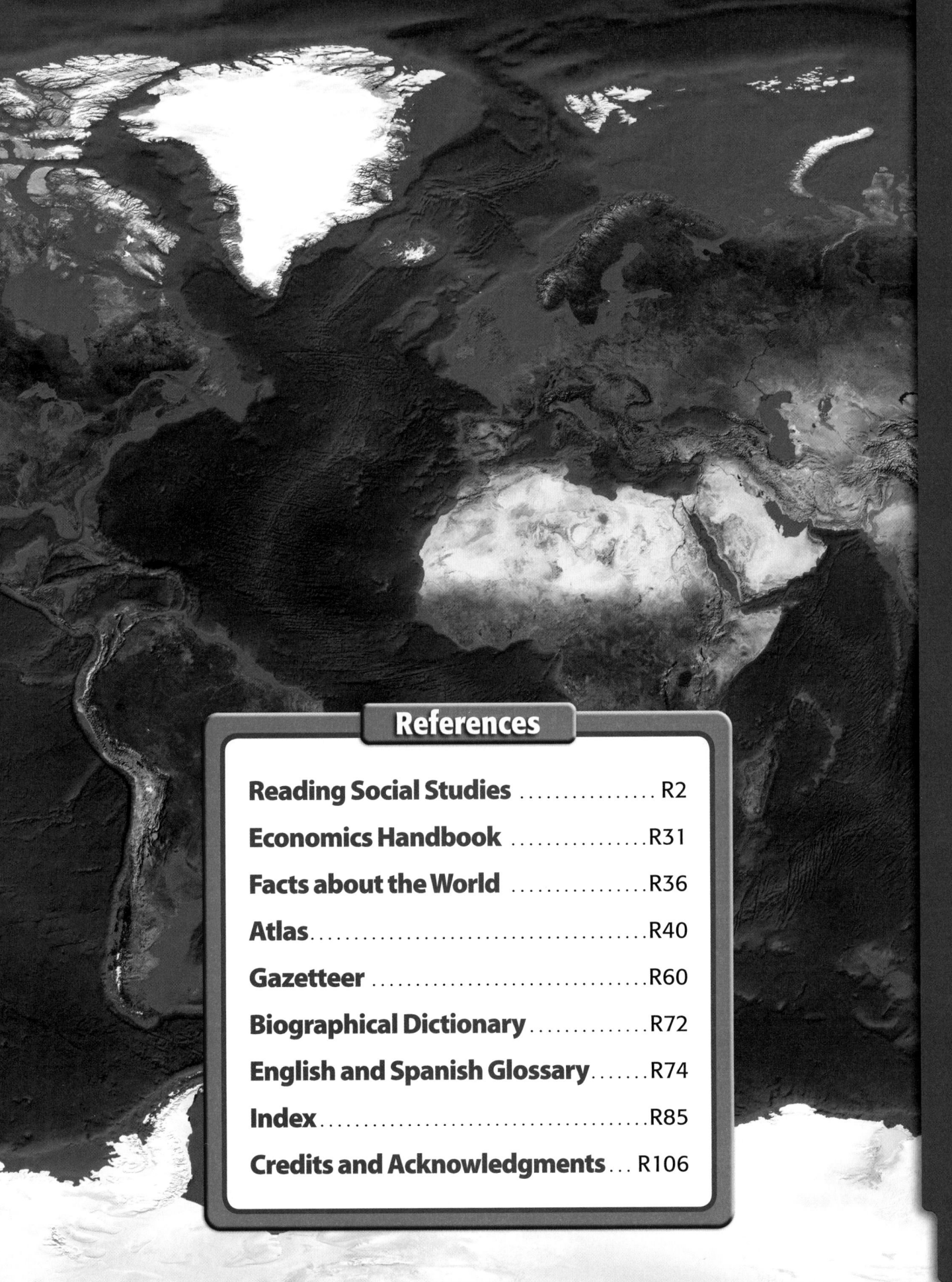

References

Using Prior Knowledge

FOCUS ON READING

When you put together a puzzle, you search for pieces that are missing to complete the picture. As you read, you do the same thing when you use prior knowledge. You take what you already know about a subject and then add the information you are reading to create a full picture. The example below shows how using prior knowledge about computer mapping helped one reader fill in the pieces about how geographers use computer mapping.

In the past, maps were always drawn by hand. Many were not very accurate. Today, though, most maps are made using computers and satellite images. Through advances in mapmaking, we can make accurate maps on almost any scale, from the whole world to a single neighborhood, and keep them up to date.

From Section 3, The Branches of Geography

Computer Mapping	
What I know before reading	What else I learned
• My dad uses the computer to get a map for trips. • I can find maps on the Internet of states and countries.	• Maps have not always been very accurate. • Computers help make new kinds of maps that are more than just cities and roads. • These computer maps are an important part of geography.

YOU TRY IT!

Draw a chart like the one above. Think about what you know about satellite images and list this prior knowledge in the left column of your chart. Then read the passage below. Once you have read it, add what you learned about satellite images to the right column.

Much of the information gathered by these satellites is in the form of images. Geographers can study these images to see what an area looks like from above Earth. Satellites also collect information that we cannot see from the planet's surface. The information gathered by satellites helps geographers make accurate maps.

From Section 1, Studying Geography

Using Word Parts

FOCUS ON READING

Many English words are made up of several word parts: roots, prefixes, and suffixes. A root is the base of the word and carries the main meaning. A prefix is a letter or syllable added to the beginning of a root. A suffix is a letter or syllable added to the end to create new words. When you come across a new word, you can sometimes figure out the meaning by looking at its parts. Below are some common word parts and their meanings.

Common Roots		
Word Root	**Meaning**	**Sample Words**
-graph-	write, writing	autograph, biography
-vid-, -vis-	see	videotape, visible

Common Prefixes		
Prefix	**Meaning**	**Sample Words**
geo-	earth	geology
inter-	between, among	interpersonal, intercom
in-	not	ineffective
re-	again	restate, rebuild

Common Suffixes		
Suffix	**Meaning**	**Sample Words**
-ible	capable of	visible, responsible
-less	without	penniless, hopeless
-ment	result, action	commitment
-al	relating to	directional
-tion	the act or condition of	rotation, selection

YOU TRY IT!

Read the following words. First separate any prefixes or suffixes and identify the word's root. Use the chart above to define the root, the prefix, or the suffix. Then write a definition for each word.

geography	visualize	movement
seasonal	reshaping	interact
regardless	separation	invisible

Understanding Cause and Effect

FOCUS ON READING

Learning to identify causes and effects can help you understand geography. A **cause** is something that makes another thing happen. An **effect** is the result of something else that happened. A cause may have several effects, and an effect may have several causes. In addition, as you can see in the example below, causes and effects may occur in a chain. Then, each effect in turn becomes the cause for another event.

First cause

The Gulf Stream is a warm current that flows north along the U.S. East Coast. It then flows east across the Atlantic to become the North Atlantic Drift. As the warm current flows along northwestern Europe, it heats the air. Westerlies blow the warmed air across Europe. This process makes Europe warmer than it otherwise would be.

From Section 1, Weather and Climate

Last effect

Cause
Gulf Stream

↓

Effect
Warm water flows along the coast of northwest Europe.

↓

Effect
Warm water raises temperature of the air above.

↓

Effect
Winds blow warm air across Europe.

↓

Effect
Warm winds make Europe warmer.

YOU TRY IT!

Read the following sentences, and then use a graphic organizer like the one below right to analyze the cause and effects. Create as many boxes as you need to list the causes and effects.

Mountains also create wet and dry areas. . . A mountain forces wind blowing against it to rise. As it rises, the air cools and precipitation falls as rain or snow. Thus, the side of the mountain facing the wind is often green and lush. However, little moisture remains for the other side. This effect creates a rain shadow.

From Section 1, Weather and Climate

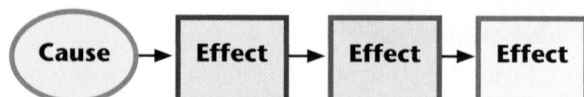

Understanding Main Ideas

FOCUS ON READING

Main ideas are like the hub of a wheel. The hub holds the wheel together, and everything circles around it. In a paragraph, the main idea holds the paragraph together and all the facts and details revolve around it. The main idea is usually stated clearly in a topic sentence, which may come at the beginning or end of a paragraph. Topic sentences always summarize the most important idea of a paragraph.

To find the main idea, ask yourself what one point is holding the paragraph together. See how the main idea in the following example holds all the details from the paragraph together.

A single country may also include more than one culture region within its borders. Mexico is one of many countries that is made up of different culture regions. People in northern Mexico and southern Mexico, for example, have different culture traits. The culture of northern Mexico tends to be more modern, while traditional culture remains strong in southern Mexico.

From Section 1, Culture

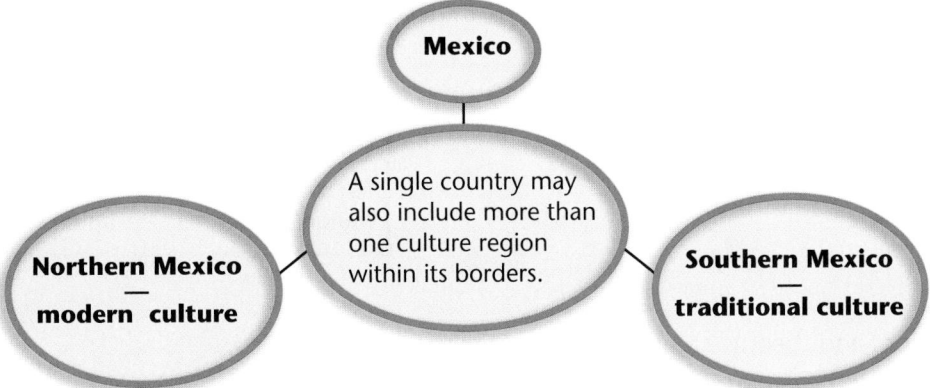

YOU TRY IT!

Read the following paragraph, and then use a graphic organizer like the one above to identify the main idea. Create as many circles as you need to list the supporting facts and details.

At the same time, the United States is influenced by global culture. Martial arts movies from Asia attract large audiences in the United States. Radio stations in the United States play music by African, Latin American, and European musicians. We even adopt many foreign words, like *sushi* and *plaza*, into English.

From Section 4, Global Connections

Categorizing

FOCUS ON READING

When you sort things into groups of similar items, you are categorizing. When you read, categorizing helps you to identify the main groups of information. Then you can find and see the individual facts in each group. Notice how the information in the paragraph below has been sorted into three main groups, with details listed under each group.

If you were traveling across the United States, you might start on the country's eastern coast. This low area, which is flat and close to sea level, is called the Atlantic Coastal Plain. As you go west, the land gradually rises higher to a region called the Piedmont. The Appalachian Mountains, which are the main mountain range in the East, rise above the Piedmont.

From Section 1, Physical Geography

Category 1:
Atlantic Coastal Plain
Details: low, flat, close to sea level

↓

Category 2:
Piedmont
Details: farther west & higher than Atlantic Coastal Plain

↓

Category 3:
Appalachian Mountains
Details: main Eastern mountain range, higher than Piedmont

YOU TRY IT!

Read the following paragraph, and then use a graphic organizer like the one above to categorize the group and details in the paragraph. Create as many boxes as you need to list the main groups.

The eastern United States has three climate regions. In the Northeast, people live in a humid continental climate with snowy winters and warm, humid summers. Southerners, on the other hand, experience milder winters and the warm, humid summers of a humid subtropical climate. Most of Florida is warm all year.

From Section 1, Physical Geography

READING SOCIAL STUDIES

Understanding Lists

FOCUS ON READING

A to-do list can keep you focused on what you need to get done. Keeping lists while you read can keep you focused on understanding the main points of a text. In the example below, a list helps the reader identify and focus on the types of cold climates found in central and northern Canada.

The farther north you go in Canada, the colder it gets. The coldest areas of Canada are located close to the Arctic Circle. Much of central and northern Canada has a subarctic climate. The far north has tundra and ice cap climates. About half of Canada lies in these extremely cold climates.

From Section 1, Physical Geography

List of cold climates
1. subarctic
2. tundra
3. ice cap

YOU TRY IT!

Read the sentences and then list the territories that make up the Canadian North region.

Northern Canada is extremely cold due to its location close to the Arctic Circle. The region called the Canadian North includes the Yukon Territory, the Northwest Territories, and Nunavut. These three territories cover more than a third of Canada but are home to only about 100,000 people.

From Section 3, Canada Today

Predicting

READING SOCIAL STUDIES *(side tab)*

FOCUS ON READING

Predicting is guessing what will happen next based on what you already know. In reading about geography, you can use what you know about the place you live to help you make predictions about other countries. Predicting helps you stay involved with your reading as you see whether your prediction was right. Your mind follows these four steps when you make predictions as you read:

Takes what you already know	→	Adds new information from your reading	→	Forms a prediction that makes sense	→	Confirms or adjusts your prediction based on what you just read

See how you might make a prediction from the following text:

> From snowcapped mountain peaks to warm, sunny beaches, Mexico has many different climates.
>
> *From Section 1, Physical Geography*

I know Mexico has warm weather and beaches.	→	Mexico has both mountains and beaches.	→	Maybe Mexico has some cool weather in the mountains.	→	The prediction was correct: "For example, the areas of high elevation on the Mexican Plateau can have surprisingly cool temperatures."

YOU TRY IT!

Read the following sentences. Then use a graphic organizer like the one below to help you predict what you will learn in your reading. Check the text in Section 3 to see if your prediction was correct.

> Mexico has a democratic government. However, Mexico is not like the United States where different political parties have always competed for power.
>
> *From Section 3, Mexico Today*

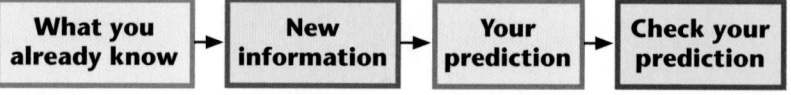

What you already know	→	New information	→	Your prediction	→	Check your prediction

Understanding Comparison-Contrast

FOCUS ON READING

Comparing shows how things are alike. Contrasting shows how things are different. You can understand comparison-contrast by learning to recognize clue words and points of comparison. Clue words let you know whether to look for similarities or differences. Points of comparison are the main topics that are being compared or contrasted.

Many Caribbean islands share a similar history and culture. However, today the islands' different economies, governments, and cultural landscapes encourage many different ways of life in the Caribbean.

From Section 3, The Caribbean Islands

Underlined words are clue words.

Highlighted words are points of comparison.

Clue Words	
Comparison	**Contrast**
share, similar, like, also, both, in addition, besides	however, while, unlike, different, but, although

YOU TRY IT!

Read the following passage to see how Haiti and the Dominican Republic are alike and different. Use a diagram like the one here to compare and contrast the two countries.

Haiti occupies the mountainous western third of the island of Hispaniola. Port-au-Prince is the capital and center of the country's limited industry. Agricultural products such as coffee and sugarcane are the country's main exports. Most Haitians farm small plots.

The Dominican Republic occupies the eastern part of Hispaniola. The Dominican Republic is not a rich country. However, its economy, health care, education, and housing are more developed than Haiti's. Agriculture is the basis of the economy

From Section 3, The Caribbean Islands

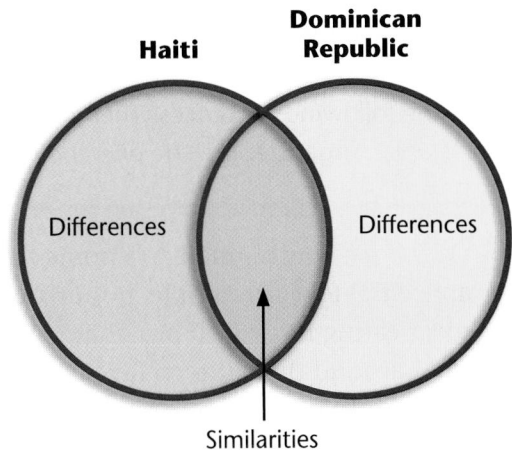

Haiti

Dominican Republic

Differences

Differences

Similarities

Identifying Supporting Details

FOCUS ON READING

Why believe what you read? One reason is because of details that support or prove the main idea. These details might be facts, statistics, examples, or definitions. In the example below, notice what kind of proof or supporting details help you believe the main idea.

Colombia's economy relies on several valuable resources. Rich soil, steep slopes, and tall shade trees produce world-famous Colombian coffee. Other major export crops include bananas, sugarcane, and cotton. Many farms in Colombia produce flowers that are exported around the world. In fact, 80 percent of the country's flowers are shipped to the United States.

From Section 2, Colombia

Main Idea
Colombia's economy relies on several valuable resources.

Supporting Details			
Example	**Fact**	**Fact**	**Statistic**
Colombian coffee	Other export crops	Export flowers	80 percent shipped to U.S.

YOU TRY IT!

Read the following sentences. Then identify the supporting details in a graphic organizer like the one above.

Caribbean South America is home to some remarkable wildlife. For example, hundreds of bird species, meat-eating fish called piranhas, and crocodiles live in or around the Orinoco River. Colombia has one of the world's highest concentrations of plant and animal species. The country's wildlife includes jaguars, ocelots, and several species of monkeys.

From Section 1, Physical Geography

Using Context Clues

FOCUS ON READING

One practical way to tackle unfamiliar words you encounter is to look at the context. Reading the words and sentences surrounding the word will often help you because they give definitions, examples, or synonyms. For example, maybe you're not sure what the word *context* means. Just from reading the previous sentences, however, you probably understood that it means the "the part of a text surrounding a word or passage that makes its meaning clear." You have relied on the context to help you define the word. In reading geography, you may forget what some of the geographical terms mean. You can use context clues to figure them out. See how this process works in the example below with the word *tributary*.

> The Amazon River is about 4,000 miles long. It extends from the Andes Mountains in Peru to the Atlantic Ocean. Hundreds of tributaries flow into it, draining an area that includes parts of most South American countries.
>
> *From Section 1, Physical Geography*

1. Look at the surrounding words or sentences.
The passage talks about the Amazon River and what flows into it.

2. Make a guess at the word's meaning.
A tributary must be a smaller river or stream that flows into a bigger river.

3. Check your guess by inserting it into the passage.
Hundreds of smaller rivers flow into it.

YOU TRY IT!

Read the following sentences, and then use the three steps described above to help you define *hydroelectric*.

> Atlantic South America also has good mineral and energy resources such as gold, silver, copper, iron, and oil. Dams on some of the region's large rivers also provide hydroelectric power.
>
> *From Section 1, Physical Geography*

Making Inferences

FOCUS ON READING

Sometimes reading effectively means understanding both what the writer tells you directly and what the writer doesn't tell you. When you fill in the gaps, you are making inferences, or educated guesses. Why worry about what the writer doesn't tell you? Making inferences can help you make connections with the text. It can also give you a fuller picture of the information. To make an inference, think about the text and what you know or can guess from the information. The example below shows you the process.

> At the southern tip of the continent, the Strait of Magellan links the Atlantic and Pacific oceans. A strait is a narrow body of water connecting two larger bodies of water. The large island south of the strait is Tierra del Fuego, or "land of fire."
>
> *From Section 1, Physical Geography*

1. Determine what the passage says:
The Strait of Magellan connects the Atlantic and Pacific oceans. There is an island south of it.

↓

2. Determine what you know about the topic or what you can connect to your experience.
This sounds like a shortcut to me. It would keep boats from having to sail all the way around the island.

↓

3. Make an inference.
Many ships probably use the Strait of Magellan because it is a shortcut.

YOU TRY IT!

Read the following sentences. Then use the three steps described above to make an inference about the Galápagos Islands.

> Chile and Ecuador both control large islands in the Pacific Ocean. Ecuador's volcanic Galápagos Islands have wildlife not found anywhere else in the world.
>
> *From Section 1, Physical Geography*

Asking Questions

FOCUS ON READING

Reading is one place where asking questions will never get you in trouble. The five W questions – who, what, when, where, and why – can help you be sure you understand the material you read. After you read a section, ask yourself the 5 Ws: **Who** was this section about? **What** did they do? **When** and **where** did they live? **Why** did they do what they did? See the example below to learn how this reading strategy can help you identify the main points of a passage.

> Many Greeks were not happy under Turkish rule. They wanted to be free of foreign influences. In the early 1800s, they rose up against the Turks. The rebellion seemed likely to fail, but the Greeks received help from other European countries and drove the Turks out. After the rebellion, Greece became a monarchy.
>
> *From Section 2, Greece*

The 5 Ws

Who? Greeks

What? Led rebellion to become independent from Turks

Where? Greece

When? Early 1800s

Why? Wanted to be free of foreign influences

YOU TRY IT!

Read the following passage and answer the 5 Ws to check your understanding of it.

> Italy remained divided into small states until the mid-1800s. At that time, a rise in nationalism, or strong patriotic feelings for a country, led people across Italy to fight for unification. As a result of their efforts, Italy became a unified kingdom in 1861.
>
> *From Section 3, Italy*

Recognizing Word Origins

FOCUS ON READING

English is a language that loves to borrow words from other languages and cultures. From the French, we took faceon and changed it to fashion. From the German, we took strollen and changed it to stroll. From the Dutch, we took koekje and changed it to cookie. Below is a list of examples of other words that come from other languages.

English Words from French	English Words from German	English Words from Latin
conquer	muffin	culture
brilliant	dollar	defeat
restaurant	rocket	general
republic	kindergarten	forces
fashion	hamburger	join
parliament	noodle	president
several	pretzel	elect
power	snorkel	control
exiled	hex	territory

YOU TRY IT!

Read the following sentences. Refer to the above word lists and make a list of the words in the passage below that originally came from other languages. After each word, list the original language.

A few years later a brilliant general named Napoleon took power. In time, he conquered much of Europe. Then in 1815 several European powers joined forces and defeated Napoleon. They exiled him and chose a new king to rule France.

France is now a republic with a parliament and an elected president. France still controls several overseas territories, such as Martinique in the West Indies.

From Section 2, France and the Benelux Countries

Using Context Clues— Synonyms

FOCUS ON READING

You have probably discovered that geography is a subject with many new words and terms. What if you don't remember or don't know what a word means? You may be able to use context clues to determine its meaning. Context clues are words near the unfamiliar word that indicate its meaning.

One helpful context clue is the synonym—words or phrases that mean the same as the new word. Look for synonyms in the words and sentences surrounding an unfamiliar term. Synonyms can help you understand the meaning of the new word. They may come in the same sentence or in the sentence following the words they define. Notice how the following passage uses synonyms to define the word urban.

> Most Swedes live in the southern part of the country in large towns and cities. In fact, more than 80 percent of Swedes live in *urban* areas. Stockholm, Sweden's capital and largest city, is located on the east coast near the Baltic Sea.
>
> *From Section 3, Scandinavia*

1. Look for words or phrases that mean the same thing.
The first sentence uses the phrase large towns and cities to describe where most Swedes live.

2. Substitute the synonym for the new word to confirm its meaning.
More than 80 percent of Swedes live in large towns and cities.

YOU TRY IT!

As you read the following sentences, look for synonyms that mean the same as the italicized words. Then use a graphic organizer like the one below to define each italicized word.

> Slow-moving sheets of ice, or *glaciers*, have left their mark on Northern Europe's coastlines and lakes.
>
> As the glaciers flowed slowly downhill, they carved long, winding channels, or *fjords*, into Norway's coastline.
>
> *From Section 1, Physical Geography*

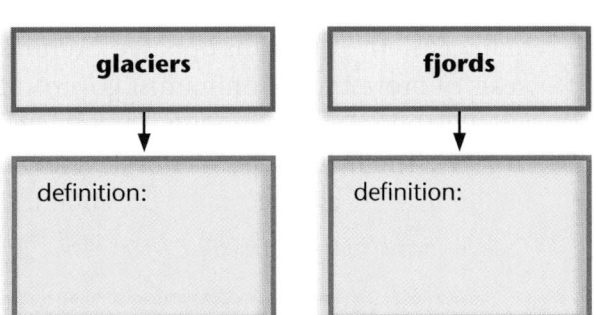

Understanding Problems and Solutions

FOCUS ON READING

Throughout history, people have faced problems and found solutions to them. As a result, writers who describe historical events often structure their writing by identifying a problem and then describing its solution. The ability to identify this pattern of writing will help you understand what you read. Notice how the following passage presents one problem with a two-pronged solution.

Estonia, Latvia, Lithuania, and Poland all still suffer from decades of Soviet rule. Under the Soviets, the economies of all four countries suffered.

Today, Poland and the Baltic Republics are working to rebuild and strengthen their economies. They are replacing the old and outdated factories built by the Soviets with new ones that take advantage of modern technology.

To further their economic growth, the countries of this region are also seeking new sources of income. One area in which they have found success is tourism.

From Section 2, Poland and the Baltic Republics

Problem:
Poor economies from Soviet rule

Solution #1:
Building new factories

Solution #2:
New source of income through tourism

YOU TRY IT!

Read the following passage, and then use the process shown above to identify the problems and solutions the writer presents. Create as many boxes as you need.

Many Eastern Europeans opposed Communist rule. After years of protest, the Communist government in the region fell. Poland rejected Communism and elected new leaders in 1989. The Baltic Republics broke away from the Soviet Union in 1991 and became independent once more.

From Section 2, Poland and the Baltic Republics

Making Generalizations

FOCUS ON READING

As you read about different people and cultures, you probably realize that people share some similarities. Seeing those similarities may lead you to make a generalization. A generalization is a broad, general idea drawn from new information combined with what you already know, such as your own experience. Notice how this process works with the following passage.

> Russians sometimes joke that winter lasts for 12 months and then summer begins. Russia is a cold country. The reason is its northern location partly within the Arctic Circle. In general, Russia has short summers and long, snowy winters. The climate is milder west of the Urals and grows colder and harsher as one goes north and east.
>
> *From Section 1, Physical Geography*

Information gathered from the passage you are reading	+	What you already know about the topic	=	Combine what you read with what you know to form a generalization.
Russians joke about the long, cold, snowy weather that they must endure.	+	My cousins in Minnesota complain about long, cold winters. My friend in New Mexico complains about hot weather.	=	**Generalization:** Living in places with very cold or very hot weather can be hard for many people.

YOU TRY IT!

Read the following passage. Using the process described above, form a general idea about holidays. Write your generalization in one sentence.

> Russian history has shaped its customs, such as holidays. Religious holidays, like Easter and Christmas, are popular. The main family holiday is New Year's Eve. To celebrate this holiday, families decorate a tree where, according to Russian folklore, Grandfather Frost and his helper the Snow Maiden leave gifts. A newer holiday is Russian Independence Day, which marks the end of the Soviet Union on June 12.
>
> *From Section 2, History and Culture of Russia*

READING SOCIAL STUDIES

Setting a Purpose

READING SOCIAL STUDIES

FOCUS ON READING

When you start on a trip, you have a purpose or a destination in mind. When you read, you should also have a purpose in mind before you start. This purpose keeps you focused and moving toward your goal. To decide on a purpose, look over the headings, pictures, and study tips before you read. Then ask yourself a question that can guide your reading. See how a heading suggested a purpose for the passage below.

Israeli Teens for Peace

Peace between Israeli Jews and Palestinian Arabs has not been easy in the past. Moreover, some believe peace in the region might be impossible ever to accomplish. But don't tell that to a group of 200 Jewish and Arab teenagers who are making a difference in Israel. These teens belong to an organization called Seeds of Peace. To learn more about each other's culture and thus understand each other better, these teens meet regularly.

From Section 3, Israel

Notice Headings, Pictures or Tips
Here's a heading about teenagers and a picture.

Set a Purpose
I wonder who these teenagers are and what they're doing for peace. I'll read to find out.

Ask Questions
What's so important about these teenagers?

YOU TRY IT!

Read the following introduction to the section on Israel. Ask yourself questions that can set a purpose for your reading. Following the steps given above, develop a purpose for reading about Israel. State this purpose in one to two sentences.

Do you know that Israel is often referred to as the Holy Land? Some people call Israel the Holy Land because it is home to sacred sites for three of the world's major religions—Judaism, Christianity, and Islam. Throughout the region's history, these three groups have fought over their right to the land.

From Section 3, Israel

Re-Reading

FOCUS ON READING

When you read about other countries, you will come across some information that is completely new to you. Sometimes it can seem difficult to keep all the people, places, dates, and events straight. Re-reading can help you absorb new information and understand the main facts of a passage. Follow these three steps in re-reading. First, read the whole passage. Look over the passage and identify the main details you need to focus on. Then re-read the passage slowly. As you read, make sure you understand the details by restating the details silently. If necessary, go back and re-read until you have the details firmly in your mind. Here's how this process works with the following passage.

> The Persian Empire was later conquered by several Muslim empires. Muslims converted the Persians to Islam, but most people retained their Persian culture. They built beautiful mosques with colorful tiles and large domes.
>
> *From Section 4, Iran*

1. Read the passage.

2. Identify the main details to focus on.
Persian Empire, Muslims, culture

3. Re-read and restate the details silently.
The Persian Empire was first. Then it was conquered by Muslims. Persian and Muslim cultures blended. Mosques show the region's culture.

YOU TRY IT!

Read the following sentences. Then, following the three steps above, write down the main details to focus on. After you re-read the paragraph, write down the information restated in your own words to show that you understood what you read.

> The Tigris and Euphrates rivers flow across a low, flat plain in Iraq. They join together before they reach the Persian Gulf. The Tigris and Euphrates are what are known as exotic rivers, or rivers that begin in humid regions and then flow through dry areas. The rivers create a narrow fertile area, which in ancient times was called Mesopotamia, or the "land between rivers."
>
> *From Section 1, Physical Geography*

Using Context Clues

FOCUS ON READING

One way to figure out the meaning of an unfamiliar word or term is by finding clues in its context, the words or sentences surrounding it. A common context clue is a restatement. Restatements simply define the new word using ordinary words you already know. Notice how the following passage uses a restatement to define nomads.

For centuries, Central Asians have made a living by raising horses, cattle, sheep, and goats. Many herders live as <u>nomads</u>, people who move often from place to place. The nomads move their herds from mountain pastures in the summer to lowland pastures in the winter.

From Section 2, History and Culture

Restatement: people who move often from place to place

YOU TRY IT!

Read the following sentences and identify the restatement for each underlined term.

Many other people in Kyrgyzstan are farmers. Fertile soils there allow a mix of irrigated crops and <u>dryland farming</u>, or farming that relies on rainfall instead of irrigation.

Even with the decline in agricultural production, Tajikistan still relies on cotton farming for much of its income. However, only 5 to 6 percent of the country's land is <u>arable</u>, or suitable for growing crops.

From Section 3, Central Asia Today

READING SOCIAL STUDIES

Summarizing

FOCUS ON READING

Learning about countries means understanding a lot of information. Summarizing is one way to help you handle large amounts of information. A summary is a short restatement of the most important ideas in a text. The example below shows three steps you can use to write a summary. First underline important details. Then write a short summary of each paragraph. Finally, combine these paragraph summaries into a short summary of the whole passage.

With more than 10 million people, Cairo is the largest urban area in North Africa. The city is crowded, poor, and polluted. Cairo continues to grow as people move into the city from Egypt's rural areas in search of work. For centuries, Cairo's location at the southern end of the Nile Delta helped the city grow. The city also lies along old trading routes.

Today the landscape of Cairo is a mixture of modern buildings, historic mosques, and small, mud-brick houses. However, there is not enough housing in Cairo for its growing population. Many people live in makeshift housing in the slums or boats along the Nile. Communities have even developed in cemeteries, where people convert tombs into bedrooms and kitchens.

From Section 3, North Africa Today

Summary of Paragraph 1
The crowded city of Cairo is North Africa's largest city and continues to grow.

Summary of Paragraph 2
Without enough housing, people in Cairo live in slums, boats and cemeteries.

Combined Summary
Cairo is North Africa's largest city, and it is so crowded that people live in houses, boats and cemeteries.

YOU TRY IT!

Read the following paragraphs. First, write a summary for each paragraph and then write a combined summary of the whole passage.

Even though Egypt is a republic, its government is heavily influenced by Islamic law. Egypt's government has a constitution and Egyptians elect their government officials. Power is shared between Egypt's president and the prime minister.

Many Egyptians debate over the role of Islam in the country. Some Egyptian Muslims believe Egypt's government, laws, and society should be based on Islamic law. However, some Egyptians worry that such a change in government would mean fewer personal freedoms.

From Section 3, North Africa Today

Understanding Comparison-Contrast

FOCUS ON READING

Comparing shows how things are alike. Contrasting shows how things are different. You can understand comparison-contrast by learning to recognize clue words and points of comparison. Clue words let you know whether to look for similarities or differences. Points of comparison are the main topics that are being compared or contrasted. Notice how the passage below compares and contrasts life in rural and urban areas.

Highlighted words are points of comparison.

> Rural homes are small and simple. Many homes in the Sahel and savanna zones are circular. Straw or tin roofs sit atop mud, mud-brick, or straw huts. Large extended families often live close together in the same village . . .
>
> In urban areas, also, members of an extended family may all live together. However, in West Africa's cities you will find modern buildings. People may live in houses or high rise apartments.
>
> *From Section 2, History and Culture*

Clue Words	
Comparison	**Contrast**
share, similar, like, also, both, in addition, besides	however, while, unlike, different, but, although

Underlined words are clue words.

YOU TRY IT!

Read the following passage about Liberia and Sierra Leone. Use a diagram like the one here to compare and contrast the two countries.

> Now, both Liberia and Sierra Leone are trying to rebuild. They do have natural resources on which to build stronger economies. Liberia has rubber and iron ore while Sierra Leone exports diamonds.
>
> *From Section 3, West Africa Today*

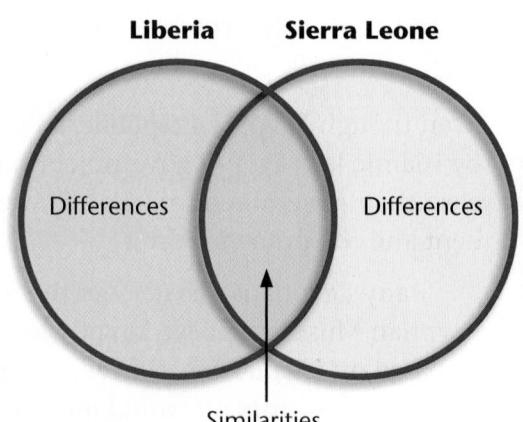

Liberia   Sierra Leone

Differences   Differences

Similarities

Identifying Supporting Details

FOCUS ON READING

Why believe what you read? One reason is because of details that support or prove the main idea. These details might be facts, statistics, examples, or definitions. In the example below, notice what kind of proof or supporting details help you believe the main idea.

> The landscape of East Africa has many high volcanic mountains. The highest mountain in Africa, Mount Kilimanjaro, rises to 19,340 feet. Despite Kilimanjaro's location near the equator, the mountain's peak has long been covered in snow. This much colder climate is caused by Kilimanjaro's high elevation.
>
> *From Section 1, Physical Geography*

Main Idea
The landscape of East Africa has many high volcanic mountains.

Supporting Details			
Example	**Statistic**	**Fact**	**Fact**
The highest mountain is Mount Kilimanjaro.	Mount Kilimanjaro is 19,340 feet high.	Kilimanjaro has a cold climate.	It is near the equator, but its peak is snow covered.

YOU TRY IT!

Read the following sentences, and then use a graphic organizer like the one above to identify the supporting details.

> Somalia is less diverse than most other African countries. Most people in the country are members of a single ethnic group, the Somali. In addition, most Somalis are Muslims and speak the same African language, also called Somali.
>
> *From Section 3, East Africa Today*

Using Word Parts

FOCUS ON READING

Many English words are made up of several word parts: roots, prefixes, and suffixes. A root is the main part of the word. A prefix is a letter or syllable added before the root. A suffix is a word part added after the root. Knowing the meanings of common prefixes and suffixes may help you figure out unfamiliar words. Below are some common prefixes and suffixes along with their meanings and examples of their use.

Common Prefixes		
Prefix	**Meaning**	**Sample Words**
en-	to cause to be	enforce
in-	not	ineffective
inter-	between, among	interpersonal
mal-	bad	malfunction
pro-	for, in front	proclaim
re-	again	rerun, rebuild

Common Suffixes		
Suffix	**Meaning**	**Sample Words**
-al	relating to	directional
-dom	state, condition	freedom
-ion	action, condition	rotation, selection
-ous	characterized by	victorious
-ment	result, action	development, entertainment

YOU TRY IT!

Read the following words from the chapter. Underline any prefixes or suffixes. Use the chart above to find the meaning of the prefix or the suffix. Then come up with a definition for each word.

> **independence,   instability,   malnutrition,**
> **interact,   re-elected,   enslaved,**
> **industrial,   endanger,   migration**

Making Generalizations

FOCUS ON READING

As you read about different people and cultures, you probably notice many similarities. Seeing those similarities may lead you to make a generalization. A generalization is a statement that applies to many different situations or people even though it is based on a few specific situations or people. In the following example, a generalization is made from combining new information with information from personal experience. Sometimes you might also make a generalization from reading about several new situations, even though you don't have personal experience with the situation.

> Several large rivers cross Southern Africa's plains. The Okavango River flows from Angola into a huge basin in Botswana. This river's water never reaches the ocean. Instead it forms a swampy inland delta that is home to crocodiles, zebras, hippos, and other animals. Many tourists travel to Botswana to see these wild animals in their natural habitat.
>
> *From Section 1, Physical Geography*

1. What you read:
Tourists will travel a long way to see wild animals.

2. What you know from personal experience:
My family loves to see wild animals in the zoo.

Generalization:
Many people enjoy seeing wild animals in person.

YOU TRY IT!

Read the following sentences about four South African countries. Then make a generalization from these four situations about political instability and a country's economy.

> Zimbabwe has suffered from a poor economy and political instability.
>
> Mozambique is one of the world's poorest countries. The economy has been badly damaged by civil war, but it is improving.
>
> Comoros suffers from a lack of resources and political instability. The government of Comoros is struggling to improve education and promote tourism.
>
> Madagascar was ruled for more than 20 years by a socialist dictator. Today the elected president is working to improve the struggling economy.
>
> *From Section 3, Southern Africa Today*

Visualizing

FOCUS ON READING

Maybe you have heard the saying "a picture is worth a thousand words." That means a picture can show in a small space what might take many words to describe. Visualizing, or creating mental pictures, can help you see and remember what you read. When you read, try to imagine what a snapshot of the images in the passage might look like. First, form the background or setting in your mind. Then keep adding specific details that can help you picture the rest of the information.

Form the background picture: I see the shape of the Indian subcontinent.

Add specific details: I see a huge diagonal line near the top left dividing the country into India and Pakistan.

> To avoid a civil war, the British agreed to the partition, or division, of India. In 1947 two independent countries were formed. India was mostly Hindu. Pakistan, which included the area that is now Bangladesh, was mostly Muslim. As a result, some 10 million people rushed to cross the border. Muslims and Hindus wanted to live in the country where their religion held a majority.
>
> *From Section 2, History and Culture of India*

Add more specific details: I see two large crowds of people moving toward the diagonal line and the number 10,000,000.

Add more specific details: I see two large arrows. The arrow pointing left says, "This way to Pakistan for Muslims." The arrow pointing right says, "This way to India for Hindus."

YOU TRY IT!

Read the following sentences. Then, using the process explained above, describe the images you see.

> Flooding is one of Bangladesh's biggest challenges. Many circumstances cause these floods. The country's many streams and rivers flood annually, often damaging farms and homes. Summer monsoons also cause flooding. For example, massive flooding in 2004 left more than 25 million people homeless. It also destroyed schools, farms, and roads throughout the country.
>
> *From Section 4, India's Neighbors*

Identifying Implied Main Ideas

FOCUS ON READING

Main ideas are often stated in a paragraph's topic sentence. When the main idea is not stated directly, however, you can find it by looking at the details in the paragraph. First, read the text carefully and think about the topic. Next, look at the facts and details and ask yourself what details are repeated. What points do those details make? Then create a statement that sums up the main idea. Examine how this process works for the paragraph below.

> Yet, other people increasingly wanted Chinese goods such as silk and tea. To gain access to the goods, some European powers forced China to open up trade in the 1800s. Europeans took over parts of the country as well. These actions angered many Chinese, some of whom blamed the emperor. At the same time, increased contact with the West exposed the Chinese to new ideas.
>
> *From Section 2, History and Culture of China*

1. What is the topic?
China's contact with Europe

2. What are the facts and details?
• Europe forced China to trade.

• Europeans took over some parts of China.

• Some Chinese blamed the emperor.

• The Chinese heard new ideas.

3. What details are repeated?
Increased contact with Europe

4. What is the main idea?
Increased contact with Europe had both positive and negative effects on China.

YOU TRY IT!

Read the following sentences. Then use the steps listed to the right to develop a statement that expresses the main idea of the paragraph.

> Only about 10 percent of China's land is good for farming. So how does China produce so much food? More than half of all Chinese workers are farmers. This large labor force can work the land at high levels. In addition, farmers cut terraces into hillsides to make the most use of the land.
>
> *From Section 3, China Today*

Understanding Fact and Opinion

FOCUS ON READING

When you read, it is important to distinguish facts from opinions. A fact is a statement that can be proved or disproved. An opinion is a personal belief or attitude, so it cannot be proved true or false. When you are reading a social studies text, you want to read only facts, not the author's opinions. To determine whether a sentence is a fact or an opinion, ask if it can be proved using outside sources. If it can, the sentence is a fact. The following pairs of statements show the difference between facts and opinions.

Fact: Hirohito was Japan's emperor for most of the 1900s. *(This fact can be proved through research.)*

Opinion: I believe Hirohito was Japan's best emperor. *(The word* best *signifies that this is the writer's judgment, or opinion.)*

Fact: One example of a long-lasting Korean food is kimchi, a dish made from pickled cabbage and various spices. *(The ingredients in kimchi can be checked for accuracy.)*

Opinion: Kimchi is a delicious dish made from pickled cabbage and various spices. *(No one can prove kimchi is delicious, because it is a matter of personal taste.)*

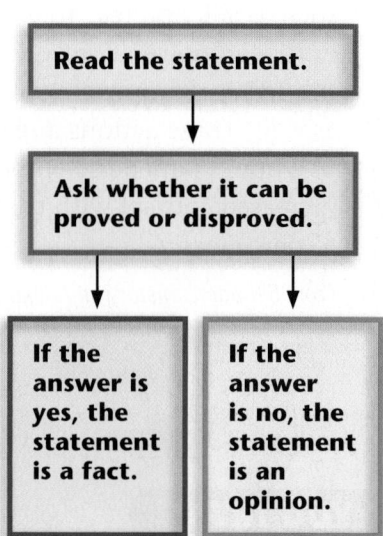

Read the statement.

Ask whether it can be proved or disproved.

If the answer is yes, the statement is a fact.

If the answer is no, the statement is an opinion.

YOU TRY IT!

Read the following sentences and identify each as a fact or an opinion.

1. The second largest city in Japan, Osaka, is located in western Honshu.

2. In Osaka—as in Tokyo and other cities—tall modern skyscrapers stand next to tiny Shinto temples.

3. Osaka is more beautiful than Tokyo.

4. Another major city is Kyoto, which all tourists should visit.

5. Once Japan's capital, Kyoto is full of historic buildings.

6. Tokyo has the country's best restaurants.

Using Context Clues— Definitions

FOCUS ON READING

One way to figure out the meaning of an unfamiliar word or term is by finding clues in its context, the words or sentences surrounding the word or term. A common context clue is a restatement. Restatements are simply a definition of the new word using ordinary words you already know. Notice how the following passage uses a restatement to define archipelago. Some context clues are not as complete or obvious. Notice how the following passage provides a description that is a partial definition of peninsula.

> The region of Southeast Asia is made up of two *peninsulas* and two large island groups. The Indochina *Peninsula* and the Malay (muh-LAY) *Peninsula* extend from the Asian mainland. . . The two island groups are the Philippines and the Malay Archipelago. An *archipelago* (ahr-kuh-PE-luh-goh) is a large group of islands.
>
> *From Section 1, Physical Geography*

Peninsula: land that extends from a mainland out into water

Archipelago: large group of islands

YOU TRY IT!

Read the following passages and identify the meaning of the italicized words by using definitions, or restatements, in context.

> The many groups that influenced Southeast Asia's history also shaped its culture. This *diverse* culture blends native, Chinese, Indian, and European ways of life.
>
> *From Section 2, History and Culture*

> The economy is based on farming, but good farmland is limited. Most people are *subsistence farmers,* meaning they grow just enough food for their families.
>
> *From Section 3, Mainland Southeast Asia Today*

Drawing Conclusions

FOCUS ON READING

You have probably heard the phrase, "Put two and two together." When people say that, they don't mean "2 + 2 = 4." They mean, "put the information together." When you put together information you already know with information you have read, you can draw a conclusion. To make a conclusion, read the passage carefully. Then think about what you already know about the topic. Put the two together to draw a conclusion.

> Off Australia's northeastern coast is the Great Barrier Reef, the world's largest coral reef. A coral reef is a collection of rocky material found in wshallow, tropical waters. The Great Barrier Reef is home to an incredible variety of marine animals.
>
> *From Section 1, Australia and New Zealand*

| **Information gathered from the passage:** Australia has the world's largest coral reef. | + | **What you already know:** I know many people like to snorkel or scuba dive at coral reefs. | = | **Add the information up to reach your conclusion:** Australia probably has many tourists who come to visit the Great Barrier Reef. |

YOU TRY IT!

Read the following paragraphs. Think about what you know about living in a very cold climate. Then use the process described above to draw a conclusion about the following passage.

> Because of Antarctica's high latitude, the continent is in almost total darkness during winter months. Seas clog with ice as a result of the extreme temperatures. In the summer, the sun shines around the clock and temperatures rise to near freezing.
>
> Plant life only survives in the ice-free tundra areas. Insects are the frozen land's only land animals. Penguins, seals, and whales live in Antarctica's waters.
>
> *From Section 3, Antarctica*

Economics Handbook

What Is Economics?

Economics may sound dull, but it touches almost every part of your life. Here are some examples of the kinds of economic choices you may have made yourself:

- Which pair of shoes to buy—the ones on sale or the ones you really like, which cost much more
- Whether to continue saving your money for the DVD player you want or use some of it now to go to a movie
- Whether to give some money to a fundraiser for a new park or to housing for the homeless

As these examples show, we can think of economics as a study of choices. These choices are the ones people make to satisfy their needs or their desires.

Glossary of Economic Terms

Here are some of the words we use to talk about economics:

ECONOMIC SYSTEMS

Countries have developed different economic systems to help them make choices, such as what goods and services to produce, how to produce them, and for whom to produce them. The most common economic systems in the world are market economies and mixed economies.

capitalism See market economy.

command economy an economic system in which the central government makes all economic decisions, such as in the countries of Cuba and North Korea

communism a political system in which the government owns all property and runs a command economy

free enterprise a system in which businesses operate with little government involvement, such as in a country with a market economy

market economy an economic system based on private ownership, free trade, and competition; the government has little to say about what, how, or for whom goods and services are produced; examples include Germany and the United States

mixed economy an economy that is a combination of command, market, and traditional economies

traditional economy an economy in which production is based on customs and tradition, and in which people often grow their own food, make their own goods, and use barter to trade

THE ECONOMY AND MONEY

People, businesses, and countries obtain the items they need and want through economic activities such as producing, selling, and buying goods or services. Countries differ in the amount of economic activity that they have and in the strength of their economies.

consumer a person who buys goods or services for personal use

consumer good a finished product sold to consumers for personal or home use

corporation a business in which a group of owners share in the profits and losses

currency paper or coins that a country uses for its money supply

demand the amount of goods and services that consumers are willing and able to buy at a given time

depression a severe drop in overall business activity over a long period of time

developed countries countries with strong economies and a high quality of life; often have high per capita GDPs and high levels of industrialization and technology

developing countries countries with less productive economies and a lower quality of life; often have less industrialization and technology

economic development the level of a country's economic activity, growth, and quality of life

economy the structure of economic life in a country

goods objects or materials that humans can purchase to satisfy their wants and needs

gross domestic product (GDP) total market value of all goods and services produced in a country in a given year; *per capita GDP* is the average value of goods and services produced per person in a country in a given year

industrialization the process of using machinery for all major forms of production

inflation an increase in overall prices

investment the purchase of something with the expectation that it will gain in value; usually property, stocks, etc.

money any item, usually coins or paper currency, that is used in payment for goods or services

producer a person or group that makes goods or provides services to satisfy consumers' wants and needs

productivity the amount of goods or services that a worker or workers can produce within a given amount of time

profit the gain or excess made by selling goods or services over their costs

purchasing power the amount of income that people have available to spend on goods and services

services any activities that are performed for a fee

standard of living how well people are living; determined by the amount of goods and services they can afford

stock a share of ownership in a corporation

supply the amount of goods and services that are available at a given time

INTERNATIONAL TRADE

Countries trade with each other to obtain resources, goods, and services. Growing global trade has helped lead to the development of a global economy.

balance of trade the difference between the value of a country's exports and imports

barter the exchange of one good or service for another

black market the illegal buying and selling of goods, often at high prices

comparative advantage the ability of a company or country to produce something at a lower cost than other companies or countries

competition rivalry between businesses selling similar goods or services; a condition that often leads to lower prices or improved products

e-commerce the electronic trading of goods and services, such as over the Internet

exports goods or services that a country sells and sends to other countries

free trade trade among nations that is not affected by financial or legal barriers; trade without barriers

imports goods or services that a country brings in or purchases from another country

interdependence a relationship between countries in which they rely on one another for resources, goods, or services

market the trade of goods and services

market clearing price the price of a good or service at which supply equals demand

one-crop economy an economy that is dominated by the production of a single product

opportunity cost the value of the next-best alternative that is sacrificed when choosing to consume or produce another good or service

scarcity a condition of limited resources and unlimited wants by people

specialization a focus on only one or two aspects of production in order to produce a product more quickly and cheaply; for example, one worker washes the wheels of the car, another cleans the interior, and another washes the body

trade barriers financial or legal limitations to trade; prevention of free trade

trade-offs the goods or services sacrificed in order to consume or produce another good or service

underground economy illegal economic activities and unreported legal economic activities

PERSONAL ECONOMICS

Individuals make personal choices in how they manage and use their money to satisfy their needs and desires. Individuals have the choice to spend, save, or invest their money.

budget a plan listing the expenses and income of an individual or organization

credit a system that allows consumers to pay for goods and services over time

debt an amount of money that is owed

financial institutions businesses that keep and invest people's money and loan money to people; include banks or credit unions

income a gain of money that comes typically from labor or capital

interest the money that a borrower pays to a lender in return for a loan

loan money given on the condition that it will be paid back, often with interest

savings money or income that is not used to purchase goods or services

tax a required payment to a local, state, or national government; different kinds of taxes include sales taxes, income taxes, and property taxes

wage the payment a worker receives for his or her labor

RESOURCES

People and businesses need resources—such as land, labor, and money—to produce goods and services.

capital generally refers to wealth, in particular wealth that can be used to finance the production of goods or services

human capital sometimes used to refer to human skills and education that affect the production of goods and services in a company or country

labor force all people who are legally old enough to work and are either working or looking for work

natural resource any material in nature that people use and value

nonrenewable resource a resource that cannot be replaced naturally, such as coal or petroleum

raw material a natural resource used to make a product or good

renewable resource a resource that Earth replaces naturally, such as water, soil, and trees

ORGANIZATIONS

Countries have formed many organizations to promote economic cooperation, growth, and trade. These organizations are important in today's global economy.

European Union (EU) an organization that promotes political and economic cooperation in Europe

International Monetary Fund (IMF) a UN agency that promotes cooperation in international trade and that works to maintain stability in the exchange of countries' currencies

Organization of Economic Cooperation and Development (OECD) an organization of countries that promotes democracy and market economies

United Nations (UN) an organization of countries that promotes peace and security around the globe

World Bank a UN agency that provides loans to countries for development and recovery

World Trade Organization (WTO) an international organization dealing with trade between nations

Economic Handbook Review

Reviewing Vocabulary and Terms

On a separate sheet of paper, fill in the blanks in the following sentences:

ECONOMIC SYSTEMS

1. **A.** Businesses are able to operate with little government involvement in a _____ system.
   B. In a _____, a central government makes all economic decisions.
   C. _____ is a political system in which the government owns all property and runs a command economy.
   D. Economies that combine parts of command, market, or traditional economies are called _____.
   E. _____ is another name for a market economy, which is based on private ownership, free trade, and competition.

THE ECONOMY AND MONEY

2. **A.** _____ are objects or materials that people can buy to satisfy their needs and wants.
   B. A _____ is any activity that is performed for a fee.
   C. A person who buys goods or services is a _____, and a person or group that makes goods or provides services is a _____.
   D. The amount of goods and services that consumers are willing and able to buy at any given time is known as _____.
   E. The total value of all the goods and services produced in the United States in one year is its _____.

INTERNATIONAL TRADE

3. A. If we have an unlimited demand for a natural resource, such as oil, and there is only so much oil in the ground, we have a condition called _____.

B. Goods or services that a country sells to other countries are _____.

C. Rivalry between producers that provide the same good or service is called _____.

D. If a country is able to produce a good or service at a lower cost than other countries, it is said to have a _____.

E. Trade among nations that is not limited by legal or economic barriers is called _____.

PERSONAL ECONOMICS

4. A. A _____ is a required payment to a local, state, or national government that is used to support public services such as education, road construction, and government aid.

B. The money we do not spend on goods or services is our _____.

C. You can use _____ to pay for goods and services over time.

D. The payment that a worker receives for his or her labor is called a _____.

E. Individuals and companies use _____ to plan and manage their expenses and income.

Activities

1. With a partner, compare prices in two grocery stores. Create a chart showing the price of five items in the two stores. Also, figure the average price of the items in each store. How do you think the fact that the stores are near each other affects prices? How might prices be different if one store went out of business? How might the prices be different or similar if the United States had a command economy? Present what you have learned about prices and competition to your class.

2. With a group, choose five countries from a unit region to research. Look up the per capita GDP and the life expectancy rates for each of these countries in the regional atlas. Then use your textbook, go to your library, or use the Internet to research the literacy rate and the number of TVs per 1,000 people for each of these countries. Organize this information in a five-column chart like the one shown here. Study the information to see if you can find any patterns. Write a brief paragraph explaining what you have learned about the five countries.

Region				
Country	Per Capita GDP (U.S. $)	Life Expectancy at Birth	Literacy Rate	TVs per 1,000 People

3. Work with a partner to identify some of the many types of currency used in either Africa, Europe, or Asia. Then imagine that you are the owners of a business in the United States. You have created a new product that you want to sell in the continent you selected, but people there do not use the same currency as you do. To sell your product, you will need to be able to exchange one type of currency for another. Search the Internet or look in a newspaper to find a list of currency exchange rates. For example, if your product sells for 1,000 dollars, what should the cost be in euros? In British pounds? In South African rand? In Japanese yen?

RESOURCES

5. A. Diamonds and gold are examples of _____, which are any materials in nature that people use and value.

B. The _____ consists of all people who are legally able to work and are working or looking for work.

C. Wealth that can be used to finance the production of goods and services is called _____.

D. Oil is an example of a _____, which is a resource that cannot be replaced naturally.

E. Water and trees are examples of _____, resources that Earth replaces naturally.

ORGANIZATIONS

6. A. Many European countries have joined the _____ to help promote political and economic cooperation across Europe.

B. The _____ consists of many agencies that promote peace and security around the world.

C. The _____ is a UN agency that provides loans to countries to help them develop their economies.

D. The _____ is a UN agency that helps protect the stability of countries' currencies.

E. Many democratic countries promote market economies through the _____.

4. With three or four partners, create a skit that illustrates one of the following basic economic concepts: scarcity and limited resources, supply and demand, or opportunity costs and trade-offs. For example, a skit might illustrate supply and demand by showing how the high demand for the best seats at a concert increases the ticket prices for those seats. Write a script for your skit. Then practice the skit and perform it for the class.

5. Conduct research to find the following information for each country in the chart below: main trading partners, exports, imports, industrial products, agricultural products, and resources. Organize the information into a second chart. Then use the information in the two charts to write a one-page report explaining how international trade, specialization, and available resources affects each country's per capita GDP and standard of living.

Facts about Countries

COUNTRY Capital	FLAG	POPULATION	AREA (sq mi)	PER CAPITA GDP (U.S. $)	LIFE EXPECTANCY AT BIRTH	TVS PER 1,000 PEOPLE
Afghanistan Kabul		29.9 million	250,001	$800	42.9	14
Ethiopia Addis Ababa		73.1 million	435,186	$800	48.8	5
Germany Berlin		82.4 million	137,847	$28,700	78.7	581
Japan Tokyo		127.4 million	145,883	$29,400	81.2	719
Kazakhstan Astana		15.2 million	1,049,155	$7,800	66.6	240
Saudi Arabia Riyadh		26.4 million	756,985	$12,000	75.5	263
United States Washington, D.C.		295.7 million	3,718,710	$40,100	77.7	844

R35

The Physical World

Inside the Earth

Earth's interior has several different layers. Deep inside the planet is the core. The inner core is solid, and the outer core is liquid. Above the core is the mantle, which is mostly solid rock with a molten layer on top. The surface layer of Earth includes the crust, which is made up of rocks and soil. Finally, the atmosphere extends from the crust into space. It supports much of the life on Earth.

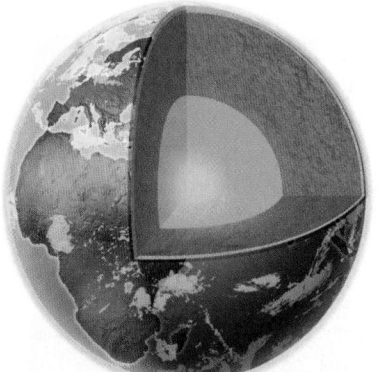

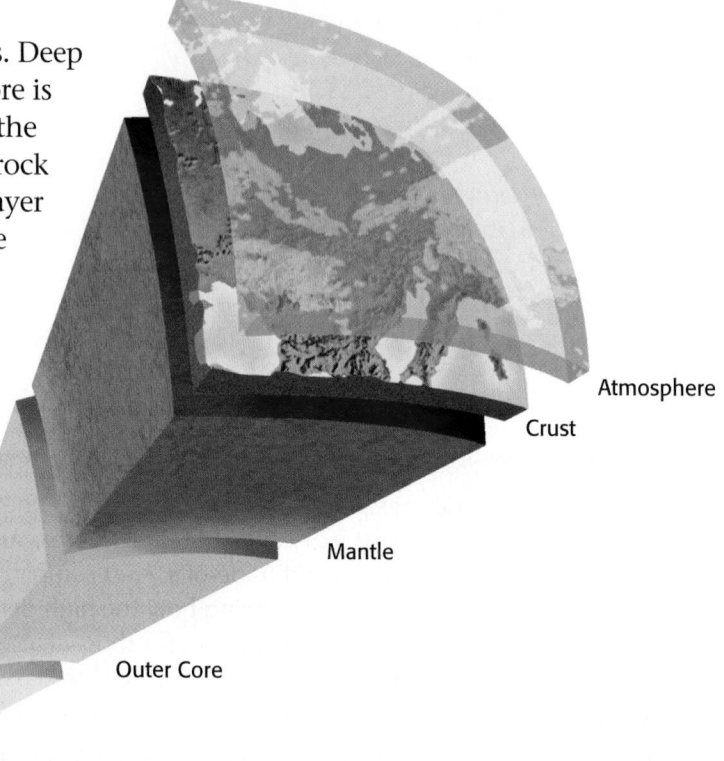

Atmosphere

Crust

Mantle

Outer Core

Inner Core

Tectonic Plates

Earth's crust is divided into huge pieces called tectonic plates, which fit together like a puzzle. As these plates slowly move, they collide and break apart, forming surface features like mountains, ocean basins, and ocean trenches.

Earth Facts	
Age:	4.6 billion years
Mass:	5,974,000,000,000,000,000,000 metric tons
Distance around the equator:	24,902 miles (40,067 km)
Distance around the poles:	24,860 miles (40,000 km)
Distance from the sun:	about 93 million miles (150 million km)
Earth's speed around the sun:	18.5 miles a second (29.8 km a second)
Percent of Earth's surface covered by water:	71%
What makes Earth unique:	large amounts of liquid water, tectonic activity, and life

The Continents

Geographers identify seven large landmasses, or continents, on Earth. Most of these continents are almost completely surrounded by water. Europe and Asia, however, are not. They share a long land boundary.

The world's continents are very different. For example, much of Australia is dry and rocky, while Antarctica is cold and icy. The information below highlights some key facts about each continent.

North America

- Percent of Earth's land: 16.5%
- Percent of Earth's population: 5.1%
- Lowest point: Death Valley, 282 feet (86 m) below sea level

Europe

- Percent of Earth's land: 6.7%
- Percent of Earth's population: 11.5%
- People per square mile: 187

South America

- Percent of Earth's land: 12%
- Percent of Earth's population: 8.6%
- Longest mountains: Andes, 4,500 miles (7,240 km)

Africa

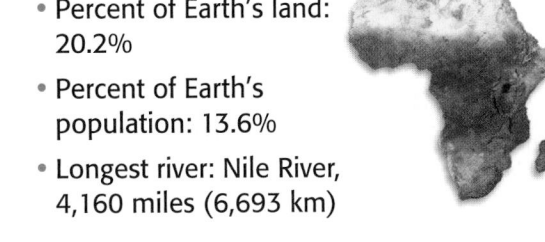

- Percent of Earth's land: 20.2%
- Percent of Earth's population: 13.6%
- Longest river: Nile River, 4,160 miles (6,693 km)

Australia

- Percent of Earth's land: 5.2%
- Percent of Earth's population: 0.3%
- Oldest rocks: 3.7 billion years

Asia

- Percent of Earth's land: 30%
- Percent of Earth's population: 60.7%
- Highest point: Mount Everest, 29,035 feet (8,850 m)

Antarctica

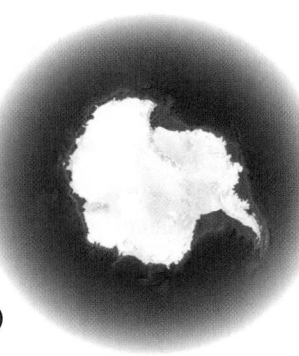

- Percent of Earth's land: 8.9%
- Percent of Earth's population: 0%
- Coldest place: Plateau Station, -56.7°C (-70.1°F) average temperature

The Human World

World Population

More than 6 billion people live in the world today, and that number is growing quickly. Some people predict the world's population will reach 9 billion by 2050. As our population grows, it is also becoming more urban. Soon, as many people will live in cities and in towns as live in rural areas.

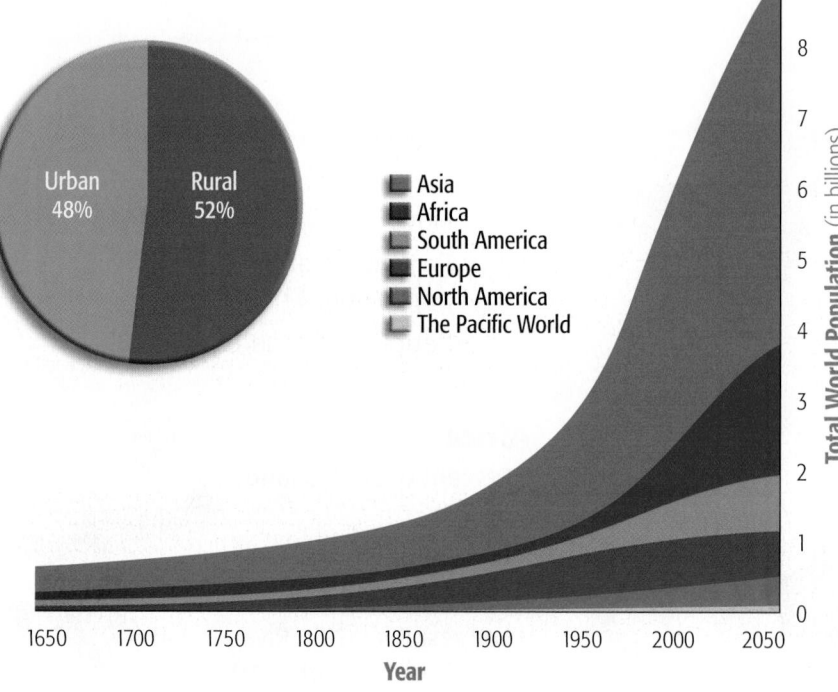

Urban 48%
Rural 52%

- Asia
- Africa
- South America
- Europe
- North America
- The Pacific World

Total World Population (in billions)

Year: 1650 1700 1750 1800 1850 1900 1950 2000 2050

As the world's population grows, people are moving to already large cities such as Shanghai (above) and Hong Kong (right) in China.

Geographers divide the world into developed and less developed regions. In general, developed countries are wealthier and more urban, have lower population growth rates and higher life expectancies. As you can imagine, life is very different in developed and less developed regions.

Developed and Less Developed Countries

	Population	Rate of Natural Increase	Life Expectancy	Percent Urban	Per Capita GNI (U.S. $)
Developed Countries	1.2 billion	0.1%	77	77%	$27,790
Less Developed Countries	5.3 billion	1.5%	65	41%	$4,950
The World	6.5 billion	1.2%	67	48%	$9,190

World Religions

A large percentage of the world's people follow one of several major world religions. Christianity is the largest religion. About 33 percent of the world's people are Christian. Islam is the second-largest religion with about 20 percent. It is also the fastest-growing religion. Hinduism and Buddhism are also major world religions.

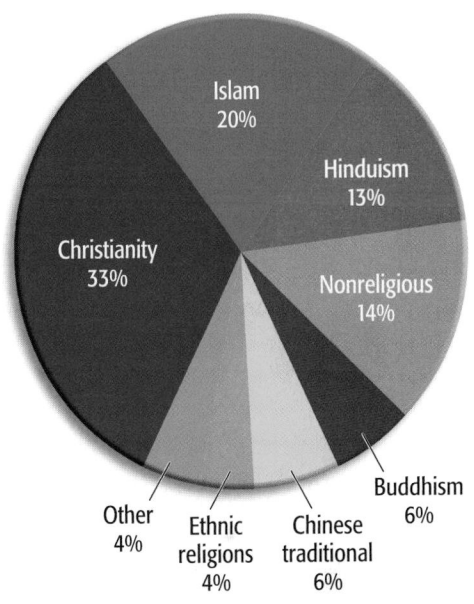

Islam 20%

Hinduism 13%

Christianity 33%

Nonreligious 14%

Buddhism 6%

Chinese traditional 6%

Ethnic religions 4%

Other 4%

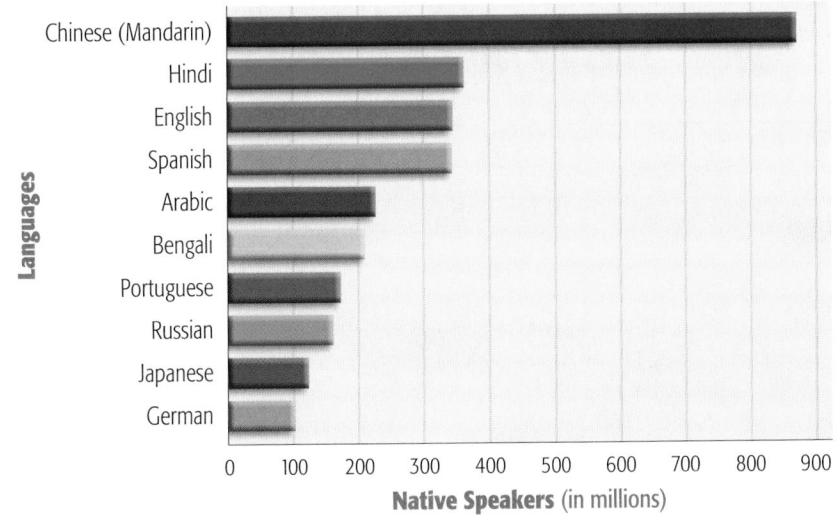

Native Speakers (in millions)

Languages: Chinese (Mandarin), Hindi, English, Spanish, Arabic, Bengali, Portuguese, Russian, Japanese, German

World Languages

Although several thousand languages are spoken today, a handful of major languages have the largest numbers of native speakers. Chinese (Mandarin) is spoken by nearly one in six people. Hindi, English, Spanish, and Arabic are next, with native speakers all over the world.

United States: Physical

Strait of Juan de Fuca

Puget Sound

Mount Rainier 14,410 ft (4,392 m)

Franklin D. Roosevelt Lake

COAST RANGES

CASCADE RANGE

Columbia River

Columbia Plateau

Bitterroot Range

Clark Fork

Flathead Lake

Lewis Range

ROCKY

Milk River

Missouri River

Lake Sakakawea

45°N

Salmon River

Salmon River Mts.

CONTINENTAL

Sawtooth Mts.

Snake River

Yellowstone River

G R E A T

Fort Peck Lake

Yellowstone Lake

Bighorn Mts.

Bighorn River

Powder River

Lake Oahe

Cape Mendocino

40°N

Klamath River

Goose Lake

Shasta Lake

Pyramid Lake

Grand Tetons

Gannett Peak 13,804 ft (4,207 m)

Wind River Range

Wind River

Black Hills

Cheyenne River

White River

James

Niobrara River

I N T E R

125°W

SIERRA NEVADA

Central Valley

Lake Tahoe

GREAT BASIN

Great Salt Lake

Utah Lake

Wasatch Range

Uinta Mts.

M O U N T A I N S

DIVIDE

Front Range

North Platte River

South Platte River

Platte River

San Francisco Bay

Sacramento River

San Joaquin River

Green River

P L A I N S

Republican River

35°N

Monterey Bay

Coast Ranges

Mount Whitney 14,494 ft (4,419 m)

Death Valley

COLORADO

Colorado River

Lake Powell

San Juan River

Mount Elbert 14,433 ft (4,400 m)

Pikes Peak 14,110 ft (4,301 m)

Smoky Hill River

Mojave Desert

Lake Mead

Grand Canyon

PLATEAU

Painted Desert

San Luis Valley

Sangre De Cristo Mts.

Canadian River

River

Salton Sea

Imperial Valley

DIVIDE

Rio Grande

PACIFIC OCEAN

Colorado River

Gila River

CONTINENTAL

30°N

Sonoran Desert

120°W

Gulf of California

Pecos River

Amistad Reservoir

Colorado River

To understand the relative locations of Alaska and Hawaii, as well as the vast distances separating them from the rest of the United States, see the world map.

Nueces River

Rio Grande

Padre Island

ARCTIC OCEAN

22°N

155°W

Kauai

Niihau

Oahu

HAWAII

Molokai

Maui

Lanai

Kahoolawe

PACIFIC OCEAN

160°W

Mauna Kea 13,796 ft (4,206 m)

Hawaii

19°N

0   75   150 Miles
0   75   150 Kilometers
Projection: Mercator

RUSSIA

Bering Strait

Arctic Circle

BROOKS RANGE

Yukon River

Kuskokwim River

Tanana River

ALASKA RANGE

Mount McKinley 20,320 ft (6,194 m)

CANADA

MEXICO

St. Lawrence Island

St. Matthew Island

Nunivak Island

Bering Sea

Attu Island

55°N

170°E

50°N

0   250   500 Miles
0   250   500 Kilometers
Projection: Albers Equal Area

ALEUTIAN ISLANDS

180°W

170°W

160°W

Kodiak Island

Gulf of Alaska

Alexander Archipelago

55°N

PACIFIC OCEAN

CANADA

Isle
Royale

Mesabi Range

Lake Superior

Red River

Minnesota River

Mississippi River

Wisconsin River

Lake Michigan

Lake Huron

St. Lawrence River

St. Lawrence Seaway

St. John River

Longfellow Mts.

Penobscot River

Lake Champlain

Green Mts.

White Mts.

Connecticut River

Adirondack Mts.

Lake Ontario

Cape Cod

Allegheny

PLATEAU

Catskill Mts.

Lake Erie

MOUNTAINS

Long Island Sound

Long Island

Des Moines River

Missouri River

Kansas R.

Illinois River

Wabash River

Scioto River

ALLEGHENY

Susquehanna River

Hudson River

Delaware River

40°N

P L A I N S

Ohio River

APPALACHIAN

Monongahela R.

Kanawha River

Potomac River

Delaware Bay

Lake of the Ozarks

OZARK PLATEAU

Cumberland River

Lake Barkley

James River

Roanoke River

Chesapeake Bay

ATLANTIC
OCEAN

70°W

Keystone Lake

Arkansas River

White River

Cumberland Plateau

Great Smoky Mts.

BLUE RIDGE MOUNTAINS

Pamlico Sound

35°N

Eufaula Lake

Lake Texoma

Ouachita Mts.

Kentucky Lake

Tennessee River

Cape Hatteras

Coosa River

PIEDMONT

Oconee River

Savannah River

Trinity River

Saline River

Red River

Tombigbee River

Alabama R.

Chattahoochee River

Altamaha River

Sea Islands

ELEVATION

Feet		Meters
13,120		4,000
6,560		2,000
1,640		500
656		200
(Sea level) 0		0 (Sea level)
Below sea level		Below sea level

Brazos River

Toledo Bend Reservoir

Pearl River

C O A S T A L

P L A I N

Okefenokee Swamp

0   100   200 Miles

0   100   200 Kilometers

Projection: Albers Equal Area

GULF

Chandeleur Islands

Mississippi Delta

N
W   E
S

Cape Canaveral

FLORIDA PENINSULA

80°W

Gulf of Mexico

85°W

90°W

95°W

Lake Okeechobee

BAHAMAS

25°N

The Everglades

Cape Sable

Florida Keys

Straits of Florida

75°W

United States: Political

Strait of
Juan de Fuca

Puget
Sound

Franklin D.
Roosevelt Lake

Pend
Oreille

Seattle
Tacoma
Olympia ★
Spokane

WASHINGTON

45°N

Portland
Columbia River

Flathead
Lake

Great Falls

Missouri River

NORTH DAKOTA

Lake
Sakakawea

★ Salem

Helena ★

MONTANA

Yellowstone River

Bismarck

Eugene

OREGON

IDAHO

Billings

Lake
Oahe

SOUTH DAKOTA

Cape
Mendocino

40°N

Goose
Lake

Shasta
Lake

★ Boise

Sun Valley

Snake River

Pocatello

Yellowstone
Lake

WYOMING

Cheyenne ★

Pierre ★

Rapid City

NEBRASKA

125°W

Sacramento River

Pyramid
Lake

Ogden

Great
Salt
Lake

Salt Lake City ★
Provo

Green River

Platte River

Berkeley
Oakland
San Francisco
San Francisco Bay
San Jose

Reno ★
★ Carson City
Lake Tahoe
★ Sacramento

NEVADA

Utah
Lake

UTAH

Boulder
Vail
Aspen

★ Denver

Colorado
Springs

Monterey
Bay

San Joaquin River

Fresno

COLORADO

Pueblo

Arkansas River

KANSAS

35°N

CALIFORNIA

Las
Vegas

Lake
Powell

Lake
Mead

Santa Barbara
Ventura
Los
Angeles
Long
Beach
Anaheim
Santa Ana
San Diego

Riverside
Palm Springs

Channel Islands

Salton
Sea

Flagstaff

ARIZONA

Colorado River

Taos
Santa Fe ★
Albuquerque

OKLAHOMA

Canadian River

Oklahoma City

PACIFIC
OCEAN

Phoenix ★

Gila River

NEW MEXICO

Amarillo

Lawton

30°N

Casa Grande

Tucson

Gulf of
California

Las Cruces

El Paso

Lubbock

Brazos River

Abilene

Fort Worth

120°W

To understand the relative locations of Alaska and
Hawaii, as well as the vast distances separating them
from the rest of the United States, see the world map.

Midland
Odessa

TEXAS

Colorado River

Pecos River

Amistad
Reservoir

Austin

Kauai
Niihau
Oahu
Honolulu ★

HAWAII

22°N

ARCTIC OCEAN

RUSSIA

Arctic Circle

San Antonio

Rio Grande

PACIFIC
OCEAN

Molokai
Lanai

Maui

Kahoolawe

155°W

Bering Strait

Nome

Yukon River

CANADA

Corpus Christi

Laredo

Hilo
Hawaii

19°N

St. Lawrence
Island

St. Matthew
Island

Fairbanks

Padre
Island

0   75   150 Miles
0   75   150 Kilometers
Projection: Mercator

160°W

Nunivak
Island

ALASKA

MEXICO

170°E

Attu Island

Bering Sea

Anchorage
Valdez

55°N

ALEUTIAN ISLANDS

50°N

0   250   500 Miles
0   250   500 Kilometers
Projection: Albers Equal Area

Kodiak Island

Gulf of Alaska

Juneau

Skagway

Alexander
Archipelago

55°N

PACIFIC
OCEAN

180°W

150°W

140°W

CANADA

MAINE

MINNESOTA

Grand Forks
Fargo
Duluth
Superior
Marquette
Sault Ste. Marie

Augusta
Burlington
Montpelier
Portland

Lake Champlain
VT
NH
Concord
Manchester

WISCONSIN
Minneapolis
St. Paul
Green Bay

Hudson R.
Lake Ontario
Rochester
Syracuse
Albany
MA
Boston
Worcester
Providence
Cape Cod

Sioux Falls
Sioux City

MICHIGAN
Lake Huron
Lake Michigan
Madison
Milwaukee
Grand Rapids
Saginaw
Lansing
Detroit
Ann Arbor

Buffalo
NEW YORK
Springfield
Hartford
CT
RI
New Haven
Long Island Sound

IOWA
Cedar Rapids
Davenport
Des Moines

Rockford
Chicago
Gary
South Bend
Toledo
Cleveland
Youngstown
Akron

Susquehanna River
Bridgeport
Jersey City
Newark
Yonkers
New York City
Long Island
40°N

naha
ncoln

Peoria
Fort Wayne
OHIO
Columbus
Dayton
Cincinnati

PENNSYLVANIA
Allentown
Harrisburg
Pittsburgh
Philadelphia
Trenton
Camden
NJ
Atlantic City

MISSOURI
Kansas City
Kansas City

INDIANA
Springfield
Indianapolis

WEST VIRGINIA
Charleston

Baltimore
MD
DE
Dover
Washington, D.C.
Annapolis
Delaware Bay

topeka

ILLINOIS
East St. Louis
St. Louis
Jefferson City

Louisville
Evansville
Frankfort
Lexington

VIRGINIA
Richmond
Chesapeake Bay

ATLANTIC OCEAN
70°W

ichita

Lake of the Ozarks
Springfield

Ohio River

KENTUCKY
Lake Barkley

Newport News
Norfolk
Virginia Beach

35°N

Keystone Lake
Tulsa

Fayetteville

Kentucky Lake
Nashville
Knoxville

Greensboro
Durham
Raleigh
Cape Hatteras

ufaula Lake

Memphis
Chattanooga

TENNESSEE
Asheville
Charlotte
NORTH CAROLINA

Lake Texoma

ARKANSAS
Little Rock
Pine Bluff

Huntsville

Greenville
SOUTH CAROLINA
Columbia

Dallas

Shreveport

MISSISSIPPI
Vicksburg
Jackson

Birmingham
ALABAMA
Meridian
Montgomery

Atlanta
GEORGIA
Macon
Columbus

Savannah River
Savannah
Charleston

Sea Islands

National capital
State capitals
Other cities

0   100   200 Miles
0   100   200 Kilometers
Projection: Albers Equal Area

Vaco

Toledo Bend Reservoir

LOUISIANA
Baton Rouge

Red River

Mobile
Pensacola
Tallahassee

Jacksonville

30°N

Beaumont
Houston

New Orleans
Biloxi
Chandeleur Islands

Chattahoochee R.
Gainesville

Galveston

Gulf of Mexico

FLORIDA
Orlando
Cape Canaveral

N
W   E
S

St. Petersburg
Tampa

Lake Okeechobee

BAHAMAS
25°N

Cape Sable
Florida Keys

Fort Myers
Fort Lauderdale
Miami

Straits of Florida

75°W
80°W
85°W
90°W
95°W

St. Lawrence River
Lake Superior
Lake Erie
Connecticut R.

Red River
Minnesota River
Mississippi River
Missouri River
Illinois River
Mississippi River

ATLAS

80°N OCEAN

ARCTIC

Beaufort Sea

Victoria Island

Baffin Bay

Greenland

Bering Strait

Yukon River

Mackenzie River

Great Bear Lake

Baffin Island

Davis Strait

Denmark Strait

Iceland

60°N

Bering Sea

Gulf of Alaska

Great Slave Lake

Hudson Bay

Aleutian Islands

Vancouver Island

MOUNTAINS

Missouri

Lake Winnipeg

Great Lakes

St. Lawrence River

Bay of Biscay

40°N

NORTH AMERICA

ROCKY

Colorado River

Mississippi

APPALACHIAN MTS.

ATLANTIC OCEAN

Strait of Gibraltar

ATL

SIERRA MADRE

Rio Grande

Gulf of Mexico

Bahamas

Tropic of Cancer

20°N

Hawaiian Islands

Greater Antilles

Caribbean Sea

Lesser Antilles

Niger

PACIFIC OCEAN

Isthmus of Panama

GUIANA HIGHLANDS

N

W E

S

0° Equator

ANDES MOUNTAINS

Amazon River

SOUTH AMERICA

BRAZILIAN HIGHLANDS

20°S

River

ATLANTIC OCEAN

Tropic of Capricorn

Parana

ANDES MOUNTAINS

40°S

Strait of Magellan

Falkland Islands

Tierra del Fuego

Cape Horn

60°S

160°W 140°W 120°W 100°W 80°W 60°W 40°W 20°W

Antarctic Circle

Weddell Sea

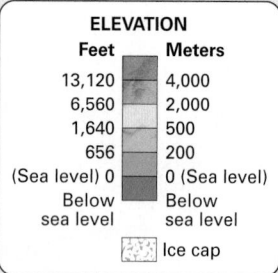

ELEVATION

Feet		Meters
13,120		4,000
6,560		2,000
1,640		500
656		200
(Sea level) 0		0 (Sea level)
Below sea level		Below sea level

Ice cap

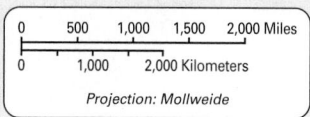

0 500 1,000 1,500 2,000 Miles

0 1,000 2,000 Kilometers

Projection: Mollweide

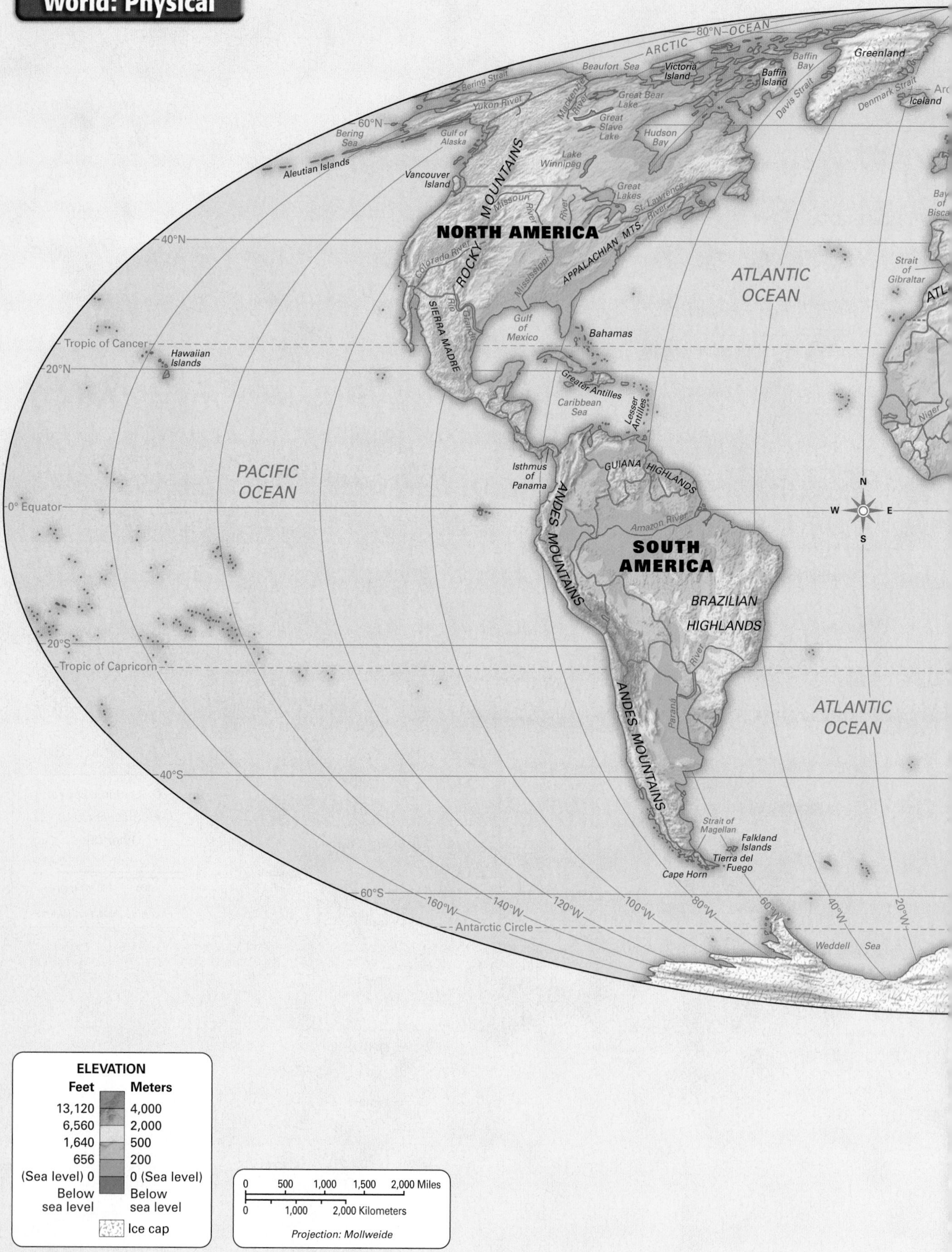

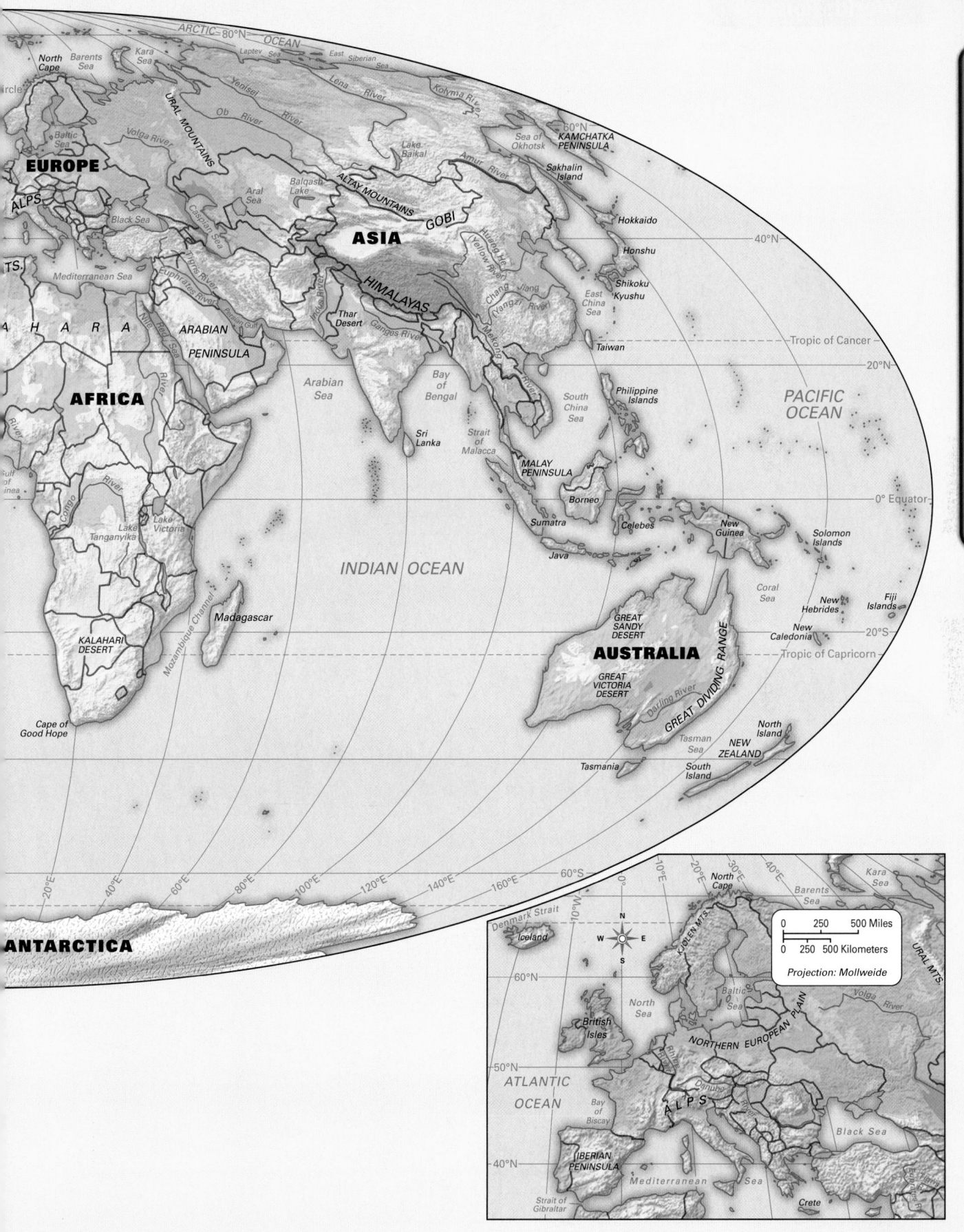

ARCTIC 80°N OCEAN

North
Cape
Barents
Sea
Kara
Sea
Laptev Sea
East Siberian
Sea

EUROPE

ALPS

Baltic
Sea

Black Sea

TS.

Mediterranean Sea

Ural Mountains
Ob
River

Volga River

Caspian Sea

Aral
Sea

Yenisei
River

Lena
River

Kolyma River

60°N

Sea of
Okhotsk

KAMCHATKA
PENINSULA

Lake
Baikal

Balqash
Lake

ALTAY MOUNTAINS

GOBI

ASIA

Amur
River

Sakhalin
Island

Hokkaido

40°N

AHARA
ARABIAN
PENINSULA

Nile River

Tigris River
Euphrates River

Persian Gulf

Indus River

Thar
Desert

HIMALAYAS

Huang He

Yellow River

Chang Jiang
(Yangzi) River

Honshu

Shikoku
Kyushu

East
China
Sea

AFRICA

Arabian
Sea

Ganges River

Bay of
Bengal

Mekong River

Taiwan
Tropic of Cancer

20°N

Congo River

Lake
Tanganyika

Lake
Victoria

Sri
Lanka

Strait
of
Malacca

MALAY
PENINSULA

South
China
Sea

Philippine
Islands

PACIFIC
OCEAN

Gulf
of
inea

Sumatra

Borneo

Celebes

New
Guinea

Solomon
Islands

0° Equator

Java

INDIAN OCEAN

Madagascar

Mozambique Channel

KALAHARI
DESERT

GREAT
SANDY
DESERT

AUSTRALIA

GREAT
VICTORIA
DESERT

Darling River

GREAT DIVIDING RANGE

Coral
Sea

New
Hebrides

New
Caledonia

Fiji
Islands

20°S
Tropic of Capricorn

Cape of
Good Hope

Tasman
Sea

NEW
ZEALAND

North
Island

Tasmania

South
Island

20°E
40°E
60°E
80°E
100°E
120°E
140°E
160°E
60°S

ANTARCTICA

Denmark Strait

Iceland

10°W

North
Cape

10°E
20°E
30°E
40°E

Barents
Sea

Kara
Sea

KJÖLEN MTS.

N
W E
S

Baltic
Sea

URAL MTS.

Volga
River

0 250 500 Miles
0 250 500 Kilometers

Projection: Mollweide

60°N

North
Sea

British
Isles

NORTHERN EUROPEAN PLAIN

ATLANTIC

OCEAN

50°N

Bay
of
Biscay

ALPS

Danube River

40°N

IBERIAN
PENINSULA

Black
Sea

Mediterranean Sea

Crete

Strait of
Gibraltar

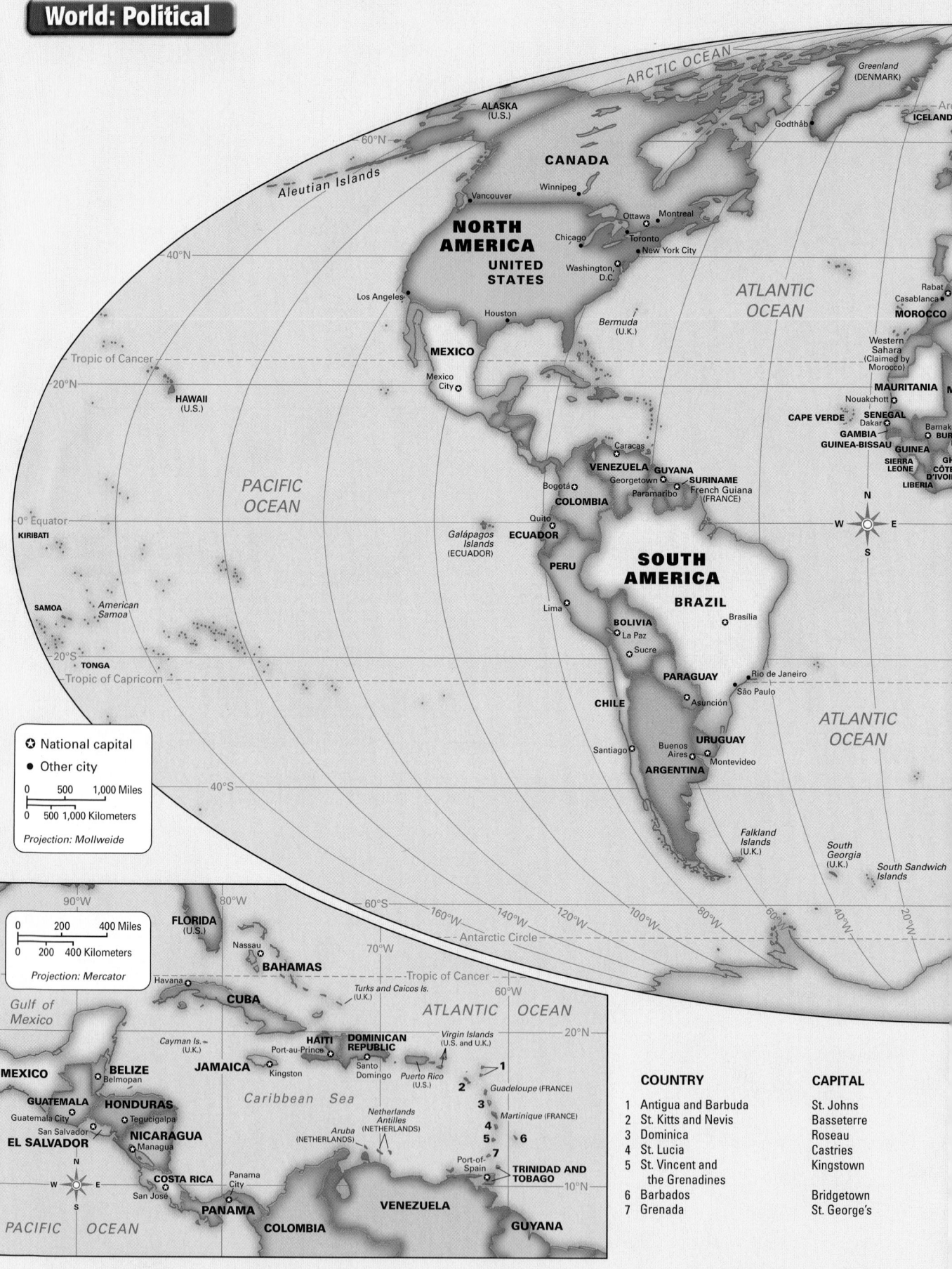

ATLAS

ARCTIC OCEAN

Greenland (DENMARK)

ICELAND

ALASKA (U.S.)

Godthåb

CANADA

NORTH AMERICA

Vancouver
Winnipeg
Ottawa · Montreal
Chicago · Toronto
New York City
Washington, D.C.

UNITED STATES

Los Angeles

Houston

Bermuda (U.K.)

ATLANTIC OCEAN

Rabat
Casablanca

MOROCCO

Western Sahara (Claimed by Morocco)

MEXICO

Mexico City

MAURITANIA

Nouakchott

HAWAII (U.S.)

CAPE VERDE

SENEGAL
Dakar
GAMBIA
GUINEA-BISSAU

Bamako
BUR

GUINEA

SIERRA LEONE
LIBERIA
CÔTE D'IVOIR
GH

Caracas

VENEZUELA GUYANA
Georgetown SURINAME
Bogotá Paramaribo French Guiana (FRANCE)

COLOMBIA

Quito
ECUADOR

Galápagos Islands (ECUADOR)

SOUTH AMERICA

BRAZIL

PACIFIC OCEAN

KIRIBATI

0° Equator

PERU

Lima

Brasília

BOLIVIA
La Paz
Sucre

SAMOA
American Samoa

PARAGUAY
Asunción

Rio de Janeiro
São Paulo

ATLANTIC OCEAN

TONGA

Tropic of Capricorn

CHILE

URUGUAY

Santiago

Buenos Aires
Montevideo

ARGENTINA

☼ National capital
● Other city

0   500   1,000 Miles
0   500 1,000 Kilometers

Projection: Mollweide

Falkland Islands (U.K.)

South Georgia (U.K.)

South Sandwich Islands

60°S

160°W 140°W 120°W 100°W 80°W 60°W 40°W 20°W

Antarctic Circle

Tropic of Cancer

60°W

90°W   80°W

FLORIDA (U.S.)

0   200   400 Miles
0   200 400 Kilometers

Projection: Mercator

Nassau

70°W

BAHAMAS

Turks and Caicos Is. (U.K.)

ATLANTIC OCEAN

20°N

Gulf of Mexico

Havana

CUBA

Cayman Is. (U.K.)

HAITI
Port-au-Prince

DOMINICAN REPUBLIC

Virgin Islands (U.S. and U.K.)

MEXICO

BELIZE
Belmopan

JAMAICA
Kingston

Santo Domingo

Puerto Rico (U.S.)

Guadeloupe (FRANCE)

GUATEMALA
Guatemala City

HONDURAS
Tegucigalpa

Caribbean Sea

Netherlands Antilles (NETHERLANDS)

Martinique (FRANCE)

San Salvador
EL SALVADOR

NICARAGUA
Managua

Aruba (NETHERLANDS)

Port-of-Spain

TRINIDAD AND TOBAGO

COSTA RICA

Panama City

San José

PANAMA

10°N

PACIFIC OCEAN

COLOMBIA

VENEZUELA

GUYANA

COUNTRY	CAPITAL
1 Antigua and Barbuda	St. Johns
2 St. Kitts and Nevis	Basseterre
3 Dominica	Roseau
4 St. Lucia	Castries
5 St. Vincent and the Grenadines	Kingstown
6 Barbados	Bridgetown
7 Grenada	St. George's

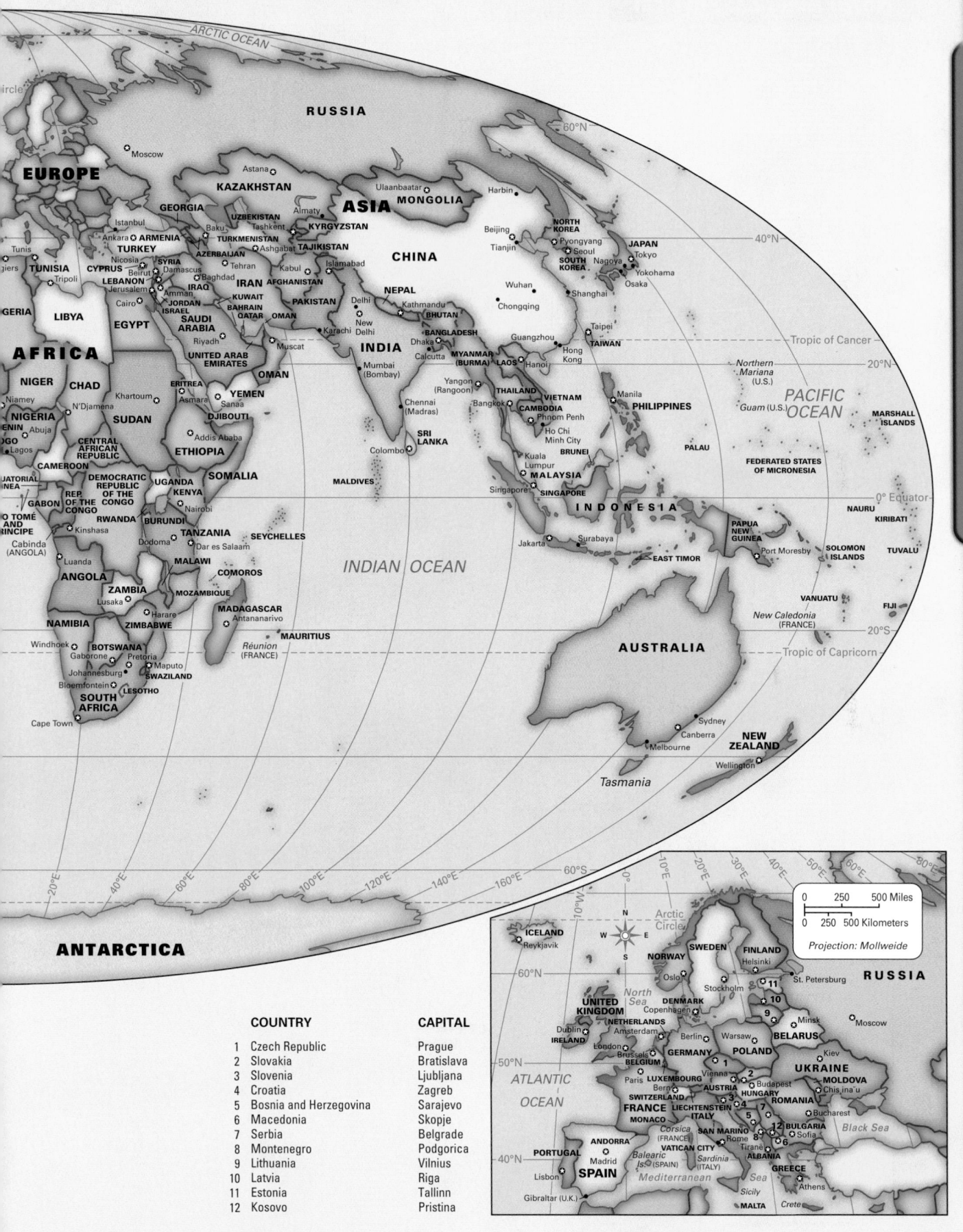

ARCTIC OCEAN

RUSSIA

60°N

EUROPE

Moscow

ASIA

Astana
KAZAKHSTAN
MONGOLIA
Ulaanbaatar
Harbin

GEORGIA
UZBEKISTAN
Almaty
KYRGYZSTAN
Beijing
NORTH KOREA
Pyongyang
JAPAN
40°N
Istanbul
Ankara **ARMENIA**
Baku
Tashkent
TAJIKISTAN
CHINA
Tianjin
Seoul
SOUTH KOREA
Tokyo
Nagoya
TURKEY
AZERBAIJAN
Ashgabat
Tehran
Kabul
AFGHANISTAN
Wuhan
Yokohama
Osaka
Tunis
TUNISIA
Nicosia
CYPRUS
Beirut
SYRIA
Damascus
Baghdad
IRAN
Islamabad
NEPAL
Shanghai
giers
LEBANON
Jerusalem
Amman
IRAQ
KUWAIT
PAKISTAN
Delhi
Kathmandu
Chongqing
ISRAEL
JORDAN
BAHRAIN
QATAR
New Delhi
BHUTAN
Guangzhou
Taipei
TAIWAN
Tropic of Cancer
GERIA
Cairo
EGYPT
SAUDI ARABIA
Riyadh
OMAN
Karachi
BANGLADESH
Dhaka
Hong Kong
LIBYA
UNITED ARAB EMIRATES
Muscat
INDIA
Calcutta
MYANMAR (BURMA)
LAOS
Hanoi
20°N
Northern Mariana (U.S.)
AFRICA
NIGER
CHAD
Khartoum
ERITREA
Asmara
YEMEN
Sanaa
Mumbai (Bombay)
Yangon (Rangoon)
THAILAND
VIETNAM
Manila
PACIFIC OCEAN
Guam (U.S.)
MARSHALL ISLANDS
Niamey
N'Djamena
SUDAN
DJIBOUTI
Chennai (Madras)
Bangkok
CAMBODIA
Phnom Penh
PHILIPPINES
ENIN
Abuja
NIGERIA
Addis Ababa
ETHIOPIA
SOMALIA
SRI LANKA
Ho Chi Minh City
PALAU
GO
Lagos
CENTRAL AFRICAN REPUBLIC
Colombo
BRUNEI
FEDERATED STATES OF MICRONESIA
CAMEROON
UGANDA
KENYA
MALDIVES
Kuala Lumpur
MALAYSIA
0° Equator
ATORIAL
NEA
DEMOCRATIC REPUBLIC OF THE CONGO
Nairobi
Singapore
SINGAPORE
NAURU
KIRIBATI
GABON
REP. OF THE CONGO
RWANDA
BURUNDI
Dodoma
TANZANIA
SEYCHELLES
INDONESIA
Kinshasa
Dar es Salaam
PAPUA NEW GUINEA
SOLOMON ISLANDS
TUVALU
Cabinda (ANGOLA)
Luanda
MALAWI
COMOROS
Jakarta
Surabaya
EAST TIMOR
Port Moresby
ANGOLA
ZAMBIA
MOZAMBIQUE
MADAGASCAR
Antananarivo
INDIAN OCEAN
Lusaka
Harare
ZIMBABWE
MAURITIUS
VANUATU
FIJI
NAMIBIA
Windhoek
Réunion (FRANCE)
New Caledonia (FRANCE)
20°S
Gaborone
BOTSWANA
Pretoria
Maputo
SWAZILAND
Tropic of Capricorn
Johannesburg
Bloemfontein
LESOTHO
AUSTRALIA
SOUTH AFRICA
Cape Town
Sydney
Canberra
NEW ZEALAND
Melbourne
Wellington

20°E 40°E 60°E 80°E 100°E 120°E 140°E 160°E 60°S

Tasmania

ANTARCTICA

COUNTRY	CAPITAL
1 Czech Republic	Prague
2 Slovakia	Bratislava
3 Slovenia	Ljubljana
4 Croatia	Zagreb
5 Bosnia and Herzegovina	Sarajevo
6 Macedonia	Skopje
7 Serbia	Belgrade
8 Montenegro	Podgorica
9 Lithuania	Vilnius
10 Latvia	Riga
11 Estonia	Tallinn
12 Kosovo	Pristina

Arctic Circle

0 250 500 Miles
0 250 500 Kilometers
Projection: Mollweide

ICELAND
Reykjavik
NORWAY
SWEDEN
FINLAND
Helsinki
St. Petersburg
RUSSIA
60°N
Oslo
Stockholm
11
Minsk
Moscow
North Sea
Copenhagen
DENMARK
10
9
UNITED KINGDOM
NETHERLANDS
Amsterdam
Berlin
Warsaw
BELARUS
Dublin
IRELAND
London
Brussels
BELGIUM
GERMANY
POLAND
Kiev
UKRAINE
50°N
Paris
LUXEMBOURG
1
Vienna
Budapest
MOLDOVA
Chisinau
ATLANTIC OCEAN
Bern
SWITZERLAND
AUSTRIA
2
HUNGARY
Bucharest
FRANCE
LIECHTENSTEIN
3
ROMANIA
MONACO
4
5
ANDORRA
Corsica (FRANCE)
SAN MARINO
ITALY
12
BULGARIA
Sofia
PORTUGAL
Madrid
VATICAN CITY
Rome
6
Black Sea
40°N
Lisbon
SPAIN
Balearic Is. (SPAIN)
Sardinia (ITALY)
Tirane
ALBANIA
GREECE
Gibraltar (U.K.)
Mediterranean
Sicily
MALTA
Crete
Athens

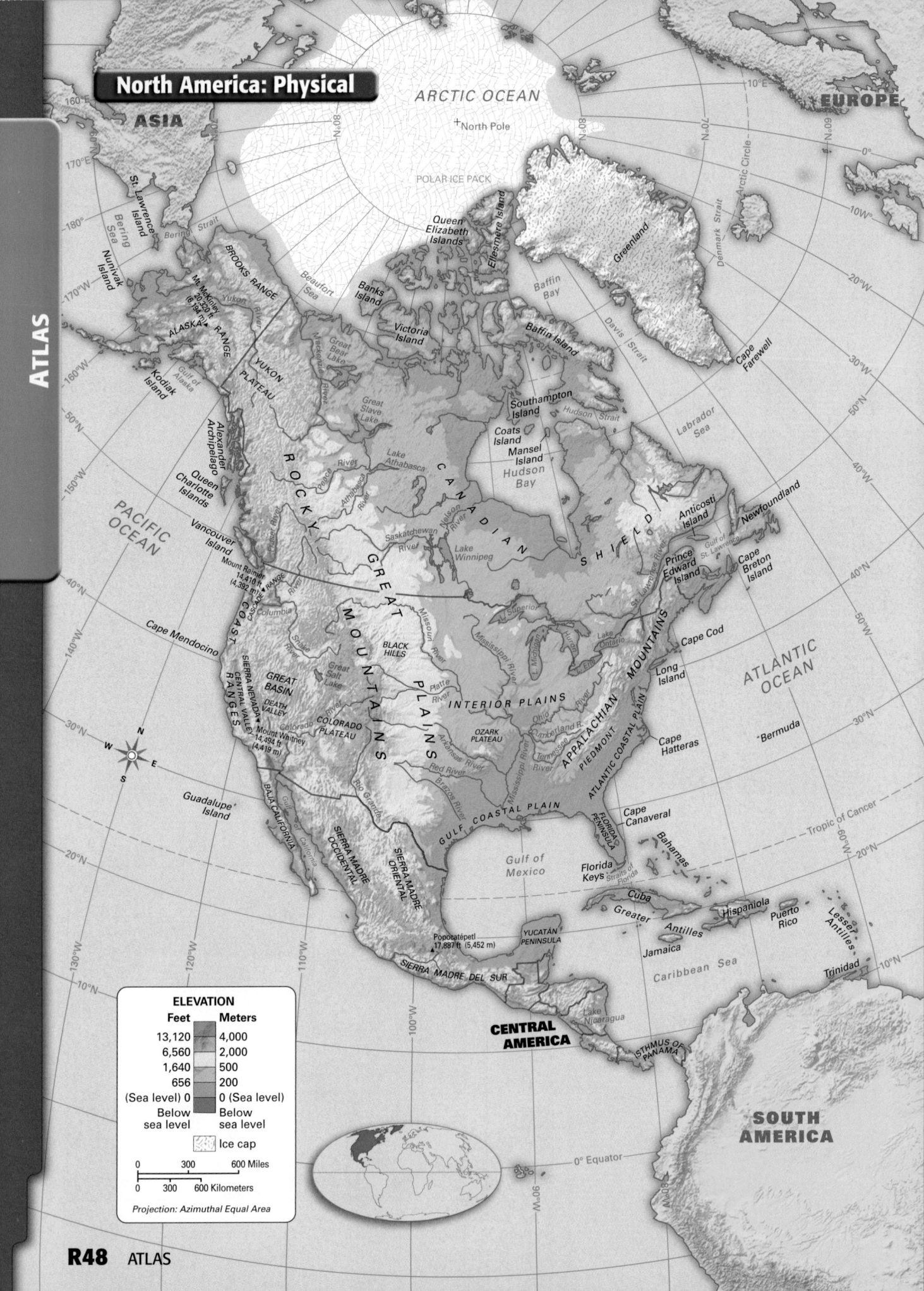

North America: Physical

ARCTIC OCEAN

+North Pole

ASIA

EUROPE

POLAR ICE PACK

Queen
Elizabeth
Islands

Ellesmere Island

Greenland

Denmark Strait

St. Lawrence
Island

Bering
Sea

Bering Strait

BROOKS RANGE

Nunivak
Island

Mt. McKinley
20,320 ft
(6,194 m)

ALASKA

Yukon River

RANGE

Beaufort
Sea

Banks
Island

Victoria
Island

Mackenzie River

Great
Bear
Lake

Baffin
Bay

Baffin Island

Davis Strait

Cape
Farewell

Arctic Circle

Kodiak
Island

Gulf
of
Alaska

YUKON
PLATEAU

Great
Slave
Lake

Southampton
Island

Hudson Strait

Labrador
Sea

Alexander
Archipelago

R
O
C
K
Y

Peace River

Lake
Athabasca

C
A
N
A
D
I
A
N

Coats
Island

Mansel
Island

Hudson
Bay

Queen
Charlotte
Islands

Athabasca River

Vancouver
Island

PACIFIC
OCEAN

Fraser River

Saskatchewan
River

Nelson River

S
H
I
E
L
D

Anticosti
Island

Newfoundland

Mount Rainier
14,410 ft
(4,392 m)

COAST
RANGE

CASCADE RANGE

G
R
E
A
T

M
O
U
N
T
A
I
N
S

Columbia
River

Lake
Winnipeg

Missouri River

Superior

St. Lawrence River

Prince
Edward
Island

Gulf of
St. Lawrence

Cape
Breton
Island

Cape
Mendocino

Snake River

BLACK
HILLS

Michigan

Lake
Ontario

Erie

Cape Cod

Long
Island

ATLANTIC
OCEAN

SIERRA NEVADA

GREAT
BASIN

Great
Salt
Lake

G
R
E
A
T

P
L
A
I
N
S

Platte
River

Mississippi River

Ohio

A
P
P
A
L
A
C
H
I
A
N

M
O
U
N
T
A
I
N
S

PIEDMONT

Cape
Hatteras

Bermuda

CENTRAL VALLEY

RANGES

DEATH
VALLEY

Mount Whitney
14,494 ft
(4,419 m)

COLORADO
PLATEAU

Colorado River

INTERIOR PLAINS

Arkansas River

OZARK
PLATEAU

Cumberland R.

Tennessee
River

ATLANTIC COASTAL PLAIN

Red River

Brazos River

Rio Grande

GULF COASTAL PLAIN

FLORIDA
PENINSULA

Cape
Canaveral

Guadalupe
Island

BAJA CALIFORNIA

Gulf of California

SIERRA MADRE
OCCIDENTAL

SIERRA MADRE
ORIENTAL

Gulf of
Mexico

Florida
Keys

Straits of
Florida

Bahamas

Cuba

Greater

Antilles

Hispaniola

Puerto
Rico

Lesser
Antilles

Popocatépetl
17,887 ft (5,452 m)

YUCATÁN
PENINSULA

Jamaica

Caribbean Sea

Trinidad

SIERRA MADRE DEL SUR

Lake
Nicaragua

CENTRAL
AMERICA

ISTHMUS OF
PANAMA

SOUTH
AMERICA

0° Equator

Tropic of Cancer

ELEVATION

Feet		Meters
13,120		4,000
6,560		2,000
1,640		500
656		200
(Sea level) 0		0 (Sea level)
Below
sea level		Below
sea level

Ice cap

0   300   600 Miles

0   300   600 Kilometers

Projection: Azimuthal Equal Area

North America: Political

ASIA
EUROPE

ARCTIC OCEAN
+ North Pole

ICELAND

Greenland
(DENMARK)

St. Lawrence
Island
Bering Strait

Point
Barrow

Queen
Elizabeth
Islands

Ellesmere Island

Nunivak
Island

Beaufort
Sea

Banks
Island

Baffin
Bay

Denmark Strait

ALASKA
(U.S.)

Victoria
Island

Baffin Island

Davis Strait

Anchorage

Great
Bear
Lake

Cape
Farewell

Kodiak
Island

Gulf of
Alaska

Labrador
Sea

Juneau

Alexander
Archipelago

Great
Slave
Lake

Southampton
Island

Hudson Strait

Queen
Charlotte
Islands

Coats
Island
Mansel
Island

PACIFIC
OCEAN

Vancouver
Island

Edmonton

Hudson
Bay

Anticosti
Island

Newfoundland

CANADA

Lake
Winnipeg

St. Pierre and
Miquelon (FRANCE)

Vancouver

Calgary

Prince
Edward
Island

Cape
Breton
Island

Gulf of St. Lawrence

Seattle

Winnipeg

Lake
Superior

Quebec

Portland

Lake
Huron

Ottawa
Toronto

Montreal

ATLANTIC
OCEAN

Minneapolis

Lake
Michigan

Lake
Ontario
Lake Erie

Boston
Cape Cod
New York City

Milwaukee
Detroit

Cleveland

Philadelphia

Chicago

Columbus

Baltimore

San Francisco
San
Jose

Great
Salt
Lake

Salt Lake
City

Indianapolis

Washington, D.C.

Denver

Kansas City

St. Louis

Norfolk

Los Angeles
San Diego
Tijuana

UNITED STATES

Bermuda
(U.K.)

Phoenix

Memphis

Atlanta
Birmingham

Dallas

Jacksonville

Austin
San
Antonio

Houston

New Orleans

Gulf of California

Tropic of Cancer

Miami
BAHAMAS

Turks and Caicos
Islands (U.K.)

ST. KITTS & NEVIS

Gulf of
Mexico

Florida
Keys

Nassau

Monterrey

DOMINICAN
REPUBLIC

Puerto Rico (U.S.)

ANTIGUA &
BARBUDA

Havana

San
Juan

Guadeloupe
(FRANCE)

MEXICO

CUBA

DOMINICA

Guadalajara

Mexico
City

Mérida

HAITI

Santo
Domingo

Virgin Is.
(U.S.-U.K.)

BARBADOS

Puebla

Cayman Is.
(U.K.)

Kingston

Port-au-
Prince

Martinique (FRANCE)

ST. LUCIA

JAMAICA

ST. VINCENT AND
THE GRENADINES

GRENADA

Belmopan
BELIZE

Netherlands
Antilles
(NETHERLANDS)

GUATEMALA
HONDURAS

Caribbean Sea

Aruba (NETHERLANDS)

TRINIDAD AND TOBAGO

Guatemala City

Tegucigalpa

San Salvador
EL SALVADOR

NICARAGUA
Managua

Panama
Canal

San José

Panama City

COSTA
RICA

PANAMA

SOUTH
AMERICA

⊕ National capital

● Other city

0   300   600 Miles

0   300   600 Kilometers

Projection: Azimuthal Equal-Area

0° Equator

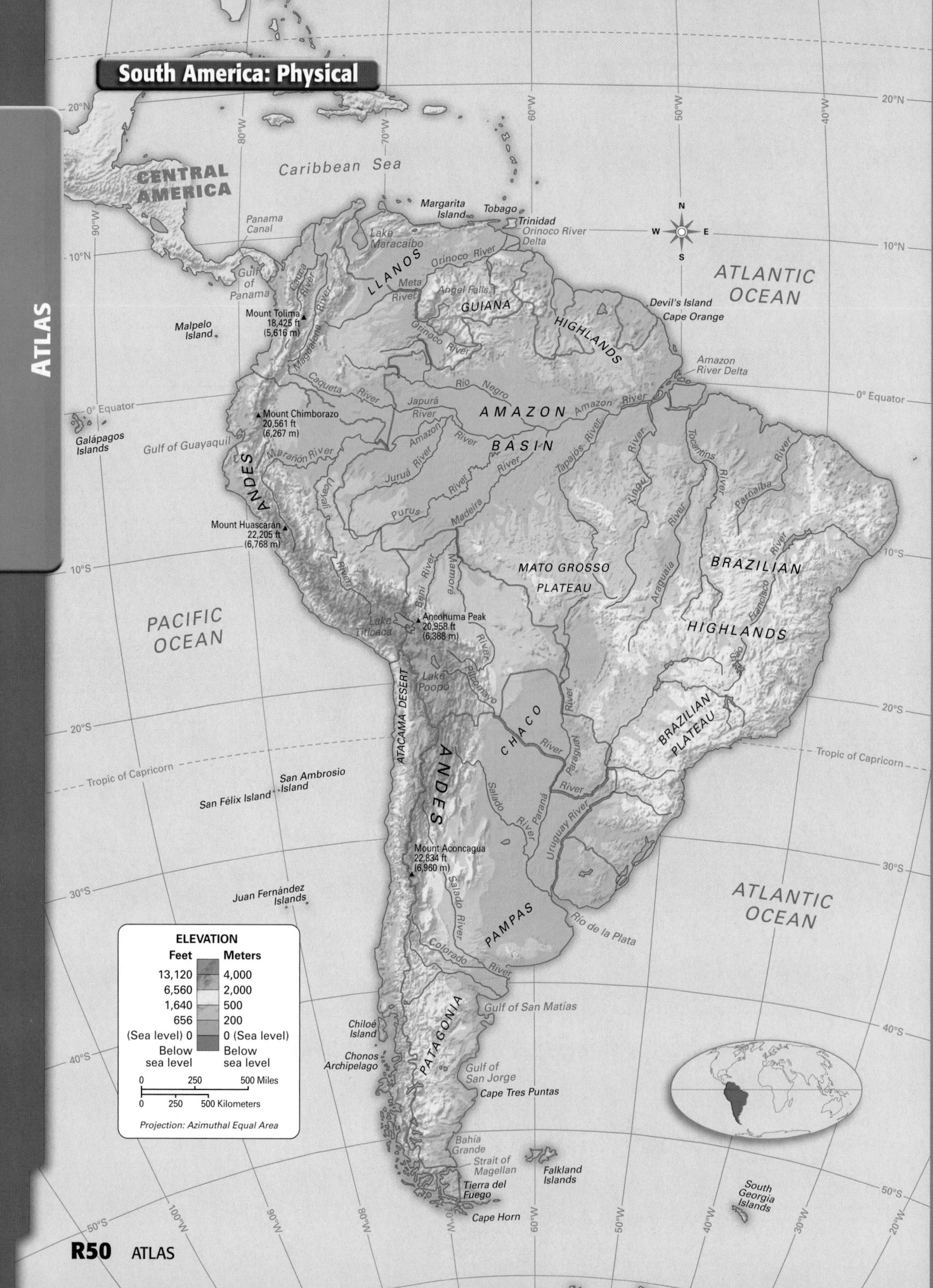

South America: Physical

CENTRAL AMERICA

Caribbean Sea

Panama Canal

Gulf of Panama

Malpelo Island

Margarita Island
Tobago
Trinidad
Orinoco River Delta

Lake Maracaibo

LLANOS

Orinoco River

Meta River

Cauca River

Magdalena River

Mount Tolima
18,425 ft
(5,616 m)

Angel Falls

GUIANA

HIGHLANDS

Devil's Island
Cape Orange

ATLANTIC OCEAN

Orinoco River

Caquetá River

Río Negro

Amazon River Delta

Mount Chimborazo
20,561 ft
(6,267 m)

Japurá River

AMAZON

Amazon River

BASIN

Amazon River

Galápagos Islands

Gulf of Guayaquil

A N D E S

Marañón River

Amazon River

Juruá River

River

River

Ucayali River

Tapajós River

River

Xingu River

Tocantins River

Parnaíba River

Purus

Madeira River

Mount Huascarán
22,205 ft
(6,768 m)

PACIFIC OCEAN

Beni River

Mamoré River

Lake Titicaca

Ancohuma Peak
20,958 ft
(6,388 m)

MATO GROSSO
PLATEAU

São Francisco River

BRAZILIAN

HIGHLANDS

BRAZILIAN
PLATEAU

Araguaia River

Lake Poopó

River

Pilcomayo River

C H A C O

Paraguay River

ATACAMA DESERT

San Félix Island

San Ambrosio Island

Salado River

Paraná River

River

Tropic of Capricorn

A N D E S

Mount Aconcagua
22,834 ft
(6,960 m)

Uruguay River

Tropic of Capricorn

ATLANTIC OCEAN

Juan Fernández Islands

Salado River

PAMPAS

Río de la Plata

Colorado River

ELEVATION

Feet		Meters
13,120		4,000
6,560		2,000
1,640		500
656		200
(Sea level) 0		0 (Sea level)
Below sea level		Below sea level

0   250   500 Miles

0   250   500 Kilometers

Projection: Azimuthal Equal Area

Chiloé Island

Chonos Archipelago

Gulf of San Matías

Gulf of San Jorge

Cape Tres Puntas

PATAGONIA

Bahía Grande

Strait of Magellan

Tierra del Fuego

Falkland Islands

South Georgia Islands

Cape Horn

South America: Political

CENTRAL
AMERICA

Caribbean Sea

Barranquilla
Cartagena
Caracas

Lake
Maracaibo
VENEZUELA

Georgetown
Paramaribo
Cayenne

GUYANA
SURINAME
French
Guiana
(FRANCE)

*ATLANTIC
OCEAN*

Medellín
Bogotá
COLOMBIA
Cali

*Malpelo
Island
(COLOMBIA)*

Quito
ECUADOR
Guayaquil

*Galápagos
Islands
(ECUADOR)*

0° Equator

Belém

Trujillo

PERU

BRAZIL

Recife

Callao Lima

*PACIFIC
OCEAN*

Arequipa

*Lake
Titicaca*
La Paz
*Lake
Poopó*
BOLIVIA
Sucre

Brasília

Salvador

Belo Horizonte

Campinas
São Paulo

PARAGUAY

Asunción

Rio de Janeiro

Tropic of
Capricorn

Tropic of Capricorn

*San Ambrosio
Island
(CHILE)*

*San Félix Island
(CHILE)*

Curitiba

Pôrto Alegre

CHILE

*Juan Fernández
Islands
(CHILE)*

Córdoba

Rosario

URUGUAY

*ATLANTIC
OCEAN*

Valparaíso
Santiago

Buenos Aires
Montevideo

ARGENTINA

☆ National capital
• Other city

0   250   500 Miles
0 250   500 Kilometers

Projection: Azimuthal Equal-Area

*Strait of
Magellan*

*Falkland
Islands (U.K.)*

*Tierra del
Fuego*

*South Georgia
Island
(U.K.)*

Europe: Physical

ELEVATION

Feet	Meters
13,120	4,000
6,560	2,000
1,640	500
656	200
(Sea level) 0	0 (Sea level)
Below sea level	Below sea level

Ice cap

0 ____ 150 ____ 300 Miles

0 ____ 150 ____ 300 Kilometers

Projection: Azimuthal Equal Area

ASIA

URAL MOUNTAINS

Ural River

Kama River

NORTHERN EUROPEAN PLAIN

Pechora River

Dvina River

North Dvina River

KOLA PENINSULA

White Sea

Lake Onega

Lake Ladoga

Rybinski Reservoir

Volga River

Caspian Sea

Mt. Elbrus 18,510 ft (5,642 m)

CAUCASUS MTS.

Sea of Azov

CRIMEAN PENINSULA

Black Sea

Don River

Dnipro River

Barents Sea

Gulf of Finland

PLAINS

BALTIC

Daugava R.

Dvina R.

Vistula River

Oder River

Elbe River

Don River

Dnister River

Nistru River

CARPATHIAN MTS.

TRANSYLVANIAN ALPS

Danube

Danube River

Sea of Marmara

Aegean Sea

Rhodes

Crete

BALKAN PENINSULA

DINARIC ALPS

Adriatic Sea

APENNINES

Tiber River

Tyrrhenian Sea

Sicily

Malta

Mediterranean

SOUTHWEST ASIA

KJØLEN MOUNTAINS

North Cape

Lake Vänern

Lake Vättern

Kattegat

Skagerrak

Gulf of Bothnia

Baltic Sea

NORTHERN

ALPS

Mont Blanc 15,781 ft (4,810 m)

Lake Geneva

Po River

Rhône River

Corsica

Sardinia

Balearic Islands

ARCTIC OCEAN

Norwegian Sea

Iceland

Faeroe Islands

Shetland Islands

Orkney Islands

Hebrides

British Isles

PENNINES

Irish Sea

North Sea

Thames River

English Channel

Seine River

Loire River

Garonne River

PYRENEES

Bay of Biscay

Cape Finisterre

IBERIAN PENINSULA

Duero River

Tagus River

Guadiana River

Guadalquivir River

Ebro River

Strait of Gibraltar

ATLANTIC OCEAN

AFRICA

Rhine River

Arctic Circle

N E S W

Europe: Political

National capital ✪
Other city ●

300 Miles
150
0

300 Kilometers
150
0

Projection: Azimuthal Equal-Area

ASIA

URAL MOUNTAINS

RUSSIA

Nizhny Novgorod

Moscow ✪

Caspian Sea

SOUTHWEST ASIA

Barents Sea

White Sea

St. Petersburg

Black Sea

UKRAINE

Kiev ✪

MOLDOVA

Chisinau ✪

Bucharest ✪

ROMANIA

BULGARIA

Sofia ✪

Belgrade ✪

SERBIA

Prishna ✪ KOSOVO

Skopje ✪ MACEDONIA

Tirana ✪ ALBANIA

GREECE

Athens ✪

Aegean Sea

Rhodes

Crete

North Cape

FINLAND

Helsinki ✪

Gulf of Finland

Tallinn ✪ ESTONIA

LATVIA

Riga ✪

LITHUANIA

Vilnius ✪

Minsk ✪

BELARUS

Warsaw ✪

POLAND

Krakow ●

RUSSIA

Baltic Sea

Gulf of Bothnia

ARCTIC OCEAN

SWEDEN

Stockholm ✪

Göteborg ●

Oslo ✪

NORWAY

Bergen ●

Copenhagen ✪

DENMARK

Hamburg ●

Berlin ✪

GERMANY

Dresden ●

Prague ✪ CZECH REPUBLIC

SLOVAKIA

Bratislava ✪

Budapest ✪

HUNGARY

Vienna ✪ AUSTRIA

SLOVENIA

Zagreb ✪ CROATIA

Ljubljana ✪

BOSNIA AND HERZEGOVINA

Sarajevo ✪

MONTENEGRO

Podgorica ✪

Adriatic Sea

SAN MARINO

San Marino ✪

ITALY

Rome ✪ VATICAN CITY

Naples ●

Sicily

MALTA

Valletta ✪

Mediterranean Sea

North Sea

Shetland Islands

Faeroe Islands (DENMARK)

ICELAND

Reykjavik ✪

Arctic Circle

SCOTLAND

Edinburgh ✪

Belfast ●

NORTHERN IRELAND

Dublin ✪

IRELAND

UNITED KINGDOM

Liverpool ●

WALES

ENGLAND

London ✪

British Isles

Channel Islands (U.K.)

English Channel

THE NETHERLANDS

Amsterdam ✪

Brussels ✪ BELGIUM

LUXEMBOURG

Luxembourg ✪

Cologne ●

Bonn ●

Paris ✪

FRANCE

Munich ●

LIECHTENSTEIN

Vaduz ✪

SWITZERLAND

Bern ✪

Lake Geneva

Milan ●

MONACO

Monaco ✪

Lyon ●

Marseille ●

Corsica (FRANCE)

Sardinia (ITALY)

Bay of Biscay

PYRENEES

ANDORRA

Andorra la Vella ✪

Barcelona ●

Balearic Islands (SPAIN)

SPAIN

Madrid ✪

Valencia ●

Seville ●

Gibraltar (U.K.)

Strait of Gibraltar

PORTUGAL

Lisbon ✪

AFRICA

ATLANTIC OCEAN

Asia: Physical

ELEVATION

Feet	Meters
13,120	4,000
6,560	2,000
1,640	500
656	200
0 (Sea level)	0 (Sea level)
Below sea level	Below sea level

Ice cap

750 Miles
500   750 Kilometers
0   250   500
0   250   500

Projection: Two-Point Equidistant

AUSTRALIA

PACIFIC OCEAN

New Guinea
MAOKE MOUNTAINS
Arafura Sea
Banda Sea
Molucca B.
Celebes Sea
Celebes
Borneo
Java Sea
Java
Sumatra
Bangka
Mentawai Islands
MALAY PENINSULA
Philippines
Mindanao
Luzon
Luzon Strait
Taiwan
Hainan
South China Sea
Gulf of Tonkin
Hong River
INDOCHINA PENINSULA
Mekong River
Chao Phraya River
Gulf of Thailand
Andaman Sea
Nicobar Islands
Andaman Islands
BOHEA HILLS
East China Sea
Okinawa
Ryukyu Islands
Korea Strait
Kyushu
Shikoku
Honshu
Hokkaido
Kuril Islands
Sakhalin Island
Sea of Japan (East Sea)
Tropic of Cancer
NORTH CHINA PLAIN
QIN LING
Huang He (Yellow River)
Yellow Sea
GREATER KHINGAN RANGE
Yangzi River (Chang)
Chang River
Brahmaputra River
PLATEAU OF TIBET
Mount Everest 29,035 ft (8,850 m)
HIMALAYAS
KUNLUN MOUNTAINS
TAKLIMAKAN DESERT
TARIM BASIN
TIAN SHAN
HINDU KUSH
Indus River
INDO-GANGETIC PLAIN
Ganges River
THAR DESERT
DECCAN PLATEAU
Godavari River
EASTERN GHATS
WESTERN GHATS
Sutlej River
Bay of Bengal
Sri Lanka
Maldives
Lakshadweep Islands
INDIAN OCEAN
Arabian Sea
Socotra Island
Gulf of Aden
Red Sea
AFRICA
RUB AL-KHALI
Gulf of Oman
Persian Gulf
Strait of Hormuz
ZAGROS MTS.
AN-NAFUD
SYRIAN DESERT
GREAT SALT DESERT
USTYURT PLATEAU
KARA KUM
Amu Darya
Aral Sea
TURAN LOWLAND
KYZYL KUM
Syr Darya
Balqash Lake
KAZAKH UPLANDS
Irtysh River
Ishim River
WEST SIBERIAN PLAIN
Ob River
Yenisey River
SAYAN MOUNTAINS
ALTAY MOUNTAINS
MONGOLIAN PLATEAU
GOBI
YABLONOV RANGE
Shilka River
Amur River
STANOVOY MOUNTAINS
Lake Baykal
Angara River
Lower Tunguska River
CENTRAL SIBERIAN PLATEAU
S I B E R I A
Lena River
Aldan River
VERKHOYANSKY RANGE
CHERSKIY RANGE
KOLYMA MTS.
CENTRAL RANGE
KAMCHATKA PENINSULA
Sea of Okhotsk
Bering Sea
Aleutian Islands
Wrangel Island
New Siberian Islands
TAYMYR PENINSULA
North Land
Laptev Sea
Kara Sea
Franz Josef Land
Novaya Zemlya
Barents Sea
North Pole
Arctic Circle
URAL MOUNTAINS
Ural River
Caspian Sea
CAUCASUS MTS.
Mount Ararat 16,945 ft (5,165 m)
ANATOLIAN PLATEAU
Cyprus
Black Sea
Bosporus
Mediterranean Sea
SINAI PENINSULA
Tigris River
Euphrates River
EUROPE

R54   ATLAS

Asia: Political

National capitals
Other cities

750 Miles
500 750 Kilometers
250 500
0
250
0

Projection: Two-Point Equidistant

EUROPE

RUSSIA

AFRICA

North Pole

Arctic Circle

Aleutian Islands

Bering Sea

Sea of Okhotsk

Sakhalin Island

Kuril Islands (RUSSIA)

URAL MOUNTAINS

Moscow

Yekaterinburg

Chelyabinsk

Omsk

Novosibirsk

Astana

KAZAKHSTAN

Lake Balkhash

Aral Sea

Caspian Sea

Black Sea

Istanbul

Izmir

Ankara

TURKEY

CYPRUS

Nicosia

LEBANON

Beirut

SYRIA

Damascus

ISRAEL

Tel Aviv

Jerusalem

Amman

JORDAN

Mecca

Jidda

Red Sea

Mediterranean Sea

GEORGIA

Tbilisi

ARMENIA

Yerevan

AZERBAIJAN

Baku

Mosul

Baghdad

IRAQ

Basra

KUWAIT

Kuwait City

BAHRAIN

Manama

QATAR

Doha

Riyadh

SAUDI ARABIA

YEMEN

Sanaa

Socotra (YEMEN)

Gulf of Aden

IRAN

Tehran

Shiraz

Abu Dhabi

UNITED ARAB EMIRATES

OMAN

Masqat (Muscat)

Persian Gulf

Arabian Sea

TURKMENISTAN

Ashgabat

UZBEKISTAN

Tashkent

TAJIKISTAN

Dushanbe

KYRGYZSTAN

Bishkek

Almaty

AFGHANISTAN

Kabul

PAKISTAN

Islamabad

Lahore

Karachi

Delhi

New Delhi

Jaipur

Ahmadabad

Mumbai (Bombay)

Bangalore

INDIA

Chennai (Madras)

Lakshadweep Islands (INDIA)

MALDIVES

Male

SRI LANKA

Colombo

Kolkata (Calcutta)

NEPAL

Kathmandu

BHUTAN

Thimphu

BANGLADESH

Dhaka

Bay of Bengal

Andaman Islands (INDIA)

Nicobar Islands (INDIA)

INDIAN OCEAN

MYANMAR (BURMA)

Naypyidaw

Yangon (Rangoon)

THAILAND

Bangkok

LAOS

Vientiane

Gulf of Thailand

CAMBODIA

Phnom Penh

VIETNAM

Hanoi

Ho Chi Minh City

South China Sea

Andaman Sea

MALAYSIA

Kuala Lumpur

SINGAPORE

Singapore

BRUNEI

Bandar Seri Begawan

Medan

Java Sea

Jakarta

Bandung

Surabaya

Ujung Pandang

INDONESIA

Celebes Sea

PHILIPPINES

Manila

Luzon Strait

EAST TIMOR

Dili

New Guinea

Arafura Sea

AUSTRALIA

Equator

PACIFIC OCEAN

Tropic of Cancer

RUSSIA

Yakutsk

Irkutsk

Lake Baykal

MONGOLIA

Ulaanbaatar

CHINA

Chengdu

Chongqing

Wuhan

Nanjing

Shanghai

Guangzhou

Hong Kong

Macao

Hainan (CHINA)

East China Sea

Yellow Sea

Beijing

Qingdao

Dalian

Fushun

Harbin

Vladivostok

NORTH KOREA

PYONGYANG

SOUTH KOREA

Seoul

Pusan

JAPAN

Sapporo

Tokyo

Yokohama

Kyoto

Osaka

Hiroshima

Nagasaki

RYUKYU ISLANDS (JAPAN)

Taipei

TAIWAN

Africa: Physical

EUROPE

SOUTHWEST ASIA

Azores

Madeira Islands

Canary Islands

Strait of Gibraltar

ATLAS MOUNTAINS

Mediterranean Sea

Gulf of Sidra

Suez Canal

Persian Gulf

Tropic of Cancer

Cape Blanc

EL DJOUF

S A H A R A

AHAGGAR MOUNTAINS

AIR MTS.

TIBESTI MOUNTAINS

LIBYAN DESERT

QATTARA DEPRESSION

Nile River

Lake Nasser

NUBIAN DESERT

Red Sea

Cape Verde Islands

Cape Verde

Senegal R.

Niger River

S A H E L

S U D A N

CHAD BASIN

Lake Chad

Blue Nile

White Nile

Lake Tana

Gulf of Aden

FOUTA DJALLON

White Volta R.

Black Volta R.

Lake Volta

Benue River

SUDAN BASIN

ETHIOPIAN HIGHLANDS

RIFT VALLEY

HORN OF AFRICA

SOMALI PENINSULA

10°N

Cape Palmas

Gulf of Guinea

ADAMAWA MTS.

Ubangi River

Congo River

Lake Albert

Lake Turkana

Mount Kenya 17,058 ft (5,199 m)

0° Equator

Cape Lopez

CONGO BASIN

Kasai River

Lake Edward

Lake Kivu

Lake Victoria

SERENGETI PLAIN

Mount Kilimanjaro 19,340 ft (5,895 m)

INDIAN OCEAN

Ascension

MITUMBA MOUNTAINS

WESTERN RIFT VALLEY

Lake Tanganyika

MASAI STEPPE

Zanzibar

EASTERN RIFT VALLEY

Seychelles

ATLANTIC OCEAN

Cuanza River

Lake Rukwa

Lake Mweru

Lake Malawi (Nyasa)

Cape Delgado

10°S

Comoro Islands

Lake Kariba

Zambezi River

Mozambique Channel

Madagascar

Okavango Delta

Victoria Falls

Mauritius

NAMIB DESERT

KALAHARI BASIN

KALAHARI DESERT

Limpopo River

Réunion

Tropic of Capricorn

Orange River

Vaal River

GREAT KARROO

DRAKENSBERG MOUNTAINS

30°S

Cape of Good Hope

ELEVATION

Feet		Meters
13,120		4,000
6,560		2,000
1,640		500
656		200
(Sea level) 0		0 (Sea level)
Below sea level		Below sea level

0   250   500 Miles

0   250   500 Kilometers

Projection: Azimuthal Equal-Area

Africa: Political

EUROPE

SOUTHWEST
ASIA

Azores
(PORTUGAL)

40°N

Madeira
(PORTUGAL)

Strait of
Gibraltar

Algiers   Tunis

Mediterranean Sea

Casablanca   Rabat

Tripoli

30°N

MOROCCO

TUNISIA

Alexandria

Giza   Cairo

Canary Islands
(SPAIN)

El Aaiún

ALGERIA

LIBYA

EGYPT

WESTERN
SAHARA
(Claimed by
Morocco)

Tropic of Cancer

20°N

MAURITANIA

Nouakchott

MALI

NIGER

CHAD

Khartoum

Red Sea

ERITREA

Asmara

Gulf of Aden

CAPE
VERDE

Praia

SENEGAL

Dakar

GAMBIA

Banjul   Bamako

Bissau

GUINEA-
BISSAU

GUINEA

Conakry

Freetown

SIERRA LEONE

Monrovia

LIBERIA

Niamey

BURKINA
FASO

Ouagadougou

BENIN

CÔTE
D'IVOIRE   GHANA
Yamoussoukro

Abidjan   Accra

TOGO

Lomé   Lagos

Porto-
Novo

NIGERIA

Abuja

CAMEROON

Bangui

Lake
Chad

N'Djamena

SUDAN

DJIBOUTI
Djibouti

ETHIOPIA

Addis Ababa

SOMALIA

Mogadishu

10°N

CENTRAL AFRICAN
REPUBLIC

Gulf of
Guinea

Malabo

EQUATORIAL GUINEA

SÃO TOMÉ AND PRÍNCIPE

São Tomé

Yaoundé

REPUBLIC
OF THE
CONGO

GABON

Libreville

Kisangani

UGANDA

Kampala

RWANDA

Kigali

KENYA

Nairobi

Lake
Victoria

0° Equator

N
W   E
S

DEMOCRATIC
REPUBLIC
OF THE CONGO

Brazzaville

CABINDA
(ANGOLA)

Kinshasa

Bujumbura   BURUNDI

TANZANIA

Lake
Tanganyika

Dodoma

Dar es Salaam

Mombasa

Pemba

Zanzibar

INDIAN
OCEAN

Victoria

SEYCHELLES

10°S

ATLANTIC
OCEAN

Luanda

St. Helena
(U.K.)

ANGOLA

Lubumbashi

ZAMBIA

Lusaka

Lake Malawi
(Nyasa)

MALAWI

Lilongwe

MOZAMBIQUE

COMOROS

Moroni

10°S

Harare

ZIMBABWE

Bulawayo

Antananarivo

MAURITIUS

MADAGASCAR

Port Louis

Réunion
(FRANCE)

Tropic of Capricorn

20°S

NAMIBIA

Windhoek

BOTSWANA

Gaborone

Pretoria

Maputo

Johannesburg   Mbabane

Bloemfontein   SWAZILAND

Maseru

Tropic of Capricorn

30°S

SOUTH AFRICA

LESOTHO

Cape Town

Key:
⊛ National capital
• Other city

0   250   500 Miles

0   250   500 Kilometers

Projection: Azimuthal Equal-Area

The Pacific: Political

ASIA

NORTH AMERICA

NORTH PACIFIC OCEAN

SOUTH PACIFIC OCEAN

INDIAN OCEAN

Philippine Sea

South China Sea

Timor Sea

Arafura Sea

Coral Sea

Tasman Sea

Tropic of Cancer

Equator

Tropic of Capricorn

International Date Line

Legend
- National capital
- Other city

1,000 Miles
1,000 Kilometers
500
500

Projection: Azimuthal Equal-Area

MICRONESIA

Bonin Islands (JAPAN)
Volcano Islands (JAPAN)
Northern Marianas (U.S.)
Guam (U.S.) • Agana
PALAU ✪ Koror
Wake Island (U.S.)
MARSHALL ISLANDS • Eniwetok I.
Kwajalein Island ✪
Majuro ✪
FEDERATED STATES OF MICRONESIA
Truk Is.
NAURU ✪
Gilbert Islands
Palikir ✪
Tarawa ✪
Midway Island (U.S.)
Johnston Island (U.S.)
Hawaiian Islands
Hawaii (U.S.)
Kingman Reef (U.S.)
Palmyra Island (U.S.)
Washington Island
Fanning Island
Howland I. (U.S.)
Baker I. (U.S.)
Jarvis I. (U.S.)
McKean I.
Gardner I.
Phoenix Islands
KIRIBATI

POLYNESIA

Marquesas Islands (FRANCE)
Tuamotu Archipelago (FRANCE)
French Polynesia
Society Islands (FRANCE)
Tahiti (FRANCE) • Papeete
Tubuai Islands (FRANCE)
Rapa Island (FRANCE)
Easter Island (CHILE)
Pitcairn (U.K.)
Pitcairn Island
Ducie Island
Starbuck Island
Manihiki Island
Cook Islands (NEW ZEALAND)
Rarotonga Island
Tokelau (N.Z.)
American Samoa
SAMOA • Apia
Pago Pago
Niue (N.Z.)
TONGA ✪ Nuku'alofa
Wallis & Futuna (Fr.)
TUVALU ✪ Funafuti
FIJI ✪ Suva
Kermadec Islands (N.Z.)
Chatham Islands (N.Z.)
Bounty Islands (N.Z.)
Auckland Islands (NEW ZEALAND)

MELANESIA

Bismarck Archipelago
PAPUA NEW GUINEA
New Guinea
Port Moresby ✪
SOLOMON ISLANDS
Honiara ✪
Guadalcanal I.
Espiritu Santo I.
VANUATU
Malekula I.
Port-Vila ✪
New Caledonia (FRANCE)
Loyalty Islands (FRANCE)
Noumea
Norfolk Island (AUSTRALIA)
North Island
NEW ZEALAND ✪ Wellington
Auckland
Christchurch
South Island

AUSTRALIA

Darwin
Perth
Adelaide
Melbourne
Sydney
Canberra ✪
Brisbane
Hobart

Christmas Island (AUSTRALIA)

120°W, 135°W, 150°W, 165°W, 180°, 165°E, 150°E, 135°E, 120°E
30°N, 15°N, 0°, 15°S, 30°S, 45°S

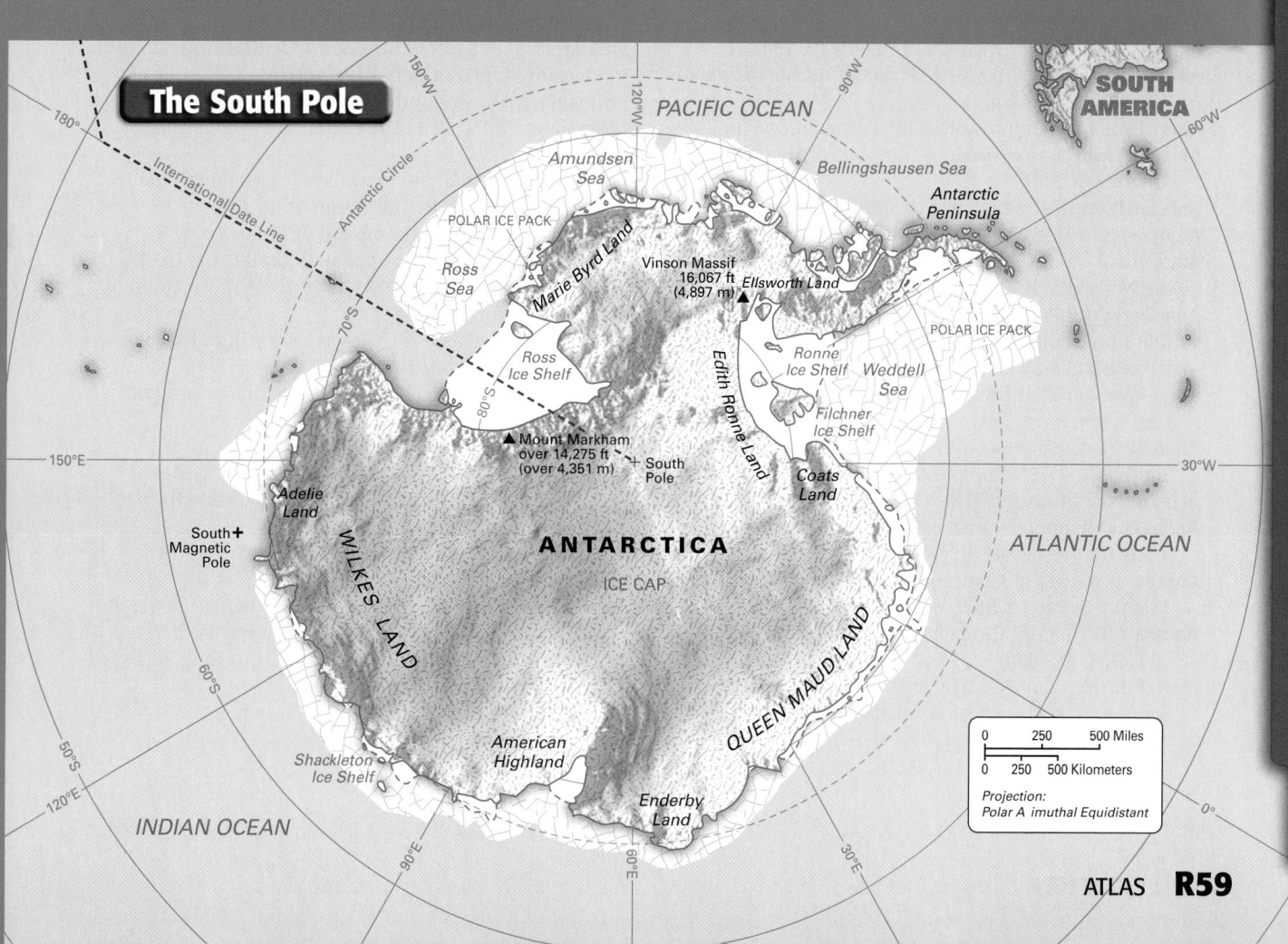

The North Pole

0   200   400 Miles
0   200   400 Kilometers

Projection:
Polar Azimuthal Equidistant

EUROPE

Barents
Sea

Kara
Sea

Norwegian
Sea

Arctic Circle

ASIA

Laptev
Sea

ARCTIC
OCEAN

North
Pole

Greenland
Sea

ATLANTIC
OCEAN

Greenland
(DENMARK)

POLAR ICE PACK

International Date Line

North
Magnetic
Pole

Baffin
Bay

Beaufort
Sea

Bering Sea

NORTH
AMERICA

ATLAS

The South Pole

PACIFIC OCEAN

SOUTH
AMERICA

International Date Line

Antarctic Circle

Amundsen
Sea

Bellingshausen Sea

Antarctic
Peninsula

POLAR ICE PACK

Ross
Sea

Marie Byrd Land

Vinson Massif
16,067 ft
(4,897 m) ▲

Ellsworth Land

POLAR ICE PACK

Ross
Ice Shelf

Ronne
Ice Shelf

Weddell
Sea

Edith Ronne Land

Filchner
Ice Shelf

▲ Mount Markham
over 14,275 ft
(over 4,351 m)

South
Pole

Coats
Land

Adelie
Land

ANTARCTICA

South
Magnetic
Pole

WILKES LAND

ICE CAP

QUEEN MAUD LAND

ATLANTIC OCEAN

American
Highland

Shackleton
Ice Shelf

Enderby
Land

INDIAN OCEAN

0   250   500 Miles
0   250   500 Kilometers

Projection:
Polar Azimuthal Equidistant

ATLAS

Gazetteer

A

Abuja (ah-BOO-jah) (9°N, 7°E) the capital of Nigeria (p. 515)

Acapulco (17°N, 100°W) a resort on the Pacific Ocean in southwest Mexico (p. 179)

Accra (6°N, 0°) the capital of Ghana (p. 515)

Addis Ababa (AH-dis AH-bah-bah) (9°N, 39°E) the capital of Ethiopia (p. 537)

Adelaide (35°S, 139°E) a city in southern Australia (p. 716)

Afghanistan a landlocked country in Central Asia (p. 459)

Africa the second-largest continent; surrounded by the Atlantic Ocean, Indian Ocean, and Mediterranean Sea (p. R56)

Alabama (AL) a state in the southern United States; admitted in 1819 (pp. R42–R43)

Alaska (AK) a state in northwestern North America; admitted in 1959 (pp. R42–R43)

Albania a country on the Balkan Peninsula in southeastern Europe (p. 353)

Alberta a province in western Canada (p. 157)

Alexandria an ancient city in Egypt built by Alexander the Great (p. 499)

Algeria a country in North Africa between Morocco and Libya (p. 493)

Algiers (37°N, 3°E) the capital of Algeria (p. 493)

Almaty (ahl-mah-TUH) (43°N, 77°E) the former capital of Kazakhstan (p. 470)

Alps a great mountain system in central Europe (p. 287)

Amazon Basin a huge basin in the heart of South America (p. R50)

Amazon River the major river in South America (p. R50)

Amman (32°N, 36°E) the capital of Jordan (p. 429)

Amsterdam (52°N, 5°E) the capital and largest city of the Netherlands (p. 319)

Amu Darya (uh-MOH duhr-YAH) a river in Central Asia that flows along Afghanistan's border with Tajikistan, Uzbekistan, and Turkmenistan to the Aral Sea (p. 461)

Amur River a river in Asia that forms part of the Russia-China border (p. 391)

Anatolia (a-nuh-TOH-lee-uh) a mountainous region in Southwest Asia forming most of Turkey; also referred to as Asia Minor (p. 412)

Andes Mountains (AN-deez) a long mountain range along the west coast of South America (p. R50)

Angola a country in Central Africa that borders the Atlantic Ocean (p. 557)

Ankara (40°N, 33°E) the capital and second-largest city of Turkey (p. 418)

An Nafud (ahn nah-FOOD) a large desert in northern Saudi Arabia; known for its giant sand dunes (p. 438)

Antananarivo (19°S, 48°E) the capital of Madagascar (p. 579)

Antarctica a continent around the South Pole (p. R59)

Antarctic Circle the line of latitude located at 66.5° south of the equator; parallel beyond which no sunlight shines on the June solstice (pp. R44–R45)

Antarctic Peninsula a large peninsula in Antarctica (p. R59)

Apennines (A-puh-nynz) the major mountain range on the Italian Peninsula (p. 287)

Apia (14°S, 172°W) the capital of Western Samoa (p. 730)

Appalachian Mountains a mountain system in eastern North America (p. 118)

Arabia or Arabian Peninsula the world's largest peninsula; located in Southwest Asia (p. 435)

Arabian Sea a large arm of the Indian Ocean between India and Arabia (p. R55)

Aral Sea an inland sea in Central Asia fed by the Syr Darya and Amu Darya rivers; it has been steadily shrinking (p. 474)

Arctic Circle the line of latitude located at 66.5° north of the equator; parallel beyond which no sunlight shines on the December solstice (pp. R44–R45)

Arctic Ocean the ocean north of the Arctic Circle; the world's fourth-largest ocean (p. R59)

Argentina a country in South America (p. 244)

Arizona (AZ) a state in the southwestern United States; admitted in 1912 (pp. R42–R43)

Arkansas (AR) a state in the south-central United States; admitted in 1836 (pp. R42–R43)

Armenia a country in the Caucasus Mountains (p. 395)

Ashgabat (38°N, 58°E) the capital of Turkmenistan (p. 459)

Asia the world's largest continent; located between Europe and the Pacific Ocean (p. R54)

Asmara (15°N, 39°E) the capital of Eritrea (p. 537)

Astana (51°N, 72°E) the capital of Kazakhstan (p. 470)

Asunción (ah-soon-SYOHN) (25°N, 58°W) the capital of Paraguay (p. 247)

Atacama Desert a desert located in northern Chile near the border with Peru (p. 257)

Athens (38°N, 24°E) an ancient city and the modern capital of Greece (p. 294)

Atlanta (33°N, 84°W) capital of Georgia (p. 136)

Atlantic Ocean the ocean between the continents of North and South America and the continents of Europe and Africa (p. R44)

Atlas Mountains a high mountain range in northwestern Africa (p. 495)

Australia a country and continent in the Pacific (p. 716)

Austria a country in West-Central Europe (p. 309)

Azerbaijan (a-zuhr-by-JAHN) a country in the Caucasus Mountains (p. 395)

Baghdad (33°N, 44°E) the capital of Iraq (p. 435)

Bahamas a country and group of islands located east of Florida in the Atlantic Ocean (p. 189)

Bahrain a small country on the Persian Gulf (p. 435)

Baja California a peninsula in Mexico (p. 168)

Baku (40°N, 48°E) the capital of Azerbaijan (p. 395)

Balkan Peninsula a peninsula in Southern Europe (p. 355)

Baltic Sea a shallow arm of the Atlantic Ocean in northern Europe (p. 335)

Baltimore (39°N, 76°W) a large city in Maryland northeast of Washington, D.C. (p. R43)

Bamako (BAH-mah-koh) (13°N, 8°W) the capital of Mali (p. 515)

Bandar Seri Begawan (5°N, 115°E) capital of Brunei (p. 691)

Bangkok (14°N, 100°E) the capital of Thailand (p. 690)

Bangladesh a country in South Asia (p. 615)

Bangui (bahn-GEE) (4°N, 19°E) the capital of the Central African Republic (p. 557)

Banjul (BAHN-jool) (13°N, 17°W) the capital of Gambia (p. 514)

Barbados island country in the Caribbean (p. 202)

Barcelona (41°N, 2°E) a large port city in Spain on the Mediterranean Sea (p. 302)

Basseterre (16°N, 62°W) the capital of St. Kitts and Nevis (p. 187)

Bavaria a state and region in southern Germany (p. 324)

Bay of Bengal a large bay of the Indian Ocean between India and Southeast Asia (p. 615)

Beijing (40°N, 116°E) the capital of China (p. 639)

Beirut (34°N, 36°E) the capital of Lebanon (p. 428)

Belarus a country in Eastern Europe (p. 353)

Belgium a country in West-Central Europe (p. 127)

Belgrade (45°N, 21°E) the capital of Serbia (p. 371)

Belize a country in Central America (p. 189)

Belmopan (17°N, 90°W) capital of Belize (p. 186)

Benelux a term that refers to Belgium, the Netherlands, and Luxembourg (p. 318)

Benin a country in West Africa between Togo and Nigeria (p. 515)

Berlin (53°N, 13°E) the capital of Germany (p. 323)

Bern (47°N, 7°E) the capital of Switzerland (p. 309)

Bhutan a country in South Asia north of India (p. 615)

Bishkek (43°N, 75°E) the capital of Kyrgyzstan (p. 459)

Bissau (bis-OW) (12°N, 16°W) the capital of Guinea-Bissau (p. 514)

Bloemfontein (BLOOM-fahn-tayn) (29°S, 26°E) the judicial capital of South Africa (p. 579)

Bogotá (4°N, 72°W) capital of Colombia (p. 210)

Bolivia a country in South America (p. 255)

Borneo the world's third-largest island; located in Southeast Asia (p. 693)

Bosnia and Herzegovina a country on the Balkan Peninsula (p. 353)

Bosporus (BAHS-puh-ruhs) a narrow strait in Turkey that connects the Mediterranean Sea with the Black Sea (p. 413)

Boston (42°N, 71°W) the capital of Massachusetts (p. 126)

Botswana a country in Southern Africa between Namibia and Zimbabwe (p. 579)

Brasília (10°S, 55°W) the capital of Brazil (p. 239)

Bratislava (48°N, 17°E) the capital of Slovakia (p. 353)

Brazil a country in South America (p. 231)

Brazilian Highlands a region of rugged, old, eroded mountains in eastern Brazil (p. 233)

Brazzaville (4°S, 15°E) the capital of the Republic of the Congo (p. 557)

British Columbia a province in Canada (p. 157)

British Isles a group of islands off the northwestern coast of Europe including Britain and Ireland (p. 335)

Brunei (brooh-NY) a country in Southeast Asia on the northern coast of Borneo (p. 691)

Brussels (51°N, 4°E) the capital of Belgium (p. 309)

Bucharest (44°N, 26°E) the capital of Romania (p. 353)

Budapest (48°N, 19°E) the capital of Hungary (p. 365)

Buenos Aires (BWAY-nohs EYE-rayz) (36°S, 60°W) the capital of Argentina (p. 244)

Bujumbura (booh-juhm-BOOHR-uh) (3°S, 29°E) the capital of Burundi (p. 537)

Bukhara (40°N, 64°E) an ancient city along the Silk Road in Central Asia; it has long been an important trade and cultural center in the region (p. 464)

Bulgaria a country in the Balkans (p. 353)

Burkina Faso (boor-KEE-nuh FAH-soh) a landlocked country in West Africa (p. 515)

Burundi (buh-ROON-dee) a landlocked country in East Africa (p. 537)

Cairo (30°N, 31°E) the capital of Egypt (p. 493)

Calgary (51°N, 114°W) a large city in the province of Alberta in Canada (p. 144)

California (CA) a state in the western United States; admitted in 1850 (pp. R42–R43)

Callao (kah-YAH-oh) (12°S, 77°W) a port city in Peru west of Lima (p. 266)

Cambodia a country in Southeast Asia (p. 690)

Cameroon a country in Central Africa south of Nigeria (p. 557)

Canada a country in North America (p. 144–45)

Canadian Shield a region of ancient rock that covers more than half of Canada (p. 147)

Canberra (35°S, 149°E) the capital of Australia (p. 716)

Cancún (21°N, 87°W) a popular resort on Mexico's Caribbean coast (p. 179)

Cape of Good Hope a cape at the southern tip of Africa (p. 581)

Cape Town (34°S, 18°E) the legislative capital of South Africa (p. 579)

Cape Verde (VUHRD) an island country off the coast of West Africa (p. 514)

Caracas (11°N, 67°W) the capital of Venezuela (p. 211)

Caribbean Islands a group of islands in the Caribbean Sea (p. 189)

Caribbean Sea an arm of the Atlantic Ocean between North and South America (p. 187)

Carpathians (kahr-PAY-thee-uhnz) a major mountain chain in central and eastern Europe (p. 354)

Cartagena (kahr-tah-HAY-nuh) (10°N, 74°W) a coastal city in northern Colombia (p. 210)

Cascade Range a mountain range in western North America (p. 119)

Caspian Sea an inland sea located between Europe and Asia; it is the largest inland body of water in the world (p. 461)

Cauca River a river in Colombia (p. 213)

Caucasus Mountains a mountain system in southeastern Europe between the Black Sea and Caspian Sea (p. 378)

Cayenne (4°N, 53°W) the capital of French Guiana (p. 211)

Central African Republic a landlocked country in Central Africa south of Chad (p. 557)

Central America a region in North America south of Mexico (p. 188)

Central Uplands an area of hills, plateaus, and valleys in central Europe (p. 311)

Chad a landlocked country in West Africa located east of Niger (p. 515)

Chang Jiang (Yangzi River) a major river in China (p. 641)

Chao Phraya (chow PRY-uh) a river in Thailand (p. R54)

Chechnya (CHECH-nyuh) a republic in Russia that is fighting a violent struggle for independence (p. 392)

Chernobyl (51°N, 30°E) a city in Ukraine; the world's worst nuclear reactor accident occurred there in 1986 (p. 357)

Chicago (42°N, 88°W) a major U.S. city and port in northeastern Illinois on Lake Michigan (p. 135)

Chile (CHEE-lay) a country in western South America (p. 253)

China a large country in East Asia (p. 639)

Chişinau (47°N, 29°E) the capital of Moldova (p. 353)

Coast Mountains a mountain range in North America along the Pacific coast (p. 147)

Colombia a country in South America (p. 210)

Colombo (7°N, 80°E) the capital of Sri Lanka (p. 615)

Colorado (CO) a state in the southwestern United States; admitted in 1876 (pp. R42–R43)

Comoros (KAH-muh-rohz) an island country in the Indian Ocean off the coast of Africa (p. 579)

Conakry (KAH-nuh-kree) (10°N, 14°W) the capital of Guinea (p. 514)

Congo Basin a large flat area on the Congo River in Central Africa (p. 559)

Congo, Democratic Republic of the the largest and most populous country in Central Africa (p. 557)

Congo, Republic of the a country in Central Africa on the Congo River (p. 557)

Congo River the major river of Central Africa (p. 559)

Connecticut (CT) a state in the northeastern United States; admitted in 1788 and one of the original 13 colonies (pp. R42–R43)

Copenhagen (56°N, 13°E) the capital of Denmark (p. 333)

Costa Rica a country in Central America (p. 186)

Côte d'Ivoire (KOHT dee-VWAHR) a country in West Africa between Liberia and Ghana (p. 515)

Croatia a country in the Balkans (p. 353)

Cuba an island country in the Caribbean Sea south of Florida (p. 187)

Czech Republic a country in Eastern Europe (p. 353)

Dakar (15°N, 17°W) the capital of Senegal (p. 514)

Dallas (33°N, 97°W) a major U.S. city and transportation and financial center in Texas (pp. R42–R43)

Damascus (34°N, 36°E) the capital of Syria (p. 411)

Danube (DAN-yoob) the second-longest river in Europe; it flows from Germany east to the Black Sea (p. 311)

Dardanelles (dahrd-uhn-ELZ) a strait between the Aegean Sea and the Sea of Marmara; part of a waterway that connects the Black Sea and the Mediterranean Sea (p. 413)

Dar es Salaam (7°S, 39°E) the capital of Tanzania (p. 537)

Darfur a region in western Sudan; because of genocide, millions of people have fled from Darfur (p. 549)

Dead Sea the saltiest lake and lowest point on Earth; located on the border between Israel and Jordan and fed by the Jordan River (p. 413)

Deccan a large plateau in southern India (p. 617)

Delaware (DE) a state in the eastern United States; admitted in 1787 and one of the original 13 colonies (pp. R42–R43)

Delhi a city in northern India that was the capital of the Mughal Empire (p. 615)

Denmark a country in Northern Europe (p. 333)

Detroit (42°N, 83°W) a large U.S. city in Michigan (p. R43)

Dhaka (DA-kuh) (24°N, 90°E) the capital of Bangladesh (p. 615)

Dili (8°N, 125°E) the capital of East Timor (p. 691)

District of Columbia (39°N, 77°W) a federal district between Maryland and Virginia; the capital of the United States (p. 117)

Djibouti (ji-BOO-tee) a country in East Africa on the Horn of Africa (p. 537)

Djibouti (12°N, 43°E) the capital of Djibouti (p. 537)

Dodoma (6°S, 36°E) the capital of Tanzania (p. 537)

Doha (26°N, 51°E) the capital of Qatar (p. 435)

Dominican Republic a country in the Caribbean (p. 187)

Drakensberg a mountain range in Southern Africa (p. 581)

Dublin (53°N, 6°W) the capital of Ireland (p. 341)

Dushanbe (39°N, 69°E) the capital of Tajikistan (p. 459)

Eastern Ghats (gawts) a mountain range in India (p. 617)

Eastern Hemisphere the half of the globe between the prime meridian and 180° longitude that includes most of Africa and Europe as well as Asia, Australia, and the Indian Ocean (p. H3)

East Timor an island country in Southeast Asia (p. 691)

Ecuador a country in South America (p. 253)

Edinburgh (56°N, 3°W) the capital of Scotland (p. 341)

Egypt a country in North Africa on the Mediterranean Sea; home to one of the world's oldest civilizations (p. 493)

Elburz Mountains a mountain range in northern Iran south of the Caspian Sea (p. 437)

El Salvador a country in Central America (p. 186)

England a part of the United Kingdom occupying most of the island of Great Britain (p. 341)

English Channel a strait of the Atlantic Ocean between England and France (p. 312)

equator the imaginary line of latitude that circles the globe halfway between the North and South Poles (p. H2)

Equatorial Guinea a country in Central Africa between Cameroon and Gabon (p. 557)

Eritrea (er-uh-TREE-uh) an East African country north of Ethiopia (p. 537)

Estonia a Baltic country in Eastern Europe (p. 353)

Ethiopia an East African country located on the Horn of Africa (p. 537)

Euphrates River a river in Southwest Asia (p. 437)

Europe the continent between the Ural Mountains and the Atlantic Ocean (p. R52)

Fergana Valley a fertile plains region of Uzbekistan in Central Asia (p. 461)

Fertile Crescent a large arc of fertile lands between the Persian Gulf and the Mediterranean Sea; the world's earliest civilizations began in the region (p. 436)

Fiji an island country in the Pacific (p. 717)

Finland a country in Northern Europe (p. 333)

Florida (FL) a state in the southeastern United States; admitted in 1845 (pp. R42–R43)

France a country in West-Central Europe (p. 309)

Freetown (9°N, 13°W) the capital of Sierra Leone (p. 514)

French Guiana (gee-A-nuh) a region of France in northern South America (p. 211)

Fuji (FOO-jee) (35°N, 135°E) a volcano and Japan's highest peak (p. 667)

Funafuti (9°S, 179°E) the capital of Tuvalu (p. 730)

Gabon (gah-BOHN) a country in Central Africa between Cameroon and the Democratic Republic of the Congo (p. 557)

Gaborone (24°S, 26°E) the capital of Botswana (p. 579)

Galápagos Islands a group of islands in the Pacific Ocean that are part of Ecuador (p. 255)

Gambia a country in West Africa surrounded on three sides by Senegal (p. 514)

Ganges River (GAN-jeez) a major river in northern India (p. 617)

Gangetic Plain a broad plain in northern India formed by the Ganges River (p. 617)

Gaza (32°N, 34°E) a city in southwestern Israel on the Mediterranean Sea (p. 423)

Georgetown (5°N, 59°W) capital of Guyana (p. 211)

Georgia (GA) a state in the southeastern United States; admitted in 1788 and one of the original 13 colonies (pp. R42–R43)

Georgia a country in the Caucasus Mountains (p. 395)

Germany a country in West-Central Europe (p. 309)

Ghana a country in West Africa between Côte d'Ivoire and Togo (p. 515)

Gobi (GOH-bee) a desert in China and Mongolia (p. 641)

Gran Chaco (grahn CHAH-koh) a region of lowlands in South America (p. 233)

Grand Banks (47°N, 52°W) a rich fishing ground near Newfoundland, Canada (p. 147)

Great Barrier Reef a huge coral reef off the northeastern coast of Australia (p. 719)

Greater Antilles an island group in the Caribbean that includes Cuba, Jamaica, Hispaniola, and Puerto Rico (p. 189)

Great Lakes a group of five large freshwater lakes in North America; they are Lake Superior, Lake Michigan, Lake Huron, Lake Erie, and Lake Ontario (p. 119)

Great Plains a large region of plains and grasslands in central North America (p. 119)

Great Rift Valley a series of valleys in East Africa caused by the stretching of Earth's crust (p. 539)

Great Zimbabwe an ancient walled town in Southern Africa (p. 585)

Greece a country in Southern Europe (p. 285)

Greenland a large island in North America controlled by Denmark (p. 145)

Guadalajara (21°N, 103°W) the second-largest city in Mexico (p. 167)

Guadeloupe a group of islands in the Caribbean that are part of France (p. 187)

Guatemala a country in Central America (p. 186)

Guatemala City (15°N, 91°W) the capital of Guatemala (p. 186)

Guayaquil (gwah-ah-KEEL) (2°S, 80°W) a city in Ecuador (p. 253)

Guiana Highlands (gee-YAH-nah) a large plateau region in northern South America (p. 213)

Guinea a country in West Africa north of Sierra Leone (p. 514)

Guinea-Bissau a country in West Africa north of Guinea (p. 514)

Gulf of Mexico a large gulf off the southeastern coast of North America (p. 167)

Gulf Stream a warm ocean current that flows north along the east coast of the United States (p. 52)

Guyana (gy-AH-nuh) a country in northern South America (p. 211)

Haiti a country in the Caribbean (p. 187)

Hanoi (21°N, 106°E) the capital of Vietnam (p. 690)

Harare (hah-RAH-ray) (18°S, 31°E) the capital of Zimbabwe (p. 579)

Havana (23°N, 82°W) the capital of Cuba (p. 187)

Hawaii (HI) state in the Pacific Ocean comprised of the Hawaiian Islands; admitted in 1959 (pp. R42–R43)

Helsinki (60°N, 25°E) the capital of Finland (p. 333)

Himalayas the highest mountains in the world; they separate the Indian Subcontinent from China (p. 617)

Hindu Kush a mountain system that stretches from northern Pakistan into northeastern Afghanistan (p. 461)

Hispaniola (ees-pah-nee-O-lah) an island in the Caribbean (p. 189)

Ho Chi Minh City a large city in southern Vietnam (p. 690)

Hokkaido (hoh-KY-doh) the northernmost of Japan's four major islands (p. 667)

Holland a region in the Netherlands (p. 318)

Honduras a country in Central America (p. 186)

Hong Kong (22°N, 115°E) a city in southern China (p. 639)

Honiara (9°S, 160°E) the capital of the Solomon Islands (p. 730)

Honshu (HAWN-shoo) the largest of Japan's four major islands (p. 667)

Houston (30°N, 95°W) a major U.S. port city in Texas (p. 135)

Huang He (Yellow River) a major river in northern China (p. 641)

Hudson Bay a large bay in central Canada (p. 147)

Hungary a country in central Europe (p. 353)

I

Iberian Peninsula a large peninsula in Southern Europe; Spain and Portugal are located there (p. 301)

Iceland an island country in Northern Europe (p. 332)

Idaho (ID) a state in the northwestern United States; admitted in 1890 (pp. R42–R43)

Illinois (IL) a state in the north-central United States; admitted in 1819 (pp. R42–R43)

India a country in South Asia (p. 615)

Indiana (IN) a state in the north-central United States; admitted in 1816 (pp. R42–R43)

Indian Ocean the world's third-largest ocean; it is located between Asia and Antarctica (p. R45)

Indochina Peninsula a large peninsula in Southeast Asia (p. 693)

Indonesia the largest country in Southeast Asia (p. 691)

Indus River a major river in Pakistan (p. 617)

Indus Valley a river valley in Pakistan that was home to the ancient Harappan civilization (p. 617)

Interior Plains a large plains region of North America (p. 119)

Iowa (IA) a state in the north-central United States; admitted in 1846 (pp. R42–R43)

Iran a country in the Persian Gulf region; it includes the ancient region of Persia (p. 435)

Iraq a country in the Persian Gulf region; it includes the ancient region of Mesopotamia (p. 435)

Ireland a country west of Britain in the British Isles (p. 332)

Islamabad (34°N, 73°E) the capital of Pakistan (p. 615)

Israel a country between the Mediterranean Sea and Jordan (p. 411)

Istanbul (41°N, 29°E) the largest city in Turkey; formerly known as Constantinople (p. 419)

Italy a country in Southern Europe (p. 285)

Jakarta (6°S, 107°E) the capital of Indonesia (p. 690)

Jamaica an island country in the Caribbean (p. 187)

Japan an island country in East Asia (p. 665)

Java a large island in Indonesia (p. 693)

Jerusalem (32°N, 35°E) the capital of Israel; it contains holy sites of Judaism, Christianity, and Islam (p. 422)

Jordan a country east of Israel and the Jordan River (p. 411)

GAZETTEER

Jordan River a river between Israel and Jordan that empties into the Dead Sea (p. 413)

Jura Mountains a mountain range in West-Central Europe in Switzerland and France (p. 311)

 K

Kabul (35°N, 69°E) the capital of Afghanistan (p. 459)

Kaliningrad (55°N, 21°E) a strategic city and port controlled by Russia (p. 389)

Kamchatka Peninsula a large, mountainous peninsula in eastern Russia on the Pacific Ocean (p. 379)

Kampala (0°, 32°E) the capital of Uganda (p. 537)

Kansas (KS) a state in the central United States; admitted in 1861 (pp. R42–R43)

Kara-Kum (kahr-uh-koom) a desert in Central Asia east of the Caspian Sea (p. 462)

Kashmir a disputed region between India and Pakistan (p. 615)

Kathmandu (kat-man-DOO) (28°N, 85°E) the capital of Nepal (p. 615)

Kazakhstan a country in Central Asia; it was part of the Soviet Union until 1991 (p. 462)

Kentucky (KY) a state in the east-central United States; admitted in 1792 (pp. R42–R43)

Kenya a country in East Africa south of Ethiopia (p. 537)

Khartoum (16°N, 33°E) the capital of Sudan (p. 537)

Kiev (50°N, 31°E) the capital of Ukraine (p. 363)

Kigali (2°S, 30°E) the capital of Rwanda (p. 537)

Kinshasa (4°S, 15°E) the capital of the Democratic Republic of the Congo (p. 557)

Kiribati an island country in the Pacific (p. 717)

Kjolen Mountains a mountain range in Scandinavia along the Norway-Sweden border (p. 334)

Kobe (KOH-bay) (35°N, 135°E) a major port city in Japan (p. 668)

Kolkata (Calcutta) a major city in eastern India (p. 615)

Kopet-Dag a group of mountains in northern Iran bordering Turkmenistan (p. 437)

Korean Peninsula a peninsula on the east coast of Asia (p. 665)

Koror (9°N, 138°E) the capital of Palau (p. 730)

Kosovo a country in the Balkans (p. 353)

Kuala Lumpur (3°N, 102°E) the capital of Malaysia (p. 690)

Kuwait a small country on the Persian Gulf (p. 435)

Kyoto (KYOH-toh) (35°N, 136°E) the ancient capital of Japan (p. 665)

Kyrgyzstan a country in Central Asia; it was part of the Soviet Union until 1991 (p. 462)

Kyushu (KYOO-shoo) the southernmost of Japan's four major islands (p. 667)

Kyzyl Kum (ki-ZIL KOOM) a vast desert region in Uzbekistan and Kazakhstan (p. 462)

 L

Lagos (6°N, 3°E) a city in Nigeria; the most populous city in West Africa (p. 515)

Lake Baikal a huge freshwater lake in Russia; it is the deepest lake in the world (p. 380)

Lake Maracaibo (mah-rah-KY-boh) (10°N, 72°W) an oil-rich body of water in Venezuela (p. 223)

Lake Victoria the largest lake in Africa (p. 539)

Laos (LOWS) a landlocked country in Southeast Asia (p. 690)

La Paz (17°S, 65°W) the capital of Bolivia (p. 265)

Latvia a Baltic country in Eastern Europe (p. 353)

Lebanon a country on the Mediterranean Sea north of Israel (p. 411)

Lena River a long river in central Russia that flows north to the Arctic Sea (p. 379)

Lesotho (luh-SOH-toh) a country completely surrounded by South Africa (p. 579)

Lesser Antilles a group of small islands in the Caribbean; they stretch from the Virgin Islands in the north to Trinidad in the south (p. 189)

Liberia a country in West Africa between Sierra Leone and Côte d'Ivoire (p. 515)

Libreville (0°, 9°E) the capital of Gabon (p. 557)

Libya a country in North Africa between Egypt and Algeria (p. 493)

Lilongwe (li-LAWN-gway) (14°S, 34°E) the capital of Malawi (p. 557)

Lima (10°S, 75°W) the capital of Peru (p. 253)

Lisbon (39°N, 9°W) the capital of Portugal (p. 284)

Lithuania a Baltic country in Eastern Europe (p. 353)

Ljubljana (46°N, 15°E) the capital of Slovenia (p. 353)

Llanos a plains region in South America (p. 213)

Lomé (6°N, 1°E) the capital of Togo (p. 515)

London (51°N, 1°W) the capital of England and the United Kingdom (p. 342)

Louisiana (LA) a state in the southeastern United States; admitted in 1812 (pp. R42–R43)

Luanda (9°S, 13°E) the capital of Angola (p. 557)

Lusaka (15°S, 28°E) the capital of Zambia (p. 557)

Luxembourg a country in West-Central Europe (p. 309)

Luxembourg City (45°N 6°E) capital of Luxembourg (p. 309)

 M

Macedonia a country on the Balkan Peninsula in southeastern Europe (p. 371)

Madagascar a large island country off the southeastern coast of Africa (p. 579)

Madrid (40°N, 4°W) the capital of Spain (p. 284)

Magdalena River a river in Colombia (p. 210)

GAZETTEER

Maghreb a region in North Africa that includes western Libya, Tunisia, Algeria, and Morocco; it means "west" in Arabic (p. 508)

Maine (ME) a state in the northeastern United States; admitted in 1820 (pp. R42–R43)

Majuro (7°N, 171°E) the capital of the Marshall Islands (p. 730)

Malabo (mah-LAH-boh) (4°N, 9°E) the capital of Equatorial Guinea (p. 557)

Malawi a landlocked country in Central Africa located south of Tanzania (p. 557)

Malay Archipelago (muh-LAY) a large group of islands in Southeast Asia (p. 693)

Malay Peninsula (muh-LAY) a narrow peninsula in Southeast Asia (p. 693)

Malaysia a country in Southeast Asia (p. 690)

Maldives an island country south of India (p. R55)

Male (5°N, 72°E) the capital of the Maldives (p. R55)

Mali a country in West Africa on the Niger River (p. 515)

Manama (26°N, 51°E) capital of Bahrain (p. 435)

Manaus (3°S, 60°W) a major port and industrial city in Brazil's Amazon rain forest (p. 231)

Manila (15°N, 121°E) the capital of the Philippines (p. 691)

Manitoba a province in central Canada (p. 145)

Maputo (27°S, 33°E) the capital of Mozambique (p. 579)

Marseille (mar-SAY) (43°N, 5°E) a port city in France on the Mediterranean Sea (p. 309)

Marshall Islands an island country in the Pacific (p. 717)

Martinique a group of islands in the Caribbean that are part of France (p. 187)

Maryland (MD) a state in the eastern United States; admitted in 1788 and one of the original 13 colonies (pp. R42–R43)

Maseru (29°S, 27°E) the capital of Lesotho (p. 579)

Massachusetts (MA) a state in the northeastern United States; admitted in 1788 and one of the original 13 colonies (pp. R42–R43)

Massif Central (ma-SEEF sahn-TRAHL) an upland region in south-central France (p. 311)

Mato Grosso Plateau a high plateau area in Brazil (p. 233)

Mauritania a country in West Africa located between Mali and the Atlantic Ocean (p. 515)

Mauritius (maw-RI-shuhs) an island country east of Madagascar (p. R57)

Mbabane (uhm-bah-BAH-nay) (26°S, 31°E) the capital of Swaziland (p. 579)

Mecca (21°N, 40°E) an ancient city in Arabia and the birthplace of Muhammad (p. 435)

Mediterranean Sea a sea between Europe and Africa (p. 287)

Mekong River a major river in Southeast Asia (p. 693)

Melanesia a huge group of Pacific islands that stretches from New Guinea to Fiji (p. 727)

Melbourne (38°S, 145°E) a city in southeastern Australia (p. 716)

Mesopotamia (mes-uh-puh-TAY-mee-uh) the region in Southwest Asia between the Tigris and Euphrates rivers; it was the site of some of the world's earliest civilizations (p. 436)

Mexican Plateau a high, mostly rugged region covering much of the interior of Mexico (p. 169)

Mexico a country in North America (p. 167)

Mexico City (23°N, 104°W) the capital of Mexico (p. 180)

Michigan (MI) a state in the north-central United States; admitted in 1837 (pp. R42–R43)

Micronesia a large group of Pacific islands located east of the Philippines (p. 727)

Micronesia, Federated States of an island country in the western Pacific (p. 716)

Mid-Atlantic Ridge a mid-ocean ridge located in the Atlantic Ocean (p. 37)

Middle East the region around the eastern Mediterranean, northeastern Africa, and Southwest Asia that links the continents of Europe, Asia, and Africa (p. 436)

Minnesota (MN) a state in the north-central United States; admitted in 1858 (pp. R42–R43)

Mississippi (MS) a state in the southeastern United States; admitted in 1817 (pp. R42–R43)

Mississippi River a major river in the United States (p. 119)

Missouri (MO) a state in the central United States; admitted in 1821 (pp. R42–R43)

Mogadishu (2°N, 45°E) the capital of Somalia (p. 537)

Moldova a country in Eastern Europe (p. 353)

Monaco a small country in West-Central Europe (p. 309)

Mongolia a landlocked country in East Asia (p. 639)

Monrovia (6°N, 11°W) the capital of Liberia (p. 515)

Montana (MT) a state in the northern United States; admitted in 1889 (pp. R42–R43)

Mont Blanc (mawn BLAHN) (46°N, 7°E) a mountain peak in France; highest of the Alps (p. 312)

Montenegro (43°N, 19°E) a country in the Balkans (p. 353)

Monterrey (26°N, 100°W) a large city and industrial center in northern Mexico (p. 167)

Montevideo (mawn-tay-vee-DAY-oh) (35°S, 56°W) the capital of Uruguay (p. 231)

Montreal (46°N, 74°W) a major Canadian city in Quebec; founded by the French in 1642 (p. 145)

Morocco a country in North Africa south of Spain (p. 492)

Moroni (12°S, 43°E) the capital of Comoros (p. 579)

Moscow (56°N, 38°E) the capital of Russia (p. 390)

Mount Elbrus (el-BROOS) the highest peak of the Caucasus Mountains (p. 379)

Mount Everest the highest mountain in the world at 29,035 feet (8,850 km); it is located in India and Nepal (p. 617)

Mount Kilimanjaro (3°S, 37°E) the highest mountain in Africa at 19,341 feet (5,895 m); it is in Tanzania near the Kenya border (p. 539)

Mount Saint Helens (46°N, 122°W) a volcano in Washington State; it erupted in 1980 (p. 43)

Mozambique a country in Southern Africa south of Tanzania (p. 579)

Mumbai (Bombay) a major city in western India (p. 615)

Muscat (24°N, 59°E) the capital of Oman (p. 435)

Myanmar (Burma) (MYAHN-mahr) a country in Southeast Asia (p. 690)

Nairobi (1°S, 37°E) the capital of Kenya (p. 537)

Namib Desert a desert in southwestern Africa (p. 581)

Namibia a country on the Atlantic coast of Southern Africa (p. 579)

Nassau (25°N, 77°W) the capital of the Bahamas (p. 187)

Nauru an island country in the Pacific (p. 717)

Naypyidaw (20°N, 98°E) the administrative capital of Myanmar (Burma) (p. 690)

N'Djamena (uhn-jah-MAY-nah) (12°N, 15°E) the capital of Chad (p. 515)

Nebraska (NE) a state in the central United States; admitted in 1867 (pp. R42–R43)

Negev (NE-gev) an arid region of southern Israel (p. 413)

Nepal a landlocked country in South Asia (p. 615)

Netherlands a country in West-Central Europe (p. 309)

Nevada (NV) a state in the western United States; admitted in 1864 (pp. R42–R43)

New Brunswick a province in Canada (p. 145)

New Delhi (29°N, 77°E) the capital of India (p. 615)

Newfoundland and Labrador an island province in eastern Canada (p. 145)

New Guinea the world's second-largest island; located in Southeast Asia (p. 693)

New Hampshire (NH) a state in the northeastern United States; admitted in 1788 and one of the original 13 colonies (pp. R42–R43)

New Jersey (NJ) a state in the northeastern United States; admitted in 1787 and one of the original 13 colonies (pp. R42–R43)

New Mexico (NM) a state in the southwestern United States; admitted in 1912 (pp. R42–R43)

New Orleans (30°N, 90°W) a major U.S. port city located in southeastern Louisiana (p. 117)

New York (NY) a state in the northeastern United States; admitted in 1788 and one of the original 13 colonies (pp. R42–R43)

New York City (41°N, 74°W) the largest city in the United States (p. 117)

New Zealand an island country southeast of Australia (p. 717)

Niamey (14°N, 2°E) the capital of Niger (p. 515)

Nicaragua a country in Central America (p. 186)

Niger (NY-juhr) a country in West Africa north of Nigeria (p. 515)

Nigeria a country on the Atlantic coast of West Africa (p. 515)

Niger River the major river of West Africa (p. 517)

Nile River the longest river in the world; located in North Africa (p. 495)

North America a continent including Canada, the United States, Mexico, Central America, and the Caribbean islands (p. R49)

North Carolina (NC) a state in the southeastern United States; admitted in 1789 and one of the original 13 colonies (pp. R42–R43)

North China Plain a plains region of northeastern China (p. 641)

North Dakota (ND) a state in the north-central United States; admitted in 1889 (pp. R42–R43)

Northern European Plain a large plain across central and northern Europe (p. 311)

Northern Hemisphere the northern half of the globe, between the equator and the North Pole (p. H3)

Northern Ireland a part of the United Kingdom occupying the northeastern portion of the island of Ireland (p. 341)

North Korea a country in East Asia (p. 665)

North Pole (90°N) the northern point of Earth's axis (p. R59)

North Sea a shallow arm of the Atlantic Ocean in Northern Europe (p. 312)

Northwest Territories a territory in Canada (p. 157)

Norway a country in Northern Europe (p. 333)

Nouakchott (nooh-AHK-shaht) (18°N, 16°W) the capital of Mauritania (p. 514)

Nova Scotia (noh-vuh SKOH-shuh) a province in eastern Canada (p. 145)

Nuku'alofa (21°N, 174°E) the capital of Tonga (p. 730)

Nunavut (NOO-nah-VOOT) a territory in northern Canada created as a homeland for Canada's Inuit people (p. 145)

Ob River a long river in central Russia (p. 379)

Ohio (OH) a state in the north-central United States; admitted in 1803 (pp. R42–R43)

Oklahoma (OK) a state in the south-central United States; admitted in 1907 (pp. R42–R43)

Oman a country on the Arabian Peninsula (p. 435)

Ontario a province in east-central Canada (p. 145)

Oregon (OR) a state in the northwestern United States; admitted in 1859 (pp. R42–R43)

Orinoco River (OHR-ee-NOH-koh) a major river in Venezuela (p. 211)

Osaka (oh-SAH-kuh) (35°N, 135°E) a city in Japan (p. 680)

Oslo (60°N, 11°E) the capital of Norway (p. 333)

Ottawa (45°N, 76°W) capital of Canada (p. 145)
Ouagadougou (wah-gah-DOO-goo) (12°N, 2°W) the capital of Burkina Faso (p. 515)
Outback the dry interior region of Australia (p. 719)

Pacific Ocean the world's largest ocean; located between Asia and the Americas (p. R58)
Pakistan a country in South Asia northwest of India (p. 615)
Palau an island country in the Pacific (p. 716)
Palestine a region between the Jordan River and the Mediterranean Sea in modern Israel (p. 421)
Palikir (6°N, 158°E) the capital of the Federated States of Micronesia (p. 730)
Pamirs a highland region in Central Asia, mainly in Tajikistan (p. 460)
Pampas a fertile plains region in southern South America located mainly in Argentina (p. 233)
Panama a country in Central America (p. 187)
Panama Canal (26°N, 80°W) a canal built by the United States in the early 1900s across the Isthmus of Panama (p. 198)
Panama City (8°N, 81°W) capital of Panama (p. 187)
Papua New Guinea a country on the island of New Guinea (p. 716)
Paraguay a country in South America (p. 246)
Paraguay River a river in South America (p. 246)
Paramaribo (6°N, 55°W) the capital of Suriname (p. 211)
Paraná River a river in South America (p. 231)
Paris (46°N, 0°) the capital of France (p. 309)
Patagonia a region of dry plains and plateaus east of the Andes in southern Argentina (p. 233)
Pennsylvania (PA) a state in the eastern United States; admitted in 1787 and one of the original 13 colonies (pp. R42–R43)
Persian Gulf a body of water located between the Arabian Peninsula and the Zagros Mountains in Iran; it has enormous oil deposits along its shores (p. 435)
Perth (32°S, 116°E) a city in western Australia (p. 716)
Peru a country in western South America (p. 253)
Philadelphia (40°N, 75°W) a major U.S. city located in southeastern Pennsylvania; it was the capital of the United States from 1790 to 1800 (p. 135)
Philippines an island country in Southeast Asia (p. 691)
Phnom Penh (puh-NAWM pen) (12°N, 105°E) the capital of Cambodia (p. 690)
Podgorica (43°N, 19°E) capital of Montenegro (p. 353)
Poland a country in Eastern Europe (p. 353)
Polynesia the largest group of islands in the Pacific Ocean (p. 727)
Pontic Mountains a group of mountains in northern Turkey bordering the Black Sea (p. 413)
Popocatépetl (poh-poh-cah-TE-pet-uhl) (19°N, 99°W) a volcano near Mexico City (p. 169)

Po River a major river in northern Italy (p. 287)
Port-au-Prince (pohr-toh-PRINS) (19°N, 72°W) the capital of Haiti (p. 187)
Port Louis (20°S, 58°E) the capital of Mauritius (p. R57)
Port Moresby (10°S, 147°E) the capital of Papua New Guinea (p. 716)
Port-of-Spain (11°N, 61°W) the capital of Trinidad and Tobago (p. 187)
Porto-Novo (6°N, 3°E) the capital of Benin (p. 515)
Portugal a country in Southern Europe on the Iberian Peninsula (p. 284)
Port-Vila (18°S, 169°E) the capital of Vanuatu (p. 730)
Prague (50°N, 14°E) capital of the Czech Republic (p. 353)
Praia (PRY-uh) (15°N, 24°W) the capital of Cape Verde (p. 514)
Pretoria (26°S, 28°E) the administrative capital of South Africa (p. 579)
prime meridian an imaginary line that runs through Greenwich, England, at 0° longitude (p. H2)
Prince Edward Island (46°N, 64°W) a small province in eastern Canada (p. 145)
Pristina (43°N, 21°E) capital of Kosovo (p. 353)
Puerto Rico an island east of Cuba and southeast of Florida; it is a U.S. territory (p. 187)
Pyongyang (pyuhng-YANG) (39°N, 126°E) the capital of North Korea (p. 665)
Pyrenees (PIR-uh-neez) a high mountain range between Spain and France (p. 287)

Qatar (KUH-tahr) a country on the Arabian Peninsula (p. 435)
Quebec a province in eastern Canada (p. 145)
Quito (2°S, 78°W) the capital of Ecuador (p. 253)

Rabat (34°N, 7°W) the capital of Morocco (p. 492)
Red Sea a sea between the Arabian Peninsula and Africa (p. 437)
Reykjavik (64°N, 22°W) the capital of Iceland (p. 332)
Rhine a major river in Europe; it begins in Switzerland and flows north to the North Sea (p. 311)
Rhode Island (RI) a state in the northeastern United States; admitted in 1790 and one of the original 13 colonies (pp. R42–R43)
Riga (57°N, 24°E) the capital of Latvia (p. 353)
Ring of Fire a region that circles the Pacific Ocean; known for its earthquakes and volcanoes (p. 42)
Río Bravo the Mexican name for the river known as the Rio Grande in the United States; it forms the border between Mexico and Texas (p. 167)

Rio de Janeiro (23°N, 43°W) the second-largest city in Brazil; it is a major port city and Brazil's former capital (p. 231)

Río de la Plata (REE-oh day lah PLAH-tah) a body of water in South America (p. 233)

Riyadh (25°N, 47°E) the capital of Saudi Arabia (p. 435)

Rocky Mountains a major mountain range in western North America (p. 119)

Romania a country in Eastern Europe (p. 353)

Rome (42°N, 13°E) the capital of Italy; it was the capital of the ancient Roman Empire (p. 285)

Ross Ice Shelf the largest ice shelf in Antarctica (p. 717)

Rub' al-Khali (ROOB ahl-KAH-lee) a huge sandy desert on the Arabian Peninsula; its name means "empty quarter" (p. 438)

Ruhr a major industrial region in Germany (p. 325)

Russia a huge country that extends from Eastern Europe to the Pacific Ocean (p. 379)

Rwanda a country in East Africa between Tanzania and the Democratic Republic of the Congo (p. 537)

Sahara the world's largest desert; it dominates much of North Africa (p. 495)

Sahel a semiarid region between the Sahara and wetter areas to the south (p. 518)

St. Kitts and Nevis country in the Caribbean (p. 187)

St. Lawrence River a river in North America that flows from the Great Lakes to the Atlantic Ocean (p. 117)

Samarqand (40°N, 67°E) an ancient city on the Silk Road in modern Uzbekistan (p. 464)

Samoa an island country in the Pacific (p. 717)

San Francisco (37°N, 122°W) a major U.S. port city in Northern California (p. 116)

San Jose (10°N, 84°W) capital of Costa Rica (p. 186)

San Salvador (14°N, 89°W) the capital of El Salvador (p. 186)

Santiago (33°S, 71°W) the capital of Chile (p. 253)

Santo Domingo (19°N, 71°W) the capital of the Dominican Republic (p. 187)

São Paulo (24°S, 47°W) the largest city in Brazil and South America (p. 231)

São Tomé (sow too-MAY) (1°N, 6°E) the capital of São Tomé and Príncipe (p. 557)

São Tomé and Príncipe (PREEN-see-pee) an island country located off the Atlantic coast of Central Africa (p. 557)

Sarajevo (44°N, 18°E) the capital of Bosnia and Herzegovina (p. 371)

Saskatchewan a province in Canada (p. 145)

Saudi Arabia a country occupying much of the Arabian Peninsula in Southwest Asia (p. 435)

Scandinavian Peninsula a large peninsula in Northern Europe that includes Norway and Sweden (p. 335)

Scotland a part of the United Kingdom located in the northern part of Great Britain (p. 332)

Seattle (48°N, 122°W) a major U.S. port and city in Washington State (p. 116)

Senegal a country in West Africa south of Mauritania (p. 514)

Seoul (38°N, 127°E) the capital of South Korea (p. 665)

Serbia a country in the Balkans (p. 353)

Serengeti Plain a large plain in East Africa that is famous for its wildlife (p. 539)

Seychelles an island country located east of Africa in the Indian Ocean (p. R57)

Shanghai (31°N, 121°E) a major port city in eastern China (p. 646)

Shikoku (shee-koh-koo) the smallest of Japan's four major islands (p. 667)

Siberia a huge region in eastern Russia (p. 379)

Sierra Leone a West African country located south of Guinea (p. 514)

Sierra Madre (SYER-rah MAH-dray) the chief mountain range in Mexico (p. 169)

Sierra Nevada a large mountain range mainly in California (p. 119)

Silk Road an ancient trade route from China through Central Asia to the Mediterranean Sea (p. 464)

Singapore an island country at the tip of the Malay Peninsula in Southeast Asia (p. 690)

Slovakia a country in Eastern Europe (p. 353)

Slovenia a country in Eastern Europe (p. 353)

Sofia (43°N, 23°E) the capital of Bulgaria (p. 353)

Solomon Islands an island country in the Pacific (p. 717)

Somalia an East African country located on the Horn of Africa (p. 537)

South Africa a country located at the southern tip of Africa (p. 579)

South America a continent in the Western and Southern hemispheres (p. R50)

South Carolina (SC) a state in the southeastern United States; admitted in 1788 and one of the original 13 colonies (pp. R42–R43)

South Dakota (SD) a state in the north-central United States; admitted in 1889 (pp. R42–R43)

Southern Hemisphere the southern half of the globe, between the equator and the South Pole (p. H3)

South Korea a country in East Asia (p. 665)

South Pole (90°S) the southern point of Earth's axis (p. R59)

Soviet Union a former country that included Russia and the former Soviet Republics; it broke up in 1991 (p. 359)

GAZETTEER

Spain a country in Southern Europe on the Iberian Peninsula (p. 284)

Sri Lanka an island country located south of India (p. 615)

Stockholm (59°N, 18°E) the capital of Sweden (p. 333)

Sucre (SOO-kray) (19°S, 65°W) the capital of Bolivia (p. 253)

Sudan a country in East Africa; it is the largest country in Africa (p. 537)

Suez Canal a canal in Egypt that links the Mediterranean and Red seas (p. 495)

Sumatra a large island in Indonesia (p. 693)

Suriname (soohr-uh-NAHM) a country in northern South America (p. 211)

Suva (19°S, 178°E) the capital of Fiji (p. 730)

Swaziland a country in Southern Africa almost completely surrounded by South Africa (p. 574)

Sweden a country in Northern Europe (p. 333)

Switzerland a country in West-Central Europe (p. 127)

Sydney (34°S, 151°E) the largest city in Australia (p. 716)

Syr Darya (sir duhr-YAH) the longest river in Central Asia; it flows through the Fergana Valley and Kazakhstan, Tajikistan, and Uzbekistan on its way to the Aral Sea (p. 461)

Syria a country on the eastern Mediterranean Sea (p. 411)

Syrian Desert a desert in Southwest Asia covering much of the Arabian Peninsula between the Mediterranean coast and the Euphrates River (p. 413)

Taipei (25°N, 122°E) the capital of Taiwan (p. 639)

Taiwan (ty-wahn) an island country southeast of China (p. 639)

Tajikistan a country in Central Asia; it was part of the Soviet Union until 1991 (p. 461)

Tallinn (59°N, 25°E) the capital of Estonia (p. 361)

Tanzania (tan-zuh-NEE-uh) an East African country south of Kenya (p. 537)

Tarawa the capital of Kiribati (p. 730)

Tashkent (41°N, 69°E) the capital of Uzbekistan (p. 459)

Tasmania a large island off the southern coast of Australia (p. 716)

Taurus Mountains a mountain range in southern Turkey along the Mediterranean Sea (p. 413)

Tbilisi (42°N, 45°E) the capital of Georgia (p. 395)

Tegucigalpa (15°N, 87°W) the capital of Honduras (p. 186)

Tehran (36°N, 51°E) the capital of Iran (p. 435)

Tennessee (TN) a state in the south-central United States; admitted in 1796 (pp. R42–R43)

Texas (TX) a state and former independent republic in the south-central United States; admitted in 1845 (pp. R42–R43)

Thailand (TY-land) a country in Southeast Asia (p. 690)

Thar Desert (TAHR) a desert in western India and eastern Pakistan (p. 617)

Thimphu (28°N, 90°E) the capital of Bhutan (p. 615)

Tierra del Fuego a group of islands in southern South America (p. 255)

Tigris River (ty-gruhs) a major river in Southwest Asia; with the Euphrates River it defined the "land between the rivers" known as Mesopotamia (p. 437)

Tirana (41°N, 20°E) the capital of Albania (p. 353)

Togo a country in West Africa between Ghana and Benin (p. 515)

Tokyo (36°N, 140°E) the capital of Japan (p. 665)

Tonga an island country in the Pacific (p. 717)

Toronto (44°N, 79°W) Canada's largest city (p. 145)

Trinidad and Tobago a country in the Caribbean just north of Venezuela (p. 187)

Tripoli (33°N, 13°E) the capital of Libya (p. 493)

Tropic of Cancer the parallel 23.5° north of the equator; parallel on the globe at which the sun's most direct rays strike Earth during the June solstice (pp. R44–R45)

Tropic of Capricorn the parallel at 23.5° south of the equator; parallel on the globe at which the sun's most direct rays strike Earth during the December solstice (pp. R44–R45)

Tunis (37°N, 10°E) the capital of Tunisia (p. 493)

Tunisia a country in North Africa on the Mediterranean Sea (p. 493)

Turkey a country on the eastern Mediterranean (p. 418)

Turkmenistan a country in Central Asia; it was part of the Soviet Union until 1991 (p. 462)

Tuvalu an island country in the Pacific (p. 717)

Uganda a country in East Africa located west of Kenya (p. 537)

Ukraine a country in Eastern Europe (p. 353)

Ulaanbaatar (oo-lahn-BAH-tawr) (48°N, 107°E) the capital of Mongolia (p. 639)

Uluru a huge natural rock formation in central Australia; also called Ayers Rock (p. 719)

United Arab Emirates a country on the Arabian Peninsula (p. 435)

United Kingdom a country in the British Isles that includes England, Wales, Scotland, and Northern Ireland (p. 341)

United States of America a country in North America located between Canada and Mexico (pp. 116–117)

Ural Mountains (YOOHR-uhl) a mountain range in Russia that separates Europe and Asia (p. 378)

Uruguay a country in South America (p. 231)

Utah (UT) a state in the western United States; admitted in 1896 (pp. R42–R43)

Uzbekistan a country in Central Asia; it was part of the Soviet Union until 1991 (p. 462)

Valley of Mexico a large plateau region in central Mexico (p. 169)

Valparaíso (bahl-pah-rah-EE-soh) (33°S, 72°W) a city and major port in Chile (p. 253)

Vancouver (49°N, 123°W) a city in western Canada just north of the U.S. border (p. 144)

Vanuatu an island country in the Pacific (p. 717)

Vatican City (42°N, 12°E) a small country in Rome that is the head of the Roman Catholic Church (p. 298)

Venezuela a country in South America (p. 211)

Vermont (VT) a state in the northeastern United States; admitted in 1791 (pp. R42–R43)

Victoria (1°S, 33°E) the capital of Seychelles (p. R57)

Vienna (45°N, 12°E) the capital of Austria (p. 309)

Vientiane (vyen-THAN) (18°N, 103°E) the capital of Laos (p. 690)

Vietnam (vee-ET-NAHM) a country in Southeast Asia (p. 690)

Vilnius (55°N, 25°E) the capital of Lithuania (p. 353)

Virginia (VA) a state in the eastern United States; admitted in 1788 and one of the original 13 colonies (pp. R42–R43)

Virgin Islands a group of small islands in the Caribbean (p. 187)

Volga (VAHL-guh) the longest river in Europe and Russia's most important commercial river (p. 379)

Wales a part of the United Kingdom located west of England on the island of Great Britain (p. 335)

Warsaw (52°N, 21°E) the capital of Poland (p. 353)

Washington (WA) a state in the northwestern United States; admitted in 1889 (pp. R42–R43)

Washington, D.C. (39°N, 77°W) the capital of the United States (p. 117)

Wellington (41°S, 175°E) the capital of New Zealand (p. 717)

West Bank a disputed territory in eastern Israel (p. 423)

Western Ghats (GAWTS) a mountain range in India (p. 617)

Western Hemisphere the half of the globe between 180° and the prime meridian that includes North and South America and the Pacific and Atlantic oceans (p. H3)

West Indies a group of more than 1,200 islands in the Caribbean Sea (p. 200)

West Virginia (WV) a state in the east-central United States; admitted in 1863 (pp. R42–R43)

Windhoek (VINT-hook) (22°S, 17°E) the capital of Namibia (p. 579)

Windsor (42°N, 83°W) a city in Canada near the U.S. border (p. 145)

Wisconsin (WI) a state in the north-central United States; admitted in 1848 (pp. R42–R43)

Wyoming (WY) a state in the northwestern United States; admitted in 1890 (pp. R42–R43)

Yamoussoukro (yah-moo-SOO-kroh) (7°N, 5°W) the capital of Côte d'Ivoire (p. 515)

Yangon (Rangoon) (17°N, 96°E) the capital of Myanmar (Burma) (p. 690)

Yaoundé (yown-DAY) (4°N, 12°E) the capital of Cameroon (p. 557)

Yellow Sea a body of water between northeastern China and the Korean Peninsula (p. 641)

Yemen a country on the Arabian Peninsula bordering the Red Sea and the Gulf of Aden (p. 435)

Yenisey River a long river in central Russia that flows north to the Arctic Ocean (p. 379)

Yerevan (40°N, 45°E) the capital of Armenia (p. 395)

Yucatán Peninsula (yoo-kah-TAHN) a large peninsula that separates the Caribbean Sea from the Gulf of Mexico (p. 168)

Yugoslavia a former country in the Balkans that broke apart in the 1990s (p. 370)

Yukon Territory a territory in Canada (p. 144)

Z

Zagreb (46°N, 16°E) the capital of Croatia (p. 371)

Zagros Mountains a mountain range in Iran; it forms the western boundary of the Plateau of Iran (p. 437)

Zambezi River a river in Central Africa that flows into the Indian Ocean (p. 559)

Zambia a country in Central Africa east of Angola (p. 557)

Zanzibar an island in Tanzania; once a major trading center (p. 539)

Zimbabwe a country in Southern Africa between Botswana and Mozambique (p. 579)

Zurich (47°N, 9°E) a city in Switzerland (p. 309)

Biographical Dictionary

A

Akbar (1542–1605) Mughal emperor, he conquered new lands and worked to make the Mughal government stronger. He also began a tolerant religious policy that helped unify the empire. (p. 622)

al-Gadhafi, Mu'ammar (1942–) Leader of Libya, he has ruled as a dictator and supported acts of violence against Israel and its neighbors. (p. 509)

Asoka (uh-SOH-kuh) (ruled 270–232 BC) Ruler of the Mauryan Empire, he extended his control over most of India and promoted the spread of Buddhism. (p. 621)

Atatürk, Kemal (1881–1938) The first president of modern Turkey, he was given the name Atatürk, which means "father of the Turks." He worked to free Turkey from foreign control and began many programs to reform and modernize the country. (p. 417)

B

Babur (bah-boor) (1483–1530) Indian emperor, he founded the Mughal Empire. (p. 622)

Bolívar, Simon (1783–1830) Latin American revolutionary leader, he inspired revolutionary movements in Bolivia, Colombia, Ecuador, and Venezuela. (p. 221)

Buddha (BOO-duh) (c. 563–483 BC) Founder of Buddhism, he was an Indian prince originally named Siddhartha Gautama. He founded the Buddhist religion after a long spiritual journey through India. (p. 624)

Bush, George W. (1946–) President of the United States, he was president on September 11, 2001, when the country suffered its worst terrorist attack. This attack led to the country's War on Terror. (p. 447)

C

Castro, Fidel (1926–) Premier of Cuba, his revolutionary movement overthrew Cuba's government in 1959 and established the first Communist government in the Western Hemisphere. (p. 204)

Charlemagne (SHAHR-luh-mayn) (c. 742–814) King of the Franks, he was brilliant warrior and a strong leader whose empire included much of Christian western Europe. (p. 315)

Chavez, Hugo (1954–) President of Venezuela, he was elected to office in 1998. He successfully changed the country's constitution to give the president more power and survived a military coup in 2002 and a recall election in 2004. (p. 223)

Chiang Kai-Shek (chang ky-SHEK) (1887–1975) Chinese general and leader of the Nationalists, he lost China's civil war and fled with his supporters to Taiwan. (p. 646)

Churchill, Sir Winston (1874–1965) Prime Minister of the United Kingdom, he led the United Kingdom through the difficult years of World War II. (p. 339)

Cleopatra (69–30 BC) Queen of Egypt, she tried to drive the Romans out of Egypt. (p. 499)

Columbus, Christopher (1451–1506) Italian sailor, he led a voyage to the Americas in 1492 while trying to find a route east to India and China. (p. 200)

Confucius (551–479 BC) Chinese philosopher, he was the most influential teacher in Chinese history. His teachings, called Confucianism, focused on morality, family, society, and government. (p. 648)

Cortés, Hernán (er-NAHN kawr-TAYS) (c.1485–1547) Spanish conquistador, he went to Mexico in search of riches and captured the Aztec capital of Tenochtitlán, causing the collapse of the Aztec Empire. (p. 174)

E, F

Ebadi, Shirin (1947–) Iranian lawyer, writer, and teacher, she was the first Muslim woman to win the Nobel Prize for Peace in 2003. She has received many awards for her work to promote democracy and human rights, especially for women and children in Iran. (p. 453)

Fox, Vicente (1942–) President of Mexico, his election in 2000 ended 71 years of one-party rule in Mexico. A populist leader, he has worked to strengthen Mexico's economy and fight poverty. (p. 178)

G

Gandhi, Mohandas (1869–1948) Indian nationalist and spiritual leader, he used nonviolence to protest British rule of India and helped the country achieve independence. (p. 622)

Genghis Khan (JENG-uhs KAHN) (c. 1162–1227) Ruler of the Mongols, he led his people in attacks against China and other parts of Asia. His name means "universal leader." (p. 656)

Gorbachev, Mikhail (GAWR-buh-chawf) (1931–) Leader of the Soviet Union, his reforms led to the breakup of the Soviet Union, a thaw in the Cold War, and the fall of Communism in Europe. (p. 384)

H

Hidalgo, Miguel (1753–1811) Mexican priest and revolutionary leader, he led a revolt against Spain that eventually led to Mexico's independence in 1821. He is known as the Father of Mexican Independence. (p. 174)

Hirohito (1901–1989) Emperor of Japan, he led the country through World War II and the transition to a democratic government. (p. 672)

Hitler, Adolf (1889–1945) German dictator and Nazi leader, his aggression launched World War II. (p. 323)

Hussein, Saddam (1937–2006) Iraqi dictator, he became president of Iraq in 1979 and led Iraq into two devastating wars. Known for his brutal suppression of opposition, Hussein was overthrown and captured by the United States in 2003 as part of the War on Terror. (p. 447)

John Paul II (1920–2005) First Polish pope, he encouraged the Polish people to protest against their Communist government and served as pope for 26 years. (p. 359)

Juárez, Benito (1806–1872) President of Mexico, he helped to establish democracy in the country and was Mexico's first president of Indian descent. He is a national hero in Mexico. (p. 175)

Kim Il Sung (1912–1994) Leader of North Korea, he established a Communist government there and attacked South Korea in 1950, launching the Korean War. (p. 684)

Kim Jong Il (1941–) Leader of North Korea, he took power after his father died in 1994. (p. 684)

L'Ouverture, Toussaint (too-sahn loo-ver-toor) (c. 1743–1803) Haitian leader, he was a former slave who became a revolutionary general and government leader in Haiti and fought for his people's freedom. (p. 201)

Lalibela (ruled late 1100s–early 1200s) Christian emperor of Ethiopia, he is best known for the 11 rock churches he built during his reign. (p. 542)

Lenin, Vladimir (1870–1924) Russian revolutionary leader, he led the overthrow of the Russian government in 1917 to create the first Communist state. (p. 383)

Mahfouz, Naguib (1911–) Egyptian writer, he became the first Arab writer to win the Nobel Prize for Literature. (p. 503)

Mandela, Nelson (1918–) South African president and Nobel Peace Prize winner, he worked to improve the living conditions of black South Africans. Before becoming president, he protested against apartheid and was imprisoned for 26 years. (p. 591)

Mao Zedong (MOW ZUH-DOOHNG) (1893–1976) Leader of China, he led the Communist takeover of China in 1949 and was head of the government until 1976. (p. 646)

Nkrumah, Kwame (1909–1972) Leader of Ghana, he believed that Africa would be better off united instead of split into separate countries after independence from European colonial powers. (p. 521)

Perón, Eva (1919–1952) Argentine political leader, she was the wife of Argentina's president Juan Perón. Known as Evita, she was a popular figure who worked to improve the lives of women, workers, and the poor. (p. 243)

Pizarro, Francisco (c.1475–1541) Spanish conquistador, he conquered the Inca Empire and captured the Inca ruler Atahualpa. (p. 261)

S

Shackleton, Ernest (1874–1922) Antarctic explorer, he led several expeditions to Antarctica, including one in which he and his companions were stranded and had to make a daring journey to get help. (p. 734)

Shi Huangdi (SHEE hwahng-dee) (259–210 BC) Ruler of China, he united China for the first time, built roads and canals, began the Great Wall of China, and imposed a standard system of laws, money, weights, and writing. (p. 645)

Soyinka, Wole (1934–) Nigerian writer, he has written plays, novels, and poems about life in West Africa. He is a winner of the Nobel Prize for Literature. (p. 531)

Suu Kyi, Aung San (1945–) Human rights advocate in Myanmar, she protested against the country's military government and won the Nobel Peace Prize in 1991. (p. 704)

T, W

Tutankhamen (too-tang-KAHM-uhn) (c. 1300 BC) Egyptian pharaoh, he died while still a young king. The discovery of his tomb in 1922 has taught archaeologists much about Egyptian culture. (p. 500)

Washington, George (1732–1799) Revolutionary general and first American president, he led American troops in their fight for independence from Britain. After the war, he served two terms as president and is known as the Father of His Country. (p. 127)

English and Spanish Glossary

Phonetic Respelling and Pronunciation Guide

Many of the key terms in this textbook have been respelled to help you pronounce them. The letter combinations used in the respelling throughout the narrative are explained in this phonetic respelling and pronunciation guide. The guide is adapted from *Merriam-Webster's Collegiate Dictionary, Eleventh Edition; Merriam-Webster's Geographical Dictionary;* and *Merriam-Webster's Biographical Dictionary.*

MARK	AS IN	RESPELLING	EXAMPLE
a	alphabet	a	*AL-fuh-bet
ā	Asia	ay	AY-zhuh
ä	cart, top	ah	KAHRT, TAHP
e	let, ten	e	LET, TEN
ē	even, leaf	ee	EE-vuhn, LEEF
i	it, tip, British	i	IT, TIP, BRIT-ish
ī	site, buy, Ohio	y	SYT, BY, oh-HY-oh
	iris	eye	EYE-ris
k	card	k	KAHRD
kw	quest	kw	KWEST
ō	over, rainbow	oh	OH-vuhr, RAYN-boh
ù	book, wood	ooh	BOOHK, WOOHD
ò	all, orchid	aw	AWL, AWR-kid
òi	foil, coin	oy	FOYL, KOYN
aù	out	ow	OWT
ə	cup, butter	uh	KUHP, BUHT-uhr
ü	rule, food	oo	ROOL, FOOD
yü	few	yoo	FYOO
zh	vision	zh	VIZH-uhn

*A syllable printed in small capital letters receives heavier emphasis than the other syllable(s) in a word.

A

Aborigines (a-buh-rij-uh-nees) the original inhabitants of Australia (p. 721)
aborígenes habitantes originales de Australia (pág. 721)

absolute location a specific description of where a place is located; absolute location is often expressed using latitude and longitude (p. 12)
ubicación absoluta descripción específica del lugar donde se ubica un punto; con frecuencia se define en términos de latitud y longitud (pág. 12)

Afrikaners (a-fri-KAH-nuhrz) Dutch, French, and German settlers and their descendants in South Africa (p. 586)
afrikaners colonizadores holandeses, franceses y alemanes y sus descendientes en Sudáfrica (pág. 586)

altiplano a broad, high plateau that lies between the ridges of the Andes (p. 255)
altiplano meseta amplia y elevada que se extiende entre las cadenas montañosas de los Andes (pág. 255)

animism the belief that bodies of water, animals, trees, and other natural objects have spirits (p. 522)
animismo creencia de que las masas de agua, los animales, los árboles y otros objetos de la naturaleza tienen espíritu (pág. 522)

apartheid South Africa's government policy of separation of races that was abandoned in the 1980s and 1990s; apartheid means "apartness" (p. 586)
apartheid política gubernamental de Sudáfrica de separar las razas, abandonada en las décadas de 1980 y 1990; apartheid significa "separación" (pág. 586)

arable land that is suitable for growing crops (p. 471)
cultivable tierra buena para el cultivo (pág. 471)

archipelago a large group of islands (pp. 189, 692)
archipiélago gran grupo de islas (págs. 189, 692)

Association of Southeast Asian Nations (ASEAN) an organization that promotes economic development and social and cultural cooperation among the countries of Southeast Asia (p. 703)
Asociación de Naciones de Asia del Sudeste (ASEAN por sus siglas en inglés) organización que promueve el desarrollo económico y social y la cooperación cultural entre los países del sureste asiático (pág. 703)

atoll a ring-shaped coral island that surrounds a lagoon (p. 728)
atolón isla de coral en forma de anillo que rodea una laguna (pág. 728)

B

basin a generally flat region surrounded by higher land such as mountains and plateaus (p. 558)
cuenca región generalmente llana rodeada de tierras más altas, como montañas y mesetas (pág. 558)

Bedouins Arabic-speaking nomads that live mostly in the deserts of Southwest Asia (p. 428)
beduinos nómadas que hablan árabe y viven principalmente en los desiertos del suroeste de Asia (pág. 428)

Berbers members of an ethnic group who are native to North Africa and speak Berber languages (p. 501)
bereberes miembros de un grupo étnico del norte de África que hablan lenguas bereberes (pág. 501)

bilingual a term used to describe people who speak two languages (p. 130)
bilingüe término utilizado para describir a las personas que hablan dos idiomas (pág. 130)

birthrate the annual number of births per 1,000 people (p. 88)
índice de natalidad número de nacimientos por cada 1,000 personas en un año (pág. 88)

Boers Afrikaner frontier farmers in South Africa (p. 586)
bóers agricultores afrikaners de la frontera en Sudáfrica (pág. 586)

Bolsheviks a radical Russian Communist group that seized power in 1917 (p. 383)
bolcheviques grupo comunista ruso radical que obtuvo el poder en 1917 (pág. 383)

Buddhism a religion based on the teachings of the Buddha that developed in India in the 500s BC (p. 624)
budismo religión basada en las enseñanzas de Buda, originada en la India en el siglo VI a. C. (pág. 624)

C

canton one of 26 districts in the republic of Switzerland (p. 327)
cantón uno de los 26 distritos de la república de Suiza (pág. 327)

cartography the science of making maps (p. 19)
cartografía ciencia de crear mapas (pág. 19)

cash crop a crop that farmers grow mainly to sell for a profit (p. 179)
cultivo comercial cultivo que los agricultores producen principalmente para vender y obtener ganancias (pág. 179)

caste system the division of Indian society into groups based on birth or occupation (p. 624)
sistema de castas división de la sociedad india en grupos basados en el nacimiento o la profesión (pág. 624)

chancellor a German prime minister (p. 325)
canciller primer ministro alemán (pág. 325)

civil war a conflict between two or more groups within a country (p. 196)
guerra civil conflicto entre dos o más grupos dentro de un país (pág. 196)

climate a region's average weather conditions over a long period of time (p. 50)
clima condiciones del tiempo promedio de una región durante un período largo de tiempo (pág. 50)

cloud forest a moist, high-elevation tropical forest where low clouds are common (p. 190)
bosque nuboso bosque tropical de gran elevación y humedad donde los bancos de nubes son muy comunes (pág. 190)

colony a territory inhabited and controlled by people from a foreign land (pp. 126, 622)
colonia territorio habitado y controlado por personas de otro país (págs. 126, 622)

command economy an economic system in which the central government makes all economic decisions (pp. 94, 651)
economía autoritaria sistema económico en el que el gobierno central toma todas las decisiones económicas (págs. 94, 651)

commonwealth a self-governing territory associated with another country (p. 203)
mancomunidad o estado libre asociado territorio autogobernado asociado con otro país (pág. 203)

Commonwealth of Independent States (CIS) a union of former Soviet republics that meets about issues such as trade and immigration (p. 364)
Comunidad de Estados Independientes (CEI) unión de ex repúblicas soviéticas que se reúne para tratar temas como el comercio y la inmigración (pág. 364)

communism a political system in which the government owns all property and dominates all aspects of life in a country (p. 92)
comunismo sistema político en el que el gobierno es dueño de toda la propiedad y controla todos los aspectos de la vida de un país (pág. 92)

Confucianism a philosophy based on the ideas of Confucius that focuses on morality, family order, social harmony, and government (p. 648)
confucianismo filosofía basada en las ideas de Confucio que se concentra en la moralidad, el orden familiar, la armonía social y el gobierno (pág. 648)

constitutional monarchy a type of democracy in which a monarch serves as head of state but a legislature makes the laws (p. 340)
monarquía constitucional tipo de democracia en la cual un monarca sirve como jefe de estado, pero una asamblea legislativa hace las leyes (pág. 340)

continent a large landmass that is part of Earth's crust; geographers identify seven continents (p. 36)
continente gran masa de tierra que forma parte de la corteza terrestre; los geógrafos identifican siete continentes (pág. 36)

ENGLISH AND SPANISH GLOSSARY

continental divide an area of high ground that divides the flow of rivers towards opposite ends of a continent (p. 120)
línea divisoria de aguas zona de terreno elevado que divide el flujo de los ríos en dos direcciones, hacia los extremos opuestos de un continente (pág. 120)

cooperative an organization owned by its members and operated for their mutual benefit (p. 204)
cooperativa organización cuyos miembros son los propietarios y que es operada para beneficio de todos (pág. 204)

coral reef a chain of rocky material found in shallow tropical waters (p. 719)
arrecife de coral cadena de material rocoso que se encuentra en aguas tropicales de poca profundidad (pág. 719)

cordillera (kawr-duhl-YER-uh) a mountain system made up of roughly parallel ranges (p. 212)
cordillera sistema de cadenas montañosas aproximadamente paralelas entre sí (pág. 212)

cosmopolitan characterized by many foreign influences (p. 319)
cosmopolita caracterizado por muchas influencias extranjeras (pág. 319)

coup (KOO) a sudden overthrow of a government by a small group of people (p. 267)
golpe de estado derrocamiento repentino de un gobierno por parte de un grupo reducido de personas (pág. 267)

Creole an American-born descendant of Europeans (p. 262)
criollo persona de ascendencia europea y nacida en América (pág. 262)

cultural diffusion the spread of culture traits from one region to another (p. 85)
difusión cultural difusión de rasgos culturales de una región a otra (pág. 85)

cultural diversity having a variety of cultures in the same area (p. 83)
diversidad cultural existencia de una variedad de culturas en la misma zona (pág. 83)

culture the set of beliefs, values, and practices that a group of people have in common (p. 80)
cultura conjunto de creencias, valores y costumbres compartidas por un grupo de personas (pág. 80)

culture region an area in which people have many shared culture traits (p. 82)
región cultural región en la que las personas comparten muchos rasgos culturales (pág. 82)

culture trait an activity or behavior in which people often take part (p. 81)
rasgo cultural actividad o conducta frecuente de las personas (pág. 81)

Cyrllic (suh-RIHL-ihk) a form of the Greek alphabet (p. 382)
cirílico forma del alfabeto griego (pág. 382)

czar (ZAHR) a Russian emperor (p. 383)
zar emperador ruso (pág. 383)

dachas Russian country houses (p. 389)
dachas casas de campo rusas (pág. 389)

Daoism a philosophy that developed in China and stressed the belief that one should live in harmony with the Dao, the guiding force of all reality (p. 648)
taoísmo filosofía que se desarrolló en China y que enfatizaba la creencia de que se debe vivir en armonía con el Tao, la fuerza que guía toda la realidad (pág. 648)

deforestation the clearing of trees (pp. 69, 235)
deforestación tala de árboles (págs. 69, 235)

delta a landform at the mouth of a river created by sediment deposits (p. 617)
delta accidente geográfico que se forma en la desembocadura de un río, creado por depósitos de sedimento (pág. 617)

demilitarized zone an empty buffer zone created to keep two countries from fighting (p. 683)
zona desmilitarizada zona vacía que se crea como barrera entre dos países para evitar que luchen (pág. 683)

democracy a form of government in which the people elect leaders and rule by majority (p. 91)
democracia sistema de gobierno en el que el pueblo elige a sus líderes y gobierna por mayoría (pág. 91)

desertification the spread of desert-like conditions (pp. 65, 518)
desertización ampliación de las condiciones desérticas (págs. 65, 518)

developed countries countries with strong economies and a high quality of life (p. 95)
países desarrollados países con economías sólidas y una alta calidad de vida (pág. 95)

developing countries countries with less productive economies and a lower quality of life (p. 95)
países en vías de desarrollo países con economías menos productivas y una menor calidad de vida (pág. 95)

dialect a regional version of a language (pp. 202, 566)
dialecto versión regional de una lengua (págs. 202, 566)

Diaspora the scattering of the Jewish population outside of Israel (p. 420)
Diáspora dispersión de la población judía fuera de Israel (pág. 420)

dictator a ruler who has almost absolute power (p. 509)
dictador gobernante que tiene poder casi absoluto (pág. 509)

Diet the name for Japan's elected legislature (p. 676)
Dieta nombre de la asamblea legislativa electa de Japón (pág. 676)

disarm to give up all weapons (p. 341)
desarmarse renunciar a todas las armas (pág. 341)

domino theory the idea that if one country fell to Communism, neighboring countries would follow like falling dominoes (p. 700)

　　teoría del efecto dominó idea de que si un país cae en manos del comunismo, los países vecinos lo seguirán como fichas de dominó que caen una tras otra (pág. 700)

droughts periods when little rain falls and crops are damaged (p. 540)

　　sequías períodos en los que los cultivos sufren daños por la falta de lluvia (pág. 540)

dryland farming farming that relies on rainfall instead of irrigation (p. 471)

　　cultivo de secano cultivo que depende de la lluvia en vez de la irrigación (pág. 471)

dynasty a series of rulers from the same family (p. 645)

　　dinastía serie de gobernantes de la misma familia (pág. 645)

earthquake a sudden, violent movement of Earth's crust (p. 38)

　　terremoto movimiento repentino y violento de la corteza terrestre (pág. 38)

ecosystem a group of plants and animals that depend on each other for survival, and the environment in which they live (p. 63)

　　ecosistema grupo de plantas y animales que dependen unos de otros para sobrevivir, y el ambiente en el que estos viven (pág. 63)

ecotourism the practice of using an area's natural environment to attract tourists (p. 196)

　　ecoturismo uso de regiones naturales para atraer turistas (pág. 196)

El Niño an ocean and weather pattern that affects the Pacific coast of the Americas; about every two to seven years, it warms normally cool ocean water and causes extreme ocean and weather events (p. 257)

　　El Niño patrón oceánico y del tiempo que afecta a la costa del Pacífico de las Américas; aproximadamente cada dos a siete años, calienta las aguas normalmente frías del océano, y provoca sucesos oceánicos y climatológicos extremos (pág. 257)

embargo a limit on trade (p. 447)

　　embargo límite impuesto al comercio (pág. 447)

empire a land with different territories and peoples under a single ruler (p. 173)

　　imperio zona que reúne varios territorios y pueblos bajo un solo gobernante (pág. 173)

enclave a small territory surrounded by foreign territory (p. 592)

　　enclave territorio pequeño rodeado de territorio extranjero (pág. 592)

environment the land, water, climate, plants, and animals of an area; surroundings (pp. 12, 62)

　　ambiente la tierra, el agua, el clima, las plantas y los animales de una zona; los alrededores (págs. 12, 62)

erosion the movement of sediment from one location to another (p. 39)

　　erosión movimiento de sedimentos de un lugar a otro (pág. 39)

escarpment a steep face at the edge of a plateau or other raised area (p. 580)

　　acantilado cara empinada en el borde de una meseta o de otra área elevada (pág. 580)

estuary a partially enclosed body of water where freshwater mixes with salty seawater (p. 233)

　　estuario masa de agua parcialmente rodeada de tierra en la que el agua de mar se combina con agua dulce (pág. 233)

ethnic cleansing the effort to remove all members of an ethnic group from a country or region (p. 368)

　　limpieza étnica esfuerzo por eliminar a todos los miembros de un grupo étnico de un país o región (pág. 368)

ethnic group a group of people who share a common culture and ancestry (p. 83)

　　grupo étnico grupo de personas que comparten una cultura y una ascendencia (pág. 83)

extended family a family group that includes the father, mother, children, and close relatives (p. 523)

　　familia extendida grupo familiar que incluye al padre, la madre, los hijos y los parientes cercanos (pág. 523)

extinct no longer here; a species that has died out has become extinct (p. 64)

　　extinto que ya no existe; una especie que ha desaparecido está extinta (pág. 64)

famine an extreme shortage of food (p. 529)

　　hambruna grave escasez de alimentos (pág. 529)

favela (fah-VE-lah) a huge slum in Brazil (p. 239)

　　favela enorme barriada en Brasil (pág. 239)

fishery a place where lots of fish and other seafood can be caught (p. 669)

　　pesquería lugar donde suele haber muchos peces y mariscos para pescar (pág. 669)

fjord (fyawrd) a narrow inlet of the sea set between high, rocky cliffs (p. 335)

　　fiordo entrada estrecha del mar entre acantilados altos y rocosos (pág. 335)

fossil fuels nonrenewable resources that formed from the remains of ancient plants and animals; coal, petroleum, and natural gas are all fossil fuels (p. 69)

　　combustibles fósiles recursos no renovables formados a partir de restos de plantas y animales antiguos; el carbón, el petróleo y el gas natural son combustibles fósiles (pág. 69)

fossil water water underground that is not being replaced by rainfall (p. 439)
    aguas fósiles agua subterránea que no es reemplazada por el agua de lluvia (pág. 439)

free port a city in which almost no taxes are placed on goods (pp. 509, 710)
    puerto libre ciudad donde hay muy pocos impuestos sobre los bienes (págs. 509, 710)

freshwater water that is not salty; it makes up only about 3 percent of our total water supply (p. 31)
    agua dulce agua que no es salada; representa sólo alrededor del 3 por ciento de nuestro suministro total de agua (pág. 31)

front the place where two air masses of different temperatures or moisture content meet (p. 53)
    frente lugar en el que se encuentran dos masas de aire con diferente temperatura o humedad (pág. 53)

gaucho (GOW-choh) an Argentine cowboy (p. 243)
    gaucho vaquero argentino (pág. 243)

genocide the intentional destruction of a people (p. 549)
    genocidio destrucción intencional de un grupo de personas (pág. 549)

geography the study of the world, its people, and the landscapes they create (p. 4)
    geografía estudio del mundo, de sus habitantes y de los paisajes creados por el ser humano (pág. 4)

geothermal energy energy produced from the heat of Earth's interior (pp. 336, 547)
    energía geotérmica energía producida a partir del calor del interior de la Tierra (págs. 336, 547)

ger a large, circular, felt tent used in Mongolia and Central Asia (p. 657)
    ger gran tienda circular de fieltro usada en Mongolia y Asia Central (pág. 657)

geyser a spring that shoots hot water and steam into the air (p. 348)
    géiser manantial que lanza agua caliente y vapor al aire (pág. 348)

glacier a large area of slow moving ice (p. 31)
    glaciar gran bloque de hielo que avanza con lentitud (pág. 31)

globalization the process in which countries are increasingly linked to each other through culture and trade (p. 97)
    globalización proceso por el cual los países se encuentran cada vez más interconectados a través de la cultura y el comercio (pág. 97)

globe a spherical, or ball-shaped, model of the entire planet (p. 8)
    globo terráqueo modelo esférico, o en forma de bola, de todo el planeta (pág. 8)

green revolution a program that encouraged farmers to adopt modern agricultural methods to produce more food (p. 629)
    revolución verde programa que animó a los agricultores a adoptar métodos de agricultura modernos para producir más alimentos (pág. 629)

gross domestic product (GDP) the value of all goods and services produced within a country in a single year (p. 95)
    producto interior bruto (PIB) valor de todos los bienes y servicios producidos en un país durante un año (pág. 95)

groundwater water found below Earth's surface (p. 32)
    agua subterránea agua que se encuentra debajo de la superficie de la Tierra (pág. 32)

guerrilla a member of an irregular military force (p. 219)
    guerrillero miembro de una fuerza militar irregular (pág. 219)

gulag a soviet labor camp (p. 384)
    gulag campo soviético de trabajos forzados (pág. 384)

habitat the place where a plant or animal lives (p. 64)
    hábitat lugar en el que vive una planta o animal (pág. 64)

hacienda (hah-see-EN-duh) a huge expanse of farm or ranch land in the Americas (p. 174)
    hacienda granja o rancho de gran tamaño en las Américas (pág. 174)

Hinduism the main religion of India; it teaches that everything is part of a universal spirit called Brahman (p. 624)
    hinduismo religión principal de la India; sus enseñanzas dicen que todo forma parte de un espíritu universal llamado Brahma (pág. 624)

human geography the study of the world's people, communities, and landscapes (p. 18)
    geografía humana estudio de los habitantes, las comunidades y los paisajes del mundo (pág. 18)

human rights rights that all people deserve, such as rights to equality and justice (p. 704)
    derechos humanos derechos que toda la gente merece como derechos a la igualdad y la justicia (pág. 704)

humanitarian aid assistance to people in distress (p. 100)
    ayuda humanitaria ayuda a personas en peligro (pág. 100)

humus (HYOO-muhs) decayed plant or animal matter; it helps soil support abundant plant life (p. 65)
    humus materia animal o vegetal descompuesta; contribuye a que crezca una gran cantidad de plantas en el suelo (pág. 65)

hydroelectric power the production of electricity from waterpower, such as from running water (p. 70)
energía hidroeléctrica producción de electricidad generada por la energía del agua, como la del agua corriente (pág. 70)

iceberg a floating mass of ice that has broken off a glacier (p. 733)
iceberg masa de hielo flotante que se ha desprendido de un glaciar (pág. 733)

ice shelf a ledge of ice that extends over the water (p. 733)
banco de hielo saliente de hielo que se extiende sobre el agua (pág. 733)

imperialism an attempt to dominate a country's government, trade, and culture (p. 543)
imperialismo intento de dominar el gobierno, el comercio y la cultura de un país (pág. 543)

inflation the rise in prices that occurs when currency loses its buying power (pp. 178, 571)
inflación aumento de los precios que ocurre cuando la moneda de un país pierde poder adquisitivo (págs. 178, 571)

informal economy a part of the economy that is based on odd jobs that people perform without government regulation through taxes (p. 245)
economía informal parte de la economía basada en trabajos pequeños que se realizan sin el pago de impuestos regulados por el gobierno (pág. 245)

infrastructure the set of resources, like roads and factories, that a country needs to support economic activities (p. 361)
infraestructura conjunto de recursos, como carre-teras o fábricas, que necesita un país para sostener su actividad económica (pág. 361)

interdependence a relationship between countries in which they rely on one another for resources, goods, or services (p. 99)
interdependencia una relación entre países en que dependen unos de otros para obtener recursos, bienes, o servicios (pág. 99)

isthmus a narrow strip of land that connects two larger land areas (p. 188)
istmo franja estrecha de tierra que une dos zonas más grandes (pág. 188)

kampong a traditional village in Indonesia; also the term for crowded slums around Indonesia's large cities (p. 709)
kampong aldea tradicional de Indonesia; término que también se usa para los barrios pobres y superpoblados que rodean las grandes ciudades de Indonesia (pág. 709)

kibbutz (kih-BOOTS) in Israel, a large farm where people share everything in common (p. 422)
kibbutz en Israel, granja grande donde las personas comparten todo (pág. 422)

kimchi a traditional Korean food made from pickled cabbage and spices (p. 675)
kimchi comida tradicional coreana hecha con repollo en vinagre y especias (pág. 675)

kimono a traditional robe worn in Japan (p. 674)
kimono bata tradicional usada en Japón (pág. 674)

klong a canal in Bangkok (p. 704)
klong canal de Bangkok (pág. 704)

kosher a term used to refer to Jewish dietary laws; it means "acceptable" in Hebrew (p. 422)
kosher término utilizado para referirse a las leyes alimenticias judías; en hebreo significa aceptable (pág. 422)

landform a shape on the planet's surface, such as a mountain, valley, plain, island, or peninsula (p. 35)
accidente geográfico forma de la superficie terrestre, como una montaña, un valle, una llanura, una isla o una península (pág. 35)

landlocked completely surrounded by land with no direct access to the ocean (pp. 246, 460)
sin salida al mar que está rodeado completamente por tierra, sin acceso directo al océano (págs. 246, 460)

landscape all the human and physical features that make a place unique (p. 4)
paisaje todas las características humanas y físicas que hacen que un lugar sea único (pág. 4)

latitude the distance north or south of Earth's equator (p. 27)
latitud distancia hacia el norte o el sur desde el ecuador (pág. 27)

lava magma that reaches Earth's surface (p. 37)
lava magma que llega a la superficie terrestre (pág. 37)

llanero (yah-NAY-roh) Venezuelan cowboy (p. 222)
llanero vaquero venezolano (pág. 222)

loess (LES) fertile, yellowish soil (p. 642)
loess suelo amarillento y fértil (pág. 642)

Magna Carta a document signed in 1215 by King John of England that required the king to honor certain rights (p. 340)
Carta Magna documento firmado por el rey Juan de Inglaterra en 1215 que exigía que el rey respetara ciertos derechos (pág. 340)

malaria a disease spread by mosquitoes that causes fever and pain (p. 572)
malaria enfermedad transmitida por los mosquitos que causa fiebre y dolor (pág. 572)

malnutrition a condition of not getting enough nutrients from food (p. 573)
desnutrición estado producido al no obtener suficientes nutrientes de los alimentos (pág. 573)

Maori (MOWR-ee) the original inhabitants of New Zealand (p. 721)
maoríes primeros habitantes de Nueva Zelanda (pág. 721)

map a flat drawing that shows all or part of Earth's surface (p. 8)
mapa representación plana que muestra total o parcialmente la superficie de la Tierra (pág. 8)

maquiladora (mah-kee-lah-DORH-ah) a U.S. or other foreign-owned factory in Mexico (p. 181)
maquiladora fábrica estadounidense o de otro país establecida en México (pág. 181)

maritime on or near the sea (p. 157)
marítimo en o cerca del mar (pág. 157)

market economy an economic system based on free trade and competition (p. 94)
economía de mercado sistema económico basado en el libre comercio y la competencia (pág. 94)

Mediterranean climate the type of climate found across Southern Europe; it features warm and sunny summer days, mild evenings, and cooler, rainy winters (p. 288)
clima mediterráneo tipo de clima de todo el sur europeo; se caracteriza por días de verano cálidos y soleados, noches templadas e inviernos lluviosos y más frescos (pág. 288)

megacity a giant urban area that includes surrounding cities and suburbs (p. 238)
megaciudad zona urbana enorme que incluye los suburbios y ciudades de alrededor (pág. 238)

megalopolis a string of large cities that have grown together (p. 135)
megalópolis serie de ciudades grandes que han crecido hasta unirse (pág. 135)

Mercosur an organization that promotes trade and economic cooperation among the southern and eastern countries of South America (p. 244)
Mercosur organización que promueve el comercio y la cooperación económica entre los países del sur y el este de América del Sur (pág. 244)

mestizo (me-STEE-zoh) a person of mixed European and Indian ancestry (p. 174)
mestizo persona de origen europeo e indígena (pág. 174)

meteorology the study of weather and what causes it (p. 20)
meteorología estudio de las condiciones del tiempo y sus causas (pág. 20)

migration the movement of people from one place to live in another (p. 89)
migración movimiento de personas de un lugar para ir a vivir a otro lugar (pág. 89)

mission a church outpost (p. 174)
misión asentamiento de la Iglesia (pág. 174)

monsoon a seasonal wind that brings either dry or moist air (p. 619)
monzón viento estacional que trae aire seco o húmedo (pág. 619)

natural resource any material in nature that people use and value (p. 68)
recurso natural todo material de la naturaleza que las personas utilizan y valoran (pág. 68)

navigable river a river that is deep and wide enough for ships to use (p. 312)
río navegable río que tiene la profundidad y el ancho necesarios para que pasen los barcos (pág. 312)

neutral not taking sides in an international conflict (p. 346)
neutral que no toma partido en un conflicto internacional (pág. 346)

newsprint cheap paper used mainly for newspapers (p. 149)
papel de prensa papel económico utilizado principalmente para imprimir periódicos (pág. 149)

nomads people who move often from place to place (p. 466)
nómadas personas que se trasladan frecuentemente de un lugar a otro (pág. 466)

nonrenewable resource a resource that cannot be replaced naturally; coal and petroleum are examples of nonrenewable resources (p. 69)
recurso no renovable recurso que no puede reemplazarse naturalmente; el carbón y el petróleo son ejemplos de recursos no renovables (pág. 69)

North Atlantic Drift a warm ocean current that brings warm, moist air across the Atlantic Ocean to Northern Europe (p. 336)
Corriente del Atlántico Norte corriente oceánica cálida que trae aire cálido y húmedo a través del océano Atlántico al norte de Europa (pág. 336)

oasis a wet, fertile area in a desert where a spring or well provides water (pp. 438, 496)
    oasis zona húmeda y fértil en el desierto con un manantial o pozo que proporciona agua (págs. 438, 496)

ocean currents large streams of surface seawater; they move heat around Earth (p. 52)
    corrientes oceánicas grandes corrientes de agua de mar que fluyen en la superficie del océano; transportan calor por toda la Tierra (pág. 52)

OPEC an international organization whose members work to influence the price of oil on world markets by controlling the supply (p. 441)
    OPEP organización internacional cuyos miembros trabajan para influenciar el precio del petróleo en los mercados mundiales controlando la oferta (pág. 441)

Orthodox Church a branch of Christianity that dates to the Byzantine Empire (p. 293)
    Iglesia ortodoxa rama del cristianismo que data del Imperio bizantino (pág. 293)

ozone layer a layer of Earth's atmosphere that protects living things from the harmful effects of the sun's ultraviolet rays (p. 734)
    capa de ozono capa de la atmósfera de la Tierra que protege a los seres vivos de los efectos dañinos de los rayos ultravioleta del sol (pág. 734)

P

pagoda a Buddhist temple based on Indian designs (p. 649)
    pagoda templo budista basado en diseños de la India (pág. 649)

pans low, flat areas (p. 582)
    depresiones áreas bajas y planas (pág. 582)

parliamentary monarchy a type of government in which a king rules with the help of an elected parliament (p. 304)
    monarquía parlamentaria tipo de gobierno en el que un rey gobierna con la ayuda de un parlamento electo (pág. 304)

partition division (p. 623)
    partición división (pág. 623)

peninsula a piece of land surrounded on three sides by water (p. 168)
    península pedazo de tierra rodeado de agua por tres lados (pág. 168)

periodic market an open-air trading market that is set up once or twice a week (p. 561)
    mercado periódico mercado al aire libre que funciona una o dos veces a la semana (pág. 561)

permafrost permanently frozen layers of soil (p. 61)
    permafrost capas de tierra congeladas permanentemente (pág. 61)

phosphate a mineral salt containing the element phosphorus (p. 415)
    fosfato sal mineral que contiene el elemento fósforo (pág. 415)

physical geography the study of the world's physical features—its landforms, bodies of water, climates, soils, and plants (p. 16)
    geografía física estudio de las características físicas de la Tierra: sus accidentes geográficos, sus masas de agua, sus climas, sus suelos y sus plantas (pág. 16)

pioneer an early settler; in the United States, people who settled the interior and western areas of the country were known as pioneers (p. 128)
    pionero poblador; en Estados Unidos, las personas que se establecieron en el interior y el oeste del país se llamaron pioneros (pág. 128)

plantation a large farm that grows mainly one crop (p. 127)
    plantación granja muy grande en la que se produce principalmente un solo tipo de cultivo (pág. 127)

plate tectonics a theory suggesting that Earth's surface is divided into a dozen or so slow-moving plates, or pieces of Earth's crust (p. 36)
    tectónica de placas teoría que sugiere que la superficie terrestre está dividida en unas doce placas, o fragmentos de corteza terrestre, que se mueven lentamente (pág. 36)

polar desert a high-latitude region that receives little precipitation (p. 733)
    desierto polar región a una latitud alta que recibe pocas precipitaciones (pág. 733)

pope the spiritual head of the Roman Catholic Church (p. 298)
    papa jefe espiritual de la Iglesia Católica Romana (pág. 298)

popular culture culture traits that are well known and widely accepted (p. 98)
    cultura popular rasgos culturales conocidos y de gran aceptación (pág. 98)

population the total number of people in a given area (p. 86)
    población número total de personas en una zona determinada (pág. 86)

population density a measure of the number of people living in an area (p. 86)
    densidad de población medida del número de personas que viven en una zona (pág. 86)

ENGLISH AND SPANISH GLOSSARY

precipitation water that falls to Earth's surface as rain, snow, sleet, or hail (p. 31)
  precipitación agua que cae a la superficie de la Tierra en forma de lluvia, nieve, aguanieve o granizo (pág. 31)

prevailing winds winds that blow in the same direction over large areas of Earth (p. 51)
  vientos preponderantes vientos que soplan en la misma dirección sobre grandes zonas de la Tierra (pág. 51)

province an administrative division of a country (p. 152)
  provincia división administrativa de un país (pág. 152)

pulp softened wood fibers; used to make paper (p. 149)
  pulpa fibras ablandadas de madera; usadas para hacer papel (pág. 149)

referendum a recall vote (p. 224)
  referéndum voto para quitar a alguien de su cargo (pág. 224)

reforestation planting trees to replace lost forestland (p. 69)
  reforestación siembra de árboles para reemplazar los bosques que han desaparecido (pág. 69)

refugee someone who flees to another country, usually for political or economic reasons (p. 203)
  refugiado persona que escapa a otro país, generalmente por razones económicas o políticas (pág. 203)

region a part of the world that has one or more common features that distinguish it from surrounding areas (p. 6)
  región parte del mundo que tiene una o más características comunes que la distinguen de las áreas que la rodean (pág. 6)

regionalism the strong connection that people feel toward the region in which they live (p. 157)
  regionalismo gran conexión que las personas sienten con la región en la que viven (pág. 157)

relative location a general description of where a place is located; a place's relative location is often expressed in relation to something else (p. 12)
  ubicación relativa descripción general de la posición de un lugar; la ubicación relativa de un lugar suele expresarse en relación con otra cosa (pág. 12)

renewable resource a resource that Earth replaces naturally, such as water, soil, trees, plants, and animals (p. 69)
  recurso renovable recurso que la Tierra reemplaza por procesos naturales, como el agua, el suelo, los árboles, las plantas y los animales (pág. 69)

revolution the 365 ¼ day trip Earth takes around the sun each year (p. 27)
  revolución viaje de 365 ¼ días que la Tierra hace alrededor del Sol cada año (pág. 27)

revolution a drastic change in a country's government and way of life (p. 451)
  revolución cambio drástico en el gobierno y la forma de vida de un país (pág. 451)

rift valleys places on Earth's surface where the crust stretches until it breaks (p. 538)
  valles de fisura puntos de la superficie de la Tierra en los que la corteza se estira hasta romperse (pág. 538)

rotation one complete spin of Earth on its axis; each rotation takes about 24 hours (p. 26)
  rotación giro completo de la Tierra sobre su propio eje; cada rotación toma 24 horas (pág. 26)

safari an overland journey to view African wildlife (p. 547)
  safari excursión por tierra con el fin de ver animales salvajes en África (pág. 547)

Sahel (SAH-hel) a strip of land that divides the Sahara from wetter areas (p. 518)
  Sahel franja de tierra que divide el Sahara de zonas más húmedas (pág. 518)

samurai (SA-muh-ry) a trained professional warrior in feudal Japan (p. 672)
  samurai guerrero profesional entrenado del Japón feudal (pág. 672)

sanctions economic or political penalties imposed by one country on another to try to force a change in policy (p. 590)
  sanciones penalizaciones económicas o políticas que un país impone a otro para obligarlo a cambiar su política (pág. 590)

savanna an area of tall grasses and scattered trees and shrubs (pp. 58, 518)
  sabana zona de pastos altos con arbustos y árboles dispersos (págs. 58, 518)

secede to break away from the main country (p. 526)
  separarse dividirse del territorio principal del país (pág. 526)

secular the separation of religion and government; nonreligious (p. 419)
  secular separación entre la religión y el gobierno; no religioso (pág. 419)

shah a Persian title that means "king" (p. 451)
  sha título persa que significa "rey" (pág. 451)

Sherpas an ethnic group from the mountains of Nepal (p. 630)
  sherpas grupo étnico de las montañas de Nepal (pág. 630)

Shia Muslims who believe that true interpretation of Islamic teaching can only come from certain religious and political leaders called imams; they make up one of the two main branches of Islam (p. 440)
   chiítas musulmanes que creen que la interpretación correcta de las enseñanzas islámicas solo puede provenir de ciertos líderes religiosos y políticos llamados imanes; forman una de las dos ramas principales del Islam (pág. 440)

shogun a general who ruled Japan in the emperor's name (p. 672)
   shogun general que gobernaba a Japón en nombre del emperador (pág. 672)

silt finely ground fertile soil that is good for growing crops (p. 494)
   cieno tierra fértil de partículas finas que es buena para el crecimiento de los cultivos (pág. 494)

slash-and-burn agriculture the practice of burning forest in order to clear land for planting (p. 179)
   agricultura de tala y quema práctica de quemar los bosques para despejar el terreno y sembrar en él (pág. 179)

smelters factories that process metal ores (p. 391)
   fundiciones fábricas que tratan menas de metal (pág. 391)

smog a mixture of smoke, chemicals, and fog (p. 180)
   smog mezcla de humo, sustancias químicas y niebla (pág. 180)

social science a field that focuses on people and the relationships among them (p. 5)
   ciencias sociales campo de estudio que se enfoca en las personas y en las relaciones entre ellas (pág. 5)

soil exhaustion the process of soil becoming infertile because it has lost nutrients needed by plants (p. 235)
   agotamiento del suelo proceso por el cual el suelo se vuelve estéril porque ha perdido los nutrientes que necesitan las plantas (pág. 235)

solar energy energy from the sun (p. 26)
   energía solar energía del Sol (pág. 26)

souk (SOOK) a marketplace or bazaar in the Islamic world (p. 509)
   zoco mercado o bazar del mundo islámico (pág. 509)

steppe a semidry grassland or prairie; steppes often border deserts (p. 59)
   estepa pradera semiárida; las estepas suelen encontrarse en el límite de los desiertos (pág. 59)

strait a narrow passageway that connects two large bodies of water (p. 255)
   estrecho paso angosto que une dos grandes masas de agua (pág. 255)

strike a work stoppage by a group of workers until their demands are met (p. 224)
   huelga interrupción del trabajo por parte de un grupo de trabajadores hasta que se cumplan sus demandas (pág. 224)

subcontinent a large landmass that is smaller than a continent (p. 616)
   subcontinente gran masa de tierra, más pequeña que un continente (pág. 616)

sultan the supreme ruler of a Muslim country (p. 711)
   sultán gobernante supremo de un país musulmán (pág. 711)

Sunni Muslims who believe in the ability of the majority of the community to interpret Islamic teachings; they make up one of the two main branches of Islam (p. 440)
   sunitas musulmanes que creen en la capacidad de la mayor parte de la comunidad de interpretar las enseñanzas islámicas; forman una de las dos ramas principales del Islam (pág. 440)

surface water water that is found in Earth's streams, rivers, and lakes (p. 31)
   agua superficial agua que se encuentra en los arroyos, ríos y lagos de la Tierra (pág. 31)

taiga (TY-guh) a forest of mainly evergreen trees covering much of Russia (p. 381)
   taiga bosque de árboles de hoja perenne principalmente que cubre gran parte de Rusia (pág. 381)

Taliban a radical Muslim group that rose to power in Afghanistan in the mid-1990s (p. 469)
   talibanes grupo radical musulmán que llegó al poder en Afganistán a mediados de la década de 1990 (pág. 469)

tariff a fee that a country charges on imports or exports (p. 677)
   arancel tarifa que impone un país a las importaciones y exportaciones (pág. 677)

territory an area that is under the authority of another government (p. 729)
   territorio zona que está bajo el control de otro go-bierno (pág. 729)

terrorism violent attacks that cause fear (p. 140)
   terrorismo ataques violentos que provocan miedo (pág. 140)

theocracy a government ruled by religious leaders (p. 452)
   teocracia gobierno dirigido por líderes religiosos (pág. 452)

townships crowded clusters of small homes in South Africa outside of cities where black South Africans live (p. 587)
   distritos segregados grupos de pequeñas viviendas amontonadas ubicadas en las afueras de las ciudades de Sudáfrica, donde vivían los sudafricanos negros (pág. 587)

trade surplus when a country exports more goods than it imports (p. 677)
   excedente comercial cuando un país exporta más bienes de los que importa (pág. 677)

ENGLISH AND SPANISH GLOSSARY

Trans-Siberian Railroad a rail line in Russia that extends about 5,800 miles (9,330 km) from Moscow to Vladivostok; it is the longest single rail line in the world (p. 391)

Ferrocarril Transiberiano línea de ferrocarril rusa de 5,800 millas (9,330 km) de largo, desde Moscú hasta Vladivostok; es la vía de ferrocarril más larga del mundo (pág. 391)

tributary a smaller stream or river that flows into a larger stream or river (p. 119)

tributario río o corriente más pequeña que fluye hacia un río o una corriente más grande (pág. 119)

tropics regions close to the equator (p. 29)

trópicos regiones cercanas al ecuador (pág. 29)

tsunami (sooh-NAH-mee) a destructive and fast-moving wave (p. 668)

tsunami ola rápida y destructiva (pág. 668)

uninhabitable unable to support human settlement (p. 347)

inhabitable que no puede sustentar asentamientos humanos (pág. 347)

United Nations an organization of countries that promotes peace and security around the world (p. 99)

Naciones Unidas organización de países que promueve la paz y la seguridad en todo el mundo (pág. 99)

urbanization the increase in the percentage of people who live in cities (p. 628)

urbanización aumento del porcentaje de personas que vive en las ciudades (pág. 628)

veld (VELT) open grassland areas in South Africa (p. 582)

veld praderas descampadas en Sudáfrica (pág. 582)

viceroy governor (p. 261)

virrey gobernador (pág. 261)

Vikings Scandinavian warriors who raided Europe in the early Middle Ages (p. 344)

vikingos guerreros escandinavos que atacaron Europa al principio de la Edad Media (pág. 344)

wadi a dry streambed (p. 439)

uadi cauce seco de un río o arroyo (pág. 439)

wat a Buddhist temple that also serves as a monastery (p. 700)

wat templo budista que sirve también como monasterio (pág. 700)

water cycle the movement of water from Earth's surface to the atmosphere and back (p. 33)

ciclo del agua circulación del agua desde la superficie de la Tierra hacia la atmósfera y de regreso a la Tierra (pág. 33)

water vapor water occurring in the air as an invisible gas (p. 32)

vapor de agua agua que se encuentra en el aire en estado gaseoso e invisible (pág. 32)

weather the short-term changes in the air for a given place and time (p. 50)

tiempo cambios a corto plazo en la atmósfera en un momento y lugar determinados (pág. 50)

weathering the process by which rock is broken down into smaller pieces (p. 39)

meteorización proceso de desintegración de las rocas en pedazos pequeños (pág. 39)

work ethic a belief that work in itself is worthwhile (p. 677)

ética de trabajo creencia de que el trabajo tiene valor propio (pág. 677)

yurt a movable round house made of wool felt mats hung over a wood frame (p. 466)

yurt tienda redonda y portátil de fieltro de lana que se coloca sobre una armazón de madera (pág. 466)

Z

Zionism a nationalist movement that began in the late 1800s and called for Jews to reestablish a Jewish state in their original homeland (p. 421)

sionismo movimiento nacionalista que comenzó a finales del siglo XIX y que alentaba a los judíos a reestablecer un estado judío en su tierra natal (pág. 421)

zonal organized by zone (p. 518)

zonal organizado por zonas (pág. 518)

Index

INDEX

INDEX

INDEX

INDEX

Credits and Acknowledgments

CREDITS AND ACKNOWLEDGMENTS

For permission to reproduce copyrighted material, grateful acknowledgment is made to the following sources:

National Geographic Society: From *Geography for Life: National Geography Standards 1994.* Copyright © 1994 by National Geographic Research & Exploration. All rights reserved.

G. P. Putnam's Sons, a division of Penguin Group (USA) Inc.: From *Time Enough for Love, the Lives of Lazarus Long* by Robert Heinlein. Copyright © 1973 by Robert Heinlein. All rights reserved.

Random House Children's Books, a division of Random House, Inc.: From *The River* by Gary Paulsen. Copyright © 1991 by Gary Paulsen.

United Nations: From the *Preamble to the Charter of the United Nations.* Copyright © 1945 by United Nations.

Atheneum Books for Young Readers, an imprint of Simon & Schuster Children's Publishing Division: From *Bearstone* by Will Hobbs. Copyright ©1989 by Will Hobbs. All rights reserved.

HarperCollins Publishers: *The Endless Steppe* by Esther Hautzig. Copyright © 1968 by Esther Hautzig.

Lonely Planet: From "Hungary" from the *Lonely Planet WorldGuide Online* Web site. Copyright © 2005 by Lonely Planet. Accessed at http://www. lonelyplanet.com/worldguide/destinations/europe/hungary/.

Naomi Shihab Nye: "Red Brocade" from *19 Varieties of Gazelle: Poems of the Middle East* by Naomi Shihab Nye. Copyright © 1994, 1995, 2002 by Naomi Shihab Nye.

Random House, Inc., www.randomhouse.com: *AKE: The Years of Childhood* by Wole Soyinka. Copyright © 1981 by Wole Soyinka.

Scribner, an imprint of Simon & Schuster Adult Publishing Group: "The Snows of Kilimanjaro" from *The Short Stories of Ernest Hemingway.* Copyright 1938 by Ernest Hemingway; copyright renewed © 1966 by Mary Hemingway.

CNN: From "Taiwan: War bill a big provocation," from *CNN.com* Web site, March 14, 2005. Copyright © 2005 by Cable News Network LP, LLLP. Accessed September 22, 2005, at http://edition.cnn.com/2005/WORLD/asiapcf/03/14/china.npc.law/

Foreign Affairs: From: "A Conversation With Lee Kuan Yew" by Fareed Zakaria from *Foreign Affairs,* March/April 1994, vol. 73, issue 2. Copyright © 2004 by Council on Foreign Relations. All rights reserved.

HarperCollins Publishers: From *Antarctic Journal: Four Months at the Bottom of the World* by Jennifer Owings Dewey. Copyright © 2001 by Jennifer Owings Dewey.

Alfred A. Knopf, Inc., a division of Random House, Inc., www.randomhouse.com: From *Shabanu: Daughter of Wind* by Suzanne Fisher Staples. Copyright ©1989 by Suzanne Fisher Staples. From *Crossing Antarctica* by Will Steger. Copyright © 1991 by Will Steger.

Sources Cited:

Quote from *Seeds of Peace* Web site, accessed August 23, 2005, at http://www.seedsofpeace.org/site/PageServer?pagename=BakerEvent.

Sources used by The World Almanac® for charts and graphs:

Eruptions in the Ring of Fire: *The World Almanac and Book of Facts, 2005;* World Energy Production: Energy Information Administration of the U.S. Department of Energy; A Developed and a Developing Country: *The World Factbook, 2005;*

U.S. Census Bureau; World Health Organization; Geographical Extremes: The Americas: *The World Almanac and Book of Facts, 2005; The World Factbook, 2005;* U.S. Bureau of the Census; The Americas: *The World Factbook, 2005;* U.S. Bureau of the Census, International Database; United Nations Statistical Yearbook; World's Largest Cities: United Nations Population Division National Censuses; Urban Populations in the Americas: United Nations Population Division; Major Food Exports of the Americas: Food and Agriculture Organization of the United Nations; Languages of the Caribbean: Joshua Project; World's Top Oil Exporters: Energy Information Administration of the U.S. Department of Energy; Argentina's Largest Cities: National Institute of Statistics and Censuses, Argentina, 2001 Census; Languages in Pacific South America: Ethnologue: Languages of the World, 15th Edition; Population of Major U.S. Cities: U.S. Census Bureau; Canadian Ethnic Groups: *The World Factbook, 2005;* Geographical Extremes: Europe and Russia: *The World Almanac and Book of Facts, 2005; The World Factbook, 2005;* U.S. Bureau of the Census; Europe and Russia: *The World Factbook, 2005;* U.S. Bureau of the Census, International Database; United Nations Statistical Yearbook; World's Highest Per Capita GDPs: *The World Factbook, 2005;* Densely Populated Countries in Europe: *The World Factbook, 2005;* U.S. Bureau of the Census, International Database; The European Union: European Union, International Programs Center; U.S. Bureau of the Census, International Database; Per Capita GDP of Greece: *The World Factbook, 2005;* Scandinavia's Per Capita GDP: *The World Factbook, 2005;* U.S. Bureau of the Census, International Database; United Nations Statistical Yearbook; Major Religions in the Balkans: World Christian Database; Russia's Population Decline, 1980–2010: U.S. Census Bureau, International Programs Center; State Statistical Committee of Russia; Eruptions in the Ring of Fire: *The World Almanac and Book of Facts, 2005;* World Energy Production: Energy Information Administration of the U.S. Department of Energy; A Developed and a Developing Country: *The World Factbook, 2005;* U.S. Census Bureau; World Health Organization; Geographical Extremes: Southwest and Central Asia: *The World Almanac and Book of Facts, 2005; The World Factbook, 2005;* World Oil Reserves: Energy Information Administration of the U.S. Department of Energy; Southwest and Central Asia: *The World Factbook, 2005;* U.S. Bureau of the Census, International Database; Largest Oil Reserves by Country: Energy Information Administration of the U.S. Department of Energy; Origin of Israel's Jewish Population: Central Bureau of Statistics, Israel; Saudi Arabia's Oil Production: Energy Information Administration of the U.S. Department of Energy; Saudi Arabia's Exports: OPEC, International Monetary Fund; Standard of Living in Central Asia: *The World Factbook, 2005;* United Nations Statistical Yearbook; Geographical Extremes: Africa: *The World Almanac and Book of Facts, 2005; The World Factbook, 2005;* Africa: *The World Factbook, 2005;* U.S. Bureau of the Census, International Database; United Nations Statistical Yearbook; Africa's Growing Population: International Programs Center, U.S. Census Bureau; Africa and the World: *The World Factbook, 2005;* U.S. Bureau of the Census, International Database; Egypt's Population, 2003: United Nations Population Division; Africa's Largest Cities: Britannica Book of the Year 2005; United Nations Population Division; Population Density in East Africa: International Programs Center, U.S. Census Bureau; *The World Factbook, 2005;* Major Religions of Central Africa: www.worldchristiandatabase.org; Kinshasa's Growing Population: United Nations Population Division; Tourism in Southern Africa: World Tourism Organization; Geographical Extremes:

South and East Asia: *The World Almanac and Book of Facts, 2005; The World Factbook, 2005;* U.S. Bureau of the Census; Food and Agriculture Organization of the United Nations—Forestry, Global Forest Watch; Geographical Extremes: The Pacific World: *The World Almanac and Book of Facts, 2005; The World Factbook, 2005;* U.S. Bureau of the Census; Marine Education Society of Australia; Food and Agriculture Organization of the United Nations—Forestry; South and East Asia and the Pacific: *The World Factbook, 2005;* U.S. Bureau of the Census, International Database; United Nations Statistical Yearbook; World's Largest Populations: International Programs Center, U.S. Census Bureau; Percent of World Population: International Programs Center, U.S. Census Bureau; Economic Powers: Japan and China: *The World Factbook, 2005;* Religions of the Indian Subcontinent: www.worldchristiandatabase.org; China's Projected Urban Population: United Nations Population Division; Population Growth in Japan: International Programs Center, U.S. Census Bureau; United Nations Population Division; Current Per Capita GDP in Island Southeast Asia and the United States: *The World Factbook, 2005;* Ethnic Groups in Australia and New Zealand: *The World Factbook, 2005*

Illustrations and Photo Credits

Frontmatter: ii, Victoria Smith/HRW; iv, Frans Lemmens/Getty Images; v (tl), Sharna Balfour/Gallo Images/Corbis; v (br), Penny Tweedie/Stone/Getty Images; viii (tl), SuperStock; viii (cr), SIME s.a.s./eStock Photo, All Rights Reserved; x, Robbie Jack/Corbis; xi, Danny Lehman/Corbis; xii, Zylberman Laurent/Corbis Sygma; xiii, Face mask with plank, Bwa People, Burkina Faso (wood & pigment), African, (20th century)/ © Indianapolis Museum of Art, USA, Gift of Mr and Mrs Harrison Eiteljorg/ Bridgeman Art Library; xiv, Lindsay Hebberd/Corbis; xv, AP Photo/Wally Santana; xvi, David Gray/Reuters/Corbis; xvii (tr), David Alan Parker/Image State; xviii, Reportage/Getty Images; xix, Donna Cox and Robert Patterson/NCSA; xx, NASA/ Corbis; H12 (t), Earth Satellite Corporation/Science Photo Library; H12 (tc), Frans Lemmens/Getty Images; H12 (c), London Aerial Photo Library/Corbis; H12 (bc), Harvey Schwartz/Index Stock Imagery; H12 (b), Tom Nebbia/Corbis. **Acetate Inserts:** (t), Gavin Hellier/Robert Harding/Getty Images; (c), Rex Butcher/Jon Arnold Images; (b), Steve McCurry/Magnum Photos.

Unit 1: A, Taxi/Getty Images; B (bl) Stephen Frink/Digital Vision/Getty Images; B (cr), Frans Lemmens/The Image Bank/Getty Images; 1 (bc), Robert Harding/Digital Vision/Getty Images; B–1 (background satellite photos), Planetary Visions.

Chapter 1: 2 (br), M. Colonel/Photo Researchers, Inc.; 2–3 (t), Age Fotostock/ SuperStock; 3 (br), Anthony Cassidy/Getty Images; 3 (bl), Tom Bean/Corbis; 5 (b), Frans Lemmens/Getty Images; 6 (b), Kim Sayer/Corbis; 7 (bl), London Aerial Photo Library/Corbis; 7 (br), ESA/K.Horgan/Getty Images; 8 (tl), Michael Newman/PhotoEdit; 11 (tl), David R. Frazier/Photo Researchers, Inc.; 11 (tr), Richard Bryand/Arcaid Picture Library; 11 (bl), David Muench/Corbis; 11 (bc), AFP/Getty Images; 11 (br), Morton Beebe/Corbis; 12–13 (b), Tom Nebbia/Corbis; 15 (l), M-SAT Ltd./Science Photo Library; 15 (r), Earth Satellite Corporation/Science Photo Library; 17 (tl), Torleif Svensson/Corbis; 17 (tr), Penny Tweedie/Stone/Getty Images; 19 (b), Donna Cox and Robert Patterson/NCSA; 20 (tl), Joe Raedle/Getty Images; 21 (tl), Frans Lemmens/Getty Images; 21 (tc), Penny Tweedie/Stone/Getty Images; 21 (tr), Donna Cox and Robert Patterson/NCSA.

R106 CREDITS AND ACKNOWLEDGMENTS

Chapter 2: 24 (br), Pete Saloutos/Corbis; 24–25 (t), Earth Satellite Corporation/Science Photo Library; 25 (br), Royalty Free/Corbis; 25 (bl), George H.H. Huey/Corbis; 29 (tr), Paul A. Souders/Corbis; 30–31 (b), Doug Wilson/Corbis; 31 (br), Terje Rakke/The Image Bank/Getty Images; 34 (tl), Rick Doyle/Corbis; 34 (tr), Alan Sirulnikoff/Photo Researchers, Inc.; 37 (bl), Bettmann/Corbis; 38 (cr), Yann Arthus-Bertrand/Corbis; 38 (br), Galen Rowell/Corbis; 39 (br), Age Fotostock/SuperStock; 40 (bl), Owaki-Kulla/Corbis; 41 (t), Age Fotostock/SuperStock; 43 (tl), David Weintraub/Photo Researchers, Inc.; 43 (tr), Gary Braasch/Corbis; 45 (tl), W.H. Mueller/Zefa Images/Corbis; 45 (tc), Rick Doyle/Corbis; 45 (tr), Galen Rowell/Corbis.

Chapter 3: 48 (br), Kate Thompson/National Geographic/Getty Images; 48–49 (t), Warren Faidley/WeatherStock; 49 (bl), L. Clarke/Corbis; 49 (br), Bill Ross/Corbis; 53 (tr), William Thomas Cain/Getty Images; 53 (br), Eric Meola/Getty Images; 56 (tl), Age FotoStock/SuperStock; 57 (tr), AlaskaStock; 57 (cr), Royalty-free/Corbis; 58 (cl), Martin Harvey/Corbis; 59 (br), Ingram/PictureQuest; 60 (t), Sharna Balfour/Gallo Images/Corbis; 64 (b), Carl and Ann Purcell/Corbis; 69 (tr), William Campbell/Peter Arnold, Inc.; 69 (c), Adrian Arbib/Corbis; 71 (tr), James L. Amos/Corbis; 71 (cr), Creatas/PictureQuest; 72 (tl), Sarah Leen/National Geographic Image Collection; 73 (tr), James Randklev/Getty Images; 75 (tl), Royalty-free/Corbis; 75 (tr), James L. Amos/Corbis.

Chapter 4: 78 (b), Liu Liqun/Corbis; 78–79 (t), Getty Images; 79 (br), Shahn Rowe/Stone/Getty Images; 79 (bl), Richard I'Anson/Lonely Planet Images; 81 (tl), Tom Wagner/Corbis; 81 (tr), Knut Mueller/Peter Arnold, Inc.; 83 (bl), Peter Armenia; 83 (br), Sebastian Bolesch/Peter Arnold, Inc.; 84 (cl), Reuters/Corbis; 84 (cr), Timothy A. Clary/AFP/Getty Images; 84–85 (t), Courtesy Library of Congress; 89 (t), The Granger Collection; 90 (cr), Marcel & Eva Malherbe/The Image Works; 90 (tr), Peter Beck/Corbis; 93 (t), Owaki-Kulla/Corbis; 93 (tc), Rosenfeld Images, Ltd./Photo Researchers, Inc.; 93 (bc), Kevin Fleming/Corbis; 93 (b), Michelle Garrett/Corbis; 94 (bl), Glen Allison/Stone/Getty Images; 94 (br), Carl & Ann Purcell/Corbis; 101 (tl), Sebastian Bolesch/Peter Arnold, Inc.; 101 (tc), Rosenfeld Images Ltd./Photo Researchers, Inc.; 101 (tr), Reuters/Corbis.

Unit 2: A, Royalty-free/Corbis; B (br), David W. Hamilton/The Image Bank/Getty Images; B (cl), Ryan/Beyer/Photographer's Choice/Getty Images; 105, John Wang/Photodisc Red/Getty Images; 107, Gavin Hellier/Robert Harding; 115 (b), Russell Gordon/Odyssey Productions, Inc.

Chapter 5: 116, eStock Photo/PictureQuest; 117 (br), Rommel Pecson/The Image Works; 117 (bl), Ron Watts/Corbis; 119, Altrendo/Getty Images; 120, NASA/Photo Researchers, Inc.; 121 (br), Dallas and John Heaton/Stock Connection/IPN; 121(cr), Alan Schein/Corbis; 125 (tr), NASA/Corbis; 125 (tl), Eric Gay/AP/Wide World Photos; 127 (b), Metropolitan Museum of Art, New York/Bridgeman Art Library; 129, *The Signing of the Constitution of the United States in 1787*, 1940, Christy, Howard Chandler (1873-1952) Hall of Representatives, Washington D.C., USA/www.bridgeman.co.uk; 131, Jeff Greenberg/ The Image Works; 133, Sam Dudgeon/HRW; 135, Alan Schein Photography/ Corbis; 137 (tl), Royalty Free/ Corbis; 137 (cl), Ray Soto/ Corbis; 138, Art Wolfe/ DanitaDelimont.com; 139, LMDC/ZUMA/Corbis; 141(tl), Altrendo/Getty Images; 141 (bl), Alan Schein Photography/ Corbis.

Chapter 6: 144, Workbook/Photolibrary; 145(bl), Steve Vidler/eStock Photo; 145 (br), Tom Bean/Corbis; 147, Joseph Sohm; Visions of America/ Corbis; 148, Simon Harris/eStock Photo; 149, CNES, 1988 Distribution Spot Image/Photo Researchers, Inc.; 150 (bl), Steve Vidler/eStock Photo; 150 (br), AKG-Images; 151(bl), Photocanada Digital Inc.; 151 (br), Photocanada Digital Inc.; 152, PhotoDisc Green, Inc./HRW; 154, Robert Frerck/Odyssey Productions, Inc.; 155, Albert Normandin/ Masterfile; 160, Index Stock Imagery, Inc.; 160 (t), Bryan & Cherry

Alexander/arcticphoto.co.uk; 161, Joseph Sohm; Visions of America/ Corbis; 163 (tl), Simon Harris/eStock Photo; 163(tc), Steve Vidler/eStock Photo.

Chapter 7: 166, Rommel/ Masterfile; 167 (br), Danny Lehman/ Corbis; 167 (bl), Age Fotostock/ SuperStock; 169, Charles & Josette Lenars/ Corbis; 170-171, Sally Brown/Index Stock Imagery, Inc.; 172, Kevin Schafer/ Corbis; 173 (bl), Fred Lengnick/ Imagestate; 173(br), Werner Forman/ Art Resource, NY; 174, Schalkwijk/Art Resource, NY; 176, Liba Taylor/ Corbis; 179, NASA; 180(tl), Edward Degginger/Bruce Coleman, Inc.; 180(c), Robert Frerck/ Odyssey/Chicago; 181 (tc), Age Fotostock/ SuperStock; 181 (cr), Macduff Everton/ Corbis; 183 (tl), Charles & Josette Lenars/ Corbis; 183 (tc), Schalkwijk/Art Resource, NY; 183 (tr), Age Fotostock/SuperStock.

Chapter 8: 186, Robert Frerck/ Odyssey/Chicago; 187 (bl) Robert Frerck/Odyssey/Chicago; 187 (br), Taxi/Getty Images; 189, Peter Treanor; 190, Galen Rowell/ Corbis; 191, Corbis; 193 (cr), Bettmann/ Corbis; 193(tl), David Alan Harvey/ Magnum Photos; 196, Look GMBH/eStock Photo; 202, Stuart Cohen/The Image Works; 203, Dave Bartruff/ DanitaDelimont.com; 204 (b), AFP/ NewsCom; 204 (cr), Hans Deryk/AP/Wide World Photos; 205, Picture Finders/Pictures Colour Library Ltd.; 207 (l), Peter Treanor/Pictures Colour Library Ltd.; 207(r), Dave Bartruff/ DanitaDelimont.com.

Chapter 9: 210, Krzysztof Dydynski/ Lonely Planet Images; 211(bl), Kevin Schafer/kevinschafer.com; 211 (br), Olivier Grunewald/Photolibrary; 213 (cl), Robert Caputo/Aurora Photos; 213 (cr), MedioImages/SuperStock; 214 (r), James Marshall/ Corbis; 214 (bc), Juan Silva/The Image Bank/Getty Images; 214 (bl), Ed Darack/D. Donne Bryant Photography; 216, Bridgeman Art Library; 217, Jane Sweeney/Lonely Planet Images; 218, Stone/Getty Images; 219 (tr), Krzysztof Dydynski/Lonely Planet Images; 219 (tl), Robert Frerck/Odyssey/Chicago; 222, Chico Sanchez/EPA/Landov; 223, John Van Hasselt/ Corbis; 224, Pablo Corral V/ Corbis; 225, Larry Luxner; 227 (tl), Jorge Silva/Reuters/NewsCom; 227 (l), James Marshall/ Corbis; 227 (c), Bridgeman Art Library; 227 (tr), Jorge Silva/Reuters/NewsCom.

Chapter 10: 230, Dario Lopez-Mills/AP/Wide World Photos; 231 (bl), Steve Vidler/eStock Photo; 231 (br), Robert Frerck/Odyssey/Chicago; 233 (cr), Kit Houghton/ Corbis; 233(br), George Hunter/Pictures Colour Library Ltd.; 237, Renzo Gostoli/AP/Wide World Photos; 238 (cl), SIME s.a.s/eStock Photo; 239 (tl), Moacyr Lopes Jr./UNEP/Peter Arnold, Inc.; 239 (tr), Wolfgang Kaehler/ Corbis; 240, Science Photo Library/Photo Researchers, Inc.; 243 (t), The British Library/Topham-HIP/The Image Works; 243 (br), Bettmann/ Corbis; 245, Marcel & Eva Malherbe/The Image Works; 246 (br), Wayne Walton/Lonely Planet Images; 246 (cr), Julio Etchart/Peter Arnold, Inc.; 248, Andrea Booher/Stone/Getty Images; 249 (cl), SIME s.a.s/eStock Photo; 249 (bl), Julio Etchart/Peter Arnold, Inc.

Chapter 11: 252, Francesc Muntada/ Corbis; 253 (br), Darrell Gulin/DanitaDelimont.com; 253 (bl), Robert Frerck/Odyssey/Chicago; 255, Graham Neden; Ecoscene/ Corbis; 257, CNES, Distribution Spot Image/Science Photo Library; 261 (t), Robert Frerck/Odyssey/Chicago; 261 (tr), Ric Ergenbright; 263 (tc), SuperStock; 265, Robert Fried/Robert Fried Photography; 266, Photodisc/Fotosearch Stock Photography; 267 (tl), Art Directors/Warren Jacobs; 267, Ron Giling/Peter Arnold, Inc.; 268, Randa Bishop/DanitaDelimont.com; 269 (tl), Graham Neden; Ecoscene/ Corbis; 269 (tc), SuperStock; 269 (tr), Art Directors/Warren Jacobs.

Unit 3: A, Peter Turnley/Corbis; B (tc), H.P. Merton/Corbis; B (bc), SIME s.a.s./eStock Photo, All Rights Reserved; 273 (tl), Wolfgang Kaehler/Corbis.

Chapter 12: 284 (br), Richard Klune/Corbis; 285 (bl), Carlos Cazalis/Corbis; 285 (br), Digital Vision/Robert Harding; 287 (br), Otto

Stadler/Peter Arnold, Inc.; 288 (tl), Charles O'Rear/Corbis; 288 (cr), Jeremy Lightfoot/Robert Harding; 289 (cl), IT Stock Free/eStock Photo; 289 (tr), SIME s.a.s./eStock Photo; 291 (cl), Vega/Taxi/Getty Images; 291 (br), Erich Lessing/Art Resource, NY; 293 (b), Roberto Meazza/IML Image Group; 294 (cl), Sylvain Grandadam/Robert Harding; 294 (cr), Mike Schroeder/Peter Arnold, Inc.; 297 (tr), Bildarchiv Preussischer Kulturbesitz/Art Resource, NY; 297 (tc), Gianni Dagli Orti/Corbis; 297 (br), Massimo Listri/Corbis; 298 (br), Giuseppe Cacace/Getty Images; 299 (bl), Steve Vidler/SuperStock; 299 (br), Martin Moos/Lonely Planet Images; 300 (tl), WorldSat; 301 (b), Dallas and John Heaton/Stock Connection; 302 (tr), AFP/Getty Images; 303 (br), Latin Focus/HRW; 304 (tl), Nigel Francis/Corbis; 305 (t), Roberto Meazza/IML Image Group; 305 (tc), Steve Vidler/SuperStock; 305 (tr), Latin Focus/HRW.

Chapter 13: 308 (br), William Manning/Corbis; 309 (bl), Brian Lawrence/Image State; 309 (br), Elfi Kluck/Index Stock Imagery/PictureQuest; 311 (br), David Barnes/PanStock/PictureQuest; 312 (cl), WorldSat; 315 (tr), SuperStock; 315 (cr), Vince Streano/Corbis; 315 (br), Corbis; 318 (t), Goos van der Veen/Hollandse Hoogte; 320 (cl), AFP/Getty Images; 321 (br), PhotoDisc Collection/Getty Images; 323, Walter Bibikow/Taxi/Getty Images; 324 (tl), Ric Ergenbright Photography; 324–325 (c), Sean Gallup/Getty Images; 325 (tr), Sean Gallup/Getty Images; 326 (bl), Ray Juno/Corbis; 326 (br), Free Agents Limited/Corbis; 329 (tl), Vince Streano/Corbis; 329 (tr), Ric Ergenbright Photography.

Chapter 14: 332 (br), Paul Harris/Stone/Getty Images; 333 (bl), Steve Vidler/Image State; 333 (br), Fredrik Naumann/Samfoto; 335 (tr), Markus Dlouhy/Peter Arnold, Inc.; 336 (cl), WorldSat; 337 (tr), Espen Bratlie/Samfoto; 338 (cr), National Portrait Gallery/SuperStock; 338 (b), Steve Vidler/Image State; 339 (tr), Time Life Images/Getty Images; 339 (bl), Hulton Archive/Getty Images; 339 (br), Hulton-Deutsch Collection/Corbis; 340 (bl), Stock Connection/PictureQuest; 342 (t), Michael Duerinckx/Image State; 346 (b), Jon Arnold/DanitaDelimont.com; 347 (cr), Dave Houser/Image State; 348 (tl), Hans Strand/Corbis; 348 (t), Hans Strand/Corbis; 349 (tl), Markus Dlouhy/Peter Arnold, Inc.; 349 (tc), Michael Duerinckx/Image State; 349 (tr), Jon Arnold/DanitaDelimont.com.

Chapter 15: 352 (br), Tom Schulze/Peter Arnold, Inc.; 353 (bl), Adam Woolfitt/Corbis; 353 (br), Stock Connection/PictureQuest; 355 (cr), Liba Taylor/Corbis; 355 (br), M. ou Me. Desjeux, Bernard/Corbis; 356 (bl), Fred Bruemmer/Peter Arnold, Inc.; 357 (tl), Reuters/Corbis; 359 (cr), Bettmann/Corbis; 360 (bl), Wally McNamee/Corbis; 361 (tr), Jon Arnold/DanitaDelimont.com; 363 (cr), Age Fotostock/SuperStock; 363 (cr), John Farrar; 367 (b), Ethel Davies/Image State; 368 (bl), Barry Lewis/Corbis; 369 (t), AP Photo/Amel Emric; 370 (bl), David Turnley/Corbis; 373 (tr), David Turnley/Corbis; 373 (tl), Jon Arnold/DanitaDelimont.com.

Chapter 16: 376 (br), Michael Yamashita/Corbis; 377 (bl), Robbie Jack/Corbis; 377 (br), Steve Vidler/Image State; 379 (b), Daisy Gilardini/DanitaDelimont.com; 380 (cl), Maxim Marmur/Getty Images; 380 (bl), Oxford Scientific/PictureQuest; 385, Kurt Scholz/SuperStock; 386 (tl), The Granger Collection, New York; 390 (tl), Yogi, Inc./Corbis; 390 (cl), Harald Sund/The Image Bank/Getty Images; 390 (cr), Maria Stenzel/National Geographic Image Collection; 393 (tr), Time Life Pictures/Getty Images; 395 (tl), Marc Garanger/Corbis; 396 (tl), Jeremy Horner/Corbis; 397 (tl), Daisy Gilardini/DanitaDelimont.com; 397 (tc), Kurt Scholz/SuperStock; 397 (tr), Marc Garanger/Corbis.

Unit 4: A, Robert Frerck/Odyssey Productions, Inc.; B (tl), Ustinenko Anatoly/ITAR-TASS/Corbis; B (bl), Hans Christian Heap/Taxi/Getty Images; 401, Gavin Hellier/Robert Harding World Imagery/Getty Images; 403, Steve Vidler/SuperStock.

DATE DUE
